TENTH EDITION

Educational Psychology

THEORY AND PRACTICE

Robert E. Slavin

Johns Hopkins University

Boston • Columbus • Indianapolis • New York • San Francisco • Upper Saddle River
Amsterdam • Cape Town • Dubai • London • Madrid • Milan • Munich • Paris • Montreal • Toronto
Delhi • Mexico City • Sao Paulo • Sydney • Hong Kong • Seoul • Singapore • Taipei • Tokyo

Editor-in-Chief: Paul A. Smith
Managing Editor: Shannon Steed
Editorial Assistant: Matthew Buchholz
Vice President, Director of Marketing: Margaret Waples
Marketing Manager: Joanna Sabella
Production Editor: Annette Joseph
Editorial Production Service: Omegatype Typography, Inc.
Manufacturing Manager: Megan Cochran
Electronic Composition: Omegatype Typography, Inc.
Interior Designer: Denise Hoffman
Photo Researcher: Annie Fuller
Cover Designer: Linda Knowles

Credits and acknowledgments borrowed from other sources and reproduced, with permission, in this textbook appear on appropriate pages within text.

Library of Congress Cataloging-in-Publication Data

Slavin, Robert E.
   Educational psychology : theory and practice / Robert E. Slavin. — 10th ed.
       p. cm.
   Includes bibliographical references and index.
   ISBN-13: 978-0-13-703435-2 (pbk.)
   ISBN-10: 0-13-703435-0 (pbk.)
  1. Educational psychology. I. Title.
   LB1051.S615 2012
   370.15—dc22

                          2010020541

10 9 8 7 6 5 4 3 2 1   WEB   14 13 12 11 10

www.pearsonhighered.com   ISBN-10: 0-13-703435-0
ISBN-13: 978-0-13-703435-2

About the Author

ROBERT SLAVIN is director of the Center for Research and Reform in Education, Johns Hopkins University, director of the Institute for Effective Education at the University of York (England), and chairman of the Success for All Foundation. He received his Ph.D. in Social Relations from Johns Hopkins in 1975, and since that time he has authored more than 200 articles and book chapters on such topics as cooperative learning, ability grouping, school and classroom organization, desegregation, mainstreaming, research review, and evidence-based reform. Dr. Slavin is the author or coauthor of 20 books, including *Cooperative Learning, School and Classroom Organization, Effective Programs for Students at Risk, Preventing Early School Failure, Show Me the Evidence: Proven and Promising Programs for America's Schools, Two Million Children: Success for All, Effective Programs for Latino Students,* and *Educational Research in the Age of Accountability.* In 1985 Dr. Slavin received the Raymond Cattell Early Career Award for Programmatic Research from the American Educational Research Association. In 1988 he received the Palmer O. Johnson Award for the best article in an AERA journal. In 1994 he received the Charles A. Dana Award, in 1998 he received the James Bryant Conant Award from the Education Commission of the States, and in 2000 he received the Distinguished Services Award from the Council of Chief State School Officers. He again received the Palmer O. Johnson award for the best article in an AERA journal in 2008, and received the AERA Review of Research award in 2009.

Brief Contents

Contents

CHAPTER 1

Educational Psychology: A Foundation for Teaching   1

CHAPTER 2

Cognitive, Language, and Literacy Development   28

CHAPTER 3

Social, Moral, and Emotional Development   52

CHAPTER 4

Student Diversity   78

CHAPTER 5

Behavioral Theories of Learning   114

CHAPTER 6

Information Processing and Cognitive Theories of Learning   142

CHAPTER 7

The Effective Lesson   182

CHAPTER 8

Student-Centered and Constructivist Approaches to Instruction   216

CHAPTER 9

Grouping, Differentiation, and Technology   248

CHAPTER 10

Motivating Students to Learn   284

CHAPTER 11

Effective Learning Environments   314

CHAPTER 12

Learners with Exceptionalities   352

CHAPTER 13

Assessing Student Learning   396

CHAPTER 14

Standardized Tests and Accountability   446

List of Features

The Intentional Teacher

21ST Century Learning

Preface

When I first set out to write *Educational Psychology: Theory and Practice,* I had a very clear purpose in mind. I wanted to give tomorrow's teachers the intellectual grounding and practical strategies they will need to be effective instructors. Most of the textbooks published then, I felt, fell into one of two categories: stuffy or lightweight. The stuffy books were full of research but were ponderously written, losing the flavor of the classroom and containing few guides to practice. The lightweight texts were breezy and easy to read but lacked the dilemmas and intellectual issues brought out by research. They contained suggestions of the "Try this!" variety, without considering evidence about the effectiveness of those strategies.

My objective was to write a text that

- Presents information that is as complete and up to date as the most research-focused texts but is also readable, practical, and filled with examples and illustrations of key ideas.

- Includes suggestions for practice based directly on classroom research (tempered by common sense) so I can have confidence that when you try what I suggest, it will be likely to work.

- Helps you transfer what you learn in educational psychology to your own teaching by making explicit the connection between theory and practice through numerous realistic examples. Even though I have been doing educational research since the mid-1970s, I find that I never really understand theories or concepts in education until someone gives me a compelling classroom example; and I believe that most of my colleagues (and certainly teacher education students) feel the same way. As a result, the word *example* or similar words appear hundreds of times in this text.

- Appeals to readers; therefore, I have tried to write in such a way that you will almost hear students' voices and smell the lunch cooking in the school cafeteria as you read.

These have been my objectives for the book from the first edition to this, the tenth edition. With every edition, I have made changes throughout the text, adding new examples, refining language, and deleting dated or unessential material. I am meticulous about keeping the text up to date, so this edition has more than 2,000 reference citations, 55 percent of which are from 2000 or later. The tenth edition is updated with more than 656 new references. Although some readers may not care much about citations, I want you and your professors to know what research supports the statements I've made and where to find additional information.

The field of educational psychology and the practice of education have changed a great deal in recent years, and I have tried to reflect these changes in this edition. Several years ago, direct instruction and related teacher effectiveness research were dominant in educational psychology. Then constructivist methods, portfolio and performance assessments, and other humanistic strategies returned. Now, the emphasis is on accountability, which requires teachers more than ever to plan outcomes and teach purposefully, qualities that I emphasize in this edition as *intentional teaching*. In the earliest editions of this text, I said that we shouldn't entirely discard discovery learning and humanistic methods despite the popularity, then, of direct instruction. In the next editions, I made just the opposite plea: that we shouldn't completely discard direct instruction despite the popularity of active, student-centered teaching and constructivist methods of instruction. I continue to advocate a balanced approach to instruction. No matter what their philosophical orientations, experienced teachers know that they must be proficient in a wide range of methods and must use them thoughtfully.

The tenth edition presents new research and practical applications of many topics. Throughout, this edition reflects the "cognitive revolution" that has transformed educational psychology and teaching. The accompanying figure presents a concept map of the book's organization.

Given the developments in education in recent years, particularly with the introduction of the No Child Left Behind legislation in 2001 and the focus on standards and accountability that continues in the Obama administration, no one can deny that teachers matter or that teachers' behaviors have a profound impact on student achievement. To make that impact positive, teachers must have both a deep understanding of the powerful principles of psychology as they apply to education and a clear sense of how these principles can be applied. The intentional teacher is one who constantly reflects on his or her practices and makes instructional decisions based on a clear conception of how these practices affect students. Effective teaching is neither a bag of tricks nor a set of abstract principles; rather, it is intelligent application of well-understood principles to address practical needs. I hope this edition will help you develop the intellectual and practical skills you need to do the most important job in the world—teaching.

New and Expanded Coverage

Among the many topics that receive new or expanded coverage in this edition are:

- 21st century skills (Chapter 1 and 21st Century Learning features throughout the text)
- Language and literacy development in the elementary years (Chapter 2)
- New research on bilingual education (Chapter 4)
- Emerging research in neuroscience (Chapter 6)
- Expanded coverage on study strategies (Chapter 6)
- The latest research on cooperative learning (Chapter 8)
- New research on tutoring and small group remediation for struggling readers (Chapter 9)
- More on differentiated instruction (Chapter 9)
- New coverage of technology applications (Chapter 9)
- New sections on bullying and classroom management (Chapter 11)
- Expanded coverage of Response to Intervention (Chapter 12)
- Expanded coverage of IEPs (Chapter 12)
- Expanded coverage of autism spectrum disorder (Chapter 12)
- Additional coverage of value-added assessments (Chapter 14)
- New information on testing accommodations for English learners (Chapter 14)
- New Appendix that correlates the content of each chapter to corresponding topics within the Praxis™ Principles of Learning and Teaching Tests
- 656 new and updated references, 55 percent of which are from 2000 or later

How This Book Is Organized

The chapters in this book address three principal themes: students, teaching, and learning (see the Concept Map). Each chapter discusses important theories and includes many examples of how these theories apply to classroom teaching.

This book emphasizes the intelligent use of theory and research to improve instruction. The chapters on teaching occupy about one-third of the total pages in the book, and the other chapters all relate to the meaning of theories and research practice. Whenever possible, the guides in this book present specific programs and strategies that have been evaluated and found to be effective, not just suggestions of things to try.

Features

■ Using Your Experience

Each chapter of the text opens with a vignette depicting a real-life situation that teachers encounter. Throughout the chapter narrative, I refer to the issues raised in the vignette. In addition, you have the opportunity to respond to the vignette in several related features, such as the Using Your Experience sections that follow each vignette. Each of these sections provides critical and creative thinking questions and cooperative learning activities that allow you to work with the issues brought up in the vignette, activate your prior knowledge, and begin thinking about the ideas the chapter will explore.

■ Personal Reflections Podcasts

In line with the emphasis on reflective, intentional practice, I've added a feature that is intended to bring a bit of myself from behind the curtain that usually divides author and readers. I've made available live interviews, called Personal Reflections, in which I reflect on my own experiences as a teacher, researcher, and parent to illuminate various aspects of the text. As a reader, it is important for you to know that behind each textbook is an author whose experiences, values, and perspectives shape the text.

■ 21st Century Learning

Throughout this book, a new feature presents information on 21st century learning that relates to the topic of the chapter. Beyond this, 21st century learning skills are discussed within the main parts of the text, as appropriate.

Educational policies and practices usually lag behind changes in society and the economy. The emphasis on 21st century learning is intended to help educators think more deeply about how each of the decisions they make about curriculum, teaching methods, use of technology, assessments, and so on contributes to helping students succeed not only by today's standards, but also in tomorrow's world.

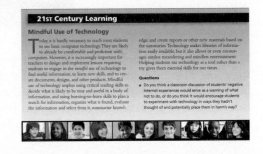

Cartoons

Throughout the text is a series of cartoons created just for this book by my colleague, James Bravo, to illustrate key concepts in educational psychology. These are intended to be humorous and also to make you reflect.

Theory into Practice

The Theory into Practice sections in each chapter help you acquire and develop the tools you need to be an effective teacher. These sections present specific strategies to apply in your classroom. New Theory into Practice sections have been added throughout this edition.

Guided Study

Each chapter offers features to help you regulate your own learning: a beginning Chapter Outline and Learning Outcomes to guide your reading, glossary and cross-reference Connections annotations in the margins, a Chapter Summary to help you review your reading, and a list of Key Terms with page references.

Certification Pointer

For teacher certification tests, you may be expected to detail various strategies for gaining students' attention, such as lowering your voice, using a gesture or surprise, or increasing the emotional content.

INTASC

3 Adapting Instruction for Individual Needs

4 Multiple Instructional Strategies

6 Communication Skills

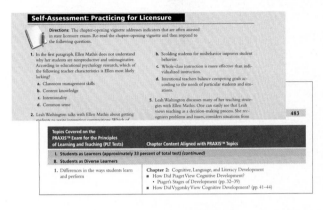

Self-Assessment: Practicing for Licensure

Directions: The chapter-opening vignette addresses indicators that are often assessed in state licensure exams. Re-read the chapter-opening vignette and then respond to the following questions.

1. In the first paragraph, Ellen Mathis does not understand why her students are nonproductive and unimaginative. According to educational psychology research, which of the following teacher characteristics is Ellen most likely lacking?
   a. Classroom management skills
   b. Content knowledge
   c. Intentionality
   d. Common sense

2. Leah Washington talks with Ellen Mathis about getting students to write interesting compositions. Which of

   b. Scolding students for misbehavior improves student behavior.
   c. Whole-class instruction is more effective than individualized instruction.
   d. Intentional teachers balance competing goals according to the needs of particular students and situations.

5. Leah Washington discusses many of her teaching strategies with Ellen Mathis. One can easily see that Leah views teaching as a decision-making process. She recognizes problems and issues, considers situations from

483

Topics Covered on the PRAXIS™ Exam for the Principles of Learning and Teaching (PLT Tests)	Chapter Content Aligned with PRAXIS™ Topics
I. Students as Learners (approximately 33 percent of total test) *(continued)*	
B. Students as Diverse Learners	
1. Differences in the ways students learn and perform	**Chapter 2:** Cognitive, Language, and Literacy Development ■ How Did Piaget View Cognitive Development? • Piaget's Stages of Development (pp. 32–39) ■ How Did Vygotsky View Cognitive Development? (pp. 41–44)

■ Licensure

This edition has multiple tools to help you apply your learning to licensure and certification. In each chapter you can both identify and practice the appropriate knowledge and skills you have attained.

- To help you assess your own learning and prepare for licensure exams, Certification Pointers identify content likely to be on certification tests.

- A special marginal icon identifies content that correlates to INTASC standards. These correspond closely to Praxis, and many state assessments are patterned on Praxis.

- In addition, Self-Assessment: Practicing for Licensure features at the end of each chapter are designed to resemble the types of questions and content typically encountered on state certification tests.

Also see the new Appendix that correlates the content of each chapter heading and features to corresponding topics within the Praxis Principles of Learning and Teaching Tests.

■ On the Web

On the Web appears within the text and lists useful websites providing further information on topics discussed in each chapter. This edition adds many new websites, as the number of sites useful to educators is rapidly expanding.

ON THE **WEB**

More information on autism spectrum disorders can be found at www.autism-society.org. Also see the CDC website (www.cdcfoundation.org/healththreats/autism.aspx) and the CEC website (www.cec.sped.org/AM/Template.cfm?Section=Autism_Asperger_s_Syndrome&Template=/TaggedPage/TaggedPageDisplay.cfm&TPLID=37&ContentID=5598).

■ The Intentional Teacher

One attribute seems to be a characteristic of all outstanding teachers: intentionality, or the ability to do things for a reason, purposefully. Intentional teachers constantly think about the outcomes they want for their students and how each decision they make moves students toward those outcomes. A key feature in each chapter, The Intentional Teacher is designed to help you develop and apply a set of strategies to carry out your intentionality. It will help you internalize a set of questions that can aid you in planning, teaching, and revising your practice in intentional ways. In each chapter, you will consider answers

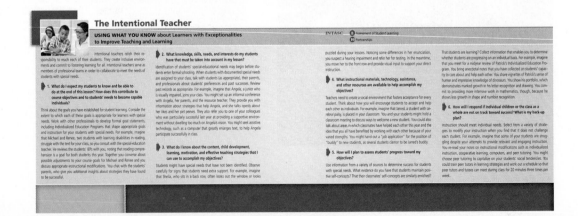

to the following questions from a new vantage point grounded in chapter content, and you will find new examples at all grade levels and in all subject areas to illustrate those answers. The Intentional Teacher focuses your attention on these questions:

1. What do I expect my students to know and be able to do at the end of this lesson? How does this contribute to course objectives and to students' needs to become capable individuals?

2. What knowledge, skills, needs, and interests do my students have that must be taken into account in my lesson?

3. What do I know about the content, child development, learning, motivation, and effective teaching strategies that I can use to accomplish my objectives?

4. What instructional materials, technology, assistance, and other resources are available to help me accomplish my objectives?

5. How will I plan to assess students' progress toward my objectives?

6. How will I respond if individual children or the class as a whole are not on track toward success? What is my backup plan?

The Intentional Teacher will help you combine your increasing knowledge of principles of educational psychology, your growing experience with learners, and your creativity to make intentional instructional decisions that will help students become enthusiastic, effective learners.

In *Preparing Teachers for a Changing World*, Linda Darling-Hammond and her colleagues point out that grounding teacher education in real classrooms—among real teachers and students and among actual examples of students' and teachers' work—is an important, and perhaps even an essential, part of training teachers for the complexities of teaching in today's classrooms. MyEducationLab is an online learning solution that provides contextualized interactive exercises, simulations, and other resources designed to help develop the knowledge and skills teachers need. All of the activities and exercises in MyEducationLab are built around essential learning outcomes for teachers and are mapped to professional teaching standards. Utilizing classroom video, authentic student and teacher artifacts, case studies, and other resources and assessments, the scaffolded learning experiences in MyEducationLab offer pre-service teachers and those who teach them a unique and valuable education tool.

For each topic covered in your course you will find most or all of the following features and resources.

■ Connection to National Standards

Now it is easier than ever to see how coursework is connected to national standards. Each topic on MyEducationLab lists intended learning outcomes connected to the appropriate national standards. And all of the activities and exercises in MyEducationLab are mapped to the appropriate national standards and learning outcomes as well.

■ Assignments and Activities

Designed to enhance student understanding of concepts covered in class and save instructors preparation and grading time, these assignable exercises show concepts in action (through video, cases, and/or student and teacher artifacts). They help students deepen content knowledge and synthesize and apply concepts and strategies they read about in the book. (Correct answers for these assignments are available to the instructor only under the Instructor Resource tab.)

■ Building Teaching Skills and Dispositions

These learning units help students practice and strengthen skills that are essential to quality teaching. After presenting the steps involved in a core teaching process, students are given an opportunity to practice applying this skill via videos, student and teacher artifacts, and/or case studies of authentic classrooms. Providing multiple opportunities to practice a single teaching concept, each activity encourages a deeper understanding and application of concepts, as well as the use of critical thinking skills.

■ IRIS Center Resources

The IRIS Center at Vanderbilt University (http://iris.peabody.vanderbilt.edu), funded by the U.S. Department of Education's Office of Special Education Programs (OSEP), develops training enhancement materials for pre-service and in-service teachers. The Center works with experts from across the country to create challenge-based interactive modules, case study units, and podcasts that provide research-validated information about working with students in inclusive settings. In your MyEducationLab course we have integrated this content where appropriate.

■ Simulations in Classroom Management

One of the most difficult challenges facing teachers today is how to balance classroom instruction with classroom management. These interactive cases focus on the classroom management issues teachers most frequently encounter on a daily basis. Each simulation presents a challenge scenario at the beginning and then offers a series of choices to solve each challenge. Along the way students receive mentor feedback on their choices and have the opportunity to make better choices if necessary. Upon exiting each simulation students will have a clear understanding of how to address these common classroom management issues and will be better equipped to handle them in the classroom.

■ Teacher Talk

This feature emphasizes the power of teaching through videos of master teachers who tell their own compelling stories of why they teach. These videos help teacher candidates see the bigger picture and consider why what they are learning is important to their career as a teacher. Each of these featured teachers has been awarded the Council of Chief State School Officers Teachers of the Year award, the oldest and most prestigious award for teachers.

■ Study Plan

A MyEducationLab Study Plan is a multiple-choice assessment tied to chapter objectives, supported by study material. A well-designed Study Plan offers multiple opportunities to fully master required course content as identified by the objectives in each chapter:

- **Chapter Objectives** identify the learning outcomes for the chapter and give students targets to shoot for as they read and study.
- **Multiple Choice Assessments** assess mastery of the content. These assessments are mapped to chapter objectives, and students can take the multiple choice quiz as many times as they want. Not only do these quizzes provide overall scores for

each objective, but they also explain why responses to particular items are correct or incorrect.

■ **Study Material: Review, Practice, and Enrichment** gives students a deeper understanding of what they do and do not know related to chapter content. This material includes text excerpts, activities that include hints and feedback, and interactive multimedia exercises built around videos, simulations, cases, or classroom artifacts.

■ Course Resources

The Course Resources section on MyEducationLab is designed to help students put together an effective lesson plan, prepare for and begin their career, navigate their first year of teaching, and understand key educational standards, policies, and laws. The Course Resources Tab includes the following:

■ The **Lesson Plan Builder** is an effective and easy-to-use tool that students can use to create, update, and share quality lesson plans. The software also makes it easy to integrate state content standards into any lesson plan.

■ The **Preparing a Portfolio** module provides guidelines for creating a high-quality teaching portfolio.

■ **Beginning Your Career** offers tips, advice, and other valuable information on

• *Resume Writing and Interviewing:* Includes expert advice on how to write impressive resumes and prepare for job interviews.

• *Your First Year of Teaching:* Provides practical tips to set up a first classroom, manage student behavior, and more easily organize for instruction and assessment.

• *Law and Public Policies:* Details specific directives and requirements teachers need to understand under the No Child Left Behind Act and the Individuals with Disabilities Education Improvement Act of 2004.

■ Certification and Licensure

The Certification and Licensure section is designed to help students pass their licensure exams by giving them access to state test requirements, overviews of what tests cover, and sample test items. The Certification and Licensure tab includes the following:

■ **State Certification Test Requirements:** Here students can click on a state and will then be taken to a list of state certification tests.

■ **Licensure Exams:** Here students can click on the exams they need to take to find

• Basic information about each test

• Descriptions of what is covered on each test

• Sample test questions with explanations of correct answers

■ **National Evaluation Series** by Pearson: Here students can see the tests in the NES, learn what is covered on each exam, and access sample test items with descriptions and rationales of correct answers. They can also purchase interactive online tutorials developed by Pearson Evaluation Systems and the Pearson Teacher Education and Development Group.

■ **ETS Online Praxis Tutorials:** Here students can purchase interactive online tutorials developed by ETS and by the Pearson Teacher Education and Development Group. Tutorials are available for the Praxis I exams and for select Praxis II exams.

Visit **www.myeducationlab.com** for a demonstration of this exciting new online teaching resource.

Instructor Resources

■ The **Instructor's Resource Manual,** written by Emilie Johnson, Lindenwood University, contains chapter overviews, suggested readings and MyEducationLab media, answers to the textbook Self-Assessment features, and handout masters. The Instructor's Manual is available for download from the Instructor Resource Center at www.pearsonhighered.com/irc.

■ The **Computerized Test Bank,** written by Rachel Green and Barbara Fuller, Northeastern State University, contains a variety of testing items. Instructors can use MyTest to create exams in just minutes by selecting from the existing database of questions, editing questions, or writing original questions. Testing items in the test bank include multiple-choice, true-false, short-answer, conceptual essay, reflective essay, and concept integration questions. Concept integration items ask students to apply a combination of concepts and principles to a written teaching scenario.

■ The **PowerPoint™ Presentation,** written by Richard Giaquinto, St. Francis College, highlights key concepts and summarizes text content. The PowerPoint™ Presentation is available for download from the Instructor Resource Center at www.pearsonhighered.com/irc.

■ The **"What Every Teacher Should Know About"** series contains short booklets that cover the basic concepts of key topics in education from assessment to IDEA and NCLB. To access this series, please contact your Pearson representative. Find your representative at **www.pearsonhighered.com/replocator.**

■ **Pearson Custom Library.** Many professors would like to add more material to their course, change the sequence of the chapters they assign, or delete chapters that they do not cover. **Pearson Custom Library** gives you that power. Featuring best-selling Pearson textbooks and case studies, the Pearson Custom Library is the largest and best resource for high-quality content tailored to your course needs.

We give you the power to assign what you actually want to use, including resources customized to your course, your state, and your teaching style and even open source and Internet materials. Every year we provide thousands of customized texts to instructors who want personalized, enhanced, and affordable products. If you've never tried it before, you will be amazed at how quick, easy, and flexible the program is.

■ Select chapters from over 600 Pearson teacher and administrator education textbooks and 600 case studies.

■ Include certification and content standards from your state (a majority of states are available).

■ Include outside content, such as readings or journal articles—Pearson will secure permissions for you.

■ Choose a cover and a title for your custom book.

■ Review the exam copy we print and send you.

■ Want to make some changes to the content or reorder the chapters? No problem! Nothing is final until your bookstore places the order.

You have the power to control the length, scope, and sequence of your book. You have the power to add or change content every semester in response to new standards, new laws, or new research. You have the power to build the book you've always wanted to use.

To build your custom book or to learn more about the program, please visit www.pearsoncustomlibrary.com, keyword search: education. If you have questions or require assistance, contact your local Pearson representative. Find your rep at **www.pearsonhighered.com/replocator.**

Acknowledgments

In this edition, I benefited from the skillful assistance of my colleague Susan Davis, who helped in particular with the rewriting of the Technology section of Chapter 9, "On the Web" material, updates to special education information in Chapter 12, and much more. My colleague Bette Chambers wrote the Certification Pointers, researched websites, and contributed content throughout the text. Steve Ross and Deborah Lowther reviewed the new technology section. I also benefited from the feedback of special content reviewers Jean Ulman, Ball State University, and Jim Persinger, Emporia State University, on Chapters 12 (Learners with Exceptionalities), 13 (Assessing Student Learning), and 14 (Standardized Tests and Accountability). I also thank the writers of the supplements: Emilie Johnson, Lindenwood University (Instructor's Resource Manual and MyEducationLab Study Plan); Rachel Green and Barbara Fuller, Northeastern State University (Assessment Package); Richard Giaquinto, St. Francis College (PowerPoint™ Presentation); and Suzanne Schellenberg, University of North Florida (Praxis Appendix).

I would like to thank the reviewers of this edition: Felicia A. B. Hanesworth, Medaille College; Pam Kidder-Ashley, Appalachian State University; E. Michael Nussbaum, University of Nevada, Las Vegas; Dr. John L. Rausch, John Carroll University; Carrie Rothstein-Fisch, California State University, Northridge; Robert J. Stevens, Pennsylvania State University; and Roger Webb, Southern Illinois University.

I also wish to thank my many colleagues who served as contributors for this edition, as well as those who participated in a special survey. Reviewers' comments provided invaluable information that helped me revise and augment the text. Contributors' work has made the features and supplements to this text first-rate.

Wallace Alexander, Thomas College

Patrick Allen, Graduate College of Union University

Ted Batson, Indiana Wesleyan University

Richard Battaglia, California Lutheran University

Elizabeth Anne Belford Horan, Methodist College

Sandra Billings, Fairfield University

Silas Born, Bethany Lutheran College

Curtis Brant, Baldwin-Wallace College

Camille Branton, Delta State University

Joy Brown, University of North Alabama

Doris Burgert, Wichita State University

Renee Cambiano, Northeastern State University

William Camp, Luzerne County Community College

Ann Caton, Rockford College

Kay Chick, Pennsylvania State University–Altoona

Martha Cook, Malone College

Faye Day, Bethel College

Christiane DeBauge, Indiana University

Donna Duellberg, Wayland Baptist University

Nick Elksnin, The Citadel

Joan Evensen, Towson University

E. Gail Everett, Bob Jones University

R. Joel Farrell, Faulkner University

Susan Frusher, Northeastern State University

Donna Gardner, William Jewell College

Michele Gill, University of Central Florida

Jennifer Gross Lara, Anne Arundel Community College

Raphael Guillory, Eastern Washington University

Jan Hayes, Middle Tennessee State University

James Hedgebeth, Elizabeth City State University

Mark Hopkin, Wiley College

John Hummel, Valdosta State University

Margaret Hurd, Anne Arundel Community College

Daniel Hursh, West Virginia University

Kathryn Hutchinson, St. Thomas Aquinas College

Karen Huxtable-Jester, University of Texas at Dallas

Gretchen Jefferson, Eastern Washington University

Carolyn Jeffries, CSU Northridge

W. Y. Johnson, Wright State University

Jeffrey Kaplan, University of Central Florida

Jack Kaufman, Bluefield State College

Robert Landry, Winston-Salem State University

Dorothea Lerman, Louisiana State University

Jupian J. Leung, University of Wisconsin–Oshkosh

Judith Levine, Farmingdale State University

Judith Luckett, University of Central Florida

Betty Magjuka, Gloucester County College

Laurell Malone, North Carolina Central University

Lloyd McCraney, Towson University

Melanie J. McGill, Stephen F. Austin State University

Lienne Medford, Clemson University

Janet Medina, McDaniel College

DeAnn Miller-Boschert, North Dakota State University

Greg Morris, Grand Rapids Community College

Pamela Nesselrodt, Dickinson College

Joe Nichols, Indiana University–Purdue University Fort Wayne

Kathryn Parr, University of Florida

Jonathan Plucker, Indiana University

Linda Robertello, Iona College

Paul Rufino, Gloucester County College

Lisa Ruiz-Lee, University of Nevada, Las Vegas

Carol Scatena, Lewis University

Tom Scheft, North Carolina Central University

Diane Serafin, Luzerne County Community College–Shamokin

Joshua S. Smith, University of Albany

Donald Snead, Middle Tennessee State University

Louise Soares, University of New Haven

Theresa Sullivan Stewart, University of Illinois at Springfield

Larry Templeton, Ferris State University

Leo Theriot, Central Bible College

Melaine Timko, National University

Diana Treahy, Point Loma Nazarene University

Kathleen Waldron-Soler, Eastern Washington University

George Watson, Marshall University

Roberta Wiener, Pace University

Betty Wood, University of Arkansas at Little Rock

Priscilla Wright, Colorado Christian University

Ronald Zigler, Pennsylvania State University–Abington

Wilkins-O'Riley Zinn, Southern Oregon University

I am also grateful to contributors to previous editions, such as Thomas Andre, Curtis Bonk, Mary Jane Caffey, Sandra Damico, Melissa Dark, Stacie Goffin, Gordon Greenwood, Chuck Greiner, Carole Grove, Andrea Guillaume, Millie Harris, Johanna Keirns, Judy Lewandowski, Elizabeth Sterling, Kathryn Wentzel, and William Zangwill.

I'd also like to thank my Pearson Vice President and Editor-in-Chief, Paul Smith, and Managing Editor, Shannon Steed, as well as Nancy Forsyth, President. I am also grateful to the editorial production team at Omegatype Typography and to the education team at Pearson who helped bring this edition to fruition: Annette Joseph, Production Editor; Joanna Sabella, Marketing Manager; Linda Knowles, Cover Administrator; and Matthew Buchholz, Editorial Assistant. I am grateful to Sharon Fox and Susan Davis of the Success for All Foundation for work on all aspects of the book—including typing, updating references, proofreading, and lending general good sense—and to James Bravo, the talented artist behind the cartoons.

This book was written while I was supported in part by grants from the Institute of Education Sciences, U.S. Department of Education (No. R305A040082). However, any opinions I have are mine alone and do not represent IES positions or policy.

R. E. S.

Educational Psychology

1

Educational Psychology: A Foundation for Teaching

GeoStock/Photodisc/Getty Images

At the end of this chapter, you should be able to:

- Identify attributes of effective teachers
- Describe the role of educational research in informing classroom practice
- Describe the research methods used in educational psychology and the rationale for each
- Discuss how you can become an intentional teacher

Ellen Mathis is baffled. She is a new teacher trying to teach creative writing to her third-grade class, but things are just not going the way she'd hoped. Her students are not producing much, and what they do write is not very imaginative and full of errors. For example, she recently assigned a composition on "My Summer Vacation," and all that one of her students wrote was "On my summer vacation I got a dog and we went swimming and I got stinged by a bee."

Ellen wonders whether her students are just not ready for writing and need several months of work on such skills as capitalization, punctuation, and usage before she tries another writing assignment. However, one day Ellen notices some compositions in the hall outside of Leah Washington's class. Leah's third-graders are just like Ellen's, but their compositions are fabulous. The students wrote pages of interesting material on an astonishing array of topics. At the end of the day, Ellen catches Leah in the hall. "How do you get your kids to write such great compositions?" she asks.

Leah explains how she first got her children writing on topics they cared about and then gradually introduced "mini-lessons" to help them become better authors. She had the students work in small groups and help one another plan compositions. Then the students critiqued and helped edit one another's drafts, before finally "publishing" final versions.

"I'll tell you what," Leah offers. "I'll schedule my next writing class during your planning period. Come see what we're doing."

Ellen agrees. When the time comes, she walks into Leah's class and is overwhelmed by what she sees. Children are writing everywhere: on the floor, in groups, at tables. Many are talking with partners. Leah is conferencing with individual children. Ellen looks over the children's shoulders and sees one student writing about

her pets, another writing a gory story about ninjas, and another writing about a dream. Marta Delgrado, a student who is Mexican American, is writing a funny story about her second-grade teacher's attempts to speak Spanish. One student is even writing a very detailed story about her summer vacation!

After school, Ellen meets with Leah. She is full of questions. "How did you get students to do all that writing? How can you manage all that noise and activity? How did you learn to do this?"

"I did go to a series of workshops on teaching writing," Leah said. "But if you think about it, everything I'm doing is basic educational psychology."

Ellen is amazed. "Educational psychology? I got an A in that course in college, but I don't see what it has to do with your writing program."

"Well, let's see," said Leah. "To begin with, I'm using a lot of motivational strategies I learned in ed psych. For instance, when I started my writing instruction this year, I read students some funny and intriguing stories written by other classes, to arouse their curiosity. I got them motivated by letting them write about whatever they wanted, and also by having 'writing celebrations' in which students read their finished compositions to the class for applause and comments. My educational psychology professor was always talking about adapting to students' needs. I do this by conferencing with students and helping them with the specific problems they're having. I first learned about cooperative learning in ed psych, and later on I took some workshops on it. I use cooperative learning groups to let students give each other immediate feedback on their writing, to let them model effective writing for each other, and to get them to encourage each other to write. The groups also solve a lot of my management problems by keeping each other on task and dealing with many classroom routines. I remember that we learned about evaluation in ed psych. I use a flexible form of evaluation. Everybody eventually gets an A on his or her composition, but only when it meets a high standard, which may take many drafts. I apply what we learned about child development just about every day. For example, I adapt to students' developmental levels and cultural styles by encouraging them to write about things that matter to them: If dinosaurs or video games are important right now, or if children are uncomfortable about being Muslim or Jewish at Christmas time, that's what they should write about!"

Ellen is impressed. She and Leah arrange to visit each other's classes a few more times to exchange ideas and observations, and in time, Ellen's writers are almost as good as Leah's. But what is particularly important to her is the idea that educational psychology can really be useful in her day-to-day teaching. She drags out her old textbook and finds that concepts that had seemed theoretical and abstract in her ed psych class actually help her think about current teaching challenges.

What is **educational psychology?** An academic definition would perhaps say that educational psychology is the study of learners, learning, and teaching (Reynolds & Miller, 2003). However, for students who are or expect to be teachers, educational psychology is something more. It is the accumulated knowledge, wisdom, and seat-of-the-pants theory that every teacher should possess to intelligently solve the daily problems of teaching. Educational psychology cannot tell you as a teacher what to do, but it can give you the principles to use in making a good decision and a language to discuss your experiences and thinking. Consider the case of Ellen Mathis and Leah Washington. Nothing in this or any other educational psychology text will tell you exactly how to teach creative writing to a particular group of third-graders. However, Leah uses concepts of educational psychology to consider how she will teach writing and then to interpret and solve problems she runs into, as well as to explain to Ellen what she is doing. Educational psychologists carry out research on the nature of students and effective methods of teaching to understand principles of learning and give educators the information they need to think critically about their craft and make teaching decisions that will work for their students (Alexander, 2004).

What Makes a Good Teacher

What makes a good teacher? Is it warmth, humor, and the ability to care about people? Is it planning, hard work, and self-discipline? What about leadership, enthusiasm, a contagious love of learning, and speaking ability? Most people would agree that all of these qualities are needed to make a good teacher, and they would certainly be correct (see Wayne & Youngs, 2003). But these qualities are not enough.

■ Knowing the Subject Matters (But So Does Teaching Skill)

There is an old joke that goes like this:

Question: What do you need to know to be able to teach a horse?
Answer: More than the horse!

educational psychology

The study of learning and teaching.

This joke makes the obvious point that the first thing a teacher must have is some knowledge or skills that the learner does not have; you must know the subject matter you plan to teach. But if you think about teaching horses (or children), you will soon realize that although subject matter knowledge is necessary, it is not enough. A rancher may have a good idea of how a horse is supposed to act and what a horse is supposed to be able to do, but if he doesn't have the skills to make an untrained, scared, and unfriendly animal into a good saddle horse, he's going to end up with nothing but broken ribs and teeth marks for his trouble. Children are a lot smarter and a little more forgiving than horses, but teaching them has this in common with teaching horses: Knowledge of how to transmit information and skills is at least as important as knowledge of the information and skills themselves. We have all had teachers (most often college professors, unfortunately) who were brilliant and thoroughly knowledgeable in their fields but who could not teach. Ellen Mathis may know as much as Leah Washington about what good writing should be, but she has a lot to learn about how to get third-graders to write well.

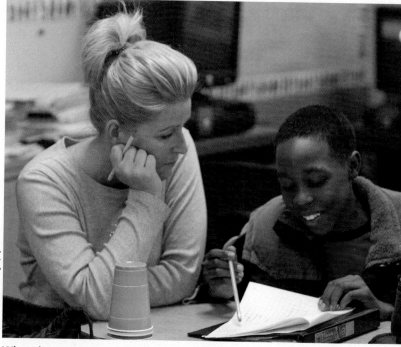

Bob Daemmrich Photography

What characteristics of good teaching might this expert teacher possess? What behaviors does she demonstrate that might make her an effective teacher?

For effective teaching, subject matter knowledge is not a question of being a walking encyclopedia. Vast knowledge is readily available. However, effective teachers not only know their subjects but also can communicate their knowledge to students. The celebrated high school math teacher Jaime Escalante taught the concept of positive and negative numbers to students in a Los Angeles barrio by explaining that when you dig a hole, you might call the pile of dirt +1, the hole −1. What do you get when you put the dirt back in the hole? Zero. Escalante's ability to relate the abstract concept of positive and negative numbers to everyday experience is one example of how the ability to communicate knowledge goes far beyond simply knowing the facts.

■ Mastering Teaching Skills

The link between what a teacher wants students to learn and students' actual learning is called *instruction*, or **pedagogy.** Effective instruction is not a simple matter of one person with more knowledge transmitting that knowledge to another. If telling were teaching, this book would be unnecessary. Rather, effective instruction demands the use of many strategies.

For example, suppose Paula Ray wants to teach a lesson on statistics to a diverse class of fourth-graders. To do so, Paula must accomplish many related tasks. She must make sure that the class is orderly and that students know what behavior is expected of them. She must find out whether students have the prerequisite skills; for example, students need to be able to add and divide to find averages. If any do not, Paula must find a way to teach students those skills. She must engage students in activities that lead them toward an understanding of statistics, such as having students roll dice, play cards, or collect data from experiments; and she must use teaching strategies that help students remember what they have been taught. The lessons should also take into account the intellectual and social characteristics of students in the fourth grade and the intellectual, social, and cultural characteristics of these particular students. Paula must make sure that students are interested in the lesson and motivated to learn statistics. To see whether students are

pedagogy

The study of teaching and learning with applications to the instructional process.

learning what is being taught, she may ask questions or use quizzes or have students demonstrate their understanding by setting up and interpreting experiments, and she must respond appropriately if these assessments show that students are having problems. After the series of lessons on statistics ends, Paula should review this topic from time to time to ensure that it is remembered.

These tasks—motivating students, managing the classroom, assessing prior knowledge, communicating ideas effectively, taking into account the characteristics of the learners, assessing learning outcomes, and reviewing information—must be attended to at all levels of education, in or out of schools. They apply as much to the training of astronauts as to the teaching of reading. How these tasks are accomplished, however, differs widely according to the ages of the students, the objectives of instruction, and other factors.

What makes a good teacher is the ability to carry out all the tasks involved in effective instruction (Burden & Byrd, 2003; Kennedy, 2006). Warmth, enthusiasm, and caring are essential (Cornelius-White, 2007; Eisner, 2006), as is subject matter knowledge and understanding of how children learn (Wiggins & McTighe, 2006). But it is the successful accomplishment of all the tasks of teaching that makes for instructional effectiveness (Shulman, 2000).

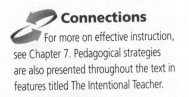

Connections

For more on effective instruction, see Chapter 7. Pedagogical strategies are also presented throughout the text in features titled The Intentional Teacher.

INTASC

5 Classroom Motivation and Management

■ Can Good Teaching Be Taught?

Some people think that good teachers are born that way. Outstanding teachers sometimes seem to have a magic, a charisma that mere mortals could never hope to achieve. Yet research has begun to identify the specific behaviors and skills that make a "magic" teacher (Borman & Kimball, 2005). An outstanding teacher does nothing that any other teacher cannot also do—it is just a question of knowing the principles of effective teaching and how to apply them. Take one small example: In a high school history class, two students in the back of the class are whispering to each other, and they are not discussing the Treaty of Paris! The teacher slowly walks toward them without looking, continuing his lesson as he walks. The students stop whispering and pay attention. If you didn't know what to look for, you might miss this brief but critical interchange and believe that the teacher just has a way with students, a knack for keeping their attention. But the teacher is simply applying principles of classroom management that anyone could learn: Maintain momentum in the lesson, deal with behavior problems by using the mildest intervention that will work, and resolve minor problems before they become major ones. When Jaime Escalante gave the example of digging a hole to illustrate the concept of positive and negative numbers, he was also applying several important principles of educational psychology: Make abstract ideas concrete by using many examples, relate the content of instruction to the students' background, state rules, give examples, and then restate rules.

"If only I could get to my ed psych text . . ."

Can good teaching be taught? The answer is definitely yes. Good teaching has to be observed and practiced, but there are principles of good teaching that teachers need to know, which can then be applied in the classroom. The major components of effective instruction are summarized in Figure 1.1.

■ The Intentional Teacher

There is no formula for good teaching, no seven steps to Teacher of the Year. Teaching involves planning and preparation, and then dozens of decisions every hour. Yet one attribute seems to be characteristic of outstanding teachers: **intentionality.** Intentionality means doing things for a reason, on purpose. Intentional teachers will constantly think about the outcomes they want for their students and about how each decision they make moves children toward those outcomes. Intentional teachers know that maximum learning does not happen by chance. Yes, children do learn in unplanned ways all the time, and many will learn from even the most chaotic lesson. But to really challenge students, to

intentionality

Doing things for a purpose; teachers who use intentionality plan their actions based on the outcomes they want to achieve.

FIGURE 1.1 Components of Good Teaching

Knowledge of subject and teaching resources

Critical-thinking and problem-solving skills

Decision Making

Self-Knowledge and Self-Regulation

GOOD TEACHING

Reflection

Application of Education Research

Knowledge of students and their learning

Teaching and communication skills

get their best efforts, to help them make conceptual leaps and organize and retain new knowledge, teachers need to be purposeful, thoughtful, and flexible, without ever losing sight of their goals for every child. In a word, they need to be *intentional*.

The idea that teachers should always do things for a reason seems obvious, and in principle it is. Yet in practice, it is difficult to constantly make certain that all students are engaged in activities that lead to important learning outcomes (Kennedy, 2008). Teachers very frequently fall into strategies that they themselves would recognize, on reflection, as being time fillers rather than instructionally essential activities. For example, an otherwise outstanding third-grade teacher once assigned seatwork to one of her reading groups. The children were given two sheets of paper with words in squares. Their task was to cut out the squares on one sheet and then paste them onto synonyms

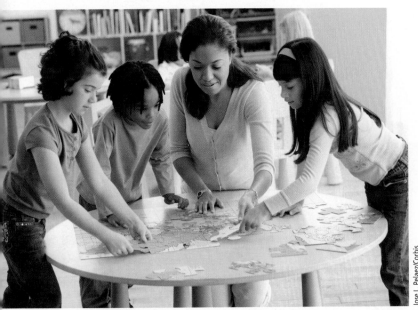

Jose L. Pelaez/Corbis

What do you need to know about your students in order to be an intentional teacher? How can you help your students achieve success?

on the other. When all the words were pasted correctly, lines on the pasted squares would form an outline of a cat, which the children were then to color. Once the children pasted a few squares, the puzzle became clear, so they could paste the remainder without paying any attention to the words themselves. For almost an hour of precious class time, these children happily cut, pasted, and colored—not high-priority skills for third-graders. The teacher would have said that the objective was for children to learn or practice synonyms, of course; but in fact the activity could not possibly have moved the children forward on that skill. Similarly, many teachers have one child laboriously work a problem on the chalkboard while the rest of the class has nothing important to do. Many secondary teachers spend most of the class period going over homework and classwork and end up doing very little teaching of new content. Again, these may be excellent teachers in other ways, but they sometimes lose sight of what they are trying to achieve and how they are going to achieve it.

Intentional teachers are constantly asking themselves what goals they and their students are trying to accomplish. Is each portion of their lesson appropriate to students' background knowledge, skills, and needs? Is each activity or assignment clearly related to a valued outcome? Is each instructional minute used wisely and well? An intentional teacher trying to build students' synonym skills during follow-up time might have them work in pairs to master a set of synonyms in preparation for individual quizzes. An intentional teacher might have all children work a given problem while one works at the board, so that all can compare answers and strategies together. An intentional teacher might quickly give homework answers for students to check themselves, ask for a show of hands for correct answers, and then review and reteach only those exercises missed by many students to save time for teaching of new content. An intentional teacher uses a wide variety of instructional methods, experiences, assignments, and materials to be sure that children are achieving all sorts of cognitive objectives, from knowledge to application to creativity, and that at the same time children are learning important affective objectives, such as love of learning, respect for others, and personal responsibility. An intentional teacher constantly reflects on his or her practices and outcomes.

Research finds that one of the most powerful predictors of a teacher's impact on students is the belief that what he or she does makes a difference. This belief, called **teacher efficacy** (Henson, 2002; Tschannen-Moran & Woolfolk Hoy, 2001), is at the heart of what it means to be an intentional teacher. Teachers who believe that success in school is almost entirely due to children's inborn intelligence, home environment, or other factors that teachers cannot influence are unlikely to teach in the same way as those who believe that their own efforts are the key to children's learning. An intentional teacher, one who has a strong belief in her or his efficacy, is more likely to put forth consistent effort, to persist in the face of obstacles, and to keep trying relentlessly until every student succeeds (Bandura, 1997). Intentional teachers achieve a sense of efficacy by constantly assessing the results of their instruction (Schmoker, 1999); trying new strategies if their initial instruction doesn't work; and continually seeking ideas from colleagues, books, magazines, workshops, and other sources to enrich and solidify their teaching skills (Corbett, Wilson, & Williams, 2005). Collective efficacy can have a particularly strong impact on student achievement (Goddard, Hoy, & Hoy, 2000). Groups of teachers, such as the entire faculty

teacher efficacy

The degree to which teachers feel that their own efforts determine the success of their students.

of an elementary school or all teachers in a given academic department, can attain collective efficacy by working together to examine their practices and outcomes, seeking professional development, and helping each other succeed (see Borko, 2004; Sachs, 2000; York-Barr, Sommerness, & Hur, 2008).

The most important purpose of this book is to give you, tomorrow's teacher, the intellectual grounding in research, theory, and practical wisdom you will need in order to become an intentional, effective teacher. To plan and carry out effective lessons, discussions, projects, and other learning experiences, teachers need to know a great deal. Besides knowing your subjects, you need to understand the developmental levels and needs of your students. You need to understand how learning, memory, problem-solving skill, and creativity are acquired and how to promote their acquisition. You need to know how to set objectives, organize activities designed to help students attain those objectives, and assess students' progress toward them. You need to know how to motivate children, how to use class time effectively, and how to respond to individual differences among students. Intentional teachers are continually experimenting with strategies to solve problems of instruction and then observing the results of their actions to see if they were effective (Duck, 2000). They pay attention to research on effective teaching and incorporate research findings in their daily teaching (Fleischman, 2006). Like Leah Washington in the vignette that opened this chapter, intentional teachers are constantly combining their knowledge of principles of educational psychology, their experience, and their creativity to make instructional decisions and help children become enthusiastic and effective learners.

This text highlights the ideas that are central to educational psychology and the related research. It also presents many examples of how these ideas apply in practice, emphasizing teaching practices, not only theory or suggestions, that have been evaluated and found to be effective. The text is designed to help you develop **critical-thinking** skills for teaching: a logical and systematic approach to the many dilemmas that are found in practice and research. No text can provide all the right answers for teaching, but this one tries to pose the right questions and to engage you by presenting realistic alternatives and the concepts and research behind them.

Many studies have looked at the differences between expert and novice teachers and between more and less effective teachers. One theme comes through these studies: Expert teachers are critical thinkers (Hogan, Rabinowitz, & Craven, 2003; Mosenthal, Lipson, Torncello, Russ, & Mekkelsen, 2004; Shulman, 2000). Intentional teachers are constantly upgrading and examining their own teaching practices, reading and attending conferences to learn new ideas, and using their own students' responses to guide their instructional decisions. There's an old saying to the effect that there are teachers with 20 years of experience and there are teachers with 1 year of experience 20 times. Teachers who get better each year are the ones who are open to new ideas and who look at their own teaching critically. Perhaps the most important goal of this book is to get you in the habit of using informed reflection to become one of tomorrow's expert teachers.

■ 21st Century Skills

Back when I was growing up, the 21st century was expected to be totally different from the 20th. The Jetsons, for example, projected an image of flying cars, robots in every home, and all sorts of amazing technology. More serious futurologists expected more or less the same. The reality has turned out to be a little more prosaic, but nevertheless, developments in technology and globalization have dramatically changed key aspects of our economy and society. In particular, economic security, for both individuals and for nations, depends more than ever on innovation, creativity, and design. The ability to work cooperatively with others, to see many solutions to problems, and to be flexible and responsive to rapid change are all becoming keys to success, as traditional "strong back" jobs disappear to be replaced by "strong mind" careers.

critical thinking
Evaluation of conclusions through logical and systematic examination of the problem, the evidence, and the solution.

All of these changes have profound significance for education. They lead educators to put a strong value on skills, attitudes, and ways of working that more closely resemble new workforce conditions. It should go without saying that students need extensive experience with technology, but that is not enough. They also need extensive experience working in groups, solving problems, and learning to read critically and think creatively. Ironically, these kinds of experiences are at the core of the progressive philosophy of John Dewey and many others, which date back to the beginning of the 20th century (Rotherham & Willingham, 2009). What has changed is that these ideas are no longer optional, as they happen to correspond to today's needs. Moreover, these skills are now needed for everyone, from the executive office to the shop floor.

Consistent with this line of reasoning, a Partnership for 21st Century Skills has been created to promote policies defining and supporting student outcomes that align with today's needs (see P. Johnson, 2009; Partnership for 21st Century Skills, 2009). The Partnership has created a framework that organizes 21st century skills in four categories, synthesizing suggestions from dozens of stakeholder groups at all levels of education:

1. Core subjects and 21st century themes (such as language arts, mathematics, science, global awareness, and financial literacy) (see Cutshall, 2009; Hersh, 2009; Trefil & O'Brien-Trefil, 2009; Zhao, 2009)

2. Learning and innovation skills (such as creativity, critical thinking, and problem solving) (see Azzam, 2009; Graseck, 2009)

3. Information, media, and technology skills (see Barab, Gresalfi, & Arici, 2009; Ferriter, 2009a,b; Sprenger, 2009)

4. Life and career skills (such as initiative and self-direction) (see Gerdes & Ljung, 2009)

Throughout this book, a new feature presents information on 21st century learning that relates to the topic of the chapter. Beyond this, 21st century skills are discussed throughout the main parts of the text, as appropriate.

Educational policies and practices usually lag behind changes in society and the economy. The emphasis on 21st century skills is intended to help you think more deeply about how each of the decisions you make about curriculum, teaching methods, use of technology, assessments, and so on contribute to helping students succeed not only by today's standards, but also in tomorrow's world.

What Is the Role of Research in Educational Psychology ?

Teachers who are intentional, critical thinkers are likely to enter classrooms equipped with knowledge about research in educational psychology. Every year, educational psychologists discover or refine principles of teaching and learning that are useful for practicing teachers. Some of these principles are just common sense backed up with evidence, but others are more surprising. One problem educational psychologists face is that almost everyone has ideas on the subject of educational psychology. Most adults have spent many years in schools watching what teachers do. Add to that a certain amount of knowledge of human nature, and *voila!* Everyone is an amateur educational psychologist. For this reason, professional educational psychologists are often accused of studying the obvious (see Ball & Forzani, 2007).

However, as we have painfully learned, the obvious is not always true. For example, most people assume that if students are assigned to classes according to their ability, the resulting narrower range of abilities in a class will let the teacher adapt instruction to the specific needs of the students and thereby increase student achievement. This assumption

Connections

For more on ability grouping, see Chapter 9, pages 253–254.

turns out to be false. Many teachers believe that scolding students for misbehavior will improve conduct. Many students will indeed respond to a scolding by behaving better, but for others, scolding may be a reward for misbehavior that actually increases it. Some "obvious" truths even conflict with one another. For example, most people would agree that students learn better from a teacher's instruction than by working alone. This belief supports teacher-centered direct instructional strategies, in which a teacher actively works with the class as a whole. However, most people would also agree that students often need instruction tailored to their individual needs. This belief, also correct, would demand that you divide your time among individuals, or at least among groups of students with differing needs, which would result in some students working independently while others received your attention. If schools could provide tutors for every student, there would be no conflict; direct instruction and individualization could coexist. In practice, however, classrooms typically have 20 or more students; as a result, more direct instruction (the first goal) almost always means less individualization (the second goal). Your task as an intentional teacher is to balance these competing goals according to the needs of particular students and situations.

Connections
For more on effectively handling misbehavior, see Chapter 5, pages 121–122.

■ The Goal of Research in Educational Psychology

The goal of research in educational psychology is to carefully examine obvious as well as less-than-obvious questions, using objective methods to test ideas about the factors that contribute to learning (Levin, O'Donnell, & Kratochwill, 2003; McComb & Scott-Little, 2003). The products of this research are principles, laws, and theories. A **principle** explains the relationship between factors, such as the effects of alternative grading systems on student motivation. Laws are simply principles that have been thoroughly tested and found to apply in a wide variety of situations. A **theory** is a set of related principles and laws that explains a broad aspect of learning, behavior, or another area of interest. Without theories the facts and principles that are discovered would be like disorganized specks on a canvas. Theories tie together these facts and principles to give us the big picture. However, the same facts and principles may be interpreted in different ways by different theorists. As in any science, progress in educational psychology is slow and uneven. A single study is rarely a breakthrough, but over time evidence accumulates on a subject and allows theorists to refine and extend their theories.

■ The Value of Research in Educational Psychology to You the Teacher

It is probably true that the most important knowledge teachers gain is learned on the job—in internships, while student teaching, or during their first years in the classroom (Darling-Hammond, Gendler, & Wise, 1990). However, you as a teacher make hundreds of decisions every day, and each decision has a theory behind it, regardless of whether you are aware of it. The quality, accuracy, and usefulness of those theories are what ultimately determine your success. For example, one teacher may offer a prize to the student with the best attendance, on the theory that rewarding attendance will increase it. Another may reward the student whose attendance is most improved, on the theory that it is poor attenders who most need incentives to come to class. A third may not reward anyone for attendance but instead try to increase attendance by teaching more interesting lessons. Which teacher's plan is most likely to succeed? This depends in large part on the ability of each teacher to understand the unique combination of factors that shape the character of her or his classroom and therefore to apply the most appropriate theory.

principle
Explanation of the relationship between factors, such as the effects of alternative grading systems on student motivation.

theory
A set of principles that explains and relates certain phenomena.

■ Teaching as Decision Making

The aim of research in educational psychology is to test the various theories that guide the actions of teachers and others involved in education. There are many common situations, such as the following example, in which a teacher might use educational psychology.

Mr. Harris teaches an eighth-grade social studies class. He has a problem with Tom, who frequently misbehaves. Today, Tom makes a paper airplane and flies it across the room when Mr. Harris turns his back, to the delight of the entire class.

What should Mr. Harris do?

As an intentional teacher, Mr. Harris considers a range of options for solving this problem, each of which comes from a theory about why Tom is misbehaving and what will motivate him to behave more appropriately.

Action	**Theory**
1. Reprimand Tom.	1. A reprimand is a form of punishment. Tom will behave to avoid punishment.
2. Ignore Tom.	2. Attention may be rewarding to Tom. Ignoring him would deprive him of this reward.
3. Send Tom to the office.	3. Being sent to the office is punishing. It also deprives Tom of the (apparent) support of his classmates.
4. Tell the class that it is everyone's responsibility to maintain a good learning environment and that if any student misbehaves, 5 minutes will be subtracted from recess.	4. Tom is misbehaving to get his classmates' attention. If the whole class loses out when he misbehaves, the class will keep him in line.
5. Explain to the class that Tom's behavior is interfering with lessons that all students need to know and that his behavior goes against the rules the class set for itself at the beginning of the year.	5. The class holds standards of behavior that conflict with both Tom's behavior in class and the class's reaction to it. By reminding the class of its own needs (to learn the lesson) and its own rules set at the beginning of the year, the teacher might make Tom see that the class does not really support his behavior.

Each of these actions is a common response to misbehavior. But which theory (and therefore which action) is correct?

The key might be in the fact that his classmates laugh when Tom misbehaves. This response is a clue that Tom is seeking their attention. If Mr. Harris scolds Tom, this might increase Tom's status in the eyes of his peers and thus reward his behavior. Ignoring misbehavior might be a good idea if a student is acting up to get your attention, but in this case it is apparently the class's attention that Tom is seeking. Sending Tom to the office does deprive him of his classmates' attention and therefore may be effective. But what if Tom is looking for a way to get out of class to avoid work? What if he struts out to confront the powers that be, to the obvious approval of his classmates? Making the entire class responsible for each student's behavior is likely to deprive Tom of his classmates' support and to improve his behavior; but some students may think that it is unfair to punish them for another student's misbehavior. Finally, reminding the class (and Tom) of its own interest in learning and its usual standards of behavior might work if the class does, in fact, value academic achievement and good behavior.

Research in education and psychology bears directly on the decision Mr. Harris must make. Developmental research indicates that as students enter adolescence, the peer group becomes all-important to them, and they try to establish their independence

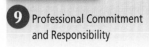

INTASC

9 Professional Commitment and Responsibility

from adult control, often by flouting or ignoring rules. Basic research on behavioral learning theories shows that when a behavior is repeated many times, some reward must be encouraging the behavior, and that if the behavior is to be eliminated, the reward must first be identified and removed. This research would also suggest that Mr. Harris consider problems with the use of punishment (such as scolding) to stop undesirable behavior. Research on specific classroom management strategies has identified effective methods to use both to prevent a student like Tom from misbehaving in the first place and to deal with his misbehavior when it does occur. Finally, research on rule setting and classroom standards indicates that student participation in setting rules can help convince each student that the class as a whole values academic achievement and appropriate behavior, and that this belief can help keep individual students in line.

Richard Hutchings/PhotoEdit

Teachers face a number of difficult, and sometimes unexpected, decisions every day and have to be able to respond quickly and appropriately. How can you become an intentional teacher?

Armed with this information, Mr. Harris can choose a response to Tom's behavior based on an understanding of why Tom is doing what he is doing and what strategies are available to deal with the situation. He may or may not make the right choice, but because he knows several theories that could explain Tom's behavior, he will be able to observe the outcomes of his strategy and, if it is ineffective, to learn from that and try something else that will work. Research does not give Mr. Harris a specific solution; that requires his own experience and judgment. But research does give Mr. Harris basic concepts of human behavior to help him understand Tom's motivations and an array of proven methods that might solve the problem. And using research to help him make teaching decisions is one way Mr. Harris can achieve a sense of his own efficacy as a teacher.

Theory into Practice
Teaching as Decision Making

If there were no educational problems to solve, there would be no need for teachers to function as professionals. Professionals distinguish themselves from nonprofessionals in part by the fact that they must make decisions that influence the course of their work.

You must decide (1) how to recognize problems and issues, (2) how to consider situations from multiple perspectives, (3) how to call up relevant professional knowledge to formulate actions, (4) how to take the most appropriate action, and (5) how to judge the consequences.

For example, Ms. O'Hara has a student named Shanika in her social studies class. Most of the time, Shanika is rather quiet and withdrawn. Her permanent record indicates considerable academic ability, but a casual observer would never know it. Ms. O'Hara asks herself the following questions:

Connections
For more on multiculturalism, see Chapter 4.

1. What problems do I perceive in this situation? Is Shanika bored, tired, uninterested, or shy, or might her participation be inhibited by something I or others are doing or not doing? What theories of educational psychology might I consider?

2. I wonder what Shanika thinks about being in this class. Does she feel excluded? Does she care about the subject matter? Is she concerned about what I or others think about her lack of participation? Why or why not? What theories of motivation will help me make a decision?

3. What do I know from theory, research, or practice that might guide my actions to involve Shanika more directly in class activities?

4. What might I actually do in this situation to enhance Shanika's involvement?

5. How would I know if I were successful with Shanika?

If Ms. O'Hara asks and tries to answer these questions—not only in the case of Shanika, of course, but at other times as well—she will improve her chances to learn about her work from doing her work. Philosopher John Dewey taught that the problems teachers face are the natural stimuli for reflective inquiry. Intentional teachers accept challenges and think productively about them.

■ Research + Common Sense = Effective Teaching

As the case of Mr. Harris illustrates, no theory, no research, no book can tell teachers what to do in a given situation. Making the right decisions depends on the context within which the problem arises, the objectives you have in mind, and many other factors, all of which must be assessed in the light of educated common sense. For example, research in mathematics instruction usually finds that a rapid pace of instruction increases achievement (Good, Grouws, & Ebmeier, 1983). Yet you may quite legitimately slow down and spend a lot of time on a concept that is particularly critical or may let students take time to discover a mathematical principle on their own. It is usually much more efficient (that is, it takes less time) to teach students skills or information directly than it is to let them make discoveries for themselves, but if you want students to gain a deeper understanding of a topic or to know how to find information or to figure things out for themselves, then the research findings about pace can be temporarily shelved.

The point is that although research in educational psychology can sometimes be translated directly to the classroom, it is best to apply the principles with a hefty dose of common sense and a clear view of what is being taught to whom and for what purpose.

■ Research on Effective Programs

Research in educational psychology not only provides evidence for principles of effective practice but also about the effectiveness of particular programs or practices (Fleischman, 2006). For example, in the vignette at the beginning of this chapter, Leah Washington uses a specific approach to creative writing instruction that has been extensively evaluated as a whole (Harris & Graham, 1996a). In other words, there is evidence that, on average, children whose teachers are using such methods learn to write better than those whose teachers use more traditional approaches. There is evidence on the effectiveness of dozens of widely used programs, from methods in particular subjects to strategies for reforming entire schools (see, for example, Dynarski, 2008/2009; Ellis, 2001b; Gunter, Estes, & Schwab, 2003; Slavin, Cheung, Groff, & Lake, 2008; Slavin & Lake, 2008; Slavin, Lake, Chambers, et al., 2009; Slavin, Lake, & Groff, 2009). An intentional teacher should be aware of research on programs for his or her subject and grade level and should be willing to seek out professional development opportunities in methods known to make a difference for children.

ON THE WEB

For educator-friendly reviews of research on effective programs, see www.bestevidence.org and www.ies.ed.gov/ncee/wwc.

■ Impact of Research on Educational Practice

Many researchers and educators have bemoaned the limited impact of research in educational psychology on teachers' practices (see, for example, Kennedy, 2008). Indeed, research in education has nowhere near as great an impact on practice as research in medicine (Riehl, 2006). Yet research in education does have a profound indirect impact on educational practice (Hattie & Marsh, 1996), even if teachers are not aware of it. It affects educational policies, professional development programs, and teaching materials. For example, the Tennessee class size study (Finn, Pannozzo, & Achilles, 2003), which found important effects of class size in the early grades on student achievement, had a direct impact on state and federal proposals for class size reduction (Wasley, 2002). Research on beginning reading (National Reading Panel, 2000) has begun to dramatically transform curriculum, instruction, and professional development for this subject. Research on the effects of career academies in high schools (Kemple, 1997) has led to a substantial increase in such programs.

It is important for you to become an intelligent consumer of research, not to take every finding or every expert's pronouncement as truth from Mount Olympus (Fleischman, 2006). The following section briefly describes the methods of research that most often produce findings of use to educators.

"In light of research on class size, we're not cutting class, we're helping our classmates get a better education!"

Theory into Practice
How to Be an Intelligent Consumer of Educational Psychology Research

INTASC

9 Professional Commitment and Responsibility

Let's say you're in the market for a new car. Before laying out your hard-earned money, you'll probably review the findings from various consumer research reports. You may want to know something about how various cars have performed in crash tests, which cars have the best gas mileage, or the trade-in values of particular models. Before embarking on this major investment, you want to feel as confident as you can about your decision. If you've been in this situation before, you probably remember that all of your research helped you make an informed decision.

Now that you are about to enter the profession of teaching, you should apply a similar consumer orientation in your decision making. As a teacher, you will be called on to make hundreds of decisions each day. Your car-buying decision is influenced by a combination of sound research findings and common sense, and your decisions about teaching and learning should follow this same pattern. Teaching and learning are complex concepts subject to a wide variety of influences, so your knowledge of relevant research will serve to guide you into making informed choices.

How can knowing the simple formula *research + common sense = effective teaching* help you to be a more intelligent consumer of educational psychology research? The following recommendations show how you can put this formula into practice:

1. *Be a consumer of relevant research.* It's obvious you can't apply what you don't know. As a professional, you have a responsibility to maintain a working knowledge of relevant research. In addition to your course textbooks, which will be excellent resources for you in the future, you should become familiar with the professional journals in your field. You may want to review the following journals, which typically present research that has direct application for classroom practices: *Educational Psychologist, Journal of Educational Psychology,* and *American Educational Research Journal.* In addition, check out *Annual Editions: Educational Psychology,* a yearly publication that reprints articles from various professional journals. Also, don't overlook the value of networking with other teachers, face to face or via the Internet. The example of Ellen Mathis and Leah Washington is an excellent illustration of how collaboration can expand your research base.

2. *Teach intentionally.* Although there is no recipe for the ingredients that make up a commonsense approach to teaching, the behaviors consistent with being an intentional teacher are about as close as we can get. Intentional teachers are thoughtful. Like Mr. Harris, you should consider multiple perspectives on classroom situations. When you take action, be purposeful and think about why you do what you do. Like other intentional teachers, you can follow your actions with careful reflection, evaluating whether your actions have resulted in the desired outcomes. You probably learned about the "scientific method" sometime during high school. Intentional teachers employ such a method in teaching, formulating a working hypothesis based on observations and background knowledge, collecting data to test the hypothesis, effectively organizing and analyzing the data, drawing sound conclusions based on the data, and taking a course of action based on the conclusions. For many experienced teachers, this cycle becomes automatic and internalized. When applied systematically, these practices can serve to validate research and theory and, as a result, increase your growing professional knowledge base.

3. *Share your experiences.* When you combine knowledge of research with your professional common sense, you will find yourself engaged in more effective practices. As you and your students experience success, share your findings. Avenues for dissemination are endless. In addition to publishing articles in traditional sources such as professional journals and organizational newsletters, don't overlook the importance of preparing schoolwide in-service demonstrations, papers for state and national professional conferences, and presentations to school boards. In addition, the Internet offers various newsgroups where teachers engage in ongoing discussions about their work.

What Research Methods Are Used in Educational Psychology?

How do we know what we know in educational psychology? As in any scientific field, knowledge comes from many sources. Sometimes researchers study schools, teachers, or students as they are, and sometimes they create special programs, or **treatments,** and study their effects on one or more **variables** (anything that can have more than one value, such as age, sex, achievement level, or attitudes). There is no one best or most useful approach to research; any method can be useful when applied to the right set of questions. The principal methods educational researchers use to learn about schools, teachers, students, and instruction are experiments, correlational studies, and descriptive research (see Henig, 2008/2009; Mertler & Charles, 2011; Slavin, 2008b).

treatment

A special program that is the subject of an experiment.

variable

Something that can have more than one value.

■ Experiments

In an **experiment,** researchers can create special treatments and analyze their effects. In one classic study, Lepper, Greene, and Nisbett (1973) set up an experimental situation in which children used felt-tipped markers to draw pictures. Children in the experimental group (the group that received a treatment) were given a prize (a "good player award") for drawing pictures. Children in a control group received no prizes. At the end of the experiment, all students were allowed to choose among various activities, including drawing with felt-tipped markers. The children who had received the prizes chose to continue drawing with felt-tipped markers about half as frequently as did those who had not received prizes. This result was interpreted as showing that rewarding individuals for doing a task they already liked could reduce their interest in doing the task when they were no longer rewarded.

The Lepper study illustrates several important aspects of experiments. First, the children were randomly assigned to receive prizes or not. For example, the children's names might have been put on slips of paper that were dropped into a hat and then drawn at random for assignment to a "prize" or "no-prize" group. **Random assignment** ensured that the two groups were essentially equivalent before the experiment began. This equivalence is critical because if we were not sure that the two groups were equal before the experiment, we would not be able to tell whether it was the prizes that made the difference in their subsequent behavior.

A second feature of this study characteristic of experiments is that everything other than the treatment itself (the prizes) was kept the same for the prize and no-prize groups. The children played in the same rooms with the same materials and with the same adults present. The researcher who gave the prize spent the same amount of time watching the no-prize children draw. Only the prize itself was different for the two groups. The goal was to be sure that it was the treatment, not some other factor, that explained the difference between the two groups.

LABORATORY EXPERIMENTS   The Lepper and colleagues (1973) study is an example of a **laboratory experiment.** Even though the experiment took place in a school building, the researchers created a highly artificial, structured setting that existed for a very brief period of time. The advantage of laboratory experiments is that they permit researchers to exert a very high degree of control over all the factors involved in the study. Such studies are high in **internal validity,** which is to say that we can confidently attribute any differences they find to the treatments themselves (rather than to other factors). The primary limitation of laboratory experiments is that they are typically so artificial and so brief that their results may have little relevance to real-life situations. For example, the Lepper et al. study, which was later repeated several times, was used to support a theory that rewards can diminish individuals' interest in an activity when the rewards are withdrawn. This theory served as the basis for attacks on the use of classroom rewards, such as grades and stars. However, later research in real classrooms using real rewards has generally failed to find such effects (see Cameron & Pierce, 1994). This finding does not discredit the Lepper and colleagues study; it does show that theories based on artificial laboratory experiments cannot be assumed to apply to all situations in real life but must be tested in the real settings.

RANDOMIZED FIELD EXPERIMENTS   Another kind of experiment that is often used in educational research is the **randomized field experiment,** in which instructional programs or other practical treatments are evaluated over relatively long periods in real classes under realistic conditions (Levin et al., 2003; Mosteller & Boruch, 2002). For example, Pinnell, Lyons, DeFord, Bryk, and Seltzer (1994) compared four approaches to reading instruction for at-risk first-graders for reading failure, including Reading Recovery, a one-to-one tutoring model for at-risk first-graders that requires extensive training. In each of 10 schools, the 10 lowest-performing students were identified. Four

experiment

Procedure used to test the effect of a treatment.

random assignment

Selection by chance into different treatment groups; intended to ensure equivalence of the groups.

laboratory experiment

Experiment in which conditions are highly controlled.

internal validity

The degree to which an experiment's results can be attributed to the treatment in question rather than other factors.

randomized field experiment

Experiment conducted under realistic conditions in which individuals are assigned by chance to receive different practical treatments or programs.

were assigned at random to the **experimental group** using Reading Recovery, and 6 were assigned to a control group. **Control group** students continued to receive the reading program and remedial services they would have received anyway.

After 4 months (in February), all children were tested. Reading Recovery children scored significantly higher than control students on each of four measures. The following October, students were tested again, and Reading Recovery students still performed significantly better than control students.

Note the similarities and differences between the Pinnell and colleagues (1994) randomized field experiment and the Lepper and colleagues (1973) laboratory experiment. Both used random assignment to make sure that the experimental and control groups were essentially equal at the start of the study. Both tried to make all factors except the treatment equal for the experimental and control groups, but the Pinnell and colleagues study was (by its very nature as a field experiment) less able to do this. For example, experimental and control students were taught by different teachers. Because many teachers were involved, this factor probably balanced out, but the fact remains that in a field setting, control is never as great as in a laboratory situation (see Pressley & Harris, 1994). On the other hand, the fact that the Pinnell and colleagues study took place over a long period of time in real classrooms means that its **external validity** (real-life validity) is far greater than that of the Lepper and colleagues study. That is, the results of the Pinnell and colleagues study have direct relevance to reading instruction for first-graders who are at risk.

Both laboratory experiments and randomized field experiments make important contributions to the science of educational psychology. Laboratory experiments are primarily important in researchers' efforts to build and test theories, whereas randomized field experiments are the acid test for evaluating practical programs or improvements in instruction. For example, the writing process approach of Leah Washington has been evaluated many times in comparison to traditional methods and found to be highly effective (Harris, Graham, & Pressley, 2001). This finding is not a guarantee that this method will work in every situation, but it does give you a good direction to follow to improve writing.

Recently, the U.S. Department of Education has begun to strongly emphasize research as a basis for practice in education. For example, in the No Child Left Behind Act of 2001, the phrase "based on scientifically-based research" appeared 110 times in reference to programs expected to be used under federal funding. In this context "scientifically-based research" primarily refers to studies in which experimental and control groups are assigned at random (see U.S. Department of Education, 2003), although well-designed studies comparing matched groups are also valued. These policies, and new funding to support randomized experiments, have greatly increased interest in this type of research. You can expect to see many more randomized studies in the coming years, and these studies will matter a great deal for policy and practice (see Mosteller & Boruch, 2002; Slavin, 2003).

Randomized field experiments are very difficult to conduct in education, as it is rare that teachers are willing to be assigned by chance to one group or another. For this reason, field experiments more often use matching, in which teachers or schools using one method would be matched with those using a different method or with a control group. For example, Calderón, Hertz-Lazarowitz, and Slavin (1998) evaluated a program called Bilingual Cooperative Integrated Reading and Composition (BCIRC) in El Paso, Texas, elementary schools. English learners in three schools using BCIRC were matched with control groups, based on prior achievement levels, socioeconomic status, and other factors. After pretesting, both sets of schools were followed for 2 years. Students in the BCIRC schools scored higher on reading measures than those in the control schools.

Matching is much more practical than random assignment, but its results must be carefully interpreted because there may be reasons that one group of educators took on one method whereas another group did not. Were the teachers in the treatment group more motivated? Did they have greater resources? On the other hand, were they more desperate to try something new? In a matched study, these possibilities need to be considered and ruled out as much as possible (Mertler & Charles, 2011).

experimental group

Group that receives treatment during an experiment.

control group

Group that receives no special treatment during an experiment.

external validity

Degree to which results of an experiment can be applied to real-life situations.

SINGLE-CASE EXPERIMENTS One experimental method occasionally used in educational research is the **single-case experiment** (see Franklin, Allison, & Gorman, 1997; Neuman & McCormick, 1995). In one typical form of this type of experiment, a single student's behavior may be observed for several days. Then a special program is begun, and the student's behavior under the new program is observed. Finally, the new program is withdrawn. If the student's behavior improves under the special program but the improvement disappears when the program is withdrawn, the implication is that the program has affected the student's behavior. Sometimes the "single case" can be several students, an entire class, or a school given the same treatment.

An example of a single-case experiment is a classic study by Barrish, Saunders, and Wolf (1969). In this study, a fourth-grade class was the single case. Observers recorded the percentage of time that at least one student in the class was talking out (talking without permission) or out of their seat during reading and math periods. After 10 days, a special program was introduced. The class was divided into two large teams, and whenever any student on a team misbehaved, the team was given a check mark. At the end of each day, the team with fewer check marks (or both teams if both received fewer than five check marks) could take part in a 30-minute free period.

The results of this study are illustrated in Figure 1.2. Before the Good Behavior Game began (baseline), at least one student in the math class was talking out 96 percent of the time, and at least one student was out of their seat without permission 82 percent of the time. When the game was instituted in math, the class's behavior improved dramatically. When the game was withdrawn, the class's behavior got worse again but improved once more when the game was reintroduced. Note that when the game was also introduced in reading class, student behaviors again improved. The fact that the program made a difference in both math and reading gives us even greater confidence that the Good Behavior Game is effective.

One important limitation of the single-case experiment is that it can be used only to study outcomes that can be measured frequently. For this reason, most single-case studies involve observable behaviors, such as talking out and being out of seat, which can be measured every day or many times per day.

■ Correlational Studies

Perhaps the most frequently used research method in educational psychology is the **correlational study.** In contrast to an experiment, in which the researcher deliberately changes one variable to see how this change will affect other variables, in correlational research the researcher studies variables as they are to see whether they are related. Variables can be positively correlated, negatively correlated, or uncorrelated. An example of a **positive correlation** is the relationship between reading achievement and mathematics achievement. In general, someone who is better than average in reading will also be better than average in math. Of course, some students who are good readers are not good in math, and vice versa; but on the average, skills in one academic area are positively correlated with skills in other academic areas: When one variable is high, the other tends also to be high. An example of a **negative correlation** is days absent and grades. The more days a student is absent, the lower his or her grades are likely to be; when one variable is high, the other tends to be low. With **uncorrelated variables,** in contrast, there is no correspondence between them. For example, student achievement in Poughkeepsie, New York, is probably completely unrelated to the level of student motivation in Portland, Oregon.

One classic example of correlational research is a study by Lahaderne (1968), who investigated the relationship between students' attentiveness in class and their achievements and IQs. She observed 125 students in 4 sixth-grade classes to see how much of the time students were paying attention (e.g., listening to the teacher and doing assigned work). She then correlated attentiveness with achievement in reading, arithmetic, and language and with students' IQs and attitudes toward school. The advantage of correlational studies is that they allow the researcher to study variables as they are, without creating artificial situations.

single-case experiment

Experiment that studies a treatment's effect on one person or one group by contrasting behavior before, during, and after application of the treatment.

correlational study

Research into the relationships between variables as they naturally occur.

positive correlation

Relationship in which high levels of one variable correspond to high levels of another.

negative correlation

Relationship in which high levels of one variable correspond to low levels of another.

uncorrelated variables

Variables for which there is no relationship between levels of one compared to another.

FIGURE 1.2   **Results of Successful Single-Case Experiments**

The effect of rewarding good behavior in fourth-grade math and reading classes is clear from these graphs. They show that misbehavior was high during the baseline period (before the Good Behavior Game was introduced) but fell during the game. For instance, in reading session 13, before the game was introduced, students were out of their seats during nearly 100 percent of the observed time intervals. In reading session 53, however, when the game was in use, the percentage of time intervals in which out-of-seat students approached zero. In single-case experiments on treatments affecting behaviors that can be frequently measured, graphs like these can prove a treatment's effectiveness.

Source: Adapted from H. H. Barrish, M. Saunders, and M. M. Wolf, "Good Behavior Game: Effects of Individual Contingencies for Group Consequences on Disruptive Behavior in a Classroom," *Journal of Applied Behavior Analysis, 2,* 1969, pp. 119–124. Copyright 1969 by the *Journal of Applied Behavior Analysis.* Reprinted by permission.

Many important research questions can be studied only in correlational studies. For example, if we wanted to study the relationship between gender and math achievement, we could hardly randomly assign students to be boys or girls! Also, correlational studies let researchers study the interrelationships of many variables at the same time.

The principal disadvantage of correlational methods is that though they may tell us that two variables are related, they do not tell us what causes what. The Lahaderne study of attentiveness, achievement, and IQ raised the question: Does student attentiveness cause high achievement, or are high-ability, high-achieving students simply more attentive than other students? A correlational study cannot answer this question completely. However, correlational researchers do typically use statistical methods to try to determine what causes what. In Lahaderne's study, it would have been possible to find out whether, among students with the same IQ, attentiveness was related to achievement.

Explanation A

Explanation B

FIGURE 1.3 Possible Explanations for Correlations between Attentiveness, Achievement, and IQ

Correlational studies can show that variables are related, but such studies cannot prove what causes what. In Lahaderne's (1968) study, for example, did the attentiveness of the students cause higher achievement scores (Explanation A), or did a third factor—intelligence—determine both attentiveness and performance on achievement tests (as diagrammed in Explanation B)? Both explanations are partially correct.

For example, given two students of average intelligence, will the one who is more attentive tend to achieve more? If not, then we may conclude that the relationship between attentiveness and achievement is simply the result of high-IQ students being more attentive and higher achieving than other students, not the result of any effect of attention on achievement.

Figure 1.3 illustrates two possible explanations for the correlation of attentiveness to achievement and IQ. In Explanation A, attentiveness causes achievement. In Explanation B, both attentiveness and achievement are assumed to be caused by a third variable, IQ. Which is correct? Evidence from other research on this relationship suggests that both explanations are partially correct—that even when the effect of IQ is removed, student attentiveness is related to achievement.

Another illustration of correlational research is a study by Lubienski and Lubienski (2006) that used data from the National Assessment of Education Progress (NAEP) to ask whether public or private schools produce better reading and math performance. Of course, students in private schools have higher achievement scores, but statistically controlling for students' ethnicity, wealth, and other background factors, the researchers found that public school students scored at least as well as similar students in private schools.

■ Descriptive Research

Experimental research and correlational research look for relationships between variables. However, some research in educational psychology simply seeks to describe a situation of interest. For example, the National Institute of Child Health and Human Development (NICHD) Early Child Care Research Network (2005) did a national observational study in 780 third-grade classrooms to describe the wide range of classroom environments children experience. Among other things, the study found that most time in third grade focuses on basic skills, with little time for higher-order skills, but there was enormous variation. In another example, Mosenthal and colleagues (2004) observed and described six schools in Vermont that consistently had extraordinary reading scores, finding that such schools had particularly focused teachers who constantly evaluated their own teaching. One type of **descriptive research** is a survey

descriptive research

Research study aimed at identifying and gathering detailed information about a topic of interest.

or interview. Another, called *ethnography,* involves observation of a social setting (such as a classroom or school) over an extended period. As an example of ethnography, Anagnostopoulos (2006) spent a year in a Chicago high school observing and interviewing teachers and students to understand their response to a new policy that required students to pass a test for promotion to the next grade. She found that both students and teachers mentally divided retained students into two categories—"true demotes" and "real students"—in which the "true demotes" were "bad kids" who deserved to be retained and the "real students" were students who, they thought, did not really deserve to be retained. Descriptive studies provide a much more complete story of what happens in schools and classrooms than could studies that boil down findings into cold, hard numbers. Descriptive research usually does not have the scientific objectivity of correlational or experimental research, but it makes up for this lack in richness of detail and interpretation (Creswell, 2002; Northcutt & McCoy, 2004; Rossman & Rallis, 2003).

Developmental psychologists use descriptive research extensively to identify characteristics of children at different ages. The most important research in developmental psychology was done by the Swiss psychologist Jean Piaget (1952b), who began by carefully observing his own children. As a result of his observations, he developed a theory that describes the cognitive development of children from infancy through adolescence (Wadsworth, 2004).

■ Action Research

Action research is a particular form of descriptive research that is carried out by educators in their own classrooms or schools (A. P. Johnson, 2009; Mills, 2007, Stringer, 2008). In action research, a teacher or principal might try out a new teaching method or school organization strategy, collect information about how it worked, and communicate this information to others. Because the people involved in the experiment are the educators themselves, action research lacks the objectivity sought in other forms of research, but it can provide deeper insight from front-line teachers or administrators than would be possible in research done by outsiders.

How Can I Become an Intentional Teacher ?

INTASC

9 Professional Commitment and Responsibility

Think about the best, most intentional teachers you ever had—the ones who seemed so confident, so caring, so skilled, so enthusiastic about their subject. Chances are, when they took educational psychology, they were as scared, uncertain, and overwhelmed about becoming a teacher as you might be today. Yet they kept at it and made themselves the great teachers you remember. You can do the same.

■ Teacher Certification

Before you can become an *intentional* teacher, you have to become a *certified* teacher. Each state, province, and country has its own requirements, but in most places you at least have to graduate from a 4-year college with a specified distribution of courses, although various alternative certification programs exist as well. You also will need to have a satisfactory student teaching experience. In most states, however, these are not enough. You also have to pass a teacher certification test, or licensure test. Many states base their requirements on the 10 principles of effective teaching shown in Figure 1.4. Developed by the Interstate New Teacher Assessment and Support Consortium (INTASC), they

action research

Research carried out by educators in their own classrooms or schools.

1. ***Knowledge of Subject Matter:*** The teacher understands the central concepts, tools of inquiry, and structures of the subject being taught and can create learning experiences that make these aspects of subject matter meaningful for students.

2. ***Knowledge of Human Development and Learning:*** The teacher understands how children learn and develop and can provide learning opportunities that support their intellectual, social, and personal development.

3. ***Adapting Instruction for Individual Needs:*** The teacher understands how students differ in their approaches to learning and creates instructional opportunities that are adapted to diverse learners.

4. ***Multiple Instructional Strategies:*** The teacher uses various instructional strategies to encourage students' development of critical thinking, problem solving, and performance skills.

5. ***Classroom Motivation and Management:*** The teacher uses an understanding of individual and group motivation and behavior to create a learning environment that encourages positive social interaction, active engagement in learning, and self-motivation.

6. ***Communication Skills:*** The teacher uses knowledge of effective verbal, nonverbal, and media communication techniques to foster active inquiry, collaboration, and supportive interaction in the classroom.

7. ***Instructional Planning Skills:*** The teacher plans instruction based upon knowledge of subject matter, students, the community, and curriculum goals.

8. ***Assessment of Student Learning:*** The teacher understands and uses formal and informal assessment strategies to evaluate and ensure the continuous intellectual, social and physical development of the learner.

9. ***Professional Commitment and Responsibility:*** The teacher is a reflective practitioner who continually evaluates the effects of his or her choices and actions on others (students, parents, and other professionals in the learning community) and who actively seeks out opportunities to grow professionally.

10. ***Partnerships:*** The teacher fosters relationships with school colleagues, parents, and agencies in the larger community to support students' learning and well-being.

FIGURE 1.4 Interstate New Teacher Assessment and Support Consortium (INTASC) Standards for Beginning Teacher Licensing and Development

Source: Council of Chief State School Officers. (1992). The Interstate New Teacher Assessment and Support Consortium (INTASC) standards were developed by the Council of Chief State School Officers and member states. Copies may by downloaded from the council's website at www.ccsso .org. Model standards for beginning teacher licensing, assessment, and development: A resource for state dialogue. Washington, DC: Author. www.ccsso.org/content/pdfs/corestrd.pdf.

form the basis for most teacher certification tests, whether developed by INTASC, by the Education Testing Service, or by individual state departments of education (see Darling-Hammond, 2008).

INTASC has developed its own Test for Teaching Knowledge (TTK). This test assesses new teachers' knowledge of child development; theories of teaching and learning, assessment, and language acquisition; the role of student background in the learning process; and other basic knowledge and skills important for teaching. Some states are beginning to use this test. To read more about the TTK, visit the Council of Chief State School Officers (CCSSO) website at www.ccsso.org/intasc.

The Praxis Series™ Professional Assessments for Beginning Teachers, developed by the Educational Testing Service, is the most common test used by states to certify teachers. The Praxis Series includes three categories of assessment that correlate to significant stages in teacher development: Praxis I: Academic Skills Assessment for entering a teacher training program, Praxis II: Subject Assessments for licensure for entering the profession, and Praxis III: Classroom Performance Assessments after the first year of teaching. Praxis II is the test you would take on completing your teacher preparation program. It offers three Principles of Learning and Teaching (PLT) tests that relate to the content in educational psychology—for grades K to 6, 5 to 9, and 7 to 12. These tests cover content in four areas: students as learners, instruction and assessment, communication techniques, and teacher professionalism.

Each PLT test presents four scenarios followed by three short-answer questions related to the scenario. There are also 24 multiple-choice questions, for a total of 36 questions. Detailed information about the Praxis series of tests can be found at www.ets .org/praxis. From this website you can access the tests-at-a-glance page, which includes test outlines, sample questions with explanations for the best answers, and test-taking strategies. There is also a list of state-by-state requirements to determine which Praxis tests each state uses, if any. Note that individual universities may also use Praxis, even if their states do not require it.

Each state, province, or institution that uses the Praxis tests sets its own passing requirements. The passing score for each test for each state is listed on the website and in a booklet you receive with your score report.

Many states, including California, Texas, Florida, and New York, have developed or are developing their own teacher certification tests. These usually include sections much like the Praxis Principles of Learning and Teaching.

Throughout this book you will find tips on topics likely to appear on teacher certification tests. These marginal notes, called *Certification Pointers,* highlight knowledge that is frequently required on state teacher licensure exams, including Praxis Principles of Learning and Teaching. Also see the new Appendix at the end of the book that correlates the content of each chapter to corresponding topics within the Praxis Principles of Learning and Teaching exam.

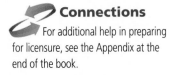

Connections

For additional help in preparing for licensure, see the Appendix at the end of the book.

■ Beyond Certification

Getting a teaching certificate is necessary but not sufficient to become an intentional teacher. Starting with your student teaching experience and continuing into your first job, you can create or take advantage of opportunities to develop your skills as an intentional teacher in a number of ways.

SEEK MENTORS Experienced teachers who are themselves intentional teachers are your best resource (Nieto, 2009). Not only are they highly effective, but they also understand and can describe what they're doing (and, hopefully, can help you learn to do those things). Talk with experienced teachers in your school, observe them teaching, and ask them to observe you and share ideas, as Ellen Mathis did in the vignette at the beginning of this chapter. Many school systems provide induction programs to help new teachers develop in the crucial first years, but even if yours does not, you can create one for yourself by seeking out experienced and helpful mentors.

SEEK PROFESSIONAL DEVELOPMENT Districts, universities, state departments of education, and other institutions provide all sorts of professional development workshops for teachers on a wide range of topics. Take advantage of every opportunity to partici-

Certification Pointer

Teacher certification tests include a section on teacher professionalism. One aspect that is emphasized is being able to read and understand research on current ideas and debates about teaching practices.

pate. The best professional development includes some sort of coaching or follow-up, in which someone who knows a given technique or program comes to your class to observe you trying to use the program and gives you feedback (see Darling-Hammond & Richardson, 2009; Hirsh & Hord, 2008; Neufield & Roper, 2003). Workshops in which many teachers from your school participate together, and then have opportunities to discuss successes and challenges, can also be very effective (see Calderón, 1999).

TALK TEACHING   Talk to your colleagues, your former classmates, your friends who teach, even your friends who don't teach. Share your successes, your failures, your questions. Teaching can be an isolating experience if it's just you and your students. Take every opportunity to share ideas and commiserate with sympathetic colleagues (Nieto, 2009). Join a book club to discuss articles and books on teaching (Hoerr, 2009).

ON THE WEB

When your friends and colleagues are worn out from your passion for teaching, try virtual colleagues on the Web. The following examples are just a few of the many teacher-oriented websites and blogs that offer opportunities to share advice, opinions, and observations (Ferriter, 2009a,b).

Blogger (www.blogger.com)

Edublogs (www.edublogs.com)

Education World (www.education-world.com)

The Knowledge Loom (www.knowledgeloom.org)

K–12 Professional Circle (www.nces.ed.gov/practitioners/teachers.asp)

Typepad (www.typepad.com)

The Vent (www.proteacher.com)

There are websites for elementary teachers (www.wmtps.org/techini/bestsite/bestsite.html), for middle school teachers (www.middleweb.com/10TeachingSites.html), and for teachers of various subjects, by topic (www.assortedstuff.com/top101/?page_id=2). Resources for middle school science teachers can be found at www.sldirectory.com/teachf/scied.html. Resources for teachers using technology in their classrooms can be found at the Networked Learning Community (http://learnweb.harvard.edu/ent/home).

PROFESSIONAL PUBLICATIONS AND ASSOCIATIONS   Intentional teachers do a lot of reading. Your school may subscribe to teacher-oriented journals, or you might choose to do so. For example, look for *Teacher Magazine, Theory Into Practice, Learning, Young Children, Phi Delta Kappan, Educational Leadership,* or subject-specific journals such as *Reading Teacher* and *Mathematics Teacher.*

In addition, check out professional associations in your subject area or area of interest. The national teachers' unions—the American Federation of Teachers (AFT) and National Education Association (NEA)—have publications, workshops, and other resources from which you can benefit greatly. Your state department of education, regional educational laboratory, or school district office may also have useful resources. A few useful websites include the following:

American Educational Research Association: www.aera.net

American Federation of Teachers: www.aft.org

Certification Pointer

The teacher professionalism section of Praxis II and other certification tests may ask you to identify the titles of several professional journals in your particular field of teaching (e.g., *Journal of Educational Psychology, Educational Leadership, Phi Delta Kappan*).

Certification Pointer

Teaching certification tests might expect you to know which professional associations offer meetings, publications, and dialogue with other teachers (e.g., American Educational Research Association, International Reading Association, American Federation of Teachers, National Education Association).

Canadian Educational Research Association: www.cea–ace.ca

Council for Exceptional Children: www.cec.sped.org

International Reading Association: www.reading.org

National Association for Bilingual Education: www.nabe.org

National Association for the Education of Young Children: www.naeyc.org

National Association of Black School Educators: www.nabse.org

National Council for the Social Studies: www.ncss.org

National Council of Teachers of English: www.ncte.org

National Council of Teachers of Mathematics: www.nctm.org

National Education Association: www.nea.org

National Institute for Literacy: www.nifl.gov

National Middle School Association: www.nmsa.org

National Science Teachers Association: www.nsta.org

Chapter 1 Summary

What Makes a Good Teacher ?

Good teachers know their subject matter and have mastered pedagogical skills. They accomplish all the tasks involved in effective instruction with warmth, enthusiasm, and caring. They are intentional teachers, and they use principles of educational psychology in their decision making and teaching. They combine research and common sense.

What Is the Role of Research in Educational Psychology ?

Educational psychology is the systematic study of learners, learning, and teaching. Research in educational psychology focuses on the processes by which information, skills, values, and attitudes are communicated between teachers and students in the classroom and on applications of the principles of psychology to instructional practices. Such research shapes educational policies, professional development programs, and teaching materials.

What Research Methods Are Used in Educational Psychology ?

Experimental research involves testing particular educational programs or treatments. Random assignment of experimental subjects into groups before the testing helps to ensure that groups are equivalent and findings will be valid. An experimental group receiving the treatment is matched with a control group whose members do not receive treatment. Laboratory experiments are highly structured and short term. All the variables involved are strictly controlled. Randomized field experiments are less structured and take place over a long period of time under realistic conditions in which not all variables can be controlled. A single-case experiment involves observation of one student or group of students over a specified period before and after treatment. Correlational studies examine variables to see whether they are related. Variables can be positively correlated, negatively correlated, or uncorrelated. Correlational studies provide information about variables without manipulating them or creating artificial situations. However, they do not indicate the causes of relationships between variables. Descriptive research uses surveys, interviews, and observations to describe behavior in social settings.

How Can I Become an Intentional Teacher?

Before you can become an intentional teacher, you have to become a certified teacher. Each state has its own requirements regarding education, student teaching, and licensure testing. These include the Test for Teaching Knowledge and the Praxis series. You can further develop your skills as an intentional teacher by seeking mentors, pursuing professional development, and talking to colleagues and friends about your experiences.

Key Terms

Review the following key terms from the chapter.

action research   20

control group   16

correlational study   17

critical thinking   7

descriptive research   19

educational psychology   2

experiment   15

experimental group   16

external validity   16

intentionality   4

internal validity   15

laboratory experiment   15

negative correlation   17

pedagogy   3

positive correlation   17

principle   9

random assignment   15

randomized field experiment   15

single-case experiment   17

teacher efficacy   6

theory   9

treatment   14

uncorrelated variables   17

variable   14

Self-Assessment: Practicing for Licensure

Directions: The chapter-opening vignette addresses indicators that are often assessed in state licensure exams. Re-read the chapter-opening vignette and then respond to the following questions.

1. In the first paragraph, Ellen Mathis does not understand why her students are nonproductive and unimaginative. According to educational psychology research, which of the following teacher characteristics is Ellen most likely lacking?
    a. Classroom management skills
    b. Content knowledge
    c. Intentionality
    d. Common sense

2. Leah Washington talks with Ellen Mathis about getting students to write interesting compositions. Which of the following statements summarizes Leah's approach to teaching writing?
    a. Select teaching methods, learning activities, and instructional materials that are appropriate and motivating for students.
    b. Have students of similar abilities work together so the teacher can adapt instruction to meet the needs of each group.
    c. When working on writing activities, consider the teacher to be the instruction center.
    d. Individualization is the first goal of instruction; direct instruction is the second goal.

3. According to research on expertise development, what characteristic separates novice teachers from expert teachers?
    a. Novice teachers tend to rely on their pedagogical skills because their content knowledge is less complex than that of experts.
    b. Expert teachers do more short-term memory processing than novices because their thinking is more complex.
    c. Novice teachers have to constantly upgrade and examine their own teaching practices, whereas experts use a "best practices" approach.
    d. Expert teachers are critical thinkers.

4. Educational psychologists are often accused of studying the obvious. However, they have learned that the obvious is not always true. All of the following statements demonstrate this idea except one. Which one is obvious *and* supported by research?
    a. Student achievement is increased when students are assigned to classes according to their ability.

b. Scolding students for misbehavior improves student behavior.
    c. Whole-class instruction is more effective than individualized instruction.
    d. Intentional teachers balance competing goals according to the needs of particular students and situations.

5. Leah Washington discusses many of her teaching strategies with Ellen Mathis. One can easily see that Leah views teaching as a decision-making process. She recognizes problems and issues, considers situations from multiple perspectives, calls on her professional knowledge to formulate action, and
    a. selects the most appropriate action and judges the consequence.
    b. chooses a strategy that agrees with her individual beliefs about teaching.
    c. consults with expert teachers and administrators to assist with her plan of action.
    d. allows students to make instructional decisions based on their interests and needs.

6. The products of research are principles, laws, and theories. Leah Washington describes many principles and theories of educational psychology as she speaks with Ellen Mathis about teaching students to write compositions. First, describe an instruction action with which Ellen Mathis is having difficulties (e.g., Ellen assigns all students the same topic), and then describe principles and theories she can use to engage her students in exciting and meaningful lessons.

7. The goal of research in educational psychology is to examine questions of teaching and learning using objective methods. These research methods include experiments, correlational studies, descriptive research, and action research. Think of a research question, and then describe how you would go about answering your question using these methods.

8. Intentional teachers are aware of resources available for professional learning. They continually refine their practices to address the needs of all students. List four actions you could take to find information to help you teach your students with limited English proficiency.

PEARSON myeducationlab

Go to the Topic **Research Methods and Teacher Reflection** in the MyEducationLab (www.myeducationlab .com) for your course, where you can:

- Find learning outcomes for **Research Methods and Teacher Reflection** along with the national standards that connect to these outcomes.

- Complete Assignments and Activities that can help you more deeply understand the chapter content.

- Apply and practice your understanding of the core teaching skills identified in the chapter with the Building Teaching Skills and Dispositions learning units.

- Access video clips of CCSSO National Teachers of the Year award winners responding to the question "Why Do I Teach?" in the Teacher Talk section.

- Check your comprehension of the content covered in the chapter by going to the Study Plan in the Book Resources for your text. Here you will be able to take a chapter quiz; receive feedback on your answers; and then access Review, Practice, and Enrichment activities to enhance your understanding of chapter content.

- Watch author Bob Slavin present Personal Reflections podcasts on *Adapting* and *Using Research to Inform Teaching* in the Book Resources for your text. Then, respond to the reflection questions that follow.

Adapting

YOUR REFLECTIONS How is my work with Mark a demonstration of critical thinking? Consider this experience as well as that of Leah Washington in the Chapter 1 opening vignette. What can you learn from these experiences that will help you become an intentional teacher?

Using Research to Inform Teaching

YOUR REFLECTIONS Why was my study ruined? What lesson can you learn from this example about using research to be an effective teacher?

2

Cognitive, Language, and Literacy Development

Shutterstock

Learning Outcomes

At the end of this chapter, you should be able to:

- Describe Vygostkian and Piagetian theories of human development
- Identify ways you can set up your classroom to promote literacy development in young children
- Identify the stages of language and literacy development during the elementary and middle school years

---

Patricia Wing is very proud of her third-grade class. Her students have done very well on state tests, and they are succeeding in all of their subjects, especially science, Patricia's own favorite. So she decides to give her students a challenge they'll really enjoy. "Class," she says, "I'm so excited to see the good work you've all done in science. Today, I'm going to give you a problem to solve in your teams that will stretch your minds, but I know you can solve it."

"At each of your tables you have a pendulum, several weights, and a stopwatch. You can change the weights on the pendulum, the length of the string, the push you give the weight to start it swinging, or anything you like. My question to you is this: What determines how many times the pendulum goes back and forth in a minute?"

The students get right to work with excitement. They try more weight and less weight, more push and less push, longer strings and shorter strings. Each team appoints a time keeper who writes down how many swings there are in a minute. The students argue with each other: "It's the weight!" "It's the push!" "It's the string!" The groups are working hard but haphazardly. None of them gets the right answer (which is that only the length of the string matters).

Patricia is astonished. The students know a lot about science, try hard, and work well together, yet they cannot solve the problem.

USING YOUR EXPERIENCE

Critical Thinking Why do you think Patricia Wing's class cannot solve the pendulum problem? What does her experience suggest to you about why teachers should consider children's stages of development in their teaching?

Over the course of their first 18 years of life, children go through astounding changes. Most of these changes are obvious—children get bigger, smarter, more socially adept, and so on. However, many aspects of development are not so obvious. Individual children develop in different ways and at different rates, and development is influenced by biology, culture, parenting, education, and other factors. Every teacher needs to understand how children grow and develop to be able to understand how children learn and how best to teach them (Comer, 2005).

How Do Children Develop Cognitively

The term **development** refers to how people grow, adapt, and change over the course of their lifetimes, through personality development, socioemotional development, cognitive

INTASC

2 Knowledge of Human Development and Learning

development

Orderly and lasting growth, adaptation, and change over the course of a lifetime.

development (thinking), and language development. This chapter begins with two major theorists of cognitive development whose ideas are widely accepted: Jean Piaget and Lev Vygotsky (see Bee & Boyd, 2010; Berk, 2009; Feldman, 2010; Keenan & Evans, 2010).

■ Aspects of Development

Children are not miniature adults. They think differently and see the world differently. One of the first requirements of effective teaching is that you understand how students think and how they view the world. Effective teaching strategies must take into account students' ages and stages of development. A bright third-grader might appear to be able to learn any kind of mathematics but in fact may not have the cognitive maturity to do the abstract thinking required for algebra. In the opening vignette, Ms. Wing's class is smart and motivated, yet the pendulum task is a classic example of a kind of thinking that usually does not appear until adolescence, when most children gain the ability to think logically about problems of this kind and to proceed in a methodical way toward a solution.

■ Issues of Development

Two central issues have been debated for decades among developmental psychologists: the degree to which development is affected by experience and whether development proceeds in stages.

NATURE–NURTURE CONTROVERSY Is development predetermined at birth, by heredity and biological factors, or is it affected by experience and other environmental factors? Today, most developmental psychologists (e.g., Bee & Boyd, 2010; Berk, 2009; Cook & Cook, 2007) believe that nature and nurture combine to influence development, with biological factors playing a stronger role in some aspects, such as physical development, and environmental factors playing a stronger role in others, such as moral development.

CONTINUOUS AND DISCONTINUOUS THEORIES A second issue revolves around the notion of how change occurs. **Continuous theories of development** assume that development occurs in a smooth progression as skills develop and experiences are provided by caregivers and the environment. Continuous theories emphasize the importance of environment rather than heredity in determining development.

A second perspective assumes that children progress through a set of predictable and invariant stages of development. In this case, change can be fairly abrupt when children advance to a new stage of development. All children are believed to acquire skills in the same sequence, although rates of progress differ from child to child. The abilities children gain in each subsequent stage are not simply "more of the same"; at each stage, children develop qualitatively different understandings, abilities, and beliefs. Skipping stages is impossible, although at any given point the same child may exhibit behaviors characteristic of more than one stage (DeVries, 2008; Zigler & Gilman, 1998). In contrast to continuous theories, these **discontinuous theories of development** focus on inborn factors rather than environmental influences to explain change over time. Environmental conditions may have some influence on the pace of development, but the sequence of developmental steps is essentially fixed. According to this perspective, the 9-year-olds in Patricia Wing's class could not have solved the pendulum problem no matter how much they had been taught, because they had not reached a developmental stage that allows people to solve problems involving many factors at the same time.

Stage theorists, such as Piaget and Vygotsky, share the belief that distinct stages of development can be identified and described. This agreement does not, however, extend to the particulars of their theories, which differ significantly in the numbers of stages and in their details (see DeVries, 2008).

continuous theories of development

Theories based on the belief that human development progresses smoothly and gradually from infancy to adulthood.

discontinuous theories of development

Theories describing human development as occurring through a fixed sequence of distinct, predictable stages governed by inborn factors.

How Did Piaget View Cognitive Development?

Jean Piaget, born in Switzerland in 1896, is the most influential developmental psychologist in the history of psychology (see Flavell, 1996; Wadsworth, 2004). After receiving his doctorate in biology, he became more interested in psychology, basing his earliest theories on careful observation of his own three children. Piaget thought of himself as applying biological principles and methods to the study of human development, and many of the terms he introduced to psychology were drawn directly from biology.

Piaget explored both why and how mental abilities change over time. For Piaget, development depends in large part on the child's manipulation of and active interaction with the environment. In Piaget's view, knowledge comes from action (see DeVries, 2008; Wadsworth, 2004). Piaget's theory of **cognitive development** proposes that a child's intellect, or cognitive ability, progresses through four distinct stages. Each stage is characterized by the emergence of new abilities and ways of processing information. Many of the specifics of Piaget's theories have been challenged in later research. In particular, many of the changes in cognitive functioning he described are now known to take place earlier, under certain circumstances. Nevertheless, Piaget's work forms an essential basis for understanding child development.

■ How Development Occurs

SCHEMES   Piaget believed that all children are born with an innate tendency to interact with and make sense of their environments. Young children demonstrate patterns of behavior or thinking, called **schemes,** that older children and adults also use in dealing with objects in the world. We use schemes to find out about and act in the world; each scheme treats all objects and events in the same way. When babies encounter a new object, how are they to know what this object is all about? According to Piaget, they will use the schemes they have developed and will find out whether the object makes a loud or soft sound when banged, what it tastes like, whether it gives milk, and whether it goes thud when dropped (see Figure 2.1).

cognitive development

Gradual, orderly changes by which mental processes become more complex and sophisticated.

schemes

Mental patterns that guide behavior.

FIGURE 2.1 Schemes

Babies use patterns of behavior called *schemes* to learn about their world.

a. Banging is a favorite **scheme** used by babies to explore their world.

b. **Assimilation** occurs when they incorporate new objects into the scheme.

c. **Accommodation** occurs when a new object does not fit the existing scheme.

Connections

For information on schema theory (a topic related to schemes) in connection with information processing and memory, see Chapter 6, pages 167–168.

ASSIMILATION AND ACCOMMODATION   According to Piaget, **adaptation** is the process of adjusting schemes in response to the environment by means of assimilation and accommodation. **Assimilation** is the process of understanding a new object or event in terms of an existing scheme. If you give young infants small objects that they have never seen before but that resemble familiar objects, they are likely to grasp them, bite them, and bang them. In other words, they will try to use existing schemes to learn about these unknown things (see Figure 2.1b). Similarly, a high school student may have a studying scheme that involves putting information on cards and memorizing the cards' contents. She may then try to apply this scheme to learn difficult concepts such as economics, for which this approach may not be effective.

> **ON THE WEB**
>
> For more on Piaget's life and work, go to www.oikos.org/Piagethom.htm and http://webspace.ship.edu/cgboer/piaget.html. For information on Piaget's theory applied to the classroom, visit www.le.ac.uk/education/resources/SocSci/piaget.html. The Jean Piaget Society's website can be found at www.piaget.org.

Sometimes, when old ways of dealing with the world simply don't work, a child might modify an existing scheme in light of new information or a new experience, a process called **accommodation.** For example, if you give an egg to a baby who has a banging scheme for small objects, what will happen to the egg is obvious (Figure 2.1c). Less obvious, however, is what will happen to the baby's banging scheme. Because of the unexpected consequences of banging the egg, the baby might change the scheme. In the future the baby might bang some objects hard and others softly. The high school student who studies only by means of memorization might learn to use a different strategy to study economics, such as discussing difficult concepts with a friend.

The baby who banged the egg and the student who tried to memorize rather than comprehend had to deal with situations that could not be fully handled by existing schemes. This, in Piaget's theory, creates a state of disequilibrium, or an imbalance between what is understood and what is encountered. People naturally try to reduce such imbalances by focusing on the stimuli that cause the disequilibrium and developing new schemes or adapting old ones until equilibrium is restored. This process of restoring balance is called **equilibration.** According to Piaget, learning depends on this process. When equilibrium is upset, children have the opportunity to grow and develop. Eventually, qualitatively new ways of thinking about the world emerge, and children advance to a new stage of development. Piaget believed that physical experiences and manipulation of the environment are critical for developmental change to occur. However, he also believed that social interaction with peers, especially arguments and discussions, helps to clarify thinking and, eventually, to make it more logical. Research has stressed the importance of confronting students with experiences or data that do not fit into their current theories of how the world works as a means of advancing their cognitive development.

Piaget's theory of development represents **constructivism,** a view of cognitive development as a process in which children actively build systems of meaning and understandings of reality through their experiences and interactions (Berk, 2006; Cook & Cook, 2007; Wadsworth, 2004). In this view, children actively construct knowledge by continually assimilating and accommodating new information.

✓ **Certification Pointer**

Most teacher certification tests will require you to know that a constructivist approach to learning emphasizes the active role that learners play in building their own understandings.

adaptation

The process of adjusting schemes in response to the environment by means of assimilation and accommodation.

assimilation

Understanding new experiences in terms of existing schemes.

accommodation

Modifying existing schemes to fit new situations.

equilibration

The process of restoring balance between present understanding and new experiences.

constructivism

View of cognitive development that emphasizes the active role of learners in building their own understanding of reality.

■ Piaget's Stages of Development

Piaget divided the cognitive development of children and adolescents into four stages: sensorimotor, preoperational, concrete operational, and formal operational. He believed that all children pass through these stages in this order and that no child can skip a stage, although different children pass through the stages at somewhat different rates. The same

---

TABLE 2.1   **Piaget's Stages of Cognitive Development**

People progress through four stages of cognitive development between birth and adulthood, according to Jean Piaget. Each stage is marked by the emergence of new intellectual abilities that allow people to understand the world in increasingly complex ways.

Stage	Approximate Ages	Major Accomplishments
Sensorimotor	Birth to 2 years	Formation of concept of "object permanence" and gradual progression from reflexive behavior to goal-directed behavior.
Preoperational	2 to 7 years	Development of the ability to use symbols to represent objects in the world. Thinking remains egocentric and centered.
Concrete operational	7 to 11 years	Improvement in ability to think logically. New abilities include the use of operations that are reversible. Thinking is decentered, and problem solving is less restricted by egocentrism. Abstract thinking is not possible.
Formal operational	11 years to adulthood	Abstract and purely symbolic thinking possible. Problems can be solved through the use of systematic experimentation.

---

individuals may perform tasks associated with different stages at the same time, particularly at points of transition into a new stage. Table 2.1 summarizes the approximate ages at which children and adolescents pass through Piaget's four stages. It also shows the major accomplishments of each stage.

SENSORIMOTOR STAGE (BIRTH TO AGE 2)   The earliest stage is called **sensorimotor** because during this stage babies and young children explore the world by using their senses and motor skills. Dramatic changes occur as infants progress through the sensorimotor period. Initially, all infants have inborn behaviors called **reflexes.** Touch a newborn's lips, and the baby will begin to suck; place your finger in the palm of an infant's hand, and the infant will grasp it. These and other innate behaviors are the building blocks from which the infant's first schemes form.

Infants soon learn to use these reflexes to produce more interesting and intentional patterns of behavior. This learning occurs initially through accident and then through more intentional trial-and-error efforts. According to Piaget, by the end of the sensorimotor stage, children have progressed from their earlier trial-and-error approach to a more planned approach to problem solving. For the first time they can mentally represent objects and events. What most of us would call "thinking" appears now. This is a major advance because it means that the child can think through and plan behavior. For example, suppose a 2-year-old is in the kitchen watching his mother prepare dinner. If the child knows where the step stool is kept, he may ask to have it set up to afford a better view of the counter and a better chance for a nibble. The child did not stumble on to this solution accidentally. Instead, he thought about the problem, figured out a possible solution that used the step stool, tried out the solution mentally, and only then tried the solution in practice (Trawick-Smith, 2010).

Another hallmark development of the sensorimotor period is the ability to grasp **object permanence.** Piaget argued that children must learn that objects are physically stable and exist even when the objects are not in the child's physical presence. For example, if you cover an infant's bottle with a towel, the child may not remove it, believing that the bottle is gone. By 2 years of age, children understand that objects exist even if they cannot be seen. Once they realize that things exist out of sight, children can start using symbols to represent these things in their minds so that they can think about them (Cohen & Cashon, 2003).

Certification Pointer

When responding to the case studies in certification tests, you may be asked to identify appropriateness of instruction according to the students' Piagetian stage of development.

sensorimotor stage

Stage during which infants learn about their surroundings by using their senses and motor skills.

reflexes

Inborn automatic responses to stimuli (e.g., eye blinking in response to bright light).

object permanence

Understanding that an object exists even if it is out of sight.

How will this child likely respond to the Piagetian conservation task she is attempting? What stage of development does she demonstrate? As a teacher, how might you help a young child discover errors caused by centration and irreversibility?

PREOPERATIONAL STAGE (AGES 2 TO 7) During the **preoperational stage,** children have greater ability to think about things and can use symbols to mentally represent objects (Massey, 2008). Their language and concepts develop at an incredible rate. Yet much of their thinking remains surprisingly primitive. One of Piaget's earliest and most important discoveries was that young children lacked an understanding of the principle of **conservation.** For example, if you pour milk from a tall, narrow container into a shallow, wide one in the presence of a preoperational child, the child will firmly believe that the tall glass has more milk (see Figure 2.2). Similarly, a preoperational child is likely to believe that a sandwich cut in four pieces is more sandwich or that a line of blocks that is spread out contains more blocks than a line that is compressed, even after being shown that the number of blocks is identical.

Several aspects of preoperational thinking help to explain the error on conservation tasks. One characteristic is **centration:** paying attention to only one aspect of a situation. In the example illustrated in Figure 2.2, children might have claimed that there was less milk after it was poured into the wide container because they centered on the height of the milk, ignoring its width. In Figure 2.3, children focus on the length of the line of blocks but ignore its density (or the actual number of blocks).

FIGURE 2.2 **The Task of Conservation**

This is a typical procedure for studying conservation of liquid quantity.

Step 1

The child agrees that containers A and B contain the same quantity of milk.

A B

Step 2

The child observes the contents of container B poured into a third, different-shaped container, C.

B

C

Step 3

The child is then asked to compare the quantity of milk in containers A and C.

A

C

Source: Robert V. Kail and Rita Wicks-Nelson, *Developmental Psychology* (5th ed.), p. 190. © 1993 Pearson Education, Inc. Reproduced by permission of Pearson Education, Inc.

preoperational stage

Stage at which children learn to represent things in the mind.

conservation

The concept that certain properties of an object (such as weight) remain the same regardless of changes in other properties (such as length).

centration

Paying attention to only one aspect of an object or situation.

FIGURE 2.3 Centration

Centration, or focusing on only one aspect of a situation, helps to explain some errors in perception that young children make.

Which row has more blocks?

Situation A

Examiner's blocks

Child's blocks

> The preoperational child is likely to say that the rows have the same number of blocks because the rows are equal in length.

Situation B

Examiner's blocks

Child's blocks

> The preoperational child may say that the examiner has fewer blocks because that row is shorter.

Source: Barry Wadsworth, *Piaget for the Classroom Teacher,* 1978, p. 225, published by Longman Publishing Group. Adapted by permission of the author.

Reversibility, the ability to change direction in one's thinking to return to a starting point, is another facet of thinking developed by preoperational children. As adults, for example, we know that if $7 + 5 = 12$, then $12 - 5 = 7$. If we add 5 items to 7 items and then take the 5 items away (reverse what we've done), we are left with 7 items. If preoperational children could think this way, then they could mentally reverse the process of pouring the milk and realize that if the milk were poured back into the tall beaker, its quantity would not change.

Another characteristic of the preoperational child's thinking is a focus on states. In the milk problem the milk is poured from one container to another. Preschoolers ignore this pouring process and focus only on the beginning state (milk in a tall glass) and end state (milk in a shallow dish). "It is as though [the child] were viewing a series of still pictures instead of the movie that the adult sees" (Phillips, 1975). Unlike adults, the young preschooler forms concepts that vary in definition from situation to situation and are not always logical. How else can we explain the 2-year-old's ability to treat a stuffed animal as an inanimate object one minute and an animate object the next? Eventually, though, the child's concepts become more consistent and less private. Children become increasingly concerned that their definitions match other people's. But they still lack the ability to coordinate one concept with another.

Finally, preoperational children are **egocentric** in their thinking. Children at this stage believe that everyone sees the world exactly as they do. For example, Piaget and Inhelder (1956) seated children on one side of a display of three mountains and asked them to describe how the scene looked to a doll seated on the other side. Children below the age of 6 or 7 described the doll's view as identical to their own, even though it was apparent to adults that this could not be so. Because preoperational children are unable to take the perspective of others, they often interpret events entirely in reference to themselves. A passage from A. A. Milne's *Winnie-the-Pooh* illustrates the young child's egocentrism. Winnie-the-Pooh is sitting in the forest and hears a buzzing sound.

> That buzzing-noise means something. You don't get a buzzing-noise like that just buzzing and buzzing, without its meaning something. If there is a buzzing-noise, somebody's making a buzzing-noise, and the only reason for making a buzzing-noise that I know of

reversibility

The ability to perform a mental operation and then reverse one's thinking to return to the starting point.

egocentric

Believing that everyone views the world as you do.

is because you're a bee . . . Then he thought for another long time, and said: And the only reason for being a bee that I know of is for making honey . . . And then he got up, and said: And the only reason for making honey is so as I can eat it.★

CONCRETE OPERATIONAL STAGE (AGES 7 TO 11)   Although the differences between the mental abilities of preoperational preschoolers and concrete operational elementary school students are dramatic, concrete operational children still do not think like adults (Davis, 2008). They are very much rooted in the world as it is and have difficulty with abstract thought. Flavell describes the concrete operational child as taking "an earthbound, concrete, practical-minded sort of problem-solving approach, one that persistently fixates on the perceptible and inferable reality right there in front of him. A theorist the elementary-school child is not" (1986, p. 103). The term **concrete operational stage** reflects this earthbound approach. Children at this stage can form concepts, see relationships, and solve problems, but only as long as they involve objects and situations that are familiar.

During the elementary school years, children's cognitive abilities undergo dramatic changes. Elementary school children no longer have difficulties with conservation problems because they have acquired the concept of reversibility. For example, they can now see that the amount of milk in the short, wide container must be the same as that in the tall, narrow container, because if the milk were poured back in the tall container, it would be at the same level as before. Another fundamental difference between preoperational and concrete operational children is that the preoperational child responds to perceived appearances, whereas the older concrete operational child responds to inferred reality. Flavell (1986) demonstrated this concept by showing children a red car and then, while they were still watching, covering it with a filter that made it appear black. When asked what color the car was, 3-year-olds responded "black," and 6-year-olds responded "red." The older concrete operational child is able to respond to **inferred reality,** seeing things in the context of other meanings; preschoolers see what they see, with little ability to infer the meaning behind what they see.

One important task that children learn during the concrete operational stage is **seriation,** or arranging things in a logical progression—for example, lining up sticks from smallest to largest. To do this, they must be able to order or classify objects according to some criterion or dimension, in this case length. Once this ability is acquired, children can master a related skill known as **transitivity,** the ability to infer a relationship between two objects on the basis of knowledge of their respective relationships with a third object. For example, if you tell preoperational preschoolers that Tom is taller than Becky and that Becky is taller than Fred, they will not see that Tom is taller than Fred. Logical inferences such as this are not possible until the stage of concrete operations, during which school-age children develop the ability to make two mental transformations that require reversible thinking. The first of these is inversion (+A is reversed by −A), and the second is reciprocity (A < B is reciprocated by B > A). By the end of the concrete operational stage, children have the mental abilities to learn how to add, subtract, multiply, and divide; to place numbers in order by size; and to classify objects by any number of criteria. Children can think about what would happen if . . . , as long as the objects are in view—for example, "What would happen if I pulled this spring and then let it go?" Children can understand time and space well enough to draw a map from their home to school and are building an understanding of events in the past.

Children in the elementary grades also are moving from egocentric thought to decentered or objective thought. Decentered thought allows children to see that others can

concrete operational stage

Stage at which children develop the capacity for logical reasoning and understanding of conservation but can use these skills only in dealing with familiar situations.

inferred reality

The meaning of stimuli in the context of relevant information.

seriation

Arranging objects in sequential order according to one aspect, such as size, weight, or volume.

transitivity

A skill learned during the concrete operational stage of cognitive development in which individuals can mentally arrange and compare objects.

★From *Winnie-the-Pooh* by A. A. Milne, illustrated by E. H. Shepard, copyright 1926 by E. P. Dutton, renewed 1954 by A. A. Milne. Used by permission of Dutton Children's Books, a division of Penguin Young Readers Group, a member of Penguin Group (USA) Inc., 345 Hudson Street, New York, NY 10014. Additional rights copyright © The Trustees of the Pooh Properties 1926. Published by Egmont UK Ltd. London and used with permission. Electronically reproduced with permission of Curtis Brown Limited, London.

have different perceptions than they do. For example, children with decentered thought will be able to understand that different children may see different patterns in clouds. Children whose thought processes are decentered are able to learn that events can be governed by physical laws, such as the laws of gravity. These changes do not all happen at the same time. Rather, they occur gradually during the concrete operational stage.

FORMAL OPERATIONAL STAGE (AGE 11 TO ADULTHOOD)   Sometime around the onset of puberty, children's thinking begins to develop into the form that is characteristic of adults (Horn, Drill, Hochberg, Heinze, & Frank, 2008; Packard & Babineau, 2008). The preadolescent begins to be able to think abstractly and to see possibilities beyond the here and now. These abilities continue to develop into adulthood. With the **formal operational stage** comes the ability to deal with potential or hypothetical situations; the form is now separate from the content.

Inhelder and Piaget (1958) described one task that is approached differently by elementary school students in the concrete operational stage than by adolescents in the formal operational stage—the pendulum problem that Patricia Wing gave to her third-graders. The children and adolescents were given a pendulum consisting of a string with a weight at the end. They could change the length of the string, the amount of weight, the height from which the pendulum was released, and the force with which the pendulum was pushed. They were asked which of these factors influenced the frequency (the number of swings per minute). Only the length of the string makes any difference in the frequency of the pendulum: The shorter the string, the more swings per minute. This experiment is illustrated in Figure 2.4. The adolescent who has reached the stage of formal operations is likely to proceed quite systematically, varying one factor at a time (e.g., leaving the string the same length and trying different weights). For example, in Inhelder and Piaget's (1958) experiment, one 15-year-old selected 100 grams with a long string and a medium-length string, then 20 grams with a long and a short string, and finally 200 grams with a long and a short string and concluded, "It's the length of the string that makes it go faster and slower; the weight doesn't play any role" (p. 75). In contrast, 10-year-olds (who can be assumed to be in the concrete operational stage) proceeded in a chaotic fashion, varying many factors at the same time and hanging on to preconceptions. One boy varied simultaneously the weight and the push; then the weight, the push, and the length; then the push, the weight, and the elevation; and so on. He first concluded, "It's by changing the weight and the push, certainly not the string."

"How do you know that the string has nothing to do with it?"

"Because it's the same string."

formal operational stage

Stage at which one can deal abstractly with hypothetical situations and reason logically.

FIGURE 2.4   A Test of Problem-Solving Abilities

The pendulum problem uses a string, which can be shortened or lengthened, and a set of weights. When children in the concrete operational stage are asked what determines frequency (the number of times per minute the pendulum swings back and forth), they will tackle the problem less systematically than will adolescents who have entered the stage for formal operations. (The answer is that only the string's length affects the frequency.)

He had not varied its length in the last several trials; previously, he had varied it simultaneously with the push, thus complicating the findings of the experiment (adapted from Inhelder and Piaget, 1958, p. 71).

The transitivity problem also illustrates the advances brought about by formal thought. Recall the concrete operational child who, when told that Tom was taller than Becky and Becky was taller than Fred, understood that Tom was taller than Fred. However, if the problem had been phrased in the following way, only an older child who had entered the formal operational stage would have solved it: "Becky is shorter than Tom, and Becky is taller than Fred. Who is the tallest of the three?" Here the younger concrete operational child might get lost in the combinations of greater-than and less-than relationships. Adolescents in the formal operational stage may also get confused by the differing relationships in this problem, but they can imagine several different relationships among the heights of Becky, Tom, and Fred and can figure out the accuracy of each until they hit on the correct one. This example shows another ability of preadolescents and adolescents who have reached the formal operational stage: They can monitor, or think about, their own thinking.

Generating abstract relationships from available information and then comparing those abstract relationships to each other is a broadly applicable skill underlying many tasks in which adolescents' competence leaps forward. Piaget (1952a) described a task in which students in the concrete operational stage were given a set of 10 proverbs and a set of statements with the same meanings as the proverbs. They were asked to match each proverb to the equivalent statement. Again, concrete operational children can understand the task and choose answers. However, their answers are often incorrect because they often do not understand that a proverb describes a general principle. For example, asked to explain the proverb "Don't cry over spilled milk," a child might explain that once milk is spilled, there's nothing to cry about but might not see that the proverb has a broader meaning. The child is likely to respond to the concrete situation of spilled milk rather than understanding that the proverb means "Don't dwell on past events that can't be changed." Adolescents and adults have little difficulty with this type of task.

HYPOTHETICAL CONDITIONS   Another ability that Piaget and others recognized in the young adolescent is an aptitude to reason about situations and conditions that have not been experienced. The adolescent can accept, for the sake of argument or discussion, conditions that are arbitrary, that are not known to exist, or even that are known to be contrary to fact. Adolescents are not bound to their own experiences of reality, so they can apply logic to any given set of conditions. One illustration of the ability to reason about hypothetical situations is found in formal debate, in which participants must be prepared to defend either side of an issue, regardless of their personal feelings or experience, with their success judged on documentation and logical consistency. For a dramatic illustration of the difference between children and adolescents in the ability to suspend their own opinions, compare the reactions of fourth- and ninth-graders when you ask them to present an argument in favor of the proposition that schools should be in session 6 days a week, 48 weeks a year. The adolescent is far more likely to be able to set aside her or his own opinions and think of reasons why more days of school might be beneficial. The abilities that make up formal operational thought—thinking abstractly, testing hypotheses, and forming concepts that are independent of physical reality—are critical to acquiring higher-order skills. For example, learning algebra or abstract geometry requires the use of formal operational thought, as does understanding complex concepts in science, social studies, and other subjects.

The thinking characteristics of the formal operations stage usually appear between ages 11 and 15, but there are many individuals who never reach this stage (Niaz, 1997; Packard & Babineau, 2008). Most individuals tend to use formal operational thinking in some situations and not others, and this remains true into adulthood.

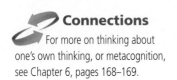

Connections

For more on thinking about one's own thinking, or metacognition, see Chapter 6, pages 168–169.

Certification Pointer

When responding to case studies in certification tests, you may be asked to design a lesson that would be considered developmentally appropriate for a group of adolescents.

How Is Piaget's Work Viewed Today ?

Piaget's theory revolutionized, and in many ways still dominates, the study of human development. However, some of his central principles have been questioned in more recent research, and modern descriptions of development have revised many of his views (see Feldman, 2010; Mercer, 2010).

■ Criticisms and Revisions of Piaget's Theory

One important Piagetian principle is that development precedes learning. Piaget held that developmental stages were largely fixed and that such concepts as conservation could not be taught. However, research has established many cases in which Piagetian tasks can be taught to children at earlier developmental stages. For example, several researchers have found that young children can succeed on simpler forms of Piaget's tasks before they reach the stage at which that task is usually achieved (Gelman, 2000; Kuhn, 2006; Larivée, Normandeau, & Parent, 2000; Siegler, 1998). Boden (1980) found that the same formal operational task produced passing rates from 19 to 98 percent, depending on the complexities of the instructions. Similarly, in simple, practical contexts, children demonstrated their ability to consider the point of view of others (Siegler, 2006) and infants have been shown to demonstrate aspects of object permanence much earlier than Piaget predicted (Baillargeon, 2002).

The result of this research has been a recognition that children are more competent than Piaget originally thought, especially when their practical knowledge is being assessed (Feldman, 2010). Piaget (1964) responded to demonstrations of this kind by arguing that the children must have been on the verge of the next developmental stage already—but the fact remains that some of the Piagetian tasks can be taught to children well below the age at which they usually appear without instruction.

Another point of criticism goes to the heart of Piaget's "stage" theory. Many researchers now doubt that there are broad stages of development affecting all types of cognitive tasks; instead, they argue that children's skills develop in different ways on different tasks and that their experience (including direct teaching in school or elsewhere) can have a strong influence on the pace of development (see Gelman, 2000; Siegler, 2006). The evidence is particularly strong that children can be taught to perform well on the Piagetian tasks assessing formal operations, such as the pendulum problem illustrated in Figure 2.4. Clearly, experience matters. De Lisi and Staudt (1980), for example, found that college students were likely to show formal operational reasoning on tasks related to their majors but not on other tasks. Watch an intelligent adult learning to sail. Initially, he or she is likely to engage in a lot of concrete operational behavior, trying everything in a chaotic order, before systematically beginning to learn how to adjust the tiller and the sail to the wind and direction (as in formal operational thought).

Theory into Practice
Educational Implications of Piaget's Theory

Piaget's theories have had a major impact on the theory and practice of education (Case, 1998; DeVries, 2008; Driscoll & Nagel, 2008). The theories focused attention on the idea of **developmentally appropriate education**—an education with environments, curriculum, materials, and instruction that are suitable for students in terms of their physical and cognitive abilities and their social and emotional needs. Piagetian theory has been influential in constructivist models of

INTASC

2 Knowledge of Human Development and Learning

3 Adapting Instruction for Individual Needs

developmentally appropriate education

Instruction felt to be adapted to the current developmental status of children (rather than to their age alone).

learning, which will be described in Chapter 8. Berk (2009) summarizes the main teaching implications drawn from Piaget as follows:

1. *A focus on the process of children's thinking, not only its products.* In addition to checking the correctness of children's answers, teachers must understand the processes children use to get to the answer. Appropriate learning experiences build on children's current level of cognitive functioning, and only when teachers appreciate children's methods of arriving at particular conclusions are they in a position to provide such experiences.

2. *Recognition of the crucial role of children's self-initiated, active involvement in learning activities.* In a Piagetian classroom the presentation of ready-made knowledge is deemphasized, and children are encouraged to discover for themselves through spontaneous interaction with the environment. Therefore, instead of teaching didactically, teachers provide a rich variety of activities that permit children to act directly on the physical world.

3. *A deemphasis on practices aimed at making children adultlike in their thinking.* Piaget referred to the question "How can we speed up development?" as "the American question." Among the many countries he visited, psychologists and educators in the United States seemed most interested in what techniques could be used to accelerate children's progress through the stages. Piagetian-based educational programs accept his firm belief that premature teaching could be worse than no teaching at all because it leads to superficial acceptance of adult formulas rather than true cognitive understanding.

4. *Acceptance of individual differences in developmental progress.* Piaget's theory assumes that all children go through the same developmental sequence but that they do so at different rates. Therefore, teachers must make a special effort to arrange classroom activities for individuals and small groups of children rather than for the total class group. In addition, because individual differences are expected, assessment of children's educational progress should be made in terms of each child's own previous course of development rather than the performances of same-age peers.

■ Neo-Piagetian Views of Development

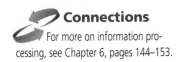
Connections

For more on information processing, see Chapter 6, pages 144–153.

Neo-Piagetian theories are modifications of Piaget's theory that attempt to overcome its limitations and address problems that critics have identified. In particular, neo-Piagetians have demonstrated that children's abilities to operate at a particular stage depend a great deal on the specific tasks involved (Massey, 2008); that training and experience, including social interactions, can accelerate children's development (Birney, Citron-Pousiy, Lutz, & Sternberg, 2005; Case, 1998; Flavell, 2004; Siegler, 1998); and that culture has an important impact on development (Gelman & Brenneman, 1994; Rogoff & Chavajay, 1995).

Neo-Piagetians see cognitive development in terms of specific types of tasks instead of overall stages. For example, different tasks described as indicators of concrete operational thinking appear at very different ages (Cohen & Cashon, 2003; Halford & Andrews, 2006). Neo-Piagetians have also described stages of development beyond Piaget's formal operations. For example, Arlin (1990) described a stage called "problem finding," in which adults are able to identify which are the important problems to solve. Other Neo-Piagetians refer to "dialectical thinking," the ability to see that real-life problems do not have a single solution (Sternberg, 2008).

How Did Vygotsky View Cognitive Development **?**

INTASC

4 Multiple Instructional Strategies

Lev Semionovich Vygotsky was a Russian psychologist who died in 1934. Although Piaget and Vygotsky never met, they were contemporaries who were aware of each other's early work (DeVries, 2008). Vygotsky's work was not widely read in English until the 1970s, however, and only since then have his theories become influential in North America. Vygotskian theory is now a powerful force in developmental psychology, and many of the critiques he made of the Piagetian perspective more than 60 years ago have come to the fore today (see Daniels, 2001; Glassman, 2001; John-Steiner & Mahn, 2003).

Vygotsky's work is based on two key ideas. First, he proposed that intellectual development can be understood only in terms of the historical and cultural contexts children experience. Second, he believed that development depends on the **sign systems** that individuals grow up with: the symbols that cultures create to help people think, communicate, and solve problems—for example, a culture's language, writing system, or counting system. In contrast to Piaget, Vygotsky proposed that cognitive development is strongly linked to input from others. Like Piaget, however, Vygotsky believed that the acquisition of sign systems occurs in an invariant sequence of steps that is the same for all children.

■ How Development Occurs

Recall that Piaget's theory suggests that development precedes learning. In other words, specific cognitive structures need to develop before certain types of learning can take place. Vygotsky's theory suggests that learning precedes development. For Vygotsky, learning involves the acquisition of signs by means of information from others and deliberate teaching. Development occurs as the child internalizes these signs so as to be able to think and solve problems without the help of others, an ability called **self-regulation.**

The first step in the development of self-regulation and independent thinking is learning that actions and sounds have a meaning. For example, a baby learns that the process of reaching toward an object is interpreted by others as a signal that the infant wants the object. In the case of language acquisition, children learn to associate certain sounds with meaning. The second step in developing internal structures and self-regulation involves practice. The infant practices gestures that will get attention. The preschooler will enter into conversations with others to master language. The final step is the use of signs to think and solve problems without the help of others. At this point, children become self-regulating, and the sign system has become internalized.

PRIVATE SPEECH   Vygotsky proposed that children incorporate the speech of others and then use that speech to help themselves solve problems. **Private speech** is easy to see in young children, who frequently talk to themselves, especially when faced with difficult tasks (Corkum, Humphries, Mullane, & Theriault, 2008; Flavell, 2004). Later, private speech becomes silent but is still very important. Studies have found that children who make extensive use of private speech learn complex tasks more effectively than do other children (Al-Namlah, Fernyhough, & Meins, 2006; Emerson & Miyake, 2003; Schneider, 2002).

THE ZONE OF PROXIMAL DEVELOPMENT   Vygotsky's theory implies that cognitive development and the ability to use thought to control our own actions require first mastering cultural communication systems and then learning to use these systems to regulate our own thought processes. The most important contribution of Vygotsky's theory is an emphasis on the sociocultural nature of learning (Karpov & Haywood, 1998;

Connections

For more on self-regulated learning, see Chapter 8.

sign systems

Symbols that cultures create to help people think, communicate, and solve problems.

self-regulation

The ability to think and solve problems without the help of others.

private speech

Children's self-talk, which guides their thinking and action; eventually internalized as silent inner speech.

"I'm sorry, Miss Scott, but this is outside of my zone of proximal development."

Connections

For more on scaffolding and cooperative learning, see Chapter 8.

zone of proximal development

Level of development immediately above a person's present level.

scaffolding

Support for learning and problem solving; might include clues, reminders, encouragement, breaking the problem down into steps, providing an example, or anything else that allows the student to grow in independence as a learner.

Roth & Lee, 2007; Vygotsky, 1978). He believed that learning takes place when children are working within their **zone of proximal development.** Tasks within the zone of proximal development are endeavors that a child cannot yet accomplish alone but could with the assistance of more competent peers or adults. That is, the zone of proximal development describes tasks that a child has not yet learned but is capable of learning at a given time. Some educators refer to a "teachable moment" when a child or group of children is exactly at the point of readiness for a given concept. Vygotsky further believed that higher mental functioning usually exists in conversation and collaboration among individuals before it exists within the individual.

SCAFFOLDING   A key idea derived from Vygotsky's notion of social learning is that of **scaffolding** (Wood, Bruner, & Ross, 1976): the assistance provided by more competent peers or adults. Typically, scaffolding means providing a child with a great deal of support during the early stages of learning and then diminishing support and having the child take on increasing responsibility as soon as she or he is able. Parents use scaffolding when they teach their children to play a new game or to tie their shoes (Rogoff, 2003). A related concept is cognitive apprenticeship, which describes the entire process of modeling, coaching, scaffolding, and evaluation that is typically seen whenever one-to-one instruction takes place (John-Steiner & Mahn, 2003; Rogoff, 2003). For example, in *Life on the Mississippi,* Mark Twain describes how he was taught to be a steamboat pilot. At first the experienced pilot talked him through every bend in the river, but gradually he was left to figure things out for himself, with the pilot there to intervene only if the boat was about to run aground.

COOPERATIVE LEARNING   Vygotsky's theories support the use of cooperative learning strategies in which children work together to help one another learn (Slavin, 2009; Webb, 2008). Because peers are usually operating within each other's zones of proximal development, they often provide models for each other of slightly more advanced thinking. In addition, cooperative learning makes children's inner speech available to others, so they can gain insight into one another's reasoning process. That is, children benefit from hearing each other "thinking out loud," especially when their groupmates talk themselves through a problem.

How is this parent playing an integral role in his child's learning development? How are scaffolding and cognitive apprenticeship similar?

Frank Siteman/PhotoEdit

a.
Learned task

b.
Assisted learning at zone of proximal development

FIGURE 2.5 Teaching Model Based on Vygotsky's Theory

In (a) the child performs a learned task; in (b) the child is assisted by a teacher or peer who interacts with the child to help him move into a new zone of proximal development (unlearned tasks at limits of learner's abilities) with a new learned task.

ON THE **WEB**

To learn more about applications of Vygotsky's theories to education practice, visit http://mathforum.org/mathed/vygotsky.html. For Vygotsky's place in the teacher education classroom, see www.subr.edu/coeducation/ejournal/Additional%20Files/Casement%20 Vygotskys%20Place%20in%20our%20Teacher%20Education%20Classroom.pdf. Vygotsky resources can be found at www.kolar.org/vygotsky.

Theory into Practice
Classroom Applications of Vygotsky's Theory

Vygotsky's theories of education have major practical implications in the classroom. The concept of a zone of proximal development implies that only instruction and activities that fall within this zone can be learned. Teaching content that is too easy or too difficult does not add to learning (see Figure 2.5). Also, according to a Vygotskian approach to instruction, teaching must emphasize scaffolding, with students taking more and more responsibility for their own learning (Daniels, 2001). Finally, students can benefit from cooperative learning arrangements among groups of learners with differing levels of ability. Tutoring by more competent peers can be effective in promoting growth within the zone of proximal development, as can interactions around complex tasks (Roth & Lee, 2007).

You can use information about Vygotsky's zone of proximal development in organizing classroom activities in the following ways:

Certification Pointer

Lev Vygotsky's work will probably be on your teacher certification test. You may be required to know that the zone of proximal development is the level of development just above where a student is presently functioning and why this is important for both teachers and students.

INTASC

2 Knowledge of Human Development and Learning

4 Multiple Instructional Strategies

- Instruction can be planned to provide practice within the zone of proximal development for individual children or for groups of children. For example, hints and prompts that helped children during a preassessment could form the basis of instructional activities.

- Scaffolding (John-Steiner & Mahn, 2003) provides hints and prompts at different levels. In scaffolding, the adult does not simplify the task, but the role of the learner is simplified "through the graduated intervention of the teacher."

- Cooperative learning activities can be planned with groups of children at different levels who can help each other learn (Slavin, 2009; Webb, 2008).

Scaffolding directly relates to the concept of a zone of proximal development. For example, a child might be shown pennies to represent each sound in a word (e.g., three pennies for the three sounds in "man"). To master this word, the child might be asked to place a penny on the table to show each sound in a word, and finally the child might identify the sounds without the pennies. When the adult provides the child with pennies, the adult provides a scaffold to help the child move from assisted to unassisted success at the task (Spector, 1992). In a high school laboratory science class, a teacher might provide scaffolding by first giving students detailed guides to carrying out experiments, then giving them brief outlines that they might use to structure experiments, and finally asking them to set up experiments entirely on their own.

How Do Language and Literacy Develop?

INTASC

2 Knowledge of Human Development and Learning

The aspects of development arguably of greatest concern to educators are language and literacy. Children who develop large vocabularies and become effective speakers, readers, and writers are likely to be successful in school and beyond. Development of language and literacy is a key objective of teaching, but there are also characteristic patterns of development over time seen in all cultures that are not the direct results of teaching.

■ Language and Literacy Development during the Preschool Years

Although there are individual differences in the rates at which children acquire language abilities, the sequence of accomplishments is similar for all children. Around age 1, children produce one-word utterances such as "bye-bye" and "Mommy." These words typically represent objects and events that are important to the child. Over the course of the second year of life, children begin to combine words into two-word sentences (e.g., "More milk"). During the preschool years, children's vocabulary increases, along with their knowledge of the rules of spoken language. By the time they start school, children have mastered most of the grammatical rules of language, and their vocabulary consists of thousands of words.

ORAL LANGUAGE   Development of oral language, or spoken language, requires not only learning words but also learning the rules of word and sentence construction (Gleason & Ratner, 2009; Hoff, 2003). For example, children learn the rules for how to form plurals before they enter kindergarten. Berko (1985) showed preschoolers a picture of a made-up bird, called a "Wug." She then showed them two such pictures and said, "Now there is another one. There are two of them. There are two _____." The children readily answered "Wugs," showing that they could apply general rules for forming plurals to a new situation. In a similar fashion, children learn to add *-ed* and *-ing* to verbs.

Interestingly, children often learn the correct forms of irregular verbs (such as "He broke the chair") and later replace them with incorrect but more rule-based constructions ("He breaked [or broked] the chair"). One 4-year-old said, "I flew my kite." He then thought for a moment and emphatically corrected himself, saying, "I flewed my kite!" These errors are a normal part of language development and should not be corrected.

Just as they learn rules for forming words, children learn rules for sentences. Their first sentences usually contain only two words ("Want milk," "See birdie," "Jessie outside"), but they soon learn to form more complex sentences and to vary their tone of voice to indicate questions ("Where doggie go?") or to indicate emphasis ("Want cookie!"). Three-year-olds can usually express rather complex thoughts, even though their sentences may still lack such words as *a, the,* and *did.*

Preschoolers often play with language or experiment with its patterns and rules (Garvey, 1990). This experimentation frequently involves changing sounds, patterns, and meanings. One 3-year-old was told by his exasperated parent, "You're impossible!" He replied, "No, I'm impopsicle!" The same child said that his baby brother, Benjamin, was a man because he was a "Benja-man." Children often rearrange word sounds to create new words, rhymes, and funny sentences. The popularity of finger plays, nonsense rhymes, and Dr. Seuss storybooks shows how young children enjoy playing with language.

Oral language development is heavily influenced by the amount and quality of talking parents do with their children. A study by Hart and Risley (1995) found that middle-class parents talked far more to their children than did working-class parents, and that their children had substantially different numbers of words in their vocabularies. The amount of parent speech was as important as socioeconomic status; children of low-income parents who spoke to their children a great deal also had large vocabularies.

READING   Learning to read in the early elementary grades is one of the most important of all developmental tasks, both because other subjects depend on reading and because in our society school success is so often equated with reading success. Children often have complex language skills that are critical in reading, and the process of learning to read can begin quite early if children are read to (Giorgis & Glazer, 2009). Research on **emergent literacy,** or preschoolers' knowledge and skills related to reading (Byrnes, 2008; Morrow, 2009; National Institute for Literacy, 2008; Pressley, 2003), has shown that children may enter school with a great deal of knowledge about reading and that this knowledge contributes to success in formal reading instruction. For example, young children have often learned concepts of print such as that print is arranged from left to right, that spaces between words have meaning, and that books are read from front to back. Many preschoolers can "read" books from beginning to end by interpreting the pictures on each page. They understand about story plots and can often predict what will happen next in a simple story. They can recognize logos on familiar stores and products; for example, very young children often know that *M* is for *McDonald's.* Children who are read to and taught letters at home start off with an advantage in reading (Hood, Conlon, & Andrews, 2008), but all children can learn concepts of print, plot, and other prereading concepts if they attend preschools or kindergartens that emphasize reading and discussing

Annie Pickert/Pearson Education

What language acquisition knowledge and skills will these children likely have by the time they enter kindergarten? As a teacher, what general approaches to formal instruction in reading and writing might you use to build on their knowledge and skills?

✓ **Certification Pointer**

For teacher certification tests you may be expected to know that children's over-generalizations of the rules of grammar are normal for young children and should not be corrected.

INTASC

3 Adapting Instruction for Individual Needs

emergent literacy

Knowledge and skills relating to reading that children usually develop from experience with books and other print media before the beginning of formal reading instruction in school.

books in class (Whitehurst et al., 1999). Similarly, young children can be taught to hear specific sounds within words (a skill called *phonemic awareness*), which contributes to later success in reading (Anthony & Lonigan, 2004; Byrne, Fielding-Barnsley, & Ashley, 2000; Cavanaugh, Kim, Wanzek, & Vaughn, 2004; National Institute for Literacy, 2008).

WRITING   Children's writing follows a developmental sequence (McCarthey, 2008; Morrow, 2009). It emerges out of early scribbles and at first is spread randomly across a page. This characteristic reflects an incomplete understanding of word boundaries as well as an inability to mentally create a line for placing letters. Children invent spellings by making judgments about sounds and by relating the sounds they hear to the letters they know. In trying to represent what they hear, they typically use letter names rather than letter sounds; short vowels are frequently left out because they are not directly associated with letter names (Snow, Burns, & Griffin, 1998). For example, one kindergartner labeled a picture of a dinosaur "DNSR."

Theory into Practice
Promoting Literacy Development in Young Children

Many of the educational implications derived from research on children's literacy development transfer findings from two sources: parental and teacher behaviors that encourage oral language development and studies of young children who learn to read without formal classroom instruction. The most frequent recommendations include reading to children; surrounding them with books and other printed materials; making various writing materials available; encouraging reading and writing; and being responsive to children's questions about letters, words, and spellings (Florez, 2008; Hood et al., 2008; Morrow, 2009; National Institute for Literacy, 2008; Rust, 2008).

You can use numerous props in the classroom, such as telephone books and office space in a dramatic play area. Classrooms can have writing centers with materials such as computers with writing programs, magnetic letters, chalkboards, pencils, crayons, markers, and paper.

You can encourage children's involvement with print by reading in small groups, having volunteers read to children individually, and allowing children to choose books to read. Intimate reading experiences allow children to turn pages, pause to look at pictures or ask questions, and read along with an adult.

Predictable books such as *The Three Little Pigs* and *There Was an Old Lady Who Swallowed a Fly* allow beginning readers to rely on what they already know about literacy while learning sound–letter relationships. Stories are predictable if a child can remember what the author is going to say and how it will be stated. Repetitive structures, rhyme and rhythm, and a match between pictures and text increase predictability.

Children's understanding of literacy is enhanced when adults point out the important features of print. Statements such as "We must start at the front, not at the back of the book"; "Move your finger; you're covering the words and I can't see to read them"; and "You have to point to each word as you say it, not to each letter, like this" help to clarify the reading process. You can indicate features in print that are significant and draw attention to patterns of letters, sounds, or phrases.

Language and Literacy Development during the Elementary and Secondary Years

Language and literacy develop at a rapid rate for children in the elementary and secondary grades. For example, Graves (2007) estimates that the average student adds 3,000 words each year to his or her vocabulary. However, these words will vary, as a student's motivations, interest, culture, and peer group come to have a huge impact. For example, a girl who talks sports with her friends and family, plays sports, reads about sports, and watches sports on television builds up an enormous sports vocabulary. A girl who loves science and is in a family and peer group who talk about science builds up an equally enormous science vocabulary. But which of these—sports or science—will be on the SAT? Obviously, the science girl is at a great advantage in school because of her interests and social context.

Literacy also develops rapidly in the elementary and middle grades. Whereas the emphasis in the early elementary grades is primarily on decoding and fluency, students from second grade onward are increasingly focused on building comprehension, vocabulary, and study skills (Deshler, Palincsar, Biancarosa, & Nair, 2007; Kamil, Borman, Dole, Kral, & Salinger, 2008). Good readers use strategies such as predicting, reviewing, summarizing, and generating their own questions, and if these strategies are directly taught to elementary and secondary students, their comprehension improves (Biancarosa & Snow, 2006; Block & Duffy, 2008; Gersten, Chard, Jayanthi, & Baker, 2006; Pressley, 2003).

INTASC

2 Knowledge of Human Development and Learning

Theory into Practice
Building Vocabulary in Elementary and Secondary Schools

Students in elementary and secondary schools are already learning a vast amount of vocabulary every year. Your task is to help them learn the specific vocabulary most likely to be useful in school and society.

Research on strategies for increasing vocabulary finds that vocabulary building should be a focus throughout the school day. An intentional teacher both creates opportunities to highlight vocabulary and takes advantage of opportunities as they arise, as in the following commonsense principles with a basis in research:

- Get students excited about words. Motivation is the key to vocabulary (Guthrie & Wigfield, 2000; Pintrich, 2003).

- Encourage students to read, especially on topics that interest them. Broad, motivated reading contributes a great deal to vocabulary (Graves, 2007).

- Teach selected words that are both frequently used and broadly useful (Beck, McKeown, & Kucan, 2002; Biemiller, 2004; Blachowicz et al., 2006).

- Give students many opportunities to use new vocabulary words in their own sentences in writing, in conversations, or in other forms that give them opportunities to put them in their own language (Biemiller, 2004; Duke et al., 2003; Headley, 2008).

- Use cooperative learning methods in which students have regular opportunities to study together and use new vocabulary words (Slavin, 2009; Webb, 2008).

Chapter 2 Summary

How Do Children Develop Cognitively

Most developmental psychologists believe nature and nurture combine to influence cognitive development. Continuous theories of development focus on social experiences that a child goes through, whereas discontinuous theories emphasize inborn factors rather than environmental influence.

How Did Piaget View Cognitive Development

Piaget postulated four stages of cognitive development through which people progress between birth and young adulthood. People adjust their schemes for dealing with the world through assimilation and accommodation. Piaget's developmental stages include the sensorimotor stage (birth to 2 years of age), the preoperational stage (2 to 7 years of age), and the concrete operational stage (ages 7 to 11). During the formal operational stage (age 11 to adulthood), young people develop the ability to deal with hypothetical situations and to monitor their own thinking.

How Is Piaget's Work Viewed Today

Piaget's theory has been criticized for relying exclusively on broad, fixed, sequential stages through which all children progress and for underestimating children's abilities. In contrast, neo-Piagetian theories place greater emphasis on social and environmental influences on cognitive development. Nevertheless, Piaget's theory has important implica-

The Intentional Teacher

USING WHAT YOU KNOW about Development to Improve Teaching and Learning

Intentional teachers use what they know about predictable patterns of moral, psychosocial, and cognitive development to make instructional decisions. They assess their students' functioning and they provide instruction that addresses the broad range of stages of development they find in their students. They modify their instruction when they find that particular students need additional challenges or different opportunities. Thinking about student development and watching for it in the classroom helps intentional teachers foster growth for each student.

 1. What do I expect my students to know and be able to do at the end of this lesson? How does this contribute to course objectives and to students' needs to become capable individuals?

You need to assess your own students' developmental functioning in light of your understanding of stages of human development. For example, if you were planning a first-grade science program, you might refer to Piaget's theory and recall that 6- and 7-year-olds have to struggle when asked to think about more than one variable at a time (centration). For that reason your science program goals might focus heavily on students' active, open-ended exploration of their world and far less on formal experimentation requiring

the control of variables. As a middle school English teacher, you might review your list of semester goals and verify that it includes not only an emphasis on a set of writing conventions but also a focus on students' moral development. You might plan to include activities that challenge students to experience characters' emotional distress or to view good and bad from different characters' perspectives.

 2. What knowledge, skills, needs, and interests do my students have that must be taken into account in my lesson?

Every class group has some common age-appropriate interests, but there is always a range of personal knowledge and interests that you can find out about to address individual needs. You might have discussions about interests, role models, sports, and so on, and then weave the information you gain into your sessions, heightening motivation and relevance.

 3. What do I know about the content, child development, learning, motivation, and effective teaching strategies that I can use to accomplish my objectives?

A broad range of individual differences can be found in each classroom, and individual students exhibit inconsistencies between their thinking and their tions for education. Piagetian principles are embedded in the curriculum and in effective teaching practices, and Piaget-influenced concepts such as cognitive constructivism and developmentally appropriate instruction have been important in education reform.

How Did Vygotsky View Cognitive Development

Vygotsky viewed cognitive development as an outgrowth of social development through interaction with others and the environment. Assisted learning takes place in children's zones of proximal development, where they can do new tasks that are within their capabilities only with a teacher's or peer's assistance. Children internalize learning, develop self-regulation, and solve problems through vocal or silent private speech. Teachers provide interactional contexts, such as cooperative learning, and scaffolding.

How Do Language and Literacy Develop

During the Preschool Years

Young children's language develops in predictable patterns as children use and play with language. Early literacy developments depend on children's experiences at home and their learning about books and letters.

During the Elementary and Secondary Years

Students make rapid progress in vocabulary and reading comprehension. Motivation is a key to both, as are opportunities to use new words and reading skills with peers and in new forms.

INTASC   **8** Assessment of Student Learning
　　　　　　 9 Professional Commitment and Responsibility

behavior. You can assess your students' developmental functioning in light of your understanding of general expectations for student development. For example, you might discuss with students problems such as those used by Piaget to assess formal operational thinking. These will give you insight into the thinking processes of your students.

 4. What instructional materials, technology, assistance, and other resources are available to help me accomplish my objectives?

How can you create a rich environment that includes a range of materials and experiences to meet a variety of needs and challenge students at all stages of development? One solution is to introduce a range of materials likely to appeal to and inform students over a broad range of developmental levels, including magazines, newspapers, children's literature, almanacs, maps, physical models, and real objects. You might invite students to suggest or bring materials. You might search out CD-ROMs, DVDs, and Internet resources relevant to the subject you teach. These resources can then be incorporated in projects and investigations that enable students of different developmental levels to find and use materials that make sense to them.

 5. How will I plan to assess students' progress toward my objectives?

Effective intentional teachers use a variety of measures to assess student growth. Students will benefit from measures that can assess psychological as well as cognitive growth. For example, you might ask secondary students to write brief analyses of current social issues and then collect their paragraphs in folders. In spring, for each student, you might pull a sampling of essays from several points in the year to allow students to examine their evolving moral and social perspectives. Students will be pleased to assess their progress over time and their growing ability to form smooth, sophisticated pieces.

 6. How will I respond if individual children or the class as a whole are not on track toward success? What is my back-up plan?

Observe your students carefully to determine whether they are working within their zones of proximal development. Are they experiencing success with the current level of support? More support can be provided for students who are working above their zones of proximal development, and additional challenges might be provided for those working below.

Key Terms

Review the following key terms from the chapter.

accommodation 32	equilibration 32
adaptation 32	formal operational stage 37
assimilation 32	inferred reality 36
centration 34	object permanence 33
cognitive development 31	preoperational stage 34
concrete operational stage 36	private speech 41
conservation 34	reflexes 33
constructivism 32	reversibility 35
continuous theories of development 30	scaffolding 42
development 29	schemes 31
developmentally appropriate education 39	self-regulation 41
	sensorimotor stage 33
discontinuous theories of development 30	seriation 36
	sign systems 41
egocentric 35	transitivity 36
emergent literacy 45	zone of proximal development 42

Self-Assessment: Practicing for Licensure

Directions: This chapter addresses indicators that are often assessed in state licensure exams. To test your understanding, respond to the following questions.

1. According to Piaget, why do preoperational children think a cut-up sandwich is more sandwich than a whole one?

2. According to Vygotsky, why does cooperative work help children to learn?

3. Write a brief description of a typical student at one of the following grade levels: K–1, 2–5, 6–8, 9–12. Use the ideas of each theorist from this chapter to guide your description.

4. Make a list of developmentally appropriate teaching strategies for one of the following grade levels: K–1, 2–5, 6–8, 9–12.

PEARSON
myeducationlab

Go to the Topic **Cognitive and Linguistic Development** in the MyEducationLab (www.myeducationlab.com) for your course, where you can:

■ Find learning outcomes for **Cognitive and Linguistic Development** along with the national standards that connect to these outcomes.

■ Complete Assignments and Activities that can help you more deeply understand the chapter content.

■ Apply and practice your understanding of the core teaching skills identified in the chapter with the Building Teaching Skills and Dispositions learning units.

■ Access video clips of CCSSO National Teachers of the Year award winners responding to the question "Why Do I Teach?" in the Teacher Talk section.

■ Check your comprehension of the content covered in the chapter by going to the Study Plan in the Book Resources for your text. Here you will be able to take a chapter quiz; receive feedback on your answers; and then access Review, Practice, and Enrichment activities to enhance your understanding of chapter content.

■ Watch author Bob Slavin present a Personal Reflections podcast on *Egocentrism in Action* in the Book Resources for your text. Then, respond to the reflection question that follows.

Egocentrism in Action

YOUR REFLECTIONS How will your understanding of egocentrism help you as a teacher?

3

Social, Moral, and Emotional Development

SW Productions/Photodisc/Getty Images

Learning Outcomes

At the end of this chapter, you should be able to:

- Discuss differing views of social, emotional, and moral development
- Identify the stages of children's social and emotional development
- Apply knowlege of social, emotional, and moral development in considering how to solve problems in the classroom

---

At Parren Elementary/Middle School, eighth-graders are encouraged to become tutors for first-graders. They help them with reading, math, and other subjects. As part of this program, Sam Stevens has been working for about a month with Billy Ames.

"Hey, shorty!" says Sam one day when he meets Billy for a tutoring session.

"Hey, Sam!" As always, Billy is delighted to see his big buddy. But today his friendly greeting turns into a look of astonishment. "What have you got in your lip?"

"Haven't you ever seen a lip ring?"

Billy is impressed. "Awesome!"

"A lot of guys are wearing them."

"Didn't it hurt to get a hole in your lip?"

"A little, but I'm tough! Boy, was my mom mad though. I have to take my lip ring off before I go home, but I put it back on while I'm walking to school."

"But didn't your mom . . ."

"Enough of that, squirt! You've got some math to do. Let's get to it!"

The interaction between Sam and Billy illustrates the enormous differences between the world of the adolescent and that of the child. Sam, at 13, is a classic young teen. His idealism and down-deep commitment to the positive are shown in his volunteering to serve as a tutor and in the caring, responsible relationship he has established with Billy. At the same time, Sam is asserting his independence by having his lip pierced and wearing a lip ring, against his mother's wishes. This independence is strongly supported by his peer group, however, so it is really only a shift of dependence from parents and teachers toward peers. His main purpose in wearing a lip ring is to demonstrate conformity to the styles and norms of his peers rather than to those of adults. Yet Sam does still depend on his parents and other adults for advice and support when making decisions that he knows have serious consequences for his future, and he does take off his lip ring at home to avoid a really serious battle with his parents.

Billy lives in a different world. He can admire Sam's audacity, but he would never go so far. Billy's world has simpler rules. He is shocked by Sam's daring to wear a lip ring. He is equally shocked by Sam's willingness to directly disobey his mother. Billy may misbehave, but within much narrower limits. He knows that rules are rules, and he fully expects to be punished if he breaks them.

USING YOUR EXPERIENCE

Critical Thinking Teenagers assert their independence in ways that often are supported by their peer group, but not their parents. In light of this, what kinds of clashes might you anticipate encountering in a secondary classroom, and how do you propose to handle them? What strategies could you use to prevent clashes in the first place?

What Are Some Views of Personal and Social Development ?

As children improve their cognitive skills, they are also developing self-concepts, ways of interacting with others, and attitudes toward the world. Understanding personal and social development is critical to your ability to motivate, teach, and successfully interact with students at various ages. Like cognitive development, personal development and social development are often described in terms of stages. We speak of the "terrible twos," not the "terrible ones" or "terrible threes"; and when someone is reacting in an unreasonable, selfish way, we accuse that person of "behaving like a 2-year-old." The words *adolescent* and *teenager* are associated in Western culture with rebelliousness, identity crises, hero worship, and sexual awakening. These associations reflect stages of development that everyone goes through. This section focuses on a theory of personal and social development proposed by Erik Erikson, which is an adaptation of the developmental theories of the great psychiatrist Sigmund Freud. Erikson's work is often called a **psychosocial theory** because it relates principles of psychological and social development.

■ Erikson's Stages of Psychosocial Development

psychosocial theory

A set of principles that relates social environment to psychological development.

psychosocial crisis

According to Erikson, the set of critical issues that individuals must address as they pass through each of the eight life stages.

Like Piaget, Erikson had no formal training in psychology, but as a young man he was trained by Freud as a psychoanalyst. Erikson hypothesized that people pass through eight psychosocial stages in their lifetimes. At each stage, there are crises or critical issues to be resolved. Most people resolve each **psychosocial crisis** satisfactorily and put it behind them to take on new challenges, but some people do not completely resolve these crises and must continue to deal with them later in life (Miller, 1993). For example, many adults have yet to resolve the "identity crisis" of adolescence. Table 3.1 summarizes the eight stages of life according to Erikson's theory. Each is identified by the central crisis that must be resolved.

TABLE 3.1 **Erikson's Stages of Personal and Social Development**

As people grow, they face a series of psychosocial crises that shape personality, according to Erik Erikson. Each crisis focuses on a particular aspect of personality and involves the person's relationship with other people.

Stage	Approximate Ages	Psychosocial Crises	Significant Relationships	Psychosocial Emphasis
I	Birth to 18 months	Trust vs. mistrust	Maternal person	To get To give in return
II	18 months to 3 years	Autonomy vs. doubt	Parental persons	To hold on To let go
III	3 to 6 years	Initiative vs. guilt	Basic family	To make (= going after) To "make like" (= playing)
IV	6 to 12 years	Industry vs. inferiority	Neighborhood, school	To make things To make things together
V	12 to 18 years	Identity vs. role confusion	Peer groups and models of leadership	To be oneself (or not to be) To share being oneself
VI	Young adulthood	Intimacy vs. isolation	Partners in friendship, sex, competition, cooperation	To lose and find oneself in another
VII	Middle adulthood	Generativity vs. self-absorption	Divided labor and shared household	To take care of
VIII	Late adulthood	Integrity vs. despair	"Mankind," "My kind"	To be, through having been To face not being

Source: "Erikson's Stages of Personality Development," from *Childhood and Society* by Erik H. Erikson. Copyright © 1950, 1963 by W. W. Norton & Company, Inc., renewed © 1978, 1991 by Erik H. Erikson. Used by permission of W. W. Norton & Company, Inc.

STAGE I: TRUST VERSUS MISTRUST (BIRTH TO 18 MONTHS)   The goal of infancy is to develop a basic trust in the world. Erikson (1968, p. 96) defined basic trust as "an essential trustfulness of others as well as a fundamental sense of one's own trustworthiness." The mother, or maternal figure, is usually the first important person in the child's world. She is the one who must satisfy the infant's need for food and affection. If the mother is inconsistent or rejecting, she becomes a source of frustration for the infant rather than a source of pleasure (Cummings, Braungart-Rieker, & Du Rocher-Schudlich, 2003; Thompson, Easterbrooks, & Padilla-Walker, 2003). The mother's behavior creates in the infant a sense of mistrust for his or her world that may persist throughout childhood and into adulthood.

STAGE II: AUTONOMY VERSUS DOUBT (18 MONTHS TO 3 YEARS)   By the age of 2, most babies can walk and have learned enough about language to communicate with other people. Children in the "terrible twos" no longer want to depend totally on others. Instead, they strive toward autonomy, the ability to do things for themselves. The child's desires for power and independence often clash with the wishes of the parent. Erikson believes that children at this stage have the dual desire to hold on and to let go. Parents who are flexible enough to permit their children to explore freely and do things for themselves, while at the same time providing an ever-present guiding hand, encourage the establishment of a sense of autonomy. Parents who are overly restrictive and harsh give their children a sense of powerlessness and incompetence, which can lead to shame and doubt in one's abilities.

STAGE III: INITIATIVE VERSUS GUILT (3 TO 6 YEARS)
During this period, children's continually maturing motor and language skills permit them to be increasingly aggressive and vigorous in the exploration of both their social and physical environment. Three-year-olds have a growing sense of initiative, which can be encouraged by parents and other family members or caregivers who permit children to run, jump, play, slide, and throw. "Being firmly convinced that he is a person on his own, the child must now find out what kind of person he may become" (Erikson, 1968, p. 115). Parents who severely punish children's attempts at initiative will make the children feel guilty about their natural urges both during this stage and later in life.

STAGE IV: INDUSTRY VERSUS INFERIORITY (6 TO 12 YEARS)   Entry into school brings with it a huge expansion in the child's social world. Teachers and peers take on increasing importance for the child, while the influence of parents decreases. Children now want to make things. Success brings with it a sense of industry, a good feeling about oneself and one's abilities. Failure creates a negative self-image, a sense of inadequacy that may hinder future learning. And "failure" need not be real; it may be merely an inability to measure up to one's own standards or those of parents, teachers, or brothers and sisters.

STAGE V: IDENTITY VERSUS ROLE CONFUSION (12 TO 18 YEARS)   The question "Who am I?" becomes important during adolescence. To answer it, adolescents increasingly turn away from parents and toward peer groups. Erikson believed that during adolescence the individual's rapidly changing physiology, coupled with pressures to make

Certification Pointer

For teacher certification tests you will probably be asked about Erik Erikson's stages of personal and social development. You should know that vigorous exploration of their physical and social behavior is a behavior typical of children in Stage III, initiative versus guilt.

According to Erikson, what is the most important question these young people are trying to answer about themselves at this stage in their development? How might it manifest itself in their behavior? What challenges can this pose for you as a teacher?

Bob Daemmrich Photography

decisions about future education and career, creates the need to question and redefine the psychosocial identity established during the earlier stages. Adolescence is a time of change. Teenagers experiment with various sexual, occupational, and educational roles as they try to find out who they are and who they can be. This new sense of self, or "ego identity," is not simply the sum of the prior identifications. Rather, it is a reassembly or "an alignment of the individual's basic drives (ego) with his or her endowment (resolutions of the previous crises) and his or her opportunities (needs, skills, goals, and demands of adolescence and approaching adulthood)" (Erikson, 1980, p. 94).

STAGE VI: INTIMACY VERSUS ISOLATION (YOUNG ADULTHOOD) Once young people know who they are and where they are going, the stage is set for the sharing of their life with another. The young adult is now ready to form a new relationship of trust and intimacy with another individual, a "partner in friendship, sex, competition, and cooperation." This relationship should enhance the identity of both partners without stifling the growth of either. The young adult who does not seek out such intimacy or whose repeated tries fail may retreat into isolation.

STAGE VII: GENERATIVITY VERSUS SELF-ABSORPTION (MIDDLE ADULT-HOOD) Generativity is "the interest in establishing and guiding the next generation" (Erikson, 1980, p. 103). Typically, people attain generativity through raising their own children. However, the crisis of this stage can also be successfully resolved through other forms of productivity and creativity, such as teaching. During this stage, people should continue to grow; if they don't, a sense of "stagnation and interpersonal impoverishment" develops, leading to self-absorption or self-indulgence (Erikson, 1980, p. 103).

STAGE VIII: INTEGRITY VERSUS DESPAIR (LATE ADULTHOOD) In the final stage of psychosocial development, people look back over their lifetime and resolve their final identity crisis. Acceptance of accomplishments, failures, and ultimate limitations brings with it a sense of integrity, or wholeness, and a realization that one's life has been one's own responsibility. The finality of death must also be faced and accepted. Despair can occur in those who regret the way they have led their lives or how their lives have turned out.

■ Implications and Criticisms of Erikson's Theory

As with Piaget's stages, not all people experience Erikson's crises to the same degree or at the same time. The age ranges stated here may represent the best times for a crisis to be resolved, but they are not the only possible times. For example, children who were born into chaotic homes that failed to give them adequate security may develop trust after being adopted or otherwise brought into a more stable environment. People whose negative school experiences gave them a sense of inferiority may find as they enter the work world that they can learn and that they do have valuable skills, a realization that may help them finally to resolve the industry versus inferiority crisis that others resolved in their elementary school years. Erikson's theory emphasizes the role of the environment, both in causing the crises and in determining how they will be resolved. The stages of personal and social development are played out in constant interactions with others and with society as a whole. During the first three stages the interactions are primarily with parents and other family members, but the school plays a central role for most children in Stage IV (industry versus inferiority) and Stage V (identity versus role confusion).

Erikson's theory describes the basic issues that people confront as they go through life. However, his theory has been criticized because it does not explain how or why individuals progress from one stage to another and also because it is difficult to confirm through research (Green, 1989; Miller, 1993).

What Are Some Views of Moral Development?

Society could not function without rules that tell people how to communicate with one another, how to avoid hurting others, and how to get along in life generally. If you are around children much, you may have noticed that they are often rigid about rules. Things are either right or wrong; there is no in-between. If you think back to your own years in middle school or high school, you may recall being shocked to find that people sometimes break rules on purpose and that the rules that apply to some people may not apply to others. These experiences probably changed your concept of rules. Your idea of laws may also have changed when you learned how they are made. People meet and debate and vote; the laws that are made one year can be changed the next. The more complexity you can see, the more you find exists. Just as children differ from adults in cognitive and personal development, they also differ in their moral reasoning. First, we will look at the two stages of moral reasoning described by Piaget and then we will discuss related theories developed by Lawrence Kohlberg. Piaget proposed that there is a relationship between the cognitive stages of development and the ability to reason about moral issues. Kohlberg believed that the development of the logical structures proposed by Piaget is necessary to, although not sufficient for, advances in the area of moral judgment and reasoning.

■ Piaget's Theory of Moral Development

Piaget's theory of cognitive development includes a theory about the development of moral reasoning. Piaget believed that cognitive structures and abilities develop first. Cognitive abilities then determine children's abilities to reason about social situations. As with cognitive abilities, Piaget proposed that moral development progresses in predictable stages, in this case from a very egocentric type of moral reasoning to one based on a system of justice based on cooperation and reciprocity. Table 3.2 summarizes Piaget's stages of moral development.

TABLE 3.2	Piaget's Stages of Personal and Moral Development
As people develop their cognitive abilities, their understanding of moral problems also becomes more sophisticated. Young children are more rigid in their views of right and wrong than older children and adults tend to be.	
Heteronomous Morality (Younger)	**Autonomous Morality (Older)**
Based on relations of constraint; for example, the complete acceptance by the child of adult prescriptions.	Based on relations of cooperation and mutual recognition of equality among autonomous individuals, as in relations between people who are equals.
Reflected in attitudes of *moral realism:* Rules are seen as inflexible requirements, external in origin and authority, not open to negotiation; and right is a matter of literal obedience to adults and rules.	Reflected in *rational* moral attitudes: Rules are viewed as products of mutual agreement, open to renegotiation, made legitimate by personal acceptance and common consent, and right is a matter of acting in accordance with the requirements of cooperation and mutual respect.
Badness is judged in terms of the objective form and consequences of actions; fairness is equated with the content of adult decisions; arbitrary and severe punishments are seen as fair.	Badness is viewed as relative to the actor's intentions; fairness is defined as equal treatment or taking account of individual needs; fairness of punishment is defined by appropriateness to the offense.
Punishment is seen as an automatic consequence of the offense, and justice is seen as inherent.	Punishment is seen as affected by human intention.

To understand children's moral reasoning, Piaget spent a great deal of time watching children play marbles and asking them about the rules of the game. The first thing he discovered was that before about the age of 6, children play by their own idiosyncratic, egocentric rules. Piaget believed that very young children were incapable of interacting in cooperative ways and therefore unable to engage in moral reasoning.

Piaget found that by age 6, children acknowledged the existence of rules, though they were inconsistent in following them. Frequently, several children who were supposedly playing the same game were observed to be playing by different sets of rules. Children at this age also had no understanding that game rules are arbitrary and something that a group can decide by itself. Instead, they saw rules as being imposed by some higher authority and unchangeable.

Piaget (1964) labeled the first stage of moral development **heteronomous morality;** it has also been called the stage of "moral realism" or "morality of constraint." *Heteronomous* means being subject to rules imposed by others. During this period, young children are consistently faced with parents and other adults telling them what to do and what not to do. Violations of rules are believed to bring automatic punishment; people who are bad will eventually be punished. Piaget also described children at this stage as judging the morality of behavior on the basis of its consequences. They judge behavior as bad if it results in negative consequences even if the actor's original intentions were good.

Piaget found that children did not conscientiously use and follow rules until the age of 10 or 12 years, when children are capable of formal operations. At this age, every child playing the game followed the same set of rules. Children understood that the rules existed to give the game direction and to minimize disputes between players. They understood that rules were something that everyone agreed on and that therefore, if everyone agreed to change them, they could be changed.

Piaget also observed that children at this age tend to base moral judgments on the intentions of the actor rather than the consequences of the actions. Children often engage in discussions of hypothetical circumstances that might affect rules. This second stage is labeled **autonomous morality** or "morality of cooperation." It arises as the child's social world expands to include more and more peers. By continually interacting and cooperating with other children, the child's ideas about rules and, therefore, morality begin to change. Rules are now what we make them to be. Punishment for transgressions is no longer automatic but must be administered with a consideration of the transgressor's intentions and extenuating circumstances.

According to Piaget, children progress from the stage of heteronomous morality to that of autonomous morality with the development of cognitive structures but also because of interactions with equal-status peers. He believed that resolving conflicts with peers weakened children's reliance on adult authority and heightened their awareness that rules are changeable and should exist only as the result of mutual consent.

Research on elements of Piaget's theories generally supports his ideas, with one key exception. Piaget is felt to have underestimated the degree to which even very young children consider intentions in judging behavior (see Bussey, 1992). However, the progression from a focus on outcomes to a focus on intentions over the course of development has been documented many times.

■ Kohlberg's Stages of Moral Reasoning

Kohlberg's (1963, 1969) stage theory of moral reasoning is an elaboration and refinement of Piaget's. Like Piaget, Kohlberg studied how children (and adults) reason about rules that govern their behavior in certain situations. Kohlberg did not study children's game playing, but rather probed for their responses to a series of structured situations or **moral dilemmas,** the most famous of which is the following:

In Europe a woman was near death from cancer. One drug might save her, a form of radium that a druggist in the same town had recently discovered. The druggist was charging $2,000, ten times what the drug cost him to make. The sick woman's husband, Heinz,

heteronomous morality
In Piaget's theory of moral development, the stage at which children think that rules are unchangeable and that breaking them leads automatically to punishment.

autonomous morality
In Piaget's theory of moral development, the stage at which a person understands that people make rules and that punishments are not automatic.

moral dilemmas
In Kohlberg's theory of moral reasoning, hypothetical situations that require a person to consider values of right and wrong.

TABLE 3.3   Kohlberg's Stages of Moral Reasoning

When people consider moral dilemmas, it is their reasoning that is important, not their final decision, according
to Lawrence Kohlberg. He theorized that people progress through three levels as they develop abilities of moral reasoning.

I. Preconventional Level	II. Conventional Level	III. Postconventional Level
Rules are set down by others.	Individual adopts rules and will sometimes subordinate own needs to those of the group. Expectations of family, group, or nation seen as valuable in own right, regardless of immediate and obvious consequences.	People define own values in terms of ethical principles they have chosen to follow.
Stage 1: Punishment and Obedience Orientation. Physical consequences of action determine its goodness or badness.		**Stage 5: Social Contract Orientation.** What is right is defined in terms of general individual rights and in terms of standards that have been agreed on by the whole society. In contrast to Stage 4, laws are not "frozen"—they can be changed for the good of society.
Stage 2: Instrumental Relativist Orientation. What is right is whatever satisfies one's own needs and occasionally the needs of others. Elements of fairness and reciprocity are present, but they are mostly interpreted in a "you scratch my back, I'll scratch yours" fashion.	**Stage 3: "Good Boy–Good Girl" Orientation.** Good behavior is whatever pleases or helps others and is approved of by them. One earns approval by being "nice."	**Stage 6: Universal Ethical Principle Orientation.** What is right is defined by decision of conscience according to self-chosen ethical principles. These principles are abstract and ethical (such as the Golden Rule), not specific moral prescriptions (such as the Ten Commandments).
	Stage 4: "Law and Order" Orientation. Right is doing one's duty, showing respect for authority, and maintaining the given social order for its own sake.	

Source: L. Kohlberg, "Stage and Sequence: The Cognitive–Developmental Approach to Socialization." In David A. Goslin (Ed.), *Handbook of Socialization Theory and Research,* pp. 347–380, 1969,
published by Rand McNally, Chicago. Reproduced with permission of David A. Goslin.

went to everyone he knew to borrow the money, but he could only get together about
half of what it cost. He told the druggist that his wife was dying and asked him to sell it
cheaper or let him pay later. But the druggist said "No." The husband got desperate and
broke into the man's store to steal the drug for his wife. Should the husband have done
that? Why? (1969, p. 379)

On the basis of the answers he received, Kohlberg proposed that people pass through
a series of six stages of moral judgment or reasoning. Kohlberg's levels and stages are
summarized in Table 3.3. He grouped these six stages into three levels: preconventional,
conventional, and postconventional. These three levels are distinguished by how the child
or adult defines what he or she perceives as correct or moral behavior. As with other stage
theories, each stage is more sophisticated and complex than the preceding one, and most
individuals proceed through them in the same order (Colby & Kohlberg, 1984). Like
Piaget, Kohlberg was concerned not so much with the child's answer as with the reasoning
behind it. The ages at which children and adolescents go through the stages in Table 3.3
may vary considerably; in fact, the same individual may behave according to one stage at
some times and according to another at other times. However, most children pass from the
preconventional to the conventional level by the age of 9 (Kohlberg, 1969).

✔ **Certification Pointer**

Teacher certification tests are likely to
require you to know the theoretical contributions of Lawrence Kohlberg to the
understanding of children's development
of moral reasoning.

ON THE WEB

The Association for Moral Education (AME) provides an interdisciplinary forum for
individuals interested in the moral dimensions of educational theory and practice at www
.amenetwork.org. For a list of web resources for children's social and ethical development, visit
http://gseacademic.harvard.edu/~tolerance/resources/sed.html. An overview of moral education
theory, by theorist, can be found at http://tigger.uic.edu/~lnucci/MoralEd/overview.html. Also see
the site for *The Journal of Moral Education* (www.tandf.co.uk/journals/titles/03057240.asp).

Stage 1, which is on the **preconventional level of morality,** is very similar in form and content to Piaget's stage of heteronomous morality. Children simply obey authority figures to avoid being punished. In Stage 2, children's own needs and desires become important, yet they are aware of the interests of other people. In a concrete sense they weigh the interests of all parties when making moral judgments, but they are still "looking out for number one." The **conventional level of morality** begins at Stage 3. Here morality is defined in terms of cooperation with peers, just as it was in Piaget's stage of autonomous morality. This is the stage at which children have an unquestioning belief that one should "do unto others as you would have them do unto you." Because of the decrease in egocentrism that accompanies concrete operations, children are cognitively capable of putting themselves in someone else's shoes. They can consider the feelings of others when making moral decisions. No longer do they simply do what will not get them punished (Stage 1) or what makes them feel good (Stage 2). At Stage 4, society's rules and laws replace those of the peer group. A desire for social approval no longer determines moral judgments. Laws are followed without question, and breaking the law can never be justified. Most adults are probably at this stage. Stage 5 signals entrance into the **postconventional level of morality,** a level of moral reasoning attained by fewer than 25 percent of adults, according to Kohlberg, in which there is a realization that the laws and values of a society are somewhat arbitrary and particular to that society. Laws are seen as necessary to preserve the social order and to ensure the basic rights of life and liberty. In Stage 6, one's ethical principles are self-chosen and based on abstract concepts such as justice and the equality and value of human rights. Laws that violate these principles can and should be disobeyed because "justice is above the law." Late in life, Kohlberg (1978, 1980) speculated that Stage 6 is not really separate from Stage 5 and suggested that the two be combined.

Kohlberg (1969) believed that moral dilemmas can be used to advance a child's level of moral reasoning, but only one stage at a time. He theorized that the way in which children progress from one stage to the next is by interacting with others whose reasoning is one or, at most, two stages above their own. Teachers can help students progress in moral reasoning by weaving discussions of justice and moral issues into lessons, particularly in response to events that occur in the classroom or in the broader society (see Nucci, 1987).

Kohlberg found that his stages of moral reasoning ability occurred in the same order and at about the same ages in the United States, Mexico, Taiwan, and Turkey. Other research throughout the world has generally found the same sequence of stages (Eckensberger, 1994), although there are clearly strong influences of culture on moral reasoning as well as moral behavior (Navaez, Getz, Rest, & Thoma, 1999).

■ Criticisms of Kohlberg's Theory

Later research generally supports Kohlberg's main sequence of development (Boom et al., 2001; Dawson, 2002; Nucci, 2009), but there have also been many critiques. One limitation of Kohlberg's early work was that it mostly involved boys. Some research on girls' moral reasoning finds patterns that are somewhat different from those proposed by Kohlberg. Whereas boys' moral reasoning revolves primarily around issues of justice, girls are more concerned about issues of caring and responsibility for others (Gilligan, 1982; Gilligan & Attanucci, 1988; Haspe & Baddeley, 1991). Carol Gilligan argued, for example, that males and females use different moral criteria: Male moral reasoning is focused on people's individual rights, whereas female moral reasoning is focused more on individuals' responsibilities for other people. This is why, she argued, females tend to suggest altruism and self-sacrifice rather than rights and rules as solutions to moral dilemmas (Gilligan, 1982). Kohlberg (Levine, Kohlberg, & Hewer, 1985) revised his theory on the basis of these criticisms. However, most research has failed to find any male–female differences in moral maturity (Bee & Boyd, 2010; Jaffee & Hyde, 2000; Tangney & Dearing, 2002; Thoma & Rest, 1999); nor is there convincing evidence that women are

preconventional level of morality

Stages 1 and 2 in Kohlberg's model of moral reasoning, in which individuals make moral judgments in their own interests.

conventional level of morality

Stages 3 and 4 in Kohlberg's model of moral reasoning, in which individuals make moral judgments in consideration of others.

postconventional level of morality

Stages 5 and 6 in Kohlberg's model of moral reasoning, in which individuals make moral judgments in relation to abstract principles.

more caring, cooperative, or helpful than men (Turiel, 2006; Walker, 2004).

Another criticism of both Piaget's and Kohlberg's work is that young children can often reason about moral situations in more sophisticated ways than a stage theory would suggest (Arnold, 2000; Rest, Edwards, & Thoma, 1997). For example, although young children often consider consequences to be more important than intentions when evaluating conduct, under certain circumstances, children as young as 3 and 4 years of age use intentions to judge the behavior of others (Bussey, 1992). Also, 6- to 10-year-olds at the stage of heteronomous morality have been shown to make distinctions between rules that parents are justified in making and enforcing and rules that are under personal or peer jurisdiction (Keenan & Evans, 2010; Laupa, 1991). Finally, Turiel (2006) has suggested that young children make a distinction between moral rules, such as not lying and stealing, that are based on principles of justice, and social-conventional rules, such as not wearing pajamas to school, that are based on social consensus and etiquette. Research has supported this view, demonstrating that children as young as 2½ to 3 years old make distinctions between moral and social-conventional rules.

The most important limitation of Kohlberg's theory is that it deals with moral reasoning rather than with actual behavior (Arnold, 2000). Many individuals at different stages behave in the same way, and individuals at the same stage often behave in different ways (Walker, 2004). In addition, the context of moral dilemmas matters. For example, a study by Einerson (1998) found that adolescents used much lower levels of moral reasoning when moral dilemmas involved celebrities than when they involved made-up characters. Similarly, the link between children's moral reasoning and moral behavior may be unclear (Thoma & Rest, 1999). For example, a study by Murdock, Hale, and Weber (2001) found that cheating among middle school students was affected by many factors, including motivation in school, success, and relationships with teachers, which have little to do with stages of moral development.

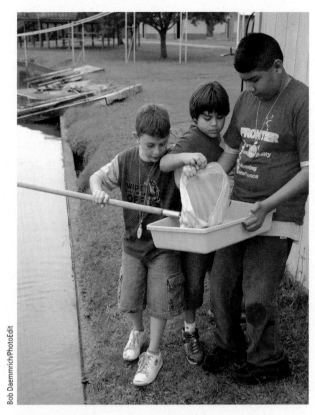

Bob Daemmrich/PhotoEdit

What influence can older children have on the development of moral reasoning in younger children? How can an understanding of moral reasoning help you as a teacher?

How Do Children Develop Socially and Emotionally?

As a teacher, you are not just responsible for the academic achievement of your children. You also strive to develop young people who are socially and emotionally healthy. Like other aspects of development, social and emotional development depend on the experiences provided by schools and families, but they also follow predictable patterns. The following sections discuss these critical areas of development.

■ Socioemotional Development during the Preschool Years

A young child's social life evolves in relatively predictable ways (see Cummings et al., 2003; McHale, Dariotis, & Kauh, 2003). The social network grows from an intimate relationship with parents or other guardians to include other family members, nonrelated adults, and peers. Social interactions extend from home to neighborhood and from preschool or other child-care arrangements to formal school. Erik Erikson's theory of personal and social development suggests that during the preschool years, children must resolve the personality crisis of initiative versus guilt. The child's successful resolution of this stage results in a sense of initiative and ambition tempered by a reasonable understanding of the permissible. Early educators can encourage this resolution by giving children opportunities to take initiative, to be challenged, and to succeed.

PEER RELATIONSHIPS   During the preschool years, **peers** (other children who are a child's equal in age) begin to play an increasingly important role in children's social and cognitive development (Hay, Payne, & Chadwick, 2004). Children's relations with their peers differ in several ways from their interactions with adults. Peer play allows children to interact with other individuals whose level of development is similar to their own. When peers have disputes among themselves, they must make concessions and cooperate in resolving them if the play is to continue; unlike in adult–child disputes, in a peer dispute no one can claim to have ultimate authority. Peer conflicts also let children see that others have thoughts, feelings, and viewpoints that are different from their own. Conflicts also heighten children's sensitivity to the effects of their behavior on others. In this way, peer relationships help young children to overcome the egocentrism that Piaget described as being characteristic of preoperational thinking, helping them see that others have perspectives that are different from their own.

PROSOCIAL BEHAVIOR   **Prosocial behaviors** are voluntary actions toward others such as caring, sharing, comforting, and cooperation. Research on the roots of prosocial behavior has contributed to our knowledge of children's moral as well as social development. Several factors seem to be associated with the development of prosocial behaviors (Eisenberg, 2001), including the following:

- Parental disciplinary techniques that stress the consequences of the child's behavior for others and that are applied within a warm, responsive parent–child relationship (Hoffman, 1993)
- Contact with adults who indicate they expect concern for others, who let children know that aggressive solutions to problems are unacceptable, and who provide acceptable alternatives (Konig, 1995)
- Contact with adults who attribute positive characteristics to children when they do well ("What a helpful boy you are!") (Grusec & Goodnow, 1994)

PLAY   Most of a preschooler's interactions with peers occur during play (Hughes, 2010). However, the degree to which play involves other children increases over the preschool years (Howes & Matheson, 1992). In a classic study of preschoolers, Mildred Parten (1932) identified four categories of play that reflect increasing levels of social interaction and sophistication. **Solitary play** is play that occurs alone, often with toys, and is independent of what other children are doing. **Parallel play** involves children engaged in the same activity side by side but with very little interaction or mutual influence. **Associative play** is much like parallel play but with increased levels of interaction in the form of sharing, turn-taking, and general interest in what others are doing. **Cooperative play** occurs when children join together to achieve a common goal, such as building a large castle with each child building a part of the structure. For example, Howes and Matheson (1992) followed a group of children for 3 years, observing their play when they were 1 to 2 years old and continuing until they were 3 to 4 years old. They found that children engage in more complex types of play as they grow older, advancing from simple forms of parallel play to complex pretend play in which children cooperate in planning and carrying out activities (Berk, 2009; Hughes, 2010).

Connections

For suggested cooperative learning activities, see Chapter 8.

peers

People who are equal in age or status.

prosocial behaviors

Actions that show respect and caring for others.

solitary play

Play that occurs alone.

parallel play

Play in which children engage in the same activity side by side but with very little interaction or mutual influence.

associative play

Play that is much like parallel play but with increased levels of interaction in the form of sharing, turn-taking, and general interest in what others are doing.

cooperative play

Play in which children join together to achieve a common goal.

Play is important for children because it exercises their linguistic, cognitive, and social skills and contributes to their general personality development (Berk, 2009; Hughes, 2010). Children use their minds when playing because they are thinking and acting as if they were another person. When they make such a transformation, they are taking a step toward abstract thinking in that they are freeing their thoughts from a focus on concrete objects. Play is also associated with creativity, especially the ability to be less literal and more flexible in one's thinking. Play has an important role in Vygotsky's theories of development, because it allows children to freely explore ways of thinking and acting that are above their current level of functioning. Vygotsky (1978) wrote, "In play a child is always above his average age, above his daily behavior; in play it is as though he were a head taller than himself" (p. 102).

Annie Pickert/Pearson Education

Are these children engaging in parallel, associative, or cooperative play? How might such play sessions benefit their development of prosocial behaviors and peer relations?

Preschoolers' play appears to be influenced by a variety of factors. For instance, preschoolers' interactions with peers are related to how they interact with their parents (Hughes, 2010). Three-year-olds who have warm and nurturing relationships with parents are more likely to engage in social pretend play and resolve conflicts with peers than are children having less secure relationships with their parents (Howes & Rodning, 1992). Children also play better with familiar peers and same-sex peers (Poulin, Cillessen, & Coie, 1997). Providing age-appropriate toys and play activities can also support the development of play and peer interaction skills.

Connections

For more on Vygotsky, see Chapter 2, pages 41–44.

■ Socioemotional Development during the Elementary Years

By the time children enter elementary school, they have developed skills for more complex thought, action, and social influence. Up to this point, children have been basically egocentric, and their world has been that of home, family, and possibly a preschool or day-care center. The early primary grades will normally be spent working through Erikson's (1963) fourth stage, industry versus inferiority. Assuming that a child has developed trust during infancy, autonomy during the early years, and initiative during the preschool years, that child's experiences in the primary grades can contribute to his or her sense of industry and accomplishment. During this stage, children start trying to prove that they are "grown up"; in fact, this is often described as the I-can-do-it-myself stage. Work becomes possible. As children's powers of concentration grow, they can spend more time on chosen tasks, and they often take pleasure in completing projects. This stage also includes the growth of independent action, cooperation with groups, and performing in socially acceptable ways with a concern for fair play (McHale et al., 2003).

SELF-CONCEPT AND SELF-ESTEEM Personal and social development for elementary school children also includes the important ideas of **self-concept** and **self-esteem** (Swann, Chang-Schneider, & McClarty, 2007). These aspects of

self-concept

A person's perception of his or her own strengths, weaknesses, abilities, attitudes, and values.

self-esteem

The value each of us places on our own characteristics, abilities, and behaviors.

children's development will be strongly influenced by experiences at home, at school, and with peers. Self-concept includes the way in which we perceive our strengths, weaknesses, abilities, attitudes, and values. Its development begins at birth and is continually shaped by experience. Self-esteem refers to how we evaluate our skills and abilities.

ON THE WEB

For an article on how to strengthen children's self-esteem, go to www.kidsource.com/kidsource/content2/strengthen_children_self.html. Also see http://kidshealth.org/parent/emotions/feelings/self_esteem.html#.

As children progress through middle childhood, their ways of thinking become less concrete and more abstract. This trend is also evident in the development of their self-concepts. Preschoolers think about themselves in terms of their physical and material characteristics, including size, gender, and possessions. In contrast, by the early elementary school years, children begin to focus on more abstract, internal qualities such as intelligence and kindness when describing themselves. They can also make a distinction between their private or inner selves and their external, public selves. This becomes especially evident as they depend more on intentions and motives and less on objective behavior in their explanations of their own and others' actions.

During middle childhood, children also begin to evaluate themselves in comparison to others. A preschooler might describe herself by saying, "I like baseball," whereas several years later this same girl is likely to say, "I like baseball more than Sally does." Ruble, Eisenberg, and Higgins (1994) have suggested that younger children use social comparison primarily to learn about social norms and the appropriateness of certain types of conduct. As children get older, they also tend to use **social comparison** to evaluate and judge their own abilities (Borg, 1998).

The trend to use social comparison information to evaluate the self appears to correspond with developmental changes in academic self-esteem. Preschoolers and young children tend to evaluate themselves very positively, in ways that bear no relationship to their school performance or other objective factors (Cole, 1991). By second or third grade, however, children who are having difficulty in school tend to have poorer self-concepts (Chapman, Tunmer, & Prochnow, 2000). This begins a declining spiral. Students who perform poorly in elementary school are at risk for developing poor academic self-concepts and subsequent poor performance in upper elementary and secondary school (Guay, Marsh, & Boivin, 2003).

The primary grades give many children their first chance to compare themselves with others and to work and play under the guidance of adults outside their family. These adults must provide experiences that let children succeed, feel good about themselves, and maintain their enthusiasm and creativity (Canfield & Siccone, 1995; Perry & Weinstein, 1998).

The key word regarding personal and social development is acceptance. The fact is, children do differ in their abilities; and no matter what teachers do, students will have figured out by the end of the elementary years (usually earlier) who is more able and who is less able. However, you can have a substantial impact on how students feel about these differences and on the value that low-achieving students place on learning even when they know they will never be class stars.

social comparison

The process of comparing oneself to others to gather information and to evaluate and judge one's abilities, attitudes, and conduct.

Theory into Practice
Promoting the Development of Self-Esteem

Our society promotes the idea that people, including students, are of equal worth. That is also the premise in a classroom. But believing students are of equal worth doesn't necessarily mean that they are equally competent. Some students are good in reading and others in math; some excel in sports and others in art.

Some classroom activities can give certain students the impression that they as individuals are of less value or worth than other students. Research findings indicate that inappropriate competition (Cohen, 1986) or inflexible ability groups within the classroom (MacIver, Reuman, & Main, 1995; Slavin, 1987a) may teach the wrong lesson to students.

This kind of research can help teachers avoid practices that may discourage children. However, it is not clear that improving self-esteem results in greater school achievement. In fact, research more strongly suggests that as a student grows more competent in school tasks, his or her self-esteem also improves, rather than the other way around (e.g., Chapman et al., 2000; Ellis, 2001b).

It is not necessary to lie and say that all students are equally good in reading or math. You can, however, recognize progress rather than level of ability, focusing your praise on the student's effort and growing competence. As the student sees success in school, a feeling of earned self-esteem will also result (Roeser, Eccles, & Sameroff, 2000).

INTASC

3 Adapting Instruction for Individual Needs

ON THE WEB

Dr. Robert Brooks has written some useful articles on promoting self-esteem in the classroom. See www.greatschools.net/LD/managing/teachers-foster-self-esteem-in-children .gs?content=773. For promoting self-esteem in children with learning disabilities, see www.greatschools.net/LD/managing/self-esteem-in-children.gs?content=759.

GROWING IMPORTANCE OF PEERS The influence of the child's family, the major force during the early childhood years, continues in importance as parents provide role models in terms of attitudes and behaviors. In addition, relationships with brothers and sisters affect relationships with peers, and routines from home either are reinforced or must be overcome in school. However, the peer group takes on added importance. Speaking of the child's entrance into the world outside the family, Ira Gordon notes the importance of peers:

> If all the world's the stage that Shakespeare claimed, children and adolescents are playing primarily to an audience of their peers. Their peers sit in the front rows and the box seats; parents and teachers are now relegated to the back rows and the balcony. (Gordon, 1957, p. 166)

In the lower elementary grades, peer groups usually consist of same-sex children who are around the same age. This preference may be because of the variety of abilities and interests among young children. By the sixth grade, however, students often form groups that include both boys and girls. Whatever the composition of peer groups, they let children compare their abilities and skills to those of others. Members of peer groups also teach one another about their different worlds. Children learn through this sharing of attitudes and values how to sort out and form their own attitudes and values.

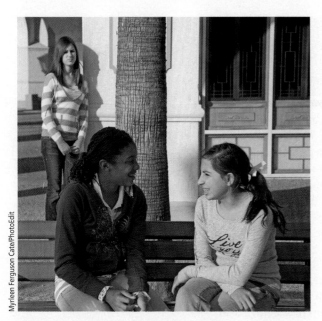

Myrleen Ferguson Cate/PhotoEdit

How do peer relationships affect one's self-concept and self-esteem? What can you as a teacher do to aid your students' emotional development?

FRIENDSHIPS IN MIDDLE CHILDHOOD   During middle childhood, children's conceptions of friendship also mature. Friendship is the central social relationship between peers during childhood, and it undergoes a series of changes before adulthood (Scharf & Hertz-Lazarowitz, 2003). Using as a basis Piaget's developmental stages and children's changing abilities to consider the perspective of others, Selman (1981) described how children's understanding of friendship changes over the years. Between the ages of 3 and 7, children usually view friends as momentary playmates. Children of this age might come home from school exclaiming, "I made a new friend today! Jamie shared her doll with me," or "Bill's not my friend anymore 'cause he wouldn't play blocks with me." These comments reveal the child's view of friendship as a temporary relationship based on a certain situation rather than on shared interests or beliefs. As children enter middle childhood, friendships become more stable and reciprocal. At this age, friends are often described in terms of personal traits ("My friend Mary is nice"), and friendships are based on mutual support, caring, loyalty, and mutual give-and-take.

Friendships are important to children for several reasons. During the elementary school years, friends are companions with whom to have fun and do things. They also serve as important emotional resources by providing children with a sense of security in new situations and when family or other problems arise. Friends are also cognitive resources when they teach or model specific intellectual skills. Social norms for conduct, social interaction skills, and how to resolve conflicts successfully are also learned within the context of friendships (McHale et al., 2003).

PEER ACCEPTANCE   One of the important aspects of peer relations in middle childhood is peer acceptance, or status within the peer group (McCallum & Bracken, 1993). A popular child is one who is named most often by peers as a person they like and least often as someone they dislike. In contrast, a rejected child is one named most often by peers as a person they dislike and least often as someone they like. A child may also be classified as neglected, neither frequently named as liked nor disliked. On the other hand, a controversial child is frequently named as someone who is liked but also frequently as someone who is disliked. Average children are those who are named as being liked and disliked with moderate frequency.

Children who are not well accepted or are rejected by their peers in elementary school are at high risk (Ladd & Troop-Gordon, 2003; Wentzel, Barry, & Caldwell, 2004). These children are more likely to drop out of school, engage in delinquent behavior, and have emotional and psychological problems in adolescence and adulthood than are their peers who are more accepted (Ladd & Troop-Gordon, 2003). Some rejected children tend to be highly aggressive; others tend to be very passive and withdrawn, and these children may be victims of bullying (Pellegrini & Bartini, 2000). Children who are rejected, whether aggressive or withdrawn, seem to be at highest risk for difficulties (Hymel et al., 1993).

Many characteristics seem to be related to peer acceptance, including physical attractiveness (Kennedy, 1990) and cognitive abilities (Wentzel et al., 2004). Studies have also linked behavioral styles to peer acceptance (see Coie, Dodge, & Kupersmidt, 1990). Well-accepted and popular children tend to be cooperative, helpful, and caring and are rarely disruptive or aggressive. Children who are disliked by their peers tend to be highly aggressive and to lack prosocial and conflict resolution skills. Neglected and controversial children display less distinct behavioral styles and often change status over short periods of time (Newcomb & Bagwell, 1998).

Theory into Practice
Helping Children Develop Social Skills

Connections

For more on systematically reinforcing prosocial skills, see Chapter 5, pages 119–124.

Because peer acceptance is such a strong predictor of current and long-term adjustment, it is important for you to try to improve the social skills and levels of acceptance of children who are unpopular or rejected by their peers. Common approaches involve the following:

1. *Reinforcing appropriate social behavior.* You should expect and praise prosocial skills such as helping and sharing. Praise for prosocial behaviors is likely to be most successful if a teacher or other adult uses it with an entire group of children. This allows the child who lacks skills to observe others being praised for positive behavior, and it draws the attention of the peer group to the target child's positive rather than negative actions.

2. *Modeling.* Children who observe models learning positive social interaction skills improve in their own skills.

3. *Coaching.* You can demonstrate positive social skills, explain why these skills are important, provide opportunities for practice, and give follow-up feedback.

The effectiveness of any intervention is likely to depend largely on the involvement of the rejected child's peers and classroom teachers. If peers and teachers notice positive changes in behavior, they are more likely to change their opinions of and accept the child than if interventions are conducted in isolation (Olweus, 1994; White & Kistner, 1992).

■ Socioemotional Development during the Middle School and High School Years

In adolescence, children undergo significant changes in their social and emotional lives as well (Rice & Dolgin, 2008). Partly as a result of their changing physical and cognitive structures, children in the upper elementary grades seek to be more grown up. They want their parents to treat them differently, even though many parents are unwilling to see them in new ways. They also report that though they believe that their parents love them, they do not think their parents understand them. For both boys and girls in the upper elementary grades, membership in groups tends to promote feelings of self-worth. Not being accepted can bring serious emotional problems. Herein lies the major cause of the preadolescent's changing relationship with parents. It is not that preadolescents care less about their parents. It is just that their friends are more important than ever. This need for acceptance by peers helps to explain why preadolescents often dress alike (Baumeister & Leary, 1995). The story of Sam Stevens's lip ring at the beginning of this chapter illustrates how young adolescents express their belongingness with other peer group members through distinctive dress or behavior.

The middle school years often also bring changes in the relationship between children and their teachers. In primary school, children easily accept and depend on teachers. During the upper elementary years, this relationship becomes more complex (see Roeser et al., 2000). Sometimes students will tell teachers personal information they would not tell their parents. Some preadolescents even choose teachers as role models. At the same time, however, some preteens talk back to teachers in ways they would never have considered several years earlier, and some openly challenge teachers. Others become deeply

"School uniforms! That'll take away our individuality!"

alienated from school, starting a pattern that may lead to delinquency and dropping out (Rice & Dolgin, 2008).

IDENTITY DEVELOPMENT One of the first signs of early adolescence is the appearance of **reflectivity,** the tendency to think about what is going on in one's own mind and to study oneself. Adolescents begin to look more closely at themselves and to define themselves differently. They start to realize that there are differences between what they think and feel and how they behave. Using the developing intellectual skills that permit them to consider possibilities, adolescents are prone to be dissatisfied with themselves. They critique their personal characteristics, compare themselves to others, and try to change the way they are.

Adolescents may also wonder whether other people see and think about the world in the same way they do (Phelan, Yu, & Davidson, 1994). They become more aware of their separateness from other people and of their uniqueness. They learn that other people cannot fully know what they think and feel. The issue of who and what one "really" is dominates personality development in adolescence. According to Erikson, the stage is set during adolescence for a major concern with one's identity.

JAMES MARCIA'S FOUR IDENTITY STATUSES On the basis of Erikson's work, James Marcia (1991) identified from in-depth interviews with adolescents four identity statuses that reflect the degree to which adolescents have made firm commitments to religious and political values as well as to a future occupation.

1. *Foreclosure.* Individuals in a state of **foreclosure** have never experienced an identity crisis. Rather, they have prematurely established an identity on the basis of their parents' choices rather than their own. They have made occupational and ideological commitments, but these commitments are more reflective of an assessment by parents or authority figures than an autonomous process of self-assessment. Foreclosure indicates a kind of "pseudo-identity" that generally is too fixed and rigid to serve as a foundation for meeting life's future crises.

2. *Identity diffusion.* Adolescents experiencing **identity diffusion** have found neither an occupational direction nor an ideological commitment of any kind, and they have made little progress toward these ends. They may have experienced an identity crisis, but if so, they were unable to resolve it.

3. *Moratorium.* Adolescents in a state of **moratorium** have begun to experiment with occupational and ideological choices but have not yet made definitive commitments to either. These individuals are directly in the midst of an identity crisis and are currently examining alternate life choices.

4. *Identity achievement.* **Identity achievement** signifies a state of identity consolidation in which adolescents have made their own conscious, clear-cut decisions about occupation and ideology. The individual is convinced that these decisions have been autonomously and freely made and that they reflect his or her true nature and deep inner commitments.

By late adolescence (18 to 22 years of age), most individuals have developed a status of identity achievement. However, adolescents' emotional development seems to be linked to their identity status. For instance, levels of anxiety tend to be highest for adolescents in moratorium and lowest for those in foreclosure (Marcia, 1991). Self-esteem also varies, with adolescents in identity achievement and moratorium reporting the highest levels and those in foreclosure and identity diffusion reporting the lowest levels (Marcia, 1991; Wallace-Broscious, Serafica, & Osipow, 1994).

reflectivity

The tendency to analyze oneself and one's own thoughts.

foreclosure

An adolescent's premature establishment of an identity based on parental choices, rather than his or her own desires.

identity diffusion

Inability to develop a clear direction or sense of self.

moratorium

Experimentation with occupational and ideological choices without definite commitment.

identity achievement

A state of consolidation reflecting conscious, clear-cut decisions concerning occupation and ideology.

In general, adolescents need to experiment and remain flexible if they are successfully to find their own identity. By trying out ways to be, then testing and modifying them, the adolescent can pick the characteristics that are most comfortable and drop the others. To do this, the adolescent must have the self-confidence to experiment and to declare an experiment over, to vary behavior, and to drop characteristics that don't fit, even if the characteristics are supported by others. It helps to have a stable and accepting set of parents, teachers, and peers who will respond positively to one's experimentation.

> ### ON THE WEB
> For explorations of many aspects of adolescent development, including identity development and self-esteem, go to the website of Nancy Darling at the University of Pennsylvania—www.oberlin.edu/faculty/ndarling/lab/ead.htm.

SELF-CONCEPT AND SELF-ESTEEM Self-concept and self-esteem also change as children enter and go through adolescence. The shift toward more abstract portrayals that began in middle childhood continues, and adolescents' self-descriptions often include personal traits (friendly, obnoxious), emotions (depressed, psyched), and personal beliefs (liberal, conservative) (Harter, 1998). In addition, the self-concept becomes more differentiated. Susan Harter's work has identified eight distinct aspects of adolescent concept: scholastic competence, job competence, athletic competence, physical appearance, social acceptance, close friendships, romantic appeal, and conduct (Harter, 1998). Marsh (1993) identified five distinct self-concepts: academic verbal, academic mathematical, parent relations, same-sex, and opposite sex.

Self-esteem also undergoes fluctuations and changes during adolescence. Self-esteem is lowest as children enter middle school or junior high school and with the onset of **puberty** (Jacobs, Lanza, Osgood, Eccles, & Wigfield, 2002). Early maturing girls tend to suffer the most dramatic and long-lasting decreases in self-esteem. In general, adolescent girls have lower self-esteem than do boys (Jacobs et al., 2002). Global self-esteem or feelings of self-worth appear to be influenced most strongly by physical appearance and then by social acceptance from peers.

SOCIAL RELATIONSHIPS As children enter adolescence, changes in the nature of friendships also take place. In general, the amount of time spent with friends increases dramatically; adolescents spend more time with their peers than they do with family members or by themselves (Ambert, 1997). Adolescents who have satisfying and harmonious friendships also report higher levels of self-esteem, are less lonely, have more mature social skills, and do better in school than adolescents who lack supportive friendships (Kerr, Stattin, Biesecker, & Ferrer-Wreder, 2003).

During adolescence, the capacity for mutual understanding and the knowledge that others are unique individuals with feelings of their own also contribute to a dramatic increase in self-disclosure, intimacy, and loyalty among friends. As early adolescents strive to establish personal identities independent of their parents, they also look increasingly to their peers for security and social support. Whereas elementary school-age children look to parents for such support, by seventh grade same-sex friends are perceived to be as supportive as parents, and by tenth grade they are perceived to be the primary source of social support (Rice & Dolgin, 2008).

RELATIONSHIPS WITH PEERS In addition to their close friends, most adolescents also place high value on the larger peer group as a source of ideas and values as well as companionship and entertainment.

puberty
Developmental stage at which a person becomes capable of reproduction.

Certification Pointer

Most teacher certification tests will require you to know how development in one domain, such as physical, may affect a student's performance in another domain, such as social.

The nature of peer relationships in adolescence has been characterized in terms of social status and peer crowds. Social status, or levels of acceptance by peers, is studied with respect to the same status groups that are identified in middle childhood. As with elementary school-age children, popular and well-accepted adolescents tend to display positive conflict resolution and academic skills, prosocial behavior, and leadership qualities, whereas rejected and poorly accepted children tend to display aggressive and antisocial behavior and low levels of academic performance (Parkhurst & Asher, 1992; Wentzel & Erdley, 1993; Zettergren, 2003). These socially rejected children appear to be at great risk for later academic and social problems (Pope & Bierman, 1999). Wentzel and Asher (1995) found, however, that rejected middle school children who were socially submissive did not display the same school-related problems as their rejected aggressive counterparts. These findings suggest that peer rejection and negative behavior together place these children at risk.

Peer relationships in adolescence have also been studied in terms of cliques and crowds with whom adolescents associate (Barber, Eccles, & Stone, 2001). A clique is a fairly small, intimate group that is defined by the common interests, activities, and friends of its members. In contrast, a crowd is a larger group defined by its reputation. Allegiance to a clique or crowd is common during adolescence but not necessarily long term or stable. Although the pressure to conform can be very powerful within these groups, only adolescents who are highly motivated to belong appear to be influenced by these norms in significant ways (Rice, 1996).

EMOTIONAL DEVELOPMENT   Most adolescents experience emotional conflicts at some point. This is hardly surprising; they are going through rapid and dramatic changes in body image, expected roles, and peer relationships. The transitions from elementary to middle school or junior high and then on to high school can also be quite stressful (Harter, Whitesell, & Kowalski, 1992; Midgley, 1993). For most adolescents, emotional distress is temporary and is successfully handled, but for some the stresses lead to delinquency, drug abuse, or suicide attempts (Fisher, 2006).

Emotional problems related to the physical, cognitive, and social development of upper elementary school-age children are common. Though preadolescents are generally happy and optimistic, they also have many fears, such as fear of not being accepted into a peer group, not having a best friend, being punished by their parents, having their parents get a divorce, or not doing well in school.

Other emotions of this age group include anger (and fear of being unable to control it), guilt, frustration, and jealousy. Preadolescents need help in realizing that these emotions and fears are a natural part of growing up. Adults must let them talk about these emotions and fears, even if they seem unrealistic to an adult. Feelings of guilt often arise when there is a conflict between children's actions (based on values of the peer group) and their parents' values. Anger is a common emotion at this age and is displayed with more intensity than many other emotions. Just as they often tell their preadolescents that they should not be afraid, parents often tell them that they should not get angry. Unfortunately, this is an unrealistic expectation, even for adults.

PROBLEMS OF ADOLESCENCE   Adolescence can be a time of great risk for many, as teenagers are now able, for the first time, to engage in behaviors or make decisions that can have long-term negative consequences (Dryfoos, 1998; National Research Council, 1995; Rice & Dolgin, 2008).

Connections

For more on emotional disorders, see Chapter 12, pages 364–366.

Emotional Disorders   Secondary school teachers should be sensitive to the stresses that adolescents face and should realize that emotional disturbances are common (Galambos & Costigan, 2003). They should understand that depressed, hopeless, or unaccountably angry behavior can be a clue that the adolescent needs help, and they should try to put such students in touch with school counselors or other psychologically trained adults (Fisher, 2006).

Bullying   Taunting, harassment, and aggression toward weaker or friendless peers occur at all age levels, but can become particularly serious as children enter early adolescence (Juvonen, Nishina, & Graham, 2000; Pellegrini & Bartini, 2000; San Antonio & Salzfass, 2007).

Dropping Out   Dropping out of secondary school can put adolescents at considerable risk, as dropouts condemn themselves to low-level occupations, unemployment, and poverty (Bracey, 2006). Of course, the factors that lead to dropping out begin early in students' school careers; school failure, retention (staying back), assignment to special education, and poor attendance all predict dropout (Battin-Pearson et al., 2000; Goldschmidt & Wang, 1999; Pallas, 2002). Dropout rates have generally been declining, especially among African American students, although African Americans are still disproportionately at risk (Balfanz & Legters, 2004; Mishel & Roy, 2006). For Latino students, however, dropout rates remain very high (Secada et al., 1998). Dropout rates among students at risk can be greatly reduced by programs that give these students individual attention, high-status roles, and assistance with academic deficits (Burt, Resnick, & Novick, 1998; Slavin & Fashola, 1998). Students in smaller and more academically focused high schools tend to drop out less frequently than other students (Lee & Burkam, 2003).

Drug and Alcohol Abuse   Substance use continues to be widespread among adolescents (Perkins & Borden, 2003). Eighty percent of high school seniors drink alcohol (Jung, 2010), and 31 percent have tried marijuana (Johnson, O'Malley, & Bachman, 2001; National Institute on Drug Abuse, 2005). Drug and alcohol abuse are strongly connected to school failure (Bryant & Zimmerman, 2002).

Delinquency   One of the most dangerous problems of adolescence is the beginning of serious delinquency. The problem is far more common among males than among females. Delinquents are usually low achievers who have been given little

Connections

To learn about prevention of delinquency, see Chapter 11, pages 342–347.

How can Gay-Straight Alliance groups in a school help to promote tolerance among young people and ease the pressure on gay and lesbian youth? What roles do teachers play in creating a safe environment for young people conflicted over sexual identity?

Robin Nelson/PhotoEdit

reason to believe that they can succeed by following the path laid out for them by the school (Hawkins et al., 2000). Delinquency in adolescence is overwhelmingly a group phenomenon; most delinquent acts are done in groups or with the active support of a delinquent subgroup (Branch, 1998; Farmer et al., 2002; Perkins & Borden, 2003).

Risk of Pregnancy Pregnancy and childbirth are serious problems among all groups of female adolescents but particularly among those from lower-income homes (Coley & Chase-Lansdale, 1998; Susman, Dorn, & Schiefelbein, 2003). Just as adolescent males often engage in delinquent behavior to try to establish their independence from adult control, adolescent females often engage in sex, and in many cases have children, to force the world to see them as adults. Because early childbearing makes it difficult for adolescent females to continue their schooling or get jobs, it is a primary cause of the continuation of the cycle of poverty into which many adolescent mothers were themselves born (Hoffman, Foster, & Furstenberg, 1993). Of course, the other side of teen pregnancy is teen fatherhood. Teen fathers also suffer behavioral and academic problems in school (Hanson, Morrison, & Ginsburg, 1989). Many programs intended to delay intercourse and reduce pregnancy exist. Research on these programs finds that sex education programs that emphasize both abstinence and use of condoms and other birth control methods are more effective than those that emphasize simply abstinence (Kirby, 2000).

The Intentional Teacher

USING WHAT YOU KNOW about Early Childhood, Middle Childhood, and Adolescent Students to Improve Teaching and Learning

Intentional teachers realize that students in their early years, in middle childhood, and in adolescence face different challenges as they develop socially, emotionally, and morally. They will relate student goals to the different levels of development and modify their instruction when they find that particular students need additional—or different—support in their growth toward independence.

1. What do I expect my students to know and be able to do at the end of this lesson? How does this contribute to course objectives and to students' needs to become capable individuals?

You need to build understanding of the issues that typically arise at your students' age levels, and you need to develop understanding of the stress that can be involved as students move from one level to the next. For example, you might build into your long-term plans activities that capitalize on the important influence of the peer culture. Examples include allowing students to study content through connections to topical interests such as fashion, music, and sports.

2. What knowledge, skills, needs, and interests do my students have that must be taken into account in my lesson?

Instruction is most appropriate when it addresses students' current functioning. Both formal and informal measures can provide information about your students' social, emotional, and moral development. For example, you might use informal conversation to assess a new student's social skills. As students work, you might listen for hints that they are becoming increasingly reflective about their inner lives.

3. What do I know about the content, child development, learning, motivation, and effective teaching strategies that I can use to accomplish my objectives?

Students' relationships with peers change over time. Observe students' peer interaction so that you can encourage prosocial behavior. For example, you might observe kindergartners during their free time, taking notes about the different forms of play you observe, or you might listen to older students' lunch table conversations, asking yourself: "Do my students compare themselves to their peers in order to evaluate themselves?" You might make a mental note to help them make appropriate comparisons.

Risk of Sexually Transmitted Diseases   Compounding the traditional risks of early sexual activity is the rise in AIDS and other sexually transmitted diseases (Kalichman, 1996). AIDS is still very rare during the adolescent years, and rates of infection have been declining (National Institute of Allergy and Infectious Diseases, 2002). However, because full-blown AIDS can take 10 years to appear, unprotected sex, needle sharing, and other high-risk behavior among teens often causes the high rates of AIDS among young adults. The appearance of AIDS has made the need for early, explicit sex education critical, potentially a life-or-death matter. However, knowledge alone is not enough; sexually active adolescents must have access to condoms and realistic, psychologically sophisticated inducements to use them (Aronson, 1995).

Sexual Identity   It is during adolescence that people begin to explore their sexual identity, including young people who begin to identify with a gay or lesbian orientation. Gay, lesbian, bisexual, and transgendered adolescents can experience great stress and difficulties with their parents. They can especially have problems with peers, who might have strong norms against homosexuality and may engage in taunting, rejection, or even violent behavior toward gay or lesbian peers (GLSEN, 2009). Teachers need to model acceptance of gay and lesbian students and strictly enforce school rules forbidding disrespect toward anyone, gay or straight (Koppelman & Goodhart, 2005).

INTASC   **7** Instructional Planning Skills   **9** Professional Commitment and Responsibility
             8 Assessment of Student Learning

 4. What instructional materials, technology, assistance, and other resources are available to help accomplish my objectives?

Classroom environments may be most likely to allow for development if they include a rich variety of materials that can foster social, linguistic, physical, and academic development. For example, if you teach young children you might include a puppet center and storytelling area to encourage oral language development. With all students, you might use classroom meetings, in which students are encouraged to share openly, to help build a sense of community and acceptance that welcomes all students, no matter what their differences.

It is important to check not only your plans and materials but also students' reaction to those plans and materials as well. Do they seem to perceive their activities as moving them forward?

You might review students' portfolios to trace their growth in self-concept as well as academic mastery. You might watch for patterns that emerge throughout the class and use that information to adjust learning opportunities. If you teach secondary grades, you might review your lesson plans to ensure that they provide opportunities for social interaction and formal problem solving, activities that help adolescents move into Piaget's stage of formal operations, and also note student comments about the assignments.

 5. How will I plan to assess students' progress toward my objectives?

Assess the information you have gathered from different sources over time. Does it suggest that students are growing in each important area of human development? For example, you might ask elementary students to write in their journals about their friends and use their entries to help you determine whether students are developing friendships that can provide social and cognitive resources for them.

 6. How will I respond if individual children or the class as a whole are not on track toward success? What is my back-up plan?

Proponents of developmentally appropriate practice urge teachers to treat each student as an individual with a unique pattern of growth. For example, you might hold a class discussion, addressing such questions as "What can you do better now than at the beginning of the year?" "What would you still like to improve?" "How can we help each other?" By listening carefully to your students' comments you might identify any areas named as trouble spots by more than one student, determining to address such topics with further instructional activities in future lessons.

Theory into Practice
Preventing Adolescents' Problems

✓ **Certification
Pointer**

On your teacher certification test,
you may be asked about the impact
on learning of students' physical,
social, emotional, moral, and cognitive
development.

Not all adolescents experience serious problems, but among those who are at risk, it is far better to prevent problems before they arise. Many programs have demonstrated success with a wide range of problem behaviors by embedding preventive strategies into the regular curriculum. For example, a number of programs have reduced high-risk behaviors by introducing "life skills training," focusing on skills such as making good decisions and resisting peer pressure (Stipek, de la Sota, & Weishaupt, 1999); others focus on building norms of cooperation, altruism, and social responsibility (Battistich, Watson, Solomon, Lewis, & Schaps, 1999). Involving community agencies to engage children in prosocial behaviors is another frequently recommended practice (Kidron & Fleischman, 2006). Comprehensive whole-school reform models can have an impact on high-risk behaviors, especially truancy and dropping out, in middle school (Balfanz & MacIver, 2000) and high school (Bottoms, Feagin, & Han, 2005; Darling-Hammond, Ancess, & Ort, 2002; Jordan, McPartland, Legters, & Balfanz, 2000; McPartland, Balfanz, Jordan, & Legters, 2002).

Chapter 3 Summary

What Are Some Views of Personal and Social Development ?

Erikson proposed eight stages of psychosocial development, each dominated by a particular psychosocial crisis precipitated through interaction with the social environment. In Stage I, trust versus mistrust, the goal is to develop a sense of trust through interaction with caretakers. In Stage II, autonomy versus doubt (18 months to age 3), children have a dual desire to hold on and to let go. In Stage III, initiative versus guilt (3 to 6 years of age), children elaborate their sense of self through exploration of the environment. Children enter school during Stage IV, industry versus inferiority (6 to 12 years of age), when academic success or failure is central. In Stage V, identity versus role confusion (12 to 18 years), adolescents turn increasingly to their peer group and begin their searches for partners and careers. Adulthood brings Stage VI (intimacy versus isolation), Stage VII (generativity versus self-absorption), and Stage VIII (integrity versus despair).

What Are Some Views of Moral Development ?

According to Piaget, children develop heteronomous morality (obedience to authority through moral realism) by around age 6 and later advance to autonomous morality (rational morality based on moral principles). Kohlberg's stages of moral reasoning reflect children's responses to moral dilemmas. In Stages 1 and 2 (the preconventional level), children obey rules set down by others while maximizing self-interest. In Stages 3 and 4 (the conventional level), the individual adopts rules, believes in law and order, and seeks the approval of others. In Stages 5 and 6 (the postconventional level), people define their own values in terms of abstract ethical principles they have chosen to follow.

How Do Children Develop Socially and Emotionally?

During the Preschool Years

Socioemotional development in early childhood can be partly described in terms of Erikson's initiative versus guilt stage. Peer relationships help children overcome the egocentrism that Piaget described as characteristic of preoperational thinking. Prosocial behavior includes caring, sharing, comforting, and cooperating. Parten identified four categories of play—solitary, parallel, associative, and cooperative—that reflect increasing levels of social interaction and sophistication. Play exercises children's linguistic, cognitive, social, and creative skills.

During the Elementary Years

In middle childhood, children may be seen as resolving Erikson's industry versus inferiority psychosocial crisis. School becomes a major influence on development, a place where the child develops a public self, builds social skills, and establishes self-esteem on the basis of academic and nonacademic competencies. In preadolescence, between ages 9 and 12, conformity in peer relations, mixed-sex peer groupings, and challenges to adult authority become more important.

During the Middle School and High School Years

Adolescents may be seen as resolving Erikson's identity versus role confusion psychosocial crisis. They pay attention to how other people view them, search the past, experiment with roles, act on feelings and beliefs, and gradually seek greater autonomy and intimacy in peer relations. Foreclosure occurs when the individual chooses a role prematurely, but by late adolescence, most individuals have developed a state of identity achievement. Many factors, such as dropping out, substance abuse, and AIDS, place adolescents at risk.

Key Terms

Review the following key terms from the chapter.

associative play 62
autonomous morality 58
conventional level of morality 60
cooperative play 62
foreclosure 68
heteronomous morality 58
identity achievement 68
identity diffusion 68
moral dilemmas 58
moratorium 68
parallel play 62
peers 62

postconventional level of morality 60
preconventional level of morality 60
prosocial behaviors 62
psychosocial crisis 54
psychosocial theory 54
puberty 69
reflectivity 68
self-concept 63
self-esteem 63
social comparison 64
solitary play 62

Self-Assessment: Practicing for Licensure

Directions: The chapter-opening vignette addresses indicators that are often assessed in state licensure exams. Re-read the chapter-opening vignette, and then respond to the following questions.

1. As noted in the interaction between Sam and Billy, there are enormous differences between students several years apart. According to the information presented in the chapter, which of the following behaviors is more likely to be exhibited by Billy than by Sam?

   a. Obey parents

   b. Conform to peer demands

   c. Assert independence

   d. Be idealistic

2. According to the information presented in the chapter, which of the following behaviors is more likely to be exhibited by Sam than by Billy?

   a. Follow simple rules

   b. Defy convention

   c. Expect punishment for disobedience

   d. Be dependent on parents

3. Typically, a young child's social life evolves in relatively predictable ways. The social network grows from an intimate relationship with parents or other guardians to

   a. nonrelated adults, peers, and then other family members.

   b. peers, nonrelated adults, and then other family members.

   c. other family members, peers, and then nonrelated adults.

   d. other family members, nonrelated adults, and then peers.

4. For students like Sam Stevens, who is entering what Piaget terms "formal operations," which of the following instructional strategies would be considered developmentally appropriate?

   a. Teach Sam to hear specific sounds as he reads (phonemic awareness)

   b. Allow Sam to invent spellings by making judgments about sounds and by relating the sounds to the letters he knows

   c. Help Sam to resolve the personality crisis of initiative versus guilt

   d. Require Sam to write assignments that require debate (argue pro or con on an issue)

5. One of the first signs of early adolescence is the appearance of reflectivity. What is this?

   a. A return to egocentric thought

   b. The development of initiative

   c. The ability to think about one's own mind

   d. Joining others in working toward a common goal

6. Design a lesson that would be considered developmentally appropriate for someone Billy's age. Include an explanation as to why you believe it is appropriate.

7. Design a lesson that would be considered developmentally appropriate for someone Sam's age. Include an explanation as to why you believe it is appropriate.

8. One of the most serious problems of adolescence is delinquency. Delinquents are usually

   a. high achievers who turn to delinquency out of boredom.

   b. socially adept at leading others into crime.

   c. low achievers who feel they can't succeed in school.

   d. late-maturing adolescents.

9. According to Kohlberg's theory of moral development, how can a teacher help her third-graders move past their belief that "rules are rules with no exceptions"?

   a. Challenge the students' reasoning with explanations from the next higher stage

   b. Discuss moral dilemmas

   c. Read books to the class about moral behavior

   d. Ask each student to write a story about someone who did not follow the rules

myeducationlab

Go to the Topic **Personal, Social, and Moral Development** in the MyEducationLab (www.myeducationlab.com) for your course, where you can:

- Find learning outcomes for **Personal, Social, and Moral Development** along with the national standards that connect to these outcomes.

- Complete Assignments and Activities that can help you more deeply understand the chapter content.

- Apply and practice your understanding of the core teaching skills identified in the chapter with the Building Teaching Skills and Dispositions learning units.

- Access video clips of CCSSO National Teachers of the Year award winners responding to the question "Why Do I Teach?" in the Teacher Talk section.

- Check your comprehension of the content covered in the chapter by going to the Study Plan in the Book Resources for your text. Here you will be able to take a chapter quiz; receive feedback on your answers; and then access Review, Practice, and Enrichment activities to enhance your understanding of chapter content.

- Watch author Bob Slavin present a Personal Reflections podcast on *Understanding Development* in the Book Resources for your text. Then, respond to the reflection questions that follow.

Understanding Development

YOUR REFLECTIONS Why was Jack unable to disconnect my voice from the image of the dinosaur? Why would an understanding of child development be helpful to an early elementary or early childhood teacher?

4

Student Diversity

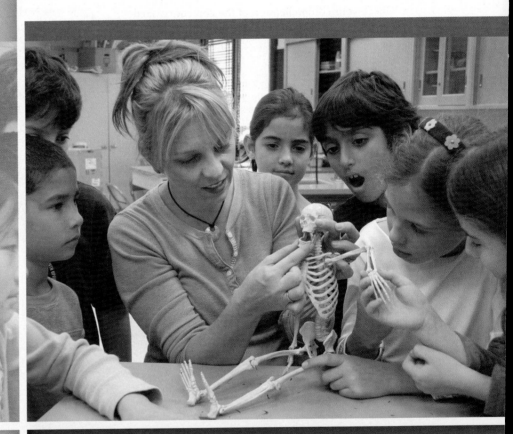

Bill Aron/PhotoEdit

Learning Outcomes

Bill Aron/PhotoEdit

At the end of this chapter, you should be able to:

- Describe the impact of culture on teaching and learning
- Discuss how socioeconomic status can affect achievement
- Discuss how race and ethnicity can affect students' school experiences
- Identify ways schools can help children from low-income families succeed
- Discuss how language differences and bilingual programs affect student achievement
- Identify ways to help English learners succeed in English-speaking classrooms
- Describe how to avoid gender bias in teaching
- Identify several theories of intelligence and learning styles

Marva Vance and John Rossi are first-year teachers at Emma Lazarus Elementary School. It's November, and Marva and John are meeting over coffee to discuss the event dreaded by many a first-year teacher: the upcoming Thanksgiving pageant.

"This is driving me crazy!" Marva starts. "Our classes are like the United Nations. How are we supposed to cast a Thanksgiving pageant? I have three Navajo children. Should I cast them as Native Americans, or would they be offended? My Vietnamese kids have probably never seen a turkey, and the idea of eating a big bird like that must be revolting to them. I wonder how meaningful this will be to my African Americans. I remember when I was in a Thanksgiving pageant and our teacher had us African American students be stagehands because she said there weren't any African American Pilgrims! Besides, what am I going to do about a narrator? José says he wants to be narrator, but his English isn't too good. Lakesha would be good, but she's often out for debate tournaments and would miss some rehearsals. I've also been worrying about the hunters. Should they all be boys? Wouldn't it be gender stereotyping if the boys were hunters and the girls were cooks? What about Mark? He uses a wheelchair. Should I make him a hunter?"

John sighs and looks into his coffee. "I know what you're talking about. I just let my kids sign up for each part in the pageant. The boys signed up as hunters, the girls as cooks, the Native Americans . . . well, you get the idea. Maybe it's too late for us to do anything about stereotyping when the kids have already bought into their roles."

USING YOUR EXPERIENCE

Critical Thinking Spend 4 or 5 minutes writing a plausible ending to the vignette. What did Marva Vance end up doing, and what were the results?

Cooperative Learning In small groups of four students, role-play Marva and John's situation. Then discuss the issues they are raising. After 6 minutes, report your group's conclusions to the class.

Students differ. They differ in ethnicity, culture, social class, and home language. They differ in gender. Some have disabilities, and some are gifted or talented in one or more areas. They differ in performance level, learning rate, and learning style. Their differences can have important implications for instruction, curriculum, and school policies and practices. Marva and John are concerned with student diversity as it relates to the Thanksgiving pageants they are planning, but diversity and its meaning for education are important issues every day, not only on Thanksgiving. This chapter discusses some of the most important ways that North American students differ and some of the methods by which teachers can accept, accommodate, and celebrate student diversity in daily teaching. However, diversity is such an important theme that almost every chapter in this book touches on it. You are more than an instructor of students. Together with your students you are one of the builders of tomorrow's society. A critical part of every teacher's role is to ensure that the equal opportunity we hold to be central to our nationhood is translated into equal opportunity in day-to-day life in the classroom. This chapter is presented with that goal in mind.

What Is the Impact of Culture on Teaching and Learning?

INTASC

2 Knowledge of Human Development and Learning

3 Adapting Instruction for Individual Needs

If you have ever traveled to a foreign country, you noticed differences in behaviors, attitudes, dress, language, and food. In fact, part of the fun of traveling is discovering these differences in **culture,** or the shared norms, traditions, behaviors, language, and perceptions of a group (King, 2002). Though we usually think of cultural differences mostly as national differences, there is probably as much cultural diversity within the United States as between the United States and other industrialized nations. The life of a middle-class family in the United States or Canada may be more like that of a middle-class family in Italy, Ireland, or Israel than like a low-income family living a mile away. Yet although we value cultural differences between nations, differences within our own society are often less valued. The tendency is to value the characteristics of mainstream high-status groups and devalue those of other groups.

By the time children enter school, they have absorbed many aspects of the culture in which they were raised, such as language, beliefs, attitudes, ways of behaving, and food preferences. More accurately, most children are affected by several cultures, in that most are members of many overlapping groups. The cultural background of an individual child is affected by his or her ethnicity, socioeconomic status, religion, home language, gender, and other group identities and experiences (see Figure 4.1). Many of the behaviors associated with growing up in a particular culture have important consequences for classroom instruction. For example, schools expect children to speak standard English. This is easy for students from homes in which standard English is spoken but difficult for those whose families speak other languages or significantly divergent dialects of English. Schools also expect students to be highly verbal, to spend most of their time working independently, and to compete with other students for grades and recognition. However, many cultures place a higher value on cooperation and peer orientation than on independence and competitiveness (Boykin, 1994a,b). Because the culture of the school reflects mainstream middle-class values, and because most teachers are from middle-class backgrounds, the child from a different culture is often at a disadvantage. Understanding students' backgrounds is critical for effectively teaching both academic material and the behaviors and expectations of the school (Asher, 2007).

How Does Socioeconomic Status Affect Student Achievement?

culture

The language, attitudes, ways of behaving, and other aspects of life that characterize a group of people.

One important student difference is social class. Even in small rural towns where almost everyone is the same in ethnicity and religion, the children of the town's bankers, doctors, and teachers probably have a different upbringing from that experienced by the children of most farmhands or domestic workers.

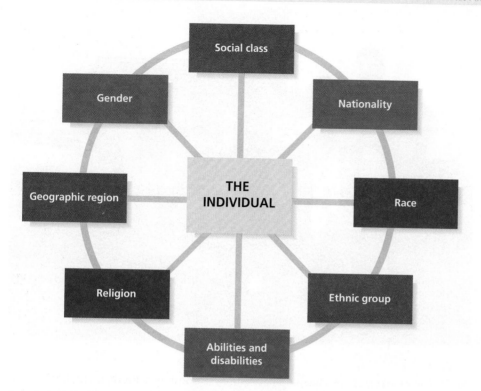

FIGURE 4.1 Cultural Diversity and Individual Identity

Source: Reprinted with permission of the author and publisher from James A. Banks, *Multiethnic Education: Theory and Practice* (3rd ed.), 1993, p. 89. Boston: Allyn & Bacon.

Sociologists define social class, or **socioeconomic status (SES),** in terms of an individual's income, occupation, education, and prestige in society (Thompson & Hickey, 2008). These factors tend to go together, so SES is most often measured as a combination of the individual's income and years of education because these are most easily quantified. Thompson and Hickey describe six class groupings in the United States, as shown in Table 4.1.

In this book the term *middle class* is used to refer to families whose wage earners are in occupations requiring significant education, *working class* to those who have relatively stable occupations not requiring higher education, and *lower class* to those in the urban or rural underclass who are often unemployed and might be living on government assistance.

However, social class indicates more than level of income and education. Along with social class goes a pervasive set of behaviors, expectations, and attitudes, which intersect with and are affected by other cultural factors. Students' social class origins are likely to have a profound effect on attitudes and behaviors in school. Students from working-class or lower-class backgrounds are less likely than middle-class students to enter school knowing how to count, to name letters, to cut with scissors, or to name colors. They are less likely to perform well in school than are children from middle-class homes (Byrnes & Miller, 2007; Natriello, 2002; Sackett, Kuncel, Arneson, Cooper, & Waters, 2009; Sirin,

socioeconomic status (SES)

A measure of prestige within a social group that is most often based on income and education.

TABLE 4.1	Class Groupings	
	Income	**% of Population**
Upper class	$150,000+	5
Upper middle class	$100,000–$150,000	15
Lower middle class	$30,000–$100,000	33
Working class	$16,000–$30,000	30
Lower class	Less than $16,000	14
Poor	Chronically unemployed or on welfare	1

Source: Based on W. Thompson and J. Hickey, 2008, *Society in Focus*, Boston: Pearson.

What additional challenges do schools and families in poor communities face with regard to educating the children of the community? What factors make their success more difficult?

David Bacon/The Image Works

2005). Their parents are less likely to have close relationships with their children's teachers or to be extensively involved with the school (Nzinga-Johnson, Baker, & Aupperlee, 2009). Of course, these differences are true only on the average; many working-class and lower-class parents do an outstanding job of supporting their children's success in school, and many working-class and lower-class children achieve at a very high level. Social class cuts across categories of race and ethnicity. Although it is true that Latino and African American families are, on average, lower in social class than white families, there is substantial overlap; the majority of all low-income families in the United States are white, and there are many middle-class nonwhite families (U.S. Census Bureau, 2001). Definitions of social class are based on such factors as income, occupation, and education, never on race or ethnicity.

Table 4.2 shows the reading performance of eighth-graders on the 2007 National Assessment of Educational Progress (National Center for Education Statistics, 2007). Note that children of more educated parents (a key component of social class) consistently scored higher than children of less educated parents. Similarly, among fourth-graders who qualified for free or reduced-price lunches, which NAEP uses as an indicator of a child's family income, only 15 percent scored at or above "proficient" on the reading portion of the NAEP, in comparison to 42 percent of fourth-graders who did not qualify (NCES, 2007).

TABLE 4.2	NAEP Reading Scores (2007) by Parents' Education: Grade 8
Parents' Education	**Percentage Scoring at or above Proficient**
Graduated college	42
Some education after high school	32
Graduated high school	19
Did not finish high school	12

Source: Based on National Center for Education Statistics (NCES), 2007, *The Condition of Education,* Washington, DC: Author.

■ The Role of Child-Rearing Practices

Average differences between middle-class and lower-class parents in child-rearing practices are the main reason for differences in school achievement. As one indicator of this, there is much evidence that lower-class children adopted into middle-class homes achieve at much higher levels than their nonadopted (usually low-income) brothers and sisters, and at similar levels to their adoptive siblings (van IJzendoorn, Juffer, & Klein Poelhuis, 2005).

Much research has focused on the differences in child-rearing practices between the average middle-class family and the average working-class or lower-class family. Many children from low-income families receive an upbringing that is less consistent with expected school behavior than do middle-class children. By the time they enter school, middle-class children are likely to be good at following directions, explaining and understanding reasons, and comprehending and using complex language, whereas working-class or lower-class children may have less experience in all these areas (Parkay, 2006). Children from disadvantaged homes are more likely to have poor access to health care and may suffer from diseases of poverty such as lead poisoning. Their mothers are less likely to have received good prenatal care (McLoyd, 1998). These factors can delay cognitive development, which also affects school readiness. Of course low-income families lack resources of all kinds to help their children succeed (Children's Defense Fund, 2009). For example, children from disadvantaged families are far more likely to have uncorrected vision, hearing problems, asthma, or other health problems that may inhibit their success in school (Natriello, 2002; Rothstein, 2004).

Another important difference between middle-class and lower-class families is in the kinds of activities parents tend to do with their children. Middle-class parents are likely to express high expectations for their children and to reward them for intellectual development. They are likely to provide good models for language use, to talk and read to their children frequently, and to encourage reading and other learning activities. They are particularly apt to provide all sorts of learning materials for children at home, such as computers, books, and educational games (Yeung, Linver, & Brooks-Gunn, 2002). They are more likely to read to their children before they enter school (Hood et al., 2008). These parents are also likely to expose their children to learning experiences outside the home, such as museums, concerts, and zoos (Duke, 2000). They are more likely to be able to help their children succeed in school and to be involved in their education (Heymann & Earle, 2000). Middle-class parents are likely to expect and demand high achievement from their children; working-class and lower-class parents are more likely to demand good behavior and obedience (Knapp & Woolverton, 1995; Trawick-Smith, 1997). Helping parents who are disadvantaged engage in more enriching interactions with their children can have a substantial impact on their children's cognitive performance. For example, the Parent–Child Home Program (PCHP) initiative provides mothers who are disadvantaged with toys for their toddlers and demonstrations of ways to play and talk with children to enhance their intellectual development. Studies have found strong and lasting effects of this simple intervention on children's cognitive skills and school success, in comparison to children whose parents did not receive PCHP services (Allen & Seth, 2004; Levenstein, Levenstein, & Oliver, 2002).

ON THE WEB

You can learn more about the Parent–Child Home Program (PCHP) by visiting their website at www.parent-child.org.

■ The Link between Income and Summer Learning

Several studies have found that although low-SES and high-SES children make similar progress in academic achievement during the school year, the high-SES children continue to make progress over the summer whereas low-SES children fall behind (Allington & McGill-Franzen, 2003; Borman, Benson, & Overman, 2005; Entwisle, Alexander, & Olson, 2001; Heyns, 2002). These findings suggest that home environment influences not only academic readiness for school but also the level of achievement throughout students' careers in school. Middle-class children are more likely to be engaged in

Connections

For more on summer school programs, see Chapter 9.

school-like activities during the summer and to have available more school-like materials. Working-class and lower-class children may be receiving less academically relevant stimulation at home and are more likely to be forgetting what they learned in school (Hill, 2001). The "summer slide" phenomenon has led many schools to offer summer school to at-risk students, and research is finding that this can be an effective strategy (Borman & Dowling, 2006).

ON THE **WEB**

For information on summer learning, see www.summerlearning.org.

■ The Role of Schools as Middle-Class Institutions

Students from backgrounds other than the mainstream middle class may have difficulties in school in part because their upbringing emphasizes different behaviors from those valued in school. Two of these characteristically middle-class values are individuality and future time orientation (see Boykin, 1994a; Jagers & Carroll, 2002). Most U.S. classrooms operate on the assumption that children should do their own work. Helping others is often defined as cheating. Students are expected to compete for grades, for your attention and praise, and for other rewards. Competition and individual work are values that are instilled early on in most middle-class homes. However, students from lower-class backgrounds (Boykin, 1994a) are less willing to compete and are more interested in cooperating with their peers than are middle-class European Americans. These students have often learned from an early age to rely on their communities, friends, and family and have always also helped and been helped by others. Not surprisingly, students who are most oriented toward cooperation with others learn best in cooperation with others, whereas those who prefer to compete learn best in competition with others (Kagan, Zahn, Widaman, Schwartzwald, & Tyrrell, 1985). Because of the mismatch between the cooperative orientation of many children who are minorities or lower class and the competitive orientation of the school environment, many researchers (e.g., Boykin, 1994a; Greenfield & Cocking, 1994; Triandis, 1995) have argued that there is a structural bias in traditional classrooms that works against these children. They recommend using cooperative learning strategies at least part of the time with these students so that they receive instruction consistent with their cultural orientations (Slavin, 2009; Webb, 2008).

■ School and Community Factors

Often, children from low-income families are placed at risk for school failure by the characteristics of the communities they live in and the schools they attend (Aikens & Barbarin, 2008; Evans, 2004; Everson & Millsap, 2004). For example, school funding in most areas of the United States is correlated with social class; middle-class children are likely to attend schools with greater resources, better-paid (and therefore better-qualified) teachers, and other advantages (Darling-Hammond, 2008). On top of these differences, schools serving low-income neighborhoods may have to spend much more on security, on services for children having difficulties, and on many other needs, leaving even less for regular education (Persell, 1997). This lack of resources can significantly affect student achievement (Land & Legters, 2002; Rothstein, 2004). In very impoverished neighborhoods, crime, a lack of positive role models, inadequate social and health services, and other factors can create an environment that undermines children's motivation, achievement, and mental health (Behrman, 1997; Black & Krishnakumar, 1998; Vernez, 1998). In addition, teachers may hold low expectations for children who are disadvantaged, and this can affect their motivation and achievement (Becker & Luthar, 2002; Borman & Overman, 2004; Hauser-Cram, Sirin, & Stipek, 2003). These factors, however, do not automatically doom children to failure. Many children placed at risk develop what is

Connections

For more on cooperative learning strategies, see Chapter 8, pages 229–236.

Certification Pointer

Teacher certification tests may require that you identify the factors outside of school that can affect student learning. These include culture, family circumstances, community environments, health, and economic conditions.

called *resilience,* the ability to succeed despite many risk factors (Borman & Overman, 2004; Glantz, Johnson, & Huffman, 2002; Waxman, Gray, & Padron, 2002). Resilience is discussed in the following section.

■ Promoting Resilience among Students Who Are Disadvantaged

Resilience refers to characteristics of learners that enable them to overcome factors such as low socioeconomic status to succeed in school and life. Borman & Overman (2004), for example, used a large, national data set to look at students from disadvantaged homes who were succeeding in mathematics. At the individual level, resilient students were not surprisingly characterized by high self-esteem, positive attitudes toward school, and high motivation. More importantly, schools that produced resilient students were places that provided a supportive school community, a safe and orderly environment, and positive teacher–student relationships. For example, resilient students were more likely to report that "most of my teachers really listen to what I have to say" and disagree that "in class I feel put down by my teachers."

Other researchers have also identified characteristics of schools that promote resilience. These include high academic standards (Jesse & Pokorny, 2001), structured schools and classes with clear rules (Pressley, Raphael, & Gallagher, 2004), and widespread participation in after-school activities (Wigfield, Byrnes, & Eccles, 2006).

■ School, Family, and Community Partnerships

If family background is a key factor for explaining differences in student achievement, then it follows that involving families in support of children's school success can be part of the solution. As a professional educator, you can reach out to families and other community members in a variety of ways to improve communication and respect between home and school and to give parents strategies to help their own children succeed. Epstein and colleagues (2002) describe six types of involvement schools might emphasize in a comprehensive partnership with parents (also see Hoover-Dempsey et al., 2005).

INTASC

10 Partnerships

1. *Parenting.*   Assist families with parenting and child-rearing skills, family support, understanding child and adolescent development, and setting home conditions to support learning at each age and grade level. Obtain information from families to help schools understand families' backgrounds, cultures, and goals for children.
2. *Communicating.*   Inform families about school programs and student progress with school-to-home and home-to-school communications. Create two-way channels so that families can easily correspond with teachers and administrators.
3. *Volunteering.*   Improve recruitment, training, activities, and schedules to involve families as volunteers and audiences at the school or in other locations to support students and school programs.
4. *Learning at home.*   Involve families with their children in academic learning activities at home, including homework, goal setting, and other curricular-linked activities and decisions.
5. *Decision making.*   Include families as participants in school decisions, governance, and advocacy activities through PTA, committees, councils, and other parent organizations. Assist family representatives to obtain information from and give information to those they represent.

"Mrs. Rogers, I think this is taking the idea of parent involvement a little too far!"

6. *Collaborating with the community.* Coordinate with community businesses, agencies, cultural and civic organizations, colleges or universities, and other groups. Enable students to contribute service to the community (adapted from Epstein et al., 2002, p. 527).

Correlational research on parent involvement has clearly shown that parents who involve themselves in their children's educations have higher-achieving children than other parents (Flouri & Buchanan, 2004; Lee & Bowen, 2006). However, there has been more debate about the impacts of school programs to increase parent involvement. Many studies have shown positive effects of parent and community involvement programs, especially those that emphasize parents' roles as educators for their own children (see Comer, 2005; Epstein et al., 2002; Hood, Conlon, & Andrews, 2008; McElvany & Artelt, 2009; Patall, Cooper, & Robinson, 2008; Sanders, Allen-Jones, & Abel, 2002), although many other studies have failed to find such benefits (Mattingly, Prisllin, McKenzie, Rodriguez, & Kayzar, 2002; Pomerantz, Moorman, & Litwak, 2007; Schutz, 2006). A recent review of research on parents' reading with their grade K–3 children by Sénéchal and Young (2008) found that parents who explicitly taught their children to read had a much larger impact than those who only listened to their children reading. What the research suggests is that building positive relations with parents and giving parents practical means of helping their children succeed in school are important in improving the achievement and adjustment of all children.

Certification Pointer

Teacher certification tests may require you to outline specific actions that you might take as a teacher to connect the school and students' home environments to benefit your students' learning.

Theory into Practice
Parent Involvement

Parents and other family members have considerable influence over their children's success in school. If you establish positive relationships with parents, you can help them see the importance of supporting the school's educational objectives by, for instance, providing an uncluttered, quiet place for their children to do homework. The more clearly you communicate your expectations for their role in their children's learning, the more likely they will be to play that role. For example, if you expect children to practice reading every evening for homework, sending a form for parents to sign each night communicates the importance of the activity. Other strategies for involving parents in their children's learning include the following (see Ramirez & Soto-Hinman, 2009; Walker & Hoover-Dempsey, 2008).

1. *Home visits.* At the beginning of the school year, it is useful to arrange for visits to your students' homes. Seeing where students come from gives you additional understanding of the supports and constraints that might affect their cognitive and emotional development.

2. *Frequent newsletters for families.* Informing families about what their children will be learning and how they might support that learning at home can increase student success. If you have English learners in your class, offering the newsletter in their first language is important both in improving communication and in showing respect.

3. *Family workshops.* Inviting parents and caregivers to your classroom so you can explain the program of study along with your expectations helps families understand how they can support their children's learning.

4. Positive calls home.   Hearing good news about their children's schoolwork or behavior helps set up a productive cycle of positive reinforcement and increases the likelihood that the behavior will continue. This is especially helpful for family members whose own experiences with the school system were less than positive.

5. Inviting family members to volunteer.   Asking family members to help out in your class by sharing their expertise, interests, or hobbies can make them feel valued. They can demonstrate their occupations, share cultural traditions, or help out with field trips or other special projects. Beyond providing extra assistance, this communicates to your students that you value the diversity of knowledge and expertise that their families bring to your class.

6. Make family members your partners.   Communicating to parents and other family members that you are a team working together to promote their children's achievement makes your job easier and greatly improves parents' attitudes toward school and willingness to work with you in difficult situations as well as good times (Epstein et al., 2002).

■ Supporting the Achievement of Children from Low-Income Groups

Schools can do a great deal to enable children from low-income families to succeed in school (Barr & Parrett, 2001; Borman, 2002/2003; Cole-Henderson, 2000; Gunter, Estes, & Schwab, 2003; Slavin, 2002). One recent study, by Aikens & Barbarin (2008), found that while social class was a strong predictor of children's starting point in kindergarten, their gains in reading from then on depended more on their schools and neighborhoods. Furthermore, there are now many intensive interventions designed to help develop children's cognitive skills early in life and to help their parents do a better job of preparing them for school. Studies of these programs have shown long-term positive effects for children growing up in very impoverished families, especially when the programs are continued into the early elementary grades (Conyers, Reynolds, & Ou, 2003; Ramey & Ramey, 1998; Reynolds, Temple, Robertson, & Mann, 2002; Zimmerman, Rodriguez, Rewey, & Heidemann, 2008). One-to-one tutoring programs for struggling first-graders, for example, have shown substantial effects on the reading achievement of children who are at risk (Cox & Hopkins, 2006; Denton, Anthony, Parker, & Hasbrouck, 2004; Morris, Tyner, & Perney, 2000; Slavin, Lake, Davis, & Madden, 2009). Success for All (Borman et al., 2007; Correnti, 2009; Slavin, Madden, Chambers, & Haxby, 2009), which combines effective instructional programs, tutoring, and family support services, has demonstrated substantial and lasting impacts on the achievement of children in high-poverty schools. Significant reductions in class size have been found to be particularly beneficial to children in high-poverty schools (Finn et al., 2003). High-quality summer school programs (Borman & Boulay, 2004; Borman, Goetz, & Dowling, 2009) and after-school programs (McComb & Scott-Little, 2003) can provide opportunities to move students who are at risk toward success. These and other programs and practices demonstrate that low achievement by lower-class children is not inevitable. Achievement can be greatly improved by use of strategies that are readily available to schools (see Datnow, Lasky, Stringfield, & Teddlie, 2005), and researchers routinely find and describe high-poverty schools that produce high achievement (Center for Public Education, 2008; Kannapel & Clements, 2005; Reeves, 2003).

■ Nonschool Solutions to Achievement Problems of Children Who Are Disadvantaged

In a 2004 book, Richard Rothstein makes an important set of observations about the gaps in achievement between children who are middle-class and children who are disadvantaged. He notes that major explanations for the difference in achievement come from problems not generally under the control of schools, which could be rectified by enlightened policies. Some of the examples he discusses include the following (also see Joe, Joe, & Rowley, 2009).

VISION   Rothstein notes that poor children have severe vision impairment at twice the normal rate. Surprisingly, juvenile delinquents have extraordinarily high rates of vision problems. Rothstein cites data indicating that more than 50 percent of children who are minorities or from low-income backgrounds have vision problems that interfere with their academic work. Some require eyeglasses, and others need eye-exercise therapies. A study by Harris (2002) found that fourth-graders from disadvantaged homes who received free eyeglasses and therapy gained substantially in achievement relative to a control group. Children in school are usually screened for nearsightedness but not for farsightedness or tracking (Gould & Gould, 2003). Even when low-income children have prescriptions for glasses, they often do not obtain them in the first place. If they have glasses, they may not wear them to school.

HEARING   Children who are disadvantaged have more hearing problems than middle-class children, in particular because of the failure to get medical care for ear infections.

LEAD EXPOSURE   Children who are disadvantaged are far more likely to live in homes where dust from old lead paint is in the air. Even small amounts of lead can lead to loss of cognitive functioning and hearing loss. Studies have found blood lead levels of poor children to be five times those of middle-class children (Brookes-Gunn & Duncan, 1997).

ASTHMA   Poor urban children have remarkably high rates of asthma (Joe et al., 2009). Studies in New York and Chicago (Whitman, Williams, & Shah, 2004) found that one in four inner-city African American children had asthma, six times the national rate. In turn, asthma is a major cause of chronic school absence, and even in school, untreated asthma interferes with academic performance.

MEDICAL CARE   Children who are disadvantaged are much less likely to receive adequate medical care than are middle-class children. This leads to problems with absenteeism; poor motivation because of poor health; and the vision, hearing, and asthma problems mentioned earlier (Starfield, 1997).

NUTRITION   Although serious malnutrition is rare in the United States, unhealthy diets are common among children who are disadvantaged, and this affects academic performance (Joe et al., 2009). One study (Neisser et al., 1996) found that simply giving children vitamin and mineral supplements improved their test scores.

Rothstein's (2004) argument is that these and other aspects of poverty could be solved, and doing so could have a significant impact on the achievement of low-income children. Even though there are health agencies and social service agencies that are charged with solving these problems (see, for example, Wulczyn, Smithgall, & Chen, 2009), schools have the advantage that they see the children every day. Simple reforms, such as improving school lunches or providing free eyeglasses that stay at school, might be as effective as much more expensive interventions, such as tutoring or special education, which may not address the root causes of children's problems.

▪ Implications for Teachers

Children enter school with varying degrees of preparation for the school behaviors that lead to success. Their conduct, attitudes, and values also vary. However, the mere fact that some children initially do not know what is expected of them and have fewer entry-level skills than others does not mean that they are destined for academic failure. Although there is a modest positive correlation between social class and achievement, it should not be assumed that this relationship holds for all children from lower-SES families. There are many exceptions. Many working-class and lower-class families can and do provide home environments that are supportive of their children's success in school. Autobiographies of people who have overcome poverty (e.g., Comer, 1990) often refer to the influence of strong parents and role models with high standards who expected nothing less than the best from their children and did what they could to help them achieve. Although you need to be aware of the struggles encountered by many pupils who are disadvantaged, you also need to avoid converting this knowledge into stereotypes. In fact, there is evidence that middle-class teachers often have low expectations for working-class and lower-class students (Borman & Overman, 2004; Persell, 1997) and that these low expectations can become a self-fulfilling prophecy, causing students to perform less well than they could have (Becker & Luthar, 2002; Hauser-Cram et al., 2003).

How Do Ethnicity and Race Affect Students' School Experiences?

One major determinant of a student's cultural background is his or her ethnic origin. An **ethnic group** is made up of individuals who have a shared sense of identity, usually because of a common place of origin (such as Swedish, Polish, or Greek Americans), religion (such as Jewish or Catholic Americans), or race (such as African or Asian Americans). Note that **ethnicity** is not the same as race; **race** refers only to physical characteristics, such as skin color. The idea that races are distinct from each other even in physical characteristics is increasingly being questioned, and there are certainly no clear boundaries, especially as the number of multiracial people increases (Williams, 2009). Ethnic groups usually share a common culture, which may not be true of all people of a given race. African Americans who are recent immigrants from Nigeria or Jamaica, for example, are from ethnic backgrounds that are quite different from those of African Americans whose families have been in the United States for many generations, even if they are of the same race (King, 2002; Mickelson, 2002). Increasingly, Americans identify with multiple ethnic groups, and this has important consequences for their self-perceptions (Shih & Sanchez, 2005).

Most European Americans identify with one or more European ethnic groups, such as Polish, Italian, Irish, Greek, Latvian, or German. Identification with these groups might affect a family's traditions, holidays, food preferences, and, to some extent, outlook on the world. However, white ethnic groups have been largely absorbed into mainstream U.S. society, so the differences among them have few implications for education (Alba, 1990).

The situation is quite different for other ethnic groups. In particular, African Americans (Loury, 2002), Latinos (Secada et al., 1998), and Native Americans (Castagno & Brayboy, 2008; Lomawaima & McCarty, 2002, 2006) have yet to be fully accepted into mainstream U.S. society and (on average) have not yet attained the economic success or security that most European and many Asian ethnic groups have achieved. Students from these ethnic groups face special problems in school and have been the focus of two of the most emotional issues in U.S. education since the mid-1960s: desegregation and bilingual education. The following sections discuss the situation of students of various ethnic backgrounds in schools today.

■ Racial and Ethnic Composition of the United States

The people who make up the United States have always come from many ethnic backgrounds, but every year the proportion of nonwhites and Latinos is increasing. Table 4.3

ethnic group

A group within a larger society that sees itself as having a common history, social and cultural heritage, and traditions, often based on race, religion, language, or national identity.

ethnicity

A history, culture, and sense of identity shared by a group of people.

race

Visible genetic characteristics of individuals that cause them to be seen as members of the same broad group (e.g., African, Asian, Caucasian).

| TABLE 4.3 | Percentage of U.S. Population by Race/Ethnicity in 1990, 2000, 2010, and Projected for 2020, 2030, 2040, and 2050 |

Race/Ethnicity	1990	2000	2010	2020	2030	2040	2050
European American	75.7	71.4	79.5	78.0	76.6	75.3	74.0
Hispanic	9.0	11.9	16.0	19.4	23.0	26.7	30.3
African American	11.8	12.2	12.9	13.0	13.0	13.1	13.0
Asian/Pacific Islander	2.8	3.8	4.9	5.7	6.6	7.4	8.1
American Indian	0.7	0.7	1.03	1.1	1.2	1.2	1.2

Note: Numbers add to more than 100 percent in 2010 to 2050 because Hispanics are also included among European Americans or African Americans.

Source: U.S. Census Bureau, 2008, www.census.gov.

shows U.S. Census Bureau estimates of U.S. population percentages according to ethnicity. Note that the proportion of non-Latino whites is declining; as recently as 1970, 83.3 percent of all Americans were in this category. In contrast, the proportion of Latinos and Asians has grown dramatically since 1990 and has continued to grow at an even more rapid rate from 2000 to 2010. The U.S. Census Bureau projects that by 2050, 48 percent of the U.S. population will be of non-Hispanic European-American background, more than 30 percent will be Hispanic, 13 percent African American, 8 percent Asian/Pacific Islander, and 1 percent American Indian. These trends, which are the result of immigration patterns and differences in birth rates, have profound implications for U.S. education. Our nation is becoming far more ethnically diverse (Hodgkinson, 2008; Lapkoff & Li, 2007).

■ Academic Achievement of Students from Underrepresented Groups

If students from all racial and ethnic groups achieved at the same level as European and Asian Americans, there would probably be little concern about ethnic group differences in U.S. schools. Unfortunately, they don't. On virtually every test of academic achievement, African American, Latino, and Native American students score significantly lower than their European and Asian American classmates. Because members of these groups are less often in situations of economic security and power, they are sometimes referred to as **underrepresented groups.**

Table 4.4 shows reading scores on the 2007 National Assessment of Educational Progress (NAEP) according to students' race or ethnicity. African American, Latino, and American Indian children scored significantly lower than non-Latino white or Asian American children at all grade levels. These differences correspond closely with differences among the groups in average socioeconomic status, which themselves translate into achievement differences (recall Table 4.2).

The achievement gap between African American, Latino, and white children may be narrowing, but not nearly rapidly enough. During the 1970s there was a substantial reduction, but since the early 1980s the gap is only slowly diminishing in both reading and math on the National Assessment of Educational Progress (NCES, 2007).

■ Barriers to the Achievement of Students from Underrepresented Groups

Why do many students from underrepresented groups score so far below European and Asian Americans on achievement tests? The reasons involve economics, society, families,

underrepresented group
An ethnic or social group, members of which are less likely than other groups to experience economic security or power.

	Percentage Scoring at or above Proficient—Grade 4	Percentage Scoring at or above Proficient—Grade 8
TABLE 4.4 **NAEP Reading Scores (2007) by Race/Ethnicity: Grades 4 and 8**		
Race/Ethnicity		
White	43	40
African American	14	13
Latino	17	15
Asian/Pacific Islander	46	41
American Indian/Alaska Native	18	18

Source: National Center for Education Statistics (NCES), 2007, *The Condition of Education,* Washington, DC: Author.

and culture, as well as inadequate responses by schools (Chatterji, 2006; Ladson-Billings, 2006; O'Connor, Hill, & Robinson, 2009; Parkay, 2006; Warikoo & Carter, 2009; Wiggan, 2007). The most important reason is that in our society, African Americans, Latinos (particularly Mexican Americans and Puerto Ricans), and Native Americans tend to occupy the lower rungs of the socioeconomic ladder. Consequently, many families in these groups are unable to provide their children with the stimulation and academic preparation that are typical of a middle-class upbringing. Neither ethnicity nor economics are destiny, of course. Our president is an African American raised by a single mother, and there are many very successful adults who overcome significant barriers. Yet those barriers do exist, and acknowledging the many exceptions, it is still the case that children do not start off with equal resources, and this affects their life chances. In particular, chronic unemployment, underemployment, and employment in very low-wage jobs, which are endemic in many communities of people from underrepresented groups, have a negative effect on family life, including contributing to high numbers of single-parent families in these communities (U.S. Census Bureau, 2001).

Another important disadvantage that many students from underrepresented groups face is academically inferior, overcrowded schools (Barton, 2003; Tate, 2008). Middle-class and many working-class families of all ethnicities throughout the United States buy their way out of inner-city schools by moving to the suburbs or sending their children to private or parochial schools, leaving the public schools to serve people who lack the resources to afford alternatives. The remaining children, who are disproportionately members of ethnic minorities, are likely to attend the lowest-quality, worst-funded schools in the country (Biddle & Berliner, 2002; Ferguson & Mehta, 2004; Lee, 2004), where they often have the least qualified and least experienced teachers (Connor, Son, Hindman, & Morrison, 2004; Darling-Hammond, 2006; Haycock, 2001).

Often, students from minority groups perform poorly because the instruction they receive is inconsistent with their cultural background (Banks, 2006; Jagers & Carroll, 2002; Latham, 1997; Lee, 2008; Ogbu, 2004; Ryan & Ryan, 2005). Academic excellence itself may be seen as inconsistent with acceptance in a student's own community; for example, Ogbu (2004), Spencer, Noll, Stoltzfus, and Harpalani (2001), Stinson (2006), Tyson, Darity, and Castellino (2005), and others have noted the tendency of many African American students to accuse their peers of "acting white" if they strive to achieve. In contrast, many Asian American parents strongly stress academic excellence as an expectation, and as a result many (though not all) Asian subgroups do very well in school (Ng, Lee, & Park, 2007). African Americans (Boykin, 1994a; Jagers & Carroll, 2002; Lee, 2000,

INTASC

8 Assessment of Student Learning

⌇ **Connections**

To learn about motivational factors that affect some students who are minorities and low achievers, including the role of teacher expectations and the phenomenon of learned helplessness, see Chapter 10, pages 298–299.

2008), Native Americans (Castagno & Brayboy, 2008; Lomawaima & McCarty, 2002, 2006; Starnes, 2006), and Mexican Americans (Padrón, Waxman, & Rivera, 2002) generally prefer to work in collaboration with others and perform better in cooperative settings than the competitive settings seen in most classrooms. Lack of respect for students' home languages and dialects can also lead to a diminishing of commitment to school (Delpit, 1995). Low expectations for students who are minorities can contribute to their low achievement (Nasir & Hand, 2006; Ogbu, 2004; Tenenbaum & Ruck, 2007; Van Laar, 2001). This is especially true if, as often happens, low expectations lead well-meaning teachers or administrators to disproportionately place students from underrepresented groups in low-ability groups or tracks (see Braddock, Dawkins, & Wilson, 1995) or in special education (O'Connor & Fernandez, 2006; Reid & Knight, 2006). It is important to note, however, that while African American students often suffer from the low expectations of teachers and others, their expectations for themselves and their academic self-concepts tend to be at least as high as those of their white classmates (Eccles, Wigfield, & Byrnes, 2003; Van Laar, 2001).

■ Stereotype Threat

Imagine that you are left-handed and someone who looks authoritative tells you that research has shown that left-handed people are terrible at math problems involving money. Then you're given a sack of assorted pennies, nickels, dimes, and quarters, and asked to divide them into piles of equal value in sixty seconds.

How would you feel, and how would you do on the task? You might be very anxious, wanting to avoid confirming the stereotype about southpaws (which has no basis whatsoever in reality). You might try to sort the coins using your right hand. In the end, you might perform less well on this simple task than you would if you didn't think left-handers had difficulties with money problems.

This phenomenon, called *stereotype threat* (Aronson, 2002; Aronson & Steele, 2005; Huguet & Régner, 2007), has been demonstrated to apply in many circumstances. Individuals who know of a stereotype about a group to which they belong are anxious about confirming the stereotype, and their anxiety causes them to perform below their real abilities. Obviously, stereotype threat is of greatest concern when members of a given ethnic, gender, or social group feel that they are not expected to do well on particular school tasks. Over time, a student might simply decide that a given activity is not for them, as when a girl decides that math is "not her thing."

To prevent or remedy stereotype threat, you must be careful never to express the belief that certain skills are easier or harder for certain people, and should give all students opportunities to shine and show leadership in all types of tasks. Individual students vary in skills and interests, of course, but teachers should never ascribe a student's success or failure on a given task to their membership in any group.

The low achievement of African American, Latino, and Native American children may well be a temporary problem. Gaps in achievement are slowly diminishing (National Assessment of Educational Progress, 2008), and as African American and Hispanic families enter the middle class, their children's achievement will probably come to resemble that of other groups. In the 1920s it was widely believed that immigrants from southern and eastern Europe (such as Italians, Greeks, Poles, and Jews) were hopelessly backward and perhaps retarded (Oakes & Lipton, 1994), yet the children and grandchildren of these immigrants now achieve as well as the descendants of the Pilgrims. However, we cannot simply wait for inequities to evaporate. The school is one institution that can break the cycle of poverty by giving children from impoverished backgrounds the opportunity to succeed. Most immediately, schools serving many African American, Latino, and Native American children can accelerate the achievement of these children by using effective instructional methods and by making a meaningful commitment to ensuring the success of all children.

■ Effects of School Desegregation

Before 1954, African American, white, and often Latino and Native American students were legally required to attend separate schools in 20 states and the District of Columbia, and segregated schools were common in the remaining states. Students from underrepresented groups were often bused miles away from their nearest public school to separate schools. In 1954, however, the Supreme Court struck down this practice in the landmark *Brown v. Board of Education of Topeka* case on the grounds that separate education was inherently unequal (Ancheta, 2006; Cose, 2004; Smith, 2002; Welner, 2006). *Brown v. Board of Education* did away with legal segregation, but it was many years before large numbers of racially different students were attending school together. In the 1970s, a series of Supreme Court decisions found that the continued segregation of many schools throughout the United States was the result of past discriminatory practices, such as deliberately drawing neighborhood boundary lines to separate schools along racial lines. These decisions forced local school districts to desegregate their schools by any means necessary (Bell, 2004; Ogletree, 2004).

Many districts were given specific standards for the proportions of students from underrepresented groups who could be assigned to any particular school. For example, a district in which 45 percent of the students were African American might be required to have an enrollment of 35 to 55 percent African Americans in each of its schools. To achieve desegregation, some school districts simply changed school attendance areas; others created special magnet schools (such as schools for the performing arts, for students who are talented and gifted, or for technology or science) to induce students to attend schools outside their own neighborhoods. However, in many large urban districts, segregation of neighborhoods is so extensive that districts must bus students to other neighborhoods to achieve racially balanced schools. School desegregation was supposed to increase the academic achievement of low-income students from underrepresented groups by giving them opportunities to interact with more middle-class, achievement-oriented peers. All too often, however, the schools to which students are bused are no better than the segregated schools they left behind, and the outflow of middle-class families from urban areas (which was well under way before busing began) often means that lower-class African American or Latino students are integrated with similarly lower-class whites (Kahlenberg, 2000). Also, it is important to note that because of residential segregation and opposition to busing, most students from underrepresented groups still attend schools in which there are few, if any, whites, and in many areas segregation is once again on the increase (Orfield, Frankenberg, & Lee, 2003; Smith, 2002). Support for busing to achieve integration has greatly diminished among African American and Latino parents (Morris, 1999; Wells & Crain, 1997), and recent Supreme Court decisions have eliminated the judicial push for desegregation (Orfield & Frankenberg, 2007; Orfield & Lee, 2004).

The overall effect of desegregation on the academic achievement of students from underrepresented groups has been small, though positive. However, when desegregation begins in elementary school, particularly when it involves busing children from underrepresented groups to high-quality schools with substantially middle-class student bodies, desegregation can have a significant positive effect on the achievement of the students from underrepresented groups (Trent, 1997; Wells, 1995; Welner, 2006). This effect is thought to result not from desegregation, but rather from attending a better school. One important outcome of desegregation is that African American and Latino students who attend desegregated schools are more likely to attend desegregated colleges, to work in integrated settings, and to attain higher incomes than their peers who attend segregated schools (Schofield, 1995; Wells & Crain, 1997).

Theory into Practice
Teaching in a Culturally Diverse School

The following recommendations can help in promoting social harmony and equal opportunity among students in racially and ethnically diverse classrooms and schools (see also Gay, 2004; Howard, 2007; Nieto & Bode, 2008; Parillo, 2008).

■ Use fairness and balance in dealing with students. Students should never have any justification for believing that "people like me [whites, African Americans, Latinos, Vietnamese] don't get a fair chance" (Banks, 2009).

■ Choose texts and instructional materials that show all ethnic groups in equally positive and nonstereotypical roles (Garcia, 1993). Make sure underrepresented groups are not misrepresented. Themes should be nonbiased, and individuals from underrepresented groups should appear in nonstereotypical high-status roles (Banks, 2008, 2009).

■ Supplement textbooks with authentic material from different cultures taken from newspapers, magazines, and other media of the culture.

■ Reach out to children's parents and families with information and activities appropriate to their language and culture (Lindeman, 2001). Avoid communicating bias, but discuss racial or ethnic relations openly and with empathy, rather than trying to pretend there are no differences (Polite & Saenger, 2003).

■ Avoid stereotyping and emphasize the diversity of individuals, not groups (Koppelman & Goodhart, 2008).

■ Let students know that racial or ethnic bias, including slurs, taunts, and jokes, will not be tolerated in the classroom or in the school. Institute consequences to enforce this standard (Wessler, 2001).

■ Help all students to value their own and others' cultural heritages and contributions to history and civilization. At the same time, avoid trivializing or stereotyping cultures merely in terms of ethnic foods and holidays. Students need more than ever to value diversity and to acquire more knowledge and appreciation of other ways of life (Villegas & Lucas, 2007).

■ Decorate classrooms, hallways, and the library/media center with murals, bulletin boards, posters, artifacts, and other materials that are representative of the students in the class or school or of the other cultures being studied (Manning & Baruth, 2009).

■ Avoid resegregation. Tracking, or between-class ability grouping, tends to segregate high and low achievers, and because of historical and economic factors, students from underrepresented groups tend to be overrepresented in the ranks of low achievers. For this and other reasons, tracking should be avoided (Ferguson & Mehta, 2004; Tyson et al., 2005).

■ Be sure that assignments are not offensive or frustrating to students of diverse cultural groups. For example, asking students to write about their Christmas experiences is inappropriate for non-Christian students (Banks, 2009).

■ Provide structure for intergroup interaction. Proximity alone does not lead to social harmony among racially and ethnically different groups. Students need opportunities to know one another as individuals and to work together toward common goals (Cooper & Slavin, 2004; Parillo, 2008). For example, students who participate in integrated sports and extracurricular activities are more likely than other students to have friends who are ethnically or racially different from themselves (Braddock et al., 1995; Slavin, 1995b).

■ Use cooperative learning, which has been shown to improve relations across racial and ethnic lines (Cooper & Slavin, 2004; National Research Council, 2000). The positive effects of cooperative learning experiences often outlast the teams or groups themselves and may extend to relationships outside of school. Cooperative learning contributes to both achievement and social harmony (Slavin, 2009) and can increase the participation of children from underrepresented groups (Cohen, 2004).

How Do Language Differences and Bilingual Programs Affect Student Achievement?

INTASC

5 Classroom Management and Motivation

In 1979, only 9 percent of Americans aged 5 to 24 were from families in which the primary language spoken was not English. In 1999, this proportion had increased to 17 percent (NCES, 2004), and projections forecast that by 2026, 25 percent of all students will come from homes in which the primary language is not English. Sixty-five percent of these students' families speak Spanish (NCES, 2004). However, many students speak any of dozens of Asian, African, or European languages. The term **language minority** is used for all such students, and **limited English proficient (LEP)** and **English learners (EL)** are terms used for the much smaller number who have not yet attained an adequate level of English to succeed in an English-only program (Garcia, Jensen, & Scribner, 2009). These students are learning English as a second language and may attend classes for English learners in their schools.

Students with limited English proficiency present a dilemma to the educational system (August & Shanahan, 2006a; Li & Wang, 2008). Bilingualism in itself is an asset for students, both cognitively and practically (Adesope, Lavin, Thompson, & Ungerleider, 2009), yet those who have limited proficiency in English need to learn English to function effectively in U.S. society. However, until students are proficient in English, should they be taught math or social studies in their first language or in English? Should they be taught to read in their first language? These questions are not simply pedagogical—they have political and cultural significance that has provoked emotional debate. One such issue is that many Latino parents want their children to be instructed in the Spanish language and culture to maintain their group identity and pride (Díaz-Rico & Weed, 2010; Macedo, 2000). Other parents whose language is neither English nor Spanish often feel the same way (Arzubiaga, Noguerón, & Sullivan, 2009).

■ Bilingual Education

The term **bilingual education** refers to programs for students who are acquiring English that teach the students in their first language part of the time while English is being learned. English learners are typically taught in one of four types of programs.

1. *English immersion.* The most common instructional placement for English learners is some form of English immersion, in which ELs are taught primarily or entirely in English. Typically, children with the lowest levels of English proficiency are placed in programs for English learners that build their oral English to help them succeed in their English-only curriculum. English immersion programs may use carefully designed strategies to build students' vocabularies, simplify instructions, and help English learners succeed in the content (see, for example, Clark, 2009; Díaz-Rico & Weed, 2010; Echevarria, Vogt, & Short, 2008; Gersten et al., 2007). Such models are often referred to as *structured English immersion*. Alternatively, ELs may simply be included in regular English instruction and

language minority
In the United States, native speakers of any language other than English.

limited English proficient (LEP)
Possessing limited mastery of English.

English learners (EL)
Students in U.S. schools who are not native speakers of English.

bilingual education
Instructional program for students who speak little or no English in which some instruction is provided in the native language.

expected to do the best they can. This "sink or swim" approach is most common when the number of ELs is small and they speak languages other than Spanish.

2. *Transitional bilingual education.*   A common but declining alternative for English learners is transitional bilingual education, programs in which children are taught reading or other subjects in their native language (most often, Spanish) for a few years and then transitioned to English, usually in second, third, or fourth grade.

3. *Paired bilingual education.*   In paired bilingual models, children are taught reading or other subjects in both their home language and in English, usually at different times of the day.

4. *Two-way bilingual education.*   Two-way, or dual language, models teach all students both in English and in another language, usually Spanish. That is, English proficient students are expected to learn Spanish as Spanish proficient students learn English (Calderón & Minaya-Rowe, 2003; Estrada, Gómez, & Ruiz-Escalante, 2009; Lessow-Hurley, 2005; Lindholm-Leary, 2004/2005). From the perspective of English learners, a two-way bilingual program is essentially a paired bilingual program, in that they are taught both in their native language and in English at different times.

Research on bilingual strategies for teaching reading generally supports bilingual approaches, especially paired bilingual methods (Greene, 1997; Slavin & Cheung, 2005). The evidence supporting paired bilingual strategies suggests that English learners need not spend many years building their oral English, but can learn English reading with a limited level of English speaking skills, and can then build their reading and speaking capabilities together (Slavin & Cheung, 2005). However, the language of instruction is only one factor in effective education for students who are EL, and the quality of instruction (whether in English only or in English and another language) is at least as important (August & Shanahan, 2006b).

Certification Pointer

In responding to a case study on a teacher certification test, you may be expected to know that conducting an assessment of students' oral language abilities in both their first language and in English would be a first step in helping English learners achieve.

ON THE **WEB**

The National Association for Bilingual Education provides support for the education of English learners at www.nabe.org. Resources for teachers of students who are ELs are presented at www.englishraven.com, teachingrecipes.com, and eflclassroom.ning.com. For a list of bilingual education associations, see: www.educationatlas.com/bilingual-education-organizations.html. Other sites that contain useful information on teaching English learners and teaching foreign languages include the American Council on the Teaching of Foreign Languages (www.actfl.org/i4a/pages/index.cfm?pageid=1), the International Association of Teachers of English as a Foreign Language (www.iatefl.org), the National Clearinghouse for English Language Acquisition and Language Instruction Educational Programs (www.ncela.gwu.edu), the National K–12 Foreign Language Resource Center (http://nflrc.iastate.edu), the Center for Applied Linguistics (www.cal.org), and Teachers of English to Speakers of Other Languages (www.tesol.org/s_tesol/index.asp).

INTASC

4 Multiple Instructional Strategies

6 Communication Skills

7 Instructional Planning Skills

Theory into Practice
Teaching English Learners

Teachers in all parts of the United States and Canada are increasingly likely to have ELs in their classes. The following general principles can help these students succeed in the English curriculum (see August & Shanahan, 2006a; Calderón, 2007; Díaz-Rico, 2004; Echevarria et al., 2008; Farrell, 2009; Garcia & Jensen, 2007;

Genesee, Lindholm-Leary, Saunders, & Christian, 2005; Gersten et al., 2007; Herrera & Murry, 2005; Hill & Flynn, 2006; Tong, Lara-Alecio, Irby, Mathes, & Kwok, 2008).

1. *Don't just say it—show it.* All students benefit from pictures, videos, concrete objects, gestures, and actions to illustrate difficult concepts, but ELs particularly benefit from teaching that includes visual as well as auditory cues (Calderón, 2001).

2. *Encourage safe opportunities to use academic English.* Many ELs are shy in class, not wanting to use their English for fear of being laughed at. Yet the best way to learn a language is to use it. Structure opportunities for students to use English in academic contexts (Reeves, 2005). For example, when asking questions, first give students an opportunity to discuss answers with a partner, and then call on partner pairs. This and other forms of cooperative learning can be particularly beneficial for students learning English (Calderón et al., 2004; Calderón et al., 1998).

3. *Develop vocabulary.* All children, but especially ELs, benefit from explicit teaching of new vocabulary. Give students many opportunities to hear new words in context and to use them in sentences they make up themselves. Learning dictionary definitions is not as useful as having opportunities to ask and answer questions, write new sentences, and discuss new words with partners (Carlo et al., 2004; Fitzgerald & Graves, 2004/2005; Snow, 2006; Zwiers, 2005).

4. *Keep instructions clear.* English learners (and other students) often know the answers but get confused about what they are supposed to do. Take extra care to see that students understand assignments and instructions, for example, by asking students to restate instructions (Díaz-Rico & Weed, 2010).

5. *Point out cognates.* If you speak the home language of your ELs, point out cases in which a word they know is similar to an English word. For example, in a class with many students learning English, you might help them learn the word *amorous* by noting the similarity to the Spanish and Portuguese word *amor*, the French word *amour*, or the Italian word *amore*, depending on the students' languages (Carlo et al., 2004; Dong, 2009).

6. *Never publicly embarrass children by correcting their English.* Instead, praise their correct answer and restate it correctly. For example, Russian students often omit *a* and *the*. If a student says, "Mark Twain was famous author," you might respond, "Right! Mark Twain was a very famous author," without calling attention to your addition of the word *a*. To encourage students to use their English, establish a classwide norm of never teasing or laughing at English errors.

7. *If students learning English are struggling in reading, provide small-group interventions.* Numerous studies have found that ELs who are struggling to learn to read English benefit from intensive small-group tutorials (August & Shanahan, 2006a; Cheung & Slavin, 2005; Gersten et al., 2007; Huebner, 2009).

Increasingly, research on bilingual education is focusing on the identification of effective forms of instruction for language-minority students rather than on the question of which is the best language of instruction (Cheung & Slavin, 2005; Christian & Genesee, 2001; Janzen, 2008; Lee, 2005; U.S. Department of Education, 2000). Cooperative learning programs have been particularly effective both in improving the outcomes of Spanish reading instruction and in helping bilingual students make a successful transition to English-only instruction in the upper elementary grades (August & Shanahan, 2006a; Calderón et al., 1998; Cheung & Slavin, 2005). Recently, there has been a movement to abandon bilingual education in favor of English-only instruction. In California, which

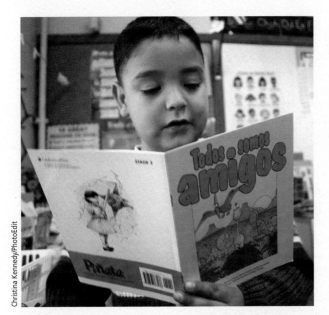

Christina Kennedy/PhotoEdit

According to research, students in a bilingual program will ultimately achieve in English as well as or better than their peers who are taught only in English. Why do you think this is true?

has the largest number of language-minority students in the United States, a referendum called Proposition 227 was passed in 1998 (Merickel et al., 2003). It mandates a maximum of 1 year for students with limited English proficiency to receive intensive assistance in learning English. After that, children are expected to be in mainstream English-only classes. This legislation has reduced but not eliminated bilingual education in California, as parents may still apply for waivers to have their children taught in their first language. Massachusetts, Arizona, and other states have also passed legislation limiting bilingual education (Hakuta, Butler, & Witt, 2000), and even in states that do not ban it, bilingual education is waning in popularity (Mora, 2009).

What Is Multicultural Education?

In recent years, multicultural education has become a much-discussed topic in U.S. education. Definitions of **multicultural education** vary broadly. The simplest definitions emphasize including non-European perspectives in the curriculum— for example, the works of African, Latino, Asian, and Native American authors in English curricula; teaching about Columbus from the point of view of Native Americans; or teaching more about the cultures and contributions of non-Western societies (Banks, 2008, 2009; Koppelman & Goodhart, 2008; Manning & Baruth, 2009). Banks (2009) defines multicultural education as encompassing all policies and practices schools might use to improve educational outcomes not only for students of different ethnic, social class, and religious backgrounds but also for students of different genders and exceptionalities (e.g., children who have mental retardation, hearing loss, or vision loss or who are gifted).

ON THE WEB

For resources and discussions of multicultural education, visit the Multicultural Pavilion at www.edchange.org/multicultural/mission.html and the North Central Regional Educational Laboratory at www.ncrel.org/sdrs/areas/issues/educatrs/presrvce/pe3lk1.htm. Also see the Center for Multilingual Multicultural Research (www.usc.edu/dept/education/CMMR/home.html), New Horizons for Learning (www.newhorizons.org/strategies/multicultural/front_multicultural.htm), the National Association for Multicultural Education (www.nameorg.org), and the National Multicultural Institute (www.nmci.org).

---

multicultural education
Education that teaches the value of cultural diversity.

content integration
Teachers' use of examples, data, and other information from a variety of cultures.

knowledge construction
Helping students understand how the knowledge we take in is influenced by our origins and points of view.

■ Dimensions of Multicultural Education

Banks (2008) discusses five key dimensions of multicultural education (see Figure 4.2).

Content integration involves your use of examples, data, and information from a variety of cultures. This is what most people think of as multicultural education: teaching about different cultures and about contributions made by individuals from diverse cultures, inclusion in the curriculum of works by members of underrepresented groups, including women, and the like (Bettmann & Friedman, 2004; Hicks-Bartlett, 2004).

Knowledge construction refers to helping children understand how knowledge is created and how it is influenced by the racial, ethnic, and social class positions of indi-

FIGURE 4.2 **Five Key Dimensions of Multicultural Education**

Source: Adapted from James A. Banks, "Historical Development, Dimensions, and Practice," in James A. Banks and Cherry A. Banks (Eds.), *Handbook of Research on Multicultural Education,* 1999, New York: Simon & Schuster Macmillan.

viduals and groups (Banks, 2008, 2009). For example, students might be asked to write a history of the early colonization of America from the perspectives of Native Americans or African Americans to learn how the knowledge we take as given is in fact influenced by our own origins and points of view (Koppelman & Goodhart, 2008; Vavrus, 2008).

Prejudice reduction is a critical goal of multicultural education. It involves both advancement of positive relationships among students of different ethnic backgrounds (Cooper & Slavin, 2004; Stephan & Vogt, 2004) and development of more democratic and tolerant attitudes toward others (Banks, 2009).

The term **equity pedagogy** refers to the use of teaching techniques that facilitate the academic success of students from different ethnic and social class groups. For example, there is evidence that members of some ethnic and racial groups, especially Mexican Americans and African Americans, learn best with active and cooperative methods (Boykin, 1994a, 1994b; Losey, 1995; Triandis, 1995).

An **empowering school culture** is one in which school organization and practices are conducive to the academic and emotional growth of all students. A school with such a culture might, for example, eliminate tracking or ability grouping, increase inclusion (and reduce labeling) of students with special needs, try to keep all students on a path leading to higher education, and consistently show high expectations. An excellent example of an empowering school culture is the AVID project (Swanson, Mehan, & Hubbard, 1995; Watt, Powell, & Mendiola, 2004), which places students from underrepresented groups who are at risk in college preparatory classes and provides them with tutors and other assistance to help them succeed in a demanding curriculum.

The first step in multicultural education is for teachers, administrators, and other school staff to learn about the cultures from which their children come and to carefully examine all the policies, practices, and curricula used in the school to identify any areas of possible bias (e.g., teaching only about European and European American culture or history). Books by Banks (2006, 2008, 2009), Koppelman and Goodhart (2008), Nieto and Bode (2008), and Manning and Baruth (2009) are good places to start. These and other books identify some of the characteristics of various cultures and teaching strategies and materials that are appropriate to each.

Certification Pointer

For your teacher certification test you should recognize the importance of connecting your instruction to your students' cultural experiences.

prejudice reduction

A critical goal of multicultural education; involves development of positive relationships and tolerant attitudes among students of different backgrounds.

equity pedagogy

Teaching techniques that facilitate the academic success of students from different ethnic and social class groups.

empowering school culture

A school culture in which the institution's organization and practices are conducive to the academic and emotional growth of all students.

21ST Century Learning

Global Awareness

Making students aware of geography and cultures throughout the world has always been important, but in the 21st century it is also crucial for students to begin to understand the perspectives of people in other countries (Zhao, 2009). How does the Amazon look to a landless Brazilian? Why are companies in India doing customer service for Americans and Europeans? How have Chile and South Africa capitalized on their locations to provide out-of-season fruits and vegetables to countries in the Northern Hemisphere, and how does this affect their societies?

Global awareness can help North American students see each other in new ways—to see differences among us as just part of the astonishing differences and the equally astonishing similarities among people and families across the globe. Knowing about the world

and feeling responsibility for the positive development of all people can help students accept each other and value diversity in all of its forms.

Questions

■ How do you think the increasing number of overseas employees for U.S. companies (e.g., people in India doing customer service for a U.S. computer company) influences the way that these countries see the United States? How do you think it affects the way they see their own country? How does it influence the way that Americans see U.S. companies?

■ What difference do you think this will make in the career choices that today's students will eventually make in the United States and abroad?

How Do Gender and Gender Bias Affect Students' School Experiences ?

A child's sex is a visible, permanent attribute. Cross-cultural research indicates that gender roles are among the first that individuals learn and that all societies treat males differently from females. Therefore, gender-role or sex-role behavior is learned behavior. However, the range of roles occupied by males and females across cultures is broad. What is considered natural behavior for each gender is based more on cultural belief than on biological necessity. Nevertheless, the extent to which biological differences and gender socialization affect behavioral patterns and achievement is still a much-debated topic. The consensus of a large body of research is that despite the inherent biological differences, virtually all of the observed differences between males and females (beyond physical characteristics) can be clearly linked to differences in early socialization experiences (Eliot, 2009).

■ Male and Female Thinking and Learning

Although there is much evidence of differences in temperament and personality between boys and girls (e.g., Else-Quest, Shibley, Goldsmith, & Van Hulle, 2006; Rose & Rudolph, 2006), there is considerable debate about differences in aptitude and achievement. The question of gender differences in intelligence or academic achievement has been debated for centuries, and the issue has taken on particular importance since the early 1970s. The most important point to keep in mind about this debate is that no responsible researcher has ever claimed that any male–female differences on any measure of intellectual ability

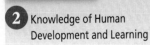

INTASC

2 Knowledge of Human Development and Learning

are large in comparison to the amount of variability within each sex. In other words, even in areas in which true gender differences are suspected, these differences are so small and variable that they have few practical consequences (Francis & Skelton, 2005; Lundeberg & Mohan, 2008; Sadker & Sadker, 2003).

A few differences are worthy of note. Twelfth-grade girls score significantly lower than boys on the quantitative section of the Scholastic Assessment Test (SAT) (Allspach & Breining, 2005) and on Advanced Placement tests in mathematics (Stumpf & Stanley, 1996). A summary of 20 major studies by Kim (2001) found that males scored better than females in math, whereas the opposite was true on English tests. Surprisingly, males scored better on multiple-choice tests but not on other formats. The most important cause is that females in our society have traditionally been discouraged from studying mathematics and, therefore, take many fewer math courses than males do (University of Wisconsin-Madison, 2009). In fact, as females have begun to take more math courses over the past 2 decades, the gender gap on the SAT and on other measures has been steadily diminishing (Allspach & Breining, 2005). A study by Hyde and Mertz (2009) found that there were no significant differences between boys and girls on state math assessments or the National Assessment of Educational Progress (NAEP, 2008). However, despite the narrowing gap between boys and girls on tests of math and science, far fewer young women than young men enter careers in math and science, especially physics, engineering, and computer science (Ceci & Williams, 2009; Halpern et al., 2007; Huebner, 2009).

Studies generally find that males score higher than females on tests of general knowledge, mechanical reasoning, and mental rotations; females score higher on language measures, including reading and writing assessments (Strand, Deary, & Smith, 2006), and on attention and planning tasks (Warrick & Naglieri, 1993). There are no male–female differences in general verbal ability, arithmetic skills, abstract reasoning, spatial visualization, or memory span (Fennema, Carpenter, Jacobs, Franke, & Levi, 1998; Halpern & LaMay, 2000). In school grades, females start out with an advantage over males and maintain this advantage into high school. Even in math and science, in which females score somewhat lower on tests, females still get better grades in class (Maher & Ward, 2002). Despite this, high school males tend to overestimate their skills in language and math (as measured by standardized tests), whereas females underestimate their skills (Herbert & Stipek, 2005; Pomerantz, Altermatt, & Saxon, 2002). In elementary school, males are much more likely than females to have reading problems (Ready, LoGerfo, Burkam, & Lee, 2005; Taylor & Lorimer, 2003) and are much more likely to have learning disabilities or emotional disorders (Smith, 2001). Kindergarten girls have been found to be higher in self-regulation than boys, and this translates into better achievement in the early grades (Matthews, Ponitz, & Morrison, 2009).

■ The Boy Crisis

Although there has been a great deal written over the past 30 years about how girls are underserved in schools, in more recent years there has been more concern about the "boy crisis" (Perkins-Gough, 2006; Von Drehle, 2007). It has long been the case that boys are more likely than girls to be assigned to special education, to be held back, to drop out, and to be in trouble with the law. Girls have become much more likely to go to college and then to graduate, and many co-ed universities and colleges are 60 percent female or more. All of these differences exist despite the advantages boys have on some aptitude tests.

Looking more closely at the data, there is indeed a "boy crisis," but it does not apply across the board. African American boys are significantly more at risk than their sisters (Thomas & Stevenson, 2009), and learning disabilities and ADHD (attention deficit hyperactive disorder) are significantly more common (and damaging) among boys. These problems are serious and need to be attended to, but they do not justify panic about the entire gender (Mead, 2006). Boys are actually improving on many indicators, such as dropout and college attendance, but girls are improving faster. In fact, our perception of a "boy crisis" may simply be the result of the effects of removing policies and practices that once discouraged girls from excelling in school.

■ Sex-Role Stereotyping and Gender Bias

If there are so few genetically based differences between males and females, why do so many behavioral differences exist? These behavioral differences originate from different experiences, including reinforcement by adults for different types of behavior.

Male and female babies have traditionally been treated differently from the time they are born. The wrapping of the infant in either a pink or a blue blanket symbolizes the variations in experience that typically greet the child from birth onward. In early studies, adults described boy or girl babies wrapped in blue blankets as being more active than the same babies wrapped in pink. Other masculine traits were also ascribed to those wrapped in blue (Baxter, 1994).

Recent research on the plasticity of the infant brain suggests that the different treatment received by boy and girl babies could actually cause brain differences (Eliot, 2009).

Although gender bias awareness has begun to have some impact on child-rearing practices, children do begin to make gender distinctions and have gender preferences by around the age of 3 or 4. Thus, children enter school having been socialized into appropriate gender-role behavior for their age in relation to community expectations (Delamont, 2002). Differences in approved gender roles between boys and girls tend to be much stronger in low-SES families than in high-SES families (Flanagan, 1993).

Socialization into this kind of approved **sex-role behavior** continues throughout life, and schools contribute to it. Though interactions between socialization experiences and achievement are complex and it is difficult to make generalizations, schools differentiate between the sexes in a number of ways. In general, males receive more attention from their teachers than females do (Jones & Dindia, 2004; Koch, 2003). Males receive more disapproval and blame from their teachers than do females, but they also engage in more interactions with teachers in such areas as approval, instruction giving, and being listened to (Jones & Dindia, 2004; Koch, 2003; Maher & Ward, 2002). Teachers tend to punish females more promptly and explicitly for aggressive behavior than males. Other differentiations are subtle, as when girls are directed to play in the house corner while boys are provided with blocks or when boys are given drums to play in music class and girls are given the triangles.

Theory into Practice
Avoiding Gender Bias in Teaching

sex-role behavior

Socially approved behavior associated with one gender as opposed to the other.

"In my science class the teacher never calls on me, and I feel like I don't exist. The other night I had a dream that I vanished" (Sadker & Sadker, 1994). Unfortunately, the girl who complained of being ignored by her teacher is not alone. Schools shortchange female students in a variety of ways, from ignoring instances of sexual harassment to interacting less frequently with females than with males (American Association of University Women, 2002). Teachers tend to choose boys, boost the self-esteem of their male students, and select literature with male protagonists. The contributions and experiences of girls and women are still often ignored in textbooks, curricula, and standardized tests (Zittleman & Sadker, 2003).

Teachers, usually without being aware of it, exhibit **gender bias** in classroom teaching in three principal ways: reinforcing gender stereotypes, maintaining sex separation, and treating males and females differently as students (see Koch, 2003; Maher & Ward, 2002). These inequities can have negative consequences for boys as well as girls (Canada, 2000; Weaver-Hightower, 2003).

AVOIDING STEREOTYPES   Avoid promoting sexual stereotypes. For example, you can assign jobs in the classroom without regard to gender, avoiding automatically appointing males as group leaders and females as secretaries, and can ask both males and females to help in physical activities. You should also refrain from stating stereotypes, such as "Boys don't cry" and "Girls don't fight," and should avoid labeling students with such terms as *tomboy*. You should encourage students who show an interest in activities and careers that do not correspond to cultural stereotypes, such as a female student who likes math and science (Sadker, Sadker, & Long, 1997).

PROMOTING INTEGRATION   One factor that leads to gender stereotyping is the tendency for boys and girls (particularly in elementary school) to have few friends of the opposite sex and to engage mostly in activities with members of their own sex. Teachers sometimes encourage this by having boys and girls line up separately, assigning them to sex-segregated tables, and organizing separate sports activities for males and females. As a result, interaction between boys and girls in schools is less frequent than between students of the same sex. However, in classes in which cross-sex collaboration is encouraged, children have less stereotyped views of the abilities of males and females (Klein, 1994).

TREATING FEMALES AND MALES EQUALLY   Too often, teachers do not treat males and females equally. Observational studies of classroom interactions have found that teachers interact more with boys than with girls and ask boys more questions, especially more abstract questions (Sadker et al., 1997). In one study, researchers showed teachers videotapes of classroom scenes and asked them whether boys or girls participated more. Most teachers responded that the girls talked more, even though in fact the boys participated more than the girls by a ratio of 3 to 1 (Sadker et al., 1997). The researchers interpreted this finding as indicating that teachers expect females to participate less and thus see low rates of participation as normal. You must be careful to allow all students equal opportunities to participate in class, to take leadership roles, and to engage in all kinds of activities (Bernard-Powers, 2001; Stein, 2000). You should use activities likely to engage the interest and perspectives of girls as well as boys (James, 2007, 2009). You need to encourage girls to study math and science, and to expect and value excellence in these subjects from girls as well as boys (Halpern et al., 2007).

How Do Students Differ in Intelligence and Learning Styles?

Intelligence is one of those words that people believe they understand until you ask them to define it. At one level, **intelligence** can be defined as a general aptitude for learning or an ability to acquire and use knowledge or skills. A consensus definition expressed by Snyderman and Rothman (1987) is that intelligence is the ability to deal with abstractions, to solve problems, and to learn.

The biggest problem comes when we ask whether there is such a thing as general aptitude (Sternberg, 2003). Many people are terrific at calculus but couldn't write a good

gender bias

Stereotypical views and differential treatment of males and females, often favoring one gender over the other.

intelligence

General aptitude for learning, often measured by the ability to deal with abstractions and to solve problems.

INTASC

4 Multiple Instructional Strategies

Connections

For more on the measurement of IQ, see Chapter 14, pages 452–454.

essay or paint a good picture if their lives depended on it. Some people can walk into a room full of strangers and immediately figure out the relationships and feelings among them; others may never learn this skill. As Will Rogers put it, "Everybody is ignorant, only on different topics." Clearly, individuals vary in their aptitude for learning any specific type of knowledge or skill taught in a specific way. A hundred students attending a lecture on a topic they knew nothing about beforehand will all walk away with different amounts and kinds of learning, and aptitude for that particular content and that particular teaching method is one important factor in explaining these differences. But would the students who learned the most in this class also learn the most if the lecture were on a different topic or if the same material were presented through hands-on experiences or in small groups?

The concept of intelligence has been discussed since before the time of the ancient Greeks, but the scientific study of this topic really began with the work of Alfred Binet, who devised the first measure of intelligence in 1904. The French government asked Binet to find a way to identify children who were likely to need special help in their schooling. His measure assessed a broad range of skills and performances but produced a single score, called **intelligence quotient (IQ),** which was set up so that the average French child would have an IQ of 100 (Hurn, 2002).

■ Definitions of Intelligence

Binet's work greatly advanced the science of intelligence assessment, but it also began to establish the idea that intelligence was a single thing—that there were "smart" people who could be expected to do well in a broad range of learning situations. Ever since Binet, debate has raged about this issue. In 1927 Charles Spearman claimed that although there were, of course, variations in a person's abilities from task to task, there was a general intelligence factor, or "g," that existed across all learning situations. Is there really one intelligence, as Spearman suggested, or are there many distinct intelligences?

The evidence in favor of "g" is that abilities are correlated with each other. Individuals who are good at learning one concept are likely, on the average, to be good at learning others. The correlations are consistent enough for us to say that there are not a thousand completely separate intelligences, but they are not nearly consistent enough to allow us to say that there is only one general intelligence (Sternberg, 2003). In recent years, much

intelligence quotient (IQ)

An intelligence test score that for people of average intelligence should be near 100.

According to Gardner's theory of multiple intelligences, which of the eight intelligences might these students use to learn? As a teacher, how would you vary your lessons to address student differences in learning style?

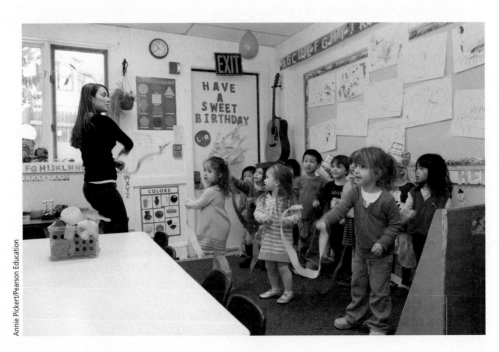

Annie Pickert/Pearson Education

FIGURE 4.3 **Gardner's Multiple Intelligences**

Linguistic. Ability to understand and use spoken and written communication. Ideal vocation: poet.*

Logical/mathematical. Ability to understand and use logic and numerical symbols and operations. Ideal vocation: computer programmer.

Musical. Ability to understand and use such concepts as rhythm, pitch, melody, and harmony. Ideal vocation: composer.

Spatial. Ability to orient and manipulate three-dimensional space. Ideal vocation: architect.

Bodily/kinesthetic. Ability to coordinate physical movement. Ideal vocation: athlete.

Naturalistic. Ability to distinguish and categorize objects or phenomena in nature. Ideal vocation: zoologist.

Interpersonal. Ability to understand and interact well with other people. Ideal vocation: politician; salesperson.

Intrapersonal. Ability to understand and use one's thoughts, feelings, preferences, and interests. Ideal vocation: autobiographer; entrepreneur. (Although high intrapersonal intelligence should help in almost any job because of its role in self-regulation, few paid positions reward a person solely for knowing himself or herself well.)

Existential. Ability to contemplate phenomena or questions beyond sensory data, such as the infinite and infinitesimal. Ideal vocation: cosmologist; philosopher.

*Most vocations involve several intelligences.

Source: S. Moran, M. Kornhaber, and H. Gardner, 2006, "Orchestrating Multiple Intelligences." *Educational Leadership, 64*(1), 22–29.

of the debate about intelligence has focused on deciding how many distinct types of intelligence there are and describing each. For example, Sternberg (2002, 2003, 2008) describes three types of intellectual abilities: analytical, practical, and creative. Moran, Kornhaber, and Gardner (2006) describe nine **multiple intelligences.** These are listed and defined in Figure 4.3.

In recent years, Gardner's (2004) multiple–intelligence (MI) theory has been very popular in education, but it has also been controversial. Waterhouse (2006), for example, notes that there is little evidence to support MI, citing findings both from brain research and from research on measurement of IQ to argue that although there are different cognitive strengths and personalities, this does not contradict the idea that there is such a thing as general intelligence (Watkins & Canivez, 2004). Chen (2004) and Gardner and Moran (2006) argue that intelligence is more than what can be measured on an IQ test but admit that the evidence for MI is indirect.

ON THE WEB

For a summary of Sternberg's work on intelligence, go to www.indiana.edu/%7Eintell/sternberg.shtml or http://wilderdom.com/personality/L2-2SternbergTriarchicTheory.html. For more on Gardner's multiple intelligences, visit www.tecweb.org/styles/gardner.html, www.thomasarmstrong.com/multiple_intelligences.htm, or www.howardgardner.com/MI/mi.html.

The precise number of intelligences is not important for you as an educator. What is important is the idea that good or poor performance in one area in no way guarantees similar performance in another. You should avoid thinking about children as smart or not smart, because there are many ways to be smart. Unfortunately, schools have traditionally recognized only a narrow set of performances, creating a neat hierarchy of students primarily in terms of what Gardner calls linguistic and logical/mathematical skills (only two of his nine intelligences). If schools want all children to be smart, they must use a

multiple intelligences

In Gardner's theory of intelligence, a person's nine separate abilities: logical/mathematical, linguistic, musical, naturalist, spatial, bodily/kinesthetic, interpersonal, intrapersonal, and existential.

broader range of activities and reward a broader range of performances than they have in the past.

Theory into Practice
Multiple Intelligences

Gardner's theory of multiple intelligences implies that concepts should be taught in a variety of ways that call on many types of intelligence (Campbell, Campbell, & Dickerson, 2004; Kornhaber, Fierros, & Veenema, 2004; Moran et al., 2006). As an illustration, Armstrong (1994) gives the following examples of different ways to teach Boyle's Law to secondary students.

- Students are provided with a verbal definition of Boyle's Law: "For a fixed mass and temperature of gas, the pressure is inversely proportional to the volume." They discuss the definition. [Linguistic]
- Students are given a formula that describes Boyle's Law: $P \times V = K$. They solve specific problems connected to it. [Logical/mathematical]
- Students are given a metaphor or visual image for Boyle's Law: "Imagine that you have a boil on your hand that you start to squeeze. As you squeeze it, the pressure builds. The more you squeeze, the higher the pressure, until the boil finally bursts and pus spurts out all over your hand!" [Spatial]
- Students do the following experiment: They breathe air into their mouths so that their cheeks puff up slightly. Then they put all the air into one side of their mouth (less volume) and indicate whether pressure goes up or down (it goes up); then they're asked to release the air in both sides of their mouth (more volume) and asked to indicate whether pressure has gone up or down (it goes down). [Bodily/kinesthetic]
- Students do lab experiments that measure air pressure in sealed containers and chart pressure against volume. [Logical/mathematical, bodily/kinesthetic]

Few lessons will contain parts that correspond to all types of intelligence, but a key recommendation of multiple-intelligence theory for the classroom is to include a variety of presentation modes in each lesson to expand the number of students who are likely to succeed (Campbell et al., 2004; Gardner, 2003; Kline, 2001).

■ Origins of Intelligence

The origins of intelligence have been debated for decades. Some psychologists (such as Toga & Thompson, 2005) hold that intelligence is overwhelmingly a product of heredity—that children's intelligence is largely determined by that of their parents and is set the day they are conceived. Others (such as Rifkin, 1998) just as vehemently hold that intelligence is shaped mostly by factors in a person's social environment, such as the amount a child is read to and talked to. Most investigators agree that both heredity and environment play an important part in intelligence (Petrill & Wilkerson, 2000). It is clear that children of high-achieving parents are, on the average, more likely to be high achievers themselves, but this is as much because of the home environment created by high-achieving parents as it is because of genetics. French studies of children of low-SES parents adopted into high-SES families find strong positive effects on the children's IQs compared to nonadopted children raised in low-SES families (Capron & Duyme, 1991; Schiff & Lewontin, 1986). One important piece of evidence in favor of the environmental view is that schooling itself clearly affects IQ scores. A review by Ceci (1991) found that the experience of being in school has a strong and systematic impact on IQ. For example, classic studies of Dutch children who entered school late because of World War II showed significant declines in IQ as a result, although their IQs increased when they finally entered school. A study of the children of mothers with mental retardation in inner-city Milwaukee (Garber, 1988) found that a program of infant stimulation and high-quality preschool could raise children's IQs substantially, and these gains were maintained at least through the end of elementary school. Studies of the Abecedarian program, which combined infant stimulation, child enrichment, and parent assistance, found lasting effects of early instruction on IQ (Ramey & Ramey, 1998). This and other evidence (see Kristof, 2009; Neuman, 2007) support the idea that IQ is not a fixed, unchangeable attribute of individuals but can change as individuals respond to changes in their environment. Furthermore, some evidence indicates that IQ can be directly changed by programs designed for this purpose (Ellis, 2001a; Feuerstein & Kozulin, 1995).

Intelligence, whether general or specific, is only one of many factors that influence the amount children are likely to learn in a given lesson or course. It is probably much less important than prior knowledge (the amount the student knew about the course beforehand), motivation, and the quality and nature of instruction. Intelligence does become important at the extremes; it is a critical issue in identifying students who have mental retardation or those who are gifted, but in the middle range, where most students fall, other factors are more important. IQ testing has very frequently been misused in education, especially when it has been used to assign students inappropriately to special education or to tracks or ability groups. Actual performance is far more important than IQ and is more directly susceptible to being influenced by teachers and schools (Sternberg, 2008). Boykin (2000) has argued that schools would do better to focus on developing talents rather than seeing them as fixed attributes of students.

■ Theories of Learning Styles

Just as students have different personalities, they also have different ways of learning. For example, think about how you learn the names of people you meet. Do you learn a name better if you see it written down? If so, you may be a visual learner, one who learns best by seeing or reading. If you learn a name better by hearing it, you may be an auditory learner. Of course, we all learn in many ways, but some of us learn better in some ways than in others (Swisher & Schoorman, 2001).

Students may also vary in preferences for different learning environments or conditions. For example, Dunn and Dunn (1993) found that students differ in preferences about such things as the amount of lighting, hard or soft seating, quiet or noisy surroundings, and working alone or with peers. These differences can predict to some extent which learning environments will be most effective for each child.

■ Aptitude–Treatment Interactions

Given the well-documented differences in learning styles and preferences, it would seem logical that different styles of teaching would have different impacts on different learners; yet this commonsense proposition has been difficult to demonstrate conclusively. Studies that have attempted to match teaching styles to learning styles have only inconsistently found any benefits for learning based on styles (Knight, Halpin, & Halpin, 1992; Snow, 1992). However, the search for such **aptitude–treatment interaction** goes on. The commonsense conclusion from research in this area is that you should be alert to detecting and responding to the differences in the ways that children learn (see Ebeling, 2000).

Connections

For a description of studies indicating that IQ can be directly changed by certain programs, see Chapter 8.

Certification Pointer

Teacher certification tests may ask you to design a lesson that would accommodate students' various learning styles, in addition to their developmental needs.

aptitude–treatment interaction

Interaction of individual differences in learning with particular teaching methods.

Theory into Practice
Understanding Diverse Thinkers

In his article "Celebrating Diverse Minds," Mel Levine of the University of North Carolina explores the importance of celebrating "all kinds of minds" as a way of making sure no child is left behind. He asks, "What becomes of students . . . who give up on themselves because they lack the kinds of minds needed to satisfy existing criteria for school success?"

Levine points out that learning differences can constitute daunting barriers, especially when they are not recognized and managed. Most importantly, these breakdowns can mislead us into undervaluing, unfairly accusing, and even undereducating students, thereby stifling their chances for success in school and life.

Many faltering students have specialized minds—brains exquisitely wired to perform certain kinds of tasks masterfully, but decidedly miswired when

The Intentional Teacher

USING WHAT YOU KNOW about Student Diversity to Improve Teaching and Learning

Intentional teachers view student diversity as a rich resource. They learn about their students' home lives, cultures, languages, and strengths, and they value each student as an individual. Intentional teachers examine data from their classrooms and question their own practices, guarding against the possibility that their perspectives may inadvertently limit students' success. Intentional teachers use what they know about their own practices and their particular students to improve the quality of education for all.

 1. What do I expect my students to know and be able to do at the end of this lesson? How does this contribute to course objectives and to students' needs to become capable individuals?

Examine the influence of your own cultural perspectives on the expectations you hold for students. Ask yourself, "Do my goals reflect only the values of a dominant group?" For example, you might curb your impulse to give stickers to the first five of your third-graders who earn 100 percent on their multiplication facts, deciding that your appreciation of individual competition may not be shared by all. You might decide to give students choices about how they do book reports, so that children with different learning strengths can express themselves in different ways.

Many educators feel that educational goals should reflect, at least to some extent, the community within which children are educated. Ask yourself, "How can we revise our classroom goals to better reflect the needs, values, and interests of all our students and families?" For example, you might begin a class with an informal discussion about what students would like

to learn and about students' definitions of success. Students' interests and cultural backgrounds should not entirely determine your goals for a given lesson or course, but they should be taken into account. Algebra is algebra, but there are many paths to proficiency in algebra. Find out the paths your students are most willing and able to travel.

 2. What knowledge, skills, needs, and interests do my students have that must be taken into account in my lesson?

Learn about your students and draw on information about your students' home lives and community resources to plan your instruction. What is your understanding of students' cultures and community? Ask yourself, "What experiences and strengths have my students gathered outside of school that can foster their learning?" For example, although you provide instruction in English, you might look for ways to value students' home language, reinforcing the idea that knowing two languages is an asset. You might design a "multilingual dictionary" activity, developing a list of classroom and family words in English, and asking students with different home languages to translate the list into their languages. You could print and distribute this short dictionary at a PTA meeting as well as to the class members, who might wish to discuss similarities and differences between the languages represented and the English equivalents. In any class, you could collect colorful expressions, sayings, or slang reflecting the cultural heritages of your students. These "dictionaries" might be exchanged online or by mail with similar efforts from classes in different regions or parts of town.

it comes to meeting other expectations. A student may be brilliant at visualizing, but embarrassingly inept at verbalizing. A classmate may reveal a remarkable understanding of people, but exhibit no insight about sentence structure.

Levine proposes addressing this problem in three ways:

- ***Broaden student assessment.***   Our understanding of learning differences often focuses on fixing deficits, rather than identifying latent or blatant talents in struggling learners.

- ***Reexamine the curriculum.***   Explore new instructional practices and curricular choices in order to provide educational opportunities for diverse learners and to prepare them for a successful life.

- ***Provide professional development for educators.***   Provide teachers with training on the insights from brain research that will help them understand and support their students' diverse minds.

INTASC   **7** Instructional Planning Skills
9 Professional Commitment and Responsibility

 3. What do I know about the content, child development, learning, motivation, and effective teaching strategies that I can use to accomplish my objectives?

Provide opportunities for students to choose ways of interacting with subject-matter content that reflects their learning style preferences. You might vary grouping structures so that students work as a whole class, individually, or in flexible small groups. You might employ principles of sheltered instruction, which make grade-level content accessible to all, for your English learners. For example, you could provide graphic organizers of the literature and bring in real examples of the items described in your readings.

 4. What instructional materials, technology, assistance, and other resources are available to help accomplish my objectives?

Work as part of an educational team. Draw on the strengths that can come from teachers and families working together. For example, you might survey families about relevant summer programs. To help students maintain academic gains, you might help them acquire library cards and suggest books for them to read over vacation. You might give them each a journal and invite them—and their families!—to write to you.

If your class includes a number of bilingual students, you might ask for volunteers to invite an older family member to talk to your art class about the particular art forms of his or her place of origin, and you might explain that the student would be asked to serve as translator and interpreter.

Use children's cultural backgrounds as a springboard to mainstream content and expectations. A Navajo child, for example, has as much need to learn about ancient Greece as any other child, but he or she comes with a rich background that an intentional teacher should evoke to help interpret Greek culture.

 5. How will I plan to assess students' progress toward my objectives?

Collect information on your teaching to ensure that your practices are equitable. An observer might gather information, or you might tape your teaching for later analysis. Key questions include the following:

Do I give equal time to interacting with males and females?

Do I praise and admonish students for the same types of behaviors, no matter what their group?

Are my expectations uniformly high for all students? Do I express this clearly?

To the extent appropriate, do I use the classroom as a forum for students to question mainstream perspectives and existing conditions? To encourage social improvement?

 6. How will I respond if individual children or the class as a whole is not on track toward success? What is my back-up plan?

You might ask yourself: "How can I confirm my current understanding of my diverse students and how can I learn more about particular groups? Have I made an effort to meet some of the adults that my students speak of as influential in their community or highly regarded by their family? Are the literature selections for class readings representative of a range of authors—by gender, nationality, ethnicity? Is my own personal reading contributing to a better understanding of diversity and individual differences?"

Chapter 4 Summary

What Is the Impact of Culture on Teaching and Learning ?

Culture profoundly affects teaching and learning. Many aspects of culture contribute to student's identity and self-concept and affect the student's beliefs and values, attitudes and expectations, social relations, language use, and other behaviors.

How Does Socioeconomic Status Affect Student Achievement ?

Socioeconomic status—based on income, occupation, education, and social prestige—can profoundly influence students' attitudes toward school, background knowledge, school readiness, and academic achievement. Working-class and low-income families experience stress that contributes to child-rearing practices, communication patterns, and lowered expectations that may challenge children when they enter school. Students from low-SES homes often learn a normative culture that is different from the middle-class culture of the school, which demands independence, competitiveness, and goal-setting. However, low achievement is not the inevitable result of low socioeconomic status. Teachers can invite families to participate in their children's education, and this can improve students' achievement.

How Do Ethnicity and Race Affect Students' School Experiences ?

Populations of underrepresented groups are growing dramatically as diversity in the United States and Canada increases. Students who are members of certain under-represented groups—self-defined by race, religion, ethnicity, origins, history, language, and culture, such as African Americans, Native Americans, and Latinos—tend to have lower scores than European and Asian Americans on standardized tests of academic achievement. The lower scores correlate with lower socioeconomic status and reflect in part a legacy of discrimination against underrepresented groups and consequent poverty. School desegregation, long intended as a solution to educational inequities as a result of race and social class, has had mixed benefits. Continuing issues include delivering fairness and equal opportunity, fostering racial harmony, and preventing segregation.

How Do Language Differences and Bilingual Programs Affect Student Achievement ?

English learners are typically taught in one of four types of programs: English immersion, transitional bilingual, paired bilingual, and two-way bilingual. Bilingual programs teach students in their native language as well as English. Research suggests that bilingual education, especially paired bilingual education, can have benefits for students. Recent legislation in states throughout the country has had a chilling effect on bilingual education.

What Is Multicultural Education ?

Multicultural education calls for the celebration of cultural diversity and the promotion of educational equity and social harmony in the schools. Multicultural education

includes content integration, knowledge construction, prejudice reduction, equity pedagogy, and an empowering school culture.

How Do Gender and Gender Bias Affect Students' School Experiences ?

Many observed differences between males and females are clearly linked to differences in early socialization, when children learn sex-role behaviors regarded as appropriate. Ongoing research shows very few genetically based gender differences in
thinking and abilities. However, gender bias in the classroom, including subtle teacher
behaviors toward male and female students and curriculum materials that contain sex-role stereotypes, has clearly affected student choices and achievement. One
outcome is a gender gap in mathematics and science, though this gap is decreasing
steadily.

How Do Students Differ in Intelligence and Learning Styles ?

Students differ in their abilities to deal with abstractions, to solve problems, and to
learn. They also differ in any number of specific intelligences, so accurate estimations
of intelligence should probably rely on broader performances than traditional IQ
tests allow. Therefore teachers should not base their expectations of students on
IQ test scores. Binet, Spearman, Sternberg, and Gardner have contributed to theories
and measures of intelligence. Both heredity and environment determine intelligence.
Research shows that home environments, schooling, and life experiences can profoundly
influence IQ.

Students differ in their prior learning and in their cognitive learning styles. Individual preferences in learning environments and conditions also affect student
achievement.

Key Terms

Review the following key terms from the chapter.

aptitude–treatment interaction   107
bilingual education   95
content integration   98
culture   80
empowering school culture   99
English learners (EL)   95
equity pedagogy   99
ethnic group   89
ethnicity   89
gender bias   103
intelligence   103
intelligence quotient (IQ)   104

knowledge construction   98
language minority   95
limited English proficient (LEP)   95
multicultural education   98
multiple intelligences   105
prejudice reduction   99
race   89
sex-role behavior   102
socioeconomic status (SES)   81
underrepresented groups   90

Self-Assessment: Practicing for Licensure

Directions: The chapter-opening vignette addresses indicators that are often assessed in state licensure exams. Re-read the chapter-opening vignette, and then respond to the following questions.

1. Marva Vance and John Rossi discuss their students' diverse norms, traditions, behaviors, languages, and perceptions. Which of the following terms best describes the essence of their conversation?

   a. Race

   b. Socioeconomic status

   c. Intelligence

   d. Culture

2. Regarding the students of Marva Vance and John Rossi, which of the following statements on socioeconomic status is most likely true?

   a. Students from working-class or lower-class backgrounds perform academically as well as or better than students from middle-class homes.

   b. Students from disadvantaged homes are more likely to have inadequate access to health care.

   c. Students from middle-class and lower-class homes are equally likely to make academic progress over the summer.

   d. Schools overwhelmingly represent the values and expectations of the working class.

3. Marva Vance and John Rossi discuss their students' tendencies to accept the stereotypical roles assigned to them by society. According to research, what should the teachers do about this stereotyping?

   a. Allow students to select their own roles, even if they make stereotypical decisions.

   b. Tell the story of Thanksgiving as realistically as possible: Native American students play Native Americans, girls play cooks, and boys play hunters.

   c. Themes should be nonbiased, and individuals from underrepresented groups should appear in non-stereotypical high-status roles.

   d. Write a Thanksgiving play that includes the contributions of all underrepresented groups.

4. José, a student in Marva Vance's class, wants to be the narrator of the Thanksgiving pageant, even though he is not proficient in English. According to research on the effectiveness of bilingual programs, which strategy might Ms. Vance use to improve all her students' English speaking and writing skills?

   a. Ms. Vance should avoid bilingual programs because they have been found to be harmful to students in their English development.

   b. Ms. Vance should learn the languages of the students in her class.

   c. Ms. Vance should support bilingual education because studies have found that students in bilingual programs ultimately achieve in English as well as or better than students taught only in English.

   d. Ms. Vance should speak out about the detrimental effects of bilingual education on a student's self-esteem.

5. Marva Vance and John Rossi discuss stereotypical gender roles in the Thanksgiving pageant. From the research reported in this section, how should the teachers assign male and female students to the roles in the pageant?

   a. The teachers should encourage students to select roles in which they are interested, not roles that society expects them to play.

   b. The teachers should reduce the interactions of males and females in the pageant.

   c. The teachers should assign males and females to authentic roles: males are hunters, females are cooks.

   d. The teachers should assign all students to nontypical racial and gender roles.

6. What is multicultural education? What steps can teachers, administrators, and other school personnel take to reach their students from underrepresented groups?

7. Students differ in their prior learning and in their cognitive learning styles. What strategies can teachers use to reach all of their students?

8. List six strategies you could implement to involve parents or caregivers in helping students meet their potential.

PEARSON myeducationlab

Go to the Topic **Student Diversity** in the MyEducationLab (www.myeducationlab.com) for your course, where you can:

- Find learning outcomes for **Student Diversity** along with the national standards that connect to these outcomes.

- Complete Assignments and Activities that can help you more deeply understand the chapter content.

- Apply and practice your understanding of the core teaching skills identified in the chapter with the Building Teaching Skills and Dispositions learning units.

- Examine challenging situations and cases presented in the IRIS Center Resources.

- Access video clips of CCSSO National Teachers of the Year award winners responding to the question "Why Do I Teach?" in the Teacher Talk section.

- Check your comprehension of the content covered in the chapter by going to the Study Plan in the Book Resources for your text. Here you will be able to take a chapter quiz; receive feedback on your answers; and then access Review, Practice, and Enrichment activities to enhance your understanding of chapter content.

- Watch author Bob Slavin present Personal Reflections podcasts on *Coping with Change* and *Being Sensitive to Race* in the Book Resources for your text. Then, respond to the reflection questions that follow.

Coping with Change

YOUR REFLECTIONS Do you remember being conflicted emotionally in middle school or high school as you adjusted to adolescence? How might the internal conflicts have differed for adolescents of different social or ethnic groups? What kind of learning challenges does this time period pose for teachers and students?

Being Sensitive to Race

YOUR REFLECTIONS What was the racial or ethnic mix of your K–12 experience? What did your school do to ensure full integration among students? Did this reflect the community efforts as a whole? What discussions about diversity have you had in your education classes? How have those discussions influenced your perspectives on classrooms and learning?

5

Behavioral Theories of Learning

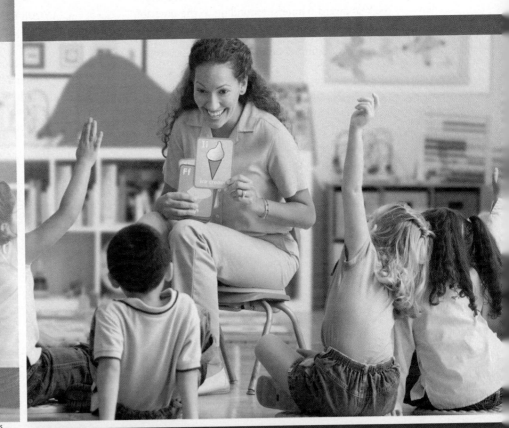

Jose Luis Pelaez/Iconica/Getty Images

At the end of this chapter, you should be able to:

- Define the concept of "learning"
- Describe principles of behavioral learning theories
- Discuss the implications of behavioral learning principles for classroom practice
- Describe social learning theories and their implications for classroom practice

Jose Luis Pelaez/Iconica/Getty Images

Julia Esteban, first-grade teacher at Tanner Elementary School, is trying to teach her students appropriate classroom behavior.

"Children," she says one day, "we are having a problem in this class that I'd like to discuss with you. Whenever I ask a question, many of you shout out your answers instead of raising your hand and waiting to be called on. Can anyone tell me what you should do when I ask the class a question?" Rebecca's hand shoots into the air. "I know, I know!" she says. "Raise your hand and wait quietly!"

Ms. Esteban sighs to herself. She tries to ignore Rebecca, who is doing exactly what she had just been told not to do, but Rebecca is the only student with her hand up, and the longer she delays, the more frantically Rebecca waves her hand and shouts her answer.

"All right, Rebecca. What are you supposed to do?"

"We're supposed to raise our hands and wait quietly for you to call on us."

"If you know the rule, why were you shouting out your answer before I called on you?"

"I guess I forgot."

"All right. Can anyone remind the class of our rule about talking out of turn?"

Four children raised their hands and shouted together.

"One at a time!"

"Take turns!"

"Don't talk when someone else is talking!"

Ms. Esteban calls for order. "You kids are going to drive me crazy!" she says. "Didn't we just talk about how to raise your hands and wait for me to call on you?"

"But Ms. Esteban," says Stephen without even raising his hand. "You called on Rebecca and she wasn't quiet!"

USING YOUR EXPERIENCE

Critical and Creative Thinking   Reflect on what Ms. Esteban might do differently in this situation to accomplish her goal.

Cooperative Learning   Discuss with another student what went wrong here. Also discuss similar ways in which you have seen inappropriate behavior reinforced in the past. Share some of these anecdotes with the class.

Children are excellent learners. What they learn, however, may not always be what we intend to teach. Ms. Esteban is trying to teach students how to behave in class, but by paying attention to Rebecca's outburst, she is actually teaching them the opposite of what she intends. Rebecca craves her teacher's attention, so being called on (even in an exasperated tone of voice) rewards her for calling out her answer. Not only does Ms. Esteban's response increase the chances that Rebecca will call out answers again but also Rebecca now serves as a model for her classmates' own calling out. What Ms. Esteban says is less important than the actual response to her students' behaviors.

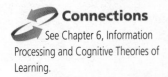

Connections

See Chapter 6, Information Processing and Cognitive Theories of Learning.

The purpose of this chapter is to define learning and then present behavioral and social learning theories, explanations for learning that emphasize observable behaviors. **Behavioral learning theories** focus on the ways that pleasurable or unpleasant consequences of behavior change individuals' behavior over time and the ways individuals model their behavior on that of others. **Social learning theories** focus on the effects of thought on action and action on thought. Later chapters present **cognitive learning theories,** which emphasize unobservable mental processes that people use to learn and remember new information or skills. In recent years, however, the boundaries between behavioral and cognitive learning theories have become increasingly indistinct as each school of thought has incorporated the findings of the other.

What Is Learning?

What is learning? This seems like a simple question until you begin to think about it. Consider the following four examples. Are they instances of learning?

1. A young child takes her first steps.
2. An adolescent male feels a strong attraction to certain females.
3. A child feels anxious when he sees the doctor coming with a needle.
4. Long after learning how to multiply, a girl realizes on her own that another way to multiply by 5 is to divide by 2 and multiply by 10 (e.g., 428×5 can be figured as follows: $428/2 = 214 \times 10 = 2,140$).

INTASC

2 Knowledge of Human Development and Learning

Learning is usually defined as a change in an individual caused by experience (Driscoll, 2000; Hill, 2002; Schunk, 2004). Mayer (2008a) defines learning as "long-lasting change in the learner's knowledge as a result of the learner's experiences" (p. 171). Changes caused by development (such as growing taller) are not instances of learning. Neither are characteristics of individuals that are present at birth (such as reflexes and responses to hunger or pain). However, humans do so much learning from the day of their birth (and some say earlier) that learning and development are inseparably linked. Learning to walk (example 1) is mostly a developmental progression but also depends on experience with crawling and other activities. The adolescent sex drive (example 2) is not learned, but learning shapes individuals' choices of desirable partners.

A child's anxiety on seeing a doctor with a needle (example 3) is definitely learned behavior. The child has learned to associate the needle with pain, and his body reacts emotionally when he sees the needle. This reaction may be unconscious or involuntary, but it is learned nonetheless.

The fourth example, the girl's insight into the multiplication shortcut, is an instance of internally generated learning, better known as thinking. Some theorists would not call this learning, because it was not caused by the environment. But it might be considered a case of delayed learning, in which deliberate instruction in multiplication plus years of experience with numbers plus mental effort on the part of the girl produced an insight.

Learning takes place in many ways. Sometimes it is intentional, as when students acquire information presented in a classroom or when they look something up on the Internet. Sometimes it is unintentional, as in the case of the child's reaction to the needle. All sorts of learning are going on all the time. As you are reading this chapter, you are learning something about learning. However, you are also learning that educational psychology is interesting or dull, useful or useless. Without knowing it, you are probably learning about where on the page certain pieces of information are to be found. You might be learning to associate the content of this chapter with unimportant aspects of your surroundings as you read it, such as the smell of books in a library or the tempera-

behavioral learning theories

Explanations of learning that emphasize observable changes in behavior.

social learning theories

Learning theories that emphasize not only reinforcement but also the effects of cues on thought and of thought on action.

cognitive learning theories

Explanations of learning that focus on mental processes.

learning

A change in an individual that results from experience.

ture of the room in which you are reading. The content of this chapter; the placement of words on the page; and the smells, sounds, and temperature of your surroundings are all **stimuli.** Your senses are usually wide open to all sorts of stimuli, or environmental events or conditions, but you are consciously aware of only a fraction of them at any one time.

The problem you face is not how to get students to learn; students are already engaged in learning every waking moment. Rather, it is how to help students learn particular information, skills, and concepts that will be useful in their lives. How do we present students with the right stimuli on which to focus their attention and mental effort so that they will acquire important skills? That is the central problem of instruction.

What Are Behavioral Learning Theories?

The systematic study of learning is relatively new. Not until the late 19th century was learning studied in a scientific manner. Using techniques borrowed from the physical sciences, researchers began conducting experiments to understand how people and animals learn. One of the most important early researchers was Ivan Pavlov. Among later researchers, B. F. Skinner was important for his studies of the relationship between behavior and consequences.

■ Pavlov: Classical Conditioning

In the late 1800s and early 1900s, Russian scientist Ivan Pavlov and his colleagues studied the digestive process in dogs. During the research, the scientists noticed changes in the timing and rate of salivation of these animals. Pavlov observed that if meat was placed in or near the mouth of a hungry dog, the dog would salivate. Because the meat provoked this response automatically, without any prior training or conditioning, the meat is referred to as an **unconditioned stimulus.** Similarly, because salivation occurred automatically in the presence of meat, also without the need for any training or experience, this response of salivating is referred to as an **unconditioned response.**

Whereas the meat will produce salivation without any previous experience or training, other stimuli, such as the ringing of a bell, will not produce salivation. Because these stimuli have no effect on the response in question, they are referred to as **neutral stimuli.** Pavlov's experiments showed that if a previously neutral stimulus is paired with an unconditioned stimulus, the neutral stimulus becomes a **conditioned stimulus** and gains the power to prompt a response similar to that produced by the unconditioned stimulus. In other words, after the bell and the meat are presented together, the ringing of the bell alone causes the dog to salivate. This process is referred to as **classical conditioning.** A diagram of Pavlov's theory is shown in Figure 5.1. In experiments such as these, Pavlov and his colleagues showed how learning could affect what were once thought to be involuntary, reflexive behaviors, such as salivating.

■ Skinner: Operant Conditioning

Some human behaviors are clearly prompted by specific stimuli. Just like Pavlov's dogs, we salivate when we are hungry and see appetizing food. However, B. F. Skinner proposed that reflexive behavior accounts for only a small proportion of all actions. Skinner proposed another class of behavior, which he labeled *operant behaviors* because they operate on the environment in the apparent absence of any unconditioned stimuli, such as food. Skinner's work focused on the relation between behavior and its consequences. For example, if an individual's behavior is immediately followed by pleasurable

Certification Pointer

Pavlov's work will probably be on your teacher certification test. Know that a ringing bell was the conditioned stimulus that he used to get dogs to salivate without the presence of meat. The bell became a conditioned stimulus because Pavlov first paired ringing with meat.

stimuli

Environmental conditions that activate the senses; the singular is *stimulus.*

unconditioned stimulus

A stimulus that naturally evokes a particular response.

unconditioned response

A behavior that is prompted automatically by a stimulus.

neutral stimuli

Stimuli that have no effect on a particular response.

conditioned stimulus

A previously neutral stimulus that evokes a particular response after having been paired with an unconditioned stimulus.

classical conditioning

The process of repeatedly associating a previously neutral stimulus with an unconditioned stimulus in order to evoke a conditioned response.

FIGURE 5.1   **Classical Conditioning**

In classical conditioning, a neutral stimulus (such as a bell) that at first prompts no response becomes paired with an unconditioned stimulus (such as meat) and gains the power of that stimulus to cause a response (such as salivation).

Before Conditioning

Unconditioned stimulus (meat)   Unconditioned response (salivation)   **And**   Neutral stimulus (bell)   No response

During Conditioning

Conditioned stimulus   **Paired with**   Unconditioned stimulus   Unconditioned response

After Conditioning

Conditioned stimulus   Conditioned response

---

operant conditioning

The use of pleasant or unpleasant consequences to control the occurrence of behavior.

Skinner box

An apparatus developed by B. F. Skinner for observing animal behavior in experiments of operant conditioning.

consequences, the individual will engage in that behavior more frequently. The use of pleasant and unpleasant consequences to change behavior is often referred to as **operant conditioning.**

Skinner's work focused on placing subjects in controlled situations and observing the changes in their behavior produced by systematic changes in the consequences of their behavior (see Alberto & Troutman, 2009; Bigge & Shermis, 2004; Malott, 2008). Skinner is famous for his development and use of the **Skinner box,** a device that contains a very simple apparatus for studying the behavior of animals, usually rats and pigeons. A Skinner box for rats consists of a bar that is easy for the rat to press, a food dispenser that can give the rat a pellet of food, and a water dispenser. The rat cannot see or hear anything outside of the box, so all stimuli are controlled by the experimenter.

In some of the earliest experiments involving Skinner boxes, the apparatus was first set up so that if the rat happened to press the bar, it would receive a food pellet. After a few accidental bar presses, the rat would start pressing the bar frequently, receiving a pellet each time. The food reward had conditioned the rat's behavior, strengthening bar pressing and weakening all other behaviors (such as wandering around the box). At this point, the experimenter might do any of several things. The food dispenser might be set up so that several bar presses were now required to obtain food, or so that some bar presses produced food but others did not, or so that bar presses no longer produced food. In each case the rat's behavior would be electronically recorded. One important advantage of the Skinner box is that it allows for careful scientific study of behavior in a controlled environment (Bigge & Shermis, 2004). Anyone with the same equipment can repeat Skinner's experiments.

Certification Pointer

Most teacher certification tests will require you to know that when a teacher reinforces a student who raises her hand to speak, she is using operant conditioning.

ON THE WEB

The B. F. Skinner Foundation website at www.bfskinner.org aims to improve the understanding of human behavior through the work of B. F. Skinner.

consequences

Pleasant or unpleasant conditions that follow behaviors and affect the frequency of future behaviors.

reinforcer

A pleasurable consequence that maintains or increases a behavior.

What Are Some Principles of Behavioral Learning?

Behavioral learning theory has its own language to describe how consequences of behavior shape later behavior (also see Alberto & Troutman, 2009; Bigge & Shermis, 2004; Kazdin, 2001; Malott, 2008; Walker, Shea, & Bauer, 2004).

■ The Role of Consequences

Skinner's pioneering work with rats and pigeons established a set of principles of behavior that have been supported in hundreds of studies involving humans as well as animals. Perhaps the most important principle of behavioral learning theories is that behavior changes according to its immediate **consequences.** Pleasurable consequences strengthen behavior; unpleasant consequences weaken it. In other words, pleasurable consequences increase the frequency with which an individual engages in a behavior, whereas unpleasant consequences reduce the frequency of a behavior. If students enjoy reading books, they will probably read more often. If they find stories boring or are unable to concentrate, they may read less often, choosing other activities instead. Pleasurable consequences are called *reinforcers;* unpleasant consequences are called *punishers.*

■ Reinforcers

A **reinforcer** is defined as any consequence that strengthens (that is, increases the frequency of) a behavior. Note that the effectiveness of the reinforcer must be demonstrated. We

How does this Skinner box work? What type of conditioning is the rat undergoing? How does that type of conditioning take place, and how is it different from the type of conditioning Pavlov studied?

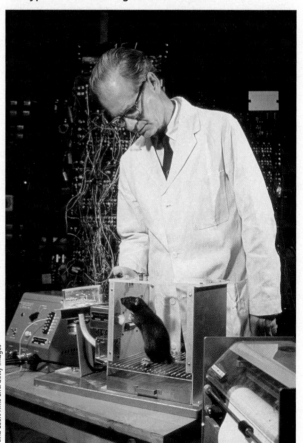

Nina Leen/Time Life/Getty Images

Teachers are a primary source of reinforcement in children's lives. What type of secondary reinforcement is this teacher demonstrating? What are the possible outcomes of this reinforcement?

David Lassman/Syracuse Newspapers/The Image Works

Connections

See Chapter 11, Effective Learning Environments, for classroom applications, including applied behavioral analysis.

primary reinforcer

Food, water, or other consequence that satisfies a basic need.

secondary reinforcer

A consequence that people learn to value through its association with a primary reinforcer.

positive reinforcer

Pleasurable consequence given to strengthen behavior.

negative reinforcer

Release from an unpleasant situation, given to strengthen behavior.

cannot assume that a particular consequence is a reinforcer until we have evidence that it strengthens behavior for a particular individual. For example, candy might generally be considered a reinforcer for young children, but after a big meal a child might not find candy pleasurable, and some children do not like candy at all. A teacher who says, "I reinforced him with praise for staying in his seat during math time, but it didn't work," may be misusing the term *reinforced* if there is no evidence that praise is in fact a reinforcer for this particular student. No reward can be assumed to be a reinforcer for everyone under all conditions (Barnhill, 2005).

PRIMARY AND SECONDARY REINFORCERS   Reinforcers fall into two broad categories: primary and secondary. **Primary reinforcers** satisfy basic human needs. Some examples are food, water, security, warmth, and sex. **Secondary reinforcers** are reinforcers that acquire their value by being associated with primary reinforcers or other well-established secondary reinforcers. For example, money has no value to a young child until the child learns that money can be used to buy things that are themselves primary or secondary reinforcers. Grades have little value to students unless their families notice and value good grades, and families' praise is of value because it is associated with love, warmth, security, and other reinforcers. There are three basic categories of secondary reinforcers. One is social reinforcers, such as praise, smiles, hugs, or attention. When Ms. Esteban recognized Rebecca, she was inadvertently giving Rebecca a social reinforcer: her own attention. Other types of secondary reinforcers are activity reinforcers (such as access to toys, games, or fun activities) and token (or symbolic) reinforcers (such as money, grades, stars, or points that individuals can exchange for other reinforcers).

POSITIVE AND NEGATIVE REINFORCERS   Most often, the reinforcers used in schools are **positive reinforcers** that include praise, grades, and stars. However, another way to strengthen a behavior is if its consequence is an escape from an unpleasant situation or a way of preventing something unpleasant from occurring. For example, a parent might release a student from doing the dishes for completing homework. If doing the dishes is seen as an unpleasant task, release from it will be reinforcing. Escapes from unpleasant situations are called **negative reinforcers** (Landrum & McDuffie, 2008).

This term is often misinterpreted to mean punishment, as in "I negatively reinforced him for being late by having him stay in during recess" (Martella, Nelson, & Marchand-Martella, 2003). One way to avoid this error in terminology is to remember that reinforcers (whether positive or negative) strengthen behavior, whereas punishment is designed to weaken behavior (see Table 5.1).

TABLE 5.1 Consequences in Behavioral Learning

Strengthens Behavior	Discourages Behavior
Positive Reinforcement *Example:* Rewarding or praising	*No Reinforcement* *Example:* Ignoring
Negative Reinforcement *Example:* Excusing from an undesirable task or situation	*Removal Punishment* *Example:* Forbidding a desirable task or situation
	Presentation Punishment *Example:* Imposing an undesirable task or situation

THE PREMACK PRINCIPLE   One important principle of behavior is that we can promote behaviors by making access to something desirable contingent on doing something less desirable. For example, you might say, "As soon as you finish your work, you may go outside" or "Clean up your art project, and then I will read you a story." These are examples of the **Premack Principle** (Premack, 1965), sometimes called "Grandma's Rule" from the age-old statement, "Eat your vegetables, and then you may play." You can use the Premack Principle by alternating more enjoyable activities with less enjoyable ones and making participation in fun activities depend on successful completion of the less enjoyable ones. For example, in elementary school it may be a good idea to schedule music, which most students consider an enjoyable activity, after a difficult subject so students will know not to fool around during the difficult subject and risk losing part of their desired music time (Martella et al., 2003).

Theory into Practice
Classroom Uses of Reinforcement

The behavioral learning principle most useful for classroom practice is also the simplest: Reinforce behaviors you wish to see repeated. This principle may seem obvious, but in practice it is not as easy as it appears. For example, some teachers take the attitude that reinforcement is unnecessary, reasoning, "Why should I reinforce them? They're just doing what they're supposed to do!"

Guidelines for the use of reinforcement to increase desired behavior in the classroom are as follows (see Alberto & Troutman, 2009; Jones & Jones, 2004; Kauffman, Mostort, Trent, & Hallahan, 2002; Malott, 2008; Marzano, 2003; Miltenberger, 2001).

1. Decide what behaviors you want from students, and reinforce these behaviors when they occur.   For example, praise or reward good work. Do not praise or reward work that is not up to students' capabilities. As students begin a new task, they will need to be reinforced at every step along the way. Close approximations of what you hope to accomplish as a final product must receive positive feedback. Break down new behaviors (classroom assignments) into smaller parts and provide adequate rewards along the way.

2. Tell students what behaviors you want; when they exhibit the desired behaviors and you reinforce them, tell them why.   Present students with a rubric that itemizes the criteria you will use when evaluating their work and include the point value for each criterion. Students then will be able to discriminate their own strengths and weaknesses from the feedback they receive from you.

✓ **Certification Pointer**

Teacher certification tests are likely to require you to know that when a teacher says, "If you get an A on tomorrow's test, you won't have to do homework the rest of the week," she's using negative reinforcement (escape from an unpleasant consequence, assuming homework is unpleasant!).

INTASC

4 Multiple Instructional Strategies

Premack Principle

Rule stating that enjoyable activities can be used to reinforce participation in less enjoyable activities.

3. Reinforce appropriate behavior as soon as possible after it occurs   Delayed reinforcement is less effective than immediate reinforcement. When you are grading an assignment, present feedback to your students as soon as possible. It is important that students know how they are doing in class, so don't delay their grades. When constructing an assignment, you should always consider the grading scheme that you will use and how long it will take you to provide the intended feedback.

Connections

For more on intrinsic and extrinsic motivation, see Chapter 10, page 301.

INTRINSIC AND EXTRINSIC REINFORCERS   Often, the most important reinforcer that maintains behavior is the pleasure inherent in engaging in the behavior. For example, most people have a hobby that they work on for extended periods without any reward. People like to draw, read, sing, play games, hike, or swim for no reason other than the fun of doing it. Reinforcers of this type are called **intrinsic reinforcers,** and people can be described as being intrinsically motivated to engage in a given activity. Intrinsic reinforcers are contrasted with **extrinsic reinforcers,** praise or rewards given to motivate people to engage in a behavior that they might not engage in without it. There is evidence that reinforcing children for certain behaviors they would have done anyway can undermine long-term intrinsic motivation (Deci & Ryan, 2002). Research on this topic finds that the undermining effect of extrinsic reinforcers occurs only in a limited set of circumstances, in which rewards are provided to children for engaging in an activity without any standard of performance, and only if the activity is one that children would have done on their own without any reward (Cameron & Pierce, 1994, 1996; Eisenberger, Pierce, & Cameron, 1999). Verbal praise and other types of feedback are extrinsic reinforcers that have been found to increase, not decrease, intrinsic interest. What this research suggests for practice is that you should be cautious about giving reinforcers to children for activities they would have done on their own. However, for most school tasks, which most students would not have done on their own, there is no basis for concern that use of extrinsic reinforcers will undermine intrinsic motivation, especially if those reinforcers are social and communicate recognition of students' growing mastery and independence. In fact, it has been argued that failure to use positive reinforcement when it would have been effective in increasing positive behaviors is unethical (e.g., Bailey & Burch, 2005; Maag, 2001). For example, consider a student who is at risk of being expelled due to fighting. If a program of positive reinforcement for avoiding fighting might have eliminated the student's fighting, then you would be ethically bound to try such a plan (or others) before considering such a serious step as expulsion.

ON THE WEB

For a debate on the issue of intrinsic versus extrinsic motivation, visit www.restud.com/PDF/intrinsicresfeb4.pdf.

intrinsic reinforcers

Behaviors that a person enjoys engaging in for their own sake, without any other reward.

extrinsic reinforcers

Praise or rewards given to motivate people to engage in behavior that they might not do otherwise.

Theory into Practice
Practical Reinforcers

Anything that children like can be an effective reinforcer, but there are obvious practical limitations on what should be used in classrooms. One general principle of positive reinforcement is that it is best to use the least elaborate or tangible reinforcer that will work. In other words, if praise or self-reinforcement will work, don't use certificates. If certificates will work, don't use small toys. If small toys will work, don't use food. One way to find out what reinforcers to use is to ask the students themselves, who are more likely to work for a reinforcer they have selected (Cote, Thompson, Hanley, & McKerchar, 2007). However, do not hesitate to use whatever practical reinforcer is necessary to motivate children to do important tasks. In particular, try all possible reinforcement strategies before even thinking of punishment (described next). A few categories of reinforcers and examples of each appear here (also see Burden, 2000; Landrum & Kauffman, 2006; Martella et al., 2003). These are arranged from least to most tangible.

1. *Self-reinforcement.* Students may be taught to praise themselves, give themselves a mental pat on the back, check off progress on a form, take a short break, or otherwise reinforce themselves for completing an assignment or staying on task.

2. *Praise.* Phrases such as "Good job," "Way to go," "I knew you could do it," and other verbal praise can be effective, but the same message can often be delivered with a smile, a wink, a thumbs-up signal, or a pat on the back. In cooperative learning and peer tutoring, students can be encouraged to praise each other for appropriate behavior (Landrum & Kauffman, 2006).

3. *Attention.* The attention of a valued adult or peer can be a very effective reinforcer for many children. Listening, nodding, or moving closer may provide a child with the positive attention she or he is seeking. For outstanding performance or for meeting goals over a longer time period, students might be allowed a special time to visit with the custodian, to help in the office, or to take a walk with the principal (Alber & Heward, 2000).

4. *Grades and recognition.* Good marks and other honors (e.g., certificates of accomplishment) can be effective both in giving students positive feedback on their efforts and in communicating progress to families, who are likely to reinforce good reports themselves. Public displays of good work, notes from the principal, and other commendations can have the same effect. Quiz scores, behavior ratings, and other feedback given frequently can be more effective than report card grades covering months of work.

5. *Call home.* Calling or sending a note to a child's caregivers to recognize success can be a powerful reinforcer.

6. *Home-based reinforcement.* Families can be effective partners in a reinforcement system. Teachers can work out an arrangement with families in which children receive special privileges at home if the children meet well-specified standards of behavior or performance.

7. *Privileges.* Children can get free time, access to special equipment (e.g., soccer balls or games), or special roles (such as running errands or distributing papers). Children or groups who have behaved well can simply be allowed to line up first for recess or dismissal or have other small privileges.

8. *Activity reinforcers.* After achieving preestablished standards, students can earn videos, games, or access to other fun activities. Activity reinforcers lend themselves particularly well to group contingencies, in which a whole class can earn free time or special activities if students collectively achieve a standard (Embry, 2002; Theodore, Bray, Kehle, & Jenson, 2001).

Connections

For more on working with parents to reinforce behavior, see Chapter 11, pages 337–338.

Connections

For more on the use of activity reinforcers, see Chapter 11, pages 334–337 and 340–341.

> **9.** *Tangible reinforcers.*   Children may earn points for achievement or good behavior that they can exchange for small toys, erasers, pencils, marbles, comic books, stickers, and so on. Tangible reinforcers usually work better if children have a choice among several options (Cruz & Cullinan, 2001; Walker et al., 2004).
>
> **10.** *Food.*   Raisins, apples, carrots, yogurt, or other healthy snacks can be used as reinforcers.

■ Punishers

Certification Pointer

For teacher certification tests you will probably need to know that unless an unpleasant consequence reduces the frequency of the behavior it follows, it may not be a punisher.

Consequences that weaken behavior are called *punishers.* Note that there is the same catch in the definition of **punishment** as in the definition of *reinforcement:* If an apparently unpleasant consequence does not reduce the frequency of the behavior it follows, it is not necessarily a punisher. For example, some students like being sent to the principal's office or out to the hall because it releases them from the classroom, which they see as an unpleasant situation (Driscoll, 2000; Kauffman et al., 2002; Martella et al., 2003). Some students like to be scolded because it gains them your attention and perhaps enhances their status among their peers. As with reinforcers, the effectiveness of a punisher cannot be assumed but must be demonstrated. Punishment can take two primary forms.

PRESENTATION PUNISHMENT   The use of unpleasant consequences, or **aversive stimuli,** characterizes **presentation punishment,** as when a student is scolded.

REMOVAL PUNISHMENT   The withdrawal of a pleasant consequence describes **removal punishment.** Examples include loss of a privilege, having to stay in during recess, or receiving detention after school. Another example, called **response cost** (Landrum & McDuffie, 2008), involves charging a cost to students who are behaving inappropriately, such as a minute of detention after school for every minute off task. One frequently used form of removal punishment in classrooms is **time out,** in which a student who misbehaves is required to sit in the corner or in the hall for several minutes (see Nelson & Carr, 2000). Teachers often use time out when they believe that the attention of other students is serving to reinforce misbehavior; time out deprives the student who has misbehaved of this reinforcer. The use of time out as a consequence for misbehavior has generally been found to reduce the misbehavior (Alberto & Troutman, 2006).

For example, White and Bailey (1990) evaluated use of a sit-and-watch consequence for physical education classes. Children who misbehaved were told what they had done wrong and were given a 3-minute sand timer and asked to sit and watch until the sand ran out. The program was first tried in an alternative class for fourth- and fifth-graders with serious behavior problems. Figure 5.2 summarizes the findings. After a baseline of up to 343 disruptive behaviors in 10 minutes was observed, a behavioral checklist program was tried, in which teachers rated each child's behavior and sent poorly behaved children to the office or deprived them of a free period. This reduced misbehavior but did not eliminate it. However, when the sit-and-watch procedure was introduced, misbehavior virtually disappeared. The same sit-and-watch method was used in a regular fourth-grade physical education class, and the results were similar.

The issue of if, when, and how to punish has been a source of considerable controversy among behavioral learning theorists. Some have claimed that the effects of punishment, especially presentation (aversive) punishment, are only temporary, that punishment produces aggression, and it causes individuals to avoid settings in which it is used (Kazdin, 2001; Landrum & Kauffman, 2006; Miltenberger, 2001). Even behavioral learning theorists who do support the use of punishment agree that it should be resorted to only when reinforcement for appropriate behavior has been tried and has failed; that when punishment is necessary, it should take the mildest possible form; and that punishment

punishment

Unpleasant consequences used to weaken behavior.

aversive stimulus

An unpleasant consequence that a person tries to avoid or escape.

presentation punishment

An aversive stimulus following a behavior, used to decrease the chances that the behavior will occur again.

removal punishment

Withdrawal of a pleasant consequence that may be reinforcing a behavior, designed to decrease the chances that the behavior will recur.

response cost

Procedure of charging misbehaving students against their free time or other privileges.

time out

Procedure of removing a student from a situation in which misbehavior was being reinforced.

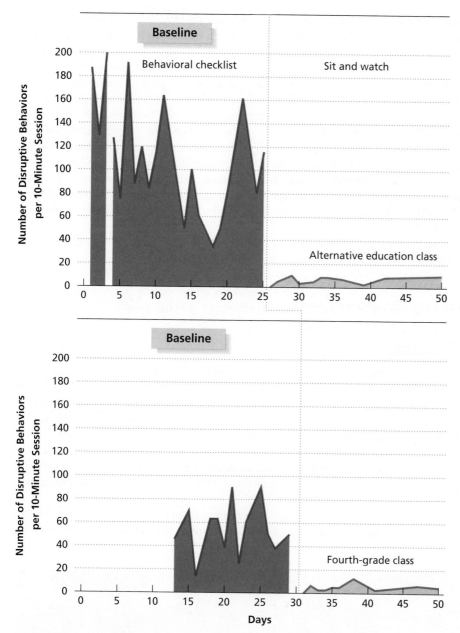

FIGURE 5.2 Reducing Disruptive Behavior with Sit and Watch

The number of disruptive behaviors per 10-minute observation period is shown here.

Source: A. G. White and J. S. Bailey, "Reducing Disruptive Behaviors of Elementary Physical Education Students with Sit and Watch," *Journal of Applied Behavior Analysis, 3,* 1990, p. 357. Adapted by permission.

should always be used as part of a careful plan, never inconsistently or out of frustration. Physical punishment in schools (such as spanking) is illegal in most places (Jones & Jones, 2007; Levin & Nolan, 2007) and is universally opposed by behavioral learning theorists on ethical as well as scientific grounds (see Bailey & Burch, 2005; Kazdin, 2001; Malott, Malott, & Trojan, 2000).

■ Immediacy of Consequences

One very important principle of behavioral learning theories is that consequences that follow behaviors closely in time affect behavior far more than delayed consequences. Waiting a few minutes to give a rat in a Skinner box its food pellet for pressing a bar will significantly increase its learning time for making the connection between bar pressing and food; by the time the food arrives, the rat may be doing something other than bar pressing. A smaller reinforcer that is given immediately generally has a much larger effect than does a large reinforcer given later (Alberto & Troutman, 2006). This concept explains much about human behavior. It suggests, for example, why people find it so difficult to give up smoking or overeating. Even though the benefits of giving up smoking or of losing weight are substantial and well known, the small but immediate reinforcement of just one cigarette or one doughnut often overcomes the behavioral effect of the large but delayed reinforcers. In the classroom the principle of immediacy of consequences is also very important. Particularly for younger students, praise for a job well done that is given immediately can be a stronger reinforcer than a good grade given much later. Moving close to a student who is misbehaving, touching his or her shoulder, or making a gesture (e.g., finger to lips to ask for silence) may be much more effective than a scolding or warning given at the end of class (Jones & Jones, 2007; Landrum & Kauffman, 2006).

Immediate feedback serves at least two purposes. First, it makes clear the connection between behavior and consequence. Second, it increases the informational value of the feedback. In dealing with misbehavior, you can apply the principle of immediacy of consequences by responding immediately and positively when students are not misbehaving—in effect, by catching them in the act of being good!

■ Shaping

Immediacy of reinforcement is important to teaching, but so is the decision of what to reinforce. Should a kindergarten teacher withhold reinforcement until a child knows the sounds of all 26 letters? Certainly not. It would be better to praise children for recognizing one letter, then for recognizing several, and finally for learning the sounds of all 26 letters. Should a music teacher withhold reinforcement until a young student has played a piano piece flawlessly? Or should the teacher praise the first halting run-through? Most students need reinforcement along the way. When you guide students toward goals by reinforcing the many steps that lead to success, you are using a technique called **shaping.**

The term *shaping* is used in behavioral learning theories to refer to the teaching of new skills or behaviors by reinforcing learners for approaching the desired final behavior

shaping

The teaching of a new skill or behavior by means of reinforcement for small steps toward the desired goal.

Whether teaching children new physical skills or academic skills, teachers and coaches begin with the basics and build from there. What techniques can they use to shape children's behaviors?

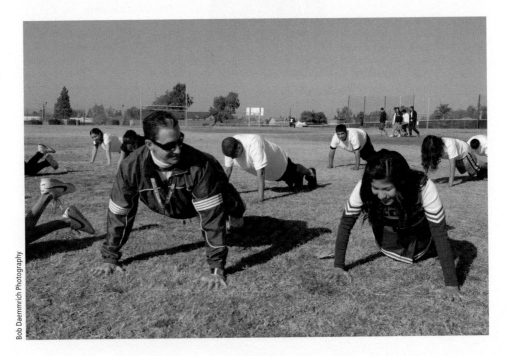

Bob Daemmrich Photography

(Bigge & Shermis, 2004; Driscoll, 2000). For example, in teaching children to tie their shoelaces, we would not simply show them how it is done and then wait to reinforce them until they do the whole job themselves. Rather, we would first reinforce them for tying the first knot, then for making the loops, and so on, until they can do the entire task. In this way we would be shaping the children's behavior by reinforcing all those steps that lead toward the final goal.

Shaping is an important tool in classroom instruction. Let's say we want students to be able to write paragraphs with a topic sentence, three supporting details, and a concluding sentence. This task has many parts: being able to recognize and then produce topic sentences, supporting details, and concluding sentences; being able to write complete sentences using capitalization, punctuation, and grammar correctly; and being able to spell. If you taught a lesson on all these skills and then asked students to write paragraphs, scoring them on content, grammar, punctuation, and spelling, most students would fail and would probably learn little from the exercise.

Instead, you might teach the skills step by step, gradually shaping the final skill. Students might be taught how to write first topic sentences, then supporting details, then concluding sentences. Early on, they might be held responsible only for paragraph content. Later, the requirement for reinforcement might be increased to include grammar and punctuation. Finally, spelling might be added as a criterion for success. At each stage, students would have a good chance to be reinforced because the criterion for reinforcement would be within their grasp. The principle here is that students should be reinforced for behaviors that are within their current capabilities but that also stretch them toward new skills.

■ Extinction

By definition, reinforcers strengthen behavior. But what happens when reinforcers are withdrawn? Eventually, the behavior will be weakened, and ultimately it will disappear. This process is called **extinction** of a previously learned behavior.

Extinction is rarely a smooth process. When reinforcers are withdrawn, individuals often increase their rate of behavior for a while. For example, think of a door that you've used as a shortcut to somewhere you go frequently. Imagine that one day the door will not open. You may push even harder for a while, shake the door, turn the handle both ways, perhaps even kick the door. You are likely to feel frustrated and angry. However, after a short time you will realize that the door is locked and go away. If the door is permanently locked (without your knowing it), you may try it a few times over the next few days and then perhaps once after a month; only eventually will you give up on it.

Your behavior when confronted by the locked door is a classic extinction pattern. Behavior intensifies when the reinforcer is first withdrawn and then rapidly weakens until the behavior disappears. Still, the behavior may return after much time has passed. For example, you could try the door again a year later to see whether it is still locked. If it is, you will probably leave it alone for a longer time, but perhaps not forever.

The characteristic **extinction burst,** the increase in levels of a behavior in the early stages of extinction, has important consequences for classroom management. For example, imagine that you have decided to extinguish a child's inappropriate calling out of answers (instead of raising her hand to be recognized) by ignoring her until she raises her hand quietly. At first, ignoring the child is likely to increase her calling-out behavior, a classic extinction burst. You might then mistakenly conclude that ignoring isn't working, when in fact continuing to ignore inappropriate call-outs is exactly the right strategy if you keep it up (Landrum & Kauffman, 2006; Martella et al., 2003). Worse, you might finally decide to give in and recognize the child after the third or fourth call-out. This would teach the worst possible message: that calling out works eventually if you keep doing it. This would probably result in an increase in the very behavior you were trying to reduce, as the child learns that "if at first you don't succeed, try, try again" (Landrum & McDuffie, 2008). This is the case in the vignette presented at the beginning of this

A dinosaur goes through extinction.

extinction

The weakening and eventual elimination of a learned behavior as reinforcement is withdrawn.

extinction burst

The increase in levels of a behavior in the early stages of extinction.

chapter. Ms. Esteban at first ignores Rebecca's calling out, so she calls out even louder. Then the teacher calls on Rebecca, unintentionally communicating to her that only loud and persistent calling out will be reinforced.

Extinction of a previously learned behavior can be hastened when some stimulus or cue informs the individual that behaviors that were once encouraged will no longer be reinforced. In the case of the locked door, a sign saying, "Door permanently locked—use other entrance" would have greatly reduced the number of times you tried the door before giving up on it. Call-outs will be reduced much more quickly if Ms. Esteban tells her class, "I will no longer respond to children unless they are silent and are raising their hand," and then ignores all other attempts to get her attention.

■ Schedules of Reinforcement

The effects of reinforcement on behavior depend on many factors, one of the most important of which is the **schedule of reinforcement** (see Alberto & Troutman, 2009; Kazdin, 2001; Miltenberger, 2001). This term refers to the frequency with which reinforcers are given, the amount of time that elapses between opportunities for reinforcement, and the predictability of reinforcement.

FIXED RATIO (FR)   One common schedule of reinforcement is the **fixed-ratio (FR) schedule,** in which a reinforcer is given after a fixed number of behaviors. For example, you might say, "As soon as you finish 10 problems, you may go outside." Regardless of the amount of time it takes, students are reinforced as soon as they finish 10 problems. This is an example of an FR10 schedule (10 behaviors for one reinforcer). One common form of fixed-ratio schedule gives reinforcement for each behavior. This is called *continuous reinforcement* (CRF), or FR1. Putting money in a soda machine is (usually) an example of continuous reinforcement because one behavior (inserting coins) results in one reinforcer (a soda). Giving correct answers in class is also usually continuously reinforced. The student gives a good answer, and you say, "Right! Good answer!"

One important process in instruction is gradually increasing reinforcement ratios. Early in a sequence of lessons, it may be necessary to reinforce students for every correct answer, such as responding to every successful math problem. However, this is inefficient in the long run. As soon as students are answering math problems correctly, it may be possible to reinforce every 5 problems (FR5), every 10 (FR10), and so on. Thinning out the reinforcement schedule in this way enhances the student's ability to work independently without reinforcement and makes the behavior more resistant to extinction. Ultimately, students might be asked to do entire projects on their own, receiving no reinforcement until the projects are completed.

Fixed-ratio schedules are effective in motivating individuals to do a great deal of work—especially if the fixed ratio starts with continuous reinforcement (FR1) to get the individual going and then moves to higher requirements for reinforcement. One reason that high requirements for reinforcement produce higher levels of behavior than low requirements is that reinforcing too frequently can make the value of the reinforcer wear off. Students who are praised for every math problem will soon grow tired of being praised, and the reinforcer might lose its value.

VARIABLE RATIO (VR)   A **variable-ratio (VR) schedule** of reinforcement is one in which the number of behaviors required for reinforcement is unpredictable, although it is certain that the behaviors will eventually be reinforced. For example, a slot machine is a variable-ratio reinforcer. It may pay off after 1 pull one time and after 200 the next, and there is no way to predict which pull will win. In the classroom teachers often use a variable-ratio schedule when students raise their hands to answer questions. Although they never know when they will be reinforced by being able to give the correct answer, students may expect to be called on about 1 time in 20 in a class of 20, called a VR20 schedule because, on the average, 20 behaviors are required for one reinforcer.

schedule of reinforcement

The frequency and predictability of reinforcement.

fixed-ratio (FR) schedule

Reinforcement schedule in which desired behavior is rewarded following a fixed number of behaviors.

variable-ratio (VR) schedule

Reinforcement schedule in which desired behavior is rewarded following an unpredictable number of behaviors.

Variable-ratio schedules tend to produce high and stable rates of behavior. In fact, almost all gambling games involve VR schedules, and so they can be quite literally addicting. Similarly, use of frequent random checks of student work can help to motivate steady, careful work.

Variable-ratio schedules are highly resistant to extinction. Even after behaviors are no longer being reinforced, people may not give up working for a long time. Because they have learned that it may take a lot of work to be rewarded, they keep on working in the mistaken belief that the next effort might just pay off.

FIXED INTERVAL (FI)   In **fixed-interval (FI) schedules,** reinforcement is available only at certain periodic times. The final examination is a classic example. Fixed-interval schedules create an interesting pattern of behavior. The individual may do very little until just before reinforcement is available and then put forth a burst of effort as the time for reinforcement approaches. This pattern can be demonstrated with rats and pigeons on fixed-interval schedules, but it is even more apparent in students who cram at the last minute before a test or who write their monthly book reports the night before they are due. These characteristics of fixed-interval schedules suggest that frequent short quizzes may be better than infrequent major exams for encouraging students to give their best effort all the time rather than putting in all-nighters before the exam (Malott, 2008).

VARIABLE INTERVAL (VI)   In a **variable-interval (VI) schedule,** reinforcement is available at some times but not at others, and we have no idea when a behavior will be reinforced. An example of this is making spot checks of students who are doing assignments in class. Students are reinforced if they are working well at the particular moment you come by. Because they cannot predict when you will check them, students must be doing good work all the time. People may obey traffic laws out of respect for the law and civic responsibility, but it also helps that the police randomly check drivers' compliance with the law. Troopers using speed cameras often hide on overpasses or behind hills so that they can get a random sampling of drivers' behavior. If they were always in plain sight, they would be a signal to drive carefully, so the necessity for driving carefully at other times would be reduced.

Like variable-ratio schedules, variable-interval schedules are very effective for maintaining a high rate of behavior while being highly resistant to extinction. For example, let's say you have a policy of having students hand in their seatwork every day. Rather than checking every paper, you pull three papers at random and give these students extra credit if their seatwork is done well. This variable-interval schedule would probably motivate students to do their seatwork carefully. If you secretly stopped spot-checking halfway through the year, the students might never know it, figuring that their own paper just hadn't been pulled to be checked rather than realizing that reinforcement was no longer available for anyone.

Table 5.2 defines and gives additional examples of schedules of reinforcement.

■ Maintenance

The principle of extinction holds that when reinforcement for a previously learned behavior is withdrawn, the behavior fades away. Does this mean that teachers must reinforce students' behaviors forever?

Not necessarily. For rats in a Skinner box, the withdrawal of reinforcement for bar pressing will inevitably lead to extinction of bar pressing. However, humans live in a much more complex world that is full of natural reinforcers for most of the skills and behaviors that we learn in school. For example, students may initially require frequent reinforcement for behaviors that lead to reading. However, once they can read, they have a skill that unlocks the entire world of written language, a world that is highly reinforcing to most students. After a certain point, reinforcement for reading may no longer be necessary because the content of reading material itself maintains the behavior.

fixed-interval (FI) schedule
Reinforcement schedule in which desired behavior is rewarded following a constant amount of time.

variable-interval (VI) schedule
Reinforcement schedule in which desired behavior is rewarded following an unpredictable amount of time.

TABLE 5.2	Schedules of Reinforcement		

Specific response patterns during reinforcement and extinction characterize each of the four types of schedules.

Schedule	Definition	Response Patterns	
		During Reinforcement	During Extinction
Fixed ratio	Constant number of behaviors for required for reinforcement	Steady response rate; pause after reinforcement	Rapid drop in response rate after required number of responses passes without reinforcement
Variable ratio	Variable number of behaviors required for reinforcement	Steady, high response rate	Response rate stays high, then drops off
Fixed interval	Constant amount of time passes before reinforcement is available	Uneven rate, with rapid acceleration at the end of each interval	Rapid drop in response rate after interval passes with no reinforcement
Variable interval	Variable amount of time passes before reinforcement is available	Steady, high response rate	Slow decrease in response rate

Similarly, poorly behaved students may need careful, systematic reinforcement for doing schoolwork. After a while, however, they will find out that doing schoolwork pays off in grades, in family approval, in ability to understand what is going on in class, and in knowledge. These natural reinforcers for doing schoolwork were always available, but the students could not experience them until their schoolwork was improved by more systematic means.

The concept of resistance to extinction, discussed earlier (in the section on schedules of reinforcement), is central to an understanding of **maintenance** of learned behavior. As was noted, when new behaviors are being introduced, reinforcement for correct responses should be frequent and predictable. However, once the behaviors are established, reinforcement for correct responses should become less frequent and less predictable. The reason for this is that variable schedules of reinforcement and schedules that require many behaviors before reinforcement is given are much more resistant to extinction than are fixed schedules or easy ones. For example, if you praise a student every time the student does a math problem but then stop praising, the student may stop doing math problems. In contrast, if you gradually increase the number of math problems a student must do to be praised and praise the student at random intervals (a variable-ratio schedule), then the student is likely to continue to do math problems for a long time with little or no reinforcement from you.

■ The Role of Antecedents

We have seen that the consequences of behavior strongly influence behavior. Yet it is not only what follows a behavior that has influence. The stimuli that precede a behavior also play an important role (Kazdin, 2001).

CUEING **Antecedent stimuli,** events that precede a behavior, are also known as **cues** because they inform us about which behavior will be reinforced and which will be punished. Cues come in many forms and give us hints as to when we should change our behavior and when we should not. For example, during a math session, most teachers will reinforce students who are working on problems. However, after the teacher has announced that math is over and it is time for music, the consequences change. The ability to behave one way in the presence of one stimulus—"It's math time"—and a different way in the presence of another stimulus—"It's time for music"—is known as *stimulus discrimination*.

maintenance

Continuation (of behavior).

antecedent stimuli

Events that precede behaviors.

cues

Signals as to which behavior(s) will be reinforced or punished.

DISCRIMINATION   When is the best time to ask your boss for a raise? When the company is doing well, the boss looks happy, and you have just done something especially good? Or when the company has just gotten a poor earnings report, the boss is glowering, and you have just made a costly error? Obviously, the first situation is more likely to lead to success. You know this because you have learned to discriminate between good and bad times to ask your boss to do something for you. **Discrimination** is the use of cues, signals, or information to know when behavior is likely to be reinforced. The company's financial condition, the boss's mood, and your recent performance are discriminative stimuli with regard to the chances that your request for a raise will be successful. For students to learn discrimination, they must have feedback on the correctness or incorrectness of their responses. Studies of discrimination learning have generally found that students need to know when their responses are incorrect as well as correct.

Learning is largely a matter of mastering more and more complex discriminations. For example, all letters, numbers, words, and mathematical symbols are discriminative stimuli. A young child learns to discriminate between the letters *b* and *d*. An older student learns the distinction between the words *effective* and *efficient*. An educational psychology student learns to discriminate negative reinforcement from punishment. A teacher learns to discriminate facial and verbal cues indicating that students are bored or interested by a lecture.

Applying the concept of discriminative stimuli to classroom instruction and management is easy: You should tell students what behaviors will be reinforced. In theory, you could wait until students did something worthwhile and then reinforce it, but this would be incredibly inefficient. Rather, you should give students messages that say, in effect, "To be reinforced (e.g., with praise, grades, or stars), these are the things you must do." In this way, you can avoid having students spend time and effort on the wrong activities. If students know that what they are doing will pay off, they will usually work hard.

GENERALIZATION   If students learn to stay in their seats and do careful work in math class, will their behavior also improve in science class? If students can subtract 3 apples from 7 apples, can they also subtract 3 oranges from 7 oranges? If students can interpret symbolism used by Shakespeare, can they also interpret symbolism used in African folktales? These are all questions of **generalization,** or transfer of behaviors learned under one set of conditions to other situations. Generalization cannot be taken for granted. For example, when a classroom management program is successfully introduced in one setting, students' behaviors do not automatically improve in other settings. Instead, students learn to discriminate among settings. Even young children readily learn what is encouraged and what is forbidden in kindergarten, at home, and at various friends' houses. Their behavior may be quite different in each setting, according to the different rules and expectations.

For generalization to occur, it usually must be planned for. A successful classroom management program used in social studies class may be transferred to English class to ensure generalization to that setting. Students may need to study the use of symbolism by many authors in many cultures before they acquire the skill to interpret symbolism in general.

Obviously, generalization is most likely to occur across similar settings or similar concepts. A new behavior is more likely to generalize from reading class to social studies class than to recess or home settings. However, even in the most similar-appearing settings, generalizations may not occur. For example, many students will demonstrate complete mastery of spelling or language mechanics and then fail to apply this knowledge to their own compositions. You should not assume that because students can perform effectively under one set of circumstances, they can also do so under a different set of circumstances.

TECHNIQUES FOR INCREASING GENERALIZATION   There are many techniques for increasing the chances that a behavior learned in one setting, such as a given class, will generalize to other settings, such as other classes or, more importantly, real-life applications (see Alberto & Troutman, 2006; Martella et al., 2003; Walker et al., 2004). Some of these strategies involve teaching in a way that makes generalization easier. For example, arithmetic lessons involving money will probably transfer better to real life if they involve manipulating real or simulated coins and bills than if they involve only problems on

discrimination
Perception of and response to differences in stimuli.

generalization
Carryover of behaviors, skills, or concepts from one setting or task to another.

paper. Another teaching strategy known to contribute to generalization is using many examples from different contexts. For example, students are more likely to be able to transfer the concept of supply and demand to new areas if they learn examples relating to prices for groceries, prices for natural resources, values of collectibles (such as baseball cards), and wages for common and rare skills than if they learn only about grocery pricing. An obvious strategy for increasing generalization is "on-the-job training": teaching a given skill in the actual environment in which it will be used, or in a simulation of such an environment.

After initial instruction has taken place, there are many ways to increase generalization. One is to repeat instruction in a variety of settings. For example, after teaching students to use a given test-taking strategy in mathematics, such as "skip difficult problems and go back to them after answering the easy ones," you might give students the opportunity to use this same strategy on a science test, a grammar test, and a health test. Another after-teaching technique is to help students make the link between a new skill and natural reinforcers in the environment so as to maintain that skill. For example, when children are learning to read, they can be given a regular homework assignment to read books or magazines that are of high interest to them, even if those materials are not "good literature." Initially, new reading skills may be better maintained by comic books than by literary classics because for some children the comic books tie their new skill more immediately to the pleasure of reading, making generalization to nonschool settings more likely. Finally, you can increase generalization by directly reinforcing generalization—for example, by praising a student who connects a new idea to a different context or uses a skill in a new application.

How Has Social Learning Theory Contributed to Our Understanding of Human Learning?

Connections

For the relation of social learning theory to social construction of meaning, see Chapter 8, page 219.

Social learning theory is a major outgrowth of the behavioral learning theory tradition. Developed by Albert Bandura, social learning theory accepts most of the principles of behavioral theories but focuses to a much greater degree on the effects of cues on behavior and on internal mental processes, emphasizing the effects of thought on action and action on thought (Bandura, 1986).

■ Bandura: Modeling and Observational Learning

Connections

For the relation of social learning theory to Vygotskian and neo-Piagetian views of development, see Chapter 2, page 41.

Bandura noted that the Skinnerian emphasis on the effects of the consequences of behavior largely ignored the phenomena of **modeling**—the imitation of others' behavior—and of vicarious experience—learning from others' successes or failures. He felt that much of human learning is not shaped by its consequences but is more efficiently learned directly from a model (Bandura, 1986; Schunk, 2000). The physical education teacher demonstrates jumping jacks, and students imitate. Bandura calls this *no-trial learning* because students do not have to go through a shaping process but can reproduce the correct response immediately.

Bandura's (1986) analysis of **observational learning** involves four phases: attentional, retention, reproduction, and motivational phases.

ON THE WEB

For more on social learning theory, go to http://tip.psychology.org/bandura.html.

modeling

Imitation of others' behavior.

observational learning

Learning by observation and imitation of others.

1. *Attentional phase.*   The first phase in observational learning is paying attention to a model. In general, students pay attention to role models who are attractive, successful, interesting, and popular. This is why so many students copy the dress, hairstyle, and mannerisms of pop culture stars. In the classroom you gain the students' attention by presenting clear and interesting cues, by using novelty or surprise, and by motivating students.

2. ***Retention phase.***   Once teachers have students' attention, it is time to model the behavior they want students to imitate and then give students a chance to practice or rehearse. For example, you might show how to write the letter *A*. Then students would imitate your model by trying to write *A*'s themselves.

3. ***Reproduction.***   During the reproduction phase, students try to match their behavior to the model's. In the classroom the assessment of student learning takes place during this phase. For example, after seeing the letter *A* modeled and practicing it several times, can the student reproduce the letter so that it looks like your model?

4. ***Motivational phase.***   The final stage in the observational learning process is motivation. Students will imitate a model because they believe that doing so will increase their own chances to be reinforced. In the classroom the motivational phase of observational learning often entails praise or grades given for matching your model. Students pay attention to the model, practicing and reproducing it because they have learned that this is what you like and they want to please you. When the child makes a recognizable *A,* you say, "Nice work!"

VICARIOUS LEARNING   Although most observational learning is motivated by an expectation that correctly imitating the model will lead to reinforcement, it is also important to note that people learn by seeing others reinforced or punished for engaging in certain behaviors (Bandura, 1986; Zimmerman & Schunk, 2003). This is why magazine distributors always include happy winners in their advertisements to induce people to enter promotional contests. We may consciously know that our chances of winning are one in several million, but seeing others so handsomely reinforced makes us want to imitate their contest-entering behavior.

Classroom teachers use the principle of **vicarious learning** all the time. When one student is fooling around, teachers often single out others who are working well and reinforce them for doing a good job. The misbehaving student sees that working is reinforced and (it is hoped) gets back to work. This technique was systematically studied in a classic study by Broden, Hall, Dunlap, and Clark (1970). Two disruptive second-graders, Edwin and Greg, sat next to each other. After a baseline period, the teacher began to notice and praise Edwin whenever he was paying attention and doing his classwork. Edwin's behavior improved markedly under this condition. Of greater interest, however, is that Greg's behavior also improved, even though no specific reinforcement for appropriate behavior was directed toward him. Apparently, Greg learned from Edwin's experience. In the case of Ms. Esteban and Rebecca at the opening of this chapter, other students saw Rebecca get Ms. Esteban's attention by calling out answers, so they modeled their behavior on Rebecca's.

One of the classic experiments in social learning theory is a study done by Bandura (1965) in which children were shown one of three films. In all three, an adult modeled aggressive behavior. In one film the model was severely punished. In another the model was praised and given treats. In a third the model was given no consequences. After viewing one of the films, the children were observed playing with toys. The children who had seen the model punished engaged in significantly fewer aggressive acts in their own play than did the children who had seen the model rewarded or had viewed the film with no consequences.

INTASC

2 Knowledge of Human Development and Learning

Certification Pointer

Teacher certification tests may require you to know that learning vicariously means that you learn from observing or hearing about another's experiences.

Theory into Practice
Observational Learning

Have you ever tried to teach someone to tie his or her shoes? Imagine explaining this task to someone without the use of a model or imitation! Learning to tie our shoes is an example of how observational learning works.

vicarious learning

Learning based on observation of the consequences of others' behavior.

Acquiring new skills by observing the behaviors of others is a common part of everyday life. In many situations children watch others talking and acting, and they witness the consequences of those activities as well. Such observations provide models that teach children strategies to use at other times and places.

Although the major focus of research on observational learning has been on specific behaviors, studies have also shown that attitudes, too, may be acquired through observation (Miller, 1993). Teachers and parents alike are concerned with the models emulated by children. The value of these models goes beyond the specific abilities they possess and includes the attitudes they represent. In the classroom you must be certain to exemplify a standard of behavior consistent with the expectations you have for the students. For instance, if promptness and politeness are characteristics you want to foster in the students, then you must be certain to be prompt and polite.

Connections

For more on self-regulated learning, see Chapter 8, page 222.

SELF-REGULATED LEARNING   Another important concept in social learning theory is **self-regulation** (Boekaerts, Pintrich, & Zeidner, 2000; Schunk & Pajares, 2004; Zimmerman, 2000). Bandura (1997) hypothesizes that people observe their own behavior, judge it against their own standards, and reinforce or punish themselves. We have all had the experience of knowing we've done a job well and mentally patting ourselves on the back, regardless of what others have said. Similarly, we all know when we've done less than our best. To make these judgments, we have to have expectations for our own performance. One student might be delighted to get 90 percent correct on a test, whereas another might be quite disappointed.

Students can be taught to use self-regulation strategies, and they can be reminded to do so in a variety of contexts so that self-regulation becomes a habit. For example, students might be asked to set goals for the amount of time they expect to study each evening and to record whether they meet their goals. Children who are studying multiplication facts might be asked to time themselves on how quickly and accurately they can complete a 50-item facts test and then to try to beat their own record. Students might be asked to grade their own essays in terms of content, mechanics, and organization, and to see whether they can match your ratings. Gureasko-Moore, DuPaul, and White (2006) asked four 12-year old boys who were frequently late and forgot materials and homework to keep a daily log of these behaviors. They met with each other daily, set goals for the group, and gradually all began coming to class on time and prepared. Each of these strategies puts students in control of their own learning goals, and each is likely to build a general strategy of setting and meeting personal goals and personal standards (Schunk & Zimmerman, 2003).

As with any skill, self-regulated learning skills are likely to remain limited to one situation or context unless they are applied in many contexts. For example, children who learn to set study goals for themselves when working alone may not transfer these skills to situations in which they are working in groups or in your presence (Schunk & Pajares, 2004; Zimmerman, 2000), although they can readily learn to make these generalizations if they are taught or reminded to do so. Similarly, children may not transfer self-regulated learning strategies from English to math, or even from computations to problem solving (Boekaerts, 1995). For this reason, students need many opportunities to use goal-setting and self-evaluation strategies in a variety of contexts; to monitor and celebrate their progress; and to understand how, when, and why they should self-regulate.

self-regulation

Rewarding or punishing one's own behavior.

cognitive behavior modification

Procedures based on both behavioral and cognitive principles for changing one's own behavior by means of self-talk and self-instruction.

■ Meichenbaum's Model of Self-Regulated Learning

Students can be taught to monitor and regulate their own behavior. Self-regulated learning strategies of this kind are often called **cognitive behavior modification** (Harris et al., 2001; Zimmerman, 2000). For example, Meichen-baum (1977) developed a strategy in which students are trained to say to themselves, "What is my problem? What is my plan? Am I using my plan? How did I do?" This strategy has been used to reduce disruptive behavior of students at many grade levels (Jones & Jones, 2007; Martella et al., 2003). Manning (1988) taught disruptive third-graders self-statements to help them remember appropriate behavior and to reinforce it for themselves. As one instance, for appropriate hand-raising, students were taught to say to themselves while raising their hands, "If I scream out the answer, others will be disturbed. I will raise my hand and wait my turn. Good for me. See, I can wait!" (Manning, 1988, p. 197). Similar strategies have been successfully applied to help students monitor their own achievement. For example, poor readers have been taught to ask themselves questions as they read and to summarize paragraphs to make sure they comprehend text (Bornstein, 1985).

The steps involved in self-instruction are described by Meichenbaum (1977) as follows:

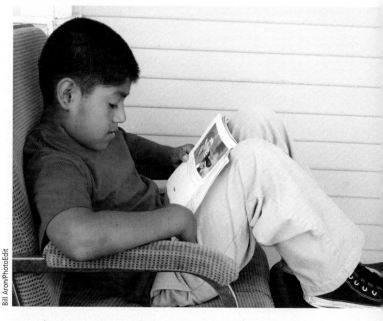

Bill Aron/PhotoEdit

How do community summer reading programs encourage young children to read? How is this a form of self-regulated learning?

1. An adult model performs a task while talking to self out loud (cognitive modeling).

2. The child performs the same task under the direction of the model's instructions (overt, external guidance).

3. The child performs the task while instructing self aloud (overt self-guidance).

4. The child whispers the instructions to self as he or she goes through the task (faded, overt self-guidance).

5. The child performs the task while guiding his or her performance via private speech (covert self-instruction). (p. 32)

Connections

For the related concept of teaching self-questioning strategies to develop metacognitive skills, see Chapter 6, pages 168–169.

Encouraging self-regulated learning is a means of teaching students to think about their own thinking. Self-regulated learning strategies not only have been found to improve performance on the task students were taught but also have generalized to other tasks (Hadwin, 2008; Harris et al., 2001; Schunk & Zimmerman, 2003).

One example of a way to help children engage in self-regulated learning is providing students, when assigning a long or complex task, with a form for monitoring their progress. For example, a teacher who assigns students to write a report on the life of Martin Luther King, Jr., might hand out the following self-monitoring checklist:

Task Completion Form

☐ Located material on Martin Luther King, Jr., in the library and online

☐ Read and took notes on material

☐ Wrote first draft of report

☐ Checked draft for sense

☐ Checked draft for mechanics:

    ☐ Spelling

    ☐ Grammar

    ☐ Punctuation

☐ Composed typed or neatly handwritten final draft

The idea behind this form is that breaking down a complex task into smaller pieces encourages students to feel that they are making progress toward their larger goal. Checking off each step allows them to give themselves a mental pat on the back that reinforces their efforts. After seeing many checklists of this kind, students might be asked to make up their own to learn how to chart their own progress toward a goal. For example, Reid and Lienemann (2006) taught a group of students with attention deficit disorders to list all of the tasks necessary to complete a writing assignment and then check them off as they completed them. This increased the length and quality of their writing. Along similar lines, Trammel, Schloss, and Alper (1994) found that having children with learning disabilities keep records and make graphs of their homework completion significantly increased the amount of homework they did. A review by Robinson, Robinson, and Katayama (1999) found that cognitive behavior modification strategies can have a substantial impact, especially on reducing hyperactive, impulsive, and aggressive behaviors (e.g., Binder, Dixon, & Ghezi, 2000). Several of the studies reviewed found these effects to be long-lasting.

SELF-REINFORCEMENT   Drabman, Spitalnik, and O'Leary (1973) designed and evaluated a classic procedure to teach students to regulate their own behavior. They asked teachers to rate student behaviors each day and reinforce students when they earned high ratings. Then they changed the program: They asked students to guess what rating the teacher had given them. The students were reinforced for guessing correctly. Finally, the reinforcers were gradually removed. The students' behavior improved under the reinforcement and guessing conditions, and it remained at its improved level long after the program was ended. The authors explained that students who were taught to match the teacher's ratings developed their own standards for appropriate behavior and reinforced themselves for meeting those standards.

Information about one's own behavior has often been found to change behavior, even when that information is self-provided. For example, researchers have increased on-task behavior by having children mark down every few minutes whether they have been studying in the last few minutes (Maag, Rutherford, & DiGangi, 1992; Webber, Scheuermann, McCall, & Coleman, 1993). Many of us use this principle in studying, saying to ourselves that we will not take a break for lunch until we have finished reading a certain amount of material. Or we might buy ourselves chocolate if we've been conscientiously going to the gym.

21ST Century Learning

Self-Reliance

In the 21st century, high-paying jobs increasingly depend on the ability to work independently or with others for long periods without a superior closely monitoring the work. More than ever, students need to learn how to break assignments into bite-sized chunks and monitor (and reinforce) their own accomplishments. Students who learn how to motivate themselves have a skill that will help them succeed with any challenge that school or life brings.

Questions

- What do you think is the biggest barrier in getting students to be self-reliant?

- Do you think that self-reliance is something that can be taught early on, or do all students have to experience failure first in order to want to experience success?

Students who feel confident in their ability to use metacognitive and self-motivational behaviors are likely to be high in self-efficacy—the belief that one's own efforts (rather than luck or other people or other external or uncontrollable factors) determine one's success or failure. Self-efficacy beliefs are perhaps the most important factor (after ability) in determining students' success in school (Bandura, 1997; Schunk & Zimmerman, 2003).

■ Strengths and Limitations of Behavioral Learning Theories

The basic principles of behavioral learning theories are as firmly established as any in psychology and have been demonstrated under many different conditions. These principles are useful for explaining much of human behavior; they are even more useful in changing behavior in the classroom.

It is important to recognize, however, that behavioral learning theories are limited in scope. With the exception of social learning theorists, behavioral learning theorists focus almost exclusively on observable behavior. This is one reason why so many of the examples presented in this chapter involve the management of behavior (see Driscoll, 2000). Less visible learning processes, such as concept formation, learning from text, problem solving, and thinking, are difficult to observe directly and have, therefore, been studied less often by behavioral learning theorists. These processes fall more into the domain of cognitive learning. Social learning theory, which is a direct outgrowth of behavioral learning theories, helps to bridge the gap between the behavioral and cognitive perspectives.

Behavioral and cognitive theories of learning are often posed as competing, opposite models. There are indeed specific areas in which these theories take contradictory positions. However, it is more accurate to see them as complementary rather than competitive—that is, as tackling different problems (Kazdin, 2001; Miltenberger, 2001).

Connections

For more on self-efficacy beliefs and student success, see Chapter 10, pages 291–292.

Certification Pointer

The idea that behavioral learning theories apply best to observable behavior (rather than thinking, for example) may appear on teacher certification tests.

Chapter 5 Summary

What Is Learning ?

Learning involves the acquisition of abilities that are not innate. Learning depends on experience, including feedback from the environment.

What Are Behavioral Learning Theories ?

Early research into learning studied the effects of stimuli on reflexive behaviors. Ivan Pavlov contributed the idea of classical conditioning, in which neutral stimuli can acquire the capacity to evoke behavioral responses through their association with unconditioned stimuli that trigger reflexes. B. F. Skinner continued the study of the relationship between behavior and consequences. He described operant conditioning, in which reinforcers and punishers shape behavior.

What Are Some Principles of Behavioral Learning ?

Reinforcers increase the frequency of a behavior, and punishers decrease its frequency. Reinforcement can be primary or secondary, positive or negative. Intrinsic reinforcers are rewards inherent in a behavior itself. Extrinsic reinforcers are praise or rewards. Punishment involves weakening behavior by either introducing aversive consequences or removing reinforcers. The Premack Principle states that a way to increase less–enjoyed activities is to link them to more–enjoyed activities.

Shaping through timely feedback on each step of a task is an effective teaching practice based on behavioral learning theory. Extinction is the weakening and gradual disappearance of behavior as reinforcement is withdrawn.

Schedules of reinforcement are used to increase the probability, frequency, or persistence of desired behavior. Reinforcement schedules may be based on ratios or intervals and may be fixed or variable.

Antecedent stimuli serve as cues indicating which behaviors will be reinforced or punished. Discrimination involves using cues to detect differences between stimulus situations, whereas generalization involves responding to similarities between stimuli. Generalization involves the transfer or carryover of behaviors learned under one set of conditions to other situations.

The Intentional Teacher

USING WHAT YOU KNOW about Behavioral and Social Learning Theory to Improve Teaching and Learning

One role of the intentional teacher is functioning as an instructional designer, carefully planning what new abilities learners will acquire. Sometimes called "behavioral" or "performance" objectives, such outcome statements often imply two performance levels. Robert Mager (1997) reminds us to "always state the *main intent*" of an objective. Many important outcomes state performances that *cannot be observed*. You can't see your students adding or composing or comparing or relating, but these "cognitive" actions are often the real goal you intend to help your students achieve. For these "covert," unobservable behaviors, Mager suggests that you, in your role as a designer of instruction, think of "indicator behaviors," observable actions that will show not only you but others, and most important the students themselves, that they can indeed "add," "compose," "compare," "relate," or perform any other meaningful mental behavior aimed at in your lesson.

 1. What do I expect my students to know and be able to do at the end of this lesson? How does this contribute to course objectives and to students' needs to become capable individuals?

In considering any plan to improve classroom behavior, remember that we tend to use the term *classroom behavior* in too limited a way, equating *behavior* with "being good" (i.e., sitting still and being quiet). Watch for indications of interest and engagement as students work individually or in groups. For example, as your students work in spirited project groups, you might briefly interrupt their work to ask questions: "Are you on task? Have you said at least one nice thing about someone else's idea?" The questions help students check their own behavior.

Before the school year begins, you should develop a discipline plan that supports appropriate behavior and seeks to extinguish negative behaviors, and then update that plan in light of student behavior. For example, before

your noisy sixth period begins, you might rehearse: "I will recognize only those who make an appropriate bid for the floor. *No matter what.* I will ignore attention-seeking behaviors. I will use praise to reinforce on-task behavior."

 2. What knowledge, skills, needs, and interests do my students have that must be taken into account in my lesson?

Particular reinforcers vary in their effectiveness for individuals and groups. Determine what kinds of reinforcers are effective for particular students. For example, you might hand out a survey early in the year that asks open-ended questions such as "If you had time to do any practical fun activity in the classroom, what would you do?" and "When you do a good job in school, what response from teachers makes you the happiest?" and "What message from your teacher to your parents would make you feel most proud?" You can then use the survey responses to determine useful consequences for various behaviors for this class and particular individuals.

Reinforcers are most effective when they immediately follow the behavior. Provide immediate feedback so that students know the results of their actions and learn to link behavior to its consequences.

 3. What do I know about the content, child development, learning, motivation, and effective teaching strategies that I can use to accomplish my objectives?

Break down complex skills and performances into smaller bits so that students learn gradually by logical steps. For example, you might give students an opportunity to discriminate and to generalize among examples and settings by suggesting the relevant characteristics and information to look for. In teaching second-graders about mammals, you might provide 40 large pictures of animals, pointing out characteristics of mammals. The students could then sort the pictures into mammals and nonmammals, and you might praise them for their accuracy. In teaching high school students about justice, you might

How Has Social Learning Theory Contributed to Our Understanding of Human Learning?

Social learning theory is based on recognition of the importance of observational learning and self-regulated learning. Bandura noted that learning through modeling—directly or vicariously—involves four phases: paying attention, retaining the modeled behavior, reproducing the behavior, and being motivated to repeat the behavior. Bandura proposed that students should be taught to have expectations for their own performances and to reinforce themselves. Meichenbaum proposed steps for self-regulated learning that represent a form of cognitive behavior modification.

Behavioral learning theories are central to the application of educational psychology in classroom management, discipline, motivation, instructional models, and other areas. Behavioral learning theories are limited in scope, however, in that they describe only observable behavior that can be directly measured.

INTASC **8** Assessment of Student Learning
9 Professional Commitment and Responsibility

have them sort a set of examples of various forms of civil disobedience into "justifiable" and "not justifiable" categories.

You can increase the likelihood of students' generalizing (transferring) their learning to new situations by using real-life applications and many examples from different contexts. For instance, after studying a variety of graphs with your students, you might prepare a bulletin board and invite students to fill it with examples of graphs from newspapers, advertisements, and other print sources.

 4. What instructional materials, technology, assistance, and other resources are available to help accomplish my objectives?

Bandura and Meichenbaum developed ideas built on modeling, observational learning, and self-directedness. Some activities that elaborate on these concepts of observational and self-regulated learning include the following suggestions.

Consider teaching cognitive behavior modification and self-regulation directly. For example, you might plan an art activity for your students designed to create an "illuminated" initial for their name. You model the tasks, describing out loud how you outline the letter, select your favorite color for the letter, and select symbols and designs to decorate it, based on your personal interests. You might guide the students through these steps, directing them with a series of statements as they perform each task.

"Make a big outline of your initial and choose your favorite color to fill it in."

"Now choose some designs that represent your own interests—sports, hobbies, et cetera—and decorate the letter."

"Next make the initial of your last name and talk yourself through it in a whisper as we just did together."

"Finally, put both your initials together, reminding yourself as you work of these steps but not saying anything out loud, just in your mind."

You might sum up the activity by pointing out that this is a process students can use to direct themselves through any task they wish to manage themselves: Think of the steps, say them to themselves in a whisper as they plan the tasks, and then do the steps, talking to themselves silently. You might say, "Talking to yourself can be a great way to get things done!" In other subject areas for this class, you might make use of similar modeling examples.

 5. How will I plan to assess students' progress toward my objectives?

In all subject areas and in all grades, you will develop a number of specific assignments with measurable expected outcomes. You might make a policy of involving students in determining the criteria for grading such tasks, informing them with each assignment of your previously decided criteria for performance.

As an intentional teacher, you should recognize that behavioral learning theories are one set of tools that can help you support positive changes in student behavior and learning. You should develop your observational skills and modify your actions in light of your perceptions of students' reactions to instruction. You should rely on constant observation of your class, developing the "withitness" that is a characteristic of effective teachers.

 6. How will I respond if individual children or the class as a whole are not on track toward success? What is my back-up plan?

Gather information on the effects of your instruction by watching students' responses, and change strategies if changes are needed. For example, you might do quick visual sweeps of your class to make note of nonverbal hints from students that they are interested or bored, getting it or lost. Check in with students who are struggling and give them additional explanations, or assign them a peer tutor.

Key Terms

Review the following key terms from the chapter.

Self-Assessment: Practicing for Licensure

Directions: The chapter-opening vignette addresses indicators that are often assessed in state licensure exams. Re-read the chapter-opening vignette, and then respond to the following questions.

1. Julia Esteban, first-grade teacher at Tanner Elementary School, calls on her students when they do not raise their hands, a practice that goes against an established rule in the class. Which of the following types of conditioning can Ms. Esteban use to teach her students about appropriate hand-raising behaviors?

   a. Classical conditioning

   b. Operant conditioning

   c. Modeled conditioning

   d. Assisted conditioning

2. Which of the following explanations best summarizes Julia Esteban's problem with her students' failure to raise their hands prior to speaking?

   a. Ms. Esteban is using negative reinforcement rather than positive reinforcement.

   b. Ms. Esteban has failed to apply the Premack Principle when her students break the hand-raising rule.

   c. Ms. Esteban allows her students to make decisions about classroom rules, a practice that research studies have shown to be unsuccessful.

   d. Ms. Esteban should note that pleasurable consequences (rewarding appropriate behaviors) increase a behavior whereas unpleasant consequences weaken the frequency of a behavior.

3. According to research on behavioral learning theories, which strategy might Ms. Esteban use to get her students to raise their hands prior to speaking?

   a. Reward those students who follow the rule.

   b. Punish those students who do not follow the rule.

   c. Ignore those students who follow the rule.

d. Wait before administering any type of consequence for rule-breakers.

4. Imagine that Ms. Esteban's students have a difficult time breaking their habit of speaking out of turn. Which of the following techniques might she use to reinforce close approximations of the behaviors she wants her students to exhibit?

 a. Extinction

 b. Maintenance

 c. Shaping

 d. Discrimination

5. Which type of reinforcement schedule is Ms. Esteban using if she reinforces her students' appropriate behavior after so many behaviors, but the students do not know when the reinforcement will be applied?

 a. Continuous

 b. Fixed-ratio schedule

 c. Fixed-interval schedule

 d. Variable-ratio schedule

6. Explain how classical conditioning and operant conditioning are alike and different. Give at least one example of each.

7. Describe Albert Bandura's social learning theory. Bandura's analysis of observational learning involves four phases—describe each phase.

PEARSON
myeducationlab

Go to the Topic **Behaviorist Perspectives** in the MyEducationLab (www.myeducationlab.com) for your course, where you can:

- Find learning outcomes for **Behaviorist Perspectives** along with the national standards that connect to these outcomes.

- Complete Assignments and Activities that can help you more deeply understand the chapter content.

- Apply and practice your understanding of the core teaching skills identified in the chapter with the Building Teaching Skills and Dispositions learning units.

- Access video clips of CCSSO National Teachers of the Year award winners responding to the question "Why Do I Teach?" in the Teacher Talk section.

- Check your comprehension of the content covered in the chapter by going to the Study Plan in the Book Resources for your text. Here you will be able to take a chapter quiz; receive feedback on your answers; and then access Review, Practice, and Enrichment activities to enhance your understanding of chapter content.

- Watch author Bob Slavin present a Personal Reflections podcast on *Modifying Behavior* in the Book Resources for your text. Then, respond to the questions that follow.

 Modifying Behavior

 YOUR REFLECTIONS Why do you think the charting strategy was so effective for Vanessa? Describe a time when you used a behavior modification strategy to change something about yourself. Was it successful? How would behavior modification strategies for elementary children differ from strategies used with middle school or high school students?

6

Information Processing and Cognitive Theories of Learning

Robin Sachs/PhotoEdit

Robin Sachs/PhotoEdit

Learning Outcomes

At the end of this chapter, you should be able to:

- Understand theories of information processing for memory and learning
- Define what we have learned from brain research regarding the practice of education
- Identify what causes people to remember and forget
- Identify memory strategies you can teach your students
- Describe how you can make classroom knowledge meaningful for your students
- Discuss how metacognitive skills help students learn
- List study strategies you can teach your students
- List cognitive teaching strategies and describe how they help students learn

Verona Bishop's biology class is doing a unit on human learning. At the start of one lesson, Ms. Bishop does an experiment with her students. For 3 seconds, using an interactive whiteboard, she flashes a diagram of a model of information processing identical to the illustration in Figure 6.1. Then she asks students to recall what they notice. Some mention that they see boxes and arrows. Some see the words *memory* and *forgotten* and infer that the figure has something to do with learning. One student even sees the word *learning,* though it isn't in the figure.

"Come now," says Ms. Bishop. "You noticed a lot more than that! You just may not have noticed what you noticed. For example, what did you smell?"

The whole class laughs. They all recall smelling the broccoli cooking in the cafeteria. The students catch on to the idea and begin to recall all the other details they noticed that had nothing to do with the diagram: the sounds of a truck going by, details of the classroom and the people in it, and so on.

After this discussion, Ms. Bishop says, "Isn't the brain amazing? In only 3 seconds you received an enormous amount of information. You didn't even know you were noticing the smell of the broccoli until I reminded you about it, but it was in your mind just the same. Also, in only 3 seconds your mind was already starting to make sense of the information in the figure. Cheryl thought she saw the word *learning,* which wasn't there at all. But her mind leaped to that word because she saw words like *memory* that relate to learning.

"Now imagine that you could keep in your mind forever everything that occurred in the 3 seconds you looked at the diagram: the arrows, the boxes, the words, the truck, the broccoli—everything. In fact, imagine that

you could keep everything that ever entered your mind. What would that be like?"

"You'd be a genius!" ventures Samphan.

"You'd go crazy!" counters Jamal.

"I think Jamal is closer to the truth," says Ms. Bishop. "If your mind filled up with all that useless junk, you'd be a blithering idiot! One of the most important things we're going to learn about learning is that it is an active process of focusing in on important information, screening out unimportant information, and using what is already in our minds to decide which is which."

Ms. Bishop turns on the interactive whiteboard again.

"When we study this diagram in more detail, you'll use what you already know about learning, memory, forgetting, and diagrams to make sense of it. I hope you'll always remember the main ideas it's trying to show you. You'll soon forget the boxes and arrows, and even the smell of the broccoli will fade from your memory, but the parts of this diagram that make sense to you and answer questions you care about may stay in your memory your whole life!"

USING YOUR EXPERIENCE

Cooperative Learning   Jot down two or three ways in which you try to memorize lists and study new concepts. Share with other students a strategy that you use to learn information better.

Cooperative Learning   What is your picture of learning, memory, and forgetting? After drafting your own picture, meet with four or five classmates to compose a summary illustration or diagram of human memory and cognition based on your individual ideas. After 10 minutes, share with the class.

INTASC

2 Knowledge of Human
Development and Learning

The human mind is a meaning maker. From the first microsecond you see, hear, taste, or feel something, you start a process of deciding what it is, how it relates to what you already know, and whether it is important to keep in your mind or should be discarded. This whole process may take place consciously, unconsciously, or both. This chapter describes how information is received and processed in the mind, how memory and forgetting work, and how you can help your students understand and remember critical information, skills, and ideas. This chapter also presents cognitive theories of learning, theories that relate to processes that go on within the minds of learners, and means of helping students use their minds more effectively to learn, remember, and use knowledge.

What Is an Information-Processing Model?

Information constantly enters our minds through our senses. Most of this information is almost immediately discarded, and we may never even be aware of much of it. Some is held in our memories for a short time and then forgotten. For example, we may remember the seat number on a theater ticket until we find our seats, at which point we will forget the number. However, some information is retained much longer, perhaps for the rest of our lives. What is the process by which information is absorbed, and how can teachers take advantage of this process to help students retain critical information and skills? These questions have been addressed by cognitive learning theorists and have led to **information-processing theory,** a dominant theory of learning and memory since the mid-1970s.

Research on human memory (e.g., Anderson, 2005; Ashcraft & Radvansky, 2010; Bransford, Brown, & Cocking, 1999; Byrnes, 2001; Elias & Saucier, 2006; Tulving & Craik, 2000) has helped learning theorists to describe the process by which information is remembered (or forgotten). This process, usually referred to as the *Atkinson–Shiffrin model of information processing* (Atkinson & Shiffrin, 1968), is illustrated in Figure 6.1.

■ Sensory Register

The first component of the memory system that incoming information meets is the sensory register, shown at the left of Figure 6.1. **Sensory registers** receive large amounts of information from each of the senses (sight, hearing, touch, smell, taste) and hold it for a very short time, no more than a couple of seconds. If nothing happens to information held in a sensory register, it is rapidly lost.

Ingenious experiments have been used to detect sensory registers. A person might be shown a display like that in Figure 6.2 for a very short period of time, say 50 milliseconds. The person is usually able to report seeing 3, 4, or 5 of the letters but not all 12 of them. In a classic early experiment, Sperling (1960) presented a display like Figure 6.2 to people. After the display disappeared, he signaled viewers to try to recall the top, middle, or bottom row. He found that people could recall any one row almost perfectly. Therefore, they must have seen all the letters in the 50 milliseconds and retained them for a short period of time. However, when people tried to recall all 12 letters, the time it took them to do so apparently exceeded the amount of time the letters lasted in their sensory registers, so they lost some of the letters.

The existence of sensory registers has two important educational implications. First, people must pay attention to information if they are to retain it. Second, it takes time to bring all the information seen in a moment into consciousness. For example, if students are bombarded with too much information at once and are not told which aspects

information-processing theory

Cognitive theory of learning that describes the processing, storage, and retrieval of knowledge in the mind.

sensory register

Component of the memory system in which information is received and held for very short periods of time.

FIGURE 6.1 The Sequence of Information Processing (Atkinson-Shiffrin Model)

Information that is to be remembered must first reach a person's senses, then be attended to and transferred from the sensory register to the working memory and then be processed again for transfer to long-term memory.

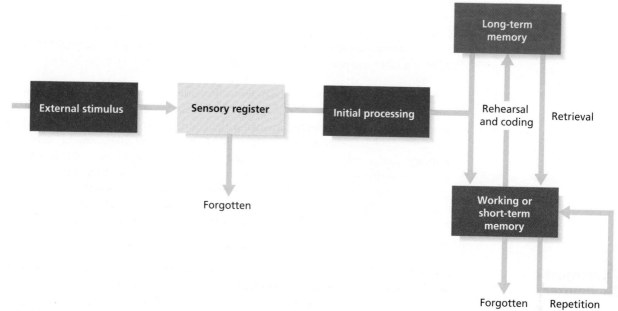

Source: Charles G. Morris, *Psychology: An Introduction* (8th ed.), p. 233. © 1993. Adapted by permission of Prentice Hall.

of the information they should pay attention to, they may have difficulty learning any of the information at all.

PERCEPTION   When the senses receive stimuli, the mind immediately begins working on some of them. Therefore, the sensory images of which we are conscious are not exactly the same as what we saw, heard, or felt; they are what our senses perceived. **Perception** of stimuli is not as straightforward as reception of stimuli. Instead, it involves mental interpretation that is influenced by our mental state, past experience, knowledge, motivations, and many other factors.

perception
A person's interpretation of stimuli.

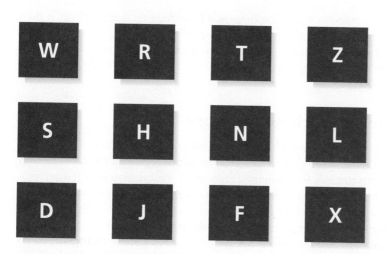

FIGURE 6.2 Display Used in Sensory Register Experiments

This is a typical display used by G. A. Sperling to detect the existence and limits of the sensory register. People who were shown the display for an instant and then asked to recall a specific row were usually able to do so. However, they were not able to recall all 12 letters.

Source: G. A. Sperling, "The Information Available in Brief Visual Presentations," *Psychological Monographs, 74,* 1960, American Psychological Association.

First, we perceive different stimuli according to rules that have nothing to do with the inherent characteristics of the stimuli. If you are sitting in a building, for example, you may not pay much attention to, or even hear, a fire engine's siren. If you are driving a car, you pay a great deal more attention. If you are standing outside a burning building waiting for the firefighters to arrive, you pay even more attention. Second, we do not perceive stimuli as we see or sense them but as we know (or assume) they really are. From across a room, a book on a bookshelf looks like a thin strip of paper, but we infer that it is a three-dimensional rectangular form with many pages. You might see just the edge of a table and mentally infer the entire table.

ATTENTION   When you say to students, "Pay attention" or "Lend me your ears," you are using the words *pay* and *lend* appropriately. Like money, **attention** is a limited resource. When you ask students to spend their limited attention capacity on whatever you are saying, students must give up actively attending to other stimuli, shifting their priorities so that other stimuli are screened out. For example, when people listen intently to an interesting speaker, they are unaware of minor body sensations (such as itches or hunger) and other sounds or sights. An experienced speaker knows that when the audience looks restless, its attention is no longer focused on the lecture but might be turning toward considerations of lunch or other activities; it is time to recapture the listeners' attention.

GAINING ATTENTION   How can you focus students' attention on the lesson at hand, and in particular on the most important aspects of what is being taught?

There are several ways to gain students' attention, all of which go under the general heading of arousing student interest. One way is to use cues that indicate "This is important." Some teachers raise or lower their voices to signal that they are about to impart critical information. Others use gestures, repetition, or body position to communicate the same message.

Another way to gain attention is to increase the emotional content of material (Armony, Chochol, Fecteau, & Belin, 2007). Attention and emotion activate some of the same parts of the brain (Vuilleumeir, 2005), which perhaps explains why people pay more attention to soap operas and reality shows (lots of emotion) than to typical classroom instruction (not so much). This is why newspaper headlines try to increase attention by saying "Senate Kills Mass Transit Proposal" rather than "Senate Votes against Mass Transit Proposal."

Unusual, inconsistent, or surprising stimuli also attract attention. For example, science teachers often introduce lessons with a demonstration or magic trick to engage student curiosity.

Finally, informing students that what follows is important to them will catch their attention. For example, you can ensure attention by telling students, "This will be on tomorrow's test." Of course, learners make their own decisions about what is important, and they learn more of what they think is important than other material because they pay more attention to it.

■ Short-Term or Working Memory

Information that a person perceives and pays attention to is transferred to the second component of the memory system: **short-term memory** (Ashcraft & Radvansky, 2010), a storage system that can hold a limited amount of information for a few seconds. It is the part of memory in which information that is currently being thought about is stored. The thoughts we are conscious of having at any given moment are being held in our short-term memory. When we stop thinking about something, it disappears from our short-term memory. Another term for short-term memory is **working memory** (Anderson, 2005; Ashcraft & Radvansky, 2010; Engle, 2001; Unsworth & Engle, 2007). This term emphasizes that the most important aspect of short-term memory is not its

Certification Pointer

For teacher certification tests, you may be expected to detail various strategies for gaining students' attention, such as lowering your voice, using a gesture or surprise, or increasing the emotional content.

INTASC

2 Knowledge of Human Development and Learning

attention

Active focus on certain stimuli to the exclusion of others.

short-term or working memory

The component of memory in which limited amounts of information can be stored for a few seconds.

duration but the fact that it is active. Working memory is where the mind operates on information, organizes it for storage or discarding, and connects it to other information. Working memory is so important that many researchers consider working memory capacity to be essentially the same as intelligence (Ackerman, Beier, & Boyle, 2005; Colom, Flores-Mendoza, & Rebello, 2003; Kane, Hambrick, & Conway, 2005).

As depicted in Figure 6.1, information may enter working memory from sensory registers or from the third basic component of the memory system: long-term memory. Usually, both processes happen at the same time. When you see a robin, your sensory register transfers the image of the robin to your working memory. Meanwhile, you may (unconsciously) search your long-term memory for information about birds so that you can identify this particular one as a robin. Along with that recognition may come a lot of other information about robins, memories of past experiences with robins, or feelings about robins—all of which have been stored in long-term memory but are brought into consciousness (working memory) by your mental processing of the sight of the robin (Gathercole, Pickering, Ambridge, & Wearing, 2004).

One way to hold information in working memory is to think about it or say it over and over. You have probably used this strategy to remember a phone number for a short time. This process of maintaining an item in working memory by repetition is called **rehearsal** (Baddeley, 1999). Rehearsal is important in learning because the longer an item remains in working memory, the greater the chance that it will be transferred to long-term memory. Recent research suggests that it is not the repeated study that makes the difference, but that repeatedly trying to remember the information brings it into working memory and then strengthens it in long-term memory (Karpicke & Roedinger, 2007). Without rehearsal, items will probably not stay in working memory for more than about 30 seconds. Because working memory has a limited capacity, information can also be lost from it by being forced out by other information. You have probably had the experience of looking up a telephone number, being interrupted briefly, and finding that you had forgotten the number.

You must allocate time for rehearsal during classroom lessons. Teaching too much information too rapidly is likely to be ineffective because, unless students are given time to mentally rehearse each new piece of information, later information is likely to drive it out of their working memories. When you stop a lesson to ask students whether they have any questions, you are also giving students a few moments to think over and mentally rehearse what they have just learned. This helps students to process information in working memory and thereby to establish it in long-term memory. This mental work is critical when students are learning new, difficult material.

WORKING MEMORY CAPACITY   Working memory is believed to have a capacity of five to nine bits of information (Thompson, 2000). That is, we can think about only five to nine distinct things at a time. However, any particular bit may itself contain a great deal of information. For example, think how difficult it would be to memorize the following shopping list:

flour	orange juice	pepper	mustard
soda pop	parsley	cake	butter
relish	mayonnaise	oregano	canned tomatoes
potatoes	milk	lettuce	syrup
hamburger	hot dogs	eggs	onions
tomato paste	apples	spaghetti	buns

This list has too many bits of information to remember easily. All 24 food items would not fit into working memory in random order. However, you could easily memorize the list by organizing it according to familiar patterns. As shown in Figure 6.3, you might mentally create three separate memory files: breakfast, lunch, and dinner. In each, you expect to find food and beverages; in the lunch and dinner files, you expect

"Mrs Lee, can I be excused? My working memory capacity is full."

rehearsal

Mental repetition of information, which can improve its retention.

Certification Pointer

On a teacher certification test, you may be required to know that organizing material into familiar patterns can help students remember concepts and vocabulary. For example, to help young students remember the names of different animals, you could help students categorize them into pets, zoo animals, and farm animals.

to find dessert as well. You can then think through the recipes for each item on the menus. In this way, you can recall what you have to buy and you need maintain only a few bits of information in your working memory. When you enter the store, you are thinking, "I need food for breakfast, lunch, and dinner." First, you bring the breakfast file out of your long-term memory. It contains food (pancakes) and a beverage (orange juice). You might think through how you make pancakes step by step and buy each ingredient, plus orange juice as a beverage. When you have done this, you can discard breakfast from your working memory and replace it with the lunch file and then the dinner file, going through the same processes. Note that all you did was to replace 24 little bits of information with 3 big bits that you could then separate into their components.

Working memory can be thought of as a bottleneck through which information from the environment reaches long-term memory. The limited capacity of working memory is one aspect of information processing that has important implications for the design and practice of instruction (Engle, 2001). For example, you cannot present students with many ideas at once unless the ideas are so well organized and well connected to information already in the students' long-term memories that their working memories (with assistance from their long-term memories) can accommodate them, as in the case of the shopping list just discussed.

As another illustration of the limited capacity of working memory, Mayer (2001) compared a lesson on lightning storms that included a number of extraneous words, pictures, and music to a lesson without these elements. The simpler lesson produced higher performance on a transfer test. Apparently, the more coherent lesson used working memory capacity more effectively (see Mayer, 2008b, 2009).

INDIVIDUAL DIFFERENCES IN WORKING MEMORY Individuals differ, of course, in the capacities of their working memories to accomplish a given learning task. One of the main factors in enhancing this capacity is background knowledge. The more a person knows about something, the better able the person is to organize and absorb new information (Engle, Nations, & Cantor, 1990; Kuhara-Kojima & Hatano, 1991). However, prior knowledge is not the only factor. Individuals also differ in their abilities to organize information and can be taught to consciously use strategies for making more efficient use of working memory capacity (Wyra, Lawson, & Hungi, 2007). Strategies of this kind are discussed later in this chapter.

FIGURE 6.3 **Example of Organization of Information to Facilitate Memory**

A 24-item shopping list that would be very hard to remember in a random order can be organized into a smaller number of familiar categories, making the list easier to recall.

Breakfast	Lunch	Dinner
Pancakes:	Hot Dogs:	Spaghetti:
■ Flour	■ Hot dogs	■ Spaghetti
■ Milk	■ Buns	■ Onions
■ Eggs	■ Relish	■ Hamburger
■ Butter	■ Mustard	■ Canned tomatoes
■ Syrup		■ Tomato paste
	Potato Salad:	■ Oregano
Beverage: Orange juice		■ Pepper
	■ Potatoes	
	■ Mayonnaise	Salad:
	■ Parsley	
		■ Lettuce
	Beverage: Soda pop	
		Beverage: Milk
	Dessert: Apple	
		Dessert: Cake

■ Long-Term Memory

Long-term memory is that part of our memory system where we keep information for long periods of time. Long-term memory is thought to be a very large-capacity, very long-term memory store. In fact, many theorists believe that we may never forget information in long-term memory; rather, we might just lose the ability to find the information within our memory (Tulving & Craik, 2000). We do not live long enough to fill up our long-term memory. The differences among sensory registers, working (short-term) memory, and long-term memory are summarized in Table 6.1.

Ericsson and Kintsch (1995) hypothesize that people store not only information but also learning strategies in long-term memory for easy access. This capacity, which Ericsson and Kintsch call *long-term working memory*, accounts for the extraordinary skills of experts (such as medical diagnosticians) who must match current information with a vast array of patterns held in their long-term memories.

Theorists divide long-term memory into at least three parts: episodic memory, semantic memory, and procedural memory (Ashcraft & Radvansky, 2010; Eichenbaum, 2003). **Episodic memory** is our memory of personal experiences, a mental movie of things we saw or heard. When you remember past events such as what you had for dinner last night or what happened at your high school prom, you are recalling information stored in your long-term episodic memory. Long-term **semantic memory** contains the facts and generalized information that we know; concepts, principles, or rules and how to use them; and our problem-solving skills and learning strategies. Most learning from class lessons is retained in semantic memory. **Procedural memory** refers to "knowing how" in contrast to "knowing that." The abilities to drive, type, and ride a bicycle are examples of skills that are retained in procedural memory.

Episodic, semantic, and procedural memory store and organize information in different ways. Information in episodic memory is stored in the form of images that are organized on the basis of when and where events happened. Information in semantic memory is organized in the form of networks of ideas. Information in procedural memory is stored as a complex of stimulus–response pairings (Anderson, 1995). Recent brain studies (e.g., Elias & Saucier, 2006) have suggested that operations relating to each of

long-term memory

The components of memory in which large amounts of information can be stored for long periods of time.

episodic memory

A part of long-term memory that stores images of our personal experiences.

semantic memory

A part of long-term memory that stores facts and general knowledge.

procedural memory

A part of long-term memory that stores information about how to do things.

TABLE 6.1 **Characteristics of Components of Cognitive Storage Systems**

Storage Structure	Processes				Cause of Failure to Recall
	Code*	Capacity	Duration	Retrieval	
Sensory "store"	Sensory features	12–20 items[†] to huge	250 msec.–4 sec.	Complete, given proper cueing	Masking or decay
Short-term memory	Acoustic, visual, semantic, sensory features identified and named	7 ± 2 items	About 12 sec.; longer with rehearsal	Complete, with each item being retrieved every 35 msec.	Displacement, interference, decay
Long-term memory	Semantic, visual knowledge; abstractions; meaningful images	Enormous, virtually unlimited	Indefinite	Specific and general information available, given proper cueing	Interference, organic dysfunctioning, inappropriate cues

*How information is represented

[†]Estimated

Source: Robert L. Solso, *Cognitive Psychology* (6th ed.), p. 240. © 2001 Allyn and Bacon, Inc. Reproduced with permission of Pearson Education, Inc.

these types of long-term memory take place in different parts of the brain. Let's examine in detail what we mean by these three kinds of memory.

EPISODIC MEMORY   Episodic memory contains images of experiences organized by when and where they happened (Rubin, 2007; Tulving & Craik, 2000). It consists of memories of personally experienced and remembered events (Ashcraft & Radvansky, 2010), which combine sensory information, spatial knowledge, language, emotions, and motor information into a sort of personal story (Rubin, 2007). For example, consider this question: What did you do on the night of your senior prom or dance? Most people answer this question by imagining themselves back on that night and describing the events. You might scan the dance floor in your mind's eye, recalling sights, sounds, and smells, and then think of the emotions you experienced, all of which are remembered together. As another example, suppose you are asked to recall the names of your high school classmates. One psychologist asked graduate students to come to a specific place for 1 hour a day and try to remember the names. Over the course of a month, the students continued to recall new names. Interestingly, they used space and time cues, which are associated with episodic memory, to imagine incidents that allowed them to recall the names. For example, they might have recalled the day their social studies teacher came to school dressed as an Arctic explorer and then mentally scanned their memory for the faces of the students who were there.

These demonstrations indicate that images are important in episodic memory and that cues related to space and time help us to retrieve information from this part of memory. You have probably taken an exam and said to yourself, "I should know this answer. I remember reading this section. It was right on the bottom left corner of the page with the diagram in the upper right."

Episodic memories are often difficult to retrieve because most episodes in our lives are repeated so often that later episodes get mixed up in memory with earlier ones, unless something happens during the episode to make it especially memorable. For example, few people remember what they had for lunch a week ago, much less years ago. However, there is a phenomenon called **flashbulb memory** in which the occurrence of an important event fixes mainly visual and auditory memories in a person's mind. For example, people who happened to be eating breakfast at the moment they first heard about the attack on the World Trade Center may well remember that particular meal (and other trivial aspects of the setting) forever. The reason for this is that the unforgettable event of that moment gives us access to the episodic (space and time) memories relating to what would usually be forgotten details.

You can improve retention of concepts and information by explicitly creating memorable events involving visual or auditory images. For example, uses of projects, plays, simulations, and other forms of active learning can give students vivid images that they can remember and then use to retrieve other information presented at about the same time. In support of this idea, there is much evidence that pictures illustrating text can help children to remember the text even when the pictures are no longer presented (Mayer, 2008b). The pictures presumably tie the semantic information to the child's episodic memory, making the information easier to retrieve. There is also evidence that students often create their own mental pictures, which then help them remember material they have studied (Robinson, Robinson, et al., 1999).

SEMANTIC MEMORY   Semantic (or declarative) memory is organized in a very different way, mentally arranged in networks of connected ideas or relationships called **schemata** (singular: *schema*) (Anderson, 2005; Bruning, Schraw, Norby, & Ronning, 2004). Recall that Piaget introduced the word *scheme* to describe a cognitive framework that individuals use to organize their perceptions and experiences. Cognitive processing theorists similarly use the terms *schema* and *schemata* to describe networks of concepts stored in individuals' memories that enable them to understand and incorporate new information. A schema is like an outline, with different concepts or

flashbulb memory

Important events that are fixed mainly in visual and auditory memory.

schemata

Mental networks of related concepts that influence understanding of new information; the singular is *schema*.

ideas grouped under larger categories. Various aspects of schemata may be related by series of propositions, or relationships. For example, Figure 6.4 illustrates a simplified schema for the concept "bison," showing how this concept is related to other concepts in memory.

In the figure, "bison" is linked to several other concepts. These may be linked to still more concepts (such as "How did Plains Indians hunt bison?") and to broader categories or concepts (such as "How have conservationists saved many species from extinction?"). Schema theory (Anderson, 2005) holds that we gain access to information held in our semantic long-term memory by mentally following paths like those illustrated in Figure 6.4. For example, you might have deep in your memory the idea that the Spanish introduction of the horse to North America revolutionized how the Plains Indians hunted bison. To get to that bit of information, you might start thinking about characteristics of bison, then think about how Plains Indians hunted bison on horseback, and then recall (or imagine) how they hunted bison before they had horses. Many pathways can be used to get at the same bit of information. In fact, the more pathways you have leading to a piece of information and the better established those pathways are, the better access you will have to information in long-term semantic memory. Recall that the problem of long-term memory is not that information is lost but that our access to information is lost.

One clear implication of schema theory is that new information that fits into a well-developed schema is retained far more readily than is information that does not fit into a schema. Schema theory will be covered in more detail later in this chapter.

Connections

For more on the concept of schemes, see Chapter 2, page 31.

FIGURE 6.4 **Schema for the Concept "Bison"**

Information in long-term semantic memory is organized in networks of related ideas. The concept "bison," for example, falls under the more general concepts "mammals" and "animals" and is related to many other ideas that help to differentiate it from other concepts in memory.

People use procedural memory to recall how to do physical tasks. This type of memory is stored in a different part of the brain from semantic and episodic memories. How can you encourage your students' procedural memory?

PROCEDURAL MEMORY   Procedural memory is the ability to recall how to do something, especially a physical task. This type of memory is apparently stored in a series of stimulus–response pairings. For example, even if you have not ridden a bicycle for a long time, as soon as you get on one, the stimuli begin to evoke responses. When the bike leans to the left (a stimulus), you "instinctively" shift your weight to the right to maintain balance (a response). Other examples of procedural memory include handwriting, typing, and running skills. Neurological studies show that procedural memories are stored in a different part of the brain than semantic and episodic memories; procedural memories are stored in the cerebellum, whereas semantic and episodic memories are stored in the cerebral cortex (Black, 2003; Bruning et al., 2004; Eichenbaum, 2003).

■ Factors That Enhance Long-Term Memory

Contrary to popular belief, people retain a large portion of what they learn in school. Semb and Ellis (1994), in reviewing research on this topic, note that laboratory studies of retention of nonsense words and other artificial material greatly underestimate the degree to which information and skills learned in school can be retained (also see Ellis, Semb, & Cole, 1998). Long-term retention of information learned in school varies a great deal according to the type of information. For example, concepts are retained much longer than names (Conway, Cohen, & Stanhope, 1991). In general, retention drops rapidly in the first few weeks after instruction but then levels off (Bahrick & Hall, 1991). Whatever students have retained about 12 to 24 weeks after instruction, they may retain forever.

Several factors contribute to long-term retention. One, not surprisingly, is the degree to which students had learned the material in the first place (Bahrick & Hall, 1991). It is interesting to note that the effects of ability on retention are unclear (Semb & Ellis, 1994). Higher-ability students score better at the end of a course but often lose the same percentage of what they had learned as lower-ability students do.

Instructional strategies that actively involve students in lessons contribute to long-term retention. For example, MacKenzie and White (1982) contrasted students in eighth and ninth grades learning geography under three conditions: traditional classroom instruction, traditional instruction plus fieldwork, and traditional instruction plus fieldwork plus active processing of information involved in fieldwork. Twelve weeks later (after summer vacation), the active processing group had lost only 10 percent of the information, whereas the other two groups had lost more than 40 percent. Similarly, Specht and Sandling (1991) contrasted undergraduates who learned accounting from traditional lectures with others who learned it through role playing. After 6 weeks, the traditionally taught students lost 54 percent of their problem-solving performance, whereas the role-playing group lost only 13 percent.

■ Other Information-Processing Models

Atkinson and Shiffrin's (1968) model of information processing outlined in Figure 6.1 is not the only one accepted by cognitive psychologists. Several alternative models do not challenge the basic assumptions of the Atkinson–Shiffrin model but elaborate aspects of it, particularly the factors that increase the chances that information will be retained in long-term memory.

LEVELS-OF-PROCESSING THEORY   One widely accepted alternative model of information processing is called **levels-of-processing theory** (Craik, 2000; Tulving & Craik, 2000), which holds that people subject stimuli to different levels of mental processing and retain only the information that has been subjected to the most thorough processing. For example, you might perceive a tree but pay little attention to it. This is the lowest level of processing, and you are unlikely to remember the tree. Second, you might give the tree a name, such as *maple* or *oak*. Once named, the tree is somewhat more likely to be remembered. The highest level of processing, however, is giving meaning to the tree. For example, you might remember climbing the tree or commenting on its unusual shape, or you might have wondered whether the tree would fall on your house if it were struck by lightning. According to levels-of-processing theory, the more you attend to the details of a stimulus, the more mental processing you must do and the more likely you are to remember it. This was illustrated in a classic study by Bower and Karlin (1974), who had Stanford undergraduates look at yearbook pictures from Yale. Some of the students were told to classify the pictures as "male" or "female," and some were told to classify them as "very honest" or "less honest." The students who had to categorize the faces as "very honest" or "less honest" remembered them far better than did those who merely categorized them as "male" or "female." Presumably, the honesty raters had to do a much higher level of mental processing with the pictures than did the gender raters, and for this reason they remembered the faces better. More recently, Kapur and colleagues (1994) had students read a series of nouns. One group was asked to identify which words contained the letter *a*. Another group had to identify the nouns as "living" or "nonliving." As in the Bower and Karlin study and many others, the students who had to sort the words into "living" and "nonliving" recalled many more words. More interesting, however, was that brain imaging revealed that the "living/nonliving" students were activating a portion of their brains associated with enhanced memory performance, whereas the other students were not. This experiment adds important evidence to the idea that the brain treats "deep processing" and "shallow processing" differently (see Craik, 2000).

DUAL CODE THEORY   A concept related to levels-of-processing theory is Paivio's **dual code theory of memory,** which hypothesizes that information is retained in long-term memory in two forms: visual and verbal (corresponding to episodic and semantic memory, respectively) (Clark & Paivio, 1991; Mayer, 2008b). This theory predicts that information represented both visually and verbally is recalled better than information held in only one format. For example, you remember a face better if you also know a name, and you remember a name better if you can connect it to a face (Mayer, 2008b).

What Is Learned from Research on the Brain ?

In the past, research on learning, memory, and other cognitive functions took place using methods one step away from the brain itself. Scientists used ingenious experiments to learn about brain function from subjects' responses to particular stimuli or tests, examined individuals with unusual brain damage, or made inferences from experiments on animals. However, in recent years neuroscientists have developed the capacity to actually watch healthy brains in operation, using brain imaging methods such as functional magnetic resonance imaging (fMRI) (Changeux, 2004; Eichenbaum, 2003; Goswami, 2004; Mitchell & Johnson, 2009; Shaywitz, 2003). Scientists can now observe what parts of the

levels-of-processing theory

Explanation of memory that links recall of a stimulus with the amount of mental processing it receives.

dual code theory of memory

Theory suggesting that information coded both visually and verbally is remembered better than information coded in only one of those two ways.

INTASC

2 Knowledge of Human
Development and Learning

brain are activated when an individual hears a symphony, reads a book, speaks a second language, or solves a math problem. This capability has led to an explosion of research on the brain (see, Banich, 2004; Elias & Saucier, 2006; Goswami, 2004).

It has long been known that specific mental functions are carried out in specific locations in the brain. For example, vision is localized in the visual cortex and hearing in the auditory cortex (see Figure 6.5). However, new research is finding that the brain is even more specialized than was thought previously. When you think about a face, you activate a different part of the brain than when you think about a chair, a song, or a feeling. If you are bilingual in, say, Spanish and English, slightly different areas of your brain are activated when you speak each language. The two hemispheres of the brain have somewhat different functions; the left hemisphere is more involved in language, whereas the right is more involved in spatial and nonverbal information. However, despite the specialization within the brain, almost all tasks we perform involve both hemispheres and many parts of the brain working together (Banich, 2004; Black, 2003; Saffran & Schwartz, 2003).

■ Implications for Education

Many findings from brain research have importance for education and child development. One has to do with early development, where studies find that the amount of stimulation early in a child's development relates to the number of neural connections, or synapses, which are the basis for higher learning and memory (Black, 2003; Elias & Saucier, 2006). The finding that the brain's capacity is not set at birth but is influenced by early experience has had an electrifying impact on the world of early childhood research and education policy. Further, some research is suggesting that extensive training can change brain structures, even into adulthood. For example, a study of London cabdrivers found that their training caused increased activity in a part of the brain that

**FIGURE 6.5 Brain
Physiology and Functions**

Each part of the brain specializes in a
particular category of functions.

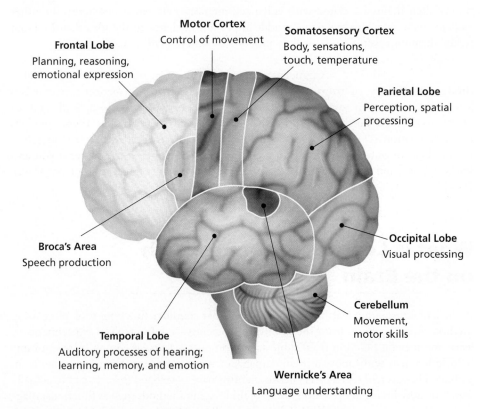

Source: Wood et al., *World of Psychology,* Figure 2.10, "The Cerebral Cortex of the Left Hemisphere," p. 64. © 2008 Pearson Education, Inc.
Reproduced by permission of Pearson Education, Inc.

processes directions (Maguire et al., 2000), and that children who receive intensive tutoring in reading develop brain structures like those of proficient readers (Shaywitz, 2003; Shaywitz & Shaywitz, 2004; Turkeltaub, Gareau, Flowers, Zeffiro, & Eden, 2003). However, there is considerable debate about what this implies for instruction (Hruby & Hynd, 2006; Shaywitz & Shaywitz, 2007; Willis, 2007).

Another important finding is initially counterintuitive. Up to the age of 18 months, infants generate enormous numbers of neurons and connections between neurons (see Figure 6.6). After that point, they begin to lose them. What is happening is that the brain sloughs off connections that are not being used, so that the remaining connections are efficient and well organized. This process is strongly affected by the environment in which the child lives and continues through early childhood. The plasticity of the brain, or its susceptibility to change by the environment, is highest at the earliest ages and diminishes over time (Elias & Saucier, 2006).

A third important finding of brain research is the discovery that as a person gains in knowledge and skill, his or her brain becomes more efficient. For example, Solso (2001) compared the brain activation of an expert artist to that of novices. On a task familiar to the artist—drawing faces—only a small portion of his brain was active, whereas novices had activity in many parts of their brains (see Figure 6.7). In another series of studies, Eden and colleagues (1996) compared the brain activation of children with dyslexia to that of normal readers while they were reading. The children with dyslexia activated auditory as well as visual areas of their brains, as though they had to laboriously translate the letters into sounds and then the sounds into meaning. The proficient readers skipped the auditory step entirely. The same difference has been documented between children just learning to read and the same children after they become good readers (Turkeltaub et al.,

FIGURE 6.6 Development of Neural Connections, from Birth through 15 Months of Age

Neural connections in children's brains develop rapidly from birth through infancy.

(a)	**(b)**	**(c)**
Newborn	3-Month-Old	15-Month-Old

Source: Richard Fabes and Carol Lynn Martin, *Exploring Child Development: Transactions and Transformations* (2nd ed.), p. 116. Published by Allyn & Bacon, Boston, MA.

H.O.

Novice

A B C D

Source: Robert L. Solso, *Cognitive Psychology* (8th ed.). © 2001 Allyn and Bacon, Inc. Reproduced by permission of Pearson Education, Inc.

FIGURE 6.7 Brain Activity of an Artist and a Nonartist While Drawing

fMRI scans made on an accomplished artist, H.O., and a nonartist control subject showing right parietal activity for both people (see column A). This area is involved in facial perception, but it appears that the nonartist is demanding more energy to process faces than H.O. In columns C and D, there is an increase in blood flow in the right frontal area of the artist, suggesting a higher-order abstraction of information.

Certification Pointer

Teacher certification tests will require you to know that as individuals learn more, their brains become more efficient. This leads to automaticity, the effortless performance that comes with the development of expertise.

2003). Research long ago noted the importance of automaticity, or seemingly effortless performance made possible by extensive experience and practice, in the development of expertise. The brain studies show how automaticity can actually allow the brain to skip steps in solving problems.

Recent studies (Shaywitz, 2003; Sousa, 2005) have found that proficient readers primarily activate three regions of the left brain. In contrast, dyslexics overactivate a region in the front of the brain called Broca's area, which controls speaking. In other words, poor readers seem to use an inefficient pathway (print to speech to understanding), whereas good readers use a more efficient pathway (print to understanding). More broadly, individuals with learning disabilities have been found to use less efficient brain processes than other learners (Blair, 2004; Halpern & Schulz, 2006).

These and many other findings of brain research reinforce the conclusion that the brain is not a filing cabinet for facts and skills but is engaged in a process of organizing information to make it efficiently accessible and usable. The process of discarding connections and selectively ignoring or excluding information, as well as the process of making orderly connections among information, is as important, or perhaps more important, than adding information.

■ Applications of Brain Research to Classroom Teaching

The progress of brain research has quite naturally led to a call for applications to the practice of education. For example, Howard (2000), Willis (2006), Sousa (2005, 2008), and Stansbury (2009) suggest that brain research justifies a shift away from linear, hierarchical teaching toward complex, thematic, and integrated activities. Gardner (2000) claims that brain research supports the importance of early stimulation, of activity in learning, and of music and emotions. All of these and other prescriptions may turn out to be valid, but at present the evidence for them, when it exists at all, comes from traditional cognitive psychology, not from brain research itself. Furthermore, the prescriptions from brain research are remarkably similar to the principles of progressive education described a century ago by John Dewey, without the benefit of modern brain research (see Ellis, 2001c). It may be that brain research will someday vindicate Dewey or lead to clear prescriptions for practice, but the rush to make grand claims for educational methods based on brain research has already led to a substantial body of cautionary literature (e.g., Coles, 2004; Jensen, 2000; Varma, McCandliss, & Schwartz, 2008).

Willingham (2006) argues that, although neuroscience has been moving forward "in leaps and bounds," significant help for classroom teachers from these advances is still well in the future for most practical purposes. After all, he points out, although fMRI images might tell us which parts of a child's brain are active when she tries to read, that information doesn't really offer anything useful for that child's teacher. According to Willingham (2006), "very exciting research is being conducted. . . . Some of it is of interest to cognitive researchers trying to figure out how the brain works. And virtually all of it is far from being able to guide teachers" (p. 177).

Willingham (2006) cautions against trying to apply emerging neuroscientific data directly to the classroom. Rather, data should be considered as pieces of a very large cognitive puzzle. This caution is supported by the way in which such data have gotten into popular culture and into the literature about teaching during the past several decades. He points, for example, to research on left-brain versus right-brain functions that is often used to support a variety of instructional strategies, although brain imaging data now confirm that both brain hemispheres participate in most cognitive tasks. He mentions as well the flurry of activity around providing stimulation for infants and young children, based on misinterpretation of data about stimulus-deprived subjects. Willingham does, however, see an immediate usefulness for neuroscientific findings in identifying children with learning disabilities, particularly dyslexia (see, e.g., the work of Espy, Molfese, Molfese, & Modglin, 2004; Lyytinen et al., 2005).

Despite any reservations about finding direct correlations between neuroscience and classroom teaching, it is clear that psychological changes, behavioral changes, and changes in cognition as a consequence of learning are all correlated with changes in the operation of the brain. We know something about *how* those changes occur, and we know something about *where* those changes occur. Neuroscience is on the cutting edge of behavioral science; it is supplying additional pieces of the cognitive puzzle all the time. A few consensus conclusions follow:

1. *Not all learning is equally likely.* Some types of learning are easier than others. For instance, humans readily acquire language and are attuned to social stimuli. Some learning seems more intuitive, or easy: For humans, this kind of learning appears to include language (Pinker, 1997), understanding about objects and the behavior of objects in space (Rosser, 1994), the geometry of three-dimensional space and the natural number system (Gelman, 2006), and the distinction between living and nonliving things (Inagaki & Hantano, 2006). Other learning can be counterintuitive, or hard to learn, and this appears to include mastering fractions, algebra, and Newtonian physics (Rosser, 2003), among other things.

This is not news, of course, to classroom teachers, who are probably very much aware that language and spatial relationships come more easily to young learners than advanced math concepts.

2. *Brain development constrains cognitive outcome.* One cannot alter a brain that is not yet ready for incoming experience to affect it. That is a point made years ago by Jean Piaget, who studied children's cognition, not their brains, and we now know that there is a correspondence between changes in the brain and cognitive development (Kuhn, 2006). Whereas brain development takes place over a long time, *behavior change through learning cannot exceed the developmental status of the neural structure.*

Developmental research also suggests that cognitive accomplishments in children and adolescents are probably best conceptualized as domain specific. Although the left and right hemispheres of the brain appear to participate together in most cognitive tasks, the brain is not entirely a general problem solver well adapted to all sorts of different challenges the person might encounter. It may be more accurate to envision the brain functioning as a series of specialized problem solvers with specific regions or circuits well adapted to handling limited kinds of problems, such as finding your way home (a geometric problem solver), figuring out language (a linguistic problem solver), or "reading" social information (a "people" problem solver).

As Willingham (2006) suggests, the classroom applicability of this is not yet clear, but future findings may uncover implications for teachers in stimulating particular domains to achieve particular goals.

3. *Some regions of the brain may be particularly important for cognitive outcomes and supporting certain sorts of neural activities related to learning and cognition.* One region that has become a primary focus of much contemporary research is the prefrontal cortex. This region has been proposed as a mediator of behavioral planning and reasoning (Grafman, 1994); attentional processes (Panskeep, 1998); impulsivity control (Murji & DeLuca, 1998; Rosser, Stevens, & Ruiz, 2006); planning and executive cognitive functioning (Grafman, Spector, & Ratterman, 2005; Huey, Krueger, & Grafman, 2006), and even the ability to use rules when engaged in cognitive tasks (Bunge & Zelazo, 2006). In short, this appears to be the seat of what we can term *deliberate cognitive activity,* which is what we try to encourage in the classroom.

Interestingly enough, this region is structurally immature even in adolescence. Gray matter in the frontal cortex peaks at about age 11 in females and at 12 years in males (Giedd, 2004), whereas white matter volume in this region increases well into adulthood (Casey, Giedd, & Thomas, 2000). This area is linked to the ability to inhibit impulses, to weigh consequences of decisions, to prioritize and strategize—in short, to act rationally. And it is still being remodeled well into early adulthood.

What does all this mean to you when facing a classroom full of students? Given what we know about brain development and brain functioning, it means those recipients of instruction are *not* empty, unformed boxes waiting to be "filled up" with information, directions, and skills. It means they are not even finished boxes—that the receptacle itself is still changing and reforming. Learners are, in fact, neural works in progress, altering themselves with every new activity, every engagement, and every new skill acquired and fact learned. That remodeling is ongoing, protracted, and continuous. As neuroscience continues to provide a wealth of new data, and those data are woven together with the data provided by sociologists, behavioral scientists, psychologists, and educators, we may indeed find that brain research provides invaluable insights—and useful strategies—for us as teachers (see Katzir & Paré-Blagoev, 2006).

What Causes People to Remember or Forget ?

Why do we remember some things and forget others? Why can we sometimes remember trivial things that happened years ago but not important things that happened yesterday? Most forgetting occurs because information in working memory was never transferred to long-term memory. However, it can also occur because we have lost our access to information in long-term memory.

■ Forgetting and Remembering

Over the years, researchers have identified several factors that make it easier or harder to remember information (see Schacter, 2001).

interference

Inhibition of recall of certain information by the presence of other information in memory.

retroactive inhibition

Decreased ability to recall previously learned information, caused by learning of new information.

INTERFERENCE   One important reason people forget is **interference** (Dempster & Corkill, 1999), which happens when information gets mixed up with, or pushed aside by, other information. One form of interference occurs when people are prevented from mentally rehearsing newly learned information. In one classic experiment, Peterson and Peterson (1959) gave subjects a simple task: the memorization of sets of three nonsense letters (such as FQB). The subjects were then immediately asked to count backward by 3s from a three-digit number (e.g., 287, 284, 281, etc.) for up to 18 seconds. At the end of that time the subjects were asked to recall the letters. They had forgotten far more of them than had subjects who learned the letters and then simply waited for 18 seconds to repeat them. The reason for this is that the subjects who were told to count backward were deprived of the opportunity to rehearse the letters mentally to establish them in their working memories. As noted earlier in this chapter, you must take into account the limited capacity of working memory by allowing students time to absorb or practice (that is, mentally rehearse) new information before giving them additional instruction.

RETROACTIVE INHIBITION   Another form of interference is called **retroactive inhibition,** which occurs when previously learned information is lost because it is mixed up with new and somewhat similar information. For example, young students may have no trouble recognizing

According to research on memory and forgetting, what factors determine how well this student remembers the information she learns in class?

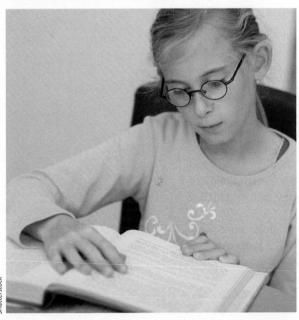
Shutterstock

the letter *b* until they are taught the letter *d*. Because these letters are similar, students often confuse them. Learning the letter *d* thus interferes with the previously learned recognition of *b*. In the same way, a traveler might know how to get around in a particular airport but then lose that skill to some extent after visiting many similar airports.

Of all the reasons for forgetting, retroactive inhibition is probably the most important. This phenomenon explains, for example, why we have trouble remembering frequently repeated episodes, such as what we had for dinner a week ago. Last night's dinner will be quickly forgotten because memories of dinners that come after it will interfere, unless something remarkable happens to clearly distinguish it from the dinners that will follow.

Theory into Practice
Reducing Retroactive Inhibition

There are two ways to help reduce retroactive inhibition for students. The first is by not teaching similar and confusing concepts too closely in time. The second is to use different methods to teach similar concepts. When addressing several confusing or similar concepts, teach the first one thoroughly before the next is introduced. For example, students should be completely able to recognize the letter *b* before the letter *d* is introduced. If these letters are introduced too closely together, learning one may interfere with learning the other. When the new letter is introduced, you must carefully point out the differences between *b* and *d,* and students must practice discriminating between them until they can unerringly say which is which.

As another example, consider the following lists of Spanish and English word pairs:

A	B
llevar—to carry	*perro*—dog
llorar—to cry	*gato*—cat
llamar—to call	*caballo*—horse

List B is much easier to learn. The similarities among the Spanish words in list A (they are all verbs, start with *ll,* end with *ar,* and have the same number of letters and syllables) make them very difficult to tell apart. The English words in list A are also somewhat difficult to discriminate among because all are verbs that start with a *c.* In contrast, the words in list B are easy to discriminate from one another. Because of the problem of retroactive inhibition, presenting all the word pairs in list A in the same lesson would be a poor instructional strategy. Students would be likely to confuse the three Spanish words because of their similar spellings. Rather, students should be completely familiar with one word pair before the next is introduced.

Another way to reduce retroactive inhibition is to use different methods to teach similar concepts or to vary other aspects of instruction for each concept. For example, in social studies you might teach about Spain by using lectures and discussion, about France by using group projects, and about Italy by using videos. This would help students avoid confusing information about one country with that of another.

Most things that are forgotten were never firmly learned in the first place. The best way to ensure long-term retention of material taught in school is to make certain that students have mastered its essential features. This means assessing students' understanding frequently and reteaching if it turns out that students have not achieved adequate levels of understanding.

PROACTIVE INHIBITION   Sometimes previous knowledge interferes with learning later information. A classic case of **proactive inhibition** is that of a North American learning to drive on the left side of the road in England. It may be easier for a North American nondriver to learn to drive in England than for an experienced North American driver because the latter has so thoroughly learned to stay to the right—a potentially fatal error in England.

INDIVIDUAL DIFFERENCES IN RESISTANCE TO INTERFERENCE   In a 1999 article, Dempster and Corkill raised the possibility that the ability to focus on key information and screen out interference is at the heart of cognitive performance. Reviewing research from many fields, including brain research, they note strong relationships between measures of resistance to interference and school performance. For example, among children with similar IQs, those with learning disabilities perform much worse on measures of resistance to interference (see Forness & Kavale, 2000). Children with attention deficit hyperactivity disorders (ADHD) are very poor at screening out irrelevant stimuli. If you think about the stereotype of the "absent-minded professor," the ability to focus one's attention on a given problem to the exclusion of all else may be a hallmark of extraordinary intellect.

FACILITATION   It should also be noted that previous learning can often help a person learn similar information, in what is called **proactive facilitation.** For example, learning Spanish first may help an English-speaking student later learn Italian, a similar language. Learning a second language can also help with an already established language. It is often the case, for example, that English-speaking students find that the study of Latin helps them understand their native language better. This would be **retroactive facilitation.**

For another example, consider teaching. We often have the experience that learning to teach a subject helps us understand the subject better. Because later learning (e.g., learning to teach addition of fractions) increases our understanding of previously learned information (addition of fractions), this is a prime example of retroactive facilitation. Table 6.2 summarizes the relationships among retroactive and proactive inhibition and facilitation.

PRIMACY AND RECENCY EFFECTS   One of the oldest findings in educational psychology is that when people are given a list of words to learn and then tested immediately afterward, they tend to learn the first few and last few much better than those in the middle of the list. The tendency to learn the first items presented is called the **primacy effect;** the tendency to learn the last elements is called the **recency effect.** The most common explanation for the primacy effect is that we pay more attention and devote more mental effort to items presented first. As was noted earlier in this chapter, mental rehearsal is important in establishing new information in long-term memory. Usually, much more mental rehearsal is devoted to the first items presented than to later components (Anderson, 2005). Recency effects, in contrast, are based on the fact that little or no other information intervenes between the final items and the test.

You should consider primacy and recency effects, which imply that material taught at the beginning or the end of the period is more likely to be retained than other infor-

proactive inhibition

Decreased ability to learn new information, caused by interference from existing knowledge.

proactive facilitation

Increased ability to learn new information based on the presence of previously acquired information.

retroactive facilitation

Increased comprehension of previously learned information because of the acquisition of new information.

primacy effect

The tendency for items at the beginning of a list to be recalled more easily than other items.

recency effect

The tendency for items at the end of a list to be recalled more easily than other items.

TABLE 6.2	Retroactive and Proactive Inhibition and Facilitation	
Summary of the effects on memory of retroactive and proactive inhibition and facilitation.		
Effect on Learning	**Effect on Memory**	
	Inhibition (Negative)	Facilitation (Positive)
Later learning affects earlier learning	Retroactive inhibition (*Example:* Learning *d* interferes with learning *b*.)	Retroactive facilitation (*Example:* Learning to teach math helps with previously learned math skills.)
Earlier learning affects later learning	Proactive inhibition (*Example:* Learning to drive in the United States interferes with learning to drive in England.)	Proactive facilitation (*Example:* Learning Spanish helps with later learning of Italian.)

mation. To take advantage of this, you might organize your lessons to put the most essential new concepts early in the lesson and then to summarize at the end. Many teachers take roll, collect lunch money, check homework, and do other noninstructional activities at the beginning of the period. However, it is probably a better idea to postpone these activities and start the period right away with important concepts, waiting until later in the period to deal with necessary administrative tasks.

AUTOMATICITY   Information or skills may exist in long-term memory but take so much time or so much mental effort to retrieve that they are of limited value when speed of access is essential. The classic case of this is reading. A child may be able to sound out every word on a page, but if he does so very slowly and laboriously, the child will lose comprehension and will be unlikely to read for pleasure (National Reading Panel, 2000). For reading and other skills in which speed and limited mental effort are necessary, long-term memory is not enough. **Automaticity** is required, that is, a level of rapidity and ease such that a task or skill involves little or no mental effort. For

> **automaticity**
>
> A level of rapidity and ease such that tasks can be performed or skills utilized with little mental effort.

a proficient reader processing simple material, decoding requires almost no mental effort. As noted earlier, neurological studies show that the brain becomes more efficient as a person becomes a skilled reader (Eden et al., 1996). A beginning reader with serious learning disabilities uses both auditory and visual parts of the brain during reading, trying laboriously to sound out new words. In contrast, a skilled reader uses only a small, well-defined portion of the brain relating to visual processing.

Automaticity is primarily gained through practice far beyond the amount needed to establish information or skills in long-term memory (Moors & De Houwer, 2006). A soccer player knows after 10 minutes of instruction how to kick a ball, but the player practices this skill thousands of times until it becomes automatic. A chess player quickly learns the rules of chess but spends a lifetime learning to quickly recognize patterns that suggest winning moves. Bloom (1986), who studied the role of automaticity in the performances of gifted pianists, mathematicians, athletes, and others, called automaticity "the hands and feet of genius."

By practicing scales far beyond the amount needed to establish the skills in his long-term memory, this young musician can gain automaticity. How will this benefit him?

Myrleen Ferguson Cate/PhotoEdit

■ Practice

The most common method for committing information to memory is also the most mundane: practice. Does practice make perfect?

Practice is important at several stages of learning. As was noted earlier in this chapter, information received in working memory must be mentally rehearsed if it is to be retained for more than a few seconds. The information in working memory must usually be practiced until it is established in long-term memory (Willingham, 2004).

MASSED AND DISTRIBUTED PRACTICE   Is it better to practice newly learned information intensively until it is thoroughly learned, a technique called **massed practice?** Or is it more effective to practice a little each day over a period of time—**distributed practice?** Massed practice allows for faster initial learning, but for most kinds of learning, distributed practice is better for retention, even over short time periods (Cepeda, Pashler, Vul, Wixted, & Rohrer, 2006). This is especially true of factual learning (Willingham, 2002); cramming factual information the night before could get you through a test, but the information probably won't be well integrated into your long-term memory. Long-term retention of all kinds of information and skills is greatly enhanced by distributed practice. This is the primary purpose of homework: to provide practice on newly learned skills over an extended period of time to increase the chances that the skills will be retained.

ENACTMENT   Everyone knows that we learn by doing. It turns out that research on **enactment** supports this commonsense conclusion. That is, in learning how to perform tasks of many kinds, individuals learn much better if they are asked to enact the tasks (to physically carry them out) than if they simply read the instructions or watch a teacher enact the task (Engelkamp & Dehn, 2000). For example, students learn much more from a lesson on drawing geometric solids (such as cubes and spheres) if they have an opportunity to draw some rather than simply watching you do so.

GENERATION   It has long been known that practice is more likely to lead to long-term retention if students create something using the new information, rather than merely rehearsing the existing information. Writing summaries, making concept maps, or teaching the content to a peer are more effective than simply reading or practicing content without creating something new from it (Bertsch, Pesta, Wiscott, & McDaniel, 2007; deWinstanley & Bjork, 2004). The generation principle is central to effective study strategies, discussed later in this chapter.

INTASC

4 Multiple Instructional Strategies

massed practice

Technique in which facts or skills to be learned are repeated often over a concentrated period of time.

distributed practice

Technique in which items to be learned are repeated at intervals over a period of time.

enactment

A learning process in which individuals physically carry out tasks.

How Can Memory Strategies Be Taught?

Much of what students learn in school are facts that must be remembered. These form the framework on which more complex concepts depend. Factual material must be learned as efficiently and effectively as possible to leave time and mental energy for meaningful learning, such as problem-solving, conceptual, and creative activities. If students can learn the routine parts more efficiently, they can free their minds for tasks that involve understanding and reasoning. Some learning involves memorization of facts or of arbitrary associations between terms. For example, *pomme,* the French word for apple, is an arbitrary term associated with an object. The capital of Iowa could just as well have been called *Iowapolis* as *Des Moines.* Students often learn ideas as facts before they understand them as concepts or skills. For instance, students may learn the formula for the volume of a cylinder as an arbitrary fact long before they understand why the formula is what it is.

 ON THE WEB

For techniques and resources for improving memory, go to www.mindtools.com.

■ Verbal Learning

In many studies psychologists have examined **verbal learning** (Ashcraft & Radvansky, 2010). For example, students might be asked to learn lists of words or nonsense syllables. Three types of verbal learning activities typically seen in the classroom have been identified and studied extensively: paired-associate, serial, and free-recall tasks.

1. **Paired-associate learning** involves learning to respond with one member of a pair when given the other member, usually from a list of pairs to be memorized. In typical experiments, the pairs are arbitrary. Educational examples of paired-associate tasks include learning the state capitals, the names and dates of Civil War battles, the addition and multiplication tables, the atomic weights of the elements, and the spellings of words.
2. **Serial learning** involves learning a list of terms in a particular order. Memorization of the notes on the musical staff, the Pledge of Allegiance, the elements in atomic weight order, and poetry and songs are serial learning tasks.
3. **Free-recall learning** tasks also involve memorizing a list, but not in a special order. Recalling the names of the 50 states, types of reinforcements, kinds of poetic feet, and the organ systems in the body are examples of free-recall tasks.

verbal learning

Learning of words (or facts expressed in words).

paired-associate learning

Learning of items in linked pairs so that when one member of a pair is presented, the other can be recalled.

serial learning

Memorization of a series of items in a particular order.

free-recall learning

Learning of a list of items in any order.

imagery

Mental visualization of images to improve memory.

PAIRED-ASSOCIATE LEARNING   In paired-associate learning, the student must associate a response with each stimulus. For example, the student is given a picture of a bone (the stimulus) and must respond "tibia," or is given the symbol Au and must respond "gold." One important aspect in the learning of paired associates is the degree of familiarity the student already has with the stimuli and the responses. For example, it would be far easier to learn to associate foreign words with English words, such as *dog—chien* (French) or *dog—perro* (Spanish), than to learn to associate two foreign words, such as *chien—perro*.

Imagery   Many powerful memory techniques are based on forming mental images to help remember associations. For example, the French word for fencing is *l'escrime,* pronounced "le scream." It is easy to remember this association (*fencing—l'escrime*) by forming a mental picture of a fencer screaming while being skewered by an opponent, as illustrated in Figure 6.8.

One ancient method of enhancing memory by use of **imagery** is the creation of stories to weave

FIGURE 6.8 **Example of the Use of Images to Aid Recall**

An English-speaking student learning French can easily remember that the French word for fencing is *l'escrime* by linking it to the English word *scream* and picturing a fencer screaming.

together information (Egan, 1989). For example, images from Greek myths and other sources have long been used to help people recall the constellations.

Theory into Practice
Keyword Mnemonics

One of the most extensively studied methods of using imagery and **mnemonics** (memory devices) to help paired-associate learning is the **keyword method,** which was originally developed for teaching foreign language vocabulary but was later applied to many other areas (Carney & Levin, 2002). The example of employing vivid imagery to recall the French word *l'escrime* is an illustration of the keyword method. In that case, the keyword was *scream*. It is called a *keyword* because it evokes the connection between the word *l'escrime* and the mental picture. The Russian word for building, *zdanie,* pronounced "zdan´-yeh," might be recalled by using the keyword *dawn* and imagining the sun coming up behind a building with an onion dome on top. Atkinson and Raugh (1975) used this method to teach students a list of 120 Russian words over a 3-day period. Other students were given English translations of the Russian words and allowed to study as they wished. At the end of the experiment, the students who used the keyword method recalled 72 percent of the words, whereas the other students recalled only 46 percent. This result has been repeated dozens of times, using a wide variety of languages (e.g., Crutcher & Ericsson, 2003; Wyra et al., 2007), with students from preschoolers to adults. However, young children seem to require pictures of the mental images they are meant to form, whereas older children (starting in upper elementary school) learn equally well making their own mental images (Willoughby, Porter, Belsito, & Yearsley, 1999). Furthermore, having students work in pairs or cooperative groups has been found to enhance vocabulary learning using mnemonic strategies (Jones, Levin, Levin, & Beitzel, 2000).

The images that are used in the keyword method work best if they are vivid and active, preferably involving interaction. For example, the German word for room, *zimmer* (pronounced "tsimmer"), might be associated with the keyword *simmer*. Recall would probably be enhanced by using an image of a distressed person immersed in a huge, steaming cauldron of water in a large bedroom than by using an image of a small pot of water simmering in the corner. The drama, action, and bizarreness of the first image make it memorable; the second is too commonplace to be easily recalled.

Similarly, Rummel, Levin, and Woodward (2002) showed students pictures to help them recall a link between various theorists of intelligence and their contributions. For example, to link Binet and measurement of higher mental processes, Rummel and colleagues showed students a race car driver protecting his *brain* with a *bonnet*. A review of many studies involving various mnemonic strategies found substantial positive effects, on average (Hattie, Bibbs, & Purdie, 1996). However, it should be noted that most of the research on mnemonic strategies has taken place under rather artificial, laboratory-like conditions, using materials that are thought to be especially appropriate for these strategies. Evaluations of actual classroom applications of these methods show more mixed results, and there are questions about the long-term retention of material learned by means of keywords (Carney & Levin, 1998; Wang & Thomas, 1995).

mnemonics

Devices or strategies for aiding the memory.

keyword method

A strategy for improving memory by using images to link pairs of items.

SERIAL AND FREE-RECALL LEARNING   Serial learning involves comprehending facts in a particular order. Learning the events on a time line, the order of operations in long division, or the relative hardnesses of minerals are examples of serial learning. Free-recall learning involves assimilating a list of items that need not be remembered in order, such as the names of the Canadian provinces.

Loci Method   A mnemonic device for serial learning that was used by the ancient Greeks employs imagery associated with a list of locations (see Anderson, 2005). In the **loci method** the student thinks of a very familiar set of locations, such as rooms in her own house, and then imagines each item on the list to be remembered in one specific location. Vivid or bizarre imagery is used to place the item in the location. Once the connections between the item and the room or other location are established, the learner can recall each place and its contents in order. The same locations can be mentally cleared and used to memorize a different list. However, they should always be used in the same order to ensure that all items on the list have been remembered.

Pegword Method   Another imagery method useful for serial learning is called the **pegword method** (Krinsky & Krinsky, 1996), in which a student memorizes a list of pegwords that rhyme with the numbers 1 to 10. To use this method, the student creates mental images relating to items on the list to be learned with particular pegwords. For example, in learning the order of the first 10 U.S. presidents, you might picture George Washington eating a *bun* (1) with his wooden teeth, John Adams tying his *shoe* (2), Thomas Jefferson hanging by his *knees* from a branch of a *tree* (3), and so on.

Initial-Letter Strategies   Another memory strategy involves a reorganization of information in which initial letters of a list to be memorized are arranged in a more easily remembered word or phrase. For example, many trigonometry classes have learned about the imaginary SOHCAHTOA tribe, whose letters help us recall that sine = opposite/hypotenuse, cosine = adjacent/hypotenuse, and tangent = opposite/adjacent. Many such **initial-letter strategies** exist for remembering the order of the planets by relative distance from the sun—Mercury, Venus, Earth, Mars, Jupiter, Saturn, Uranus, and Neptune. Students are taught a sentence in which the first letters of the words are the first letters of the planets in order, such as "My very educated monkey just served us nachos."

In a similar fashion, acronyms help people remember the names of organizations, such as NATO (North Atlantic Treaty Organization), and computer components, such as ROM (read-only memory). Initial-letter strategies may also help students remember procedural knowledge, such as steps in a process.

What Makes Information Meaningful

Consider the following sentences:

1. Enso flrs hmen matn snoi teha erso iakt siae otin tnes esna nrae.
2. Easier that nonsense information to makes than sense is learn.
3. Information that makes sense is easier to learn than nonsense.

Which sentence is easiest to learn and remember? Obviously, sentence 3. All three sentences have the same letters, and sentences 2 and 3 have the same words. Yet to learn sentence 1, you would have to memorize 52 separate letters, and to learn sentence 2, you would have to learn 10 separate words. Sentence 3 is easiest because to learn it you need only learn one concept, a concept that readily fits your common sense and prior knowledge about how learning takes place. You know the individual words; you know

loci method

A strategy for remembering lists by picturing items in familiar locations.

pegword method

A strategy for memorization in which images are used to link lists of facts to a familiar set of words or numbers.

initial-letter strategies

Strategies for learning in which initial letters of items to be memorized are made into a more easily remembered word or phrase.

the grammar that connects them; and you already have in your mind a vast store of information, experiences, and thoughts about the same topic. For these reasons, sentence 3 slides smoothly into your understanding.

The message in sentence 3 is what this chapter is all about. Most human learning, particularly school learning, involves making sense out of information, sorting it in our minds until it fits in a neat and orderly way, and using old information to help assimilate new learning. We have limited ability to recall rote information—how many telephone numbers can you remember for a month? However, we can retain meaningful information far more easily. Recall that most of the mnemonic strategies discussed in the previous section involve adding artificial meaning to arbitrary associations in order to take advantage of the much greater ease of learning meaningful information.

The message in sentence 3 has profound implications for instruction. One of your most important tasks is to make information meaningful to students by presenting it in a clear, organized way; by relating it to information already in students' minds; and by making sure that students have truly understood the concepts being taught and can apply them to new situations.

■ Rote versus Meaningful Learning

INTASC

4 Multiple Instructional Strategies

Rote learning refers to the memorization of facts or associations, such as the multiplication tables, the chemical symbols for the elements, words in foreign languages, or the names of bones and muscles in the human body. Much of rote learning involves associations that are essentially arbitrary. For example, the chemical symbol for gold (Au) could just as well have been *Go* or *Gd*. In contrast, **meaningful learning** is not arbitrary, and it relates to information or concepts learners already have. For example, if we learn that silver is an excellent conductor of electricity, this information relates to our existing information about silver and about electrical conductivity. Furthermore, the association between "silver" and "electrical conductivity" is not arbitrary. Silver really is an excellent conductor, and although we could state the same principle in many ways or in any language, the meaning of the statement "Silver is an excellent conductor of electricity" could not be arbitrarily changed.

USES OF ROTE LEARNING   We sometimes get the impression that rote learning is "bad" and meaningful learning is "good." This is not necessarily true. For example, when the doctor tells us we have a fractured tibia, we hope that the doctor has mastered the rote association between the word *tibia* and the leg bone it names. The mastery of foreign language vocabulary is an important case of rote learning. It is mainly due to overuse that rote learning has such a bad name in education. We can all remember being taught to parrot supposedly meaningful facts that we were forced to learn as rote, meaningless information. Long ago, William James (1912) gave an excellent example of this kind of false learning:

rote learning

Memorization of facts or associations that might be essentially arbitrary.

meaningful learning

Mental processing of new information that relates to previously learned knowledge.

inert knowledge

Learned information that could be applied to a wide range of situations but whose use is limited to restricted, often artificial, applications.

> A friend of mine, visiting a school, was asked to examine a young class in geography. Glancing at the book, she said: "Suppose you should dig a hole in the ground, hundreds of feet deep, how should you find it at the bottom—warmer or colder than on top?" None of the class replying, the teacher said: "I'm sure they know, but I think you don't ask the question quite rightly. Let me try." So, taking the book, she asked: "In what condition is the interior of the globe?" and received the immediate answer from half the class at once. "The interior of the globe is in a condition of igneous fusion." (p. 150)

Clearly, the students had memorized the information without learning its meaning. The information was useless to them because it did not tie in with other information they had.

INERT KNOWLEDGE   The "igneous fusion" information that students had memorized is an example of what Bransford, Burns, Delclos, and Vye (1986) call **inert knowledge.**

This is knowledge that could and should be applicable to a wide range of situations but is applied only to a restricted set of circumstances. Usually, inert knowledge consists of information or skills learned in school that we cannot apply in life. For example, you may know people who could pass an advanced French test but would be unable to communicate in Paris, or who can solve volume problems in math class but have no idea how much sand to order to fill a sandbox. Many problems in life arise not from a lack of knowledge but from an inability to use the knowledge we already have.

A classic experiment by Perfetto, Bransford, and Franks (1983) illustrates the concept of inert knowledge. In the experiment, college students were given problems such as the following: "Uriah Fuller, the famous Israeli superpsychic, can tell you the score of any baseball game before the game starts. What is his secret?"

Before seeing the problems, some of the students were given a list of sentences to memorize that were clearly useful in solving the problems; among the sentences was "Before it starts, the score of any game is 0 to 0." Students who were told to use the memorized sentences as clues performed much better on the problem-solving task than did other students, whereas students who memorized the clues but were not told to use them did no better than students who never saw the clues. What this experiment tells us is that having information in your memory does not guarantee that you can retrieve and use it when appropriate. Rather, you need to know how and when to use the information you have.

You can help students learn information in a way that will make it useful as well as meaningful to them. Effective teaching requires an understanding of how to make information accessible to students so that they can connect it to other information, think about it, and apply it outside of the classroom (Willingham, 2003).

■ Schema Theory

As noted earlier, meaningful information is stored in long-term memory in networks of connected facts or concepts called *schemata*. Recall the representation of the concept "bison" presented in Figure 6.4, showing how this one concept was linked to a wide range of other concepts. The most important principle of **schema theory** (Anderson, 2005; McVee, Dunsmore, & Gavelek, 2005) is that information fitting into an existing schema is more easily understood, learned, and retained than information that does not fit into an existing schema (Anderson & Bower, 1983). The sentence "Bison calves can run soon after they are born" is an example of information that will be easily incorporated into your "bison" schema because you know that (1) bison rely on speed to escape from predators, and (2) more familiar animals (such as horses) that also rely on speed have babies that can run very early. Without all this prior knowledge, "Bison calves can run soon after they are born" would be more difficult to assimilate mentally and more easily forgotten.

HIERARCHIES OF KNOWLEDGE   It is thought that most well-developed schemata are organized in hierarchies similar to outlines, with specific information grouped under general categories, which are grouped under still more general categories. Recall Figure 6.4. Note that in moving from the top to the bottom of the figure, you are going from general (animals and Native Americans) to specific (how Native Americans hunted bison). The concepts in the figure are well anchored in the schema. Any new information relating to this schema will probably be learned and incorporated into the schema much more readily than would information relating to less established schemata or rote learning that does not attach to any schema.

One important insight of schema theory is that meaningful learning requires the active involvement of the learner, who has a host of prior experiences and knowledge to bring to understanding and incorporating new information (Alexander, 1992). What you learn from any experience depends in large part on the schema you apply to the experience.

schema theory

Theory stating that information is stored in long-term memory in schemata (networks of connected facts and concepts), which provide a structure for making sense of new information.

THE IMPORTANCE OF BACKGROUND KNOWLEDGE   One of the most important determinants of how much you can learn about something is how much you already know about it (Alexander, Kulikowich, & Jetton, 1994; Schneider, 1993). A study in Japan by Kuhara-Kojima and Hatano (1991) illustrates this clearly. College students were taught new information about baseball and music. Those who knew a great deal about baseball but not about music learned much more about baseball; the converse was true of those who knew a lot about music and little about baseball. In fact, background knowledge was much more important than general learning ability in predicting how much the students would learn. Learners who know a great deal about a subject have more well-developed schemata for incorporating new information. Not surprisingly, interest in a given subject contributes to background knowledge in it as well as to depth of understanding and willingness to use background knowledge to solve new problems (Perfetti, 2003). However, learners often do not spontaneously use their prior understanding to help them learn new material. Teachers must link new learning to students' existing background knowledge (Bruning et al., 2004).

How Do Metacognitive Skills Help Students Learn ?

The term **metacognition** means knowledge about one's own learning (McCormick, 2003) or about how to learn. Thinking skills and study skills are examples of **metacognitive skills.** Students can be taught strategies for assessing their own understanding, figuring out how much time they will need to study something, and choosing an effective plan of attack to examine or solve problems (McCormick, 2003). For example, in reading this book, you are bound to come across a paragraph that you don't understand on first reading. What do you do? Perhaps you re-read the paragraph more slowly. Perhaps you look for other clues, such as pictures, graphs, or glossary terms to help you understand. Perhaps you read further back in the chapter to see whether your difficulty arose because you did not fully understand something that came earlier. These are all examples of metacognitive skills; you have learned how to know when you are not understanding and how to correct yourself (Martinez, 2006). Another metacognitive strategy is the ability to predict what is likely to happen or to tell what is sensible and what is not. For example, when you first read the word *modeling* in Chapter 5, you knew right away that this did not refer to building models of ships or airplanes because you knew that meaning would not fit in the context of this book.

Connections

The term *modeling* is discussed in Chapter 5, page 132, in relation to Bandura's social learning theory.

metacognition

Knowledge about one's own learning or about how to learn ("thinking about thinking").

metacognitive skills

Methods for learning, studying, or solving problems.

self-questioning strategies

Learning strategies that call on students to ask themselves *who, what, where,* and *how* questions as they read material.

ON THE WEB

For an overview of metacognition, visit www.ncrel.org/sdrs/areas/issues/students/learning/lr1metn.htm.

Although most students gradually do develop adequate metacognitive skills, some do not. Teaching metacognitive strategies to students can lead to a marked improvement in their achievement (Alexander, Graham, & Harris, 1998). Students can learn to think about their own thinking processes and apply specific learning strategies to think themselves through difficult tasks (Schunk, 2000). **Self-questioning strategies** are particularly effective (Zimmerman, 1998). In self-questioning, students look for common elements in a given type of task and ask themselves questions about these elements. For example, many researchers (e.g., Stevens, Madden, Slavin, & Farnish, 1987) have taught students to look for characters, settings, problems, and problem solutions in stories. Instructors start with specific questions and then let students find these critical elements on their own. Paris, Cross, and Lipson (1984) and King (1992) found that students comprehend better if they are taught to ask themselves *who, what, where,* and *how* questions as they read. Englert, Raphael, Anderson, Anthony, and Stevens (1991) gave students planning sheets with questions to ask themselves in planning their creative writing assignments. For whom am I writing? What is being explained? What are the steps? Essentially, students are taught to talk themselves through the activities they are engaged in, asking themselves or each other the questions a teacher would ask. Students have been successfully taught to talk themselves through mathematics problem solving (Cardelle-Elawar, 1990), spelling (Block & Peskowitz, 1990), creative writing (Zeller-mayer, Salomon, Globerson, & Givon, 1991), reading (Chin, 1998; Kucan & Beck, 1997), and many other subjects.

What Study Strategies Help Students Learn ?

INTASC

4 Multiple Instructional Strategies

How are you reading this book? Are you underlining or highlighting key sentences? Are you taking notes or summarizing? Are you discussing the main ideas with a classmate? Are you putting the book under your pillow at night and hoping the information will somehow seep into your mind? Students have used these and many other strategies ever since the invention of reading, and such strategies have been studied almost as long. Even Aristotle wrote on the topic. Yet educational psychologists are still debating which study strategies are most effective.

Research on effective study strategies is confusing at best. Few forms of studying are found to be always effective, and fewer still are never effective. Clearly, the value of study strategies depends on their specifics and on the uses to which they are put (Weinstein & Hume, 1998; Zimmerman, 1998). A generalization about effective study strategies is that effective methods involve learners in reshaping the information (Kiewra, 1991), not just rereading (Callender & McDaniel, 2009) or highlighting without consciously choosing the most important information to highlight (Gaddy, 1998). Research on the most common study strategies is summarized in the following sections.

■ Practice Tests

Perhaps the most effective study strategy is taking practice tests aligned with the real test to come. Test taking, especially when tests require constructed responses rather than multiple choice or fill-in-the-blank, causes test takers to engage in high-level processing of the content, thereby enhancing understanding and memory (Carpenter & Pashler, 2007; Marsh, Roediger, Bjork, & Bjork, 2007; McDaniel, Roediger, & McDermott, 2007; Roediger & Karpicke, 2006). Furthermore, the practice test reminds you what you know and do not know, so that you can focus your studying most efficiently. Working in a study group that makes up practice tests for each other can be particularly effective (Ashcraft & Radvansky, 2010).

■ Note-Taking

A common study strategy used both in reading and in learning from lectures, **note-taking** can be effective for certain types of material because it requires mental processing of main ideas as one makes decisions about what to write. However, the effects of note-taking have been found to be inconsistent. Positive effects are most likely when note-taking is used for complex conceptual material in which the critical task is to identify the main ideas (Kobayashi, 2005; Peverly et al., 2007). Also, note-taking that requires some mental processing is more effective than simply writing down what was read

note-taking

A study strategy that requires decisions about what to write.

(Igo, Bruning, & McCrudden, 2005). For example, Bretzing and Kulhavy (1981) found that writing paraphrase notes (stating the main ideas in different words) and taking notes in preparation to teach others the material are effective note-taking strategies because they require a high degree of mental processing of the information.

One apparently effective means of increasing the value of students' note-taking is for you to provide partial notes before a lecture or reading, giving students categories to direct their own note-taking. Several studies have found that this practice, combined with student note-taking and review, increases student learning (Robinson, Katayama, Beth, Odom, & Hsieh, 2004).

■ Underlining

Perhaps the most common study strategy is underlining or highlighting. Yet despite the widespread use of this method, research on underlining generally finds few benefits (Anderson & Armbruster, 1984; Gaddy, 1998). The problem is that most students fail to make decisions about what material is most critical and simply underline too much. When students are asked to underline the one sentence in each paragraph that is most important, they do retain more, probably because deciding which is the most important sentence requires a higher level of processing (Snowman, 1984).

■ Summarizing

Summarizing involves writing brief statements that represent the main ideas of the information being read. The effectiveness of this strategy depends on how it is used (Slotte & Lonka, 1999). One effective way is to have students write one-sentence summaries after reading each paragraph (Wittrock, 1991). Another is to have students prepare summaries that are intended to help others learn the material—partly because this activity forces the summarizer to be brief and to consider seriously what is important and what is not. However, it is important to note that several studies have found no effects of summarization, and the conditions under which this strategy increases comprehension or retention of written material are not well understood (Wittrock, 1991; Wittrock & Alesandrini, 1990).

■ Writing to Learn

A growing body of evidence supports the idea that having students explain in writing the content they are learning helps them understand and remember it (Klein, 1999). For example, Fellows (1994) had sixth-graders in a 12-week science unit on states of matter write about their understandings of the concepts at several points in the unit. A control group studied the same content without writing. The writing group retained substantially more of the content at post-test. This and other studies find that focused writing assignments help children learn the content about which they are writing. However, evidence is much more mixed regarding the effects of less focused "journal writing," in which students keep logs of their ideas and observations.

summarizing

Writing brief statements that represent the main idea of the information being read.

outlining

Representing the main points of material in hierarchical format.

concept mapping

Diagramming main ideas and the connections between them.

■ Outlining and Concept Mapping

A related family of study strategies requires the student to represent the material studied in skeletal form. These strategies include outlining, networking, and concept mapping. **Outlining** presents the main points of the material in a hierarchical format, with each detail organized under a higher-level category. In networking and **concept mapping,** students identify main ideas and then diagram connections between them (Hyerle, 1995; Robinson & Skinner, 1996). For example, the schematic representation of the concept "bison" shown in Figure 6.4 might have been produced by students themselves as a network to summarize factual material about bison and their importance to Plains Indians (see Clark, 1990; Rafoth, Leal, & De Fabo, 1993).

Research on outlining, networking, and concept mapping is limited and inconsistent but generally finds that these methods are helpful as study aids (Nebsit & Adesope, 2006).

■ The PQ4R Method

One of the best-known study techniques for helping students understand and remember what they read is the **PQ4R method** (Thomas & Robinson, 1972), which is based on an earlier version known as SQ3R, developed by F. P. Robinson (1961). The acronym stands for *preview, question, read, reflect, recite,* and *review.*

Research has shown the effectiveness of the PQ4R method for older children (Adams, Carnine, & Gersten, 1982), and the reasons seem clear. Following the PQ4R procedure focuses students on the meaningful organization of information and involves them in other effective strategies, such as question generation, elaboration, and distributed practice (opportunities to review information over a period of time) (Anderson, 1990).

Theory into Practice
Teaching the PQ4R Method

Explain and model the steps of the PQ4R method for your students, using the following guidelines:

1. *Preview.*   Survey or scan the material quickly to get an idea of the general organization and major topics and subtopics. Pay attention to headings and subheadings, and identify what you will be reading about and studying.

2. *Question.*   Ask yourself questions about the material before you read it. Use headings to invent questions using the *wh* words: *who, what, why, where.*

3. *Read.*   Read the material. Do not take extensive written notes. Try to answer the questions that you posed prior to reading.

4. *Reflect on the material.*   Try to understand and make meaningful the presented information by (1) connecting it to what you already know, (2) relating the subtopics in the text to primary concepts or principles, (3) trying to resolve contradictions within the presented information, and (4) using the material to solve problems suggested by the material.

5. *Recite.*   Practice remembering the information by stating points out loud and asking and answering questions. Use headings, highlighted words, and notes on major ideas to generate those questions.

6. *Review.*   In the final step, actively review the material, focusing on asking yourself questions; re-read the material only when you are not sure of the answers.

How Do Cognitive Teaching Strategies Help Students Learn?

In *Alice's Adventures in Wonderland* the White Rabbit is unsure how to give his evidence in the trial of the Knave of Hearts. The King of Hearts gives him a bit of advice: "Begin at

Certification Pointer

When responding to the case studies in certification tests, you may be asked to design a lesson that includes strategies for helping students learn relationships between ideas using concept mapping.

PQ4R method

A study strategy that has students preview, question, read, reflect, recite, and review material.

21ST Century Learning

Learning How to Learn

A key skill in the 21st century is self-direction. The Internet has made vast amounts of information easily available on Google, Wikipedia, and so on. The problem is that learners need to know how to organize their thinking to make effective use of all this information. They need to know how to identify what they already know about a topic along with what they need to know, and have a strategy for extracting the relevant information. Teaching students to take control of their own learning process helps them to use their time efficiently in reading for information, whether the material is on paper or online.

In a world awash in data, knowing learning strategies such as use of graphic organizers, outlining, and organizing information in hierarchies is essential.

Questions

- What are some issues you can discuss with your students in order to make sure their online research is effective?

- Anyone can post anything on the Internet, even false information. How can students know that the information they are obtaining online is accurate and true?

INTASC

3 Adapting Instruction for Individual Needs

4 Multiple Instructional Strategies

6 Communication Skills

Connections

See, for example, "How Is a Direct Instruction Lesson Taught?" in Chapter 7, pages 185–202.

the beginning . . . and go on until you come to the end: then stop." The "King of Hearts method" is a common means of delivering lectures, especially at the secondary and college levels. However, you can do more to help your students understand lessons. You can prepare students to learn new material by reminding them of what they already know, asking questions, and helping students link and recall new information (Carver & Klahr, 2001; McCormick, 2003). Many aspects of effective lesson presentation are covered in Chapter 7, but the following sections discuss practices derived from cognitive psychology that can help students understand, recall, and apply essential information, concepts, and skills.

■ Making Learning Relevant and Activating Prior Knowledge

Read the following passage:

> With the hocked gems financing him our hero bravely defied all scornful laughter that tried to prevent his scheme. Your eyes deceive he had said. An egg, not a table, correctly typifies this unexplored planet. Now three sturdy sisters sought proof. Forging along, sometimes through calm vastness, yet more often through turbulent peaks and valleys, days became weeks as many doubters spread fearful rumors about the edge. At last, from nowhere, welcome winged creatures appeared signifying momentous success. (Dooling & Lachman, 1971, p. 217)

Now read the paragraph again with the following information: The passage is about Christopher Columbus. Before you knew what the passage was about, it probably made little sense to you. You could understand the words and grammar and could probably infer that the story involved a voyage of discovery. However, once you learned that the story was about Columbus, you could bring all your prior knowledge about Columbus to bear on comprehending the paragraph, so that seemingly obscure references made sense. The "hocked gems" (Queen Isabella's jewelry), the egg (the shape of the earth), the three sturdy sisters (the *Niña, Pinta,* and *Santa Maria*), and the winged creatures (birds) become comprehensible when you know what the story is about.

In terms of schema theory, advance information that the story concerns Columbus activates your schema relating to Columbus. You are ready to receive and incorporate information relating to Columbus, to Isabella and Ferdinand, and to the ships. It is as though you had a filing cabinet with a drawer labeled "Columbus." When you know you are about to hear about Columbus, you mentally open the drawer, which contains files marked "Isabella," "ships," and "scoffers and doubters." You are now ready to file new information in the proper places. If you learned that the *Santa Maria* was wrecked in a storm, you would mentally file that information in the "ships" file. If you learned that most of the educated world agreed with Columbus that the earth was round, you would file that information in the "scoffers and doubters" file. The file drawer analogy is not completely appropriate, however, because the files of a schema are all logically connected with one another. Also, you are actively using the information in your files to interpret and organize the new information.

ADVANCE ORGANIZERS   David Ausubel (1963) developed a method called **advance organizers** to orient students to material they were about to learn and to help them recall related information that could assist them in incorporating the new information. An advance organizer is an initial statement about a subject to be learned that provides a structure for the new information and relates it to knowledge students already possess (Joyce, Weil, & Calhoun, 2000). For example, in one classic study (Ausubel & Youssef, 1963), college students were assigned to read a passage on Buddhism. Before reading the passage, some students were given an advance organizer comparing Buddhism to Christianity, whereas others read an unrelated passage. The students who were given the advance organizer retained much more of the material than did the other students. Ausubel and Youssef maintain that the reason for this is that the advance organizer activates most students' knowledge of Christianity, and the students were able to use that knowledge to incorporate information about a less familiar religion.

Many studies have established that advance organizers increase students' understanding of certain kinds of material (see Schwartz, Ellsworth, Graham, & Knight, 1998). Advance organizers seem to be most useful for teaching content with a well-organized

advance organizers

Activities and techniques that orient students to the material before reading or class presentation.

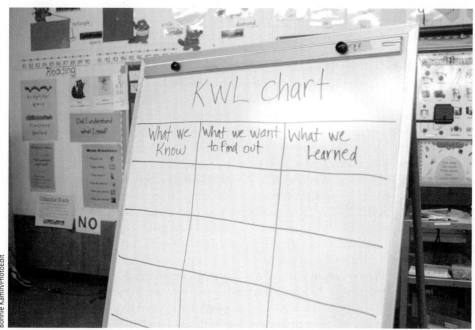

Using advance organizers with students can help activate their prior knowledge before an assignment or lesson. With what types of materials and in what situations do advance organizers work best?

Bonnie Kamin/PhotoEdit

Certification Pointer

On a teacher certification test, you may be asked to propose a strategy for stimulating the prior knowledge of students described in a particular case.

structure that might not be immediately apparent to students. However, they have not generally been found to help students learn factual information that does not lend itself to a clear organization or subjects that consist of a large number of separate topics (Corkill, 1992). In addition, methods designed to activate prior knowledge, such as advance organizers, can be counterproductive if the prior knowledge is weak or lacking (Alvermann, Smith, & Readence, 1985). If students know little about Christianity, relating Buddhism to Christianity may confuse rather than help them.

The use of advance organizers is a valuable strategy in its own right, but research on advance organizers also illustrates a broader principle that is extremely important: Activating prior knowledge enhances understanding and retention (Pressley, Harris, & Marks, 1992). Strategies other than advance organizers draw on this same principle. For example, having students discuss what they already know about a topic before they learn it (Pressley, Tannenbaum, McDaniel, & Wood, 1990) and having them make predictions about material to be learned (Fielding, Anderson, & Pearson, 1990) are additional ways to encourage students to make conscious use of prior knowledge.

ANALOGIES   Like advance organizers, use of explanatory analogies (comparisons or parallels) can contribute to understanding by linking new information to well-established background knowledge. For example, you could introduce a lesson on the human body's disease-fighting mechanisms by telling students to imagine a battle and to consider it as an analogy for the body's fight against infection. Similarly, you could preface a lesson on termite societies by asking students to think of the hierarchy of citizens within a kingdom, using that as an analogy for such insect societies. **Analogies** can help students learn new information by relating it to concepts they already know (Bulgren, Deshler, Schumaker, & Lenz, 2000; McDaniel & Dannelly, 1996).

One interesting study (Halpern, Hansen, & Riefer, 1990) found that analogies work best when they are most different from the process being explained. For example, college students' learning about the lymph system was aided more by an analogy of the movement of water through a sponge than by one involving the movement of blood through veins. What this probably illustrates is that it is more important that analogies be thoroughly familiar to the learner than that they relate in any direct way to the concepts being taught.

ELABORATION   Cognitive psychologists use the term **elaboration** to refer to the process of thinking about material to be learned in a way that connects the material to information or ideas that are already in the learner's mind (Ayaduray & Jacobs, 1997). As an example of the importance of elaboration, Stein, Littlefield, Bransford, and Persampieri (1984) conducted a series of experiments in which students were given lists of phrases to learn, such as "The gray-haired man carried the bottle." Some students were given the same phrases embedded in a more elaborate sentence, such as "The gray-haired man carried the bottle of hair dye." These latter students recalled the phrases much better than those who did not receive the elaboration, because the additional words tied the phrase to a well-developed schema that was already in the students' minds. The connection between *gray-haired man* and *bottle* is arbitrary until we give it meaning by linking these words with the *hair dye* idea.

You can apply this principle—that elaborated information is easier to understand and remember—to help students comprehend lessons. Students may be asked to think of connections between ideas or to relate new concepts to their own lives. For example, it might help students to understand the U.S. annexation of Texas and California if they consider these events from the perspective of Mexicans or if they compare the events to a situation in which a friend borrows a bicycle and then decides not to give it back. Elaboration can be taught as a skill to help students comprehend what they read (Willoughby et al., 1999). In discussing a story or novel, you might ask students from time to time to stop and visualize what is happening or what's about to happen as a means of helping them to elaborate their understanding of the material.

analogies

Images, concepts, or narratives that compare new material to information students already understand.

elaboration

The process of connecting new material to information or ideas already in the learner's mind.

■ Organizing Information

Recall the shopping list discussed earlier in this chapter. When the list was presented in random order, it was very difficult to memorize, partly because it contained too many items to be held in working memory all at once. However, when the list was organized in a logical way, it was meaningful and therefore easy to learn and remember. The specific foods were grouped according to familiar recipes (e.g., flour, eggs, and milk were grouped under "pancakes"), and the recipes and other foods were grouped under "breakfast," "lunch," and "dinner."

Material that is well organized is much easier to learn and remember than material that is poorly organized (Durso & Coggins, 1991). Hierarchical organization, in which specific issues are grouped under more general topics, seems particularly helpful for student understanding. For example, in a classic study by Bower, Clark, Lesgold, and Winzenz (1969), one group of students was taught 112 words relating to minerals in random order. Another group was taught the same words, but in a definite order. Figure 6.9 shows the hierarchy within which the words were organized. The students were taught the words at levels 1 and 2 in the first of four sessions; those at levels 1, 2, and 3 in the second session; and those at levels 1 through 4 in the third and fourth sessions. The students in this second group recalled an average of 100 words, in comparison to only 65 for the group that received the random presentation—demonstrating the effectiveness of a coherent, organized presentation. In teaching complex concepts, not only is it necessary that material be well organized but it is also important that the organizing framework itself be made clear to students (Kallison, 1986). For example, in teaching about the minerals shown in Figure 6.9, you might refer frequently to the framework and mark transitions from one part of it to another, as follows:

"Recall that alloys are combinations of two or more metals."

"Now that we've covered rare and common metals and alloys, let's move on to the second category of minerals: stones."

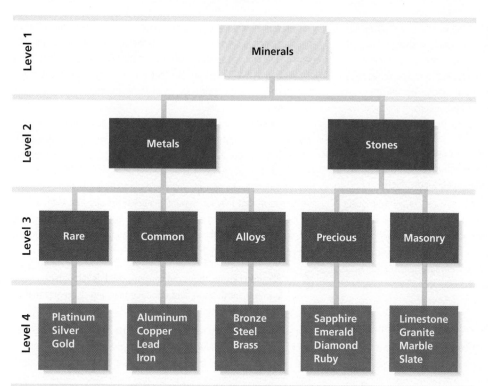

FIGURE 6.9

The Hierarchical Structure of Minerals

Source: "Hierarchical Retrieval Schemes in Recall of Categorized Word Lists" by G. H. Bower et al., from *Journal of Verbal Learning and Verbal Behavior*, Volume 8, 323–343. Copyright © 1969. Reprinted by permission of Elsevier.

USING QUESTIONING TECHNIQUES   One strategy that helps students learn from written texts, lectures, and other sources of information is the insertion of questions requiring students to stop from time to time to assess their own understanding of what the text or teacher is saying (Pressley et al., 1990; Sadker & Sadker, 2006). Presenting questions before the introduction of the instructional material can also help students learn material related to the questions, as can having students generate their own questions (Rosenshine, Meister, & Chapman, 1996).

USING CONCEPTUAL MODELS   Another means that you can use to help students comprehend complex topics is the introduction of conceptual models, or diagrams showing how elements of a process relate to one another. Figure 6.1, which illustrates information processing, is a classic example of a conceptual model. Use of such models organizes and integrates information. Examples of topics that lend themselves to use of conceptual models are electricity, mechanics, computer programming, and the processes by which laws are passed. When models are part of a lesson, not only do students learn more but they also are better able to apply their learning to creatively solve problems (Mayer, 2008b). Knowledge maps, a variation on conceptual models, can be used to teach a wider variety of content. A knowledge map graphically shows the main concepts of a topic of study and the links between them. Giving students knowledge maps after a lesson has been shown to increase their retention of the lesson's content (Nesbit & Adesope, 2006; O'Donnell, Dansereau, & Hall, 2002).

The Intentional Teacher

USING WHAT YOU KNOW about Cognitive Theories of Learning to Improve Teaching and Learning

Intentional teachers know how information is received, processed, and stored in memory. They demonstrate that teaching is more than telling; they help students connect new information with what they already know and encourage students to apply information in other contexts. Incorporating research findings about cognition into the classroom allows intentional teachers to help students build lasting and meaningful understandings.

 1. **What do I expect my students to know and be able to do at the end of this lesson? How does this contribute to course objectives and to students' needs to become capable individuals?**

Meaningful information tends to be remembered best. Review your goals and objectives to ensure that you plan for meaningful learning. For example, if you are teaching about the human body, you might make sure to focus on functions and connections among organs, not only identification. If you are teaching about parts of speech, you might ask students to generate their own examples of sentences using adjectives or adverbs, not only locate adjectives and adverbs in sentences you create.

 2. **What knowledge, skills, needs, and interests do my students have that must be taken into account in my lesson?**

The more students know about a subject, the better they can organize and relate new information. Find out what your students already know about the topics you study.

In your history class, you might begin a unit on the Vietnam War by spending a period charting what students already know about the war. Recognizing that emotion and personal meaning and relevance can help students process information deeply so that they can remember better, you might invite them to share personal stories of family members who might have participated in that combat.

For your science unit on sea life, you might determine in the initial class session that your students are fascinated by whales. You might discuss with them how scientists differentiate among species of whales and help them generate a list of characteristics common to all whales that vary according to the species. You could guide their selection of categories to ensure that they list relevant characteristics and give them a reading passage from the text as homework, asking them to write down the questions that come to their minds as they read for discussion in the next session.

 3. **What do I know about the content, child development, learning, motivation, and effective teaching strategies that I can use to accomplish my objectives?**

To make information meaningful and memorable, you should engage students in using new knowledge and skills to create their own new products. In teaching a foreign language, for instance, you might have students make up their own sentences and dialogues using new vocabulary or verb forms. For example, you might ask students in teams to make up gossip

Graphs, charts, tables, matrices, and other means of organizing information into a comprehensible, visual form, have all been found to aid comprehension, memory, and transfer (Carney & Levin, 2002; Mayer, 2008a,b). However, these devices lose their effectiveness if they contain too much information that is not quickly communicated by the visuals (Butcher, 2006; Schnotz, 2002; Vekiri, 2002). Atkinson et al. (1999) described a method to confront this problem by combining mnemonics with tables. To teach about the characteristics of various sharks, teachers made tables in which humorous pictures linked the names of the sharks with their characteristics. For example, dogfish sharks live near shore in moderate depth and have sawlike teeth, so the mnemonic showed dogs emerging from a submarine in shallow water holding saws to cut down a "No Dogs Allowed" sign on shore. Fifth-graders retained much more about the characteristics of nine sharks using this method than did students who saw other kinds of displays.

Chapter 6 Summary

What Is an Information-Processing Model?

The three major components of memory are the sensory register, short-term or working memory, and long-term memory. The sensory registers are very short-term memories

 INTASC **8** Assessment of Student Learning
9 Professional Commitment and Responsibility

about a boy, a girl, a couple, a group of girls, and a school principal, enabling them to use different pronouns, verbs, and adjectives in realistic contexts.

 4. What instructional materials, technology, assistance, and other resources are available to help accomplish my objectives?

Schema theory suggests that new information is added to existing networks of connected ideas. With the computer lab teacher, you might explore software for diagramming information and for building databases. You could plan to demonstrate the use of these programs and then provide follow-up lab time or classroom opportunities for the students to use these tools to develop materials for their portfolios in appropriate content areas. Many current software programs allow inclusion of visual as well as verbal material, addressing more than one form of information processing and encouraging students to think about and monitor their learning of the material being manipulated.

 5. How will I plan to assess students' progress toward my objectives?

Students need to demonstrate different kinds of understanding: rote learning, meaningful learning, and the ability to use information in new contexts. Give them tasks that allow you to check for different uses of knowledge: Are they forgetting? Are they transferring? Are they applying? Adjust your

instruction based on your results. For example, as the teacher of an advanced foreign language class, you could assess students' recall of vocabulary terms, their ability to describe rules and structures of the language, and their ability to communicate in the language you are teaching. You might find that students have good recall of vocabulary but struggle with expressing their own thoughts, so you could plan opportunities for them to speak in simulated realistic contexts, such as a party, a restaurant, an airport, or a picnic.

6. How will I respond if individual children or the class as a whole are not on track toward success? What is my back-up plan?

Students demonstrate success when they show they can control their own learning. Check to see that students use self-questioning strategies and metacognition to assess their own learning. For example, before you hand your fourth-graders a reading passage on reptiles, you might prompt them to ask themselves questions as they read and suggest they record their findings. After they complete the passage, you could ask them which sections of text were difficult and what they do when they encounter difficult text. Their answers tell you how far they have progressed toward actively monitoring their own learning.

linked to the senses. Information received by the senses but not attended to will be quickly forgotten. Once information is received, it is processed by the mind in accord with our experiences and mental states. This activity is called *perception*.

Short-term or working memory is a storage system that holds five to nine bits of information at any one time. Information enters working memory from both the sensory register and the long-term memory. Rehearsal is the process of repeating information in order to hold it in working memory.

Long-term memory is the part of the memory system in which a large amount of information is stored for an indefinite time period. Cognitive theories of learning stress the importance of helping students relate information being learned to existing information in long-term memory.

The three parts of long-term memory are episodic memory, which stores our memories of personal experiences; semantic memory, which stores facts and generalized knowledge in the form of schemata; and procedural memory, which stores knowledge of how to do things. Schemata are networks of related ideas that guide our understanding and action. Information that fits into a well-developed schema is easier to learn than information that cannot be so accommodated. Levels-of-processing theory suggests that learners will remember only what they process. Students are processing information when they manipulate it, look at it from different perspectives, and analyze it. Dual code theory further suggests the importance of using both visual and verbal coding to learn bits of information.

What Is Learned from Research on the Brain ?

Technology that enables scientists to observe the brain in action has led to rapid advances in brain science. Findings have shown how specific parts of the brain process specific types of information in concert with other specific brain sites. As individuals gain expertise, their brain function becomes more efficient. Early brain development is a process of adding neural connections and then sloughing off those that are not used. Neuroscience is discovering much about how the brain operates, but this research does not yet have direct applications to teaching.

What Causes People to Remember or Forget ?

Interference theory helps explain why people forget. It suggests that students can forget information when it gets mixed up with, or pushed aside by, other information. Interference theory states that two situations cause forgetting: retroactive inhibition, when learning a second task makes a person forget something that was learned previously, and proactive inhibition, when learning one thing interferes with the retention of things learned later. The primacy and recency effects state that people best remember information that is presented first and last in a series. Automaticity is gained by practicing information or skills far beyond the amount needed to establish them in long-term memory so that using such skills requires little or no mental effort. Practice strengthens associations of newly learned information in memory. Distributed practice, which involves practicing parts of a task over a period of time, is usually more effective than massed practice. Enactment also helps students to remember information.

How Can Memory Strategies Be Taught ?

Teachers can help students remember facts by presenting lessons in an organized way and by teaching students to use memory strategies called *mnemonics*. Three types of verbal learning are paired-associate learning, serial learning, and free-recall learning. Paired-associate learning is learning to respond with one member of a pair when given the other member. Students can improve their learning of paired associates by using imagery techniques such as the keyword method. Serial learning involves recalling a list of items in a specified order. Free-recall learning involves recalling a list in any order. Helpful strategies are the loci method, the pegword method, rhyming, and initial-letter strategies.

What Makes Information Meaningful ?

Information that makes sense and has significance to students is more meaningful than inert knowledge and information learned by rote. According to schema theory, individuals' meaningful knowledge is constructed of networks and hierarchies of schemata.

How Do Metacognitive Skills Help Students Learn ?

Metacognition helps students learn by thinking about, controlling, and effectively using their own thinking processes.

What Study Strategies Help Students Learn ?

Note-taking, selective directed underlining, summarizing, writing to learn, outlining, and mapping can effectively promote learning. The PQ4R method is an example of a strategy that focuses on the meaningful organization of information.

How Do Cognitive Teaching Strategies Help Students Learn ?

Advance organizers help students process new information by activating background knowledge. Analogies, information elaboration, organizational schemes, questioning techniques, and conceptual models are other examples of teaching strategies that are based on cognitive learning theories.

Key Terms

Review the following key terms from the chapter.

advance organizers   173
analogies   174
attention   146
automaticity   161
concept mapping   170
distributed practice   162
dual code theory of memory   153
elaboration   174
enactment   162
episodic memory   149
flashbulb memory   150
free-recall learning   163
imagery   163
inert knowledge   166
information-processing theory   144
initial-letter strategies   165
interference   158
keyword method   164
levels-of-processing theory   153
loci method   165
long-term memory   149

massed practice   162
meaningful learning   166
metacognition   168
metacognitive skills   168
mnemonics   164
note-taking   169
outlining   170
paired-associate learning   163
pegword method   165
perception   145
PQ4R method   171
primacy effect   160
proactive facilitation   160
proactive inhibition   160
procedural memory   149
recency effect   160
rehearsal   147
retroactive facilitation   160
retroactive inhibition   158
rote learning   166
schemata   150

Self-Assessment: Practicing for Licensure

Directions: The chapter-opening vignette addresses indicators that are often assessed in state licensure exams. Re-read the chapter-opening vignette, and then respond to the following questions.

1. According to information-processing theory, which component of the memory system did Verona Bishop's students first use during the 3-second experiment?

   a. Sensory register

   b. Short-term memory

   c. Working memory

   d. Long-term memory

2. Verona Bishop asks her students to "imagine that you could keep everything that ever entered your mind. What would that be like?" One student responds, "You'd be a genius!" Another responds, "You'd go crazy!" Why does Ms. Bishop side with the second student?

   a. Genius is an inherited trait not associated with memory.

   b. There is no correlation between genius and paying attention to environmental clues.

   c. Being bombarded with too much information at once decreases learning.

   d. People with mental illness absorb more environmental information than do people without mental illness.

3. During the 3-second memory experiment, Verona Bishop asks her students to recall information not associated with the overhead information she presented. What type of memory are students using when they recall smells, sounds, and details of the classroom and the people in it?

   a. Semantic memory

   b. Procedural memory

   c. Dual code memory

   d. Episodic memory

4. Cheryl, one of Verona Bishop's students, recalled seeing the word *learning* on the overhead screen, even though it was not there. How does Ms. Bishop explain this phenomenon?

   a. Ms. Bishop actually said the word during the 3-second experiment, so Cheryl picked it up there.

   b. Humans have a tendency to learn the first and last bits of information presented, so Cheryl thought of the word *learning* after the 3-second experiment.

   c. *Learning* and *memory,* a word that was actually presented, are closely related and most likely stored closely together in memory. When one is recalled, so is the other.

   d. Because the students had only 3 seconds to review the information, Cheryl's report of what she remembered contained guesses.

5. Consider that some of Verona Bishop's students attempted to memorize the information on the overhead screen in a random fashion. Which of the following learning strategies were they using?

   a. Free-recall learning

   b. Serial learning

   c. Paired-associate learning

   d. Process learning

6. Verona Bishop summarizes her experiment by telling her students that they will forget some details of the experiment but remember others. Why is this so?

   a. According to levels-of-processing theory, we tend to retain information that has been subject to thorough processing. If the students gave meaning to the information, it is likely to be remembered.

b. According to dual code theory, visual information is more likely to be retained than verbal information. If the students saw the information, it is more likely to be remembered than if they heard it.

7. Describe several memory strategies that you can teach your students to help them remember the facts, concepts, and ideas presented in a lesson.

PEARSON
myeducationlab

Go to the Topic **Cognition and Memory** in the MyEducationLab (www.myeducationlab.com) for your course, where you can:

- Find learning outcomes for **Cognition and Memory** along with the national standards that connect to these outcomes.

- Complete Assignments and Activities that can help you more deeply understand the chapter content.

- Apply and practice your understanding of the core teaching skills identified in the chapter with the Building Teaching Skills and Dispositions learning units.

- Access video clips of CCSSO National Teachers of the Year award winners responding to the question "Why Do I Teach?" in the Teacher Talk section.

- Check your comprehension of the content covered in the chapter by going to the Study Plan in the Book Resources for your text. Here you will be able to take a chapter quiz; receive feedback on your answers; and then access Review, Practice, and Enrichment activities to enhance your understanding of chapter content.

- Watch author Bob Slavin present a Personal Reflections podcast on *Defining Effective* in the Book Resources for your text. Then, respond to the reflection questions that follow.

Defining **Effective**

YOUR REFLECTIONS Make a case for why the Chinese method for processing information might be effective. In studying for your classes, do you memorize or do you learn? What have you found to be the best way for you to learn new information and retain it?

7

The Effective Lesson

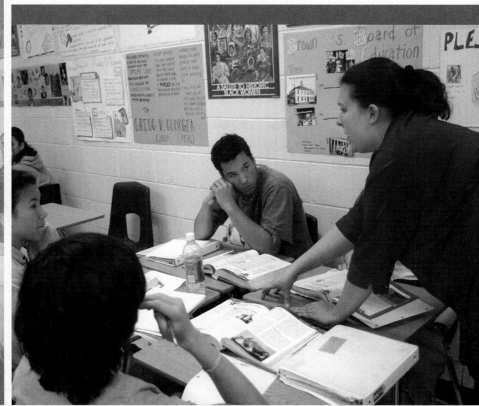

Billy E. Barnes/PhotoEdit

Learning Outcomes

At the end of this chapter, you should be able to:

- Define direct instruction and when it is appropriate to use
- Describe how a direct instruction lesson is taught
- Discuss what research on direct instruction suggests for classroom practice
- Describe how to best teach for transfer of learning
- Identify instructional situations in which discussion is most useful

Billy E. Barnes/PhotoEdit

Jennifer Logan's eighth-grade physical science class is a happy mess. Students are working in small groups at lab stations, filling all sorts of bottles with water and then tapping them to see how various factors affect the sound. One group has set up a line of identical bottles and put different amounts of water in each one so that tapping the bottles in sequence makes a crude musical scale. "The amount of water in the bottle is all that matters," one group member tells Ms. Logan, and her groupmates nod in agreement. Another group has an odd assortment of bottles and has carefully measured the same amount of water into each. "It's the shape and thickness of the bottles that make the difference," says one group member. Other groups are working more chaotically, filling and tapping large and small, narrow and wide, and thick and thin bottles with different amounts of water. Their theories are wild and varied.

After a half hour of experimentation, Ms. Logan calls the class together and asks group members to describe what they did and what they concluded. Students loudly uphold their group's point of view. "It's the amount of water!" "It's the height of the bottles!" "It's the thickness of the bottles!" "No, it's their shape!" "It's how hard you tap the bottles!" Ms. Logan moderates the conversation but lets students confront each other's ideas and give their own arguments.

The next day, Ms. Logan teaches a lesson on sound. She explains how sound causes waves in the air and how the waves cause the eardrum to vibrate, transmitting sound information to the brain. She has two students come to the front of the class with a Slinky and uses the Slinky to illustrate how sound waves travel. She asks many questions of students, both to see whether they understand and to get them to take the next mental step. She then explains how sound waves in a tube become lower in pitch the longer the tube is. To illustrate this,

she plays a flute and a piccolo. Light bulbs are starting to click on in the students' minds, and Ms. Logan can tell from the responses to her questions that the students are starting to get the idea. At the end of the period, Ms. Logan lets the students get back into their groups to discuss what they have learned and to try to apply their new knowledge to the bottle problem.

When the students come into class on the third day of the sound lesson, they are buzzing with excitement. They rush to their lab stations and start filling and tapping bottles to test out the theories they came up with the day before. Ms. Logan walks among the groups, listening in on their conversations. "It's not the amount of water, it's the amount of air," she hears one student say. "It's not the bottle; it's the air," says a student in another group. She helps one group that is still floundering to get on track. Finally, Ms. Logan calls the class together to discuss their findings and conclusions. Representatives of some of the groups demonstrate the experiments they used to show how it was the amount of air in each bottle that determined the sound.

"How could we make one elegant demonstration to show that it's only the amount of air that controls the sound?" asks Ms. Logan.

The students buzz among themselves and then assemble all their bottles into one experiment. They make one line of identical bottles with different amounts of water. Then to demonstrate that it is the air, not the water, that matters, they put the same amount of water in bottles of different sizes. Sure enough, in each case, the more air space left in the bottle, the lower the sound.

Ms. Logan ends the period with a homework assignment: to read a chapter on sound in a textbook. She tells the students that they will have an opportunity to work in their groups to make certain that every group member understands everything in the sound lesson, and then there will be a quiz in which students will have to show individually that they can apply their new knowledge. She reminds them that their groups can be "super-teams" only if everyone knows the material.

The bell rings, and the students pour into the hallway, still talking excitedly about what they have learned. Some groupmates promise to call each other that evening to prepare for the group study the next day. Ms. Logan watches them file out. She's exhausted, but she knows that this group of students will never forget the lessons they've learned about sound, about experiments, and, most important, about their ability to use their minds to figure out difficult concepts.

The lesson is where education takes place. All other aspects of schooling, from buildings to buses to administration, are designed to support teachers in delivering effective lessons; they do not educate in and of themselves. If you are like most teachers, you will spend most of your class time teaching lessons. The typical elementary or secondary school teacher may teach 800 to 1,000 class lessons each year!

Conducting effective lessons is at the heart of the teacher's craft. Some aspects of lesson presentation have to be learned on the job; good teachers get better at it every year. Yet educational psychologists have studied the elements that go into effective lessons, learning a great deal that is useful in day-to-day teaching at every grade level and in every subject (Arends, 2004; Good & Brophy, 2008; Marzano, Pickering, & Pollock, 2001; Rosenshine, 2008; Schmoker, 2006). This chapter and the four that follow it present the principal findings of this research and translate them into ways of thinking about the practical demands of everyday teaching.

As Ms. Logan's lesson illustrates, effective lessons use many teaching methods. In four periods on one topic, she used direct instruction as well as discussion, cooperative learning, and other constructivist techniques. These methods are often posed as different philosophies, and the ideological wars over which is best go on incessantly (see Joyce, Weil, & Calhoun, 2004; Kirschner, Sweller, & Clark, 2006; Pressley et al., 2003). Yet few experienced teachers would deny that teachers must be able to use all of them as well as know when each is appropriate.

This chapter focuses on the strategies that teachers apply to transmit information in ways that are most likely to help students understand, incorporate, and use new concepts and skills. Chapter 8 focuses on student-centered methods, in which students play an active role in structuring learning for themselves and for each other. However, the teaching strategies presented in these two chapters should be seen not as representing two sharply conflicting philosophies of education, but as complementary approaches to be used at different times for different purposes.

What Is Direct Instruction

At times, the most effective and efficient way to teach students is for you to present information, skills, or concepts in a direct fashion (Bligh, 2000; Good & Brophy, 2008; Gunter et al., 2003; Hollingsworth & Ybarra, 2009; Kirschner et al., 2006; Rosenshine, 2008). The term **direct instruction** is used to describe lessons in which you transmit information

direct instruction

Approach to teaching in which the teacher transmits information directly to the students; lessons are goal oriented and structured by the teacher.

184

directly to students, structuring class time to reach a clearly defined set of objectives as efficiently as possible. Direct instruction is particularly appropriate for teaching a well-defined body of information or skills that all students must master (Gunter et al., 2003). It is held to be less appropriate when deep conceptual change is an objective or when exploration, discovery, and open-ended objectives are the objects of instruction. However, recent research has supported the idea that direct instruction can be more efficient than discovery in conceptual development as well. Klahr and Nigam (2004) compared third-graders directly taught to do experiments that isolate the effects of one variable to those who carried out their own experiments without direct instruction. Those who received direct instruction performed much better in setting up new experiments.

A great deal of research was done in the 1970s and 1980s to discover the elements of effective direct instruction lessons. Although different authors describe these elements differently (see Evertson & Poole, 2008; Good & Brophy, 2008; Hunter, 1995; Rosenshine, 2008), researchers and teachers generally agree as to the sequence of events that characterize effective direct instruction lessons. First, you bring students up to date on any skills they might need for the lesson (e.g., you might briefly review yesterday's lesson if today's is a continuation) and tell students what they are going to learn. Then you devote most of the lesson time to teaching the skills or information, giving students opportunities to practice the skills or express the information, and questioning or quizzing students to determine whether they are learning the objectives.

A brief description of the parts of a direct instruction lesson follows. The next section of this chapter will cover each part in detail.

1. ***State learning objectives and orient students to the lesson.***   Tell students what they will be learning and what performance will be expected of them. Whet students' appetites for the lesson by informing them how interesting, important, or personally relevant it will be to them.

2. ***Review prerequisites.***   Go over any skills or concepts students need in order to understand the lesson.

3. ***Present new material.***   Teach the lesson, presenting information, giving examples, demonstrating concepts, and so on.

4. ***Conduct learning probes.***   Pose questions to students to assess their level of understanding and correct their misconceptions.

5. ***Provide independent practice.***   Give students an opportunity to practice new skills or use new information on their own.

6. ***Assess performance and provide feedback.***   Review independent practice work or give a quiz. Give feedback on correct answers, and reteach skills if necessary.

7. ***Provide distributed practice and review.***   Assign homework to provide distributed practice on the new material. In later lessons, review material and provide practice opportunities to increase the chances that students will remember what they learned and also be able to apply it in different circumstances.

How Is a Direct Instruction Lesson Taught?

The general lesson structure takes vastly different forms in different subject areas and at different grade levels. Teachers of older students may take several days for each step of the process, ending with a formal test or quiz. Teachers of younger students may go through the entire cycle in a class period, using informal assessments at the end. Tables 7.1 and 7.2 present two quite different lessons to illustrate how direct instruction would be applied to

INTASC

6 Communication Skills

TABLE 7.1	**Sample Lesson for Basic Math: Subtraction with Renaming**
Lesson Part	**Teacher Presentation**
1. State learning objective and orient students to lesson.	"There are 32 students in this class. Let's say we were going to have a party, and I was going to get one cupcake for each student in the class. But 5 of you said you didn't like cupcakes. How many cupcakes would I need to get for the students who do like cupcakes? Let's set up the problem on the chalkboard the way we have before, and mark the tens and ones . . ." <table><tr><td>tens</td><td>ones</td><td></td></tr><tr><td>3</td><td>2</td><td>Students</td></tr><tr><td>−</td><td>5</td><td>Don't like cupcakes</td></tr></table> "All right, let's subtract: 2 take away 5 is . . . *hey!* We can't do that! Five is more than 2, so how can we take 5 away from 2? We can't! "In this lesson we are going to learn how to subtract when we don't have enough ones. By the end of this lesson, you will be able to show how to rename tens as ones so that you can subtract."
2. Review prerequisites.	"Let's review subtraction when we have enough ones." Put on the chalkboard and have students solve: <table><tr><td>47</td><td>56</td><td>89</td></tr><tr><td>− 3</td><td>− 23</td><td>− 8</td></tr></table> How many tens are in 23? ____ How many ones are in 30? ____ Give answers, discuss all items missed by many students.
3A. Present new material (first subskill).	Have table monitors help hand out five bundles of 10 popsicle sticks each and 10 individual sticks to each student. Using an overhead projector, explain how to use sticks to show 13, 27, and 30. Have students show each number at their own desks. Walk around to check.
4A. Conduct learning probes (first subskill).	Have students show 23 using their sticks. Check desks. Then have students show 40. Check desks. Continue until all students have the idea.
3B. Present new material (second subskill).	Using an overhead projector, explain how to use sticks to show 6 minus 2 and 8 minus 5. Then show 13 and try to take away 5. Ask for suggestions on how this could be done. Show that by removing the rubber band from the tens bundle, we have a total of 13 ones and can remove 5. Have students show this at their desks. Walk around to check.
4B. Conduct learning probes (second subskill).	Have students show 12 (check) and then take away 4 by breaking apart the ten bundle. Then have students show 17 and take away 9. Continue until all students have the idea.
3C. Present new material (third subskill).	Give students worksheets showing tens bundles and single units. Explain how to show renaming by crossing out a bundle of ten and rewriting it as 10 units and then subtracting by crossing out units.
4C. Conduct learning probes (third subskill).	Have students do the first items on the worksheet one at a time until all students have the idea.
5. Provide independent practice.	Have students continue, completing the worksheet on their own.
6. Assess performance and provide feedback.	Show correct answers to worksheet items on overhead projector. Have students mark their own papers. Ask how many got item 1, item 2, and so on, and discuss all items missed by more than a few students. Have students hand in papers.
7. Provide distributed practice and review.	Hand out homework, and explain how it is to be done. Review lesson content at start of following lesson and in later lessons.

TABLE 7.2	Sample Lesson for History: The Origins of World War II
Lesson Part	**Teacher Presentation**
1. State learning objective and orient students to lesson.	"Today we will begin to discuss the origins and causes of World War II—perhaps the most important event in the 20th century. The political situation of the world today—the map of Europe, the political predominance of the United States, the problems of the Eastern European countries formerly under Soviet domination, even the problems of the Middle East—all can be traced to the rise of Hitler and the bloody struggle that followed. I'm sure many of you have relatives who fought in the war or whose lives were deeply affected by it. Raise your hand if a relative or someone you know well fought in World War II." ■ "Germany today is peaceful and prosperous. How could a man like Hitler have come to power? To understand this, we must first understand what Germany was like in the years following its defeat in World War I and why an unemployed Austrian painter could come to lead one of the largest countries in Europe." ■ "By the end of this lesson you will understand the conditions in Germany that led up to the rise of Hitler, the reasons he was successful, and the major events of his rise to power."
2. Review prerequisites.	Have students recall from the previous lesson: ■ The humiliating provisions of the Treaty of Versailles —Reparations —Demilitarization of the Ruhr —Loss of territory and colonies ■ The lack of experience with democracy in Germany
3. Present new material.	Discuss with students: ■ Conditions in Germany before the rise of Hitler —Failure of the Weimar Republic —Economic problems, inflation, and severe impact of the U.S. Depression —Belief that Germany lost World War I because of betrayal by politicians —Fear of Communism ■ Events in Hitler's rise to power —Organization of National Socialist (Nazi) Party —Beer-Hall Putsch and Hitler's imprisonment —*Mein Kampf* —Organization of Brown Shirts (S.A.) —Election and appointment as chancellor
4. Conduct learning probes.	Questions to students throughout lesson should assess student comprehension of the main points.
5. Provide independent practice.	Have students independently write three reasons why the situation in Germany in the 1920s and early 1930s might have been favorable to Hitler's rise, and have students be prepared to defend their answers.
6. Assess performance and provide feedback.	Call on randomly selected students to read and justify their reasons for Hitler's success. Discuss well-justified and poorly justified reasons. Have students hand in papers.
7. Provide distributed practice and review.	Review lesson content at start of next lesson and in later lessons.

different subjects and grade levels. The first lesson, "Subtraction with Renaming," is an example of the first of a series of lessons directed at a basic math skill. In contrast, the second lesson, "The Origins of World War II," is an example of a lesson directed at higher-order understanding of critical events in history and their causes and interrelationships. Note that the first lesson (Table 7.1) proceeds step by step and emphasizes frequent learning probes and independent practice to help students thoroughly learn the concepts being taught, whereas the second lesson (Table 7.2) is characterized by an alternation between new information, discussion, and questions to assess comprehension of major concepts.

Connections

For in-depth coverage of instructional objectives, writing lesson plans, and using taxonomies, see Chapter 13, pages 398–407.

✓ **Certification Pointer**

For teacher certification tests, you may be asked to suggest techniques for building bridges between curriculum objectives and students' experiences.

The sequence of activities outlined in these two lessons flows along a logical path, from arousing student interest to presenting new information to allowing students to practice their new knowledge or skills to assessment. This orderly progression is essential to direct instruction lessons at any grade level and in any subject, although the various components and how they are implemented would, of course, look different for different subjects and grades.

■ State Learning Objectives

The first step in presenting a lesson is planning it in such a way that the reasons for teaching and learning the lesson are clear. What do you want students to know or be able to do at the end of the lesson? Setting out objectives at the beginning of the lesson is an essential step in providing a framework into which information, instructional materials, and learning activities will fit (Gronlund & Brookhart, 2009).

🖱 **ON THE WEB**

For tips on writing quality learning objectives, visit http://park.edu/cetl/quicktips/ writinglearningobj.html.

Theory into Practice
Planning a Lesson

The first step of a lesson, stating learning objectives or outcomes, represents a condensation of much advance **lesson planning** (see Burden & Byrd, 2010; Dick, Carey, & Carey, 2009; Karges-Bone, 2000). As a teacher planning a lesson, you will need, at the least, to answer the following questions:

1. What will students know or be able to do after the lesson? What will be the outcomes of their learning? How will you know when and how well students have achieved these learning outcomes or objectives?

2. What prerequisite skills are needed to learn this content? How will you make sure students have these skills?

3. What information, activities, and experiences will you provide to help students acquire the knowledge and skills they need in order to attain the learning outcomes? How much time will be needed? How will you use in-class and out-of-class time? How will seatwork and homework assignments help students achieve the learning objectives?

4. How will you arouse students' interest in the content? How will you motivate them to learn? How will you give them feedback on their learning?

5. What books and materials will you use to present the lesson? When will you preview or test all the materials and create guidelines for students' responses to them? Are all materials accurate, pedagogically sound, fair to different cultures, and appropriate in content and grade level?

6. What methods of teaching will you incorporate? For example, will you use reading, lecture, role playing, video viewing, demonstration, or writing assignments?

7. What participation structures will you use: whole-group or small-group discussions, cooperative learning groups, ability groups, or individual assign-

lesson planning

Procedure that includes stating learning objectives such as what the students should know or be able to do after the lesson; what information, activities, and experiences the teacher will provide; how much time will be needed to reach the objective; what books, materials, and media support the teacher will provide; and what instructional method(s) and participation structures will be used.

ments? What learning tasks will groups and individuals perform? How will you organize, monitor, and evaluate groups?

■ Orient Students to the Lesson

At the beginning of a lesson, you need to establish a positive **mental set,** or attitude of readiness, in students: "I'm ready to get down to work. I'm eager to learn the important information or skills the teacher is about to present, and I have a rough idea of what we will be learning." This mental set can be established in many ways. First, you should require students to be on time to class and should start the lesson immediately when the period begins (Emmer & Evertson, 2009; Evertson, Emmer, & Worsham, 2009). This establishes a sense of seriousness of purpose that is lost in a ragged start. Second, you need to arouse students' curiosity or interest in the lesson they are about to learn. The teacher in the first sample lesson (Table 7.1) does this by introducing subtraction with renaming as a skill that would be necessary in connection with counting cupcakes for a class party, a situation of some reality and interest to young students. In the second sample lesson (Table 7.2), the teacher advertises the importance of the lesson on the basis that understanding the origins and events of World War II will help students understand events today and makes the lesson personally relevant to students by having them think of a relative who either fought in World War II or was deeply affected by it. In the chapter-opening vignette, Ms. Logan whets students' curiosity about sound by giving them an opportunity to experiment with it before the formal lesson.

"Dang. I'm not even ready for fifth period!"

A lesson on genetics might be introduced as follows:

> Did you ever wonder why tall parents have taller-than-average children and red-haired children usually have at least one red-haired parent? Think of your own family. If your father and mother are both taller than average, then you will probably be taller than average. Well, today we are going to have a lesson on the science called genetics, in which we will learn how characteristics of parents are passed on to their children.

This introduction might be used to grab students' interest because it makes the subject personally relevant.

Humor or drama can also establish a positive mental set. An English teacher may use a top hat and a wand to capture student interest by "magically" transforming adjectives into adverbs (e.g., *sad* into *sadly*). Popular and instructionally effective children's television programs, such as "Sesame Street" and "Between the Lions," use this kind of device constantly to get young children's attention and hold their interest in basic skills. Finally, in starting a lesson, you must give students a road map of where the lesson is going and what they will know at the end. Stating lesson objectives clearly has generally been found to enhance student achievement of those objectives (Gronlund & Brookhart, 2009). Giving students an outline of the lesson in advance may also help them to incorporate new information (Bligh, 2000).

Theory into Practice
Communicating Objectives to Students

Teacher education programs include training in creating lesson plans, beginning with a consideration of instructional objectives and learning outcomes.

mental set

Students' attitude of readiness to begin a lesson.

Sharing lesson plans with students is a good idea, because research suggests that knowledge of objectives can lead to improvements in student achievement. Use the following practical suggestions for sharing lesson objectives with your students.

1. The objectives you communicate to students should be broad enough to encompass everything the lesson will teach. Research suggests that giving students too narrow a set of objectives may lead them to devalue or ignore other meaningful aspects of a lesson. In addition, broad objectives provide greater flexibility for adapting instruction as needed once the lesson is underway.

2. The objectives you communicate should be specific enough in content to make clear to students what the outcomes of their learning will be—what they will know and be able to do and how they will use their new knowledge and skills.

3. Consider stating objectives both orally and in writing and repeating them during the lesson to remind students why they are learning. Teachers often use verbal and written outlines or summaries of objectives. Providing demonstrations or models of learning products or outcomes is also effective. For example, an art teacher might show a student's drawing that demonstrates use of perspective to illustrate what students will be able to produce themselves, or a math teacher might show a math problem that students could not do at the beginning of a series of lessons but will be able to do at the end.

4. Consider using questioning techniques to elicit from students their own statements of objectives or outcomes. Their input will likely both reflect and inform your lesson plan. Some teachers ask students to express their ideas for meeting objectives or demonstrating outcomes, because research suggests that students who have a stake in the lesson plan and a sense of control over their learning will be more motivated to learn.

■ Review Prerequisites

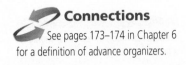

Connections

For more about the importance of activating students' prior knowledge, see Chapter 6, page 172.

For the next major task in a lesson, you need to ensure that students have mastered prerequisite skills and to link information that is already in their minds to the information you are about to present. If today's lesson is a continuation of yesterday's and you are reasonably sure that students understood yesterday's lesson, then the review might simply remind them about the earlier lesson and ask a few quick questions before beginning the new one. For instance, you might say, "Yesterday we learned how to add the suffix *-ed* to a word ending in *y*. Who will tell us how this is done?"

As today's lesson—adding other suffixes to words ending in *y*—is a direct continuation of yesterday's, this brief reminder is adequate. However, if you are introducing a new skill or concept that depends on skills learned much earlier, then more elaborate discussion and assessment of prerequisite skills may be needed.

Sometimes you need to assess students on prerequisite skills before starting a lesson. In the first sample lesson (Table 7.1), the teacher briefly quizzes students on subtraction without renaming and numeration skills in preparation for a lesson on subtraction with renaming. If students show poor understanding of either prerequisite skill, the teacher will review those skills before going on to the new lesson.

Connections

See pages 173–174 in Chapter 6 for a definition of advance organizers.

Another reason you should review prerequisites is to provide advance organizers. As defined in Chapter 6, advance organizers are introductory statements by the teacher that remind students of what they already know and give them a framework for understanding the new material to be presented. In the second sample lesson (Table 7.2), the teacher sets the stage for the new content (Hitler's rise to power) by reviewing the economic, political, and social conditions in Germany that made Hitler's success possible.

■ Present New Material

Here begins the main body of the lesson, the point at which you present new information or skills.

Connections

See page 173 in Chapter 6 for a discussion of retention of well-organized information.

LESSON STRUCTURE   Lessons should be logically organized. Recall from Chapter 6 that information that has a clear, well-organized structure is retained better than less clearly presented information (Fuchs et al., 1997). A lesson on the legislative branch of the U.S. government might be presented as follows:

The Legislative Branch of the Federal Government (First Lesson)

I. Functions and nature of the legislative branch (Congress)

A. Passes laws

B. Approves money for executive branch

C. Has 2 houses—House of Representatives and Senate

II. House of Representatives

A. Designed to be closest to the people—representatives elected to 2-year terms—proportional representation

B. Responsible for originating money bills

III. Senate

A. Designed to give greater continuity to legislative branch—senators elected to 6-year terms—each state has two senators

B. Approves appointments and treaties made by executive branch

This would be a beginning lesson; subsequent lessons would discuss how laws are introduced and passed, checks and balances on legislative power, and so on. The lesson has a clear organization that you should point out to students. For example, you might pause at the beginning of the second topic and say, "Now we are going to learn about the lower house of Congress, the House of Representatives." This helps students form a mental outline that will help them remember the material. Research finds that a clearly laid out structure and transitional statements about the structure of the lesson increase student understanding (Lorch, Lorch, & Inman, 1993).

LESSON EMPHASIS   In addition to making clear the organization of a lesson by noting when the next subtopic is being introduced, instructionally effective teachers give clear indications about the most important elements of the lesson by saying, for example, "It is particularly important to note that . . ." (Alexander & Jetton, 1996). Repeat important points and bring them back into the lesson whenever appropriate. For example, in teaching about the presidential veto in the lesson on the legislative branch of government, you might say:

Here again, we see the operation of the system of checks and balances we discussed earlier. The executive can veto legislation passed by the Congress, which in turn can withhold funds for actions of the executive. Remember, understanding how this system of checks and balances works is critical to an understanding of how the U.S. government works.

In this way, you emphasize one of the central concepts of the U.S. government—the system of checks and balances among the executive, legislative, and judicial branches—by bringing it up whenever possible and by labeling it as important.

LESSON CLARITY One consistent feature of effective lessons is clarity—the use of direct, simple, and well-organized language to present concepts (Land, 1987; McCaleb & White, 1980; Smith & Land, 1981). Wandering off into digressions or irrelevant topics or otherwise interrupting the flow of the lesson detracts from clarity. Clear presentations avoid the use of vague terms that do not add to the meaning of the lesson, such as the italicized words in the following sentence (from Smith & Land, 1981): "*Maybe* before we get to *probably* the main idea of the lesson, you should review a few prerequisite concepts."

EXPLANATIONS Effective explanations are at the core of effective teaching (Wragg & Brown, 2001). A recent review of research on explanations by Wittwer and Renkl (2008) concluded that effective explanations take into account and link to what students already know (Bolhuis, 2003; Leinhardt & Steele, 2005) and emphasize concepts and principles rather than just facts and skills. Effective explanations make use of strategies that help students visualize and organize complex ideas, such as embedded multimedia (Mayer, 2008a,b, 2009), and they give students opportunities to discuss their current understandings with peers in cooperative learning groups (Webb & Mastergeorge, 2003).

Research finds that effective teachers also use many explanations and explanatory words (such as *because, in order to,* and *consequently*) and frequently use a pattern of **rule–example–rule** when presenting new concepts (Van Patten, Chao, & Reigeluth, 1986), as in the following example.

> Matter may change forms, but it is never destroyed. If I were to burn a piece of paper, it would appear that the paper was gone, but in fact it would have been combined with oxygen atoms from the air and changed to a gas (mostly carbon dioxide) and ash. If I could count the atoms in the paper plus the atoms from the air before and after I burned the paper, we could see that the matter involved did not disappear, but merely changed forms.

Note that the teacher stated the rule ("Matter . . . is never destroyed"), gave an example, and restated the rule in the explanation of how the example illustrates the rule. Also note that a rule–example–rule sequence was used here to illustrate the rule–example–rule pattern!

WORKED EXAMPLES Worked examples are an established strategy for teaching certain kinds of problem solving, especially in mathematics (Atkinson, Derry, Renkl, & Wortham, 2000). For example, you might pose a problem and then work it out on a chalkboard or overhead, explaining your thinking at each step. In this way, you model the strategies an expert would use to solve the problem so that students can use similar strategies on their own. Research on worked examples generally finds that they are effective if they alternate with problems students do on their own (e.g., one worked example followed by several problems of the same type) (Atkinson et al., 2000; Sweller, van Merrienboer, & Paas, 1998). Teaching students to stop during worked examples to explain to themselves or to explain to a partner what is going on in each step enhances the effects of worked examples (Renkl, 2002). Worked examples are particularly effective for students who are new to a given topic or skill (Kalyuga, Chandler, Tuovinen, & Sweller, 2001).

DEMONSTRATIONS, MODELS, AND ILLUSTRATIONS Cognitive theorists emphasize the importance of students' seeing and, when appropriate, having hands-on experience with concepts and skills. Visual representations are maintained in long-term memory far more readily than information that is only heard (Hiebert, Wearne, & Taber, 1991; Sousa, 2001). Showing, rather than simply telling, is particularly essential for children who are acquiring English (August & Shanahan, 2006b). Recall how Ms. Logan gave her students both hands-on experience (filling and tapping bottles) and a visual

rule–example–rule

Patterned teaching of concepts involving first presenting a rule or definition, then giving examples, and finally showing how examples illustrate the rule.

analogy (the Slinky representing sound waves) to give the students clear and lasting images of the main principles of sound. However, manipulatives (such as counting blocks) can be counterproductive to learning if they do not clearly relate to the concept being taught (Campbell & Mayer, 2004).

EMBEDDED VIDEO   Video, television, and DVD have long been used in education. However, a new use is showing particular promise—video or DVD material that is embedded in on-screen text or class lessons used to illustrate key concepts. Research on embedded video finds that it helps children learn and retain information to the degree that it is easy to understand and it clearly links to the main content (Mayer, 2008a, 2009). For example, two year-long studies by Chambers and colleagues (Chambers, Cheung, Madden, Slavin, & Gifford, 2006; Chambers et al., 2008) found that adding brief animations and puppet videos to illustrate letter sounds and sound blending significantly increased first-graders' progress in reading.

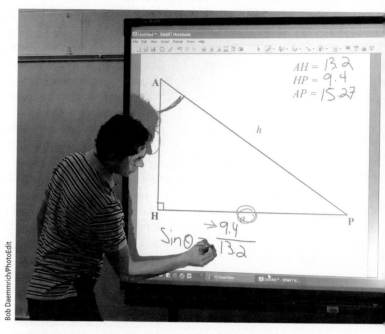

Bob Daemmrich/PhotoEdit

By working through examples with students, you can demonstrate problem solving and decision making. Why is this an important instructional strategy? Why is hands-on experience important for your students?

MAINTAINING ATTENTION   Straight, dry lectures can be boring, and bored students soon stop paying attention to even the most carefully crafted lesson. For this reason you should introduce variety, activity, or humor to enliven the lecture and maintain student attention. For example, the use of humor has been found to increase student achievement (Droz & Ellis, 1996; Ziv, 1988), and illustrating a lecture with easily understood graphics can help to hold students' attention (Mayer, 2008b). Although too much variation in mode of presentation can hurt achievement if it distracts students from the lesson content, several studies have established that students learn more from lessons that are presented with enthusiasm and expressiveness than from dry lectures (Patrick, Hisley, & Kempler, 2000). In one sense, teaching is performing, and it appears that some of the qualities we would look for in a performer are also helpful in increasing teachers' effectiveness.

Connections

For more on the importance of attention in learning, see Chapter 6, page 146.

CONTENT COVERAGE AND PACING   One of the most important factors in effective teaching is the amount of content covered. In general, students whose teachers cover more material learn more than other students do (e.g., Barr, 1987). This does not necessarily mean that you should teach faster; obviously, there is such a thing as going too fast and leaving students behind. Yet research on instructional pace does imply that most teachers could increase their pace of instruction (Good et al., 1983), as long as degree of understanding is not sacrificed. In addition to increasing content coverage, a relatively rapid pace of instruction can also help with classroom management.

Connections

For more on the impact of time on learning, see Chapter 11, page 317.

■ Conduct Learning Probes

Imagine an archer who shoots arrows at a target but never finds out how close to the bull's-eye the arrows fall. The archer wouldn't be very accurate to begin with and would certainly never improve in accuracy. Similarly, effective teaching requires you to be constantly aware of the effects of your instruction. All too often, teachers mistakenly believe that if they have covered a topic well and students appear to be paying attention, then instruction has been successful. Students often believe that if they have listened intently to an interesting lecture, they know the material presented. This might not be true. If you do not regularly probe students' understanding of the material being presented, students might be left with serious misunderstandings or gaps in knowledge (Hattie & Timperley, 2007; McMillan, 2007; Safer & Fleischman, 2005).

The term **learning probe** refers to any of a variety of ways of asking for brief student responses to lesson content. Learning probes give you feedback on students' levels of understanding and allow students to try out their understanding of a new idea to find out whether they have it right. Learning probes can take the form of questions to the class, as in the sample lesson on World War II presented in Table 7.2, or brief written or physical demonstrations of understanding, as in the sample subtraction lesson in Table 7.1.

CHECKS FOR UNDERSTANDING   Whether the response to the learning probe is written, physical, or oral, the purpose of the probe is checking for understanding (Black, Harrison, Lee, Marshall, & Wiliam, 2004; Brookhart, Moss, & Long, 2008; Fisher & Frey, 2008; Reeves, 2007; Stiggins, 2007). That is, use learning probes not so much to teach or to provide practice as to find out whether students have understood what they just heard. Use the probes to set the pace of instruction. If students are having trouble, you must slow down and provide additional explanation. If all students show understanding, you can move on to new topics. The following interchange shows how you might use learning probes to uncover student strengths and misunderstandings and then adjust instruction accordingly. The teacher, Mr. Swift, has written several sentences containing conversation on an overhead projector transparency, and students are learning the correct use of commas and quotation marks.

> *Mr. Swift:* Now we are ready to punctuate some conversation. Everyone get out a sheet of paper and copy this sentence, adding punctuation where needed: *Take the criminal downstairs Tom said condescendingly.* Is everyone ready? . . . Carl, how did you punctuate the sentence?
>
> *Carl:* Quote take the criminal downstairs quote comma Tom said condescendingly period.
>
> *Mr. Swift:* Close, but you made the most common error people make with quotation marks. Maria, what did you write?
>
> *Maria:* I think I made the same mistake Carl did, but I understand now. It should be: Quote take the criminal downstairs comma quote Tom said condescendingly period.
>
> *Mr. Swift:* Good. How many got this right the first time? [Half of class raises hands.] OK, I see we still have some problems with this one. Remember, commas and periods go inside the quotation mark. I know that sometimes this doesn't make much sense, but if English always made sense, a lot of English teachers would be out of work! Think of quotation marks as wrappers for conversation, and the conversation, punctuation and all, goes inside the wrapper. Let's all try another. *Drive carefully Tom said recklessly.* Samphan?
>
> *Samphan:* Quote drive carefully comma quote Tom said recklessly period.
>
> *Mr. Swift:* Great! How many got it? [All but one or two raise hands.] Wonderful, I think you're all with me. The quotation marks "wrap up" the conversation, including its punctuation. Now let's all try one that's a little harder: *I wonder Tom said quizzically whether quotation marks will be on the test.*

This interchange contains several features worth noting. First, Mr. Swift had all students work out the punctuation, called on individuals for answers, and then asked all students whether they got the right answers. This is preferable to asking only one or two students to work (say, on the chalkboard) while the others watch, thus wasting the time of most of the class. When all students have to figure out the punctuation and no one knows whom Mr. Swift will call on to answer, all students actively participate and

learning probe
A method, such as questioning, that helps teachers find out whether students understand a lesson.

test their own knowledge, and Mr. Swift gets a quick reading on the level of understanding of the class as a whole.

Note also that when Mr. Swift found that half the class missed the first item, he took time to reteach the skill students were having trouble with, using a different explanation from the one he had used in his first presentation. By giving students the mental image of quotation marks as wrappers, he helped them to remember the order of punctuation in conversation. When almost all students got the second item, he moved to the next step, because the class had apparently mastered the first one.

Finally, note that Mr. Swift had plenty of sentences prepared on the overhead projector, so he did not have to use class time to write out sentences. Learning probes should always be brief and should not be allowed to destroy the tempo of the lesson. By being prepared with sentences for learning probes, Mr. Swift was able to maintain student involvement and interest. In fact, he might have done even better if he had given students photocopies with unpunctuated sentences on them to reduce the time used in copying the sentences.

QUESTIONS   Questions to students in the course of the lesson serve many purposes (Dantonio & Beisenherz, 2001; Walsh & Sattes, 2005). You can use questions as Socrates used them, to prompt students to take the next mental step—for example, "Now that we've learned that heating a gas makes it expand, what do you suppose would happen if we cool a gas?" You can also use questions to encourage students to think further about information they learned previously or to get a discussion started—for example, "We've learned that if we boil water, it becomes water vapor. Now, water vapor is a colorless, odorless, invisible gas. In that case, why do you suppose we can see steam coming out of a tea kettle?" With guidance, a class discussion would eventually arrive at the answer, which is that the water vapor recondenses when it hits the relatively cool air and that what is visible in steam is water droplets, not vapor. You will often find it helpful to have students generate their own questions, either for themselves or for each other (Brookhart, 2007/2008). A great deal of evidence indicates that students gain from generating their own questions (Foos, Mora, & Tkacz, 1994; Rosenshine et al., 1996; Sadker & Sadker, 2006), especially questions that relate to students' existing background knowledge about a topic they are studying (King, 1994).

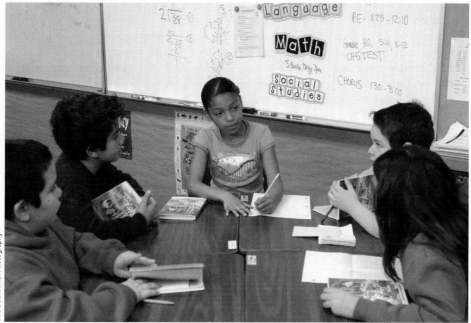

Why are questions valuable learning probes? What value can students gain by learning to ask good questions of each other?

Finally, you can use questions as learning probes (Fisher & Frey, 2007). In fact, any question is to some degree a learning probe, in that the quality of response will indicate to you how well students are learning the lesson. Research on the frequency of questions indicates that asking more questions related to the lesson at hand is more instructionally effective than asking relatively few questions (Dunkin & Biddle, 1974; Gall et al., 1978; Stallings & Kaskowitz, 1974). At all levels of schooling, factual questions generally help with factual skills (Clark et al., 1979) and questions that encourage students to think about concepts help with conceptual skills (Sadker & Sadker, 2006).

Theory into Practice
Assessment for Learning

Formative assessment within class lessons is at the heart of an important movement called Assessment for Learning, established by two British researchers, Paul Black and Dylan Wiliam (Black, Harrison, Lee, Marshall, & Wiliam, 2003, 2004; Wiliam, 2007, 2007/2008). Its authors emphasize the word *for* in the name; there is already too much assessment *of* learning, they argue, but not enough assessment during lessons that can inform teachers and students themselves of students' levels of understanding in ways that are both meaningful enough and timely enough to be useful in improving learning and teaching (Leahy, Lyon, Thompson, & Wiliam, 2005; also see Brookhart, 2007/2008; Chappuis, 2005; Popham, 2006). Assessment for Learning suggests dozens of strategies for helping students understand criteria for success, providing feedback, asking peers to provide feedback to each other, and letting students assess and report their own levels of understanding (Leahy et al., 2005; Wiliam, 2007), as in the following list of examples.

1. In any class with a writing component, distribute anonymous writing products (e.g., essays, lab reports, book reports) from the previous year's class, and ask students to judge their quality before asking students to create their own writing products.

2. Ask "big questions" that are at the core of the learning objective and give students time to talk among themselves and then share ideas with the class. For example, a math teacher might ask students to list fractions between one-half and one-fourth, both to understand students' grasp of fractional concepts and to spur their thinking. Students might be off the mark entirely, or they might think that three-eighths is the only possible answer, but with time and hints from the teacher, students might eventually realize that there are an infinite number of fractions between one-half and one-fourth. Similarly, you might ask why France supported Napoleon's wars throughout Europe, or why many plants have fruits surrounding seeds.

3. Avoid asking for volunteers to respond to questions (because it's always the same students who volunteer). Instead, put students' names on popsicle sticks or cards and call on them at random (Weinstein, 2007; Weinstein & Mignano, 2007).

4. When appropriate, ask students to respond at once, perhaps by writing an answer on a small chalkboard and holding it up on cue, showing a letter card to answer a multiple-choice question, or giving a choral (unison) response.

5. Use "traffic lights": Ask students to assess their own understanding of a lesson and hold up a green card if they are solid, yellow if they are not sure, or red if they are not getting it. You can quickly scan the class, and move on if there is a sea of green or stop and reteach if there's a lot of red and yellow. Use cooperative learning strategies to let students work together to help each other master content, assess each other's learning, and lead each other toward productive lines of thinking.

WAIT TIME   One issue related to questioning that has received much research attention is **wait time,** the length of time you wait for a student to answer a question before giving the answer or going on to another student. Research has found that teachers tend to give up too rapidly on students whom they perceive to be low achievers, a practice that tells those students that the teacher expects little from them (Sadker & Sadker, 2006; Tobin & Capie, 1982).

Waiting approximately 3 seconds after asking a student a question obtains better learning results than giving up more rapidly (Tobin, 1986). Furthermore, following up with students who do not respond has been associated with higher achievement (Anderson, Evertson, & Brophy, 1979; Larrivee, 1985). Waiting for students to respond or staying with them when they do not communicates positive expectations for them. However, there is such a thing as waiting too long. A study by Duell (1994) found that a wait time as long as 6 seconds had a small negative effect on the achievement of university students.

CALLING ORDER   In classroom questioning, **calling order** is a concern. Calling on volunteers is perhaps the most common method, but this allows some students to avoid participating in the lesson by keeping their hands down (Good & Brophy, 2008). Common sense would suggest that when the question is a problem to be worked (as in math), all students should attempt the problem before any individual is called on. For questions that are not problems to be worked, it is probably best to pose the question to the class as a whole and then ask a randomly chosen student (not necessarily a volunteer) to answer. Some teachers even carry around a class list on a clipboard and check off the students called on to make sure that all get frequent chances to respond or put students' names on popsicle sticks and draw them at random from a can (Freiberg & Driscoll, 2005; Weinstein, 2007; Weinstein & Mignano, 2007). One teacher put her students' names on cards, shuffled them before class, and randomly selected cards to decide which student to call on. This system worked well until one student found the cards after class and removed his name from the deck!

In conducting learning probes, you might find it especially important to ask questions of students who usually perform above, at, and below the class average to be sure that all students understand the lesson.

ALL-PUPIL RESPONSE   Many teachers ask students for **all-pupil responses** when there is only one possible correct answer. For example, you might say, "Class, in the words listed on the board [*write, wring, wrong*], what sound does the *wr* make?" To which the class responds together, "Rrrr!" This is called a **choral response.** Similarly, when appropriate, you can ask all students to use hand signals to indicate true or false, to hold up a certain number of fingers to indicate an answer in math, or to write a short answer on a small chalkboard and hold it up on cue (Black et al., 2004). Research finds this type of all-pupil response has a positive effect on student learning (McKenzie, 1979; McKenzie & Henry, 1979). In the subtraction with renaming example used earlier in this chapter, recall that all students worked with popsicle sticks at their desks, and the teacher walked around to check their work. All-student responses give students many opportunities to respond and give you information on the entire class's level of knowledge and confidence.

wait time
Length of time that a teacher waits for a student to answer a question.

calling order
The order in which students are called on by the teacher to answer questions during the course of a lesson.

all-pupil responses
Responses to questions made by the entire class.

choral responses
Responses to questions spoken by an entire class in unison.

Theory into Practice
Questioning Strategies to Avoid

As a teacher, you ask a lot of questions, and it is easy for you to fall into bad habits, as demonstrated by the following common pitfalls (see Freiberg & Driscoll, 2005; Good & Brophy, 2008; Walsh & Sattes, 2005).

1. *Leading questions.* Your phrasing can give or strongly suggest the answer to a question, as in "You don't think the Pilgrims believed in religious toleration, do you?" Your tone of voice can easily give away the answer as well. If students know that they can tell the answer from your question, they do not need to pay attention to instruction to be prepared.

2. *Always asking the same students.* Many teachers only ask questions of the students who they believe will probably give right answers, avoiding those who might be slow to respond, unlikely to get the question right, or prone to make trouble if questioned. Yet when students know it is unlikely they will be called on, they may stop paying attention, so it is imperative that all students believe that they could be selected at any moment. Using a random questioning pattern (by, for example, putting students' names on popsicle sticks and drawing them at random) not only ensures that all students are called on, but seeing the process of drawing names makes it clear to students that they must always be ready to respond.

3. *Asking questions all at one level.* Some teachers ask only factual questions. Others never ask factual questions. It is important to ask questions at all levels, simple and difficult, factual and conceptual.

4. *Engaging one student at length while others have nothing to do.* It's fine to ask complex questions that may take a while to answer, but avoid having nothing for the other students to do while one student is responding. You can avoid this by asking a question of the whole class, giving them time to work out their answers or discuss them with partners, and only then calling on students at random to give their answers. Following up on one student's answer with a question based on it helps ensure that students are paying attention to each other's answers, as in this example:

Teacher: Can anyone give me an example of a mammal that lives in the sea? Tony?

Tony: A dolphin?

Teacher: Thank you, Tony, that's a good example. Can anyone give another example besides the one Tony gave? . . . Natalia?

Natalia: A whale.

Teacher: Right again. Now class, if you saw an animal in the sea other than the ones Tony and Natalia mentioned, what facts about that animal would tell you that it's a mammal?

5. *Failing to correct wrong answers.* Some teachers, not wanting to embarass students, do not correct wrong answers. It is important not to humiliate students who give wrong answers, but it is also important not to leave the class with the wrong impression, as in the following:

Teacher: Before the Russian Revolution, why do you think the Germans sent Lenin to Russia in a sealed train? . . . Marta?

Marta: They wanted to get him out of Germany.

Teacher: Perhaps, but remember, Germany and Russia were at war. Can anyone give me the main reason the Germans sent Lenin to Russia? Ahmed?

6. *Ignoring answers.* Every student who knows the answer to your question wants to say that answer. Calling on many students and being sure to acknowledge all answers give students a sense that it was beneficial to be prepared. Having students briefly discuss answers with a partner ensures that even if you can't call on everyone, all students at least got to share their good answers with someone.

7. *Asking too many yes–no questions.* Questions that have only two possible answers are sometimes unavoidable, but they should not be overused. A guesser will be right 50 percent of the time, and so a correct answer may or may not indicate knowledge. One way to avoid this problem is to ask a follow-up question after the correct answer to get at why the answer is correct, as in the following:

Teacher: If I multiply a fraction less than one by another fraction less than one, will the product be larger or smaller than the first fraction? . . . Louisa?

Louisa: Less.

Teacher: Class, raise your hand if you agree with Louisa (most do). All right, you're in the majority. Now Louisa, tell me why you think the product would be less.

8. *Unclear questions.* Sometimes, students do not know what they are being asked. For example, an English teacher might point to a sentence and ask, "What's wrong with this sentence?" without making it clear whether students are being asked to look at the grammar, the punctuation, the phrasing, or the meaning.

■ Provide Independent Practice

The term **independent practice** refers to work students do in class on their own to practice or express newly learned skills or knowledge. For example, after hearing a lesson on solving equations in algebra, students need an opportunity to work several equations on their own without interruptions, both to crystallize their new knowledge and to help you assess their knowledge. Practice is an essential step in the process of transferring new information in working memory to long-term memory.

Independent practice is most critical when students are learning skills, such as mathematics, reading, grammar, composition, map interpretation, or a foreign language (Topping, Samuels, & Paul, 2007). Students can no more learn arithmetic, writing, or Spanish without practicing than they could learn to ride a bicycle from lectures alone. By contrast, independent practice is less necessary for certain concept lessons, such as the lesson on the origins of World War II outlined in Table 7.2 or a science lesson on the concept of magnetic attraction. In lessons of this kind, you can use independent practice to let students rehearse knowledge or concepts on their own, as the teacher did in the World War II lesson, but rehearsal is not as central to this type of lesson as practice of skills is to a subtraction lesson.

SEATWORK Research on **seatwork,** or in-class independent practice, suggests that it is typically both overused and misused (Good & Brophy, 2008; Tate, 2003; Weinstein, 2007; Weinstein & Mignano, 2007). Several researchers have found that student time

Connections
For more on working memory and long-term memory, see Chapter 6, pages 146 and 149.

independent practice
Component of instruction in which students work by themselves to demonstrate and rehearse new knowledge.

seatwork
Work that students are assigned to do independently during class.

spent receiving instruction directly from the teacher is more productive than time spent in seatwork (Evertson, Emmer, & Brophy, 1980; Good & Brophy, 2008). For example, Evertson and colleagues (1980) found that the most effective seventh- and eighth-grade math teachers in their study spent about 16 minutes on lecture–demonstration and 19 minutes on seatwork, whereas the least effective teachers spent less than 7 minutes on lecture–demonstration and about 25 minutes on seatwork. Yet studies of elementary mathematics and reading classes have found students spending 50 to 70 percent of their class time doing seatwork (Fisher et al., 1978; Rosenshine, 1980). Anderson, Brubaker, Alleman-Brooks, and Duffy (1985) have noted that time spent on seatwork is often wasted for students who lack the motivation, reading skills, or self-organization abilities to work well on their own. Yet a review of research on the teaching of reading to students with disabilities found that 40 percent of their time, on average, was spent on seatwork (Vaughn, Levy, Coleman, & Bos, 2002). Many students simply give up when they run into difficulties. Others fill out worksheets with little care for correctness, apparently interpreting the task as finishing the paper rather than learning the material.

EFFECTIVE USE OF INDEPENDENT PRACTICE TIME   The following recommendations for effective use of independent practice time are derived from the work of Anderson (1985), Evertson and colleagues (2009), and Good and Brophy (2008).

Certification Pointer

Your teacher certification test may require you to choose the least effective teaching strategy to achieve a particular curriculum objective. You should know that one of the least effective strategies for practicing a skill students have just learned is lengthy independent seatwork for which students do not receive feedback.

   1. *Do not assign independent practice until you are sure students can do it.* This is probably the most important principle. Independent practice is practice, not instruction, and the students should be able to do most of the items they are assigned to do on their own (Freiberg & Driscoll, 2005). In cognitive terms, practice serves as rehearsal for transferring information from working memory to long-term memory. For this to work, the information must first be established in students' working memories (Ashcraft & Radvansky, 2010).

   A high success rate on independent practice work can be accomplished in two ways. First, assignments should be clear and self-explanatory and cover content on which all students can succeed. Second, students should rarely be given independent practice worksheets until they have indicated in learning probes that they can handle the material. For example, you might use the first items of a class assignment as learning probes, assigning them one at a time and discussing each one after students have attempted it until it is clear that all or almost all students have the right idea. You may prepare a series of questions on an overhead projector or interactive whiteboard and introduce them one at a time until most of the class is on the right track, only then revealing the rest of the items.

   2. *Keep independent practice assignments short.* There is rarely a justification for long independent practice assignments. About 10 minutes of work is adequate for most objectives, but this is far less than most teachers usually assign (Rosenshine, 1980). Massed practice (e.g., many items at one sitting) has a limited effect on retention. Students are more likely to profit from relatively brief independent practice in class supplemented by distributed practice such as homework (Dempster, 1989; Krug, Davis, & Glover, 1990).

   3. *Give clear instructions.* Make sure that all students understand the instructions and know what they are supposed to do. In the lower grades, ask students to read aloud or paraphrase the instructions to be sure that they have understood them.

   4. *Get students started, and then avoid interruptions.* When students start on their independent practice work, circulate among them to be sure that everyone is under way before attending to the problems of individual students or other tasks. Once students have begun, avoid interrupting them.

   5. *Monitor independent work.* It is important to monitor independent work, for example, by walking around the class while students are doing their assignments. This helps to keep students working and increases your availability for questions. You can also look in on students who may be struggling to give them additional assistance.

6. Collect independent work and include it in student grades. Many students see no reason to do their best on seatwork because it usually has little or no bearing on their grades. Students should know that their seatwork will be collected and count toward their grade. To this end, it is a good idea to save a few minutes at the end of each class period to briefly read answers to assigned questions and allow students to check their own papers or exchange papers with partners. Then students may pass in their papers for spot checking and recording. This procedure gives students immediate feedback on their seatwork and relieves you of having to check all papers every day. Make this checking time brief to avoid taking time from instruction.

■ Assess Performance and Provide Feedback

Every lesson should contain an assessment of the degree to which students have mastered the objectives set for the lesson (Fisher & Frey, 2007; Reeves, 2007). Assessment can range from informally questioning students to using independent work as an assessment to giving a separate quiz. One way or another, however, you should assess the effectiveness of the lesson and give the results of the assessment to students as soon as possible (Guskey, 2003; Hattie & Timperley, 2007; Safer & Fleischman, 2005; Stiggins, 2007). For example, research has found frequent use of classroom assessment of the content of instruction improves children's reading skills (Taylor, Pearson, Clark, & Walpole, 2000). Further, there is evidence that testing itself improves students' retention of what they have learned, because the testing process makes it more likely that students will deeply process the information (Haynie & Haynie, 2008). Students need to know when they are right and when they are wrong if they are to use feedback to improve their performance. In addition to assessing the results of each lesson, you need to test students from time to time on their learning of larger units of information. In general, more frequent testing results in greater achievement than does less frequent testing, but any testing is much more effective than none at all (Bangert-Drowns, Kulik, & Kulik, 1986). Feedback to students is important, but feedback to you on student performance is probably even more important. If students are learning everything they are taught, it might be possible to pick up the pace of instruction. However, if assessment reveals serious misunderstandings, you can reteach the lesson or take other steps to get students back on track. If some students have mastered the lesson and some have not, it might be appropriate to give more instruction only to the students who need it.

Connections
For in-depth coverage of assessment, see Chapter 13.

INTASC

8 Assessment of Student Learning

■ Provide Distributed Practice and Review

Practice or review spaced out over time increases retention of many kinds of knowledge (Dempster, 1989). This has several implications for teaching. First, it implies that reviewing and recapitulating important information from earlier lessons enhances learning. Students particularly need to review important material at long intervals (e.g., monthly) to maintain previous skills. In addition, you should assign homework in most subjects, especially at the secondary level. Homework gives students a chance to practice skills learned in one setting at one time (school) in another setting at a different time (home). Homework can be used as formative assessment, providing both you and your students information on current levels of understanding of key concepts (Christopher, 2007/2008). Research on homework finds that it generally does increase achievement, particularly if teachers check it and give comments to students (Cooper, Robinson, & Patall, 2006; Trautwein, 2007). However, the effects of homework are not as clear in elementary schools as they are at the secondary level (Cooper et al., 2006; Cooper & Valentine, 2001), and assigning excessively lengthy or boring homework can actually be detrimental to learning and motivation (Corno, 2000). Making homework interesting and worthwhile

21ST Century Learning

Enhancing Classroom Lessons with Technology

In the past, almost all teaching has been directed to the same part of the brain. Both reading and hearing lectures address the same semantic processes, and only the occasional picture or video addresses equally important episodic learning processes. In the 21st century, this is changing, as interactive whiteboards, DVDs, and other devices make it easy for teachers to incorporate brief bits of video or still pictures into their daily lessons, adding intrinsic motivation as well as strengthening learning by pairing pictures and spoken words or text (Mayer, 2008a, 2009). Students today are increasingly visual learners outside

of school, and teachers can capitalize on these skills in school as well.

Questions

- What are some visual learning activities students experience outside of school that can be capitalized on in the classroom?

- Do you think it is ethical to give students extra credit to do these kinds of activities if they enhance classroom learning?

is critical to its value (Darling-Hammond & Ifill-Lynch, 2006; Marzano & Pickering, 2007). Good and Brophy (2003) recommend 5 to 10 minutes of homework per subject for fourth-graders, increasing to 30 minutes or more per subject for college-bound high school students. Homework can provide a means for parents to become constructively engaged in their children's schooling (Epstein & Van Voorhis, 2001; Xu & Corno, 2003), but it can also become a significant source of conflict in the home, especially for children having difficulty with the content (Walker & Hoover-Dempsey, 2001).

How Does Research on Direct Instruction Methods Inform Teaching?

Most of the principles of direct instruction discussed in this chapter have been derived from **process–product studies,** in which observers record the teaching practices of teachers whose students consistently achieve at a high level and compare them to teachers whose students make less progress. These principles have been assembled into specific direct instruction programs and evaluated in field experiments; that is, other teachers have been trained in the methods used by successful teachers, and their students' achievement has been compared to that of students whose teachers did not receive the training.

Many studies have found a correlation between student achievement and teachers' use of strategies associated with direct instruction (e.g., Gage & Needels, 1989; Weinert & Helmke, 1995). However, experimental studies that compare the achievement of students whose teachers have been trained in specific direct instruction strategies to that of students whose teachers have not received this training show more mixed results. In classic studies of a direct instruction math approach called the Missouri Mathematics Program (MMP), Good and Grouws (1979) and Good and colleagues (1983) found that fourth-graders whose teachers used the MMP methods learned more than students

process–product studies

Research approach in which the teaching practices of effective teachers are recorded through classroom observation.

whose teachers were not trained in MMP. Evaluations of another direct instruction model, Madeline Hunter's (1982, 1995) Mastery Teaching program, did not generally find that the students of teachers trained in the model learned more than other students (Mandeville, 1992; Mandeville & Rivers, 1991; Slavin, 1986). A study of explicit teaching, a form of direct instruction, found that this method made no difference in reading achievement of low achievers unless the method was supplemented by peer tutoring (Simmons, Fuchs, Fuchs, Mathes, & Hodge, 1995). More successful have been direct instruction models that place a greater emphasis on building teachers' classroom management skills (e.g., Evertson, Weade, Green, & Crawford, 1985) and models that improve teachers' use of reading groups (Anderson et al., 1979).

Studies of Direct Instruction (DI), a program built around specific teaching materials and structured methods, have found strong positive effects of this approach in elementary schools, particularly with low achievers and students at risk (Adams & Engelmann, 1996; Ellis, 2001b). One study (Meyer, 1984) following the progress of students from an inner-city Brooklyn, New York, neighborhood who had been in DI classes in first through third grades found that these students were considerably more likely to graduate from high school than were students in a similar Brooklyn school who had not been taught with DI.

Although the research on direct instruction models has produced mixed conclusions, most researchers agree that the main elements of these models are essential minimum skills that all teachers should have (see Gage & Needels, 1989). In fact, most of the recommendations from direct instruction research are so commonsensical that they seem obvious. A study by Wong (1995), however, found that some methods contrary to direct instruction principles also seemed obvious to teachers and university students. When studies find no differences between teachers trained in the models and other teachers, it is often because both groups of teachers already had most of the direct instruction skills before the training took place (see Slavin, 1986).

It is clear that direct instruction methods can improve the teaching of certain basic skills, but it is equally clear that much is yet to be learned about how and when they should be used. The prescriptions derived from studies of effective teachers cannot be applied uncritically in the classroom and expected to make a substantial difference in student achievement. Structured, systematic instructional programs based on these prescriptions can markedly improve student achievement in basic skills, but it is important to remember that the research on direct instruction has focused mostly on basic reading and mathematics, mostly in the elementary grades. For other subjects and at other grade levels we have less of a basis for believing that direct instruction methods will improve student learning (see Arends, 2004).

How Do Students Learn and Transfer Concepts?

A very large proportion of all lessons focus on teaching concepts. A **concept** is an abstract idea that is generalized from specific examples. For example, a red ball, a red pencil, and a red chair all illustrate the simple concept "red." A green book is not an instance of the concept "red." If you were shown the red ball, pencil, and chair and asked to say what they have in common, you would produce the concept "red objects." If the green book were also included, you would have to fall back on the much broader concept "objects."

Of course, many concepts are far more complex and less well defined than the concept "red." For example, the concept "justice" is one that people might spend a lifetime trying to understand. This book is engaged primarily in teaching concepts; in fact, at this very moment you are reading about the concept "concept"!

INTASC

2 Knowledge of Human Development and Learning

4 Multiple Instructional Strategies

concept

An abstract idea that is generalized from specific examples.

■ Concept Learning and Teaching

Concepts are generally learned in one of two ways. Most concepts that we learn outside of school we learn by observation. For example, a child learns the concept "car" by hearing certain vehicles referred to as "cars." Initially, the child might include SUVs or motorcycles under the concept "car," but as time goes on, the concept is refined until the child can clearly differentiate "car" from "noncar." Similarly, the child learns the more difficult concepts "naughty," "clean," and "fun" by observation and experience.

Other concepts are typically learned by definition. For example, it is very difficult to learn the concepts "aunt" or "uncle" by observation alone. One could observe hundreds of "aunts" and "nonaunts" without deriving a clear concept of "aunt." In this case the concept is best learned by definition: To be an aunt, one must be a female whose brother or sister (or brother- or sister-in-law) has children. With this definition, instances and noninstances of "aunt" can be readily differentiated.

DEFINITIONS   Just as children can learn concepts in two ways, instructors can teach them in two ways. You might give students instances and noninstances of a concept and later ask them to derive or infer a definition. Or you might give students a definition and then ask them to identify instances and noninstances. Some concepts lend themselves to the example–definition approach. For most concepts that are taught in school, it makes most sense to state a definition, present several instances (and noninstances, if appropriate), and then restate the definition, showing how the instances typify the definition. For example, we might define the concept "learning" as "a change in an individual caused by experience." Instances might include learning of skills, of information, of behaviors, and of emotions. Noninstances might include maturational changes, such as changes in behaviors or emotions caused by the onset of puberty. Finally, we might restate the definition and discuss it in light of the instances and noninstances.

EXAMPLES   Teaching concepts involves extensive and skillful use of examples. Tennyson and Park (1980, p. 59) suggest that you follow three rules when presenting examples of concepts:

1. Order the examples from easy to difficult.
2. Select examples that differ from one another.
3. Compare and contrast examples and nonexamples.

Consider the concept "mammal." Easy examples are dogs, cats, and humans, and nonexamples are insects, reptiles, and fish. No problem so far. But what about dolphins? Bats? Snakes that bear live young? Kangaroos? Each of these is a more difficult example or nonexample of the concept "mammal"; each challenges the simplistic belief, based on experience, that terrestrial animals that bear live young are mammals and that aquatic animals, birds, and other egg-layers are not. The easy examples (dogs versus fish) establish the concept in general, but the more difficult examples (snakes versus whales) test the true boundaries of the concept. Students should thoroughly understand simple examples before tackling more complex cases.

■ Teaching for Transfer of Learning

Students often get so wrapped up in preparing for tests, and teachers in preparing students to take tests, that both forget the primary purpose of school: to give students the skills and knowledge necessary for them to function effectively as adults. If a student can fill in blanks on a language arts test but cannot write a clear letter to a friend or a prospective employer, or can multiply with decimals and percents on a math test but cannot figure sales tax, then that student's education has been sadly misdirected. Yet all too frequently, students who do very well in school or on tests are unable to transfer their knowledge or skills to real-life situations.

REAL-LIFE LEARNING   **Transfer of learning** from one situation to another depends on the degree to which the information or skills were learned in the original situation and on the degree of similarity between the situation in which the skill or concept was learned and the situation to which it is to be applied (Bransford et al., 1999; Hall & Greeno, 2008; Smagorinsky & Smith, 1992). These principles, known since the beginning of the 20th century, have important implications for teaching. We cannot simply assume that students will be able to transfer their school learning to practical situations, so we must teach them to use skills in situations like those they are likely to encounter in real life or in other situations to which we expect learning to transfer. Students must receive specific instruction in how to use their skills and information to solve problems and encounter a variety of problem-solving experiences if they are to be able to apply much of what they learned in school.

The most important thing to know about transfer of learning is that it cannot be assumed (Cox, 1997). Just because a student has mastered a skill or concept in one setting or circumstance, there is no guarantee whatsoever that the student will be able to apply this skill or concept to a new setting, even if the setting seems (at least to the teacher) to be very similar (Mayer & Wittrock, 1996). Classic examples are people who score well on tests of grammar and punctuation but cannot apply these skills in their own compositions (Smagorinsky & Smith, 1992) and people who can solve all sorts of math problems in school but do not apply their math knowledge in real life. As an example of this, Lave (1988) describes a man in a weight-loss program who was faced with the problem of measuring out a serving of cottage cheese that was three-quarters of the usual two-thirds cup allowance. The man, who had passed college calculus, measured out two-thirds of a cup of cottage cheese, dumped it out in a circle on a cutting board, marked a cross on it, and scooped away one quadrant. It never occurred to him to multiply $\frac{2}{3} \times \frac{3}{4} = \frac{1}{2}$, an operation that almost any sixth-grader could do on paper (but few might apply in a practical situation).

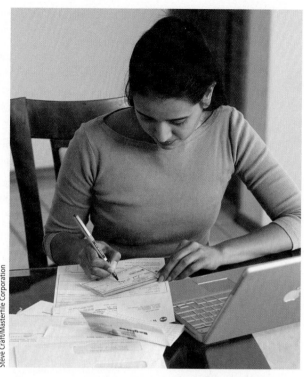

This woman has been able to transfer knowledge about math concepts to help with her personal finances. As a teacher, how will you ensure that your students are able to transfer what they have learned in the classroom to real-life situations?

INITIAL LEARNING AND UNDERSTANDING   Not surprisingly, one of the most important factors in transfer of a skill or concept from one situation to another is how well the skill or concept was learned in the first place (Pressley & Yokoi, 1994). However, it also matters a great deal how well students understood the material and to what degree it was taught in a meaningful way (Bereiter, 1995; Mayer & Wittrock, 1996). In other words, material that is memorized by rote is unlikely to transfer to new situations no matter how thoroughly it was mastered.

LEARNING IN CONTEXT   If transfer of learning depends in large part on similarity between the situation in which information is learned and that in which it is applied, then how can we teach in the school setting so that students will be able to apply their knowledge in the very different setting of real life?

One important principle of transfer is that the ability to apply knowledge in new circumstances depends in part on the variety of circumstances in which we have learned or practiced the information or skill (Bereiter, 1995). For example, a few weeks' experience

transfer of learning

The application of knowledge acquired in one situation to new situations.

TABLE 7.3   Teaching of Concepts

Research demonstrates that to teach a new concept, teachers should first present examples of the concept used in similar contexts and then offer examples in widely different contexts. This approach promotes the students' abilities to transfer the concept to new situations. The example here comes from a classic study in which students learned new concepts from the traditional culture of cowboys.

Concept to be taught: *Minge*
Definition: To gang up on a person or thing

Same-Context Examples	Varied-Context Examples
The three riders decided to converge on the cow.	The band of sailors angrily denounced the captain and threatened a mutiny.
Four people took part in branding the horse.	A group in the audience booed the inept magician's act.
They circled the wolf so it would not escape.	The junk dealer was helpless to defend himself from the three thieves.
All six cowboys fought against the rustler.	All six cowboys fought against the rustler.

Source: John D. Bransford, *Human Cognition,* Wadsworth Publishing, 1979. (Adapted from an unpublished doctoral thesis titled *Structuring Decontextualized Forms of Knowledge* by K. E. Nitsch, 1977.) Reprinted by permission of John D. Bransford.

as a parking attendant, driving all sorts of cars, would probably be better than years of experience driving one kind of car for enabling a person to drive a completely new and different car (at least in a parking lot!).

In teaching concepts, one way to increase the chance that students will appropriately apply the concepts to new situations is to give examples from a range of situations. A set of classic experiments by Nitsch (1977) illustrated this principle. Students were given definitions of words and then presented with examples to illustrate the concepts. Some received several examples in the same context; others received examples from mixed contexts. Table 7.3 shows examples for *minge,* a cowboy word meaning "to gang up on." Students who received only the same-context examples could identify additional examples in the same context but were less successful in applying the concepts to new contexts. By contrast, the students who learned with the varied-context examples had some difficulties in learning the concept at first but, once they did, were able to apply it to new situations. The best strategy was a hybrid in which students received the same-context examples first and then the varied-context examples.

You can use many other methods to increase the probability that information or skills learned in one context will transfer to other contexts, particularly to real-life applications. For example, simulations can approximate real-life conditions, as when secondary students prepare for job interviews by role-playing with teachers or peers pretending to be interviewers. You can also facilitate transfer by introducing skills learned in one setting into a new setting. For example, a history teacher might do well to find out what writing or grammar skills are being taught in English classes and then remind students to use these same skills in history essays (Anderson, Reder, & Simon, 1996; White & Frederiksen, 1998).

TRANSFER VERSUS INITIAL LEARNING   What makes transfer tricky is that some of the most effective procedures for enhancing transfer are exactly the opposite of those for initial learning. As the Nitsch (1977) study illustrated, teaching a concept in many different contexts confuses students when done at the beginning of a sequence of instruction, but it enhances transfer if it occurs after students understand the concept in one setting. This principle holds important implications for teaching. In introducing a new concept, you should use similar examples until your students understand the concept and then use diverse examples that still demonstrate the essential aspects of the concept (Reimann & Schult, 1996).

As one example of this, consider a series of lessons on evolution. In introducing the concept, you should first use clear examples of how animals have evolved in ways that increase their chances of survival in their environments, using such examples as the evolution of flippers in seals or of humps in camels. Then you might present evolution in plants (e.g., evolution of a waxy skin on desert plants), somewhat broadening the concept. Next, you might discuss the evolution of social behaviors (such as cooperation in lions, baboons, and humans); finally, you might explore phenomena that resemble the evolutionary process (such as the modification of businesses in response to selective pressures of free-market economies). In this way, you first establish the idea of evolution in one clear context (animals) and then gradually broaden the concept until your students can see how processes in quite different contexts demonstrate the principles of selective adaptation. If you had begun the lessons with a mixed discussion of animals, plants, societies, and businesses, it would have been too confusing. If you never moved beyond the evolution of animals, the concept would not have had much chance of transferring to different contexts. After learning about the concept of evolution in many different contexts, students are much more likely to be able to distinguish scientific and metaphorical uses and apply the concept to a completely new context, such as the evolution of art in response to changes in society (Bransford et al., 1999).

"I wasn't copying. I was transferring knowledge from one context to another!"

It is important in teaching for transfer not only to provide many examples but also to point out in each example how the essential features of the concept are reflected (Kosonen & Winne, 1995). In the evolution lessons you might explain the central process as it applies to each particular case. The development of cooperation among lions, for instance, shows how a social trait evolved because groups of lions that cooperated were better able than others to catch game, to survive, and to ensure that their offspring would survive. Pointing out the essential elements in each example helps students apply a concept to new instances they have never encountered (Anderson et al., 1996). Similarly, comparing cases or situations illustrates a given concept, and pointing out similarities and differences between them can enhance transfer (Bulgren, Lenz, Schumaker, Deshler, & Marquis, 2002; Gentner, Loewenstein, & Thompson, 2002).

EXPLICIT TEACHING FOR TRANSFER   Students can be explicitly taught to transfer skills to new circumstances. For example, Fuchs and colleagues (Fuchs, Fuchs, Finelli, Courey, & Hamlett, 2003) evaluated an "explicit transfer" technique in third-grade math classes. Children in the explicit transfer condition were taught what transfer means and given examples of how the same kind of story problems could be changed using different language, different contexts, and different numbers. They were also taught to look at story problems to see if they resembled problems they had done before. For example, one problem asked how many packages of lemon drops (10 to a package) you'd have to buy to get 32 lemon drops. They then presented the same problem worded differently, with additional questions added, with different contexts, and so on. Teaching students how to look for commonalities among story problems significantly enhanced their success on transfer tasks.

How Are Discussions Used in Instruction ?

INTASC

4 Multiple Instructional Strategies

You can use discussions as part of instruction for many reasons. Discussions lend themselves to controversial topics, to questions for which there may be many right answers, and to affective or attitudinal objectives. They may be moderated by the teacher in the class as a whole or may take place in small student-led groups.

■ Subjective and Controversial Topics

Questions in many subjects do not have simple answers. There may be one right answer to an algebra problem or one right way to conjugate a German verb, but is there one right set of factors that explains what caused the Civil War? How were Shakespeare's writings influenced by the politics of his day? Should genetic engineering be banned as a danger to world health? These and many other questions have no clear-cut answers, so it is important for students to discuss and understand these issues instead of simply receiving and rehearsing information or skills. Such subjects as history, government, economics, literature, art, and music include many issues that lend themselves to discussion and multiple and diverse explanations. Research finds that discussing controversial issues increases knowledge about the issues while encouraging deeper understanding of the various sides of an issue (Johnson & Johnson, 1999).

■ Difficult and Novel Concepts

In addition to subjective and controversial subjects, discussions can clarify topics that do contain single right answers but which involve difficult concepts that force students to see something in a different way. For example, a science teacher could simply give a lesson on buoyancy and specific gravity. However, because this lesson would challenge a simplistic view of why things float ("Things float because they are light"), students might understand buoyancy and specific gravity better if they had an opportunity to make and defend their own theories about why things float and if they faced such questions as "If things float because they are light, then why does a battleship float?" and "If you threw certain objects in a lake, they would sink part way but not to the bottom. Why would they stop sinking?" In searching together for theories to explain these phenomena, students might gain an appreciation for the meaning of buoyancy and specific gravity that a lecture alone could not provide.

■ Affective Objectives

You might also use discussions when affective objectives (objectives that are concerned with student attitudes and values) are of particular importance. For example, a course on civics or government contains much information about how our government works but also involves important values to be transmitted, such as civic duty and patriotism. You could teach "six reasons why it is important to vote," but the real objective here is not to teach reasons for voting, but rather to instill respect for the democratic process and a commitment to register and vote when the time comes. Similarly, a discussion of peer pressure might be directed at giving students the skills and the willingness to say no when classmates pressure them to engage in illegal, unhealthy, or undesirable behaviors. A long tradition of research in social psychology has established that group discussion, particularly when group members must publicly commit themselves, is far more effective at changing individuals' attitudes and behaviors than is even the most persuasive lecture.

■ Whole-Class Discussions

Discussions take two principal forms. In one, the entire class discusses an issue, with the teacher as moderator (Connolly & Smith, 2002; Gunter et al., 2003). In the other, students form small groups to examine a topic. A **whole-class discussion** differs from a usual lesson because the teacher plays a less dominant role. You may guide the discussion and help the class avoid dead ends but should encourage the students to come up with their own ideas. The following vignette illustrates an inquiry-oriented discussion led (but not dominated) by Ms. Wilson, who wants students to explore and develop their own ideas about the American Revolution using information they have recently learned.

> *Ms. Wilson:* In the past few weeks we've been learning about the events leading up to the American Revolution. Of course, because we are all Americans, we tend to take the side of the revolutionaries. We use the term *Patriots* to describe them; King George probably used a less favorable term. Yet many of the colonists were Loyalists, and at times, the Loyalists outnumbered the Patriots. Let's think about how Loyalists would have argued against the idea of independence from Britain.
>
> *Beth:* I think they'd say King George was a good king.
>
> *Vinnie:* But what about all the things he did to the colonists?
>
> *Ms. Wilson:* Give some examples.
>
> *Vinnie:* Like the Intolerable Acts. The colonists had to put up British soldiers in their own houses, and they closed Boston Harbor.
>
> *Tanya:* But those were to punish the colonists for the Boston Tea Party. The Loyalists would say that the Patriots caused all the trouble in the first place.
>
> *Ms. Wilson:* Good point.
>
> *Frank:* I think the Loyalists would say, "You may not like everything he does, but King George is still our king."
>
> *Richard:* The Loyalists probably thought the Sons of Liberty were a bunch of thugs.
>
> *Ms. Wilson:* Well, I wouldn't put it quite that way, but I think you're right. What did they do that makes you think that?
>
> *Ramon:* They destroyed things and harassed the Loyalists and the British troops. Like they called them names and threw things at them.
>
> *Ms. Wilson:* How do you think Loyalists would feel about the Boston Massacre?
>
> *Beth:* They'd say those thugs got what they deserved. They'd think that it was Sam Adams's fault for getting everyone all stirred up.
>
> *Ms. Wilson:* Let's think about it another way. We live in California. Our nation's capital, Washington, is three thousand miles away. We have to pay all kinds of taxes, and a lot of those taxes go to help people in Boston or Baltimore rather than people here. Many of the things our government does make people in California mad. We've got plenty of food, and we can make just about anything we want to right here. Why don't we have a California Revolution and have our own country?
>
> *Sara:* But we're part of America!
>
> *Tanya:* We can't do that! The army would come and put down the revolution!
>
> *Ms. Wilson:* Don't you think that the Loyalists thought some of the same things?
>
> *Vinnie:* But we can vote and they couldn't.
>
> *Ramon:* Right. Taxation without representation!
>
> *Beth:* I'll bet a lot of Loyalists thought the British would win the war and it would be better to stay on the side of the winners.

whole-class discussion

A discussion among all the students in the class with the teacher as moderator.

In this discussion Ms. Wilson was not looking for any particular facts about the American Revolution, but rather was trying to get students to use the information they had learned previously to discuss issues from a different perspective. Ms. Wilson let the students determine the direction of the discussion to a substantial degree. Her main tasks were to keep the discussion rolling, to get students to use specifics to defend their positions, to ensure that many students participated, and to help the students avoid dead ends or unproductive avenues.

ON THE WEB

For an example of how to conduct an effective class discussion, go to www.ncrel.org/sdrs/areas/issues/students/learning/lr1jungl.htm.

Certification Pointer

For your teacher certification test you will need to demonstrate your understanding of the principles and techniques associated with a variety of instructional strategies. For example, you might be asked to identify the curricular goals for which whole-class discussion would be appropriate and how you would structure the discussion so it would be effective.

INFORMATION BEFORE DISCUSSION   Before beginning a discussion, you must ensure that students have an adequate knowledge base. There is nothing so dreary as a discussion in which the participants don't know much about the topic. The American Revolution discussion depended on students' knowledge of the main events preceding the Revolution. Teachers can sometimes use a discussion before instruction as a means of generating interest in a topic, but at some point you must give students information. In the chapter-opening vignette, for example, Ms. Logan let students discuss and experiment not only before presenting a formal lesson but also after the lesson, when they had more information.

■ Small-Group Discussions

In a **small-group discussion,** students work in four- to six-member groups to discuss a particular topic, and the teacher moves from group to group, aiding the discussion (Cook & Tashlik, 2004; Spiegel, 2005). Because small-group discussions require that students work independently of the teacher most of the time, young or poorly organized students need a great deal of preparation and, in fact, might not be able to benefit from them at all. However, most students at or above the fourth-grade level can profit from small-group discussions.

Like any discussion, most small-group discussions should follow the presentation of information through teacher-directed lessons, books, or videos, or following an opportunity for students to find information for themselves in the library or online. When students know something about a subject, they might start to work in their groups, pulling desks together if necessary to talk and hear one another more easily.

Each group should have a leader that you appoint. Leaders should be responsible, well-organized students but not necessarily the highest-achieving students. Groups may all discuss the same topic, or each may discuss a different subtopic of a larger topic that the whole class is studying. For example, in a unit on the Great Depression, one group might focus on causes of the Depression, another on the collapse of the banking system, a third on the social consequences of the Depression, and a fourth on the New Deal. You should give each group a series of questions to answer on the topic to be discussed. For example, if the topic were the collapse of the banking system, the questions might include the following:

1. What was the connection between the stock market crash of 1929 and the failures of so many banks?

2. What caused savers to lose confidence in the banks?

3. Why did the banks not have enough funds to pay savers who wished to withdraw their money?

4. Why is a widespread run on banks unlikely today?

---

small-group discussion

A discussion among four to six students in a group working independently of a teacher.

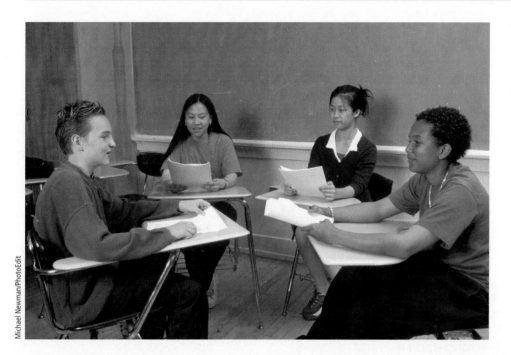

These students are involved in a small-group discussion. What does research tell us about the effectiveness of small-group discussions?

The leader's role in each discussion group is to make sure that the group stays on the topic and questions assigned to it and to ensure that all group members participate. A group recorder could be appointed to write down the group's ideas. At the end of the discussion, the group members prepare a report on their activities or conclusions to present to the rest of the class.

Research on small-group discussions indicates that these activities can increase student achievement more than traditional lessons if the students are well prepared to work in small groups and if the group task is well organized (Sharan et al., 1984; Sharan & Shachar, 1988). Also, some research suggests that small-group discussions have greater effects on student achievement if students are encouraged to engage in controversy (Johnson & Johnson, 1999). Correlational studies by Applebee and colleagues (Applebee, Langer, Nystrand, & Gameran, 2003) and Knapp (1995) found that high-achieving classrooms were more likely to make extensive use of discussions.

Certification Pointer

A certification test question may ask you to respond to a case study by identifying the strengths and weaknesses of the instructional strategies employed in the case.

Chapter 7 Summary

What Is Direct Instruction?

Direct instruction is a teaching approach that emphasizes teacher control of most classroom events and the presentation of structured lessons. Direct instruction programs call for active teaching; clear lesson organization; step-by-step progression between subtopics; and the use of many examples, demonstrations, and visual prompts.

How Is a Direct Instruction Lesson Taught?

The first part of a lesson is stating learning objectives and orienting students to the lesson. The principal task is to establish both a mental set, so that students are ready to work and learn, and a "road map," so that students know where the lesson is going.

Part two of a lesson is to review prerequisites or pretest to ensure that students have mastered required knowledge and skills. The review might function as an advance organizer for the lesson.

Part three involves presenting the new material in an organized way, providing explanations and demonstrations and maintaining attention.

Part four, conducting learning probes, elicits students' responses to lesson content. This practice gives you feedback and lets students test their ideas. Questioning techniques are important, including the uses of wait time and calling order.

Part five of a lesson is independent practice, or seatwork, in which students apply their new skill. Research shows that independent practice should be given as short assignments with clear instructions and no interruptions and that it should be given only when students can do the assignments. You should monitor work, collect it, and include it in assessments.

Part six is to assess performance and provide feedback. Every lesson should include an assessment of student mastery of the lesson objectives.

The Intentional Teacher

USING WHAT YOU KNOW about Direct Instruction to Improve Teaching and Learning

Intentional teachers select their instructional strategies with purpose. They understand the benefits and shortcomings of the strategies they select and then choose strategies based on their students, the content, and the context.

Intentional teachers capitalize on their power as directors of learning by using the components of effective instruction. They take responsibility for presenting clear lessons that carefully lead students toward mastery of objectives. They use their time well by providing a quick instructional pace, by checking for student understanding frequently, and by providing meaningful practice in which students learn to transfer information and skills to new settings. Intentional teachers relish their role as designers of learning experiences.

1. **What do I expect my students to know and be able to do at the end of this lesson? How does this contribute to course objectives and to my students' need to become capable individuals?**

Effective instruction requires careful preparation, which begins with thoughtful selection and phrasing of learning objectives. Think in specific terms about content students are to master and plan your lesson to focus directly on those objectives. For example, you might begin planning a series of lessons on spiders for your second-graders with the goal: "Students will learn about spiders' bodies and behaviors." From that goal you would develop specific objectives to frame your lessons. You might list as your first objective "Students will be able to point to, label, and describe at least three features of a spider's anatomy."

Stating the objective and purpose for a lesson helps students prepare mentally for the information that follows. Begin your lessons with a clear declaration of *what* and *why* students are to learn. For example, you could begin a lesson as follows: "Take a look at the two rocks here on my table. By the time you leave today, you'll be able to state how each of these rocks was formed. That's important information, because it can give us clues about the conditions of the earth far back in time."

2. **What knowledge, skills, needs, and interests do my students have that must be taken into account in my lesson?**

Use preassessments to ensure that objectives and instruction are appropriate for students' needs. For example, before teaching a unit on the metric system, you might give a 10-item pretest to determine their current knowledge of metrics, such as "Which unit would you use to measure how long something is: liter, meter, or gram?"

Effective lessons include a review of prerequisite skills. Briefly review previous learnings that students will need in the current lesson. For example, in a unit on persuasive speech, you might ask students what they have learned about making an effective speech. After noting their ideas on the board, you could add any points they might have missed that you think are especially important for persuasive speeches—such as organization, clarity, poise, or effective use of gestures.

3. **What do I know about the content, child development, learning, motivation, and effective teaching strategies that I can use to accomplish my objectives?**

Effective presentation of information will require you to call on all your skills in incorporating appropriate humor, novelty, and variety. It is important to consider means other than text for presenting information. Use pictures, music, video, and real objects or models when the content permits. Clarity of speech and pronunciation and a pleasant tone are important when you are speaking or reading aloud to present information. (In doing so, you are also modeling your expectations for student speaking.) For example, in a lesson on trees for young children, you might bring in a variety of leaf forms. To introduce the concept of "conifers" you might bring not only pictures of the cone and foliage of a variety of conifers but also actual cones and sample foliage. Learners can then use their tactile sense as well as their eyes to discriminate between the types of cones. They can use their beginning number awareness to differentiate between conifers by the number of needles

Part seven of a lesson is to provide distributed practice through homework and review. Information is retained better when practice is spaced out over a period of time.

How Does Research on Direct Instruction Methods Inform Teaching

Research on particular direct instruction models shows mostly positive but inconsistent effects on student achievement. One program, DI (direct instruction), has proven to be particularly successful for teaching reading and mathematics to low achievers and students at risk.

INTASC   **7** Instructional Planning Skills   **9** Professional Commitment and Responsibility
             8 Assessment of Student Learning

in the "bundles" of their foliage. You could make a point of clarifying the new words in these lessons to help build vocabulary and develop linguistic skills.

Practice by the students should include variety. You help your students develop the ability to apply ideas in new contexts when you provide a range of activities. For example, you might offer your students a choice of activities to practice applying their new knowledge of explorers of the New World. You could direct them to select three of the explorers they have studied. They might map their general routes, write an imaginary journal entry for a member of the party after seeing an important landmark, or write an imaginary dialogue between two different explorers, comparing their experiences.

 4. What instructional materials, technology, assistance, and other resources are available to help accomplish my objectives?

Effective instruction maintains a high degree of student attention. Visual input is especially important for students who are acquiring English. Pace lessons rapidly (without sacrificing student understanding) and use humor, novelty, and variety to support the lesson focus. For example, imagine a lesson on descriptive writing. Rather than rely on mental images, you might bring in an assortment of odd kitchen utensils and toolbox treasures. Students could pass the items around, conjecturing about their uses. The objects' novelty might enhance students' written descriptions.

Students need time to process information. Use wait time after you ask a question, and follow through with students who do not express understanding. For example, you might pose a question to your literature students: "What emotion do you suppose our main character was experiencing at this point?" Instead of calling on the first student to raise a hand, you could say: "I see three hands up. I think I'll wait for more." After a few seconds, many hands might be in the air, and you could select three or four students to share their responses.

 5. How will I plan to assess students' progress toward my objectives?

During direct instruction, teachers conduct many learning probes. Check for understanding frequently, and modify your instruction based on results. For example, in a geometry lesson for young children, you might arrange students in small groups and give each group a set of large shapes. You could ask, "Please hold up a shape that has four corners. Please hold up a shape that reminds you of a stop sign. Please hold up the shape that has the fewest number of sides." You might note that students struggle with your last prompt but easily respond to the first two and make a note to provide additional work on problem solving and vocabulary terms such as *least, most, more,* and *fewer.*

Active participation devices allow teachers to assess all of their students' understandings. Use strategies that provide feedback on every student's progress. For example, after working on different spellings of the long /a/ sound (as in *made*), you might distribute individual chalkboards, chalk, and erasers. You could recite a few words that students silently write on their boards and then raise the boards for you to check. You would quickly—and silently—assess each student's mastery of spelling patterns and then make a list of students who require further instruction.

6. How will I respond if individual children or the class as a whole are not on track toward success? What is my back-up plan?

As follow-up to any unit of instruction, you might plan for a review and question session in which homework assignments for the unit are reviewed and corrected by peers. Then you can actively encourage and answer questions about the content of the unit's lessons. You should have watched for the level of student understanding throughout the unit in the "learning probe" activities you have conducted, and your notes from these "probes" can serve as a guide for your review of content.

How Do Students Learn and Transfer Concepts ?

Students learn concepts through observation and definition. Concepts are taught through examples and nonexamples and through the rule–example–rule approach, in which you first state a definition, then give examples, and finally restate the definition. Unambiguous examples should be given before less obvious ones, and you should compare and contrast examples and nonexamples. Students first transfer their learning to similar situations and then must be taught to transfer concepts to different contexts and real-life situations. Material memorized by rote is unlikely to transfer.

How Are Discussions Used in Instruction ?

In whole-group discussion the teacher plays a less dominant role than in a regular lesson. Students need an adequate knowledge base before beginning a discussion. In small-group discussion, each group should have a leader and a specific focus.

Key Terms

Review the following key terms from the chapter.

all-pupil responses 197	mental set 189
calling order 197	process–product studies 202
choral responses 197	rule–example–rule 192
concept 203	seatwork 199
direct instruction 184	small-group discussion 210
independent practice 199	transfer of learning 205
learning probe 194	wait time 197
lesson planning 188	whole-class discussion 209

Self-Assessment: Practicing for Licensure

Directions: The chapter-opening vignette addresses indicators that are often assessed in state licensure exams. Re-read the chapter-opening vignette, and then respond to the following questions.

1. In the chapter-opening vignette, Ms. Logan uses a variety of instructional strategies in the lesson on sound. Which of the following statements from the vignette is an example of Ms. Logan using direct instruction?

   a. Students are working in small groups at lab stations.

   b. After a half hour of experimentation, Ms. Logan calls the class together.

   c. Representatives from some of the groups demonstrate the experiment.

   d. Ms. Logan teaches a lesson on sound.

2. If Ms. Logan were to use a direct instruction approach to teach a science lesson on gravity, which of the following steps would come first?

   a. Conduct learning probes

   b. State the learning objective

   c. Present new material

   d. Provide independent practice

3. According to research on direct instruction, why should Ms. Logan conduct learning probes during her lesson on sound?

   a. To facilitate in teaching the lesson

   b. To provide students practice with the concepts presented

   c. To give the teacher feedback on the students' level of understanding

d. To catch students who are not paying attention

4. Ms. Logan plays a flute and a piccolo to demonstrate how sound waves travel through air. She hopes this demonstration will help her students understand the experiment with the bottles of water. What principle of instruction is she using?

   a. Reciprocal teaching

   b. Distributed practice

   c. Transfer of learning

   d. Alternative assessment

5. After Ms. Logan's students work in groups to finish the lesson on sound, she tells them they will be tested

individually to demonstrate their knowledge; however, their group can only be called "superteam" if everyone knows the material. What instructional strategy is the teacher using?

   a. Cooperative learning

   b. Small-group discussion

   c. Direct instruction

   d. Inquiry learning

6. Create a lesson using all of the steps of a direct instruction lesson.

7. What are some advantages and disadvantages of small-group discussions and whole-group discussions?

PEARSON myeducationlab

Go to the Topic **Planning and Instruction** in the MyEducationLab (www.myeducationlab.com) for your course, where you can:

- Find learning outcomes for **Planning and Instruction** along with the national standards that connect to these outcomes.

- Complete Assignments and Activities that can help you more deeply understand the chapter content.

- Apply and practice your understanding of the core teaching skills identified in the chapter with the Building Teaching Skills and Dispositions learning units.

- Examine challenging situations and cases presented in the IRIS Center Resources.

- Access video clips of CCSSO National Teachers of the Year award winners responding to the question "Why Do I Teach?" in the Teacher Talk section.

- Check your comprehension of the content covered in the chapter by going to the Study Plan in the Book Resources for your text. Here you will be able to take a chapter quiz; receive feedback on your answers; and then access Review, Practice, and Enrichment activities to enhance your understanding of chapter content.

- Watch author Bob Slavin present a Personal Reflections podcast on *Balancing Instruction* in the Book Resources for your text. Then, respond to the reflection questions that follow.

   Balancing Instruction

   YOUR REFLECTIONS What subjects might lend themselves more to discovery learning? As the teacher of this class, how could I turn this lesson around to teach students to arrive at the correct answer?

8

Student-Centered and Constructivist Approaches to Instruction

Bob Daemmrich Photography

Learning Outcomes

At the end of this chapter, you should be able to:

- Identify key concepts of the constructivist view of learning and their implications for classroom practice
- Discuss how to most effectively use cooperative learning in the classroom
- Describe how you can teach your students problem-solving and thinking skills

Bob Daemmrich Photography

"You'll all recall," begins Mr. Dunbar, "how last week we figured out how to compute the area of a circle and the volume of a cube. Today you're going to have a chance to discover how to compute the volume of a cylinder. This time, you're really going to be on your own. At each of your lab stations you have five unmarked cylinders of different sizes. You also have a metric ruler and a calculator, and you may use water from your sink. The most important resources you'll have to use, however, are your minds and your partners. Remember, at the end of this activity, everyone in every group must be able to explain not only the formula for volume of a cylinder but also precisely how you derived it. Any questions? You may begin!"

The students in Mr. Dunbar's middle school math and science class get right to work. They are seated around lab tables in groups of four. One of the groups, the Master Minds, starts off by filling all its cylinders with water.

"OK," says Miguel, "we've filled all of our cylinders. What do we do next?"

"Let's measure them," suggests Margarite. She takes the ruler and asks Dave to write down her measurements.

"The water in this little one is 36 millimeters high and . . . just a sec . . . 42 millimeters across the bottom."

"So what?" asks Yolanda. "We can't figure out the volume this way. Let's do a little thinking before we start measuring everything."

"Yolanda's right," says Dave. "We'd better work out a plan."

"I know," says Miguel, "let's make a hypo . . . , hypotha . . . , what's it called?"

"Hypothesis," says Yolanda. "Yeah! Let's guess what we think the solution is."

"Remember how Mr. Dunbar reminded us about the area of a circle and the volume of a cube? I'll bet that's an important clue."

"You're right, Miguel," says Mr. Dunbar, who happens to be passing by. "But what are you guys going to do with that information?"

The Master Minds are quiet for a few moments. "Let's try figuring out the area of the bottom of one of these cylinders," ventures Dave. "Remember that Margarite said the bottom of the little one was 42 millimeters? Give me the calculator . . . now how do we get the area?"

Yolanda says, "I think it was pi times the radius squared."

"That sounds right. So 42 squared—"

"Not 42; 21 squared," interrupts Margarite. "If the diameter is 42, the radius is 21."

"OK, OK, I would have remembered. Now, 21 squared is . . . 441, and pi is about 3.14, so my handy-dandy calculator says . . . 13,847."

"Can't be," says Miguel. "Four hundred times three is twelve hundred, so 441 times 3.14 can't be thirteen thousand. I think you did something wrong."

"Let me do it again . . . 441 times 3.14 . . . you're right. Now it's about 1,385."

"So what?" says Yolanda.

"That doesn't tell us how to figure the volume!"

Margarite jumps in excitedly. "Just hang on for a minute, Yolanda. Now, I think we should multiply the area of the bottom by the height of the water."

"But why?" asks Miguel.

"Well," said Margarite, "when we did the volume of a cube, we multiplied length times width times height. Length times width is the area of the bottom. I'll bet we could do the same with a cylinder!"

"The girl's brilliant!" says Miguel. "Sounds good to me. But how could we prove it?"

"I've got an idea," says Yolanda. She empties the water out of all the cylinders and fills the smallest one to the top. "This is my idea. We don't know what the volume of this cylinder is, but we do know that it's always the same. If we pour the same amounts of water into all four cylinders and use our formula, it should always come out to the same amount!"

"Let's try it!" says Miguel. He pours the water from the small cylinder into a larger one, refills it, and pours it into another of a different shape.

The Master Minds measure the bases and the heights of the water in their cylinders, write down the measurements, and try out their formula. Sure enough, their formula always gives the same answer for the same volume of water. In great excitement they call Mr. Dunbar to come see what they are doing. Mr. Dunbar asks each of the students to explain what he or she has done.

"Terrific!" he says. "Not only did you figure out a solution, but everyone in the group participated and understood what you did. Now I'd like you to help me out. I've got a couple of groups that are really stumped. Do you suppose you could help them? Don't give them the answer, but help them get on track. How about Yolanda

and Miguel help with the Brainiacs, and Dave and Margarite help with the Dream Team. OK? Thanks!"

USING YOUR EXPERIENCE

Cooperative Learning and Critical Thinking   After reading this case, randomly select or appoint a four- to eight-member panel of "experts" on constructivism who sit in front of the class to explain why this method of teaching worked so well for Mr. Dunbar in his middle school math and science classroom. (Students might want to volunteer for the panel.) Members of the audience can ask questions once each panelist has spoken.

Critical Thinking   Reflect on Mr. Dunbar's teaching style. How would you characterize it (e.g., Piagetian, Vygotskian, discovery, other)? How does he frame the task and interact with students? His addressing of students' prior learning and questioning is critical from a constructivist point of view. Why?

Learning is much more than memory. For students to really understand and be able to apply knowledge, they must work to solve problems, to discover things for themselves, to wrestle with ideas. Mr. Dunbar could have told his students that the formula for the volume of a cylinder is $\pi r^2 h$. With practice the students would have been able to feed numbers into this formula and grind out correct answers. But how much would it have meant to them, and how well could they have applied the ideas behind the formula to other problems? The task of education is not to pour information into students' heads, but to engage students' minds with powerful and useful concepts. The focus of this chapter is to examine ways of doing this.

What Is the Constructivist View of Learning ❓

INTASC

4 Multiple Instructional Strategies

constructivist theories of learning

Theories that state learners must individually discover and transform complex information, checking new information against old rules and revising rules when they no longer work.

One of the most important principles of educational psychology is that teachers cannot simply give students knowledge. Students must construct knowledge in their own minds. You can facilitate this process by teaching in ways that make information meaningful and relevant to students, by giving students opportunities to discover or apply ideas themselves, and by teaching students to be aware of and consciously use their own strategies for learning. You can give students ladders that lead to higher understanding, but the students themselves must climb these ladders (Guskey & Anderman, 2008).

Theories of learning based on these ideas are called **constructivist theories of learning.** The essence of constructivist theory is the idea that learners must individually discover and transform complex information if they are to make it their own (Anderson, Greeno, Reder, & Simon, 2000; Fosnot, 2005; Waxman, Padrón, & Arnold, 2001). Constructivist theory sees learners as constantly checking new information against old rules and then revising rules when they no longer work. This view has profound implications for teaching because it suggests a far more active role for students in their own learning than is typical in many classrooms. Because of the emphasis on students as active learners, constructivist strategies are often called *student-centered instruction* (Cornelius-White, 2007). In a student-centered classroom the teacher becomes the "guide on the side" instead of the "sage on the stage," helping students to discover their own meaning instead of lecturing and controlling all classroom activities (Noddings, 2008; Weinberger & McCombs, 2001; Zmuda, 2008).

■ Historical Roots of Constructivism

The constructivist revolution has deep roots in the history of education. It draws heavily on the work of Piaget and Vygotsky (recall Chapter 2), both of whom emphasized that cognitive change takes place only when previous conceptions go through a process of disequilibration in light of new information. Piaget and Vygotsky also stressed the social nature of learning, and both suggested the use of mixed-ability learning groups to promote conceptual change. Modern constructivist thought draws most heavily on Vygotsky's theories (see John-Steiner & Mahn, 1996; Karpov & Bransford, 1995), which have been used to support classroom instructional methods that emphasize cooperative learning, project-based learning, and discovery. Four key principles derived from Vygotsky's ideas have played an important role: social learning, the zone of proximal development, cognitive apprenticeship, and mediated learning.

SOCIAL LEARNING Vygotsky emphasized the social nature of learning (Hall & Greeno, 2008; O'Connor, 1998; Salomon & Perkins, 1998). Children learn, he proposed, through joint interactions with adults and more capable peers. On cooperative projects, such as in Mr. Dunbar's class, children are exposed to their peers' thinking processes; this method not only makes the learning outcome available to all students, but also makes other students' thinking processes available to all. Vygotsky noted that successful problem-solvers talk themselves through difficult problems. In cooperative groups, children can hear this inner speech out loud and learn how successful problem-solvers are thinking through their approaches.

ZONE OF PROXIMAL DEVELOPMENT A second key concept is the idea that children learn best the concepts that are in their zones of proximal development. As discussed in Chapter 2, a child's zone of proximal development marks the range of tasks the child might not be able to do alone but can do with the assistance of peers or adults. For example, if a child cannot find the median of a set of numbers by herself but could do so with some assistance from her teacher, then finding medians is probably in her zone of proximal development. When children are working together, most of them will be performing on the given tasks at slightly higher or lower cognitive levels but still within each child's zone of proximal development.

COGNITIVE APPRENTICESHIP Another concept derived from Vygotsky that emphasizes both the social nature of learning and the zone of proximal development is **cognitive apprenticeship** (Greeno, Collins, & Resnick, 1996; Harpaz & Lefstein, 2000). This term refers to the process by which a learner gradually acquires expertise through interaction with an expert, either an adult or an older or more advanced peer. In many occupations, new workers learn their jobs through a process of apprenticeship in which they work closely with experts who provide models, give feedback to less experienced workers, and gradually socialize new workers into the norms and behaviors of the profession. Student teaching is a form of apprenticeship. Constructivist theorists suggest that teachers transfer this long-standing and highly effective model of teaching and learning to day-to-day activities in classrooms, by engaging students in complex tasks and helping them through these tasks (as a master electrician would help an apprentice rewire a house) (Hamman, Berthelot, Saia, & Crowley, 2000) and also by engaging students in

"2 + 2 = 4? What kind of constructivist answer is that?"

Connections

The work of Piaget and of Vygotsky is discussed on pages 31–44 of Chapter 2.

Connections

For more on the zone of proximal development, see Chapter 2, pages 41–42.

cognitive apprenticeship

The process by which a learner gradually acquires expertise through interaction with an expert, either an adult or an older or more advanced peer.

heterogeneous, cooperative learning groups in which more advanced students help less advanced peers through complex tasks.

> **ON THE WEB**
>
> For more on cognitive apprenticeship go to http://mathforum.org/~sarah/Discussion.Sessions/Collins.html. To see examples of cognitive apprenticeship in two fourth-grade classrooms go to http://projects.coe.uga.edu/epltt/index.php?title=Cognitive_Apprenticeship and www.21learn.org/archive/articles/brown_seely.php.

MEDIATED LEARNING   Finally, Vygotsky's emphasis on scaffolding, or mediated learning (Kozulin & Presseisen, 1995), is important in modern constructivist thought. Current interpretations of Vygotsky's ideas emphasize the idea that students should be given complex, difficult, realistic tasks and then be given enough help to achieve these tasks (rather than being taught little bits of knowledge that are expected someday to build up to complex tasks). This principle is used to support the classroom use of projects, simulations, explorations in the community, writing for real audiences, and other authentic tasks (Byerly, 2001; Holt & Willard-Holt, 2000; Levy, 2008). The term *situated learning* (Anderson et al., 2000) is used to describe learning that takes place in real-life, authentic tasks. This perspective emphasizes learning in depth, rather than learning that is a mile wide and an inch deep (Egan, 2008).

■ Top-Down Processing

Constructivist approaches to teaching emphasize top-down rather than bottom-up instruction. The term *top-down* means that students begin with complex problems to solve and then work out or discover (with your guidance) the basic skills required. For example, students might be asked to write compositions and only later learn about spelling, grammar, and punctuation. This top-down processing approach is contrasted with the traditional bottom-up strategy, in which basic skills are gradually built into more complex skills. In top-down teaching, the tasks students begin with are complex, complete, and authentic, meaning that they are not parts or simplifications of the tasks that students are ultimately expected to perform but are the actual tasks. As one instance of a constructivist approach to mathematics teaching, consider an example from Lampert (1986). The traditional, bottom-up approach to teaching the multiplication of two-digit numbers by one-digit numbers (e.g., $4 \times 12 = 48$) is to teach students a step-by-step procedure to get the right answer. Only after students have mastered this basic skill are they given simple application problems, such as "Sondra saw some pencils that cost 12 cents each. How much money would she need to buy four of them?"

The constructivist approach works in exactly the opposite order, beginning with problems (often proposed by the students themselves) and then helping students figure out how to do the operations. Lampert's example of this appears in Figure 8.1. In the chapter-opening vignette, Mr. Dunbar used cooperative groups to help students derive a formula for the volume of a cylinder. Recall how the Master Minds bounced ideas off of each other, tried out and discarded false leads, and ultimately came up with a solution and a way to prove that their solution was correct. None of the students could have solved the problem alone, so the groupwork was helpful in arriving at a solution. More important, the experience of hearing others' ideas, trying out and receiving immediate feedback on proposed solutions, and arguing about different ways to proceed gave the Master Minds the cognitive scaffolding that Vygotsky, Bruner, and other constructivists hold to be essential to higher-order learning (Fosnot, 2005).

■ Cooperative Learning

Constructivist approaches to teaching typically make extensive use of cooperative learning, on the theory that students will more easily discover and comprehend difficult

INTASC

5 Classroom Management and Motivation

FIGURE 8.1   Mathematical Stories for Teaching Multiplication

Teacher: Can anyone give me a story that could go with this multiplication . . . 12 × 4?

Student 1: There were 12 jars, and each had 4 butterflies in it.

Teacher: And if I did this multiplication and found the answer, what would I know about those jars and butterflies?

Student 1: You'd know you had that many butterflies altogether.

Teacher: Okay, here are the jars. *[Draws a picture to represent the jars of butterflies—see diagram.]* Now, it will be easier for us to count how many butterflies there are altogether if we think of the jars in groups. And, as usual, the mathematician's favorite number for thinking about groups is?

Student 2: 10

Teacher: Each of these 10 jars has 4 butterflies in it. *[Draws a loop around 10 jars.]*

Teacher: Suppose I erase my circle and go back to looking at the 12 jars again all together: Is there any other way I could group them to make it easier for us to count all the butterflies?

Student 3: You could do 6 and 6.

Teacher: Now, how many do I have in this group?

Student 4: 24

Teacher: How did you figure that out?

Student 4: 8 and 8 and 8. *[He puts the 6 jars together into 3 pairs, intuitively finding a grouping that made the figuring easier for him.]*

Teacher: That's 3 × 8. It's also 6 × 4. Now how many are in this group?

Student 3: 24. It's the same. They both have 6 jars.

Teacher: And how many are there altogether?

Student 5: 24 and 24 is 48.

Teacher: Do we get the same number of butterflies as before? Why?

Student 5: Yeah, because we have the same number of jars and they still have 4 butterflies in each.

concepts if they can talk with each other about the problems. Again, the emphasis on the social nature of learning and the use of groups of peers to model appropriate ways of thinking and expose and challenge each other's misconceptions are key elements of Piaget's and Vygotsky's conceptions of cognitive change (Webb, 2008). Cooperative learning methods are described in more detail later in this chapter.

▪ Discovery Learning

Discovery learning is an important component of modern constructivist approaches that has a long history in education innovation. In **discovery learning** (Bergstrom & O'Brien, 2001; Wilcox, 1993), students are encouraged to learn largely on their own through active involvement with concepts and principles, and teachers encourage students to have experiences and conduct experiments that permit them to discover principles for themselves. Bruner (1966), an advocate of discovery learning, put it this way: "We teach a subject not to produce little living libraries on that subject, but rather to get a student to think ... for himself, to consider matters as an historian does, to take part in the process of knowledge-getting. Knowing is a process, not a product" (1966, p. 72).

Discovery learning has applications in many subjects. For example, some science museums have a series of cylinders of different sizes and weights, some hollow and some solid. Students are encouraged to race the cylinders down a ramp. By careful experimentation the students can discover the underlying principles that determine the cylinders' speed. Computer simulations can create environments in which students can discover scientific principles (DeJong & van Joolingen, 1998). After-school enrichment programs (Bergstrom & O'Brien, 2001) and innovative science programs (Singer, Marx, Krajcik, & Chambers, 2000) are particularly likely to be based on principles of discovery learning.

Discovery learning has several advantages. It arouses students' curiosity, motivating them to continue to work until they find answers. Students also learn independent problem-solving and critical-thinking skills, because they must analyze and manipulate information. However, discovery learning can also lead to errors and wasted time. For this reason, *guided* discovery learning is more common than pure discovery learning (Hmelo-Silver, Duncan, & Chinn, 2007; Kirschner & van Merrienboer, 2008; Pressley et al., 2003). In guided discovery the teacher plays a more active role, giving clues, structuring portions of an activity, or providing outlines.

▪ Self-Regulated Learning

A key concept of constructivist theories of learning is a vision of the ideal student as a **self-regulated learner** (Greene & Azevedo, 2007; Hadwin, 2008; Paris & Paris, 2001), one who has knowledge of effective learning strategies and how and when to use them (Bandura, 2001; Dembo & Eaton, 2000; Hadwin, 2008; Zimmerman & Schunk, 2001). For example, self-regulated learners know how to break complex problems into simpler steps or to test out alternative solutions (Hall & Greeno, 2008), they know how and when to skim and how and when to read for deep understanding, and they know how to write to persuade and how to write to inform (Zimmerman & Schunk, 2001). Furthermore, self-regulated learners are motivated by learning itself, not only by grades or others' approval (Boekaerts, 2006), and they are able to stick to a long-term task until it is done. When students have both effective learning strategies and the motivation and persistence to apply these strategies until a job is done to their satisfaction, then they are likely to be effective learners (Williams, 1995; Zimmerman, 1995) and to have a lifelong motivation to learn (Corno & Kanfer, 1993). Programs that teach children self-regulated learning strategies have been found to increase students' achievement (Cho & Bergin, 2009; Cleary & Zimmerman, 2004; Fuchs et al., 2003; Mason, 2004; Torrance, Fidalgo, & Garcia, 2007).

▪ Scaffolding

As was noted in Chapter 2, scaffolding is a practice based on Vygotsky's concept of assisted learning. According to Vygotsky, higher mental functions, including the ability to

Connections

For more on the motivational aspects of self-regulated learning, see Chapter 10, page 293.

Connections

For more on scaffolding, see Chapter 2, page 42.

discovery learning

A constructivist approach to teaching in which students are encouraged to discover principles for themselves.

self-regulated learners

Students who have knowledge of effective learning strategies and how and when to use them.

Michael Newman/PhotoEdit

Early in the scaffolding process, the teacher provides more structure and then gradually turns responsibility over to the student. What are the possible benefits of this strategy?

direct memory and attention in a purposeful way and to think in symbols, are mediated behaviors (DeVries, 2008). Mediated externally by culture, these and other behaviors become internalized in the learner's mind as psychological tools. In assisted learning, or **mediated learning,** the teacher is the cultural agent who guides instruction so that students will master and internalize the skills that permit higher cognitive functioning. This ability to internalize cultural tools is a function of the learner's age or stage of cognitive development. Once acquired, internal mediators allow greater self-mediated learning.

In practical terms, scaffolding might include giving students more structure at the beginning of a set of lessons and gradually turning responsibility over to them to operate on their own (Good & Brophy, 2008; Puntambekar & Hübscher, 2005; Shepard, 2005). For example, students can be taught to generate their own questions about material they are reading. Early on, you might suggest the questions, modeling the kinds of questions students might ask, but students later take over the question-generating task (Fisher & Frey, 2008). For another example of scaffolding, see Figure 8.2.

■ APA's Learner-Centered Psychological Principles

In 1992 the American Psychological Association's Task Force on Psychology in

mediated learning

Assisted learning; an approach in which the teacher guides instruction by means of scaffolding to help students master and internalize the skills that permit higher cognitive functioning.

FIGURE 8.2 **Scaffolding**

Here is a brief example of an adult scaffolding a young child's efforts to put a difficult puzzle together.

Jason: I can't get this one in. *(Tries to insert a piece in the wrong place)*

Adult: Which piece might go down here? *(Points to the bottom of the puzzle)*

Jason: His shoes. *(Looks for a piece resembling the clown's shoes but tries the wrong one)*

Adult: Well, what piece looks like this shape? *(Points again to the bottom of the puzzle)*

Jason: The brown one. *(Tries it and it fits; then attempts another piece and looks at the adult)*

Adult: There you have it! Now try turning that piece just a little. *(Gestures to show him)*

Jason: There! *(Puts in several more, commenting to himself, "Now a green piece to match," "Turn it [meaning the puzzle piece]," as the adult watches)*

Source: Laura E. Berk, *Infants, Children, and Adolescents* (2nd ed.), p. 328. © 1996 Allyn and Bacon. Reproduced by permission of Pearson Education, Inc.

Education published a document called *Learner-Centered Psychological Principles: Guidelines for School Redesign and Reform* (American Psychological Association, 1992, 1997; see also Alexander & Murphy, 1994). Revised in 1997, this publication presents a consensus view of principles of learning and motivation among prominent educational psychologists primarily working within the constructivist tradition. Table 8.1 shows the APA's 14 principles.

TABLE 8.1	**Learner-Centered Psychological Principles: Cognitive and Metacognitive Factors**
Principle	**Explanation**
Principle 1 Nature of the learning process	The learning of complex subject matter is most effective when it is an intentional process of constructing meaning from information and experience.
Principle 2 Goals of the learning process	The successful learner, over time and with support and instructional guidance, can create meaningful, coherent representations of knowledge.
Principle 3 Construction of knowledge	The successful learner can link new information with existing knowledge in meaningful ways.
Principle 4 Strategic thinking	The successful learner can create and use a repertoire of thinking and reasoning strategies to achieve complex learning goals.
Principle 5 Thinking about thinking	Higher-order strategies for selecting and monitoring mental operations facilitate creative and critical thinking.
Principle 6 Context of learning	Learning is influenced by environmental factors, including culture, technology, and instructional practices.
Principle 7 Motivational and emotional influences on learning	What and how much is learned is influenced by the learner's motivation. Motivation to learn, in turn, is influenced by the individual's emotional states, beliefs, interests and goals, and habits of thinking.
Principle 8 Intrinsic motivation to learn	The learner's creativity, higher-order thinking, and natural curiosity all contribute to motivation to learn. Intrinsic motivation is stimulated by tasks that are of optimal novelty and difficulty, are relevant to personal interests, and provide for personal choice and control.
Principle 9 Effects of motivation on effort	Acquisition of complex knowledge and skills requires extended learner effort and guided practice. Without learners' motivation to learn, the willingness to exert this effort is unlikely without coercion.
Principle 10 Developmental influences on learning	As individuals develop, they encounter different opportunities and experience different constraints for learning. Learning is most effective when differential development within and across physical, intellectual, emotional, and social domains is taken into account.
Principle 11 Social influences on learning	Learning is influenced by social interactions, interpersonal relations, and communication with others.
Principle 12 Individual differences in learning	Learners have different strategies, approaches, and capabilities for learning that are a function of prior experience and heredity.
Principle 13 Learning and diversity	Learning is most effective when differences in learners' linguistic, cultural, and social backgrounds are taken into account.
Principle 14 Standards and assessment	Setting appropriately high and challenging standards and assessing the learner and learning progress—including diagnostic, process, and outcome assessment—are integral parts of the learning process.

The Learner-Centered Psychological Principles paint a picture of the learner as actively seeking knowledge by (1) reinterpreting information and experience for himself or herself, (2) feeling self-motivated by the quest for knowledge (rather than by grades or other rewards), (3) working with others to socially construct meaning, and (4) becoming aware of his or her own learning strategies and capable of applying them to new problems or circumstances.

■ Constructivist Methods in the Content Areas

Constructivist and student-centered methods have come to dominate current thinking in all areas of curriculum (see Gabler & Schroeder, 2003; Gagnon & Collay, 2001; Henson, 2004). The following sections describe constructivist approaches in reading, mathematics, and science.

RECIPROCAL TEACHING IN READING One well-researched example of a constructivist approach based on principles of question generation is **reciprocal teaching** (Palincsar & Brown, 1984). This approach, designed primarily to help low achievers in elementary and middle schools learn reading comprehension, involves the teacher working with small groups of students. Initially, you model questions students might ask as they read, but students are soon appointed to act as "teacher" to generate questions for each other. Figure 8.3 presents an example of reciprocal teaching in use. Note in the example how the teacher directs the conversation about crows at first but then turns the responsibility over to Jim (who is about to turn it over to another student as the example ends). The teacher is modeling the behaviors she wants the students to be able to do on their own and then changes her role to that of facilitator and organizer as the students begin to generate the actual questions. Research on reciprocal teaching has generally found this strategy to increase the success of low achievers (Alfassi, 1998; Carter, 1997; Lysynchuk, Pressley, & Vye, 1990; Palincsar & Brown, 1984; Rosenshine & Meister, 1994).

Theory into Practice
Introducing Reciprocal Teaching

In introducing reciprocal teaching to students, you might begin as follows: "For the coming weeks we will be working together to improve your ability to understand what you read. Sometimes we are so busy figuring out what the words are that we fail to pay much attention to what the words and sentences mean. We will be learning a way to pay more attention to what we are reading. I will teach you to do the following activities as you read:

1. To think of important questions that might be asked about what is being read and to be sure that you can answer those questions

2. To summarize the most important information that you have read

3. To predict what the author might discuss next in the passage

4. To point out when something is unclear in the passage or doesn't make sense and then to see if we can make sense of it

"These activities will help you keep your attention on what you are reading and make sure that you are understanding it.

reciprocal teaching

A small-group teaching method based on principles of question generation; through instruction and modeling, teachers foster metacognitive skills primarily to improve the reading performance of students who have poor comprehension.

FIGURE 8.3 **Example of a Reciprocal Teaching Lesson**

Teacher: The title of this story is "Genius with Feathers." Let's have some predictions. I will begin by guessing that this story will be about birds that are very smart. Why do I say that?

First student: Because a genius is someone very smart.

Second student: Because they have feathers.

Teacher: That's right. Birds are the only animals that have feathers. Let's predict now the kind of information you might read about very smart birds.

Third student: What kinds of birds?

Teacher: Good question. What kinds would you guess are very smart?

Third student: Parrots or blue jays.

First student: A cockatoo.

Teacher: What other information would you want to know? *[No response from students]*

Teacher: I would like to know what these birds do that is so smart. Any ideas?

Second student: Some birds talk.

Fourth student: They can fly.

Teacher: That's an interesting one. As smart as people are, they can't fly. Well, let's read this first section now and see how many of our predictions were right. I will be the teacher for this section. *[All read the section silently.]*

Teacher: Who is the genius with feathers?

First student: Crows.

Teacher: That's right. We were correct in our prediction that this story would be about birds, but we didn't correctly guess which kind of bird, did we? My summary of the first section would be that it describes the clever things that crows do, which make them seem quite intelligent.

Let's read on. Who will be the teacher for this section? Jim?

Jim: How do crows communicate with one another?

Teacher: Good question! You picked right up on our prediction that this is about the way crows communicate. Whom do you choose to answer your question?

Jim: Barbara.

Barbara: Crows have built-in radar and a relay system.

Jim: That's a good part of it. The answer I wanted was how they relay the messages from one crow to the other crow.

Teacher: Summarize now.

Jim: This is about how crows have developed a system of communication.

Teacher: That's right. The paragraph goes on to give examples of how they use pitch and changes in interval, but these are supporting details. The main idea is that crows communicate through a relay system, Jim?

Jim: It says in this section that crows can use their communication system to play tricks, so I predict the next section will say something about the tricks crows play. I would like Sue to be the next teacher.

Teacher: Excellent prediction. The last sentence of a paragraph often suggests what the next paragraph will be about. Good, Jim.

Source: Annemarie Palincsar, "The Role of Dialogue in Providing Scaffolded Instruction," *Educational Psychologist, 21,* pp. 73–98. Copyright 1986 by Taylor and Francis Informa UK Ltd.–Journals. Reproduced with permission of Taylor and Francis Informa UK Ltd. via Copyright Clearance Center.

"The way in which you will learn these four activities is by taking turns in the role of teacher during our reading group sessions. When I am the teacher, I will show you how I read carefully by thinking of questions I have while reading, by summarizing the most important information I read, and by predicting what I think the author might discuss next. I will also tell you if I found anything I read to be unclear or confusing and how I made sense out of it.

"When you are the teacher, you will first ask the rest of us the questions you made up while reading. You will tell us if our answers are correct. You will summarize the most important information you learned while reading. You will also tell us if you found anything in the passage to be confusing. Several times throughout the story you will also be asked to predict what you think might be discussed next in the passage. When you are the teacher, the rest of us will answer your questions and comment on your summary.

"These are activities that we hope you will learn and use, not only when you are here in reading class but also whenever you want to understand and remember what you are reading—for example, in social studies, science, or history."

Daily Procedures

1. Pass out the passage for the day.

2. Explain that you will be the teacher for the first segment.

3. Instruct the students to read silently whatever portion of the passage you determine is appropriate. At the beginning, it will probably be easiest to work paragraph by paragraph.

4. When everyone has completed the first segment, model the following:
   - "The question that I thought a teacher might ask is . . ."
   - Have the students answer your question. They may refer to the text if necessary. "I would summarize the important information in this paragraph in the following way . . ."
   - "From the title of the passage, I would predict that the author will discuss . . ."
   - If appropriate, "When I read this part, I found the following to be unclear . . ."

5. Invite the students to make comments regarding your teaching and the passage with prompts such as the following:
   - "Was there more important information?"
   - "Does anyone have more to add to my prediction?"
   - "Did anyone find something else confusing?"

6. Assign the next segment to be read silently. Choose a student to act as teacher for this segment. Begin with the more verbal students who you think will have less difficulty with the activities.

7. Coach the student teacher through the activities as necessary. Encourage the other students to participate in the dialogue, but always give the student teacher for that segment the opportunity to go first and lead the dialogue. Be sure to give the student teacher plenty of feedback and praise for his or her participation.

8. As the training days go by, try to remove yourself more and more from the dialogue so that the student teacher initiates the activities with students providing feedback. Your role will continue to be monitoring, keeping students on track, and helping them over obstacles. Throughout the training, however, continue to take your turn as teacher, modeling at least once a session.

QUESTIONING THE AUTHOR   Another constructivist approach for reading is Questioning the Author (Beck & McKeown, 2001; McKeown & Beck, 2004; Salinger & Fleischman, 2005). In this method, children in grades 3–9 are taught to see the authors of factual material as real, fallible people and to then engage in simulated "dialogues" with the authors. As the students are reading a text, stop them from time to time to ask questions such as "What is the author trying to say, or what does she want us to know?" and then follow up with questions such as "How does that fit in with what she said before?" Ultimately, the students themselves take responsibility for formulating questions of the author's intent and meaning. A study of fifth- and sixth-graders found that students who experienced this technique recalled more from texts than did a comparison group, and were far more likely to describe the purpose of reading as *understanding* rather than simply memorizing the text (McKeown & Beck, 1998). A study of low-achieving kindergartners and first-graders also found positive effects of a similar strategy on vocabulary development (Beck & McKeown, 2007).

WRITING PROCESS MODELS   A widely used set of approaches to the teaching of creative writing, writing process models (Calkins, 1983; Graves, 1983) engage students in small peer-response teams in which they work together to help one another plan, draft, revise, edit, and "publish" compositions. That is, children may review each other's drafts and give helpful ideas for improvements in content as well as mechanics (e.g., spelling, punctuation), ultimately presenting compositions for some authentic purpose (such as a poetry reading or a literary review). In the process of responding to others' compositions, children gain insight into the process of writing and revision.

Research on writing process methods has found positive effects of these strategies (Harris & Graham, 1996b). Strategies that provide specific scaffolding, such as instruction in graphic organizers to help children use metacognitive strategies for planning and evaluating their own work, have been particularly effective (de La Paz & Graham, 2002; Glaser & Brunstein, 2007; Graham, 2006; Harris, Graham, & Mason, 2006). There is also evidence that teaching writing in various content areas increases content learning in these subjects (Bangert-Drowns, Hurley, & Wilkinson, 2004; Headley, 2008). Adding strategy instruction to writing instruction further adds to outcomes (Fidalgo, Torrance, & Garcia, 2008).

CONSTRUCTIVIST APPROACHES TO MATHEMATICS TEACHING IN THE PRIMARY GRADES   Carpenter and colleagues (1994) describe four approaches to mathematics instruction for the early elementary grades. In all four, students work together in small groups; teachers pose problems and then circulate among groups to facilitate the discussion of strategies, join students in asking questions about strategies they have proposed, and occasionally offer alternative strategies when students appear to be stuck. In Supporting Ten-Structured Thinking (STST) (Fuson, 1992), children use base-10 blocks to invent procedures for adding and subtracting large numbers. Conceptually Based Instruction (CBI) (Hiebert & Wearne, 1993) makes extensive use of physical, pictorial, verbal, and symbolic presentations of mathematical ideas and gives students opportunities to solve complex problems using these representations and to contrast different representations of the same concepts. Similarly, the Problem Centered Mathematics Project (PCMP) (Murray, Olivier, & Human, 1992) leads children through stages, from modeling with counters to solving more abstract problems without counters. Cognitively Guided Instruction (CGI) (Carpenter & Fennema, 1992; Fennema, Franke, Carpenter, & Carey, 1993), unlike STST and CBI, does not have a specific curriculum or recommended set of activities but provides extensive professional development for teachers of primary mathematics, focusing on principles similar to those used in the other programs. There is good evidence that this program increases student achievement not only on measures related to higher-level thinking in mathematics, which is the program's focus, but also on computational skills (Carpenter & Fennema, 1992; Carpenter, Fennema, Peterson, Chiang, & Loef, 1989).

In these and other constructivist approaches to mathematics, the emphasis is on beginning with real problems for students to solve intuitively and letting students use their existing knowledge of the world to solve problems any way they can (Greeno & Goldman, 1998; Hiebert et al., 1996; Schifter, 1996). The problem and solutions in Figure 8.1 illustrate this approach. Only at the end of the process, when students have achieved a firm conceptual understanding, are they taught formal, abstract representations of the mathematical processes they have been working with (see Clements & Battista, 1990).

CONSTRUCTIVIST APPROACHES IN SCIENCE   Discovery, groupwork, and conceptual change have long been emphasized in science education, so it is not surprising that many elementary and secondary science educators have embraced constructivist ideas (see Greeno & Goldman, 1998). In this subject, constructivism translates into an emphasis on hands-on, investigative laboratory activities (Pine & Aschbacher, 2006; Singer et al., 2000; White & Frederiksen, 1998), identifying misconceptions and using experimental approaches to correct these misconceptions (Hand & Treagust, 1991; Sandoval, 1995), cooperative learning (Pea, 1993; Wheatley, 1991), and teaching of metacognitive skills (Zohar & Peled, 2008).

■ Research on Constructivist Methods

Research comparing constructivist and traditional approaches to instruction is often difficult to interpret because constructivist methods are themselves very diverse and usually intended to produce outcomes that are qualitatively different from those of traditional methods. For example, many researchers argue that acquisition of skills and basic information must be balanced against the deeper learning possible in constructivist approaches (Egan, 2008; Jensen & Nickelsen, 2008). But what is the appropriate balance, and for which objectives (Harris & Alexander, 1998; von Glaserfeld, 1996; Waxman et al., 2001)? Also, much of the research on constructivist methods is descriptive rather than comparative. However, there are studies showing positive effects of constructivist approaches on traditional achievement measures in mathematics (e.g., Carpenter & Fennema, 1992), science (e.g., Neale, Smith, & Johnson, 1990), reading (e.g., Duffy & Roehler, 1986), and writing (e.g., de La Paz & Graham, 2002). Furthermore, a study by Knapp (1995) found a correlation between use of more constructivist approaches and achievement gains in high-poverty schools. Weinberger and McCombs (2001) and Cornelius-White (2007) observed that students who reported more learner-centered methods being used in their classrooms performed at a higher level than other students. Langer (2001) found that secondary schools performing better than expected used more constructivist approaches than lower-achieving schools. However, other studies reported better results for explicit teaching than for constructivist approaches (Baker, Gersten, & Lee, 2002; Kirschner et al., 2006; Klahr & Nigam, 2004; Kroesbergen, Van Luit, & Maas, 2004). Much more research is needed to establish the conditions under which constructivist approaches are effective for enhancing student achievement. However, it is only reasonable to seek a balance between direct instruction and constructivist approaches and to use them to accomplish a wide range of objectives (Huebner, 2008.)

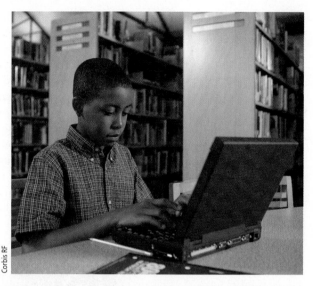

Corbis RF

Technology can help you provide students with multiple representations of concepts. How does technology reinforce constructivist learning?

✓ Certification Pointer

For teacher certification tests, you may be expected to choose alternative teaching strategies to achieve particular instructional goals.

How Is Cooperative Learning Used in Instruction?

In **cooperative learning** instructional methods, or peer-assisted learning (Rohrbeck, Ginsburg-Block, Fantuzzo, & Miller, 2003; Slavin, in press; Webb, 2008), students work together in small groups to help each other learn. Many quite different approaches to cooperative learning are used. Most involve students in four-member mixed-ability groups (e.g., Slavin, 1994b), but some methods use dyads (e.g., Fantuzzo, Polite, & Grayson, 1990; Maheady, Harper, & Mallette, 1991; O'Donnell & Dansereau, 1992) and some

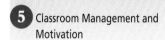

INTASC

4 Multiple Instructional Strategies

5 Classroom Management and Motivation

cooperative learning

Instructional approaches in which students work in small mixed-ability groups.

use varying group sizes (e.g., Cohen, 1994b; Johnson & Johnson, 1999; Kagan, 1992; Sharan & Sharan, 1992). Typically, students are assigned to cooperative groups and stay together for many weeks or months. They are usually taught specific skills that will help them work well together, such as listening actively, giving good explanations, avoiding putdowns, and including other people.

Cooperative learning activities can play many roles in lessons (Webb, 2008). Recall the chapter-opening vignette in Chapter 7: Ms. Logan used cooperative learning for three distinct purposes. At first, students worked as discovery groups, helping each other figure out how water in bottles could tell them about principles of sound. After the formal lesson, students worked as discussion groups. Finally, students had an opportunity to work together to make sure that all group members had learned everything in the lesson in preparation for a quiz, working in a group study format. In the vignette at the beginning of this chapter, Mr. Dunbar used cooperative groups to solve a complex problem.

> **ON THE WEB**
>
> For newsletters and resources for cooperative learning, visit the website of the International Association for the Study of Cooperation in Education at www.iasce.net. Information on STAD, TGT, CIRC, and other cooperative learning methods developed at Johns Hopkins University is available at www.successforall.org. For the University of Minnesota Cooperative Learning Center, see www.co-operation.org. For PALS, see www.vanderbilt.edu/cft/resources/teaching_resources/activities/cooperative.htm.

■ Cooperative Learning Methods

Many quite different cooperative learning methods have been developed and researched. The most extensively evaluated cooperative learning methods are described in the following sections.

STUDENT TEAMS–ACHIEVEMENT DIVISIONS (STAD)   Students are assigned to four-member learning teams in **Student Teams–Achievement Divisions (STAD)** (Slavin, 1994b). The groups are mixed in performance level, gender, and ethnicity. The teacher presents a lesson, and then students work within their teams to make sure that all team members have mastered the lesson. Finally, all students take individual quizzes on the material, at which time they may not help one another.

Students' quiz scores are compared to their own past averages, and points are awarded on the basis of the degree to which students meet or exceed their own earlier performances. These points are then summed to form team scores, and teams that meet certain criteria may earn certificates or other rewards. In a related method called Teams–Games–Tournaments (TGT), students play games with members of other teams to add points to their team scores.

STAD and TGT have been used in a wide variety of subjects, from mathematics to language arts to social studies, and have been used from second grade through college. The STAD method is most appropriate for teaching well-defined objectives, such as mathematical computations and applications, language usage and mechanics, geography and map skills, and science facts and concepts. However, it can easily be adapted for use with less well-defined objectives by incorporating more open-ended assessments, such as essays or performances. Many studies have found positive effects of STAD on learning of a variety of subjects (e.g., Barbato, 2000; Mevarech, 1991; Slavin & Karweit, 1984). STAD is described in more detail in the following Theory into Practice feature.

Certification Pointer

On your teacher certification test, you may be required to suggest an appropriate way of assigning students in a case study to cooperative learning groups.

Connections

To learn about the benefits of cooperative learning methods for promoting harmony in culturally diverse classrooms, see Chapter 4, page 94.

Student Teams–Achievement Divisions (STAD)

A cooperative learning method for mixed-ability groupings involving team recognition and group responsibility for individual learning.

Theory into Practice
Student Teams–Achievement Divisions (STAD)

Student Teams–Achievement Divisions (Slavin, 1994b, 1995a) is an effective co-operative learning method that consists of a regular cycle of teaching, cooperative study in mixed-ability teams, and quizzes, with recognition or other rewards provided to teams whose members excel.

STAD consists of a regular cycle of instructional activities, as follows:

- **Teach.**   Present the lesson.
- **Team study.**   Students work on worksheets in their teams to master the material.
- **Test.**   Students take individual quizzes or other assessments (such as essays or performances).
- **Team recognition.**   Team scores are computed on the basis of team members' scores, and certificates, a class newsletter, or bulletin board display recognizes high-scoring teams.

The following steps describe how to introduce students to STAD:

1. Assign students to teams of four or five members each. Groups of four are preferable; make five-member teams only if the class is not divisible by four. To assign the students, rank them from top to bottom on some measure of academic performance (e.g., past grades, test scores) and divide the ranked list into quarters, placing any extra students in the middle quarters. Then put one student from each quarter on each team, making sure that the teams are well balanced in gender and ethnicity. Extra (middle) students may become fifth members of teams.

2. Make a worksheet and a short quiz for the lesson you plan to teach. Tell the class that during team study (one or two class periods), the team members' tasks are to master the material you have presented in your lesson and to help their teammates master the material. Inform students that they will have worksheets or other study materials that they can use to practice the skill being taught and to assess themselves and their teammates.

3. Have teammates move their desks together or move to team tables and allow students about 10 minutes to decide on a team name. Then hand out worksheets or other study materials (two of each per team). Make sure students understand the following points before they begin:

- Suggest that students on each team work in pairs or threes. If they are working problems (as in math), each student in a pair or threesome should work the problem and then check with his or her partner(s). If anyone misses a question, that student's teammates have a responsibility to explain it. If students are working on short-answer questions, they might quiz each other, with partners taking turns holding the answer sheet or attempting to answer the questions.

- Emphasize to students that they are not finished studying until they are sure that all their teammates will make 100 percent on the quiz.

- Make sure that students understand that the worksheets are for studying—not for filling out and handing in. That is why it is important for students to have the answer sheets to check themselves and their teammates as they study.

- Have students explain answers to one another instead of only checking each other against the answer sheet.

- When students have questions, they should ask a teammate before asking you.

4. While students are working in teams, circulate through the class, praising teams that are working well and sitting in with each team to hear how the members are doing.

5. Distribute the quiz or other assessment, and give students adequate time to complete it. Do not let students work together on the quiz; at this point they must show what they have learned as individuals. Have students move their desks apart if this is possible. Either allow students to exchange papers with members of other teams or collect the quizzes to score after class.

6. Figure individual and team scores. Team scores in STAD are based on team members' improvements over their own past records. As soon as possible after each quiz, you should compute individual team scores and write a class newsletter (or prepare a class bulletin board) to announce the team scores. If at all possible, the announcement of team scores should be made in the first period after the quiz. This makes the connection between doing well and receiving recognition clear to students, increasing their motivation to do their best. Compute team scores by adding up the improvement points earned by the team members and dividing the sum by the number of team members who are present on the day of the quiz.

7. Recognize team accomplishments. As soon as you have calculated points for each student and figured team scores, you should provide some sort of recognition to any teams that average 20 improvement points or more. You might give certificates to team members or prepare a bulletin board display. It is important to help students value team success. Your own enthusiasm about team scores will help. If you give more than one quiz in a week, combine the quiz results into a single weekly score. After 5 or 6 weeks of STAD, reassign students to new teams. This allows students to work with other classmates and keeps the program fresh.

Cooperative Integrated Reading and Composition (CIRC)

A comprehensive program for teaching reading and writing in the upper elementary grades; students work in four-member cooperative learning teams.

Jigsaw

A cooperative learning model in which students are assigned to six-member teams to work on academic material that has been broken down into sections for each member.

COOPERATIVE INTEGRATED READING AND COMPOSITION (CIRC) A comprehensive program for teaching reading and writing in the upper elementary grades, **Cooperative Integrated Reading and Composition (CIRC)** (Stevens & Slavin, 1995b) involves students working in four-member cooperative learning teams. They engage in a series of activities with one another, including reading to one another; making predictions about how narrative stories will come out; summarizing stories to one another; writing responses to stories; and practicing spelling, decoding, and vocabulary. They also work together to master main ideas and other comprehension skills. During language arts periods, students engage in writing drafts, revising and editing one another's work, and preparing for publication of team books. Several studies of the CIRC program have found positive effects on students' reading skills, including improved scores on standardized reading and language tests (Calderón et al., 1998; Slavin, Madden, & Stevens, 1994; Stevens et al., 1987; Stevens & Slavin, 1995b).

JIGSAW In classes using **Jigsaw** (Aronson, Blaney, Stephen, Sikes, & Snapp, 1978), students are assigned to six-member teams to work on academic material that has been broken down into sections. For example, a biography might be divided into early life,

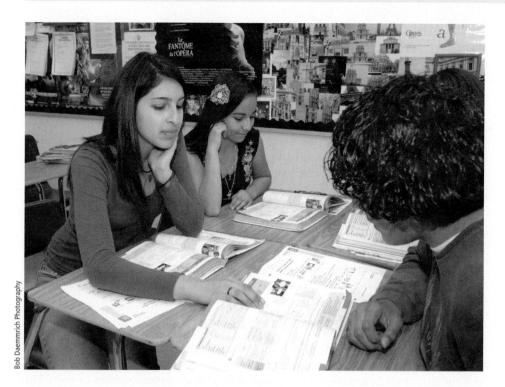

By working together, these students learn from each other. What are some advantages of cooperative learning?

first accomplishments, major setbacks, later life, and impact on history. Each team member reads his or her section. Next, members of different teams who have studied the same sections meet in expert groups to discuss their parts. Then the students return to their teams and take turns teaching their teammates about their sections. Because the only way students can learn sections other than on their own is to listen carefully to their teammates, they are motivated to support and show interest in one another's work. In a modification of this approach called Jigsaw II (Slavin, 1994b), students work in four- or five-member teams, as in STAD. Instead of each student being assigned a unique section, all students read a common text, such as a book chapter, a short story, or a biography, and then each student receives a topic on which to become an expert. Students with the same topics meet in expert groups to discuss them, after which they return to their teams to teach what they have learned to their teammates. The students take individual quizzes, which result in team scores, as in STAD.

LEARNING TOGETHER   A model of cooperative learning developed by David Johnson and Roger Johnson (1999), **Learning Together** involves students working in four- or five-member heterogeneous groups on assignments. The groups hand in a single completed assignment and receive praise and rewards based on the group product. This method emphasizes team-building activities before students begin working together and regular discussions within groups about how well they are working together.

GROUP INVESTIGATION   **Group Investigation** (Sharan & Sharan, 1992) is a general classroom organization plan in which students work in small groups using cooperative inquiry, group discussion, and cooperative planning and projects. In this method, students form their own two- to six-member groups. After choosing subtopics from a unit that the entire class is studying, the groups break their subtopics into individual tasks and carry out the activities that are necessary to prepare group reports. Each group then makes a presentation or display to communicate its findings to the entire class.

PEER-ASSISTED LEARNING STRATEGIES (PALS)   **PALS** is a structured cooperative learning method in which students work in pairs, taking turns as teacher and learner,

Learning Together

A cooperative learning model in which students in four- or five-member heterogeneous groups work together on assignments.

Group Investigation

A cooperative learning model in which students work in small groups using cooperative inquiry, group discussion, and cooperative planning and projects, afterward making presentations to the whole class on their findings.

peer-assisted learning strategies (PALS)

A structured cooperative learning method in which students work in pairs taking turns as teacher and learner, using specific metacognitive strategies.

Bob Daemmrich Photography

using specific metacognitive strategies. Several studies of PALS have found positive effects of this approach in reading (e.g., Calhoon, Al Otaiba, Cihak, King, & Aralos, 2007; Mathes & Babyak, 2001) and math (e.g., Fuchs, Fuchs, & Karns, 2001).

COOPERATIVE SCRIPTING   Many students find it helpful to get together with classmates to discuss material they have read or heard in class. A formalization of this age-old practice has been researched by Dansereau (1985) and his colleagues in which students work in pairs and take turns summarizing sections of the material for one another. While one student summarizes, the other listens and corrects any errors or omissions. Then the two students switch roles, continuing in this manner until they have covered all the material to be learned. A series of studies of this **cooperative scripting** method has consistently found that students who study this way learn and retain far more than students who summarize on their own or who simply read the material (Newbern, Dansereau, Patterson, & Wallace, 1994). It is interesting that although both participants in the cooperative pairs gain from the activity, the larger gains are seen in the sections that students teach to their partners rather than those in which they serve as listeners (King, 1997, 1998; Fuchs & Fuchs, 1997; Webb, 2008).

■ Research on Cooperative Learning

Cooperative learning methods fall into two broad categories (Slavin, 2010) defined by the goals of study. Group study methods are used primarily when students work together to help one another master a relatively well-defined body of information or skills. The other category, often called *project-based learning* or *active learning* (David, 2008; Zmuda, 2008), involves students working in groups to create a report, experiment, mural, or other product (Webb & Palincsar, 1996). Project-based learning methods such as those described by Blumenfeld, Marx, Soloway, and Krajcik (1996), Cohen (1994a), and Sharan and Sharan (1992) focus on problems that typically have less clear expected outcomes or instructional objectives than other approaches. Methods of this kind are often referred to as *collaborative learning methods* (Webb & Palincsar, 1996).

Most research comparing cooperative learning to traditional teaching methods has evaluated group study methods such as STAD, Jigsaw II, CIRC, and Johnson's methods. More than 100 studies have compared achievement in classrooms using such methods to traditional classrooms over periods of at least 4 weeks (Slavin, 1995a). The results have consistently favored cooperative learning as long as two essential conditions are met. First, some kind of recognition or small reward must be provided to groups that do well, so that group members can see that it is in their interest to help their groupmates learn. Second, there must be individual accountability. That is, the success of the group must depend on the individual learning of all group members, not on a single group product. For example, groups might be evaluated on the basis of the average of their members' scores on individual quizzes or essays (as in STAD), or students might be individually responsible for a unique portion of a group task (as in Group Investigation). Without this individual accountability there is a danger that one student might do the work of the others, or that some students might be shut out of group interaction because they are thought to have little to contribute (Chapman, 2001; Slavin, in press; Webb, 2008).

Studies of cooperative learning methods that incorporate group goals and individual accountability show substantial positive effects on the achievement of students in grades 2 through 12 in all subjects and in all types of schools (Ellis, 2001b; Rohrbeck et al., 2003; Slavin, 1995a, 2010). A review of group learning with technology also found positive effects for well-structured methods (Lou, Abrami, & d'Apollonia, 2001). Effects are similar for all grade levels and for all types of content, from basic skills to problem solving. Cooperative learning methods are usually used for only a portion of a student's school day and school year (Antil, Jenkins, Wayne, & Vadasy, 1998), but one study found that students in schools using a variety of cooperative learning methods in almost all subjects for a 2-year period achieved significantly better than did students in traditionally organized

Connections

For more on how cooperative learning methods benefit the social integration of students with special-education needs in the general education classroom, see Chapter 12, page 389.

cooperative scripting

A study method in which students work in pairs and take turns orally summarizing sections of material to be learned.

schools (Stevens & Slavin, 1995a). Studies generally show equal effects of cooperative learning for high, average, and low achievers and for boys and girls (Roseth, Johnson, & Johnson, 2008; Slavin, 1995a). There is some evidence that these methods are particularly effective for African American and Latino students (Boykin, 1994a; Calderón et al., 1998; Hurley, 2000). A review of peer-assisted learning by Rohrbeck and colleagues (2003) reported that effects were strongest on younger, urban, and low-income students and/or students who are minorities. More informal cooperative learning methods, lacking group goals and individual accountability, have not generally had positive effects on student achievement (Chapman, 2001; Klein & Schnackenberg, 2000; Slavin, 1995a, in press).

In addition to group goals and individual accountability, a few classroom practices can contribute to the effectiveness of cooperative learning. For example, cooperative groups who are taught communication and helping skills (Fuchs, Fuchs, Kazdan, & Allen, 1999; Kutnick, Ota, & Berdondini, 2008; Prichard, Bizo, & Stratford, 2006; Webb & Mastergeorge, 2003) or are given specific structured ways of working with each other learn more than students in cooperative groups without these enhancements (Baker et al., 2002; Emmer & Gerwels, 2002; Mathes et al., 2003; Saleh, Lazonder, & deJon, 2007). In addition, students who are taught metacognitive learning strategies (Friend, 2001; Jones et al., 2000; King, 1999; Kramarski & Mevarech, 2003) learn more than do students in usual cooperative groups. For example, King (1999) taught students generic question forms to ask each other as they studied, such as "compare and contrast _____ and _____ ," or "how does _____ affect _____?" Students that used these discourse patterns learned more than students using other forms of cooperative learning. A great deal of research has shown that students who give extensive explanations to others learn more in cooperative groups than those who give or receive short answers or no answers (Webb, 1992; Webb, Trooper, & Fall, 1995).

There is less research on the effects of project-based forms of cooperative learning focused on ill-structured problems, but the studies that do exist generally show equally favorable results of cooperative methods designed for such problems (Blumenfeld et al., 1996; David, 2008; Thousand & Villa, 1994). A study by Sharan and Shachar (1988)

✓ Certification Pointer

On your teacher certification test, you may be asked to determine when you would *not* employ a particular cooperative learning strategy.

21ST Century Learning

Cooperative Learning

In the 21st century, teamwork and the ability to solve problems and learn in groups are increasingly important in the world of work, and every student should know how to work productively with others. A great deal of research, summarized in this chapter, has shown that working in cooperative groups with group goals and individual accountability increases students' learning of traditional academic content. Along the way, they are likely to acquire equally important teamwork skills, such as the ability to teach and learn with partners, to support and encourage partners' efforts, to disagree with dignity and hold to a reasoned opinion without putting others down, and to resolve interpersonal conflicts and create a positive working environ-

ment within teams. All of these skills will help young people thrive in today's workforce while helping create a more peaceful and prosocial environment.

Questions

- What kinds of problems might you encounter in the workplace in which the experience of working in groups in school could help participants facilitate a solution?

- Taking it a step further, looking at the clashing of political factions, which skills gained in cooperative learning groups might be applicable to conflict resolution on a widespread scale?

found substantial positive effects of the Group Investigation method on higher-order objectives in language and literature. Methods incorporating "constructive conflict," in which students are taught positive ways to debate controversial issues, can also increase learning about the issues discussed (Johnson & Johnson, 2009; Lin & Anderson, 2008; Nussbaum, 2008). In addition to boosting achievement, cooperative learning methods have had positive effects on such outcomes as improved intergroup relations (Slavin, 1995b), self-esteem, attitudes toward school, and acceptance of children with special educational needs (Ginsburg-Block, Rohrbeck, & Fantuzzo, 2006; Roseth, Johnson, & Johnson, 2008; Shulman, Lotan, & Whitcomb, 1998; Slavin, 1995a). Studies find that co-operative learning is widely used (e.g., Antil et al., 1998; Puma et al., 1997), but the forms most often seen are informal methods lacking group goals and individual accountability, which research has found to be less effective than more structured methods.

How Are Problem-Solving and Thinking Skills Taught ?

INTASC

4 Multiple Instructional Strategies

Students cannot be said to have learned anything useful unless they have the ability to use information and skills to solve problems. For example, a student might be quite good at adding, subtracting, and multiplying but have little idea of how to solve this problem: "Sylvia bought four hamburgers at $1.25 each, two orders of french fries at 65 cents, and three large sodas at 75 cents. How much change did she get from a 10-dollar bill?"

Sylvia's situation is not unusual in real life, and the computations involved are not difficult. However, many students (and even some otherwise-competent adults) would have difficulty solving this problem. The difficulty of most application problems in mathematics lies not in the computations but in knowing how to set the problem up so that it can be solved. **Problem solving** is a skill that can be taught and learned (Fuchs et al., 2006).

■ The Problem-Solving Process

GENERAL PROBLEM-SOLVING STRATEGIES   Students can be taught several well-researched strategies to use in solving problems (see, for example, Beyer, 1998; Kirschner & van Merrienboer, 2008). Bransford and Stein (1993) developed and evaluated a five-step strategy called IDEAL:

I   Identify problems and opportunities

D   Define goals and represent the problem

E   Explore possible strategies

A   Anticipate outcomes and act

L   Look back and learn

IDEAL and similar strategies begin with carefully identifying the problem that needs to be solved, defining the resources and information that are available, determining a way that the problem can be represented (e.g., in a drawing, outline, or flowchart), and then breaking the process into steps that lead to a solution. For example, the first step is to identify the goal and figure out how to proceed. Newell and Simon (1972) suggest that the problem-solver repeatedly ask, "What is the difference between where I am now and where I want to be? What can I do to reduce that difference?" In solving Sylvia's problem, the goal is to find out how much change she will receive from a 10-dollar bill after buying food and drinks. We might then break the problem into substeps, each with its own subgoal:

problem solving

The application of knowledge and skills to achieve certain goals.

1. Figure how much Sylvia spent on hamburgers.

2. Figure how much Sylvia spent on french fries.

3. Figure how much Sylvia spent on sodas.

4. Figure how much Sylvia spent in total.

5. Figure how much change Sylvia gets from $10.00.

MEANS–ENDS ANALYSIS   Deciding what the problem is and what needs to be done involves a **means–ends analysis.** Learning to solve problems requires a great deal of practice with different kinds of problems that demand thought. All too often, textbooks in mathematics and other subjects that include many problems fail to present examples that will make students think. They might give students a set of word problems whose solutions require the multiplication of two numbers. Students soon learn that they can solve such problems by looking for any two numbers and multiplying them. In real life, however, problems do not line themselves up neatly in categories. We might hear, "Joe Smith got a 5 percent raise last week, which amounted to $1,200." If we want to figure out how much Joe was making before his raise, the hard part is not doing the calculation, but knowing what calculation is called for. In real life this problem would not be on a page titled "Dividing by Percents." The more different kinds of problems students learn to solve, and the more they have to think to solve the problems, the greater the chance that, when faced with real-life problems, students will be able to transfer their skills or knowledge to the new situation.

EXTRACTING RELEVANT INFORMATION   Realistic problems are rarely neat and tidy. Imagine that Sylvia's problem involved the following scenario:

Sylvia walked into the fast-food restaurant at 6:18 with three friends. Between them, they bought four hamburgers at $1.25 each, two orders of french fries at 65 cents, and three large sodas at 75 cents. Onion rings were on sale for 55 cents. Sylvia's mother told her to be in by 9:00, but she was already 25 minutes late by the time she and her friends left the restaurant. Sylvia drove the 3 miles home at an average of 30 miles per hour. How long was Sylvia in the restaurant?

means–ends analysis

A problem-solving technique that encourages identifying the goal (ends) to be attained, the current situation, and what needs to be done (means) to reduce the difference between the two conditions.

What problem-solving strategies might this pair of students use?

Ellen B. Sensi/The Image Works

The first part of this task is to clear away all the extraneous information to get to the important facts. The means–ends analysis suggests that only time information is relevant, so all the money transactions and the speed of Sylvia's car can be ignored. Careful reading of the problem reveals that Sylvia left the restaurant at 9:25. This and her arrival time of 6:18 are all that matters for solving the problem. Once we know what is relevant and what is not, the solution is easy.

REPRESENTING THE PROBLEM   For many kinds of problems, graphic representation might be an effective means of finding a solution. Adams (1974) provides an illustrative story.

> A Buddhist monk has to make a pilgrimage and stay overnight in a temple that is at the top of a high mountain. The road spirals around and around the mountain. The monk begins walking up the mountain at sunrise. He walks all day long and finally reaches the top at about sunset. He stays all night in the temple and performs his devotions. At sunrise the next day the monk begins walking down the mountain. It takes him much less time than walking up, and he is at the bottom shortly after noon. The question is: Is there a point on the road when he was coming down that he passed at the same time of day when he was coming up the mountain?

This can seem to be a difficult problem because people begin to reason in a variety of ways as they think about the man going up and down. Adams points out one representation that makes the problem easy: Suppose there were two monks, one leaving the top at sunrise and one starting up at sunrise. Would they meet? Of course they would.

In addition to drawings, there are many other ways of representing problems. Students may be taught to make diagrams, flowcharts, outlines, and other means of summarizing and depicting the critical components of a problem (Jitendra et al., 2009; Van Meter, 2001).

■ Teaching Creative Problem Solving

Most of the problems students encounter in school might require careful reading and some thought, but little creativity. However, many of the problems we face in life are not so cut-and-dried. Life is full of situations that call for creative problem solving, as in figuring out how to change or end a relationship without hurt feelings or how to repair a machine with a bent paper clip (Plucker, Beghetto, & Dow, 2004). The following strategies can help in teaching creative problem solving (Beyer, 1998; Fleith, 2000).

INCUBATION   Creative problem solving is quite different from the analytical step-by-step process used to solve Sylvia's problems. In creative problem solving, one important principle is to avoid rushing to a solution; instead, it is useful to pause and reflect on the problem and think through, or incubate, several alternative solutions before choosing a course of action. Consider the following simple problem:

> Roger baked an apple pie in his oven in three-quarters of an hour. How long would it take him to bake three apple pies?

Many students would rush to multiply 45 minutes by 3. However, if they took some time to reflect, most would realize that baking three pies in the same oven would actually take about the same amount of time as baking one pie! In teaching this process, you must avoid putting time pressures on students. Instead of speed, they should value ingenuity and careful thought. A review of research on incubation (setting aside time to reflect on problems) by Sio and Ormerod (2009) found that time for incubation made the most difference on problems with many possible solutions where creativity was most important.

SUSPENSION OF JUDGMENT   In creative problem solving, students should be encouraged to suspend judgment and consider all possibilities before trying out a solution. One specific method based on this principle is called *brainstorming*, in which two or more individuals suggest as many solutions to a problem as they can think of, no matter how seemingly ridiculous. Only after they have thought of as many ideas as possible is any idea evaluated as a possible solution. The point of brainstorming is to avoid focusing on one solution too early and perhaps ignoring better ways to proceed.

APPROPRIATE CLIMATES   Creative problem solving is enhanced by a relaxed, even playful environment (Tishman, Perkins, & Jay, 1995). Perhaps even more important, students who are engaging in creative problem solving must feel that their ideas will be accepted. People who do well on tests of creative problem solving seem to be less afraid of making mistakes and appearing foolish than those who do poorly. Successful problem solvers also seem to treat problem-solving situations more playfully (Benjafield, 1992), implying that a relaxed, fun atmosphere is important in the process. Students should certainly be encouraged to try different solutions and not criticized for taking a wrong turn.

ANALYSIS   One frequently suggested method of creative problem solving is to analyze and juxtapose major characteristics or specific elements of a problem (Chen & Daehler, 2000). For example, careful analysis of the situation might help solve the following problem:

> A tennis tournament was set up with a series of rounds. The winner of each match advanced to the next round. If there were an odd number of players in a round, one player (chosen at random) would advance automatically to the next round. In a tournament with 147 players, how many matches would take place before a single winner would be declared?

We might solve this problem the hard way, making diagrams of the various matches. However, careful analysis of the situation would reveal that each match would produce exactly one loser. Therefore it would take 146 matches to produce 146 losers (and one winner).

ENGAGING PROBLEMS   One key to teaching problem solving is providing problems that intrigue and engage children. The same problem-solving skills can be presented in boring contexts or compelling scenarios to students, and this matters in the outcomes. For example, Bottge (2001) found that low-achieving secondary students, many with serious learning disabilities, could learn complex problem-solving skills relating to building a cage for a pet or setting up a car racing track. Since John Dewey proposed it a hundred years ago, the motivational value of connecting problem solving to real life or simulations of real life has been demonstrated many times (Holt & Willard-Holt, 2000; Westwater & Wolfe, 2000).

FEEDBACK   Perhaps the most effective way to teach problem solving is to provide students with a great deal of practice on a wide variety of problem types, giving feedback not only on the correctness of their solutions but also on the process by which they arrived at the solutions (Fisher & Frey, 2007). The role of practice with feedback (Hattie & Timperley, 2007) in solving complex problems cannot be overemphasized. Mr. Dunbar's students, in the chapter-opening vignette, could not have arrived at the solution to their problem if they had not had months of practice and feedback on simpler problems.

Certification Pointer

Teacher certification tests will require you to know appropriate strategies for engaging students in active learning to promote the development of creative problem-solving skills.

■ Teaching Thinking Skills

One of the oldest dreams in education is finding a way to make students smarter—not only more knowledgeable or skillful but actually better able to learn new information of all kinds (Costa, 2008). Perhaps someday someone will come up with a "smart pill" that will have this effect; in the meantime, several groups of researchers have been developing and evaluating instructional programs designed to increase students' general thinking skills.

The most widely known and extensively researched of several thinking-skills programs was developed by an Israeli educator, Reuven Feuerstein (1980). In this program, called **Instrumental Enrichment,** students work through a series of paper-and-pencil exercises intended to build such intellectual skills as categorization, comparison, orientation in space, and numerical progression. Figure 8.4 shows an activity designed to increase analytic perception. The Instrumental Enrichment treatment is meant to be administered for 3 to 5 hours per week over a period of at least 2 years, usually to adolescents who are underachievers or have learning disabilities. Studies of this duration have found that the program has positive effects on tests of aptitude, such as IQ tests, but generally not on achievement (Savell, Twohig, & Rachford, 1986; Sternberg & Bhana, 1986).

Instrumental Enrichment

A thinking skills program in which students work through a series of paper-and-pencil exercises that are designed to develop various intellectual abilities.

FIGURE 8.4 **Examples from Analytic Perception**

Look at the three columns. For each drawing in the left column, there is a drawing in the right column that completes it to make the form shown in the middle column. Write the number of the form in the right column needed to complete the form in the first column. The task requires representation, internalization and labeling of the model, definition of the missing parts, systematic work, and comparison to the model for self-criticism.

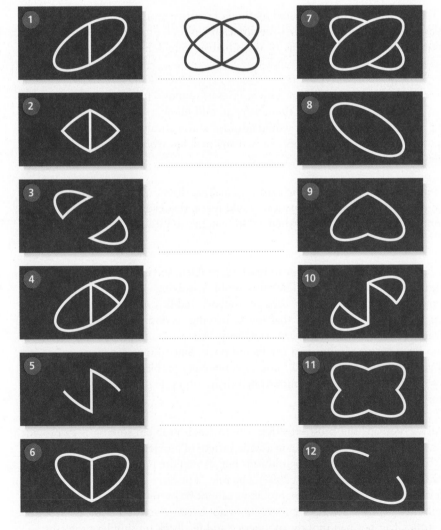

Source: Reuven Feuerstein, "Instrumental Enrichment: A Selected Sample of Material for Review Purposes." Jerusalem: The Hadassah-Wizo-Canada Research Institute, May 1973, p. 5. Reprinted by permission of the author.

Another approach to teaching thinking skills is to incorporate them in daily lessons and classroom experiences—to create a "culture of thinking" (Costa, 2008; Ivey & Fisher, 2006; Ritchhart & Perkins, 2008; Sternberg, 2002; Swartz, 2009). As an example of integrating thinking skills into daily lessons, Tishman and colleagues (1995) describe an impromptu discussion in a class that has been taught a generic strategy for problem solving. Built around the four-step process (state, search, evaluate, and elaborate) summarized in Table 8.2, the strategy provides a framework for Ms. Mandly's sixth-graders to discuss why plants in terrariums the class planted a month earlier are starting to die and what they might do about it. The class has learned the steps shown in Table 8.2 and can refer to a poster identical to the table that is posted in the classroom.

Ms. Mandly: Let's take a look at the poster. How can we build a strategy to deal with this situation? Which building blocks can we use?

Rory: We should use the search step, to search for a solution to the problem.

Marc: Yeah, but we're not even exactly sure what the problem is. We don't know if the plants in the terrarium are wilted because they have too much water or too little.

Ms. Mandly: Are you suggesting we also need a state step, Marc?

TABLE 8.2 Thinking Skills: Build a Strategy

Strategy Building Blocks		
When . . .	**Strategy Step**	**Tactics**
When you need to be clear about what you're doing or where you're going . . .	**State** . . . either the problem, the situation, or your goal(s).	■ Identify the different dimensions of the situation. ■ Identify the parts of the situation you will focus on. ■ State precisely what you want to change or what you want your outcome to be. ■ Be specific!
When you need to think broadly about something . . .	**Search** . . . for ideas, options, possibilities, purposes, features, assumptions, causes, effects, questions, dimensions, hypotheses, facts, or interpretations.	■ Brainstorm. ■ Look for different kinds of ideas. ■ Look at things from different points of view. ■ Look for hidden ideas. ■ Build on other people's ideas. ■ Use categories to help you search.
When you need to assess, rate, or decide something . . .	**Evaluate** . . . options, plans, ideas, theories, or objects.	■ Look for lots of reasons. ■ Consider the immediate and long-term consequences. ■ List all the pros and cons, paying attention to both. ■ Try to be objective; avoid bias. ■ Use your imagination: How will it affect others?
When you need to think about the details of something . . .	**Elaborate** . . . possibilities, plans, options, hypotheses, or ideas.	■ Make a detailed plan: Say what will happen at each step. ■ Visualize what it will look/feel/seem like *in detail*. ■ Ask yourself: What resources will be used? ■ How will it happen? ■ Who will be affected? ■ How long will it take? ■ Think about the different parts. ■ Draw a picture or write a description; imagine *telling* someone about it.

Source: Shari Tishman, David N. Perkins, and Eileen Jay, *The Thinking Classroom.* Copyright © 1995 by Allyn & Bacon. Reprinted by permission.

Marc (after a moment of looking at the poster): Yes. In two ways: I think we need to state the problem and we need to state our goal.

Ms. Mandly: That sounds reasonable. Any other building blocks we can use?

Marc: Yeah, that might not be enough. What if you take care of a terrarium, and it still wilts? Other people in your group will want to know what went wrong.

Ms. Mandly: It sounds like we have two goals here. One, decide how to care for the terrarium. And two, make a plan for keeping track of the terrarium's care.

After more discussion, students agree on exactly which outcomes they want and move to the "search" step. Looking at the search tactics, they decided to brainstorm lots of different possible solutions. Ms. Mandly keeps track of their ideas on the blackboard and occasionally reminds them to keep in mind some key tactics: to look for hidden ideas and to look for different kinds of ideas. Among the students' ideas are the following:

1. Have a sign-up list.
2. Let the teacher decide who should water.
3. Have one person volunteer to do it all.
4. Make a rotating schedule for each group.
5. Make a rotating schedule, plus have weekly group meetings to discuss progress.

After students review and evaluate their brainstormed list, they unanimously agree that option 5—rotating schedule plus weekly meetings—is best.

They then continue to step 4: Elaborate and make a plan. They design a rotation schedule for each terrarium group, and with Ms. Mandly's help they pick a time for weekly group meetings. Working through the "elaborate" step, they invent a detailed checklist for the designated weekly waterer to help track factors that might contribute to the terrarium's health, such as how much water has been given, the date of watering, the temperature of the classroom, and so on (Tishman et al., 1995).

In the course of discussing the terrarium problem, the students are learning a broadly applicable strategy for approaching and solving complex problems. By calling on this and other strategies frequently as they are appropriate in a classroom context, Ms. Mandly not only gives students useful strategies but also communicates the idea that strategy use is a normal and expected part of daily life.

■ Critical Thinking

One key objective of schooling is enhancing students' abilities to think critically and make rational decisions about what to do or what to believe (Abrami et al., 2008; Marzano et al., 2001). Examples of **critical thinking** include identifying misleading advertisements, weighing competing evidence, and identifying assumptions or fallacies in arguments. As with any other objective, learning to think critically requires practice; students can be given many dilemmas, logical and illogical arguments, valid and misleading advertisements, and so on. Effective teaching of critical thinking depends on setting a classroom tone that encourages the acceptance of divergent perspectives and free discussion (Epstein, 2008). There should be an emphasis on giving reasons for opinions rather than only giving correct answers. Skills in critical thinking are best acquired in relation to topics with which students are familiar. For example, students will learn more from a unit evaluating Nazi propaganda if they know a great deal about the history of Nazi Germany and the culture of the 1930s and 1940s. Perhaps most important, the goal of teaching critical thinking is to create a critical spirit, which encourages students to question what they hear and to examine their own thinking for logical inconsistencies or fallacies.

Beyer (1988) identifies 10 critical-thinking skills that students might use in judging the validity of claims or arguments, understanding advertisements, and so on:

Certification Pointer

When responding to the case studies in certification tests, you may be asked to design a lesson that includes strategies for teaching critical-thinking skills.

critical thinking

The ability to make rational decisions about what to do or what to believe.

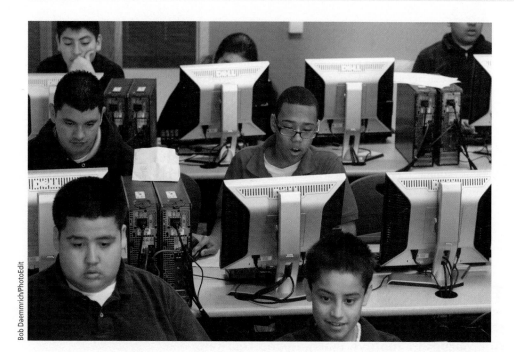

Why is critical thinking particularly important when using the Internet for research or help with homework?

1. Distinguishing between verifiable facts and value claims
2. Distinguishing relevant from irrelevant information, claims, or reasons
3. Determining the factual accuracy of a statement
4. Determining the credibility of a source
5. Identifying ambiguous claims or arguments
6. Identifying unstated assumptions
7. Detecting bias
8. Identifying logical fallacies
9. Recognizing logical inconsistencies in a line of reasoning
10. Determining the strength of an argument or claim (p. 57)

Beyer notes that this is not a sequence of steps but rather a list of possible ways a student might approach information to evaluate whether it is true or sensible. The key task in teaching critical thinking to students is to help them learn not only how to use each of these strategies but also how to tell when each is appropriate.

> **ON THE WEB**
>
> For articles and resources on critical thinking go to www.criticalthinking.org, the website of the Foundation for Critical Thinking.

Chapter 8 Summary

What Is the Constructivist View of Learning?

Constructivists believe that knowing is a process and that learners must individually and actively discover and transform complex information to make it their own. Constructivist approaches emphasize top-down processing, in which students begin with complex problems or tasks and discover the basic knowledge and skills needed to solve the problems or perform the tasks. Constructivist approaches also emphasize cooperative learning, questioning or inquiry strategies, and other metacognitive skills.

Discovery learning and scaffolding are constructivist learning methods based on cognitive learning theories. Bruner's discovery learning highlights students' active self-learning, curiosity, and creative problem solving. Scaffolding, based on Vygotsky's views, calls for teacher assistance to students at critical points in their learning.

How Is Cooperative Learning Used in Instruction

In cooperative learning, small groups of students work together to help one another learn. Cooperative learning groups are used in discovery learning, discussion, and study for assessment. Cooperative learning programs such as Student Teams–Achievement Divisions (STAD) are successful because they reward both group and individual effort and

The Intentional Teacher

USING WHAT YOU KNOW about Student-Centered and Constructivist Approaches to Improve Teaching and Learning

Intentional teachers keep sight of one of the overarching goals of education: to foster students' ability to solve real, complex problems. Intentional teachers work toward this lofty goal by ensuring that schooling provides more than a series of lectures and discrete workbook exercises. Intentional teachers furnish opportunities for students to build their own knowledge, to work with others in discovering important ideas, and to attack challenging real-life issues.

 1. What do I expect my students to know and to be able to do at the end of this lesson? How does this contribute to course objectives and to my students' need to become capable individuals?

Build in regular opportunities for students to approach complex, difficult, and realistic tasks. Check your goals and curriculum: Where and how often do you encourage students to construct knowledge through student-centered approaches? For example, you might provide regular opportunities for students to study and use mathematics in realistic settings. The class might, for instance, develop, administer, analyze, and act on a school-wide survey about a current issue, such as the purchase of playground equipment.

Think about the balance between direct, teacher-centered instructional approaches and constructivist, student-centered approaches. Select teaching strategies based on your goals for students, and realize that a balance of both kinds of approaches might be best for promoting a variety of learning outcomes. For example, imagine that you feel pressed to cover a great deal of information in your government class; as a result, you find yourself lecturing almost daily. Then you recall that your major goal is to help your students become citizens who make informed decisions about complicated issues. Therefore, you review your plan book to ensure that you are using discovery approaches regularly. You begin with a discovery lesson the very next day by distributing nickels and asking students to draw inferences about the culture that created them.

2. What knowledge, skills, needs, and interests do my students have that must be taken into account in my lesson?

Background knowledge affects students' abilities to build meaning and solve problems. Gather information about your students' earlier school experiences by conversing with last year's teacher or teachers. Do your learners come with previous experiences in groupwork? What do their records suggest about their preferences and attitudes toward novelty?

Make use of top-down processing by beginning instruction with holistic problems or issues and moving to analysis of their parts. You might begin your lessons with real problems in the context of a supportive atmosphere. For example, you might start a math class with a question: "If there are five flavors of fruity candies in this bag, how many flavor combinations can I create?" You could note the students' widely varying initial guesses and then pass out bags of candy and allow them to get to work on the problem. When it becomes evident that they are stymied, you could suggest that they try a charting strategy to work on a single part of the problem: How many combinations of *just two* flavors are there? You and your class could devise the chart below, quickly finding patterns and discovering that there are 10 flavor combinations of two candies. Students should discern that they simply need to make similar charts for 3-, 4-, and 5-flavor combinations to arrive at their answer.

Flavor 1	1-1	1-2	1-3	1-4	1-5	(flavor 1 with flavors 2, 3, 4, and 5)
Flavor 2	2-1	2-2	2-3	2-4	2-5	
Flavor 3	3-1	3-2	3-3	3-4	3-5	
Flavor 4	4-1	4-2	4-3	4-4	4-5	
Flavor 5	5-1	5-2	5-3	5-4	5-5	

Teach strategies for problem solving, including drawing pictures, acting out situations, and making diagrams. Model a variety of problem-solving strategies, using them as scaffolds to keep students working within their zones of proximal development.

improvement and because groups are responsible for the individual learning of each group member.

How Are Problem-Solving and Thinking Skills Taught

Problem-solving skills are taught through a series of steps, including, for example, means–ends analysis and problem representation. Creative problem solving requires incubation time, suspension of judgment, conducive climates, problem analysis, the application of thinking skills, and feedback. Thinking skills include, for example, planning, classifying, divergent thinking, identifying assumptions, recognizing misleading information, and generating questions. Thinking skills can be taught through programs such

---

INTASC **7** Instructional Planning Skills   **9** Professional Commitment and Responsibility
8 Assessment of Student Learning

 3. What do I know about the content, child development, learning, motivation, and effective teaching strategies that I can use to accomplish my objectives?

As students work on a cooperative project, watch them. What does their nonverbal behavior tell you about how well they are working with peers? How willing are they to take risks? When you see unwillingness to accept peers' ideas, you might stop the lesson and provide instruction on working well with others: "When someone gives a new idea, wait before you say no. Think for 20 seconds about how that idea might work. Watch, I'll pretend I'm in your group and you tell me a new idea . . ."

 4. What instructional materials, technology, assistance, and other resources are available to help accomplish my objectives?

Emotion, personal meaning, and relevance can help students process information deeply so that they remember better. Begin your lesson in ways that capture student interest, and provide instruction that focuses on developing understanding beyond surface-level features.

You begin a lesson on density by displaying two bottles of soda (one full, one with some air in it) in an aquarium: One sinks, but the other floats! The students' curiosity is piqued and they actively engage themselves in discovering the rule that allows for the bottles' behavior. At the lesson's close, you create a powerful visual image of an immense iceberg floating in the chilling sea. You ask students to explain, using their new understanding of density, why the iceberg floats despite its vast size.

Your discussions with colleagues, both in the current setting in which you work and with former classmates, can serve to help you identify new materials and other resources that will benefit your efforts to become a more intentional, student-centered teacher.

 5. How will I plan to assess students' progress toward my objectives?

Student output provides information about success. Examine students' work for evidence of sense-making, of critical thinking, and of creativity. Imagine that you've just collected a stack of essays on students' analysis of a current environmental issue: destruction of the rain forests. You might begin your assessment by listing two questions to help you focus on students' knowledge construction: (a) How well do students marshal factual details to support their positions? (b) What evidence is there of creative, inventive thinking?

One of the most challenging aspects of a student-centered orientation to teaching is how to determine whether students have met learning goals and attained intended objectives. Assess your instruction using multiple measures. Review your plan book and check to see how many realistic opportunities you provided in the past week. Make an audio or video of your teaching and analyze the kinds of questions and prompts you use. Ask your students for feedback on your teaching, using survey questions like the following: "The teacher _____ [never/sometimes/often/always] gives us opportunities to figure things out on our own."

 6. How will I respond if individual children or the class as a whole are not on track toward success? What is my back-up plan?

How can you, as an intentional teacher seeking to incorporate constructivist approaches, help prepare your students for this change from "tell me what I'm supposed to do" to the practices of group learning, inquiry, and open-ended thinking?

To help your students become more self-directed, not only utilize cooperative approaches wherever possible but also furnish direct instruction in helping and communication skills at the start of cooperative learning lessons. You can provide instruction on how to give feedback in groupwork, recalling that research has shown that students who give and/or receive extensive explanations learn more in cooperative settings. These techniques will help students to reach group goals.

as Instrumental Enrichment; creating a culture of thinking in the classroom is another useful technique.

Key Terms

Review the following key terms from the chapter.

cognitive apprenticeship   219
constructivist theories of learning   218
Cooperative Integrated Reading and
   Composition (CIRC)   232
cooperative learning   229
cooperative scripting   234
critical thinking   242
discovery learning   222
Group Investigation   233
Instrumental Enrichment   240
Jigsaw   232

Learning Together   233
means–ends analysis   237
mediated learning   223
peer-assisted learning strategies
   (PALS)   233
problem solving   236
reciprocal teaching   225
self-regulated learners   222
Student Teams–Achievement Divisions
   (STAD)   230

Self-Assessment: Practicing for Licensure

Directions: The chapter-opening vignette addresses indicators that are often assessed in state licensure exams. Re-read the chapter-opening vignette, and then respond to the following questions.

1. Mr. Dunbar, in his lesson on the volume of a cylinder, asks his students to figure out how to measure volume through experimentation. What type of learning strategy is he using?

  a. Direct instruction

  b. Classical conditioning

  c. Discovery learning

  d. Teacher-mediated discussion

2. Why didn't Mr. Dunbar just tell his students that the formula for finding the volume of a cylinder is $\pi r^2 h$?

  a. He believes that students will gain deeper understanding if they work it out for themselves.

  b. He thought the lesson would take less time if the students could figure it out.

  c. He knows that discovery learning is superior to direct instruction.

  d. He is applying teaching strategies suggested by B. F. Skinner and other behaviorists.

3. In which of the following examples is Mr. Dunbar demonstrating Vygotsky's "zone of proximal development" concept?

  a. Mr. Dunbar says, "Today we are going to have a chance to discover how to compute the volume of a cylinder."

  b. Mr. Dunbar assigns his students to sit around the lab tables in groups of four.

  c. Mr. Dunbar, as he is passing by the Master Minds group, says, "You're right, Miguel, but what are you going to do with that information?"

  d. Mr. Dunbar praises the Master Minds group for figuring out the answer on its own.

4. Mr. Dunbar effectively uses cooperative learning strategies in his lesson on the volume of cylinders. He does all of the following except

  a. give recognition to the groups when they solve the problem.

  b. assure that each group contains members who have similar abilities.

  c. make certain that each group member learns.

  d. mixes students in terms of race, ethnicity, gender, and special needs.

5. Which of the following cooperative learning strategies is Mr. Dunbar using?

   a. Group Investigation

   b. Learning Together

   c. Jigsaw

   d. STAD

6. Describe an example of discovery learning. What is the teacher's role in a discovery lesson? What strengths and limitations are found in discovery learning?

7. How can teachers improve students' problem-solving abilities?

PEARSON myeducationlab

Go to the Topics **Planning and Instruction** and **Constructing Knowledge** in the MyEducationLab (www.myeducationlab.com) for your course, where you can:

- Find learning outcomes for **Planning and Instruction** and **Constructing Knowledge** along with the national standards that connect to these outcomes.

- Complete Assignments and Activities that can help you more deeply understand the chapter content.

- Apply and practice your understanding of the core teaching skills identified in the chapter with the Building Teaching Skills and Dispositions learning units.

- Examine challenging situations and cases presented in the IRIS Center Resources.

- Access video clips of CCSSO National Teachers of the Year award winners responding to the question "Why Do I Teach?" in the Teacher Talk section.

- Check your comprehension of the content covered in the chapter by going to the Study Plan in the Book Resources for your text. Here you will be able to take a chapter quiz; receive feedback on your answers; and then access Review, Practice, and Enrichment activities to enhance your understanding of chapter content.

- Watch author Bob Slavin present a Personal Reflections podcast on *Working Together* in the Book Resources for your text. Then, respond to the reflection question that follows.

Working Together

YOUR REFLECTIONS How might the math teacher have structured the cooperative learning to ensure that all students would be involved and all would learn to solve similar problems?

9

Grouping, Differentiation, and Technology

Bob Daemmrich/PhotoEdit

Learning Outcomes

At the end of this chapter, you should be able to:

- Describe different types of grouping used to accommodate achievement differences
- List several ways to differentiate instruction for diverse learners
- Identify types of programs for students placed at risk of academic difficulties
- Describe how technology can be used effectively in education

Mr. Arbuthnot is in fine form. He is presenting a lesson on long division to his fourth-grade class and feels that he's never been so clear, so interesting, and so well organized. When he asks questions, several students raise their hands; when he calls on them, they always know the answers. "Arbuthnot, old boy," he says to himself, "I think you're really getting to these kids!"

At the end of the period he passes out a short quiz to see how well his students have learned the long-division lesson. When the papers are scored, he finds to his shock and disappointment that only about a third of the class got every problem right. Another third missed every problem; the remaining students fell somewhere in between. "What went wrong?" he thinks. "Well, no matter, I'll set the situation right in tomorrow's lesson."

The next day, Mr. Arbuthnot is even better prepared, uses vivid examples and diagrams to show how to do long division, and gives an active, exciting lesson. Even more hands than before go up when he asks questions, and the answers are usually correct. However, some of the students are beginning to look bored, particularly those who got perfect papers on the quiz and those who got none right.

Toward the end of the period, he gives another brief quiz. The scores are better this time, but there is still a group of students who got none of the problems correct. He is crestfallen. "I had them in the palm of my hand," he thinks. "How could they fail to learn?"

To try to find out what went wrong, Mr. Arbuthnot goes over the quiz papers of the students who missed all the problems. He immediately sees a pattern. By the second lesson, almost all students were proceeding correctly in setting up the long-division problems. However, some were making consistent errors in subtraction. Others had apparently forgotten their multiplication facts. Their problems were not with division at all; the students simply lacked the prerequisite skills.

"Well," thinks Mr. Arbuthnot, "at least I was doing great with some of the kids." It occurs to him that one of the students who got a perfect paper after the first lesson might be able to give him an idea about how to teach the others better. He asks Teresa how she grasped long division so quickly.

"It was easy," she says. "We learned long division last year!"

USING YOUR EXPERIENCE

Critical Thinking   List all of the ways in which Mr. Arbuthnot could be more effective in addressing student individual differences. Then list all of the ways in which he is effective in addressing student needs.

Cooperative Learning   Work with a group of four or five classmates. Pass a sheet of paper around the group, and ask each member to write down an idea to help Mr. Arbuthnot become more effective in addressing students' needs. After one idea is added, the sheet is passed to the next person in the group, who adds an idea and passes the sheet and so on. Share some of these ideas with the class.

What Are Elements of Effective Instruction beyond a Good Lesson?

INTASC

3 Adapting Instruction for
Individual Needs

6 Communication Skills

7 Instructional Planning Skills

As Mr. Arbuthnot learned to his chagrin, effective instruction takes a lot more than good lectures. He gave a great lesson on long division, yet it was appropriate for only some of the students, those who had the needed prerequisites but had not already learned long division. To make his lesson effective for all of the students, he needed to adapt it to meet their diverse needs. Furthermore, the best lesson in the world won't work if students are not motivated to learn it or if inadequate time is allotted to allow all students to learn.

If the quality of lectures were all that mattered in effective instruction, we could probably find the best lecturers in the world, record their lessons, and show the videos to students. If you think about why video lessons would not work very well by themselves, you will realize how much more is involved in effective instruction than simply giving good lectures. First, the video teacher would have no idea what students already know. A particular lesson might be too advanced or too easy for a particular group of students. Second, some students might be learning the lesson quite well, whereas others would be missing key concepts and falling behind. The video teacher would have no way of knowing which students needed additional help and, in any case, would have no way of providing it. There would be no way to question students to find out whether they were getting the main points and then to reteach any concept they had missed. Third, the video teacher would have no way of motivating students to pay attention to the lesson or to really try to learn it. If students failed to pay attention or misbehaved, the video teacher could not do anything about it. Finally, the video teacher would never know at the end of a lesson whether students had actually learned the main concepts or skills.

This analysis of video teaching illustrates why you must be concerned with many elements of instruction in addition to the presentation of information. You must know how to adapt your instruction to the students' levels of knowledge. You must motivate students to learn, manage student behavior, group students for instruction, and assess the students' learning.

To help make sense of all these elements of effective instruction, educational psychologists have proposed models of effective instruction. These models explain the critical features of high-quality lessons and how they relate to one another to enhance learning.

■ Carroll's Model of School Learning and QAIT

One of the most influential articles ever published in the field of educational psychology was a paper by John Carroll titled "A Model of School Learning" (1963, 1989). In it he describes teaching in terms of the management of time, resources, and activities to ensure student learning. Carroll proposes that learning is a function of (1) time actually spent on learning and (2) time needed to learn. Time needed is a product of aptitude, prior knowledge, and ability to learn; time spent depends on clock time available for learning, quality of instruction, and student perseverance.

Slavin (1995b) describes a model focusing on the alterable elements of Carroll's model, those that the teacher or school can directly change. It is called the **QAIT model,** for quality, appropriateness, incentive, and time.

QAIT model

A model of effective instruction that focuses on elements teachers can directly control: quality, appropriateness, incentive, and time.

1. *Quality of instruction.*   The degree to which presentation of information or skills helps students easily learn the material. Quality of instruction is largely a product of the quality of the curriculum and of lesson presentation.

2. *Appropriate levels of instruction.*   The degree to which the teacher makes sure that students are ready to learn a new lesson (that is, have the necessary skills and knowledge to learn it) but have not already learned the lesson. In other words, the

level of instruction is appropriate when a lesson is neither too difficult nor too easy for students.

3. **Incentive.** The degree to which the teacher makes sure that students are motivated to work on instructional tasks and to learn the material being presented.

4. **Time.** The degree to which students are given enough time to learn the material being taught.

For instruction to be effective, each of these four elements must be adequate. No matter how high the quality of instruction, students will not learn a lesson if they lack the necessary prior skills or information, if they lack the motivation, or if they lack the time they need to learn the lesson. However, if the quality of instruction is low, then it makes no difference how much students already know, how motivated they are, or how much time they have. Figure 9.1 illustrates the relationships among the elements in the QAIT model.

FIGURE 9.1 **The QAIT Model**

Each of the elements of the QAIT model is like a link in a chain, and the chain is only as strong as the weakest link.

Quality of Instruction

Incentive

EFFECTIVE INSTRUCTION

Time

Appropriate Levels of Instruction

QUALITY OF INSTRUCTION Quality of instruction refers to the set of activities most people first picture when they think of teaching: lecturing, calling on students, discussing, helping students with seatwork, and so on. When instruction is high in quality, the information presented makes sense to students, interests them, and is easy to remember and apply.

The most important aspect of quality of instruction is the degree to which the lesson makes sense to students, which you ensure by presenting material in an orderly, organized way. You need to relate new information to what students already know. You need to use examples, demonstrations, pictures, and diagrams to make ideas vivid for students. You might use such cognitive strategies as advance organizers and memory strategies. Sometimes a concept will not make sense to students until they discover it or experience it themselves or until they discuss it with others.

Another important aspect of quality of instruction is the degree to which the teacher monitors how well students are learning and adapts the pace of instruction so that it is neither too fast nor too slow. For example, you should ask questions frequently to determine how much students have grasped. If the answers show that students are keeping up with the lesson, you might move along a little more rapidly. But if students' answers show that they are having trouble keeping up, you might review parts of the lesson and slow down the pace.

APPROPRIATE LEVELS OF INSTRUCTION Perhaps the most difficult problem of classroom organization is the fact that students come into class with different levels of prior knowledge, skills, and motivation as well as with different learning rates (Tomlinson, 2004, 2008). This was Mr. Arbuthnot's main dilemma. Student diversity requires teachers to

What are some of the challenges to the effectiveness of the QAIT model in a crowded classroom?

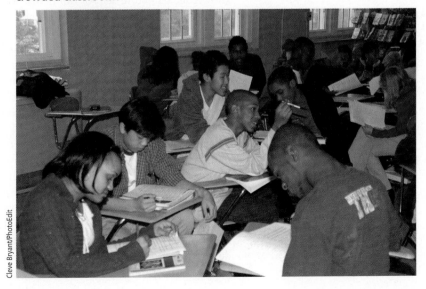

Cleve Bryant/PhotoEdit

provide appropriate levels of instruction. Teaching a class of 30 students (or even a class of 10) is fundamentally different from one-to-one tutoring because of the inevitability of student-to-student differences that affect the success of instruction. You can always be sure that if you teach one lesson to the whole class, some students will learn the material much more quickly than others. In fact, some students might not learn the lesson at all; they might lack important prerequisite skills or adequate time (because to give them enough time would waste too much of the time of students who learn rapidly). Recognition of these instructionally important differences leads many teachers to search for ways of individualizing or differentiating instruction, adapting instruction to meet students' different needs, or grouping students according to their abilities.

However, some of these solutions create problems of their own that could be more serious than the ones they are meant to solve. For example, you might give all students materials appropriate to their individual needs and allow students to work at their own rates. This solves the problem of providing appropriate levels of instruction but creates serious new problems of managing the activities of 20 or 30 students doing 20 or 30 different things. Alternatively, you might group students within a relatively narrow range of abilities (e.g., Redbirds, Bluebirds, and Yellowbirds). However, this creates problems, too, because when you are working with the Redbirds, the Bluebirds and Yellowbirds must work without supervision or help. Effective ways of adapting instruction to meet student needs are discussed later in this chapter.

INTASC

5 Classroom Management and Motivation

INCENTIVE Thomas Edison once wrote that "genius is one per cent inspiration and ninety-nine per cent perspiration." The same could probably be said of learning. Learning is work. This is not to say that learning isn't or can't be fun or stimulating—far from it. But it is true that students must exert themselves to pay attention, to conscientiously perform the tasks required of them, and to study; moreover, students must somehow be motivated to do these things. This incentive, or motivation, might come from characteristics of the tasks themselves (e.g., the interest value of the material being learned), from characteristics of students (such as their curiosity or positive orientation toward learning), or from rewards provided by the teacher or the school (such as grades and certificates).

If students want to know something, they will be motivated to exert the necessary effort to learn it. This is why there are students who can rattle off the names, batting averages, number of home runs, and all sorts of other information about every player of the Chicago Cubs but know little about science or history or math. To such students, baseball facts are of great interest, so they are willing to invest substantial effort to master them. Some information is naturally interesting to some or all students, but you can do much to create interest in a topic by arousing students' curiosity or by showing how knowledge gained in school can be useful outside of school. For example, baseball fans might be much more interested in learning about understanding proportions if they are convinced that this information is necessary for computing batting averages.

Connections

The rewards and general principles of motivation are discussed throughout Chapter 10.

However, not every subject can be made fascinating to all students at all times. Most students need some kind of recognition or reward if they are to exert maximum effort to learn skills or concepts that might seem unimportant at the moment but will be critical for later learning. For this reason, schools use praise, feedback, grades, certificates, stars, prizes, and other rewards to increase student motivation.

Connections

Principles of classroom management and discipline are discussed throughout Chapter 11.

TIME The final element of the QAIT model is time. Instruction takes time. More time spent teaching something does not necessarily mean more learning; but if instructional quality, appropriateness of instruction, and incentive are all high, then more time on instruction will pay off in greater learning. The amount of time available for learning depends largely on two factors. The first is the amount of time that you schedule for instruction and then actually use to teach. The other is the amount of time students pay attention to the lesson. Both kinds of time are affected by classroom management and discipline strategies. If students are well behaved, well motivated, and have a sense of purpose and direction and if you are well prepared and well organized, then there is plenty of time for students to learn whatever you want to teach. However, many factors such as interruptions, behavior problems, and poor transitions between activities eat away at the time available for learning (see Hong, 2001).

How Are Students Grouped to Accommodate Achievement Differences?

From the day they walk into school, students differ in their knowledge, skills, motivations, and predispositions toward what is about to be taught. Some students are already reading when they enter kindergarten; others need much time and support to learn to read well. When starting a new lesson you can usually assume that some students already know a great deal about the lesson's content, some know less but will master the content early on, and some might not be able to master the content at all within the time provided. Some have the prerequisite skills and knowledge to learn the lesson, whereas others do not. This was Mr. Arbuthnot's problem: Some of his students were not ready to learn long division, whereas others had already learned it before he began. Some of his students lacked basic multiplication and subtraction skills crucial for long division. Others learned it during the first lesson and did not need the second. If Mr. Arbuthnot stops to review multiplication and division, he will be wasting the time of the better-prepared students. If he sets his pace of instruction according to the needs of his more able students, those with learning problems will never catch up. How can Mr. Arbuthnot teach a lesson that will work for all of his students, who are performing within the normal range but differ in prior knowledge, skills, and learning rates?

Accommodating instruction to student differences is one of the most fundamental problems of education and often leads to politically and emotionally charged policies (Atkins & Ellsesser, 2003; Loveless, 1998). One solution, which some advocate, is simply to retain more children in a grade until they meet grade-level requirements. Some countries outside of North America attempt to deal with the problem of student differences, or student heterogeneity, by testing children at around 10 to 12 years of age and assigning them to different types of schools, only one of which is meant to prepare students for higher education. In the United States a similar function is sometimes carried out by assignment of secondary students to college preparatory, general, and vocational **tracks,** in which students are assigned to a specified curriculum sequence within which they take all their academic courses. Tracking rapidly diminished in the 1980s and 1990s, however. Today, most secondary schools place students in ability-grouped classes separately by subject area; a student may be in a high-level math class but in a middle- or low-level English class (Lucas & Gamoran, 2002). Many secondary schools allow students, in consultation with counselors, to choose the level of each class, perhaps changing levels if a course turns out to be too difficult or too easy. All of these strategies, which result in students' attending classes that are more or less homogeneous in performance level, are forms of **between-class ability grouping** (Slavin, 1991). The predominant form of ability grouping in middle, junior high, and high schools, it is also sometimes used in elementary schools.

Another common means of accommodating instruction to student differences in elementary schools is **within-class ability grouping,** as in the use of reading groups (Bluebirds, Redbirds, Yellowbirds) that divide students according to their reading performance (Lou et al., 1996). The problem of accommodating student differences is so important that many educators have suggested completely individualized instruction so that students can work independently at their own rates, which has led to the creation of several individualized instructional programs. In recent years computer-assisted instruction has been the primary method of individualized instruction.

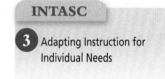

Connections
To learn more about student differences in general intelligence, specific aptitudes, and abilities and learning styles, see Chapter 4, page 103.

INTASC
3 Adapting Instruction for Individual Needs

tracks
Curriculum sequences to which students of specified achievement or ability level are assigned.

between-class ability grouping
The practice of grouping students in separate classes according to ability level.

within-class ability grouping
A system of accommodating student differences by dividing a class of students into two or more ability groups for instruction in certain subjects.

Each of the many ways of accommodating students' differences has its own benefits, but each introduces its own problems, which sometimes outweigh the benefits. Some student differences can be easily accommodated (see Gregory & Chapman, 2001; Tomlinson, 2004, 2008). For example, you can support different learning styles by augmenting oral presentations with visual cues—perhaps writing on a whiteboard or showing pictures and diagrams to emphasize important concepts (Mayer, 2008a). You can accommodate other differences in learning styles by varying classroom activities, as in alternating active and quiet tasks or individual and groupwork. You can sometimes work with students on an individual basis and adapt instruction to their learning styles—for example, by reminding impulsive students to take their time or by teaching overly reflective students strategies for skipping problematic items so that they can complete tests on time.

Differences in prior knowledge and learning rates are more difficult to deal with. Sometimes the best way to deal with these differences is to ignore them and teach the whole class at a single pace, perhaps offering additional help to low-achieving students and giving extra extension or enrichment activities to students who tend to finish assignments rapidly (see Meyer & Rose, 2000; Pettig, 2000; Tomlinson, 2008; Tomlinson, Kaplan, & Renzulli, 2001). You can consciously vary the examples and questions used to accommodate a range of students in each lesson. Appropriate use of cooperative learning methods, in which students of different performance levels help each other, can be an effective means of helping all children learn (Slavin, 1995a, 2010; Webb, 2008). Some subjects lend themselves more than others to a single pace of instruction for all. For example, it is probably less important to accommodate student achievement differences in social studies, science, and English than in mathematics, reading, and foreign languages. In the latter subjects, skills build directly on one another, so teaching at one pace to a heterogeneous class might do a disservice to both low and high achievers; low achievers might fail because they lack prerequisite skills, and high achievers might become bored at what is for them a slow pace of instruction.

■ Between-Class Ability Grouping

Probably the most common means of dealing with instructionally important differences is to assign students to classes according to their abilities. This between-class ability grouping can take many forms. High schools may use college preparatory and general tracks that divide students on the basis of measured ability. In some middle schools, students are assigned to one class by general ability, and they then stay with that class, moving from teacher to teacher. For example, the highest-performing seventh-graders might be assigned to class 7-1, middle-performing students to 7-5, and low-performing students to 7-12. In other middle schools (and in many high schools), students are grouped separately by ability for each subject, so a student might be in a high-performing math class and an average-performing science class. In high schools this is accomplished by course placements. For example, some ninth-graders take Algebra I, whereas others who do not qualify for Algebra I take general mathematics. Elementary schools use a wide range of strategies for grouping students, including many of the patterns found in secondary schools. Often, students in elementary schools will be assigned to a mixed-ability class for homeroom, social studies, and science but regrouped by ability for reading and math. Elementary schools are less likely than secondary schools to use ability grouping between classes but more likely to use ability grouping within classes, especially in reading. At any level, however, the establishment of separate special-education programs for students with serious learning problems is one common form of between-class ability grouping, as is provision of separate programs for students who are academically gifted and talented.

RESEARCH ON BETWEEN-CLASS ABILITY GROUPING Despite the widespread use of between-class ability grouping, research on this strategy does not support its use.

Connections

Programs for students who are gifted and who have special needs are discussed in Chapter 12, page 368.

Certification Pointer

For teacher certification tests, you may be asked to describe the strengths and weaknesses of between-class ability grouping. You should know that research does not support most forms of between-class ability grouping.

Cindy Charles/PhotoEdit

Some of these students are reading well above grade level, whereas others are still only learning to read. As a teacher, how might you accommodate instruction to your students' differing abilities? What are the advantages and disadvantages of such strategies as between-class and within-class ability groupings?

Researchers have found that although ability grouping might have slight benefits for students assigned to high-track classes, these benefits are balanced by losses for students in low-track classes (Ireson & Hallam, 2001; Oakes & Wells, 1998; Slavin, 1987b, 1990).

ON THE WEB

The National Association for Gifted Children's position statement on ability grouping can be found at www.nagc.org/index.aspx?id=382. Also see NEA's Research Spotlight on Academic Ability Grouping (www.nea.org/tools/16899.htm).

Why is between-class ability grouping so ineffective? Several researchers have explored this question. The primary purpose of ability grouping is to reduce the range of student performance levels that teachers must deal with so they can adapt instruction to the needs of a well-defined group. However, grouping is often done on the basis of standardized test scores or other measures of general ability rather than according to performance in a particular subject. As a result, the reduction in the range of differences that are actually important for a specific class may be too small to make much difference (Oakes, 1995). Furthermore, concentrating low-achieving students in low-track classes seems to be harmful because it exposes them to too few positive role models (Page, 1991). Many teachers do not like to teach such classes and might subtly (or not so subtly) communicate low expectations for students in them (Weinstein, 1996). Studies find that teachers actually do not make many adaptations to the needs of students in low-ability groups (Ross, Smith, Lohr, & McNelis, 1994). Several studies have found that the quality of instruction is lower in low-track classes than in middle- or high-track classes. For example, teachers of low-track classes are less enthusiastic and less organized, teaching more facts and fewer concepts than teachers of high-track classes (Gamoran, Nystrand, Berends, & LePore, 1995; Oakes, 1995; Raudenbush, Rowan, & Cheong, 1993). Instruction in untracked mixed-ability classes more closely resembles teaching in high- and middle-track classes than that in low-track classes (Goodlad, 1983; Oakes, 1985). Perhaps the most damaging effect of tracking is its stigmatizing effect on students who are assigned to the low tracks; the message these students get is that academic success is not within their capabilities (Oakes & Guiton, 1995; Page, 1991). Schafer and Olexa (1971) interviewed one noncollege-prep girl who said that she carried her general-track books upside down to avoid being humiliated while walking down the hall.

Students in lower-track classes are far more likely to become delinquent and truant and drop out of school than are students of similar ability in middle-track or mixed placements (Goodlad, 1983; Oakes, 1985). Although these problems certainly exist in part because students in low-track classes are low in academic performance to begin with, this cannot be the whole story. For example, students who are assigned to the low track in middle or junior high school experience a rapid loss of self-esteem (Goodlad, 1983). Slavin and Karweit (1982) found that fifth- and sixth-graders in urban elementary schools were absent about 8 percent of the time. When these same students entered the tracked junior high school, absenteeism rose almost immediately to 26 percent, and the truancy was concentrated among students assigned to the bottom-track classes. The change happened too rapidly to be attributed entirely to characteristics of students. Something about the organization of the junior high school apparently convinced a substantial number of students that school was no longer a rewarding place to be.

One of the most insidious aspects of tracking is that low-track classes are often composed predominantly of students from lower socioeconomic backgrounds and from minority groups, whereas upper-track classes are more often composed of children from higher socioeconomic levels (Braddock & Dawkins, 1993; Cooper, 1998; Dornbusch, 1994). There is evidence that this difference is in part a result of discrimination (intended or not) against African American and Latino students (Hoffer & Nelson, 1993). A study by Yonezawa, Wells, and Serna (2002) found that even in high schools where students are theoretically given a "free choice" of academic levels, African American and Latino students disproportionately ended up in low-level classes. The creation of groupings that are so often associated with social class and race is impossible to justify in light of the lack of evidence that such groupings are educationally necessary.

Although individual teachers can rarely set policies on between-class ability grouping, it is useful for you to know that research does not support this practice at any grade level, and tracking should be avoided whenever possible. This does not mean that all forms of between-class grouping should be abandoned, however. For example, there is probably some justification for acceleration programs, such as offering Algebra I to mathematically talented seventh-graders or providing advanced placement classes in high school (see Chapter 12). Also, some between-class grouping is bound to occur in secondary schools, because some students choose to take advanced courses and others do not. However, the idea that having high, middle, and low sections of the same course can help student achievement has not been supported by research. Mixed-ability classes can be successful at all grade levels, particularly if other, more effective means of accommodating student differences are used, such as within-class ability grouping, tutoring for low achievers, and cooperative learning strategies.

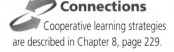

Connections

Cooperative learning strategies are described in Chapter 8, page 229.

Connections

Various forms of cooperative and project-based learning are described in Chapter 8, page 230.

untracking

A focus on having students in mixed-ability groups and holding them to high standards but providing many ways for students to reach those standards.

■ Untracking

For many years, educators and researchers have challenged between-class ability grouping at all levels. Influential groups such as the National Governors' Association (1993) and the Carnegie Corporation of New York (1989) have recommended moving away from traditional ability grouping practices, and a number of guides to untracking and examples of successful untracking have been published (e.g., Burris, Heubert, & Levin, 2004; Cooper, 1998; Fahey, 2000; Hubbard & Mehan, 1998; Kugler & Albright, 2005; Oakes, Quartz, Ryan, & Lipton, 2000). **Untracking** recommendations focus on placing students in mixed-ability groups and holding them to high standards but providing many ways for them to reach those standards, including extra assistance for students who are having difficulties keeping up (Burris, Heubert, & Levin, 2006; Hubbard & Mehan, 1998). Appropriate forms of cooperative learning and project-based approaches have often been recommended as a means of opening up more avenues to high performance for all children (Cohen, 1992; Hubbard & Mehan, 1998; Pool & Page, 1995). Yet the road to untracking is far from easy, especially in middle and high schools (Cooper, 1998; Oakes et al., 2000; Rubin, 2003). In particular, untracking often runs into serious opposition from the parents of high achievers. Oakes and colleagues (2000) and Wells, Hirshberg, Lipton, and Oakes (1995) have pointed out that untracking requires changes in thinking about children's potentials, not only changes in school or classroom practices. Teachers, parents, and students themselves, these researchers claim, must come to see the goal of schooling as success for every child, not as sorting students into categories, if untracking is to take hold (Hubbard & Mehan, 1997; Oakes et al., 2000). This change in perception is difficult to bring about; perhaps, as a result, the move toward untracking is going slowly at the secondary level (Hallinan, 2004).

■ Regrouping for Reading and Mathematics

Regrouping is a form of ability grouping often used in the elementary grades. In regrouping plans, students stay in mixed-ability classes most of the day but are assigned to reading and/or math classes on the basis of their performance in these subjects. For example, at 9:30 A.M. the fourth-graders in a school may move to different teachers so that they can receive reading instruction appropriate to their reading levels. One form of regrouping for reading, the **Joplin Plan,** regroups students across grade lines. For example, a reading class at the fourth grade, first semester reading level may contain third-, fourth-, and fifth-graders.

One major advantage of regrouping over all-day ability grouping is that students spend most of the day in a mixed-ability class. Thus, low achievers are not separated out as a class and potentially stigmatized. Perhaps for these reasons, regrouping plans, especially the Joplin Plan, have generally been found to increase student achievement (Gutiérrez & Slavin, 1992; Slavin, 1987b).

■ Nongraded (Cross-Age Grouping) Elementary Schools

A form of grouping sometimes seen in elementary schools, **nongraded programs,** or cross-age grouping programs (Fogarty, 1993; Pavan, 1992), combine children of different ages in the same classes. Most often, students aged 5 to 7 or 6 to 8 may be mixed in a nongraded primary program. Students work across age lines but are often flexibly grouped for some instruction according to their needs and performance levels (Kasten & Lolli, 1998). Reviews of research on nongraded programs have found a positive effect on achievement when the focus is on flexible grouping for instruction but less effectiveness when they have a strong focus on individualized instruction (Gutiérrez & Slavin, 1992; Pavan, 1992). Research on the open classroom, which usually incorporates nongraded organization, similarly has failed to find achievement benefits (Giaconia & Hedges, 1982).

Sometimes cross-grade grouping is used out of necessity because there are too few children at a given grade level to make up a whole class. Such combination classes (e.g., grades 3–4 or 5–6) have not been found to enhance student achievement and might even be harmful (Burns & Mason, 2002; Veenman, 1995, 1997).

■ Within-Class Ability Grouping

Another way to adapt instruction to differences in student performance levels is to group students within classes, as is typical in elementary school reading classes. For example, a third-grade teacher might have the Rockets group using a 3–1 (third-grade, first-semester) text, the Stars group using a 3–2 (third-grade, second-semester) text, and the Planets group using a 4–1 (fourth-grade, first-semester) text.

Within-class ability grouping is very common in elementary reading classes (Chorzempa & Graham, 2006). Surveys of principals have found that more than 90

regrouping

A method of ability grouping in which students in mixed-ability classes are assigned to reading or math classes on the basis of their performance levels.

Joplin Plan

A regrouping method in which students are grouped across grade lines for reading instruction.

nongraded programs

Programs, generally at the primary level, that combine children of different ages in the same class. Also called *cross-age grouping programs.*

Certification Pointer

You may be asked on your teacher certification test to describe a technique for grouping students within a reading class to meet a wide range of student reading abilities.

percent of elementary reading teachers use multiple reading groups (Puma et al., 1997), whereas only 15 to 18 percent of elementary math teachers do so (Good, Mulryan, & McCaslin, 1992; Mason, 1995). Within-class ability grouping is rare in subjects other than reading or mathematics. In reading, teachers typically have each group working at a different point in a series of reading texts and allow each group to proceed at its own pace. In many math classes the teacher presents a lesson to the whole class and then meets with two or more ability groups while other students are doing seatwork to reinforce skills or provide enrichment as needed.

RESEARCH ON WITHIN-CLASS ABILITY GROUPING   Research on the achievement effects of within-class ability grouping has taken place almost exclusively in elementary mathematics classes. The reason is that researchers want to look at teaching situations in which some teachers use within-class ability grouping and others do not, and this is typically true only in elementary math; almost all elementary teachers differentiate reading groups, some do in math, and few group in subjects other than reading and math. Most studies that have evaluated within-class ability grouping methods in math (in which the different groups proceed at different paces on different materials) have found that students in the ability-grouped classes learned more than students in classes without grouping (Slavin, 1987b). Students of high, average, and low achievement levels seem to benefit equally from within-class ability grouping (Lou et al., 1996). One study by Mason and Good (1993) found that teachers who flexibly grouped and regrouped students according to their needs had better math achievement outcomes than did those who used permanent within-class groups.

The research suggests that small numbers of ability groups are better than large numbers (Slavin & Karweit, 1984). A smaller number of groups has the advantage of allowing more direct instruction from the teacher and using less seatwork time and transition time. With only three groups seatwork time rises to at least two-thirds of class time. Teachers who try to teach more than three reading or math groups might also have problems with classroom management. Dividing the class into more than three groups does not decrease the magnitude or range of differences within each group enough to offset these problems (see Hiebert, 1983).

The main point to be drawn from research on within-class ability grouping is not that it is desirable but that if some form of grouping is thought to be necessary, grouping within the class is preferable to grouping between classes. Beyond its more favorable achievement outcomes, within-class grouping can be more flexible and less stigmatizing and occupies a much smaller portion of the school day than between-class grouping does (Rowan & Miracle, 1983).

■ Retention

One of the most controversial issues in education is whether low-achieving students should be required to repeat grades. Primarily as a result of accountability pressures, retention rates have risen dramatically. In recent years, Florida held back 24,000 students, New York City failed 16,000 third-graders, and Miami had 2,000 students in third grade for the third time (McGill-Franzen & Allington, 2006).

Proponents of holding back low-achieving students argue that this gives them a "gift of time" to catch up and sets clear standards that students must strive to achieve. Students being considered for retention are usually given the opportunity to catch up in summer school or to receive other assistance leading to promotion, and it may be that the threat of retention brings many students into such services (March, Gershwin, Kirby, & Xia, 2009; McCombs, Kirby, & Mariano, 2009). Opponents note that students who are held back lose motivation; in fact, having been retained is one of the strongest predictors of dropping out (Allensworth, 2005; Jimerson, Anderson, & Whipple, 2002). Retention is concentrated among male students who are minorities and/or from disadvantaged homes (Beebe-Frankenberger, Bocian, MacMillan, & Gresham, 2004).

Is retention beneficial or harmful? In the short term, holding students back increases scores in a given school or district, not because students are learning more but because they are older when they take the test. For this reason, states and districts often report "dramatic gains" on state tests following a new policy of holding students back unless they meet a given test standard (Bali, Anagnostopoulos, & Roberts, 2005; McGill-Franzen, & Allington, 2006). In long-term studies, however, students who were retained end up learning less than similar low achievers of the same age who were not retained (Burkam, Logerfo, Ready, & Lee, 2007; Hong & Raudenbush, 2005; Hong & Yu, 2007; Roderick & Nagaoka, 2005).

The best solutions to the problems of low-achieving students are neither retention nor "social promotion" (promoting students without regard to their levels of achievement). Instead, such children should be given special attention, diagnosis, and intensive interventions, such as tutoring, until their achievement falls within the normal range. An extra year of education is a very expensive intervention—for that amount of money, students can be given much more effective assistance (Reeves, 2006; Slavin, Lake, Davis, & Madden, 2009).

What Are Some Ways of Differentiating Instruction?

The problem of providing all students with appropriate levels of instruction could be completely solved if schools simply assigned each student his or her own teacher. Not surprisingly, studies of one adult–one student tutoring find substantial positive effects of tutoring on student achievement (Slavin, Lake, Davis, & Madden, 2009). One major reason for the effectiveness of tutoring is that the tutor can provide **differentiated instruction,** tailoring instruction precisely to a student's needs. If the student learns quickly, the tutor can move to other tasks; if not, the tutor can figure out what the problem is, try another explanation, or simply spend more time on the task.

There are situations in which tutoring by adults is feasible and necessary. Cross-age peer tutors (older students working with younger ones) can also be very effective. In addition, educational innovators have long tried to simulate the one-to-one teaching situation by individualizing instruction. Teachers have found a variety of ways to informally accommodate the needs of different learners in heterogeneous classrooms (Corno, 2008; Tomlinson, 2008). Individualized instruction, or programmed instruction methods, in which students work at their own level and pace, were popular in the 1960s and 1970s (Fletcher, 1992), and this type of instruction continues in many forms of computer-based instruction. Differentiation strategies are discussed in the following sections.

■ Differentiated Instruction

Differentiated instruction (George, 2005; Tomlinson, 2004, 2008) is an approach to teaching that adapts the content, level, pace, and products of instruction to accommodate the different needs of diverse students in regular classes. The philosophy behind differentiated instruction emphasizes that all children can reach high standards, but some may need tailored assistance to do so.

For example, you might ask a diverse class to write a biography of Gandhi but provide materials on Gandhi at different reading levels. Or you might create a common math test for a heterogeneous class but include a few "challenge questions" for students with stronger preparation in math. During seatwork, you might focus on students known to have difficulties with prerequisite skills or provide them preteaching on those skills before class; for example, before a unit on decimals, you might arrange an extra

INTASC

3 Adapting Instruction for Individual Needs

differentiated instruction

An approach to teaching that adapts the content, level, pace, and products of instruction to accommodate different needs of diverse students in regular classes.

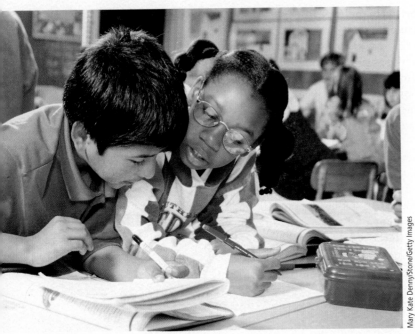

Mary Kate Denny/Stone/Getty Images

What type of tutoring is taking place in this picture? What other means of individualizing instruction are available to you as a teacher?

INTASC

6 Communication Skills

Connections

For more on reciprocal teaching, see Chapter 8, page 225.

session to review fractions with students who are not solid with fractional concepts central to decimals.

■ Peer Tutoring

Students can help one another learn. In **peer tutoring,** one student teaches another. There are two principal types of peer tutoring: **cross-age tutoring,** in which the tutor is several years older than the student being taught, and same-age peer tutoring, in which a student tutors a classmate. Cross-age tutoring is recommended by researchers more often than same-age tutoring—partly because of the obvious fact that older students are more likely to know the material, and partly because students might accept an older student as a tutor but resent having a classmate in that role (Topping & Ehly, 1998). Sometimes peer tutoring is used with students who need special assistance, in which case a few older students might work with a few younger students. Other tutoring schemes have involved, for example, entire fifth-grade classes tutoring entire second-grade classes. In these cases, half of the younger students might be sent to the older students' classroom while half of the older students go to the younger students' classroom. Otherwise, peer tutoring may take place in the cafeteria, the library, or another school facility.

Peer tutoring among students of the same age can be easier to arrange and has also been found to be very effective (Rohrbeck et al., 2003). Among classmates of the same age and performance level, reciprocal peer tutoring, in which students take turns as tutors and tutees, can be both practical and effective (Fantuzzo, King, & Heller, 1992; Greenwood, Terry, Utley, Montagna, & Walker, 1993; Mathes, Torgeson, & Allor, 2001).

Adequate training and monitoring of tutors are essential. Tutors who have been taught specific tutoring strategies produce much better results than those who have not had such training (Fuchs, Fuchs, Bentz, Phillips, & Hamlett, 1994; Merrill, Reiser, Merrill, & Landes, 1995).

RESEARCH ON PEER TUTORING   Research evaluating the effects of peer tutoring on student achievement has generally found that this strategy increases the achievement of both tutees and tutors (Fantuzzo et al., 1992; King, Staffieni, & Adelgais, 1998; Simmons et al., 1995; Van Keer, 2004). In fact, some studies have found greater achievement gains for tutors than for tutees (Rekrut, 1992). As many teachers have noted, the best way to learn something thoroughly is to teach it to someone else. High achievers who tutor other students usually enjoy and value this activity (Thorkildsen, 1993).

ON THE WEB

For more on peer tutoring, see an article by the Northwest Regional Educational Laboratory (www.nwrel.org/request/oct96/article3.html). You can also access Kids as Helpers: A Peer-Tutoring Training Manual (free) at www.interventioncentral.org/htmdocs/interventions/rdngfluency/prtutor.php. Another article by NWREL on peer and cross-age tutoring is found at www.nwrel.org/archive/sirs/9/c018.html. Information for families on classwide peer tutoring by the Center for Effective Collaboration and Practice is available at http://cecp.air.org/familybriefs/docs/PeerTutoring.pdf.

peer tutoring

Tutoring of one student by another.

cross-age tutoring

Tutoring of a younger student by an older one.

■ Tutoring by Teachers

One-to-one adult-to-child tutoring is one of the most effective instructional strategies known, and it essentially solves the problem of appropriate levels of instruction. The principal drawback to this method is cost. However, it is often possible, on a small scale, to provide adult tutors for students who are having problems learning in the regular class setting. For example, adult volunteers such as parents, college students, or senior citizens are often willing to tutor students (Hopkins, 1998; Juel, 1996; Neuman, 1995). Volunteer tutors who are well supervised and use well-structured materials can have a positive effect on children's reading performance (Baker, Gersten, & Keating, 2000; Tingley, 2001). Tutoring is an excellent use of school aides (Hock, Schumaker, & Deshler, 2001); some school districts hire large numbers of paraprofessional aides precisely for this purpose. In fact, research has found few achievement benefits of classroom aides unless they are doing one-to-one tutoring (see Slavin, 1994a).

There are some circumstances in which one-to-one tutoring is particularly justifiable, despite the cost, such as for first-graders who are having difficulties learning to read. Failing to learn to read in the lower grades of elementary school is so detrimental to later school achievement that an investment in tutors who can prevent reading failure is worthwhile. A recent review of research on programs for struggling readers in the elementary grades found substantial positive effects of a variety of tutoring and small-group interventions (Slavin, Lake, Davis, & Madden, 2009). One-to-one tutoring was very effective, but tutoring models that use structured phonetic methods were much more effective than other tutoring methods (Blachman et al., 2004; Brown, Morris, & Fields, 2005; Ehri, 2007). Phonetic programs delivered by paraprofessionals were almost as effective (Jenkins, Peyton, Sanders, & Vadasy, 2004; Vadasy, Sanders, & Tudor, 2007). Smaller positive effects were found in studies of phonetic tutoring to groups of three to eight children (Hempenstall, 2008; Mathes et al., 2003, 2005). Whole-class use of cooperative learning methods was also almost as effective as one-to-one tutoring with struggling readers (Mathes & Babyak, 2001; Nelson & Stage, 2007; Stevens & Slavin, 1995b; Stevens et al., 2008). Success for All, which uses both cooperative learning and tutoring, has had substantial and lasting effects on the learning of students at risk (Borman et al., 2007; Correnti, 2009; Slavin, Madden, Chambers, & Haxby, 2009). These findings suggest that a large proportion of children who are struggling in reading can be substantially helped with some combination of tutoring and cooperative learning.

Theory into Practice
Effectively Using Peer Tutoring Methods to Meet Individual Needs

Peer tutoring is an effective way to improve learning for both the tutee and the tutor, and no one doubts the value of this strategy for meeting individual needs within a classroom. However, it takes more than simply pairing off students for peer tutoring to result in improved learning.

Although you are likely to use informal tutoring practices in your classroom every day (e.g., asking one student to help another student with a problem), establishing a formalized tutoring program requires more involved planning. The following strategies can help you create and sustain an effective program within your classroom. As with most initiatives, if you can work with your building administrator and other teachers to establish a schoolwide tutoring program, you will be able to serve the needs of all students more successfully.

✓ Certification Pointer

For your teacher certification test, you will probably need to demonstrate your understanding of appropriate applications of cross-age tutoring. For example, you might be asked to identify the curricular goals that cross-age tutoring would be appropriate for and how you would structure the tutoring so that it would be effective.

To establish a tutoring program, recognize that specific skills need to be developed in both the tutors and tutees. Whether the tutors are same-age peers, older students, or even adults, use care in selecting tutors. It is always wise to begin with volunteers. Consider not only the knowledge base of the tutors (i.e., their proven proficiency with the subject matter) but also their ability to convey knowledge clearly.

Typically, training will include basic instruction in modeling, prompting responses from tutees, using corrective feedback and praise/reinforcement, alternating teaching methods and materials (i.e., using multisensory methods), and recording and reporting progress. If this is a schoolwide initiative, classroom teachers or even parents or paraprofessionals can train students who will tutor as part of an extracurricular service activity.

Students receiving tutoring need to be clear about their role in this process. It would be counterproductive to force any student into a tutorial relationship. Therefore, initially select only students who express a willingness to work with a tutor. Steadily make tutoring a part of the natural learning activities within a classroom or an entire school. In this collaborative model, every student at some point in time will have the opportunity to be both tutor and tutee. Even students with less knowledge and skills might be able to find peers or younger students with whom they can work. Many students with special-education needs have gained confidence and improved their own abilities by working with younger students.

During the training process help all students to understand that the tutor represents the teacher and, therefore, should be respected accordingly. In addition, tutees and tutors must understand that the goal of the activity is to have each tutee reach a clear understanding of the concepts, not merely complete an assignment. To augment the preparation, you might want to use various role-playing activities during the training process. Demonstrate appropriate and inappropriate forms of instruction, feedback, reinforcement, and so on; then allow the participants to practice under supervised conditions. Corrective feedback within this controlled environment will allow you to feel more confident as the tutor–tutee pairs work together without your direct supervision.

Whether you decide to begin this process solely within your own classroom or to develop a schoolwide tutorial program, keep the following issues in mind:

1. Tutors need to be trained in specific instructional practices.

2. Tutors and tutees need to have a clear understanding of their roles and expectations.

3. Tutors and tutees need to receive supervision and feedback about their work, particularly during the early stages of the tutoring process.

4. Teachers need to work with the tutors to create effective and efficient ways of recording and reporting the progress of the sessions.

What Educational Programs Exist for Students Placed at Risk ?

Any child can succeed in school. Any child can fail. The difference between success and failure depends primarily on what the school, the parents, community agencies, and the child himself or herself do to create conditions that are favorable for learning (Thomas & Bainbridge, 2001). Before school entry we cannot predict very well which individual children will succeed or fail, but there are factors in a child's background that make success or failure more likely (on the average). For example, students who come from impoverished or single-parent homes, those who have marked developmental delays, or those who exhibit aggressive or withdrawn behavior are more likely to experience problems in school than are other students. These children are often referred to as **students at risk** (Barr & Parrett, 1995; Manning & Baruth, 1995). The term *at risk* is borrowed from medicine, in which it has long been used to describe individuals who do not have a given disease but are more likely than average to develop it. For example, a heavy smoker or a person with a family history of cancer might be at risk for lung cancer, even though not all heavy smokers or people with family histories of cancer actually get the disease. High blood pressure is a known risk factor for heart attacks, even though most people with high blood pressure do not have heart attacks. Similarly, a given child from an impoverished home might do well in school, but 100 such children are likely to perform significantly worse, on the average, than 100 children from middle-class homes (Rossi & Stringfield, 1995). Boykin (2000) introduced the term "placed at risk" rather than "at risk," to emphasize the fact that it is often an inadequate response to a child's needs by school, family, or community that places the child at risk. For example, a child who could have succeeded in reading if he or she had been given appropriate instruction, a reading tutor, or eyeglasses could be said to be placed at risk by lack of these services.

Before children enter school, the most predictive risk factors relate to their socioeconomic status and family structure. After they begin school, however, such risk factors as poor reading performance, grade repetition, and poor behavior become more important predictors of later school problems (such as dropping out) than family background factors (Ensminger & Slusarcick, 1992).

Educational programs for students who are at risk fall into three major categories: compensatory education, early intervention programs, and special education. **Compensatory education** is the term used for programs designed to prevent or remediate learning problems among students who are from low-income families or who attend schools in low-income communities. Some intervention programs target infants and toddlers who are at risk to prevent possible later need for remediation. Other intervention programs are aimed at keeping children in school. Compensatory and early intervention programs are discussed in the following sections. Special education, discussed in Chapter 12, is designed to serve children who have more serious learning problems as well as children with physical or psychological problems.

■ Compensatory Education Programs

Compensatory education programs are designed to overcome the problems associated with being brought up in low-income communities. Compensatory education supplements the education of students from disadvantaged backgrounds who are experiencing trouble in school or who are thought to be in danger of having school problems. Two such programs, Head Start and Follow Through, are designed to give preschool and primary school children from disadvantaged homes the skills they need for a good start in school. However, the largest compensatory education program, and the one that is most likely to affect regular classroom teachers, is called **Title I** (formerly "Chapter 1"), a federally funded program that gives schools money to provide extra services for students from low-income families who are having trouble in school (see Borman, Stringfield, & Slavin, 2001; Manna, 2008).

Title I is not merely a transfer of money from the federal government to local school districts. According to federal guidelines, these funds must be used to "supplement, not supplant" local educational efforts. This means that school districts cannot use the money to increase teachers' salaries or purchase ordinary supplies. Instead, funds must go directly toward increasing the academic achievement of low achievers in schools that serve many students who are disadvantaged. The exception is that schools that serve very disadvantaged neighborhoods—neighborhoods in which at least 40 percent of the students

Connections
For more on factors such as poverty and limited English proficiency that might place students at risk of school failure, see Chapter 4, pages 80 and 95.

Connections
To learn about factors such as problems of childhood and adolescence that might place students at risk of school failure, see Chapter 3, pages 66 and 69–70.

Connections
Special education is discussed in detail in Chapter 12.

students at risk
Students who are subject to school failure because of their own characteristics and/or because of inadequate responses to their needs by school, family, or community.

compensatory education
Programs designed to prevent or remediate learning problems among students from lower socioeconomic status communities.

Title I
Compensatory programs reauthorized under Title I of the Improving America's Schools Act (IASA) in 1994; formerly known as *Chapter 1*.

qualify for free lunch—can use Title I money to improve the school as a whole (but still not for basic costs, only for improving outcomes).

TITLE I PROGRAMS   Title I programs can take many forms. Most often, a special Title I teacher provides remedial help to students who are experiencing difficulties in reading and, in many cases, in other subjects as well (Borman et al., 2001). Programs of this type are called **pull-out programs** because the students are pulled out of their general education classes to take part in the programs.

Pull-out programs have been criticized for many years. One major problem is that often the regular teacher and the Title I teacher do not coordinate their efforts, so the very students who need the most consistent and structured instruction may have to deal with two completely different approaches (Allington & McGill-Franzen, 1989; Meyers, Gelzheiser, Yelich, & Gallagher, 1990). Title I programs should be directed at ensuring the success of students in the general education classroom and should therefore be closely coordinated with the general education teacher's instructional activities. For example, if a student is having trouble in the general education class with finding the main ideas of paragraphs, the Title I teacher should be working on main ideas, perhaps using the same instructional materials that the classroom teacher is using.

Many other innovative programs have been found to accelerate the achievement gains of students who are disadvantaged. Among these are tutoring programs or other structured instructional programs that have clear objectives and frequent assessments of students' attainment of these objectives (see Slavin & Madden, 1987; Slavin, Madden, & Karweit, 1989). The most effective approaches, however, are those that prevent students from ever having academic difficulties in the first place (Hamburg, 1992; Slavin, Karweit, & Wasik, 1994). These include high-quality preschool and kindergarten programs (Berrueta-Clement, Schweinhart, Barnett, Epstein, & Weikart, 1984; Reynolds, 1991) as well as comprehensive school reform programs that help all children succeed the first time they are taught (Borman, 2003; Comprehensive School Reform Quality Center, 2006a,b; Kidron & Darwin, 2007).

RESEARCH ON THE EFFECTS OF TITLE I   Two major nationwide studies of the achievement effects of the programs offered under Title I have been carried out. The first, called the Sustaining Effects Study (Carter, 1984), found that Title I students did achieve better in reading and math than did similar low-achieving students who did not receive Title I services, but that these effects were not large enough to enable Title I students to close the gap with students performing at the national average. The greatest gains were for first-graders, whereas the benefits of Title I participation for students in fourth grade and above were slight.

The other major study of the effects of the compensatory services funded under Title I, called *Prospects,* also compared elementary and middle school children receiving compensatory education services both to similar children at risk who were not receiving services and to children who were never at risk. *Prospects* did not find any achievement benefits for children receiving Title I services (Puma, Jones, Rock, & Fernandez, 1993). A more detailed analysis by Borman, D'Agostino, Wong, and Hedges (1998) found similarly disappointing outcomes, although there were some positive effects for children who were less disadvantaged and for those who received services during some years but not others. However, the lowest-achieving students from the most disadvantaged backgrounds were not narrowing achievement gaps with agemates who were less disadvantaged.

Although the *Prospects* study did not find overall positive effects of receiving compensatory services, results were positive in some situations. One particularly influential factor was the degree to which Title I services were closely coordinated with other school services (Borman, 1997; Borman, D'Agostino, Wong, & Hedges, 1998). In other words, schools that closely integrated remedial or instructional Title I services with the school's main instructional program, and especially schools that used Title I dollars to

pull-out programs

Compensatory education programs in which students are placed in separate classes for remediation.

enhance instruction for all students in schoolwide projects, obtained the best outcomes. This kind of integration contrasts with the traditional practice of sending low-achieving students to remedial classes where instruction is poorly coordinated with the classes they are leaving.

Although a review of many studies did find positive effects on average (Borman, Hewes, Overman, & Brown, 2003; Borman & D'Agostino, 2001), no one familiar with the data would argue that Title I impacts are large (Manna, 2008). This is not a surprising conclusion, given that for most students Title I means no more than a 30-minute daily remedial session (Stringfield et al., 1997).

Research on effective practices in compensatory pull-out classes finds that, in general, effective approaches in regular classes are also effective in pull-out classes. For example, more instructional time, more time on task, and other indicators of effective classroom management are important predictors of achievement gain in compensatory program classes (Crawford, 1989; Stein, Leinhardt, & Bickel, 1989). A large study of programs for students from high-poverty areas (Knapp, 1995; Knapp, Shields, & Turnbull, 1995) found that students in schools emphasizing instruction for deep understanding and meaning achieved significantly better than students whose teachers emphasized drill and practice (also see Waxman et al., 2001). Another large study, by Stringfield and colleagues (1997), evaluated a range of programs used in high-poverty schools. Two comprehensive school reform programs were particularly effective: Success for All and Comer's School Development Program, both of which are discussed later in this chapter. These and other findings have led Title I policy-makers increasingly to favor schoolwide programs in which Title I funds are used to improve instruction for all children in the school (see Borman et al., 2001; Slavin & Fashola, 1998).

■ Early Intervention Programs

Traditionally, Title I and other compensatory education programs have overwhelmingly emphasized remediation. They typically provide services to children only after the children have already fallen behind. Such children might also end up in special education or might be retained. It makes more sense to focus on prevention and **early intervention** rather than remediation in serving children placed at risk of school failure (see Chambers, Cheung, Slavin, Smith, & Laurenzano, 2010; Powell, 1995; Slavin, Karweit, & Wasik, 1994).

Programs that emphasize infant stimulation, parent training, and other services for children from birth to age 5 have been found to have long-term effects on the school success of students who are at risk. An example is the Carolina Abecedarian program (Campbell & Ramey, 1994), which found long-term achievement effects of an intensive program for children from low-income homes who receive services from infancy through school entry. The Perry Preschool program has also demonstrated long-term effects of an intensive program for 4-year-olds (Schweinhart & Weikart, 1998). Other programs have had similar effects (Chambers et al., 2010). In addition to such preventive programs, there is evidence that early intervention can keep children from falling behind in the early grades. For example, Whitehurst and colleagues (1999) found lasting effects of an early intervention program emphasizing phonemic awareness (knowledge of how sounds blend into words) and other preliteracy strategies. A program called **Reading Recovery** (Lyons, Pinnell, & DeFord, 1993; Pinnell, DeFord, & Lyons, 1988) provides one-to-one tutoring from specially trained teachers to first-graders who are not reading adequately. This program has been found to bring most children placed at risk to adequate levels of performance and can have long-lasting positive effects. Reading Recovery is used in thousands of elementary schools in the United States, Canada, the United Kingdom, and other countries. Although there is little disagreement that Reading Recovery has a positive effect on the reading success of first-graders who are at risk (see Slavin et al., 2009), there are conflicting findings concerning maintenance of these gains beyond first grade. A major long-term evaluation of Reading Recovery in London

Connections

For more on prevention and early intervention, see Chapter 12, page 386.

early intervention

Programs that target infants and toddlers who are at risk to prevent possible later need for remediation.

Reading Recovery

A program in which specially trained teachers provide one-to-one tutoring to first-graders who are not reading adequately.

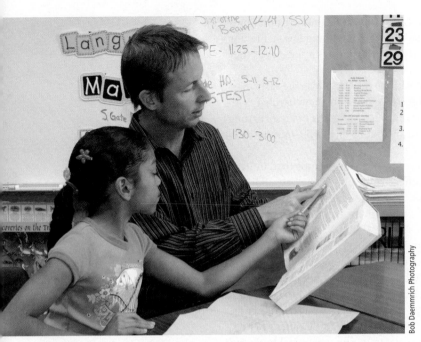

Reading Recovery is particularly helpful for working with students who are English learners. How do such programs differ from traditional compensatory programs?

found strong immediate effects that had faded away by the time the children were 10 years old (Hurry & Sylva, 2007). There have also been questions about the cost-effectiveness of Reading Recovery (Hiebert, 1996; Shanahan, 1998) and whether positive effects for small numbers of first-graders represent the best use of limited funds for an entire age group of children (see Hiebert, 1996; Schacter, 2000).

In addition to Reading Recovery, several other programs have successfully used certified teachers, paraprofessionals, and even well-trained and well-supervised volunteers to improve the reading achievement of first-graders (Morris et al., 2000; Slavin, Lake, Davis, & Madden, 2009). A phonetic tutoring program called Reading Rescue has produced substantially better outcomes for first-graders than either a small-group remedial program or no intervention (Ehri, Dreyer, Flugman, & Gross, 2007). An Australian program that used a combination of curricular reform, one-to-one tutoring (Reading Recovery), family support, and other elements showed significant effects on first-graders' reading performance (Crévola & Hill, 1998).

Research on tutoring programs, the Carolina Abecedarian program, and other preventive strategies shows that children who are at risk can succeed if we are willing to give them high-quality instruction and intensive services early in their school careers (Slavin, 1997/1998). Early intervention also ensures that children who do turn out to need long-term services are identified early—and that those whose problems can be solved early on are not needlessly assigned to special education (see Vellutino et al., 1996).

■ Comprehensive School Reform Programs

Comprehensive school reform (CSR) programs are schoolwide approaches that introduce research-based strategies into every aspect of school functions: curriculum, instruction, assessment, grouping, accommodations for children having difficulties, parent involvement, and other elements (Borman, Hewes, Overman, & Brown, 2003; CSRQ, 2006a,b; Kidron & Darwin, 2007; Slavin, 2008a). Comprehensive reform models vary widely. Some, such as Success for All (Slavin et al., 2009) and Direct Instruction (Adams & Engelmann, 1996) provide specific student materials in each subject and detailed guides to using them, whereas others, such as Accelerated Schools (Hopfenberg & Levin, 1993) and the School Development Program (Comer, Haynes, Joyner, & Ben-Avie, 1996), provide more general guidelines for practice and then help school staffs develop their own approaches. America's Choice (Supovitz, Poglinco, & Snyder, 2001) and Modern Red Schoolhouse (Kilgore, Doyle, & Linkowsky, 1996) focus on infusing standards into school practices. Collectively, these comprehensive school reform models are used in about 3,000 U.S. schools (Slavin, 2008a).

The most widely used and extensively researched of the CSR programs is **Success for All** (Slavin, Madden, Chambers, et al., 2009), a program that focuses on prevention and early intervention for elementary schools serving disadvantaged communities. Success for All provides research-based reading programs for preschool, kindergarten, and grades 1 through 8; one-to-one tutoring for first-graders who need it; family support services; and other changes in instruction, curriculum, and school organization designed to ensure that students do not fall behind in the early grades. Longitudinal studies of Suc-

Success for All

A comprehensive approach to prevention and early intervention for preschool, kindergarten, and grades 1 through 8, with one-to-one tutoring, family support services, and changes in instruction designed to prevent students from falling behind.

cess for All have shown that students in this program read substantially better than do students in matched control schools throughout the elementary and middle grades and that they are far less likely to be assigned to special education or to fail a grade (see Borman & Hewes, 2003; Borman et al., 2007; Correnti, 2009; Muñoz, Dossett, & Judy-Gullans, 2004; Slavin, Lake, Davis, & Madden, 2009; Slavin, Madden, Chambers, & Haxby, 2009). In 2009–2010, Success for All was used in about 1,000 Title I schools in 48 states.

Another widely researched comprehensive school reform model is James Comer's School Development Program (Comer et al., 1996). Comer's model emphasizes building connections with parents and communities and organizing school staff into collaborative teams to create engaging, effective instruction (Ramirez-Smith, 1995). Two randomized experiments evaluating the Comer model found that schools making the most extensive use of the principles underlying the approach had the greatest achievement gains (Cook et al., 1999; Cook, Murphy, & Hunt, 2000).

■ After-School and Summer School Programs

Increasingly, Title I and other federal, state, and local education agencies are funding programs that extend learning time for students beyond the school day. Both after-school and summer school programs are expanding rapidly.

After-school programs typically combine some sort of academic activity, such as homework help, with sports, drama, and cultural activities (Friedman, 2003). However, studies of after-school programs generally find that for such programs to enhance student achievement, they need to incorporate well-organized coursework, such as individual or small-group tutoring, to extend the academic day (Fashola, 2002; McComb & Scott-Little, 2003).

Summer school sessions are also increasingly seen in schools, particularly as a last chance for students to avoid being retained in their grade. Summer school has long been advocated as a solution to the "summer loss" phenomenon, in which children from families that are low in socioeconomic status tend to lose ground over the summer, whereas middle-class students tend to gain (Entwisle et al., 2001). Research on summer school generally finds benefits for children's achievement (Borman & Boulay, 2004). One recent study by Kim (2006) found that simply sending books home with fourth-graders and encouraging them to read with their parents increases their reading performance in the fall.

A review by Lauer, Akiba, Wilkerson, Apthorp, Snow, and Martin-Glenn (2006) looked at the research on both types of out-of-school programs, summer school and after school. They found small positive effects of out-of-school programs for reading and math when children who attend these programs are compared to those who do not. When the programs include tutoring, effects are much more positive. Effects are the same for after-school as for summer school programs. The importance of these findings is the indication that struggling children can be helped by extending instructional time for them, especially if the additional time is used for targeted instructional activities.

For more on summer school, see Cooper, Charlton, Valentine, and Muhlenbruck (2000). For more on after-school programs, see McComb and Scott-Little (2003).

How Is Technology Used in Education

Watch children of any age playing video games, sending text messages to their friends, or looking up information on the Internet. Adults who see this, or experience it themselves, ask themselves why the obvious power of technology, which is transforming every aspect of life, hasn't transformed education. This is not to say that technology is not present in classrooms. Computers, DVDs, interactive whiteboards, and all sorts of other technology are present to one degree or another in every school, and most middle-class children,

INTASC

6 Communication Skills

at least, go home to an array of technology as well (DeBell & Chapman, 2006; Thorsen, 2009). Yet only gradually is technology truly changing the core of teaching and learning in America's schools (Borgman et al., 2008).

ON THE **WEB**

The International Society for Technology in Education (ISTE) has developed standards for technology use in education. It provides guidance for teachers in the following areas:

- Facilitating and inspiring student learning and creativity
- Designing and developing digital-age learning experiences and assessments
- Modeling digital-age work and learning
- Promoting and modeling digital citizenship and responsibility
- Engaging in professional growth and leadership

The complete ISTE National Educational Technology Standards for Teachers (NETS-T) is found at www.iste.org/Content/NavigationMenu/NETS/ForTeachers/2008Standards/NETS_T_Standards_Final.pdf. Link to the International Technology Education Association from www.iteaconnect .org. Another website for teachers about integrating technology into their classrooms is online at www.4teachers.org.

There are three general types of technology applications in education. First, teachers use technology in classroom teaching to plan instruction and present content to classes. Second, students use technology to explore, practice, communicate with others, and prepare papers and presentations. Finally, teachers and administrators use technology to accomplish associated administrative tasks, such as assessment, record keeping, reporting, and management (see Bitter & Legacy, 2008; Lever-Duffy & McDonald, 2008; Thorsen, 2009). Examples of these three types of technology applications are described in the next sections.

■ Technology for Teaching

In order for technology to be beneficial in the classroom, you have to use its various tools effectively. Just providing a computer to a student is not sufficient to promote adequate, meaningful learning with technology. Let's look at some ways technology can be effectively applied to class lessons.

COMPUTERS   Word processors, electronic spreadsheets, and presentation software are the most common electronic technologies utilized for instruction. You can use word processors for numerous teaching tasks, such as preparing student worksheets, tests, rubrics, classroom signs, and posters. In addition, the "Review" tools in word processing enable you to provide individualized feedback through the use of "tracked changes" and "inserted comments." Simple desktop publishing features allow teachers to use color, graphics, and art to make texts appealing to students. The editing features of word processing programs make it easy for you to adapt documents to meet specific student needs.

Electronic spreadsheets organize and compute numerical data, producing charts and graphs to illustrate information. Spreadsheets are particularly helpful for teaching mathematics because they allow you to display numeric data visually, such as the impact of changes on variable values.

Presentation software helps you make professional expositions with a prearranged group of electronic slides. These presentations can include multimedia elements such as graphics, sound, special effects, animation, and video clips that make the displays more appealing. They can also be printed to provide students with an outline of the presentation. More advanced multimedia and Web authoring systems help you create your own multimedia tutorials and Web pages to support their lessons.

Increasingly, technology is being used to combine text and visual content, such as animations or video. This multimedia approach has been found to enhance students' learning as long as the text and visuals directly support each other (Hoeffler & Leutner, 2006; Reed, 2006). For example, adding diagrams or animations to show how lightning works has been found to enhance the text, but adding motivational but nonexplanatory text (such as a picture of an airplane being hit by lightning) can actually detract from learning (Mayer, 2008b, 2009). Similarly, recent studies of first-grade reading found that adding video content on letter sounds, sound blending, and vocabulary to teacher-led reading lessons significantly increases students' learning (Chambers et al., 2006, 2008).

The many technological tools available make your lessons more dynamic. Initial fears that computers might replace teachers are unfounded. Effective use of computer simulations, presentation software, spreadsheets, and other software enhances rather than replaces teacher instruction.

INTERACTIVE WHITEBOARDS AND LEARNER RESPONSE DEVICES

An **interactive whiteboard** is a large screen, visible to a whole class, on which it is possible to display anything that can be shown on a computer screen (Betcher & Lee, 2009). Teachers or children can also write on the board and manipulate content already there, using either a finger or a special pen (depending on the brand). In addition, students can be provided with **electronic response devices,** or **clickers,** on which they can electronically answer your questions. You can then quickly assess the concepts your class has mastered and which concepts you need to spend more time teaching (Becker & Lee, 2009; Marzano, 2009).

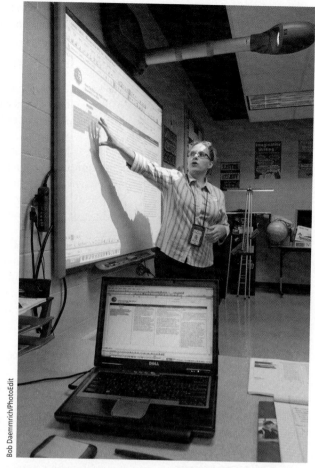

Bob Daemmrich/PhotoEdit

Interactive whiteboards are used in about 25 percent of U.S. classrooms to help teachers solve the problems of orchestrating complex lessons. How will you use technology such as interactive whiteboards to help in organizing your lessons?

At present, interactive whiteboards are widely used in Britain, in perhaps 75 percent of classrooms, but are only found in about 25 percent of U.S. classrooms. However, their availability is growing very rapidly. Interactive whiteboards can help teachers solve the problems of orchestrating complex lessons. All lesson elements can be loaded into the computer and projected on the whiteboard, including PowerPoints, video clips, still pictures, letters, words, and other prepared content. Moreover, you can create, add to, or modify lessons using the vast digital resources available on the Internet. The whiteboard does not replace the teacher, but instead provides visual aids at the right time to facilitate teaching of exciting, varied, and effective lessons.

Because the technology is fairly recent, there is little U.S. research on interactive whiteboards. Studies in Britain have found promising outcomes. Somekh and colleagues (2007) showed a positive correlation between months of access to interactive whiteboards and achievement on national reading and math tests. Higgins and colleagues (2005) found similar results in another correlational study. Reviews by Pittard, Bannister, and Dunn (2003), and by Smith, Higgins, Wall, and Miller (2005) reported that early findings from research on interactive whiteboards show positive effects of the approach on student learning. Descriptive research on applications of interactive whiteboards (e.g., Latham, 2002; Miller, Glover, Averis, & Door, 2005) demonstrates both the potential and the difficulties of whiteboard use and universally recommends extensive professional development

interactive whiteboard

Large touchscreen that teachers can use to display and modify digital content for an entire class.

electronic response devices (clickers)

Electronic devices on which students enter answers to questions and have them registered on a computer or interactive whiteboard.

and follow-up, development of content specifically for the whiteboards, and integration of interactive whiteboards with other instructional activities and resources.

■ The Internet for Teachers

The Internet can provide rich resources for lesson planning. Teacher-related websites enable teachers to exchange information, support each other, share ideas, and problem solve. Online resources for teachers include a variety of Web tools.

E-MAIL   The advent of e-mail in the classroom has made it possible for teachers to communicate with each other and with parents quickly and easily. From an administrative perspective, e-mail can reduce the need for meetings because teachers can communicate via e-mail. Some schools use e-mail to take attendance. E-mail can also be used within the classroom to communicate with other classes in different states and countries.

DISCUSSION BOARDS   A discussion board is similar to e-mail in that users respond to each other's comments, but on a discussion board an organizer provides topics for discussion on the initial screen, and then participants can choose the topic they wish to discuss. In this way, you can facilitate student debates on classroom-related issues and provided a forum for opinions.

WEB AUTHORING   It is becoming common practice for teachers to post homework assignments, calendars, and general messages onto a website for parents to access.

■ Technology for Learning

Technology is used for a wide variety of purposes to help students learn. The applications of learning technology fall into the following categories: word processing and publishing, spreadsheets and databases, computer-assisted instruction, the Internet, multimedia, integrated learning systems, and computer programming (Bitter & Legacy, 2008; Goldman-Segall & Maxwell, 2003; Shuler, 2007; Thorsen, 2009; Zhao & Frank, 2003). See Chapter 12 for a discussion of the use of technology in special education and mainstreaming (Lever-Duffy & McDonald, 2008).

WORD PROCESSING AND PUBLISHING   One of the most common application of computers, especially in grades 4 through 12, is **word processing** or **desktop publishing.** Increasingly, students are asked to write compositions on classroom computers. A key advantage of word processing over paper-and-pencil composition is the ease of revision. Spell checkers and other utilities help students to worry less about mechanics and focus on the meaning and organization of their compositions. As writing instruction has moved toward an emphasis on the process of revision and editing, this capability has become very important. Word processing is probably the best-researched application of computers to instruction, and studies have shown that students who use computers write more, revise more, and take greater pride in their writing than do paper-and-pencil writers (Cochran-Smith, 1991). Writing quality also tends to be somewhat better when students have access to word processors (Goldberg, Russell, & Cook, 2003; Kamil, Intrator, & Kim, 2000). This writing effect may be enhanced when each student has a laptop, instead of having to share a small number of computers (Lowther, Ross, & Morrison, 2003). Of course, word processing itself has become an essential skill in a vast range of occupations, so teaching students to use word processing programs (e.g., in high school business courses) has obvious value.

SPREADSHEETS   As with word processing, **spreadsheets** in education are extensions of software widely used by adults. Typically, spreadsheets can convert raw data into graphs, charts, and other data summaries so that students can easily organize information

---

Connections

To learn about the use of computers for students with disabilities, see Chapter 12, page 387.

word processing or desktop publishing

A computer application for writing compositions that lends itself to revising and editing.

spreadsheets

Computer programs that convert data into tables, charts, and graphs.

and see the effects of various variables on outcomes (see Figure 9.2). For example, a student could enter data for the number of daily visitors to Wilbur the pig in a petting zoo. By assigning a formula to a given column, the student could customize the spreadsheet program to total the number of visits to Wilbur by day of the week, time of day, age of visitors, and so forth. Changing any number automatically changes row and column totals. The spreadsheet program could then show the data in raw numeric form or convert the data into a graph. Students are increasingly using spreadsheets to record data from science experiments and to reinforce mathematics skills.

DATABASES A **database** is a computer program that keeps a lot of information available for reference or possible manipulation. Students can learn to search CD-ROM (ROM stands for *read-only memory*) databases such as encyclopedias, atlases, road maps, catalogs, and so on to find information for a variety of instructional purposes. Databases of current information are readily available on the Internet. Databases of archived or current information can be particularly important in project-based learning because they may put a great deal of information into easy reach for open-ended reports and other projects.

In many databases, students can use **hypertext** and **hypermedia** to search a database (such as an encyclopedia) by clicking on a word or picture. This leads the student to related or more detailed information on a specific portion of the text (see Figure 9.3). Hypermedia can similarly provide pictures, music, video footage, or other information to illuminate and extend the information on a CD-ROM or online database. Hypermedia

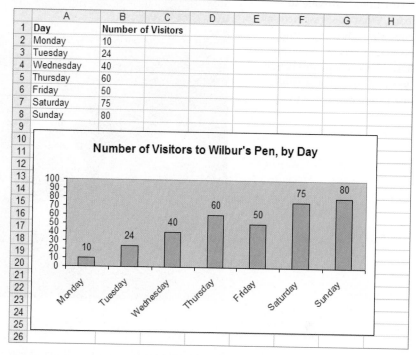

FIGURE 9.2 **Example of a Spreadsheet and Resulting Graph**

databases

Computer programs that contain large volumes of information, such as encyclopedias and atlases.

hypertext and hypermedia

Related information that appears when a computer user clicks on a word or picture.

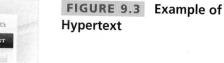

FIGURE 9.3 **Example of Hypertext**

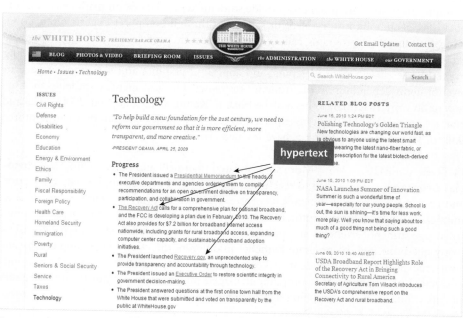

Source: www.whitehouse.gov/issues/technology

These students are using instructional software to learn. What does research say about the advantages and disadvantages of computer-based instruction? Are certain types of computer-assisted instruction more effective?

Bob Daemmrich Photography

has exciting possibilities for allowing learners to follow their interests or resolve gaps in understanding more efficiently than with traditional text, but so far, research on use of hypermedia finds limited and inconsistent effects on student learning that depend on both the type of material being studied and the nature of the learners (Dillon & Gabbard, 1998; Kamil et al., 2000).

COMPUTER-ASSISTED INSTRUCTION

Applications of **computer-assisted instruction (CAI)** range in complexity from simple drill and practice software to complex problem-solving programs.

DRILL AND PRACTICE

One of the most common applications of computers in education is to furnish students with **drill and practice** on skills or knowledge. For example, many software programs provide students with practice on math facts or computations, geography, history facts, or science. Although computer experts often frown on drill and practice programs, calling them "electronic page turning," drill and practice programs used to replace independent seatwork have several major advantages, including immediate feedback, record keeping, and appealing graphics and variations in pace or level of items depending on the student's responses. This can increase students' motivation to do work that might otherwise be boring (Kamil et al., 2000; Leu, 2000). Drill and practice programs should not be expected to teach by themselves, but they can reinforce skills or knowledge that students have learned elsewhere.

TUTORIAL PROGRAMS

More sophisticated than drill and practice programs, **tutorial programs** are intended to teach new material and present appropriate correction and review based on the student's responses. The best tutorial programs come close to mimicking a patient human tutor. Increasingly, tutorial programs use speech and graphics to engage students' attention and present new information. Students are typically asked many questions, and the program branches in different directions depending on the answers, reexplaining if the student makes mistakes or moving on if the student responds correctly. Very sophisticated computer-managed programs that simulate the behaviors of expert human tutors are being developed and applied in a variety of settings (Lever-Duffy, McDonald, & Mizell, 2003).

computer-assisted instruction (CAI)

Individualized instruction administered by computer.

drill and practice

Application of computer technology to provide students with practice of skills and knowledge.

tutorial programs

Computer programs that teach new material, varying their content and pace according to the student's responses.

INSTRUCTIONAL GAMES Most children are first introduced to computers through video games, and many educators (and parents) have wondered whether the same intensity, motivation, and perseverance that they see in children playing video games could be brought to the classroom (Gee & Levine, 2009; Shaffer, Squire, Halverson, & Gee, 2005; Shuler, 2007). Many **instructional games** have been designed; most are simple extrapolations of drill and practice designs into a game format, but some are more creative. For example, the popular program "Where in the World Is Carmen Sandiego?" is designed to teach geography by engaging children in tracking a gang of criminals through various countries. Computer games are among the most common applications of computer software in schools (Becker, 2001).

■ The Internet for Students

Perhaps the fastest-growing technology applications in U.S. schools involve the **Internet** (Leu, 2000; Lewin, 2001; March, 2005/2006). Internet access for schools, which is becoming virtually universal (NCES, 2007), gives schools access to vast stores of information, including databases on every imaginable subject, libraries throughout the world, and other specialized information (Jukes, Dosaj, & Macdonald, 2000). This information can be used to help students become active, creative learners (Martinez & Harper, 2008). For example, students can use the Internet to do WebQuests, in which they search the Internet on a given topic or theme. The Internet can also enable students to communicate with peers in other schools, regardless of distance. Through this capability students can create international projects or carry out cooperative projects with other schools (Lewin, 2001; Means, 2001). Many classes and schools have set up their own Web pages (Havens, 2003) and have created their own virtual museums or encyclopedias by collecting and synthesizing information from many sources. Students can contribute to **wikis** (online encyclopedias), podcasts, and other virtual publications that give them authentic opportunities to communicate their work (Dlott, 2007; Ohler, 2006; Valenza, 2005/2006).

SIMULATIONS As an interactive model of some sort of reality, **simulation software** allows students to operate within a simulated environment and, by doing so, learn about that environment from the inside. For example, one of the earliest simulations, "Oregon Trail," gives students limited allocations of food, water, money, and horses. Students must use these resources wisely to successfully move their wagon trains to the West. Modern simulations include Sim City Societies, Rise of Nations, Age of Mythology, Civilization, Zoo Tycoon, and Local Journey of the Zoominis (Gee & Levine, 2009).

WEBQUESTS WebQuests are like simulations, with the additional element of having users seek information on the Web to enhance their ability to play their role or contribute to a discussion or combined product. For example, Global Education (www .globaleducation.edna.edu.au) allows students to take any of a variety of roles related to the expansion of the desert in Mongolia. In order to participate meaningfully, students need to do research to understand issues from the perspective they have taken on. In Urban Science (http://epistemicgames.org), middle school students learn about urban planning, economics, and social policy to plan a new city. In Quest Atlantic (http://atlantis.crlt.indiana.edu), students find and use scientific information to solve simulated problems, such as pollution in fish habitats.

PROBLEM-SOLVING PROGRAMS The goal of developing students' critical-thinking skills has led to the creation of numerous programs that are designed as problem-solving activities. One innovative **problem-solving program** is the Jasper series, developed and researched at Vanderbilt University (Cognition and Technology Group at Vanderbilt, 1996). In this program, students are shown videos in which a character, Jasper Woodbury, faces a series of challenges that require applications of mathematics and thinking skills. Students must solve the problems Jasper faces before they see his solution. In addition to

---

instructional games

Drill and practice exercises presented in a game format.

Internet

A large and growing telecommunications network of computers around the world that communicate electronically.

wiki

A website, such as Wikipedia, containing content to which the user can add or make modifications.

simulation software

Computer programs that model real-life phenomena to promote problem-solving abilities and motivate interest in the areas concerned.

problem-solving program

Program designed specifically to develop students' critical-thinking skills.

Certification Pointer

A teacher certification question may ask you to suggest a strategy for using technology to help students learn various instructional objectives.

using computers, students work in cooperative groups on offline activities that are related to the stories. Evaluations have found that in comparison to matched controls, students in classes using the Jasper program perform similarly in math computations and concepts but better in word problems and planning.

ON THE WEB

Resources that can help you effectively use simulations, games, and lessons to engage students with technology include Classroom 2.0 Wiki (http://wiki.classrooms20.com), Route 21 (www.21stcenturyskills.org/route21), Technology in Education Resource Center (www.rtec.org), Universal Design for Learning (www.cast.org), Edutopia (www.edutopia.org), and the Apple Learning Interchange (http://edcommunity.apple.com/ali).

Theory into Practice
Helping Students Judge Internet Sources

The easy availability of information (and misinformation) on the Internet means that students need to become critical readers, able to judge the truthfulness, impartiality, and usefulness of the information they find (Badke, 2009; David, 2009; Richardson, 2009; Weigel & Gardner, 2009). Harris (2007) created a checklist for students to use in evaluating research sources (see Figure 9.4).

You can use Internet-based communications such as e-mail, conferencing, listservs (electronic mailing lists), chat rooms, and video conferencing to connect students to others in other areas of the world. Through these interactions students are exposed to perspectives different from their own (Lever-Duffy et al., 2003).

FIGURE 9.4 **Summary of the CARS Checklist for Research Source Evaluation**

Credibility
Trustworthy source, author's credentials, evidence of quality control, known or respected authority, organizational support. Goal: An authoritative source, a source that supplies some good evidence that allows you to trust it.

Accuracy
Up-to-date, factual, detailed, exact, comprehensive; audience and purpose reflect intentions of completeness and accuracy. Goal: A source that is correct today (not yesterday), a source that gives the whole truth.

Reasonableness
Fair, balanced, objective, reasoned, no conflict of interest, absence of fallacies or slanted tone. Goal: A source that engages the subject thoughtfully and reasonably, concerned with the truth.

Support
Listed sources, contact information, available corroboration, claims supported, documentation supplied. Goal: A source that provides convincing evidence for the claims made, a source you can triangulate (find at least two other sources that support it).

Source: "Evaluating Internet Research Sources" by Robert Harris, www.virtualsalt.com/evalu8it.htm. Text copyright © 2007 by Robert Harris.

ON THE WEB

For an example of a website that provides information for WebQuests, see www.edhelper.com.

There is little research on the achievement outcomes of Internet involvement (Leu, 2000; Wallace, 2004). There are also serious concerns about how to limit children's access to pornography or other inappropriate materials that can be found on the Web (see National Research Council, 2001; Wartella & Jennings, 2000). Yet the Internet is here to stay, at least as a tool to supplement school libraries with a broad range of information.

MULTIMEDIA PROJECTS   Students can be encouraged to make their own **multimedia** projects—an update of the old-fashioned group report (Ohler, 2009; Simpkins, Cole, Tavalin, & Means, 2002). In project-based multimedia learning, students design, plan, and produce a product or performance, integrating media objects such as graphics, video, animation, and sound. An example is a seventh-grade class that created a social studies and science multimedia presentation about the Black Plague, integrating animations of how the plague virus attacks and the perspectives of 14th-century farmers (Simkins et al., 2002).

Students can use a wide array of graphics tools to create their multimedia presentations, including CD-ROMs, digital photos, concept mapping, and graphic organizers. **CD-ROM** and online databases include clip art, photographs, illustrations, music, and sometimes video. Students can use them to create multimedia reports, projects, or explorations that combine audio, video, music, and pictures. **Digital video and photographs** can be used as a stimulus for writing or to illustrate projects. For example, students might take digital video or photographs of animals on a field trip to the zoo. Back in the classroom, these serve as a reminder to students of what they saw and also are used to illustrate their reports on the trip.

INTEGRATED LEARNING SYSTEMS   Schools often purchase **integrated learning systems**—entire packages of hardware and software, including most of the types of software described previously. Integrated learning systems provide many terminals

multimedia

Electronic material such as graphics, video, animation, and sound, which can be integrated into classroom projects.

CD-ROM

A computer database designed for "read-only memory" that provides massive amounts of information, including pictures and audio; it can be of particular importance to students doing projects and research activities.

digital video and photographs

Video and photographs that can be loaded into a computer and shared electronically.

integrated learning systems

Commercially developed comprehensive, multipurpose packages of interlinked management instructional software, running on a computer network.

Bob Daemmrich/PhotoEdit

In project-based multimedia learning, students design, plan, and produce a product or performance, integrating media objects such as graphics, video, animation, and sound. How can multimedia projects enhance your students' learning?

that are linked to each other and to computers that you can use to monitor individual student work (Lever-Duffy et al., 2003). Web versions of integrated learning systems are also available and add the benefit of providing online learning to students who need alternative schooling options. Research on the effectiveness of commercial integrated learning systems has found modest positive effects on mathematics achievement (Kulik, 2003; Slavin & Lake, 2008; Slavin, Lake, & Groff, 2009), but few effects on reading achievement (Kulik, 2003; Slavin, Cheung, Groff, & Lake, 2008; Slavin, Lake, Chambers, et al., 2009).

■ Web 2.0

Web 2.0 refers to the modern use of the World Wide Web that incorporates free collaborative online communication using a template for users to enter their comments and responses (Bitter & Legacy, 2008; Ferriter, 2009a; Knobel & Wilber, 2009; Reeves, 2009; Richardson, 2008). The groups of people who communicate this way are referred to as *virtual communities* or *social networkers.*

WEBLOGS (BLOGS) Weblogs, commonly called *blogs,* are like online diaries, where authors, or bloggers, post their thoughts and opinions. You can find a tutorial on how to start a blog and a sample blog on www.blogger.com. In education, blogs can be used as online storage for assignments and projects, for resources the students will need to download, as readers' guides for classroom books, or as a place where students can create and post content.

WIKIS A wiki is a website where visitors can add or change the information on the site. The most widely known example is Wikipedia (www.wikipedia.org), a free online encyclopedia written (and constantly updated) by volunteers who submit whole articles or edit existing articles. In the classroom, wikis can be used during group projects for online collaboration and organizing a group's arsenal of information. You can reference sites such as WikiEd (http://wik.ed.uiuc.edu/index.php/Main_Page) to access a wide variety of educational resources.

RSS FEEDS RSS stands for Real Simple Syndication or Rich Site Summary. RSS lets users know when something new is posted on a blog, wiki, or RSS-capable website in which they're interested. For example, *Education Week* provides educational RSS feeds from their publications, online discussion, and blogs on many topics (www.edweek.org/ew/section/feeds/index.html).

PODCASTS Podcasts are multimedia files available on the Internet for playback on computers and mobile devices. There are podcasts on many topics, including TV newscasts and college lectures. You can use podcasts in the classroom to supplement lessons you are teaching. One source is the Education Podcast Network, which lists podcasts by grade level and subject areas (http://epnweb.org).

SOCIAL NETWORKING Social networking is the use of websites to communicate with or to meet others who share the same interests. Facebook and LinkedIn are examples. The National Education Association has a social website for teachers to communicate with each other at www.nea.org.

■ Instructional Television and Embedded Multimedia

An old technology, educational television, is being used in new ways (see Shore, 2008). Research has long established the learning benefits of watching educational television shows such as "Sesame Street" (Fisch & Truglio, 2000) and "Between the Lions" (Line-

21st Century Learning

Mindful Use of Technology

Today, it is hardly necessary to teach most students to use basic computer technology. They are likely to already be comfortable and proficient with computers. However, it is increasingly important for teachers to design and implement lessons requiring students to engage in the *mindful* use of technology to find useful information, to learn new skills, and to create documents, designs, and other products. Mindful use of technology implies using critical reading skills to decide what is likely to be true and useful in a body of information, and using learning-to-learn skills to plan a search for information, organize what is found, evaluate the information and select from it, summarize knowl-edge, and create reports or other new materials based on the summaries. Technology makes libraries of information easily available, but it also allows or even encourages aimless meandering and mindless entertainment. Helping students use technology as a tool rather than a toy gives them essential skills for our times.

Question

■ Do you think a classroom discussion of students' negative Internet experiences would serve as a warning of what not to do, or do you think it would encourage students to experiment with technology in ways they hadn't thought of and potentially place them in harm's way?

barger, Kosanic, Greenwood, & Doku, 2004). Children who watch a lot of educational television become better readers, whereas those who watch a lot of noneducational television become worse-than-average readers (Ennemoser & Schneider, 2007; Wright et al., 2001).

A new application of video in the classroom is called **embedded multimedia** (Chambers, Cheung, Madden, Slavin, & Gifford, 2006). In this approach, brief segments of video content are threaded into lessons. In two large experiments, Chambers and colleagues (2006, 2008) found that adding to daily reading instruction 5 minutes of animations and puppet skits illustrating letter sounds and sound blending significantly increases children's reading performance. A review of research contrasting use of animations and static pictures in lessons found that students learn better from animated content (Höffler & Leutner, 2006).

ASSISTIVE TECHNOLOGY   Assistive technology helps students with physical disabilities such as hearing loss or deafness, speech disorders, vision impairment, or limited dexterity as well as learning or cognitive delay that impairs performance of target skills. Some examples of assistive technology are adaptive keyboards, screen readers, or screen magnifiers. Assistive technology is discussed further in Chapter 12.

■ Technology for Administration

You can use a variety of technologies to accomplish the many administrative tasks associated with your work, such as grading, creating reports, writing class newsletters, making invitations, and sending individual notes to parents. E-mail makes it easier for you to communicate with teaching assistants, administrators, parents, and others. Part of every teacher's job involves organizing, maintaining, and retrieving different types of data. This ranges from creating student rosters and logging students' contact information to tracking coverage of the district's language arts objectives (Archer, 2007). You can use

embedded multimedia

Video content woven into teachers' lessons.

portfolio assessment software to document student achievement. These programs allow you to collect and display the information when it comes time to report to parents.

As schools are being held more accountable for their students' achievements, school districts are using technology to monitor the progress of individual students, teachers, and schools using database management systems. In addition to tracking students' achievements, these school management systems allow districts to monitor enrollment, attendance, and school expenditures. Data management software makes it easier for you to enter, retrieve, and update records and to create accurate, customized, professional reports for administrators or parents. You can track which students are mastering what content areas so that you can better target specific instruction to the students who need it the most.

AUDIO AND VIDEO CONFERENCING   Audio and video conferencing make it possible for groups of people, each in front of their respective computers, to see and hear each other anywhere in the world (Thorsen, 2009). For administrators, this can eliminate the need to travel to as many meetings. In the classroom, this allows students to witness historic moments or to talk to an expert on a topic they're studying who lives far away.

■ Challenges of Integrating Technology

EQUAL ACCESS TO TECHNOLOGY   It is clear that students do not all have the same access to computers. Middle-class children are considerably more likely than children of a lower socioeconomic status to have access to computers at home (Becker, 2000; Bitter & Legacy, 2008; Education Commission of the States, 2000; Holloway, 2000; Thorsen, 2009), although the digital divide is rapidly diminishing in schools (Thorsen, 2009). Home computer access is associated with higher math and reading scores (Attewell & Battle, 1999). Within schools, boys tend to spend much more time on computers than do girls (Volman & van Eck, 2001). To the extent that computers become increasingly effective and important in providing state-of-the-art instruction, these inequities must be addressed.

SETTING LIMITS

Cyberbullying   Cyberbullying refers to threats or insults one person makes to another via instant or text messaging or over e-mail. Students may post insulting or damaging information about each other where others are sure to see it as one form of bullying. Students who are cyberbullied should be encouraged to print out the offensive messages as proof of their harassment and provide it to their teachers or principal. If possible, they should obtain the e-mail address of the bully. If students don't know who the bully is, it is recommended that they change their screen name and only tell it to trusted friends (Thorsen, 2009).

Cell Phones in Class   The popularity of the cell phone for sending text messages has yielded both positives and negatives in the classroom (Trotter, 2009). On the positive side, the latest technology allows you to project instant messages onto a screen so the entire class can benefit from a teacher/student instant message exchange. Text messages can be archived, allowing students to later refer to links or to answers they've received. On the negative side, text messaging can be an in-class distraction, can transmit computer viruses, could potentially be used for cheating, and can be a forum for cyberbullying. Given these drawbacks, you need to set limits on the use of cell phones in the classroom.

Safety and Security of Students   Students using the Internet can place themselves in harm's way, ranging from accidentally stumbling on inappropriate material to interacting with Internet predators.

There are several ways you can protect your students from viewing inappropriate material online. Although the best way to protect students is via responsible adult supervision, children can encounter objectionable material inadvertently, and Internet filtering software can help prevent many inappropriate sites from being viewed (Bitter & Legacy, 2008).

In addition, cybercrime, which is any illegal activity involving computers, is on the rise. Criminals now make more money via cybercrime than drug-related crimes (Vamosi, 2005). Even more frighteningly, studies have shown that one in five students received an online sexual solicitation in a 1-year period, and that 29 percent of children provide their home address when asked (Bitter & Legacy, 2008).

There are some general online safety guidelines students can follow to protect themselves from cybercrime and Internet predators:

- Never give out personal information to a person you've met online.

- Never, ever, ever meet with a person you have met online.

- Never say anything online you wouldn't want the world to know you've said.

- Do not give out your user name or password, or any financial information in response to an e-mail, even if it appears to be initiated from a business whose name you recognize.

- Only give out credit card or account information over a secure website or telephone.

■ Research on Computer-Assisted Instruction

Can computers teach? Most large evaluations and reviews of research on the effects of CAI conclude that computer-based instruction has few effects on reading achievement (Kulik, 2003; Slavin et al., 2008; Slavin, Lake, Chambers, et al., 2009) and small positive effects on math and other subjects (Aviram, 2000; Dynarski et al., 2007; Kulik, 2003; Slavin et al., 2008; Slavin & Lake, 2008; Texas Center for Educational Research, 2007). As was noted earlier, evidence does favor other uses of technology, such as use of interactive whiteboards (Somekh et al., 2007), embedded multimedia (Chambers et al., 2006, 2008), and word processing (Bangert-Drowns, 1993; Goldberg et al., 2003).

The potential of computers to improve achievement outcomes remains unclear. Some reviewers have argued that when the content of instruction is carefully controlled, computers are no more effective than other instructional methods (Bebell, O'Dwyer, Russell, & Seeley, 2004; Clark, 2001) or have small and variable effects (Blok, Oostdam, Otter, & Overmaat, 2002). Researchers today generally agree that the computer itself is not magic. What matters is the curriculum, instruction, and social context surrounding the use of the computer (Winne, 2006). Asking whether computers enhance learning is like asking whether chalkboards enhance learning. In either case, it depends on how they are used.

A review of research by Lou, Abrami, and d'Apollonia (2001) found that having students work on computers in small groups is, on average, more effective than having them work individually, as long as students use well-specified cooperative learning approaches such as those described in Chapter 8. Simply asking students to work together, however, produces no benefit. Outcomes are also enhanced when students work in pairs rather than in larger groups.

Use of computers and research on technology use are developing so rapidly that it is difficult to anticipate what the future will bring. At this time, however, computers are rarely being used to provide basic instruction. In fact, many studies find that even in technology-rich schools, computers are turned off most of the day, and computer use occupies a tiny portion of each student's academic time (e.g., Cuban, Kirkpatrick, & Peck, 2001; Ganesh & Berliner, 2004). In secondary schools, computers are used primarily to teach programming and word processing, and in elementary schools they are used chiefly for enrichment. Many schools that originally bought computers for CAI have ended up using them to teach computer programming or computer literacy, giving students hands-on experience with the computer but not depending on it to achieve major instructional objectives (Dugger, 2001; Zhao & Frank, 2003). Of course, as computers become ubiquitous in the world of work, exposure to them becomes important in its own right (Prensky, 2005/2006; Thornburg, 2002); but in helping students learn traditional subjects, computers continue to play a supporting role to teachers (Borja, 2007).

Chapter 9 Summary

What Are Elements of Effective Instruction beyond a Good Lesson ?

Teachers must know how to adapt instruction to students' levels of knowledge. According to Carroll's Model of School Learning, effectiveness of instruction depends on time needed (a function of student aptitude and ability to understand instruction) and time actually spent learning (which depends on time available, quality of instruction, and student perseverance).

Slavin's QAIT model of effective instruction identifies four elements that are subject to the teacher's direct control: quality of instruction, appropriate level of instruction, incentive, and amount of time. The model proposes that instruction deficient in any of these elements will be ineffective.

How Are Students Grouped to Accommodate Achievement Differences ?

Many schools manage student differences in ability and academic achievement through between-class ability grouping, tracking, or regrouping into separate classes for particular subjects during part of a school day. However, research shows that within-class groupings

The Intentional Teacher

USING WHAT YOU KNOW about Differentiating Instruction to Meet Individual Needs

Intentional teachers see students' needs, not textbooks, as the starting point for planning and providing instruction. They expect students to have varied areas of strength and struggle and plan instruction that meets the needs of individual students. They monitor student progress carefully and use resources beyond the classroom to meet the needs of students with varying capabilities. Intentional teachers expect to continue learning and mastering strategies that encourage all students to succeed.

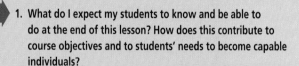

▶ 1. **What do I expect my students to know and be able to do at the end of this lesson? How does this contribute to course objectives and to students' needs to become capable individuals?**

Think about instructional quality in terms of many components. As you plan and assess your lessons, analyze the extent to which they focus on providing high-quality, appropriate instruction; student motivation; and appropriate use of classroom time (this chapter's QAIT). For example, imagine that you view a video of yourself teaching and are pleased to see that student levels of enthusiasm and engagement are high during most parts of the lesson. However, you note with dismay that you spent nearly 20 minutes of the 50-minute period handling routines and interruptions. You might resolve to try a few management strategies that will allow you and your students to use instructional time to fuller advantage.

▶ 2. **What knowledge, skills, needs, and interests do my students have that must be taken into account in my lesson?**

All students bring a range of experiences and achievements to the classroom. Check students' prerequisite knowledge through strategies such as informal discussion, student drawings, and pre-tests. Then decide whether and how your instruction in specific instances should be modified to reflect differences in students' experiences. For example, you might discover that your math and science students display a wide range of reading achievement. These reading differences have little bearing on your mathematics instruction, but you might modify your science teaching carefully to accommodate students' diverse reading abilities. You might arrange for a variety of print materials and for peer tutoring and also devise skeleton outlines to guide students' reading.

▶ 3. **What do I know about the content, child development, learning, motivation, and effective teaching strategies that I can use to accomplish my objectives?**

Use a variety of approaches and resources to accommodate student differences. When you find relevant student differences, consider a wide variety of strategies that can help you meet needs. Examples include mastery learning, grouping strategies, tutoring, and computer-based instruction. For example, imagine that one-third of your students are working substantially above your grade-level mathematics curriculum, but more than half are wrestling with most concepts and skills. Over coffee, you and an experienced colleague discuss your options.

are more effective, especially in reading and math, and are clearly preferable to groupings that segregate or stigmatize low achievers. Untracking recommends placing students in mixed-ability groups. The students are held to high standards and provided with assistance to reach those goals. Nongraded elementary schools combine children of different ages in the same classroom. Students are flexibly grouped according to their needs and performance levels.

What Are Some Ways of Differentiating Instruction

Differentiation, peer tutoring, and tutoring by teachers are all methods for individualizing instruction. Research supports all of these solutions.

What Educational Programs Exist for Students Placed at Risk

Students defined as at risk are any students who are likely to fail academically for any reason stemming from the student or from the student's environment. Reasons are diverse and might include poverty.

Educational programs for students who are at risk include compensatory education, early intervention programs, and special education. Federally funded compensatory education programs include, for example, Head Start, which aims to help preschool-age children

---

INTASC   **3** Adapting Instruction for Individual Needs   **8** Assessment of Student Learning
                      7 Instructional Planning Skills   **9** Professional Commitment and Responsibility

You consider four strategies that might work: (1) combining your students with your colleague's class for peer tutoring; (2) spending a portion of each period in mastery learning, in which you and your colleague would divide students into those who have or have not mastered particular skills; (3) calling in volunteer tutors from a local senior center; (4) arranging for tutorial and drill and practice work in mathematics at your school's computer lab.

 4. What instructional materials, technology, assistance, and other resources are available to help accomplish my objectives?

Use grouping practices that are supported by research. Think about alternatives to between-class ability grouping. Consider options such as regrouping, within-class grouping, and cross-age grouping. For example, you might ask the principal of your high school to put you on a faculty meeting agenda to discuss alternatives to your school's traditional tracks for college preparatory, basic, and remedial courses. You could provide an overview of the research on ability grouping; share some descriptions of schools that have engaged in untracking; and suggest that a committee of teachers, parents, and administrators explore the issue further.

5. How will I plan to assess students' progress toward my objectives?

Use a variety of ongoing assessments to monitor how well students are learning and apply this information to adapt instruction to accommodate indi-

vidual needs. Assess student progress frequently and be prepared to modify future lessons based on your findings. For example, you might use semiweekly journal entries and weekly objective quizzes to check student progress in your biology class. To students who demonstrate that they have quickly mastered objectives, you might provide enrichment opportunities to study the content through websites, software packages, readings, and investigations. For students who need additional scaffolding, you can provide more intensive instruction.

6. How will I respond if individual children or the class as a whole are not on track toward success? What is my back-up plan?

Assumptions that accommodations are uniformly effective could prove faulty. Gather data to determine the extent to which your accommodations are having the desired effect. Check effects on attitude and self-esteem as well as achievement. For example, you might continually assess children's progress within their reading groups and accelerate students doing well, so that over time students not progressing as fast as others can receive more individual attention.

from low-income backgrounds achieve school readiness, and Title I, which mandates extra services to low-achieving students in schools that have many low-income students. Extra services include pull-out programs, tutoring, and continuous-progress plans.

Research supports the effectiveness of many prevention and intervention efforts such as Reading Recovery and comprehensive school reform programs such as Success for All, the School Development Program, America's Choice, and Direct Instruction.

After-school and summer school arrangements are increasingly funded by federal, state, and local education agencies to extend students' learning time. Research is mixed regarding the effectiveness of compensatory education programs.

How Is Technology Used in Education ?

Technology in education is used for three general purposes. First, teachers use technology, such as word processors, multimedia, and presentation software, for planning and presenting lessons. Research supports use of presentation technologies such as embedded multimedia, forms of instructional television, and interactive whiteboards. Second, students use technology, such as word processing and CD-ROM reference software, for learning and preparing presentations. Computer-assisted instruction in the form of drill and practice, tutorials, instructional games, simulations, and the Internet is widespread. Third, teachers and administrators use technology for administrative tasks. Research on computer-assisted instruction demonstrates small to moderate positive effects on achievement.

Key Terms

Review the following key terms from the chapter.

between-class ability grouping 253
CD-ROM 275
compensatory education 263
computer-assisted instruction
  (CAI) 272
cross-age tutoring 260
databases 271
desktop publishing 270
differentiated instruction 259
digital photographs 275
digital video 275
drill and practice 272
early intervention 265
electronic response devices
  (clickers) 269
embedded multimedia 277
hypermedia 271
hypertext 271
instructional games 273
integrated learning systems 275
interactive whiteboard 269

Internet 273
Joplin Plan 257
multimedia 275
nongraded programs 257
peer tutoring 260
problem-solving program 274
pull-out programs 264
QAIT model 250
Reading Recovery 265
regrouping 257
simulation software 273
spreadsheets 270
students at risk 263
Success for All 266
Title I 263
tracks 253
tutorial programs 272
untracking 256
wiki 273
within-class ability grouping 253
word processing 270

Directions: The chapter-opening vignette addresses indicators that are often assessed in state licensure exams. Re-read the chapter-opening vignette, and then respond to the following questions.

1. How does Mr. Arbuthnot, the fourth-grade teacher in the chapter-opening vignette, incorporate John Carroll's Model of School Learning into his lesson?

    a. Mr. Arbuthnot tries to match the time spent on learning with the time students need to learn.

    b. Mr. Arbuthnot groups students according to their ability level.

    c. Mr. Arbuthnot expects students to learn the concepts of long division through group discussion and inquiry.

    d. Mr. Arbuthnot equates quality of instruction with quantity of instruction.

2. Imagine that Mr. Arbuthnot decides to divide his class into three groups: those who know long division, those who know some long division, and those who do not know long division. What type of ability group would he be using?

    a. Tri-grade ability grouping

    b. High–low ability grouping

    c. Within-class ability grouping

    d. Between-class ability grouping

3. In the opening of the vignette, Mr. Arbuthnot teaches an engaging lesson on long division and then gives students a quiz on the content learned. What type of evaluation is this?

    a. Norm-referenced

    b. Standardized

    c. Minimum competency

    d. Formative

4. Mr. Arbuthnot decides that he cannot work individually with all the students who have not yet mastered long division. He decides that some sort of tutoring might solve his problem. If he selects the type of tutoring that is most effective, according to research, which of the following will he use?

    a. Cross-age peer tutoring

    b. Same-age peer tutoring

    c. Tutoring by certified teachers

    d. Computer tutoring

5. Describe programs that exist for students placed at risk.

6. Explain how Mr. Arbuthnot could integrate technology into his teaching. What does the research on computer-based instruction say?

PEARSON myeducationlab

Go to the Topic **Planning and Instruction** in the MyEducationLab (www.myeducationlab.com) for your course, where you can:

- Find learning outcomes for **Planning and Instruction** along with the national standards that connect to these outcomes.

- Complete Assignments and Activities that can help you more deeply understand the chapter content.

- Apply and practice your understanding of the core teaching skills identified in the chapter with the Building Teaching Skills and Dispositions learning units.

- Examine challenging situations and cases presented in the IRIS Center Resources.

- Access video clips of CCSSO National Teachers of the Year award winners responding to the question "Why Do I Teach?" in the Teacher Talk section.

- Check your comprehension of the content covered in the chapter by going to the Study Plan in the Book Resources for your text. Here you will be able to take a chapter quiz; receive feedback on your answers; and then access Review, Practice, and Enrichment activities to enhance your understanding of chapter content.

- Watch author Bob Slavin present a Personal Reflections podcast on *Computers in Education* in the Book Resources for your text. Then, respond to the reflection questions that follow.

Computers in Education

YOUR REFLECTIONS How were computers used in your classes when you were in grade school? High school? How do you see technology changing in schools? Do you think access to technology is equal across all social groups? What might be the impact of differences across social groups on student learning?

10

Motivating Students to Learn

Shutterstock

At the end of this chapter, you should be able to:

- Describe theories of motivation
- Describe how goals and attributions enhance achievement motivation
- Discuss how teachers can increase their students' motivation to achieve

The students in Cal Lewis's tenth-grade U.S. history class are all in their seats before the bell rings, eagerly awaiting the start of the period. After the bell, in he walks dressed as George Washington, complete with an 18th-century costume and powdered wig and carrying a gavel. He gravely takes his seat, raps the gavel, and says, "I now call to order this meeting of the Constitutional Convention."

The students have been preparing for this day for weeks. Each of them represents one of the 13 original states. In groups of two and three, they have been studying all about their states, the colonial era, the American Revolution, and the United States under the Articles of Confederation. Two days ago, Mr. Lewis gave each group secret instructions from their "governor" on the key interests of their state. For example, the New Jersey and Delaware delegations are to insist that small states be adequately represented in the government, whereas New York and Virginia are to demand strict representation by population.

In preparing for the debate, each delegation had to make certain that any member of the delegation could represent the delegation's views. To ensure this, Mr. Lewis assigned each student a number from one to three at random. When a delegation asks to be recognized, he will call out a number, and the student with that number will respond for the group.

Mr. Lewis, staying in character as George Washington, gives a speech on the importance of the task they are undertaking and then opens the floor for debate. First, he recognizes the delegation from Georgia, represented by Beth Andrews. Beth is a shy girl, but she has been well prepared by her fellow delegates and knows that they are rooting for her.

"The great state of Georgia wishes to raise the question of a Bill of Rights. We have experienced the tyranny of government, and we demand that the people have a guarantee of their liberties!"

Beth goes on to propose elements of the Bill of Rights that her delegation has drawn up. While she is talking, Mr. Lewis is rating her presentation on historical accuracy, appropriateness to the real interests of her state, organization, and delivery. He will use these ratings in evaluating each delegation at the end of the class period. The debate goes on. The North Carolina delegates argue in favor of the right of states to expand to the west; the New Jersey delegation wants western territories made into new states. Wealthy Massachusetts wants taxes to remain in the states where they are collected; poor Delaware wants national taxes. Between debates, the delegates have an opportunity to do some "horse trading," promising to vote for proposals important to other states in exchange for votes on issues important to them. At the end of the week, the class votes on 10 key issues. After the votes are taken and the bell rings, the students pour into the hall still arguing about issues of taxation, representation, and powers of the executive.

After school, Rikki Ingram, another social studies teacher, drops into Mr. Lewis's classroom. "I see you're doing your Constitutional Convention again this year. It looks great, but how can you cover all of U.S. history if you spend a month on only the Constitution?"

Cal smiles. "I know I'm sacrificing some coverage to do this unit, but look how motivated these kids are!" He picks up a huge sheaf of notes and position papers written by the South Carolina delegation. "These kids are working their tails off, and they're learning that history is fun and useful. They'll remember this material for the rest of their lives!"

USING YOUR EXPERIENCE

Critical Thinking   Rikki Ingram seems concerned that Mr. Lewis's class is not covering the material well enough. What do you think are the advantages, disadvantages, and interesting or unclear aspects of Mr. Lewis's teaching strategy?

Cooperative Learning   With another student, relate stories of a social studies or other high school teacher who tried methods similar to Mr. Lewis's method of teaching. As a pair, retell your stories to a student from another pair.

Motivation is one of the most important ingredients of effective instruction. Students who want to learn can learn just about anything. But how can you ensure that every student wants to learn and will put in the effort needed to master complex material?

Mr. Lewis knows the value of motivation, so he has structured a unit that taps many aspects of motivation. By placing students in groups and evaluating them on the basis of presentations made by randomly selected group members, he has created a situation in which students are encouraging each other to excel. Social motivation of this kind is very powerful, especially for adolescents. Mr. Lewis is rating students' presentations according to clear, comprehensive standards and giving them feedback each day. He is tying an important period in history to students' daily lives by putting them into active roles of debating and trading votes. These strategies are designed not only to make history fun but also to give students many sources of motivation to learn and remember the history they have studied. Mr. Lewis is right. The students will probably never forget their experience in his class and are likely to approach new information about the American Revolution, the Constitution, and perhaps history in general with enthusiasm throughout their lives.

This chapter presents the many ways that you can enhance students' desire to learn academic material and the theories and research behind each method.

What Is Motivation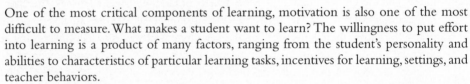

One of the most critical components of learning, motivation is also one of the most difficult to measure. What makes a student want to learn? The willingness to put effort into learning is a product of many factors, ranging from the student's personality and abilities to characteristics of particular learning tasks, incentives for learning, settings, and teacher behaviors.

All students are motivated. The question is: Motivated to do what? Some students are motivated more to socialize or watch television than to do schoolwork. Your job is not to increase motivation per se but to discover, prompt, and sustain students' motivations to learn the knowledge and skills needed for success in school and in life, and to engage in activities that lead to this learning. Imagine that Cal Lewis had come to class in 18th-century costume but had not structured tasks and evaluations to encourage students to study U.S. history. The students might have been amused and interested, but we cannot assume that they would have been motivated to do the work necessary to learn the material.

Psychologists define **motivation** as an internal process that activates, guides, and maintains behavior over time (Murphy & Alexander, 2000; Pintrich, 2003; Schunk, 2000; Stipek, 2002). In plain language, motivation is what gets you going, keeps you going, and determines where you're trying to go.

Motivation can vary in both intensity and direction (Ryan & Deci, 2000). Two students might be motivated to play video games, but one of them might be more strongly motivated to do so than the other. Or one student might be strongly motivated to play video games, and the other equally strongly motivated to play football. Actually, though, the intensity and direction of motivations are often difficult to separate. The intensity of a motivation to engage in one activity might depend in large part on the intensity and direction of motivations to engage in alternative activities. If someone has only enough time and money to go to the movies or to play video games, but not both, motivation to engage in one of these activities is strongly influenced by the intensity of motivation to engage in the other (Fries, Dietz, & Schmid, 2008). Motivation is important not only in getting students to engage in academic activities but also in determining how much students will learn from the activities they perform or from the information to which they are exposed. Students who are motivated to learn something use higher

motivation

The influence of needs and desires on the intensity and direction of behavior.

cognitive processes in learning about it and absorb and retain more from it (Driscoll, 2005; Jetton & Alexander, 2001; Pintrich, 2003). They are more likely to transfer their learning to new situations (Pugh & Bergin, 2006).

Motivation to do something can come about in many ways (Stipek, 2002). Motivation can be a personality characteristic; individuals might have lasting, stable interests in participating in such broad categories of activities as academics, sports, or social activities. Motivation can come from intrinsic characteristics of a task: By making U.S. history fun, social, active, and engaging, Cal Lewis made students eager to learn it. Motivation can also come from sources extrinsic to the task, as when Cal Lewis rated students' performances in the Constitutional Convention simulation.

What Are Some Theories of Motivation?

The first half of this chapter presents contemporary theories of motivation, which seek to explain why people are motivated to do what they do. The second half discusses the classroom use of incentives for learning and presents strategies for increasing students' motivations to learn and to do schoolwork.

■ Motivation and Behavioral Learning Theory

The concept of motivation is closely tied to the principle that behaviors that have been reinforced in the past are more likely to be repeated than are behaviors that have not been reinforced or that have been punished (see Bandura, 1986; Bigge & Shermis, 2004). Why do some students persist in the face of failure whereas others give up? Why do some students work to please the teacher, others to make good grades, and still others out of interest in the material they are learning? Why do some students achieve far more than would be predicted on the basis of their ability and some achieve far less? Examination of reinforcement histories and schedules of reinforcement might provide answers to such questions, but it is usually easier to speak in terms of motivations to satisfy various needs.

Connections

For more on reinforcement of behaviors, see Chapter 5, page 119.

REWARDS AND REINFORCEMENT   One reason that reinforcement history is an inadequate explanation for motivation is that human motivation is highly complex and context-bound. With very hungry animals we can predict that food will be an effective reinforcer. With humans, even hungry ones, we can't be sure what will be a reinforcer and what will not because the reinforcing value of most potential reinforcers is largely determined by personal or situational factors. As an example of this, think about the value of $50 in exchange for one hour of light work. Most of us would view $50 as a powerful reinforcer, more than adequate to get us to do an hour of work. But consider these four situations:

1. Mr. Scrooge offers Bill $60 to paint his fence. Bill thinks this is more than enough for the job, so he does his best work. However, when he is done, Mr. Scrooge says, "I don't think you did 60 dollars' worth of work. Here's 50."

2. Now consider the same situation, except that Mr. Scrooge originally offers Bill $40 and, when Bill is finished, praises him for an excellent job and gives him $50.

3. Dave and Barbara meet at a party, like each other immediately, and after the party take a long walk in the moonlight. When they get to Barbara's house, Dave says, "Barbara, I enjoyed spending time with you. Here's 50 dollars I'd like you to have."

4. Marta's aunt offers her $50 to give little Pepa a piano lesson next Saturday. However, if Marta agrees to do so, she will miss her chance to try out for the school baseball team.

In situations 1, 3, and 4, $50 is not a good reinforcer at all. In situation 1, Bill's expectations have been raised and then dashed by Mr. Scrooge. In situation 2, the amount of monetary reward is the same, but this situation is much more likely to make Bill want to paint Mr. Scrooge's fence again, because in this case his reward exceeds his expectation. In situation 3, Dave's offer of $50 is insulting and would certainly not increase Barbara's interest in going out with him in the future. In situation 4, although Marta's aunt's offer would seem generous to Marta under most circumstances, it is insufficient reinforcement this particular Saturday because it interferes with a more highly valued activity.

DETERMINING THE VALUE OF AN INCENTIVE These situations illustrate an important point: The motivational value of an incentive cannot be assumed, because it might depend on many factors. When you say, "I want you all to be sure to hand in your book reports on time because they will count toward your grade," you might be assuming that grades are effective incentives for most students. However, some students might not care about grades, perhaps because their parents don't or because they have a history of failure in school and have decided that grades are unimportant. If you say to a student, "Good work! I knew you could do it if you tried!" this might be motivating to a student who had just completed a task he or she thought was difficult, but insulting to one who thought the task was easy (because your praise implies that he or she had to work especially hard to complete the task). As in the case of Bill and Mr. Scrooge, students' expectations for rewards determine the motivational value of any particular reward. And it is often difficult to determine students' motivations from their behavior because many different motivations can influence behavior. Sometimes, one type of motivation clearly determines behavior; at other times, several (perhaps conflicting) motivations are influential.

■ Motivation and Human Needs

Motivation can be thought of as a drive to satisfy needs, such as needs for food, shelter, love, and maintenance of positive self-esteem. People differ in the degree of importance they attach to each of these needs. Some need constant reaffirmation that they are loved or appreciated; others have a greater need for physical comfort and security. Also, the same person has different needs at different times. A drink of water would be much more appreciated after a 4-mile run than after a 4-course meal.

MASLOW'S HIERARCHY OF NEEDS Given that people have many needs, which will they try to satisfy at any given moment? To predict this, Maslow (1954) proposed a hierarchy of needs, which is illustrated in Figure 10.1. In Maslow's theory, needs that are lower in this hierarchy must be at least partially satisfied before a person will try to satisfy higher-level needs. For example, a hungry person or someone who is in physical danger will be less concerned about maintaining a positive self-image than about obtaining food or safety; but once that person is no longer hungry or afraid, self-esteem needs might become paramount. One critical concept that Maslow introduced is the distinction between deficiency needs and growth needs. **Deficiency needs** (physiological, safety, love, and esteem) are those that are critical to physical and psychological well-being. These needs must be satisfied, but once they are, a person's motivation to satisfy them diminishes. In contrast, **growth needs,** such as the need to know and understand things, to appreciate beauty, or to grow and develop in appreciation of others, can never be satisfied completely. In fact, the more people are able to meet their need to know and understand the world around them, the greater their motivation might become to learn still more.

INTASC

2 Knowledge of Human Development and Learning

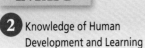

✓ **Certification Pointer**

Teacher certification tests will require you to identify which needs Maslow identified as deficiency needs and which he identified as growth needs.

deficiency needs

Basic requirements for physical and psychological well-being as identified by Maslow.

growth needs

Needs for knowing, appreciating, and understanding, which people try to satisfy after their basic needs are met.

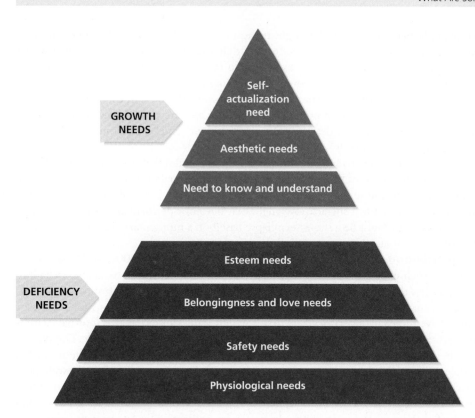

FIGURE 10.1 Maslow's Hierarchy of Needs

Maslow identifies two types of needs: deficiency needs and growth needs. People are motivated to satisfy needs at the bottom of the hierarchy before seeking to satisfy those at the top.

SELF-ACTUALIZATION   Maslow's theory includes the concept of **self-actualization,** which he defines as "the desire to become everything that one is capable of becoming" (Maslow, 1954, p. 92). Self-actualization is characterized by acceptance of self and others, spontaneity, openness, relatively deep but democratic relationships with others, creativity, humor, and independence—in essence, psychological health.

IMPLICATIONS OF MASLOW'S THEORY FOR EDUCATION   The importance of Maslow's theory for education is in the relationship between deficiency needs and growth needs. Obviously, students who are very hungry or in physical danger will have little psychological energy to put into learning. Schools and government agencies recognize that if students' basic needs are not met, learning will suffer. They have responded by providing free breakfast and lunch programs. The most important deficiency needs, however, are those for love and self-esteem. Students who do not feel that they are loved and that they are capable are unlikely to have a strong motivation to achieve the higher-level growth objectives (Martin & Dowson, 2009; Stipek, 2006). A student who is unsure of his or her worth or capability will tend to make the safe choice: Go with the crowd, study for the test without interest in learning the ideas, write a predictable but uncreative essay, and so on. If you can put students at ease and make them feel accepted and respected as individuals, you are more likely (in Maslow's view) to help them become eager to learn for the sake of learning and willing to risk being creative and open to new ideas. A school that emphasizes social-emotional learning might, in this view, create an environment that is more conducive to academic as well as social-emotional learning (see Greenberg et al., 2003; Hoffman, 2009; Jennings & Greenberg, 2009).

■ Motivation and Attribution Theory

Teresa usually gets good grades but just received a D on her first quiz in a new class. The mark is inconsistent with her self-image and causes her discomfort. To resolve this discomfort, Teresa might decide to work harder to make certain that she never gets such

Connections

Motivational factors affecting the academic performance of students who are at risk of school failure are discussed in Chapter 9, page 262.

self-actualization

A person's ability to develop his or her full potential.

a low grade again. However, she might try to rationalize her low grade: "The questions were tricky. I wasn't feeling well. The teacher didn't tell us the quiz was coming. I wasn't really trying. It was too hot." These excuses help Teresa account for one D—but suppose she gets several poor grades in a row. Now she might decide that she never did like this subject anyway or that the teacher shows favoritism to the boys in the class or is a hard grader. All of these changes in opinions and excuses are directed at avoiding an unpleasant pairing of inconsistent ideas: "I am a good student" and "I am doing poorly in this class, and it is my own fault."

Teresa is struggling to find a reason for her poor grades that does not require her to change her perception of herself as a good student. She attributes her poor performance to her teacher, to the subject matter, or to other students—external factors over which she has no control. Or if she acknowledges that her poor performance is her own fault, she decides that it must be a short-term lapse based on a momentary (but reversible) lack of motivation or attention regarding this unit of instruction.

Attribution theory (see Hareli & Weiner, 2002; Weiner, 2000) seeks to understand just such explanations and excuses, particularly when applied to success or failure (wherein lies the theory's greatest importance for education, in which success and failure are recurrent themes). Weiner (2000) suggests that most explanations for success or failure have three characteristics. The first is whether the cause is seen as internal (within the person) or external. The second is whether it is seen as stable or unstable. The third is whether it is perceived as controllable. A central assumption of attribution theory is that people will attempt to maintain a positive self-image. Therefore, when they do well in an activity, they are likely to attribute their success to their own efforts or abilities; but when they do poorly, they will believe that their failure is based on factors over which they had no control (Vispoel & Austin, 1995). In particular, students who experience failure will try to find an explanation that enables them to save face with their peers (Juvonen, 2000). It has been demonstrated that if groups of people are given a task and then told that they either failed or succeeded (even though all, in fact, were equally successful), those told that they failed will say their failure was because of bad luck, whereas those told that they succeeded will attribute their success to skill and intelligence (Weiner, 2000).

Attributions for others' behavior are also important. For example, students are more likely to respond to a classmate's request for help if they believe that the classmate needs help because of a temporary uncontrollable factor (such as getting hurt in a basketball game) than if they believe that help is needed because of a controllable factor (such as failure to study) (Juvonen & Weiner, 1993).

attribution theory

A theory of motivation that focuses on how people explain the causes of their own successes and failures.

ATTRIBUTIONS FOR SUCCESS AND FAILURE Attribution theory deals primarily with four explanations for success and failure in achievement situations: ability, effort, task difficulty, and luck. Ability and effort attributions are internal to the individual; task difficulty and luck attributions are external. Ability is taken to be a relatively stable, unalterable state. In contrast, effort can be altered. Similarly, task difficulty is essentially a stable characteristic, whereas luck is unstable and uncontrollable. These four attributions and representative explanations for success and failure are presented in Table 10.1.

Table 10.1 shows how students often seek to explain success and failure differently. When students succeed, they would like to believe that it was because they are smart (an internal, stable attribution), not because they were lucky

TABLE 10.1 Attributions for Success and Failure

Attribution theory describes and suggests the implications of people's explanations of their successes and failures.

Attribution	Stability	
	Stable	**Unstable**
Internal	*Ability*	*Effort*
Success	"I'm smart."	"I tried hard."
Failure	"I'm stupid."	"I didn't really try."
External	*Task Difficulty*	*Luck*
Success	"It was easy."	"I lucked out."
Failure	"It was too hard."	"I had bad luck."

Source: Bernard Weiner, "A Theory of Motivation for Some Classroom Experiences," *Journal of Educational Psychology, 71,* pp. 3–25. Copyright © 1979 by the American Psychological Association.

or because the task was easy or even because they tried hard (because "trying hard" says little about their likelihood of success in the future). In contrast, students who fail would like to believe that they had bad luck (an external, unstable attribution), which allows for the possibility of succeeding next time (Weiner, 2000). Of course, over time, these attributions might be difficult to maintain. As in the case of Teresa, a student who gets one bad grade is likely to blame it on bad luck or some other external, unstable cause. After several bad grades, though, an unstable attribution becomes difficult to maintain; no one can be unlucky on tests week after week. Therefore, a student like Teresa might switch to a stable but still external attribution. For example, she could decide that the course is too difficult or the teacher is unfair or make some other stable, external attribution that lets her avoid making a stable, internal attribution that would shatter her self-esteem: "I failed because I don't have the ability" (Juvonen, 2000). She might even reduce her level of effort so that she can maintain the belief that she could succeed if she really wanted to (Jagacinski & Nicholls, 1990).

LOCUS OF CONTROL AND SELF-EFFICACY   One concept central to attribution theory is **locus of control** (Rotter, 1954). The word *locus* means "location." A person with an internal locus of control believes that success or failure is the result of his or her own efforts or abilities. Someone with an external locus of control is more likely to believe that other factors, such as luck, task difficulty, or other people's actions, cause success or failure. Internal locus of control is often called *self-efficacy,* the belief that one's behavior makes a difference (Bandura, 1997; Goddard, Hoy, & Woolfolk Hoy, 2004; Schunk & Pajares, 2004; Skinner & Greene, 2008). Figure 10.2 shows items from a widely used measure of locus of control. Locus of control or self-efficacy can be very important in explaining a student's school performance. For example, several researchers have found that students who are high in internal locus of control have better grades and test scores than do students of the same intelligence who are low in internal locus of control (Cappella & Weinstein, 2001; Caprara et al., 2008; Zimmerman, 2000). Studies have found locus of control to be the second most important predictor (after ability) of a student's academic achievement (e.g., Bong, 2001; Dweck, 2007; Pietsch, Walker, & Chapman, 2003). The reason is easy to comprehend. Students who believe that success in school

Connections

Attributions for success or failure that are related to the socioemotional factors of self-esteem and peer relations are discussed in Chapter 3, pages 62, 63, 66, and 69–70.

locus of control

A personality trait that determines whether people attribute responsibility for their own failure or success to internal or external factors.

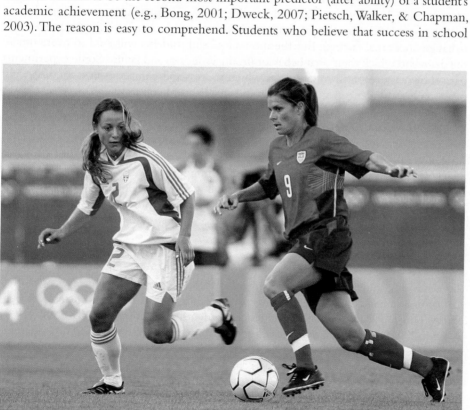

STR/AFP/Getty Images

Despite being one of the world's most accomplished athletes, Mia Hamm often fought off self-doubt. Why is locus of control important to an athlete? How do locus of control and self-efficacy translate to the classroom? As a teacher, how can you influence self-efficacy?

FIGURE 10.2 **Items from the Intellectual Achievement Responsibility Questionnaire**

1. If a teacher passes you to the next grade, would it probably be
   a. because she liked you, or
   b. because of the work you did? [*internal*]

2. When you do well on a test at school, is it more likely to be
   a. because you studied for it, or [*internal*]
   b. because the test was especially easy?

3. When you have trouble understanding something in school, is it usually
   a. because the teacher didn't explain it clearly, or
   b. because you didn't listen carefully? [*internal*]

4. Suppose your parents say you are doing well in school. Is it likely to happen
   a. because your school work is good, or [*internal*]
   b. because they are in a good mood?

5. Suppose you don't do as well as usual in a subject in school. Would this probably happen
   a. because you weren't as careful as usual, or [*internal*]
   b. because somebody bothered you and kept you from working?

Source: V. C. Crandall, W. Katkovsky, and V. J. Crandall, "Children's Beliefs in Their Own Control of Reinforcement in Intellectual–Academic Achievement Situations," *Child Development, 36,* 1965, pp. 91–109. © The Society for Research in Child Development, Inc. Reprinted by permission.

is due to luck, the teacher's whims, or other external factors are unlikely to work hard. They tend to procrastinate or avoid difficult tasks (Steel, 2007). In contrast, students who believe that success and failure are primarily due to their own efforts can be expected to work hard (Pressley et al., 2003). In reality, success in a particular class is a product of both students' efforts and abilities (internal factors) and luck, task difficulty, and teacher behaviors (external factors). But the most successful students will tend to overestimate the degree to which their own behavior produces success and failure. Some experiments have shown that even in situations in which success and failure are in fact completely based on luck, students who are high in internal locus of control will believe that it was their efforts that made them succeed or fail (see Weiner, 1992).

It is important to note that locus of control can change and depends somewhat on the specific activity or situation. One difficulty in studying the effects of locus of control on achievement is that achievement has a strong effect on locus of control (Bong & Skaalvik, 2003). For example, the same student might have an internal locus of control in academics (because of high academic ability) but an external locus of control in sports (because of low athletic ability). If this student discovered some unsuspected skill in a new sport, he or she might develop an internal locus of control in that sport (but probably still not in other sports).

IMPLICATIONS OF ATTRIBUTIONS AND SELF-EFFICACY FOR EDUCATION In the classroom, students receive constant information concerning their level of performance on academic tasks, either relative to others or relative to some norm of acceptability. This feedback ultimately influences students' self-perceptions (Bandura, 1997; Schunk, 2004). Attribution theory is important in helping you understand how students might interpret and use feedback on their academic performance and in suggesting how you might give feedback that has the greatest motivational value (see Tollefson, 2000). In particular, it suggests that you should always praise students for their effort (which is controlled by them) rather than their intelligence (which is not) (see Dweck, 2007).

■ Motivation and Self-Regulated Learning

Self-regulated learning, discussed in Chapter 5, refers to "learning that results from students' self-generated thoughts and behaviors that are systematically oriented toward their learning goals" (Schunk & Zimmerman, 2003, p. 59). As this definition makes clear, self-regulated learning is closely related to students' goals. Students who are highly motivated to learn something are more likely than other students to consciously organize their learning, carry out a learning plan, and retain the information they obtain (Radosevich, Vaidyanathan, Yeo, & Radosevich, 2004; Summers, 2008; Zimmerman, 2008). For example, students with high reading motivation are more likely to read on their own and to use effective comprehension strategies (Miller, Partelow, & Sen, 2004). This motivation can come from many sources. One is social modeling (Zimmerman & Kitsantas, 2002), such as seeing other students use self-regulated strategies. Another is goal-setting, in which students are encouraged to establish their own learning goals. A third is feedback that shows students that they are making good progress toward their learning goals, especially if the feedback emphasizes students' efforts and abilities (Zimmerman, 2008). Schunk and Zimmerman (2003) argue that motivation to engage in self-regulated learning is not the same as achievement motivation in general because self-regulated learning requires the learner to take independent responsibility for learning, not to simply comply with the teacher's demands. Fredericks, Blumenfeld, and Paris (2004) use the terms *engagement* and *investment* to describe motivation that leads students to engage in self-regulated learning, rather than simply doing the work and following the rules. Algozzine, Browder, Karvonen, Test, and Wood (2001) use the similar term *self-determination* and describe a set of successful strategies for building self-determination among individuals with disabilities.

Connections

For more on self-regulated learning, see Chapter 5, page 134.

Connections

For more on successful strategies for building self-determination, see Chapter 12, page 386.

Theory into Practice
Giving Students Motivating Feedback

Students who believe that their past failures on tasks were because of lack of ability are unlikely to expect to succeed in similar tasks and are, therefore, unlikely to exert much effort (Juvonen, 2000; Weiner, 2000). Obviously, the belief that you will fail can be self-fulfilling. Students who believe that they will fail will be poorly motivated to do academic work, and this might in turn cause them to fail. Therefore, the most damaging idea you can communicate to a student is that the student cannot learn.

Few teachers would say such a thing directly to a student, but the idea can be communicated just as effectively in several other ways. One is to use a competitive grading system (e.g., grading on the curve) and to make grades public and emphasize relative student rankings. This practice can make small differences in achievement level seem large, and students who receive the poorest grades might decide that they can never learn.

Alternatively, deemphasizing grades and relative rankings but expressing the (almost always correct) expectation that all students in the class can learn is likely to help students see that their chances of success depend on their efforts—an internal but alterable attribution that lets students anticipate success in the future if they do their best.

A stable, internal attribution for success ("I succeed because I am smart") is also a poor motivator. Able students, too, need to believe that it is their effort, not their ability, that leads to academic success. Teachers who emphasize the amount

Connections

For more on individualized instruction, see Chapter 9, page 259.

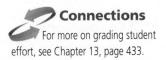

Connections
For more on grading student effort, see Chapter 13, page 433.

of effort as the cause of success as well as failure and who reward effort rather than ability are more likely to motivate all their students to do their best than are teachers who emphasize ability alone (Resnick, 1998). Some formal means of rewarding students for effort rather than ability are the use of rewards for improvement; the use of differentiated instruction, in which the basis of success is progress at the student's own level; and the inclusion of effort as a component of grading or as a separate grade.

■ Motivation and Expectancy Theory

Expectancy theory is a theory of motivation based on the belief that people's efforts to achieve depend on their expectations of reward. Atkinson (1964) developed theories of motivation based on the following formula:

Motivation (M) = Perceived probability of success (Ps) × Incentive value of success (Is).

The formula is called an expectancy model, or **expectancy–valence model,** because it largely depends on the person's expectations of reward (see Pintrich, 2003; Stipek, 2006; Wigfield & Eccles, 2000). What this theory implies is that people's motivation to achieve something depends on the product of their estimation of the chance of success (perceived probability of success, Ps) and the value they place on success (incentive value of success, Is). For example, if Mark says, "I think I can make the honor roll if I try, and it is very important to me to make the honor roll," then he will probably work hard to make the honor roll. However, one very important aspect of the $M = Ps × Is$ formula is that it is multiplicative, meaning that if people believe that their probability of success is zero or if they do not value success, then their motivation will be zero. If Mark would like very much to make the honor roll but believes that he hasn't a prayer of doing so, he will be unmotivated. If his chances are actually good but he doesn't care about making the honor roll, he will also be unmotivated. Wigfield (1995) found that students' beliefs that they were capable and their valuing of academic success were, taken together, more important than their actual ability in predicting their achievement.

Atkinson (1964) adds an important aspect to expectancy theory in pointing out that under certain circumstances an overly high probability of success can be detrimental to motivation. If Mark is very able, it might be so easy for him to make the honor roll that he need not do his best. Atkinson (1958) explains this by arguing that there is a relationship between probability of success and incentive value of success such that success in an easy task is not as valued as success in a difficult task. Therefore, motivation should be at a maximum at moderate levels of probability of success. For example, two evenly matched tennis players will probably play their hardest. Unevenly matched players will not play as hard; the poor player might want very much to win but will have too low a probability of success to try very hard, and the better player will not value winning enough to exert his or her best effort. Confirming Atkinson's theory, more recent research has shown that a person's motivation increases as task difficulty increases up to a point at which the person decides that success is very unlikely or that the goal isn't worth the effort (DeBacker & Nelson, 1999). This and other research findings indicate that moderate to difficult (but not impossible) tasks are better than easy ones for learning and motivation (Brophy, 1999; Wigfield & Eccles, 2000).

IMPLICATIONS OF EXPECTANCY THEORY FOR EDUCATION   The most important implication of expectancy theory is the commonsense proposition that tasks for students should be neither too easy nor too difficult. If some students believe that they are likely to get an A no matter what they do, then their motivation will not be at a maximum. Similarly, if some students feel certain to fail no matter what they do, their

expectancy theory

A theory of motivation based on the belief that people's efforts to achieve depend on their expectations of reward.

expectancy–valence model

A theory that relates the probability and the incentive value of success to motivation.

motivation will be minimal. Therefore, grading systems should be set up so that earning an A is difficult (but possible) for as many students as feasible and so that earning a low grade is possible for students who exert little effort. Success must be within the reach, but not the easy reach, of all students.

How Can Achievement Motivation Be Enhanced?

INTASC

2 Knowledge of Human Development and Learning

One of the most important types of motivation for education is **achievement motivation** (McClelland & Atkinson, 1948), or the generalized tendency to strive for success and to choose goal-oriented success/failure activities. For example, French (1956) found that given a choice of work partners for a complex task, achievement-motivated students tend to choose a partner who is good at the task, whereas affiliation-motivated students (who express the need for love and acceptance) are more likely to choose a friendly partner. Even after they experience failure, achievement-motivated students will persist longer at a task than will students who are lower in achievement motivation and will attribute their failures to lack of effort (an internal but alterable condition) rather than to external factors such as task difficulty or luck. In short, achievement-motivated students want and expect to succeed; when they fail, they redouble their efforts until they do succeed (see Weiner, 1992).

Not surprisingly, students who are high in achievement motivation tend to succeed at school tasks (Stipek, 2006). However, it is unclear which causes which: Does high achievement motivation lead to success in school, or does success in school (based on ability or other factors) lead to high achievement motivation? Initially, achievement motivation is strongly affected by family experiences (Turner & Johnson, 2003), but after children have been in school for a few years, success and motivation cause each other. Success breeds the desire for more success, which in turn breeds success (Dotterer, McHale, & Crouter, 2009; Wigfield, Eccles, & Rodriguez, 1998). In contrast, students who do not experience success in achievement settings will tend to lose the motivation to succeed in such settings and will turn their interest elsewhere (perhaps to social activities, sports, or even delinquent activities in which they might succeed). Achievement motivation tends to diminish over the school years, but it appears that this trend is due both to the nature of children and to the nature of middle and high schools (Dotterer et al., 2009; Hidi & Harackiewicz, 2000; Stipek, 2006).

■ Motivation and Goal Orientations

Some students are motivationally oriented toward **learning goals** (also called *task* or *mastery goals*); others are oriented toward **performance goals** (Brophy, 2005; Harackiewicz & Linnenbrink, 2005; Pintrich, 2000). Students with learning goals see the purpose of schooling as gaining competence in the skills being taught, whereas students with performance goals primarily seek to gain positive judgments of their competence (and avoid negative judgments). Students who are striving toward learning goals are likely to take difficult courses and to seek challenges. In contrast, students with performance goals focus on getting good grades, taking easy courses, and avoiding challenging situations (Urdan & Mestas, 2006).

LEARNING VERSUS PERFORMANCE GOALS   Students with learning goals and those with performance goals do not differ in overall intelligence, but their classroom performances can differ markedly. When they run into obstacles, performance-oriented students tend to become discouraged, and their performance is seriously hampered. In contrast, when learning-oriented students encounter obstacles, they tend to keep trying, and their motivation and performance might actually increase (Pintrich, 2000; Schunk, 2005; Sins, va Joolingnen, Savelsbergh, & van Hout-Wolters, 2008). Learning-oriented

achievement motivation

The desire to experience success and to participate in activities in which success depends on personal effort and abilities.

learning goals

The goals of students who are motivated primarily by desire for knowledge acquisition and self-improvement. Also called *mastery goals*.

performance goals

The goals of students who are motivated primarily by a desire to gain recognition from others and to earn good grades.

students are more likely to use metacognitive or self-regulated learning strategies (Greene, Miller, Crowson, Duke, & Akey, 2004; Pajares, Britner, & Valiante, 2000; Radosevich et al., 2004; Usher & Pajares, 2008). They are likely to learn more than performance-oriented students of the same abilities (Shih, 2005). On the other hand, they may not get grades that reflect their learning, as they may focus their studying on what interests them rather than what gets them good grades (Hulleman, Durik, Schweigert, & Harackiewicz, 2008; Senko & Miles, 2008). Performance-oriented students who perceive their abilities to be low are likely to fall into a pattern of helplessness, for they believe that they have little chance of earning good grades (Midgley & Urdan, 2001; Pajares et al., 2000; Usher & Pajares, 2008). There is some evidence that such students are more prone to cheat (Murdock & Anderman, 2006). Learning-oriented students who perceive their ability to be low are concerned with how much they themselves can learn without regard for the performance of others (Fuchs et al., 1997; Thorkildsen & Nicholls, 1998). Unfortunately, there is evidence that over their years in school, students tend to shift from learning or mastery goals to performance goals (Harackiewicz, Barron, Tauer, & Carter, 2000; Stipek, 2002). However, there is also evidence that teachers who emphasize learning and developing competence (rather than grades) as the goals of the class obtain better learning results from their students (Maruyama & Elliot, 2009; Usher & Pajares, 2008, 2009).

The most important implication of research on learning goals versus performance goals is that you should try to convince students that learning, rather than grades, is the purpose of academic work (Anderman et al., 2001; Ryan & Patrick, 2001; Wentzel, 2000). This can be done by emphasizing the interest value and practical importance of material students are studying and by deemphasizing grades and other rewards. For example, you might say, "Today we're going to learn about events deep in the earth that cause the fiery eruptions of volcanoes!" rather than "Today we're going to learn about volcanoes. Pay attention so that you can do well on tomorrow's test." In particular, use of highly competitive grading or incentive systems should be avoided. When students perceive that there is only one standard of success in the classroom and that only a few people can achieve it, those who lack confidence in their ability will be likely to give up in advance (Summers, 2006). Table 10.2 (from Ames & Archer, 1988) summarizes the differences between the achievement goals of students with mastery (learning) goals and those of students with performance goals. Studies indicate that the types of tasks that are used in classrooms have a strong influence on students'

TABLE 10.2	Achievement Goal Analysis of Classroom Climate	
Climate Dimensions	**Mastery Goal**	**Performance Goal**
Success defined as . . .	Improvement, progress	High grades, high normative performance
Value placed on . . .	Effort/learning	Normatively high ability
Reasons for satisfaction . . .	Working hard, challenge	Doing better than others
Teacher oriented toward . . .	How students are learning	How students are performing
View of errors/mistakes . . .	Part of learning	Anxiety eliciting
Focus of attention . . .	Process of learning	Own performance relative to others'
Reasons for effort . . .	Learning something new	High grades, performing better than others
Evaluation criteria . . .	Absolute progress	Normative

Source: C. Ames and J. Archer, "Achievement Goals in the Classroom," *Journal of Educational Psychology, 80,* p. 261. Copyright © 1988 by the American Psychological Association.

TABLE 10.3	School and Teacher Policies That Are Likely to Promote Learning or Task Goals	
Area	**Objectives**	**Examples of Possible Strategies**
Task	Enhance intrinsic attractiveness of learning tasks. Make learning meaningful.	Encourage instruction that relates to students' backgrounds and experience. Avoid payment (monetary or other) for attendance, grades, or achievement. Foster goal setting and self-regulation. Use extra classroom programs that make learning experiences relevant.
Autonomy/ Responsibility	Provide optimal freedom for students to make choices and take responsibility.	Give alternatives in making assignments. Ask for student comments on school life—and take them seriously. Encourage instructional programs that encourage students to take initiatives and evaluate their own learning. Establish leadership opportunities for *all* students.
Recognition	Provide opportunities for *all* students to be recognized for learning. Recognize *progress* in goal attainment. Recognize challenge seeking and innovation.	Foster personal-best awards. Reduce emphasis on honor rolls. Recognize and publicize a wide range of school-related activities of students.
Resources	Encourage the development and maintenance of strategies that enhance task–goal emphases.	Underwrite action taken by staff that is in accord with a task–goal emphasis.
Grouping	Build an environment of acceptance and appreciation of all students. Broaden the range of social interaction, particularly of students placed at risk. Enhance social skills development.	Provide opportunities for cooperative learning, problem solving, and decision making. Allow time and opportunity for peer interaction. Foster the development of subgroups (teams, schools within schools, etc.) within which significant interaction can occur. Encourage multiple group membership to increase range of peer interaction. Eliminate ability-grouped classes.
Evaluation	Grading and reporting processes. Practices associated with use of standardized tests. Definition of goals and standards.	Reduce emphasis on social comparisons of achievement by minimizing public reference to normative evaluation standards (e.g., grades, test scores). Establish policies and procedures that give students opportunities to improve their performance (e.g., study skills, classes). Establish grading/reporting practices that portray student progress in learning. Encourage student participation in the evaluation process.
Time	Allow the learning task and student needs to dictate scheduling. Provide opportunities for extended and significant student involvement in learning tasks.	Allow students to *progress at their own rate* whenever possible. Encourage flexibility in the scheduling of learning experiences. Give teachers greater control over time usage through, for example, block scheduling.

Source: M. L. Maehr and E. M. Anderman, "Reinventing Schools for Early Adolescents: Emphasizing Task Goals," *The Elementary School Journal, 93*(5), 1993, pp. 593–610. Copyright © 1993 by The University of Chicago Press. Adapted by permission.

adoption of learning goals. Use of tasks that are challenging, meaningful, and related to real life are more likely to lead to learning goals than are other tasks (Cushman, 2006; Darling-Hammond & Ifill-Lynch, 2006). Table 10.3 (from Maehr & Anderman, 1993) summarizes strategies that you can use to promote learning or task goals among students.

Certification Pointer

For a case study on your teacher certification test, you may be required to suggest an appropriate strategy for improving student motivation by training students to attribute their successes to controllable causes, especially effort.

■ Learned Helplessness

An extreme form of the motive to avoid failure is called **learned helplessness,** which is a perception that no matter what one does, one is doomed to failure or ineffectuality: "Nothing I do matters." In academic settings, learned helplessness can be related to an internal, stable explanation for failure: "I fail because I'm stupid, and that means I will always fail." Students who experience repeated failures might develop a "defensive pessimism" to protect themselves from negative feedback (Martin, Marsh, & Debus, 2001).

Learned helplessness can arise from inconsistent, unpredictable use of rewards and punishments by parents or teachers—a pattern that can lead students to believe that there is little they can do to be successful. Students with learning disabilities, for example, are more likely than other students to respond to failure with helpless behavior (Pintrich & Schunk, 2002). You can prevent or alleviate learned helplessness by giving students (1) opportunities for success in small steps; (2) immediate feedback; and (3) most important, consistent expectations and follow-through.

Theory into Practice
Helping Students Overcome Learned Helplessness

The concept of learned helplessness derives from the theory that students might become academic failures through a conditioning process based on negative feedback from teachers, school experiences, peers, and students themselves. Numerous studies show that when students consistently fail, they eventually give up. They become conditioned to helplessness.

Teachers at both the elementary and secondary levels can help to counter this syndrome in a variety of ways, including attribution training, goal restructuring, self-esteem programs, success-guaranteed approaches, and positive feedback systems. The following general principles are helpful for all students, especially students who have shown a tendency to accept failure.

1. *Accentuate the positive.* Get to know the student's strengths and then use these as building blocks. Every student has something she or he does well. But be careful that the strength is authentic; don't make up a strength. For example, a student might like to talk a lot but write poorly. Have the student complete assignments by talking rather than writing. As confidence is restored, slowly introduce writing.

2. *Eliminate the negative.* Do not play down a student's weaknesses. Deal with them directly but tactfully. In the preceding example, talk to the student about problems with writing. Then have the student develop a plan to improve on the writing. Discuss the plan, and together make up a contract about how the plan will be completed.

3. *Go from the familiar to the new, using advance organizers or guided discovery.* Some students have difficulties with concepts, skills, or ideas with which they are not familiar. Also, students relate better to lessons that are linked to their own experiences. For example, a high school math teacher might begin a lesson with a math problem that students might face in the real world, such as calculating the sales tax when purchasing an iPod. Further, the teacher can ask students to bring to class math problems they have encountered outside of school. The whole class can become involved in solving a student's math problem.

4. *Create challenges in which students actively create problems and solve them using their own knowledge and skills.*

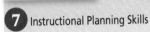
INTASC

7 Instructional Planning Skills

learned helplessness

The expectation, based on experience, that one's actions will ultimately lead to failure.

■ Teacher Expectations and Achievement

On the first day of class, Mr. Erhard called roll. Soon he got to a name that looked familiar. "Wayne Clements?"

"Here!"

"Do you have a brother named Victor?"

"Yes."

"I remember Victor. He was a terror. I'm going to keep my eye on you!"

As he neared the end of the roll, Mr. Erhard saw that several boys were starting to whisper to one another in the back of the room. "Wayne! I asked the class to remain silent while I read the roll. Didn't you hear me? I knew I'd have to watch out for you!"

This dialogue illustrates how teachers can establish expectations for their students and how these expectations can be self-fulfilling. Mr. Erhard doesn't know it, but Wayne is generally a well-behaved, conscientious student, quite unlike his older brother, Victor. However, because of his experience with Victor, Mr. Erhard expects that he will have trouble with Wayne. When he sees several boys whispering, it is Wayne he singles out for blame, confirming for himself that Wayne is a troublemaker. After a few episodes of this treatment, we can expect Wayne to begin playing the role Mr. Erhard has assigned to him.

Research on teachers' expectations for their students has generally found that students live up (or down) to the expectations that their teachers have for them (Hinnant, O'Brien & Ghazarian, 2009; Jussim & Harber, 2005; Rubie-Davies, 2007, 2008), particularly in the younger grades and when teachers know relatively little about their students' actual achievement levels. Furthermore, there is evidence that students in schools whose teachers have high expectations achieve more than those in other schools (Marks, Doane, & Secada, 1998). Of course, students' expectations for themselves are at least as important as those of their teachers. One study found that students whose self-perceptions exceeded their current performance later tended to improve in grades, whereas those whose self-perceptions were lower than their performance tended to drop in grades (Anderman, Anderman, & Griesinger, 1999).

COMMUNICATING POSITIVE EXPECTATIONS It is important to communicate to students the expectation that they can learn. Obviously, it is a bad idea to state the contrary—that a particular student cannot learn—and few teachers would explicitly do so. There are several implicit ways to communicate positive expectations of your students (or avoid negative ones).

1. *Wait for students to respond.* Rowe (1974) and others have noted that teachers wait longer for answers from students for whom they have high expectations than from other students. Longer wait times may communicate high expectations and increase student achievement (Tobin, 1987).

2. *Avoid unnecessary achievement distinctions among students.* Assessment results and grades should be a private matter between students and their teacher, not public information. Students usually know who is good in school and who is not, but you can still successfully communicate the expectation that all students, not only the most able ones, are capable of learning (Weinstein, Madison, & Kuklinski, 1995).

3. *Treat all students equally.* Call on students at all achievement levels equally often, and spend equal amounts of time with them. In particular, guard against bias.

Connections

For more on grouping students, see Chapter 9, page 253.

■ Anxiety and Achievement

Anxiety is a constant companion of education. Every student feels some anxiety at some time while in school; but for certain students, anxiety seriously inhibits learning or performance, particularly on tests (Cassady & Johnson, 2002).

The recent focus on high-stakes testing and achievement leaves students, administrators, and teachers anxious over the outcome of text scores. What can you do to alleviate some of that pressure from your students?

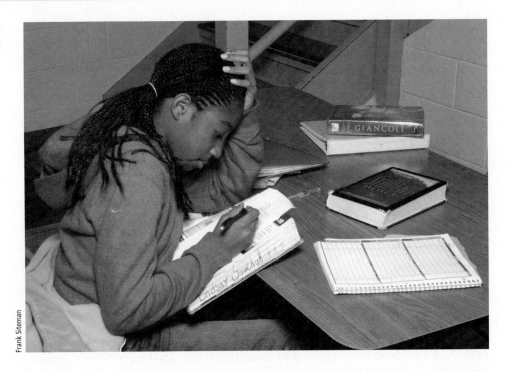

Frank Siteman

The main source of anxiety in school is the fear of failure and, with it, loss of self-esteem (Pintrich & Schunk, 2002). Low achievers are particularly likely to feel anxious in school, but they are by no means the only ones. We all know very able, high-achieving students who are also very anxious, maybe even terrified to be less than perfect at any school task.

Anxiety can block school performance in several ways. Anxious students might have difficulty learning in the first place, difficulty using or transferring knowledge they do have, and difficulty demonstrating their knowledge on tests (Bandalos, Yates, & Thorndike-Christ, 1995). Anxious students are likely to be overly self-conscious in performance settings, a feeling that distracts attention from the task at hand (Tobias, 1992). One particularly common form of debilitating anxiety is math anxiety. Many students (and adults) simply freeze up when given math problems, particularly word problems (Everson, Tobias, Hartman, & Gourgey, 1993).

You can apply many strategies to reduce the negative impact of anxiety on learning and performance. Clearly, creating a classroom climate that is accepting, comfortable, and noncompetitive helps. Giving students opportunities to correct errors or improve their work before handing it in also helps anxious children, as does providing clear, unambiguous instructions (Wigfield & Eccles, 1989). In testing situations, teachers have many ways to help anxious students to do their best. You can avoid time pressure, giving students plenty of time to complete a test and check their work. Tests that begin with easy problems and only gradually introduce more difficult ones are better for anxious students, and tests with standard, consistent answer formats also help such students. Test-anxious children can be trained in test-taking skills and relaxation techniques, and these can have a positive impact on their test performance (Spielberger & Vagg, 1995).

Connections

Programs designed to train test-anxious children in test-taking skills are discussed in Chapter 14, page 470.

How Can Teachers Increase Students' Motivation to Learn ❓

Learning takes work. Euclid, a Greek mathematician who lived around 300 B.C. and wrote the first geometry textbook, was asked by his king whether there were any shortcuts he could use to learn geometry, as he was a very busy man. "I'm sorry," Euclid replied, "but there is no royal road to geometry." The same is true of every other subject: Students get out of any course of study only what they put into it.

The remainder of this chapter discusses the means by which students can be motivated to exert the effort learning requires.

■ Intrinsic and Extrinsic Motivation

Sometimes a course of study is so fascinating and useful to students that they are willing to do the work required to learn the material with no incentive other than the interest level of the material itself. For example, many students would gladly take auto mechanics or photography courses and work hard in them, even if the courses offered no credit or grades. For these students the favorite subject itself has enough **intrinsic incentive** value to motivate them to learn. Other students love to learn about particular topics such as insects, dinosaurs, or famous people in history and need little encouragement or reward to do so (Gottfried & Fleming, 2001; Schraw, Flowerday, & Lehman, 2001). Students who have a strong "future time perspective" (i.e., are willing to do things today that may benefit them in the future) are often particularly motivated to learn, even without immediate incentives (Husman & Lens, 1999).

However, much of what must be learned in school is not inherently interesting or useful to most students in the short run. Students receive about 900 hours of instruction every year, and intrinsic interest alone will not keep them enthusiastically working day in and day out. In particular, students' intrinsic motivation generally declines from early elementary school through secondary school (Gottfried & Fleming, 2001; Sethi, Drake, Dialdin, & Lepper, 1995). It also declines over the course of each school year (Corpus, McClintic-Gilbert, & Hayenga, 2009). For this reason, schools apply a variety of **extrinsic incentives,** rewards for learning that are not inherent in the material being learned (Brophy, 1998). Extrinsic rewards might range from praise to grades to recognition to prizes or other rewards.

In the vignette at the beginning of this chapter, Cal Lewis tried to enhance both intrinsic and extrinsic motivation. His simulation of the Constitutional Convention was intended to arouse students' intrinsic interest in the subject, and his ratings of students' presentations and his feedback at the end of each period were intended to provide extrinsic motivation.

LEPPER'S EXPERIMENT ON THE IMPACT OF REWARDS ON MOTIVATION   An important question in research on motivation concerns whether the providing of extrinsic rewards diminishes intrinsic interest in an activity. In a classic experiment exploring this topic, Lepper and colleagues (1973) gave preschoolers an opportunity to draw with felt-tip markers, which many of them did quite enthusiastically. Then the researchers randomly divided the children into three groups: One group was told that its members would receive a reward for drawing a picture for a visitor (a Good Player Award), one was given the same reward as a surprise (not dependent on the children's drawing), and one received no reward. Over the next 4 days, observers recorded the children's free-play activities. Children who had received a reward for drawing spent about half as much time drawing with felt-tip markers as did those who had received the surprise reward and those who had gotten no reward. The authors suggested that promising extrinsic rewards for an activity that is intrinsically interesting might undermine intrinsic interest by inducing children to expect a reward for doing what they had previously done for nothing. In a later study (Greene & Lepper, 1974), it was found that simply telling children that they would be watched (through a one-way mirror) had an undermining effect similar to that of a promised reward.

DO REWARDS DESTROY INTRINSIC MOTIVATION?   In understanding the results of these studies, it is important to recall the conditions of the research. The students

"The school board decided not to raise teachers' salaries. We didn't want to undermine their intrinsic motivation."

intrinsic incentive

An aspect of an activity that people enjoy and, therefore, find motivating.

extrinsic incentive

A reward that is external to the activity, such as recognition or a good grade.

who were chosen for the studies showed an intrinsic interest in using marking pens. Those who did not were excluded from the experiments. Also, drawing with felt-tip pens does not resemble most school tasks. Many children love to draw at home, but few, even those who are most interested in school subjects, would independently study grammar and punctuation, work math problems, or learn the valences of chemical elements. Further, many of our most creative and self-motivated scientists (for example) were frequently rewarded as students with grades, science fair prizes, and scholarships for doing science, and virtually all successful artists have been rewarded at some point for their artistic creations. Bill Cosby attributes his early interest in storytelling to his grandfather, who told him stories from the Bible and then gave him a quarter from an old sock if he'd listened well. These rewards certainly did not undermine his intrinsic interest in storytelling or listening to stories. Research on older students doing more school-like tasks has generally failed to replicate the results of the Lepper and colleagues (1973) experiment (Cameron & Pierce, 1994, 1996; Eisenberger & Cameron, 1998). In fact, the use of rewards more often increases intrinsic motivation, especially when rewards are contingent on the quality of performance rather than on mere participation in an activity (Cameron, Pierce, Banko, & Gear, 2005; Lepper, 1983; Ryan & Deci, 2000), when the rewards are seen as recognition of competence (Rosenfield, Folger, & Adelman, 1980), when the task in question is not very interesting (Morgan, 1984), or when the rewards are social (e.g., praise) rather than material (Cameron, 2001; Cameron & Pierce, 1994; Ryan & Deci, 2000). Cameron (2001) summarizes the situation in which extrinsic rewards undermine intrinsic interest as follows: "A negative effect occurs when a task is of high interest, when the rewards are tangible and offered beforehand, and when the rewards are delivered without regard to success on the task or to any specified level of performance" (p. 40). This is a very narrow set of conditions, characterized by Bandura (1986, p. 246) as "of no great social import because rewards are rarely showered on people regardless of how they behave." However, Deci, Koestner, and Ryan (2001), while acknowledging that there are many forms of extrinsic rewards that have a positive or neutral impact on motivation, nevertheless argue that "the use of rewards as a motivational strategy is clearly a risky proposition, so we continue to argue for thinking about educational practices that will engage students' interest and support the development of their self-regulation" (2001, p. 50).

The research on the effects of extrinsic rewards on intrinsic motivation does counsel caution in the use of material rewards for engaging in tasks that students would do without rewards (see Lepper, 1998; Ryan & Deci, 2000; Sansone & Harackiewicz, 2000). You should attempt to make everything you teach as intrinsically interesting as possible and should avoid handing out material rewards when they are unnecessary, but you should not refrain from using extrinsic rewards when they are needed (Ryan & Deci, 2000). Often, extrinsic rewards may be necessary to get students started in a learning activity but may be phased out as students come to enjoy the activity and succeed at it (Stipek, 2006). Also, remember that in any given class, there are students who are intrinsically motivated to do a given activity and those who are not. To ensure that all students learn, strategic use of both intrinsic and extrinsic motivators is likely to be necessary.

■ Enhancing Intrinsic Motivation

Classroom instruction should enhance intrinsic motivation as much as possible. Increasing intrinsic motivation is always helpful for learning, regardless of whether extrinsic incentives are also in use (Covington, 1999; Vansteenkiste, Lens, & Deci, 2006). This means that you must try to get your students interested in the material you are presenting and then present it in an appealing way that both satisfies and increases students' curiosity about the material itself. A discussion of some means of doing this

Certification Pointer

On your teacher certification test, you should recognize the value of intrinsic motivation in promoting students' life-long growth and learning.

follows (see also Brophy, 1999, 2008; Burden & Byrd, 2003; Covington, 1999; Stipek, 2006).

AROUSING INTEREST   It is important to convince students of the importance and interest level of the material that is about to be presented to show (if possible) how the knowledge to be gained will be useful to students (Bergin, 1999; Brophy, 2008; Tomlinson, 2002). For example, intrinsic motivation to learn a lesson on percents might be increased by introducing the lesson as follows:

> Today we will begin a lesson on percents. Percents are important in our daily lives. For example, when you buy something at the store and a salesperson figures the sales tax, he or she is using percents. When we leave a tip for a waiter or waitress, we use percents. We often hear in the news things like "Prices rose seven percent last year." In a few years, many of you will have summer jobs, and if they involve handling money, you'll probably be using percents all the time.

Introducing lessons with examples relating the material to students' cultures can be particularly effective. For example, in introducing astronomy to a class with many Latino children, you could say, "Thousands of years ago, people in Mexico and Central America had calendars that accurately predicted the movement of the moon and stars for centuries into the future. How could they do this? Today we will learn about how planets, moons, and stars move in predictable paths." The purpose of these statements is to arouse student curiosity about the lesson to come, thereby enhancing intrinsic motivation to learn the material (Vacca, 2006).

Another way to enhance students' intrinsic interest is to give them some choice about what they will study or how they will study it (Cordova & Lepper, 1996; Stipek, 2006). Choices need not be unlimited to be motivational. For example, students might be given a choice of writing about ancient Athens or Sparta, or a choice of working independently or in pairs.

MAINTAINING CURIOSITY   A skillful teacher uses a variety of means to further arouse or maintain curiosity in the course of the lesson. Science teachers, for instance, often use demonstrations that surprise or baffle students and induce them to want to understand why. A floating dime makes students curious about the surface tension of liquids. "Burning" a dollar bill covered with an alcohol–water solution (without harming the dollar bill) certainly increases curiosity about the heat of combustion. Guthrie and Cox (2001) found that giving students hands-on experience with science activities greatly increased their learning from books on related topics.

Less dramatically, surprising or challenging students with a problem they can't solve with their current knowledge can arouse curiosity, and, therefore, intrinsic motivation (see Bottge, 2001). A seventh-grade teacher in England used this principle in a lesson on equivalent fractions. First, he had his students halve and then halve again $\frac{8}{13}$ and $\frac{12}{20}$. Working in pairs they instantly agreed on $\frac{4}{13}$ and $\frac{2}{13}$, $\frac{6}{20}$ and $\frac{3}{20}$. Then he gave them $\frac{13}{20}$. After a moment of hesitation, students came back with $6\frac{1}{2}/20$ and then $3\frac{1}{4}/20$! "Crikey!" he said. "All these fractions inside fractions are making me nervous! Isn't there some other way we can do this?" "Round off?" suggested one student. "Use decimals?" suggested another. Finally, after much discussion and argument, the students realized that they could use their knowledge about equivalent fractions to find the solutions: $\frac{13}{40}$ and $\frac{13}{80}$. Getting the students into a familiar pattern and then breaking that pattern excited and engaged the whole class, engaging them far more effectively than would have been possible by simply teaching the algorithm in the first place. The element of surprise, challenging the students' current understanding, made them intensely curious about an issue they'd never before considered.

Connections

The importance of student interest in creative problem solving and other constructivist approaches is discussed in Chapter 8, page 238.

INTASC

4 Multiple Instructional Strategies

Connections

The importance of student interest in lesson content and presentation is discussed in Chapter 7, page 189.

USING A VARIETY OF INTERESTING PRESENTATION MODES   The intrinsic motivation to learn something is enhanced by the use of interesting materials, as well as by variety in mode of presentation. For example, you can maintain student interest in a subject by alternating use of films, guest speakers, demonstrations, and so on, although the use of each resource must be carefully planned to be sure it focuses on the course objectives and complements the other activities. Use of computers can enhance most students' intrinsic motivation to learn (Lepper, 1985). What makes materials interesting are elements such as the use of emotional content (e.g., danger, sex, money, heartbreak, disaster), concrete rather than abstract examples, cause-and-effect relationships, and clear organization (Jetton & Alexander, 2001; Schraw et al., 2001; Wade, 2001).

One excellent means of increasing interest in a subject is to use games or simulations. A simulation, or role play, is an exercise in which students take on roles and engage in activities appropriate to those roles. Cal Lewis used a simulation to teach students about the Constitutional Convention. Programs exist that simulate many aspects of government; for example, students may take roles as legislators who must negotiate and trade votes to satisfy their constituents' interests or the roles of economic actors (farmers, producers, consumers) who run a minieconomy. Creative teachers have long used simulations that they designed themselves. For example, you can have students write their own newspaper; design, manufacture, and market a product; or set up and run a bank.

The advantage of simulations is that they allow students to learn about a subject from the inside. Although research on use of simulations (see Van Sickle, 1986) finds that they are usually no more effective than traditional instruction for teaching facts and concepts, studies do consistently find that simulations increase students' interest, motivation, and affective learning (Dukes & Seidner, 1978). They certainly impart a different affective knowledge of a subject.

Nonsimulation games can also increase motivation to learn a given subject. The spelling bee is a popular example of a nonsimulation game. Teams–Games–Tournament, or TGT (Slavin, 1995a), uses games that can be adapted to any subject. Team games are usually better than individual games. A form of cooperative learning (recall Chapter 8), team games provide an opportunity for teammates to help one another and avoid one problem of individual games—that of more-able students consistently winning. If all students are put on mixed-ability teams, all have a good chance of success.

HELPING STUDENTS MAKE CHOICES AND SET THEIR OWN GOALS   One fundamental principle of motivation is that people work harder for goals that they themselves set than for goals set for them by others (Ryan & Deci, 2000). For example, a student might set a minimum number of books she expects to read at home or a score she expects to attain on an upcoming quiz. At the next goal-setting conference you might discuss student attainment of (or failure to attain) goals and set new goals for the following week. During these meetings you might help students learn to set ambitious but realistic goals and would praise them for setting and then achieving their goals. Goal-setting strategies of this kind have been found to increase students' academic performance and self-efficacy (Page-Voth & Graham, 1999; Shih & Alexander, 2000). Similarly, there is much evidence that children are more highly motivated to engage in activities that they choose, even if the choice is just between two alternatives (Patall et al., 2008; Vokoun & Bigelow, 2008).

Shutterstock

This student has intrinsic incentive to learn about art projects. As a teacher, how can you maintain or extend her motivation? How can you present the same task to a student for whom the task does not have intrinsic value?

21st Century Learning

Intrinsic Motivation

In traditional teaching, it has long been necessary to use extrinsic incentives, such as grades and praise, to motivate students to do their best. Incentives are still likely to be important in the future, but new classroom teaching technologies can help increase intrinsic motivation for learning. Video clips, animations, demonstrations, and interactive technologies can add variety and fun to lessons and give students more active roles. This is not only useful for learning school subjects but also prepares students for a world in which they will increasingly need to take responsibility for motivation themselves and maintain high productivity in less structured, more flexible workplaces.

Question

■ Given what you now know about intrinsic and extrinsic motivation, what are some ways you might motivate students to learn about technology applications?

■ Principles for Providing Extrinsic Incentives to Learn

Teachers should always try to enhance students' intrinsic motivation to learn academic materials but should at the same time be concerned about extrinsic incentives for learning (Brophy, 2008; Hidi & Harackiewicz, 2000). Not every subject is intrinsically interesting to all students, and students must be motivated to do the hard work necessary to master difficult subjects. The following sections discuss a variety of incentives that can help motivate students to learn academic material.

EXPRESSING CLEAR EXPECTATIONS   Students need to know exactly what they are supposed to do, how they will be evaluated, and what the consequences of success will be. Often, students' failures on particular tasks stem from confusion about what they are being asked to do (see Anderson et al., 1985; Brophy, 2008). Communicating clear expectations is important. For example, you might introduce a writing assignment as follows:

> Today, I'd like you all to write a composition about what Thomas Jefferson would think of government in the United States today. I expect your compositions to be about two pages long, and I want them to compare and contrast the plan of government laid out by the nation's founders with the way government actually operates today. Your compositions will be graded on the basis of your ability to describe similarities and differences between the structure and function of the U.S. government in Thomas Jefferson's time and today, as well as on the originality and clarity of your writing. This will be an important part of your 6 weeks' grade, so I expect you to do your best!

Note that you are clear about what students are to write, how much material is expected, how the work will be evaluated, and how important the work will be for the students' grades. This clarity assures students that efforts directed at writing a good composition will pay off. If you had just said, "I'd like you all to write a composition about what Thomas Jefferson would think about government in the United States today," students might write the wrong thing, write too much or too little, or perhaps emphasize the if-Jefferson-were-alive-today aspect of the assignment rather than the comparative-government aspect. They would be unsure how much importance you intended to place on the mechanics of the composition as compared to its content. Finally, they would have no way of knowing how their efforts would pay off, lacking any indication of how much emphasis you would give to the compositions in computing grades.

A study by Graham, MacArthur, and Schwartz (1995) shows the importance of specificity. Low-achieving fifth- and sixth-graders were asked to revise compositions either to "make [your paper] better" or to "add at least three things that will add information to your paper." The students with the more specific instructions wrote higher-quality, longer revisions because they had a clearer idea of exactly what was being asked of them.

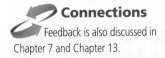

Connections

Feedback is also discussed in Chapter 7 and Chapter 13.

PROVIDING CLEAR FEEDBACK   The word **feedback** means information on the results of one's efforts. The term has been used throughout this book to refer both to information students receive on their performance and to information teachers obtain on the effects of their instruction. Feedback can serve as an incentive. Research on feedback has found that provision of information on the results of one's actions can be an adequate reward in many circumstances (Gibbons, Duffin, Robertson, & Thompson, 1998). However, to be an effective motivator, feedback must be clear, specific, and given close in time to performance (Hattie & Timperley, 2007). This is important for all students, but especially for young ones. For example, praise for a job well done should specify what the student did well:

- "Good work! I like the way you used the guide words in the dictionary to find your target words."

- "I like that answer. It shows you've been thinking about what I've been saying about freedom and responsibility."

- "This is an excellent essay. It started with a statement of the argument you were going to make and then supported the argument with relevant information. I also like the care you took with punctuation and word usage."

Specific feedback is both informative and motivational (Kulhavy & Stock, 1989). It tells students what they did right, so that they will know what to do in the future, and helps give them an effort-based attribution for success ("You succeeded because you worked hard"). In contrast, if students are praised or receive a good grade without any explanation, they are unlikely to learn from the feedback what to do next time to be successful and might form an ability attribution ("I succeeded because I'm smart") or an external attribution ("I must have succeeded because the teacher likes me, the task was easy, or I lucked out"). As noted earlier in this chapter, effort attributions are most conducive to continuing motivation (Pintrich & Schunk, 2002). Similarly, feedback about mistakes or failures can add to motivation if it focuses only on the performance itself (not on students' general abilities) and if it is alternated with success feedback (see Clifford, 1990).

PROVIDING IMMEDIATE FEEDBACK   Immediacy of feedback is also very important (Kulik & Kulik, 1988). If students complete a project on Monday and don't receive any feedback on it until Friday, the informational and motivational value of the feedback will be diminished. First, if they made errors, they might continue all week making similar errors on related material that might have been averted by feedback on the performance. Second, a long delay between behavior and consequence confuses the relationship between the two. Young students, especially, might have little idea why they received a

feedback

Information on the results of one's efforts.

particular grade if the performance on which the grade is based occurred several days earlier.

PROVIDING FREQUENT FEEDBACK   Feedback should be delivered frequently to students to maintain their best efforts. For example, it is unrealistic to expect most students to work hard for 6 or 9 weeks in hope of improving their grade unless they receive frequent feedback. Research in the behavioral learning theory tradition has established that no matter how powerful a reward is, it might have little impact on behavior if it is given infrequently; small, frequent rewards are more effective incentives than are large, infrequent ones. Research on frequency of testing has generally found that it is a good idea to give frequent brief quizzes to assess student progress rather than infrequent long tests (Dempster, 1991). Research also indicates the importance of asking many questions in class so that students can gain information about their own level of understanding and can receive reinforcement (such as praise and recognition) for paying attention to lessons.

INCREASING THE VALUE AND AVAILABILITY OF EXTRINSIC MOTIVATORS Expectancy theories of motivation, discussed earlier in this chapter, hold that motivation is a product of the value an individual attaches to success and the individual's estimate of the likelihood of success (see Wigfield & Eccles, 2000). One implication of this is that students must value incentives if they are to be effective motivators. Some students are not particularly interested in teacher praise or grades but might value notes sent home to their parents, a little extra recess time, or a special privilege in the classroom.

Another implication of expectancy theory is that although all students should have a chance to be rewarded if they do their best, no student should have an easy time achieving the maximum reward. This principle is violated by traditional grading practices, because some students find it easy to earn A's and B's, whereas others believe that they have little chance of academic success no matter what they do. In this circumstance, neither high achievers nor low achievers are likely to exert their best efforts. This is one reason that it is important to reward students for effort, for doing better than they have done in the past, or for making progress, rather than only for getting a high score. For example, students can build a portfolio of compositions, projects, reports, or other work and can then see how their work is improving over time. Not all students are equally capable of achieving high scores, but all are equally capable of exerting effort, exceeding their own past record, or making progress, so these are often better, more equally available criteria for reward (see Chapter 13).

■ Using Praise Effectively

Praise serves many purposes in classroom instruction but is primarily used to reinforce appropriate behaviors and to give feedback to students on what they are doing right. Overall, it is a good idea to use praise frequently, especially with young children and in classrooms with many low-achieving students (Brophy, 1998; Evans, 1996). However, what is more important than the amount of praise given is the way it is given. Praise is effective as a classroom motivator to the extent that it is contingent, specific, and credible (Sutherland, Wehby, & Copeland, 2000). **Contingent praise** depends on student performance of well-defined behaviors. For example, if you say, "I'd like you all to open your books to page 92 and work problems one to ten," then only give praise to the students who follow directions. Praise should be given only for appropriate behaviors.

Connections

For grading methods that recognize progress and effort, see Chapter 13, page 439.

Connections

For more on student portfolios, see Chapter 13, page 430.

Connections

For more on the use of praise as a reinforcer, see Chapter 11, page 331.

contingent praise

Praise that is effective because it refers directly to specific task performances.

FIGURE 10.3
Guidelines for Effective Praise

If used properly, praise can be an effective motivator in classroom situations.

Effective Praise

1. Is delivered contingently.
2. Specifies the particulars of the accomplishment.
3. Shows spontaneity, variety, and other signs of credibility; suggests clear attention to the student's accomplishment.
4. Rewards attainment of specified performance criteria (which can include effort criteria, however).
5. Provides information to students about their competence or the value of their accomplishments.
6. Orients students toward better appreciation of their own task-related behavior and thinking about problem solving.

7. Uses students' own prior accomplishments as the context for describing present accomplishments.
8. Is given in recognition of noteworthy effort or success at difficult tasks (for *this* student).
9. Attributes success to effort and ability, implying that similar successes can be expected in the future.
10. Focuses students' attention on their own task-relevant behavior.
11. Fosters appreciation of, and desirable attributions about, task-relevant behavior after the process is completed.

Source: Jere Brophy, "Teacher Praise: A Functional Analysis," *Review of Educational Research, 51,* p. 26.

Certification Pointer

When responding to a case study on your certification test, you should know that providing praise that is contingent, specific, and credible can increase student motivation.

Specificity means to praise students for specific behaviors, not for general "goodness." For example, you might say, "Susan, I'm glad you followed my directions to start work on your composition," rather than "Susan, you're doing great!"

When praise is *credible,* it is given sincerely for good work. Brophy (1981) notes that when praising low-achieving or disruptive students for good work, teachers often contradict their words with tone, posture, or other nonverbal cues. Brophy's (1981) list of guidelines for effective praise appears in Figure 10.3.

Praise is an effective classroom motivator when it is contingent, specific, and credible. As a teacher, how will you use praise to motivate your students?

Jose Luis Pelaez/Corbis

In addition to contingency, specificity, and credibility, Brophy's list includes several particularly important principles that reinforce topics discussed earlier in this chapter. For example, guidelines 7 and 8 emphasize that praise should be given for good performance relative to a student's usual level of performance. That is, students who usually do well should not be praised for a merely average performance, but students who usually do less well should be praised when they do better. This relates to the principle of accessibility of reward discussed earlier in this chapter; rewards should be neither too easy nor too difficult for students to obtain. Guideline 9 emphasizes the importance of praising effort, rather than intelligence or other factors that students do not control (see Dweck, 2007).

■ Teaching Students to Praise Themselves

There is increasing evidence that students can learn to praise themselves and that this increases their academic success. For example, children can learn to mentally give themselves a pat on the back when they finish a task or to stop at regular intervals to notice how much they have done (Corno & Kanfer, 1993; Ross, Rolheiser, & Hogaboam-Gray, 1998). This strategy is a key component of self-regulated learning (see Schunk & Zimmerman, 1997; Zimmerman, 2008).

ON THE WEB

The Northwest Regional Laboratory has resources on sparking students' motivation at www.nwrel.org/request/oct00. In *Tools for Teaching,* Barbara Gross Davis devotes a chapter to motivating students. You can find it online at http://honolulu.hawaii.edu/intranet/committees/FacDevCom/guidebk/teachtip/motiv.htm.

Chapter 10 Summary

What Is Motivation?

Motivation is an internal process that activates, guides, and maintains behavior over time. There are different kinds, intensities, aims, and directions of motivation.

What Are Some Theories of Motivation?

In behavioral learning theory, motivation is a consequence of reinforcement. However, the value of a reinforcer depends on many factors, and the strength of motivation may be different in different students.

In Maslow's human needs theory, which is based on a hierarchy of needs, people must satisfy their lower-level (deficiency) needs before they will be motivated to try to satisfy their higher-level (growth) needs. Maslow's concept of the need for self-actualization, the highest need, is defined as the desire to become everything one is capable of becoming.

Attribution theory seeks to understand people's explanations for their success or failure. A central assumption is that people will attempt to maintain a positive self-image; when good things happen, people attribute them to their own abilities, whereas they tend to attribute negative events to factors beyond their control. Locus of control might be internal (success or failure is based on personal effort or ability) or external (success or failure is the result of luck or task difficulty). Students who are self-regulated learners perform better than those who are externally motivated. Self-regulated learners consciously plan and monitor their learning and thus retain more.

Expectancy theory holds that a person's motivation to achieve a goal depends on the product of that person's estimation of his or her chance of success and the value he or she places on success. Motivation should be at a maximum at moderate levels of probability of success. An important educational implication is that learning tasks should be neither too easy nor too difficult.

How Can Achievement Motivation Be Enhanced ?

You can emphasize learning goals and positive or empowering attributions. Students with learning goals see the purpose of school as gaining knowledge and competence; these students tend to have higher motivation to learn than do students whose performance goals are positive judgments and good grades. Use special programs such as

The Intentional Teacher

USING WHAT YOU KNOW about Motivation to Improve Teaching and Learning

Intentional teachers know that, although students might be motivated by different incentives and to varying degrees, every student is motivated. They understand that many elements of motivation can be influenced by the teacher, and they capitalize on their ability to unearth and direct student motivation. They provide instruction that helps students find meaning in learning and in taking pride in their own accomplishments.

1. What do I expect my students to know and be able to do at the end of this lesson? How does this contribute to course objectives and to students' needs to become capable individuals?

Plan how you will support student motivation. Think about how you will discover and sustain your students' drive to participate in learning. Consider principles of motivation in your long- and short-term planning. You might review major findings on motivation and jot down some guiding ideas on an index card that you clip to your plan book.

2. What knowledge, skills, needs, and interests do my students have that must be taken into account in my lesson?

Motivation varies by student, situation, and domain. Determine your students' current motivation. You can gather information about your students' motivation from a variety of sources. For instance, you could ob-

serve the students during informal conversations and during instruction, or ask them to write journal entries on such prompts as "What accounts for your score on this test?" You could analyze their answers and your observations to gather information about three areas of motivation: (1) Where do students seem to be functioning in terms of Maslow's hierarchy of needs? (2) Do students seem to be seeking success or avoiding failure? (3) Do students use internal or external causal attributions? Stable or unstable? Controllable or uncontrollable? (4) Are students primarily oriented toward mastery, or learning, or only toward performance or grades?

3. What do I know about the content, child development, learning, motivation, and effective teaching strategies that I can use to accomplish my objectives?

For motivation to be high, students need to perceive that with effort, success is possible. Provide tasks that require effort but allow students to see that success is within reach. For example, imagine that you check your grade book at the end of the first marking period and find that some of your students have earned D's and F's across the board but that others have a string of apparently easy A's. You could begin your quest to improve instruction by meeting with students individually. You might ask how they earned their grades and what they expect to earn in the future. Based on your conversations, you could develop research projects at the student's correct level of difficulty and attribution training to help students out of learned helplessness, in which students feel that they are doomed to fail despite their actions. Your expectations significantly affect students' motivation and achievement. You can communicate positive expectations for student learning and for reduced anxiety.

How Can Teachers Increase Students' Motivation to Learn

An incentive is a reinforcer that people can expect to receive if they perform a specific behavior. Intrinsic incentives are aspects of certain tasks that in themselves have enough value to motivate students to do the tasks on their own. Extrinsic incentives include grades, gold stars, and other rewards. You can enhance intrinsic motivation by arousing students' interest, maintaining curiosity, using a variety of presentation modes, and letting students set their own goals. Ways to offer extrinsic incentives include stating clear expectations; giving clear, immediate, and frequent feedback; and increasing the value and availability of rewards. Classroom rewards include praise, which is most effective when it is contingent, specific, and credible.

INTASC **7** Instructional Planning Skills   **9** Professional Commitment and Responsibility
        8 Assessment of Student Learning

devise careful contracts so that students who have yet to achieve see that success is possible.

Some students display a performance orientation instead of the more useful learning orientation. Help students shift their focus from completion to mastery by emphasizing the practical importance of content. Deemphasize grades and rewards. For example, imagine that your secondary students seem overly concerned with their scores on essays and the grading curve. You might employ portfolio assessments and require students to analyze their growth over time. Students could grade themselves on improvement rather than on how their work compares to that of their peers.

Praise needs to be used effectively. Be certain that your praise is sincere, specific, and contingent on students' behavior. Try to reserve your praise for good performance, to focus on the behavior and not the student, and to be specific about what constitutes good performance: "Jamal, I like the way you blended those two colors. That really adds depth to the painting. It looks real!"

 4. What instructional materials, technology, assistance, and other resources are available to help accomplish my objectives?

Always be on the lookout for additional sources of motivation, intrinsic as well as extrinsic. For example, bring in parents or other speakers with life experience relevant to your lesson to excite students about the content. Students will be more interested in trigonometry if they hear a former artilleryman explain how he used trig every day in the army, or they might be more interested in persuasive essays if they hear a volunteer for Amnesty International describe how she writes letters to attempt to gain freedom for prisoners of conscience.

 5. How will I plan to assess students' progress toward my objectives?

Students need to develop accurate attributions for their success. Observe your students to note whether they perceive that their efforts contribute to their learning. Intervene when students' attributions are inaccurate. Step up your efforts to help students set goals, take responsibility for their progress, and evaluate their work. Together, you and your students might devise a grading system that rewards performance, effort, and improvement.

6. How will I respond if individual children or the class as a whole are not on track toward success? What is my back-up plan?

Maslow asserted that the goal of psychological health is self-actualization. Review your instruction and your students' learning to determine the extent to which you and the students are meeting the broad span of their needs and reaching their full potential. Consider the following. What evidence is there that (1) the environment is safe and comfortable and encourages students to take risks, (2) instruction is meaningful and lively, and (3) students are active participants in analyzing their growth and setting plans?

Key Terms

Review the following key terms from the chapter.

achievement motivation   295
attribution theory   290
contingent praise   307
deficiency needs   288
expectancy theory   294
expectancy–valence model   294
extrinsic incentive   301
feedback   306

growth needs   288
intrinsic incentive   301
learned helplessness   298
learning goals   295
locus of control   291
motivation   286
performance goals   295
self-actualization   289

Self-Assessment: Practicing for Licensure

Directions: The chapter-opening vignette addresses indicators that are often assessed in state licensure exams. Re-read the chapter-opening vignette, and then respond to the following questions.

1. According to behavioral learning theorists, why are Cal Lewis's students motivated to learn about the Constitutional Convention?

  a. To obtain reinforcers

  b. To satisfy growth needs

  c. To eliminate deficiency needs

  d. To maximize expectancy effects

2. Mr. Lewis's students see the purpose of lessons about the Constitutional Convention as a way to gain information about the history of the United States. What type of goal orientation is this?

  a. Performance goal

  b. Learning goal

  c. Expectancy goal

  d. Self-regulated goal

3. Beth Andrews, a shy girl in Mr. Lewis's class, proposes elements of the Bill of Rights to the convention members. If Beth has an internal locus of control, she is most likely to attribute her successful presentation to which of the following factors?

  a. The presentation requirements being easy

  b. Favoritism by the teacher

  c. Careful preparation

  d. Good luck

4. Mr. Lewis wants his students to work hard regardless of their ability level or task difficulty. What type of attributions will he attempt to instill in his students?

  a. Internal–stable

  b. Internal–unstable

  c. External–stable

  d. External–unstable

5. Under what circumstances is it most important for Mr. Lewis to avoid the use of external incentives?

  a. When students are doing challenging work

  b. When the task communicates feedback about students' competence

  c. When students are motivated to do the work without extrinsic incentives

  d. When students have experienced a great deal of failure

6. Analyze Mr. Lewis's lesson and his students' willingness to participate from the four theories of motivation presented in the chapter: behavioral, human needs, attribution, and expectancy.

7. Describe ways that you can increase students' motivation to learn.

PEARSON myeducationlab

Go to the Topic **Motivation and Affect** in the MyEducationLab (www.myeducationlab.com) for your course, where you can:

- Find learning outcomes for **Motivation and Affect** along with the national standards that connect to these outcomes.

- Complete Assignments and Activities that can help you more deeply understand the chapter content.

- Apply and practice your understanding of the core teaching skills identified in the chapter with the Building Teaching Skills and Dispositions learning units.

- Access video clips of CCSSO National Teachers of the Year award winners responding to the question "Why Do I Teach?" in the Teacher Talk section.

- Check your comprehension of the content covered in the chapter by going to the Study Plan in the Book Resources for your text. Here you will be able to take a chapter quiz; receive feedback on your answers; and then access Review, Practice, and Enrichment activities to enhance your understanding of chapter content.

- Watch author Bob Slavin present a Personal Reflections podcast on *Using Different Styles* in the Book Resources for your text. Then, respond to the reflection questions that follow.

Using Different Styles

YOUR REFLECTIONS Why do you think Mary was unable to use the same strategies with her students and athletes that her parents had used with her? Identify a teacher or coach from your K–12 school days from whom you learned a lot or who brought out the best in you. What methods did this person use? Do you see yourself using some of those same methods as a teacher?

11

Effective Learning Environments

Bob Daemmrich Photography

Learning Outcomes

At the end of this chapter, you should be able to:

- Describe an effective learning environment
- Understand the impact of time on learning
- Identify several practices to promote classroom management
- Describe strategies for handling routine student misbehavior
- Discuss how applied behavior analysis can be used to manage more serious student behavior problems
- Discuss how to prevent serious behavior problems

The bell rings outside of Julia Cavalho's tenth-grade English class. The sound is still echoing in the hall when Ms. Cavalho starts her lesson.

"Today," she begins, "you will become thieves. Worse than thieves. Thieves steal only your money or your property. You—" (she looks around the class and pauses for emphasis) "—will steal something far more valuable. You will steal an author's style. An author builds his or her style, word by word, sentence by sentence, over many years. Stealing an author's style is like stealing a work of art that someone took years to create. It's despicable, but you're going to do it."

During her speech the students sit in rapt attention. Two students, Mark and Gloria, slink in late. Mark makes a funny "Oops, I'm late" face and does an exaggerated tiptoe to his desk. Ms. Cavalho ignores both of them, as does the class. She continues her lesson.

"To whom are you going to do this dirty deed? Papa Hemingway, of course. Hemingway of the short, punchy sentence. Hemingway of the almost excessive attention to physical detail. You've read *The Old Man and the Sea*. You've read parts of *The Sun Also Rises* and *For Whom the Bell Tolls*."

While Ms. Cavalho talks, Mark makes an exaggerated show of getting out his books. He whispers to a neighboring student. Without stopping her lesson, Ms. Cavalho moves near Mark. He stops whispering and pays attention.

"Today you will become Hemingway. You will steal his words, his pace, his meter, his similes, his metaphors, and put them to work in your own stories."

Ms. Cavalho has students review elements of Hemingway's style, which the class has studied before.

"Everyone think for a moment. How would Hemingway describe an old woman going up the stairs at the end of a long day's work? Mai, what do you think?"

Mai gives her short description of the old woman.

"Sounds great to me. I like your use of very short sentences and physical description. Any other ideas? Kevin?"

Ms. Cavalho lets several students give Hemingway-style descriptions, using them as opportunities to reinforce her main points.

"In a moment," she says, "you're going to get your chance to become Ernest Hemingway. As usual, you'll be working in your writing response groups. Before we start, however, let's go over our rules about effective group work. Who can tell me what they are?"

The students volunteer several rules: Respect others, explain your ideas, be sure everyone participates, stand up for your opinion, keep voices low.

"All right," says Ms. Cavalho. "When I say begin, I'd like you to move your desks together and start planning your compositions. Ready? Begin."

The students move their desks together smoothly and quickly and get right to work. During the transition, Ms. Cavalho calls Mark and Gloria to her desk to discuss their lateness. Gloria has a good excuse, but Mark is developing a pattern of lateness and disruptiveness.

"Mark," says Ms. Cavalho, "I'm concerned about your lateness and your behavior in class. I've spoken to some of your other teachers, and they say you're behaving even worse in their classes than you do in mine. Please come here after school, and we'll see if we can come up with a solution to this problem."

Mark returns to his group and gets to work. Ms. Cavalho circulates among the groups, giving encouragement to students who are working well. When she sees two girls who are goofing off, she moves close to them and puts her hand on one girl's shoulder while looking at the plan for her composition. "Good start," she says. "Let's see how far you can get with this by the end of the period."

The students work in a controlled but excited way through the end of the period, thoroughly enjoying "stealing" from Hemingway. The classroom sounds like a beehive with busy, involved students sharing ideas, reading drafts to each other, and editing each other's compositions. At the end of the day, Mark returns to Ms. Cavalho's classroom.

"Mark," she says, "we need to do something about your lateness and your clowning in class. How would you suggest that we solve this problem?"

"Gloria was late, too," Mark protests.

"We're not talking about Gloria. We're talking about you. You are responsible for your own behavior."

"OK, OK, I promise I'll be on time."

"That's not good enough. We've had this conversation before. We need a different plan this time. I know you can succeed in this class, but you're making it hard on yourself as well as disrupting your classmates."

"Let's try an experiment," Ms. Cavalho goes on. "Each day, I'd like you to rate your own behavior. I'll do the same. If we both agree at the end of each week that you've been on time and appropriately behaved, fine. If not, I'll need to call your parents and see whether we can make a plan with them. Are you willing to give it a try?"

"OK, I guess so."

"Great. I'm expecting to see a new Mark starting tomorrow. I know you won't let me down!"

USING YOUR EXPERIENCE

Critical Thinking   What methods of classroom management does Ms. Cavalho use? What potential problems is she preventing?

Creative Thinking   Suppose Mark continues to be late for class. Plan a conference with his parents. What are the goals? How will they be implemented?

Critical and Creative Thinking   Analyze two variables, grade level and classroom management strategies, in a matrix. Using Ms. Cavalho's classroom as a starter, create this matrix with grade level on the horizontal (e.g., elementary, middle, and high school), and then brainstorm classroom management strategies down the vertical column. Finally, check off which management strategies are influential at different grade levels.

What Is an Effective Learning Environment?

INTASC

5 Classroom Management and Motivation

6 Communication Skills

classroom management

Methods used to organize classroom activities, instruction, physical structure, and other features to make effective use of time; to create a happy and productive learning environment; and to minimize behavior problems and other disruptions.

Providing an effective learning environment includes strategies that teachers use to create a positive, productive classroom experience. Often called **classroom management,** strategies for providing effective learning environments include not only preventing and responding to misbehavior but also, more importantly, using class time well, creating an atmosphere that is conducive to interest and inquiry, and permitting activities that engage students' minds and imaginations (Kunter, Baumert, & Köller, 2007; Martin, 2008). A class with no behavior problems can by no means be assumed to be a well-managed class.

The most effective approach to classroom management is effective instruction (Evertson & Poole, 2008). Students who are participating in well-structured activities that engage their interests, who are highly motivated to learn, and who are working on tasks that are challenging yet within their capabilities rarely pose any serious management problems. The vignette involving Ms. Cavalho illustrates this. She has a well-managed class not because she behaves like a drill sergeant, but because she teaches interesting lessons, engages students' imaginations and energies, makes efficient use of time, and communicates a sense of purpose, high expectations, and contagious enthusiasm. However, even a well-managed class is sure to contain individual students who will misbehave. Although Ms. Cavalho's focus is on preventing behavior problems, she is also ready to intervene when necessary to see that students' behaviors are within acceptable limits (see Emmer & Stough, 2008). For some students a glance, physical proximity, or a hand on the shoulder is enough. For others, consequences might be necessary. Even in these cases, Ms. Cavalho does not let behavior issues disrupt her lesson or her students' learning activities.

This chapter focuses on the creation of effective learning environments, classroom management, and discipline. Creating an effective learning environment involves organizing classroom activities, instruction, and the physical classroom to provide for effective use of time; to create a happy, productive classroom; and to minimize disruptions. **Discipline** refers to methods used to prevent behavior problems or to respond to existing behavior problems so as to reduce their occurrence in the future (see Charles, 2008; Levin & Nolan, 2010; Marzano, 2003).

There is no magic or charisma to make you an effective classroom manager. Setting up an effective learning environment is a matter of knowing a set of techniques that any teacher can learn and apply. This chapter takes an approach to classroom management and discipline that emphasizes prevention of misbehavior, based on the theory that effective instruction itself is the best means of avoiding discipline problems. Still, every teacher, no matter how effective, will encounter discipline problems sometimes, and this chapter also presents means of handling these problems when they arise.

What Is the Impact of Time on Learning?

INTASC

7 Instructional Planning Skills

Obviously, if no time is spent teaching a subject, students will not learn it. However, within the usual range of time allocated to instruction, how much difference does time make? This has been a focus of considerable research (see Adelman, Haslam, & Pringle, 1996; National Education Commission on Time and Learning, 1994). Although it is clear that more time spent in instruction has a positive impact on student achievement, the effects of additional time are often modest or inconsistent (Gijselaers & Schmidt, 1995; Karweit, 1989). In particular, the typical differences in lengths of school days and school years among different districts have only a minor impact on student achievement (Karweit, 1989). What seems to be more important is how time is used in class. **Engaged time,** or **time on task,** the number of minutes actually spent learning, is the time measure that is most frequently found to contribute to learning (e.g., Bodovski & Farkas, 2007; Marks, 2000; Rowan, Correnti, & Miller, 2002). In other words, the most important aspect of time is the one that is under your direct control as the teacher: the organization and use of time in the classroom (Jones & Jones, 2010; Marzano, 2003).

■ Using Allocated Time for Instruction

Time is a limited resource in schools. A typical U.S. school is in session about 6 hours a day for 180 days each year. Time for educational activities can be expanded by means of homework assignments or (for some students) participation in after-school activities or summer school, but the total time available for instruction is essentially set. Out of these 6 hours (or so) must come time for teaching a variety of subjects plus time for lunch, recess, and physical education; transitions between classes; announcements; and so on. Over a 40- to 60-minute period in a particular subject, many quite different factors reduce the time available for instruction. Figure 11.1 illustrates how time scheduled for mathematics instruction in 12 second- to fifth-grade classes observed by Karweit and Slavin (1981) was whittled away.

The classes that Karweit and Slavin (1981) observed were in schools in and around a rural Maryland town. Overall, the classes were well organized and businesslike, with dedicated and hardworking teachers. Students were generally well behaved and respectful

discipline

Methods used to prevent behavior problems from occurring or to respond to behavior problems so as to reduce their occurrence in the future.

engaged time or time on task

Time students spend actively engaged in learning the task at hand.

FIGURE 11.1 **Where Does the Time Go?**

Observations of elementary school mathematics classes showed that the time students actually spend learning in class is only about 60 percent of the time allocated for instruction.

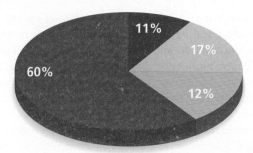

No math lesson occurred on 11% of days scheduled

Examples: field trips, teacher absence, standardized tests, school events

Noninstructional activities occupied an additional 17% of scheduled time

Examples: late starts, announcements, passing out of materials

Students not engaged in learning cost an additional 12% of total minutes

Examples: pencil sharpening, daydreaming, goofing off, assignments finished early

Students engaged in instructional activities 60% of total scheduled time

Source: Based on data from N. L. Karweit and R. E. Slavin, "Measurement and Modeling Choices in Studies of Time and Learning," *American Educational Research Journal, 18*(2).

of authority. However, even in these very good schools, the average student spent only 60 percent of the time scheduled for mathematics instruction actually learning mathematics. First of all, about 20 class days were lost to such activities as standardized testing, school events, field trips, and teacher absences. On days when instruction was given, class time was lost because of late starts and noninstructional activities such as discussions of upcoming events, announcements, passing out of materials, and disciplining of students. Finally, even when math was being taught, many students were not actually engaged in the instructional activity. Some were daydreaming during lecture or seatwork times, goofing off, or sharpening pencils; others had nothing to do, either because they were finished with their assigned work or because they had not yet been assigned a task. The 60 percent figure estimated by Karweit and Slavin is, if anything, a high estimate. In a much larger study, Weinstein and Mignano (1993) found that elementary school students spent only about one-third of their time engaged in learning tasks (see also Hong, 2001; Meek, 2003).

Available instructional time is called **allocated time,** the time during which students have an opportunity to learn. When you are lecturing, students can learn by paying attention. When students have written assignments or other tasks, they can learn by doing them. There are several ways that allocated time can be maximized (see Jones & Jones, 2010).

PREVENTING LOST TIME   One way that instructional time disappears is through losses of entire days or periods. Many of these losses are inevitable because of events such as standardized testing days and snow days, and we certainly would not want to abolish important field trips or school assemblies simply to get in a few more periods of instruction. However, frequent losses of instructional periods interrupt the flow of instruction and can ultimately deprive students of sufficient time to master the curriculum.

Making good use of all classroom time is less a matter of squeezing out a few more minutes or hours of instruction each year than of communicating to students that learning is an important business that is worth their time and effort. If you find excuses not to

allocated time

Time during which students have the opportunity to learn.

Frank Siteman

Teachers' time for instruction is limited by the amount of time used for routine management concerns such as taking attendance. As a teacher, how will you prevent loss of instruction time?

teach, students might learn that learning is not a serious enterprise. In studying an outstandingly effective inner-city Baltimore elementary school, Salganik (1980) describes a third-grade teacher who took her class to the school library, which she found locked. She sent a student for the key, and while the class waited, the teacher whispered to her students, "Let's work on our doubles. Nine plus nine? Six plus six?" The class whispered the answers back in unison. Did a couple of minutes working on addition facts increase the students' achievement? Of course not. But it probably did help to develop a perception that school is for learning, not for marking time.

PREVENTING LATE STARTS AND EARLY FINISHES   A surprising amount of allocated instructional time is lost because you may not start teaching at the beginning of the period. This can be a particular problem in self-contained elementary classes, in which there are no bells or fixed schedules to structure the period. It is also a problem in departmentalized secondary schools, where you might spend a long time dealing with late students or other problems before starting the lesson. A crisp, on-time start to a lesson is important for setting a purposive tone to instruction. If students know that you do not start on time, they might be lackadaisical about getting to class on time; this attitude makes future on-time starts increasingly difficult. In Ms. Cavalho's class, students know that if they are late, they will miss something interesting, fun, and important. As a result, almost all of them are in class and ready to learn when the bell rings.

You can also shortchange students by not teaching until the end of the period. This is less damaging than a ragged or late start but is still worth avoiding by planning more instruction than you think you'll need, in case you finish the lesson early.

PREVENTING INTERRUPTIONS   One important cause of lost allocated time for instruction is interruptions, which may be externally imposed, such as announcements or the need to sign forms sent from the principal's office, or may be caused by teachers or students themselves. Interruptions not only directly cut into the time for instruction but also break the momentum of the lesson, which reduces students' attention to the task at hand.

Avoiding interruptions takes planning. For example, some teachers put a "Do not disturb—learning in progress!" sign on the door to inform would-be interrupters to come back later. One teacher wore a special hat during small-group lessons to remind her other second-graders not to interrupt her during that time. Rather than signing forms or dealing with other "administrivia" at once, some teachers keep a box where students and others can put any forms for attention later while students are doing independent or group work or after the lesson is over.

Anything you can postpone doing until after a lesson should be postponed. For example, if you have started a lesson and a student walks in late, go on with the lesson and deal with the tardiness issue later.

HANDLING ROUTINE PROCEDURES   You can spend too much time on simple classroom routines. For example, some elementary teachers spend many minutes getting students ready for lunch or dismissal because they call students by name, one at a time. This is unnecessary. Early in the school year, many teachers establish a routine that only when the entire table (or row) is quiet and ready to go are students called to line up. Lining up for lunch then takes seconds, not minutes.

Other procedures should also become routine for students. They must know, for example, when they may go to the washroom or sharpen a pencil and not ask to do these things at other times. You may collect papers by having students pass them to the front or to the left or by having table monitors collect the table's papers. Distribution of materials must also be planned for. Exactly how these tasks are done is less important than that students know clearly what they are to do. Many teachers assign regular classroom helpers to take care of distribution and collection of papers, taking messages to the office, erasing the blackboard, and other routine tasks that are annoying interruptions for teachers but that students love to do. Use student power as much as possible.

MAINTAINING A RAPID PACE OF INSTRUCTION.   Research finds that students learn more from teachers who cover a lot of content in each lesson (Good & Brophy, 2008). A rapid pace also contributes to students' interest and time on task.

MINIMIZING TIME SPENT ON DISCIPLINE   Methods of disciplining students are discussed at length later in this chapter. However, one aspect of disciplining should be mentioned at this point. Whenever possible—which is almost always—disciplinary statements or actions should not interrupt the flow of the lesson. A sharp glance, silently moving close to an offending student, or a hand signal, such as putting finger to lips to remind a student to be silent, is usually effective for the kind of minor behavior problems that you must constantly deal with, and they allow the lesson to proceed without interruption. For example, Ms. Cavalho could have interrupted her lesson to scold Mark and Gloria, but that would have wasted time and disrupted the concentration and focus of the whole class. If students need talking to about discipline problems, the time to do it is after the lesson or after school, not in the middle of a lesson. If Diana and Martin are talking during a quiet reading time instead of working, it would be better to say, "Diana and Martin, see me at three o'clock," than to launch into an on-the-spot speech about the importance of being on task during seatwork times.

■ Using Engaged Time Effectively

Engaged time (or time on task) is the time individual students actually spend doing assigned work. It differs from allocated time, which refers to the opportunity for the entire class to engage in learning activities, because engaged time may be different for each student, depending on individual attentiveness and willingness to work. Strategies for maximizing student time on task are discussed in the following sections. Several studies have found teacher training programs based on principles presented in the following sections to increase student engagement and, in some cases, learning (Epstein, 2008; Good & Brophy, 2008; Jones & Jones, 2010).

TEACHING ENGAGING LESSONS   The best way to increase students' time on task is to teach lessons that are so interesting, engaging, and relevant to their interests that

Connections

For more information about the importance of time use and time management in effective teaching, see Chapter 9, page 252.

students will pay attention and eagerly do what is asked of them (Emmer & Evertson, 2009; Evertson et al., 2009; Weinstein & Mignano, 2003). Part of this strategy calls for you to emphasize active, rapidly paced instruction with varied modes of presentation and frequent opportunities for student participation and to deemphasize independent seatwork, especially unsupervised seatwork (as in follow-up time in elementary reading classes). Research has consistently shown that student engagement is much higher when you are teaching than during individual seatwork (Evertson & Harris, 1992). Engaged time is also much higher in well-structured cooperative learning programs than in independent seatwork (Slavin, 1990), and giving students many opportunities to participate actively in lessons is associated with greater learning as well (Finn & Cox, 1992),

MAINTAINING MOMENTUM   Maintaining momentum during a lesson is a key to keeping task engagement high. The term *momentum* refers to the avoidance of interruptions or slowdowns (Kounin, 1970). In a class that maintains good momentum, students always have something to do and, once started working, are not interrupted. Anyone who has tried to write a term paper only to be interrupted by telephone calls, knocks on the door, and other disturbances knows that these interruptions cause much more damage to concentration and progress than the amount of time they take.

Kounin (1970) gives the following example of teacher-caused slowdowns and interruptions:

> The teacher is just starting a reading group at the reading circle while the rest of the children are engaged in seatwork with workbooks. She sat in front of the reading group and asked, "All right, who can tell me the name of our next chapter?" Before a child was called on to answer, she looked toward the children at seatwork, saying: "Let's wait until the people in Group Two are settled and working." (Actually most were writing in their workbooks.) She then looked at John, who was in the seatwork group, naggingly asking, "Did you find your pencil?" John answered something which was inaudible. The teacher got up from her seat, saying, "I'd like to know what you did with it." Pause for about two seconds. "Did you eat it?" Another pause. "What happened to it? What color was it? You can't do your work without it." The teacher then went to her desk to get a pencil to give to John, saying, "I'll get you a pencil. Make sure the pencil is here tomorrow morning. And don't tell me you lost that one too. And make it a new one, and see that it's sharpened." (p. 104)

This teacher destroyed the momentum of a reading lesson by spending more than a minute dealing with a behavior that could easily have been ignored. Of course, during this interchange, the entire class—both the reading group and the seatwork group—were off task, but what is worse, they required much more time to get resettled and back to work after the incident.

Kounin found momentum to be strongly related to total time on task, and Brophy and Evertson (1976) and Anderson, Evertson, and Brophy (1979) found momentum to be related to student achievement.

MAINTAINING SMOOTHNESS OF INSTRUCTION   *Smoothness* is another term Kounin (1970) uses to refer to continued focus on a meaningful sequence of instruction. Smooth instruction avoids jumping without transitions from topic to topic or from the lesson to other activities, which produces "jarring breaks in the activity flow" (Kounin, 1970, p. 97), as in the following example.

> The teacher was conducting a recitation with a subgroup. She was walking toward a child who was reciting when she passed by the fish bowl. She suddenly stopped walking toward the boy, and stopped at the fish bowl, saying: "Oh my, I forgot to feed the fish!" She then got some fish food from a nearby shelf and started to feed the fish, saying: "My, see how hungry it is." She then turned to a girl, saying: "See, Margaret, you forgot to feed the fish. You can see how hungry it is. See how quickly it comes up to eat." (Kounin, 1970, pp. 98–99)

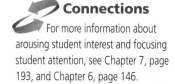

Connections

For more information about arousing student interest and focusing student attention, see Chapter 7, page 193, and Chapter 6, page 146.

Connections

For more information about active learning, see Chapter 8, page 234.

INTASC

4 Multiple Instructional Strategies

This example illustrates how smoothness and momentum are related. The teacher jumped from her lesson to housekeeping to (unnecessary) disciplining, interrupting one student's recitation and making it impossible for the other students to focus on the lesson. As with momentum, smoothness has been found to be strongly associated with student time on task (Kounin, 1970) and achievement (Anderson et al., 1979; Brophy & Evertson, 1976).

MANAGING TRANSITIONS   Transitions are changes from one activity to another—for example, from lecture to seatwork, from subject to subject, or from lesson to lunch. Elementary school classes have been found to average 31 major transitions a day, occupying 15 percent of class time (Burns, 1984). Transitions are the seams of class management at which classroom order is most likely to come apart; Anderson and colleagues (1979) and Evertson and colleagues (1980) found that teachers' efficiency at managing transitions between activities was positively related to their students' achievement.

Following are three rules for the management of transitions:

1. When making a transition, you should give a clear signal to which your students have been taught to respond. For example, in the elementary grades, some teachers use a bell or a hand signal to indicate to students that they should immediately be quiet and listen to instructions.

2. Before the transition is made, students must be certain about what they are to do when the signal is given. For example, you might say, "When I say 'Go,' I want you all to put your books away and get out the compositions you started yesterday. Is everyone ready? All right, go!" When giving instructions to students to begin independent seatwork, you can help them get started with the activity before letting them work independently, as in the following example:

> *Teacher:* Today we are going to find guide words for different pages in the dictionary. Everyone should have an assignment sheet with the words on it and a dictionary. Class, hold up your assignment sheet. [They do.] Now hold up your dictionary. [They do.] Good. Now turn to page 82. [The teacher walks around to see that everyone does so.] Look at the top of the page, and put your finger on the first guide word. [The teacher walks around to check on this.] Class, what is the first guide word?
>
> *Class:* Carrot!
>
> *Teacher:* Good. The first guide word is *carrot*. Now look to the right on the same page. Class, what word do you see there?
>
> *Class:* Carve!
>
> *Teacher:* Right. The guide words are *carrot* and *carve*. Now turn to page 555 and find the guide words. [Students do this.] Class, what is the first guide word on 555?
>
> *Class:* Scheme!
>
> *Teacher:* Class, what is the second guide word?
>
> *Class:* Scissors!
>
> *Teacher:* Great! Now do the first problem on your assignment sheet by yourselves, and then check with a partner to see if you agree.

The teacher will then check whether all or almost all students have the first item correct before telling them to complete the worksheet. The idea, of course, is to make sure that students know exactly what they are to do before they start doing it.

3. Make transitions all at once. Students should be trained to make transitions as a group, rather than one student at a time (Charles, 2008). You should give directions to

Certification Pointer

You may be asked on your teacher certification test to discuss why it is important for a teacher to plan carefully for transitions and describe what can happen if transitions are not implemented with care.

the class as a whole or to well-defined groups: "Class, I want you all to put away your laboratory materials and prepare for dismissal as quickly and quietly as you can. . . . I see that Table Three is quiet and ready. Table Three, please line up quietly. Table Six, line up. Table One . . . Table Four. Everyone else may line up quietly. Let's go!"

MAINTAINING GROUP FOCUS DURING LESSONS   Maintaining group focus means using classroom organization strategies and questioning techniques to ensure that all students in the class stay involved in the lesson, even when only one student is called on by the teacher. Two principal components of Kounin's concept of maintaining group focus were found to be significantly related to students' on-task behavior: accountability and group alerting.

Kounin (1970) uses the term **accountability** to mean "the degree to which the teacher holds the children accountable and responsible for their task performances during recitation sessions" (p. 119). Examples of tactics for increasing accountability are using choral responses, having all students hold up their work so you can see it, circulating among the students to see what they are doing, and drawing other children into the performance of one child (e.g., "I want you all to watch what Suzanne is doing so you can tell me whether you agree or disagree with her answer"). Ms. Cavalho increased involvement and accountability by having all students prepare a Hemingway-like description and only then asking for a few of them to be read.

The idea behind these tactics is to maintain the involvement of all students in all parts of the lesson. A study of third- and fourth-graders found that students raised their hands an average of once every 6 minutes and gave an answer only once every 15 minutes, with some students hardly ever participating (Potter, 1977). This is not enough participation to ensure student attention. You should be concerned not only about drawing all students into class activities but also about avoiding activities that relegate most students to the role of spectator for long periods. For example, a very common teaching error is for one or two students to work out a lengthy problem on the chalkboard or electronic whiteboard or read an extended passage while the rest of the class has nothing to do. Such methods waste the time of much of the class, break the momentum of the lesson, and leave the door open for misbehavior (Gump, 1982).

Group alerting refers to questioning strategies that are designed to keep all students on their toes during a lecture or discussion. One example of group alerting is creating suspense before calling on a student by saying, "Given triangle *ABC,* if we know the measures of sides *A* and *B* and of angle *AB,* what else can we find out about the triangle? . . . [Pause] . . . Maria?" Note that this keeps the whole class thinking until Maria's name is called. The opposite effect would have been created by saying, "Maria, given triangle *ABC* . . . ," because only Maria would have been alerted. Calling on students in a random order is another example of group alerting, as is letting students know that they may be asked questions about the preceding reciter's answers. For example, you might follow up Maria's answer with "What is the name of the postulate that Maria used? . . . Ralph?"

MAINTAINING GROUP FOCUS DURING SEATWORK   When students are doing seatwork and you are available to work with them, it is important to monitor activities and to informally check individual students' work. That is, you should circulate among your students' desks to see how they are doing. This allows you to identify any problems students are having before they waste seatwork time practicing errors or giving up in frustration. If students are engaged in cooperative groupwork, students can check each other's work, but you still need to check frequently with each group to see that students are on the right track.

Seatwork times are excellent opportunities for providing individual help to students who are struggling to keep up with the class, but you should resist the temptation to work too long with an individual student. Interactions with students during seatwork

accountability

The degree to which people are held responsible for their task performances or decision outcomes.

group alerting

Questioning strategies that encourage all students to pay attention during lectures and discussions.

should be as brief as possible because if you get tied down with any one student, the rest of the class may drift off task or run into problems of their own.

WITHITNESS   Another term coined by Kounin (1970), **withitness** describes teachers' actions that indicate awareness of students' behavior at all times. Kounin calls this awareness "having eyes in the back of one's head." Teachers who are with-it can respond immediately to student misbehavior and know who started what. Teachers who lack withitness can make the error of scolding the wrong student, as in the following instance:

> Lucy and John, who were sitting at the same table as Jane, started to whisper. Robert watched this, and he too got into the act. Then Jane giggled and said something to John. Then Mary leaned over and whispered to Jane. At this point, the teacher said, "Mary and Jane, stop that!" (adapted from Kounin, 1970, p. 80)

By responding only to Mary and Jane, who were the last to get involved in the whispering and giggling incident, the teacher indicated that she did not know what was going on. A single incident of this kind might make little difference, but after many such incidents, students recognize the teacher's tendency to respond inappropriately to their behavior.

Another example of a lack of withitness is responding too late to a sequence of misbehavior. Lucy and John's whispering could have been easily nipped in the bud, perhaps with simply a glance or a finger to the lips. By the time the whispering had escalated to giggling and spread to several students, a full stop in the lesson was needed to rectify the situation.

A major component of withitness is scanning the class frequently and establishing eye contact with individual students. Several studies have found that more effective classroom managers frequently scan the classroom visually, monitoring the pace of activity as well as individual students' behaviors (Brooks, 1985; Evertson & Emmer, 1982). Effective classroom managers have the ability to interpret and act on the mood of the class as a whole. They notice when students are beginning to fidget or are otherwise showing signs of flagging attention, and they act on this information to change activities to recapture student engagement (Levin & Nolan, 2010).

OVERLAPPING   A teacher's ability to attend to interruptions or behavior problems while continuing a lesson or other instructional activity is known as **overlapping.** For example, while teaching a lesson on reading comprehension, a teacher sees a student looking at a book unrelated to the lesson. Without interrupting his lesson, the teacher walks over to the student, takes her book, closes it, and puts it on her desk, all while continuing to speak to the class. This takes care of the student's misbehavior without slowing the momentum of the lesson, and the rest of the class hardly notices that the event occurred. Similarly, Ms. Cavalho squelched a whispering incident just by moving closer to the whispering students while continuing her lesson. The following incident shows another example of a teacher doing a good job of overlapping.

> The teacher is at the reading circle and Lucy is reading aloud while standing. Johnny, who was doing seatwork at his desk, walks up toward the teacher, holding his workbook. The teacher glances at Johnny, then looks back at Lucy, nodding at Lucy, as Lucy continues to read aloud. The teacher remains seated and takes Johnny's workbook. She turns to Lucy, saying, "That was a hard word, Lucy, and you pronounced it right." She checks about three more answers in Johnny's book saying, "That's fine, you can go ahead and do the next page now," and resumes looking at the reading book as Lucy continues reading. (Kounin, 1970, p. 84)

Johnny's interruption of the reading group might have been avoided altogether by a good classroom manager, who would have assigned enough work to keep all students

Certification Pointer

For your teacher certification test, you may be asked to make suggestions for helping students stay on task in a particular case.

withitness

The degree to which the teacher is aware of and responsive to student behavior at all times.

overlapping

A teacher's ability to respond to behavior problems without interrupting a classroom lesson productively busy during reading circle time and given clear instructions on what they were to do when they finished their seatwork. For example, Johnny's work could have been checked by a partner or teammate. However, interruptions are sometimes unavoidable, and the ability to keep the main activity going while handling them is strongly related to overall classroom order (Copeland, 1983; Kounin, 1970) and to achievement (Anderson et al., 1979; Brophy & Evertson, 1976).

■ Overdoing Time On Task

A class that is rarely on task is certainly not a well-managed class. However, it is possible to go too far in the other direction, emphasizing time on task to the exclusion of all other considerations. For example, in a study of time on task in elementary mathematics, one teacher's class was found to be engaged essentially 100 percent of the time. The teacher accomplished this by walking up and down the rows of desks looking for the slightest flicker of inattention. This class learned very little math over the course of the year. An overemphasis on engaged time rather than on engaging instruction can produce what Bloome, Puro, and Theodorou (1989) called **mock participation,** in which students appear to be on task but are not really engaged in learning.

Several studies have found that increasing time on task in classrooms where students were already reasonably well behaved did not increase student achievement (Blackadar & Nachtigal, 1986; Slavin, 1986; Stallings & Krasavage, 1986). An overemphasis on time on task can be detrimental to learning in several ways. For example, complex tasks involving creativity and uncertainty tend to produce lower levels of time on task than do simple cut-and-dried tasks (Evertson & Randolph, 1995; Weinstein & Mignano, 2003). Yet it would clearly be a poor instructional strategy to avoid complex or uncertain tasks just to keep time on task high. Maintaining classroom order is an important goal of teaching, but it is only one of many (see Charles, 2008; Levin & Nolan, 2010).

■ Classroom Management in the Student-Centered Classroom

It is important to note that most research on classroom management has taken place in traditionally organized classrooms, in which students have few choices as to what they do and few interactions with each other. In more student-centered classrooms, children are likely to be spending much of their time working with each other, doing open-ended projects, writing, and experimenting. Evertson and Randolph (1995) have discussed the shift that must take place in thinking about classroom management for such classrooms. Clearly, classroom management is more participatory in a student-centered classroom, with students fundamentally involved in setting standards of behavior. Equally clearly, the type of behavior to be expected will be different. It is impossible to imagine a student-centered classroom that is silent, for example. Yet in other respects the requirements for managing student-centered classrooms are not so different from those of traditional ones. Rules are still needed and must be consistently communicated to students and consistently enforced (Freiberg, Connell, & Lorentz, 2001; Freiberg & Lamb, 2009). If students in student-centered classrooms are deeply involved and motivated by the variety, activity, and social nature of classroom activities, then disciplinary actions will be less necessary (Weinstein & Mignano, 2003). Inevitably, however, certain students' misbehavior will disrupt others' learning, and you must have strategies to help students live up to norms to which all members of the class have agreed.

The following sections describe strategies for preventing misbehavior in any classroom context and responding effectively to misbehavior when it does occur.

mock participation

Situation in which students appear to be on task but are not engaged in learning.

What Practices Contribute to Effective Classroom Management?

Research has consistently shown that basic commonsense planning and groundwork go a long way toward preventing discipline problems from ever developing. Simple measures include starting the year properly, arranging the classroom for effective instruction, setting class rules and procedures, and making expectations of conduct clear to students (Marzano, 2003). Further, establishing caring connections between teachers and students helps establish a cooperative tone in the classroom that reduces discipline problems (Crowe, 2008; Freiberg & Lamb, 2009; McNeely, Nonnemaker, & Blum, et al., 2002; Osher & Fleishman, 2005).

Different grade levels and student groups present different management concerns. For instance, with younger students, teachers need to be concerned about socializing students to the norms and behaviors that are expected in school (Epstein, 2008; Evertson, Emmer, & Worsham, 2009; Weinstein & Mignano, 2003). Programs focusing on establishing consistent schoolwide behavior expectations and on building positive relationships and school success through the use of cooperative learning have been effective in improving the behavior of elementary school children (Freiberg et al., 2001; O'Donnell, Hawkins, Catalano, Abbott, & Day, 1995).

In middle school and high school, students can grasp the principles that underlie rules and procedures and can rationally agree to observe them (Emmer & Evertson, 2009; Evertson et al., 2009; Weinstein, 2003). At the same time, some adolescents resist authority and place greater importance on peer norms. Aggressive behavior, truancy, and delinquency also increase as students enter adolescence. In the upper grades, departmentalization, tracking, and class promotion might become management issues, especially with students who have established patterns of learned helplessness or academic failure. Teachers of older students need to be more concerned with motivating them toward more self-regulation in observing rules and procedures and in learning the course material. Programs that increase the clarity of rules, consistency of rule enforcement, and frequency of communication with the home have been very effective in improving adolescents' behavior (Gottfredson, Gottfredson, & Hybl, 1993).

INTASC

7 Instructional Planning Skills

The relationship you establish with your students will set the tone for learning in your classroom. What do you anticipate being the biggest challenge to establishing a productive classroom?

Rob Marmion/Shutterstock

■ Starting Out the Year Right

Emmer, Evertson, and Anderson (1980) and Evertson and Emmer (1982) studied teachers' actions at the beginning of the school year and correlated them with students' behaviors later in the year. They found that the first days of school are critical in establishing classroom order. They compared teachers whose classes were mostly on task over the course of the school year with teachers whose classes were less consistently on task and found that the better classroom managers engage in the following activities during the first days of school significantly more often than do the less effective managers (Evertson et al., 2009; see also Wong & Wong, 2004).

1. More-effective managers have a clear, specific plan for introducing students to classroom rules and procedures and spend as many days as necessary carrying out their plan until students know how to line up, ask for help, and so on.

2. More-effective managers work with the whole class initially (even if they plan to group students later). They remain involved with the whole class at all times, rarely leaving any students without something to do or without supervision. For example, more-effective managers seldom work with an individual student unless the rest of the class is productively occupied (Doyle, 1984; Sanford & Evertson, 1981).

3. More-effective managers spend extra time during the first days of school introducing procedures and discussing class rules (often encouraging students to suggest rules themselves). These teachers usually remind students of class rules every day for at least the first week of school (Weinstein & Mignano, 2003).

4. More-effective managers teach students specific procedures. For example, some have students practice lining up quickly and quietly; others teach students to respond to a signal, such as a bell, a flick of the light switch, or a call for attention.

5. More-effective managers use simple, enjoyable tasks as first activities. Materials for the first lessons are well prepared, clearly presented, and varied. These teachers ask students to get right to work on the first day of school and give them instructions on procedures gradually, to avoid overloading them with too much information at a time.

6. More-effective managers respond immediately to stop any misbehavior.

■ Setting Class Rules

One of the first management-related tasks at the start of the year is setting class rules. Three principles govern this process. First, class rules should be few in number. Second, they should make sense and be seen as fair by students. Third, they should be clearly explained and deliberately taught to students (Metzger, 2002). A major purpose of clearly explaining general class rules is to give a moral authority for specific procedures (Kagan, Kyle, & Scott, 2004). For example, all students will understand and support a rule such as "Respect others' property." This simple rule can be invoked to cover such obvious misbehaviors as stealing or destroying materials but also gives a reason for putting materials away, cleaning up litter, and refraining from marking up textbooks. Students may be asked to help set the rules, or they may be given a set of rules and asked to give examples of these rules. Class discussions give students a feeling of participation in setting rational rules that everyone can live by (Gathercoal, 2001; Strout, 2005). When the class as a whole has agreed on a set of rules, offenders know that they are transgressing community norms, not the teacher's arbitrary regulations, as in the following all-purpose set of class rules.

1. *Be courteous to others.*   This rule forbids interrupting others or speaking out of turn, teasing or laughing at others, bullying, fighting, and so on.

2. *Respect others' property.*

3. *Be on task.*   This includes listening when the teacher or other students are talking, working on seatwork, continuing to work during any interruptions, staying in one's seat, being at one's seat and ready to work when the bell rings, and following directions.

4. *Raise hands to be recognized.*   This is a rule against calling out or getting out of one's seat for assistance without permission.

21ST Century Learning

Effective Use of Time

New technologies are making it easier for teachers to create productive learning environments. In addition to adding intrinsic motivation through use of brief videos, interactive devices, and other means of making lessons fun and engaging, it is now becoming possible to use electronic response devices to constantly obtain feedback on students' levels of learning, so that you can target lessons to the exact needs of your students, and students can immediately see their own levels of learning. Using these devices, all students can quickly answer a question or enter an opinion at the same time. You can display the answers or the percentage of answers that were correct on a chart or graph to display to the class. You can immediately find out what students know or what they

are thinking, so you can adjust your lessons in light of student learning. Students know that their knowledge will always be assessed, instead of hoping that someone else will be called on. These and other technologies can focus classroom activities on the most productive content and tasks and motivate students to pay attention and work enthusiastically individually and in groups.

Question

■ Think of as many ways as possible of using electronic response devices in teaching students at the age level and subject you expect to teach. Which of these seem most and least likely to increase learning?

What Are Some Strategies for Managing Routine Misbehavior?

The preceding sections of this chapter discussed means of organizing classroom activities to maximize time for instruction and minimize time for such minor disturbances as students talking out of turn, getting out of their seats without permission, and not paying attention. Interesting lessons, efficient use of class time, and careful structuring of instructional activities will prevent most such minor behavior problems—and many more serious ones as well (Barr & Parrett, 2001; Freiberg & Lapointe, 2006). For example, Kounin (1970) found that teacher behaviors associated with high time on task are also associated with fewer serious behavior problems. Time off task can lead to more serious problems; many behavior issues arise because students are frustrated or bored in school. Instructional programs that actively involve students and provide all of them with opportunities for success can help prevent such problems.

However, effective lessons and good use of class time are not the only means of preventing or dealing with inappropriate behavior. Besides structuring classes to reduce the frequency of misconduct, teachers must have strategies for dealing with such problems when they do occur (Emmer & Stough, 2001).

The great majority of behavior problems with which a teacher must deal are relatively minor disruptions, such as failing to follow class rules or procedures—nothing really serious, but behaviors that must be minimized for learning to occur. Before considering disciplinary strategies, it is important to reflect on their purpose. Students should learn much more in school than the "three Rs." They should learn that they are competent learners and that learning is enjoyable and satisfying. A classroom environment that is warm, supportive, and accepting fosters these attitudes (Fay, 2001). Furthermore, there is a strong link between attentive, nondisruptive behavior and student achievement (Finn, Pannozzo, & Voelkl, 1995; Wentzel, 1993).

A healthy classroom environment cannot be created if students do not respect teachers or teachers do not respect students. Though you should involve students in setting class rules and take student needs or input into account in organizing the classroom, you are ultimately the leader who establishes and enforces rules by which students must live. These class rules and procedures should become second nature to students. If you have not established your authority in the classroom, you are likely to spend too much time dealing with behavior problems or yelling at students to be instructionally effective. Furthermore, the clearer the structure and routine procedures in the classroom, the more freedom you can allow students. The following sections discuss strategies for dealing with typical discipline problems.

■ The Principle of Least Intervention

In dealing with routine classroom behavior problems, the most important principle is that you should correct misbehaviors by using the simplest intervention that will work (Gathercoal, 2001; Kyle & Rogien, 2004). Many studies have found that the amount of time spent disciplining students is negatively related to student achievement (Crocker & Brooker, 1986; Evertson et al., 1980). Your main goal in dealing with routine misbehavior is to do so in a way that is both effective and avoids unnecessarily disrupting the lesson (Charles, 2008; Evertson et al., 2009; Jones & Jones, 2010). If at all possible, the lesson must go on while any behavior problems are dealt with. A continuum of strategies for dealing with minor misbehaviors, from least disruptive to most, is listed in Table 11.1 and discussed in the following sections.

■ Prevention

The easiest behavior problems to deal with are those that never occur in the first place. As illustrated earlier in this chapter, teachers can prevent behavior problems by presenting interesting and lively lessons, making class rules and procedures clear, keeping students busy on meaningful tasks, and using other effective techniques of basic classroom

TABLE 11.1	**Principle of Least Intervention**	
Step	**Procedure**	**Example**
1	Prevention	Teacher displays enthusiasm, varies activities, keeps students interested.
2	Nonverbal cues	Tanya turns in paper late: teacher frowns.
3	Praise of correct behavior that is incompatible with misbehavior	"Tanya, I hear you completed your science fair project on time for the judging. That's great!"
4	Praise for other students	"I see most of you turned your papers in on time today. I really appreciate that."
5	Verbal reminders	"Tanya, please turn in your next paper on time."
6	Repeated reminders	"Tanya, it's important to turn your paper in on time."
7	Consequences	Tanya spends 10 minutes after class starting on the next paper assignment.

management (Colvin, 2004; Fay, 2001; Jones & Jones, 2010; Levin & Nolan, 2010). Ms. Cavalho's class is an excellent example of this. Her students rarely misbehave because they are interested and engaged.

Varying the content of lessons, using a variety of materials and approaches, displaying humor and enthusiasm, and instituting cooperative learning or project-based learning can all reduce boredom-caused behavior problems. You can avert frustration caused by material that is too difficult or assignments that are unrealistically long by breaking assignments into smaller steps and doing a better job of preparing students to work on their own. Fatigue can be reduced if short breaks are allowed, activities are varied, and difficult subjects are scheduled in the morning, when students are fresh.

Theory into Practice
Consistency Management and Cooperative Discipline

One of the most extensively evaluated schoolwide approaches to classroom management is Consistency Management and Cooperative Discipline (Freiberg, Huzinec, & Templeton, 2009; Freiberg & Lapointe, 2006; Freiberg et al., 2001). CMCD focuses on preventing behavior problems by engaging all students in leadership roles within the class, using timers to ensure that transitional activities are quickly dealt with, and establishing predictable routines. Students have opportunities to share opinions and resolve disputes in classroom meetings. Teachers randomly draw students' names on popsicle sticks to ensure fairness in questioning during lessons. Several studies of CMCD have found that the program not only improves students' behaviors but also their learning of reading and math skills (Freiberg et al., 2009; Freiberg et al., 2001).

ON THE WEB

To learn more about classroom management, go to the Teacher Talk Forum on the Center for Adolescent and Family Studies website, www.indiana.edu/~cafs. Also check out the website of the Center for the Prevention of School Violence, www.ncdjjdp.org/cpsv. To see a teacher-created website, go to www.theteachersguide.com/ClassManagement.htm. Also see www.education-world.com/a_curr/archives/classmanagement.shtml. Information for new and future teachers can be seen at www.adprima.com/managing.htm and www.nea.org/tools/ClassroomManagement.html.

■ Nonverbal Cues

INTASC

6 Communication Skills

nonverbal cues

Eye contact, gestures, physical proximity, or touching that a teacher uses to communicate without interrupting verbal discourse.

You can eliminate much routine classroom misbehavior without breaking the momentum of the lesson by using simple **nonverbal cues** (Levin & Nolan, 2007). Making eye contact with a misbehaving student might be enough to stop misbehavior. For example, if two students are whispering, you might simply catch the eye of one or both of them. Moving close to a student who is misbehaving also usually alerts the student to shape up. If these techniques fail, a light hand on the student's shoulder is likely to be effective (although touch should be used cautiously with adolescents, who may be sensitive about being touched). These nonverbal strategies all clearly convey the same message: "I see what you are doing and don't like it. Please get back to work." The advantage of communicating this message nonverbally is that the lesson need not be interrupted. In contrast, verbal reprimands can cause a ripple effect; many students stop working while one is being reprimanded (Kounin, 1970). Instead of interrupting the flow of concentration for many to deal with the behavior of one, nonverbal cues usually have an effect only on the student who is misbehaving, as illustrated earlier in this chapter by the example of the teacher who continues his lesson while silently closing and putting away a book one student is reading. That student is the only one in the class who pays much attention to the whole episode.

■ Praising Behavior That Is Incompatible with Misbehavior

Praise can be a powerful motivator for many students. One strategy for reducing misbehavior in class is to make sure to praise students for behaviors that are incompatible with the misbehavior you want to reduce. That is, catch students in the act of doing right. For example, if students often get out of their seats without permission, praise them on the occasions when they do get to work right away.

■ Praising Other Students

It is often possible to get one student to behave by praising others for behaving. For example, if Polly is goofing off, you might say, "I'm glad to see so many students working so well—Jake is doing a good job, Carol is doing well, and José and Michelle are also working nicely." When Polly finally does get to work, you should praise her, too, without dwelling on her past inattention: "I see James and Walter and Polly doing such good work."

■ Verbal Reminders

If a nonverbal cue is impossible or ineffective, a simple verbal reminder might help to bring a student into line. The reminder should be given immediately after the student misbehaves; delayed reminders are usually ineffective. If possible, the reminder should state what students are supposed to be doing rather than dwelling on what they are doing wrong. For example, it is better to say, "John, please attend to your own work" than "John, stop copying off of Alfredo's paper." Stating the reminder positively communicates more positive expectations for future behavior than does a negative statement (Evertson, Emmer, & Worsham, 2006). Also, the reminder should focus on the behavior, not on the student. Although a particular student behavior may be intolerable, the student himself or herself is always accepted and welcome in the classroom.

■ Repeated Reminders

Most often a nonverbal cue, reinforcement of other students, or a simple reminder will be enough to end minor misbehavior. However, sometimes students test your resolve by failing to do what has been asked of them or by arguing or giving excuses. This testing will diminish over time if students learn that you mean what you say and will use appropriate measures to enforce an orderly, productive classroom environment.

When a student refuses to comply with a simple reminder, one strategy to attempt first is a repetition of the reminder, ignoring any irrelevant excuse or argument. Canter and Canter (2002) call this strategy the *broken record*. If a student has a legitimate issue to discuss, you might deal with it, but all too often students' arguments or excuses are nothing more than a means of drawing out an interaction with you to avoid getting down to work (see Walker, Ramsey, & Gresham, 2003a,b). Recall, for example, how Ms. Cavalho refused to be drawn into a discussion of Gloria's lateness when it was Mark's behavior that was at issue.

■ Applying Consequences

When all previous steps have been ineffective in getting the student to comply with a clearly stated and reasonable request, the final step is to pose a choice to the student: Either comply or suffer the consequences (Axelrod & Mathews, 2003; Colvin, 2004). Examples of consequences are sending the student out of class, making the student miss a few minutes of recess or some other privilege, keeping the student after school, or calling the student's parents. A consequence for not complying with the teacher's request should be mildly unpleasant, short in duration, and applied as soon as possible after the behavior occurs. Certainty is far more important than severity; students must know that consequences follow misbehavior as night follows day. One disadvantage of using severe or long-lasting punishment (e.g., no recess for a week) is that it can create resentment in the student and a defiant attitude. Also, it might be difficult to follow through on severe or long-lasting consequences. Mild but certain consequences communicate, "I cannot tolerate that sort of behavior, but I care about you and want you to rejoin the class as soon as you are ready."

Before presenting a student with a consequence for noncompliance, you must be absolutely certain you can and will follow through if necessary. When you say, "You may choose to get to work right away, or you may choose to spend 5 minutes of your recess doing your work here," you must be certain that someone will be available to monitor the student in the classroom during recess. Vague or empty threats ("You stop that or I'll make you wish you had!" or "You get to work or I'll have you suspended for a month!") are worse than useless. If you are not prepared to follow through with consequences, students will learn to shrug them off.

After a consequence has been applied, you should avoid referring to the incident. For example, when the student returns from a 10-minute exclusion from class, you should accept her or him back without any sarcasm or recriminations. The student now deserves a fresh start.

How Is Applied Behavior Analysis Used to Manage More Serious Behavior Problems ?

The previous section discussed how to deal with behaviors that might be appropriate on the playing field but are out of line in the classroom. Some other behaviors are not appropriate anywhere, including fighting, stealing, destruction of property, and gross disrespect for teachers or other school staff. These are far less common than routine classroom misbehavior but far more serious. Behavioral learning theories, described in Chapter 5, have direct application to effective responses to serious misbehavior. Simply put, behavioral learning theories hold that behaviors that are not reinforced or are punished will diminish in frequency. The following sections present **applied behavior analysis,** an analysis of classroom behavior in terms of behavioral concepts, and give specific strategies for preventing and dealing with misbehavior (Alberto & Troutman, 2009; Malott, 2008).

> **ON THE WEB**
>
> For articles on applied behavior analysis, visit the website for the Cambridge Center for Behavioral Studies at www.behavior.org and click on About Behavior Analysis.

applied behavior analysis

The application of behavioral learning principles to understanding and changing behavior.

■ How Student Misbehavior Is Maintained

A basic principle of behavioral learning theories is that if any behavior persists over time, it is being maintained by some reinforcer. To reduce misbehavior in the classroom, we must understand which reinforcers maintain misbehavior in the first place (Chandler & Dahlquist, 2006; Epstein, 2008; Kauffman, Mostert, Trent, & Pullen, 2006).

The most common reinforcer for classroom misbehavior is attention—from the teacher, the peer group, or both. Students receiving one-to-one tutoring rarely misbehave, both because they already have the undivided attention of an adult and because no classmates are present to attend to any negative behavior. In the typical classroom, however, students have to go out of their way to get the teacher's personal attention, and they have an audience of peers who might encourage or applaud their misdeeds.

TEACHER'S ATTENTION

Sometimes students misbehave because they want the teacher's attention, even if it is negative. This is a more common reason for misbehavior than many teachers think. A puzzled teacher might say, "I don't know what is wrong with Nathan. I have to stay with him all day to keep him working! Sometimes I get exasperated and yell at him. My words fall off him like water off a duck's back. He even smiles when I'm scolding him!"

When students appear to misbehave to gain your attention, the solution is relatively easy: Pay attention to these students when they are doing well, and ignore them (as much as possible) when they misbehave. When ignoring their actions is impossible, imposing time out (e.g., sending these students to a quiet corner or to the principal's office) might be effective.

PEERS' ATTENTION

Another very common reason that students misbehave is to get the attention and approval of their peers. The classic instance of this is the class clown, who is obviously performing for the amusement of his or her classmates. However, many other forms of misbehavior are motivated primarily by peer attention and approval—in fact, few students completely disregard the potential impact of their behavior on their classmates. For example, students who refuse to do what you ask are consciously or unconsciously weighing the effect of their defiance on their standing among classmates (Hartup, 2005).

Even preschoolers and early elementary school students misbehave to gain peer attention, but beginning around the third grade (and especially during the middle and high school years), it is particularly likely that student misbehavior is linked to peer attention and support. As students enter adolescence, the peer group takes on extreme importance, and peer norms begin to favor independence from authority. When older children and teenagers engage in serious delinquent acts (such as vandalism, theft, and assault), they are usually supported by a delinquent peer group.

Strategies for reducing peer-supported misbehavior are quite different from those for dealing with misbehavior that is meant to capture the teacher's attention. Ignoring misbehavior will be ineffective if the misbehavior is reinforced by peers. For example, if a student is balancing a book on his head and the class is laughing, the behavior can hardly be ignored because it will continue as long as the class is interested (and will encourage others to behave likewise). Furthermore, scolding might only attract more attention from classmates or, worse, enhance the student's standing among peers. Similarly, if two students are whispering or talking to each other, they are reinforcing each other for misbehaving, and ignoring their behavior will only encourage more of it.

The two primary responses to peer-supported misbehavior, if simple reminders (such as moving close to the student) are not working, are to remove the offender from

Bob Daemmrich Photography

Some students misbehave to get attention from their peers. Which responses to peer-supported misbehavior will you use in the classroom?

Connections

For more information about behavioral theory, see Chapter 5, page 117.

INTASC

4 Multiple Instructional Strategies

the classroom to deprive her of peer attention or to use **group contingencies,** strategies in which the entire class (or groups of students within the class) is rewarded on the basis of everyone's behavior. Under group contingencies, all students benefit from their classmates' good behavior, so peer support for misbehavior is removed. Group contingencies and other behavior management strategies for peer-supported misbehavior are described in more detail in the following sections.

RELEASE FROM UNPLEASANT STATES OR ACTIVITIES   A third important reinforcer for misbehavior is release from boredom, frustration, fatigue, or unpleasant activities. As was explained in Chapter 5, escaping from or avoiding an unpleasant stimulus is a reinforcer. Some students see much of what happens in school as unpleasant, boring, frustrating, or tiring. This is particularly true of students who experience repeated failure in school. But even the most able and motivated students feel bored or frustrated at times. Students often misbehave simply to escape from unpleasant activities. This can be clearly seen with students who frequently ask permission to get a drink of water, go to the washroom, or sharpen their pencils. Such students are more likely to make these requests during independent seatwork than during cooperative learning activities or even a lecture because seatwork can be frustrating or anxiety provoking for students who have little confidence in their academic abilities. More serious misbehaviors can also be partially or completely motivated by a desire for release from boredom, frustration, or fatigue. A student might misbehave just to stir things up. Sometimes students misbehave precisely so that they will be sent out of the classroom. Obviously, sending such a student to the hall or the principal's office can be counterproductive.

The best solution for misbehaviors arising from boredom, frustration, or fatigue is prevention. Students rarely misbehave during interesting, varied, engaging lessons. Actively involving students in lessons can head off misbehaviors that are the result of boredom or fatigue. Use of cooperative learning methods or other means of involving students in an active way can be helpful. You can prevent frustration by using materials that ensure a high success rate for all, thus making sure that all students are challenged but none are overwhelmed. Changing instruction and assessments to help students succeed can be an effective means of resolving frustration-related behavior problems.

■ Principles of Applied Behavior Analysis

The behavior management strategies outlined earlier (e.g., nonverbal cues, reminders, mild but certain punishment) might be described as informal applications of behavioral learning theories. These practices, plus the prevention of misbehavior by the use of efficient class management and engaging lessons, will be sufficient to create a good learning environment in most classrooms.

However, more systematic methods are sometimes needed. In classrooms in which most students are well behaved but a few have persistent behavior problems, individual behavior management strategies can be effective. In classrooms in which many students have behavior problems, particularly when there is peer support for misbehavior, whole-class strategies or group contingencies might be needed. Such strategies are most often required when many low-achieving students or students who lack motivation are put in one class, as often happens in special-education classes and in schools that use tracking or other between-class ability grouping methods.

Setting up and using any applied behavior analysis program requires following a series of steps proceeding from the observation of the behavior through program implementation to program evaluation (see Alberto & Troutman, 2009; Jones & Jones, 2010; Malott, 2008; Walker, Colvin, & Ramsey, 2003). The steps listed here are, to a greater or lesser extent, part of all applied behavior analysis programs:

1. Identify target behavior(s) and reinforcer(s).
2. Establish a baseline for the target behavior.

Connections

For more information about the problems of tracking, see Chapter 9, pages 253–256.

group contingencies

Class rewards that depend on the behavior of all students.

3. Choose a reinforcer and criteria for reinforcement.

4. If necessary, choose a punisher and criteria for punishment.

5. Observe behavior during program implementation, and compare it to baseline.

6. When the behavior management program is working, reduce the frequency of reinforcement.

Individual behavior management strategies are useful for coping with individual students who have persistent behavior problems in school. **Behavior modification** is a systematic application of antecedents and consequences to change behavior (Alberto & Troutman, 2009; Malott, 2008; Walker, Shea, & Bauer, 2007).

IDENTIFY TARGET BEHAVIORS AND REINFORCERS   The first step in implementing a behavior management program is to observe the misbehaving student: Identify one behavior or a small number of behaviors to target first and see which reinforcers maintain the behavior(s). Another purpose of this observation is to establish a baseline against which to compare improvements. A structured individual behavior management program should aim to change only one behavior or a small set of closely related behaviors. Tackling too many behaviors at a time risks failure with all of them because the student might not clearly see what he or she must do to be reinforced.

The first behavior targeted should be one that is serious, easy to observe, and most important, occurs frequently. For example, if a child gets into fights on the playground every few days but gets out of his or her seat without permission several times per hour, you might start with the out-of-seat behavior and deal with the fighting later. Ironically, the more frequent and persistent a behavior, the easier it is to extinguish. This is because positive or negative consequences can be applied frequently, making the connection between behavior and consequence clear to the student.

In observing a student, try to determine what reinforcer(s) are maintaining the target behavior. If a student misbehaves with others (e.g., talks without permission, swears, or teases) or if a student's misbehavior usually attracts the attention of others (e.g., clowning), then you might guess that the behavior is peer supported. If the behavior does not attract much peer attention but always requires teacher attention (e.g., getting out of seat without permission), then you might guess that the behavior is supported by your own attention.

ESTABLISH BASELINE BEHAVIOR   Observe the student to see how often the target behavior occurs. Before you do this, you will need to clearly define exactly what constitutes the behavior. For example, if the target behavior is "bothering classmates," you will have to decide what specific behaviors constitute "bothering" (perhaps teasing, interrupting, and taking materials).

SELECT REINFORCERS AND CRITERIA FOR REINFORCEMENT   Typical classroom reinforcers include praise, privileges, and tangible rewards. Praise is especially effective for students who misbehave to get your attention. It is often a good idea to start a behavior management program by using attention and praise for appropriate behavior to see whether this is sufficient. However, be prepared to use stronger reinforcers if praise is not enough (see Alberto & Troutman, 2009; Walker et al., 2007). In addition to praise, you may find it useful to give stars, "smilies," or other small rewards when students behave appropriately. Some teachers use a rubber stamp to mark students' papers with a symbol indicating good work. These small rewards make your praise more concrete and visible and let students take their work home and receive praise from their parents. Figure 11.2 provides suggestions for social reinforcers and preferred activities to encourage positive behavior.

SELECT PUNISHERS AND CRITERIA FOR PUNISHMENT, IF NECESSARY   Behavioral learning theories strongly favor the use of reinforcers for appropriate behavior

behavior modification
Systematic application of antecedents and consequences to change behavior.

FIGURE 11.2 Social Reinforcers and Preferred Activities

Social Reinforcers

Praising Words and Phrases

"That's clever."

"Good thinking."

"That shows a great deal of work."

"You really pay attention."

"You should show this to your father."

"That was very kind of you."

"I'm pleased with that."

"Keep up the good work."

"I appreciate your help."

"Now you've got the hang of it."

"That's an interesting point."

"You make it look easy."

"I like the way you got started on your homework."

Nearness

Walking together

Sitting together

Eating lunch together

Playing games with the student

Working after school together

Physical Contact

Touching

Hugging

Shaking hands

Holding hands

Expressions

Smiling

Winking

Nodding up and down

Looking interested

Laughing

Preferred Activities

Going first

Running errands

Getting to sit where he or she wants to

Telling a joke to the class

Having a party

Doing artwork related to studies

Choosing the game for recess

Earning an extra or longer recess

Helping the teacher

Visiting another class

Playing a short game: connect the dots, tic-tac-toe

Taking a class pet home for the weekend

Being team captain

Seeing a movie

Playing with a magnet or other science equipment

Reading with a friend

Getting free time in the library

Being asked what he or she would like to do

Planning a class trip or project

Source: Vernon F. Jones and Louise S. Jones, *Comprehensive Classroom Management* (4th ed.), p. 363. Copyright © 1995 by Allyn & Bacon. Adapted by permission.

rather than punishers for inappropriate behavior. The reasons for this are practical as well as ethical. Punishment often creates resentment; so even if it solves one problem, it could create others. Even if punishment would work as well as reinforcement, it should be avoided because it is not conducive to the creation of a happy, healthy classroom environment (Walker et al., 2007). Punishment of one kind or another is necessary in some circumstances, and it should be used without qualms when reinforcement strategies are impossible or ineffective. However, a program of punishment for misbehavior (e.g., depriving a student of privileges, never physical punishment) should always be the last option considered, never the first. A punisher is any unpleasant stimulus that an individual will try to avoid. Common punishers used in schools are reprimands, being sent out of class or to the principal's office, and detention or missed recess. Corporal punishment (e.g., spanking) is illegal in some states and districts and highly restricted in others, but regardless of laws or policies, it should never be used in schools. It is neither a necessary nor an effective response to misbehavior in school (Jones & Jones, 2010).

O'Leary and O'Leary (1972) list seven principles for the effective and humane use of punishment:

1. Use punishment sparingly.
2. Make it clear to the child why he or she is being punished.
3. Provide the child with an alternative means of obtaining positive reinforcement.
4. Reinforce the child for behaviors that are incompatible with those you wish to weaken (e.g., if you punish for being off task, also reinforce for being on task).
5. Never use physical punishment.
6. Never punish when you are in a very angry or emotional state.
7. Punish when a behavior starts rather than when it ends.

One effective punisher is called **time out.** The teacher tells a misbehaving student to go to a separate part of the classroom, the hall, the principal's or vice principal's office, or another teacher's class. If possible, the place where the student is sent should be uninteresting and out of view of classmates. One advantage of time-out procedures is that they remove the student from the attention of classmates. Therefore, time out may be especially effective for students whose misbehavior is motivated primarily by peer attention. The sit-and-watch procedure described in Chapter 5 is a good example of the use of time out. Students who misbehaved in a physical education class were given a sand timer and asked to sit and watch for 3 minutes. This consequence, applied immediately and consistently, soon virtually eliminated misbehavior (White & Bailey, 1990).

Assign time outs infrequently. When you do assign them, do so calmly and surely. The student is to go straight to the time-out area and stay there until the prescribed time is up. Time-out assignments should be brief; about 5 minutes is usually adequate. However, timing should begin only after the student settles down; if the student yells or argues, that time should not count. During time out, no one should speak to the student. Do not scold the student during time out. Students should be told why they are being given time out but should not otherwise be lectured. If the principal's office is used, the principal should be asked not to speak to the student.

REDUCE THE FREQUENCY OF REINFORCEMENT   Once a reinforcement program has been in operation for a while and the student's behavior has improved and stabilized at a new level, the frequency of reinforcement can be reduced. Initially, reinforcers might be applied to every instance of appropriate behavior; as time goes on, every other instance and then every several instances might be reinforced. Reducing the frequency of reinforcement helps to maintain the new behaviors over the long run and aids in extending the behaviors to other settings.

■ Applied Behavior Analysis Programs

Home-based reinforcement strategies and daily report card programs are examples of applied behavioral analysis involving individual students. A group contingency program is an example of an applied behavioral analysis in which the whole class is involved.

HOME-BASED REINFORCEMENT   Some of the most practical and effective classroom management methods are **home-based reinforcement strategies** (see Barth, 1979; Rhode, Jenson, & Reavis, 1993; Walker et al., 2007). Teachers give students a daily or weekly report card to take home, and parents are instructed to provide special privileges or rewards to students on the basis of these teacher reports. Home-based re-

Connections

For more information about sit-and-watch as a punishment for misbehavior, see Chapter 5, page 125 and Figure 5.2.

✓ Certification Pointer

For your teacher certification test you will need to demonstrate your understanding of appropriate applications of applied behavioral analysis.

time out

Removal of a student from a situation in which misbehavior was reinforced.

home-based reinforcement strategies

Behavior modification strategies in which a student's school behavior is reported to parents, who supply rewards.

FIGURE 11.3 **Example of a Daily Report Card**

Teachers who use a home-based reinforcement program must set up a daily report card so that a student's work and behavior can be assessed and reported to the student's parents.

STUDENT *Homer H.*	DAILY REPORT CARD	DATE *March 21*	
PERIOD	**BEHAVIOR**	**SCHOOLWORK**	**TEACHER**
Reading	1 2 ③ 4	1 ② 3 4	*Ms. Casa*
Math	1 2 3 ④	1 2 3 ④	*Ms. Casa*
Lunch	1 2 ③ 4		*Mr. Mason*
Recess	1 2 ③ 4		*Ms. Hauser*
Language	1 2 3 ④	1 2 3 ④	*Ms. Casa*
Science/Soc. Stud.	1 2 ③ 4	1 2 ③ 4	*Ms. Casa*

1 = Poor	1 = Assignments not completed
2 = Fair	2 = Assignments completed poorly
3 = Good	3 = Assignments completed adequately
4 = Excellent	4 = Assignments completed—excellent!

Total rating *33* ☺ **Score needed** *30*

Source: E. Dougherty and A. Dougherty, "The Daily Report Card," *Psychology in the Schools, 14,* pp. 191–195. Copyright © 1977 by the Clinical Psychology Publishing Co., Inc., Brandon, Vermont. Reprinted with permission of John Wiley and Sons, Inc.

inforcement is not a new idea; a one-room schoolhouse museum in Vermont displays weekly report cards from the 1860s.

Home-based reinforcement has several advantages over other equally effective behavior management strategies. First, parents can give much more potent rewards and privileges than schools can. For example, parents control access to such activities as television, computers, video games, trips to the store, and going out with friends. Parents also know what their own children like and, therefore, can provide more individualized privileges than the school can. Second, home-based reinforcement gives parents frequent good news about their children. Parents of disruptive children usually hear from the school only when their child has done something wrong. This is bad for parent–school relations and can lead to much blame and finger-pointing. Third, home-based reinforcement is easy to administer. You can involve any adults who deal with the child (other teachers, bus drivers, playground or lunch monitors) in the program by having the student carry a daily report card all day. Finally, over time, daily report cards can be replaced by weekly report cards and then biweekly report cards without loss in effectiveness, until just the school's usual 6- or 9-week report cards are used.

DAILY REPORT CARDS Figure 11.3 presents a daily report card for Homer Heath, an elementary school student. His teacher, Ms. Casa, rates his behavior and schoolwork at the end of each academic period, and she arranges to have the lunch monitor and the recess monitor rate his behavior when Homer is with them. Homer is responsible for carrying his report card with him at all times and for making sure that it is marked and initialed at the end of each period. Whenever he makes at least 30 points, his parents have agreed to give him a special privilege: His father is to read him an extra story before bedtime and let him stay up 15 minutes longer than usual. Whenever he forgets to bring home his report card, his parents are to assume that he does not meet the criterion. If Homer were a middle or high school student or in a departmentalized elementary school (where he changes classes for each subject), he would carry his report card to every class, and each teacher would mark it. Obviously, this approach requires some coordination among teachers, but the effort is certainly worthwhile if the daily report card dramatically reduces a student's misbehaviors and increases his or her academic output, as it has in dozens of studies evaluating this method (Barth, 1979).

Theory into Practice
Using a Daily Report Card System

Setting up and implementing a daily report card system requires the following steps:

1. ***Decide which behaviors to include in the daily report card.*** Choose a behavior or set of behaviors on which the daily report card is to be based. Devise a rating scheme for each behavior, and construct a standard report card form. Your daily report card might be more or less elaborate than Figure 11.3. For example, you might break behavior down into more precise categories, such as getting along with others, staying on task, and following class rules.

2. ***Explain the program to parents.*** Home-based reinforcement programs depend on parent participation, so it is critical to inform parents about the program and to obtain their cooperation. Parents should be told what the daily report card means and asked to reward their children whenever they bring home a good report card. In presenting the program to parents, teachers should explain what parents might do to reward their children. Communications with parents should be brief, positive, and informal and should generate a feeling that "we're going to solve this together." The program should focus on rewarding good behavior rather than punishing bad behavior. The following examples demonstrate rewards parents might use at home (adapted from Walker et al., 2003):

- Special activities with a parent (e.g., reading, flying a kite, building a model, shopping, playing a game, going to the zoo)
- Special foods
- Baking cookies or cooking
- Operating equipment that is usually reserved for adults (e.g., the dishwasher or vacuum cleaner)
- Access to special games, toys, technology, or equipment
- Small rewards (such as coloring books, paper, comic books, erasers, or stickers)
- Additional play time, television time, video game time, and the like
- Having a friend spend the night
- Later bedtime or curfew

Parents should be encouraged to choose rewards that they can give every day (that is, nothing too expensive or difficult).

The best rewards are those that build closeness between parent and child, such as doing special activities together. Many children who have behavior problems in school also have problems at home and might have relationships with their parents that are less than ideal. Home-based reinforcement programs provide an opportunity for parents to show their love for their child at a time when the child has something of which to be proud. A special time with Dad can be especially valuable as a reward for good behavior in school and for building the father–son or father–daughter relationship.

3. ***When behavior improves, reduce the frequency of the report.*** When home-based reinforcement works, it often works dramatically. Once the student's behavior has improved and stabilized, it is time to decrease the frequency of the reports to parents (of course, keep the parents informed about this change). Report cards might then be issued only weekly (for larger but less frequent rewards). As was noted in Chapter 5, the best way to ensure maintenance is to thin out the reinforcement schedule—that is, to increase the interval between reinforcers.

GROUP CONTINGENCY PROGRAMS   A reinforcement system in which an entire group is rewarded on the basis of the behavior of the group members is called a **group contingency program.** Teachers have always used group contingencies, as in "We'll go to lunch as soon as all students have put their work away and are quiet." When the teacher says this, any one student can cause the entire class to be late to lunch. Or you might say, "If the class averages at least 90 on tomorrow's quiz, then you'll all be excused from homework for the rest of the week." This group contingency will depend on the average performance of all group members rather than on any single student's performance.

One important advantage of group contingencies is that they are relatively easy to administer. Most often, the whole class is either rewarded or not rewarded, freeing you from applying different contingencies with different students. For example, suppose you say, "If the whole class follows the class rules this morning, we will have 5 extra minutes of recess." If the class does earn the extra recess, they all get it together; you do not have to arrange to have some students stay out longer while others are called inside.

The theory behind group contingencies is that when a group is rewarded on the basis of its members' behavior, the group members will encourage one another to do whatever helps the group gain the reward (Slavin, 1990). Group contingencies can turn the same peer pressure that often supports misbehaviors to pressure opposing misbehavior. When the class can earn extra recess only if all students are well behaved all morning, no one is liable to find it funny when Joan makes silly faces or Quinn speaks disrespectfully to the teacher.

Group contingencies have been used successfully in many forms and for many purposes (Epstein, 2008; Kauffman et al., 2006; Marzano, 2003). For example, Barrish and colleagues (1969) divided a fourth-grade class into two teams during math period. When the teacher saw any member of a team disobeying class rules, the whole team received a check mark on the chalkboard. If a team had five or fewer check marks at the end of the period, all team members would take part in a free-time activity at the end of the day. If both teams got more than five check marks, the one with fewer would receive the free time. Long-term follow-up studies of first-graders who experienced this approach have found remarkable lasting impacts on children's lives (Bradshaw, Zmuda, Kellam, & Ialongo, 2009; Ialongo, Poduska, Wethamer, & Keller, 2001).

Certification Pointer

Your teacher certification test may require you to describe types of classroom management procedures that would tend to make class discussions more productive.

group contingency program

A program in which rewards or punishments are given to a class as a whole for adhering to or violating rules of conduct.

Theory into Practice
Establishing a Group Contingency Program

As noted earlier, a group contingency behavior management program can be as simple as the statement "Class, if you are all in your seats, on task, and quiet this morning, you may have 5 extra minutes of recess." However, having a little more structure can increase the effectiveness of the group contingency.

   1. *Decide which behaviors will be reinforced.*   As in any whole-class behavior modification program, the first step in instituting a group contingency is to establish a set of class rules.

   2. *Set up a developmentally appropriate point system.*   There are essentially three ways to implement a group contingency behavior management program. One is simply to rate class behavior each period or during each activity. That is, an elementary school class might receive 0 to 5 points during each individual instructional period such as reading, language arts, and math. A secondary school class might receive one overall rating each period or separate ratings for behavior and completed assignments. The class would then be rewarded each day or week if they exceeded a preestablished number of points.

Another way to set up a group contingency program is to rate the class at various times during the day. For example, you might set a timer to ring on the average of once every 10 minutes (but varying randomly from 1 to 20 minutes). If the whole class is conforming to class rules when the timer rings, then the class earns a point. The same program can be used without the timer by giving the class a point every 10 minutes or so if all students are conforming to class rules. Some teachers put a marble into a jar from time to time whenever the class is following rules. Each marble would be worth 30 seconds of extra recess. The sound of marbles going into the jar tells the students they are doing well. In secondary schools, where extra recess is not possible, each marble might represent 30 seconds of break time held at the end of the period on Friday.

3. *Consider deducting points for serious misbehavior.* The group contingency reward system by itself should help to improve student behavior. However, it might still be necessary to react to occasional serious misbehavior. For example, you might deduct 10 points for any instance of fighting or of serious disrespect for the teacher. When points must be deducted, do not negotiate with students about it. Simply deduct them, explaining why they must be deducted and reminding students that they may earn them back if they follow class rules.

4. *When behavior improves, reduce the frequency of the points and reinforcers.* Initially, the group contingency should be applied every day. When the class's behavior improves and stabilizes at a new level for about a week, you may change to giving rewards once a week. Ultimately, the class may graduate from the point-and-reward system entirely, though feedback and praise based on class behavior should continue.

5. *Combine group and individual contingencies if necessary.* The use of group contingencies need not rule out individual contingencies for students who need them. For example, students who continue to have problems in a class using a group contingency might still receive daily or weekly report cards to take home to their parents.

■ Ethics of Behavioral Methods

The behavior analysis strategies described in this chapter can be powerful. Properly applied, they will usually bring the behavior of even the most disruptive students to manageable levels. However, there is a danger that teachers might use such techniques to overcontrol students. They could be so concerned about getting students to sit down, stay quiet, and look productive that they lose sight of the fact that school is for learning, not for social control. Many years ago, Winett and Winkler (1972) wrote an article titled "Current Behavior Modification in the Classroom: Be Still, Be Quiet, Be Docile," in which they warned that behavior modification–based classroom management systems are being misused if teachers mistakenly believe that a quiet class is a learning class. Behavior management systems can increase time for learning; however, unless the quality of instruction, appropriate levels of instruction, and incentives for learning are also adequate, the additional time might be wasted (Emmer & Aussiker, 1990).

Some people object to applied behavior analysis on the basis that it constitutes bribing students to do what they ought to do anyway. However, all classrooms use rewards and punishers (such as grades, praise, scolding, suspension). Applied behavior analysis strategies simply apply these rewards in a more systematic way and avoid punishers as much as possible.

Applied behavior analysis methods should be instituted only when it is clear that preventive or informal methods of improving classroom management are not enough to create a positive environment for learning. It is unethical to overapply these methods, but it might be equally unethical to fail to apply them when they could avert serious problems. For example, it might be unethical to refer a child to special education or to suspend, expel, or retain a child on the basis of a pattern of behavior problems before using positive behavior management methods long enough to see whether they can resolve the problem without more draconian measures.

How Can Serious Behavior Problems Be Prevented?

Everyone misbehaves. There is hardly a person on earth who has not at some time done something he or she knew to be wrong or even illegal. However, some people's misbehavior is far more frequent or serious than others', and students in this category cause their teachers and school administrators (not to mention their parents and themselves) a disproportionate amount of trouble and concern.

Serious behavior problems are not evenly distributed among students or schools. Most students identified as having severe behavior problems are male; from three to eight times as many boys as girls are estimated to have serious conduct problems (Perkins & Borden, 2003). Serious delinquency is far more common among students from impoverished backgrounds, particularly in urban locations. Students with poor family relationships are also much more likely than other students to become involved in serious misbehavior and delinquency, as are students who are low in achievement and those who have attendance problems (see Hawkins et al., 2000; Herrenkohl, Maguin, Hill, Hawkins, & Abbott, 2001; Perkins & Borden, 2003).

The school has an important role to play in preventing or managing serious misbehavior and delinquency, but the student and the school are only one part of the story. Delinquent behavior often involves the police, courts, and social service agencies, as well as students' parents and peers. However, there are some guidelines for prevention of delinquency and serious misbehaviors.

■ Preventive Programs

As noted earlier in this chapter, the easiest behavior problems to deal with are those that never occur. There are many approaches that have promise for preventing serious behavior problems. One is simply creating safe and prosocial classroom environments and openly discussing risky behaviors and ways to avoid them (Learning First Alliance, 2001; Osher, Dwyer, & Jackson, 2004; Stipek et al., 1999). Another is giving students opportunities to play prosocial roles as volunteers, tutors, or leaders in activities that benefit their school and community (Allen, 2003; Freiberg & Lapointe, 2006). Creating democratic, participatory classrooms can give students ways of achieving recognition and control in a positive environment, reducing the need to act out (Hyman & Snook, 2000). Smaller, less impersonal schools have been found to reduce bullying and violence (Pellegrini, 2002). Programs that improve academic achievement also often affect behavior as well (Barr & Parrett, 2001). These kinds of strategies embed preventive activities in the day-to-day lives of students, rather than singling them out for special treatment.

■ Identifying Causes of Misbehavior

Even though some types of students are more prone to misbehavior than others, these characteristics do not cause misbehavior. Some students misbehave because they perceive that the rewards for misbehavior outweigh the rewards for good behavior. For example, students who do not experience success in school might perceive that the potential rewards for hard work and good behavior are small, so they turn to other sources of rewards. Some, particularly those who are failing in many different domains, find their niche in groups that hold norms that devalue achievement and other prosocial behavior (Wentzel, 2003). The role of the delinquent peer group in maintaining delinquent behavior cannot be overstated. Delinquent acts among adolescents and preadolescents are usually done in groups and are supported by antisocial peer norms (Gardner & Steinberg, 2005; Perkins & Borden, 2003).

■ Enforcing Rules and Practices

Expectations that students will conform to school rules must be consistently expressed. For example, graffiti or other vandalism must be repaired at once so that other students do not get the idea that misbehavior is common or accepted. However, rules should be enforced firmly but fairly; rigid applications of "zero tolerance" policies have often been found to be counterproductive (Freiberg & Reyes, 2008; Skiba, 2000).

■ Enforcing School Attendance

Truancy and delinquency are strongly related; when students are out of school, they are often in the community making trouble. There are many effective means of reducing truancy (Haslinger, Kelly, & O'Lara, 1996; Lehr, Hansen, Sinclair, & Christenson, 2003; Minke & Bear, 2000). Brooks (1975) had high school students with serious attendance problems carry cards to be signed by their teachers at the end of each period they attended. Students received a ticket for each period attended, plus bonus tickets for good behavior in class and for going 5 days without missing a class. The tickets were used in a drawing for a variety of prizes. Before the program began, the target students were absent 60 percent of all school days. During the program, absences dropped to 19 percent of school days. Over the same period, truancy among other students with attendance problems who were not in the program increased from 59 percent to 79 percent.

Barber and Kagey (1977) markedly increased attendance in an entire elementary school by making full participation in once-a-month parties dependent on student attendance. Several activities were provided during the parties, and students could earn access to some or all of them according to the number of days they attended class.

Fiordaliso, Lordeman, Filipczak, and Friedman (1977) increased attendance among chronically truant junior high school students by having the school call their parents whenever the students were present several days in a row. The number of days before calling depended on how severe the student's truancy had been. Parents of the most truant students, who had been absent 6 or more days per month, were called after the student attended for only 3 consecutive days.

Theory into Practice
Check and Connect

Check and Connect is a model in which school-based "monitors" work with students, families, and school personnel to improve the attendance and engagement of students in schools. The program has documented significant gains on attendance in elementary schools (Lehr, Sinclair, & Christenson, 2004) and on dropout reduction and overall school success in middle schools (Sinclair, Christenson, Evelo, &

INTASC

 10 Partnerships

Hurley, 1998). Check and Connect includes the following elements (Lehr et al., 2004, p. 284):

- *Relationship building.*   Fostering mutual trust and open communication, nurtured through a long-term commitment that is focused on students' educational success
- *Routine monitoring of alterable indicators.*   Systemically checking warning signs of withdrawal (attendance, academic performance, behavior) that are readily available to school personnel and that can be altered through intervention
- *Individualized and timely intervention.*   Providing support that is tailored to individual student needs, based on level of engagement with school, associated influences of home and school, and the leveraging of local resources
- *Long-term commitment.*   Committing to stay with students and families for at least 2 years, including following students during transitions across school levels and following highly mobile youth from school to school and program to program
- *Persistence plus.*   Maintaining a persistent source of academic motivation, a continuity of familiarity with the youth and family, and a consistency in the message that "education is important for your future"
- *Problem solving.*   Promoting the acquisition of skills to resolve conflict constructively and to look for solutions rather than a source of blame
- *Affiliation with school and learning.*   Facilitating students' access to and active participation in school-related activities and events.

■ Practicing Intervention

Classroom management strategies should be used to reduce inappropriate behavior before it escalates into delinquency. Improving students' behavior and success in school can prevent delinquency (Gresham, 2005; Walker, Ramsey, & Gresham, 2003a,b). For example, Hawkins, Guo, Hill, Battin-Pearson, and Abbott (2001) used preventive classroom management methods such as those emphasized in this chapter along with interactive teaching and cooperative learning to help low-achieving seventh-graders. In comparison with control-group students, the students in the program were suspended and expelled less often, had better attitudes toward school, and were more likely to expect to complete high school. Freiberg and Lapointe (2006) reviewed research on several promising preventive approaches of this kind. Use of applied behavior analysis programs for misbehavior in class can also contribute to the prevention of delinquency (Walker & Gresham, 2003). Group contingencies can be especially effective with predelinquent students because this strategy can deprive students of peer support for misbehavior.

■ Requesting Family Involvement

Involve the student's home in any response to serious misbehavior. When misbehavior occurs, parents should be notified. If misbehavior persists, parents should be involved in establishing a program, such as a home-based reinforcement program, to coordinate home and school responses to misbehavior.

Certification Pointer

A teacher certification question may ask you to respond to a case study by suggesting ways of helping students develop the social skills that would help resolve conflicts presented in the case.

■ Using Peer Mediation

Students can be trained to serve as peer mediators, particularly to resolve conflicts between fellow students. Students who are having problems with other students might be asked to take these problems to peer mediators rather than to adults for resolution, and the peer mediators themselves might actively look for interpersonal problems among their classmates and offer help when they occur. Peer mediators have been found to be effective in resolving a variety of interpersonal problems, from insults and perceptions of unfairness among students to stealing to physical aggression (Johnson & Johnson, 2001; Troop & Asher, 1999). However, peer mediators need to be carefully trained and monitored if they are to be effective (Latham, 1997). Figure 11.4 shows a guide for peer mediators used in one conflict management program.

FIGURE 11.4 **Peer Conflict Management**

1. Introduce yourselves: "Hi, my name is _____. I'm conflict manager and this is my partner _____."

2. Ask the parties: "Do you want to solve the problem with us or with a teacher?" If necessary, move to a quiet place to solve the problem.

3. Explain to the parties: "First you have to agree to four rules":

   a. Agree to solve the problem.

   b. No name-calling.

   c. Do not interrupt.

   d. Tell the truth.

4. Conflict Manager 1 asks Person 1: "What happened? How do you feel?" Conflict Manager 1 repeats what Person 1 said, using active listening: "So, what you're saying is . . ."

5. Conflict Manager 2 asks Person 2: "What happened? How do you feel?" Conflict Manager 2 repeats what Person 2 said, using active listening: "So, what you're saying is . . ."

6. Ask Person 1: "Do you have a solution?" Ask Person 2: "Do you agree with the solution?" If no: "Do you have another solution?" and so on until disputants have reached a solution agreeable to both of them.

7. Have disputants tell each other what they have just agreed to: "So will you tell each other what you've just agreed to?"

8. Congratulate them both: "Thank you for working so hard to solve your problem. Congratulations."

9. Fill out Conflict Manager Report Form.

Source: Classroom Law Project, 6318 S. W. Corbett, Portland, OR 97201. Adapted by permission.

These students are demonstrating peer mediation as a way to resolve a conflict. As a teacher, how will you advise student mediators to handle conflicts with a group of students?

Bob Daemmrich Photography

■ Confronting Bullying

A widespread problem in schools at all levels is bullying, where students repeatedly torment weaker peers. Bullying is particularly common among boys; a 1998 survey by the National Institute of Child Health and Human Development found that boys were more likely to report being bullies (26%) or victims (21%). Rates for girls were 14 percent for both categories (Levin & Nolan, 2010). Rates were much higher in middle and high school than in elementary school (Sampson, 2002). Bullying can have serious negative effects on both the bully and the victim, leading to escalating violence as well as depression and anxiety. Recently, bullying online, or cyberbullying, has become increasingly common, including put-downs, nasty rumors, and humiliating pictures posted on social networking sites (Patchin & Hinduja, 2006).

Effective approaches to preventing bullying in schools include the following components (see Emmer & Evertson, 2009; Levin & Nolan, 2010; Murawski, Lockwood, Khalili, & Johnston, 2010; Olweus & Limber, 1999).

1. Develop and publicize a schoolwide antibullying policy.
2. Educate all students about bullying and its negative effects on the whole school.
3. Provide training in social skills and recognize students who engage in prosocial activites. Particularly important skills are empathy, impulse control, and anger management (Frey, Hirschstein, & Guzzo, 2000).
4. Monitor locations and activities in which bullying occurs.
5. Establish consequences for bullying behavior.

ON THE **WEB**

For information on programs to confront bullying in school, see www.stopbullyingnow.com, www.clemson.edu/olweus, and www.cfchildren.org/programs/str/overview.

■ Judiciously Applying Consequences

Avoid the use of suspension (or expulsion) as punishment for all but the most serious misbehavior (see Curwin & Mendler, 1999). Suspension often exacerbates truancy problems, both because it makes students fall behind in their work and because it gives them experience with time out of school. In-school suspension, detention, and other penalties are more effective (Axelrod & Mathews, 2003).

When students misbehave, they should be punished; but when punishment is applied, it should be brief. Being sent to a time-out area or detention room is a common punishment that is effective for most students. Loss of privileges may also be used. However, any punishment should not last too long. It is better to make a misbehaving student miss 2 days of football practice than to throw him off the team, in part because once the student is off the team, the school would have little else of value to offer or withhold. Every child has within himself or herself the capacity for good behavior as well as for misbehavior. The school must be the ally of the good in each child at the same time that it is the enemy of misbehavior. Overly harsh penalties or penalties that do not allow the student to reenter the classroom on an equal footing with others risk pushing students into the antisocial, delinquent subculture. When a student has paid her or his debt by losing privileges, experiencing detention, or whatever the punishment might be, he or she must be fully reaccepted as a member of the class.

Chapter 11 Summary

What Is an Effective Learning Environment ?

Creating effective learning environments involves strategies that teachers use to maintain appropriate behavior and respond to misbehavior in the classroom. Keeping students interested and engaged and showing enthusiasm are important in preventing misbehavior. Creating an effective learning environment is a matter of knowing a set of techniques that teachers can learn and apply.

What Is the Impact of Time on Learning ?

Methods of maximizing allocated time include preventing late starts and early finishes, preventing interruptions, handling routine procedures smoothly and quickly, minimizing time spent on discipline, and using engaged time effectively. Engaged time, or time on task, is the time individual students spend actually doing assigned work. Teachers can maximize engaged time by teaching engaging lessons, sustaining momentum, establishing smoothness of instruction, managing transitions, maintaining group focus, practicing withitness, and overlapping. In a student-centered classroom, classroom management is more participatory, with students involved in setting standards of behavior; however, rules are still needed and must be consistently communicated and enforced.

What Practices Contribute to Effective Classroom Management ?

Practices that contribute to effective classroom management include starting the year properly and developing rules and procedures. Class rules and procedures should be explicitly presented to students and applied promptly and fairly.

What Are Some Strategies for Managing Routine Misbehavior ?

One principle of classroom discipline is good management of routine misbehavior. The principle of least intervention means using the simplest methods that will work. There is a continuum of strategies from least to most disruptive: prevention of misbehavior; nonverbal cues such as eye contact, which can stop a minor misbehavior; praise of incompatible, correct behavior; praise of other students who are behaving; simple verbal reminders given immediately after students misbehave; repetition of verbal reminders; and application of consequences when students refuse to comply. For serious behavior problems, swift and certain consequences must be applied. A call to the student's parents can be effective.

How Is Applied Behavior Analysis Used to Manage More Serious Behavior Problems ?

The most common reinforcer for both routine and serious misbehavior is attention from teacher or peers. When the student misbehaves to get the teacher's attention, one effective strategy is to pay attention to correct behavior while ignoring misbehavior as much as possible; scolding often acts as a reinforcer of misbehavior.

Individual behavior management strategies are useful for students with persistent behavior problems in school. After establishing baseline behavior, select reinforcers such as verbal praise or small, tangible rewards and punishers such as time outs (removing a child from a situation that reinforces misbehavior). Also establish criteria for applying reinforcement and punishment.

The Intentional Teacher

USING WHAT YOU KNOW about Effective Learning Environments to Improve Teaching and Learning

Intentional teachers are leaders in their classrooms who take responsibility for managing time, activities, and behaviors. At the core of their success as classroom managers is high-interest, meaningful instruction. Intentional teachers use instructional time to its fullest by structuring a positive, consistent environment with reasonable rules and time-conscious procedures. They proactively prevent misbehavior and have a planned range of responses to misbehavior should it occur despite prevention. Intentional teachers' actions reflect their understanding that effective learning environments result from careful planning and vigilant monitoring.

 1. **What do I expect my students to know and be able to do at the end of this lesson? How does this contribute to course objectives and to students' needs to become capable individuals?**

Students learn best when they are productively engaged in instruction. Develop a management plan that aims to prevent misbehavior. Before the school year begins, list some of the strategies that you can employ to help your students make good choices about their behavior. At the top of your list type in bold: **Provide instruction that taps students' curiosity and creativity!** Next, list key terms and brief reminders about actions that can help to prevent misbehavior, such as

Fairness. Show genuine concern for the students and consider their perspectives. Apply consequences consistently and without emotion.

Withitness. Remember to monitor all corners of the room.

Research indicates that some teachers lose half—or more—of their instructional time. Make a plan to use your students' time well, and guard your instructional minutes carefully. Commit to teach bell-to-bell, beginning your lessons with an opener—usually a practice exercise or a brain teaser—that is on the overhead projector as students arrive, and closing the lessons with a brief period of independent work during which you can work with students who had difficulties with the lesson.

 2. **What knowledge, skills, needs, and interests do my students have that must be taken into account in my lesson?**

Bored or frustrated students might find greater rewards in avoiding schoolwork than in completing it. Provide instruction that engages students' curiosity and attends to the various preparation levels students bring to the classroom. For example, imagine that a small cluster of students has been unruly during the beginning of your unit on computation with decimals. You could do a task analysis of the concepts and skills required in the unit and find that this small group of students is missing some prerequisite skills: They have not yet committed basic math facts to memory. So that students can succeed with decimal computations, you might allow them to use their fact tables. At the same time, you could plan to introduce math facts games to help your students master basic operations.

 3. **What do I know about the content, child development, learning, motivation, and effective teaching strategies that I can use to accomplish my objectives?**

Different kinds of misbehavior require different levels of intervention. Develop a range of responses to misbehavior, beginning with the lowest level of inten-

Home-based reinforcement strategies might involve giving students daily or weekly report cards to take home and instructing parents to provide rewards on the basis of these reports. The steps to setting up such a program include deciding on behaviors to use for the daily report card and explaining the program to parents.

Group contingency programs are those in which an entire group is rewarded on the basis of the behavior of the group members.

One objection to behavior management techniques is that they can be used to overcontrol students. Behavior management strategies should always emphasize praise and reinforcement, reserving punishment as a last resort.

How Can Serious Behavior Problems Be Prevented

There are few sure methods of preventing delinquency, but some general principles include clearly expressing and consistently enforcing classroom rules, reducing truancy however possible, avoiding the use of between-class ability grouping, instituting preventive classroom management strategies, involving parents in any response to serious misbehavior, using peer mediation, refraining from the use of suspension, applying only

INTASC **7** Instructional Planning Skills

9 Professional Commitment and Responsibility

sity. When students exhibit serious misbehaviors, consider the motivation for their behavior, and respond in ways that take into account the individual and the problem. You can address most misbehavior through low-level interventions such as nonverbal cues, physical proximity, and hints. A few students, though, demonstrate persistent misbehavior. You might develop home-based reinforcement programs in which students can earn added time at their favorite activities if their school behavior improves.

 4. What instructional materials, technology, assistance, and other resources are available to help accomplish my objectives?

Effective managers start the year by teaching and reinforcing classroom rules and procedures. Spend time during the first days of school teaching students your expectations for behavior. Perhaps you could interview a few experienced colleagues about their first-day-of-school plans. From their suggestions, you might develop a plan to (1) devise a set of classroom rules through class discussion; (2) develop consequences for instances when students choose to violate or ignore those rules; and (3) teach the students procedures for submitting homework, collecting work for an absent paper, and working effectively in small groups.

 5. How will I plan to assess students' progress toward my objectives?

Collect ongoing information about your use of allocated and engaged time. Ask yourself whether you are devoting enough time to each subject and whether students are engaged during that time in experiences that result in meaningful learning. Review your use of time by, first, examining your sched-

ule to determine whether allocated time is appropriate. Then, for a week, you might track start and end times for each of your lessons to determine where minutes may be lost. Finally, examine students' work to assess the degree to which students demonstrate that their on-task behavior has resulted in significant learning.

Review students' responses to your efforts to redirect behavior. Consider changing strategies when misbehavior persists or when you are spending too much time correcting it. For example, when you overhear some of your students bragging about being members of your Three O'Clock Club (after-school detention), you are forced to reconsider its effectiveness as a punishment.

 6. How will I respond if individual children or the class as a whole is not on track toward success? What is my back-up plan?

Take frequent "temperature readings" of the motivational climate of your classroom environment. Gather information from several sources to determine that your strategies are productive and that students are happy and learning. For example, ask students to write an anonymous journal entry on their perceptions of how the class is going. You might ask, in particular, whether they feel they have enough say in what happens in the classroom. After searching for patterns in the entries, you might spend a class period on a classroom meeting to set new goals.

brief punishment, and reintegrating students after punishment. Check and Connect is one program that incorporates many of these principles.

Key Terms

Review the following key terms from the chapter.

accountability 323	group contingency program 340
allocated time 318	home-based reinforcement
applied behavior analysis 332	strategies 337
behavior modification 335	mock participation 325
classroom management 316	nonverbal cues 330
discipline 317	overlapping 324
engaged time 317	time on task 317
group alerting 323	time out 337
group contingencies 334	withitness 324

Self-Assessment: Practicing for Licensure

Directions: The chapter-opening vignette addresses indicators that are often assessed in state licensure exams. Re-read the chapter-opening vignette, and then respond to the following questions.

1. Ms. Cavalho works hard to prevent behavior problems and disruption in her classroom. Which of the following terms refers to her interaction with Mark?

   a. Management

   b. Discipline

   c. Learning environment

   d. Instruction

2. According to research, how could Ms. Cavalho increase student achievement in her classroom?

   a. Increase allocated time for instruction by 10 percent above what is normal

   b. Increase engaged time to 100 percent of the allocated classroom time

   c. Increase engaged time by 10 percent above what is normal

   d. Decrease allocated time by starting late and finishing early

3. Ms. Cavalho continues her lesson on writing style even as Mark attempts to interrupt. This is called

   a. engaged time.

   b. allocated time.

   c. momentum.

   d. overlapping.

4. Ms. Cavalho uses the principle of least intervention in her classroom. She works to prevent inappropriate behavior first, and if that does not work, she gives nonverbal cues and verbal reminders about how to act. She has used these strategies with Mark. Assume that Mark's behavior does not change after their discussion. What should she do next?

   a. Apply consequences

   b. Give praise for appropriate behavior

   c. Ask students to solve the problem

   d. Ignore the behavior

5. Daily report cards, group contingency programs, home-based reinforcement programs, and individual behavior management programs are all based on

   a. assertive discipline practices.

   b. delinquency prevention.

   c. behavioral learning theory.

   d. the principle of least intervention.

6. Discuss ethical considerations in the use of individual and group behavior management programs.

7. Explain how you would prevent the following misbehaviors: speaking out of turn, teasing, physical fighting.

PEARSON
myeducationlab

Go to the Topic **Classroom Management** in the MyEducationLab (www.myeducationlab.com) for your course, where you can:

- Find learning outcomes for **Classroom Management** along with the national standards that connect to these outcomes.

- Complete Assignments and Activities that can help you more deeply understand the chapter content.

- Apply and practice your understanding of the core teaching skills identified in the chapter with the Building Teaching Skills and Dispositions learning units.

- Examine challenging situations and cases presented in the IRIS Center Resources.

- Access video clips of CCSSO National Teachers of the Year award winners responding to the question "Why Do I Teach?" in the Teacher Talk section.

- Check your comprehension of the content covered in the chapter by going to the Study Plan in the Book Resources for your text. Here you will be able to take a chapter quiz; receive feedback on your answers; and then access Review, Practice, and Enrichment activities to enhance your understanding of chapter content.

- Watch author Bob Slavin present a Personal Reflections podcast on *Maintaining Control* in the Book Resources for your text. Then, respond to the reflection question that follows.

  Maintaining Control

  YOUR REFLECTIONS Think of examples from your own experience as a student. How did your best teachers create effective learning environments?

12

Learners with Exceptionalities

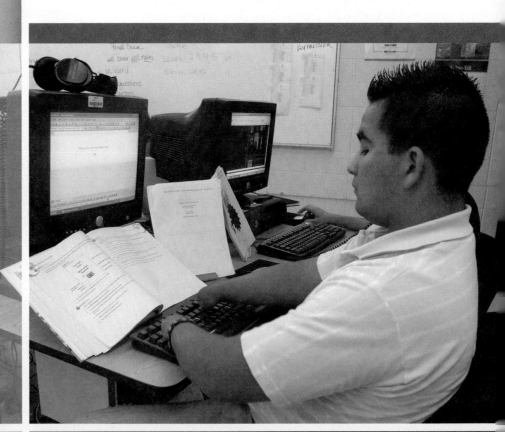

Bob Daemmrich/PhotoEdit

At the end of this chapter, you should be able to:

- Identify the most common types of learners with exceptionalities
- Describe laws and policies that define special education
- Discuss response to intervention strategies for students placed at risk
- Discuss inclusion and methods that teachers can use to facilitate learning in inclusion situations

Bob Daemmrich/PhotoEdit

laine Wagner, assistant principal at Dover Elementary School, comes in to work one day and is stopped by the school secretary.

"Good morning," the secretary says. "There's a Helen Ross here to see you. She is interested in enrolling her children. She's waiting in your office. Looks nervous—I gave her some coffee and settled her down."

"Thanks, Beth," says Ms. Wagner. She goes into her office and introduces herself to Ms. Ross.

"I appreciate your seeing me," says Ms. Ross. "We're planning to move to Dover next fall, and I wanted to look at the schools before we move. We have one child, Tommy, going into second grade, and Annie is going into kindergarten. I'm really concerned about Tommy. In the school he's in now, he's not doing very well. It's spring, and he's hardly reading at all. His teacher says he might have a learning disability, and the school wants to put him in special education. I don't like that idea. He's a normal, happy kid at home, and it would crush him to find out he's 'different,' but I want to do what's best for him. I guess the main thing I want to see is what you do for kids like Tommy."

"Well," says Ms. Wagner, "the most important thing I can tell you about our school is that our philosophy is that every child can learn, and it is our job to find out how to reach each one. I can't tell you exactly what we'd do with Tommy, of course, because I don't know him, but I can assure you of a few things. First, we'll attend to his reading problem right away. We believe in preventing problems if we can, and if problems still show up despite our best efforts, we use the most intensive help there is as early as possible. If Tommy is having serious reading problems, we'll probably arrange to give him one-to-one tutoring so that he can catch up quickly with the other second-graders. Second, we'll try to keep him in his regular classroom if we possibly can. If he needs special-ed-

ucation services, he'll get them, but in this school we try everything to solve a child's learning problems before we refer him or her for testing that might lead to special-education placement. Even if Tommy does qualify for special education, we'll structure his program so that he is with his regular class as much as possible. We will develop an individualized education plan for him. Finally, I want to assure you that you will be very much involved in all decisions that have to do with Tommy and that we'll talk with you frequently about his progress and ask for your help at home to make sure that Tommy is doing well."

"Ms. Wagner, that all sounds great. But how can you give Tommy the help he needs and still let him stay in his regular class?"

"Why don't I take you to see some of our classes in operation right now?" says Ms. Wagner. "I think you'll see what I mean."

Ms. Wagner leads the way through the brightly lit corridors lined with student projects, artwork, and compositions. She turns in at Mr. Esposito's second-grade class. There, she and Ms. Ross are met by a happy, excited buzz of activity. The children are working in small groups, measuring each other's heights and the lengths of fingers and feet. Some children are trying to figure out how to measure the distance around each other's heads. Another teacher, Ms. Park, is working with some of the groups.

Ms. Wagner and Ms. Ross step back into the hall. "What I wanted to show you," says Ms. Wagner, "is how we integrate our students with special needs into the general education classroom. Could you tell which students were students with special needs?"

"No," admits Ms. Ross.

"That's what we hope to create—a classroom in which children with special needs are so well integrated

353

that you can't pick them out. Ms. Park is the special-education teacher for the younger grades, and she teams with Mr. Esposito during math and reading periods to serve all of the second-graders who need special services. Ms. Park will help any child who is having difficulty, not only students with special needs, because a large part of her job is to prevent students from ever needing special education. Sometimes she'll work with individual kids or small groups that need help. She often teaches skills children will be learning in advance, so they will be better prepared in class. For example, she might have gone over measurement with some of the kids before this lesson so that they'd have a leg up on the concept."

Ms. Wagner leads the way to a small room near the library room. She points through a window at a teacher working with one child. "What you see there is a tutor working with a first-grader who is having difficulty in reading. If your Tommy were here, he might do this as well. We try to do anything we can to keep kids from falling behind in the first place so that they can stay out of special education and progress along with their classmates."

Ms. Wagner shows Ms. Ross all over the school. In one class a child with a visual disability is reading text from a computer that has inch-high letters. In another they see a child with Down syndrome working in a cooperative learning group on a science project. In a third classroom a child using a wheelchair is leading a class discussion.

Ms. Ross is fascinated.

"I had no idea a school could be like this. I'm so excited that we're moving to Dover. This looks like the perfect school for both of my children. I only wish we could have moved here 2 years ago!"

Cooperative Learning In groups of five, discuss Tommy Ross and students like him. One person assumes the role of Ms. Wagner; one is his future homeroom teacher, Mr. Esposito; one is Ms. Ross; one is the special-education teacher, Ms. Park; and one is the special-education director for the district. Discuss how Tommy will be screened for a potential learning disability in reading, and list some strategies that his teachers might use if, in fact, he does have a learning disability.

Cooperative Learning Divide groups of four classmates into pairs. Each student interviews her partner about what a learning disability in reading might look like (i.e., how a reading disability might be identified) and what a teacher might do to address this situation. The two interviewers share what they have learned within their group. Roles are then reversed. The two new interviewers tell their group what they have learned about reading disabilities.

D over Elementary School is organized around two key ideas: that all children can learn and that it is the school's responsibility to find ways to meet each child's needs in the general education classroom to the maximum extent possible. Dover Elementary is committed to identifying children's strengths as well as their problems and to provide the best program it can for each child. Every school has children with exceptionalities who can do well in school when they are given the specific supports they need to learn. This chapter describes children with exceptionalities and programs that are designed to help them achieve their full potential.

Who Are Learners with Exceptionalities

 Certification Pointer

Teacher certification tests will require you to identify areas of exceptionality in learning, including learning disabilities, visual and perceptual difficulties, and specific physical challenges.

In one sense, every child is exceptional. No two children are exactly alike in their ways of learning and behaving, in their activities and preferences, in their skills and motivations. All students would benefit from programs uniquely tailored to their individual needs.

However, schools cannot practically meet the precise needs of every student. For the sake of efficiency, students are grouped into classes and given common instructional experiences designed to provide the greatest benefit to the largest number at a moderate cost. This system works reasonably well for the great majority of students. However, some students do not fit easily into this mold. Some students have physical or sensory disabilities, such as hearing or vision loss or orthopedic disabilities, that restrict their ability to participate in the general education classroom program without special assistance. Other students have mental retardation, emotional or behavioral disorders, or learning disabilities that make it difficult for them to learn in the general education classroom without assistance. Finally, some students have such outstanding talents that the general education classroom teacher is unable to meet their unique needs without help.

To receive special-education services, a student must have one of a few designated categories of disabilities or disorders. These general labels, such as "specific learning disabilities," "mental retardation," and "orthopedic impairments," cover a wide diversity of problems.

Labels tend to stick, making change difficult, and the labels themselves can become handicaps for the student. Education professionals must avoid using labels in a way that unintentionally stigmatizes students, dehumanizes them, segregates them socially from their peers, or encourages discrimination against them in any form (Hehir, 2007). The term **learners with exceptionalities** may be used to describe any individuals whose physical, mental, or behavioral performance is so different from the norm—either higher or lower—that additional services are needed to meet the individuals' needs.

The terms *disability* and *handicap* are not interchangeable. A **disability** is a functional limitation a person has that interferes with the person's physical or cognitive abilities. A **handicap** is a condition imposed on a person with disabilities by society, the physical environment, or the person's attitude. For example, a student who uses a wheelchair is handicapped by a lack of access ramps (Hallahan, Kauffman, & Pullen, 2009).

■ "People-First" Language

It is important to ensure that our language and choice of vocabulary and terminology in referring to people with disabilities convey the appropriate message of respect. There are two basic principles to keep in mind (Smith, 2001). The first is to *put people first*. An example of this would be to refer to Frankie as a student with a learning disability, not a "learning disabled child." He is a student first; the fact that he has a learning disability is secondary. The second principle is to *avoid making the person equal the disability* (Smith & Tyler, 2010). Each student has many characteristics and the disability is only one. To define the child in terms of the disability does him or her an injustice. The following sections discuss characteristics of students with the types of exceptionalities that are most commonly seen in schools.

■ Types of Exceptionalities and the Numbers of Students Served

Some exceptionalities, such as loss of vision and hearing, are relatively easy to define and measure. Others, such as mental retardation, learning disabilities, and emotional disorders, are much harder to define, and their definitions have evolved over time. In fact, recent decades have seen dramatic changes in these categories (Hallahan et al., 2009). Since the mid-1970s, the numbers of children in categories of disabilities that are most easily defined, such as physical impairments, have remained fairly stable. However, the number of students categorized as learning disabled has steadily increased, and the use of the category "mentally retarded" has diminished.

Figure 12.1 shows the percentages of all students, ages 6 to 21, receiving special-education services in 2004. There are several important pieces of information in this figure. First, notice that the overall percentage of students receiving special education was about 9 percent; that is, 1 out of 11 students, ages 6 to 21, was categorized as exceptional.

learners with exceptionalities

Any individuals whose physical, mental, or behavioral performance is so different from the norm—either higher or lower—that additional services are needed to meet the individuals' needs.

disability

The limitation of a function, such as cognitive processing or physical or sensory abilities.

handicap

A condition imposed on a person with disabilities by society, the physical environment, or the person's attitude.

FIGURE 12.1   **Percentage of Children Ages 6 to 21 Served under IDEA, Part B, by Disability during the 2004 School Year**

■ Students without disabilities	90.84%
▨ Specific learning disabilities	4.24%
■ Speech or language impairments	1.73%
▨ Mental retardation	0.84%
▨ Orthopedic impairments	0.10%
■ Multiple disabilities	0.20%
▨ Hearing impairments	0.11%
■ Other	1.21%
▨ Other health impairments	0.77%
▨ Visual impairments	0.04%
▨ Autism and traumatic brain injury	0.29%
■ Developmental delay	0.11%

Source: U.S. Department of Education, Office of Special Education and Rehabilitative Services, *Annual Report to Congress on the Implementation of the Individuals with Disabilities Education Act,* Washington, DC, 2006.

Of these, the largest proportion was categorized as having specific learning disabilities (4.2 percent of all students) or speech disabilities (1.7 percent). Figure 12.2 shows the percentages of students ages 6 to 21 receiving special-education services who had various disabilities in 2004 (U.S. Department of Education, 2006). Specific learning disabilities (46.2 percent of all students with disabilities), speech and language impairments (18.9 percent), and mental retardation (9.2 percent) are far more common than physical or sensory disabilities. In a class of 25 a teacher might, on the average, have one or two students with learning disabilities and one with a speech impairment. In contrast, only about 1 class in 40 is likely to have a student who has hearing or vision loss or a physical disability.

FIGURE 12.2

Percentage of All Students with Disabilities Ages 6 to 21 Served under IDEA, Part B, by Disability, 2004

Type of Disability	Percentage of All Students with Disabilities
Specific learning disabilities	46.4
Speech or language impairments	18.8
Mental retardation	9.3
Emotional disturbance	7.9
Multiple disabilities	2.2
Hearing impairments	1.2
Orthopedic impairments	1.1
Other health impairments	8.4
Visual impairments	0.4
Autism	2.7
Deaf blindness	<0.1
Traumatic brain injury	0.4
Developmental delay	0.8
Other disabilities	0.3
All disabilities	100.0

Source: U.S. Department of Education, *Annual Report to Congress on the Implementation of the Individuals with Disabilities Act,* Washington, DC, 2006.

■ Students with Mental Retardation

Just over 1 percent of all students ages 6 to 21 have mental retardation (U.S. Department of Education, 2005). There are several definitions of **mental retardation.** In 2002 the American Association on Mental Retardation (AAMR) defined it as follows:

> Mental retardation is a disability characterized by significant limitations both in intellectual functioning and in adaptive behavior as expressed in conceptual, social, and practical adaptive skills. This disability originates before age 18. (AAMR, 2002, p. 1)

This definition means that people with mental retardation have low scores on tests of intelligence and also show difficulty in maintaining the standards of personal independence and social responsibility that would be expected based on age (Hallahan et al., 2009; Smith & Tyler, 2010). In addition, these impairments in intelligence and adaptive behavior become apparent sometime between conception and age 18.

CAUSES OF MENTAL RETARDATION   Among the many causes of mental retardation are genetic inheritance; chromosomal abnormalities, such as Down syndrome (Turner & Alborz, 2003); diseases passed from mother to fetus in utero, such as rubella (German measles) and syphilis; fetal chemical dependency syndromes caused by a mother's abuse of alcohol or cocaine during pregnancy; birth accidents that result in oxygen deprivation; childhood diseases and accidents, such as encephalitis or traumatic brain injury; and toxic contamination from the environment, such as lead poisoning (McDonnell, Hardman, & McDonnell, 2003).

INTELLIGENCE QUOTIENT (IQ)   To understand how severity of impairment in children with mental retardation is classified, it is first important to recall from Chapter 4 the concept of **intelligence quotient (IQ),** derived from scores on standardized tests. Students with IQs above 70 are generally regarded as being in the normal range. Slightly more than 2 percent of students have IQs below this range. However, consistent with AAMR recommendations, education professionals do not use IQ alone to determine the severity of cognitive impairment. They take into account a student's school and home performance, scores on other tests, and cultural background.

Connections

For more on IQ, see Chapter 4, page 103.

Connections

For more about IQ testing, see Chapter 14, page 452.

CLASSIFICATIONS OF MENTAL RETARDATION   In the past, individuals with mental retardation were largely categorized according to their IQ scores. For example, the 1983 AAMR manual listed four degrees of severity of mental retardation in terms of ranges of IQ, including mild retardation (IQs 50–55 to 70–75), moderate retardation (IQs 35–40 to 50–55), severe retardation (IQs 20–25 to 35–40), and profound retardation (IQs below 20–25) (Luckasson et al., 1992). This IQ-based classification system has been challenged by some professionals who believe that the emphasis in present-day special education is that all people can learn and that education and training cannot be clearly differentiated (Smith, Polloway, Patton, & Dowdy, 2008). However, many school districts use this or a similar simplified system of classification.

Current AAMR definitions emphasize the capabilities of individuals with mental retardation in two main areas—intellectual functioning and adaptive skills—and categorize individuals on the basis of the supports they need (Smith & Tyler, 2010). Table 12.1 defines four categories of services people with mental retardation might need and gives examples of these services.

However the categories are defined, children with mild retardation, who need intermittent or limited support, are rarely identified before school entry (Hallahan et al., 2009). Approximately 90 percent of children with mental retardation have mild mental retardation (U.S. Department of Education, 1994).

There is increasing evidence that as many as 50 percent of all cases of mental retardation could have been prevented by improving prenatal care; ensuring proper

mental retardation

A condition, usually present at birth, that results in below-average intellectual skills and poor adaptive behavior.

intelligence quotient (IQ)

An intelligence test score that should be near 100 for people of average intelligence.

TABLE 12.1	Definitions and Examples of Intensities of Supports
Type of Support	**Definition and Examples**
Intermittent	Supports on an as-needed basis. Characterized by episodic nature, person not always needing the support(s), or short-term supports needed during life span transitions (e.g., job loss or an acute medical crisis). Intermittent supports may be high or low intensity when provided.
Limited	An intensity of supports characterized by consistency over time, time-limited but not of an intermittent nature, might require fewer staff members and less cost than more intense levels of support (e.g., time-limited employment training or transitional supports during the school to adult period).
Extensive	Supports characterized by regular involvement (e.g., daily) in at least some environments (such as work at home) and not time-limited (e.g., long-term support and long-term home living support).
Pervasive	Supports characterized by their constancy, high intensity; provided across environments; potential life-sustaining nature. Pervasive supports typically involve more staff members and intrusiveness than do extensive or time-limited supports.

Source: AAMR, *Mental Retardation: Definitions, Classification, and Systems of Supports,* p. 26. Copyright 2002 by American Association on Mental Retardation. Reprinted by permission.

nutrition; preventing accidents, diseases, and ingestions of poisons (such as lead paint) among children; and providing children with safe, supportive, and stimulating environments in early childhood (Smith et al., 2008). Studies of intensive early intervention programs emphasizing infant stimulation, effective preschool programs, parent support programs, and other services have shown lasting impacts on the performance of children who are at risk for mental retardation (Bradley et al., 1994; Campbell & Ramey, 1994; Garber, 1988; Noonan & McCormick, 1993; Ramey & Ramey, 1992). Even children with more pervasive mental retardation benefit substantially from intensive prevention programs in their early childhood years (Casto & Mastropieri, 1986).

The following Theory into Practice section suggests ways in which general education classroom teachers can help students who have mental retardation to acquire adaptive behavior skills. Specific ways of modifying instruction for students with special needs are discussed later in this chapter.

Theory into Practice
Teaching Adaptive Behavior Skills

Instructional objectives for helping students who have mental retardation to acquire adaptive behavior skills are not very different from those that are valuable for all students. Every student needs to cope with the demands of school, develop interpersonal relationships, learn language skills, grow emotionally, and take care of personal needs. Teachers can help students by directly instructing or supporting students in the following areas (see Hardman, Drew, Egan, & Wolf, 1996; Wehmeyer, 2001):

1. ***Coping with the demands of school.*** Attending to learning tasks, organizing work, following directions, managing time, and asking questions.

2. *Developing interpersonal relationships.*   Learning to work cooperatively with others, responding to social cues in the environment, using socially acceptable language, responding appropriately to teacher directions and cues, and enhancing social awareness.

3. *Developing language skills.*   Understanding directions, communicating needs and wants, expressing ideas, listening attentively, and using appropriate voice modulation and inflection.

4. *Socioemotional development.*   Seeking out social participation and interaction (decreasing social withdrawal) and being motivated to work (decreasing work avoidance, tardiness, and idleness).

5. *Personal care.*   Practicing appropriate personal hygiene, dressing independently, taking care of personal property, and moving successfully from one location to another.

■ Students with Learning Disabilities

Learning disabilities (LD) are not a single condition but a wide variety of specific disabilities that are presumed to stem from some dysfunction of the brain or central nervous system. The following definition is adapted from the National Joint Committee on Learning Disabilities (1988, p. 1):

> Learning disabilities is a general term for a diverse group of disorders characterized by significant difficulties in the acquisition and use of listening, speaking, reading, writing, reasoning, or computing. These disorders stem from the individual and may occur across the life span. Problems in self-regulatory behaviors, social perception, and social interaction may exist with learning disabilities but do not by themselves constitute a learning disability. Learning disabilities may occur with other handicapping conditions but are not the result of those conditions.

IDENTIFYING STUDENTS WITH LEARNING DISABILITIES   Different interpretations of the many definitions of *learning disability* have led state and local school districts to vary widely in their eligibility requirements and provisions for students with learning disabilities (Bender, 2008). The increasing numbers of students identified as having learning disabilities have contributed to the confusion. In 2004, for example, 46.2 percent of all students ages 6 to 21 with disabilities were identified as having specific learning disabilities (U.S. Department of Education, 2006). However, the growing numbers of students in this category are the result of a shift in its definition, not because of a change in the total number of children at risk.

In some school districts a student who falls more than two grade levels behind expectations and has an IQ in the normal range is likely to be called *learning disabled*. Students with learning disabilities have some or all of the following characteristics:

- Normal intelligence or even giftedness
- Discrepancy between intelligence and performance
- Delays in achievement
- Attention deficit or high distractibility
- Hyperactivity or impulsiveness
- Poor motor coordination and spatial relation ability
- Difficulty solving problems
- Perceptual anomalies, such as reversing letters, words, or numbers
- Difficulty with self-motivated, self-regulated activities

learning disabilities (LD)

Disorders that impede academic progress of people who are not mentally retarded or emotionally disturbed.

- Overreliance on teacher and peers for assignments
- Specific disorders of memory, thinking, or language
- Immature social skills
- Disorganized approach to learning

Definitions of learning disabilities have historically required evidence of a serious discrepancy between actual performance and the performance that might have been predicted on the basis of one or more tests of cognitive functioning, such as an IQ test (Meyer & Rose, 2000; Siegel, 2003). In practice, many children are identified as having a learning disability as a result of having substantial differences between some subscales of an IQ test and others or between one ability test and another. This emphasis on discrepancies has increasingly come under attack in recent years, however. For example, Fletcher and colleagues (1994) studied children ages 7.5 to 9.5 who were failing in reading. Some of these children had major discrepancies between their IQs and performance; others had (low) IQ scores consistent with poor performance. On an extensive battery of assessments, the discrepant and "nondiscrepant" children were nearly identical. In either case, what they lacked were skills closely related to reading. A similar pattern has been found for students with mathematics disabilities (Swanson & Jerman, 2006). Many other studies (e.g., Francis, Shaywitz, Shaywitz, Stuebing, & Fletcher, 1996; Metsala, Stanovich, & Brown, 1998; Stanovich, Siegel, & Gottard, 1997) have found similar results. These studies have undermined the idea that there is a sharp-edged definition of learning disabilities distinct from low achievement (see Hessler, 2001; Stuebing et al., 2002).

Based on this research, the 2004 reauthorization of the main U.S. special-education law, IDEA, eliminated the use of discrepancy as part of the definition of learning disabilities and asked that states develop new definitions defining learning disabilities as a failure to respond to high-quality instruction based on well-validated principles.

CHARACTERISTICS OF STUDENTS WITH LEARNING DISABILITIES   On average, students with learning disabilities tend to have lower academic self-esteem than do students who are nondisabled, although in nonacademic arenas their self-esteem levels are like those of other children (Elbaum & Vaughn, 2001; Kelly & Norwich, 2004; Manning, Bear, & Minke, 2001). On most social dimensions, children with learning disabilities resemble other low achievers (Bender, 2008). Boys are more likely than girls to be labeled as learning disabled. African Americans, Latinos, and children from families in which the head of the household has not attended college tend to be over-represented in special-education classes, whereas female students are under-represented (Harry & Klingner, 2007; O'Connor & Fernandez, 2006). There is a great deal of concern about the overidentification of boys and students who are minorities in special education (Waitoller, Artiles, & Cheney, 2010). The 2004 reauthorization of IDEA requires states and the federal government to monitor racial differences in special-education placements and to change policies that perpetuate them.

Theory into Practice
Teaching Students with Learning Disabilities

INTASC

5 Classroom Management and Motivation

7 Instructional Planning Skills

There are many types of learning disabilities, and issues in teaching students with learning disabilities differ by age level. However, a few broad principles apply across many circumstances. In general, effective teaching for students with learning disabilities uses the same strategies that are effective with other students, except that there might be less margin for error. In other words, a student with learning disabilities is less likely than other students to learn from poor instruction. The following general concepts apply to effective teaching for students with learning disabilities (see Bender, 2008):

1. Emphasize prevention.   Many of the learning deficits that cause a child to be categorized as having learning disabilities can be prevented. For example, high-quality early childhood programs and primary-grades teaching significantly reduce the number of children identified with learning disabilities (Conyers et al., 2003; Slavin, 1996; Snow et al., 1998). One-to-one tutoring for first-graders struggling with reading can be particularly effective in preventing reading disabilities (Morris et al., 2000; Slavin, Lake, Davis, & Madden, 2009). Early reading strategies emphasizing phonics, beneficial to most children, are essential to a large proportion of children at risk for reading disabilities (Cavanaugh et al., 2004; Schneider, Roth, & Ennemoser, 2000). Clearly, the easiest learning disabilities to deal with are those that never appear in the first place.

Recognizing that the great majority of children labeled as having learning disabilities experience problems in reading, the 2004 reauthorization of IDEA encourages schools to provide scientifically validated reading programs to students who are at risk, and it allows schools to spend up to 15 percent of their IDEA funding for prevention and early intervention to help struggling students before they fall far enough behind to require a disability diagnosis.

2. Teach learning-to-learn skills.   Many students with learning disabilities lack good strategies for studying, test-taking, and so on. These skills can be taught. Many studies have shown that students with learning disabilities who are directly taught study strategies and other cognitive strategies perform significantly better in school (Bryant, Ugel, Thompson, & Hampff, 1999; Deshler, Ellis, & Lenz, 1996; Gersten, Fuchs, Williams, & Baker, 2001; Harris et al., 2001; Jitendra, Edwards, Sacks, & Jacobson, 2004; Swanson, 2001).

3. Give frequent feedback.   Students with learning disabilities are less likely than other students to be able to work productively for long periods of time with little or no feedback. They do better in situations in which they get frequent feedback on their efforts, particularly feedback about how they have improved or how they have worked hard to achieve something. For example, children with learning disabilities are likely to do better with brief, concrete assignments that are immediately scored than with long-term assignments. If long-term projects or reports are assigned, the students should have many intermediate goals and get feedback on each (see Deshler et al., 1996).

4. Use teaching strategies that engage students actively in lessons.   Students with learning disabilities are particularly unlikely to learn from long lectures. They tend to do best when they are actively involved. This implies that teachers who have such students in their classes should make extensive use of hands-on projects, cooperative learning, and other active learning methods, although it is important that these activities are well structured and have clear goals and roles (see Putnam, 1998; Slavin, 1995a; Slavin, Lake, Davis, & Madden, 2009; Swanson & Hoskyn, 1998).

5. Use effective classroom management methods.   Because of their difficulties with information processing and language, many students with learning disabilities experience a great deal of frustration in school and respond by engaging in minor (or major) misbehavior. Effective classroom management methods can greatly reduce this misbehavior, especially strategies that emphasize prevention. For example, students with learning disabilities are likely to respond well to a rapid pace of instruction with much variety and many opportunities to participate and respond successfully (Bender, 2008; Mather & Goldstein, 2001).

6. Coordinate supplementary services with classroom instruction. Many students with learning disabilities will need some sort of supplementary services, such as small-group tutorials, resource teachers, one-to-one tutoring, or computer-assisted instruction. Whatever these services are, they should be closely aligned with the instruction being given in academic classes (Vaughn, Bos, & Schumm, 2007). For example, if a student is working on *Treasure Island* in class, a tutor should also work on *Treasure Island*. If a student's math class is working on fractions, so should the resource teacher. Of course, there are times when supplementary services cannot be coordinated fully with classroom instruction, as when a student needs work on study strategies or prerequisite skills. However, every effort should be made to create as much linkage as possible so that the student can see an immediate learning payoff for his or her efforts in the supplementary program. The students having the greatest difficulties in learning should not have to balance two completely different kinds of teaching on different topics.

■ Students with Attention Deficit Hyperactivity Disorder

Students with **attention deficit hyperactivity disorder (ADHD)** have difficulties maintaining attention because of a limited ability to concentrate (Mash & Wolfe, 2003). ADHD includes impulsive actions, attention deficits, and sometimes hyperactive behavior. These characteristics differentiate students with ADHD from students with learning disabilities, who have attention deficits for other unknown reasons (American Psychiatric Association, 1994). Children with ADHD do not qualify for special education unless they also have some other disability condition that is defined in the law (Aleman, 1990). There is much debate about whether ADHD exists as a distinct diagnostic category (Swanson, Mink, & Bocian, 1999). About 7.8 percent of children ages 4 to 17 have been diagnosed with ADHD (Brown, 2007). Research indicates that males with ADHD outnumber females in ratios varying from 4:1 to 9:1 (Kauffman & Landrum, 2009). Children with ADHD may be impulsive, acting before they think or without regard for the situation they are in, and often can be inattentive and may find it hard to sit still. Medications for ADHD are widely prescribed, and a variety of drugs have been found to make hyperactive children more manageable and improve their academic performance (Brown, 2007; Evans et al., 2000). They can also have side effects, such as insomnia, weight loss, and blood pressure changes (Wilens, 1998), and should not be prescribed unless other strategies for helping children focus their attention have been tried.

Theory into Practice
Students with ADHD: The Role of the Teacher

Attention deficit hyperactivity disorder (ADHD) is usually associated with inattention, impulsivity, and hyperactivity. Educational implications of ADHD for students can include significant academic, behavior, and social problems stemming from the inability to pay attention. Specific suggestions for the general education classroom teacher who has students with ADHD include the following (see Brown, 2007; Kauffman & Landrum, 2009; Smith, 2001; Teeter, 2000):

attention deficit hyperactivity disorder (ADHD)

A disorder characterized by difficulties maintaining attention because of a limited ability to concentrate; includes impulsive actions and hyperactive behavior.

- Make sure students understand all classroom rules and procedures.

- Consider carefully the seating arrangements of students with ADHD to prevent distractions and to keep these students in proximity to the teacher.

- Adhere to the principles of effective classroom management described in Chapter 11.

- Understand that certain behaviors, although not desirable, are not meant to be noncompliant—students might not be able to control their behaviors.

- Allow students who are hyperactive to have many opportunities to be active.

- Refrain from implementing a behavior management system that is predicated mostly on the use of punishment or threats.

- Group students with ADHD wisely, taking into consideration the purpose of the group and the other students who will be members of the group.

- Teach students to manage their own behaviors—including self-monitoring, self-evaluation, self-reinforcement, and self-instruction (Binder et al., 2000; Robinson, Smith, Miller, & Brownell, 1999).

- Maintain ongoing communication with the students' homes by using daily report cards or other instruments to convey information (see Chapter 11).

- Collaborate with special-education personnel to develop behavioral and instructional plans for dealing with attention problems.

INTASC

3 Adapting Instruction for Individual Needs

5 Classroom Management and Motivation

7 Instructional Planning Skills

✓ Certification Pointer

For a case study on your teacher certification test, you may be asked to suggest how to help a student with a very limited attention span to focus on a lecture and organize the concepts.

Students with Speech or Language Impairments

Some of the most common disabilities are problems with speech and language. About 1 in every 40 students has a communication disorder serious enough to warrant speech therapy or other special-education services.

Although the terms *speech* and *language* are often used interchangeably, they are not the same. Language is the communication of ideas using symbols and includes written language, sign language, gesture, and other modes of communication in addition to oral speech. Speech refers to the formation and sequencing of sounds. It is quite possible to have a speech disorder without a language disorder or to have a language disorder without a speech disorder (Bernstein & Tiegerman-Farber, 2009).

STUDENTS WITH SPEECH DISORDERS   There are many kinds of **speech disorders.** The most common are articulation (or phonological) disorders, such as omissions, distortions, or substitutions of sounds. For example, some students have difficulty pronouncing *r*'s, saying "sowee" for "sorry." Others have lisps, substituting *th* for *s,* saying "thnake" for "snake."

Misarticulated words are common and developmentally normal for many children in kindergarten and first grade but drop off rapidly through the school years. Moderate and extreme deviations in articulation diminish over the school years, with or without speech therapy. For this reason, speech therapists often decide not to work with a child who has a mild articulation problem. However, speech therapy is called for if a student cannot be understood or if the problem is causing the student psychological or social difficulties (such as being teased).

Speech disorders of all kinds are diagnosed and treated by speech pathologists or speech therapists. The classroom teacher's role is less important here than with other disability areas. However, the classroom teacher does have one crucial role to play: displaying acceptance of students with speech disorders. Most speech disorders will eventually resolve themselves. The lasting damage is more often psychological than phonological; students with speech disorders often are subjected to a great deal of teasing and social

speech disorders

Oral articulation problems, occurring most frequently among children in the early elementary school grades.

rejection. Teachers can model acceptance of the child with speech disorders in several ways. First, teachers should be patient with students who are stuttering or having trouble producing words and never finish a student's sentence or allow others to do so. Second, teachers should avoid putting students who have speech problems into high-pressure situations that require quick verbal responses. Third, teachers should refrain from correcting students' articulation in class.

Connections

Problems that result from limited English proficiency are discussed in Chapter 4, page 95.

Connections

For more on preschool and primary programs that help overcome problems of children from disadvantaged homes, see Chapter 9, page 263.

STUDENTS WITH LANGUAGE DISORDERS   Impairments of the ability to understand language or to express ideas in one's native language constitute **language disorders** (Bernstein & Tiegerman-Farber, 2009). Problems that result from limited English-speaking proficiency (LEP) of students whose first language is not English are not considered language disorders.

Difficulties in understanding language (receptive language disorders) or in communicating (expressive language disorders) might result from such physical problems as hearing or speech impairment. If not, they are likely to indicate mental retardation or learning disabilities. Many students come to school with what appear to be receptive or expressive language disorders but that in fact result from a lack of experience with standard English because they speak either a language other than English or a dialect of English (Bonner-Tompkins, 2001). Preschool programs that are rich in verbal experience and direct instruction in the fundamentals of standard English have been found effective in overcoming language problems that are characteristic of children from disadvantaged homes.

■ Students with Emotional and Behavioral Disorders

All students are likely to have emotional problems at some point in their school careers; however, about 1 percent have such serious, long-lasting, and pervasive emotional or psychiatric disorders that they require special education. As in the case of learning disabilities, students with serious emotional and behavioral disorders are far more likely to be boys than girls, by a ratio of more than 3 to 1 (Kauffman & Landrum, 2009; U.S. Department of Education, 2005).

Students with **emotional and behavioral disorders** have been defined as those whose educational performance is adversely affected over a long period of time to a marked degree by any of the following conditions:

1. An inability to learn that cannot be explained by intellectual, sensory, or health factors
2. An inability to build or maintain satisfactory interpersonal relationships with peers and teachers
3. Inappropriate types of behavior or feelings under normal circumstances
4. A general, pervasive mood of unhappiness or depression
5. A tendency to develop physical symptoms, pains, or fears associated with personal or school problems

language disorders

Impairments in one's ability to understand language or to express ideas in one's native language.

emotional and behavioral disorders

Exceptionalities characterized by problems with learning, interpersonal relationships, and control of feelings and behavior.

CAUSES OF EMOTIONAL AND BEHAVIORAL DISORDERS   Serious and long-term emotional and behavioral disorders may be the result of numerous potential causal factors in the makeup and development of an individual (Jones, Dohrn, & Dunn, 2004). Neurological functioning, psychological processes, a history of maladaptations, self-concept, and lack of social acceptance all play a role (Smith et al., 2008). Some of the same factors, including family dysfunction and maltreatment (Thompson & Wyatt, 1999), also play a role in disturbances that might temporarily affect a child's school performance.

Many factors that affect families can disrupt a student's sense of security and self-worth for a period of time. Changes in the family structure, for example, might leave a child depressed, angry, insecure, defensive, and lonely, especially in the case of divorce, relocation to a new community, the addition of a new sibling, the addition of a step-parent, or the death or serious illness of a family member.

One problem in identifying serious emotional and behavioral disorders is that the term covers a wide range of behaviors, from aggression or hyperactivity to withdrawal or inability to make friends to anxiety and phobias (Kauffman & Landrum, 2009). Also, children with emotional disorders quite frequently have other disabilities, such as learning disabilities or mental retardation, and it is often hard to tell whether an emotional problem is causing the diminished academic performance or school failure is causing the emotional problem.

CHARACTERISTICS OF STUDENTS WITH EMOTIONAL AND BEHAVIORAL DISORDERS   Scores of characteristics are associated with emotional and behavioral disorders (Rosenberg, Wilson, Maheady, & Sindelar, 2004). The important issue is the degree of the behavior problem. Virtually any behavior that is exhibited excessively over a long period of time might be considered an indication of emotional disturbance. However, most students who have been identified as having emotional and behavioral disorders share some general characteristics. These include poor academic achievement, poor interpersonal relationships, and poor self-esteem (Lewis & Sullivan, 1996). Quay and Werry (1986) noted four general categories: conduct disorder, anxiety–withdrawal, immaturity, and socialized–aggressive disorder. For example, children with **conduct disorders** are frequently characterized as disobedient, distractible, selfish, jealous, destructive, impertinent, resistive, and disruptive. Quay and Werry noted that the first three of these general categories represent behaviors that are maladaptive or sources of personal distress. However, socialized–aggressive behavior, which relates to frequent aggression against others, seems to be tied more to poor home conditions that model or reward aggressive behavior and, therefore, might be adaptive (though certainly not healthy or appropriate). The inclusion of conduct disorders in classifications of emotional and behavioral disorders is controversial. By law, students with conduct disorders must also have some other recognized disability or disorder to receive special-education services. IDEA has long protected children who have emotional and behavioral disorders from ordinary punishments (such as suspension) for disruptive behavior. The 2004 reauthorization maintains this protection for behaviors related to the child's disability but not for unrelated behaviors.

STUDENTS EXHIBITING AGGRESSIVE BEHAVIOR   Students with conduct disorders and socialized–aggressive behaviors might frequently fight, steal, destroy property, and refuse to obey teachers (Jones et al., 2004). These students tend to be disliked by their peers, their teachers, and sometimes their parents. They typically do not respond to punishment or threats, though they might be skilled at avoiding punishment. Aggressive children not only pose a threat to the school and to their peers but also put themselves in grave danger. Aggressive children, particularly boys, often develop serious emotional problems later in life, have difficulty holding jobs, and become involved in criminal behavior (Loeber & Stouthamer-Loeber, 1998; van Goozen, Fairchild, Snoek, & Harold, 2007). Effective approaches for these children include behavior management strategies like those described in Chapter 11 (see Jones & Jones, 2007)

STUDENTS WITH WITHDRAWN AND IMMATURE BEHAVIOR   Children who are withdrawn, immature, low in self-esteem, or depressed typically have few friends or play with children much younger than themselves. They often have elaborate fantasies or daydreams and either very poor or grandiose self-images. Some might be overly anxious about their health and feel genuinely ill when under stress. Some students exhibit school phobia by refusing to attend or by running away from school.

> **Connections**
> Behavior management programs for students exhibiting aggressive behavior are described in Chapter 11, page 334.

> **conduct disorders**
> Socioemotional and behavioral disorders that are indicated in individuals who, for example, are chronically disobedient or disruptive.

Unlike children who are aggressive, who can appear quite normal when they are not being aggressive, children who are withdrawn and immature often appear odd or awkward at all times. They almost always suffer from a lack of social skills (see Troop & Asher, 1999).

■ Students with Autism Spectrum Disorder

In 1990, autism became a formal category of disability. The U.S. Department of Education defined **autism** as a developmental disability that significantly affects social interaction and verbal and nonverbal communication. It is usually evident before age 3 and has an adverse affect on educational performance. Children with autism are typically extremely withdrawn and have such severe difficulties with language that they might be entirely mute. They often engage in self-stimulation activities such as rocking, twirling objects, or flapping their hands. However, they might have normal or even outstanding abilities in certain areas.

The term *autism spectrum disorder* is now being used to describe a broad range of severity, including a mild form of autism called *Asperger syndrome* (National Research Council, 2001; Sweeney & Hoffman, 2004). Children with Asperger syndrome may be able to function in society and can be successful in school, but they have significant problems with social relations, perhaps avoiding eye contact, misinterpreting social cues, and behaving in odd ways. Approximately 1 in 166 children is estimated to have autistim spectrum disorder, although the number of children with autism is much less than this (Hallahan et al., 2009). For unknown reasons, autism is far more prevalent among boys than girls (Friend & Bursuck, 2008). It is thought to be caused by brain damage or other brain dysfunction (Volkmar & Pauls, 2003).

There is no cure for autism, and appropriate interventions depend on the child's level of functioning. The main focus should be on teaching these children social skills that might be taken for granted in other children, such as making eye contact, smiling, and greeting others. The National Research Council (2001), in a review of the literature, concluded that successful strategies include systematic teaching of communication skills, social skills, and cognitive skills in a step-by-step progression. Children with autism spectrum disorders who are in general education classes may benefit from working in small groups, or being assigned a peer partner to help with social and academic problems.

ON THE **WEB**

More information on autism spectrum disorders can be found at www.autism-society.org. Also see the CDC website (www.cdcfoundation.org/healththreats/autism.aspx) and the CEC website (www.cec.sped.org/AM/Template.cfm?Section=Autism_Asperger_s_Syndrome&Template=/TaggedPage/TaggedPageDisplay.cfm&TPLID=37&ContentID=5598).

■ Students with Sensory, Physical, and Health Impairments

Sensory impairments are problems with the ability to see or hear or otherwise receive information through the body's senses. Physical disorders include conditions such as cerebral palsy, spina bifida, spinal cord injury, and muscular dystrophy. Health disorders include, for example, acquired immune deficiency syndrome (AIDS); seizure disorders; diabetes; cystic fibrosis; sickle-cell anemia (in African American students); and bodily damage from chemical addictions, child abuse, or attempted suicide (Hardman et al., 1996).

STUDENTS WITH VISUAL DISABILITIES   Most students' visual problems are correctable by glasses or other types of corrective lenses. A **vision loss** is considered a disability only if it is not correctable. It is estimated that approximately 1 out of every 1,000

autism

A category of disability that significantly affects social interaction, verbal and nonverbal communication, and educational performance.

sensory impairments

Problems with the ability to receive information through the body's senses.

vision loss

Degree of uncorrectable inability to see well.

children has a visual disability. Such disabilities are usually referred to as *blindness* or *visual impairment*. A child defined as legally blind is one whose vision is judged to be 20/200 or worse in the better eye, even with correction, or whose field of vision is significantly narrower than that of a person with normal vision. Persons with partial sight, according to this classification system, are those whose vision is between 20/70 and 20/200 in the better eye with correction (Rogow, 1988).

It is a misconception to assume that individuals who are legally blind have no sight. More than 80 percent of students who are legally blind can read large- or regular-print books (Levin, 1996). Assistive technology used to enlarge and clarify text has further expanded the numbers of students who can participate normally in class (Boone & Higgins, 2007). This implies that many students with vision loss can be taught by means of a modification of usual teaching materials. Classroom teachers should be aware of the signs indicating that a child has a vision problem. Undoubtedly, children who have difficulty seeing also have difficulty in many areas of learning because classroom lessons typically use a tremendous amount of visual material. Several possible signs of vision loss include the following: (1) child often tilts head; (2) child rubs eyes often; (3) child's eyes are red, inflamed, crusty, or water excessively; (4) child has difficulty reading small print or can't discriminate letters; (5) child complains of dizziness or headaches after a reading assignment (Sornson, 2001). If you notice any of these problems, you should refer the student for appropriate vision screening. It is crucial to catch vision problems early, before they adversely affect students' learning and motivation.

STUDENTS WHO ARE DEAF OR HARD OF HEARING   The range of **hearing disabilities** spans complete deafness to problems that can be alleviated with a hearing aid. The appropriate classification of an individual with hearing loss depends on the measures required to compensate for the problem. Simply having a student sit at the front of the classroom might be enough to compensate for a mild hearing loss. Many children can communicate adequately by listening to your voice and watching your lips. Others might need a hearing aid, and those with more severe problems

hearing disabilities
Degree of deafness; uncorrectable inability to hear well.

will need to use a nonverbal form of communication such as sign language (see Radziewicz & Antonellis, 2002). Approaches to reading instruction also need to be modified (Schirmer & McGough, 2005). Flexner (2001) argues that a broad range of children can benefit from amplification of the teacher's voice or the use of assistive technology on computers to amplify and clarify speech (Boone & Higgins, 2007). Following are several suggestions to keep in mind:

1. Seat children with hearing problems in the front of the room, slightly off center toward the windows. This will allow them to see your face in the best light.

2. If the hearing problem is predominantly in one ear, students should sit in a front corner seat so that their better ear is toward you.

3. Speak at the student's eye level whenever possible.

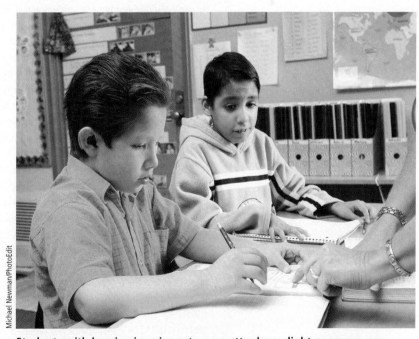

Michael Newman/PhotoEdit

Students with hearing impairments, no matter how slight or severe, can easily fall through the cracks in a busy classroom. As a teacher, what considerations might you need to make in order to fully support the needs of a student who is hearing impaired?

4. Give important information and instructions while facing the class. Avoid talking while facing the chalkboard.

5. Do not use exaggerated lip movements when speaking.

6. Learn how to assist a child who has a hearing aid.

■ Students Who Are Gifted and Talented

Who are the gifted and talented? Almost all children, according to their parents; and in fact many students do have outstanding talents or skills in some area. **Giftedness** was once defined almost entirely in terms of superior IQ or demonstrated ability, such as outstanding performance in mathematics or chess, but the definition now encompasses students with superior abilities in a wide range of activities, including the arts (Colangelo & Davis, 2009; Olszewski-Kubilius, 2003; Sternberg, 2007). High IQ is still considered part of the definition of gifted and talented (Steiner & Carr, 2003), and most students who are so categorized have IQs above 130. However, some groups are underidentified as gifted and talented, including females, students with disabilities, underachievers, and students who are members of racial or ethnic minority groups (Sternberg, 2007). Approximately 3 to 5 percent of students are considered gifted or talented (Heller, Monks, Sternberg, & Subotnik, 2000).

ON THE WEB

There are many Web-based resources for special needs educators. Family Friendly Fun with Special Needs (www.family-friendly-fun.com) offers a great collection of resources for use with children with special needs on a variety of topics. The Special Needs Resource site (www.edbydesign.com/specneedsres/links.html) showcases international students, assistive technologies, and other resources for special learners. Internet Resources for Special Children (www.irsc.org) is an organization dedicated to providing information, activities, and support for learners with special needs. Visit Special Needs Opportunity Windows (http://snow.utoronto.ca) for professional development, student activities, and parent resource materials, which are only a few of the many areas contained on this site. DREAMMS for Kids, Inc. (www.dreamms.org) is a site created by Developmental Research for the Effective Advancement of Memory and Motor Skills, which is a nonprofit parent and professional service agency that specializes in assistive technology (AT)–related research, development, and information dissemination. CAST (Center for Applied Special Technology) (www.cast.org) is an educational not-for-profit organization that uses technology to expand opportunities for all people, including those with disabilities. The National Center to Improve Practice in Special Education (www2.edc.org/NCIP) was federally funded from 1992 to 1998 to improve educational outcomes for students with disabilities by promoting the effective use of assistive and instructional technologies among educators and related personnel serving these students. The Alliance for Technology Access (ATA) at www.ataccess.org is a network of community-based resource centers, developers and vendors, affiliates, and associates dedicated to providing information and support services to children and adults with disabilities and increasing their use of standard, assistive, and information technologies. Closing the Gap (www.closingthegap.com) is a rich source for information on innovative applications of computer technology for persons with disabilities. This site provides a comprehensive examination of the most current uses of technology by persons with disabilities and the professionals who work with them. Internet Special Education Resources (www.iser.com) is a nationwide directory of professionals who serve the learning disabilities and special-education communities. ISER helps parents and caregivers find local special-education professionals to help with learning disabilities and attention deficit hyperactivity disorder assessment, therapy, advocacy, and other special needs. The University of Washington's Adaptive Technologies site (www.washington.edu/doit) has an extensive collection of publications and videos concerning technologies to help people with disabilities.

giftedness

Exceptional intellectual ability, creativity, or talent.

CHARACTERISTICS OF STUDENTS WHO ARE GIFTED AND TALENTED   Children who are intellectually gifted typically have strong motivation (Colangelo & Davis, 2009; Gottfried & Gottfried, 2004). They also are academically superior, usually learn to read early, and generally do excellent work in most school areas (Gallagher, 1992). One of the most important studies of children with intellectual gifts, begun by Lewis Terman in 1926, followed 1,528 individuals who had IQs higher than 140 as children. Terman's research exploded the myth that high-IQ individuals were brainy but physically and socially inept. In fact, Terman found that children with outstanding IQs were larger, stronger, and better coordinated than other children and became better adjusted and more emotionally stable adults (Terman & Oden, 1959). Students who are gifted also have high self-concepts (Hoge & Renzulli, 1993), although they can suffer from perfectionism (Parker, 1997).

EDUCATION OF STUDENTS WHO ARE GIFTED   How to educate students who are gifted is a matter of debate (see Karnes & Bean, 2001; Smutny, 2003; Willard-Holt, 2003; Winebrenner, 2000). Some programs for those with gifts and talents involve special secondary schools for students who are gifted in science or in the arts. Some programs include special classes for high achievers in regular schools (see Olszewski-Kubilius, 2003). One debate in this area concerns acceleration versus enrichment. Advocates of acceleration (e.g., Colangelo, Assouline, & Gross, 2005; Pendarvis & Howley, 1996) argue that students with intellectual gifts should be encouraged to move through the school curriculum rapidly, perhaps skipping grades and going to college at an early age. Others (e.g., Feldhusen, 1996; Gallagher, 1992; Renzulli & Reis, 1997) maintain that rather than merely moving students through school more rapidly, programs for those who are gifted should engage them in more creative and problem-solving activities.

Research on giftedness provides more support (in terms of student achievement gains) for acceleration than for enrichment (Kulik & Kulik, 1997; Rogers, 2009). However, this could be because the outcomes of enrichment, such as creativity or problem-solving skills, are difficult to measure. **Acceleration programs** for students who are gifted often involve the teaching of advanced mathematics to students at early ages. A variation on the acceleration theme is a technique called curriculum compacting, in which teachers may skip over portions of the curriculum that the students who are very able do not need (Willard-Holt, 2003).

Enrichment programs take many forms. Renzulli and Reis (2000) suggest an emphasis on three types of activities: general exploratory activities, such as projects that allow students to find out about topics on their own; group training activities, such as games and simulations to promote creativity and problem-solving skills; and individual and small-group investigations of real problems, such as writing books or newspapers, interviewing elderly people to write oral histories, and conducting geological or archaeological investigations.

One problem with enrichment programs for students who are gifted and talented is simply that most of the activities suggested for these students would benefit all students (Borland, 2008). In recognition of this, many schools are now infusing activities that are characteristic of enrichment programs into the curriculum for all students, thereby meeting the needs of students who are gifted and talented without physically separating them from their peers (see Colangelo & Davis, 2009; Holloway, 2003; Page, 2000; Renzulli & Reis, 2000; Van Tassel-Baska, 1989). Examples of such activities include increased use of projects, experiments, independent study, and cooperative learning.

What Is Special Education

Special education is any program provided for children with disabilities instead of, or in addition to, the general education classroom program. The practice of special

---

acceleration programs

Rapid promotion through advanced studies for students who are gifted or talented.

enrichment programs

Programs in which assignments or activities are designed to broaden or deepen the knowledge of students who master classroom lessons quickly.

special education

Programs that address the needs of students with mental, emotional, or physical disabilities.

education has changed dramatically in recent years and is still evolving (see Hallahan et al., 2009; Smith et al., 2008; Sorrells, Rieth, & Sindelar, 2004). Federal legislation has been critical in setting standards for special-education services administered by states and local districts.

■ Public Law 94-142 and IDEA

As recently as the mid-1960s, education of children with exceptionalities was quite different from what it is today. Many "handicapped" students received no special services at all. Those who did get special services usually attended separate schools or institutions for people with mental retardation, emotional disturbances, or vision or hearing loss. In the late 1960s the special-education system came under attack (see Semmel, Gerber, & MacMillan, 1994). Critics argued that people who had serious disabilities were too often shut away in state institutions with inadequate educational services or were left at home with no services at all and that children with mild disabilities (particularly those with mild mental retardation) were being isolated in special programs that failed to teach them the skills they needed to function in society. Four million of the eight million students of school age who had disabilities were not in school.

As a result, in 1975, Congress passed **Public Law 94-142,** the Education for the Handicapped Act. P.L. 94-142, as it is commonly called, profoundly affected both special and general education throughout the United States. It prescribed the services that all children who had disabilities must receive and gave the children and their parents legal rights that they had not previously possessed. A basic tenet of P.L. 94-142 was that every child who is disabled is entitled to special education appropriate to the child's needs at public expense. This means, for example, that school districts or states must provide special education to children who are severely retarded or disabled.

P.L. 94-142 was extended beyond its original focus in two major pieces of legislation. In 1986, Public Law 99-457 extended the entitlement for free, appropriate education to children ages 3 to 5. It also added programs for infants and toddlers who are seriously disabled. Public Law 101-476, which passed in 1990 and changed the name of the special-education law to the **Individuals with Disabilities Education Act (IDEA),** required that schools plan for the transition of adolescents with disabilities into further education or employment starting at age 16, and replaced the term *handicapped children* with the term *children with disabilities.*

In 1997, Public Law 105-17, the Individuals with Disabilities Education Act Amendments of 1997, or IDEA '97, was passed to reauthorize and strengthen the original act (National Information Center for Children and Youth with Disabilities, 1998). Among the goals of this law were raising educational expectations for children with disabilities, increasing the role of parents in the education of their children with disabilities, assuring that regular classroom teachers are involved in planning for and assessment of these children, including students with disabilities in local and state assessments, and supporting professional development for all who educate children with disabilities (U.S. Department of Education, 1998).

IDEA was further updated in 2004 under Public Law 108-446, known as the Individuals with Disabilities Education Improvement Act. This revision emphasized prevention and early intervention, allowing schools to spend special-education funds to prevent children from needing special-education services. It changed the definition of learning disabilities to eliminate from it the concept of discrepancy between IQ and achievement, asked states to monitor and correct racial disparities in assignment to special education, and coordinated IDEA with other reforms, especially No Child Left Behind. The major provisions of IDEA 2004 are summarized in Table 12.2.

LEAST RESTRICTIVE ENVIRONMENT   The provision of IDEA that is of greatest importance to general education classroom teachers is that students with disabilities must be assigned to the **least restrictive environment** that is appropriate to their needs. This provision gives a legal basis for the practice of **mainstreaming,** a

Public Law 94-142

Federal law enacted in 1975 requiring provision of special-education services to eligible students.

Individuals with Disabilities Education Act (IDEA)

P.L. 101-476, a federal law enacted in 1990 that changed the name of P.L. 94-142 and broadened services to adolescents with disabilities.

least restrictive environment

Provision in IDEA that requires students with disabilities to be educated alongside peers without disabilities to the maximum extent appropriate.

mainstreaming or inclusion

The temporal, instructional, and social integration of eligible children having exceptionalities with peers who do not have exceptionalities based on an ongoing, individually determined educational planning and programming process.

TABLE 12.2 — Key Components of the Individuals with Disabilities Education Act (IDEA) (2004)

Provisions	Description
Least restrictive environment	Children with disabilities are educated with children who do not have disabilities as much as possible.
Individualized Education Program	All children served in special education must have an Individualized Education Program.
Due-process rights	Children and their parents must be involved in decisions about special education.
Due-process hearing	Parents and schools can request an impartial hearing if there is a conflict over special-education services.
Nondiscriminatory assessment	Students must be given a comprehensive assessment that is nondiscriminatory in nature.
Related services	Schools must provide related services, such as physical therapy, counseling, and transportation, if needed.
Free appropriate public education	The primary requirement of IDEA is the provision of a free appropriate public education to all school-age children with disabilities.
Mediation/resolution	Parents have a right, if they choose, to mediation or a resolution session to resolve differences with the school. Using mediation should not deny or delay a parent's request for a due-process hearing.
Transfer of rights	When the student reaches the age of majority, as defined by the state, the school shall notify both the parents and the student and transfer all rights of the parents to the child.
Discipline	A child with a disability cannot be expelled or suspended for 10 or more cumulative days in a school year without a manifest determination as to whether the child's disability is related to the inappropriate behavior.
State assessments	Children with disabilities must be included in districtwide and statewide assessment programs with appropriate accommodations. Alternative assessment programs must be developed for children who cannot participate in districtwide or statewide assessment programs.
Transition	Transition planning and programming must begin when students with disabilities reach age 16.

Source: Tom E. K. Smith, Edward A. Polloway, James R. Patton, & Carol A. Dowdy, *Teaching Students with Special Needs in Inclusive Settings* (5th ed.), Table 1.5, p. 16. © 2008 Pearson Education, Inc. Reproduced by permission of Pearson Education, Inc.

term that has now been replaced with the word *inclusion* (Friend & Bursuck, 2008; Friend & Shamberger, 2008). This means that general education classroom teachers are likely to have in their classes students with mild disabilities (such as learning disabilities, mild mental retardation, physical disabilities, or speech problems) who might leave class for special instruction part of the day. It also means that classes for students with more serious disabilities are likely to be located in general education school facilities and that these students will probably attend some activities with their peers without disabilities.

INDIVIDUALIZED EDUCATION PROGRAM (IEP)   Another important requirement of IDEA is that every student with a disability must have an **Individualized Education Program (IEP)** that guides the services the student receives. The IEP describes a student's problems and delineates a specific course of action to address these problems. Generally, it is prepared by a special services committee composed of school professionals such as special-education teachers, special-education supervisors, school psychologists, the principal, counselors, and/or classroom teachers. Special services teams go by different names in different states; for example, they may be called child study teams or appraisal and review teams. The student's parent must consent to the IEP. The idea behind the use of IEPs is to give everyone concerned with the education of a child with a disability an opportunity to help formulate the child's instructional program. The requirement that a parent sign the IEP is designed to ensure parental awareness of and

Certification Pointer

On your teacher certification test, you should know that the placement of students in the "least restrictive" educational environment developed as a result of efforts to normalize the lives of children with disabilities.

Individualized Education Program (IEP)

A program tailored to the needs of a learner with exceptionalities.

IEP meetings are an outgrowth of IDEA. What is the purpose of an IEP meeting? What will your role be at these types of meetings?

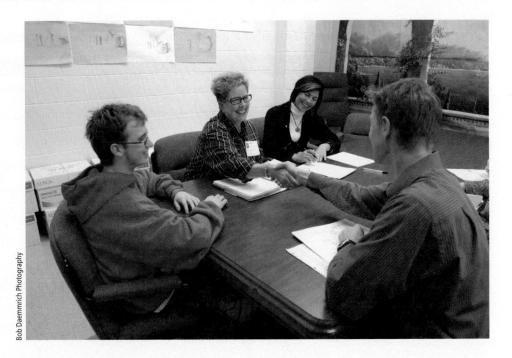

Bob Daemmrich Photography

approval of what the school proposes to do for the child. A parent might hold the school accountable if the child does not receive the promised services.

The law requires that evaluations of students for possible placement in special-education programs be done by qualified professionals. Although general education classroom and special-education teachers will typically be involved in the evaluation process, teachers are not generally allowed to give the psychological tests (such as IQ tests) that are used for placement decisions.

IDEA gives children with disabilities and their parents legal safeguards with regard to special-education placement and programs. For example, if parents believe that a child has been diagnosed incorrectly or assigned to the wrong program or if they are unsatisfied with the services a child is receiving, they may bring a grievance against the school district. Also, the law specifies that parents be notified about all placement decisions, conferences, and changes in program.

For children with special needs who are under the age of 3, a specialized plan focusing on the child and his or her family is typically prepared, called an Individualized Family Service Plan (IFSP). At the other end of the education system, an Individualized Transition Plan (ITP) is often written for adolescents with special needs before their 17th birthday (Sax & Thoma, 2002). The ITP anticipates the student's needs as he or she makes the transition from school to work and to adult life.

■ An Array of Special-Education Services

An important aspect of an IEP is a special-education program that is appropriate to the student's needs. Every school district offers children with special needs an array of services intended to be flexible enough to meet the unique needs of all. In practice, these services are often organized as a continuum going from least to most restrictive, as follows:

1. Direct or indirect consultation and support for general education teacher
2. Special education up to 1 hour per day
3. Special education 1 to 3 hours per day; resource program
4. Special education more than 3 hours per day; self-contained special education

5. Special day school

6. Special residential school

7. Home/hospital

In general, students with more severe disabilities receive more restrictive services than do those with less severe disabilities. For example, a student with severe mental retardation is unlikely to be placed in a general education classroom during academic periods, whereas a student with a speech problem or a mild learning disability is likely to be in a general education classroom for most or all of the school day. However, severity of disability is not the sole criterion for placement; also considered is the appropriateness of the various settings for an individual student's needs. For example, a student in a wheelchair with a severe orthopedic disability but no learning problems could easily attend and profit from general education classes, whereas a student with a hearing deficit might not.

With the exception of students who have physical or sensory disabilities, few students receive special education outside of the school building. The great majority of students who have learning disabilities or speech impairments attend general education classes part or most of the day, usually supplemented by 1 or more hours per day in a special-education resource room. This is also true for the majority of students with physical disabilities and almost half of all students with emotional disorders. Most other students with special needs attend special classes located in their school buildings. The continuum of services available to students with disabilities, from least to most restrictive, is described in the following sections.

GENERAL EDUCATION CLASSROOM PLACEMENT   The needs of many students with disabilities can be met in the general education classroom with little or no outside assistance. For example, students who have mild vision or hearing loss may simply be seated near the front of the room. Students with mild to moderate learning disabilities may have their needs met in the general education classroom if the teacher uses strategies for accommodating instruction to student differences. For example, the use of instructional aides, tutors, or parent volunteers can allow exceptional students to remain in the general education classroom. You can often adapt your instruction to make it easier for students to succeed. For example, one teacher noticed that a student with perceptual problems was having difficulties with arithmetic because he could not line up his numbers. She solved the problem by giving him graph paper to work on.

Research generally shows that the most effective strategies for dealing with students who have learning and behavior problems are those used in the general education classroom (Lloyd, Singh, & Repp, 1991). Special-education options should usually be explored only after serious efforts have been made to meet students' needs in the general education classroom (see Smith et al., 2008; Vaughn et al., 2007).

COLLABORATION WITH CONSULTING TEACHERS AND OTHER PROFESSIONALS   In **collaboration,** several professionals work cooperatively to provide educational services. Students with disabilities who are included in the general education classroom benefit from professionals such as the consulting resource room teacher, school psychologist, speech and language specialists, and other professionals who collaborate with the general education teacher to develop and implement appropriate educational experiences for the students. Many school districts provide classroom teachers with consultants to help them adapt their instruction to the needs of students with disabilities. Consulting teachers typically are trained in special education as well as general education. They might come into the classroom to observe the behavior of a student, but most often they suggest solutions to the general education teacher rather than work directly with students (Warger & Pugach, 1996). Research finds that well-designed consulting models can be effective in assisting teachers to maintain students with mild disabilities,

Connections

Strategies for accommodating instruction to student differences are discussed in Chapter 9.

INTASC

10 Partnerships

collaboration

Process in which professionals work cooperatively to provide educational services.

particularly those with learning disabilities, in the general education classroom (Rosenfield & Gravois, 1996; Snell & Janney, 2000).

For some types of disabilities, itinerant (traveling) teachers provide special services to students a few times a week. This pattern of service is typical of programs for students with speech and language disorders.

RESOURCE ROOM PLACEMENT   Many students with disabilities are assigned to general education classes for most of their school day but participate in resource programs at other times. Most often, resource programs focus on teaching reading, language arts, mathematics, and occasionally other subjects. A resource room program usually involves a small number of students working with a special-education teacher. Ideally, the resource teacher meets regularly with the classroom teacher to coordinate programs for students and to suggest ways in which the general education classroom teacher can adapt instruction when the students are in the general education class (Smith et al., 2008; Vaughn et al., 2007).

Sometimes resource teachers work in the general education classroom. For example, a resource teacher might work with one reading group while the general education classroom teacher works with another. This arrangement avoids pulling students out of class—which is both inefficient (because of the transition time required) and potentially demeaning because the students are excluded from class for some period of time. Team teaching involving general education and special-education teachers also enhances communication between the teachers (Friend, 2007).

SPECIAL-EDUCATION CLASS PLACEMENT WITH PART-TIME INCLUSION   Many students with disabilities are assigned to special classes taught by a special-education teacher but are integrated alongside students without disabilities part of the school day. These students join other students most often for music, art, and physical education; somewhat less often for social studies, science, and mathematics; and least often for reading. One important difference between this category of special services and the resource room model is that in the resource room, the student's primary placement is in the general education class; the classroom teacher is the homeroom teacher and generally takes responsibility for the student's program, with the resource teacher providing extra support. In the case of a student who is assigned to special education and is integrated part of the day, the situation is reversed. The special-education teacher generally serves as the homeroom teacher and takes primary responsibility.

SELF-CONTAINED SPECIAL EDUCATION   A self-contained special-education program is a class located in a school separately from the general education instructional program. Until the mainstreaming movement began in the early 1970s, this (along with separate schools for children with mental retardation) was the typical placement for students with disabilities. Students in self-contained programs are taught by special-education teachers and have relatively few contacts with the general education instructional program.

Some students attend separate special day schools. These are typically students with severe disabilities, such as severe retardation or physical disabilities, or students whose presence might be disruptive to the general education school, such as those with serious emotional disturbances. In addition, small numbers of students with disabilities attend special residential schools for students with profound disabilities who require special treatment.

RELATED SERVICES   IDEA 2004 guarantees "related services" for children with disabilites, constituting services required by a child with a disability to benefit from general or special education. For example, school psychologists are often involved in the process of diagnosing students with disabilities and sometimes participate in the preparation of IEPs (Reschly, 2003). In addition, they may counsel the student or consult with the teacher about behavioral and learning problems. Speech and language therapists generally work with students on a one-to-one basis, though they may provide some small-group instruction for students with similar problems. These therapists also consult with teachers about ways to address student difficulties. Physical and occupational therapists treat motor difficulties under the direction of a physician. School social workers and pupil personnel workers serve as a major link between the school and the family and are likely to become involved when problems at home are affecting students' school performance or behavior.

Classroom teachers have important roles in the education of children with disabilities. They are important in referring students to receive special services, in participating in the assessment of students, and in preparing and implementing IEPs. The Theory into Practice section that follows describes the process by which classroom teachers seek special-education services for students (see Hallahan et al., 2009; Smith & Tyler, 2010).

Theory into Practice
Preparing IEPs

INITIAL REFERRAL The process of preparing an Individualized Education Program begins when a student is referred for assessment. Referrals for special-education assessment can be made by parents, physicians, principals, or teachers. Classroom teachers most often initiate referrals for children with suspected learning disabilities, mental retardation, speech impairment, or emotional disturbance. Most other disabilities are diagnosed before students enter school. In most schools, initial referrals are made to the building principal, who contacts the relevant school district staff.

SCREENING AND ASSESSMENT As soon as the student is referred for assessment, an initial determination is made to accept or reject the referral. In practice, almost all referrals are accepted. The evaluation and placement team may look at the student's school records and interview classroom teachers and others who know the student. If the team members decide to accept the referral, they must obtain parental permission to do a comprehensive assessment.

Members of the special services team include professionals designated by the school district plus the parents of the referred student and, if appropriate, the referred student. If the referral has to do with learning or emotional problems, a school psychologist or guidance counselor will usually be involved. If the referral has to do with speech or language problems, a speech pathologist or speech teacher will typically serve on the team. The building principal usually chairs the team but may designate a special-education teacher or other professional to do so.

The referred student is then given tests to assess strengths and weaknesses. For learning and emotional problems, these tests are usually given by a school psychologist. Specific achievement tests (such as reading or mathematics assessments) are often given by special-education or reading teachers. Parents must give permission for any specialized assessments. Increasingly, portfolios of student work, teacher evaluations, and other information collected over extended time periods are becoming important parts of the assessment process (Smith & Tyler, 2010).

If appropriate, the school may try a prereferral intervention before deciding on placement in special education. For example, a child having serious reading problems might be given a tutor for a period of time before being determined to have a reading disability. For a child with a behavior problem, a home-based

INTASC

8 Assessment of Student Learning

reinforcement program or other behavior management program might be set up. If these interventions work, the child might not be assigned to special education but could be served within the general education program. Even if a child does need special-education services, the prereferral intervention is likely to provide important information about the kind of services most likely to work. Prereferral interventions are becoming far more common under current policies favoring Response to Intervention, discussed later in this chapter.

WRITING THE IEP   When the comprehensive assessment is complete, the special services team members meet to consider the best placement for the student. If they determine that special education is necessary, they will prepare an IEP. In Figure 12.3 a flowchart shows how the IEP process operates. Figure 12.4 on pages 378–379 is an example of an IEP. Usually, the special-education teacher and/or the classroom teacher prepares the IEP. The student's parent(s) must sign a consent form regarding the placement decision, and in many school districts a parent must also sign the IEP. This means that parents can (and in some cases do) refuse to have their children placed in special-education programs. At a minimum, the IEP must contain the following information (see Bateman & Linden, 1998).

1. *Statements indicating the child's present level of performance.*   Statements typically include the results of specific tests as well as descriptions of classroom functioning. Behavior rating checklists, work samples, or other observation forms may be used to clarify a student's strengths and weaknesses.

2. *Goals indicating anticipated progress during the year.*   For example, a student might have goals of reading at a fourth-grade level as measured by a standardized test, of improving classroom behavior so that disciplinary referrals are reduced to zero, or of completing a bricklaying course in a vocational education program.

3. *Intermediate (shorter-term) instructional objectives.*   A student who is having difficulties in reading might be given a short-term objective (STO) of completing a certain number of individualized reading comprehension units per month, or a student with emotional and behavior problems might be expected to get along with peers better and avoid fights.

4. *A statement of the specific special-education and related services to be provided as well as the extent to which the student will participate in general education programs.*   The IEP might specify, for example, that a student would receive two 30-minute sessions with a speech therapist each week. An IEP for a student with a learning disability might specify 45 minutes per day of instruction from a resource teacher in reading plus consultation between the resource teacher and the classroom teacher on ways to adapt instruction in the general education classroom. A student with mental retardation might be assigned to a self-contained special-education class, but the IEP might specify that the student participate in the general physical education program. The IEP would specify any adaptations necessary to accommodate students in the general education class, such as wheelchair ramps, large-type books, or CDs.

5. *The projected date for the initiation of services and the anticipated duration of services.*   Once the IEP has been written, the student must receive services within a reasonable time period. Students may not be put on a waiting list; the school district must provide or contract for the indicated services.

6. *Evaluation criteria and procedures for measuring progress toward goals on at least an annual basis.*   The IEP should specify a strategy for remediating the student's deficits. In particular, the IEP should state the objectives the student is to achieve and how those objectives are to be attained and measured. It is critical to direct special-education services toward a well-specified set of learning or behavior

Connections

For more on home-based reinforcement strategies, see Chapter 11, page 337.

Source: Diane Pedrotty Rivera and Deborah Deutsch Smith, *Teaching Students with Learning and Behavior Problems* (3rd ed.), p. 52. Copyright © 1997 by Allyn & Bacon. Reprinted by permission.

FIGURE 12.3 **Flowchart for the Individualized Education Program Process**

objectives rather than simply deciding that a student falls into some category and, therefore, should receive some service. Ideally, special education for students with mild disabilities should be a short-term, intensive treatment to give students the skills needed in a general education classroom. All too often, a student who is assigned to special education remains there indefinitely, even after the problem for which the student was initially referred has been remediated.

IEPs must be updated at least once a year. The updating provides an opportunity for the team to change programs that are not working or to reduce or terminate special-education services when the student no longer needs them.

FIGURE 12.4 Sample Individualized Education Program

Individualized Education Program Team Report: 10/01/2011

Student's Last Name: _Smith_   First: _Joe_   MI: _____   DOB: _04/18/2001_   Grade: _4_

Parent's Last Name: _Smith_   First: _Juan_   Relationship: _Father_

Native Language or Other Communication Mode: _None_   Interpreter Needed _No_

The Purpose of This IEP Team Meeting is to Discuss (check one of the following):

__ Initial Eligibility _X_ Review/Revise IEP __ Reevaluation __ Change of Disability Reevaluation

Parent Invitations and Contacts:

Method of contact: _Phone_ by: _Principal_   Date: _09/20/2011_   Result: _Contacted_

Eligibility for Special Education:

The IEP Team determined this student to be: __ Ineligible   _X_ Eligible

Primary disability: _Learning disability/dyslexia_   Secondary disability: _none_

Factors to Consider in Order to Provide a Free and Appropriate Public Education (FAPE)

Consider (check) each of the following:

_X_ Strengths of the student	_X_ Communication needs of the student
_X_ Parent input and concerns for enhancing student's education	_n/a_ Positive behavior interventions, supports, and strategies for students whose behavior impedes learning
_X_ Results of an initial evaluation or the most recent reevaluation of the student	_n/a_ Language needs for students with limited English proficiency
_n/a_ Progress on the current IEP annual goals and objectives	_n/a_ Need for assistive technology devices or services
_X_ Student's anticipated needs or other matters	

Annual Goals and Short-Term Objectives

Data used to determine present level of academic achievement and functional performance:

Evaluation S: Student's Daily Work D: Documented Observation R: Rating Scale T: Standardized Test O: Other (specify above)	**Criterion** __% Accuracy __ of __ Rate __ Achievement Level Other (specify above)	**Schedule** Weekly Daily Monthly Other (specify above)	**Status of Progress on Objectives** **1** Achieved/Maintained **2** Progressing at a rate sufficient to meet the annual goal **3** Progressing below a rate sufficient to meet the annual goal **4** Not applicable **5** Other (specify above)

Annual Goal: _Joe will read short stories at a third-grade level independently to demonstrate improved decoding and reading comprehension skills._

Short-Term Objectives (at least two per goal)	Evaluation	Criterion	Schedule
1. _Joe will demonstrate comprehension of reading strategies by utilizing them independently 80% of the time when reading single paragraphs and short reading items from daily living (e.g., ads, jokes, etc.)._	_S, D, O (informal reading inventory)_	_80% accuracy independently_	_M_
2. _Joe will answer questions about a paragraph he reads with 80% accuracy independently_	_S, O (informal reading inventory)_	_80% accuracy independently_	_M_
3. _Joe will answer questions about a 3-paragraph story with 80% accuracy given minimal cues._	_S, O (informal reading inventory)_	_80% accuracy, minimal cues_	_M_

Date	Status Obj 1	Status Obj 2	Status Obj 3	Comments/Data on Progress
_10/01/2010_	_1_	_1_	_2_	_Joe is able to use his strategies independently at the 1–2 paragraph level. Needs prompts on longer passages._

Reporting Progress

_X_ Parents will be informed in writing of progress on goals and objectives of this IEP at the regular reporting periods applicable to general education students.

Additional Reporting: How: _____ When: _____

Supplementary Aids/Services/Personnel Supports

_X_ The IEP Team has considered supplementary aids/services and supports. Needed services are listed below.

Supplementary Aids/Services/Supports	Amount of Time/Frequency/Conditions	Location
Tutoring by paraprofessional	*3 times per week for 20 minutes*	*Room 3*

Special Education Programs/Related Services

Is there a need for a teacher with a particular endorsement? Y / (N)   If yes, please specify:_____

Special Education Program/Services Rule No.	Frequency and Duration	Initiation Date and Location

Special Transportation

_X_ No __ Yes, specifics: _____

Commitment Signatures

_____
Student

_____
Parent

_____
Parent

_____
Public Education Agency Representative/Designee

_____
General Education Teacher

_____
Special Education Teacher/Provider

What Is Response to Intervention?

The emphasis in IDEA 2004 for students with learning disabilities is on **Response to Intervention,** an approach in which students are identified for special-education services not primarily based on tests, but rather based on their ability to profit from increasingly intensive instruction (Fuchs & Fuchs, 2006; Mellard & Johnson, 2008; Smith et al., 2008).

In particular, children who are struggling in reading might be given small-group remediation, one-to-one tutoring, computer-assisted instruction, or other assistance to help them get on track. Only if intensive and long-term interventions have

Response to Intervention

Policies in which struggling children are given intensive assistance and evaluated for possible special-education services only if they fail to respond.

been consistently applied and found to be ineffective might a child be evaluated for potential learning disabilities, and even at this stage, the child's response to the additional assistance would be as diagnostically important as any test scores (Hoover, 2009).

Response to Intervention is intended to replace the longstanding emphasis on IQ-performance discrepancy, which has been found to be a poor predictor of actual performance (Fuchs, Fuchs, & Compton, 2004), with a criterion that focuses directly on the reading problems that cause most referrals in the first place. It also emphasizes immediate preventive services rather than waiting until children are far behind.

Response to Intervention often involves a three-tier model of services to struggling students. Figure 12.5 illustrates the concept, and the following sections describe each of the tiers.

■ Tier 1: Prevention

Tier 1 refers to whole-class strategies designed to help all children succeed. Examples of Tier 1 strategies include giving clear, simple directions to ensure that all students know what to do, teaching study strategies and metacognitive skills, using cooperative learning in small groups, and applying effective classroom management strategies (see Fuchs & Fuchs, 2006; Smith et al., 2008). The idea behind Tier 1 is to use effective teaching methods and to broaden the range of students who can succeed without any special interventions. Perhaps 80 percent of students never need anything more than such preventive strategies.

■ Tier 2: Immediate Intervention

Even with the best preventive efforts, some students will still fall behind and need assistance. The idea in Response to Intervention is to provide such students with assistance targeted to their needs, rather than considering special education. For example, a student who is struggling in reading might receive individual or small-group tutoring from teachers, aides, or volunteers, so that the problem is resolved as quickly as possible and the student can continue in the regular class. Tier 2 interventions may involve adding time (such as after-school or summer school programs), assigning students to computer-assisted instruction, or other means of solving the immediate problem. Perhaps 15 percent of students ever need Tier 2 assistance.

FIGURE 12.5 **Response to Intervention: Three-Tier Model of Support**

Tier 1 Prevention	Tier 2 Immediate Intervention	Tier 3 Intensive Intervention
• Improve whole-class teaching • Use proven whole-class reforms • Improve classroom management	• Provide proven 1-1 or small-group tutoring • Provide additional time (e.g., after school or summer school) • Provide behavioral supports	• Provide proven, high-intensity 1-1 or small-group tutoring • Provide additional time (e.g., after school or summer school) • Provide intensive behavioral supports

■ Tier 3: Intensive Intervention

Tier 3 refers to more intensive interventions for students who have not made sufficient progress in Tiers 1 and 2, perhaps 5 percent of struggling students. These individuals are at risk for special education or retention, both of which are very expensive and disruptive interventions, so Tier 3 strategies should be as intensive and long-lasting as necessary to keep students on track. Tier 3 strategies are not different from Tier 2 strategies except in intensity and duration. They might include one-to-one tutoring by teachers or aides, extended small-group tutoring, or extra time. Outcomes of these services should be carefully monitored to see that students are making good progress, so that any problems are identified and resolved right away.

In concept, Tier 3 services could be provided indefinitely, as an alternative to assessing students for possible placement in special education. Only when every plausible service has been tried and has failed to resolve the student's problems might special education be considered.

■ Research on Response to Intervention

At present, Response to Intervention is a philosophy more than a set of methods, but there has been some research on particular three-tier models in practice. To date, Response to Intervention has only been evaluated in small, controlled studies (e.g., Speece, Case, & Molloy, 2003; Vaughn et al., 2007), and outcomes generally appear positive. Evaluations in more realistic settings have produced conflicting conclusions (Stahl, Keane, & Vukovic, 2009; Struzziero, 2009). However, there is a long way to go in establishing what this policy means for classroom practice as well as national policy (Fuchs & Fuchs, 2006; Gersten & Dimino, 2006; Klingner & Edwards, 2006).

What Is Inclusion ?

The least restrictive environment clause of P.L. 94-142 revolutionized the practice of special education as well as general education. As has already been noted, it requires that students who are exceptional be assigned to the least restrictive environment that is appropriate to their needs (Friend & Shamberger, 2008). Refer to Figure 12.6 for definitions of least restrictive environment and inclusion. This provision has resulted in greatly increased contact between students with disabilities and students without disabilities. In general, students with all types of disabilities have moved one or two notches up the continuum of special-education services. Students who were once placed in special schools are now generally put in separate classrooms in general education schools. Students who were once placed in separate classrooms in general education schools, particularly students with mild retardation and learning disabilities, are now most often assigned to general education classes for most of their instruction.

A movement for **full inclusion** calls for including all children in general education classes, with appropriate assistance (see Artiles, Kozleski, Dorn, & Christensen, 2006; Sapon-Shevin, 2001, 2003). Proponents of full inclusion argue that pull-out programs discourage effective partnerships between general and special educators in implementing IEPs and that students in pull-out programs are stigmatized when they are segregated from other students. These proponents suggest that special-education teachers or paraprofessionals team with classroom teachers and provide services in the general education classroom (Fisher, Sax, & Grove, 2000; Hanline & Daley, 2002; McLeskey & Waldron, 2002; Ruder, 2000; Sapon-Shevin, 2001; Vaughn et al., 2007). Opponents of full inclusion argue that general education classroom teachers lack appropriate training and materials and are already overburdened with large class sizes and inadequate support services, and

full inclusion

Arrangement whereby students who have disabilities or are at risk receive all their instruction in a general education setting; support services are brought to the student.

FIGURE 12.6

Terminology: Inclusive Education

Mainstreaming:
"The temporal, instructional, and social integration of eligible exceptional children with normal peers based on an ongoing, individually determined educational planning and programming process" (Kaufman et al., 1975, pp. 40–41).

Least restrictive environment:
The provision in Public Law 94-142 (renamed the Individuals with Disabilities Education Act, or IDEA) that requires students with disabilities to be educated to the maximum extent appropriate alongside their peers without disabilities.

Inclusive education:
"Students attend their home school with their age and grade peers. It requires that the proportion of students labeled for special services is relatively uniform for all of the schools within a particular district. . . . Included students are not isolated into special classes or wings within the school" (National Association of State Boards of Education, 1992, p. 12).

Full inclusion:
Students who are disabled or at risk receive all their instruction in a general education setting; support services come to the student.

Partial inclusion:
Students receive most of their instruction in general education settings, but the student may be pulled out to another instructional setting when such a setting is deemed appropriate to the student's individual needs.

they worry that children with special needs might not receive necessary services (Kauffman, Lloyd, Baker, & Riedel, 1995; Shanker, 1994/1995).

Many (perhaps most) classroom teachers have students with disabilities, who are usually receiving some type of special-education services part of the day. Most of these integrated students are categorized as having learning disabilities, speech impairments, mild retardation, or emotional disorders. High-quality inclusion models can improve the achievement and self-confidence of these students. Inclusion also allows students with disabilities to interact with peers and to learn conventional behavior. However, inclusion also creates challenges. When integrated students are performing below the level of the rest of the class, some teachers struggle to adapt instruction to these students' needs—and to cope with the often negative attitudes of students without disabilities toward their classmates with disabilities (McLeskey & Waldron, 2002; Pearl et al., 1998), which might defeat attempts at social integration. Unfortunately, some classroom teachers are uncomfortable about having students with disabilities in their classes, and many feel poorly prepared to accommodate these students' needs (Vaughn et al., 2007). Inclusion provides an opportunity for more effective services but is by no means a guarantee that better services will actually be provided (see Kauffman, McGee, & Brigham, 2004; Riehl, 2000).

This student with physical impairments is in a full inclusion program. According to research, how effective are full inclusion and mainstreaming compared to other approaches? As a teacher, how will you foster this boy's social acceptance by peers?

Bill Bachmann/PhotoEdit

■ Research on Inclusion

Research on inclusion, often referred to as *mainstreaming,* has focused on students with learning disabilities, mild retardation, and mild emotional disorders, whose deficits can be termed "mild academic disabilities" (Holloway, 2001; Smith et al., 2008). Several studies have compared students with mild academic disabilities in special-education classes to those in general education classes. When the general education teacher uses an instructional method that is designed to accommodate a wide range of student abilities, students with mild disabilities generally learn much better in the general education classroom than in special-education classes. One classic study on this topic was done by Calhoun and Elliott (1977), who compared students with mild mental retardation and emotional disorders in general education classes to students with the same disabilities in special-education classes. General education classes as well as special-education classes used the same individualized materials, and teachers (trained in special education) were rotated across classes to ensure that the only difference between the general and special programs was the presence of classmates without disabilities. The results of the Calhoun and Elliott (1977) study, depicted in Figure 12.7, suggest the superiority of general education class placement. A study by Roach and Elliott (2006) found that, controlling for many factors, access to the central curriculum was strongly correlated with achievement for students with cognitive disabilities. Other studies (e.g., Gottlieb & Weinberg, 1999; Reynolds & Wolfe, 1999; Saleno & Garrick-Duhaney, 1999) have found more mixed results.

Research on programs for general education classrooms that contain students with learning disabilities indicates that one successful strategy is to use individualized instructional programs. For example, the Cooperative Integrated Reading and Composition (CIRC) program described in Chapter 8 has been found to improve the achievement of mainstreamed students with learning disabilities, in comparison to mainstreamed students in traditionally organized classes (Slavin, Madden, & Leavey, 1984a,b; Stevens & Slavin, 1995b).

Improving the social acceptance of students with academic disabilities is a critical task of inclusion. One consistently effective means of doing this is to involve the students in cooperative learning teams with their classmates without disabilities (Nevin, 1998; Putnam, 1998). For example, a study of Student Teams–Achievement Divisions (STAD) in classes containing students with learning disabilities found that STAD reduces the social rejection of the students with learning disabilities while significantly increasing their achievement (Madden & Slavin, 1983). Other cooperative learning programs have found similar effects on the social acceptance of students with mild academic disabilities (Slavin et al., 1984b; Slavin & Stevens, 1991; Stevens & Slavin, 1995b).

FIGURE 12.7 **Achievement of Students in General Education and Special-Education Classes**

In a classic study, placement in general education classes rather than special-education classes resulted in higher achievement levels over 3 years for students who were emotionally disturbed (ED) and educable mentally retarded (EMR).

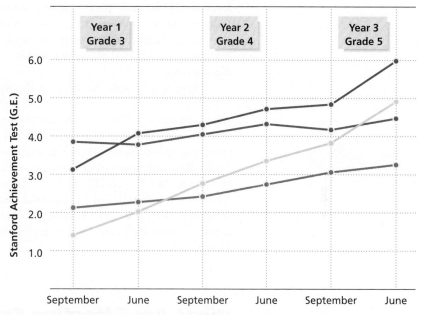

Source: "Self-Concept and Academic Achievement of Educable Retarded and Emotionally Disturbed," *Exceptional Children, 43*(6), pp. 379–380. Copyright © 1977 by The Council for Exceptional Children. Reprinted with permission.

Connections

Cooperative Integrated Reading and Composition (CIRC) is discussed in Chapter 8, page 232.

Connections

For more on STAD, see Chapter 8, page 230.

INTASC

10 Partnerships

A key element in effective inclusion is maintaining close coordination between classroom and special-education teachers (Choate, 2004; Friend & Bursuck, 2008; Smith et al., 2008). An experiment by Fuchs, Fuchs, and Fernstrom (1993) shows how coordination can improve student performance and accomplish full integration of all students with learning disabilities into general education classes over a period of time. In this study, children in pull-out math programs were given frequent curriculum-based measures assessing their progress relative to the school's math program. Special-education teachers examined the requirements for success in the general education class and prepared children specifically to succeed in that setting. As the children reached a criterion level of skills in math, they were transitioned into the general education class and then followed up to ensure that they were succeeding there. Over the course of a school year, all 21 students involved in the study were successfully transitioned to full-time general education class placement and learned significantly more than matched control students did.

There is very little research on the outcomes of full inclusion programs that integrate children who generally would not have been integrated in traditional mainstreaming models. There are descriptions of outstanding full inclusion programs (e.g., Mahony, 1997; Raison, Hanson, Hall, & Reynolds, 1995; Villa & Thousand, 2003), but there have also been reports of full inclusion disasters (e.g., Baines, Baines, & Masterson, 1994). Research comparing inclusive and special-education programs finds few differences (e.g., Mock & Kauffman, 2005; Zigmond, 2003). However, the goals of including students with even the most profound disabilities in general education classrooms are difficult to measure (see McLeskey & Waldron, 2002). Full inclusion is a goal worth striving toward with care, caution, and flexibility (Capper, Kampschroer, & Keyes, 2000; Downing, 2001).

What Are Effective Strategies for Students with Disabilities in General Education ?

The great majority of students with disabilities attend general education classes for part or all of the day. You can help these students succeed by using the strategies described in the following sections: adapting their instruction to accommodate individual needs, teaching learning strategies, using preventive methods to keep students from running into trouble in the first place, and providing intensive early interventions when learning problems first appear.

■ Adapting Instruction

INTASC

3 Adapting Instruction for Individual Needs

Teacher behaviors that are associated with effective teaching for students with disabilities in the general education classroom are essentially the same as those that improve achievement for all students (Swanson & Hoskyn, 1998). Nevertheless, some adaptations in instructional strategies will help you better meet the needs of students with disabilities. When students have difficulty with instruction or materials in learning situations, the recommendation is frequently to adapt or modify the instruction or the materials (see Carolan & Guinn, 2007; Giangreco, 2007). The particular adaptation that is required depends on the student's needs and could be anything from format adaptation to the rewriting of textbook materials. The following Theory into Practice describes four common types of adaptations for accommodating integrated students (also see Browder, 2001; Choate, 2004; Smith et al., 2008; Vaughn et al., 2007).

Theory into Practice
Adapting Instruction for Students with Special Needs

FORMAT ADAPTATIONS FOR WRITTEN ASSIGNMENTS You can change the format by which a task is presented without changing the actual task. Such a change might be needed for a variety of reasons: (1) An assignment is too long; (2) the spacing on the page is too close to allow the student to focus on individual items; (3) the directions for the task are insufficient or confusing; or (4) the models or examples for the task are either absent, misleading, or insufficient. The critical concept here is that although task and response remain the same, you can make adaptations in the way the material is presented (Kleinert & Kearns, 2001).

Occasionally, the directions for a task or assignment must be simplified. For example, you might substitute in a set of directions the word *circle* for *draw a ring around*. You could also teach students the words that are commonly found in directions (Bender, 2008; Smith et al., 2008). By teaching students how to understand such words, you will help them become more independent learners. Models or examples presented with a task may also be changed to more closely resemble the task.

CONTENT ADAPTATIONS In some instances, students might require an adaptation in the content being presented, such as when so much new information is presented that the student cannot process it quickly or when the student lacks a prerequisite skill or concept necessary to complete a task.

One way to adapt the amount of content being presented is to isolate each concept (Bryant, Smith, & Bryant, 2008) and require mastery of each concept as a separate unit before teaching the next concept. Although this type of adaptation involves smaller units of material, the same content will be covered in the end.

Adaptations that are required because students lack essential prerequisites might be as simple as explaining vocabulary or concepts before teaching a lesson. More complex adaptations are required when students lack prerequisite skills or concepts that cannot be explained easily or when students do not have a skill they need to learn the lesson. For example, if the math lesson involves solving word problems that require the division of three-digit numerals and a student has not yet learned how to divide three-digit numerals, this skill will have to be taught before the student can address the word problems.

ADAPTATIONS IN MODES OF COMMUNICATION Some students require adaptations in either the way by which they receive information or the way they demonstrate their knowledge of specific information (Bender, 2008). Many students cannot learn information when their only means of getting it is through reading but can learn if the information is made available in other forms. Be creative in considering the possibilities. You might have students watch a demonstration, filmstrip, film, video, television program, computer program, or play. Or you might have them listen to an audiorecording, lecture/discussion, or debate.

A different type of adaptation might be required if a student cannot respond as the task directs. If a student has a writing problem, for example, you might ask the student to tell you about the concept in a private conversation and record the student's response with an audio recorder or ask the student to present an oral report to the class. Or you might let the student represent the knowledge by drawing a picture or diagram or by constructing a model or diorama.

EXTENDING TIME   Extending time for students to complete activities and take tests may be all that is necessary for many students, who may simply be slow workers or anxious in testing circumstances (Sireci, Scarpati, & Li, 2005).

■ Teaching Learning Strategies and Metacognitive Awareness

Many students do poorly in school because they have failed to learn how to learn. Programs that are directed at helping students learn such strategies as note-taking, summarization, and memorization methods have been very successful with children and adolescents who have learning disabilities (Deshler, 2005; Mastropieri, Scruggs, & Berkeley, 2007). Increasingly, research is identifying a variety of strategies for teaching students with learning disabilities to use metacognitive strategies to comprehend what they read (Gersten et al., 2001, 2009) and to build "self-determination" skills, such as the ability to work independently (Algozzine et al., 2001).

■ Prevention and Early Intervention

INTASC

4 Multiple Instructional Strategies

6 Communication Skills

The debate over inclusion versus special education for children with learning problems revolves around concerns about children whose academic performance is far below that of their agemates. However, many of these children could have succeeded in school in the first place if they had had effective prevention and early intervention programs (Snow, Burns, & Griffin, 1998). Slavin (1996) proposed a policy of "never-streaming," which avoids the mainstreaming/special-education dilemma by focusing attention on intensive early intervention that is capable of bringing students who are at risk to performance levels high enough to remove any need for special-education services.

There is strong evidence that a substantial portion of students who are now in the special-education system could have been kept out of it if they had had effective early intervention. Studies of high-quality early childhood programs such as the Perry Preschool (Berrueta-Clement et al., 1984), the Abecedarian Project (Ramey & Ramey, 1992), and the Milwaukee Project (Garber, 1988) all showed substantial reductions in special-education placements for students with learning disabilities and mild mental retardation (Siegel, 2003). Programs that provide one-to-one tutoring to first-graders who are struggling in reading have also shown reductions in the need for special-education services for students with learning disabilities (see the following section). Success for All, which combines effective early childhood programs, curriculum reform, and one-to-one tutoring, has reduced special-education placement by more than half (Borman & Hewes, 2003; Slavin, 1996; Slavin & Madden, 2001) and has substantially increased the reading achievement of children who have already been identified as needing special-education services (Ross, Smith, Casey, & Slavin, 1995; Smith, Ross, & Casey, 1994). These and other findings suggest that the number of children who need special-education services could be greatly reduced if prevention and early intervention programs were more widely applied.

Connections

For more on the Success for All approach, see Chapter 9, page 266.

■ Tutoring and Small-Group Interventions for Struggling Readers

Because reading difficulties are almost always involved in assignments to special education for learning disabilities, preventing reading failure and helping children who are already behind in reading is essential. Research on a variety of one-to-one and small-group tutoring models, reviewed in Chapter 9, has shown substantial positive effects on the reading performance of struggling readers (see Slavin, Lake, Davis, & Madden, 2009). Tutoring should almost always be tried before a child is assessed for a possible reading disability.

Computers and Students with Disabilities

Computers provide opportunities to individualize instruction for students with disabilities. The use of computers to help children with exceptionalities has four major advantages (Curry, 2003; Hasselbring & Williams-Glaser, 2000; Kamil et al., 2000; Silver-Pacuilla & Fleischman, 2006). First, computers can help to individualize instruction in terms of method of delivery, type and frequency of reinforcement, rate of presentation, and level of instruction (Anderson-Inman & Horney, 2007; McKenna & Walpole, 2007). Second, computers can give immediate corrective feedback and emphasize the active role of the child in learning (Boone & Higgins, 2007). Third, computers can hold the attention of children who are easily distractible. Fourth, computer instruction is motivating and patient. For students with physical disabilities, computers can permit greater ease in learning and communicating information. For example, computers can enlarge text or read text aloud for children with visual disabilities (Kamil et al., 2000; Poel, 2007).

Children in special-education programs seem to like learning from computers. Students who lack motivation have become more enthusiastic about their studies. They feel more in control because they are being taught in a context that is positive, reinforcing, and nonthreatening. However, findings as to the actual learning benefits of computer-assisted instruction for students with disabilities have been inconsistent (MacArthur, Ferretti, Okolo, & Cavalier, 2001; Malouf, Wizer, Pilato, & Grogan, 1990).

One valuable approach using computers is to provide children who are academically disabled with activities in which they can explore, construct, and communicate. Word processors serve this purpose (Bender, 2008), and other programs have been specifically designed for children with disabilities (Meyer & Rose, 2000; Wagmeister & Shifrin, 2000). Refer to Figure 12.8 for examples of computers and other technology for students with disabilities. Also, Chapter 9 describes many additional applications of technology in education.

Buddy Systems and Peer Tutoring

One way to help meet the needs of students with disabilities in the general education classroom is to provide these students with assistance from classmates without disabilities, using either a buddy system for noninstructional needs or peer tutoring to help with learning problems (Mastropieri et al., 2007).

A student who volunteers to be a special-education student's buddy can help that student cope with the routine tasks of classroom life. For example, a buddy can guide a student with vision loss, help a student who is academically disabled to understand directions, or deliver cues or prompts as needed in some classes. In middle school and high school settings, a buddy can take notes for a student with hearing loss or learning disabilities or make photocopies of his or her own notes. The buddy can also ensure that the student with a disability has located the correct textbook page during a lesson and has the materials necessary for a class. The buddy's primary responsibility is to help the student with special needs adjust to the general education classroom, to answer questions, and to provide direction for activities. Use of this resource allows the general education classroom teacher to address more important questions related to instructional activities.

Connections

For more on computer-based instruction, see Chapter 9, page 267.

Certification Pointer

When responding to a case study on your certification test, you should be familiar with adaptive technologies for assisting students with disabilities.

INTASC

6 Communication Skills

Peers helping peers can provide multiple benefits for all parties involved, including the teacher. What do you think is most beneficial about these relationships?

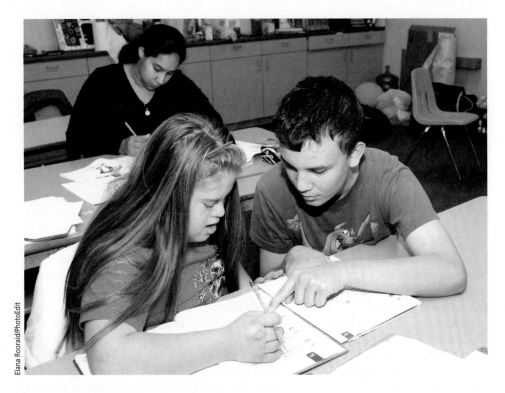

Elana Rooraid/PhotoEdit

FIGURE 12.8   **Adaptive Technologies for Students with Disabilities**

For Students with Limited Motor Control

- Cursor and mouse enhancements allow students who do not have sufficient fine motor control to use a keyboard. Mouse enhancement utilities can be trained to recognize gestures made with mouse commands. Other features include high visibility, color, and animated cursors.

- Key definition programs allow students to define function keys on their keyboard to complete common tasks with fewer keystrokes.

- Virtual keyboard software displays a picture of a computer keyboard on the screen. Students can "type" on this virtual keyboard using a mouse, trackball, or similar pointing device, instead of pushing keys on a real keyboard.

For Students with Visual Impairments

- Magnification software programs ease reading on a computer monitor by displaying text in large fonts (from 2 to 16 times the normal view) and with foreground and background colors of the user's choice.

- Scanners allow students to scan documents that are then converted into editable word processing and spreadsheet documents. These can be magnified and edited on the screen or read aloud by a speech synthesizer.

- Speech synthesizers read aloud what is displayed on the screen—the contents of the active window, menu options, or text that has been typed. They can save documents in audio format as well. There are speaking calendars and talking calculators that read out every operation, as well as mathematical results.

- Braille readers and writers permit students to access the Internet, send and receive e-mail, and create documents by converting text into Braille.

For Students with Hearing Impairments

- Voice recognition software converts spoken words into written text. It can be programmed to execute particular commands, for example, taking a user to favorite websites with a single voice command.

For Students with Learning Disabilities

- Some word processing programs have a word prediction and abbreviation–expansion program that makes writing faster and easier for those with physical or learning disabilities who use a keyboard to write. Both features help reduce the number of keystrokes needed for typing and can make writing more productive.

- Concept mapping software helps students understand the relationship between concepts by constructing, navigating, sharing, and criticizing knowledge models represented as concept maps.

Another way of helping students within the general education classroom is peer tutoring (Fantuzzo et al., 1992; Watkins & Wentzel, 2008). Teachers who use peers to tutor in the classroom should ensure that they are carefully trained. This means that the peer tutor must be taught how to provide assistance by modeling and explaining, how to give specific positive and corrective feedback, and when to allow the student to work alone. Peer tutors and tutees may both benefit: the special-education student by acquiring academic concepts and the tutor by gaining a better acceptance and understanding of students with disabilities. Sometimes, older students with disabilities tutor younger ones; this generally benefits both students (Osguthorpe & Scruggs, 1986; Top & Osguthorpe, 1987).

Special-Education Teams

When a student with disabilities is integrated into the general education classroom, the classroom teacher often works with one or more special educators to ensure success (Friend, 2007; Friend & Bursuck, 2008; Smith et al., 2008; Snell & Janney, 2000). The classroom teacher might participate in conferences with special-education personnel, a special educator might at times be present in the classroom, or the classroom teacher might consult with a special educator at regular intervals. Whatever the arrangement, classroom teachers and special educators must recognize that each has expertise crucial to the student's success. The classroom teacher is the expert on classroom organization and operation on a day-to-day basis, the curriculum of the classroom, and the expectations placed on students for performance. The special educator is the expert on the characteristics of a particular group of students with disabilities, the learning and behavioral strengths and deficits of the mainstreamed student, and instructional techniques for a particular kind of disability. All this information is important to the successful integration of students, which is why communication between general education and special-education teachers is so necessary (Pawlowski, 2001; Tucker, 2001).

Communication should begin before students are placed in the general education classroom and should continue throughout the placement. Both teachers must have

Connections

For more on peer tutoring, see Chapter 9, page 260.

Certification Pointer

For teacher certification tests you may be expected to suggest ways of structuring peer tutoring to help meet the needs of students with disabilities.

INTASC

10 Partnerships

21ST Century Learning

Including All Learners

Advances in assistive technologies are revolutionizing the educational possibilities for students with disabilities. Computer programs able to enlarge text have long existed to help students with visual impairments, but increasing use of interactive whiteboards and other whole-class lesson technologies now make it easy to provide enlarged text and pictures that enable students with visual impairments to follow regular class lessons. Similarly, the opportunity to make far greater use of visual and interactive content to supplement lessons is likely to provide alternative pathways to success in school for students with learning disabilities and other special needs. In the 21st century, standards for educational attainment will rise, but there will be a greater diversity of ways students can meet these standards.

Question

■ Make a chart showing the types of disabilities your students may have. Which technologies seem particularly appropriate for each?

Connections

For more on teaching adaptive skills to help students in their socio-emotional development, see Chapter 3, page 67.

up-to-date information about the student's performance in each setting to plan and coordinate an effective program. Only then can instruction targeted at improving the student's performance in the general education classroom be designed and presented. In addition, generalization of skills and behaviors from one setting to the other will be enhanced (see Fuchs, Fuchs, Bahr, Fernstrom, & Stecker, 1990).

■ Social Integration of Students with Disabilities

Placement of students in the general education classroom is only one part of their integration into that environment. These students must be integrated socially as well as instructionally (see Wilkins, 2000). As the classroom teacher, you play a critical role in this process. Much has been written about the effects of teacher expectations on student achievement and behavior. In the case of students with disabilities, your attitude toward these students is important not only for teacher–student interactions but also as a model for the students without disabilities in the classroom. The research on attitudes toward individuals with disabilities provides several strategies that might be useful to the general education classroom teacher who wants to promote successful social integration by influencing the attitudes of students without disabilities. One strategy is to use cooperative learning methods (Nevin, 1998; Slavin & Stevens, 1991;

FIGURE 12.9 **Including Secondary Students with Disabilities in the General Education Classroom**

Consider these tips for including secondary students in the general education classroom:

Secondary Students with Learning Disabilities

1. Specifically teach self-recording strategies such as asking, "Was I paying attention?"

2. Relate new material to knowledge that the student with learning disabilities already has, drawing specific implications from familiar information.

3. Teach the use of external memory enhancers (e.g., lists and note-taking).

4. Encourage the use of other devices to improve class performance (e.g., tape recorders).

Secondary Students with Emotional or Behavioral Disorders

1. Create positive relationships within your classroom through the use of cooperative learning teams and group-oriented assignments.

2. Use all students in creating standards for conduct as well as consequences for positive and negative behaviors.

3. Focus your efforts on developing a positive relationship with the student with behavior disorders by greeting him or her regularly, informally talking with him or her at appropriate times, attending to improvement in his or her performance, and becoming aware of his or her interests.

4. Work closely with the members of the teacher assistance team to be aware of teacher behaviors that might adversely or positively affect students' performance.

5. Realize that changes in behavior often occur very gradually, with periods of regression and sometimes tumult.

Source: Michael L. Hardman, Clifford J. Drew, and M. Winston Egan, *Human Exceptionality* (5th ed.). Copyright © 1996 by Allyn & Bacon. Adapted by permission.

Stevens & Slavin, 1995b). Social skills training has also been found to improve the social acceptance of children with disabilities (Troop & Asher, 1999). For practical ways to include secondary students with disabilities in the general education classroom, see Figure 12.9.

Chapter 12 Summary

Who Are Learners with Exceptionalities?

Learners with exceptionalities are students who have special-educational needs in relation to societal or school norms. An inability to perform appropriate academic tasks for any reason inherent in the learner makes that learner exceptional. A handicap is a condition or barrier imposed by the environment or the self; a disability is a functional limitation that interferes with a person's mental, physical, or sensory abilities. The often arbitrary classification systems for learners with exceptionalities are widely debated, and the use of labels may lead to inappropriate treatment or damage students' self-concepts.

About 9 percent of students ages 6 to 21 in the United States receive special education. Examples of learners with exceptionalities are students with mental retardation, specific learning disabilities, speech or language disorders, emotional and behavioral disorders, and vision or hearing loss. Students who are gifted and talented are also regarded as exceptional and may be eligible for special accelerated or enrichment programs. Clearly identifying learners with exceptionalities and accommodating instruction to meet their needs are continual challenges.

What Is Special Education?

Special-education programs serve children with disabilities instead of, or in addition to, the general education classroom program.

Public Law 94-142 (1975), which was amended by P.L. 99-457 (1986) to include preschool children and infants with serious disabilities, is now called the Individuals with Disabilities Education Act (IDEA). It mandates that every child with a disability is entitled to appropriate special education at public expense. The current version of the law, IDEA 2004, calls for greater involvement of parents and classroom teachers in the education of children with disabilities. The least restrictive environment clause means that students with special needs must be mainstreamed into general education classes as much as possible. A requirement of IDEA is that every student with a disability must have an Individualized Education Program (IEP). The idea behind the use of IEPs is to give everyone concerned with the education of a child with a disability an opportunity to help formulate the child's instruction program. An array of services is available for students who are exceptional, including support for the general education teacher, special education for part of the day in a resource room, special education for more than 3 hours per day in a special-education classroom, special day schools, special residential schools, and homes/hospitals.

What Is Response to Intervention?

Response to Intervention (RTI) means using modifications to instruction or intensive services in the general education classroom before referring a struggling student for special education. RTI approaches generally provide struggling students with three tiers of intervention: prevention (whole class), immediate assistance (small group or individual), and intensive, extended assistance.

What Is Inclusion

Inclusion means placing students with special needs in general education class-rooms for at least part of the time. Full inclusion of all children in general education classes with appropriate assistance is a widely held goal. Research has shown that inclusion is effective in raising many students' performance levels, especially when cooperative learning, buddy systems, peer tutoring, computer instruction, modifications in lesson presentation, and training in social skills are regular parts of classroom learning. Research has also shown that some disabilities, especially reading disabilities, can be prevented through programs of prevention and early intervention.

What Are Effective Strategies for Students with Disabilities in General Education

Teachers in inclusive classrooms can help their students with disabilities succeed by adapting instruction and modifying materials, teaching students specific learning strategies, and providing tutoring and computer practice.

The Intentional Teacher

USING WHAT YOU KNOW about Learners with Exceptionalities to Improve Teaching and Learning

Intentional teachers relish their responsibility to reach each of their students. They create inclusive environments and commit to fostering learning for all. Intentional teachers serve as members of professional teams in order to collaborate to meet the needs of students with special needs.

 1. What do I expect my students to know and be able to do at the end of this lesson? How does this contribute to course objectives and to students' needs to become capable individuals?

Think about the goals you have established for student learning. Consider the extent to which each of these goals is appropriate for learners with special needs. Work with other professionals to develop formal goal statements, including Individualized Education Programs that shape appropriate goals and instruction for your students with special needs. For example, imagine that Michael and Renee, two students with learning disabilities in reading, struggle with the text for your class, so you consult with the special-education teacher. He reviews the students' IEPs with you, noting that reading comprehension is a goal for both students this year. Together you converse about possible adjustments to your course goals for Michael and Renee and you discuss appropriate instructional modifications. You chat with the students' parents, who give you additional insights about strategies they have found to be successful.

2. What knowledge, skills, needs, and interests do my students have that must be taken into account in my lesson?

Identification of students' special-educational needs may begin before students enter formal schooling. When students with documented special needs are assigned to your class, talk with students (as appropriate), their parents, and professionals about students' preferences and past successes. Review past records as appropriate. For example, imagine that Angela, a junior who is visually impaired, joins your class. You might set up an informal conference with Angela, her parents, and the resource teacher. They provide you with information about strategies that help Angela, and she talks openly about her likes and her pet peeves. They also refer you to one of your colleagues who was particularly successful last year at providing a supportive environment without dwelling too much on Angela's vision. You might seek assistive technology, such as a computer that greatly enlarges text, to help Angela participate successfully in class.

3. What do I know about the content, child development, learning, motivation, and effective teaching strategies that I can use to accomplish my objectives?

Students might have special needs that have not been identified. Observe carefully for signs that students need extra support. For example, imagine that Sheila, who sits in a back row, often looks out the window or looks

Key Terms

Review the following key terms from the chapter.

INTASC   **8** Assessment of Student Learning
          10 Partnerships

puzzled during your lessons. Noticing some differences in her enunciation, you suspect a hearing impairment and refer her for testing. In the meantime, you move her to the front row and provide visual input to support your direct instruction.

 4. What instructional materials, technology, assistance, and other resources are available to help accomplish my objectives?

Teachers need to create a social environment that fosters acceptance for every student. Think about how you will encourage students to accept and help each other as individuals. For example, imagine that Jarred, a student with cerebral palsy, is placed in your classroom. You and your students might hold a classroom meeting to discuss ways to welcome a new student. You could also talk about areas in which classmates have helped each other this year and the idea that you all have benefited by working with each other because of your varied strengths. You might hand out a "job application" for the position of "buddy" to new students, as several students clamor to be Jarred's buddy.

 5. How will I plan to assess students' progress toward my objectives?

Use information from a variety of sources to determine success for students with special needs. What evidence do you have that students maintain positive self-concepts? That their classmates' self-concepts are similarly enriched?

That students are learning? Collect information that enables you to determine whether students are progressing on an individual basis. For example, imagine that you meet for a midyear review of Patrick's Individualized Education Program. You bring anecdotal notes that you have collected on students' capacity to care about and help each other. You share vignettes of Patrick's sense of humor and impressive knowledge of dinosaurs. You show his portfolio, which demonstrates marked growth in his letter recognition and drawing. You commit to providing more intensive work in mathematics, though, because he shows less growth in shape and number recognition.

 6. How will I respond if individual children or the class as a whole are not on track toward success? What is my back-up plan?

Instruction should meet individual needs. Select from a variety of strategies to modify your instruction when you find that it does not challenge each student. For example, imagine that some of your students are struggling despite your attempts to provide relevant and engaging instruction. You re-read your notes on instructional modifications such as individualized instruction, cooperative learning, computers, and peer tutoring. You might choose peer tutoring to capitalize on your students' social tendencies. You could train peer tutors in learning strategies and work out a schedule so that peer tutors and tutees can meet during class for 20 minutes three times per week.

Self-Assessment: Practicing for Licensure

Directions: The chapter-opening vignette addresses indicators that are often assessed in state licensure exams. Re-read the chapter-opening vignette, and then respond to the following questions.

1. Elaine Wagner, assistant principal at Dover Elementary School, meets with Helen Ross about her son, Tommy, who is having a difficult time in another school. She explains to Ms. Ross that Tommy would need to meet certain criteria to receive special-education services. Which of the following examples is an indication that someone needs special-education services?

   a. The student must have an IQ at or below 120.

   b. The student must have at least one of a few designated categories of disabilities.

   c. The student must be below the 50th percentile in his or her academic work.

   d. All parents who request special-education services for their children must receive them.

2. Suppose you are going to be Tommy's new teacher. If his mother were to ask you about the difference between handicap and disability, what would you say?

   a. A disability is a condition in which a person has difficulty with cognitive functioning, whereas a handicap is a condition in which a person has difficulty with physical functioning.

   b. A disability is a condition in which a person has barriers placed on him or her by society, whereas a handicap is the disabling condition.

   c. A disability is a functional limitation a person has that interferes with her or his physical or cognitive abilities. A handicap is a condition imposed on a person with disabilities by society, the physical environment, or the person's attitude.

   d. The terms *disability* and *handicap* are synonymous.

3. Which of the following public laws gave parents like Helen Ross an increased role in making decisions about the education of their children?

   a. Public Law 94-142, the Education for the Handicapped Act

   b. Public Law 99-457, the amendment to P.L. 94-142

   c. Public Law 101-476, the Individuals with Disabilities Education Act

   d. Public Law 105-17, the Individuals with Disabilities Education Act Amendments

4. Assistant Principal Elaine Wagner tells Helen Ross that even if Tommy needs special-education services, he will be placed in the "least restrictive environment." What does this mean for Tommy?

   a. Tommy will be placed in the general education classes as much as possible and only removed for special-education services if necessary.

   b. Tommy will be placed in a special-education room that does not restrict his movements or academic choices.

   c. Tommy will be eligible for any and all special-education services.

   d. Tommy will receive public funds to pay for his private special-education services.

5. Helen Ross, Tommy's mother, asks Elaine Wagner, "Your school's philosophy on inclusion sounds just right for Tommy. Why don't all schools adopt it? What disadvantages are there?" Ms. Wagner, who is current on her knowledge about inclusion, would most likely make which of the following responses?

   a. Data show that students enrolled in inclusion programs do not do as well academically as those who are enrolled in special-education classrooms.

   b. General education classroom teachers sometimes lack appropriate training and materials and are already overburdened with large class sizes and inadequate support services.

   c. Special-education experts are not convinced that there is such a thing as a learning disability. They believe that all students should be in a general education classroom.

   d. Many parents of general education students do not feel it is fair to adapt instruction to meet the needs of students with disabilities.

6. How would you go about developing an individualized learning plan for Tommy if it is determined that he has a reading disability?

7. Describe the advantages and disadvantages of enrolling students with special needs in the general education classroom.

PEARSON myeducationlab

Go to the Topic **Students with Special Needs** in the MyEducationLab (www.myeducationlab.com) for your course, where you can:

- Find learning outcomes for **Students with Special Needs** along with the national standards that connect to these outcomes.

- Complete Assignments and Activities that can help you more deeply understand the chapter content.

- Apply and practice your understanding of the core teaching skills identified in the chapter with the Building Teaching Skills and Dispositions learning units.

- Examine challenging situations and cases presented in the IRIS Center Resources.

- Access video clips of CCSSO National Teachers of the Year award winners responding to the question "Why Do I Teach?" in the Teacher Talk section.

- Check your comprehension of the content covered in the chapter by going to the Study Plan in the Book Resources for your text. Here you will be able to take a chapter quiz; receive feedback on your answers; and then access Review, Practice, and Enrichment activities to enhance your understanding of chapter content.

- Watch author Bob Slavin present a Personal Reflections podcast on *The Struggle over Inclusion* in the Book Resources for your text. Then, respond to the reflection questions that follow.

The Struggle over Inclusion

YOUR REFLECTIONS What are the possible positive benefits this teacher's children might realize as a result of her belief? What are the potential negative ramifications of her approach? What do you consider to be the best approach to inclusion, and what do you see as your biggest challenge as the classroom teacher?

13

Assessing Student Learning

Bob Daemmrich/The Image Works

Learning Outcomes

Bob Daemmrich/The Image Works

At the end of this chapter, you should be able to:

- Describe instructional objectives and their use
- Understand why evaluation is important
- Identify different types of evaluation
- Write different types of test questions
- Discriminate between authentic, portfolio, and performance assessments
- Identify different methods of grading

Mr. Sullivan is having a great time teaching about the Civil War, and his eleventh-grade U.S. history class is having fun, too. Mr. Sullivan is relating all kinds of anecdotes about the war. He describes a battle fought in the nude (a group of Confederates was caught fording a river), the time Stonewall Jackson lost a battle because he took a nap in the middle of it, and several stories about women who disguised their gender to fight as soldiers. He tells the story of a Confederate raid (from Canada) on a Vermont bank. He passes around real minié balls and grapeshot. In fact, Mr. Sullivan has gone on for weeks about the battles, the songs, and the personalities and foibles of the generals. Finally, after an interesting math activity in which students have to figure out how much Confederate money they would need to buy a loaf of bread, Mr. Sullivan has students put away all their materials to take a test.

The students are shocked. The only question is: What were the main causes, events, and consequences of the Civil War?

Mr. Sullivan's lessons are fun. They are engaging. They use varied presentation modes. They integrate skills from other disciplines. They are clearly accomplishing one important objective of social studies: building enjoyment of the topic. However, as engaging as Mr. Sullivan's lessons are, there is little correspondence between what he is teaching and what he is testing. He and his students are on a happy trip, but where are they going?

USING YOUR EXPERIENCE

Cooperative Learning In a group of four or five students, draw a value line from 1 to 100, with 1 representing poor teaching and 100 representing great teaching. Take turns marking where you would place Mr. Sullivan on this scale. Let each person explain his or her rating. Now review the ratings and change them as appropriate. Discuss better methods that Mr. Sullivan might use to teach and then assess his students.

In teaching lessons, units, and courses, how do you know where you are going and whether or not you and your students are getting there? This chapter discusses objectives and assessments as well as the goals of teaching and ways of determining whether goals are being achieved. Objectives are the learning plan for what students should know and be able to do at the end of a course of study; lessons must be designed to accomplish these objectives. Evaluations of students must indicate the extent to which each student has actually mastered those objectives by the end of the course (Carr & Harris, 2001; Marzano et al., 2001). Every teacher should have a clear idea of where the class is going, how it will get there, and how to know whether it has arrived.

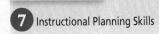

INTASC

7 Instructional Planning Skills

What Are Instructional Objectives and How Are They Used?

What do you want your students to know or be able to do at the end of today's lesson? What should they know at the end of a series of lessons on a particular subject? What should they know at the end of the course? Knowing the answers to these questions is one of the most important prerequisites for intentional, high-quality instruction. A teacher is like a wilderness guide with a troop of tenderfeet. If you do not have a map or a plan for getting the group where it needs to go, the whole group will surely be lost. Mr. Sullivan's students are having a lot of fun, but because their teacher has no plan for how his lessons will give them essential concepts relating to the Civil War, they will be unlikely to learn these concepts.

Setting out objectives at the beginning of a course is an essential step in providing a framework into which individual lessons will fit. Without such a framework it is easy to wander off the track, to spend too much time on topics that are not central to the course. One high school biology teacher spent most of the year teaching biochemistry; her students knew all about the chemical makeup of DNA, red blood cells, chlorophyll, and starch but little about zoology, botany, anatomy, or other topics that are usually central to high school biology. Then in late May the teacher panicked because she realized that the class had to do a series of laboratory exercises before the end of the year. On successive days they dissected a frog, an eye, a brain, and a pig fetus! Needless to say, the students learned little from those hurried labs and little about biology in general. This teacher did not have a master plan but was deciding week by week (or perhaps day by day) what to teach, thereby losing sight of the big picture—the scope of knowledge that is generally agreed to be important for a high school student to learn in biology class. Few teachers follow a plan rigidly once they make it, but the process of making it is still very helpful.

An **instructional objective,** sometimes called a *behavioral objective,* is a statement of skills or concepts that students are expected to know at the end of some period of instruction. Typically, an instructional objective is stated in such a way as to make clear how the objective will be measured (see Mager, 1997). Some examples of instructional objectives are as follows:

- Given 100 division facts (such as 27 divided by 3), students will give correct answers to all 100 in 3 minutes.
- When asked, students will name at least five functions that characterize all living organisms (respiration, reproduction, etc.).
- In an essay, students will be able to compare and contrast the artistic styles of van Gogh and Gauguin.
- Given the statement "Resolved: The United States should not have entered World War I," students will be able to argue persuasively either for or against the proposition.

Note that despite varying enormously in the type of learning involved and in the performance levels they address, these objectives have several things in common. Mager (1997), whose work began the behavioral objectives movement, described objectives as having three parts: performance, conditions, and criteria. Explanations and examples are given in Table 13.1.

Connections

For more on lesson planning and lesson objectives as components of effective instruction, see Chapter 7, page 188.

instructional objective

A statement of skills or concepts that students should master after a given period of instruction.

■ Planning Lesson Objectives

In practice, the skeleton of a behavioral objective is condition–performance–criterion. First, state the conditions under which learning will be assessed, as in the following:

TABLE 13.1   **Parts of a Behavioral Objectives Statement**

	Performance	Conditions	Criterion
Definition	An objective always says what a learner is expected to do.	An objective always describes the conditions under which the performance is to occur.	Whenever possible, an objective describes the criterion of acceptable performance.
Question Answered	What should the learner be able to do?	Under what conditions do you want the learner to be able to do it?	How well must it be done?
Example	Correctly use adjectives and adverbs.	Given 10 sentences with missing modifiers, . . .	. . . the student will correctly choose an adjective or adverb in at least 9 of the 10 sentences.

- Given a 10-item test, students will be able to . . .
- In an essay, the student will be able to . . .
- Using a compass and protractor, the student will be able to . . .

The second part of an objective is usually an action verb that indicates what students will be able to do, for example (from Gronlund & Brookhart, 2009):

- Write
- Distinguish between
- Identify
- Match
- Compare and contrast

Finally, a behavioral objective generally states a criterion for success, such as the following:

- . . . all 100 multiplication facts in 3 minutes.
- . . . at least five of the nations that sent explorers to the New World.
- . . . at least three similarities and three differences between the U.S. government under the Constitution and under the Articles of Confederation.

Sometimes a criterion for success cannot be specified as the number correct. Even so, success should be specified as clearly as possible, as in the following:

- The student will write a two-page essay describing the social situation of women as portrayed in *A Doll's House.*
- The student will think of at least six possible uses for an eggbeater other than beating eggs.

WRITING SPECIFIC OBJECTIVES   Instructional objectives must be adapted to the subject matter being taught. When students must learn well-defined skills or information with a single right answer, specific instructional objectives can be written as follows:

- Given 10 problems involving addition of two fractions with like denominators, students will solve at least 9 correctly.
- Given 10 sentences lacking verbs, students will correctly choose verbs that agree in number in at least 8 sentences. Examples: My cat and I [has, have] birthdays in May. Each of us [want, wants] to go to college.

■ Given a 4-meter rope attached to the ceiling, students will be able to climb to the top in less than 20 seconds.

Some material, of course, does not lend itself to such specific instructional objectives, and it would be a mistake in such cases to adhere to objectives that have numerical criteria. For example, the following objective could be written:

■ The student will list at least five similarities and five differences between the situation of immigrants to the United States in the early 1900s and that of immigrants today.

Note that this objective asks for lists, which might not demonstrate any real understanding of the topic. A less specific but more meaningful objective might be the following:

■ In an essay, the student will compare and contrast the situation of immigrants to the United States in the early 1900s and that of immigrants today.

This general instructional objective would allow students more flexibility in expressing their understanding of the topic and promote comprehension rather than memorization of lists of similarities and differences.

WRITING CLEAR OBJECTIVES   Instructional objectives should be specific enough to be meaningful. For example, an objective concerning immigrants might be written as follows:

■ Students will develop a full appreciation for the diversity of peoples who have contributed to the development of U.S. society.

This sounds nice, but what does "full appreciation" mean? Such an objective neither helps you prepare lessons nor helps students understand what is to be taught and how they will be assessed. Mager (1997, p. 20) lists more slippery and less slippery words used to describe instructional objectives:

Words Open to Many Interpretations	**Words Open to Fewer Interpretations**
to know	to write
to understand	to recite
to appreciate	to identify
to fully appreciate	to sort
to grasp the significance	to solve
to enjoy	to construct

PERFORMING A TASK ANALYSIS   In planning lessons, it is important to consider the skills required in the tasks to be taught or assigned. For example, you might ask students to use the school library to write a brief report on a topic of interest. The task seems straightforward enough, but consider the separate skills involved:

■ Knowing alphabetical order
■ Using library information resources to find books on a subject
■ Knowing how to use the library's information resources and book indexes

- Getting the main idea from expository material
- Planning or outlining a brief report
- Writing expository paragraphs
- Understanding language mechanics skills (such as capitalization, punctuation, and usage)

These skills could themselves be broken down into subskills. You must be aware of the subskills involved in any learning task to be certain that students know what they need to know to succeed. Before assigning the library report task, you would need to be sure that students knew how to use the library's information resources and book indexes, among other things, and could comprehend and write expository material. You might teach or review these skills before sending students to the library.

Similarly, in teaching a new skill, it is important to consider all the subskills that go into it. Think of all the separate steps involved in long division, in writing chemical formulas, or in identifying topic sentences and supporting details. For that matter, consider the skills that go into making a pizza, as illustrated in Figure 13.1.

This process of breaking tasks or objectives down into their simpler components is called **task analysis.** In planning a lesson, a three-step process for task analysis may be used:

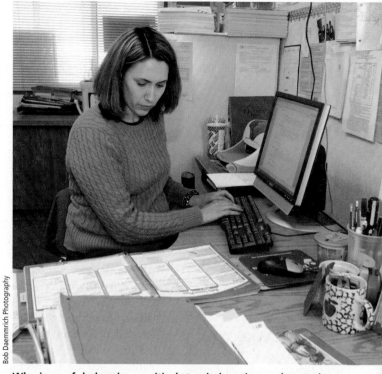

Bob Daemmrich Photography

Why is careful planning a critical step in learning and assessing learning? What kinds of ongoing assessment can you build into your lessons that will help you determine whether your students are meeting the objectives you establish?

1. *Identify prerequisite skills.* What should students already know before you teach the lesson? For example, for a lesson on long division, students must know their subtraction, multiplication, and division facts and must be able to subtract and multiply with renaming.

task analysis

Breaking tasks down into fundamental subskills.

FIGURE 13.1 **Example of a Skill Hierarchy**

Before students can practice the main skill (making pizza), they must be able to use an oven, make dough, and make sauce. These skills must all be learned before the main skill can be mastered. They are independent of one another and can be learned in any order. Before making dough or making sauce, students must be able to read a recipe and measure ingredients. Finally, to read a recipe the learner first has to learn how to decode abbreviations.

Source: The Center for Effective Performance, Inc. www.cepworldwide.com, 800-558-4237. Reprinted from *Preparing Instructional Objectives,* 3rd edition, by Robert Mager, copyright © 1997, with permission. All rights reserved.

2. *Identify component skills.*   In the actual lesson, what subskills must students be taught before they can learn to achieve the larger objective? To return to the long-division example, students will need to learn estimating, dividing, multiplying, subtracting, checking, bringing down the next digit, and then repeating the process. Each of these steps must be planned for, taught, and assessed during the lesson.

3. *Plan how component skills will be assembled into the final skill.*   The final step in task analysis is to assemble the subskills back into the complete process being taught. For example, students might be able to estimate, to divide, and to multiply, but this does not necessarily mean that they can do long division. The subskills must be integrated into a complete process that students can understand and practice.

BACKWARD PLANNING   Just as lesson objectives are more than the sum of specific task objectives, the objectives of a course of study are more than the sum of specific lesson objectives. For this reason it makes sense to start by writing broad objectives for the course as a whole, then objectives for large units, and only then specific behavioral objectives (see Gronlund & Brookhart, 2009). This is known as **backward planning.** For example, Mr. Sullivan would have done well to have identified the objective of his Civil War unit as follows: "Students will understand the major causes, events, and consequences of the Civil War." Then he might have written more detailed objectives relating to causes, events, and consequences and planned units and individual lessons around these objectives. A detailed example of the backward planning process is illustrated in Table 13.2 and described in the next Theory into Practice.

backward planning

Planning instruction by first setting long-range goals, then setting unit objectives, and finally planning daily lessons.

TABLE 13.2   **Example of Objectives for a Course in Life Science**

Teachers can allocate instructional time for a course by (a) deciding what topics to cover during the year or semester, (b) deciding how many weeks to spend on each topic, (c) choosing units within each topic, (d) deciding how many days to spend on each, and (e) deciding what each day's lesson should be.

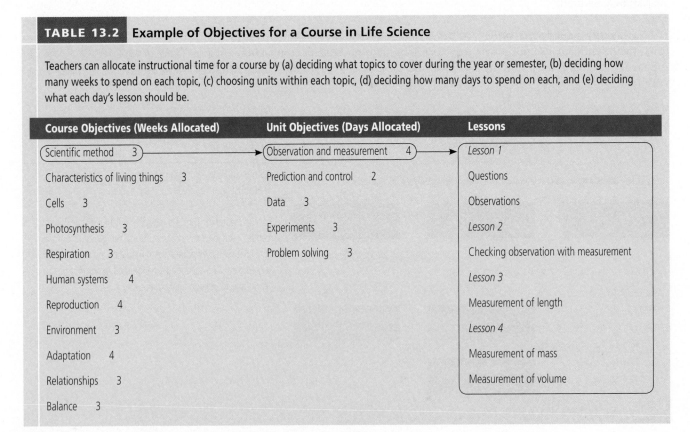

Course Objectives (Weeks Allocated)	Unit Objectives (Days Allocated)	Lessons
Scientific method 3	Observation and measurement 4	Lesson 1
Characteristics of living things 3	Prediction and control 2	Questions
Cells 3	Data 3	Observations
Photosynthesis 3	Experiments 3	Lesson 2
Respiration 3	Problem solving 3	Checking observation with measurement
Human systems 4		Lesson 3
Reproduction 4		Measurement of length
Environment 3		Lesson 4
Adaptation 4		Measurement of mass
Relationships 3		Measurement of volume
Balance 3		

Source: Objectives adapted from Wong, Bernstein, and Shevick, *Life Science* (2nd ed.), 1978.

Theory into Practice
Planning Courses, Units, and Lessons

In planning a course, it is important to set long-term, middle-term, and short-term objectives before starting to teach. Before the students arrive for the first day of class, you need to have a general plan of what will be covered all year, a more specific plan for what will be in the first unit (a connected set of lessons), and a very specific plan for the content of the first lessons (as shown in Table 13.2). All states have established standards for each subject, and these standards should help guide your planning.

Table 13.2 implies a backward planning process. First the course objectives are established. Then unit objectives are designated. Finally, specific lessons are planned. The course objectives list all the topics to be covered during the year. You might divide the number of weeks in the school year by the number of major topics to figure what each will require. More or less time could be reserved for any particular topic, as long as adequate time is allowed for the others. A whole semester could be spent on any one of the topics in Table 13.2, but this would be inappropriate in a survey course on life science. You must make hard choices before the first day of class about how much time to spend on each topic to avoid spending too much time on early topics and not having enough time left to do a good job with later ones. Some history teachers always seem to find themselves still on World War I in mid-May and have to compress most of the 20th century into a couple of weeks!

Table 13.2 shows approximate allocations of weeks to each of the topics to be covered. These are only rough estimates to be modified as time goes on.

UNIT OBJECTIVES AND UNIT TESTS   After course objectives have been laid out, the next task is to establish objectives for the first unit and to estimate the number of class periods to spend on each objective. It is a good idea to write a unit test as part of the planning process. Writing a test in advance helps you to focus on the important issues to be covered. For example, in a 4-week unit on the Civil War, Mr. Sullivan might have decided that the most important concepts students should learn are the causes of the war, a few major points about the military campaigns, the importance of the Emancipation Proclamation, Lincoln's assassination, and the history of the Reconstruction period. These topics would be central to the unit test on the Civil War. Writing this test could have helped him put into proper perspective the importance of the various issues that should be covered. It's not that he shouldn't have shared anecdotes and shown students Civil War weapons, but preparing the unit test would have helped him keep the big picture in mind.

The test that you prepare as part of your course planning might not be exactly the test that you give at the end of the unit. You may decide to change, add, or delete items to reflect the content you actually covered. But this does not diminish the importance of having decided in advance exactly what objectives you wanted to achieve and how you were going to assess them.

Many textbooks provide unit tests and objectives, making your task easier. However, even if you have ready-made objectives and tests, it is still important to review their content and change them as necessary to match what you expect to teach.

If you prepare unit tests from scratch, use the guide to test construction presented later in this chapter. Be sure that the test items cover the various objectives

✓ Certification Pointer

For your teacher certification test, you may be asked to take a goal from a state curriculum standard and write a behavioral objective to meet that standard.

in proportion to their importance to the course as a whole (that is, that the more important objectives are covered by more items), and include items that assess higher-level thinking as well as factual knowledge.

LESSON PLANS AND LESSON ASSESSMENTS The final step in backward planning is to plan daily lessons. Table 13.2 shows how a given unit objective might be broken down into daily lessons. The next step is to plan the content of each lesson. A lesson plan consists of an objective, a plan for presenting information, a plan for giving students practice (if appropriate), a plan for assessing student understanding, and, if necessary, a plan for reteaching students (or whole classes) if their understanding is inadequate.

■ Aligning Objectives and Assessment

INTASC

8 Assessment of Student Learning

Because instructional objectives are stated in terms of how they will be measured, it is clear that objectives are closely aligned with **assessment,** which is a measure of the degree to which students have learned the objectives set out for them. Most assessments in schools are tests or quizzes or informal verbal assessments such as questions in class. However, students can also show their learning by writing an essay, painting a picture, doing a car tune-up, or baking a pineapple upside-down cake.

One critical principle of assessment is that assessments and objectives must be clearly linked. Students learn some proportion of what they are taught; the greater the overlap between what was taught and what is tested, the better students will score on the test and the more accurately any need for additional instruction can be determined (Carr & Harris, 2001; Marzano et al., 2001; Squires, 2009). Teaching should be closely linked to instructional objectives, and both should clearly relate to assessment (Buhle & Blachowicz, 2008/2009). If any objective is worth teaching, it is worth testing, and vice versa. This idea is illustrated by Mager as follows:

> During class periods of a seventh grade algebra course, a teacher provided a good deal of skillful guidance in the solution of simple equations. . . . When it came time for an examination, however, the test items consisted mainly of word problems, and the students did rather poorly. The teacher's justification for this "sleight of test" was that the students didn't "really understand" algebra if they could not solve word problems. Perhaps the teacher was right. But the skill of solving equations is considerably different from the skill of solving word problems; if he wanted his students to learn how to solve word problems, he should have taught them how to do so. (Mager, 1975, p. 82)

Mager's algebra teacher really had one objective in mind (solving word problems) but taught according to another (solving equations). If he had coordinated his objectives, his teaching, and his assessment, he and his students would have been a lot happier, and the students would have had a much better opportunity to learn to solve algebra word problems.

One way to specify objectives for a course is to actually prepare test questions before the course begins (see Gronlund & Waugh, 2009). This allows you to write general **teaching objectives** (clear statements of what students are expected to learn through instruction) and then to clarify them with very specific **learning objectives** (specific behaviors students are expected to exhibit at the end of a series of lessons), as in the following examples:

assessment

A measure of the degree to which instructional objectives have been attained.

teaching objectives

Clear statements of what students are intended to learn through instruction.

learning objectives

Specific behaviors students are expected to exhibit at the end of a series of lessons.

Teaching Objective	Specific Learning Objective (Test Questions)
a. Ability to subtract three-digit numbers renaming once or twice	a1. $\begin{array}{r} 237 \\ -184 \end{array}$ a2. $\begin{array}{r} 412 \\ -298 \end{array}$ a3. $\begin{array}{r} 596 \\ -448 \end{array}$
b. Understanding use of language to set mood in Edgar Allan Poe's "The Raven"	b1. How does Poe reinforce the mood of "The Raven" after setting it in the first stanza?
c. Ability to identify the chemical formulas for common substances	Write the chemical formulas for the following: c1. Water ____ c2. Carbon dioxide ____ c3. Coal ____ c4. Table salt ____

■ Using Taxonomies of Instructional Objectives

In writing objectives and assessments, it is important to consider different skills and different levels of understanding. For example, in a science lesson on insects for second-graders, you might want to impart both information (the names of various insects) and a set of attitudes (e.g., the importance of insects to the ecosystem and the idea that science is fun). In other subjects you might try to convey facts and concepts that differ by type. For example, in teaching a lesson on topic sentences in reading, you might have students first recall the definition of topic sentences, then identify topic sentences in paragraphs, and finally write their own topic sentences for original paragraphs. Each of these activities demonstrates a different kind of understanding of the concept "topic sentence," and this concept has not been adequately taught if students can do only one of these activities. These various lesson goals can be classified by type and degree of complexity. A taxonomy, or system of classification, helps you to categorize instructional activities.

BLOOM'S TAXONOMY   In 1956, Benjamin Bloom and some fellow research-ers (Bloom, Englehart, Furst, Hill, & Krathwohl, 1956) published a **taxonomy of educational objectives** that has been influential in the research and prac-tice of education ever since. Bloom and his colleagues categorized objectives from simple to complex or from factual to conceptual. The following key elements (from simple to complex) constitute what is commonly called Bloom's taxon-omy for the cognitive domain (Badgett & Christmann, 2009; Marzano & Kendall, 2007):

1. *Knowledge (recalling information).*   The lowest level of objectives in Bloom's hierarchy, knowledge refers to objectives such as memorizing math facts or formulas, scientific principles, or verb conjugations.

2. *Comprehension (translating, interpreting, or extrapolating information).*   Com-prehension objectives require that students show an understanding of information as well as the ability to use it. Examples include interpreting the meaning of a diagram, graph, or parable; inferring the principle underlying a science experiment; or predicting what might happen next in a story.

3. *Application (using principles or abstractions to solve novel or real-life prob-lems).*   Application objectives require students to use knowledge or principles to solve practical problems. Examples include using geometric principles to figure out how many gallons of water to put into a swimming pool of given dimensions or using knowledge of the relationship between temperature and pressure to explain why a balloon is larger on a hot day than on a cold day.

Connections

For information on thinking skills and critical thinking, see Chapter 8, page 242.

taxonomy of educational objectives

Bloom's ordering of objectives from simple learning tasks to more complex ones.

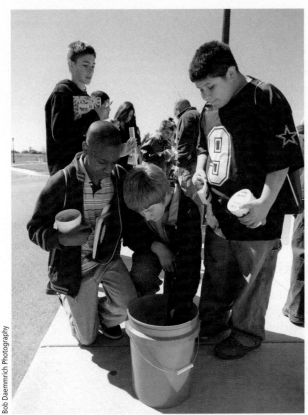

Bob Daemmrich Photography

What stage in Bloom's taxonomy might these students be taking part in here? How could a teacher incorporate all of Bloom's stages into this lesson?

4. *Analysis (breaking down complex information or ideas into simpler parts to understand how the parts relate or are organized).*   Analysis objectives require students to see the underlying structure of complex information or ideas. Examples of analysis objectives include contrasting schooling in the United States with education in Japan, understanding how the functions of the carburetor and distributor are related in an automobile engine, or identifying the main idea of a short story.

5. *Synthesis (creation of something that did not exist before).*   Synthesis objectives involve using skills to create completely new products. Examples include writing a composition, deriving a mathematical rule, designing a science experiment to solve a problem, or making up a new sentence in a foreign language.

6. *Evaluation (judging something against a given standard).*   Evaluation objectives require making value judgments against some criterion or standard. For example, students might be asked to compare the strengths and weaknesses of two home computers in terms of flexibility, power, and available software.

Because Bloom's taxonomy is organized from simple to complex, some people interpret it as a ranking of objectives from trivial (knowledge) to important (synthesis, evaluation). However, this is not the intent of the taxonomy. Different levels of objectives are appropriate for different purposes and for students at different stages of development (Marzano & Kendall, 2007).

The primary importance of Bloom's taxonomy is in its reminder that we want students to have many levels of skills. All too often, teachers focus on measurable knowledge and comprehension objectives and forget that students cannot be considered proficient in many skills until they can apply or synthesize those skills (see Iran-Nejad & Stewart, 2007). On the other side of the coin, some teachers fail to make certain that students are well rooted in the basics before heading off into higher-order objectives.

USING A BEHAVIOR CONTENT MATRIX   One way to be sure that your objectives cover many levels is to write a **behavior content matrix.** This is simply a chart that shows how a particular concept or skill will be taught and assessed at different cognitive levels. Examples of objectives in a behavior content matrix appear in Table 13.3. Note that for each topic, objectives are listed for some but not all levels of Bloom's taxonomy. Some topics do not lend themselves to some levels of the taxonomy, and there is no reason that every level should be covered for every topic. However, using a behavior content matrix in setting objectives forces you to consider objectives above the knowledge and comprehension levels.

OBJECTIVES BEYOND THE BASICS.   Learning facts and skills is not the only important goal of instruction. Sometimes the feelings that students have about a subject or about their own skills are at least as important as how much information they learn. Instructional goals related to attitudes and values are called **affective objectives.** Many people would argue that a principal purpose of a U.S. history or civics course is to promote values of patriotism and civic responsibility and one purpose of any mathematics course is to give students confidence in their ability to use mathematics. In planning instruction, it is important to consider affective as well as cognitive objectives. Love of

behavior content matrix

A chart that classifies lesson objectives according to cognitive level.

affective objectives

Objectives that have to do with student attitudes and values.

TABLE 13.3 Examples of Objectives in a Behavior Content Matrix

A behavior content matrix can remind teachers to develop instructional objectives that address skills at various cognitive levels.

Type of Objective	Example 1: The Area of a Circle	Example 2: Main Idea of a Story	Example 3: The Colonization of Africa
Knowledge	Give the formula for area of a circle.	Define *main idea*.	Make a time line showing how Europeans divided Africa into colonies.
Comprehension		Give examples of ways to find the main idea of a story.	Interpret a map of Africa showing its colonization by European nations.
Application	Apply the formula for area of a circle to real-life problems.		
Analysis		Identify the main idea of a story	Contrast the goals and methods used in colonizing Africa by the different European nations.
Synthesis	Use knowledge about the areas of circles and volumes of cubes to derive a formula for the volume of a cylinder.	Write a new story based on the main idea of the story read.	Write an essay on the European colonization of Africa from the perspective of a Bantu chief.
Evaluation		Evaluate the story.	

learning, confidence in learning, and development of prosocial, cooperative attitudes are among the most important objectives you should have for your students. Sternberg (2008) suggests that schools supplement objectives relating to the 3R's (reading, 'riting, and 'rithmetic) with three more R's: reasoning, resilience, and responsibility (also see Rothstein & Jacobsen, 2009).

■ Research on Instructional Objectives

Three principal reasons are given for writing instructional objectives. One is that this exercise helps to organize your planning. As Mager (1997) puts it, if you're not sure where you're going, you're liable to end up someplace else and not even know it. Another is that establishing instructional objectives helps to guide evaluation. Finally, it is hypothesized that development of instructional objectives improves student achievement.

Although it would be a mistake to overplan or to adhere rigidly to an inflexible plan, most experienced teachers create, use, and value objectives and assessments that are planned in advance. Perhaps the most convincing support for the establishment of clear instructional objectives is indirect. Cooley and Leinhardt (1980) found that the strongest single factor predicting student reading and math scores was the degree to which students were actually taught the skills that were tested. This implies that instruction is effective to the degree to which objectives, teaching, and assessment are coordinated with one another. Specification of clear instructional objectives is the first step in ensuring that classroom instruction is directed toward giving students critical skills, those that are important enough to test.

It is important to make sure that instructional objectives that are communicated to students are broad enough to encompass everything the lesson or course is supposed to teach. There is some danger that giving students too narrow a set of objectives might focus them on some information to the exclusion of other facts and concepts.

Why Is Evaluation Important

Evaluation, or assessment, refers to all the means used in schools to formally measure student performance (Gronlund & Waugh, 2009; McMillan, 2008; Popham, 2005). These include quizzes and tests, written evaluations, and grades. Student evaluation usually focuses on academic achievement, but many schools also assess behaviors and attitudes. Many elementary schools provide descriptions of student behaviors (such as "follows directions," "listens attentively," "works with others," "uses time wisely"). In upper elementary, middle, and high school the prevalence of behavior reports diminishes successively, but even many high schools rate students on such criteria as "works up to ability," "is prepared," and "is responsible."

Why do teachers use tests and grades? You use them because, one way or another, you must periodically check and communicate about students' learning. Tests and grades tell teachers, students, and parents how students are doing in school. You can use tests to determine whether your instruction was effective and to find out which students need additional help. Students can use tests to find out whether their studying strategies are paying off. Parents need grades to learn how their children are doing in school; grades usually serve as the one consistent form of communication between school and home. Schools sometimes need grades and tests to make student placements. States and school districts need tests to evaluate schools and, in some cases, teachers. Ultimately, colleges use grades and standardized test scores to decide who to admit and employers use grade-based evidence of attainment such as diplomas and other credentials in hiring decisions. Teachers, therefore, must evaluate student learning; few would argue otherwise. Research on the use of tests finds that students learn more in courses that test students than in those that do not (Dempster, 1991; Haynie & Haynie, 2008).

Student evaluations serve six primary purposes (see Gronlund & Waugh, 2009):

1. Feedback to students
2. Feedback to teachers
3. Information to parents
4. Information for selection and certification
5. Information for accountability
6. Incentives to increase student effort

■ Evaluation as Feedback

Imagine that a store owner tried several strategies to increase business—first advertising in the newspaper, then sending fliers to homes near the store, and finally holding a sale. However, suppose that after trying each strategy, the store owner failed to record and compare the store's revenue. Without taking stock this way, the owner would learn little about the effectiveness of any of the strategies and might well be wasting time and money. The same is true of teachers and students. They need to know as soon as possible whether their investments of time and energy in a given activity are paying off in increased learning.

FEEDBACK FOR STUDENTS   Like the store owner, students need to know the results of their efforts (Hattie & Timperley, 2007; Scriffiny, 2008). Regular evaluation gives them feedback on their strengths and weaknesses (Sato & Atkin, 2006/2007). For example, suppose you had students write compositions and then gave back written evaluations. Some students might find out that they needed to work more on content, others on the use of modifiers, and still others on language mechanics. This information would help students to improve their writing much more than would a grade with no explanation (Chappuis, Chappuis, & Stiggins, 2009; Leahy, Lyon, Thompson, & Wiliam, 2005).

Connections

For more on feedback as a component of effective teaching, see Chapter 7, page 201.

INTASC

8 Assessment of Student Learning

9 Professional Commitment and Responsibility

evaluation

Measurement of student performance in academic and, sometimes, other areas; used to determine appropriate teaching strategies.

To be useful as feedback, evaluations should be as specific as possible. For example, Cross and Cross (1980/1981) found that students who received written feedback in addition to letter grades were more likely than other students to believe that their efforts, rather than luck or other external factors, determined their success in school.

FEEDBACK TO TEACHERS   One of the most important (and often overlooked) functions of evaluating student learning is to provide feedback to teachers on the effectiveness of their instruction. You cannot expect to be optimally effective if you do not know whether students have grasped the main points of your lessons. Asking questions in class and observing students as they work gives you some idea of how well students have learned; but in many subjects brief but frequent quizzes, writing assignments, and other student products are necessary to provide more detailed indications of students' progress. Well-crafted questions can help you understand students' thinking and uncover misconceptions (Burns, 2005; Salend, 2009). Evaluations also give information to the principal and the school as a whole, which can be used to guide overall reform efforts by identifying where schools or subgroups within schools are in need of improvement (Hanna & Dettmer, 2004; Kallick & Colosimo, 2009; Lane & Beebe-Frankenberger, 2004; Trumbull & Farr, 2000).

■ Evaluation as Information

A report card is called a report card because it reports information on student progress. This reporting function of evaluation is important for several reasons.

INFORMATION TO PARENTS   First, routine school evaluations of many kinds (test scores, stars, and certificates as well as report card grades) keep parents informed about their children's schoolwork. For example, if a student's grades are dropping, the parents might know why and may be able to help the student get back on track. Second, grades and other evaluations set up informal home-based reinforcement systems. Recall from Chapter 11 that many studies have found that reporting regularly to parents when students do good work and asking parents to reinforce good reports improve student behavior and achievement. Without much prompting, most parents naturally reinforce their children for bringing home good grades, thereby making grades important and effective as incentives.

Connections
For more on information for parents, see Chapter 11, page 337.

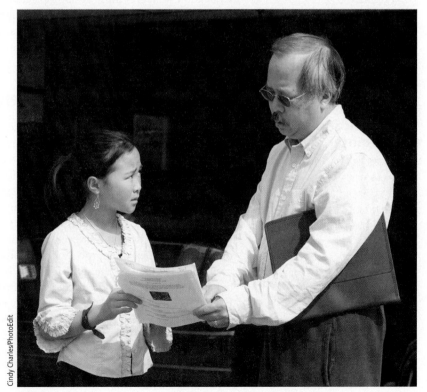

This student discusses her report card with her father. As a teacher, how can you ensure that report cards provide feedback, information, and incentive?

Cindy Charles/PhotoEdit

INFORMATION FOR SELECTION Some sociologists see the sorting of students into societal roles as a primary purpose of schools: If schools do not actually determine who will be a butcher, a baker, or a candlestick maker, they do substantially influence who will be a laborer, a skilled worker, a white-collar worker, or a professional. This sorting function takes place gradually over years of schooling. In the early grades, students are sorted into reading groups. Later, for example, some ninth-graders take algebra whereas

Connections

For more information on ability grouping, see Chapter 9.

others take prealgebra or general mathematics. In high school, students are often steered toward advanced, basic, or remedial levels of particular courses, and of course a major sorting takes place when students are accepted into various colleges and training programs. Moreover, throughout the school years, some students are selected into special-education or gifted programs or into other special programs with limited enrollments.

Closely related to selection is certification, a use of tests to qualify students for promotion or for access to various occupations. For example, many states and local districts have minimum competency tests that students must pass to advance from grade to grade or to graduate from high school. Bar exams for lawyers, board examinations for medical students, and tests for teachers such as the National Teachers' Examination are examples of certification tests that control access to professions.

INFORMATION FOR ACCOUNTABILITY   Often, evaluations of students serve as data for the evaluation of teachers, schools, districts, or even states. Every state has some form of statewide testing program that allows the states to rank every school in terms of student performance (Gandal & Vranek, 2001; Linn, 2000). These test scores are also often used in evaluations of principals, teachers, and superintendents. Consequently, these tests are taken very seriously.

■ Evaluation as Incentive

One important use of evaluations is to motivate students to give their best efforts. In essence, high grades, stars, and prizes are given as rewards for good work. Students value grades and prizes primarily because their parents value them. Some high school students also value grades because they are important for getting into selective colleges.

How Is Student Learning Evaluated

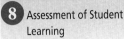

INTASC

8 Assessment of Student Learning

Evaluation strategies must be appropriate for the uses that are made of them (McMillan, 2008; O'Connor, 2007, 2009; Oosterhof, 2009; Salend, 2009). To understand how assessments can be used most effectively in classroom instruction, it is important to know the differences between formative and summative evaluations and between norm-referenced and criterion-referenced interpretations.

■ Formative and Summative Evaluations

Certification Pointer

For your teacher certification test, you may be given a case illustrating an evaluation of student performance and you will need to categorize that evaluation as formative or summative.

Assessments can be divided into two categories: formative and summative. Essentially, a formative evaluation asks, "How well are you doing and how can you be doing better?" A summative evaluation asks, "How well did you do?" A **formative evaluation** is designed to tell teachers whether additional instruction is needed and to tell students whether additional learning is needed (Marzano, 2010; Tomlinson, 2007/2008). Formative, or diagnostic, tests are given to discover strengths and weaknesses in learning and to make midcourse corrections in pace or content of instruction (Fisher & Frey, 2009). Formative evaluations might even be made "on the fly" during instruction through oral or brief written learning probes or by listening to students during groupwork. Formative evaluation is useful to the degree that it is informative, closely tied to the curriculum being taught, timely, and frequent (Ainsworth & Viegut, 2006; Dunn & Mulvenon, 2009; Fogarty & Kerns, 2009; McMillan, 2008). For example, frequent quizzes that are given and scored immediately after specific lessons might serve as formative evaluations, providing feedback to help both teachers and students improve students' learning. Effective uses of formative assessments in lessons was discussed in Chapter 7.

In contrast, **summative evaluation** refers to tests of student knowledge at the end of instructional units (such as final exams). Summative evaluations may or may not be

formative evaluations

Evaluations designed to determine whether additional instruction is needed.

summative evaluations

Final evaluations of students' achievement of an objective.

frequent, but they must be reliable and (in general) should allow for comparisons among students. Summative evaluations should also be closely tied to formative evaluations and to course objectives (Gronlund & Brookhart, 2009).

Connections

For more on standardized testing, see Chapter 14.

■ Norm-Referenced and Criterion-Referenced Evaluations

Interpretation in order to attach a degree of value to a student's performance is an important step in an evaluation. The distinction between norm referencing and criterion referencing refers to how students' scores are interpreted.

Norm-referenced interpretations focus on comparisons of a student's scores with those of other students. Within a classroom, for example, grades commonly are used to give teachers an idea of how well a student has performed in comparison with classmates. A student might also have a grade-level or school rank; in standardized testing, student scores might be compared with those of a nationally representative norm group.

Criterion-referenced interpretations focus on assessing students' mastery of specific skills, regardless of how other students did on the same skills. Criterion-referenced evaluations are best if they are closely tied to specific objectives or well-specified domains of the curriculum being taught. Table 13.4 compares the principal features and purposes of criterion-referenced and norm-referenced testing (see also Gronlund & Waugh, 2009; Popham, 2008).

Formative evaluation is almost always criterion referenced. In formative testing, teachers want to know, for example, who is having trouble with Newton's laws of thermodynamics, not which student is first, fifteenth, or thirtieth in the class in physics knowledge. Summative testing, in contrast, can be either criterion referenced or norm referenced. Even if it is criterion referenced, however, teachers usually want to know on a summative test how each student did in comparison with other students.

Certification Pointer

Your teacher certification test may require you to evaluate when it would be more appropriate to use a criterion-referenced versus a norm-referenced test.

norm-referenced interpretations

Assessments that compare the performance of one student against the performance of others.

criterion-referenced interpretations

Assessments that rate how thoroughly students have mastered specific skills or areas of knowledge.

TABLE 13.4	**Comparison of Two Approaches to Achievement Testing**	
Norm-referenced tests and criterion-referenced tests serve different purposes and have different features.		
Feature	**Norm-Referenced Testing**	**Criterion-Referenced Testing**
Principal use	Survey testing	Mastery testing
Major emphasis	Measures individual differences in achievement	Describes tasks students can perform
Interpretation of results	Compares performance to that of other individuals	Compares performance to a clearly specified achievement domain
Content coverage	Typically covers a broad area of achievement	Typically focuses on a limited set of learning tasks
Nature of test plan	Table of specifications is commonly used	Detailed domain specifications are favored
Item selection procedures	Items selected to provide maximum discrimination between individuals (to obtain high score variability); easy items typically eliminated from the test	Includes all items needed to adequately describe performance; no attempt is made to alter item difficulty or to eliminate easy items to increase score variability
Performance standards	Level of performance determined by *relative* position in some known group (e.g., student ranks fifth in a group of 20)	Level of performance commonly determined by *absolute* standards (e.g., student demonstrates mastery by defining 90 percent of the technical terms)

Source: Adapted from Gronlund, *How to Make Achievement Tests and Assessments* (5th ed.), Figure 1.2, "Comparison of Two Approaches to Achievement Testing," p. 13. © 1993 by Pearson Education, Inc. Reproduced by permission of Pearson Education, Inc.

■ Matching Evaluation Strategies with Goals

Considering all the factors discussed up to this point, what is the best strategy for evaluating students? The first answer is that there is no one best strategy (Popham, 2005, 2009). The best means of accomplishing any one objective of evaluation might be inappropriate for other objectives. Therefore, you should choose different types of evaluation for different purposes. At a minimum, two types of evaluation should be used: one directed at providing incentive and feedback and the other directed at ranking individual students relative to the larger group.

INTASC

5 Classroom Management and Motivation

6 Communication Skills

Connections

Rewards and motivation are discussed in Chapter 5, page 119.

Connections

For more on which rewards make poor motivators, see Chapter 10, page 301.

Connections

For more on rewards that are too easy to attain, see Chapter 10, page 307.

EVALUATION FOR INCENTIVE AND FEEDBACK   Traditional grades are often inadequate as incentives to encourage students to give their best efforts and as feedback to teachers and students. The principal problems are that grades are given too infrequently, are too far removed in time from student performance, and are poorly tied to specific student behaviors. Research has found that achievement is higher in classrooms where students receive immediate feedback on their quizzes than in classrooms where feedback is delayed (Bangert-Drowns, Kulik, Kulik, & Morgan, 1991; Crooks, 1988).

Another reason that grades are less than ideal as incentives is that they are usually based on comparative standards. In effect, it is relatively easy for high-ability students to achieve A's and B's but very difficult for low achievers to do so. As a result, some high achievers do less work than they are capable of doing, and some low achievers give up. As was noted in Chapter 10, a reward that is too easy or too difficult to attain, or that is felt to be a result of ability rather than of effort, is a poor motivator (Chapman & King, 2005; Wigfield & Eccles, 2000).

For these reasons, traditional grades should be supplemented by evaluations that are better designed for incentive and feedback. For example, teachers might give daily quizzes of 5 or 10 items that are scored in class immediately after completion, or they might have students write daily "mini-essays" on a topic the class is studying. These give both students and teachers the information they need to adjust their teaching and learning strategies and to rectify any deficiencies revealed by the evaluations (Shepard, 2005). If teachers make quiz results important by having them count toward course grades or by giving students with perfect papers special recognition or certificates, then quiz scores also serve as effective incentives, rewarding effective studying behavior soon after it occurs. It is important to have a clear and objective set of criteria that student work is compared with so students can see exactly why they scored as they did. If the criteria are illustrated using a rubric that has descriptions of different levels of achievement (scores) as well as examples of student work at the highest levels of achievement (or better yet, that is typical of each possible score students might receive according to the rubric), then students can see exactly how their achievement compares with the criteria (see Stiggins, 2007).

Connections

For more on grades and standardized tests, see Chapter 14.

EVALUATION FOR COMPARISON WITH OTHERS   There are times when you need to know and to communicate how well students are doing in comparison to others. This information is important to give parents (and students themselves) a realistic picture of student performance. For example, students who have outstanding skills in science ought to know that they are exceptional, not only in the context of their class or school, but also in a broader state or national context. In general, students need to form accurate perceptions of their strengths and weaknesses to guide their decisions about their futures.

Comparative evaluations are traditionally provided by grades and by standardized tests. Unlike incentive/feedback evaluations, comparative evaluations need not be conducted frequently. Rather, the emphasis in comparative evaluations must be on fair, unbiased, reliable assessment of student performance.

To be fair, comparative evaluations and other summative assessments of student performance must be firmly based on the objectives established at the beginning of the course and consistent with the formative incentive/feedback evaluations in format as

21st Century Learning

Creativity and Authentic Problem Solving

Since the progressive era began a hundred years ago, educators have advocated creativity and authentic problem-solving skills as key outcomes of education. Yet because these outcomes are difficult and time-consuming to measure reliably, they are often downplayed in comparison to relatively easy-to-assess facts and skills. New assessment software, especially adaptive testing, is beginning to make regular assessment of creativity and authentic problem solving more practical, using computers to pose complex, open-ended problems at the student's precise level of functioning. Such solutions, used as frequent benchmark assessments as well as summative assessments, may soon help teachers both focus more on these essential 21st century skills and monitor students' development as creative problem-solvers.

Questions

- What are the potential difficulties in judging creativity?
- Do you think it is ethical to penalize a student based on what is judged to be a lack of creativity?
- Do you think creativity should count towards grades?
- Is creativity a necessary life skill?
- How might a lack of creativity be a problem in the workplace?

well. No teacher wants a situation in which students do well on week-to-week assessments but then fail the summative evaluations because there is a lack of correspondence between the two forms of evaluation. For example, if the summative test uses essay questions, then the formative tests leading up to it should also include essay questions (Tileston & Darling, 2008).

There are two keys to reliable summative assessment. First, you should use multiple assessment opportunities (Brookhart, 2007/2008; Popham, 2008). No student should receive a grade based on only one test because too much can go wrong with only one assessment. Second, you should test learning when it is completed, not as it is developing. It is better to collect summative evaluation information as students complete instructional units as well as to use major unit and final tests.

How Are Tests Constructed

Once you know the concept domains to be assessed in a test of student learning, it is time to write test items. Writing good achievement tests is a critical skill for effective teaching. This section presents some basic principles of achievement testing and practical tools for test construction (see Popham, 2008; Oosterhof, 2009). Achievement testing is taken up again in Chapter 14 in relation to standardized tests.

■ Principles of Achievement Testing

Gronlund & Brookhart (2009) listed six principles to keep in mind in preparing achievement tests, paraphrased as follows:

1. *Achievement tests should measure clearly defined learning objectives that are in harmony with instructional objectives.* Perhaps the most important principle of

Connections

For more on achievement testing in relation to standardized tests, see Chapter 14, page 454.

Connections

For more on the characteristics and uses of standardized achievement tests, see Chapter 14, page 459.

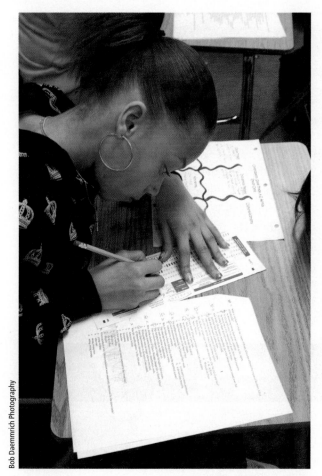

This student is taking an achievement test. What are the principles for preparing achievement tests?

achievement testing is that the tests should correspond with the course objectives and with the instruction that is actually provided (Carr & Harris, 2001; Gorin & Blanchard, 2004; Gronlund & Waugh, 2009; Hanna & Dettmer, 2004; Squires, 2009). An achievement test should never be a surprise for students; rather, it should assess the students' grasp of the most important concepts or skills the lesson or course is supposed to teach.

2. Achievement tests should measure a representative sample of the learning tasks included in the instruction. With rare exceptions (such as multiplication facts), achievement tests do not assess every skill or fact students are supposed to have learned. Rather, they sample from among all the learning objectives. If students do not know in advance what questions will be on a test, then they must study the entire course content to do well. However, the test items must be representative of all the objectives (contents and skills) that were covered. For example, if an English literature course spent 8 weeks on Shakespeare and 2 weeks on other Elizabethan authors, the test should have about four times as many items relating to Shakespeare as to the others. Items that are chosen to represent a particular objective must be central to that objective. There is no place in achievement testing for tricky or obscure questions. For example, a unit test on the American Revolution should ask questions relating to the causes, principal events, and outcomes of that struggle, not who rowed George Washington across the Delaware. (*Answer:* John Glover and his Marblehead Marines.)

3. Achievement tests should include the types of test items that are most appropriate for measuring the desired learning outcomes. Items on achievement tests should correspond as closely as possible to the ultimate instructional objectives (Carr & Harris, 2001; Flippo, 2008; Strong, Silver, & Perini, 2001). For example, in mathematics problem solving, one of your goals might be to enable students to solve problems like the ones they will encounter outside of school. Matching items or multiple choice might be inappropriate for this kind of exam, because in real life we do not select from a menu of possible solutions to a problem.

4. Achievement tests should fit the particular uses that will be made of the results. Each type of achievement test has its own requirements. For example, a test that is used for diagnosis would focus on particular skills with which students might need help. A diagnostic test of elementary arithmetic might contain items on subtraction involving zeros in the minuend (e.g., 307 minus 127), a skill with which many students have trouble. In contrast, a test that is used to predict future performance might assess a student's general abilities and breadth of knowledge. Formative tests should be very closely tied to material that has recently been presented, whereas summative tests should survey broader areas of knowledge or skills.

Connections

For more on the reliability of achievement tests, see Chapter 14, page 465.

5. Achievement tests should be as reliable as possible but nevertheless interpreted with caution. A test is reliable to the degree that students tested a second time fall in the same rank order. In general, writers of achievement tests increase reliability by using relatively large numbers of items and by including few items that almost all students get right or that almost all students miss (O'Connor, 2009). The use of clearly written items that focus directly on the objectives that are actually taught also enhances test reliability. Still, no matter how rigorously reliability is built into a test, there will always be some error of measurement. Students have good and bad days or can be lucky or unlucky guessers. Some students are test-wise and usually test well; others are test-anxious and test far below their actual knowledge or potential. Therefore, no single test score should be viewed with excessive confidence. Any test score is only an approximation of a student's true knowledge or skills and should be interpreted as such.

6. *Achievement tests should improve learning.*   Achievement tests of all kinds, particularly formative tests, provide important information on students' learning progress. Stiggins (2004), for example, urges that assessments *for* learning are more important than assessments *of* learning. Achievement testing should be seen as part of the instructional process and used to improve instruction and guide student learning (Ainsworth & Viegut, 2006; Black et al., 2004; Chappuis et al., 2009). This means that achievement test results should be clearly communicated to students soon after the test is taken; in the case of formative testing, students should be given the results immediately. Teachers should use the results of formative and summative tests to guide instruction, to locate strong and weak points in students' understandings, and to set an appropriate pace of instruction.

Theory into Practice
Making Assessments Fair

INTASC

8 Assessment of Student Learning

Although fairness in assessment is something everyone believes in, defining fairness in assessment is not straightforward. Indeed, the latest edition of the *Standards for Educational and Psychological Testing* gives four definitions and acknowledges that many more are in the literature (AERA/APA/NCME, 1999). Fairness means being honest, impartial, and free from discrimination. Besides being ethical, fairness makes good instructional sense. Fair testing encourages students to spend more effort on learning because they will come to see that success depends only on what they know and can do (Oosterhof, 2009).

Fairness in assessment arises from good practice in four phases of testing: writing, administering, scoring, and interpreting assessments. Practices that lead to fairness in these areas are considered separately below.

WRITING ASSESSMENTS   Base assessments on course objectives. Students expect a test to cover what they have been learning. They also have a right to a test that neither "tricks" them into wrong answers nor rewards them with a high score for guessing or bluffing.

Avoid contexts and expressions that are more familiar or intriguing to some students than to others. One challenge in writing tests is to make sure none of your students are advantaged or disadvantaged because of their different backgrounds. For example, music, sports, or celebrity-related examples might be appealing to some students but not others. Language or topics should not be used if they are more well known or interesting to some students than to others. If that proves impossible, then at least make sure the items that favor some students are balanced with others that favor the rest.

GIVING ASSESSMENTS   Make sure students have had equal opportunities to learn the material on the assessment. Regardless of whether students have learned as much as they can, at least they should have had equal chances to do so. If some students are given extra time or materials that are withheld from others, the others likely will not feel they have been treated fairly.

Make sure students are familiar with the formats they will be using to respond. If some students are not comfortable with the types of questions on an assessment, they will not have an equal chance to show what they can do. If that might be the case, some practice with the format beforehand is recommended to help them succeed.

Give plenty of time. Most tests in education do not cover content that will eventually be used under time pressure. Thus, most assessments should reward quality instead of speed. Only by allowing enough time so virtually all students have an opportunity to answer every question will the effects of speed be eliminated as a barrier to performance.

SCORING ASSESSMENTS   Make sure the rubric used to score responses awards full credit to an answer that is responsive to the question asked as opposed to requiring more information than requested for full credit. If the question does not prompt the knowledgeable student to write an answer that receives full credit, then it should be changed. It is unfair to reward some students for doing more than has been requested in the item; not all students will understand the real (and hidden) directions because they have not been told.

INTERPRETING ASSESSMENTS   Base grades on summative end-of-unit assessments rather than formative assessments that are used to make decisions about learning as it is progressing. The latter are intended to be diagnostic and used to help accomplish learning. Because grades certify attainment, they should be determined based on assessments made after learning has taken place.

Base grades on several assessment formats. Because students differ in their preferred formats, some are advantaged by selected-response tests, others by essay tests, others by performance assessments, and still others by papers and projects. Also, base grades on several assessments over time. As with assessment formats, grades should also depend on multiple assessments taken at different times. Finally, make sure factors that might result in atypical performance for a student are recognized to minimize the importance of the student's score on that assessment. If it is known that a student has not done her or his best, then basing a grade or other important decision on that assessment is not only unfair but also inaccurate.

ON THE WEB

DiscoverySchool.com has rubrics for every kind of assessment imaginable, as well as lesson plans and other useful information for educators: http://school.discoveryeducation.com/schrockguide/assess.html. For student project assessment rubrics, see http://eduscapes.com/tap/topic53.htm. The website of Educate America (NREL) discusses testing reform at www.maec.org/educate/11.html. Resources for student assessment can be found at www.iste.org/source/orders/excerpts/netssa.pdf. For a website on creating a rubric, see http://assessment.aas.duke.edu/documents/CreatingaRubric.pdf. For developing classroom performance assessments and scoring rubrics, see www.ericdigests.org/2005-2/scoring.html.

■ Using a Table of Specifications

table of specifications

A list of instructional objectives and expected levels of understanding that guides test development.

Achievement tests should measure well-specified objectives. The first step in the test development process is to decide which concept domains the test will measure and how many test items will be allocated to each concept. Gronlund & Waugh (2009) suggest that teachers make up a **table of specifications** for each instructional unit, listing the various objectives taught and different levels of understanding to be assessed (also see

TABLE 13.5 Table of Specifications for a Chemistry Unit

This table of specifications classifies test items (circled numbers) and objectives according to six categories ranging from knowledge of terms to ability to apply knowledge.

A. Knowledge of Terms	B. Knowledge of Facts	C. Knowledge of Rules and Principles	D. Skill in Using Processes and Procedures	E. Ability to Make Translations	F. Ability to Make Applications
Atom ①		Boyle's law ⑫			
Molecule ②		Properties of a gas ⑬		Substance into diagram ㉒	
Element ③		Atomic theory ⑯			Writing and solving equations to fit experimental situations
Compound ④	Diatomic gases ⑪	Chemical formula ⑲		Compound into formula ㉑	㉘
Diatomic ⑤					㉓
Chemical formula ⑥		Avogadro's hypothesis ⑭			㉔
Avogadro's number ⑦		Gay-Lussac's law ⑮			㉕
Mole ⑧		Grams to moles ⑱			㉖
Atomic weight ⑨		Molecular weight ⑰	Molecular weight ⑳		㉗
Molecular weight ⑩					㉙

Guskey, 2005). The levels of understanding might correspond to Bloom's taxonomy of educational objectives (Bloom et al., 1956; Marzano & Kendall, 2009). Bloom, Hastings, and Madaus (1971) recommend classifying test items for each objective according to six categories, as shown in Table 13.5, a table of specifications for a chemistry unit.

The table of specifications varies for each type of course and is nearly identical to behavior content matrixes, discussed earlier in this chapter. This is as it should be; a behavior content matrix is used to lay out objectives for a course, and the table of specifications tests those objectives.

Once you have written items corresponding to your table of specifications, look over the test in its entirety and evaluate it against the following standards:

1. Do the items emphasize the same concepts you have emphasized in day-to-day instruction? (Recall how Mr. Sullivan, in the chapter-opening vignette, ignored this commonsense rule.)
2. Has an important area of content or any objective been overlooked or underemphasized?
3. Does the test cover all levels of instructional objectives included in the lessons?

4. Does the language of the items correspond to the language and reading level you used in the lessons?

5. Are the instructions clear, even for students who have difficulty with instructions?

6. Is there a reasonable balance between what the items measure and the amount of time that will be required for students to develop a response?

7. Did you write model answers or essential component outlines for the short essay items? Does the weighting of each item reflect its relative value among all the other items?

Evaluation that is restricted to information acquired from paper-and-pencil tests provides only certain kinds of information about students' progress in school. Other sources and strategies for appraisal of student work must be used, including checklists, interviews, classroom simulations, role-playing activities, and anecdotal records. To do this systematically, you may keep a journal or log to record concise and cogent evaluative information on each student throughout the school year.

■ Writing Selected-Response Test Items

Test items that can be scored correct or incorrect without the need for interpretation are referred to as **selected-response items.** Multiple-choice, true–false, and matching items are the most common forms. Note that the correct answer appears on the test and the student's task is to select it. There is no ambiguity about whether the student has or has not selected the correct answer. Each type, however, has its own advantages and disadvantages.

MULTIPLE-CHOICE ITEMS   Considered by some educators to be the most useful and flexible of all test forms (Badgett & Christmann, 2009; Gronlund & Waugh, 2009), **multiple-choice items** can be used in tests for most school subjects. The basic form of the multiple-choice item is a **stem** followed by choices, or alternatives. The stem may be a question or a partial statement that is completed by one of several choices. No perfect number of choices exists, but four or five are most common—one correct response and wrong but plausible answers referred to as **distractors** or **foils.**

The following examples demonstrate two types of multiple-choice items, one with a question stem and the other with a completion stem:

1. What color results from the mixture of equal parts of yellow and blue paint?
   a. Black
   b. Gray
   c. Green [*correct choice*]
   d. Red

2. U.S. presidents are actually elected to office by
   a. all registered voters.
   b. our congressional representatives.
   c. the Electoral College. [*correct choice*]
   d. the Supreme Court.

When writing a multiple-choice item, keep two goals in mind. First, a capable student should be able to choose the correct answer and not be distracted by the wrong alternatives. Second, you should minimize the chance that a student who is ignorant of the subject matter can guess the correct answer. To achieve this, the distractors must look possible to the uninformed; their wording and form must not identify them readily as bad answers. Hence, one of the tasks in writing a good multiple-choice item is to identify two, three, or four plausible, but not tricky, distractors.

selected-response items

Test items in which respondents can select from one or more possible answers, without requiring the scorer to interpret their response.

multiple-choice items

Test items that usually consist of a stem followed by choices or alternatives.

stem

A question or partial statement in a test item that is completed by one of several choices.

distractors or foils

Incorrect responses that are offered as alternative answers to a multiple-choice question.

Theory into Practice
Writing Multiple-Choice Tests (Format Suggestions)

The following guidelines are useful resources for constructing effective multiple-choice items (see Badgett & Christmann, 2009; McMillan, 2008):

1. Make the stem sufficiently specific to stand on its own without qualification. In other words, the stem should contain enough information to set the context for the concepts in it. The following example shows a stem for which insufficient context has been established:

Applied behavior analysis can be
a. classical conditioning.
b. punishment.
c. reinforcement contingencies.
d. self-actualization.

An improved version of this stem is the following:

What is the main emphasis of modern classroom use of applied behavior analysis?
a. Classical conditioning
b. Punishment
c. Reinforcement contingencies [*correct choice*]
d. Self-actualization

2. Avoid long and complicated stems unless the purpose of the item is to measure a student's ability to deal with new information or to interpret a paragraph. The stem should not be too wordy; a test is not the place to incorporate instruction that should have been given in the lessons.

3. The stem and every choice in the list of potential answers ought to fit grammatically. In addition, avoid repeating phrases or words to begin each of the alternatives; instead, these should be part of the stem. It is also a sound idea to have the same grammatical form (say, a verb) at the beginning of each choice, as in the following example.

The task of statistics is to
a. *make* the investigation of human beings more precise and rigorous.
b. *promote* the social sciences to a status of being as respectable as the physical sciences.
c. *predict* human behavior.
d. *reduce* large masses of data to an interpretable form. [*correct choice*]

4. Take special care in using no-exception words such as *never, all, none,* or *always.* These words are most commonly found in incorrect statements because the requirement of no exceptions usually makes statements wrong. In multiple-choice items these words often give clues to the test-wise but concept-ignorant student. Words allowing qualification, such as *often, sometimes, seldom, usually, typically, generally,* and *ordinarily,* are most often found in correct statements (or responses that are true) and, along with no-exception words, such specific determiners should be avoided whenever possible, or at least distributed among both correct answers and distractors.

5. Avoid making the correct choice the only one that is qualified (e.g., by an "if" clause). Also, it should be neither the longest nor shortest of the alternatives (the longest can be guessed to be right because absolutely correct answers often require qualification and precision). These features make a choice stand out.

6. Do not use an item that can be answered on the basis of information contained in another item on the same test.

7. Avoid overly inclusive options that contain other options. For example, the choices "dogs" and "setters" should not be in the same item because a setter is a type of dog. Similarly, be cautious in using "all of the above" as an alternative because it also often reduces the possible correct choices to one or two alternatives. The following example illustrates how a student might know very little and get the correct answer. By knowing that only one of the choices is incorrect, a student will reduce the number of plausible choices from four to two.

What type of research is best for investigating the effects of a new instructional program on mathematics achievement?

a. Correlational

b. Experimental [*correct choice*]

c. Historical

d. All of the above

The student who knows that "historical" is not a good choice also knows that item d must be incorrect, and the answer must be a or b.

8. After a test, discuss the items with students, and note their interpretations of the wording of each. Students often understand certain phrases quite differently from the way you may have intended. Such feedback will help you revise items for the next test, as well as informing you about students' understandings.

9. Do not include a choice that is transparently absurd. All choices should seem plausible to a student who has not studied.

Besides these guidelines for writing multiple-choice items, here are some suggestions about format:

■ List the choices vertically rather than side by side.

■ Use letters rather than numerals to label the choices, especially on scientific and mathematical tests.

■ Use word structures that make the stem agree with the choices according to acceptable grammatical practice. For example, a completion-type stem would require that each of the choices begin with a lowercase letter (unless it begins with a proper noun).

■ Avoid repeating the same word or phrase in the stem and in only one alternative.

■ Avoid overusing one letter position as the correct choice, as well as any patterns in the correct answers. Instead, correct choices should appear in random letter positions.

As an illustration of how test "wiseness" rather than knowledge can help students pass an exam, take the brief test in Figure 13.2.

TRUE–FALSE ITEMS   Another form of multiple choice is the **true–false item.** The main drawback of the true–false format is that students have a 50 percent chance of guessing correctly. For this reason, it should rarely be used.

MATCHING ITEMS   As commonly presented, **matching items** usually take the form of two lists, say *A* and *B*. For each item in list *A,* the student has to select one item in list *B*. The basis for choosing must be clearly explained in the directions. Matching items can be used to cover a large amount of content; that is, a large (but not unmanageably so) number of concepts should appear in the two lists. Each list should cover related content (use more than one set of matching items for different types of material). The primary cognitive skill that matching exercises test is recall.

Matching items can often be answered by elimination because many teachers maintain a one-to-one correspondence between the two lists. To engage students in the content, not the format, teachers should either include more items in list *B* than in list *A* or allow re-use of the items in list *B*.

true–false items

A form of multiple-choice test items, most useful when a comparison of two alternatives is called for.

matching items

Test items that are presented in two lists, each item in one list matching one or more items in the other list.

FIGURE 13.2   A Test of "Test Wiseness"

The following test is about a made-up country, Quizzerland. Use your test wiseness to guess the answers to these very bad items.

1. What is the main currency used in Quizzerland?
   a. Dollar
   b. Peso
   c. Quark
   d. Pound

2. Describe the pattern of annual rainfall in Quizzerland.
   a. Mostly rainy in the highlands, dry in the lowlands
   b Rainy
   c. Dry
   d. Snowy

3. How many children are there in Quizzerlandian families?
   a. Never more than 2
   b. Usually 2–3
   c. Always at least 3
   d. None

4. What would be the correct response to any question asked here?
   a.
   b.
   c.
   d.

Answers:
1. c (process of elimination)
2. a (longer item with qualifications is usually correct)
3. b ("always" and "never" items are usually wrong)
4. d (this response hasn't been used yet)

■ Writing Constructed-Response Items

Constructed-response items require the student to supply rather than to select the answer. The simplest form is fill-in-the-blank items, which can often be written to reduce or eliminate ambiguity in scoring. Still, unanticipated responses might lead to ambiguous answers, causing questions in the mind of the instructor on how to score them. Constructed-response items also come in short and long essay forms.

FILL-IN-THE-BLANK ITEMS   When there is clearly only one possible correct answer, an attractive format is completion, or "fill in the blank," as in the following examples:

1. The largest city in Germany is _____.

2. What is 15 percent of $198.00? _____

3. The measure of electric resistance is the _____.

The advantage of these **completion items** is that they can reduce the element of test-wiseness to near zero. For example, compare the following items:

1. The capital of Maine is _____.

2. The capital of Maine is
   a. Sacramento.
   b. Augusta.
   c. Juneau.
   d. Boston.

A student who has no idea what the capital of Maine is could pick Augusta from the list in item 2 because it is easy to rule out the other three cities. In item 1, however, the student has to know the answer. Completion items are especially useful in math, because multiple-choice items may help to give the answer away or reward guessing, as in the following example:

$$\begin{array}{r} 4037 \\ -\ 159 \\ \hline \end{array}$$

   a. 4196
   b. 4122
   c. 3878 [*correct answer*]
   d. 3978

If students subtract and get an answer other than any of those listed, they know that they have to keep trying. In some cases they can narrow the alternatives by estimating rather than knowing how to compute the answer.

It is critical to avoid ambiguity in completion items. In some subject areas this can be difficult because two or more answers can reasonably fit a fragment that does not specify the context, as in the next two examples.

1. The Battle of Hastings was in _____. [Date or place?]

2. "H_2O" represents _____. [Water or two parts hydrogen and one part oxygen?]

If there is any ambiguity possible, it is probably best to move to a selection type of item such as multiple choice.

completion items

Fill-in-the-blank test items.

■ Writing and Evaluating Essay Tests

Short essay questions allow students to respond in their own words. The most common form for a **short essay item** provides a question for the student to answer. The answer may range from a sentence or two to a page of, say, 100 to 150 words. A **long essay item** requires more length and more time, allowing greater opportunity for students to demonstrate organization and development of ideas. Although they differ in length, the methods available to write and score them are similar.

The essay form can elicit a wide variety of responses, from giving definitions of terms to comparing and contrasting important concepts or events. These items are especially suited for assessing students' ability to analyze, synthesize, and evaluate. Hence, you might use them to appraise students' progress in organizing data and applying concepts at the highest levels of instructional objectives. Of course, these items depend heavily on writing skills and the ability to phrase ideas, so exclusive use of essays might cause the teacher to underestimate the knowledge and effort of a student who has learned the material but is a poor writer.

One of the crucial mistakes teachers make in writing essay items is failing to specify clearly the approximate detail required in the response and its expected length. Stating how much weight an item has relative to the entire test is generally not sufficient to tell students how much detail must be incorporated in a response. The following example illustrates this point.

Poor Essay Item

Discuss the role of the prime minister in Canadian politics.

Improvement

In five paragraphs or less, identify three ways in which the Canadian prime minister and the U.S. president differ in their obligations to their respective constituencies. For each of the three, explain how the obligations are different.

Note that the improved version expresses a length (five paragraphs or less), the aspect to be treated (differences between the prime minister and the president), the number of points to be covered (three; if you write "at least three," that would introduce ambiguity into the task), how the points should be selected (differ in their obligations to their respective constituencies), and the direction and degree of elaboration needed (explain how the obligations are different). This item points the student toward the desired response and allows you greater opportunity to explain the criteria by which student responses will be judged.

An essay item should contain specific information that students are to address. Some teachers are reluctant to name the particulars they want students to discuss because they believe that supplying a word or phrase in the instructions is giving away too much information. But if an item is ambiguous, different students will interpret it differently. Consequently, they will be responding to different questions and the test will almost surely not be fair to all of them.

Essay items have a number of advantages in addition to letting students state ideas in their own words. For example, essay items are not susceptible to correct guesses. They can promote efficient assessment by requiring students to combine several concepts in one response. They can also be used to measure creative abilities, such as writing talent or imagination in constructing hypothetical events, as well as assessing organization and fluency.

On the negative side is the problem of reliability in scoring essay responses. Some studies demonstrate that independent marking of the same essay response by different teachers can result in appraisals ranging from excellent to a failing grade (Popham,

short essay item

A test question the answer to which may range from a sentence or two to a page of 100 to 150 words.

long essay item

A test question requiring an answer of more than a page.

2005). A second drawback is that essay responses take considerable time to evaluate. The time you save by writing one essay item instead of several other kinds of items must be paid back when grading the essays. Third, essay items in general take considerable response time from students. Consequently, they typically cannot be used to cover broad ranges of content. Nevertheless, essay items allow teachers the opportunity to see how well students can use the material they have been taught. Breadth is sacrificed for depth.

The following suggestions provide additional guidelines for writing effective essay items:

1. As with any item format, match the items with the instructional objectives.

2. Do not use such general directives in an item as "discuss," "give your opinion about," or "tell all you know about." Rather, carefully choose specific response verbs such as "compare," "contrast," "identify," "list and define," and "explain the difference."

3. Write a response to the item before you give the test to estimate the time students will need to respond. About four times your response time is a fair estimate.

4. Rewrite the item to point students clearly toward the desired response.

5. Require all students to answer all items. Although it seems attractive to allow student choice in which items to answer, that is fundamentally an unfair practice. First, students differ in their ability to make the best selections. Second, the items will not be of equivalent difficulty. And third, students who know they will have a choice can increase their score by studying very carefully only part of the material.

After writing an essay item—and clearly specifying the content that is to be included in the response—you must have a clear idea of how you will score various elements of a student's response. The first step is to write a model response or a detailed outline of the essential elements students are being directed to include in their responses to which you can compare students' responses. If you intend to use evaluative comments but not letter grades, your outline or model will serve as a guide for pointing out to students any omissions and errors in their responses, as well as the good points of their answers. If you are using letter grades to score the essays, you should compare elements of students' responses with the contents of your model and give suitable credit to responses that match the relative weights of elements in the model.

If possible, you should ask a colleague to assess the validity of the elements and their weights in your model response. Going a bit further and having the colleague apply the model criteria to one or more student responses will increase the reliability of your scoring (see Langer & Colton, 2005). Be sure to offer to do the same for them!

One issue relating to essay tests is whether and how much to count grammar, spelling, and other technical features. If you do count these factors, give students separate grades in content and in mechanics so that they will know the basis on which their work is being evaluated.

A powerful use of assessment in instruction is to generate one or more scoring rubrics that can be shared with students well in advance of the test. The rubrics, like the example, should be generic, in that they can be applied to a broad range of essays. Students can see which aspects of their achievement will contribute to a positive evaluation and can practice to make sure their work illustrates those critical elements. You might show students (anonymous) essays from previous years to illustrate the rubric. One rubric for high school math problem solving appears in Figure 13.3.

FIGURE 13.3 **Generic Rubric for Brief Constructed-Response Items in High School Mathematics in Maryland**

Level 3

The response indicates application of a reasonable strategy that leads to a correct solution in the context of the problem. The representations are essentially correct. The explanation and/or justification is logically sound, clearly presented, fully developed, supports the solution, and does not contain significant mathematical errors. The response demonstrates a complete understanding and analysis of the problem.

Level 2

The response indicates application of a reasonable strategy that may be incomplete or undeveloped. It may or may not lead to a correct solution. The representations are fundamentally correct. The explanation and/or justification supports the solution and is plausible, although it may not be well developed or complete. The response demonstrates a conceptual understanding and analysis of the problem.

Level 1

The response indicates little or no attempt to apply a reasonable stategy or applies an inappropriate strategy. It may or may not have the correct answer. The representations are incomplete or missing. The explanation and/or justification

reveals serious flaws in reasoning. The explanation and/or justification may be incomplete or missing. The response demonstrates a minimal understanding and analysis of the problem.

Level 0

The response is completely incorrect or irrelevant. There may be no response, or the response may state, "I don't know."

Explanation refers to the student using the language of mathematics to communicate how the student arrived at the solution.

Justification refers to the student using mathematical principles to support the reasoning used to solve the problem or to demonstrate that the solution is correct. This could include the appropriate definitions, postulates, and theorems.

Essentially correct representations may contain several minor errors such as missing labels, reversed axes, or scales that are not uniform.

Fundamentally correct representations may contain several minor errors such as missing labels, reversed axes, or scales that are not uniform.

Source: W. D. Schafer, G. Swanson, N. Bené, & G. Newberry, "Effects of Teacher Knowledge of Rubrics on Student Achievement in Four Content Areas," *Applied Measurement in Education, 14,* 2001, pp. 151–170.

Theory into Practice
Detecting Bluffing in Students' Essays

Students who are not well prepared for essay tests are likely to try to bluff their way through. Credit should not be given unless the question is specifically answered. Some common types of bluffing are as follows:

1. Student repeats the question in statement form (slightly paraphrased) and tells how important the topic is. ("The role of assessment in teaching is extremely important. It is hard to imagine effective instruction without it.")

2. Student writes on a topic he or she knows about and fits it to the question. (A student who knows testing well but knows little about performance assessment and is asked to compare testing and performance assessment might describe testing in considerable detail and frequently state that performance assessment is much superior for evaluating the type of learning measured by the test.)

3. Student liberally sprinkles the answer with basic concepts whether they are understood or not. (Asked to write about any assessment technique, a student responds by frequently mentioning the importance of "validity" and "reliability.")

4. Student includes the teacher's basic beliefs wherever possible. ("The intended learning outcomes must be stated in performance terms before this type of test is constructed or selected.")

■ Writing and Evaluating Problem-Solving Items

Connections

For more on problem solving, see Chapter 8, page 236.

In many subjects, such as mathematics and the physical and social sciences, instructional objectives include the development of skills in problem solving, so it is important to assess students' performance in solving problems (Badgett & Christmann, 2009; McMillan, 2008). A **problem-solving assessment** requires students to organize, select, and apply complex procedures that have at least several important steps or components. It is important to appraise the students' work in each of these steps or components.

The following example shows a seventh-grade-level mathematical problem and a seventh-grader's response to it. The discussion of evaluating problem solving that follows can be applied to any discipline.

Problem

Suppose two gamblers are playing a game in which the loser must pay an amount equal to what the other gambler has at the time. If Player *A* won the first and third games, and Player *B* won the second game, and they finished the three games with $12 each, with how much money did each begin the first game? How did you get your answer?

A student's response:

After game	A had	B had
3	$12.00	$12.00
2	6.00	18.00
1	15.00	9.00
In the beginning	$ 7.50	$16.50

When I started with Game 1, I guessed and guessed, but I couldn't make it come out to 12 and 12.

Then I decided to start at Game 3 and work backward. It worked!

How will you objectively evaluate such a response? As in evaluating short essay items, you should begin your preparation for appraising problem-solving responses by writing either a model response or, perhaps more practically, an outline of the essential components or procedures that are involved in problem solving. As with essays, problem solving responses may take several different yet valid approaches. The outline must be flexible enough to accommodate all valid possibilities.

problem-solving assessment

Test that calls for organizing, selecting, and applying complex procedures that have at least several important steps or components.

Theory into Practice
Peer Evaluations

An evaluation technique often used in cooperative learning, especially in creative writing and (less often) mathematics problem solving, is to have students rate each

Criterion	Partner	Teacher
Content		
1. Shows how concepts are similar		
2. Shows how concepts are different		
3. Well organized		
4. Good opening sentence		
5. Good concluding sentence		
Mechanics		
1. Spelling correct		
2. Grammar correct		
3. Punctuation correct		
4. At least 2 pages		

FIGURE 13.4

Example of a Partner Response Form for a Comparison–Contrast Assignment

INTASC

6 Communication Skills

other's work on a specific set of criteria before the teacher rates them on the same criteria (Reynolds, 2009; Smith, 2009). The peer evaluation does not contribute to a student's score or grade but gives the student feedback to use in revising the composition or product. Figure 13.4 shows a peer response guide that might be used for a comparison–contrast writing assignment. The partner, and then the teacher, puts a check mark for each category in which the student has done an adequate job. The partner and the teacher would also mark the student's paper to make suggestions for improvement. Peer evaluation provides a formative evaluation for the writer, but it also gives the evaluator an invaluable opportunity to take the teacher's perspective and gain insight into what constitutes good writing.

EVALUATING PROBLEM-SOLVING ITEMS   Problem solving involves several important components that fit most disciplines, including understanding the problem to be solved, attacking the problem systematically, and arriving at a reasonable answer. Following is a detailed checklist of elements common to most problem solving that can guide the weighting of elements in your evaluation of a student's problem-solving abilities.

Problem-Solving Evaluation Elements

☐ 1. Problem organization

 ☐ a. Representation made by table, graph, chart, etc.

 ☐ b. Representation shown fits the problem.

 ☐ c. Global understanding of the problem demonstrated.

☐ 2. Procedures (mathematical: trial and error, working backward, experimental process, empirical induction)

 ☐ a. A viable procedure was attempted.

 ☐ b. The procedure was carried to a final solution.

 ☐ c. Computation (if any) was correct.

☐ 3. Solution (mathematical: a table, number, figure, graph, etc.)

 ☐ a. Answer was reasonable.

☐ b. Answer was checked.

☐ c. Answer was correct.

☐ 4. Logic specific to the detail or application of the given information was sound.

If you wish to give partial credit for an answer that contains correct elements or want to inform students about the value of their responses, you must devise ways to do this consistently. The following points offer some guidance:

1. Write model responses before giving partial credit for such work as essay writing, mathematical problem solving, laboratory assignments, or any work that you evaluate according to the quality of its various stages.

2. Tell students in sufficient detail the meaning of the grades you give to communicate the value of the work.

The following examples illustrate outlines of exemplary student work from mathematics and social studies or literature.

FROM MATHEMATICS   Students are given the following problem:

In a single-elimination tennis tournament, 40 players are to play for the singles championship. Determine how many matches must be played.

Evaluation

☐ a. Evidence that the student understood the problem, demonstrated by depiction of the problem with a graph, table, chart, equation, etc. (*3 points*)

☐ b. Use of a method for solving the problem that had potential for yielding a correct solution—for example, systematic trial and error, empirical induction, elimination, working backward. (*5 points*)

☐ c. Arrival at a correct solution. (*3 points*)

The three components in the evaluation were assigned points according to the weight the teacher judged each to be worth in the context of the course of study and the purpose of the test. You can give full credit for a correct answer even if all the work is not shown in the response, provided that you know that students can do the work in their heads. But it is important to guard against the **halo effect,** which occurs when you know which student wrote which response and you alter the grading of the paper depending on your opinion of the student. The same response should receive the same score no matter who wrote it. Use of a detailed rubric, or scoring guide, in evaluation is a way to make scoring more objective and thus to avoid any halo effects.

FROM SOCIAL STUDIES OR LITERATURE   Students are asked to respond with a 100-word essay to the following item:

Compare and contrast the development of Inuit and Navajo tools on the basis of the climates in which these two peoples live.

Evaluation

☐ a. The response gives evidence of specific and accurate recall of the climates in which the Inuit and Navajos live (*1 point*) and of Inuit and Navajo tools. (*1 point*)

halo effect

Bias due to carryover of a general attitude about a respondent, as when a teacher knows which student wrote which response and alters the grading depending on his or her opinion of the student.

☐ b. The essay develops with continuity of thought and logic. (*3 points*)

☐ c. An accurate rationale is provided for the use of the various tools in the respective climates. (*3 points*)

☐ d. An analysis comparing and contrasting the similarities and differences between the two groups and their tool development is given. (*8 points*)

☐ e. The response concludes with a summary and closure. (*1 point*)

These two examples should suggest ways to evaluate items in other subject areas as well. Giving partial credit for much of the work students do certainly results in a more complete evaluation of student progress than does scoring the work as merely right or wrong. The examples show how to organize objective assessments for evaluating work that does not lend itself to the simple forms of multiple-choice, true–false, completion, and matching items. Points do not have to be used to evaluate components of the responses. In many situations, some kind of evaluative descriptors might be more meaningful. **Evaluative descriptors** are statements describing strong and weak features of a response to an item, a question, or a project. In the mathematics example a teacher's evaluative descriptor for item a might read, "You have drawn an excellent chart showing that you understand the meaning of the problem, and that is very good, but it seems you were careless when you entered several important numbers in your chart."

Note that each of these examples is much like a rubric and can be generalized to broad ranges of topics. If teachers and students discuss these during instruction, students will have a device that helps them understand what they are working toward and both teachers and students will have a common language that they can use during instruction and in their formative assessments.

What Are Authentic, Portfolio, and Performance Assessments?

INTASC

8 Assessment of Student Learning

After much criticism of traditional testing (e.g., Rotberg, 2001; Shepard, 2000; Thompson, 2001), critics have developed and implemented alternative assessment systems that are designed to avoid the problems of typical multiple-choice tests. The key idea behind the testing alternatives is that students should be asked to document their learning or demonstrate that they can actually do something real with the information and skills they have learned in school (Burke, 2009; Carey, 2001; Marzano et al., 2001). For example, students might be asked to keep a portfolio, design a method of measuring wind speed, draw a scale model of a racing car, or write something for a real audience. Such tests are referred to as *authentic assessments* or *performance assessments* (Belgrad, Burke, & Fogarty, 2008). One goal of these "alternative assessments" is to demonstrate achievement in realistic contexts. In reading, for example, the authentic assessment movement has led to the development of tests in which students are asked to read and interpret longer sections and show their metacognitive awareness of reading strategies (Roeber & Dutcher, 1989; Valencia, Pearson, Peters, & Wixson, 1989). In science, authentic assessments might involve having students set up and carry out an experiment. In writing, students might be asked to write real letters or newspaper articles. In math, students might solve complex physical problems that require insight and creativity. Authentic tests sometimes require students to integrate knowledge from different domains—for example, to use algebra in the context of reading about and performing a science experiment and to write up the results.

evaluative descriptors

Statements describing strong and weak features of a response to an item, question, or project.

■ Portfolio Assessment

One popular form of alternative assessment is called **portfolio assessment:** the collection and evaluation of samples of student work over an extended period (Burke, 2009; McMillan, 2008). You may collect student compositions, projects, and other evidence of higher-order functioning and use this evidence to evaluate student progress over time. For example, many teachers have students maintain portfolios of their writings that show the development of a composition from first draft to final product; portfolios can also be used for journal entries, book reports, artwork, computer printouts, or papers showing development in problem solving (Belgrad, Burke, & Fogarty, 2008). Portfolios are increasingly being maintained on computers to supplement paper files (Diehm, 2004; Niguidula, 2005). Refer to Figure 13.5 for sample criteria in evaluating student writing portfolios.

portfolio assessment

Assessment of a collection of the student's work to show growth, self-reflection, and achievement.

FIGURE 13.5

Sample of Criteria for Evaluating Students' Writing Ability through Portfolio Assessment

Continua of Descriptors		
Strong Performance ◄──────────────────► Needs Improvement		
Versatility		
Wide variety of reading and writing across genre	Some variety	Little or no variety Collection shows little breadth or depth
Process		
Samples reveal discoveries or pivotal learning experiences	Process illustrated in inflexible or mechanistic ways	Minimal use of process to reflect on achievements
Response		
Engaged with story Discusses key issues Evidence of critical questioning	Personal reflection but focus is narrow	Brief retelling of isolated events
Self-Evaluations		
Multidimensional Wide variety of observations Establishing meaningful goals Notes improvement	Developing insights Some specifics noted Limited goal setting Vague idea of improvement	Single focus, global in nature Goal setting too broad or nonexistent
Individual Pieces		
Strong control of a variety of elements: organization, cohesion, surface features, etc.	Growing command evidenced; some flaws, but major ideas clear	Needs to improve: sophistication of ideas, text features, and surface features
Problem Solving		
Wrestles with problems using various resources Enjoys problem solving and learning new ways	Uses limited resources Wants quick fix	Seems helpless Frustrated by problems
Purposefulness/Uses		
Uses reading and writing to satisfy various goals including sharing with others	Uses reading and writing to meet others' goals	Apathetic, resistant

Source: Cathy Collins Block, *Teaching the Language Arts: Expanding Thinking through Student Centered Instruction.* Copyright © 1993 by Allyn & Bacon. Reprinted by permission.

Portfolio assessment has important uses when you want to evaluate students for reports to parents or other within-school purposes. When combined with on-demand assessments and used with consistent and public rubrics, portfolios showing improvement over time can provide powerful evidence of change to parents and to students themselves (Burke, 2009).

Certification Pointer

A teacher certification question may ask you to respond to a case study by suggesting a way to implement portfolio assessment that would be appropriate for the case.

ON THE WEB

For reports, newsletters, and other publications about assessment, particularly performance and portfolio assessment, visit www.cresst.org, the National Center for Research on Evaluation, Standards, and Student Testing (CRESST), located at UCLA. To view articles and multimedia related to assessment and other education topics, go to the website of the George Lucas Educational Foundation at www.edutopia.org/assessment. Also visit the Education Commission of the States' website, which contains a list of assessment-related sites, at www.ecs.org/html/IssueSection.asp?issueid=12&s=Other+Web+Sites.

Theory into Practice
Using Portfolios in the Classroom

PLANNING AND ORGANIZATION

- Develop an overall flexible plan for student portfolios. What purposes will the portfolios serve? What items will be required? When and how will they be obtained? What criteria will be applied for reflection and evaluation?

- Plan sufficient time for students to prepare and discuss portfolio items. Portfolio assessments take more time and thought than correcting paper-and-pencil tests does.

- Begin with one aspect of student learning and achievement, and gradually include others as you and the students learn about portfolio procedures. The writing process, for instance, is particularly well suited to documentation through portfolios.

- Choose items to be included in portfolios that will show developing proficiency on important goals and objectives. Items that address multiple objectives help to make portfolio assessments more efficient.

- Collect at least two types of items: required indicators (Arter & McTighe, 2001; Murphy & Underwood, 2000) or core items and optional work samples. Required or core indicators are items collected for every child that will show how each is progressing. Optional work samples show individual student's unique approaches, interests, and strengths.

- Place a list of goals and objectives in the front of each portfolio along with a list of required indicators and also include a place for recording optional items, so that you and the students can keep track of contents.

IMPLEMENTATION

- In order to save time, to ensure that portfolio items are representative of students' work, and to increase authenticity, embed the development of portfolio items into ongoing classroom activities.

- Give students responsibility for preparing, selecting, evaluating, and filing portfolio items and keeping portfolios up to date. Young children will need guidance with this.

- For selected portfolio items, model reflection and self-assessment for students to help them become aware of the processes they used, what they learned and have yet to learn, and what they might need to do differently next time.

- Be selective. A portfolio is not a haphazard collection of work samples, audio or videorecordings, pictures, websites, and other products. It is a thoughtful selection of items that exemplify children's learning. Random inclusion of items quickly becomes overwhelming.

- Use information in portfolios to place learners on a sequence of developing skills.

- Analyze portfolio items for insight into students' knowledge and skills. As you do this, you will understand more of the students' strengths and needs, thinking processes, preconceptions, misconceptions, error patterns, and developmental benchmarks.

- Use portfolio information to document and celebrate students' learning, to share students' accomplishments with parents and other school personnel, and to improve and target classroom instruction. If portfolios are not linked to improving instruction, they are not working. (For guides to portfolio evaluation, see Belgrad et al.; 2008; Burke, 2009; Stiggins, 2000.)

■ Performance Assessment

performance assessments

Assessments of students' ability to perform tasks in real-life contexts rather than just showing knowledge. Also called *authentic assessments*.

Tests that involve actual demonstrations of knowledge or skills in real life are called **performance assessments** (Foster & Noyce, 2004; McMillan, 2008; Popham, 2005). For example, ninth-graders might be asked to conduct an oral history project, reading about a significant recent event and then interviewing the individuals involved. The quality of the oral histories, done over a period of weeks, indicates the degree of the students' mastery of the social studies concepts involved. Wiggins (1993) also describes assessments used in the last 2 weeks of school in which students must apply everything they have learned all year to analyze a sludge that mixes a variety of solids and liquids. Some schools are requiring elaborate "exhibitions," such as projects developed over many months, as demonstrations of competence. More time-limited performance assessments might ask students to set up experiments, respond to extended text, write in various genres, or solve realistic math problems.

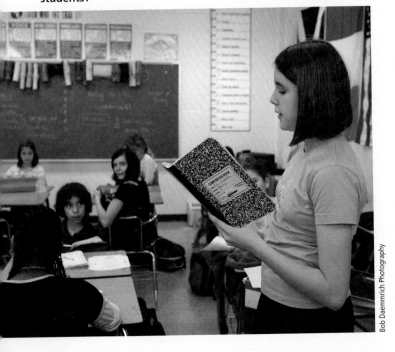

This student's performance is being evaluated by classmates. What are the advantages and disadvantages of using a performance or group activity as a method for evaluating students?

Bob Daemmrich Photography

■ Effectiveness of Performance Assessments

One of the most important criticisms of traditional standardized tests is that they can focus teachers on teaching a narrow range of skills that happen to be on the test (see Popham, 2004). How might performance assessments be better? At least in theory, it should be possible to create tests that would require such a broad understanding of subject matter that the test would be worth teaching to.

For example, consider the performance test in science shown in Figure 13.6. Imagine that your students will have to conduct an experiment to solve a problem like the one posed in the figure (but not that exact problem). The only way to teach such a test will be to expose students to a broad range of information about electricity, experimentation, and problem-solving strategies (see Shepard, 1995).

Beyond all the practical problems and expense of administering and scoring performance tests, it is not yet clear whether performance tests will solve all the problems of standardized testing. For example, Shavelson, Baxter, and Pine (1992) studied performance assessments in science (Figure 13.6 is taken from their study). They found that student performance on such assessments could be reliably rated, but different performance assessments produced very different patterns of scores, and student scores were still related more closely to student aptitude than to what students were actually taught (see also Educational Testing Service, 1995; Linn, 1994; Supovitz & Brennan, 1997).

■ Scoring Rubrics for Performance Assessments

Performance assessments are typically scored according to rubrics that specify in advance the type of performance that is expected for each activity (Andrade, 2007/2008; Burke, 2009; Popham, 2005). Figure 13.7 shows one rubric (from Taylor, 1994) that was developed for an essay on character development in stories students have read.

Performance assessment tasks are similar to essay items in that students might approach them in multiple ways. It is, therefore, also important for performance assessments that the criteria for scoring be understood by students. One way to do this is to write a few generic rubrics that are flexible enough to apply to the full range of student performance. Figure 13.3 gave an example of a generic rubric that has been applied to outcomes in high school mathematics. It has been suggested that using rubrics such as this in classroom instruction can enhance student achievement (Schafer, Swanson, Bené, & Newberry, 2001).

Planning for performance assessments takes time, and avoiding the pitfalls of subjectivity in rating performances takes practice. However, a few well-thought-out, well-written items for a performance assessment could serve, for example, as a summative evaluation for all or most of your educational objectives for an entire unit (see Figure 13.8, p. 435).

FIGURE 13.6 **Example of a Performance Assessment Activity**

Find out what is in the mystery boxes. They have five different items or sets of items inside, shown below.

a. Two batteries:

b. Wire:

c. Bulb:

d. Battery and a bulb:

e. Nothing:

For each box, connect it in a circuit to help you figure out what is inside. You can use the bulbs, batteries, and wires any way you like.

Source: R. J. Shavelson, G. P. Baxter, and J. Pine, "Performance Assessments: Political Rhetoric and Measurement Reality," *Educational Researcher, 21*(2), p. 23, 1992.

Certification Pointer

You may be asked on your teacher certification test to give an example of a performance goal and then to write a behavioral objective, an activity, and an assessment of student learning that would accomplish the goal.

How Are Grades Determined

One of the most perplexing and often controversial tasks you face is grading student work (Guskey & Bailey, 2001; Marzano, 2000; O'Connor, 2007, 2009; Scriffiny, 2008). Is grading necessary? It is clear that some form of summative student evaluation is necessary, and grading of one kind or another is the predominant form used in most schools.

INTASC

5 Classroom Management and Motivation

FIGURE 13.7

**Sample Scoring Rubric:
Targeted Performance,
Performance Criteria,
and a Description of
Performances at Different
Score Points**

Performance

Essay on Character Development in Literature

Performance Criteria

■ Character is identified.

■ At least three aspects of the character's development during the course of the story are described.

■ Appropriate support for each character aspect is given using excerpts from the story.

■ Character's contribution to the story's plot is described.

■ At least three excerpts from the story are given as support for writer's ideas about the character's contribution to the story.

■ Text references used for support are appropriate.

Scoring Rubric

4 points	Essay is complete, thorough, and insightful in describing the character's development and contribution to the story. Adequate support is given to encourage us to consider the writer's point of view. All excerpts from the text enhance our understanding of the writer's view of the character.
3 points	Essay is complete in describing the character's development and contribution to the story. Adequate support is given to encourage us to consider the writer's point of view. Most excerpts from the text enhance our understanding of the writer's view of the character.
2 points	Essay is complete in its description of either the character's development *or* the character's contribution to the story. Some support is given to help us consider the writer's point of view. Most excerpts from the text enhance our understanding of the writer's view of the character for the element described.
1 point	Essay is mostly complete in its description of either the character's development or the character's contribution to the story. Support is given for the writer's point of view, but it is not always convincing. Few excerpts from the text enhance our understanding of the writer's view of the character for the element described.
0 points	The written essay was not completed, is significantly lacking in performance of all criteria, or is off task.

Source: Catherine Taylor, "Assessment for Measurement or Standards," *American Educational Research Journal, 31*(2), pp. 231–262, 1994.

■ Establishing Grading Criteria

Many sets of grading criteria exist, but regardless of the level of school that teachers teach in, they generally agree on the need to explain the meaning of grades they give (Guskey & Bailey, 2001; Marzano, 2000). Grades should communicate at least the relative value of a student's work in a class. They should also help students to understand better what is expected of them and how they might improve.

Teachers and schools that use letter grades attach the following general meanings to the letters:

A = superior; exceptional; outstanding attainment

B = very good, but not superior; above average

C = competent, but not remarkable work or performance; average

FIGURE 13.8 Semester-Long Assessment

Psychology Fair Rubric

✓ **Our Psychology Project . . .**

☐ (25 pts) Provides background information—it cites other studies, explains our interest in the topic, and presents a rationale for the topic. [The better the background information, the more detailed, and the more it "fits," the more points you earn.]

Brief example: "We are interested in how dress affects behavior. We always felt better when we were dressed up and also thought that less violence occurs between people who 'dress up.' Cohen and Cohen (1987) found that students who wore uniforms performed 10 percent better on exams and were cited for fewer office referrals. Thus we wanted to look into this topic further."

☐ (25 pts) Gives a description of the study (an abstract—a *general* statement in 100 words or fewer about your project).

Brief example: "This study investigates the relationship between academic performance and the use of uniforms in schools. Three schools in Derry County, Pennsylvania, were surveyed on issues of academic performance and office referrals. The use of uniforms showed an increase in achievement and decreased behavioral problems."

☐ (40 pts) Has a measurable hypothesis with specific variables defined and identified.

☐ (25 pts) Includes at least one graph, chart, or other visual aid which *summarizes the data*. Someone should be able to look at your graph/chart and clearly see what the variables and results were.

☐ (10 pts) Includes a clean copy of any survey or other scale that was used to gather data.

☐ (40 pts) Includes a written procedure that tells the observer *exactly* what we did.
Brief example: "We took 3 days to survey 100 students and 30 teachers."

☐ (30 pts) Includes a section that explains the data and tells whether the hypothesis was accurate.

Brief example: "Our data reflect that our hypothesis was correct: The 30 percent increase in scores reflects the improved achievement of students while . . ." [Again, develop your explanation. If you only say "We were right" or "Our hypothesis is correct/wrong" you will not receive more than half the points.]

☐ (30 pts) Includes a section explaining the significance of the study—why it is important.

Brief example: "This is an important study because it reflects a bias that many people may not be aware of, as well as a way in which students can improve scores and reduce their own behavioral problems. It further . . ."

☐ (50 pts) Is interactive. That is, observers can take the test, view the screen, do the quiz, and so on. [This can be done in a variety of ways. For instance, if the test is long, have observers do part of it or show a video of your procedure.]

Total Points Possible: 275

Source: Chuck Greiner, high school psychology teacher, James M. Bennett High School, Salisbury, MD.

D = minimum passing, but serious weaknesses are indicated; below average

F = failure to pass; serious weaknesses demonstrated

■ Assigning Letter Grades

All school districts have a policy or common practice for assigning report card grades. Most use A-B-C-D-F or A-B-C-D-E letter grades, but many (particularly at the elementary school level) use various versions of outstanding-satisfactory-unsatisfactory

(Marzano, 2000; O'Connor, 2009). Some simply report percentage grades. The criteria on which grades are based vary enormously from district to district. Secondary schools usually give one grade for each subject taken, but most elementary schools and some secondary schools include ratings on effort or behavior as well as on performance.

The criteria for giving letter grades might be specified by a school administration, but grading criteria are most often set by individual teachers using very broad guidelines. In practice, few teachers could get away with giving half their students A's or with failing too many students; but between these two extremes, teachers may have considerable leeway (see Guskey, 2009; O'Connor, 2009).

ABSOLUTE GRADING STANDARDS   Grades may be given according to absolute or relative standards. Absolute grading standards might consist of preestablished percentage scores required for a given grade, as in the following example:

Grade	Percentage Correct
A	90–100 percent
B	80–89 percent
C	70–79 percent
D	60–69 percent
F	Less than 60 percent

In another form of absolute standards, called *criterion-referenced grading,* you decide in advance which performances constitute outstanding (A), above-average (B), average (C), below-average (D), and inadequate (F) mastery of the instructional objective.

Absolute percentage standards have one important disadvantage: Student scores might depend on the difficulty of the tests they are given. For example, a student can pass a true–false test (if a passing grade is 60 percent) by knowing only 20 percent of the answers and guessing on the rest (getting half of the remaining 80 percent of the items by chance). On a difficult test on which guessing is impossible, however, 60 percent could be a very high score. For this reason, use of absolute percentage criteria should be tempered with criterion-referenced standards. That is, you might use a 60–70–80–90 percent standard in most circumstances but establish (and announce to students) tougher standards for tests that students are likely to find easy and easier standards for more difficult tests.

Another disadvantage is that the ranges of the grades are typically different, especially for F's. A student who receives an F may be very close to a D or may be hopelessly far from "passing." This is true for the other grades, too, but the large range of F (0 to 60 percent) emphasizes the uncertainty. Moreover, the consequences of an F are often quite severe.

RELATIVE GRADING STANDARDS   A **relative grading standard** is a system whereby a teacher gives grades according to the students' rank in their class or grade. The classic form of relative grading is specifying what percentage of students will be given A's, B's, and so on. A form of this practice is called *grading on the curve* because students are given grades on the basis of their position on a predetermined distribution of scores.

Relative grading standards have the advantage of placing students' scores in relation to one another without regard to the difficulty of a particular test. However, relative grading standards also have serious drawbacks (see O'Connor, 2009). One is that because they hold the number of A's and B's constant, students in a class of high achievers must get much higher scores to earn A's or B's than students in low-achieving classes—a situation that is likely to be seen as unfair. Teachers often deal with this problem by giving relatively more A's and B's in high-achieving classes than in others. Another disadvantage of relative grading is that it creates competition among students; when one student earns an A, this diminishes the chances that others may do so. Competition can inhibit students from helping one another and hurt social relations among classmates (Krumboltz & Yeh, 1996).

relative grading standard

Grades given according to a student's rank in his or her class or grade.

Strict grading on the curve and guidelines for numbers of A's and B's have been disappearing in recent years. For one thing, there has been a general grade inflation; more A's and B's are given now than in the past, and C is no longer the expected average grade but often indicates below-average performance. Anderson (1994) summarized a national survey of eighth-graders who were asked to report their English grades since sixth grade. The results were as follows:

Mostly A's: 31 percent

Mostly B's: 38 percent

Mostly C's: 23 percent

Mostly D's: 6 percent

Mostly less than D's: 2 percent

Results were similar in mathematics, and grades were only slightly lower in high-poverty schools than in middle-class schools. It is likely that these self-reported grades are somewhat higher than those students actually received, but it is nevertheless likely that the average grade today is B, not C.

The most common approach to grading involves looking at student scores on a test, taking into account test difficulty and the overall performance of the class, and assigning grades in such a way that about the "right number" of students earn A's and B's and the "right number" fail. Teachers vary considerably in their estimates of what these right numbers should be, but schools often have unspoken norms about how many students should be given A's and how many should fail.

■ Performance Grading

One of the most important limitations of traditional grades is that although they might give some indication of how students are doing in comparison to others, they provide no information about what students know and can do. A student who gets a B in English might be disappointed or breathe a sigh of relief, depending on what she expected. However, this grade does not tell her or her parents or teachers what she can do, what she needs to do to progress, or where her strengths or weaknesses are. Furthermore, giving a single grade in each subject can reinforce the idea that students are more able or less able, or perhaps more motivated or less motivated, rather than the idea that all students are growing.

Some schools have responded to these limitations with an alternative approach to grading called *performance grading* (Guskey, 2009), in which teachers determine what children know and can do and then report this in a way that is easy for parents and students to understand (Guskey, 2006). Figure 13.9 (from Wiggins, 1994) shows one page of a language arts assessment keyed to fifth-grade exit standards, or expectations of what a fifth-grader should know. A parent who receives a form like this can see how the student is progressing toward the kind of performance the school district has defined as essential. Note that although the form does provide information on how the student is doing in comparison to other students, the emphasis is on growth over time.

SCORING RUBRICS FOR PERFORMANCE GRADING   A key requirement for the use of performance grading is collection of work samples from students that indicate their level of performance on a developmental sequence. Collecting and evaluating work that students are already doing in class (such as compositions, lab reports, or projects) is called *portfolio assessment* (Burke, 2009), discussed earlier in this chapter. An alternative is to give students tests in which they can show their abilities to apply and integrate knowledge, skills, and judgment. Most performance grading schemes use some combination of portfolios and on-demand performance tests. In either case, student performance is usually evaluated against rubrics, which describe, for example, partially proficient,

FIGURE 13.9   **Sample Performance Grading Criteria**

**Cherry Creek School District
Polton Community Elementary
School Fairplay Progress Report
(Language Arts Section)**

Student Name _____   Grade 3 _____   4 _____
Teacher _____   School Year _____

Performance-based graduation requirements focus on student mastery of the proficiencies. The curriculum and written progress report are geared toward preparing students for this task. A date (for example, 3/12) indicates where a student is performing on a continuum of progress based on the fifth-grade exit standards.

	Basic	Proficient	Advanced
Language Arts Proficiency 1 Listens, interpreting verbal and nonverbal cues to construct meaning.	Actively listens, demonstrates understanding, and clarifies with questions and para-phrasing.	Actively listens for purpose, demonstrates understanding, and clarifies with questions and paraphrasing.	Actively listens for purpose, demonstrates understanding, clarifies with questions and paraphrasing, classifies, ana-lyzes, and applies information.
Language Arts Proficiency 2 ◄————————————————————————————► Conveys meaning clearly and coherently through speech in both formal and informal situations.	Appropriately speaks to in-form, explain, demonstrate, or persuade. Organizes a speech and uses vocabulary to convey a message.	Appropriately speaks to in-form, explain, demonstrate, or persuade. Organizes a for-mal speech and uses vocabu-lary to convey a message.	Appropriately speaks to in-form, explain, demonstrate, or persuade. Organizes a formal speech with details and transi-tions adapting subject and vocabulary. Uses eye contact, gestures, and suitable expres-sion for an audience and topic.
Language Arts Proficiency 3 ◄————————————————————————————► Reads to construct meaning by interacting with the text, by recognizing the different requirements of a variety of printed materials, and by using appropriate strategies to in-crease comprehension.	Reads varied material, com-prehends at a literal level. Recalls and builds knowledge through related information. Begins to use strategies to develop fluency, adjusting rate when reading different material.	Reads varied material, comprehends literally and interpretively. Synthesizes and explores information, drawing inferences. Critiques author's intent, analyzes ma-terial for meaning and value. Applies strategies to increase fluency, adjusting rate when reading different material.	Reads varied material, compre-hends and draws inferences, recalls and builds knowledge through related information. Applies strategies to increase fluency, adjusting rate when reading different material.
Language Arts Proficiency 4 ◄————————————————————————————► Produces writing that conveys purpose and meaning, uses ef-fective writing strategies, and incorporates the conventions of written language to com-municate clearly.	Appropriately writes on as-signed or self-selected topics. Clear main ideas, few details. Weak elements in the begin-ning, middle, end. Sentence structure lacks variety and contains errors.	Appropriately writes on as-signed or self-selected topics. Clear main ideas, interesting details, clear organization, sequencing, varied sentence structure, edits to reduce er-rors. Appropriate voice and word choice.	Appropriately writes on as-signed or self-selected topics. Connects opinions, details, and examples. Effective organiza-tion and sequencing, meaning-ful sentence structure, edits to eliminate most errors. Appro-priate voice and word choice.

As compared to the class in the area of Language Arts, your child

Note: The teacher places a check in one box per marking period to indicate child's status in language arts.

1	2	3	Marking Periods
			Displays strong performance
			Demonstrates appropriate development
			Needs practice and support

Source: Grant Wiggins, "Toward Better Report Cards," *Educational Leadership, 52*(2), 1994, pp. 28–37. Copyright © 1994 by the Center on Learning, Assessment, and School Structure. Reprinted by permission of the author.

proficient, and advanced performance, or which indicate a student's position on a developmental sequence.

Other Alternative Grading Systems

Several other approaches to grading are used in conjunction with innovative instructional approaches. In the system called *contract grading,* students negotiate a particular amount of work or level of performance that they will achieve to receive a certain grade. For example, a student might agree to complete five book reports of a given length in a marking period to receive an A. **Mastery grading** involves establishing a standard of mastery, such as 80 or 90 percent correct on a test. All students who achieve that standard receive an A; students who do not achieve it the first time receive corrective instruction and then retake the test to try to achieve the mastery criterion (Guskey, 2009). Finally, many teachers give grades based on improvement or effort, usually in combination with traditional grades. In this way a student who is performing at a low level relative to others can nevertheless receive feedback indicating that he or she is on a path leading to higher performance (see Tomlinson, 2008).

LETTING STUDENTS RETAKE TESTS   Many teachers allow students to retake tests, especially if they failed the first time. This can be a good idea if it gives students an opportunity to do additional studying and master the material the class is studying. For example, a student might be given 2 days to study the content that was tested and then take an alternative form of the test. (Giving the same test to the student is not recommended because that would allow the student to study only the questions that were asked.) The student might then be given a grade that is one letter grade lower than he or she scored on the second test because the student had an advantage in having an extra opportunity to study. There is some danger that if students know that they can retake tests, they might not study until after attempting the first test, but in general, allowing students a second chance is a good way to allow those who are willing to put in extra effort to improve a poor grade. Some schools give grades of A, B, C, or incomplete, permitting additional time and support until all students are able to earn at least a C (Kenkel, Hoelscher, & West, 2006).

Assigning Report Card Grades

Most schools give report cards four or six times per year, that is, every 6 or 9 weeks. Report card grades are most often derived from some combination of the following factors (Guskey & Bailey, 2001; Marzano, 2000; O'Connor, 2007; Reeves, 2008):

- Scores on quizzes and tests
- Scores on papers and projects
- Scores on homework
- Scores on seatwork
- Class participation (academic behaviors in class, answers to class questions, and so on)
- Deportment (classroom behavior, tardiness, attitude)
- Effort

These are listed in order from the most formal and reliable measures of achievement to those considered least valid as a learning indicator. The first two factors listed are summative assessments and virtually everyone would consider them appropriate for grading. The next two are typically formative and thus indicate how learning is progressing when it is still incomplete. They are less appropriate because they do not convey information about status at the end of instructional units. The final three might

mastery grading

Grading requiring an established standard of mastery, such as 80 or 90 percent correct on a test. Students who do not achieve it the first time may receive corrective instruction and then retake the test to try to achieve mastery.

contribute to achievement, but they are not achievement. Basing grades on them could miscommunicate information to others about students (see O'Connor, 2007). Teachers often give different weights to various factors, stating (for example) that grades will be based 30 percent on quizzes, 30 percent on a final test, 20 percent on homework, and 20 percent on class participation. This helps communicate to students what is most important to the teacher.

One important issue arises when scores are to be combined for grading—how to treat missing work, such as homework assignments (O'Connor, 2009; Reeves, 2008). Some teachers assign a "zero" to missing work. But a zero can be devastating (it is so far from even a passing grade that it is virtually impossible for the student to recover). This practice can only be viewed as punitive. A better strategy would be to use a system whereby grades are converted to a reasonable set of numerical grades (e.g., A = 4, B = 3, etc.), with 0 given for any missing work. To illustrate the difference in these two strategies, consider a student who misses one assignment out of five. If she is given a zero for the missing work and her scores for the assignments are 92, 86, 0, 73, and 91, her average score would be 68.4, or a D in a 60-70-80-90 grading scheme. Converting the scores using the letter grades, on the other hand, would give her a mean of 2.6, which would be a solid C.

Sometimes a student's performance on a test or a quiz seems unusually poor for him or her. Such atypical assessments might be because of nonacademic reasons such as a disruption at home or in school. A private conversation with the student about

The Intentional Teacher

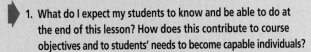

USING WHAT YOU KNOW about Assessing Student Learning to Improve Teaching and Learning

Intentional teachers assess student learning in ways that align with both their goals and their instruction. They use assessment results to adjust their instruction and to provide important feedback to students, families, and communities. Intentional teachers know that no one measure is ideal for every circumstance, and they implement a range of assessments that fits their purposes and circumstances.

▶ **1. What do I expect my students to know and be able to do at the end of this lesson? How does this contribute to course objectives and to students' needs to become capable individuals?**

One cardinal rule of assessing learning is that tests should be tied directly to learning goals and to instruction. Specify in advance what students are to learn. Design instruction to help students achieve those results and then assess their learning in relation to the specified goals.

Due to the variety and range of objectives to which teachers should teach, you must have an organized approach. Write objectives in different domains (for example, cognitive and affective) and at different levels of specificity (for example, long-term goals and lesson objectives as well as goals for different levels of understanding according to Bloom's taxonomy). For example, you might begin your year-long planning by examining your state's and district's expected outcomes for the grade and subject you teach. Then you might spread out the teacher's editions of your five texts, flipping each open to the scope and sequence chart that specifies content and learning

objectives. This process allows you to examine and evaluate the variety and levels of understanding set by your curricular materials.

▶ **2. What knowledge, skills, needs, and interests do my students have that must be taken into account in my lesson?**

Formative assessments allow you to discover your students' experiences, preferences, and needs. Use frequent formative assessments to gather information about students' attitudes and prior knowledge. For example, to begin a unit on geology, you might conduct interviews with small groups. You could display a variety of rocks and minerals and listen as students converse about the rocks. Your notes could document students' enthusiasm about the topic and their extensive out-of-class experiences studying rocks. You could then use this information to create a more sophisticated unit than you might have if students had no prior knowledge of rocks and minerals.

▶ **3. What do I know about the content, child development, learning, motivation, and effective teaching strategies that I can use to accomplish my objectives?**

Students' levels of preparation might affect their performance on tests and other measures. Check to see that your measures truly assess the objective you intended to assess. For example, imagine that a cluster of students who typically are highly successful in solving the challenging word problems you present in mathematics each week scores surprisingly low on the problem-the test or quiz might uncover a problem that should be looked into and the student might be given an opportunity to retake the test. Some teachers drop the lowest score a student receives on quizzes to avoid penalizing the student for one unusual slippage.

One important principle in report card grading is that grades should never be a surprise. Students should always know how their grades will be computed, whether classwork and homework are included, and whether class participation and effort are taken into account. Being clear about standards for grading helps you avert many complaints about unexpectedly low grades and, more important, lets students know exactly what they must do to improve their grades (Guskey, 2009; Reeves, 2008).

Many schools give an "interim" grade at the middle of a marking period, which gives students an early idea of how they are doing and a warning if they seem headed for trouble. A variation on this practice is to provide an interim grade only if students are heading for a D or F. Furthermore, adding comments to the grade to explain what the student needs to do to earn a higher grade can be very helpful in maintaining motivation and improving performance (Black et al., 2004).

Another important principle is that grades should be private. There is no need for students to know one another's grades; making grades public only invites invidious comparisons among students. Finally, it is important to restate that grades are only one method of student evaluation. Written evaluations that add information can provide

solving items of a school-based achievement test. When you review the items, you wonder whether students' reading abilities—and not their problem-solving abilities—accounted for their low scores. To test your hunch, you read similar problems aloud to the students, which they solve accurately. This leads you to seek tutorial or other assistance for these students.

4. What instructional materials, technology, assistance, and other resources are available to help accomplish my objectives?

Assessments should be challenging for all but impossible for none. Use assessments that are fair measures of the objectives and not of general aptitude. Check that your assessments are applied consistently to all students. For example, you might write weekly quizzes with a general format in mind: Put recall-level items first, reasoning that they provide immediate success for all or most students in demonstrating knowledge. Subsequent items test higher levels of understanding and stretch even the best-prepared students to apply content to new situations.

5. How will I plan to assess students' progress toward my objectives?

Assessment equals feedback. Use information from assessments to adjust your instruction and future assessments. Imagine that in reviewing your students' writing portfolios, you discern some trends that offer strong guidance for your instruction. For instance, students' reflections indicate that they

seem to find particular meaning in writing autobiographical pieces but less relevance in other forms of writing. You might build on their interests in autobiography by including prewriting experiences that tap into students' life experiences, no matter what the genre.

Evaluations need to be important to students if they are to serve as incentives for effort. Ensure that your students perceive the objectives as important and the assessments as fair, consistent, and driven by clear criteria. For example, if you were assigning a shelf-building project in a woodworking class, you might display a set of samples of varying quality. You could ask the students to brainstorm the qualities of a well-made shelf and discuss the real-life consequences of poorly constructed shelves, with students laughing at the imagined disasters that accompany shoddy work. You might develop a scoring rubric based on the criteria they have generated and distribute it as students begin their work.

6. How will I respond if individual children or the class as a whole are not on track toward success? What is my back-up plan?

Successful assessments are valid and reliable for the setting. Check the validity and reliability of your measures with the help of students and peers. For example, after writing a summative exam for a given unit, ask a peer to assess whether the questions appropriately emphasize particular sections of content. When students complete the exam, ask them to turn over their test papers and evaluate the exam for fairness. You might invite them to write the concepts they know from the unit that were *not* assessed in your test.

useful information to parents and students (Marzano, 2000). Computerized gradebooks are now widely available and widely used. Guskey (2009), however, warns that you should be careful when using this time-saving software and avoid letting the program make decisions that you should make.

Chapter 13 Summary

What Are Instructional Objectives and How Are They Used?

Research supports the use of instructional, or behavioral, objectives, which are clear statements about what students should know and be able to do at the end of a lesson, unit, or course. These statements also specify the conditions of performance and the criteria for assessment. In lesson planning, task analysis contributes to the formulation of objectives, and backward planning facilitates the development of specific objectives from general objectives in a course of study. Objectives are closely linked with assessment. Bloom's taxonomy of educational objectives classifies educational objectives from simple to complex, including knowledge, comprehension, application, analysis, synthesis, and evaluation. A behavior content matrix helps to ensure that objectives cover many levels.

Why Is Evaluation Important?

Formal measures of student performance or learning are important as feedback for students and teachers, as information for parents, as guidance for selection and certification, as data for assessing school accountability, and as incentives for increasing student effort.

How Is Student Learning Evaluated?

Strategies for evaluation include formative evaluation; summative evaluation; norm-referenced evaluation, in which a student's scores are compared with other students' scores; and criterion-referenced evaluation, in which students' scores are compared to a standard of mastery. Students are evaluated through tests or performances. The appropriate method of evaluation is based on the goal of evaluation. For example, if the goal of testing is to find out whether students have mastered a key concept in a lesson, a criterion-referenced formative quiz or a performance would be the most appropriate.

How Are Tests Constructed?

Tests are constructed to elicit evidence of student learning in relation to the instructional objectives. Achievement tests should be constructed in keeping with six principles: They should (1) measure clearly defined learning objectives, (2) examine a representative sample of the learning tasks included in instruction, (3) include the types of test items most appropriate for measuring the desired learning outcomes, (4) fit the uses that will be made of the results, (5) be as reliable as possible and interpreted with caution, and (6) improve learning. A table of specifications helps in the planning of tests that correspond to instructional objectives. Types of test items include multiple-choice, true–false, completion, matching, short essay, and problem-solving items. Each type of test item has optimal uses, along with advantages and disadvantages. For example, if you want to learn how students think about, analyze, synthesize, or evaluate some aspect of course content, a short essay test might be most appropriate, provided that you have time to administer it and evaluate students' responses.

What Are Authentic, Portfolio, and Performance Assessments ?

Portfolio assessment and performance assessment avoid the negative aspects of pencil-and-paper multiple-choice tests by requiring students to demonstrate their learning through work samples or direct real-world applications. Performance assessments are usually scored according to rubrics that specify in advance the type of performance expected.

How Are Grades Determined ?

Grading systems differ in elementary and secondary education. For example, informal assessments might be more appropriate at the elementary level, whereas letter grades become increasingly important at the secondary level. Grading standards might be absolute or relative (grading on the curve). Performance grading is a way for teachers to determine what children know and can do. A key requirement for performance grading is judicious collection of work samples from students that indicate level of performance. Another approach is to give students tests in which they can show their abilities. Other systems include contract grading and mastery grading. Report card grades typically average scores on tests, homework, seatwork, class participation, deportment, and effort.

Key Terms

Review the following key terms from the chapter.

Self-Assessment: Practicing for Licensure

Directions: The chapter-opening vignette addresses indicators that are often assessed in state licensure exams. Re-read the chapter-opening vignette and then respond to the following questions.

1. Mr. Sullivan is having a difficult time connecting what he is teaching and what he is testing. Which of the following evaluation tools will most likely help Mr. Sullivan make the connection?

   a. Multiple-choice test

   b. Instructional objectives

   c. Traditional teaching strategies

   d. Open-book testing

2. Mr. Sullivan might use a chart showing how a concept or skill will be taught at different cognitive levels in relation to an instructional objective. What is this chart called?

   a. Task analysis

   b. Backward planning

   c. Behavior content matrix

   d. Table of specifications

3. Mr. Sullivan might improve the connection between what he teaches and what he tests by following which of the following pieces of advice?

   a. Include all instructional content in the test.

   b. Make a test that includes all item types: true–false, multiple choice, matching, short answer, essay, and problem solving.

   c. Be free from the confines of instructional objectives.

   d. Design a test that fits the particular uses that will be made of the results.

4. Which of the following types of evaluation is Mr. Sullivan using?

   a. Summative

   b. Aptitude

   c. Affective

   d. Task analysis

5. Why would Mr. Sullivan choose to construct a table of specifications?

   a. To indicate the type of learning to be assessed for different instructional objectives

   b. To measure a student's performance against a specified standard

   c. To make comparisons among students

   d. To identify conditions of mastery

6. In a brief essay explain why evaluation is important.

7. Write instructional objectives, create a table of specifications using Bloom's taxonomy, develop a lesson plan, and write a short test for a topic of study.

PEARSON myeducationlab

Go to the Topic **Assessment** in the MyEducationLab (www.myeducationlab.com) for your course, where you can:

- Find learning outcomes for **Assessment** along with the national standards that connect to these outcomes.

- Complete Assignments and Activities that can help you more deeply understand the chapter content.

- Apply and practice your understanding of the core teaching skills identified in the chapter with the Building Teaching Skills and Dispositions learning units.

- Examine challenging situations and cases presented in the IRIS Center Resources.

- Access video clips of CCSSO National Teachers of the Year award winners responding to the question "Why Do I Teach?" in the Teacher Talk section.

- Check your comprehension of the content covered in the chapter by going to the Study Plan in the Book Resources for your text. Here you will be able to take a chapter quiz; receive feedback on your answers; and then access Review, Practice, and Enrichment activities to enhance your understanding of chapter content.

- Watch author Bob Slavin present a Personal Reflections podcast on *Assigning Grades* in the Book Resources for your text. Then, respond to the reflection questions that follow.

Assigning Grades

YOUR REFLECTIONS Why do you think a teacher might feel he or she "failed" when a student fails a class? What can you do to make sure you can always justify the grades you give students?

14

Standardized Tests and Accountability

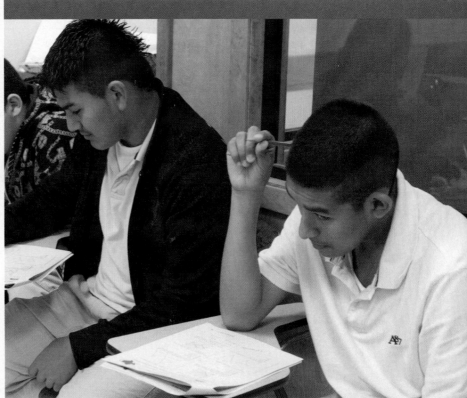

Bob Daemmrich/PhotoEdit

Learning Outcomes

At the end of this chapter, you should be able to:

- Define standardized tests and their use
- Identify different types of standardized tests
- Describe how standardized tests are interpreted
- Address issues concerning standardized testing and in-class testing
- Discuss how teachers are held accountable for their students' achievement

Bob Daemmrich/PhotoEdit

Jennifer Tranh is a fifth-grade teacher at Lincoln Elementary School. She is meeting with the parents of one of her students, Anita McKay.

"Hello, Mr. and Mrs. McKay," says Ms. Tranh when Anita's parents arrive. "I'm so glad you could come. Please take a seat, and we'll start right in. First, I wanted to tell you what a delight it is to have Anita in my class. She is always so cheerful, so willing to help others. Her work is coming along very well in most subjects, although there are a few areas I'm a bit concerned about. Before I start, though, do you have any questions for me?"

Mr. and Mrs. McKay explain to Ms. Tranh that they think Anita is having a good year and that they are eager to hear how she is doing.

"All right. First of all, I know you've seen the results of Anita's California Achievement Tests. We call those 'CATs' for short. Most parents don't understand these test scores, so I'll try to explain them to you. First, let's look at math. As you know, Anita has always been a good math student, and her scores and grades reflect this. She got an A on her last report card and a percentile score of 90 on math computations. That means that she scored better than 90 percent of all fifth-graders in the country. She did almost as well on math concepts and applications—her score is in the 85th percentile."

"What does this 'grade equivalent' mean?" asks Mrs. McKay.

"That's a score that's supposed to tell how a child is achieving in relation to his or her grade level. For example, Anita's grade equivalent of 6.9 means that she is scoring more than a year ahead of the fifth-grade level."

"Does this mean she could skip sixth-grade math?" asks Mr. McKay.

Ms. Tranh smiles. "I'm afraid not. It's hard to explain, but a grade equivalent score of 6.9 is supposed to be what a student at the end of sixth grade would score on a fifth-grade test. It doesn't mean that Anita already knows sixth-grade material. Besides, we take any student's testing information with a grain of salt. We rely much more on day-to-day performance and classroom tests to tell how each student is doing. In this case the standardized CAT scores are pretty consistent with what we see Anita doing in class. But let me show you another example that shows less consistency. I'm sure you noticed that even though Anita's reading grades have been pretty good, her scores in reading comprehension were much lower than her scores in most other areas. She got a percentile score of only 30. This is almost a year below grade level. I think Anita is a pretty good reader, so I was surprised. I gave her another test, the Gray Oral Reading Test. This test is given one-on-one, so it gives you a much better indication of how well students are reading. On the Gray, Anita scored at grade level. This score is more indicative of where I see her reading in class, so I'm not concerned about her in this area.

"On the other hand, there is a concern I have about Anita that is not reflected in her standardized tests. She scored near the 70th percentile in both language mechanics and language expression. This might make you think Anita's doing great in language arts, and she is doing well in many ways. However, I'm concerned about Anita's writing. I keep a portfolio of student writing over the course of the year. This is Anita's here. She's showing some development in writing, but I think she could do a lot better. As you can see, her spelling, punctuation, and grammar are excellent, but her stories are very short and factual. As you know, we don't give grades in writing. We use a rating form that shows the student's development toward proficient writing. Based on her portfolio I rated her at proficient, but to go to advanced, I'd like to see her write more and really let her imagination loose. She

447

tells great stories orally, but I think she's so concerned about making a mistake in mechanics that she writes very conservatively. On vacation you might encourage her to write a journal or to do other writing wherever it makes sense."

"But if her standardized test scores are good in language," says Mrs. McKay, "doesn't that mean that she's doing well?"

"Test scores tell us some things, but not everything," says Ms. Tranh. "The CAT is good on simple things such as math computations and language mechanics, but it is not so good at telling us what children can actually do. That's why I keep portfolios of student work in writing, in math problem solving, and in science. I want to see how children are really developing in their ability to apply their skills to doing real things and solving real problems. In fact, now that we've gone over Anita's grades and standardized tests, let's look at her portfolios,

and I think you'll get a much better idea of what she's doing here in school."

Jennifer Tranh's conversation with the McKays illustrates some of the uses and limitations of grades and standardized tests. The CATs and the Gray Oral Reading Test give Ms. Tranh information that does relate Anita's performance in some areas to national norms, and Anita's grades give Ms. Tranh some idea of how Anita is doing relative to her classmates, but neither standardized tests nor grades provide the detail or comprehensiveness reflected in the portfolios of work and other observations of Anita's performance. Taken together, cautiously interpreted standardized tests, grades, portfolios of work, and other classroom assessments provide a good picture of Anita's performance. Each has value and all the information should be evaluated in making educational decisions.

What Are Standardized Tests and How Are They Used?

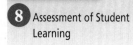

standardized tests

Tests that are usually commercially prepared for nationwide use and designed to provide accurate and meaningful information on students' performance relative to that of others at their age or grade levels.

Do you remember taking SATs, ACTs, or other college entrance examinations? Did you ever wonder how those tests were constructed, what the scores meant, and the degree to which your scores represented what you really knew or could really do? The SATs and other college entrance examinations are examples of **standardized tests.** Unlike the teacher-made tests discussed in Chapter 13, a standardized test is typically given under the same "standardized" conditions to thousands of similar students for whom the test is designed, allowing the test publisher to establish norms for comparing any individual score. For example, if a representative national sample of fourth-graders had an average score of 37 items correct on a 50-item standardized test, then 37 would be the fourth-grade "national norm" on this test, the score dividing those above or below "the norm."

Traditional standardized tests have been subjected to a great deal of criticism and controversy, and today a wide variety of alternative assessments are used. However, standardized tests of many kinds continue to be given for a wide range of purposes at all levels of education. This chapter discusses how and why standardized tests are implemented and how scores on these tests can be interpreted and applied to important educational decisions. It discusses why standardized tests are used to hold districts, schools, and teachers accountable for student performance, and how No Child Left Behind, a major federal initiative focused primarily on accountability, has increased the stakes. It also includes information on criticisms of standardized testing and on alternatives that are being developed, debated, and applied.

Standardized tests are usually meant to offer a yardstick against which to compare individuals or groups of students that teacher-made tests cannot provide. For example, suppose a child's parents ask you how their daughter is doing in math. You say, "Fine, she got a score of 81 percent on our latest math test." For some purposes this information would be adequate. But for others the parents might want to know much more. How does 81 percent compare to the scores of other students in this class? How about other students in the school, the district, the state, or the whole country? In some contexts the score of 81 percent might help to qualify the girl for a special program for students with mathematical gifts; in others it might suggest the need for remedial instruction. Also, suppose you found that the class averaged 85 percent correct on the math test. How is this class doing compared to other math classes or to students nationwide? A teacher-made test cannot yield this information.

Standardized tests are typically carefully constructed to provide accurate information about students' levels of performance. Most often, curriculum experts establish what students at a particular age should know and be able to do in a particular subject. Then questions are written to assess the various skills or information students are expected to possess. The questions are tried out on various groups of students. Items that almost all students get right or almost all miss are usually dropped, as are items that students find unclear or confusing. Patterns of scores are carefully examined. If students who score well on most items do no better than lower-scoring students on a particular item, then that item will probably be dropped.

Eventually, a final test is developed and given to a large selected group of students from all over the country. Attempts are usually made to ensure that this group resembles the larger population of students who will ultimately use the test. For example, a test of geometry for eleventh-graders might be given to a sampling of eleventh-graders in urban, rural, and suburban locations; in different regions of the country; in private as well as public schools; and to students with different levels of preparation in mathematics. Care will be taken to include students of all ethnic backgrounds. This step establishes the **norms** for the test, which provide an indication of how an average student will score (Aiken & Groth-Marnat, 2006; Popham, 2008). Finally, a testing manual is prepared, explaining how the test is to be given, scored, and interpreted. The test is now ready for general use. The test development process has created a test whose scores have meaning outside of the confines of a particular classroom or school and can be used in a variety of ways. Important functions of standardized testing include placement, diagnosis, evaluation, and school improvement.

■ Selection and Placement

Standardized tests are often used to select students for entry or placement in specific programs. For example, the SAT (Scholastic Assessment Test) or ACT (American College Testing Program) that you probably took in high school might have been considered by your college admissions board in deciding whether to accept you as a student. Similarly, admission to special programs for students who are gifted and talented might depend on standardized test scores. Along with other information, standardized tests can provide information to help you decide whether to place students in special-education programs or to assign students to ability groups. High schools may use standardized tests in deciding which students to place or counsel into college preparatory, general, or vocational programs. Elementary schools may apply such scores for placing students in reading groups. Some colleges base prerequisites for certain courses on meeting certain scores. Standardized tests are sometimes used to determine eligibility for grade-to-grade

Connections

For discussions of between- and within-class ability grouping, see Chapter 9, pages 254 and 257.

---

norms

Standards that are derived from the test scores of a sample of people who are similar to those who will take the test and that can be used to interpret scores of future test takers.

promotion, graduation from high school, or entry into an occupation. For example, most states make standardized test scores part of the teacher certification process.

■ Diagnosis

Standardized tests are often used to diagnose individual students' learning problems or strengths. For example, a student who is performing poorly in school might be given a battery of tests to determine whether he or she has a learning disability or mental retardation. At the same time the testing might identify specific deficits that need remediation. Teachers frequently employ diagnostic tests of reading skills, such as the Gray Oral Reading Test that Ms. Tranh used, to identify a student's particular reading problem. For example, a diagnostic test might indicate that a student's decoding skills are fine but that reading comprehension is poor; or that a student has good computation skills but lacks problem-solving skills. More fine-grained diagnostic tests might tell a teacher that a physics student is doing well in states of matter but not scientific measurement, or that a foreign language student has a good understanding of grammar but still lacks in expression. Sophisticated assessments can help you determine students' cognitive styles and the depth of their understanding of complex concepts.

■ Evaluation and Accountability

Perhaps the most common application of standardized testing is to evaluate students' progress and teachers' and schools' effectiveness. For example, districts and states use tests to hold educators accountable for the achievement of their students by evaluating the gains that schools make in overall student performance. Parents often want to know how their children are doing in comparison with the typical achievement of children at their grade level. For individual students, standardized test scores are meaningful as evaluation only if you use them along with other information, such as students' actual performance in school and in other contexts, as Ms. Tranh did. Many students who score poorly on standardized tests often excel in school, college, or occupations; either they have trouble taking tests or have important skills that are not measured by such tests. However, some students demonstrate their achievement best on standardized tests. For an extended dis-

The primary goal of the No Child Left Behind program was to level the playing field for students throughout the country, no matter where they attend school. How can high-stakes testing accomplish this goal?

Bob Daemmrich Photography

cussion of accountability and related educational policies, see "How Are Educators Held Accountable for Student Achievement?" later in the chapter.

■ School Improvement

Standardized tests can contribute to improving the schooling process. The results of some standardized tests provide information about appropriate student placement and diagnostic information that is important in remediation. In addition, achievement tests can guide curriculum development and revision when areas of weakness appear (see Kallick & Colosimo, 2009). Standardized tests can play a role in guidance and counseling as well. This is true not only for achievement and aptitude testing but also for more specialized types of measures, such as vocational interest inventories and other psychological scales employed for counseling students.

Schools often turn to academic achievement tests to evaluate the relative success of competing educational programs or strategies. For example, if a teacher or school tries out an innovative teaching strategy, tests can help reveal whether it was more successful than previous methods. Statewide and districtwide test results often serve as a yardstick by which citizens can judge the success of their local schools. Tests are sometimes used to indicate the relative teaching strengths and weaknesses of the school's faculty. However, educating students is a complex process, and standardized tests provide only a small portion of the information necessary for evaluating teachers, programs, or schools.

What Types of Standardized Tests Are Given?

Three kinds of standardized tests are commonly used in school settings: aptitude tests, norm-referenced achievement tests, and criterion-referenced achievement tests (Aiken & Groth-Marnat, 2006; Popham, 2008). An **aptitude test** is designed to assess students' abilities. It is meant to predict the ability of students to learn or to perform particular types of tasks rather than to measure how much the students have already learned. The most widely used aptitude tests measure general intellectual aptitude, but many other, more specific tests measure particular aptitudes, such as mechanical or perceptual abilities or reading readiness. The SAT, for example, is meant to predict a student's aptitude for college studies. An aptitude test is successful to the degree that it predicts performance. For example, a reading readiness test given to kindergartners that did not accurately predict how well the students would read when they reached first or second grade would be of little use.

Achievement tests are used to (1) predict students' future performance in a course of study, (2) diagnose students' difficulties, (3) serve as formative tests of students' progress, and (4) serve as summative tests of learning.

Norm-referenced achievement tests are assessments of a student's knowledge of a particular content area, such as mathematics, reading, or Spanish. The norms that are referenced are the results from a representative group of students to which scores can be compared. The tests are purposely constructed to reveal differences among students. Those differences are expected to be the result of quality of instruction and student learning rather than differences from school to school in curricula, thus assessing some but not all of the skills that are taught in any one school. A norm-referenced achievement test cannot range too broadly because it is designed for nationwide use and the curricula for any given subject vary from district to district. For example, if some seventh-graders learn about base-2 arithmetic or Venn diagrams but others do not, then these topics will be unlikely to appear on a national mathematics test.

Certification Pointer

You may be asked on your teacher certification test to define standardized tests and discuss their purposes.

---

aptitude test

A test designed to measure general abilities and to predict future performance.

---

achievement tests

Standardized tests measuring how much students have learned in a given context.

A criterion-referenced achievement test also assesses a student's knowledge of subject matter, but rather than comparing the achievement of an individual student against national norms, it is designed to measure the degree to which the student has mastered certain well-specified skills. The information that a criterion-referenced test produces is quite specific: "Thirty-seven percent of Ontario fifth-graders can fill in the names of the major Western European nations on an outline map" or "Ninety-three percent of twelfth-graders at Alexander Hamilton High School know that increasing the temperature of a gas in a closed container increases the gas's pressure." Sometimes criterion-referenced test scores are used in comparisons between schools or between districts, but typically no representative norming group is used. If a group of curriculum experts decides that every fifth-grader in Illinois should be able to fill in an outline map of South America, then the expectation for that item is 100 percent; it is of less interest whether Illinois fifth-graders score better or worse on this item than students in other states. What is more important is that, overall, students improve each year on this item.

■ Aptitude Tests

Although aptitude tests, norm-referenced achievement tests, and criterion-referenced tests are distinct from one another in theory, there is in fact considerable overlap among them. For example, aptitudes are usually measured by evaluating achievement over a very broadly defined domain. School learning can thus affect students' aptitude test scores, and a student who scores well on one type of test will usually score well on another (Popham, 2008).

GENERAL INTELLIGENCE TESTS   The most common aptitude tests given in school are tests of **intelligence,** or general aptitude for school learning. The intelligence quotient, or IQ, is the score that is most often associated with intelligence testing, but other types of scores are also calculated.

Intelligence tests are designed to provide a general indication of individuals' aptitudes in many areas of intellectual functioning. Intelligence itself is seen as the ability to deal with abstractions, to learn, and to solve problems (Sternberg, Jarvin, & Grigorenko, 2009), and tests of intelligence focus on these skills. Intelligence tests give students a wide variety of questions to answer and problems to solve.

THE MEASUREMENT OF IQ   The measurement of the intelligence quotient (IQ) was introduced in the early 1900s by Alfred Binet, a French psychologist, to identify children with such serious learning difficulties that they were unlikely to profit from regular classroom instruction. The scale that Binet developed to measure intelligence assessed a wide range of mental characteristics and skills, such as memory, knowledge, vocabulary, and problem solving. Binet tested a large number of students of various ages to establish norms (expectations) for overall performance on his tests. He then expressed IQ as a ratio of **mental age** (the average test scores of students at a particular age) to **chronological age,** multiplied by 100. For example, 6-year-olds (chronological age [CA] = 6) who scored at the average for all 6-year-olds (mental age [MA] = 6) would have an IQ of 100 (6/6 × 100 = 100). Any 6-year-olds who scored at a level typical of 7-year-olds (MA = 7) would have IQs of about 117 (7/6 × 100 = 117).

Over the years the mental age/chronological age comparison has been dropped, and IQ is now defined as having a mean of 100 and a standard deviation of 15 (a standard deviation is a measure of how spread out scores are, defined later in this chapter) at any age. Most scores fall near the mean, with small numbers of scores extending well above and below the mean. In theory, about 68 percent of all individuals will have IQs within one standard deviation of the mean; that is, from 85 (one standard deviation below the mean) to 115 (one standard deviation above), and 95 percent will be found in the range up to two standard deviations from the mean (between 70 and 130).

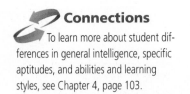

Connections
To learn more about student differences in general intelligence, specific aptitudes, and abilities and learning styles, see Chapter 4, page 103.

"According to your vocational aptitude test, you're best suited to a job filling in bubbles with a #2 pencil."

intelligence

General aptitude for learning, often measured by ability to deal with abstractions and to solve problems.

mental age

The average test score received by individuals of a given chronological age.

chronological age

The age of an individual in years.

Intelligence tests are designed to provide a general indication of an individual's aptitudes in many areas of intellectual functioning. The most widely used tests contain many different scales. Figure 14.1 shows items like those used on the Wechsler Adult Intelligence Scale (Wechsler, 1955). Each scale measures a different component of intelligence. Most often, a person who scores well on one scale will also do well on others, but this is not always so. The same person might do very well on general comprehension and similarities, less well on arithmetic reasoning, and poorly on block design, for example.

Intelligence tests are administered either to individuals or to groups. Tests such as the Otis-Lennon Mental Ability Tests, the Lorge-Thorndike Intelligence Tests, and the California Test of Mental Maturity, are often given to large groups of students as general assessments of intellectual aptitude. These tests are not as accurate or detailed as intelligence tests administered individually to people by trained psychologists, such as the Wechsler Intelligence Test for Children–Fourth Edition (WISC-IV) or the Stanford-Binet test. For example, students who are being assessed for possible placement in special education usually take an individually administered test (most often the WISC-IV), along with other tests.

IQ scores are important because they are correlated with school performance. That is, students who have higher IQs tend, on the average, to get better grades, score higher on achievement tests, and so on. By the time a child is about age 6, IQ estimates tend to become relatively stable, and most people's IQs remain about the same into adulthood.

Connections

For a discussion of the use of IQ scores in the classification of learners with exceptionalities or for special-education services, see Chapter 12, page 357.

FIGURE 14.1 Illustrations of Items Used in Intelligence Testing

Intelligence tests focus on skills such as dealing with abstractions and solving problems. This sample of items resembles those used on the Wechsler Adult Intelligence Scale.

Verbal Subscale

1. General comprehension

Why do people buy fire insurance?

2. Arithmetic reasoning

If eggs cost 60 cents a dozen, what does one egg cost?

3. Similarities

In what way are wool and cotton alike?

4. Digit span

Listen carefully, and when I am through, say the numbers right after me.

> 7 - 3 - 4 - 1 - 8 - 6

Now I am going to say some more numbers, but I want you to say them backward.

> 3 - 8 - 4 - 1 - 6

Performance Subscale

5. Digit–symbol substitution

Code   △ ○ ⧸ ✕ 8
          1 2 3 4 5

Test   △ 8 ✕ ○ △ ⧸ 8 ✕ △ 8

6. Block design

Using the four blocks, make one just like this:

However, some people will experience substantial changes in their estimated IQ, often because of schooling or other environmental influences (Ceci, 1991).

MULTIFACTOR APTITUDE TESTS   Another form of aptitude test that provides a breakdown of more specific skills is the **multifactor aptitude battery.** Many such tests are available, with a range of content and emphases. They include scholastic abilities tests such as the SAT; elementary and secondary school tests, such as the Differential Aptitude Test, the Cognitive Abilities Test, and the Test of Cognitive Skills; reading readiness tests, such as the Metropolitan Reading Readiness Test; and various developmental scales for preschool children. At a minimum, most of these tests provide not only overall aptitude scores but also subscores for verbal and nonverbal aptitudes. Often, subscores are even more finely divided to describe more specific abilities.

■ Norm-Referenced Achievement Tests

Whereas aptitude tests focus on general learning potential and knowledge acquired both in school and out, achievement tests focus on skills or abilities that are traditionally taught in schools. In general, standardized achievement tests fall into one of four categories: achievement batteries, diagnostic tests, single-subject achievement measures, and criterion-referenced achievement measures (Aiken & Groth-Marnat, 2006; Popham, 2008).

ACHIEVEMENT BATTERIES   Standardized **achievement batteries,** such as the California Achievement Test, the Iowa Tests of Basic Skills, the Comprehensive Test of Basic Skills, the Stanford Achievement Test, and the Metropolitan Achievement Tests, are used to measure individual or group achievement in a variety of subject areas. These survey batteries include several small tests, each in a different subject area, and are usually administered to a group over a period of several days. Many of the achievement batteries available for use in schools are similar in construction and content. However, because of slight differences among the tests in the instructional objectives and subject matter sampled within the subtests, it is important before selecting a particular test to examine it carefully for its match with a specific school curriculum and for its appropriateness relative to school goals. Achievement batteries usually have several forms for various age or grade levels so that achievement can be monitored over a period of several years.

DIAGNOSTIC TESTS   Differing from achievement batteries in that they generally focus on a specific content area and emphasize the skills that are thought to be important for mastery of that subject matter, **diagnostic tests** produce much more detailed information than other achievement tests. For example, a standardized mathematics test often produces scores for math computations, concepts, and applications, whereas a diagnostic test would give scores on more specific skills, such as adding decimals or solving two-step word problems. Diagnostic tests are available mostly for reading and mathematics and are intended to show specific areas of strength and weakness in these skills. The results can be used to guide remedial instruction or to structure learning experiences for students who are expected to learn the skill.

SUBJECT AREA ACHIEVEMENT TESTS   Teachers make up most classroom tests for assessing skills in specific subjects. However, school districts can purchase specific achievement tests for almost any subject. A problem with such tests is that unless they are tied to the particular curriculum and instructional strategies used in the classroom, they might not adequately represent the content that has been taught. If standardized achievement tests are considered for evaluating learning in specific areas, the content of the test should be closely examined for its match with the district curriculum, the instruction the students have received, and the district's or state's standards and assessments.

multifactor aptitude battery

A test that predicts ability to learn a variety of specific skills and types of knowledge.

achievement batteries

Standardized tests that include several subtests designed to measure knowledge of particular subjects.

diagnostic tests

Tests of specific skills used to identify students' needs and to guide instruction.

◼ Criterion-Referenced Achievement Tests

Criterion-referenced tests differ from norm-referenced standardized tests in several ways (Aiken, 2003; McMillan, 2007; Popham, 2008). Such tests can take the form of a survey battery, a diagnostic test, or a single-subject test. In contrast to norm-referenced tests, which are designed for schools with varying curricula, criterion-referenced tests are most meaningful when constructed around a well-defined set of objectives. For many tests, these objectives can be chosen by the school district, building administrator, or teacher. The items on the test are selected to match specific instructional objectives, often with three to five items measuring each objective. Therefore, the tests can indicate which objectives individual students or the class as a whole have mastered. Test results can be used to guide future instruction or remedial activities. For this reason these tests are sometimes referred to as objective-referenced tests.

Criterion-referenced tests differ from other achievement tests in the way they are scored and how the results are interpreted. On criterion-referenced tests, it is generally the score for each objective that is important. Results could show, for example, how many students can multiply two digits by two digits or how many can write a business letter correctly. Moreover, students' scores on the total test or on specific objectives are interpreted with respect to some criterion of adequate performance independent of group performance. Examples of criterion-referenced tests include tests for drivers and pilots, designed to determine who can drive or fly, not who is in the top 20 percent of drivers or pilots. Tests for teachers are also criterion referenced.

Score reports for criterion-referenced tests are frequently in the form of the number of items that the student got correct on each objective. From these data you can gauge whether the student has mastered the objective.

◼ Standard Setting

When tests are used for making decisions about mastery of a subject or topic, some procedure must be employed to determine the test cutoff scores indicating various proficiency levels (Popham, 2008). Most methods of establishing a **cutoff score** rely on the professional judgment of representative groups of teachers and other educators. Qualified professionals might examine each item in a test and judge the probability that a student with a given level of proficiency would get the item correct. They then base the cutoff score for mastery or proficiency on these probabilities. Standards set using procedures like this are common in licensing exams as well as in many state and district accountability programs.

How Are Standardized Tests Interpreted ?

After students take a standardized test, the tests are usually sent for computer scoring to the central office or the test publisher. The students' raw scores (the number correct on each subtest) are translated into one or more **derived scores**, such as percentiles, grade equivalents, or normal curve equivalents, which relate the students' scores to those of the group on which the test was normed. These statistics are described in the following sections (see Aiken, 2003; McMillan, 2008; Popham, 2008).

◼ Percentile Scores

A **percentile score**, or percentile rank (sometimes abbreviated in test reports as % ILE), indicates the percentage of students in the norming group who scored lower than a

Connections

For more on the definitions of norm-referenced and criterion-referenced testing, see Chapter 13, page 411.

Certification Pointer

On your teacher certification test you may need to know that a criterion-referenced test would give you better information about how much each student has learned about a particular aspect of the curriculum than a norm-referenced test.

cutoff score

The score designated as the minimum necessary to demonstrate mastery of a subject.

derived scores

Values computed from raw scores that relate students' performances to those of a norming group (e.g., percentiles and grade equivalents).

percentile score

A derived score that designates what percentage of the norming group earned raw scores lower than a particular score.

particular score. For example, if a student achieved at the median for the norming group (that is, if equal numbers of students scored better and worse than that student), the student would have a percentile rank of 50 because his or her scores exceeded those of 50 percent of the others in the norming group. If you ranked a group of 30 students from bottom to top on test scores, the 25th student from the bottom would score in the 83rd percentile ($25/30 \times 100 = 83.3$).

■ Grade-Equivalent Scores

Grade-equivalent scores relate students' scores to the average scores obtained by students at a particular grade level. Let's say a norming group achieved an average raw score of 70 on a reading test at the beginning of fifth grade. This score would be established as a grade equivalent of 5.0. If a sixth-grade norming group achieved a test score of 80 in September, this would be established as a grade equivalent of 6.0. Now let's say that a fifth-grader achieved a raw score of 75. This is halfway between the score for 5.0 and that for 6.0, so this student would be assigned a grade equivalent of 5.5. The number after the decimal point is referred to as "months," so a grade equivalent of 5.5 would be read "five years, five months." In theory, a student in the third month of fifth grade should have a score of 5.3 (five years, three months), and so on. Only the 10 months of the regular academic year, September to June, are counted.

The advantage of grade equivalents is that they are easy to interpret and make some intuitive sense. For example, if an average student gains one grade equivalent each year, we call this achieving at expected levels. If we know that a student is performing 2 years below grade level (say, a ninth-grader is scoring at a level typical of seventh-graders), this gives us some understanding of how poorly the student is doing.

However, grade-equivalent scores should be interpreted as only a rough approximation (Gronlund, 2003). For one thing, students do not gain steadily in achievement from month to month. For another, scores that are far from the expected grade level do not mean what they appear to mean. A fourth-grader who scores at, say, the 7.4 grade equivalent is by no means ready for seventh-grade work; this score simply means that the fourth-grader has thoroughly mastered fourth-grade work and has scored as well as a seventh-grader would on the fourth-grade test. Obviously, the average seventh-grader knows a great deal more than what is assessed on a fourth-grade test, so there is no real comparison between a fourth-grader who scores at a 7.4 grade equivalent and a seventh-grader who does so. The two tests they took are very different.

Shifting definitions of grade-level expectations can also confuse the interpretation of scores. For example, New York City school administrators were pleased during the late 1980s to report that 67 percent of students were reading at or above grade level. This redefinition of *average* is called the "Lake Wobegon Effect." (In humorist Garrison Keillor's mythical town of Lake Wobegon, "All the children are above average.") Far more than 50 percent of students in New York were scoring "above average" (Cannell, 1987). Test makers renormed their tests, and as a result, administrators in New York City could then claim that only 49 percent of their students were reading at or above grade level (Fiske, 1989). Today, the Lake Wobegon Effect is again in full force, and most standardized tests again produce scores that put many more than 50 percent of students "at grade level" or "above national norms." Because the norms vary from test to test, statements about how many students are at a given level should always be taken with a grain of salt. What is more meaningful is how students are changing over time, or how one district, school, or subgroup compares to another on the same test.

■ Standard Scores

Several kinds of scores describe test results according to their positions on the normal curve. A normal curve describes a distribution of scores in which most fall near the mean, or average, with a symmetrically smaller number of scores appearing the farther we go

FIGURE 14.2 **Frequency of Scores Forming a Normal Curve**

If 100 people take a test and the score for each is marked by an x on a graph, the result could suggest a normal curve. In a normal distribution, most scores are at or near the mean (in this case, 50), and the number of scores progressively decreases farther from the mean.

above or below the mean. A frequency plot of a **normal distribution** produces a bell-shaped curve. For example, Figure 14.2 shows a frequency distribution from a test with a mean score of 50. Each × indicates one student who got a particular score; there are 10 ×'s at 50, so we know that 10 students got this score. Nine students got 49s and nine got 51s, and so on, and very few students made scores above 60 or below 40. Normal distributions like the one shown in Figure 14.2 are common in nature; for example, height and weight are normally distributed throughout the general adult population. Standardized tests are designed so that extremely few students will get every item or no item correct, so scores on them are typically normally distributed.

STANDARD DEVIATION   One important concept related to normal distributions is the **standard deviation,** a measure of the dispersion of scores. The standard deviation is, roughly speaking, the average amount that scores differ from the mean. For example, consider these two sets of scores:

Set A		Set B
85		70
70		68
65	< Mean >	65
60		62
45		60
Standard deviation: 14.6		Standard deviation: 4.1

Note that both sets have the same mean (65) but that otherwise they are quite different, Set *A* being more spread out than Set *B*. This is reflected in the fact that Set *A* has a much larger standard deviation (14.6) than does Set *B* (4.1). The standard deviation of a set of scores indicates how spread out the distribution will be. Furthermore, when scores or other data are normally distributed, we can predict how many scores will fall a given number of standard deviations from the mean. This is illustrated in Figure 14.3, which shows that in any normal distribution, about 34 percent of all scores fall between the mean and one standard deviation above the mean (+1 SD), and a similar number fall between the mean and one standard deviation below the mean (−1 SD). If you go out two standard deviations from the mean, about 95 percent of the scores are included.

normal distribution

A bell-shaped symmetrical distribution of scores in which most scores fall near the mean, with progressively fewer occurring as the distance from the mean increases.

standard deviation

A statistical measure of the degree of dispersion in a distribution of scores.

FIGURE 14.3 **Standard Deviation**

When test scores are normally distributed, knowledge of how far a given score lies from the mean in terms of standard deviations indicates what percentage of scores are higher and lower.

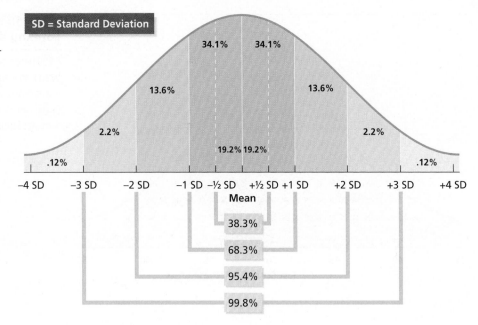

Scores on standardized tests are often reported in terms of how far they lie from the mean as measured in standard deviation units. For example, IQ scores are normed so that there is a mean of 100 and a standard deviation of 15. This means that the average person will score 100, someone scoring one standard deviation above the mean will score 115, someone scoring one standard deviation below will score 85, and so on. Therefore, in theory about 68 percent of all IQ scores (that is, a little more than two-thirds) fall between 85 (–1 SD) and 115 (+1 SD). SAT scores are also normed according to standard deviations, with the mean for the Verbal and Quantitative scales set at 500 and a standard deviation of 100. That puts more than two-thirds of all scores between 400 and 600. For IQ, 95 percent will be between 70 (–2 SD) and 130 (+2 SD); for the SAT scale, the comparable range is from 300 to 700.

STANINES   A standard score that is sometimes used is the **stanine score** (from the words <u>sta</u>ndard <u>nine</u>). Stanines have a mean of 5 and a standard deviation of 2, so each stanine represents a 0.5 standard deviation. Stanine scores are reported as whole numbers, so a person who earned a stanine score of 7 (+1 SD) actually fell somewhere between 0.75 SD and 1.25 SD above the mean.

NORMAL CURVE EQUIVALENTS   Another form of a standard score that is sometimes used is the **normal curve equivalent** (NCE). A normal curve equivalent can range from 1 to 99, with a mean of 50 and a standard deviation of approximately 21. NCE scores are similar to percentiles, except that intervals between NCE scores are equal (which is not the case with percentile scores). Another standard score, used more often in statistics than in reporting standardized test results, is the **z-score,** which sets the mean of a distribution at 0 and the standard deviation at 1. Figure 14.4 shows how a set of normally distributed raw scores with a mean percent correct of 70 percent and a standard deviation of 5 would be represented in *z*-scores, stanines, normal curve equivalents, percentile scores, and equivalent IQ and SAT scores.

Note the difference in the figure between percentile scores and all standard scores (*z*-score, stanine, NCE, IQ, and SAT). Percentile scores are bunched up around the middle of the distribution because most students score near the mean. This means that small changes in raw scores near the mean can produce large changes in percentiles (percentages of students below the score). In contrast, changes in raw scores that are far above or below the mean make a smaller difference in percentiles. For example, an increase of 5

stanine score

A type of standardized score ranging from 1 to 9, having a mean of 5 and a standard deviation of 2.

normal curve equivalent

A set of standard scores ranging from 1 to 99, having a mean of 50 and a standard deviation of about 21.

z-score

A standard score having a mean of 0 and a standard deviation of 1.

SD = Standard Deviation

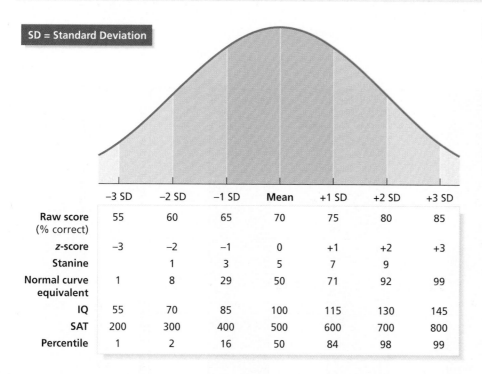

	–3 SD	–2 SD	–1 SD	**Mean**	+1 SD	+2 SD	+3 SD
Raw score (% correct)	55	60	65	70	75	80	85
z-score	–3	–2	–1	0	+1	+2	+3
Stanine		1	3	5	7	9	
Normal curve equivalent	1	8	29	50	71	92	99
IQ	55	70	85	100	115	130	145
SAT	200	300	400	500	600	700	800
Percentile	1	2	16	50	84	98	99

FIGURE 14.4

Relationships among Various Types of Scores

Raw scores that are normally distributed can be reported in a variety of ways. Each reporting method is characterized by its mean, by the range between high and low scores, and by the standard deviation interval.

points on the test from 70 to 75 moves a student from the 50th to the 84th percentile, an increase of 34 percentile points; but 5 more points (from 75 to 80) increases the student's percentile rank by only 14 points. At the extreme, the same 5-point increase, from 80 to 85, results in an increase of only 1 percentile point, from 98 to 99.

This characteristic of percentile ranks means that changes in percentiles should be interpreted cautiously. For example, one teacher might brag, "My average kids increased 23 percentile points [from 50 to 73], while your supposedly smart kids gained only 15 percentile points [from 84 to 99]. I really did a great job with them!" In fact, the bragging teacher's students gained only 3 points in raw score, or 0.6 standard deviations, whereas the other teacher's students gained 10 points in raw score, or 2 standard deviations!

Theory into Practice

Interpreting Standardized Test Scores

This section presents a guide to interpreting test reports for one widely used standardized test of academic performance, the Terra Nova, published by CTB/ McGraw-Hill (1997). Other widely used nationally standardized tests (such as the CAT, the Iowa, and the Stanford) use similar report formats.

CLASS RECORD SHEET   Figure 14.5 on pages 460–461 shows portions of an actual Terra Nova (CTBS/5) pre/post class record sheet for children (whose names have been changed) in a Title I second-grade reading class.

Identification Data   Look first at the top of the form. It identifies the tests taken at the end of the previous year (pre) and at the end of the current year (post). The grade (2.7) indicates that at the time of post-testing, students were in month 7 of second grade (April; September is month 0). Information at the bottom left

FIGURE 14.5 Sample Class Record Sheet for a Standardized Test

When a class of students takes a standardized test as a pre-test and a post-test, the results may be compared by means of a form similar to the one shown here.

CTB MACMILLAN/MCGRAW-HILL

170508
170
PAGE 1

PRE-POST CLASS RECORD SHEET
CLASS: GRD.2 TCH 3

PRE-TEST: CTBS/5 MA
POST-TEST: CTBS/5 MA

GRADE 2.7

TITLE 1 READING

STUDENTS	FORM/LEVEL	SCORES	READING READ	READING VOCAB	READING CMPST	LANGUAGE LANG	LANGUAGE MECH	LANGUAGE CMPST	MATHEMATICS MATH	MATHEMATICS COMPU	MATHEMATICS CMPST	TOTAL SCORE ++	SCI	SOCIAL STDY	SPELL	WORD ANLYS
BEACHY JULIA M		PRE NP	98			94			76			94				
BIRTH DATE: 5/ 4/90		POST NP	55			81			62			70				
PRE GRADE: 1.7	A-11	PRE NCE	94			83			65			82				
POST GRADE: 2.7	A-12	POST NCE	53			69			57			61				
CODES/PRE: 3916720000.......1.....		DIFF	-41			-14			-8			-21				
CODES/POST: 3916721.........1.....																
DUPHILY BRITTN D		PRE NP	79			70			88			82				
BIRTH DATE: 9/25/90		POST NP	53			58			70			62				
PRE GRADE: 1.7	A-11	PRE NCE	67			61			74			70				
POST GRADE: 2.7	A-12	POST NCE	52			54			61			57				
CODES/PRE: 6613080000.......		DIFF	-15			-7			-13			-13				
CODES/POST: 661308.........1.....																
HARRISON ROBERT L		PRE NP	44			30			19			28				
BIRTH DATE: 5/23/90		POST NP	63			34			42			46				
PRE GRADE: 1.7	A-11	PRE NCE	47			39			32			37				
POST GRADE: 2.7	A-12	POST NCE	57			41			46			48				
CODES/PRE: 4039710000.......1.....		DIFF	10			2			14			11				
CODES/POST: 403971.........1.....																
KNOX CARLY M		PRE NP	99			* 99			99			99				
BIRTH DATE: 7/ 9/90		POST NP	84			64			56			71				
PRE GRADE: 1.7	A-11	PRE NCE	99			99			99			99				
POST GRADE: 2.7	A-12	POST NCE	71			57			53			62				
CODES/PRE: 8441620000.......		DIFF	-28			-42			-46			-37				
CODES/POST: 844162.........1.....																
MILLER MARVIN R		PRE NP	49			85			70			73				
BIRTH DATE: 5/11/90		POST NP	76			86			39			71				
PRE GRADE: 1.7	A-11	PRE NCE	49			72			61			63				
POST GRADE: 2.7	A-12	POST NCE	65			73			44			62				
CODES/PRE: 2905390000.......		DIFF	16			1			-17			-1				
CODES/POST: 290539.........1.....																
MOORE RICHAR J		PRE NP	58			66			86			75				
BIRTH DATE: 8/26/90		POST NP	54			76			80			72				
PRE GRADE: 1.7	A-11	PRE NCE	54			59			73			64				
POST GRADE: 2.7	A-12	POST NCE	52			65			68			63				
CODES/PRE: 352384.........1.....		DIFF	-2			6			-5			-1				
CODES/POST: 352384.........1.....																

PRE-TEST DATE: 4/14/97
QUARTER MONTH: 31
NORMS: CTBS/5 1996
PATTERN (IRT)
POST-TEST DATE: 4/22/98
QUARTER MONTH: 31
NORMS: CTBS/5 1996
PATTERN (IRT)

SCHOOL: SCHOOL 1
DISTRICT: ANY DISTRICT
CITY: ANY CITY
STATE: CA

++ TOTAL SCORE CONSISTS OF READING, LANGUAGE, MATHEMATICS

NP: NATIONAL PERCENTILE
NCE: NORMAL CURVE EQUIVALENT
DIFF: DIFFERENCE (POST-SCORE MINUS PRE-SCORE)
DIFFERENCES ARE NOT REPORTED FOR NATIONAL PERCENTILES

*: MAXIMUM OR MINIMUM SCORE

CTBID: 9826802735490001-03-00094-000051

FIGURE 14.5 Continued

PRE-POST CLASS RECORD SHEET
DISTRICT: ANY DISTRICT

PRE-TEST: CTBS/5 MA
POST-TEST: CTBS/5 MA

GRADE 2

CTB MACMILLAN/MCGRAW-HILL

TITLE 1 READING

170508
170
PAGE 1

| DISTRICT SUMMARY | SCORES | READING | | | LANGUAGE | | | MATHEMATICS | | | TOTAL SCORE ++ | SCI | SOCIAL STDY | SPELL | WORD ANLYS |
		READ	VOCAB	CMPST	LANG	MECH	CMPST	MATH	COMPU	CMPST					
	PRE MDNP	40.4			39.2			34.3			33.0				
	POST MDNP	35.3			32.5			36.3			34.0				
	PRE NPMN	36			39			36			36				
	POST NPMN	35			35			38			36				
	PRE MNCE	42.5			44.0			42.5			42.5				
	POST MNCE	41.6			42.1			43.4			42.3				
	DIFF	-0.9			-1.9			0.9			-0.2				
** NUMBER OF STUDENTS =	95	91			91			93			90				

PRE-TEST FORM/LEVEL
A-11

POST-TEST FORM/LEVEL
A-12

++ TOTAL SCORE CONSISTS OF READING, LANGUAGE, MATHEMATICS

MDNP: MEDIAN NATIONAL PERCENTILE
NPMN: NATIONAL PERCENTILE OF MEAN NORMAL CURVE EQUIVALENT
MNCE: MEAN NORMAL CURVE EQUIVALENT
DIFF: DIFFERENCE (POST-SCORE MINUS PRE-SCORE)
DIFFERENCES ARE NOT REPORTED FOR NATIONAL PERCENTILES

**: SUMMARIES DO NOT INCLUDE
STUDENTS WHO WERE RETAINED
OR WHO SKIPPED A GRADE

PRE-TEST DATE: 4/14/97
QUARTER MONTH: 31
NORMS: CTBS/5 1996
PATTERN (IRT)
POST-TEST DATE: 4/22/98
QUARTER MONTH: 31
NORMS: CTBS/5 1996
PATTERN (IRT)
CITY: ANY CITY
STATE: CA

CTBID: 9826Q273549001-03-00078-000002

Source: Reproduced with permission of The McGraw-Hill Companies.

461

shows testing dates, school, district, test norm, and "quarter month" (i.e., weeks since school began).

Scores   Under each column, test scores are shown in two metrics. NP refers to national percentiles; NCE, to normal curve equivalent. For example, look at the fifth child, Marvin Miller. At the end of first grade, his national percentile score in reading was 49, indicating that he scored better than 49 percent of all first-graders. By second grade, his percentile score had increased to 76. In NCEs, however, he increased from 49 to 65. The test form shows a gain of 16 NCEs; NCE scores can be added and subtracted, because they are on an equal interval scale, whereas percentile scores cannot. Now look at the second student, Brittany Duphily. In reading, her percentile scores (and NCEs) dropped from first to second grade. Does this mean that she knows less in second grade than she did in first? Not at all. However, she did perform less well in second grade compared to other second-graders. To understand this, consider a girl who is the third-fastest runner in the fourth grade, but a year later is the twelfth fastest in the fifth grade. The girl has not slowed down, and probably can run faster than before, but other runners are making better progress.

Summary   At the bottom of the form is a summary of the test scores for second-graders in the entire district (a class or school summary would look the same). The scores are presented as median percentiles (the score of the middle child in the district) and the national percentile of the median, which indicates how well the district is doing among all districts. In this district, for example, the middle second-grader is scoring better than 35.3 percent of all second-graders in reading. The last set of numbers shows the mean NCEs for all second-graders and the difference between first-grade NCEs (42.5) and second-grade NCEs (41.6). The difference, a loss of 0.9 NCEs, is very small, essentially indicating that children in this district score at about the same reading level in first and second grades, in comparison to children in other districts.

INDIVIDUAL PROFILE REPORT   Like most standardized tests, the Terra Nova provides a detailed analysis of the test performance of each child. Figure 14.6 shows an example for a third-grader, Maria Olthof (a real report, but not her real name).

Norm-Referenced Scores   At the top of the report is a list of Maria's scores on 14 scales listed six ways. The first is grade equivalent. In reading, Maria's grade equivalent is 2.0, indicating that her score is typically obtained by an average child just starting second grade. Her NCE of 35 also shows that she is performing significantly below grade level. (In general, an NCE of 50 is considered "at grade level.") Skip over scale score, which is not interpretable. Maria's local percentile indicates that she is reading extremely poorly in comparison to other children in her class, school, or district (however "local" was defined). A percentile of 1 is the lowest possible score.

Number correct is self-explanatory. In reading, Maria's national percentile indicates that she is scoring better than only 24 percent of all third-graders in the United States. "NP range" indicates the likely range of national percentile scores that Maria might receive if she took the same test many times. That is, there is always a range of scores a student might get, depending on luck, inadvertent errors, testing conditions, motivation, and so on—all factors that could vary each time a student took a test even if his or her level of knowledge or skill stayed the same. The chart on the upper right shows this national percentile range with a diamond

FIGURE 14.6 Sample Individual Test Record for a Standardized Test

Reports for individuals who take standardized tests may include overall scores and scores on specific content objectives.

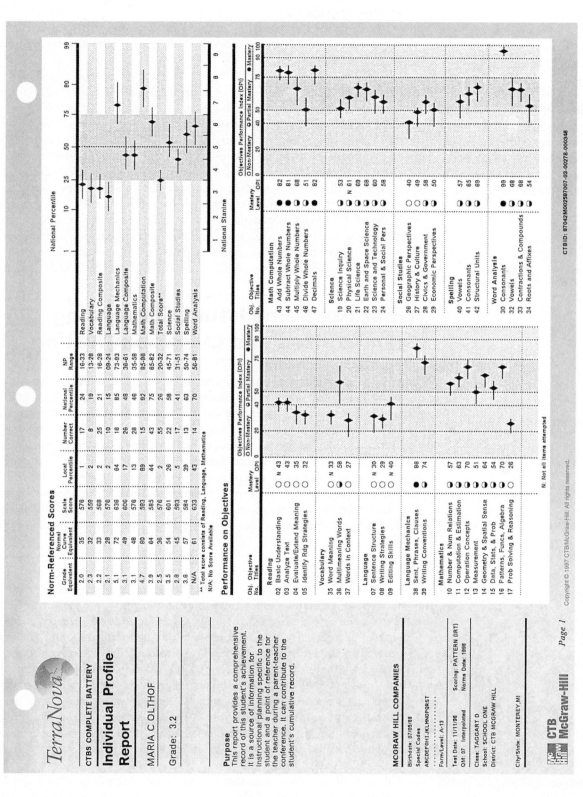

Source: Reproduced with permission of The McGraw-Hill Companies.

463

indicating the actual percentile score. The shading between the 25th and 75th percentiles indicates the "normal range"; Maria's reading score is below that range, although her own "NP range" suggests that on a very good day she might score within the normal range.

Note that at the bottom of the national percentile chart is a scale indicating stanines. Recall that stanine scores range from 1 to 9, with a score of 5 indicating the national average.

Performance on Objectives The remainder of the individual profile report breaks Maria's test down into subskills in each area. This breakdown can provide some useful information to explain overall scores. For example, look at Maria's mathematics scores. She scores very well on an "objectives performance index" in every subscale of math but one: problem solving. For Maria, this one low score could be because of her reading problems; or she might need additional work with this skill. However, subscale analyses of this kind should be interpreted very cautiously. The small number of items involved and the lack of a clear connection to the material Maria is studying mean that classroom assessments, perhaps supplemented by more fine-tuned diagnostic tests in mathematics, would be a much better indicator of Maria's strengths, weaknesses, and instructional needs.

Certification Pointer

For your teacher certification test, you may need to be able to select, construct, and use assessment strategies and instruments appropriate to the learning outcomes being evaluated.

What Are Some Issues Concerning Standardized and Classroom Testing?

The use of standardized tests to assess teachers, schools, and districts has increased dramatically in recent years. As noted earlier, all states now have statewide testing programs in which students at selected grade levels take criterion-referenced performance tests and/or standardized achievement tests. State education departments analyze scores on these tests to evaluate the state's educational program as a whole and to compare the performance of individual school districts, schools, and teachers as part of accountability programs. Accountability is one of several issues related to uses and abuses of standardized tests. Issues concerning testing, standards, and related topics are among the most hotly debated questions in U.S. education (Chatterji, 2002; Gallagher, 2003). In recent years there have been many developments and proposals for changes in testing.

■ Test Validity

We use test scores to make inferences about the students we are measuring. The **validity** of a test is the extent to which those inferences are justified (Aiken & Groth-Marnat, 2006; McMillan, 2008; Moss, Girard, & Haniford, 2006; Popham, 2008). The types of evidence that are used to evaluate the validity of a test vary according to the test's purpose. For example, if a test is being selected to help teachers and administrators determine which students are likely to have some difficulty with one or more aspects of instruction, primary interest will be in how well the test predicts future academic performance. However, if the aim is to describe the current achievement levels of a group of students, primary interest will focus on the accuracy of that description. In short, validity deals with the relevance of a test for its intended purpose (Aiken & Groth-Marnat, 2006).

Because of the various roles that tests are expected to play in schools and in the education process, three classes of evidence of validity are of concern to test users: content, criterion, and consequential.

validity

A measure of the degree to which a test is appropriate for its intended use.

CONTENT EVIDENCE OF VALIDITY   The most important criterion for the usefulness of a test—especially an achievement test—is whether it assesses what the user wants it to assess (Popham, 2008). The criterion called **content evidence** is an assessment of the degree of overlap between what is taught (or what should be taught) and what is tested. It is determined by content experts through careful comparison of the content of a test with state or district standards or with the objectives of a course or program. For example, a test that emphasizes dates and facts in history while curricula and state or local standards emphasize key ideas of history could not be considered valid.

CRITERION-RELATED EVIDENCE OF VALIDITY   Gathered by looking at relationships between scores on the test and other sets of scores, **criterion-related evidence** compares test results with expectations based on understandings about these various assessments. For example, **predictive evidence** of a test's validity might be a measure of its ability to help predict future behavior. If we are using a test to predict students' future school performance, one way to examine the test's validity is to relate the test scores to some measure of students' subsequent performance. If an appropriate level of correspondence exists between the test and later performance, the test can then be used to provide predictive information for students. For example, test scores on SATs and ACTs have been shown to relate reasonably well to performance in college; many college admissions officers therefore use these scores (along with high school grades and other information) in deciding which applicants to accept.

Another criterion-related form called **concurrent evidence** of validity determines whether the test measures the same domain as another test. For example, if a group IQ test were to be substituted for an individual IQ test, one would first want to know whether they yielded comparable scores. By giving the two tests to the same students in a study, the relationship between their scores could be evaluated.

Another form of concurrent evidence is called **discriminant evidence.** Achievement tests, for example, might be expected to show a relative *lack* of relationship with some variables. For example, a test of mechanical aptitude should relate to a test taker's ability to assemble a machine but should *not* correlate too well with verbal aptitude, which is a different skill, or with gender, which has nothing to do with the skill being measured.

■ Test Reliability

Whereas validity relates to the skills and knowledge measured by a test, the **reliability** of a test relates to the accuracy with which these skills and knowledge are measured (Aiken & Groth-Marnat, 2006; Popham, 2008). Test scores are supposed to result from the knowledge and skill of the students being measured. But when a test is administered, aspects related to both the test itself and the circumstances surrounding its administration could cause the results to be inaccurate. In theory, if a student were to take equivalent tests twice, he or she should obtain the same score both times. The extent to which this would not occur involves the subject of reliability. Random features of the assessment such as ambiguous test items, differences in specific item content, lucky or unlucky guessing, inconsistent motivation, and anxiety all affect test scores and could cause results for different administrations of equivalent tests to differ. In addition, on essays or other performance measures, differences between raters reduce reliability. If it could be shown that individuals received similar scores on two administrations of the same test, then some confidence could be placed in the test's reliability. If the scores were greatly inconsistent, it would be difficult to place much faith in a particular test score. Generally, the longer the test and the more similar the items are to each other, the greater is the reliability.

Reliability is commonly measured using a coefficient that has a theoretical range from 0 to 1. The higher the number, the more reliable the test. In general, good

content evidence

A measure of the match between the content of a test and the content of the instruction that preceded it.

criterion-related evidence

A type of evidence of validity that exists when scores on a test are related to scores from another measure of an associated trait.

predictive evidence

A type of criterion-related evidence of validity demonstrated when scores on a test are related to scores from a measure of a trait that the test could be used to predict.

concurrent evidence

A type of criterion-related evidence of validity that exists when scores on a test are related to scores from another measure of the same or a very similar trait.

discriminant evidence

A type of evidence of validity shown when scores on a test are unrelated to scores from one or more measures of other traits when educational or psychological theory about these traits predicts they should be unrelated.

reliability

A measure of the consistency of test scores obtained from the same students at different times.

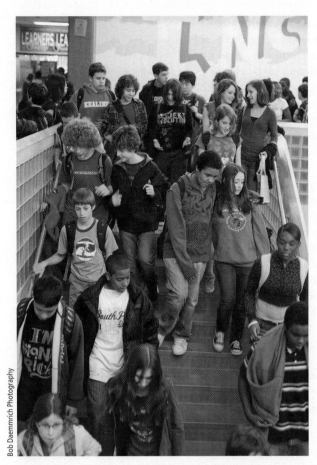

Bob Daemmrich Photography

These students will take nationwide standardized aptitude and achievement tests this year. Will the results be equally fair to them all? Why or why not?

bias

An undesirable characteristic of tests in which item content discriminates against certain students.

standardized achievement tests should have coefficients of .90 or higher. The question of reliability might be thought of as how consistently the test measures something about students. Validity relates to the question of how meaningful a test score is for something we care about. Thus, a test cannot have validity without reliability, but a test can be reliable without being valid. As an example of reliability without validity, consider your reaction if your instructor assigned course grades on the basis of student height. He or she would have a highly reliable assessment (height can be determined quite accurately), but the scores would not be valid indicators of your knowledge or skill. Now, imagine a test of creativity in which students were asked to describe innovative uses for a can opener. If raters could not agree on how to score students' responses, or if scores varied a great deal when students took the same test 6 months later, then the scale would lack reliability and, therefore, could not be considered valid.

■ Test Bias

Some major criticisms of traditional standardized tests relate to issues of validity and reliability (see Linn, 2000). Critics argue that such tests

- Provide false information about the status of learning in the nation's schools (Bracey, 2003)
- Are unfair to (or biased against) some kinds of students (e.g., students from diverse backgrounds, those with limited proficiency in English, females, and students from low-income families) (see Lissitz & Schafer, 2002; Orfield & Kornhaber, 2001; Scheurich, Skrla, & Johnson, 2000; Suzuki, Ponterotto, & Meller, 2000)
- Tend to corrupt the processes of teaching and learning, often reducing teaching to mere preparation for testing (Cizek, 1999; Darling-Hammond & Falk, 1997; Rotberg, 2001)
- Focus time, energy, and attention on the simpler skills that are easily tested and away from higher-order thinking skills and creative endeavors (Campbell, 2000; Popham, 2008)

One major issue in the interpretation of standardized test scores is the possibility of **bias** against students from low-income or diverse backgrounds (Lissitz & Schafer, 2002; Suzuki et al., 2000). In one sense, this is a question of test validity: A test that gives an unfair advantage to one or another category of student cannot be considered valid. Of greatest concern is the possibility that tests could be biased because their items assess knowledge or skills that are common to one group or culture but not another. For example, a test that includes a reading comprehension passage about a trip to the beach could be biased against students who live far from a beach or cannot afford to travel to a beach. A passage about Halloween could be unfair to Jehovah's Witnesses, who do not celebrate Halloween.

Test publishers routinely assess bias in test items (called *item bias*). Items that exhibit lower (or higher) scores for student demographic groups (e.g., gender or race groups) than expected on the basis of the test as a whole are flagged for evaluation. These items are usually referred to a committee with representatives from a broad range of demographic groups, which is likely to exclude the item. A related issue is sensitivity. It should go without saying that test items with any kind of overt cultural or gender stereotyping should be rejected. For example, a test whose items always refer to doctors as "he" or give Hispanic names only to menial workers should not be used.

■ Computer Test Administration

The use of computers to administer tests is becoming more common. In its simplest form, the same multiple-choice items (in the same order) are presented to students as they would take them if they sat for the typical paper-and-pencil test. However, the computer makes it possible to tailor the selection of items to the performance of the student. In **computer–adaptive** administration (Olson, 2005; Wainer, 2000), follow-up to any single item depends on the student's success in answering, with harder items following correct responses and easier items presented after wrong answers. As the test progresses, a running estimate of the student's performance over the entire test is continually updated. This can result in real time savings; students can commonly take tests in less than one-third the time for a paper-and-pencil administration with the same degree of accuracy. Also, computer-adaptive testing can zero in on a particular set of skills at the forward edge of what a student knows, giving more accurate information on those skills while avoiding wasting time on items that are very easy or impossible for the student.

ON THE WEB

For more on issues related to the principles of educational assessment go to the website of the National Council on Measurement in Education (NCME) (www.ncme.org), the website of James McMillan of Virginia Commonwealth University on Fundamental Assessment Principles for Teachers and Administrators (http://pareonline.net/getvn.asp?v=7&n=8), and 9 Principles for Good Practice for Assessing Student Learning by the Center for Teaching, Learning, and Assessment (www.iuk.edu/~koctla/assessment/9principles.shtml). Also see the NCREL website on Rethinking Assessment and Its Role in Supporting Educational Reform (www.ncrel.org/sdrs/areas/issues/methods/assment/as700.htm), the National Center for the Improvement of Educational Assessment (www.nciea.org), and the National Board on Educational Testing and Public Policy (www.bc.edu/research/nbetpp).

How Are You as an Educator Held Accountable for Student Achievement?

A growing trend in recent years has been the effort to hold teachers, schools, and districts accountable for what students learn. All U.S. states, most Canadian provinces, and England (among other countries) have implemented regular standardized testing programs and publish the results on a school-by-school basis. Many districts supplement these state tests with additional tests, including "benchmark assessments" that are given several times each year to help guide instruction toward meeting state standards. Not surprisingly, principals and other administrators watch these scores the way business owners watch their profit sheets. Standardized tests have become "high-stakes" tests, which means that their results have serious consequences for educators and (increasingly) for students themselves. For example, many states and districts now require that students score at a given level on state tests in order to be promoted from grade to grade or to graduate from high school. Many states and districts issue school report cards listing such data as test scores, attendance, retentions, and suspensions; these might be reported in newspapers or otherwise publicized. Test scores are frequently used in decisions about

computer-adaptive

An approach to assessment in which a computer is used to present items and each item presented is chosen to yield the best new information about the examinee based on prior responses to earlier items.

hiring, firing, promotion, and transfer of principals and superintendents, and sometimes teachers.

> ### ON THE **WEB**
>
> To learn more about accountability and state-level assessment issues, visit the website for the Council of Chief State School Officers (CCSSO) at www.ccsso.org. CCSSO is an organization of public officials who lead K–12 education in the 50 states. For information on accountability for charter schools, see www.uscharterschools.org/pub/uscs_docs/r/account.htm. For accountability and assessment issues for students with disabilities, see www.cehd.umn.edu/NCEO/OnlinePubs/NCLBdisabilities.html. For historical context for state-level assessment issues in higher education, visit www.stanford.edu/group/ncpi/unspecified/assessment_states/pdf/Metropolitan.pdf. A list of links to state assessment sites is available at www.bc.edu/research/nbetpp/weblinks.html. Also see the website for the National Center for Educational Accountability (www.ecs.org/html/project.asp?projectID=26).

The accountability movement stems in part from the public's loss of confidence in education. Legislators (among others), upset by examples of students graduating from high school unable to read or compute, have demanded that schools establish higher standards and that students achieve them (McDermott, 2007).

The accountability movement has many critics, however (Hamilton, Stecher, & Yuan, 2008; Rotberg, 2001; Ryan & Shepard, 2008; Sirotnik, 2002; Thompson, 2001). Many argue that schools will teach only what is tested, emphasizing reading and mathematics at the expense of, for instance, science and social studies (Marx & Harris, 2006), and emphasizing easily measured objectives (such as punctuation) over more important hard-to-measure objectives (such as composition). Many educators point out that accountability assessments fail to take into account differences in the challenges faced by schools (Barton, 2007/2008). A school or classroom might test low because the students are from disadvantaged backgrounds or do not yet speak English well rather than because they were given poor instruction. Students in high-poverty schools may have fewer opportunities to learn because their funding is often lower than that of other schools (Orfield & Kornhaber, 2001; Starratt, 2003). High student mobility, especially prevalent in low-SES urban areas, might mean that schools are held accountable for students they have only had for a few weeks or months. School performance year-to-year is unstable, and schools may be rewarded or punished based on minor variations of no statistical importance (Fuller, Wright, Gesicki, & Kang, 2007; Hess, 2008/2009; Ho, 2008; Kelly & Monczunski, 2007; Linn & Haug, 2002). High-stakes testing can lead schools and districts to try to adopt policies that artificially inflate scores by removing potentially low-scoring students from the testing pool, such as assigning more children to special education, categorizing more students as limited English proficient, or retaining more students (Booher-Jennings & Beveridge, 2007; Linn, 2000). Many observers have noted that teachers, under extraordinary pressure, sometimes use unethical strategies to increase students' scores (Hamilton et al., 2008; Popham, 2005).

Several researchers (e.g., Amrein & Berliner, 2003; Bracey, 2003; Ellmore & Fuhrman, 2001; Neill, 2003) have questioned whether increased accountability actually leads to higher achievement. Carnoy and Loeb (2002) found only slight differences in NAEP score gains favoring states with strong accountability systems in comparisons with other states, whereas Neill and Gaylor (2001) and Amrein and Berliner (2003) found that states with strong accountability systems had *lower* gains on NAEP than did other states. Chicago studies of grade-to-grade promotion standards found higher student motivation (Roderick & Engel, 2001) and higher achievement (Roderick, Jacob, & Bryk, 2002) than before the standards were implemented.

Regardless of the criticisms, the demand for accountability is here to stay (Gandal & Vranek, 2001; Scherer, 2001). One advantage of accountability is that it does increase the pressure on schools and teachers to pay attention to students who might otherwise fall through the cracks and to help those who need help the most. States are increasingly reporting "disaggregated" scores, meaning that they are separately held accountable for gains of students of each ethnicity, limited English proficient students, and so on. This can focus school leaders on means of ensuring that all groups are making progress (Scheurich et al., 2000). Another advantage is that accountability encourages schools to search out improved instructional methods and guarantees routine evaluation of any innovations schools try (Kennedy, 2003; Streifer, 2002; Gandal & McGiffert, 2003; Lane & Beebe-Frankenberger, 2004).

State accountability tests are based on state standards (Strong et al., 2001). For a teacher, a principal, or a subject matter specialist, knowing what these standards are is a key to helping students achieve higher test performance (Carr & Harris, 2001). Goals that are understood are more likely to be reached than goals that are unclear.

The standards on which accountability tests are based are usually developed by diverse groups of stakeholders, including teachers, parents, employers, and researchers who express their judgments about what should be taught and learned. Through a consensus-building process, a state or district pools the thinking of educators and noneducators in defining the content domains it demands through its assessments. This process forces education leaders and policymakers to make clear what it is they want children to learn, which can then help them set policies in line with these objectives (Gandal & Vranek, 2001).

■ No Child Left Behind

The **No Child Left Behind (NCLB)** legislation was the main education policy of the Bush Administration. NCLB is currently being substantially revised and will certainly have a new name once revisions are passed; check www.ed.gov for updates.

The assessment provisions of NCLB were set up as follows (see Center on Education Policy, 2003; The Education Trust, 2003; Stecher, Hamilton, & Gonzales, 2003; U.S. Department of Education, 2002).

1. *Annual testing.* Under NCLB, all states must test students in reading and math. Before NCLB, most states tested children for accountability purposes only in selected grades. Under NCLB, states test in grades 3 through 8, plus one high school grade. Some states have developed their own tests, some have contracted with companies to create customized tests, and some have purchased commercial tests such as those described in this chapter.

2. *Disaggregated reporting of scores.* Under NCLB, states have to report test scores for each school according to each subgroup in the school: each ethnic group, students in special education, students living in poverty, and limited English proficient students. There has to be a minimum number of students in a given category for it to be considered a subgroup for NCLB, and this number varies from state to state. Schools and districts are held accountable for each subgroup, so it is no longer possible to look successful by succeeding on average even though one or more subgroups may be failing to make good progress.

3. *Adequate yearly progress.* All subgroups in all schools are expected to make adequate yearly progress (AYP) on all state assessments. This is defined differently in each state, but in essence each subgroup has to either be scoring at a high level or have an increasing percentage of students scoring at the proficient level each year. Further, subgroups are not considered to be making adequate progress if too many students are missing (to avoid situations in which schools fail to obtain tests from some low-achieving students). The AYP requirement is, for most schools, the most important aspect of NCLB, and school and district leaders are very anxious to ensure that every group is making progress.

"Well now, let's see who made adequate yearly progress this year . . ."

No Child Left Behind (NCLB)

Federal legislation that requires annual testing in grades 3 through 8 plus high school, requires schools to make adequate yearly progress, and provides assistance to schools not meeting standards.

"Of course we still make time for art. Right now, for example, we're practicing shading in boxes."

4. Consequences for not meeting AYP.   Schools with one or more subgroups not meeting their state's AYP standards are subject under NCLB to various consequences, depending on how many years they fail to meet AYP. Schools not meeting AYP for 2 years or more have to offer their children supplemental educational services, usually small-group tutorials held after school or over the summer. Also, such schools are supposed to offer parents the opportunity to transfer their children to more successful schools, although in practice very few parents take advantage of this. If schools fail to meet AYP for further years, they are subject to more severe consequences, eventually leading to the possibility of reconstitution (replacing the staff with a new staff), closure, or takeover by the state, although these consequences are rarely applied in practice.

CRITICISMS OF NCLB   Although the NCLB Act was supported by Republicans and Democrats, and the Obama administration continues to support test-based accountability, NCLB's accountability provisions have unleashed a firestorm of criticism from educators, much of which can be grouped under the following major headings:

1. Excessive and narrow testing.   Many educators have expressed concern that NCLB continues a trend toward excessive testing of children on standardized, mostly multiple-choice tests (McGill-Franzen & Allington, 2006; Popham, 2003; Sadker & Zittleman, 2004). In particular, because NCLB focuses on reading and math, many educators have been concerned that science, social studies, art, music, and anything involving creativity or deep understanding will be pushed out (Cawelti, 2006; Guilfoyle, 2006).

2. State-to-state variations in standards.   Because NCLB left up to the states the testing, passing standards, and other elements that determine whether schools have met AYP, there is enormous variation from state to state. For example, a study by the Northwest Evaluation Association (NWEA, 2003) found that an eighth-grader performing at the proficient level in Montana is at the 36th percentile on an NWEA exam, whereas a similar student in Wyoming must score at the 89th percentile on the same test. In addition, states vary in how many students are needed to constitute a subgroup, so states with high requirements (some require 50 students, some as few as 5) are not held accountable for their students in special education or other small subgroups, whereas other states with identical test scores might have many schools not meeting AYP because they are accountable for a larger number of subgroups. As a result, some states have the majority of their schools not meeting AYP, whereas others have hardly any in trouble. A major focus of the Obama administration's reform of federal education laws is on reducing these state-by-state variations and focusing on national standards.

3. Underfunding of NCLB.   NCLB has brought with it a substantial increase in federal education funding but far less than the amount many of its advocates had hoped (Center on Education Policy, 2004). The problem is that much of the new funding is taken up by the requirements for additional testing, supplemental educational services, and assistance to parents in transfering their children to new schools.

Connections
See Chapter 4 for a description of the achievement gap between majority and minority students.

Connections
For more on teaching test-taking skills in the context of teaching metacognitive awareness and study skills, see Chapter 6, page 168.

Theory into Practice
Teaching Test-Taking Skills

As standardized testing has taken on increasing importance in the evaluation of students, teachers, and schools, so too has the preparation of students to take these tests. Of course, the best way to get students ready for tests is to do a good job of teaching them the material (Salend, 2009; Schmidt & Cogan, 2009; Tileston & Darling, 2008). However, schools also need to help many students to become test-wise so they can show what they really know on standardized tests and get the highest scores possible.

Many ethical issues are involved in helping students do well on standardized tests (Popham, 2008; Salend, 2009). For example, one way to help students score well would be to know the test items in advance and teach students the answers. Clearly, this would be cheating. A much more ethically ambiguous case arises when teachers know what subjects will be on the test and teach only material that they know will be tested. For example, if a standardized test does not assess Roman numerals, a math teacher might skip this topic to spend more time on an objective that will be tested. This practice is criticized as "teaching to the test." However, it could also be argued that it is unfair to test students on material that they have not been taught and that instruction, therefore, should be closely aligned with tests (Popham, 2008; Tileston & Darling, 2008). The issue is that a standardized test can assess only a small sample of all objectives that are taught in school and gearing instruction toward the objectives that will be on the test, to the exclusion of all others, would produce a very narrow curriculum. Because of this temptation to limit instruction to the content of upcoming tests, it is important to maintain test security. Specific items on a test should never be shared with teachers in advance of the administration date.

Beyond matching instructional content with general test objectives, there are many ways to help students learn to do well on tests in general. Research has found that students can be taught to be test-wise and that this increases their standardized test scores (Bangert-Drowns, Kulik, Kulik, & Morgan, 1991; Scruggs, White, & Bennion, 1986). Students can also be taught coping strategies to deal with their anxiety about testing. These strategies can sometimes help children approach tests with more confidence and less stress (Flippo, 2008; Schutz & Davis, 2000).

Questions have been raised about the effectiveness of programs that prepare students for the SAT. Because the SAT measures cognitive skills, it is perhaps to be expected that instructional programs can improve scores. The consensus among researchers is that coaching (especially long-term coaching) is effective for the SAT, particularly for students who are minorities and/or low-achieving students (Becker, 1990), when it focuses on the skills the SAT measures.

Some ways of helping students to prepare for standardized tests include the following (see Flippo, 2008; Tileston & Darling, 2008):

1. Give students practice with similar item formats. For example, if a test will use multiple-choice formats, give students practice with similar formats in routine classroom quizzes and tests. If a test will use an unusual format such as verbal analogies (e.g., Big:Small::Honest: ____), give students practice with this type of item.

2. Suggest that students skip over difficult or time-consuming items and return to them later.

3. If there is no penalty for guessing on a test, suggest to students that they always fill in some answer. If there is a penalty for guessing, students should be encouraged to guess only if they can narrow down the options by eliminating one or more choices.

4. Suggest that students read all options on a multiple-choice test before choosing one. Sometimes more than one answer is correct but one of them should always be the better answer.

5. Suggest to students that they use all available time. If they finish early, they should go back over their answers.

IMPACTS OF NCLB   No Child Left Behind (NCLB) has significantly changed the landscape of American education. Jennings and Rentner (2006) describe 10 "big effects" of NCLB, drawn from their surveys at the Center on Education Policy.

1. *State and district officials have reported rising achievement on state tests, but it is not clear if this is meaningful.*   Scores on state tests have gone up under NCLB (Center on Education Policy, 2009a,b). However, for 20 years state test scores have gone up in most states, whereas scores on the National Assessment of Academic Progress (NAEP) have hardly changed, leading critics to claim that factors other than actual improvements in student learning have caused state test scores to appear to rise (e.g., McGill-Franzen & Allington, 2006).

2. *Schools spend more time on reading and math, sometimes at the expense of subjects not tested.*   Because NCLB accountability focuses only on reading and math, many schools (71 percent, according to Jennings and Rentner, 2006) have reduced time in other subjects, such as social studies and science.

3. *Schools pay much more attention to test scores and alignment.*   School leaders have learned to watch their test scores carefully and to try to get teachers to focus their instruction on the objectives and even the test formats most likely to be on the state test.

4. *Low-performing schools have undergone makeovers rather than radical restructuring.*   NCLB anticipated that schools failing to make adequate yearly progress would make major changes, from adopting new schoolwide reform models to complete reconstitution. This has not happened. Instead, most schools continue to muddle through, making modest improvements in hopes of better luck next time.

5. *Teachers have made progress in demonstrating academic qualifications.*   NCLB introduced minimum standards for qualifications of teachers and instructional aides. For Title I teachers this meant holding at least a bachelor's degree and demonstrating subject area competency (Berry, Hoke, & Hirsch, 2004; Rebell & Hunter, 2004; U.S. Department of Education, 2002). Unavailability of highly qualified teachers, especially in inner-city and rural areas, has hindered administrators' attempts to meet this requirement, and a survey by the Center on Education Policy (2007) found that this part of NCLB is not perceived by state officials to be working.

6. *Students have taken a lot more tests.*   To comply with NCLB, all states have to test annually in grades 3 through 8, plus one high school year (usually 11). Previously, most states had only tested in selected grades. In addition, pressure to improve end-of-year test scores has led to the rapidly increasing use of benchmark assessments, tests given three to five times per year to give educators information about how well their students are likely to do on state assessments.

7. *Schools have paid much more attention to the achievement of particular groups of students.*   Under NCLB, schools are held accountable for the achievement of each of several subgroups of students: African American, Hispanic, and white students; students in special education; and low-income students. Because of this, school leaders report paying a lot more attention to the scores of each of these groups (see Haycock, 2006). This provision of NCLB has also led to a great deal of controversy about assessment of students with disabilities and of English learners.

8. *The percentage of schools on state "needs improvement" lists is substantial.*   About 10 percent of all schools have been designated as being "in need of improvement," meaning that they have not met their adequate yearly progress goals for 2 years in a row. However, states vary widely in the percentages of schools meeting standards because of substantial differences in the difficulty of their tests and their procedures for computing adequate yearly progress.

Under NCLB, students in schools in need of improvement are given the opportunity to transfer to more successful schools. This has rarely happened; only 2 percent of eligible students have transferred to new schools. Students in schools in need of improvement are also eligible for "supplemental educational services," usually after-school instruction in small groups. Only 20 percent of eligible students take advantage of these services. School leaders are skeptical about the benefits of both of these remedies, and research has failed to find any positive effects.

9. *The federal government plays a more significant role in education.* According to the U.S. Constitution, education is a state responsibility, and by tradition it is a local responsibility. NCLB has enormously increased the federal government's involvement in education at all levels, and the U.S. Department of Education is seen to be strictly enforcing the provisions of NCLB. The active federal role in education is being continued by the Obama administration.

10. *Under NCLB, states and districts have expanded roles in the operation of individual schools, but do not have adequate funds to carry out their new duties.* State departments of education have increased responsibilities to monitor compliance with NCLB and to help schools and districts in need of improvement. Districts also have an increased role. However, neither states nor districts receive sufficient funding to perform their new roles adequately, or so they report. Still, NCLB has led to diminished authority and autonomy for principals and school staffs, while increasing district and state authority.

ON THE WEB

For more on the Center for Education Policy's surveys of No Child Left Behind, see www.cep-dc.org. For the official U.S. Department of Education site on NCLB, see www.ed.gov/nclb/landing.jhtml. For criticisms of NCLB, see http://nochildleft.com; www.educationsector.org.

The bottom line is that NCLB has greatly increased accountability pressures on schools, districts, and states. Progress on national tests has increased only a small amount since NCLB went into effect (Bracey, 2006; Fuller, Wright, Gesicki, & Kang, 2007), although there have been some gains on state tests (Center on Education Policy, 2007). Overall, *Time* magazine gave NCLB an F in helping schools to improve (Wallis & Steptoe, 2007) but praised its focus on accountability for all students.

■ Education Policies of the Obama Administration

As of this writing, the Obama administration, under Education Secretary Arne Duncan, is continuing many of the policies introduced in NCLB, but the administration and Congress are also working on many changes. Elements of the current Administration's policies can be characterized as follows.

1. Accountability for students' test scores remains strong, and Secretary Duncan is pressuring states to link student test score data to their individual teachers, so that this information can be used in decisions about teacher retention and promotion.

2. The administration is pressuring states to form regional or national consortia to agree on standards and assessments and remove some or all of the state-to-state variations in definitions of success.

3. The administration is encouraging states to make major changes in persistently failing schools, such as closing them, firing some or all of the staff, adopting proven

"turnaround" models, or allowing them to become charter schools. A charter school is a public school run by an organization separate from any school district that has greater freedom to hire and fire teachers, choose curricula, and set its own policies.

4. The administration strongly favors charter schools and is pressuring states to raise caps on the number of charters that can be issued in a given year.

5. Because of the huge amount of money being put into education as part of the Obama administration's American Reinvestment and Reform Act (ARRA), the administration is able to pressure states and districts to follow its priorities, as they will not receive ARRA funding if they do not.

For most teachers, the Obama administration's policies will not bring about major changes. Major new funding for schools is being offset in most places by the recession, and test-based accountability remains very important.

■ Benchmark Assessments

In test-obsessed American schools, you'd think the last thing we'd need is more tests. Yet many districts and states are administering **benchmark assessments** that assess children three, five, or even eight times a year, usually in reading and math.

The popularity of benchmark assessments is easy to understand. NCLB increased the already substantial pressure on schools to improve scores on their state tests. Yet state tests are given too infrequently and the scores arrive too late to be of much use in adjusting instructional policies or practices. For example, most states test in the spring. By the time scores are reported, it is summer or fall. A school might find out in July that its math scores are in trouble. Yet by July, schools have already committed their resources and made their plans for the coming year. Information from fourth-grade test scores, for example, cannot benefit the fourth-graders who took the test and may be too late to be of much value to fifth-graders or to the next group of fourth-graders.

Educators have long understood this problem and have long looked for solutions. Today, a wide array of benchmark assessments designed to give you useful early information on students' progress are available. Many districts and even individual teachers have designed and used their own benchmark assessments. Benchmark assessments allow you to identify how each student, class, subgroup, and school is doing on each of the objectives assessed by the state and emphasized in state and district standards, so you can target professional development and reform where they are needed most (Ainsworth & Viegut, 2006; Fogarty & Kerns, 2009; Odden & Archibald, 2009).

Benchmark assessments can allow schools to take their achievement "pulse," but as in medicine, taking a pulse does not constitute a cure. It's what the doctor and patient do next that matters. Similarly, a benchmark assessment tells schools where they're headed and where they need to focus, but use of benchmark assessments has not yet been shown in itself to increase student achievement.

Benchmark assessments are useful tools in the hands of enlightened educators, but they are nothing more than indicators of children's current achievement. As part of a comprehensive strategy for district and school reform, benchmark assessments can play a key supporting role, but only a supporting role (Chappuis & Chappuis, 2007/2008). If we're going to take even more of our children's precious class time for testing, we must use the results intelligently and proactively to improve core teaching and learning.

■ Data-Driven Reform

The movement toward the use of benchmark assessments is part of a broader trend toward using data to drive reforms in schools and districts. **Data-driven reform** goes beyond simply looking at scores on state tests. School leaders involved in such reforms organize information from state tests and benchmark assessments by subskill, subgroup,

benchmark assessments
Brief tests given every few months to help you know whether students are on track toward success on state standards.

data-driven reform
School reform strategies emphasizing careful analysis of data and implementation of proven programs to strengthen areas of need.

grade level, and other categories, adding information on attendance, dropout programs in use in schools, and so on to find "root causes" for the school's problems (Hamilton et al., 2008). They then carefully consider potential solutions to their problems, ideally programs with strong evidence of effectiveness (see Coalition for Evidence Based Policy, 2003; Slavin et al., 2010; Odden, 2009; Towne, Wise, & Winters, 2005), implement those solutions, and then continue to monitor benchmark and test data to see that they are working.

Heritage and Chen (2005) discuss an approach to data-driven reform that uses a Web-based tool called the Quality School Portfolio (QSP) to help school leaders organize and make sense of data. They then describe a process for using data to guide school reform:

1. *Determine what you want to know.* Data-based reform should begin with a problem that the educators involved want to solve or a question they want answered. No one pays attention to data that do not tell them something they want to know.

2. *Collect data.* Educators involved in data-based reform organize existing data and collect new data to answer the questions they have posed. The data could include state and benchmark tests, additional assessments (such as writing or math problem-solving assessments not part of the state test), information on materials and programs being used by teachers, teachers' and students' attitudes, or whatever else might inform decisions about reforms being considered (Bernhardt, 2003, 2005).

3. *Analyze results.* The next step is to organize the data, first simply computing averages and then using the data to test ideas about what is causing the problems the school is trying to solve. For example, imagine that a school has lower math scores than it likes. A school committee reviews the state test scores and quarterly benchmark scores, and they all tell the same story: Scores are low and not improving. Could it be that the teachers are not focusing on all skills tested? The committee looks at scores on portions of the test (e.g., fractions, geometry, word problems) and finds that the scores are low across the board. Could the problem be isolated to certain subgroups? The committee looks at scores for boys and girls, African Americans, Hispanics, and whites. They see one surprising pattern: Girls seem to be doing particularly poorly. The committee arranges to visit classes and see what is happening. When they return to discuss their findings, they have a whole new perspective on the data. Teachers throughout the school are making extensive use of traditional lectures and problem solving, as suggested by their textbooks. In many classes, an aggressive group of boys dominates the discussions, whereas most girls are bored and feel left out of the class activities. They found classes in which most girls never participated and did not say a single thing in a 50-minute lesson. Linking their quantitative data with their observations, the committee decides that the problem might be that teaching methods are not engaging all students.

4. *Set priorities and goals.* In data-based reform, it is not enough simply to know the data. The school must take action based on the data. This begins with setting priorities and goals for solutions the school might try. The goals should be measurable, focused on student achievement, realistic, and attainable (Bernhardt, 2005). In the case of the school with the math problem, the committee sets a goal of improving the math performance of all students, with a particular focus on the girls, and organizes a plan to closely monitor quarterly benchmark data.

5. *Develop strategies.* The most important step in data-driven reform is to develop specific strategies to solve identified problems. School leaders need to consider potential solutions for the problems they have observed. For example, to solve an achievement problem, the school might look at the federal What Works Clearinghouse (www.ies .ed.gov/ncee/wwc) or the *Best Evidence Encyclopedia* (www.bestevidence.org), both of which summarize scientific reviews of research on educational programs for grades pre-K to 12.

In the case of the school with the math problem, committee members look at the *Best Evidence Encyclopedia* and find that there is good evidence for cooperative learning in elementary math. They reason that this could increase the participation of all students. They find a local trainer to prepare the teachers in using cooperative learning in math, and over time, they begin to see their math benchmark scores improve. Later, when the state test scores came back, the committee is glad to see that math scores have improved for all students, but especially for girls, who are now fully engaged with math in all classrooms.

Allan Odden and his colleagues (Odden, 2009; Odden & Archibald, 2009) have done studies of schools and districts that make exceptional gains on state accountability tests. They found that successful schools and districts follow a path like the one just laid out. They look carefully at their own data, identify areas of need, select and carefully implement proven programs, and continuously use data to track their success in implementing new strategies. The Johns Hopkins University Center for Data-Driven Reform in Education (CDDRE) evaluated a district reform program of this kind in 59 high-poverty districts in seven states and found significant gains, especially in reading (Slavin et al., 2010). However, the gains did not appear when data analysis tools began to be used, but when schools in the districts began to select and implement proven reading and math programs.

▪ Value-Added Assessment Systems

A key issue in all assessment for accountability is dealing with the fact that schools are not equal in their student inputs. Those serving areas with many students who are disadvantaged or English learners face greater difficulties in reaching standards than do schools serving middle-class areas. One solution to this problem adopted by several states is to focus on what are called *value-added assessments,* determinations of how much learning a school has added to its students. The most widely known of these is the Educational Value-Added Assessment System (EVAAS), first used in Tennessee (as TVAAS) and later extended to several other states. The idea is that while not every school has an equal challenge in getting its students to pass state tests, they can be more legitimately compared on the degree to which they can move students forward from whatever baseline level of learning they start with (Sanders, 2000). As appealing as this idea is, value-added models have been criticized on technical grounds (e.g., Amrein-Beardsley, 2008, 2009; McCaffrey, Lockwood, Koretz, Louis, & Hamilton, 2004) as being potentially inaccurate, failing to account for student risk factors, and other problems. The concern is that using value-added scores as a basis for accountability will not solve the problem of inequalities in starting points, as high-poverty schools are still less likely to score well on value-added measures.

> **ON THE WEB**
>
> For more on data-driven reform, visit the What Works Clearinghouse (www.ies.ed.gov/ncee/wwc), Best Evidence Encyclopedia (www.bestevidence.org), the Center for Data-Driven Reform in Education (www.cddre.org), the Center for Research on Evaluation, Standards, and Student Testing (CRESST) (www.cse.ucla.edu), The Education Trust (www2.edtrust.org/edtrust), the Consortium for Policy Research in Education (www.cpre.wceruw.org), or the Education Resource Strategies (ERS) District Resource Allocation Modeler (DREAM) (www.erstools.org/mydream).

▪ Testing Accommodations for Students with Disabilities

How should students with disabilities participate in standardized testing? This question has taken on greater importance under No Child Left Behind, which requires progress in test scores for students with disabilities as a subgroup for schools to meet their adequate yearly progress standards.

Some kinds of accommodations, such as enlarging text for students with vision problems, are not controversial. Far more controversial are accommodations for students with learning disabilities, such as extending testing time and reading items to students. A review of many studies by Sireci and colleagues (2005) examined research on the effects of various accommodations. They found that extending testing time increases scores for all students (not only those with disabilities), although students with disabilities benefit more than other students. Reading items to students, however, is primarily beneficial to students with disabilities. Given these findings, it is important for policymakers to establish clear guidelines in accountability systems for when accommodations may and may not be used, to avoid biasing scores one way or the other.

■ Testing Accommodations for English Learners

NCLB, with its focus on accountability for the achievement of all subgroups, has heightened concern about the testing of English learners. Obviously, students who speak no English cannot respond meaningfully on tests given in English, but if English learners are excused from testing, there is a danger that their needs will not be addressed sufficiently (Kieffer, Lesaux, Rivera, & Francis, 2009). State accountability systems (as in Texas) have used tests in Spanish in the early grades. Other accommodations include rewriting tests to simplify the instructions or the items themselves, providing extra time, or presenting tests in two languages at the same time (English and the native language).

Chapter 14 Summary

What Are Standardized Tests and How Are They Used ?

The term *standardized* describes tests that are uniform in content, administration, and scoring and, therefore, allow for the comparison of results across classrooms, schools, and school districts. Standardized tests such as the SAT and CTBS measure individual performance or ability against standards, or norms, that have been established for many other students in the school district, state, or nation for which each test is designed. Standardized test scores are used for selection and placement, such as grade promotion or college admission; for diagnosis and remediation; for evaluation of student proficiency or progress in content areas; and for evaluation of teaching strategies, teachers, and schools.

What Types of Standardized Tests Are Given ?

Aptitude tests, such as tests of general intelligence and multifactor batteries, predict students' general abilities and preparation to learn. IQ tests administered to individuals or groups attempt to measure individual aptitude in the cognitive domain. Achievement tests assess student proficiency in various subject areas. Diagnostic tests focus on specific subject matter to discover strengths or weaknesses in mastery. Norm-referenced testing interprets scores in comparison with the scores of other people who took the test, and criterion-referenced testing interprets scores based on fixed performance criteria.

How Are Standardized Tests Interpreted ?

Scores that are derived from raw scores include percentiles, the percentage of scores in the norming group that fall below a particular score; grade equivalents, the grade and month at which a particular score is thought to represent typical performance; and standard scores, the students' performance in relation to the normal distribution of scores. Standard scores include stanines (based on the standard deviation of scores), normal curve equivalents (based on a comparison of scores with the normal distribution), and z-scores (the location of scores above or below the mean).

What Are Some Issues Concerning Standardized and Classroom Testing ?

Tests and test items must have validity, the quality of testing what is intended to be tested. Predictive validity means that the test accurately predicts future performance. Reliability means that test results are consistent when the test is administered at different places or times. Test bias in any form compromises validity. Other issues related to standardized testing include ethics in the content of tests, student preparation for testing, the uses of test scores, the relationship of tests to the curriculum, and computer administration of tests.

How Are You as an Educator Held Accountable for Student Achievement ?

Educators are increasingly held accountable for student achievement. Test scores are often used in decisions about hiring, firing, and promoting educators. Critics say that holding teachers accountable for student gains is unfair because of different student starting points and may encourage teaching to the test or adopting policies that artificially inflate standardized scores. An advantage of accountability is that it increases pressures on schools to pay attention to students who might otherwise fall through the cracks. Because accountability tests are based on standards about what should be learned, they can help clarify learning objectives.

The Intentional Teacher

USING WHAT YOU KNOW about Standardized Tests to Improve Teaching and Learning

Intentional teachers know that standardized tests can provide some—albeit limited—information about how teachers, schools, and students are performing. They can interpret standardized scores and use results from standardized tests for decision making. Intentional teachers rely on other assessment measures to complete the complicated picture of student learning.

1. What do I expect my students to know and be able to do at the end of this lesson? How does this contribute to course objectives and to students' needs to become capable individuals?

Explore the role of standardized testing in your locale. Talk with experienced colleagues and your administrators to determine the extent to which standardized tests play a role in your professional practice. Ask about district and local expectations for your use of standardized tests. Imagine that after a lunchtime conversation with some experienced peers, you (a first-year teacher in this district) perceive a sense of urgency surrounding standardized testing in this district. Knowing that parents and community members are highly interested in year-end results, you might take some time to reflect on your own position on standardized testing. You might ask yourself, "To what extent do standardized tests measure what we value here? What information do stan-

dardized tests provide that can be useful to my school? How do we continue to teach complex thinking and still help our students prepare for tests?" You might call your experienced colleagues and arrange a second lunch date to discuss your answers to tough questions such as these.

2. What knowledge, skills, needs, and interests do my students have that must be taken into account in my lesson?

Use formal standardized tests to provide information about your students' needs, such as diagnostic tests to identify learning problems and cognitive strengths. For example, imagine that Mindy reads at a level that appears to be far above that of her peers. She gives sophisticated analyses of the stories she reads, and although she is a willing learner, she sometimes appears bored with the curriculum. You might call the school psychologist to learn the procedure for obtaining formal testing to determine whether special services for students who are gifted and talented would be appropriate for Mindy.

3. What do I know about the content, child development, learning, motivation, and effective teaching strategies that I can use to accomplish my objectives?

The assessments that you use should provide information about each of your students in several domains. Ask yourself about one of your students—pick

Key Terms

Review the following key terms from the chapter.

achievement batteries   454
achievement tests   451
aptitude test   451
benchmark assessments   474
bias   466
chronological age   452
computer–adaptive   467
concurrent evidence   465
content evidence   465
criterion–related evidence   465
cutoff score   455
data-driven reform   474
derived scores   455
diagnostic tests   454
discriminant evidence   465
grade–equivalent scores   456

intelligence   452
mental age   452
multifactor aptitude battery   454
No Child Left Behind (NCLB)   469
normal curve equivalent   458
normal distribution   457
norms   449
percentile score   455
predictive evidence   465
reliability   465
standard deviation   457
standardized tests   448
stanine score   458
validity   464
z-score   458

INTASC   **7** Instructional Planning Skills   **9** Professional Commitment and Responsibility
8 Assessment of Student Learning

one at random—and consider how much you understand about this student's progress. Adjust your use of standardized tests, grades, and other assessment measures to provide more complete information about student learning. Although you might have taken a quick glance at each of your students' standardized scores from the previous year and you have your gradebook filled with letter grades at hand, you might still find yourself unable to give an accurate, trustworthy picture of many students' efforts to date. To round out your understanding of student learning, you could resolve to collect performance-based data through observations and attitudinal data through journal entries and interest inventories.

4. What instructional materials, technology, assistance, and other resources are available to help accomplish my objectives?

The public is increasingly interested in maintaining teachers' and schools' accountability. Check current sources such as your school's annual statement and newspaper reports to determine public perceptions of your success. To what extent do you consider public information a valid measure of schools' (and your!) success? Imagine that a recent newspaper article puts your mean students' districtwide performance at the 48th percentile. The headline of the article is "Pleasant City's Seventh-Graders Score Well on Standardized Tests!" How should you interpret this?

5. How will I plan to assess students' progress toward my objectives?

You should be a careful consumer when using standardized measures. Check information related to the content and the predictive and construct validity of the tests employed in your district. Ask for information related to test bias. If the information booklet that accompanies the teacher's packet on the state-wide test does not provide information about test bias, call the question hot line and ask how the authors have screened for bias against students from minority groups and students acquiring English.

6. How will I respond if individual children or the class as a whole are not on track toward success? What is my back-up plan?

If your students take a standardized test that has consequences for them (such as grade-to-grade promotion), be sure to examine test scores to ascertain that they make sense. If a test score seems too low for a student who you see doing well in class, ask whether the student can be retested, perhaps using a different test format.

Self-Assessment: Practicing for Licensure

Directions: The chapter-opening vignette addresses indicators that are often assessed in state licensure exams. Re-read the chapter-opening vignette and then respond to the following questions.

1. Ms. Tranh speaks to Anita's parents about the many measures of achievement available to assess Anita's academic ability. Which of the following types of assessment would Ms. Tranh use to predict Anita's future performance?

   a. Placement test

   b. Achievement test

   c. Aptitude test

   d. Diagnostic test

2. Which of the following interpretations would Ms. Tranh make if Anita were to score at the mean of a standardized test?

   a. percentile = 90, stanine = 0, z = 20

   b. NCE = 50, z = 0, percentile = 50

   c. GE = 7.2, stanine = 5, NCE = 45

   d. z = 1, NCE = 60, percentile = 50

3. Ms. Tranh tells Mr. and Mrs. McKay that Anita's grade equivalent score on the CAT is 6.9. What does this mean?

   a. Anita is almost ready for seventh-grade work.

   b. Anita found the test very easy.

   c. Anita has done as well as an end-of-year sixth-grader.

   d. Anita scored at the 6.9 percentile.

4. Ms. Tranh compares her students' scores on a math test with those of another class. She finds that the students' average score in both classes is 75, but the students in her class have scores that are much more spread out. This means that Ms. Tranh's results will have a larger

   a. mean.

   b. median.

   c. standard deviation.

   d. normal curve.

5. If Anita scored consistently on the CAT over multiple applications, it can be said that the test has

   a. predictive validity.

   b. content validity.

   c. construct validity.

   d. reliability.

6. Write a short essay describing the advantages and major criticisms of standardized tests.

7. What are the advantages and disadvantages of absolute grading and relative grading standards?

PEARSON
myeducationlab

Go to the Topic **Assessment** in the MyEducationLab (www.myeducationlab.com) for your course, where you can:

- Find learning outcomes for **Assessment** along with the national standards that connect to these outcomes.

- Complete Assignments and Activities that can help you more deeply understand the chapter content.

- Apply and practice your understanding of the core teaching skills identified in the chapter with the Building Teaching Skills and Dispositions learning units.

- Examine challenging situations and cases presented in the IRIS Center Resources.

- Access video clips of CCSSO National Teachers of the Year award winners responding to the question "Why Do I Teach?" in the Teacher Talk section.

- Check your comprehension of the content covered in the chapter by going to the Study Plan in the

Book Resources for your text. Here you will be able to take a chapter quiz; receive feedback on your answers; and then access Review, Practice, and Enrichment activities to enhance your understanding of chapter content.

- Watch author Bob Slavin present a Personal Reflections podcast on *Mixed Messages* in the Book Resources for your text. Then, respond to the reflection questions that follow.

Mixed Messages

YOUR REFLECTIONS What are some potential negative ramifications of cutbacks to non-core-curricular programs in schools? Who has to pick up the slack in these areas when schools no longer offer such programs? Do you think all communities are affected equally by such cutbacks, regardless of socioeconomic conditions?

Appendix

Using This Text to Prepare for the Praxis™ Principles of Learning and Teaching Exam

Topics Covered on the Praxis™ Exam for the Principles of Learning and Teaching (PLT Tests)	Chapter Content Aligned with Praxis™ Topics
I. Students as Learners (approximately 33 percent of total test)	
A. Student Development and the Learning Process	
1. Theoretical foundations about how learning occurs: how students construct knowledge, acquire skills, and develop habits of mind	**Chapter 2:** Cognitive, Language, and Literacy Development ■ How Do Children Develop Cognitively? (pp. 29–30) ■ How Did Piaget View Cognitive Development? (pp. 31–40) ■ How Did Vygotsky View Cognitive Development? (pp. 41–44) **Chapter 5:** Behavioral Theories of Learning (Entire Chapter) **Chapter 6:** Information Processing and Cognitive Theories of Learning (Entire Chapter) **Chapter 8:** Student-Centered and Constructivist Approaches to Instruction (Entire Chapter) *Important terms related to learning theory:* Chapter 2 Key Terms (p. 50) Chapter 5 Key Terms (p. 140) Chapter 6 Key Terms (p. 179) Chapter 8 Key Terms (p. 246)

2. Human development in the physical, social, emotional, moral, and cognitive domains	**Chapter 2:** Cognitive, Language, and Literacy Development (Entire Chapter)
	
	Chapter 3: Social, Moral, and Emotional Development
	■ What Are Some Views of Personal and Social Development?
	  • Erickson's Stages of Psychosocial Development (pp. 54–56)
	■ What Are Some Views of Moral Development?
	  • Piaget's Theory of Moral Development (pp. 57–58)
	  • Kohlberg's Stages of Moral Reasoning (pp. 58–60)
	■ How Do Children Develop Socially and Emotionally? (pp. 61–72)
	
	Chapter 5: Behavioral Theories of Learning
	■ What Are Behavioral Learning Theories?
	  • Pavlov: Classical Conditioning (p. 117)
	  • Skinner: Operant Conditioning (pp. 117–119)
	■ How Has Social Learning Theory Contributed to Our Understanding of Human Learning?
	  • Bandura: Modeling and Observational Learning (pp. 132–134)
	  • Meichenbaum's Model of Self-Regulated Learning (pp. 134–136)
	
	Chapter 6: Information Processing and Cognitive Theories of Learning
	■ What Is Learned from Research on the Brain?
	  • Applications of Brain Research to Classroom Teaching (pp. 156–158)
	■ What Makes Information Meaningful?
	  • Schema Theory (pp. 167–168)
	■ How Do Cognitive Teaching Strategies Help Students Learn?
	  • Making Learning Relevant and Activating Prior Knowledge (pp. 172–175)
	
	Chapter 8: Student-Centered and Constructivist Approaches to Instruction
	■ What Is the Constructivist View of Learning?
	  • Self-Regulated Learning (p. 222)

Topics Covered on the Praxis™ Exam for the Principles of Learning and Teaching (PLT Tests)	Chapter Content Aligned with Praxis™ Topics
I. Students as Learners (approximately 33 percent of total test) *(continued)*	
B. Students as Diverse Learners	

1. Differences in the ways students learn and perform	**Chapter 2:** Cognitive, Language, and Literacy Development
	■ How Did Piaget View Cognitive Development?
	  • Piaget's Stages of Development (pp. 32–39)
	■ How Did Vygotsky View Cognitive Development? (pp. 41–44)
	
	Chapter 4: Student Diversity
	■ How Does Socioeconomic Status Affect Student Achievement? (pp. 80–89)
	■ How Do Ethnicity and Race Affect Students' School Experiences? (pp. 89–94)
	■ How Do Language Differences and Bilingual Programs Affect Student Achievement? (pp. 95–98)
	■ *Theory into Practice:* Teaching English Learners (pp. 96–97)
	■ How Do Gender and Gender Bias Affect Students' School Experiences? (pp. 100–102)
	■ How Do Students Differ in Intelligence and Learning Styles?
	  • Definitions of Intelligence (p. 104)
	  • Theories of Learning Styles (p. 107)
	
	Chapter 6: Information Processing and Cognitive Theories of Learning
	■ What Is an Information-Processing Model? (pp. 144–153)
	■ How Can Memory Strategies be Taught?
	  • Verbal Learning (p. 163)
	
	Chapter 12: Learners with Exceptionalities
	■ What Are Effective Strategies for Students with Disabilities in General Education?
	  • Teaching Learning Strategies and Metacognitive Awareness (p. 386)

2. Areas of exceptionality in students' learning	**Chapter 12:** Learners with Exceptionalities
	■ Who Are Learners with Exceptionalities?
	  • Types of Exceptionalities and the Numbers of Students Served (pp. 355–356)
	  • Students with Mental Retardation (pp. 357–358)
	  • Students with Learning Disabilities (pp. 359–362)
	  • Students with Attention Deficit Hyperactivity Disorder (pp. 362–363)
	  • Students with Speech or Language Impairments (pp. 363–364)
	  • Students with Emotional and Behavioral Disorders (pp. 364–366)
	  • Students with Autism Spectrum Disorder (p. 366)
	  • Students with Sensory, Physical, and Health Impairments (pp. 366–368)
	  • Students Who Are Gifted and Talented (pp. 368–369)

3. Legislation and institutional responsibilities relating to exceptional students	**Chapter 12:** Learners with Exceptionalities
	■ What Is Special Education?
	  • Public Law 94-142 and IDEA (pp. 370–372)
	  • An Array of Special-Education Services (pp. 372–375)
	■ What Is Inclusion? (pp. 381–384)

4. Approaches for accommodating various learning styles, intelligences, or exceptionalities	**Chapter 8:** Student-Centered and Constructivist Approaches to Instruction
	■ What Is the Constructivist View of Learning?
	  • Discovery Learning (p. 222)
	  • Scaffolding (pp. 222–223)

Topics Covered on the Praxis™ Exam for the Principles of Learning and Teaching (PLT Tests)	Chapter Content Aligned with Praxis™ Topics
I. Students as Learners (approximately 33 percent of total test) *(continued)*	
B. Students as Diverse Learners *(continued)*	

4. Approaches for accommodating various learning styles, intelligences, or exceptionalities *(continued)*	**Chapter 9:** Grouping, Differentiation, and Technology ■ How Are Students Grouped to Accommodate Achievement Differences? (pp. 253–259) ■ What Are Some Ways of Differentiating Instruction? (pp. 259–262) **Chapter 12:** Learners with Exceptionalities ■ What Are Effective Strategies for Students with Disabilities in General Education? • Adapting Instruction (pp. 384–386) • Teaching Learning Strategies and Metacognitive Awareness (p. 386) • Prevention and Early Intervention (p. 386) • Tutoring and Small-Group Interventions for Struggling Readers (p. 386) • Computers and Students with Disabilities (pp. 387–388) • Buddy Systems and Peer Tutoring (pp. 387–389) • Special-Education Teams (p. 389) • Social Integration of Students with Disabilities (pp. 390–391) **Chapter 13:** Assessing Student Learning ■ What Are Authentic, Portfolio, and Performance Assessments? (pp. 429–433) **Chapter 14:** Standardized Tests and Accountability ■ What Are Standardized Tests and How Are They Used? (pp. 448–451) ■ What Are Some Issues Concerning Standardized and Classroom Testing? (pp. 464–467) ■ *Theory into Practice:* Teaching Test-Taking Skills (p. 470) ■ How Are You as an Educator Held Accountable for Student Achievement? • Testing Accommodations for Students with Disabilities (p. 476) • Testing Accommodations for English Learners (p. 477)
5. Process of second language acquisition and strategies to support the learning of students for whom English is not a first language	**Chapter 2:** Cognitive, Language, and Literacy Development ■ How Do Language and Literacy Develop? (pp. 44–47) **Chapter 4:** Student Diversity ■ How Do Language Differences and Bilingual Programs Affect Student Achievement? • Bilingual Education (pp. 95–96) ■ *Theory into Practice:* Teaching English Learners (pp. 96–98)
6. Understanding of influences of individual experiences, talents, and prior learning, as well as language, culture, family, and community values on students' learning	**Chapter 2:** Cognitive, Language, and Literacy Development ■ How Did Piaget View Cognitive Development? (pp. 31–40) ■ How Did Vygotsky View Cognitive Development? (pp. 41–44) ■ How Do Language and Literacy Develop? (pp. 44–47) **Chapter 3:** Social, Moral, and Emotional Development ■ What Are Some Views of Personal and Social Development? • Erickson's Stages of Psychosocial Development (pp. 54–56) ■ What Are Some Views of Moral Development? • Piaget's Theory of Moral Development (pp. 57–58) • Kohlberg's Stages of Moral Reasoning (pp. 58–61) ■ How Do Children Develop Socially and Emotionally? (pp. 61–74) **Chapter 4:** Student Diversity ■ What Is the Impact of Culture on Teaching and Learning? (p. 80) ■ How Does Socioeconomic Status Affect Student Achievement? (pp. 80–89) ■ How Do Ethnicity and Race Affect Students' School Experiences? (pp. 89–95) ■ How Do Language Differences and Bilingual Programs Affect Student Achievement? (pp. 95–98)

Topics Covered on the Praxis™ Exam for the Principles of Learning and Teaching (PLT Tests)	Chapter Content Aligned with Praxis™ Topics
I. Students as Learners (approximately 33 percent of total test) *(continued)*	
B. Students as Diverse Learners *(continued)*	
	Chapter 6: Information Processing and Cognitive Theories of Learning ■ What Makes Information Meaningful? • Schema Theory (p. 167) ■ How Do Cognitive Teaching Strategies Help Students Learn? • Making Learning Relevant and Activating Prior Knowledge (pp. 172–176) **Chapter 8:** Student-Centered and Constructivist Approaches to Instruction ■ What Is the Constructivist View of Learning? (pp. 218–225)
C. Student Motivation and the Learning Environment	
1. Theoretical foundations about human motivation behavior	**Chapter 3:** Social, Moral, and Emotional Development ■ What Are Some Views of Personal and Social Development? • Erickson's Stages of Psychosocial Development (pp. 54–56) ■ How Do Children Develop Socially and Emotionally? (pp. 61–72) **Chapter 5:** Behavioral Theories of Learning ■ What Are Behavioral Learning Theories? • Pavlov: Classical Conditioning (p. 117) • Skinner: Operant Conditioning (pp. 117–119) **Chapter 10:** Motivating Students to Learn ■ What Is Motivation? (p. 286) ■ What Are Some Theories of Motivation? • Motivation and Behavioral Learning Theory (pp. 287–288) • Motivation and Human Needs (pp. 288–289) • Motivation and Attribution Theory (pp. 289–292) • Motivation and Self-Regulated Learning (pp. 293–294) • Motivation and Expectancy Theory (pp. 294–295)
2. How knowledge of human motivation and behavior should influence strategies for organizing and supporting individual and group work in the classroom	**Chapter 7:** The Effective Lesson ■ How Are Discussions Used in Instruction? • Subjective and Controversial Topics (p. 208) • Whole-Class Discussions (pp. 209–210) • Small-Group Discussions (pp. 210–211) **Chapter 8:** Student-Centered and Constructivist Approaches to Instruction ■ How Is Cooperative Learning Used in Instruction? • Cooperative Learning Methods (pp. 230–234) • Research on Cooperative Learning (pp. 234–236) ■ How Are Problem-Solving and Thinking Skills Taught? (pp. 236–239) **Chapter 10:** Motivating Students to Learn ■ How Can Achievement Motivation Be Enhanced? (pp. 295–300) ■ How Can Teachers Increase Students' Motivation to Learn? (pp. 300–309)
3. Factors and situations that are likely to promote or diminish students' motivation to learn; how to help students become self-motivated	**Chapter 3:** Social, Moral, and Emotional Development ■ How Do Children Develop Socially and Emotionally? (pp. 61–74) **Chapter 4:** Student Diversity ■ What Is the Impact of Culture on Teaching and Learning? (p. 80) ■ How Does Socioeconomic Status Affect Student Achievement? • Promoting Resilience among Students Who Are Disadvantaged (p. 85) **Chapter 5:** Behavioral Theories of Learning ■ How Has Social Learning Theory Contributed to Our Understanding of Human Learning? • Meichenbaum's Model of Self-Regulated Learning (pp. 134–137)

Topics Covered on the Praxis™ Exam for the Principles of Learning and Teaching (PLT Tests)	Chapter Content Aligned with Praxis™ Topics

II. Instruction and Assessment (approximately 33 percent of total test)

A. Instructional Strategies

1. The major cognitive processes associated with student learning

Chapter 2: Cognitive, Language, and Literacy Development (Entire Chapter)
- *Theory into Practice:* Educational Implications of Piaget's Theory (pp. 39–40)
- *Theory into Practice:* Classroom Applications of Vygotsky's Theory (pp. 43–44)
- *Theory into Practice:* Promoting Literacy Development in Young Children (pp. 46–47)

Chapter 5: Behavioral Theories of Learning
- How Has Social Learning Theory Contributed to Our Understanding of Human Learning?
  - Bandura: Modeling and Observational Learning (pp. 132–134)
  - Meichenbaum's Model of Self-Regulated Learning (pp. 134–136)

Chapter 6: Information Processing and Cognitive Theories of Learning
- What Is an Information-Processing Model?
  - Short-Term or Working Memory (pp. 146–149)
  - Long-Term Memory (pp. 149–152)
  - Factors That Enhance Long-Term Memory (p. 152)
  - Other Information-Processing Models (pp. 152–153)
- How Can Memory Strategies Be Taught?
  - Verbal Learning (pp. 163–165)
- How Do Metacognitive Skills Help Students Learn? (pp. 168–169)

Chapter 7: The Effective Lesson
- How Do Students Learn and Transfer Concepts? (pp. 203–207)

Chapter 8: Student-Centered and Constructivist Approaches to Instruction
- How Are Problem-Solving and Thinking Skills Taught?
  - The Problem-Solving Process (pp. 236–238)
  - Teaching Creative Problem Solving (pp. 238–239)
  - Teaching Thinking Skills (pp. 240–242)
  - Critical Thinking (pp. 242–243)

2. Major categories, advantages, and appropriate uses of instructional strategies

Chapter 1: Educational Psychology: A Foundation for Teaching
- What Makes a Good Teacher? (pp. 2–8)

Chapter 6: Information Processing and Cognitive Theories of Learning
- *The Intentional Teacher:* Using What You Know about Cognitive Theories of Learning to Improve Teaching and Learning (pp. 176–177)

Chapter 7: The Effective Lesson
- What Is Direct Instruction? (p. 184)
- How Is a Direct Instruction Lesson Taught? (pp. 185–203)
- How Do Students Learn and Transfer Concepts? (pp. 203–207)
- How Are Discussions Used in Instruction?
  - Whole-Class Discussions (p. 209)
  - Small-Group Discussions (pp. 210–211)

Chapter 8: Student-Centered and Constructivist Approaches to Instruction
- What Is the Constructivist View of Learning?
  - Constructivist Methods in the Content Areas (pp. 225–229)

Chapter 12: Learners with Exceptionalities
- What Are Effective Strategies for Students with Disabilities in General Education? (pp. 384–391)

Chapter 13: Assessing Student Learning
- What Are Instructional Objectives and How Are They Used? (pp. 398–407)
- What Are Authentic, Portfolio, and Performance Assessments? (pp. 429–433)

Topics Covered on the Praxis™ Exam for the Principles of Learning and Teaching (PLT Tests)	Chapter Content Aligned with Praxis™ Topics
II. Instruction and Assessment (approximately 33 percent of total test) *(continued)*	
A. Instructional Strategies *(continued)*	

3. Principles, techniques, and methods associated with major instructional strategies, especially direct instruction and student-centered models	**Chapter 7:** The Effective Lesson
	■ What Is Direct Instruction? (pp. 184–185)
	■ How Is a Direct Instruction Lesson Taught? (pp. 185–203)
	■ How Do Students Learn and Transfer Concepts? (pp. 203–207)
	■ How Are Discussions Used in Instruction?
	  • Whole-Class Discussions (pp. 209–210)
	  • Small-Group Discussions (pp. 210–211)
	■ *The Intentional Teacher:* Using What You Know about Direct Instruction to Improve Teaching and Learning (pp. 212–213)
	
	Chapter 8: Student-Centered and Constructivist Approaches to Instruction
	■ What Is the Constructivist View of Learning?
	  • Constructivist Methods in the Content Areas (pp. 225–229)
	■ How Is Cooperative Learning Used in Instruction? (pp. 229–236)
	■ *The Intentional Teacher:* Using What You Know about Student-Centered and Constructivist Approaches to Improve Teaching and Learning (pp. 244–245)

4. Methods for enhancing student learning through the use of a variety of resources and materials	**Chapter 2:** Cognitive, Language, and Literacy Development
	■ *Theory into Practice:* Educational Implications of Piaget's Theory (pp. 39–40)
	■ *Theory into Practice:* Classroom Applications of Vygotsky's Theory (pp. 43–44)
	■ *Theory into Practice:* Building Vocabulary in Elementary and Secondary Schools (p. 47)
	■ *The Intentional Teacher:* Using What You Know about Development to Improve Teaching and Learning (pp. 48–49)
	
	Chapter 7: The Effective Lesson
	■ *The Intentional Teacher:* Using What You Know about Direct Instruction to Improve Teaching and Learning (pp. 212–213)
	
	Chapter 8: Student-Centered and Constructivist Approaches to Instruction
	■ *The Intentional Teacher:* Using What You Know about Student-Centered and Constructivist Approaches to Improve Teaching and Learning (pp. 244–245)
	
	Chapter 9: Grouping, Differentiation, and Technology
	■ How Is Technology Used in Education?
	  • Technology for Teaching (pp. 268–270)
	  • The Internet for Teachers (p. 270)
	  • Technology for Learning (pp. 270–273)
	  • The Internet for Students (pp. 273–276)
	  • Web 2.0 (p. 276)
	  • Instructional Television and Embedded Multimedia (p. 276)
	
	Chapter 12: Learners with Exceptionalities
	■ What Are Effective Strategies for Students with Disabilities in General Education?
	  • Computers and Students with Disabilities (pp. 387–388)

B. Planning Instruction	
1. Techniques for planning instruction, including addressing curriculum goals, incorporating learning theory, subject matter, curriculum development, and student development and interests	**Chapter 2:** Cognitive, Language, and Literacy Development (Entire Chapter) ■ *Theory into Practice:* Educational Implications of Piaget's Theory (pp. 39–40) ■ *Theory into Practice:* Classroom Applications of Vygotsky's Theory (pp. 43–44) ■ *Theory into Practice:* Promoting Literacy Development in Young Children (p. 46)

Topics Covered on the Praxis™ Exam for the Principles of Learning and Teaching (PLT Tests)	Chapter Content Aligned with Praxis™ Topics
II. Instruction and Assessment (approximately 33 percent of total test) *(continued)*	
B. Planning Instruction *(continued)*	

Chapter 4: Student Diversity
- *Theory into Practice:* Teaching in a Culturally Diverse School (pp. 94–95)

Chapter 5: Behavioral Theories of Learning
- How Has Social Learning Theory Contributed to Our Understanding of Human Learning? (pp. 132–136)

Chapter 6: Information Processing and Cognitive Theories of Learning
- How Do Cognitive Teaching Strategies Help Students Learn? (pp. 171–176)
- *The Intentional Teacher:* Using What You Know about Cognitive Theories of Learning to Improve Teaching and Learning (pp. 176–177)

Chapter 7: The Effective Lesson
- *Theory into Practice:* Planning a Lesson (pp. 188–189)
- *The Intentional Teacher:* Using What You Know about Direct Instruction to Improve Teaching and Learning (pp. 212–213)

Chapter 8: Student-Centered and Constructivist Approaches to Instruction
- *The Intentional Teacher:* Using What You Know about Student-Centered and Constructivist Approaches to Improve Teaching and Learning (pp. 244–245)

Chapter 9: Grouping, Differentiation, and Technology
- What Are Elements of Effective Instruction beyond a Good Lesson? (pp. 250–253)

Chapter 13: Assessing Student Learning
- What Are Instructional Objectives and How Are They Used?
  - Planning Lesson Objectives (pp. 398–403)
  - Aligning Objectives and Assessment (pp. 404–405)
  - Using Taxonomies of Instructional Objectives (pp. 405–407)
- Why Is Evaluation Important? (pp. 408–410)

Chapter 14: Standardized Tests and Accountability
- How Are You as an Educator Held Accountable for Student Achievement? (pp. 467–478)

2. Techniques for creating effective bridges between curriculum goals and students' experiences

Chapter 5: Behavioral Theories of Learning
- What Are Some Principles of Behavioral Learning? (pp. 119–132)
- How Has Social Learning Theory Contributed to Our Understanding of Human Learning?
  - Bandura: Modeling and Observational Learning (pp. 132–134)

Chapter 6: Information Processing and Cognitive Theories of Learning
- How Do Metacognitive Skills Help Students Learn? (pp. 168–169)
- What Study Strategies Help Students Learn? (pp. 169–171)
- How Do Cognitive Teaching Strategies Help Students Learn? (pp. 171–176)
- *The Intentional Teacher:* Using What You Know about Cognitive Theories of Learning to Improve Teaching and Learning (pp. 176–177)

Chapter 7: The Effective Lesson
- *Theory into Practice:* Planning a Lesson (pp. 188–189)
- How Is a Direct Instruction Lesson Taught?
  - Review Prerequisites (pp. 190–191)
  - Present New Material (pp. 191–193)
  - Conduct Learning Probes (pp. 193–199)
  - Provide Independent Practice (pp. 199–201)
- *The Intentional Teacher:* Using What You Know about Direct Instruction to Improve Teaching and Learning (pp. 212–213)

Topics Covered on the Praxis™ Exam for the Principles of Learning and Teaching (PLT Tests)	Chapter Content Aligned with Praxis™ Topics

II. Instruction and Assessment (approximately 33 percent of total test) *(continued)*

B. Planning Instruction *(continued)*

Chapter 8: Student-Centered and Constructivist Approaches to Instruction
- What Is the Constructivist View of Learning? (pp. 218–229)
- How Is Cooperative Learning Used in Instruction?
  - Cooperative Learning Methods (pp. 230–234)
- How Are Problem-Solving and Thinking Skills Taught? (pp. 236–243)
- *The Intentional Teacher:* Using What You Know about Student-Centered and Constructivist Approaches to Improve Teaching and Learning (pp. 244–245)

Chapter 9: Grouping, Differentiation, and Technology
- What Are Elements of Effective Instruction beyond a Good Lesson? (pp. 250–253)
- What Are Some Ways of Differentiating Instruction?
  - Peer Tutoring (p. 260)
  - Tutoring by Teachers (p. 261)

Chapter 12: Learners with Exceptionalities
- What Are Effective Strategies for Students with Disabilities in General Education?
  - Adapting Instruction (pp. 384–386)
  - Teaching Learning Strategies and Metacognitive Awareness (p. 386)
  - Prevention and Early Intervention (p. 386)
  - Tutoring and Small-Group Interventions for Struggling Readers (pp. 386–387)
  - Computers and Students with Disabilities (pp. 387–388)
  - Buddy Systems and Peer Tutoring (pp. 387–389)
  - Special-Education Teams (p. 389)
  - Social Integration of Students with Disabilities (pp. 390–391)

Chapter 13: Assessing Student Learning
- *Theory into Practice:* Making Assessments Fair (pp. 415–418)

C. Assessment Strategies

1. Types of assessments

Chapter 7: The Effective Lesson
- How Is a Direct Instruction Lesson Taught?
  - Assess Performance and Provide Feedback (p. 201)
- *Theory into Practice:* Assessment for Learning (pp. 196–197)

Chapter 13: Assessing Student Learning
- How Are Tests Constructed?
  - Writing Selected-Response Test Items (pp. 418–421)
  - Writing Constructed-Response Items (p. 422)
  - Writing and Evaluating Essay Tests (pp. 423–426)
  - Writing and Evaluating Problem-Solving Items (pp. 426–429)
- What Are Authentic, Portfolio, and Performance Assessments?
  - Portfolio Assessment (p. 430)
  - Performance Assessment (pp. 432–433)

Chapter 14: Standardized Tests and Accountability
- What Are Standardized Tests and How Are They Used? (pp. 448–451)
- What Types of Standardized Tests Are Given?
  - Aptitude Tests (pp. 452–454)
  - Norm-Referenced Achievement Tests (pp. 454–455)
  - Criterion-Referenced Achievement Tests (p. 455)
- How Are You as an Educator Held Accountable for Student Achievement?
  - Benchmark Assessments (p. 474)
  - Data-Driven Reform (pp. 474–476)
  - Value-Added Assessment Systems (p. 476)

Topics Covered on the Praxis™ Exam for the Principles of Learning and Teaching (PLT Tests)	Chapter Content Aligned with Praxis™ Topics
II. Instruction and Assessment (approximately 33 percent of total test) *(continued)*	
C. Assessment Strategies *(continued)*	

2. Characteristics of assessments

Chapter 13: Assessing Student Learning
- How Are Tests Constructed? (pp. 413–429)
- What Are Authentic, Portfolio, and Performance Assessments?
  - Effectiveness of Performance Assessments (pp. 432–433)

Chapter 14: Standardized Tests and Accountability
- What Types of Standardized Tests Are Given? (pp. 451–455)

3. Scoring assessments

Chapter 7: The Effective Lesson
- How Is a Direct Instruction Lesson Taught?
  - Assess Performance and Provide Feedback (p. 201)
- *Theory into Practice:* Assessment for Learning (pp. 196–197)

Chapter 13: Assessing Student Learning
- *Theory into Practice:* Peer Evaluations (pp. 426–429)
- What Are Authentic, Portfolio, and Performance Assessments?
  - Scoring Rubrics for Performance Assessments (p. 433)
- How Are Grades Determined? (pp. 433–442)

Chapter 14: Standardized Tests and Accountability
- How Are Standardized Tests Interpreted?
  - Standard Setting (p. 455)

4. Uses of assessments

Chapter 7: The Effective Lesson
- *Theory into Practice:* Assessment for Learning (pp. 196–197)

Chapter 9: Grouping, Differentiation, and Technology
- How Are Students Grouped to Accommodate Achievement Differences? (pp. 253–259)

Chapter 10: Motivating Students to Learn
- *Theory into Practice:* Giving Students Motivating Feedback (pp. 293–294)
- How Can Achievement Motivation Be Enhanced? (pp. 295–300)

Chapter 13: Assessing Student Learning
- Why Is Evaluation Important?
  - Evaluation as Feedback (pp. 408–409)
  - Evaluation as Information (pp. 409–410)
  - Evaluation as Incentive (p. 410)

Chapter 14: Standardized Tests and Accountability
- What Are Standardized Tests and How Are They Used?
  - Diagnosis (p. 450)
  - School Improvement (p. 451)

5. Understanding of measurement theory and assessment-related issues

Chapter 13: Assessing Student Learning
- Why Is Evaluation Important? (pp. 408–410)
- How Is Student Learning Evaluated? (pp. 410–413)
- How Are Tests Constructed? (pp. 413–429)

Chapter 14: Standardized Tests and Accountability
- What Are Standardized Tests and How Are They Used?
  - Selection and Placement (p. 449)
  - Diagnosis (p. 450)
  - Evaluation and Accountability (p. 450)
  - School Improvement (p. 451)
- What Are Some Issues Concerning Standardized and Classroom Testing? (pp. 464–467)

Topics Covered on the Praxis™ Exam for the Principles of Learning and Teaching (PLT Tests)	Chapter Content Aligned with Praxis™ Topics

II. Instruction and Assessment (approximately 33 percent of total test) *(continued)*

C. Assessment Strategies *(continued)*

5. Understanding of measurement theory and assessment-related issues *(continued)*	■ How Are You as an Educator Held Accountable for Student Achievement?
	  • No Child Left Behind (pp. 469–474)
	  • Benchmark Assessments (p. 474)
	  • Testing Accommodations for Students with Disabilities (pp. 476–477)
	  • Testing Accommodations for English Learners (p. 477)

6. Interpreting and communicating results of assessments	**Chapter 7:** The Effective Lesson
	■ How Is a Direct Instruction Lesson Taught?
	  • Assess Performance and Provide Feedback (p. 201)
	
	Chapter 13: Assessing Student Learning
	■ Why Is Evaluation Important? (p. 408)
	■ How Is Student Learning Evaluated?
	  • Formative and Summative Evaluations (pp. 410–411)
	  • Norm-Referenced and Criterion-Referenced Evaluations (p. 411)
	  • Matching Evaluation Strategies with Goals (pp. 412–413)
	
	Chapter 14: Standardized Tests and Accountability
	■ How Are Standardized Tests Interpreted?
	  • Percentile Scores (p. 455)
	  • Grade-Equivalent Scores (p. 456)
	  • Standard Scores (p. 456)
	■ *Theory into Practice:* Interpreting Standardized Test Scores (pp. 459–464)

III. Communication Techniques (approximately 11 percent of total test)

A. Basic, effective verbal and nonverbal communication techniques	**Chapter 2:** Cognitive, Language, and Literacy Development (Entire Chapter)
	■ How Do Language and Literacy Develop? (pp. 44–46)
	■ *Theory into Practice:* Promoting Literacy Development in Young Children (p. 46)
	
	Chapter 3: Social, Moral, and Emotional Development
	■ How Do Children Develop Socially and Emotionally? (pp. 61–74)
	■ *Theory into Practice:* Helping Children Develop Social Skills (p. 67)
	
	Chapter 7: The Effective Lesson
	■ How Are Discussions Used in Instruction? (pp. 208–211)
	■ *The Intentional Teacher:* Using What You Know about Direct Instruction to Improve Teaching and Learning (pp. 212–213)
	
	Chapter 8: Student-Centered and Constructivist Approaches to Instruction
	■ What Is the Constructivist View of Learning? (pp. 218–225)
	■ *The Intentional Teacher:* Using What You Know about Student-Centered and Constructivist Approaches to Improve Teaching and Learning (pp. 244–245)
	
	Chapter 11: Effective Learning Environments
	■ What Practices Contribute to Effective Classroom Management? (pp. 326–328)
	■ What Are Some Strategies for Managing Routine Misbehavior?
	  • Prevention (pp. 329–330)
	  • Nonverbal Cues (pp. 330–331)
	  • Praising Behavior That Is Incompatible with Misbehavior (p. 331)
	  • Praising Other Students (p. 331)
	  • Verbal Reminders (p. 331)

Topics Covered on the Praxis™ Exam for the Principles of Learning and Teaching (PLT Tests)	Chapter Content Aligned with Praxis™ Topics

III. Communication Techniques (approximately 11 percent of total test) *(continued)*

B. Effect of cultural and gender differences on communications in the classroom

Chapter 4: Student Diversity
- What Is the Impact of Culture on Teaching and Learning? (p. 80)
- How Does Socioeconomic Status Affect Student Achievement? (pp. 80–89)
- How Do Ethnicity and Race Affect Students' School Experiences? (p. 89–95)
- How Do Language Differences and Bilingual Programs Affect Student Achievement? (pp. 95–98)
- How Do Gender and Gender Bias Affect Students' School Experiences? (pp. 100–103)

C. Types of communication and interactions that can stimulate discussion in different ways for particular purposes

Chapter 3: Social, Moral, and Emotional Development
- How Do Children Develop Socially and Emotionally? (pp. 61–74)

Chapter 6: Information Processing and Cognitive Theories of Learning
- How Do Cognitive Teaching Strategies Help Students Learn?
  - Making Learning Relevant and Activating Prior Knowledge (pp. 172–174)

Chapter 7: The Effective Lesson
- How Is a Direct Instruction Lesson Taught?
  - Present New Material (pp. 191–193)
  - Conduct Learning Probes (pp. 193–196)
- How Do Students Learn and Transfer Concepts? (pp. 203–207)
- How Are Discussions Used in Instruction? (pp. 208–211)

Chapter 8: Student-Centered and Constructivist Approaches to Instruction
- What Is the Constructivist View of Learning?
  - Cooperative Learning (pp. 220–221)
  - Discovery Learning (p. 222)
- *Theory into Practice:* Introducing Reciprocal Teaching (pp. 225–229)
- How Are Problem-Solving and Thinking Skills Taught? (pp. 236–243)

Chapter 11: Effective Learning Environments
- What Is the Impact of Time on Learning?
  - Using Engaged Time Effectively (pp. 320–325)
- What Practices Contribute to Effective Classroom Management?
  - Setting Class Rules (p. 327)
- *Theory into Practice:* Using a Daily Report Card System (pp. 339–340)

Chapter 12: Learners with Exceptionalities
- What Are Effective Strategies for Students with Disabilities in General Education? (pp. 384–391)

Chapter 13: Assessing Student Learning
- Why Is Evaluation Important?
  - Evaluation as Feedback (pp. 408–409)
  - Evaluation as Information (pp. 409–410)
  - Evaluation as Incentive (p. 410)

Topics Covered on the Praxis™ Exam for the Principles of Learning and Teaching (PLT Tests)	Chapter Content Aligned with Praxis™ Topics
IV. Profession and Community (approximately 11 percent of total test)	
A. The Reflective Practitioner	
1. Types of resources available for professional development and learning	**Chapter 1:** Educational Psychology: A Foundation for Teaching ■ What Is the Role of Research in Educational Psychology? (pp. 8–14) ■ How Can I Become an Intentional Teacher? (pp. 20–23)
2. Ability to read and understand articles and books about current views, ideas, and debates regarding best teaching practices	**Chapter 1:** Educational Psychology: A Foundation for Teaching ■ What Makes a Good Teacher? • Knowing the Subject Matters (But So Does Teaching Skill) (pp. 2–3) • Mastering Teaching Skills (pp. 3–4) • Can Good Teaching Be Taught? (p. 4) ■ What Is the Role of Research in Educational Psychology? (pp. 8–14) ■ How Can I Become an Intentional Teacher? • Beyond Certification (pp. 22–23) **Chapter 7:** The Effective Lesson ■ How Does Research on Direct Instruction Methods Inform Teaching? (pp. 202–203) **Chapter 14:** Standardized Tests and Accountability ■ How Are You as an Educator Held Accountable for Student Achievement? • No Child Left Behind (pp. 469–473) • Education Policies of the Obama Administration (pp. 473–474) • Benchmark Assessments (p. 474) • Data-Driven Reform (pp. 474–475) • Value Added Assessment Systems (p. 476) ■ *The Intentional Teacher:* Using What You Know about Standardized Tests to Improve Teaching and Learning (pp. 478–479)
3. Ongoing personal reflection on teaching practices as a basis for making professional decisions	**Chapter 1:** Educational Psychology: A Foundation for Teaching ■ What Makes a Good Teacher? • The Intentional Teacher (pp. 4–7) ■ *Theory into Practice:* How to Be an Intelligent Consumer of Educational Psychology Research (pp. 13–14) **Chapter 4:** Student Diversity ■ What Is the Impact of Culture on Teaching and Learning? (p. 80) ■ How Does Socioeconomic Status Affect Student Achievement? • Promoting Resilience among Students Who Are Disadvantaged (p. 85) ■ How Do Ethnicity and Race Affect Students' School Experiences? (pp. 89–95) ■ How Do Language Differences and Bilingual Programs Affect Student Achievement? (pp. 95–98) ■ How Do Sudents Differ in Intelligence and Learning Styles? (pp. 103–109) **Chapter 11:** Effective Learning Environments ■ What Practices Contribute to Effective Classroom Management? (pp. 326–328) ■ What Are Some Strategies for Managing Routine Misbehavior? (pp. 328–332) ■ How Is Applied Behavior Analysis Used to Mange More Serious Behavior Problems? • Ethics of Behavioral Methods (pp. 341–342) ■ How Can Serious Behavior Problems Be Prevented? • Identifying Causes of Misbehavior (pp. 342–343) • Confronting Bullying (pp. 346–347)

Topics Covered on the Praxis™ Exam for the Principles of Learning and Teaching (PLT Tests)	Chapter Content Aligned with Praxis™ Topics
IV. Profession and Community (approximately 11 percent of total test) *(continued)*	
B. The Larger Community	

1. The role of the school as a resource to the larger community

Chapter 4: Student Diversity
- How Does Socioeconomic Status Affect Student Achievement?
  • The Role of Schools as Middle-Class Institutions (p. 84)
  • School and Community Factors (pp. 84–85)
  • School, Family, and Community Partnerships (pp. 85–86)

2. Factors in the students' environment outside of school (family circumstances, community environments, health and economic conditions) that may influence students' life and learning

Chapter 1: Educational Psychology: A Foundation for Teaching
- What Makes a Good Teacher?
  • 21st Century Skills (pp. 7–8)

Chapter 4: Student Diversity
- What Is the Impact of Culture on Teaching and Learning? (p. 80)
- How Does Socioeconomic Status Affect Student Achievement?
  • The Role of Child-Rearing Practices (p. 82)
  • The Link between Income and Summer Learning (p. 83)
  • The Role of Schools as Middle-Class Institutions (p. 84)
  • School and Community Factors (p. 84)
  • Nonschool Solutions to Achievement Problems of Children Who Are Disadvantaged (pp. 87–88)
- How Do Ethnicity and Race Affect Students' School Experiences? (pp. 89–95)
- How Do Language Differences and Bilingual Programs Affect Student Achievement? (pp. 95–98)

Chapter 9: Grouping, Differentiation, and Technology
- What Educational Programs Exist for Students Placed at Risk? (pp. 262–267)

Chapter 11: Effective Learning Environments
- How Can Serious Behavior Problems Be Prevented?
  • Enforcing School Attendance (p. 343)
  • Requesting Family Involvement (pp. 344–345)
- *Theory into Practice:* Check and Connect (pp. 343–345)

3. Develop and utilize creative partnerships among teachers, parents/guardians, and leaders in the community in the educational process

Chapter 4: Student Diversity
- How Does Socioeconomic Status Affect Student Achievement?
  • School and Community Factors (pp. 84–85)
  • Promoting Resilience among Students Who Are Disadvantaged (p. 85)
  • School, Family, and Community Partnerships (pp. 85–86)
  • Implications for Teachers (pp. 88–89)

Chapter 11: Effective Learning Environments
- *Theory into Practice:* Using a Daily Report Card System (p. 339)

Chapter 12: Learners with Exceptionalities
- What Is Special Education?
  • Public Law 94-142 and IDEA (pp. 370–372)

IV. Profession and Community (approximately 11 percent of total test) *(continued)*

B. The Larger Community *(continued)*

References

Abrami, P., Bernard, R., Borokovski, E., Wade, A., Surkes, M., Tamim, R., & Zhang, D. (2008). Instructional interventions affecting critical thinking skills and dispositions: A State 1 meta-analysis. *Review of Educational Research, 78*(4), 1102–1134.

Ackerman, P., Beier, M., & Boyle, M. (2005). Working memory and intelligence: The same or different constructs? *Psychological Bulletin, 131*(1), 30–60.

Adams, A., Carnine, D., & Gersten, R. (1982). Instructional strategies for studying content area texts in the intermediate grades. *Reading Research Quarterly, 18,* 27–53.

Adams, G. L., & Engelmann, S. (1996). *Research on Direct Instruction: 25 years beyond DISTAR.* Seattle, WA: Educational Achievement Systems.

Adams, J. L. (1974). *Conceptual blockbusting.* San Francisco: Freeman.

Adelman, N. E., Haslam, M. B., & Pringle, B. A. (1996). *The uses of time for teaching and learning.* Washington, DC: U.S. Department of Education.

Adesope, O., Lavin, T., Thompson, T., & Ungerleider, C. (2009, April). *A systematic review and meta-analysis on the cognitive benefits of bilingualism.* Paper presented at the annual meeting of the American Educational Research Association, San Diego, CA.

AERA/APA/NCME. (1999). *Standards for educational and psychological testing.* Washington, DC: American Educational Research Association.

Aiken, L. R. (2003). *Psychological testing and assessment* (11th ed.). Boston: Allyn & Bacon.

Aiken, L. R., & Groth-Marnat, G. (Eds.). (2006). *Psychological testing and assessment* (12th ed.). Boston: Pearson Education Group.

Aikens, N., & Barbarin, O. (2008). Socioeconomic differences in reading trajectories: The contribution of family, neighborhood, and school contexts. *Journal of Educational Psychology, 100*(2), 235–251.

Ainsworth, L., & Viegut, D. (2006). *Common formative assessments.* Thousand Oaks, CA: Corwin.

Alba, R. D. (1990). *Ethnic identity.* New Haven, CT: Yale University Press.

Alber, S. R., & Heward, W. L. (2000). Teaching students to recruit positive attention: A review and recommendations. *Journal of Behavioral Education, 10,* 177–204.

Alberto, P., & Troutman, A. (2009). *Applied behavior analysis for teachers* (8th ed.). Upper Saddle River, NJ: Merrill.

Alberto, P., & Troutman, A. C. (2006). *Applied behavior analysis for teachers* (7th ed.). Upper Saddle River, NJ: Prentice-Hall/Merrill.

Aleman, S. R. (1990). *Attention deficit disorder.* Washington, DC: Education and Public Welfare Division of the Congressional Research Service.

Alexander, G. A., Graham, S., & Harris, K. R. (1998). A perspective on strategy research: Progress and prospects. *Educational Psychology Review, 10*(2), 129–154.

Alexander, P. (2004). In the year 2020: Envisioning the possibilities for educational psychology. *Educational Psychologist, 39*(3), 149–156.

Alexander, P. A. (1992). Domain knowledge: Evolving themes and emerging concerns. *Educational Psychologist, 27,* 33–51.

Alexander, P. A., & Jetton, T. L. (1996). The role of importance and interest in the processing of text. *Educational Psychology Review, 8*(1), 89–121.

Alexander, P. A., Kulikowich, J. M., & Jetton, T. L. (1994). The role of subject-matter knowledge and interest in the processing of linear and nonlinear texts. *Review of Educational Research, 64,* 201–252.

Alexander, P. A., & Murphy, P. K. (1994, April). *The research base for APA's learning-centered psychological principles.* Paper presented at the annual meeting of the American Educational Research Association, San Francisco.

Alfassi, M. (1998). Reading for meaning: The efficacy of reciprocal teaching in fostering reading comprehension in high school students in remedial reading classes. *American Educational Research Journal, 35*(2), 309–332.

Algozzine, B., Browder, D., Karvonen, M., Test, D. W., & Wood, W. M. (2001). Effects of interventions to promote self-determination for individuals with disabilities. *Review of Educational Research, 71*(2), 219–277.

Allen, L., & Seth, A. (2004). Bridging the gap between poor and privileged. *American Educator, 28*(2), 34–42.

Allen, R. (2003). The democratic aims of service learning. *Educational Leadership, 60*(6), 51–54.

Allensworth, E. (2005). Dropout rates after high-stakes testing in elementary school: A study of the contradictory effects of Chicago's efforts to end social promotion. *Evaluation and Policy Analysis, 27*(4), 341–364.

Allington, R., & McGill-Franzen, A. (2003). The impact of summer setback on the reaching achievement gap. *Phi Delta Kappan, 85*(1), 68–75.

Allington, R. L., & McGill-Franzen, A. (1989). School response to reading failure: Instruction for Chapter 1 and special education students in grades two, four, and eight. *Elementary School Journal, 89*(5), 529–542.

Allspach, J., & Breining, K. (2005). *Gender differences and trends over time for the SAT reasoning test.* Princeton, NJ: Educational Testing Service.

Al-Namlah, A. S., Fernyhough, C., & Meins, E. (2006). Sociocultural influences on the development of verbal mediation: Private speech and phonological decoding in Saudi Arabian and British samples. *Developmental Psychology, 42,* 117–131.

Alvermann, D. E., Smith, L., & Readence, J. (1985). Prior knowledge activation and the comprehension of compatible and incompatible text. *Reading Research Quarterly, 20,* 420–436.

Ambert, A. M. (1997). *Parents, children, and adolescents: Interactive relationships and development in context.* New York: Haworth.

American Association of University Women. (2002). *Harrassment-free hallways: How to stop sexual harassment in schools.* Washington, DC: Author.

American Association on Mental Retardation (AAMR). (2002). *Mental retardation: Definition, classification, and systems of supports* (10th ed.). Washington, DC: Author.

American Psychiatric Association. (1994). *Diagnostic and statistical manual of mental disorders* (4th ed.). Washington, DC: Author.

American Psychological Association. (1992). *Working draft report of the APA Presidential Task Force on Psychology in Education.*

American Psychological Association. (1997). *Learner-centered psychological principles: A framework for school redesign and reform.* Washington, DC: Author.

Ames, C., & Archer, J. (1988). Achievement goals in the classroom: Students' learning strategies and motivation processes. *Journal of Educational Psychology, 80,* 260–267.

Amrein, A., & Berliner, D. (2003). The effects of high-stakes testing on student motivation and learning. *Educational Leadership, 60*(5), 32–38.

Amrein-Beardsley, A. (2008). Methodological concerns about the education value-added assessment system. *Educational Researcher, 37*(2), 65–75.

Amrein-Beardsley, A. (2009). The unintended, pernicious consequences of staying the course. *International Journal of Education Policy and Leadership, 4*(6), 1–13.

Anagnostopoulos, D. (2006). "Real Students" and "True Demotes": Ending social promotion and the moral ordering of urban high schools. *American Educational Research Journal, 43*(1), 5–42.

Ancheta, A. (2006). Civil rights, education research, and the courts. *Educational Researcher, 35*(1), 26–29.

Anderman, E. M., Anderman, L. H., & Griesinger, T. (1999). The relation of present and possible academic selves during early adolescence to grade point average and achievement goals. *The Elementary School Journal, 100*(1), 3–18.

Anderman, E. M., Eccles, J. S., Yoon, K. S., Roeser, R., Wigfield, A., & Blumenfeld, P. (2001). Learning to value mathematics and reading: Relations to mastery and performance-oriented instructional practices. *Contemporary Educational Psychology, 26*(1), 76–95.

Anderson, J. (1994). *What do student grades mean? Differences across schools.* Washington, DC: U.S. Department of Education, Office of Educational Research and Improvement.

Anderson, J. R. (1985). *Cognitive psychology and its implications* (2nd ed.). San Francisco: Freeman.

Anderson, J. R. (1990). *Cognitive psychology and its implications* (3rd ed.). New York: Freeman.

Anderson, J. R. (1995). *Learning and memory: An integrated approach.* New York: Wiley.

Anderson, J. R. (2005). *Cognitive psychology and its implications* (6th ed.). New York: Worth.

Anderson, J. R., & Bower, G. (1983). *Human associative memory.* Washington, DC: Winston.

Anderson, J. R., Greeno, J. G., Reder, L. M., & Simon, H. (2000). Perspectives on learning, thinking, and activity. *Educational Researcher, 29*(4), 11–13.

Anderson, J. R., Reder, L. M., & Simon, H. A. (1996). Situated learning and education. *Educational Researcher, 25*(4), 5–11.

Anderson, L. M., Brubaker, N. L., Alleman-Brooks, J., & Duffy, G. G. (1985). A qualitative study of seatwork in first-grade classrooms. *Elementary School Journal, 86,* 123–140.

Anderson, L. M., Evertson, C. M., & Brophy, J. E. (1979). An experimental study of effective teaching in first-grade reading groups. *Elementary School Journal, 79,* 193–223.

Anderson, T. H., & Armbruster, B. B. (1984). Studying. In P. D. Pearson (Ed.), *Handbook of reading research.* New York: Longman.

Anderson-Inman, L., & Horney, M. (2007). Supported eText: Assistive technology through text transformations. *Reading Research Quarterly, 42*(1), 153–160.

Andrade, H. (2007/2008). Self-assessment through rubrics. *Educational Leadership, 65*(4), 60–63.

Anthony, J. L., & Lonigan, C. J. (2004). The nature of phonological awareness: Converging evidence from four studies of preschool and early grade school children. *Journal of Educational Psychology, 96*(1), 43–55.

Antil, L., Jenkins, J., Wayne, S., & Vadasy, P. (1998). Cooperative learning: Prevalence, conceptualizations, and the relation between research and practice. *American Educational Research Journal, 35*(3), 419–454.

Applebee, A. Langer, J., Nystrand, M., & Gameran, A. (2003). Discussion-based approaches to developing understanding: Classroom instruction and student performance in middle and high school English. *American Educational Research Journal, 40,* 685–730.

Archer, J. (2007). Information exchange. *Technology counts 2007,* 37–41. Retrieved June 1, 2007, from www.edweek/go/tc07

Arends, R. I. (2004). *Learning to teach* (6th ed.). New York: Worth.

Arlin, M. (1990). Wisdom: The art of problem finding. In R. J. Sternberg (Ed.), *Wisdom: Its nature, origins, and development* (pp. 230–243). New York: Cambridge University Press.

Armony, J., Chochol, C., Fecteau, S., & Belin, P. (2007). Laugh (or cry) and you will be remembered. *Psychological Science, 18,* 1027–1029.

Armstrong, T. (1994). *Multiple intelligences in the classroom.* Alexandria, VA: Association for Supervision and Curriculum Development.

Arnold, M. L. (2000). Stage, sequence, and sequels: Changing conceptions of morality, post-Kohlberg. *Educational Psychology Review, 12,* 365–383.

Aronson, E., Blaney, N., Stephan, C., Sikes, J., & Snapp, M. (1978). *The jigsaw classroom.* Beverly Hills, CA: Sage.

Aronson, E. A. (1995). *The social animal.* New York: Freeman.

Aronson, J. (2002). Stereotype threat: Contending and coping with unnerving expectations. In J. Aronson & D. Cordova (Eds.), *Improving education: Classic and contemporary lessons from psychology* (pp. 279–301). New York: Academic Press.

Aronson, J., & Steele, C. (2005). Stereotypes and the fragility of human competence, motivation, and self-concept. In C. Dweck & E. Elliot (Eds.), *Handbook of competence and motivation.* New York: Guilford.

Arter, J., & McTighe, J. (2001). *Scoring rubrics in the classroom.* Thousand Oaks, CA: Corwin.

Artiles, A., Kozleski, E., Dorn, S., & Christensen, C. (2006). Chapter 3: Learning in inclusive education research—Re-mediating theory and methods with a transformative agenda. *Review of Research in Education, 30*(1), 65–108.

Arzubiaga, A., Noguerón, S., & Sullivan, A. (2009). The education of children in immigrant families. *Review of Research in Education, 33,* 246–271.

Ashcraft, M. H., & Radvansky, G. A. (Eds.). (2010). *Cognition* (5th ed.). Boston: Prentice Hall.

Asher, N. (2007). Made in the (multicultural) U.S.A.: Unpacking tensions of race, culture, gender, and sexuality in education. *Educational Researcher, 36*(2), 65–73.

Atkins, J., & Ellsesser, J. (2003). Tracking: The good, the bad, and the questions. *Educational Leadership, 61*(2), 44–47.

Atkinson, J. W. (1958). Towards experimental analysis of human motivation in terms of motive expectancies and incentives. In J. W. Atkinson (Ed.), *Motives in fantasy, action, and society.* Princeton, NJ: Van Nostrand.

Atkinson, J. W. (1964). *An introduction to motivation.* Princeton, NJ: Van Nostrand.

Atkinson, R., Levin, J., Atkinson, L., Kiewra, K., Meyers, T., Kim, S., Renandya, W., & Hwang, Y. (1999). Matrix and mnemonic text-processing adjuncts: Comparing and combining their components. *Journal of Educational Psychology, 91*(2), 342–357.

Atkinson, R. C., & Raugh, M. R. (1975). An application of the mnemonic keyword method to the acquisition of Russian vocabulary. *Journal of Experimental Psychology: Human Learning and Memory, 104,* 126–133.

Atkinson, R. C., & Shiffrin, R. M. (1968). Human memory: A proposed system and its component processes. In K. Spence & J. Spence (Eds.), *The psychology of learning and motivation* (Vol. 2). New York: Academic Press.

Atkinson, R. K., Derry, S. J., Renkl, A., & Wortham, D. (2000). Learning from examples: Instructional principles from the worked examples research. *Review of Educational Research, 70*(2), 181–214.

Attewell, P., & Battle, J. (1999). Home computers and school performance. *The Information Society, 15*(1), 1–10.

August, D., & Shanahan, T. (Eds.). (2006a). *Developing literacy in second-language learners.* Mahwah, NJ: Erlbaum.

August, D., & Shanahan, T. (2006b). Synthesis: Instruction and professional development. In D. August & T. Shanahan (Eds.), *Developing literacy in second-language learners* (pp. 351–364). Mahwah, NJ: Erlbaum.

Ausubel, D. P. (1963). *The psychology of meaningful verbal learning.* New York: Grune and Stratton.

Ausubel, D. P., & Youssef, M. (1963). Role of discriminability in meaningful parallel learning. *Journal of Educational Psychology, 54,* 331–336.

Aviram, A. (2000). From "computers in the classroom" to mindful radical adaptation by education systems to the emerging cyber culture. *Journal of Educational Change, 1*(4), 331–352.

Axelrod, S., & Matthews, S. (2003). *How to manage behavior.* Austin, TX: Pro-Ed.

Ayaduray, J., & Jacobs, G. M. (1997). Can learner strategy instruction succeed? The case of higher order questions and elaborate responses. *System, 25*(4), 561–570.

Azzam, A. (2009). Why creativity now? A conversation with Sir Ken Robinson. *Educational Leadership, 67,* 22–26.

Baddeley, A. (1999). *Essentials of human memory.* Philadelphia: Psychology Press.

Badgett, J., & Christmann, E. (2009). *Designing elementary instruction and assessment.* Thousand Oaks, CA: Corwin.

Badke, W. (2009). Stepping beyond Wikipedia. *Educational Leadership, 66*(6), 54–58.

Bahrick, H. P., & Hall, L. K. (1991). Lifetime maintenance of high school mathematics. *Journal of Experimental Psychology, 120,* 20–33.

Bailey, J., & Burch, M. (2005). *Ethics for behavior analysis.* Mahwah, NJ: Erlbaum.

Baillargeon, R. (2002). The acquisition of physical knowledge in infancy: A summary in eight lessons. In U. Goswami, (Ed.), *Blackwell handbook of childhood cognitive development* (pp. 47–83). Malden, MA: Blackwell.

Baines, L., Baines, C., & Masterson, C. (1994). Mainstreaming: One school's reality. *Phi Delta Kappan, 76*(1), 39–40, 57–64.

Baker, S., Gersten, R., & Keating, T. (2000). When less may be more: A two-year longitudinal evaluation of a volunteer tutoring program requiring minimal training. *Reading Research Quarterly, 35*(4), 494–519.

Baker, S., Gersten, R., & Lee, D. S. (2002). A synthesis of empirical research on teaching mathematics to low-achieving students. *The Elementary School Journal, 103*(1), 51–73.

Balfanz, R., & Legters, N. (2004). *Locating the dropout crisis.* Baltimore, MD: Johns Hopkins University, Center for Social Organization of Schools.

Balfanz, R., & MacIver, D. (2000). Transforming high-poverty urban middle schools into strong learning institutions: Lessons from the first five years of the Talent Development Middle School. *Journal of Education for Students Placed at Risk, 5*(1 & 2), 137–158.

Bali, V., Anagnostopoulos, D., & Roberts, R. (2005). Toward a political explanation of grade retention. *Evaluation and Policy Analysis, 27*(3), 133–155.

Ball, D., & Forzani, F. (2007). What makes education research "educational"? *Educational Researcher, 36*(9), 529–540.

Bandalos, D. L., Yates, K., & Thorndike-Christ, T. (1995). Effects of math self-concept, perceived self-efficacy, and attributions for failure and success on test anxiety. *Journal of Educational Psychology, 87*(4), 611–623.

Bandura, A. (1965). Influence of models' reinforcement contingencies on the acquisition of imitative responses. *Journal of Personality and Social Psychology, 28*(2), 117–148.

Bandura, A. (1986). *Social foundations of thought and action: A social-cognitive theory.* Englewood Cliffs, NJ: Prentice-Hall.

Bandura, A. (1997). *Self-efficacy: The exercise of control.* New York: Freeman.

Bandura, A. (2001). Social cognitive theory: An agentic perspective. *Annual Review of Psychology, 52,* 1–26.

Bangert-Drowns, R. L. (1993). The word processor as an instructional tool: A meta-analysis of word processing in writing instruction. *Review of Educational Research, 63*(1), 69–93.

Bangert-Drowns, R. L., Hurley, M., & Wilkinson, B. (2004). The effects of school-based writing-to-learn interventions on academic achievement: A meta-analysis. *Review of Educational Research, 74*(1), 29–58.

Bangert-Drowns, R. L., Kulik, C. C., Kulik, J. A., & Morgan, M. (1991). The instructional effect of feedback in test-like events. *Review of Educational Research, 61*(2), 213–238.

Bangert-Drowns, R. L., Kulik, J. A., & Kulik, C. L. (1986, April). *Effects of frequent classroom testing.* Paper presented at the annual meeting of the American Education Research Association, San Francisco.

Banich, M. T. (2004). *Cognitive neuroscience and neuropsychology* (2nd ed.). Boston: Houghton-Mifflin.

Banks, J. A. (2006). *Cultural diversity and education: Foundations, curriculum, and teaching* (5th ed.). Boston: Pearson.

Banks, J. A. (2008). *An introduction to multicultural education* (4th ed.). Boston: Pearson.

Banks, J. A. (Ed.). (2009). *Teaching strategies for ethnic studies* (8th ed.). Boston: Pearson.

Barab, S., Gresalfi, M., & Arici, A. (2009). Why educators should care about games. *Educational Leadership, 67*(1), 76.

Barbato, R. (2000). *Policy implications of cooperative learning on the achievement and attitudes of secondary school mathematics students.* Unpublished doctoral dissertation, Fordham University.

Barber, B., Eccles, J., & Stone, M. (2001). Whatever happened to the jock, the brain, and the princess? Young adult pathways linked to adolescent activity involvement and social identity. *Journal of Adolescent Research, 16,* 429–455.

Barber, R. M., & Kagey, J. R. (1977). Modification of school attendance for an elementary population. *Journal of Applied Behavior Analysis, 10,* 41–48.

Barnhill, G. P. (2005). Functional behavioral assessment in schools. *Intervention in school and clinic, 40,* 131–143.

Barr, R. (1987). Content coverage. In M. J. Dunkin (Ed.), *International encyclopedia of teaching and teacher education.* New York: Pergamon.

Barr, R. D., & Parrett, W. H. (1995). *Hope at last for at-risk youth.* Boston: Allyn & Bacon.

Barr, R. D., & Parrett, W. H. (2001). *Hope fulfilled for at-risk and violent youth* (2nd ed.). Boston: Allyn & Bacon.

Barrish, H. H., Saunders, M., & Wolf, M. M. (1969). Good behavior game: Effects of individual contingencies for group consequences on disruptive behavior in a classroom. *Journal of Applied Behavior Analysis, 2,* 119–124.

Barth, R. (1979). Home-based reinforcement of school behavior: A review and analysis. *Review of Educational Research, 49,* 436–458.

Barton, P. (2003). *Parsing the achievement gap: Baselines for tracking progress.* Princeton, NJ: Educational Testing Service.

Barton, P. (2007/2008). The right way to measure growth. *Educational Leadership, 65*(4), 70–73.

Bateman, B., & Linden, M. (1998). *Better IEPs* (3rd ed.). Longmont, CO: Sopris West.

Battin-Pearson, S., Newcomb, M., Abbott, R., Hill, K., Catalano, R., & Hawkins, D. (2000). Predictors of early high school dropout: A test of five theories. *Journal of Educational Psychology, 92*(3), 568–582.

Battistich, V., Watson, M., Solomon, D., Lewis, C., & Schaps, E. (1999). Beyond the three R's: A broader agenda for school reform. *The Elementary School Journal, 99*(5), 415–432.

Baumeister, R. F., & Leary, M. R. (1995). The need to belong: Desire for interpersonal attachments as a fundamental human motivation. *Psychological Bulletin, 117*(3), 497–529.

Baxter, S. (1994). The last word on gender differences. *Psychology Today, 27*(2), 51–53.

Bebell, D., O'Dwyer, L., Russell, M., & Seeley, K. (2004). *Estimating the effect of computer use at home and in school on student achievement.* Paper presented at the annual meeting of the American Educational Research Association, San Diego, CA.

Beck, I., & McKeown, M. (2001). Inviting students into the pursuit of meaning. *Educational Psychology Review, 13*(3), 225–242.

Beck, I., & McKeown, M. (2007). Increasing young low-income children's oral vocabulary repertoires through rich and focused instruction. *The Elementary School Journal, 107*(3), 251–272.

Beck, I., McKeown, M., & Kucan, L. (2002). *Bringing words to life: Robust vocabulary instruction.* New York: Guilford Press.

Becker, B. E., & Luthar, S. S. (2002). Social-emotional factors affecting achievement outcomes among disadvantaged students: Closing the achievement gap. *Educational Psychologist, 37*(4), 197–214.

Becker, C., & Lee, M. (2009). *The interactive whiteboard revolution: Teaching with IWBs.* Victoria, Australia: ACER Press.

Becker, H. J. (1990). Coaching for the scholastic aptitude test: Further synthesis and appraisal. *Review of Educational Research, 60*(3), 373–417.

Becker, H. J. (2000). Who's wired and who's not: Children's access to and use of computer technology. *Children and Computer Technology, 10*(2), 44–75.

Becker, H. J. (2001, April). *How are teachers using computers in instruction?* Paper presented at the annual meeting of the American Educational Research Association, Seattle, WA.

Bee, H., & Boyd, D. (Eds.). (2010). *The developing child* (12th ed.). Boston: Allyn & Bacon.

Beebe-Frankenberger, M., Bocian, K. L., MacMillan, D. L., & Gresham, F. M. (2004). Sorting second grade students with academic deficiencies: Characteristics differentiating those retained in grade from those promoted to third grade. *Journal of Educational Psychology, 96,* 204–215.

Behrman, R. E. (1997). Children and poverty. *The Future of Children, 7*(2), 4–16.

Belgrad, S., Burke, K., & Fogarty, R. (2008). *The portfolio connection: Student work linked to standards* (3rd ed.). Thousand Oaks, CA: Corwin.

Bell, D. (2004). *Silent covenants: Brown v. Board of Education and the unfulfilled hopes for racial reform.* New York: Oxford University Press.

Bender, W. N. (Ed.). (2008). *Learning disabilities: Characteristics, identification, and teaching strategies* (6th ed.). Boston: Pearson.

Benjafield, J. G. (1992). *Cognition.* Englewood Cliffs, NJ: Prentice-Hall.

Bereiter, C. (1995). A dispositional view of transfer. In A. McKeough, J. Lupart, & A. Marini (Eds.), *Teaching for transfer: Fostering generalization in learning.* Mahwah, NJ: Erlbaum.

Bergin, D. (1999). Influences on classroom interest. *Educational Psychologist, 34*(2), 87–98.

Bergstrom, J. M., & O'Brien, L. A. (2001). Themes of discovery. *Educational Leadership, 58*(7), 29–33.

Berk, L. E. (2006). *Child development* (7th ed.). Boston: Allyn & Bacon.

Berk, L. E. (Ed.). (2009). *Child development* (8th ed.). Boston: Pearson.

Berko, J. (1985). The child's learning of English morphology. *Word, 14,* 150–177.

Bernard-Powers, J. (2001). Gender effects in schooling. In C. F. Diaz (Ed.), *Multicultural education for the 21st century.* New York: Longman.

Bernhardt, V. (2003). No schools left behind. *Educational Leadership, 60*(5), 26–30.

Bernhardt, V. (2005). Data tools for school improvement. *Educational Leadership, 62*(5), 66–69.

Bernstein, D. K., & Tiegerman-Farber, E. (Eds.) (2009). *Language and communication disorders in children* (6th ed.). Boston: Allyn & Bacon.

Berrueta-Clement, J. R., Schweinhart, L. J., Barnett, W. S., Epstein, A. S., & Weikart, D. P. (1984). *Changed lives.* Ypsilanti, MI: High/Scope.

Berry, B., Hoke, M., & Hirsch, E. (2004). The search for highly qualified teachers. *Phi Delta Kappan, 85*(9), 684–689.

Bertsch S., Pesta B. J., Wiscott R., & McDaniel M. A. (2007). The generation effect: A meta-analytic review. *Memory & Cognition, 35,* 201–210.

Bettmann, E. H., & Friedman, L. J. (2004). The Anti-Defamation League's A Word of Difference Institute. In W. G. Stephan & W. P. Vogt (Eds.), *Education programs for improving intergroup relations.* New York: Teachers College Press.

Beyer, B. K. (1988). *Developing a thinking skills program.* Boston: Allyn & Bacon.

Beyer, B. K. (1998). *Improving student thinking: A comprehensive approach.* Boston: Allyn & Bacon.

Biancarosa, C., & Snow, C. E. (2006). *Reading next—A vision for action and research in middle and high school literacy: A report to Carnegie Corporation of New York* (2nd ed.). Washington, DC: Alliance for Excellent Education.

Biddle, B., & Berliner, D. (2002). Unequal school funding in the United States. *Educational Leadership, 59*(8), 48–59.

Biemiller, A. (2004). Teaching vocabulary in the primary grades: Vocabulary instruction needed. In J. F. Baumann & E. J. Kame'enui (Eds.), *Vocabulary instruction: Research to practice* (pp. 28–40). New York: Guilford Press.

Bigge, M. L., & Shermis, S. S. (2004). *Learning theories for teachers* (6th ed.). Boston: Pearson.

Binder, L. M., Dixon, M. R., & Ghezi, P. M. (2000). A procedure to teach self-control to children with attention deficit hyper-activity disorder. *Journal of Applied Behavior Analysis, 33,* 233–237.

Birney, D., Citron-Pousiy, J., Lutz, D., & Sternberg, R. (2005). The development of cognitive and intellectual abilities. In M. Borstein & M. Lamb (Eds.), *Developmental science: An advanced textbook* (5th ed., pp. 327–358). Hillsdale, NJ: Erlbaum.

Bitter, G. G., & Legacy, J. M. (2008). *Using technology in the classroom* (7th ed.). Boston: Pearson.

Blachman, B., Schatschneider, C., Fletcher, J., Francis, D., Clonan, S., Shaywitz, B., & Shaywitz, C. (2004). Effects of intensive reading remediation for second and third graders and a one year followup. *Journal of Educational Psychology, 96*(3), 444–461.

Blachowicz, C., Fisher, P., Ogle, D., & Watts-Taffe, S. (2006). Vocabulary: Questions from the classroom. *Reading Research Quarterly, 41*(4), 524–539.

Black, J. (2003). Environment and development of the nervous system. In M. Gallagher & R. J. Nelson (Eds.), *Handbook of psychology: Vol. 3. Biological psychology* (pp. 655–665). Hoboken, NJ: Wiley.

Black, M. M., & Krishnakumar, A. (1998). Children in low-income, urban settings. Interventions to promote mental health and well-being. *American Psychologist, 53*(6), 635–646.

Black, P., Harrison, C., Lee, C., Marshall, B., & Wiliam, D. (2003). Working inside the black box: Assessment for learning in the classroom. *Phi Delta Kappan, 86*(1), 8–21.

Black, P., Harrison, C., Lee, C., Marshall, B., & Wiliam, D. (2004). *Assessment for learning.* New York: Open University Press.

Blackadar, A. R., & Nachtigal, P. (1986). *Cotapaxi/Westcliffe follow-through project: Final evaluation report.* Denver, CO: Mid-Continental Regional Educational Laboratory.

Blair, C. (2004). Learning disability, intelligence, and fluid cognitive functions of the prefrontal cortex: A developmental neuroscience approach. *Learning Disabilities: A Contemporary Journal, 2*(1), 22–29.

Bligh, D. (2000). *What's the use of lectures?* San Francisco: Jossey-Bass.

Block, C., & Duffy, G. (2008). Research on teaching comprehension. In C. Block & S. Parris (Eds.), *Comprehension instruction: Research-...* New York: Guilford.

Bonner-Tompkins, E. (2001, May/June). Effective practices for serving limited English proficient students with disabilities. *Gaining Ground.* Washington, DC: Council of Chief State School Officers.

Booher-Jennings, J., & Beveridge, A. (2007). Who counts for accountability? High-stakes test exemptions in a large urban school district. In A. Sadovnik, J. O'Day, G. Bohrnstedt, & K. Borman (Eds.), *No Child Left Behind and the reduction of the achievement gap: Sociological perspectives on federal education policy.* New York: Routledge.

Boom, J., Brugman, D., & van der Heijden, P. G. M. (2001). Hierarchical structure of moral stages assessed by a sorting task. *Child Development, 72,* 535–548.

Boone, R., & Higgins, K. (2007). The role of instructional design in assistive technology research and development. *Reading Research Quarterly, 42*(1), 134–160.

Borg, M. (1998). Tests of the internal/external frames of reference model with subject-specific academic self-efficacy and frame-specific academic concepts. *Journal of Educational Psychology, 90*(1), 102–110.

Borgman, C., Abelson, H., Dirks, L., Johnson, R., Koedinger, K., Linn, M., Lynch, C., et al. (2008). *Fostering learning in the networked world: The cyberlearning opportunity and challenge: A 21st century agenda for the National Science Foundation.* Washington, DC: National Science Foundation.

Borja, R. R. (2007). Teaching assistants. *Technology counts 2007,* 18–22. Retrieved Dec. 1, 2007, from www.edweek/go/tc07

Borko, H. (2004). Professional development and teacher learning: Mapping the terrain. *Educational Researcher, 33*(8), 3–15.

Borland, J. H. (2008). Gifted students. In T. L. Good (Ed.), *21st century learning* (Vol. 2, pp. 141–149). Thousand Oaks, CA: Sage.

Borman, G. (2002/2003). How can Title I improve achievement? *Educational Leadership, 60*(4), 49–53.

Borman, G., Benson, J., & Overman, L. (2005). Families, schools, and summer learning. *The Elementary School Journal, 106*(2), 131–150.

Borman, G., & Dowling, N. M. (2006). Longitudinal achievement effects of multiyear summer school: Evidence from the Teach Baltimore randomized field trial. *Educational Evaluation and Policy Analysis, 28*(1), 25–48.

Borman, G., & Hewes, G. (2003). Long-term effects and cost effectiveness of Success for All. *Educational Evaluation and Policy Analysis, 24*(2), 243–266.

Borman, G., & Kimball, S. (2005). Teacher quality and educational quality: Do teachers with higher standards-based evaluation ratings close student achievement gaps? *The Elementary School Journal, 106*(1), 3–20.

Borman, G., Stringfield, S., & Slavin, R. (Eds.). (2001). *Title I: Compensatory education at the crossroads.* Mahwah, NJ: Erlbaum.

Borman, G. D. (1997). *A holistic model of the organization of categorical program students' total educational opportunities.* Unpublished doctoral dissertation, University of Chicago.

Borman, G. D., & Boulay, M. (2004). *Summer learning: Research, policies, and programs.* Mahwah, NJ: Erlbaum.

Borman, G. D., & D'Agostino, J. V. (2001). Title I and student achievement: A quantitative synthesis. In G. D. Borman, S. C. Stringfield, & R. E. Slavin (Eds.), *Title I: Compensatory education at the crossroads* (pp. 25–57). Mahwah, NJ: Erlbaum.

Borman, G. D., D'Agostino, J. V., Wong, K. K., & Hedges, L. V. (1998). The longitudinal achievement of Chapter I students: Preliminary evidence from the Prospects study. *Journal of Education for Students Placed at Risk, 3*(4), 363–399.

Borman, G. D., Goetz, M., & Dowling, N. (2009). Halting the summer achievement slide: A randomized field trial of the kindergARTen summer camp. *Journal of Education for Students Placed at Risk, 14*(2), 133–147.

Borman, G. D., Hewes, G. M., Overman, L. T., & Brown, S. (2003). Comprehensive school reform and achievement: A meta-analysis. *Review of Educational Research, 73*(2), 125–230.

Borman, G. D., & Overman, L. T. (2004). Academic resilience in mathematics among poor and minority students. *The Elementary School Journal, 104*(3), 177–195.

Borman, G. D., Slavin, R. E., Cheung, A., Chamberlain, A., Madden, N. A., & Chambers, B. (2007). Final reading outcomes of the national randomized field trial of Success for All. *American Educational Research Journal, 44*(3), 701–731.

Bornstein, P. H. (1985). Self-instructional training: A commentary and state-of-the-art. *Journal of Applied Behavior Analysis, 18,* 69–72.

Bottge, B. A. (2001). Using intriguing problems to improve math skills. *Educational Leadership, 58*(6), 68–72.

Bottoms, J. E., Feagin, C. H., & Han, L. (2005). *Making high schools and middle grades schools work.* Atlanta, GA: Southern Regional Education Board.

Bower, G. H., Clark, M. C., Lesgold, A. M., & Winzenz, D. (1969). Hierarchical retrieval schemes in recall of categorized word lists. *Journal of Verbal Learning and Verbal Behavior, 8,* 323–343.

Bower, G. H., & Karlin, M. B. (1974). Depth of processing pictures of faces and recognition memory. *Journal of Experimental Psychology, 103,* 751–757.

Boykin, A. W. (1994a). Afrocultural expression and its implications for schooling. In E. R. Hollins, J. E. King, & W. C. Hayman (Eds.), *Teaching diverse populations.* Albany: State University of New York Press.

Boykin, A. W. (1994b). Harvesting culture and talent: African American children and educational reform. In R. Rossi (Ed.), *Schools and students at risk* (pp. 116–130). New York: Teachers College Press.

Boykin, A. W. (2000). The talent development model of schooling: Placing students at promise for academic success. *Journal of Education for Students Placed at Risk, 5*(1 & 2), 3–25.

Bracey, G. (2003). The 13th Bracey report on the condition of education. *Phi Delta Kappan, 84*(8), 616–621.

Bracey, G. (2006). Dropping in on dropouts. *Phi Delta Kappan, 87*(10), 798.

Braddock, J. H., & Dawkins, M. P. (1993). Ability grouping, aspirations, and attainments: Evidence from the National Educational Longitudinal Study of 1988. *Journal of Negro Education, 62*(3), 1–13.

Braddock, J. H., Dawkins, M. P., & Wilson, G. (1995). Intercultural contact and race relations among American youth. In W. D. Hawley & A. W. Jackson (Eds.), *Toward a common destiny: Improving race and ethnic relations in America.* San Francisco: Jossey-Bass.

Bradley, R. H., Whiteside, L., Mundfrom, D. J., Casey, P. H., Caldwell, B. M., & Barrett, K. (1994). Impact of the Infant Health and Development Program (IHDP) on the home environments of infants born prematurely and with low birthweight. *Journal of Educational Psychology, 80,* 531–541.

Bradshaw, C., Zmuda, J., Kellam, S., & Ialongo, N. (2009). Longitudinal impact of two universal preventive interventions in first grade on educational outcomes in high school. *Journal of Educational Psychology, 101*(4), 926–937.

Branch, C. (1998). *Adolescent gangs: Old issues, new approaches.* Philadelphia: Brunner/Mazel.

Bransford, J., Brown, A., & Cocking, R. (Eds.). (1999). *How people learn: Brain, mind, experience, and school.* Washington, DC: National Academies Press.

Bransford, J. D., Burns, M. S., Delclos, V. R., & Vye, N. J. (1986). Teaching thinking: Evaluating evaluations and broadening the data base. *Educational Leadership, 44*(2), 68–70.

Bransford, J. D., & Stein, B. S. (1993). *The ideal problem solver* (2nd ed.). New York: W. H. Freeman.

Bretzing, B. B., & Kulhavy, R. W. (1981). Note taking and passage style. *Journal of Educational Psychology, 73,* 242–250.

Broden, M., Hall, R. V., Dunlap, A., & Clark, R. (1970). Effects of teacher attention and a token reinforcement system in a junior high school special education class. *Exceptional Children, 36,* 341–349.

Brookes-Gunn, J., & Duncan, G. (1997). The effects of poverty on children. *Children and Poverty, 7*(2) 55–71.

Brookhart, S. (2007/2008). Feedback that fits. *Educational Leadership, 65*(4), 54–59.

Brookhart, S., Moss, C., & Long, B. (2008). Formative assessment that empowers. *Educational Leadership, 66*(3), 52–57.

Brooks, B. D. (1975). Contingency management as a means of reducing school truancy. *Education, 95,* 206–211.

Brooks, D. M. (1985). Beginning of the year in junior high: The first day of school. *Educational Leadership, 42,* 76–78.

Brophy, J. (1981). Teacher praise: A functional analysis. *Review of Educational Research, 51,* 5–32.

Brophy, J. (1999). Toward a model of the value aspects of motivation in education: Developing appreciation for particular learning domains and activities. *Educational Psychologist, 34*(2), 75–85.

Brophy, J. (2005). Goal theorists should move on from performance goals. *Educational Psychologist, 40*(3), 167–176.

Brophy, J. (2008). Developing students' appreciation for what is taught in school. *Educational Psychologist, 43*(3), 132–141.

Brophy, J. E. (1998). *Motivating students to learn.* Boston: McGraw-Hill.

Brophy, J. E., & Evertson, C. M. (1976). *Learning from teaching: A developmental perspective.* Boston: Allyn & Bacon.

Browder, D. M. (2001). *Curriculum and assessment for students with moderate and severe disabilities.* New York: Guilford.

Brown, K., Morris, D., & Fields, M. (2005). Intervention after grade 1: Serving increased numbers of struggling readers effectively. *Journal of Literacy Research, 37*(1), 61–94.

Brown, T. (2007). A new approach to attention deficit disorder. *Educational Leadership, 64*(5), 22–28.

Bruner, J. S. (1966). *Toward a theory of instruction.* New York: Norton.

Bruning, R. H., Schraw, G. J., Norby, M. M., & Ronning, R. R. (2004). *Cognitive psychology and instruction* (4th ed.). Columbus, OH: Merrill.

Bryant, A. L., & Zimmerman, M. A. (2002). Examining the effects of academic beliefs and behaviors on changes in substance use among urban adolescents. *Journal of Educational Psychology, 94*(3), 621–637.

Bryant, D. P., Smith, D. D., & Bryant, B. R. (2008). *Teaching students with special needs in inclusive classrooms.* Boston: Allyn & Bacon.

Bryant, D. P., Ugel, N., Thompson, S., & Hampff, A. (1999). Instructional strategies for content-area reading instruction. *Intervention in School and Clinic, 34*(5), 293–302.

Buhle, R., & Blachowicz, C. (2008/2009). The assessment double play. *Educational Leadership, 66*(4), 42–47.

Bulgren, J., Deshler, D., Schumaker, J., & Lenz, B. (2000). The use and effectiveness of analogical instruction in diverse secondary content classrooms. *Journal of Educational Psychology, 92*(3), 426–441.

Bulgren, J. A., Lenz, B. K., Schumaker, J. B., Deshler, D. D., & Marquis, J. G. (2002). The use and effectiveness of a comparison routine in diverse secondary content classrooms. *Journal of Educational Psychology, 94*(2), 356–371.

Bunge, S. A., & Zelazo, P. D. (2006). A brain-based account of the development of rule use in childhood. *Current Directions in Psychological Science, 15*(3), 118–121.

Burden, P. R. (2000). *Powerful classroom management strategies: Motivating students to learn.* Thousand Oaks, CA: Corwin.

Burden, P. R., & Byrd, D. (2003). *Methods for effective teaching.* Boston: Allyn & Bacon.

Burden, P., & Byrd, D. (2010). *Methods for effective teaching* (5th ed.). Boston: Allyn & Bacon.

Burkam, D., LoGerfo, L., Ready, D., & Lee, V. (2007). The differential effects of repeating kindergarten. *Journal of Education for Students Placed at Risk, 12*(2), 103–136.

Burke, K. (2009). *How to assess authentic learning.* Thousand Oaks, CA: Corwin.

Burns, M. (2005). Looking at how students reason. *Educational Leadership, 63*(3), 26–31. Retrieved November 29, 2006, from www.ascd.org/authors/ed_lead/el200511_burns.html

Burns, R. B. (1984). How time is used in elementary schools: The activity structure of classrooms. In L. W. Anderson (Ed.), *Time and school learning: Theory, research, and practice.* London: Croom Helm.

Burns, R. B., & Mason, D. A. (2002). Class composition and student achievement in elementary schools. *American Educational Research Journal, 39*(1), 207–233.

Burris, C., Heubert, J., & Levin, H. (2004). Math acceleration for all. *Educational Leadership, 61*(5), 68–71.

Burris, C., Heubert, J., & Levin, H. (2006). Accelerating mathematics achievement using heterogeneous grouping. *American Educational Research Journal, 43*(1), 105–136.

Burt, M. R., Resnick, G., & Novick, E. R. (1998). *Building supportive communities for at-risk adolescents.* Washington, DC: American Psychological Association.

Bussey, K. (1992). Lying and truthfulness: Children's definitions, standards, and evaluative reactions. *Child Development, 63,* 129–137.

Butcher, K. (2006). Learning from text with diagrams: Promoting mental model development and inference generation. *Journal of Educational Psychology, 98*(1), 182–197.

Byerly, S. (2001). Linking classroom teaching to the real world through experiential instruction. *Phi Delta Kappan, 82*(9), 697–699.

Byrne, B., Fielding-Barnsley, R., & Ashley, L. (2000). Effects of preschool phoneme identity training after six years: Outcome level distinguished from rate of response. *Journal of Educational Psychology, 92*(4), 659–667.

Byrnes, J. (2001). *Cognitive development and learning* (2nd ed.). Boston: Allyn & Bacon.

Byrnes, J., & Miller, D. (2007). The relative importance of predictors of math and science achievement: An opportunity-propensity analysis. *Contemporary Educational Psychology, 32*(4), 599–629.

Byrnes, J. P. (2008). *Cognitive development and learning in instructional contexts* (3rd ed.). Boston: Pearson.

Calderón, M. (1999). Teacher learning communities for cooperation in diverse settings. *Theory into Practice, 38*(2), 94–99.

Calderón, M. (2001). Curricula and methodologies used to teach Spanish-speaking limited English proficient students to read English. In R. Slavin and M. Calderón (Eds.), *Effective programs for Latino students.* Mahwah, NJ: Erlbaum.

Calderón, M. (2007). *Teaching reading to English language learners, grades 6–12.* Thousand Oaks, CA: Corwin.

Calderón, M., August, D., Slavin, R. E., Durán, D., Madden, N. A., & Cheung, A. (2004). *The evaluation of a bilingual transition program for Success for All.* Baltimore, MD: Johns Hopkins University, Center for Research on the Education of Students Placed at Risk.

Calderón, M., Hertz-Lazarowitz, R., & Slavin, R. E. (1998). Effects of bilingual cooperative integrated reading and composition on students making the transition from Spanish to English reading. *Elementary School Journal, 99*(2), 153–165.

Calderón, M. E., & Minaya-Rowe, L. (2003). *Designing and implementing two-way bilingual programs.* Thousand Oaks, CA: Corwin.

Calhoon, M., Al Otaiba, S., Cihak, D., King, A., & Avalos, A. (2007). The effects of a peer-mediated program on reading skill acquisition for two-way bilingual first-grade classrooms. *Learning Disability Quarterly, 30*(3), 169–184.

Calhoun, G., & Elliott, R. (1977). Self-concept and academic achievement of educable retarded and emotionally disturbed children. *Exceptional Children, 44,* 379–380.

Calkins, L. M. (1983). *Lessons from a child: On the teaching and learning of writing.* Exeter, NH: Heinemann.

Callender, A., & McDaniel, M. (2009). The limited benefits of rereading educational texts. *Contemporary Educational Psychology, 34*(1), 30–41.

Cameron, J. (2001). Negative effects of reward on intrinsic motivation—a limited phenomenon: Comment on Deci, Koestner, and Ryan (2001). *Review of Educational Research, 71*(1), 29–42.

Cameron, J., & Pierce, W. D. (1994). Reinforcement, reward, and intrinsic motivation: A meta-analysis. *Review of Educational Research, 64,* 363–423.

Cameron, J., & Pierce, W. D. (1996). The debate about rewards and intrinsic motivation: Protests and accusations do not alter the results. *Review of Educational Research, 66*(1), 39–51.

Cameron, J., Pierce, W. D., Banko, K., & Gear, A. (2005). Achievement-based rewards and intrinsic motivation: A test of cognitive mediators. *Journal of Educational Psychology, 97*(4), 641–655.

Campbell, D. (2000). Authentic assessment and authentic standards. *Phi Delta Kappan, 81*(5), 405–407.

Campbell, F. A., & Ramey, C. T. (1994). Effects of early intervention on intellectual and academic achievement: A follow-up study of children from low-income families. *Child Development, 65,* 684–698.

Campbell, J., & Mayer, R. E. (2004, April). *Concrete manipulatives: For whom are they beneficial?* Paper presented at the annual meeting of the American Educational Research Association, San Diego, CA.

Campbell, L., Campbell, B., & Dickerson, D. (2004). *Teaching and learning through multiple intelligences.* Boston: Pearson.

Canada, G. (2000). Raising better boys. *Educational Leadership, 57*(4), 14–17.

Canfield, J., & Siccone, F. (1995). *101 ways to develop students' self-esteem and responsibility.* Boston: Allyn & Bacon.

Cannell, J. J. (1987). *Nationally normed elementary achievement testing in America's public schools: How all fifty states are above the national average.* Daniels, WV: Friends for Education.

Canter, L., & Canter, M. (2002). *Assertive discipline: Positive behavior management for today's schools.* Seal Beach, CA: Lee Canter & Associates.

Cappella, E., & Weinstein, R. (2001). Turning around reading achievement: Predictors of high school students' academic resilience. *Journal of Educational Psychology, 93*(4), 758–771.

Capper, C. A., Kampschroer, E. F., & Keyes, M. W. (2000). *Meeting the needs of students of all abilities: How leaders go beyond inclusion.* Bloomington, IN: Phi Delta Kappan.

Caprara, G., Fida, R., Vecchione, M., Del Bove, G., Vecchio, G., Barbaranelli, C., & Bandura, A. (2008). Longitudinal analysis of the role of perceived self-efficacy for self-regulated learning in academic continuance and achievement. *Journal of Educational Psychology, 100*(3), 525–534.

Capron, C., & Duyme, M. (1991). Children's IQ's and SES of biological and adoptive parents in a balanced cross-fostering study. *Cahiers de Psychologie Cognitive, II,* 323–348.

Cardelle-Elawar, M. (1990). Effects of feedback tailored to bilingual students' mathematics needs on verbal problem solving. *Elementary School Journal, 91,* 165–175.

Carey, L. M. (2001). *Measuring and evaluating school learning* (3rd ed.). Boston: Allyn & Bacon.

Carlo, M. S., August, D., McLaughlin, B., Snow, C. E., Dressler, C., Lippman, D., Lively, T., & White, C. (2004). Closing the gap: Addressing the vocabulary needs of English language learners in bilingual and mainstream classrooms. *Reading Research Quarterly, 39*(2), 188–215.

Carnegie Corporation of New York. (1989). *Turning points: Preparing American youth for the 21st century.* New York: Author.

Carney, R. N., & Levin, J. R. (1998). Do mnemonic memories fade as time goes by? Here's looking anew! *Contemporary Educational Psychology, 23*(3), 276–297.

Carney, R. N., & Levin, J. R. (2002). Pictorial illustrations still improve students' learning from text. *Educational Psychology Review, 14*(1), 5–26.

Carnoy, M., & Loeb, S. (2002). Does external accountability affect student outcomes? A cross-state analysis. *Educational Evaluation and Policy Analysis, 24*(4), 305–331.

Carolan, J., & Guinn, A. (2007). Differentiation: Lessons from master teachers. *Educational Leadership, 64*(5), 44–47.

Carpenter, S., & Pashler, H. (2007). Testing beyond words: Using tests to enhance visuospatial map learning. *Psychonomic Bulletin & Review, 14,* 474–478.

Carpenter, T. P., & Fennema, E. (1992). Cognitively guided instruction: Building on the knowledge of students and teachers. *International Journal of Educational Research, 17,* 457–470.

Carpenter, T. P., Fennema, E., Fuson, K., Hiebert, J., Human, P., Murray, H., Olivier, A., & Wearne, D. (1994, April). *Teaching mathematics for learning with understanding in the primary grades.* Paper presented at the annual meeting of the American Educational Research Association, New Orleans, LA.

Carpenter, T. P., Fennema, E., Peterson, P. L., Chiang, C. P., & Loef, M. (1989). Using knowledge of children's mathematics thinking in classroom teaching: An experimental study. *American Educational Research Journal, 26,* 499–531.

Carr, J. F., & Harris, D. E. (2001). *Succeeding with standards: Linking curriculum, assessment, and action planning.* Alexandria, VA: ASCD.

Carroll, J. B. (1963). A model of school learning. *Teachers College Record, 64,* 723–733.

Carroll, J. B. (1989). The Carroll model: A 25-year retrospective and prospective view. *Educational Researcher, 18,* 26–31.

Carter, C. J. (1997). Why reciprocal teaching? *Educational Leadership, 54*(6), 64–68.

Carter, L. F. (1984). The sustaining effects study of compensatory and elementary education. *Educational Researcher, 13*(7), 4–13.

Carver, S. M., & Klahr, D. (2001). *Cognition and instruction: Twenty five years of progress.* Mahwah, NJ: Erlbaum.

Case, R. (1998). The development of conceptual structures. In W. Damon (Ed.), *Handbook of child psychology* (Vol. 2, pp. 851–898). Hoboken, NJ: Wiley.

Casey, B., Giedd, J., & Thomas, K. (2000). Structural and functional brain development and its relation to cognitive development. *Biological Psychology, 54,* 241–257.

Cassady, J. C., & Johnson, R. E. (2002). Cognitive anxiety and academic performance. *Contemporary Educational Psychology, 27,* 270–295.

Castagno, A., & Brayboy, B. (2008). Culturally responsive schooling for indigenous youth: A review of the literature. *Review of Educational Research, 78*(4), 941–993.

Casto, G., & Mastropieri, M. A. (1986). The efficacy of early intervention programs: A meta-analysis. *Exceptional Children, 52,* 417–424.

Cavanaugh, C., Kim, A.-H., Wanzek, J., & Vaughn, S. (2004). Kindergarten reading interventions for at-risk students: Twenty years of research. *Learning Disabilities: A Contemporary Journal, 2*(1), 1–8.

Cawelti, G. (2006). The side effects of NCLB. *Educational Leadership, 64*(3), 64–68.

Ceci, S. & Williams, W. (Eds.). (2009). *Why aren't more women in science? Top researchers debate the evidence* (pp. 47–55). Washington, DC: American Psychological Association.

Ceci, S. J. (1991). How much does schooling influence general intelligence and its cognitive components? A reassessment of the evidence. *Developmental Psychology, 27,* 703–722.

Center for Public Education. (2008). *High-performing, high-poverty schools: Research review.* Fairfax, VA: Caliber Associates.

Center on Education Policy. (2003). *State and federal efforts to implement the No Child Left Behind Act.* Washington, DC: Author.

Center on Education Policy. (2004). *From the Capitol to the classroom: Year 2 of the No Child Left Behind Act.* Washington, DC: Author.

Center on Education Policy. (2007). *Has student achievement increased since No Child Left Behind?* Washington, DC: Author.

Center on Education Policy. (2009a). *Answering the question that matters most: Has student achievement increased since No Child Left Behind?* Washington, DC: Author.

Center on Education Policy. (2009b). *State test score trends through 2007–08: Are achievement gaps closing and is achievement rising for all?* Washington, DC: Author.

Cepeda, N. J., Pashler, H., Vul, E., Wixted, J. T., & Rohrer, D. (2006). Distributed practice in verbal recall tasks: A review and quantitative synthesis. *Psychological Bulletin, 132,* 354–380.

Chambers, B., Cheung, A., Madden, N., Slavin, R. E., & Gifford, R. (2006). Achievement effects of embedded multimedia in a Success for All reading program. *Journal of Educational Psychology, 98*(1), 232–237.

Chambers, B., Cheung, A., Slavin, R., Smith, D., & Laurenzano, M. (2010). *Effective early childhood programmes: A best-evidence synthesis.* York, England: Institute for Effective Education, University of York.

Chambers, B., Slavin, R. E., Madden, N. A., Abrami, P. C., Tucker, B. J., Cheung, A., & Gifford, R. (2008). Technology infusion in Success for All: Reading outcomes for first graders. *Elementary School Journal, 109*(1), 1–15.

Chandler, L., & Dahlquist, C. (2006). *Functional assessment: Strategies to prevent and remediate challenging behavior in school settings.* Upper Saddle River, NJ: Prentice-Hall.

Changeux, J.-P. (2004). [Review of the book *The physiology of truth: Neuroscience and human knowledge.*] *Educational Leadership, 62*(4), 92.

Chapman, C., & King, R. (2005). *Differentiated assessment strategies.* Thousand Oaks, CA: Corwin.

Chapman, E. (2001, April). *More on moderations in cooperative learning outcomes.* Paper presented at the annual meeting of the American Educational Research Association, Montreal, Canada.

Chapman, J., Tunmer, W., & Prochnow, J. (2000). Early reading-related skills and performance, reading self-concept, and the development of academic self-concept: A longitudinal study. *Journal of Educational Psychology, 92*(4), 703–708.

Chappuis, J. (2005). Helping students understand assessment. *Educational Leadership, 63*(3), 39–43.

Chappuis, S., & Chappuis, J. (2007/2008). The best value in formative assessment. *Educational Leadership, 65*(4), 14–19.

Chappuis, S., Chappuis, J., & Stiggins, R. (2009). The quest for quality. *Educational Leadership, 67*(3), 14–20.

Charles, C. M. (2008). *Building classroom discipline* (9th ed.). Boston: Allyn & Bacon.

Chatterji, M. (2002). Models and methods for examining standards-based reforms and accountability initiatives: Have the tools of inquiry answered pressing questions on improving schools? *Review of Educational Research, 72*(3), 345–386.

Chatterji, M. (2006). Reading achievement gaps, correlates, and moderators of early reading achievement: Evidence from the Early Childhood Longitudinal Study (ECLS) kindergarten to first grade sample. *Journal of Educational Psychology, 98*(3), 489–507.

Chen, J.-Q. (2004). Theory of multiple intelligences: Is it a scientific theory? *Teachers College Record, 106,* 17–23.

Chen, Z., & Daehler, M. (2000). External and internal instantiation of abstract information facilitates transfer in insight problem solving. *Contemporary Educational Psychology, 25*(4), 423–449.

Cheung, A., & Slavin, R. E. (2005). Effective reading programs for English language learners and other language-minority students. *Bilingual Research Journal, 29*(2), 241–267.

Children's Defense Fund. (2009). *Child poverty.* Washington, DC: Author. Also available at www.childrensdefense.org

Chin, C. W. T. (1998, April). *Synthesizing metacognitive interventions: What training characteristics can improve reading performance?* Paper presented at the annual meeting of the American Educational Research Association, San Diego, CA.

Cho, M.-H., & Bergin, D. (2009, April). *Review of self-regulated learning models and implications for theory development.* Paper presented at the annual meeting of the American Educational Research Association, San Diego, CA.

Choate, J. (2004). *Successful inclusive teaching* (4th ed.). Boston: Pearson.

Chorzempa, B., & Graham, S. (2006). Primary-grade teachers' use of within-class ability grouping in reading. *Journal of Educational Psychology, 98*(3), 529–541.

Christian, D., & Genesee, F. (Eds.). (2001). *Bilingual education.* Alexandria, VA: TESOL.

Christopher, S. (2007/2008). Homework: A few practice arrows. *Educational Leadership, 65*(4), 74.

Cizek, G. J. (1999). *Cheating on tests: How to do it, detect it, and prevent it.* Mahwah, NJ: Erlbaum.

Clark, C. M., Gage, N. L., Marx, R. W., Peterson, P. L., Stayrook, N. G., & Winne, P. H. (1979). A factorial experiment on teacher structuring, soliciting, and reacting. *Journal of Educational Psychology, 71,* 534–552.

Clark, J. (1990). *Patterns of thinking: Integrating learning skills with content teaching.* Boston: Allyn & Bacon.

Clark, J. M., & Paivio, A. (1991). Dual coding theory and education. *Educational Psychology Review, 3*(3), 149–210.

Clark, K. (2009). The case for structured English immersion. *Educational Leadership, 66*(7), 42–47.

Clark, R. E. (Ed.). (2001). *Learning from media: Arguments, analysis, and evidence.* Greenwich, CT: Information Age.

Cleary, T. J., & Zimmerman, B. J. (2004). Self-regulation empowerment program: A school-based program to enhance self-regulated and self-motivated cycles of student learning. *Psychology in the Schools, 41,* 537–550.

Clements, D. H., & Battista, M. T. (1990). Constructivist learning and teaching. *Arithmetic Teacher, 38,* 34–37.

Clifford, M. M. (1990). Students need challenge, not easy success. *Educational Leadership, 48*(1), 22–26.

Coalition for Evidence Based Policy. (2003). *Identifying and implementing educational practices supported by rigorous evidence: A user friendly guide.* Washington, DC: U.S. Department of Education.

Cochran-Smith, M. (1991). Word processing and writing in elementary classrooms: A critical review of related literature. *Review of Educational Research, 61*(1), 107–155.

Cognition and Technology Group at Vanderbilt. (1996). Looking at technology in context: A framework for understanding technology and education research. In D. C. Berliner & R. C. Calfee (Eds.), *Handbook of educational psychology* (pp. 807–840). New York: Macmillan.

Cohen, E. G. (1986). *Designing groupwork: Strategies for the heterogeneous classroom.* New York: Teachers College Press.

Cohen, E. G. (1992, April). *Complex instruction in the middle school.* Paper presented at the annual meeting of the American Educational Research Association, San Francisco.

Cohen, E. G. (1994a). *Designing groupwork: Strategies for the heterogeneous classroom* (2nd ed.). New York: Teachers College Press.

Cohen, E. G. (1994b). Restructuring the classroom: Conditions for productive small groups. *Review of Educational Research, 64*(1), 1–35.

Cohen, E. G. (2004). Producing equal-status interaction amidst classroom diversity. In W. G. Stephan & W. P. Vogt (Eds.), *Education programs for improving intergroup relations.* New York: Teachers College Press.

Cohen, L. B., & Cashon, C. H. (2003). Infant perception and cognition. In R. M. Lerner, M. A. Easterbrooks, & J. Mistry (Eds.), *Handbook of psychology: Vol. 6. Developmental psychology* (pp. 65–89). Hoboken, NJ: Wiley.

Coie, J. D., Dodge, K. A., & Kupersmidt, J. (1990). Peer group behavior and social status. In S. R. Asher & J. D. Coie (Eds.), *Peer rejection in children* (pp. 17–59). New York: Cambridge University Press.

Colangelo, N., Assouline, S., & Gross, M. U. M. (2005). *A nation deceived: How schools hold back America's brightest students.* Iowa City, IA: International Center for Gifted Education and Talent Development.

Colangelo, N., & Davis, G. A. (Eds.). (2009). *Handbook of gifted education* (3rd ed.) Boston: Allyn & Bacon.

Colby, C., & Kohlberg, L. (1984). Invariant sequence and internal consistency in moral judgment stages. In W. Kurtines & J. Gewirts (Eds.), *Morality, moral behavior, and moral development.* New York: Wiley-Interscience.

Cole, D. A. (1991). Change in self-perceived competence as a function of peer and teacher evaluation. *Developmental Psychology, 27,* 682–688.

Cole-Henderson, B. (2000). Organizational characteristics of schools that successfully service low-income African American students. *Journal of Education for Students Placed at Risk, 5*(1–2), 77–91.

Coles, G. (2004). Danger in the classroom: "Brain Glitch" research and learning to read. *Phi Delta Kappan, 85*(5), 344–357.

Coley, R. L., & Chase-Lansdale, P. L. (1998). Adolescent pregnancy and parenthood. *American Psychologist, 53*(2), 152–166.

Colom, R., Flores-Mendoza, C., & Rebello, I. (2003). Working memory and intelligence. *Personality and Individual Differences, 34,* 33–39.

Colvin, G. (2004). *Managing the cycle of acting-out behavior in the classroom.* Longmont, CO: Sopris West.

Comer, J. (2005). Child and adolescent development: The critical missing focus in school reform. *Phi Delta Kappan, 86*(10), 757–763.

Comer, J. P. (1990). *Maggie's American dream.* New York: Plume.

Comer, J. P., Haynes, N. M., Joyner, E. T., & Ben-Avie, M. (1996). *Rallying the whole village: The Comer process for reforming education.* New York: Teachers College Press.

Comprehensive School Reform Quality Center (CSRQ). (2006a). *CSRQ center report on elementary comprehensive school reform models.* Washington, DC: American Institutes for Research.

Comprehensive School Reform Quality Center (CSRQ). (2006b). *CSRQ center report on middle and high school comprehensive school reform models.* Washington, DC: American Institutes for Research.

Connolly, B., & Smith, M. W. (2002). Teachers and students talk about talk: Class discussions and the way it should be. *Journal of Adolescent and Adult Literacy, 46*(1), 16–26.

Connor, C. M., Son, S. H., Hindman, A. H., & Morrison, F. J. (2004). *Teacher qualifications, classroom practices, and family characteristics: Complex effects on first-graders' vocabulary and early reading outcomes.* Ann Arbor: University of Michigan, Department of Psychology.

Conway, M. A., Cohen, G., & Stanhope, N. (1991). Very long-term memory of knowledge acquired through formal education: Twelve years of cognitive psychology. *Journal of Experimental Psychology: General, 120,* 395–409.

Conyers, L., Reynolds, A., & Ou, S. (2003). The effect of early childhood intervention and subsequent special education services: Findings from the Chicago child–parent centers. *Educational Evaluation and Policy Analysis, 25*(1), 75–95.

Cook, A., & Tashlik, P. (2004). *Talk, talk, talk,: Discussion based classrooms.* New York: Teachers College Press.

Cook, J. L., & Cook, G. (2007). *The world of children.* Boston: Allyn & Bacon.

Cook, T., Murphy, R. F., & Hunt, H. D. (2000). Comer's school development program in Chicago: A theory-based evaluation. *American Educational Research Journal, 37*(2), 535–597.

Cook, T. D., Habib, F., Phillips, M., Settersten, R. A., Shagle, S., & Degirmencioglu, M. (1999). Comer's school development program in Prince George's County, Maryland: A theory-based evaluation. *American Educational Research Journal, 36*(3), 543–597.

Cooley, W. W., & Leinhardt, G. (1980). The instructional dimensions study. *Educational Evaluation and Policy Analysis, 2,* 7–26.

Cooper, H., Charlton, K., Valentine, J. C., & Muhlenbruck, L. (2000). Making the most of summer school: A meta-analytic and narrative review. *Monographs of the Society for Research in Child Development, 65*(1, Serial No. 260), 1–118.

Cooper, H., Robinson, J. C., & Patall, E. (2006). Does homework improve academic achievement? *Review of Educational Research, 76*(1), 1–62.

Cooper, H., & Valentine, J. C. (2001). Using research to answer practical questions about homework. *Educational Psychologist, 36*(3), 143–153..

Cooper, R. (1998). Urban school reform: Student responses to detracking in a racially mixed high school. *Journal of Education for Students Placed at Risk, 4*(3), 259–275.

Cooper, R., & Slavin, R. E. (2004). Cooperative learning: An instructional strategy to improve intergroup relations. In W. G. Stephan & W. P. Vogt (Eds.), *Education programs for improving intergroup relations.* New York: Teachers College Press.

Copeland, W. D. (1983, April). *Classroom management and student teachers' cognitive abilities: A relationship.* Paper presented at the annual convention of the American Educational Research Association, Montreal, Canada.

Corbett, D., Wilson, B., & Williams, B. (2005). No choice but success. *Educational Leadership, 62*(6), 8–13.

Cordova, D. I., & Lepper, M. R. (1996). Intrinsic motivation and the process of learning: Beneficial effects of contextualization, personalization, and choice. *Journal of Educational Psychology, 88*(4), 715–730.

Corkill, A. J. (1992). Advance organizers: Facilitators of recall. *Educational Psychology Review, 4,* 33–67.

Corkum, P., Humphries, K., Mullane, J., & Theriault, F. (2008). Private speech in children with ADHD and their typically developing peers during problem-solving and inhibition tasks. *Contemporary Educational Psychology, 33*(1), 97–115.

Cornelius-White, J. (2007). Learner-centered teacher-student relationships are effective: A meta-analysis. *Review of Educational Research, 77*(1), 113–143.

Corno, L. (2000). Looking at homework differently. *The Elementary School Journal, 100*(5), 529–548.

Corno, L. (2008). On teaching adaptively. *Educational Psychologist, 43*(3), 161–173.

Corno, L., & Kanfer, R. (1993). The role of volition in learning and performance. *Review of Research in Education, 19,* 301–341.

Corpus, J., McClintic-Gilbert, M., & Hayenga, A. (2009). Within-year changes in children's intrinsic and extrinsic motivational orientations: Contextual predictors and academic outcomes. *Contemporary Educational Psychology, 34*(2), 154–166.

Correnti, R. (2009, March). *Examining CSR Program effects on student achievement: Causal explanation through examination of implementation rates and student mobility.* Paper presented at the 2nd annual conference of the Society for Research on Educational Effectiveness, Washington, DC.

Cose, E. (2004). *Beyond Brown v. Board: The final battle for excellence in American education.* A report by Ellis Cose to the Rockefeller Foundation.

Costa, A. (2008). The thought-filled curriculum. *Educational Leadership, 65*(5), 20–25.

Cote, C., Thompson, R., Hanley, G., & McKerchar, P. (2007). Teacher report and direct assessment of preferences for identifying reinforcers for young children. *Journal of Applied Behavior Analysis, 40,* 157–166.

Covington, M. (1999). Caring about learning: The nature and nurturing of subject-matter appreciation. *Educational Psychologist, 34*(2), 127–136.

Cox, B., & Hopkins, C. (2006). Building on theoretical principles gleaned from Reading Recovery to inform classroom practice. *Reading Research Quarterly, 41*(2), 254–267.

Cox, B. D. (1997). The rediscovery of the active learner in adaptive contexts: A developmental-historical analysis of transfer of training. *Educational Psychologist, 32,* 41–55.

Craik, F. I. M. (2000). Memory: Coding processes. In A. Kazdin (Ed.), *Encyclopedia of psychology.* Washington, DC: American Psychological Association.

Crawford, J. (1989). Instructional activities related to achievement gain in Chapter I classes. In R. E. Slavin, N. L. Karweit, & N. A. Madden (Eds.), *Effective programs for students at risk.* Boston: Allyn & Bacon.

Creswell, J. W. (2002). *Research design: Qualitative, quantitative, and mixed methods approaches* (2nd ed.). Thousand Oaks, CA: Sage.

Crévola, C. A., & Hill, P. W. (1998). Evaluation of a whole-school approach to prevention and intervention in early literacy. *Journal of Education for Students Placed at Risk, 3*(2), 133–157.

Crocker, R. K., & Brooker, G. M. (1986). Classroom control and student outcomes in grades 2 and 5. *American Educational Research Journal, 23,* 1–11.

Crooks, T. J. (1988). The impact of classroom evaluation practices on students. *Review of Educational Research, 58,* 438–481.

Cross, L. H., & Cross, G. M. (1980/1981). Teachers' evaluative comments and pupil perception of control. *Journal of Experimental Education, 49,* 68–71.

Crowe, C. (2008). Solving behavior problems together. *Educational Leadership, 66*(3), 44–47.

Crutcher, R. J., & Ericsson, K. A. (2003). The effects of practice on mnemonic encodings involving prior knowledge and semantic memory. *Journal of Experimental Psychology: Learning Memory and Cognition, 29*(6), 1387–1389.

Cruz, L., & Cullinan, D. (2001). Awarding points, using levels to help children improve behavior. *Teaching Exceptional Children, 33*(3), 16–23.

Cuban, L., Kirkpatrick, H., & Peck, C. (2001). High access and low use of technology in high school classrooms: Explaining an apparent paradox. *American Educational Research Journal, 38*(4), 813–834.

Cummings, E. M., Braungart-Rieker, J. M., & Du Rocher-Schudlich, T. (2003). Emotion and personality development in childhood. In R. M. Lerner, M. A. Easterbrooks, & J. Mistry (Eds.), *Handbook of psychology: Vol. 6. Developmental psychology* (pp. 211–239). Hoboken, NJ: Wiley.

Curry, C. (2003). Universal design accessibility for all learners. *Educational Leadership, 61*(2), 55–60.

Curwin, R. E., & Mendler, A. N. (1999). Zero tolerance for zero tolerance. *Phi Delta Kappan, 81*(2), 119–120.

Cushman, K. (2006). Help us care enough to learn. *Educational Leadership, 63*(5), 34–37.

Cutshall, S. (2009). Clicking across cultures. *Educational Leadership, 67*(1), 40–44.

Daniels, H. (2001). *Vygotsky and pedagogy.* New York: Routledge.

Dansereau, D. F. (1985). Learning strategy research. In J. Segal, S. Chipman, & R. Glaser (Eds.), *Thinking and learning skills: Relating instruction to basic research, Vol. 1.* Hillsdale, NJ: Erlbaum.

Dantonio, M., & Beisenherz, P. (2001). *Learning to question, questioning to learn.* Boston: Allyn & Bacon.

Darling-Hammond, L. (2006). Securing the right to learn: Policy and practice for powerful teaching and learning. *Educational Researcher, 35*(7), 13–24.

Darling-Hammond, L. (2008). Teacher quality definition debates: What is an effective teacher? In T. L. Good (Ed.), *21st century learning: Vol. 2* (pp. 12–22). Thousand Oaks, CA: Sage.

Darling-Hammond, L., Ancess, J., & Ort, S. W. (2002). Reinventing high school: Outcomes of the coalition campus schools project. *American Educational Research Journal, 39*(3), 639–673.

Darling-Hammond, L., & Falk, B. (1997). Using standards and assessments to support student learning. *Phi Delta Kappan, 79*(3), 190–201.

Darling-Hammond, L., Gendler, T., & Wise, A. D. (1990). *The teaching internship: Practical preparation for a licensed profession.* Santa Monica, CA: RAND.

Darling-Hammond, L., & Ifill-Lynch, O. (2006). If they'd only do their work! *Educational Leadership, 63*(5), 8–13.

Darling-Hammond, L., & Richardson, N. (2009). Teacher learning: What matters? *Educational Leadership, 66*(5), 46–55.

Datnow, A., Lasky, S., Stringfield, S., & Teddlie, C. (2005). Systemic integration for educational reform in racially and linguistically diverse contexts: A summary of the evidence. *Journal of Education for Students Placed at Risk, 10*(4), 441–453.

David, J. (2008). Project-based learning. *Educational Leadership, 65*(5), 80–84.

David, J. (2009). Teaching media literacy. *Educational Leadership, 66*(6), 84–86.

Davis, H. (2008). Development: 3–5. In T. L. Good (Ed.), *21st century learning* (Vol. 1, pp. 82–92). Thousand Oaks, CA: Sage.

Dawson, T. L. (2002). New tools, new insights: Kohlberg's moral judgement stages revisited. *International Journal of Behavioral Development, 26,* 154–166.

DeBacker, T., & Nelson, R. M. (1999). Variations on an expectancy-value model of motivation in science. *Contemporary Educational Psychology, 24*(2), 71–94.

DeBell, M., & Chapman, C. (2006). *Computer and internet use by students in 2003.* Washington, DC: National Center for Education Statistics, U.S. Department of Education.

Deci, E., Koestner, R., & Ryan, R. (2001). Extrinsic rewards and intrinsic motivation in education: Reconsidered once again. *Review of Educational Research, 71*(1), 1–27.

Deci, E. L., & Ryan, R. M. (Eds.). (2002). *Handbook of self-determination research.* Rochester, NY: University of Rochester Press.

De Jong, T., & van Joolingen, W. R. (1998). Scientific discovery learning with computer simulations of conceptual domains. *Review of Educational Research, 68*(2), 179–201.

Delamont, S. (2002). Gender and education. In D. L. Levinson, P. W. Cookson, Jr., & A. R. Sadovnik (Eds.), *Education and sociology: An encyclopedia* (pp. 273–279). New York: Routledge Falmer.

de La Paz, S., & Graham, S. (2002). Explicitly teaching strategies, skills, and knowledge: Writing instruction in middle school classrooms. *Journal of Educational Psychology, 94*(2), 687–698.

De Lisi, R., & Staudt, J. (1980). Individual differences in college students' performance on formal operations tasks. *Journal of Applied Developmental Psychology, 1,* 201–208.

Delpit, L. (1995). *Other people's children: Cultural conflict in the classroom.* New York: New Press.

Dembo, M., & Eaton, M. (2000). Self-regulation of academic learning in middle-level schools. *The Elementary School Journal, 100*(5), 472–490.

Dempster, F. N. (1989). Spacing effects and their implications for theory and practice. *Educational Psychology Review, 1,* 309–330.

Dempster, F. N. (1991). Synthesis of research on reviews and tests. *Educational Leadership, 72*(8), 71–76.

Dempster, F. N., & Corkill, A. J. (1999). Interference and inhibition in cognition and behavior: Unifying themes for educational psychology. *Educational Psychology Review, 11*(1), 1–74.

Denton, C. A., Anthony, J. L., Parker, R., & Hasbrouck, J. E. (2004). Effects of two tutoring programs on the English reading development of Spanish-English bilingual students. *The Elementary School Journal, 104*(4), 289–305.

Deshler, D., Palincsar, A., Biancarosa, G., & Nair, M. (2007). *Informed choices for struggling adolescent readers.* Newark, DE: International Reading Association.

Deshler, D. D. (2005). Adolescents with learning disabilities. *Learning Disabilities Quarterly, 28*(2), 122–123.

Deshler, D. D., Ellis, E. S., & Lenz, B. K. (1996). *Teaching students with learning disabilities: Strategies and methods* (2nd ed.). Denver: Love.

DeVries, R. (2008). Piaget and Vygotsky: Theory and practice in early education. In T. L. Good (Ed.), *21st century learning* (Vol. 1, pp. 184–193). Thousand Oaks, CA: Sage.

deWinstanley, P. A., & Bjork, E. L. (2004). Processing strategies and the generation effect: Implications for making a better reader. *Memory & Cognition, 32*(6), 945–955.

Díaz-Rico, L. T. (2004). *Teaching English learners: Strategies and methods.* Boston: Allyn & Bacon.

Díaz-Rico, L. T., & Weed, K. Z. (2010). *The crosscultural, language, and academic development handbook: A complete K–12 reference guide* (4th ed.). Boston: Allyn & Bacon.

Dick, W., Carey, L., & Carey, J. O. (Eds.). (2009). *The systematic design of instruction* (7th ed.). Upper Saddle River, NJ: Merrill.

Diehm, C. (2004). From worn-out to web-based: Better student portfolios. *Phi Delta Kappan, 85*(10), 792–795.

Dillon, A., & Gabbard, R. (1998). Hypermedia as an educational technology: A review of the quantitative research literature on learner comprehension, control, and style. *Review of Educational Research, 68*(3), 322–349.

Dlott, A. (2007). A (pod)cast of thousands. *Educational Leadership, 64*(7), 80–82.

Dong, Y. (2009). Linking to prior learning. *Educational Leadership, 66*(7), 26–31.

Dooling, D. J., & Lachman, R. (1971). Effects of comprehension on retention of prose. *Journal of Experimental Psychology, 8,* 216–222.

Dornbusch, S. (1994). *Off the track*. Paper presented at the annual meeting of the Society for Research on Adolescence, San Diego, CA.

Dotterer, A., McHale, S., & Crouter, A. (2009). The development and correlates of academic interests from childhood through adolescence. *Journal of Educational Psychology, 101*(2), 509–519.

Downing, J. E. (2001). *Including students with severe and multiple disabilities in typical classrooms*. Baltimore: Brookes.

Doyle, W. (1984). How order is achieved in classrooms: An interim report. *Journal of Curriculum Studies, 16*, 259–277.

Drabman, R., Spitalnik, R., & O'Leary, K. (1973). Teaching self-control to disruptive children. *Journal of Abnormal Psychology, 82*, 10–16.

Driscoll, A., & Nagel, N. G. (2008). *Early childhood education, birth–8: The world of children, families, and educators* (4th ed.). Boston: Pearson.

Driscoll, M. P. (2000). *Psychology of learning for instruction* (2nd ed.). Boston: Allyn & Bacon.

Driscoll, M. P. (2005). *Psychology of learning for instruction* (3rd ed.). Boston: Allyn & Bacon.

Droz, M., & Ellis, L. (1996). *Laughing while learning: Using humor in the classroom*. Longmont, CO: Sopris West.

Dryfoos, J. G. (1998). *Safe passage: Making it through adolescence in a risky society*. New York: Oxford University Press.

Duck, L. (2000). The ongoing professional journey. *Educational Leadership, 57*(8), 43–45.

Duell, O. K. (1994). Extended wait time and university student achievement. *American Educational Research Journal, 31*(2), 397–414.

Duffy, G. G., & Roehler, L. R. (1986). The subtleties of instructional mediation. *Educational Leadership, 43*(7), 23–27.

Dugger, W. (2001). Standards for technological literacy. *Phi Delta Kappan, 82*(7), 513–517.

Duke, N., Bennett-Armistead, V., & Roberts, E. (2003). Bridging the gap between learning to read and reading to learn. In D. Barone & L. Morrow (Eds.), *Literacy and young children: Research-based practices* (pp. 226–242). New York: Guilford.

Duke, N. K. (2000). For the rich it's richer: Print experiences and environments offered to children in very low- and very high-socioeconomic status first-grade classrooms. *American Educational Research Journal, 37*(2), 441–478.

Dukes, R., & Seidner, C. (1978). *Learning with simulations and games*. Beverly Hills, CA: Sage.

Dunkin, M. J., & Biddle, B. J. (1974). *A study of teaching*. New York: Holt, Rinehart and Winston.

Dunn, K., & Mulvenon, S. (2009). A critical review of research on formative assessment: The limited scientific evidence of the impact of formative assessment in education. *Practical Assessment, Research & Evaluation, 14*(7), 1–11.

Dunn, R., & Dunn, K. (1993). *Teaching secondary students through their individual learning styles*. Boston: Allyn & Bacon.

Durso, F. T., & Coggins, K. A. (1991). Organized instruction for the improvement of word knowledge skills. *Journal of Educational Psychology, 83*, 108–112.

Dweck, C. (2007). The perils and promises of praise. *Educational Leadership, 65*(2), 34–39.

Dynarski, M. (2008/2009). Researchers and educators: Allies in learning. *Educational Leadership, 66*(4), 48–53.

Dynarski, M., Agodini, R., Heaviside, S., Novak, T., Carey, N., Campuzzano, L., Means, B., et al. (2007). *Effectiveness of reading and mathematics software products: Findings from the first student cohort*. Washington, DC: Institute of Education Sciences.

Ebeling, D. G. (2000). Adapting your teaching to any learning style. *Phi Delta Kappan, 82*(3), 247–248.

Eccles, J. S., Wigfield, A., & Byrnes, J. (2003). Cognitive development in adolescence. In R. M. Lerner, M. A. Easterbrooks, & J. Mistry (Eds.), *Handbook of psychology: Vol. 6. Developmental psychology* (pp. 325–350). Hoboken, NJ: Wiley.

Echevarria, J., Vogt, M. E., & Short, D. (Eds.). (2008). *Making content comprehensible for English learners: The SIOP model*. Boston: Allyn & Bacon.

Eckensberger, L. H. (1994). Moral development and its measurement across cultures. In W. J. Lonner & R. S. Malpass (Eds.), *Psychology and culture* (pp. 75–79). Boston: Allyn & Bacon.

Eden, G. F., Van Meter, J. W., Rumsey, J. M., Maisog, J. M., Woods, R. P., & Zeffiro, T. A. (1996). Abnormal processing of visual motion in dyslexia revealed by functional brain imaging. *Nature, 382*, 66–69.

Educational Testing Service. (1995). *Performance assessment: Different needs, difficult answers*. Princeton, NJ: Author.

Education Commission of the States. (2000). *Technology: Equitable access in schools*. Denver, CO: Author.

The Education Trust. (2003). *ESEA: Myths versus realities. Answers to questions about the No Child Left Behind Act*. Washington, DC: Author.

Egan, K. (1989). Memory, imagination, and learning: Connected by the story. *Phi Delta Kappan, 70*, 455–459.

Egan, K. (2008). Learning in depth. *Educational Leadership, 66*(3), 58–64.

Ehri, L. C., Dreyer, L. G., Flugman, B., & Gross, A. (2007). Reading Rescue: An effective tutoring intervention model for language-minority students who are struggling readers in first grade. *American Educational Research Journal, 44*, 414–448.

Eichenbaum, H. (2003). Memory systems. In M. Gallagher & R. J. Nelson (Eds.), *Handbook of psychology: Vol. 3. Biological psychology* (pp. 543–558). Hoboken, NJ: Wiley.

Einerson, M. (1998). Fame, fortune, and failure: Young girls' moral language surrounding popular culture. *Youth and Society, 30*, 241–257.

Eisenberg, N. (2001). The core and correlates of affective social competence. *Social Development, 10*, 120–124.

Eisenberger, R., & Cameron, J. (1998). Reward, intrinsic interest, and creativity: New findings. *American Psychologist, 53*(6), 676–679.

Eisenberger, R., Pierce, W. D., & Cameron, J. (1999). Effects of rewards on intrinsic motivation—negative, neutral, and positive: Comment on Deci, Koestner, and Ryan (1999). *Psychological Bulletin, 125*, 677–691.

Eisner, E. (2006). The satisfactions of teaching. *Educational Leadership, 63*(6), 44–47.

Elbaum, B., & Vaughn, S. (2001). School-based interventions to enhance the self-concept of students with learning disabilities: A meta-analysis. *The Elementary School Journal, 101*(3), 303–330.

Elias, L. J., & Saucier, D. M. (2006). *Neuropsychoogy: Clinical and experimental foundations*. Boston: Allyn & Bacon.

Eliot, L. (2009). *Pink brain, blue brain*. Boston: Houghton Mifflin Harcourt.

Ellis, A. K. (2001a). Authentic and performance assessment. In A. K. Ellis (Ed.), *Research on educational innovations*. Larchmont, NY: Eye on Education.

Ellis, A. K. (2001b). Cooperative learning. In A. K. Ellis (Ed.), *Research on educational innovations*. Larchmont, NY: Eye on Education.

Ellis, A. K. (2001c). Innovations from brain research. In A. K. Ellis (Ed.), *Research on educational innovations*. Larchmont, NY: Eye on Education.

Ellis, J., Semb, G. B., & Cole, B. (1998). Very long-term memory for information taught in school. *Contemporary Educational Psychology, 23*, 419–433.

Ellmore, R. F., & Fuhrman, S. H. (2001). Holding schools accountable: Is it working? *Phi Delta Kappan, 83*(1), 67–72.

Else-Quest, N., Shibley, J., Goldsmith, H., & Van Hulle, C. (2006). Gender differences in temperament: A meta-analysis. *Psychological Bulletin, 132*(1), 33–72.

Embry, D. D. (2002). The good behavior game: A best practice candidate as universal behavior vaccine. *Clinical Child and Family Psychology Review, 5,* 273–297.

Emerson, M. J., & Miyake, A. (2003). The role of inner speech in task switching: A dual-task investigation. *Journal of Memory and Language, 48,* 148–168.

Emmer, E. T., & Aussiker, A. (1990). School and classroom discipline programs: How well do they work? In O. C. Moles (Ed.), *Student discipline strategies.* Albany: State University of New York Press.

Emmer, E. T., & Evertson, C. M. (Eds.). (2009). *Classroom management for middle and high school teachers.* Upper Saddle River, NJ: Pearson.

Emmer, E. T., Evertson, C. M., & Anderson, L. M. (1980). Effective classroom management at the beginning of the school year. *Elementary School Journal, 80,* 219–231.

Emmer, E. T., & Gerwels, M. C. (2002). Cooperative learning in elementary classrooms: Teaching practices and lesson characteristics. *The Elementary School Journal, 103*(1), 75–91.

Emmer, E. T., & Stough, L. M. (2001). Classroom management: A critical part of educational psychology, with implications for teacher education. *Educational Psychologist, 36*(2), 103–112.

Emmer, E. T., & Stough, L. M. (2008). Responsive classroom management. In T. L. Good (Ed.), *21st century learning: Vol. 1* (pp. 140–148). Thousand Oaks, CA: Sage.

Engelkamp, J., & Dehn, D. M. (2000). Item and order information in subject-performed tasks and experimenter-performed tasks. *Journal of Experimental Psychology: Learning, Memory, & Cognition, 26,* 671–682.

Engle, R. W. (2001). What is working memory capacity? In H. L. Roediger, J. S. Nairne, I. Neath, & A. M. Suprenant (Eds.), *The nature of remembering: Essays in honor of Robert G. Crowder* (pp. 297–314). Washington, DC: American Psychological Association.

Engle, R. W., Nations, J. K., & Cantor, J. (1990). Is "working memory capacity" just another name for word knowledge? *Journal of Educational Psychology, 82*(4), 799–804.

Englert, C. S., Raphael, T. E., Anderson, L. M., Anthony, H. M., & Stevens, D. D. (1991). Making strategies and self-talk visible: Writing instruction in regular and special education classrooms. *American Educational Research Journal, 28,* 337–372.

Ennemoser, M., & Schneider, W. (2007). Relations of television viewing and reading: Findings from a 4-year longitudinal study. *Journal of Educational Psychology, 99*(2), 349–368.

Ensminger, M. E., & Slusarcick, A. L. (1992). Paths to high school graduation or dropout: A longitudinal study of a first grade cohort. *Sociology of Education, 65,* 95–113.

Entwisle, D., Alexander, L., & Olson, L. S. (2001). Keep the faucet flowing: Summer learning and home environment. *American Educator, 25*(3), 10–15.

Epstein, A. (2008). An early start on thinking. *Educational Leadership, 65*(5), 38–43.

Epstein, J. L., & Van Voorhis, F. L. (2001). More than minutes: Teachers' roles in designing homework. *Educational Psychologist, 36*(3), 181–193.

Epstein, J. L., Sanders, M. G., Salinas, K., Simon, B., Van Voorhis, F., & Jansorn, N. (2002). *School, family and community partnerships: Your handbook for action* (2nd ed.). Thousand Oaks, CA: Corwin.

Ericsson, K. A., & Kintsch, W. (1995). Long-term working memory. *Psychological Review, 102,* 211–245.

Erikson, E. H. (1963). *Childhood and society* (2nd ed.). New York: Norton.

Erikson, E. H. (1968). *Identity, youth and crisis.* New York: Norton.

Erikson, E. H. (1980). *Identity and the life cycle* (2nd ed.). New York: Norton.

Espy, K. A., Molfese, D. L., Molfese, V. J., & Modglin, A. (2004). Development of auditory event-related potentials in young children and relations to word-level reading abilities at age 8 years. *Annals of Dyslexia, 54*(1), 9–38.

Estrada, V., Gómez, L., & Ruiz-Escalante, J. (2009). Let's make dual language the norm. *Educational Leadership, 66*(7), 54–58.

Evans, G. (2004). The environment of childhood poverty. *American Psychologist, 59,* 77–92.

Evans, S. W., Pelham, W. E., Smith, B. H., Bukstein, O., Gnagy, E. M., Greiner, A. R., Altenderfer, L., & Baron-Myak, C. (2000). Dose-response effect of methylphenidate on ecologically valid measures of academic performance and classroom behavior in adolescents with ADHD. *Experimental and Clinical Psychopharmacology, 9*(2), 163–175.

Evans, T. D. (1996). Encouragement: The key to reforming the classrooms. *Educational Leadership, 54*(1), 81–85.

Everson, H., & Millsap, R. (2004). Beyond individual differences: Exploring school effects on SAT scores. *Educational Psychologist, 39*(3), 157–172.

Everson, H., Tobias, S., Hartman, H., & Gourgey, A. (1993). Test anxiety and the curriculum: The subject matters. *Anxiety, Stress, and Coping, 6,* 1–8.

Evertson, C., Emmer, E., & Worsham, M. E. (2006). *Classroom management for elementary teachers* (7th ed.). Boston: Allyn & Bacon.

Evertson, C. M., & Emmer, E. T. (1982). Effective management at the beginning of the year in junior high classes. *Journal of Educational Psychology, 74,* 485–498.

Evertson, C. M., Emmer, E. T., & Brophy, J. E. (1980). Predictors of effective teaching in junior high mathematics classrooms. *Journal for Research in Mathematics Education, 11,* 167–178.

Evertson, C. M., & Harris, A. H. (1992). What we know about managing classrooms. *Educational Leadership, 49*(7), 74–78.

Evertson, C. M., & Poole, I. R. (2008). Proactive classroom management. In T. L. Good (Ed.), *21st century learning: Vol. 1* (pp. 131–139). Thousand Oaks, CA: Sage.

Evertson, C. M., & Randolph, C. H. (1995). Classroom management in the learning-centered classroom. In A. C. Ornstein (Ed.), *Teaching: Theory into practice.* Boston: Allyn & Bacon.

Evertson, C. M., Weade, R., Green, J., & Crawford, J. (1985). *Effective classroom management and instruction: An exploration of models.* Nashville, TN: Vanderbilt University.

Evertson, E., Emmer, E., & Worsham, M. (2009). *Classroom management for middle and high school teachers.* Boston: Allyn & Bacon.

Fahey, J. A. (2000). Who wants to differentiate instruction? We did. . . . *Educational Leadership, 58*(1), 70–72.

Fantuzzo, J. W., King, J. A., & Heller, L. R. (1992). Effects of reciprocal peer tutoring on mathematics and school adjustment: A component analysis. *Journal of Educational Psychology, 84,* 33–39.

Fantuzzo, J. W., Polite, K., & Grayson, N. (1990). An evaluation of reciprocal peer tutoring across elementary school settings. *Journal of School Psychology, 28,* 309–323.

Farmer, T., Leung, M.-C., Pearl, R., Rodkin, P., Cadwallader, T., & Van Acker, R. (2002). Deviant or diverse peer groups? The peer affiliations of aggressive elementary students. *Journal of Educational Psychology, 94*(3), 611–620.

Farrell, T. (2009). *Teaching reading to English language learners: A reflective guide.* Thousand Oaks, CA: Corwin.

Fashola, O. S. (2002). *Building effective after school programs.* Thousand Oaks, CA: Corwin.

Fay, J. (2001). The classroom of your dreams. In B. Sornson (Ed.), *Preventing early learning failure.* Alexandria, VA: ASCD.

Feldhusen, J. F. (1996). How to identify and develop special talents. *Educational Leadership, 53*(5), 66–69.

Feldman, R. S. (Ed.). (2010). *Child development.* Upper Saddle River, NJ: Prentice-Hall.

Fellows, N. J. (1994). A window into thinking: Using student writing to understand conceptual changes in science learning. *Journal of Science Teaching, 31,* 985–1001.

Fennema, E., Carpenter, T. P., Jacobs, V. R., Franke, M. L., & Levi, L. W. (1998). A longitudinal study of gender differences in young children's mathematical thinking. *Educational Researcher, 27*(5), 6–11.

Fennema, E., Franke, M. L., Carpenter, T. P., & Carey, D. A. (1993). Using children's mathematical knowledge in instruction. *American Educational Research Journal, 30*(3), 555–583.

Ferguson, R., & Mehta, J. (2004). An unfinished journey: The legacy of Brown and the narrowing of the achievement gap. *Phi Delta Kappan, 85*(9), 656–669.

Ferriter, B. (2009a). Learning with blogs and wikis. *Educational Leadership, 66*(5), 34–39.

Ferriter, B. (2009b). Taking the digital plunge. *Educational Leadership, 67*(1), 85.

Feuerstein, R. (1980). *Instrumental enrichment: An intervention program for cognitive modifiability.* Baltimore: University Park Press.

Feuerstein, R., & Kozulin, A. (1995). The bell curve: Getting the facts right. *Educational Leadership, 52*(7), 71–74.

Fidalgo, R., Torrance, M., & Garcia, J.-N. (2008). The long-term effects of strategy-focused writing instruction for grade six students. *Contemporary Educational Psychology, 33*(4), 672–693.

Fielding, L. G., Anderson, R. C., & Pearson, P. D. (1990). *How discussion questions influence children's story understanding* (Tech. Rep. No. 490). Champaign: University of Illinois, Center for the Study of Reading.

Finn, J. D., & Cox, D. (1992). Participation and withdrawal among fourth-grade pupils. *American Educational Research Journal, 29*(1), 141–162.

Finn, J. D., Pannozzo, G. M., & Achilles, C. M. (2003). The "whys" of class size: Student behavior in small classes. *Review of Educational Research, 73*(3), 321–368.

Finn, J. D., Pannozzo, G. M., & Voelkl, K. E. (1995). Disruptive and inattentive-withdrawn behavior and achievement among fourth graders. *The Elementary School Journal, 95*(5), 421–434.

Fiordaliso, R., Lordeman, A., Filipczak, J., & Friedman, R. M. (1977). Effects of feedback on absenteeism in the junior high school. *Journal of Educational Research, 70,* 188–192.

Fisch, S., & Truglio, R. (2000). *G is for growing: 30 years of research on Sesame Street.* Mahwah, NJ: Erlbaum.

Fisher, C. W., Berliner, D. C., Filby, N. N., Marliave, R., Cahen, L. S., Dishaw, M. M., & Moore, J. E. (1978). *Teaching behaviors, academic learning time, and student achievement: Final report of Phase III-B, beginning teacher evaluation study* (Tech. Rep. V-1). San Francisco: Far West Laboratory for Educational Research and Development.

Fisher, D. (2006). Keeping adolescents "alive and kickin' it: Addressing suicide in schools. *Phi Delta Kappan, 87*(10), 784–786.

Fisher, D., & Frey, N. (2007). *Checking for understanding: Formative assessment techniques for your classroom.* Alexandria, VA: ASCD.

Fisher, D., & Frey, N. (2008). Releasing responsibility. *Educational Leadership, 66*(3), 32–37.

Fisher, D., & Frey, N. (2009). Feed up, back, forward. *Educational Leadership, 67*(3), 20–25.

Fisher, D., Sax, C., & Grove, K. (2000). The resilience of changes promoting inclusiveness in an urban elementary school. *The Elementary School Journal, 100*(3), 213–228.

Fiske, E. B. (1989, July 12). The misleading concept of "average" on reading tests changes, and more students fall below it. *The New York Times.*

Fitzgerald, J., & Graves, M. (2004/2005). Reading supports for all. *Educational Leadership, 62*(4), 68–71.

Flanagan, C. (1993). Gender and social class: Intersecting issues in women's achievement. *Educational Psychologist, 28*(4), 357–378.

Flavell, J. (2004). Theory-of-mind development: Retrospect and prospect. *Merrill-Palmer Quarterly, 50,* 21–45.

Flavell, J. H. (1986, January). Really and truly. *Psychology Today, 20*(1), 38–44.

Flavell, J. H. (1996). Piaget's legacy. *Psychological Science, 7*(4), 200–203.

Fleischman, S. (2006). Moving to evidence-based professional practice. *Educational Leadership, 63*(6), 87–90.

Fleith, D. (2000). Teacher and student perceptions of creativity in the classroom environment. *Roeper Review, 22,* 148–153.

Fletcher, J. D. (1992). Individualized systems of instruction. In M. C. Alkin (Ed.), *Encyclopedia of educational research* (6th ed., pp. 612–620). New York: Macmillan.

Fletcher, J. M., Shaywitz, S. E., Shankweiler, D. P., Katz, L., Liberman, I. Y., Stvebing, K. K., Francis, D. J., Fowler, A. E., & Shaywitz, B. A. (1994). Cognitive profiles of reading disability: Comparisons of discrepancy and low achievement definitions. *Journal of Educational Psychology, 86,* 6–23.

Flexner, C. (2001). Enhancing the listening environment for early learning success. In B. Sornson (Ed.), *Preventing early learning failure.* Alexandria, VA: ASCD.

Flippo, R. (2008). *Preparing students for testing and doing better in school.* Thousand Oaks, CA: Corwin.

Florez, I. R. (2008). Early childhood education: The developmentally appropriate practice debate. In T. L. Good (Ed.), *21st century learning* (Vol. 1, pp. 396–404). Thousand Oaks, CA: Sage.

Flouri, E., & Buchanan, A. (2004). Early father's and mother's involvement and child's later educational outcomes. *British Journal of Educational Psychology, 74*(2), 141–153.

Fogarty, R. (Ed.). (1993). *The multiage classroom.* Palatine, IL: IRI/Skylight.

Fogarty, R., & Kerns, G. (2009). *inFormative assessment: When it's not about a grade.* Thousand Oaks, CA: Corwin.

Foos, P. W., Mora, J. J., & Tkacz, S. (1994). Student study techniques and the generation effect. *Journal of Educational Psychology, 86*(4), 567–576.

Forness, S. R., & Kavale, K. A. (2000). What definitions of disabilities say and don't say: A critical analysis. *Journal of Learning Disabilities, 33*(3), 239–256.

Fosnot, C. (Ed.). (2005). *Constructivism: Theory, perspectives, and practice* (2nd ed.). New York: Teachers College Press.

Foster, D., & Noyce, P. (2004). The mathematics assessment collaborative: Performance testing to improve instruction. *Phi Delta Kappan, 85*(5), 367–374.

Francis, B., & Skelton, C. (2005). *Reassessing gender and achievement.* New York: Routledge.

Francis, D. J., Shaywitz, S. E., Shaywitz, B. A., Stuebing, K. K., & Fletcher, J. M. (1996). Developmental lag versus deficit models of reading disability: A longitudinal, individual growth curves analysis. *Journal of Educational Psychology, 88*(1), 3–17.

Franklin, R. D., Allison, D. B., & Gorman, B. S. (Eds.). (1997). *Design and analysis of single-case research.* Mahwah, NJ: Erlbaum.

Fredricks, J. A., Blumenfeld, P. C., & Paris, A. H. (2004). School engagement: Potential of the concept, state of the evidence. *Review of Educational Research, 74*(1), 59–109.

Freiberg, H., Huzinec, C., & Templeton, S. (2009). Classroom management—a pathway to student achievement: A study of fourteen inner-city elementary schools. *The Elementary School Journal, 110*(1), 63–80.

Freiberg, H., & Lamb, S. (2009). Dimensions of person-centered classroom management. *Theory into Practice, 48,* 99–105.

Freiberg, H., & Lapointe, J. (2006). Research-based programs for preventing and solving disciplinary problems. In C. Evertson & C. Weinstein (Eds.), *Handbook of classroom management: Research, practice, and contemporary issues.* Mahwah, NJ: Erlbaum.

Freiberg, H. J., Connell, M. L., & Lorentz, J. (2001). Effects of consistency management on student mathematics achievement on seven Chapter I elementary schools. *Journal of Education for Students Placed at Risk, 6*(3), 249–270.

Freiberg, H. J., & Driscoll, A. (Eds.). (2005). *Universal teaching strategies* (4th ed.). Boston: Pearson.

Freiberg, H. J., & Reyes, A. (2008). Zero tolerance: A reconsideration of practice and policy. In T. L. Good (Ed.), *21st century learning* (Vol. 1, pp. 149–160). Thousand Oaks, CA: Sage.

French, E. G. (1956). Motivation as a variable in work partner selection. *Journal of Abnormal and Social Psychology, 55,* 96–99.

Frey, K., Hirschstein, M., & Guzzo, B. (2000). Second step: Preventing aggression by promoting social competence. *Journal of Emotional and Behavioral Disorders, 8,* 102–112.

Friedman, L. (2003). Promoting opportunity after school. *Educational Leadership, 60*(4), 79–82.

Friend, M. (2007). The coteaching partnership. *Educational Leadership, 64*(5), 48–53.

Friend, M., & Bursuck, W. D. (Eds.). (2008). *Including students with special needs: A practical guide for classroom teachers* (5th ed.). Upper Saddle River, NJ: Pearson.

Friend, M., & Shamberger, C. T. (2008). Inclusion. In T. L. Good (Ed.), *21st century learning* (Vol. 2, pp. 124–131). Thousand Oaks, CA: Sage.

Friend, R. (2001). Effects of strategy instruction on summary writing of college students. *Contemporary Educational Psychology, 26*(1), 3–24.

Fries, S., Dietz, F., & Schmid, S. (2008). Motivational interference in learning: The impact of leisure alternatives on subsequent self-regulation. *Contemporary Educational Psychology, 33*(2), 119–133.

Fuchs, D., & Fuchs, L. (2006). Introduction to response to intervention: What, why, and how valid is it? *Reading Research Quarterly, 41*(1), 92–128.

Fuchs, D., & Fuchs, L. S. (1997). Peer-assisted learning strategies: Making classrooms more responsive to diversity. *American Educational Research Journal, 34*(1), 174–206.

Fuchs, D., Fuchs, L. S., Bahr, M. W., Fernstrom, P., & Stecker, P. M. (1990). Mainstream assistance teams: A scientific basis for the art of consultation. *Exceptional Children, 56,* 493–513.

Fuchs, D., Fuchs, L. S., & Compton, D. L. (2004). Identifying reading disability by responsiveness to instruction: Specifying measures and criteria. *Learning Disability Quarterly, 27,* 216–227.

Fuchs, D., Fuchs, L. S., & Fernstrom, P. (1993). A conservative approach to special education reform: Mainstreaming through trans environmental programming and curriculum-based measurement. *American Educational Research Journal, 30,* 149–177.

Fuchs, L., Fuchs, D., Finelli, R., Courey, S., & Hamlett, C. (2003). Expanding schema-based transfer instruction to help third graders solve real-life mathematical problems. *American Educational Research Journal, 41*(2), 419–445.

Fuchs, L., Fuchs, D., Finelli, R., Courey, S., Hamlett, C., Sones, E., & Hope, S. (2006). Teaching third graders about real-life mathematical problem solving: A randomized controlled study. *The Elementary School Journal, 106*(4), 293–312.

Fuchs, L. S., Fuchs, D., Bentz, J., Phillips, N. B., & Hamlett, C. L. (1994). The nature of student interactions during peer tutoring with and without prior training and experience. *American Educational Research Journal, 31*(1), 75–103.

Fuchs, L. S., Fuchs, D., & Karns, K. (2001). Enhancing kindergartners' mathematical development: Effects of peer-assisted learning strategies. *The Elementary School Journal, 101*(5), 495–510.

Fuchs, L. S., Fuchs, D., Karns, K., Hamlett, C. L., Katzaroff, M., & Dutka, S. (1997). Effects of task-focused goals on low-achieving students without learning disabilities. *American Educational Research Journal, 34*(3), 513–543.

Fuchs, L. S., Fuchs, D., Kazdan, S., & Allen, S. (1999). Effects of peer-assisted learning strategies in reading with and without training in elaborated help giving. *The Elementary School Journal, 99*(3), 201–221.

Fuller, B., Wright, J., Gesicki, K., & Kang, E. (2007). Gauging growth: How to judge NCLB? *Educational Researcher, 36*(5), 268–278.

Fuson, K. C. (1992). Research on whole number addition and subtraction. In D. Grouws (Ed.), *Handbook of research on mathematics teaching and learning* (pp. 243–275). New York: Macmillan.

Gabler, I. C., & Schroeder, M. (2003). *Constructivist methods for the secondary classroom.* Boston: Allyn & Bacon.

Gaddy, M. L. (1998, April). *Reading and studying from highlighted text: Memory for information highlighted by others.* Paper presented at the annual meeting of the American Educational Research Association, San Diego, CA.

Gage, N. L., & Needels, M. C. (1989). Process-product research on teaching: A review of criticism. *Elementary School Journal, 89,* 253–300.

Gagnon, G. W., & Collay, M. (2001). *Designing for learning: Six elements in constructivist classrooms.* Thousand Oaks, CA: Corwin.

Galambos, N. L., & Costigan, C. L. (2003). Emotional and personality development in adolescence. In R. M. Lerner, M. A. Easterbrooks, & J. Mistry (Eds.), *Handbook of psychology: Vol. 6. Developmental psychology* (pp. 351–372). Hoboken, NJ: Wiley.

Gall, M., Ward, B., Berliner, D., Cahen, L., Winne, P., Glashoff, J., & Stanton, G. (1978). Effects of questioning techniques and recitation on student learning. *American Educational Research Journal, 15,* 175–199.

Gallagher, C. J. (2003). Reconciling a tradition of testing with a new learning paradigm. *Educational Psychology Review, 15*(1), 83–99.

Gallagher, J. J. (1992). Gifted persons. In M. C. Alkin (Ed.), *Encyclopedia of educational research* (6th ed., pp. 544–549). New York: Macmillan.

Gamoran, A., Nystrand, M., Berends, M., & LePore, P. C. (1995). An organizational analysis of the effects of ability grouping. *American Educational Research Journal, 32,* 687–715.

Gandal, M., & McGiffert, L. (2003). The power of testing. *Educational Leadership, 60*(5), 39–42.

Gandal, M., & Vranek, J. (2001). Standards: Here today, here tomorrow. *Educational Leadership, 59*(1), 6–13.

Ganesh, T., & Berliner, D. (2004, April). *Practices of computer use in elementary education: Perceived and missed opportunities.* Paper presented at the annual meeting of the American Educational Research Association, San Diego, CA.

Garber, H. L. (1988). *The Milwaukee Project: Preventing mental retardation in children at risk.* Washington, DC: American Association on Mental Retardation.

Garcia, E., & Jensen, B. (2007). Helping young Hispanic learners. *Educational Leadership, 64*(6), 34–39.

Garcia, E., Jensen, B., & Scribner, K. (2009). The demographic imperative. *Educational Leadership, 66*(7), 8–13.

Garcia, J. (1993). The changing image of ethnic groups in textbooks. *Phi Delta Kappan, 75*(1), 29–35.

Gardner, H. (2000). *Intelligence reframed: Multiple intelligences for the 21st century.* New York: Basic Books.

Gardner, H. (2003, April). *Multiple intelligences after twenty years.* Paper presented at the annual meeting of the American Educational Research Association, Chicago.

Gardner, H. (2004). *Multiple intelligences: New horizons, in theory and practice.* New York: Basic Books.

Gardner, H., & Moran, S. (2006). The science of multiple intelligences theory: A response to Lynn Waterhouse. *Educational Psychologist, 41*(4), 227–232.

Gardner, M., & Steinberg, L. (2005). Peer influence on risk taking, risk preference, and risky decision making in adolescence and adulthood: An experimental study. *Developmental Psychology, 41,* 625–635.

Garvey, C. (1990). *Play* (enlarged ed.). Cambridge, MA: Harvard University Press.

Gathercoal, F. (2001). *Judicious discipline* (5th ed.). San Francisco: Caddo Gap Press.

Gathercole, S. E., Pickering, S. J., Ambridge, B., & Wearing, H. (2004). The structure of working memory from 4 to 15 years of age. *Developmental Psychology, 40,* 177–190.

Gay, G. (2004). The importance of multicultural education. *Educational Leadership, 61*(4), 30–34.

Gee, J., & Levine, M. (2009). Welcome to our virtual worlds. *Educational Leadership, 66*(6), 48–53.

Gelman, R. (2000). Domain specificity and variability in cognitive development. *Child Development, 71,* 854–856.

Gelman, R. (2006). Young natural-number arithmeticians. *Current Directions in Psychological Science, 15*(4), 193–197.

Gelman, R., & Brenneman, K. (1994). Domain specificity and cultural variation are not inconsistent. In L. A. Hirschfeld & S. Gelman (Eds.), *Mapping the mind: Domain specificity in cognition and culture.* New York: Cambridge University Press.

Genesee, F., Lindholm-Leary, K., Saunders, W., & Christian, D. (2005). English language learners in U.S. schools: An overview of research findings. *Journal of Education for Students Placed at Risk, 10*(4), 363–385.

Gentner, D., Loewenstein, J., & Thompson, L. (2002). Learning and transfer: A general role for analogical encoding. *Journal of Educational Psychology, 94*(2), 393–408.

George, P. S. (2005). A rationale for differentiated instruction in the regular classroom. *Theory into Practice, 44,* 185–193.

Gerdes, D., & Ljung, E. J. (2009). The students have the answers. *Educational Leadership, 67*(1), 71–75.

Gersten, R., Baker, S., Shahahan, T., Linan-Thompson, S., Collins, P., & Scarcella, R. (2007). *Effective literacy and English language instruction for English learners in the elementary grades* (NCEE 2007–4011). Washington, DC: Institute of Education Sciences, U.S. Department of Education.

Gersten, R., Chard, D., Jayanthi, M., & Baker, S. (2006). *Experimental and quasi-experimental research on instructional approaches for teaching mathematics to students with learning disabilities: A research synthesis.* Signal Hill, CA: Center on Instruction/RG Research Group.

Gersten, R., Chard, D., Jayanthi, M., Baker, S., Morphy, P., & Flojo, J. (2009). Mathematics instruction for students with learning disabilities: A meta-analysis of instructional components. *Review of Educational Research, 79*(3), 1202–1242.

Gersten, R., & Dimino, J. (2006). RTI (response to intervention): Rethinking special education for students with reading difficulties (yet again). *Reading Research Quarterly, 41*(1), 99–107.

Gersten, R., Fuchs, L. S., Williams, J. P., & Baker, S. (2001). Teaching reading comprehension strategies to students with learning disabilities: A review of research. *Review of Educational Research, 71*(2), 279–320.

Giaconia, R. M., & Hedges, L. V. (1982). Identifying features of effective open education. *Review of Educational Research, 52,* 579–602.

Giangreco, M. (2007). Extending inclusive opportunities. *Educational Leadership, 64*(5), 34–38.

Gibbons, A. S., Duffin, J. R., Robertson, D. J., & Thompson, B. (1998, April). *Effects of administering feedback following extended problem solving.* Paper presented at the annual meeting of the American Educational Research Association, San Diego, CA.

Giedd, J. N. (2004). Structural magnetic resonance imaging of the adolescent brain. In R. E. Dahl & L. P. Spear (Eds.), *Adolescent brain development. Vulnerabilities and opportunities. Annals of the New York Academy of Sciences* (Vol. 1021). New York: The New York Academy of Science.

Gijselaers, W. H., & Schmidt, H. G. (1995). Effects of quantity of instruction on time spent on learning and achievement. *Educational Research and Evaluation, 1*(2), 183–201.

Gilligan, C. (1982). *In a different voice: Sex differences in the expression of moral judgment.* Cambridge, MA: Harvard University Press.

Gilligan, C., & Attanucci, J. (1988). Two moral orientations: Gender differences and similarities. *Merrill-Palmer Quarterly, 34,* 223–237.

Ginsburg-Block, M., Rohrbeck, C., & Fantuzzo, J. (2006). A meta-analytic review of social, self-concept, and behavioral outcomes of peer-assisted learning. *Journal of Educational Psychology, 98*(4), 732–749.

Giorgis, C., & Glazer, J. I. (2009). *Literature for young children: Supporting emergent literacy, ages 0–8* (6th ed.). Boston: Allyn & Bacon.

Glantz, M. D., Johnson, J., & Huffman, L. (Eds.). (2002). *Resilience and development: Positive life adaptations.* New York: Kluwer.

Glaser, C., & Brunstein, J. (2007). Improving fourth-grade students' composition skills: Effects of strategy instruction and self-regulation procedures. *Journal of Educational Psychology, 99*(2), 297–310.

Glassman, M. (2001). Dewey and Vygotsky: Society, experience, and inquiry in educational practice. *Educational Researcher, 30*(4), 3–14.

Gleason, J. B., & Ratner, N. B. (Eds.). (2009). *The development of language* (7th ed.). Boston: Pearson.

GLSEN. (2009). *The experiences of lesbian, gay, bisexual, and transgender middle school students.* New York: Author.

Goddard, R. D., Hoy, W. K., & Hoy, A. W. (2000). Collective teacher efficacy: Its meaning, measure, and impact on student achievement. *American Educational Research Journal, 37*(2), 479–507.

Goddard, R. D., Hoy, W. K., & Woolfolk Hoy, A. (2004). Collective efficacy beliefs: Theoretical developments, empirical evidence, and future directions. *Educational Researcher, 33*(3), 1–13.

Goldberg, A., Russell, M., & Cook, A. (2003). The effect of computers on student writing: A meta-analysis of studies from 1992 to 2002. *Journal of Technology, Learning, and Assessment, 2*(1), 1–51. Available at www.jtla.org

Goldman-Segall, R., & Maxwell, J. W. (2003). Computers, the Internet, and new media for learning. In W. M. Reynolds & G. E. Miller (Eds.), *Handbook of psychology: Vol. 7. Educational psychology* (pp. 393–427). Hoboken, NJ: Wiley.

Goldschmidt, P., & Wang, J. (1999). When can schools affect dropout behavior? A longitudinal multilevel analysis. *American Educational Research Journal, 36*(4), 715–738.

Good, T., & Brophy, J. (2003). *Looking in classrooms* (9th ed.). Boston: Allyn & Bacon.

Good, T., & Brophy, J. (2008). *Looking in classrooms* (10th ed.). Boston: Allyn & Bacon.

Good, T., & Grouws, D. (1979). The Missouri Mathematics Effectiveness Project: An experimental study in fourth-grade classrooms. *Journal of Educational Psychology, 71,* 355–362.

Good, T., Grouws, D., & Ebmeier, H. (1983). *Active mathematics teaching.* New York: Longman.

Good, T. L., & Brophy, J. E. (2008). *Looking in classrooms* (10th ed.). Boston: Allyn & Bacon.

Good, T. L., Mulryan, C., & McCaslin, M. (1992). Grouping for instruction in mathematics: A call for programmatic research on small group processes. In D. Grouws (Ed.), *Handbook of research on mathematics teaching and learning* (pp. 165–196). New York: Macmillan.

Goodlad, J. I. (1983). *A place called school.* New York: McGraw-Hill.

Gordon, P. (1957). *The social system of the high school: A study in the sociology of adolescence.* Glencoe, IL: Free Press.

Gorin, J. S., & Blanchard, J. S. (2004, April). *The effect of curriculum alignment on elementary mathematics and reading achievement.* Paper presented at the annual meeting of the American Educational Research Association, San Diego, CA.

Goswami, U. (2004). Neuroscience and education. *British Journal of Educational Psychology, 74*(1), 1–14.

Gottfredson, D. C., Gottfredson, G. D., & Hybl, L. G. (1993). Managing adolescent behavior: A multiyear, multi-school study. *American Educational Research Journal, 30*(1), 179–215.

Gottfried, A. E., & Fleming, J. S. (2001). Continuity of academic intrinsic motivation from childhood through late adolescence: A longitudinal study. *Journal of Educational Psychology, 93*(1), 3–13.

Gottfried, A. E., & Gottfried, A. W. (2004). Toward the development of a conceptualization of gifted motivation. *Gifted Child Quarterly, 48*(2), 121–132.

Gottlieb, J., & Weinberg, S. (1999). Comparison of students referred and not referred for special education. *The Elementary School Journal, 99*(3), 187–200.

Gould, M., & Gould, H. (2003). A clear vision for equity and opportunity. *Phi Delta Kappan, 85*(4), 324–328.

Grafman, J. (1994). Alternative frameworks for the conceptualization of frontal lobe functions. In F. Boller & J. Grafman (Eds.), *Handbook of neuropsychology* (Vol. 9). San Diego, CA: Elsevier.

Grafman, J., Spector, L., & Ratterman, M. (2005). Planning and the brain. In R. Morris & G. Ward (Eds.), *The cognitive psychology of planning* (pp. 181–198). Hove, England: Psychology Press.

Graham, S. (2006). Strategy instruction and the teaching of writing: A meta-analysis. In C. MacArthur, S. Graham, & J. Fitzgerald (Eds.), *Handbook of writing research* (pp. 187–207). New York: Guilford Press.

Graham, S., MacArthur, C., & Schwartz, S. (1995). Effects of goal setting and procedural facilitation on the revising behavior and writing performance of students with writing and learning problems. *Journal of Educational Psychology, 87*(2), 230–240.

Graseck, S. (2009). Teaching with controversy. *Educational Leadership, 67*(1), 45–49.

Graves, D. (1983). *Writing: Teachers and children at work.* Exeter, NH: Heinemann.

Graves, M. (2007). Conceptual and empirical bases for providing struggling readers with multifaceted and long-term vocabulary instruction. In B. M. Taylor & J. E. Ysseldyke (Eds.), *Effective instruction for struggling readers, K–6* (pp. 55–83). New York: Teachers College Press.

Green, M. (1989). *Theories of human development.* New York: Prentice-Hall.

Greenberg, M. T., Weissberg, R., O'Brien, M., Zins, J., Fredericks, L., Resnick, H., & Elias, M. (2003). Enhancing school-based prevention and youth development through coordinated social, emotional, and academic learning. *American Psychologist, 58,* 466–474.

Greene, B. A., Miller, R. B., Crowson, M., Duke, B. L., & Akey, K. L. (2004). Predicting high school students' cognitive engagement and achievement: Contributions of classroom perceptions and motivation. *Contemporary Educational Psychology, 29*(4), 462–482.

Greene, D., & Lepper, M. R. (1974). How to turn play into work. *Psychology Today, 8,* 49–54.

Greene, J., & Azevedo, R. (2007). A theoretical review of Winne and Hadwin's model of self-regulated learning: New perspectives and directions. *Review of Educational Research, 77*(3), 334–372.

Greene, J. P. (1997). A meta-analysis of the Rossell & Baker review of bilingual education research. *Bilingual Research Journal, 21,* 2–3.

Greenfield, P., & Cocking, R. (Eds.). (1994). *Cross-cultural roots of minority child development.* Hillsdale, NJ: Erlbaum.

Greeno, J., & Goldman, S. (Eds.). (1998). *Thinking practices in mathematics and science learning.* Mahwah, NJ: Erlbaum.

Greeno, J. G., Collins, A. M., & Resnick, L. R. (1996). Cognition and learning. In D. C. Berliner & R. C. Calfe (Eds.), *Handbook of educational psychology* (pp. 15–46). New York: Macmillan.

Greenwood, C. R., Terry, B., Utley, C. A., Montagna, D., & Walker, D. (1993). Achievement, placement, and services: Middle school benefits of Classwide Peer Tutoring used at the elementary level. *School Psychology Review, 22*(3), 497–516.

Gregory, G. H., & Chapman, C. (2001). *Differentiated instructional strategies: One size doesn't fit all.* Thousand Oaks, CA: Corwin.

Gresham, F. (2005). Methodological issues in evaluating cognitive-behavioral treatments for students with behavioral disorders. *Behavioral Disorders, 30*(3), 213–225.

Gronlund, N. E. (2003). *Assessment of student achievement* (7th ed.). Boston: Allyn & Bacon.

Gronlund, N. E., & Brookhart, S. M. (2009). *Gronlund's writing instructional objectives* (8th ed.). Upper Saddle River, NJ: Pearson.

Gronlund, N. E., & Waugh, C. K. (2009). *Assessment of student achievement.* Upper Saddle River, NJ: Pearson.

Grusec, J. E., & Goodnow, J. J. (1994). Impact of parental discipline methods on the child's internalization of values. *Developmental Psychology, 30,* 4–19.

Guay, F., Marsh, H. W., & Boivin, M. (2003). Academic self-concept and academic achievement: Developmental perspectives on their causal ordering. *Journal of Educational Psychology, 95*(1), 124–136.

Guilfoyle, C. (2006). NCLB: Is there life beyond testing? *Educational Leadership, 64*(3), 8–13.

Gump, P. V. (1982). School settings and their keeping. In D. L. Duke (Ed.), *Helping teachers manage classrooms* (pp. 98–114). Alexandria, VA: ASCD.

Gunter, M. A., Estes, T. H., & Schwab, J. (2003). *Instruction: A models approach* (4th ed.). Boston: Allyn & Bacon.

Gureasko-Moore, S., DuPaul, G., & White, G. (2006). The effects of self-management in general education classrooms on the organizational skills of adolescents with ADHD. *Behavior Modification, 30,* 159–183.

Guskey, T. (2003). How classroom assessments improve learning. *Educational Leadership, 60*(5), 7–11.

Guskey, T. (2005). Mapping the road to proficiency. *Educational Leadership, 63*(3), 32–37.

Guskey, T. (2006). Making high school grades meaningful. *Phi Delta Kappan, 87*(9), 670–675.

Guskey, T. (Ed.). (2009). *Practical solutions for serious problems in standards-based grading.* Thousand Oaks, CA: Corwin.

Guskey, T., & Anderman, E. (2008). Students at bat. *Educational Leadership, 66*(3), 8–15.

Guskey, T. R., & Bailey, J. M. (2001). *Developing grading and reporting systems for student learning.* Thousand Oaks, CA: Corwin.

Guthrie, J., & Wigfield, A. (2000). Engagement and motivation in reading. In M. Kamil, P. Mosenthal, P. Pearson, & R. Barr (Eds.), *Handbook of reading research* (Vol. 3, pp. 403–422). Mahwah, NJ: Erlbaum.

Guthrie, J. T., & Cox, K. (2001). Classroom conditions for motivation and engagement in reading. *Educational Psychology Review, 13*(3), 283–302.

Gutiérrez, R., & Slavin, R. E. (1992). Achievement effects of the nongraded elementary school: A best evidence synthesis. *Review of Educational Research, 62*(4), 333–376.

Hadwin, A. F. (2008). Self-regulated learning. In T. L. Good (Ed.), *21st century learning* (Vol. 1, pp. 175–183). Thousand Oaks, CA: Sage.

Hakuta, K., Butler, Y. G., & Witt, D. (2000). *How long does it take English learners to attain proficiency?* The University of California Linguistic Minority Research Institute, Policy Report 2000/1.

Halford, G., & Andrews, G. (2006). Reasoning and problem solving. In D. Kuhn & R. Siegler (Eds.), *Handbook of child psychology: Vol. 2* (6th ed., pp. 557–608). Hoboken, NJ: Wiley.

Hall, R., & Greeno, J. (2008). Conceptual learning. In T. L. Good (Ed.), *21st century learning* (Vol. 1, pp. 212–224). Thousand Oaks, CA: Sage.

Hallahan, D. P., Kauffman, J. M., & Pullen, P. C. (2009). *Exceptional learners: Introduction to special education* (11th ed.). Boston: Pearson.

Hallinan, M. T. (2004). *The detracking movement.* Palo Alto, CA: Stanford University, The Hoover Institute.

Halpern, D., Aronson, J., Reimer, N., Simpkins, S., Star, J., & Wentzel, K. (2007). Encouraging girls in math and science: IES practice guide (NCER 2007-2003). Washington, DC: Institute of Education Sciences, U.S. Department of Education.

Halpern, D. F., Hansen, C., & Riefer, D. (1990). Analogies as an aid to understanding and memory. *Journal of Educational Psychology, 82,* 298–305.

Halpern, D. F., & LaMay, M. L. (2000). The smarter sex: A critical review of sex differences in intelligence. *Educational Psychology Review, 12*(2), 229–246.

Halpern, J. M., & Schulz, K. P. (2006). Revisiting the role of the prefrontal cortex in the pathophysiology of ADHD. *Psychological Bulletin, 132,* 560–581.

Hamburg, D. A. (1992). *Today's children: Creating a future for a generation in crisis.* New York: Times Books.

Hamilton, L., Stecher, B., & Yuan, K. (2008). *Standards-based reform in the United States: History, research, and future directions.* Washington, DC: Center on Education Policy.

Hamman, D., Berthelot, J., Saia, J., & Crowley, E. (2000). Teachers' coaching of learning and its relation to students' strategic learning. *Journal of Educational Psychology, 92*(2), 342–348.

Hand, B., & Treagust, D. F. (1991). Student achievement and science curriculum development using a constructive framework. *Schools, Science, and Mathematics, 91,* 172–176.

Hanline, M. F., & Daley, S. (2002). "Mom, will Haelie always have possibilities?" *Phi Delta Kappan, 84*(1), 73–76.

Hanna, G. S., & Dettmer, P. A. (2004). *Assessment for effective teaching: Using context-adaptive planning.* Boston: Pearson.

Hanson, S. L., Morrison, D. R., & Ginsburg, A. L. (1989). The antecedents of teenage fatherhood. *Demography, 26,* 579–596.

Harackiewicz, J., Barron, K., Tauer, J., & Carter, S. (2000). Short-term and long-term consequences of achievement goals: Predicting interest and performance over time. *Journal of Educational Psychology, 92*(2), 316–330.

Harackiewicz, J., & Linnenbrink, E. (2005). Multiple achievement goals and multiple pathways for learning: The agenda and impact of Paul R. Pintrich. *Educational Psychologist, 40*(2), 75–84.

Hardman, J. L., Drew, C., Egan, M., & Wolf, B. (1996). *Human exceptionality: Society, school, and family* (5th ed.). Boston: Allyn & Bacon.

Hareli, S., & Weiner, B. (2002). Social emotions and personality inferences: A scaffold for a new direction in the study of achievement motivation. *Educational Psychologist, 37*(3), 183–189.

Harpaz, Y., & Lefstein, A. (2000). Communities of thinking. *Educational Leadership, 58*(3), 54–57.

Harris, K. R., & Alexander, P. A. (1998). Integrated, constructivist education: Challenge and reality. *Education Psychology Review, 10*(2), 115–127.

Harris, K. R., & Graham, S. (1996a). *Making the writing process work: Strategies for composition and self-regulation.* Cambridge, MA: Brookline.

Harris, K. R., & Graham, S. (1996b). Memo to constructivists: Skills count, too. *Educational Leadership, 53*(5), 26–29.

Harris, K. R., Graham, S., & Mason, L. (2006). Improving the writing, knowledge, and motivation of struggling young writers: Effects of self-regulated strategy development with and without peer support. *American Educational Research Journal, 43*(2), 295–340.

Harris, K. R., Graham, S., & Pressley, M. (2001). Cognitive strategies in reading and written language. In N. N. Singh & I. Beale (Eds.), *Current perspectives in learning disabilities: Nature, theory and treatment.* New York: Springer-Verlag.

Harris, P. (2002). Learning-related visual problems in Baltimore City: A long-term program. *Journal of Optometric Vision Development, 33*(2), 75–115.

Harris, R. (2007). Virtual salt. Retrieved January 5, 2010, from www.virtualsalt.com/evalu8it.htm

Harry, B., & Klingner, J. (2007). Discarding the deficit model. *Educational Leadership, 64*(5), 16–21.

Hart, B., & Risley, T. R. (1995). *Meaningful differences in the everyday experience of young American children.* Baltimore: Brookes.

Harter, S. (1998). The development of self-representations. In W. Damon (Ed.), *Handbook of child psychology* (Vol. 3, pp. 553–618). New York: Wiley.

Harter, S., Whitesell, N. R., & Kowalski, P. (1992). Individual differences in the effects of educational transitions on young adolescents' perceptions of competence and motivational orientation. *American Educational Research Journal, 29,* 777–807.

Hartup, W. W. (2005). Peer Intraction: What causes what? *Journal of Abnormal Child Psychology, 33,* 387–394.

Haslinger, J., Kelly, P., & O'Lara, L. (1996). Countering absenteeism, anonymity, and apathy. *Educational Leadership, 54*(1), 47–49.

Haspe, H., & Baddeley, J. (1991). Moral theory and culture: The case of gender. In W. Kurtines & J. L. Gewirtz (Eds.), *Handbook of moral behavior and development* (Vol. 1, pp. 223–250). Mahwah, NJ: Erlbaum.

Hasselbring, T., & Williams-Glaser, C. H. (2000). Use of computer technology to help students with special needs. *Children and Computer Technology, 10*(2), 102–122.

Hattie, J., Bibbs, J., & Purdie, N. (1996). Effects of learning skills interventions on student learning: A meta-analysis. *Review of Educational Research, 66*(2), 99–136.

Hattie, J., & Marsh, H. W. (1996). The relationship between research and teaching: A meta-analysis. *Review of Educational Research, 66*(4), 507–542.

Hattie, J., & Timperley, H. (2007). The power of feedback. *Review of Educational Research, 77*(1), 81–112.

Hauser-Cram, P., Sirin, S. R., & Stipek, D. (2003). When teachers' and parents' values differ: Teachers' ratings of academic competence in children from low-income families. *Journal of Educational Psychology, 95*(4), 813–820.

Havens, J. (2003). Student web pages—a performance assessment they'll love. *Phi Delta Kappan, 84*(9), 710–711.

Hawkins, J. D., Guo, J., Hill, K., Battin-Pearson, S., & Abbott, R. (2001). Long-term effects of the Seattle social development intervention on school bonding trajectories. *Applied Developmental Sciences, 5,* 225–236.

Hawkins, J. D., Herrenkohl, T. I., Farrington, D. P., Brewer, D., Catalano, R. F., Harachi, T. W., & Cothern, L. (2000). *Predictors of youth violence.* Washington, DC: Office of Juvenile Justice and Delinquency Prevention.

Hay, D., Payne, A., & Chadwick, A. (2004). Peer relations in childhood. *Journal of Child Psychology and Psychiatry, 45,* 84–108.

Haycock, K. (2001). Closing the achievement gap. *Educational Leadership, 58*(6), 6–11.

Haycock, K. (2006). No more invisible kids. *Educational Leadership, 64*(3), 38–42.

Haynie, W., III, & Haynie, G. (2008). *Effects of test taking on retention learning: A meta-analysis of eight quasi-experiments.* Paper presented at the annual meeting of the American Educational Research Association, San Diego, CA.

Headley, K. (2008). Improving reading comprehension through writing. In C. Block & S. Parris (Eds.), *Comprehension instruction: Research-based best practices* (2nd ed., pp. 214–225). New York: Guilford.

Hehir, T. (2007). Confronting abelism. *Educational Leadership, 64*(5), 8–15.

Heller, K. A., Monks, F. J., Sternberg, R. S., & Subotnik, R. F. (2000). *International handbook of giftedness and talent* (2nd ed.). New York: Pergamon.

Hempenstall, K. (2008). Corrective reading: An evidence-based remedial reading intervention. *Australasian Journal of Special Education, 32*(1), 23–54.

Henig, J. (2008/2009). The spectrum of education research. *Educational Leadership, 66*(4), 6–11.

Henson, K. T. (2004). *Constructivist teaching strategies for diverse middle-level classrooms.* Boston: Pearson.

Henson, R. K. (2002). From adolescent angst to adulthood: Substantive implications and measurement dilemmas in the development of teacher efficacy research. *Educational Psychologist, 37*(3), 137–150.

Herbert, J., & Stipek, D. (2005). The emergence of gender differences in children's perceptions of their academic competence. *Applied Developmental Psychology, 26,* 276–295.

Heritage, M., & Chen, E. (2005). Why data skills matter in school improvement. *Phi Delta Kappan, 86*(9), 707–710.

Herrenkohl, T. I., Maguin, E., Hill, K. G., Hawkins, J. D., & Abbott, R. D. (2001). Developmental risk factors for youth violence. *Journal of Adolescent Health, 26,* 176–186.

Herrera, S. G., & Murry, K. G. (2005). *Mastering ESL and bilingual methods.* Boston: Allyn & Bacon.

Hersh, R. (2009). A well-rounded education for a flat world. *Educational Leadership, 67*(1), 50–53.

Hess, F. (2008/2009). The new stupid. *Educational Leadership, 66*(4), 12–17.

Hessler, G. L. (2001). Who is really learning disabled? In B. Sornson, (Ed.), *Preventing early learning failure.* Alexandria, VA: ASCD.

Heymann, S. J., & Earle, A. (2000). Low-income parents: How do working conditions affect their opportunity to help school-age children at risk? *American Educational Research Journal, 37*(3), 833–848.

Heyns, B. (2002). Summer learning. In D. L. Levinson, P. W. Cookson, Jr., & A. R. Sadovnik (Eds.), *Education and sociology: An encyclopedia* (pp. 645–650). New York: Routledge Falmer.

Hicks-Bartlett, S. (2004). Forging the chain: "Hands across the campus" in action. In W. G. Stephan & W. P. Vogt (Eds.), *Education programs for improving intergroup relations.* New York: Teachers College Press.

Hidi, S., & Harackiewicz, J. M. (2000). Motivating the academically unmotivated: A critical issue for the 21st century. *Review of Educational Research, 70*(2), 151–179.

Hiebert, E. (1983). An examination of ability groupings for reading instruction. *Reading Research Quarterly, 18,* 231–255.

Hiebert, E. H. (1996). Revisiting the question: What difference does Reading Recovery make to an age cohort? *Educational Researcher, 25*(7), 26–28.

Hiebert, J., Carpenter, T. P., Fennema, E., Fuson, K., Human, P., Murray, H., Olivier, A., & Wearne, D. (1996). Problem solving as a basis for reform in curriculum and instruction: The case of mathematics. *Educational Researcher, 25*(4), 12–21.

Hiebert, J., & Wearne, D. (1993). Instructional tasks, classroom discourse, and student learning in second grade. *American Educational Research Journal, 30,* 393–425.

Hiebert, J., Wearne, D., & Taber, S. (1991). Fourth graders' gradual construction of decimal fractions during instruction using different physical representations. *Elementary School Journal, 91,* 321–341.

Higgins, S., Falzon, C., Hall, L., Moseley, D., Smith, F., Smith, H., & Wall, K. (2005). *Embedding ICT in the literacy and numeracy strategies: Final report.* Newcastle, UK: University of Newcastle.

Hill, J., & Flynn, K. (2006). *Classroom instruction that works with English language learners.* Alexandria, VA: ASCD.

Hill, N. E. (2001). Parenting and academic socialization as they relate to school readiness: The roles of ethnicity and family income. *Journal of Educational Psychology, 93*(4), 686–697.

Hill, W. F. (2002). *Learning: A survey of psychological interpretations* (7th ed.). Boston: Allyn & Bacon.

Hinnant, J., O'Brien, M., & Ghazarian, S. (2009). The longitudinal relations of teacher expectations to achievement in the early school years. *Journal of Educational Psychology, 101*(3), 662–670.

Hirsh, S. A., & Hord, S. M. (2008). Role of professional learning in advancing quality teaching and student learning. In T. L. Good (Ed.), *21st century learning* (Vol. 2, pp. 337–350). Thousand Oaks, CA: Sage.

Hmelo-Silver, C., Duncan, R., & Chinn, C. (2007). Scaffolding and achievement in problem-based inquiry learning: A response to Kirschner, Sweller, and Clark (2006). *Educational Psychologist, 42*(2), 99–107.

Ho, A. (2008). The problem with "proficiency": Limitations of statistics and policy under No Child Left Behind. *Educational Researcher, 37*(6), 351–360.

Hock, M., Schumaker, J., & Deshler, D. D. (2001). The case for strategic tutoring. *Educational Leadership, 58*(7), 50–52.

Hodgkinson, H. (2008). *Demographic trends and the federal role in education.* Washington, DC: Center on Education Policy.

Hoerr, T. (2009). How book groups bring change. *Educational Leadership, 66*(5), 80–84.

Hoff, E. (2003). Language development in childhood. In R. M. Lerner, M. A. Easterbrooks, & J. Mistry (Eds.), *Handbook of psychology: Vol. 6. Developmental psychology* (pp. 171–193). Hoboken, NJ: Wiley.

Hoffer, T., & Nelson, C. (1993, April). *High school effects on coursework in science and mathematics.* Paper presented at the annual meeting of the American Educational Research Association, Chicago.

Höffler, T., & Leutner, D. (2006). *Instructional animation versus static picture: A meta-analysis.* Poster presented at the annual meeting of the American Educational Research Association, San Francisco.

Hoffman, D. (2009). Reflecting on social emotional learning: A critical perspective on trends in the United States. *Review of Educational Research, 79*(2), 533–556.

Hoffman, M. L. (1993). Affective and cognitive processes in moral internalization. In E. T. Higgins, D. Ruble, & W. Hartup (Eds.), *Social cognition and social development* (pp. 236–274). Cambridge, England: Cambridge University Press.

Hoffman, S. D., Foster, E. M., & Furstenberg, F. F. (1993). Reevaluating the costs of teenage childbearing. *Demography, 30,* 1–13.

Hogan, T., Rabinowitz, M., & Craven, J. A., III. (2003). Representation in teaching: Inferences from research of expert and novice teachers. *Educational Psychologist, 38*(4), 235–247.

Hoge, R. D., & Renzulli, J. S. (1993). Exploring the link between giftedness and self-concept. *Review of Educational Research, 63,* 449–465.

Hollingsworth, J., & Ybarra, S. (2009). *Explicit Direct Instruction (EDI): The power of the well-crafted, well-taught lesson.* Thousand Oaks, CA: Corwin.

Holloway, J. (2003). Grouping gifted students. *Educational Leadership, 61*(2), 89–91.

Holloway, J. H. (2000). The digital divide. *Educational Leadership, 58*(2), 90–91.

Holloway, J. H. (2001). Inclusion and students with learning disabilities. *Educational Leadership, 58*(6), 88–89.

Holt, D. G., & Willard-Holt, C. (2000). Let's get real: Students solving authentic corporate problems. *Phi Delta Kappan, 82*(3), 243–246.

Hong, G., & Raudenbush, S. (2005). Effects of kindergarten retention policy on children's cognitive growth in reading and mathematics. *Evaluation and Policy Analysis, 27*(3), 205–244.

Hong, G., & Yu, B. (2007). Early-grade retention and children's reading and math learning in elementary years. *Educational Evaluation and Policy Analysis, 29*(4), 239–261.

Hong, L. K. (2001). Too many intrusions on instructional time. *Phi Delta Kappan, 82*(9), 712–714.

Hood, M., Conlon, E., & Andrews, G. (2008). Preschool home literacy practices and children's literacy development: A longitudinal analysis. *Journal of Educational Psychology, 100*(2), 252–271.

Hoover, J. (2009). *RTI assessment essentials for struggling learners.* Thousand Oaks, CA: Corwin.

Hoover-Dempsey, K., Walker, J., Sandler, H., Whetsel, D., Green, C., Wilkins, A., & Closson, K. (2005). Parental involvement: Model revision through scale development. *The Elementary School Journal, 106*(2), 85–104.

Hopfenberg, W. S., & Levin, H. M. (1993). *The accelerated schools resource guide.* San Francisco: Jossey-Bass.

Hopkins, C. J. (1998). "I'm here to help—what do you want me to do?" A primer for literacy tutors. *The Reading Teacher, 52*(3), 310–312.

Horn, S. S., Drill, K. L., Hochberg, M. J., Heinze, J., & Frank, T. (2008). Development: 6–8. In T. L. Good (Ed.), *21st century learning* (Vol. 1, pp. 93–102). Thousand Oaks, CA: Sage.

Howard, G. (2007). As diversity grows, so must we. *Educational Leadership, 64*(6), 16–22.

Howard, P. (2000). *The owner's manual for the brain: Everyday applications from mind-brain research.* Austin, TX: Bard.

Howes, C., & Matheson, C. C. (1992). Sequences in the development of competent play with peers: Social and social pretend play. *Developmental Psychology, 28,* 961–974.

Howes, C., & Rodning, C. (1992). Attachment security and social pretend play negotiations: Illustrative study #5. In C. Howes, O. Unger, & C. C. Matheson (Eds.), *The collaborative construction of pretend: Social pretend play functions* (pp. 89–98). Albany: State University of New York Press.

Hruby, G., & Hynd, G. (2006). Decoding Shaywitz: The modular brain and its discontents. [Review of the book *Overcoming dyslexia: A new and complete science-based program for reading problems at any level.*] *Reading Research Quarterly, 41*(4), 544–566.

Hubbard, L., & Mehan, H. (1997, March). *Scaling up an untracking program: A co-constructivist process.* Paper presented at the annual meeting of the American Educational Research Association, Chicago.

Hubbard, L., & Mehan, H. (1998). Scaling up an untracking program: A co-constructed process. *Journal of Education for Students Placed at Risk, 4*(1), 83–100.

Huebner, T. (2008). Balancing the concrete and the abstract. *Educational Leadership, 66*(3), 86–88.

Huebner, T. (2009). Encouraging girls to pursue math and science. *Educational Leadership, 67*(1), 90–92.

Huey, E. D., Krueger, F., & Grafman, J. (2006). Representations in the human prefrontal cortex. *Current Directions in Psychological Science, 15*(4), 167–171.

Hughes, F. (2010). *Children, play, and development.* Thousand Oaks, CA: Sage.

Huguet, P., & Regner, I. (2007). Stereotype threat among schoolgirls in quasi-ordinary classroom circumstances. *Journal of Educational Psychology, 99,* 345–360.

Hulleman, C., Durik, A., Schweigert, S., & Harackiewicz, J. (2008). Task values, achievement goals, and interest: An integrative analysis. *Journal of Educational Psychology, 100*(2), 398–416.

Hunter, M. (1982). *Mastery teaching.* El Segundo, CA: TIP Publications.

Hunter, M. (1995). Mastery teaching. In J. H. Block, S. T. Everson, & T. R. Guskey (Eds.), *School improvement programs* (pp. 181–204). New York: Scholastic.

Hurley, E. (2000, April). *The interaction of culture with math achievement and group processes among African American and European American children.* Paper presented at the annual meeting of the American Educational Research Association, New Orleans, LA.

Hurn, C. J. (2002). IQ. In D. L. Levinson, P. W. Cookson, Jr., & A. R. Sadovnik (Eds.), *Education and sociology: An encyclopedia* (pp. 399–402). New York: Routledge Falmer.

Hurry, J., & Sylva, K. (2007). Long-term outcomes of early reading intervention. *Journal of Research in Reading, 30*(3), 227–248.

Husman, J., & Lens, W. (1999). The role of the future in student motivation. *Educational Psychologist, 34*(2), 113–125.

Hyde, J., & Mertz, J. (2009). Gender, culture, and mathematics performance. *Proceedings of the National Academy of Sciences, 106*(8), 801–807.

Hyerle, D. (1995). Thinking maps: Seeing is understanding. *Educational Leadership, 53*(4), 85–89.

Hyman, I. A., & Snook, P. A. (2000). Dangerous schools and what you can do about them. *Phi Delta Kappan, 81*(7), 488–501.

Hymel, S., Bowker, A., & Woody, E. (1993). Aggressive versus withdrawn unpopular children: Variations in peer and self-perceptions in multiple domains. *Child Development, 64,* 879–896.

Ialongo, N., Poduska, J., Wethamer, L., & Keller, S. (2001). The digital impact of two first-grade preventive interventions on conduct problems and disorder in early adolescence. *Journal of Emotional and Behavioral Disorders, 9*(3), 146–160.

Igo, L. B., Bruning, R., & McCrudden, M. (2005). Exploring differences in students' copy-and-paste decision making and processing: A mixed-methods study. *Journal of Educational Psychology, 72*(3), 165–178.

Inagaki, K., & Hantano, G. (2006). Young children's conception of the biological world. *Current Directions in Psychological Science, 15*(4), 177–181.

Inhelder, B., & Piaget, J. (1958). *The growth of logical thinking from childhood to adolescence.* New York: Basic Books.

Iran-Nejad, A., & Stewart, W. (2007, April). *What's wrong with Bloom's cognitive taxonomy of educational objectives?* Paper presented at the annual meeting of the American Educational Research Association, Chicago.

Ireson, J., & Hallam, S. (2001). *Ability grouping in education.* London: Sage.

Ivey, G., & Fisher, D. (2006). Then thinking skills trump reading skills. *Educational Leadership, 64*(2), 16–21.

Jacobs, J., Lanza S., Osgood, D., Eccles, J., & Wigfield, A. (2002). Changes in children's self-competence and values: Gender and domain differences across grades one through twelve. *Child Development, 73,* 509–527.

Jaffee, S., & Hyde, J. S. (2000). Gender differences in moral orientation: A meta-analysis. *Psychological Bulletin, 126,* 703–726.

Jagacinski, C. M., & Nicholls, J. G. (1990). Reducing effort to protect perceived ability: "They'd do it but I wouldn't." *Journal of Educational Psychology, 82,* 15–21.

Jagers, R. J., & Carroll, G. (2002). Issues in educating African American children and youth. In S. Stringfield & D. Land (Eds.), *Educating at-risk students* (pp. 48–65). Chicago: National Society for the Study of Education.

James, A. (2007). *Teaching the male brain: How boys think, feel, and learn in school.* Thousand Oaks, CA: Corwin.

James, A. (2009). *Teaching the female brain: How girls learn math and science.* Thousand Oaks, CA: Corwin.

James, W. (1912). *Talks to teachers on psychology: And to students on some of life's ideals.* New York: Holt.

Janzen, J. (2008). Teaching English language learners in the content areas. *Review of Educational Research, 78*(4), 1010–1038.

Jenkins, J. R., Peyton, J. A., Sanders, E. A., & Vadasy, P. F. (2004). Effects of reading decodable texts in supplemental first–grade tutoring. *Scientific Studies of Reading, 8,* 53–85.

Jennings, J., & Rentner, D. (2006). Ten big effects of the No Child Left Behind Act on public schools. *Phi Delta Kappan, 88*(2), 110–113.

Jennings, P., & Greenberg, M. (2009). The prosocial classroom: Teacher social and emotional competence in relation to student and classroom outcomes. *Review of Educational Research, 79*(1), 491–525.

Jensen, E. (2000). Brain-based learning: A reality check. *Educational Leadership, 57*(7), 76–80.

Jensen, E., & Nickelsen, L. (2008). *Deeper learning: Seven powerful strategies for in-depth and longer-lasting learning.* Thousand Oaks, CA: Corwin.

Jesse, D., & Pokorny, N. (2001, April). *Understanding high achieving middle schools for Latino students in poverty.* Paper presented at the annual meeting of the American Educational Research Association, Seattle.

Jetton, T. L., & Alexander, P. A. (2001). Interest assessment and the content area literacy environment: Challenges for research and practice. *Educational Psychology Review, 13*(3), 303–318.

Jimerson, S. R., Anderson, G. E., & Whipple, A. D. (2002). Winning the battle and losing the war: Examining the relation between grade retention and dropping out of high school. *Psychology in the Schools, 39,* 441–457.

Jitendra, A., Edwards, L., Sacks, G., & Jacobson, L. (2004, April). *What research says about vocabulary instruction for students with learning disabilities.* Paper presented at the annual meeting of the American Educational Research Association, San Diego, CA.

Jitendra, A., Star, J., Starosta, K., Leh, J., Sood, S., Caskie, G., Hughes, C., & Mack, T. (2009). Improving seventh grade students' learning of ratio and proportion: The role of schema-based instruction. *Contemporary Educational Psychology, 34*(3), 250–264.

Joe, S., Joe, E., & Rowley, L. (2009). Consequences of physical health and mental illness risks for academic achievement in grades K–12. *Review of Research in Education, 33,* 283–309.

Johnson, A. P. (2009). *What every teacher should know about action research.* Upper Saddle River, NJ: Pearson.

Johnson, D. W., & Johnson, R. T. (1999). *Learning together and alone: Cooperative, competitive, and individualistic learning.* Boston: Allyn & Bacon.

Johnson, D. W., & Johnson, R. T. (2001). *Teaching students to be peacemakers: A meta-analysis.* Paper presented at the annual convention of the American Educational Research Association, Seattle, WA.

Johnson, L. D., O'Malley, P. M., & Bachman, J. G. (2001). *Monitoring the future: National survey results on drug use, 1975–2000: Vol. 1, secondary school students.* Bethesda, MD: National Institute on Drug Abuse.

Johnson, P. (2009). The 21st century skills movement. *Educational Leadership, 67*(1), 8–15.

John-Steiner, V., & Mahn, H. (1996). Sociocultural approaches to learning and development: A Vygotskian framework. *Educational Psychologist, 31*(3 & 4), 191–206.

John-Steiner, V., & Mahn, H. (2003). Sociocultural contexts for teaching and learning. In W. M. Reynolds & G. E. Miller (Eds.), *Handbook of psychology: Vol. 7. Educational psychology* (pp. 125–151). Hoboken, NJ: Wiley.

Jones, M., Levin, M., Levin, J., & Beitzel, B. (2000). Can vocabulary-learning strategies and pair-learning formats be profitably combined? *Journal of Educational Psychology, 92*(2), 256–262.

Jones, S., & Dindia, K. (2004). A meta-analytic perspective on sex equity in the classroom. *Review of Educational Research, 74*(4), 443–472.

Jones, V., Dohrn, E., & Dunn, C. (2004). *Creating effective programs for students with emotional and behavior disorders.* Boston: Pearson.

Jones, V., & Jones, L. (Eds.). (2010). *Comprehensive classroom management* (9th ed.). Upper Saddle River, NJ: Merrill.

Jones, V. F., & Jones, L. S. (2004). *Comprehensive classroom management* (7th ed.). Boston: Allyn & Bacon.

Jones, V. F., & Jones, L. S. (2007). *Comprehensive classroom management* (8th ed.). Boston: Allyn & Bacon.

Jordan, W. J., McPartland, J. M., Legters, N. E., & Balfanz, R. (2000). Creating a comprehensive school reform model: The talent development high school with career academies. *Journal of Education for Students Placed at Risk, 5*(1 & 2), 159–181.

Joyce, B. R., Weil, M., & Calhoun, E. (2004). *Models of teaching* (7th ed.). Boston: Allyn & Bacon.

Juel, C. (1996). What makes literacy tutoring effective? *Reading Research Quarterly, 31,* 268–289.

Jukes, I., Dosaj, A., & Macdonald, B. (2000). *NetSavvy: Building information literacy in the classroom* (2nd ed.). ERIC No. ED450685.

Jung, J. (2010). *Alcohol, other drugs, and behavior* (2nd ed.). Thousand Oaks, CA: Sage.

Jussim, L., & Harber, K. D. (2005). Teacher expectations and self-fulfilling prophecies: Knowns and unknowns, resolved and unresolved controversies. *Personality and Social Psychology Review, 9,* 131–155.

Juvonen, J. (2000). The social functions of attributional face-saving tactics among early adolescents. *Educational Psychology Review, 12*(1), 15–32.

Juvonen, J., Nishina, A., & Graham, S. (2000). Peer harassment, psychological adjustment, and school functioning in early adolescence. *Journal of Educational Psychology, 92*(2), 349–359.

Juvonen, J., & Weiner, B. (1993). An attributional analysis of students' interactions: The social consequences of perceived responsibility. *Educational Psychology Review, 5,* 325–345.

Kagan, S. (1992). *Cooperative learning resources for teachers.* San Juan Capistrano, CA: Resources for Teachers.

Kagan, S., Kyle, P., & Scott, S. (2004). *Win-win discipline.* San Clemente, CA: Kagan Publishing.

Kagan, S., Zahn, G. L., Widaman, K. F., Schwartzwald, J., & Tyrrell, G. (1985). Classroom structural bias: Impact of cooperative and competitive classroom structures on cooperative and competitive individuals and groups. In R. E. Slavin, S. Sharan, S. Kagan, R. Hertz-Lazarowitz, C. Webb, & R. Schmuck, (Eds.), *Learning to cooperate, cooperating to learn.* New York: Plenum.

Kahlenberg, R. E. (2000). The new economic school desegregation. *Educational Leadership, 57*(7), 16–19.

Kalichman, S. C. (1996). *Answering questions about AIDS.* Washington, DC: American Psychological Association.

Kallick, B., & Colosimo, J. (2009). *Using curriculum mapping and assessment data to improve learning.* Thousand Oaks, CA: Corwin.

Kallison, J. M. (1986). Effects of lesson organization on achievement. *American Educational Research Journal, 23,* 337–347.

Kalyuga, S., Chandler, P., Tuovinen, J., & Sweller, J. (2001). When problem solving is superior to studying worked examples. *Journal of Educational Psychology, 93*(3), 579–588.

Kamil, M. L., Borman, G. D., Dole, J., Kral, C. C., & Salinger, T. (2008). *Improving adolescent literacy: Effective classroom and intervention practices* (NCEE 2008-4027). Washington, DC: Institute of Education Sciences, U.S. Department of Education.

Kamil, M. L., Intrator, S. M., & Kim, H. S. (2000). The effects of other technologies on literacy and literacy learning. In M. L. Kamil, P. B. Mosenthal, P. D. Pearson, & R. Barr (Eds.), *Handbook of reading research* (Vol. 3, pp. 771–788). Mahwah, NJ: Erlbaum.

Kane, M. S., Hambrick, D. Z., & Conway, A. R. A. (2005). Working memory capacity and fluid intelligence are strongly related concepts: Comment on Ackerman, Beier, & Boyle (2005). *Psychological Bulletin, 131*(1), 66–71.

Kannapel, P. J., & Clements, S. K. (2005). *Inside the black box of high-performing high-poverty schools: A report from the Prichard Committee for Academic Excellence.* Lexington, KY: Prichard Committee for Academic Excellence.

Kapur, S., Craik, F. I. M., Tulving, E., Wilson, A. A., Hoyle, S., & Brown, G. M. (1994). Neuroanatomical correlates of encoding in episodic memory: Levels of processing effect. *Proceedings of the National Academy of Sciences, 91,* 2008–2011.

Karges-Bone, L. (2000). *Lesson planning: Long-range and short-range models for grades K–6.* Boston: Allyn & Bacon.

Karnes, F. A., & Bean, M. (Eds.). (2001). *Methods and materials for teaching the gifted.* Waco, TX: Prufrock Press.

Karpicke, J. D., & Roediger, H. L. (2007). Repetition during retrieval is the key to long-term retention. *Journal of Memory and Language, 43,* 508–529.

Karpov, Y. V., & Bransford, J. D. (1995). L. S. Vygotsky and the doctrine of empirical and theoretical learning. *Educational Psychologist, 30,* 61–66.

Karpov, Y. V., & Haywood, H. C. (1998). Two ways to elaborate Vygotsky's concept of mediation. *American Psychologist, 53*(1), 27–36.

Karweit, N. (1989). Time and learning: A review. In R. E. Slavin (Ed.), *School and classroom organization.* Hillsdale, NJ: Erlbaum.

Karweit, N. L., & Slavin, R. E. (1981). Measurement and modeling choices in studies of time and learning. *American Educational Research Journal, 18,* 157–171.

Kasten, W. C., & Lolli, E. M. (1998). *Implementing multiage education.* Norwood, MA: Christopher–Gordon.

Katzir, T., & Paré-Blagoev, J. (2006). Applying cognitive neuroscience research to education: The case of literacy. *Educational Psychologist, 41*(1), 53–74.

Kauffman, J., McGee, K., & Brigham, M. (2004). Enabling or disabling? Observations on changes in special education. *Phi Delta Kappan, 85*(8), 613–620.

Kauffman, J. M., & Landrum, T. J. (2009). *Characteristics of emotional and behavioral disorders of children and youth* (9th ed.). Upper Saddle River, NJ: Pearson.

Kauffman, J. M., Lloyd, J. W., Baker, J., & Riedel, T. M. (1995). Inclusion of all students with emotional or behavioral disorder? Let's think again. *Phi Delta Kappan, 76*(7), 542–546.

Kauffman, J. M., Mostert, M. P., Trent, S. C., & Hallahan, D. P. (2002). *Managing classroom behavior: A reflective case-based approach* (3rd ed.). Boston: Allyn & Bacon.

Kauffman, J. M., Mostert, M. P., Trent, S. C., & Pullen, P. L. (2006). *Managing classroom behavior: A reflective case-based approach* (4th ed.). Boston: Allyn & Bacon.

Kazdin, A. E. (2001). *Behavior modification in applied settings* (6th ed.). Belmont, CA: Wadsworth.

Keenan, T., & Evans, S. (2010). *An introduction to child development.* Thousand Oaks, CA: Sage.

Kelly, N., & Norwich, B. (2004). Pupils' perceptions of self and of labels: Moderate learning difficulties in mainstream and special schools. *British Journal of Educational Psychology, 74*(3), 411–435.

Kelly, S., & Monczunski, L. (2007). Overcoming the volatility in school-level gain scores: A new approach to identifying value added with cross-sectional data. *Educational Researcher, 36*(5), 279–287.

Kemple, J. J. (1997). *Career academies: Communities of support for students and teachers: Further findings from a 10-site evaluation.* New York: MDRC.

Kenkel, S., Hoelscher, S., & West, T. (2006). Leading adolescents to mastery. *Educational Leadership, 63*(7), 33–37.

Kennedy, E. (2003). *Raising test scores for all students: An administrator's guide to improving standardized test performance.* Thousand Oaks, CA: Corwin.

Kennedy, J. H. (1990). Determinants of peer social status: Contributions of physical appearance, reputation, and behavior. *Journal of Youth and Adolescence, 19,* 233–244.

Kennedy, M. (2006). From teacher quality to quality teaching. *Educational Leadership, 63*(6), 14–19.

Kennedy, M. M. (2008). Teachers thinking about their practice. In T. L. Good (Ed.), *21st century learning* (Vol. 1, pp. 21–30). Thousand Oaks, CA: Sage.

Kerr, M., Stattin, H., Biesecker, G., & Ferrer-Wreder, L. (2003). Relationships with parents and peers in adolescence. In R. M. Lerner, M. A. Easterbrooks, & J. Mistry (Eds.), *Handbook of psychology: Vol. 6. Developmental psychology* (pp. 395–419). Hoboken, NJ: Wiley.

Kidron, Y., & Darwin, M. (2007). A systematic review of whole-school improvement models. *Journal of Education for Students Placed at Risk, 12*(1), 9–35.

Kidron, Y., & Fleischman, S. (2006). Promoting adolescents' prosocial behavior. *Educational Leadership, 63*(7), 90–91.

Kieffer, M., Lesaux, N., Rivera, M., & Francis, D. (2009). Accommodations for English language learners taking large-scale assessments: A meta-analysis on effectiveness and validity. *Review of Educational Research, 79*(3), 1168–1201.

Kiewra, K. A. (1991). Aids to lecture learning. *Educational Psychologist, 26,* 37–53.

Kilgore, S., Doyle, D., & Linkowsky, L. (1996). The modern red schoolhouse. In S. Stringfield, S. Ross, & L. Smith (Eds.), *Bold plans for school restructuring: The new American schools development corporation designs.* Mahwah, NJ: Erlbaum.

Kim, J. (2006). Effects of a voluntary summer reading intervention on reading achievement: Results from a randomized field trial. *Educational Evaluation and Policy Analysis, 28*(4), 335–355.

Kim, S. E. (2001, April). *Meta-analysis of gender differences in test performance using HLM.* Paper presented at the annual meeting of the American Educational Research Association, Seattle, WA.

King, A. (1992). Facilitating elaborative learning through guided student-generated questioning. *Educational Psychologist, 27,* 111–126.

King, A. (1994). Guiding knowledge construction in the classroom: Effects of teaching children how to question and how to explain. *American Educational Research Journal, 31*(2), 338–368.

King, A. (1997). Ask to think—tell why: A model of transactive peer tutoring for scaffolding higher level complex learning. *Educational Psychologist, 32*(4), 221–235.

King, A. (1998). Transactive peer tutoring: Distributing cognition and metacognition. *Educational Psychology Review, 10*(1), 57–74.

King, A. (1999). Teaching effective discourse patterns for small-group learning. In R. J. Stevens (Ed.), *Teaching in American schools.* Upper Saddle River, NJ: Merrill/Prentice-Hall.

King, A., Staffieni, A., & Adelgais, A. (1998). Mutual peer tutoring: Effects of structuring tutorial interaction to scaffold peer learning. *Journal of Educational Psychology, 90*(1), 134–152.

King, E. W. (2002). Ethnicity. In D. L. Levinson, P. W. Cookson, Jr., & A. R. Sadovnik (Eds.), *Education and sociology: An encyclopedia* (pp. 247–253). New York: Routledge Falmer.

Kirby, D. (2000). What does the research say about sexuality education? *Educational Leadership, 58*(2), 72–75.

Kirschner, P., Sweller, J., & Clark, R. (2006). Why minimal guidance during instruction does not work: An analysis of the failure of constructivist, discovery, problem-based, experiential, and inquiry-based teaching. *Educational Psychologist, 41*(2), 75–86.

Kirschner, P., & van Merrenboer, J. J. G. (2008). In T. L. Good (Ed.), *21st century learning* (Vol. 1, pp. 244–253). Thousand Oaks, CA: Sage.

Klahr, D., & Nigam, M. (2004). The equivalence of learning paths in early science instruction: Effects of direct instruction and discovery learning. *Psychological Science, 15*(10), 661–667.

Klein, J. D., & Schnackenberg, H. L. (2000). Effects of informal cooperative learning and the affiliation motive on achievement, attitude, and student interactions. *Contemporary Educational Psychology, 25*(1), 332–341.

Klein, P. D. (1999). Reopening inquiry into cognitive processes in writing-to-learn. *Educational Psychology Review, 11*(3), 203–270.

Klein, S. F. (1994). Continuing the journey toward gender equity. *Educational Researcher, 23*(8), 13–21.

Kleinert, H. L., & Kearns, J. F. (2001). *Alternate assessment: Measuring outcomes and supports for students with disabilities.* Baltimore: Paul H. Brookes.

Kline, P. (2001). Teaching to all of a child's intelligences. In B. Sornson (Ed.), *Preventing early learning failure.* Alexandria, VA: ASCD.

Klingner, J., & Edwards, P. (2006). Cultural considerations with response to intervention models. *Reading Research Quarterly, 41*(1), 108–117.

Knapp, M. S. (1995). *Teaching for meaning in high-poverty classrooms.* New York: Teachers College Press.

Knapp, M. S., Shields, P. M., & Turnbull, B. S. (1995). Academic challenge in high-poverty classrooms. *Phi Delta Kappan, 76*(10), 770–776.

Knapp, M. S., & Woolverton, S. (1995). Social class and schooling. In J. A. Banks & C. A. M. Banks (Eds.), *Handbook of research on multicultural education.* New York: Macmillan.

Knight, C. B., Halpin, G., & Halpin, G. (1992, April). *The effects of learning environment accommodations on the achievement of second graders.* Paper presented at the annual meeting of the American Educational Research Association, San Francisco.

Knobel, M., & Wilber, D. (2009). Let's talk 2.0. *Educational Leadership, 66*(6), 20–25.

Kobayashi, K. (2005). What limits the encoding effect of note-taking? A meta-analytic examination. *Contemporary Educational Psychology, 30*(2), 242–262.

Koch, J. (2003). Gender issues in the classroom. In W. M. Reynolds & G. E. Miller (Eds.), *Handbook of psychology: Vol. 7. Educational psychology* (pp. 259–281). Hoboken, NJ: Wiley.

Kohlberg, L. (1963). The development of children's orientations toward moral order. I: Sequence in the development of human thought. *Vita Humana, 6,* 11–33.

Kohlberg, L. (1969). Stage and sequence: The cognitive–developmental approach to socialization. In D. A. Golsin (Ed.), *Handbook of socialization theory and research* (pp. 347–380). Chicago: Rand McNally.

Kohlberg, L. (1978). Revisions in the theory and practice of moral development. In W. Damon (Ed.), *New directions for child development* (No. 2, pp. 83–87). San Francisco: Jossey-Bass.

Kohlberg, L. (1980). High school democracy and educating for a just society. In M. L. Mosher (Ed.), *Moral education: A first generation of research and development* (pp. 20–57). New York: Praeger.

Konig, A. (1995, March/April). *Maternal discipline and child temperament as contributors to the development of internalization in your children.* Paper presented at the biennial meeting of the Society for Research in Child Development, Indianapolis, IN.

Koppelman, K., & Goodhart, L. (2005). *Understanding human differences: Multicultural education for a diverse America.* Boston: Pearson.

Koppelman, K., & Goodhart, L. (2008). *Understanding human differences: Multicultural education for a diverse America* (2nd ed.). Boston: Pearson.

Kornhaber, M., Fierros, E., & Veenema, S. (2004). *Multiple intelligences: Best ideas from research and practice.* Boston: Allyn & Bacon.

Kosonen, P., & Winne, P. H. (1995). Effects of teaching statistical laws of reasoning about everyday problems. *Journal of Educational Psychology, 87*(1), 33–46.

Kounin, J. (1970). *Discipline and group management in classrooms.* New York: Holt, Rinehart and Winston.

Kozulin, A., & Presseisen, B. Z. (1995). Mediated learning experience and psychological tools: Vygotsky's and Feuerstein's perspectives in a study of student learning. *Educational Psychologist, 30,* 67–75.

Kramarski, B., & Mevarech, Z. R. (2003). Enhancing mathematical reasoning in the classroom: The effects of cooperative learning and metacognitive training. *American Educational Research Journal, 40*(1), 281–310.

Krinsky, R., & Krinsky, S. G. (1996). Pegword mnemonic instruction: Retrieval times and long-term memory performance among fifth grade children. *Contemporary Educational Psychology, 21*(2), 193–207.

Kristof, N. D. (2009, April 15). How to raise our I.Q. *The New York Times.* Retrieved July 27, 2009, from www.nytimes.com/2009/04/16/opinion/16kristof.html

Kroesbergen, E. H., Van Luit, J. E. H., & Maas, C. J. M. (2004). Effectiveness of explicit and constructivist mathematics instruction for low-achieving students in the Netherlands. *The Elementary School Journal, 104*(3), 233–251.

Krug, D., Davis, T. B., & Glover, J. A. (1990). Massed versus distributed reading: A case of forgetting helping recall? *Journal of Educational Psychology, 82,* 366–371.

Krumboltz, J. D., & Yeh, C. J. (1996). Competitive grading sabotages good teaching. *Phi Delta Kappan, 78*(4), 324–326.

Kucan, L., & Beck, I. L. (1997). Thinking aloud and reading comprehension research: Inquiry, instruction, and social interaction. *Review of Educational Research, 67*(3), 271–299.

Kugler, E., & Albright, E. (2005). Increasing diversity in challenging classes. *Educational Leadership, 62*(5), 42–45.

Kuhara-Kojima, K., & Hatano, G. (1991). Contribution of content knowledge and learning ability to the learning of facts. *Journal of Educational Psychology, 83*(2), 253–263.

Kuhn, D. (2006). Do cognitive changes accompany developments in the adolescent brain? *Perspectives on Psychological Science, 1*(1), 59–67.

Kulhavy, R. W., & Stock, W. A. (1989). Feedback in written instruction: The place of response certitude. *Educational Psychology Review, 1*(4), 279–308.

Kulik, J. A. (2003). *Effects of using instructional technology in elementary and secondary schools: What controlled evaluation studies say* (SRI Project Number P10446.001). Arlington, VA: SRI International.

Kulik, J. A., & Kulik, C.-L. (1988). Timing of feedback and verbal learning. *Review of Educational Research Journal, 21*, 79–97.

Kulik, J. A., & Kulik, C.-L. (1997). Ability grouping. In N. Colangelo & G. A. Davis (Eds.), *Handbook of gifted education* (2nd ed., pp. 230–242). Boston: Allyn & Bacon.

Kunter, M., Baumert, J., & Köller, O. (2007). Effective classroom management and the development of subject-related interest. *Learning and Instruction, 17*(5), 494–509.

Kutnick, P., Ota, C., & Berdondini, L. (2008). Improving the effects of group working in classrooms with young school-aged children: Facilitating attainment, interaction and classroom activity. *Learning and Instruction, 18*(1), 83–95.

Kyle, P., & Rogien, L. (2004). *Opportunities and options in classroom management*. Boston: Pearson.

Ladd, G. W., & Troop-Gordon, W. (2003). The role of chronic peer difficulties in the development of children's psychological adjustment problems. *Child Development, 55*, 1958–1965.

Ladson-Billings, G. (2006). From the achievement gap to the education debt: Understanding achievement in U.S. schools. *Educational Researcher, 35*(7), 3–12.

Lahaderne, H. (1968). Attitudinal and intellectual correlates of attention: A study of four sixth-grade classrooms. *Journal of Educational Psychology, 59*, 320–324.

Lampert, M. (1986). Knowing, doing, and teaching multiplication. *Cognition and Instruction, 3*, 305–342.

Land, D., & Legters, N. (2002). The extent and consequences of risk in U.S. education. In S. Stringfield & D. Land (Eds.), *Educating at-risk students* (pp. 1–28). Chicago: National Society for the Study of Education.

Land, M. L. (1987). Vagueness and clarity. In M. J. Dunkin (Ed.), *International encyclopedia of teaching and teacher education*. New York: Pergamon.

Landrum, T. J., & Kauffman, J. M. (2006). Behavioral approaches to classroom management. In C. M. Evertson & C. S. Weinstein (Eds.), *Handbook of classroom management*. Mahwah, NJ: Erlbaum.

Landrum, T. J., & McDuffie, K. A. (2008). Behavioral. In T. L. Good (Ed.), *21st century learning* (Vol. 1, pp. 161–167). Thousand Oaks, CA: Sage.

Lane, K. L., & Beebe-Frankenberger, M. (2004). *School-based interventions: The tools you need to succeed*. Boston: Pearson.

Langer, G., & Colton, A. (2005). Looking at student work. *Educational Leadership, 62*(5), 22–27.

Langer, J. A. (2001). Beating the odds: Teaching middle and high school students to read and write well. *American Educational Research Journal, 38*(4), 837–880.

Lapkoff, S., & Li, R. (2007). Five trends for schools. *Educational Leadership, 64*(6), 8–17.

Larivée, S., Normandeau, S., & Parent, S. (2000). The French connection: Some contributions of French-language research in the post-Piagetian era. *Child Development, 71*, 823–839.

Larrivee, B. (1985). *Effective teaching behaviors for successful mainstreaming*. New York: Longman.

Latham, A. S. (1997). Peer counseling: Proceed with caution. *Educational Leadership, 55*(2), 77–78.

Latham, P. (2002). Teaching and learning primary mathematics: The impact of interactive whiteboards. *BEAM Research Papers*. Retrieved September 23, 2004, from www.beam.co.uk/pdfs/RES03.pdf

Lauer, P. A., Akiba, M., Wilkerson, S., Apthorp, H., Snow, D., & Martin-Glenn, M. L. (2006). Out-of-school-time programs: A meta-analysis of effects for at-risk students. *Review of Educational Research, 76*(2), 275–313.

Laupa, M. (1991). Children's reasoning about three authority attributes: Adult status, knowledge, and social position. *Developmental Psychology, 27*, 321–329.

Lave, J. (1988). *Cognition in practice*. Boston: Cambridge Press.

Leahy, S., Lyon, C., Thompson, M., & Wiliam, D. (2005). Looking at how students reason. *Educational Leadership, 63*(3), 26–31.

Learning First Alliance. (2001). *Every child learning: Safe and supportive schools*. Washington, DC: Author.

Lee, C. (2008). Synthesis of research on the role of culture in learning among African American youth: The contributions of Asa G. Hillard, III. *Review of Educational Research, 78*(4), 797–827.

Lee, C. D. (2000, April). *The state of knowledge about the education of African Americans*. Paper presented at the annual meeting of the American Educational Research Association, New Orleans, LA.

Lee, J. (2004). Multiple facets of inequity in racial and ethnic achievement gaps. *Peabody Journal of Education, 79*(2), 51–73.

Lee, J., & Bowen, N. (2006). Parent involvement, cultural capital, and the achievement gap among elementary school children. *American Educational Research Journal, 43*(2), 193–218.

Lee, O. (2005). Science education with English language learners: Synthesis and research agenda. *Review of Educational Research, 75*(4), 491–530.

Lee, V. E., & Burkam, D. T. (2003). Dropping out of high school: The role of school organization and structure. *American Educational Research Journal, 40*(2), 353–393.

Lehr, C. A., Hansen, A., Sinclair, M. F., & Christenson, S. L. (2003). Moving beyond dropout prevention to school completion: An integrative review of data based interventions. *School Psychology Review, 32*, 342–364.

Lehr, C. A., Sinclair, M. F., & Christenson, S. L. (2004). Addressing student engagement and truancy prevention during the elementary school years: A replication study of the Check & Connect model. *Journal of Education for Students Placed at Risk, 9*(3), 279–301.

Leinhardt, G., & Steele, M. D. (2005). Seeing the complexity of standing to the side: Instructional dialogues. *Cognition and Instruction, 23*, 87–163.

Lepper, M. R. (1983). Extrinsic reward and intrinsic motivation: Implications for the classroom. In J. M. Levine & M. C. Wang (Eds.), *Teacher and student perceptions: Implications for learning* (pp. 281–317). Hillsdale, NJ: Erlbaum.

Lepper, M. R. (1985). Microcomputers in education. Motivational and social issues. *American Psychologist, 40*, 1–18.

Lepper, M. R. (1998). A whole much less than the sum of its parts. *American Psychologist, 53*(6), 675–676.

Lepper, M. R., Greene, D., & Nisbett, R. E. (1973). Undermining children's intrinsic interest with extrinsic rewards: A test of the overjustification hypothesis. *Journal of Personality and Social Psychology, 28*, 129–137.

Lessow-Hurley, J. (2005). *The foundations of dual language instruction*. Boston: Pearson.

Leu, D. J., Jr. (2000). Literacy and technology: Deictic consequences for literacy education in an information age. In M. L. Kamil, P. B. Mosenthal, P. D. Pearson, & R. Barr (Eds.), *Handbook of reading research* (Vol. 3, pp. 743–770). Mahwah, NJ: Erlbaum.

Levenstein, P., Levenstein, S., & Oliver, D. (2002). First grade school readiness of former participants in a South Carolina replication of the Parent-Child Home Program. *Journal of Applied Developmental Psychology, 23,* 331–353.

Lever-Duffy, J., McDonald, J., & Mizell, A. (2003). *Teaching and learning with technology.* Boston: Pearson.

Lever-Duffy, J., & McDonald, J. B. (2008). *Teaching and learning with technology* (3rd ed.). Boston: Allyn & Bacon.

Levin, A. V. (1996). Common visual problems in the classroom. In R. H. A. Haslam & P. J. Valletutti (Eds.), *Medical problems in the classroom: The teacher's role in diagnosis and management* (pp. 161–180). Austin, TX: Pro-Ed.

Levin, J., & Nolan, J. F. (2007). *Principles of classroom management* (5th ed.). Boston: Allyn & Bacon.

Levin, J., & Nolan, J. F. (Eds.). (2010). *Principles of classroom management: A professional decision-making model* (6th ed.). Boston: Pearson.

Levin, J. R., O'Donnell, A. M., & Kratochwill, T. R. (2003). Educational/psychological intervention research. In W. M. Reynolds & G. E. Miller (Eds.), *Handbook of psychology: Vol. 7. Educational psychology* (pp. 557–581). Hoboken, NJ: Wiley.

Levine, C., Kohlberg, L., & Hewer, A. (1985). The current formulation of Kohlberg's theory and a response to critics. *Human Development, 28,* 94–100.

Levy, S. (2008). The power of audience. *Educational Leadership, 66*(3), 75–79.

Lewin, L. (2001). *Using the Internet to strengthen curriculum.* Alexandria, VA: ASCD.

Lewis, M., & Sullivan, M. W. (Eds.). (1996). *Emotional development in atypical children.* Mahwah, NJ: Erlbaum.

Li, G., & Wang, W. (2008). English language learners. In T. L. Good (Ed.), *21st century learning* (Vol. 2, pp. 97–104). Thousand Oaks, CA: Sage.

Lin, T., & Anderson, R. (2008). Reflections on collaborative discourse, argumentation, and learning. *Contemporary Educational Psychology, 33*(3), 443–448.

Lindeman, B. (2001). Reaching out to immigrant parents. *Educational Leadership, 58*(6), 62–66.

Lindholm-Leary, K. (2004/2005). The rich promise of two-way immersion. *Educational Leadership, 62*(4), 56–59.

Linebarger, D., Kosanic, A., Greenwood, C., & Doku, N. (2004). Effects of viewing the television program *Between the Lions* on the emergent literacy skills of young children. *Journal of Educational Psychology, 96,* 297–308.

Linn, R. L. (1994). Performance assessment: Policy promises and technical measurement standards. *Educational Researcher, 23*(9), 4–14.

Linn, R. L. (2000). Assessments and accountability. *Educational Researcher, 29*(2), 4–15.

Linn, R. L., & Haug, C. (2002). Stability of school-building accountability scores and gains. *Educational Evaluation and Policy Analysis, 24*(1), 29–36.

Lissitz, R., & Schafer, W. (2002). *Assessment in educational reform: Both means and ends.* Boston: Allyn & Bacon.

Lloyd, J. W., Singh, N. N., & Repp, A. C. (Eds.). (1991). *The Regular Education Initiative: Alternative perspectives on concepts, issues, and models.* DeKalb, IL: Sycamore.

Loeber, R., & Stouthamer-Loeber, M. (1998). Development of juvenile aggression and violence. *American Psychologist, 53*(2), 242–259.

Lomawaima, K. T., & McCarty, T. L. (2002). When tribal sovereignty challenges democracy: American Indian education and the democratic ideal. *American Educational Research Journal, 39*(2), 279–305.

Lomawaima, T., & McCarty, T. (2006). *To remain an Indian: Lessons in democracy from a century of Native American education.* New York: Teachers College Press.

Lorch, R. F., Lorch, E. P., & Inman, W. E. (1993). Effects of signaling topic structure on text recall. *Journal of Educational Psychology, 85,* 281–290.

Losey, K. M. (1995). Mexican American students and classroom interaction: An overview and critique. *Review of Educational Research, 65,* 283–318.

Lou, Y., Abrami, P. C., & d'Apollonia, S. (2001). Small group and individual learning with technology: A meta-analysis. *Review of Educational Research, 71*(3), 449–521.

Lou, Y., Abrami, P. C., Spence, J. C., Poulsen, C., Chambers, B., & D'Apollonia, S. (1996). Within-class grouping: A meta-analysis. *Review of Educational Research, 66*(4), 423–458.

Loury, G. C. (2002). *The anatomy of racial inequality.* Cambridge, MA: Harvard University Press.

Loveless, T. (1998). The tracking and ability grouping debate. *Fordham Report, 2*(8), 1–27.

Lowther, D., Ross, S., & Morrison, G. (2003). *When each one has one: The influences on teaching strategies and student achievement of using laptops in the classroom.* Paper presented at the annual meeting of the American Educational Research Association, Seattle, WA.

Lubienski, S., & Lubienski, T. (2006). School sector and academic achievement: A multilevel analysis of NAEP mathematics data. *American Educational Research Journal, 43*(4), 651–698.

Lucas, S. R., & Gamoran, A. (2002). Tracking and the achievement gap. In J. E. Chubb & T. Loveless (Eds.), *Bridging the achievement gap* (pp. 171–198). Washinton, DC: Brookings.

Luckasson, R., Coulter, D., Polloway, E., Reiss, S., Schalock, R., Snell, M., Spitalnik, D., & Stark, J. (1992). *Mental retardation: Definitions, classification, and systems of supports* (9th ed.). Washington, DC: American Association on Mental Retardation.

Lundeberg, M., & Mohan, L. (2008). Gender issues and schooling. In T. L. Good (Ed.), *21st century learning* (Vol. 2, pp. 288–296). Thousand Oaks, CA: Sage.

Lyons, C. A., Pinnell, G. S., & DeFord, D. E. (1993). *Partners in learning: Teachers and children in reading recovery.* New York: Teachers College Press.

Lysynchuk, L. M., Pressley, M., & Vye, N. J. (1990). Reciprocal teaching improves standardized reading-comprehension performance in poor comprehenders. *Elementary School Journal, 90,* 469–484.

Lyytinen, H., Guttorm, T. K., Huttunen, T., Hamalainen, J., Leppanen, P. H. T., & Vesterinen, M. (2005). Psychophysiology of developmental dyslexic: A review of findings including studies of children at risk for dyslexia. *Journal of Neurolinguistics, 18,* 167–195.

Maag, J. (2001). Rewarded by punishment: Reflections on the disuse of positive reinforcement in schools. *Exceptional Children, 67,* 173–186.

Maag, J. W., Rutherford, R. B., & DiGangi, S. A. (1992). Effects of self-monitoring and contingency reinforcement on on-task behavior and academic productivity of learning disabled students: A social validation study. *Psychology in the Schools, 29,* 157–172.

MacArthur, C., Ferretti, R., Okolo, C., & Cavalier, A. (2001). Technology applications for students with literacy problems: A critical review. *The Elementary School Journal, 101*(3), 273–302.

Macedo, D. (2000). The illiteracy of English-only literacy. *Educational Leadership, 57*(4), 63–67.

MacIver, D. J., Reuman, D. A., & Main, S. R. (1995). Social structuring of the school: Studying what is, illuminating what could be. *Annual Review of Psychology, 46,* 375–400.

MacKenzie, A. A., & White, R. T. (1982). Fieldwork in geography and long-term memory. *American Educational Research Journal, 19,* 623–632.

Madden, N. A., & Slavin, R. E. (1983). Effects of cooperative learning on the social acceptance of mainstreamed academically handicapped students. *Journal of Special Education, 17,* 171–182.

Maehr, M. L., & Anderman, E. M. (1993). Reinventing schools for early adolescents: Emphasizing task goals. *The Elementary School Journal, 93*(5), 593–610.

Mager, R. F. (1975). *Preparing instructional objectives.* Belmont, CA: Fearon.

Mager, R. F. (1997). *Preparing instructional objectives.* Atlanta, GA: CEP.

Maguire, E. A., Gadian, D. G., Johnsrude, I. S., Good, C. D., Ashburner, J., Frackowiak, R. S. J., & Frith, C. D. (2000). Navigation-related structural change in the hippocampi of taxi drivers. *Proceedings of the National Academy of Sciences, 97*(8), 4398–4403.

Maheady, L., Harper, G. F., & Mallette, B. (1991). Peer-mediated instruction: Review of potential applications for special education. *Reading, Writing, and Learning Disabilities, 7,* 75–102.

Maher, F. A., & Ward, J. V. (2002). *Gender and teaching.* Mahwah, NJ: Erlbaum.

Mahony, M. (1997). Small victories in an inclusive classroom. *Educational Leadership, 54*(7), 59–62.

Malott, R., Malott, M., & Trojan, E. (2000). *Punishment.* In R. Malott, M. Malott, & E. Trojan, *Elementary principles of behavior* (4th ed., pp. 56–79). Upper Saddle River, NJ: Prentice Hall.

Malott, R. W. (Ed.). (2008). *Principles of behavior* (6th ed.). Upper Saddle River, NJ: Pearson.

Malouf, D. B., Wizer, D. R., Pilato, V. H., & Grogan, M. M. (1990). Computer-assisted instruction with small groups of mildly handicapped students. *Journal of Special Education, 24,* 51–68.

Mandeville, G. K. (1992). Does achievement increase over time? Another look at the South Carolina PET program. *The Elementary School Journal, 93*(2), 117–129.

Mandeville, G. K., & Rivers, J. L. (1991). The South Carolina PET study: Teachers' perceptions and student achievement. *The Elementary School Journal, 91,* 377–407.

Manna, P. (2008). *Federal aid to elementary and secondary education: Premises, effects, and major lessons learned.* Washington, DC: Center on Education Policy.

Manning, B. H. (1988). Application of cognitive behavior modification: First and third graders' self-management of classroom behaviors. *American Educational Research Journal, 25,* 193–212.

Manning, M. A., Bear, G. G., & Minke, K. M. (2001, April). *The self-concept of students with learning disabilities: Does educational placement matter?* Paper presented at the annual meeting of the American Educational Research Association, Seattle, WA.

Manning, M. L., & Baruth, L. G. (1995). *Students at risk.* Boston: Allyn & Bacon.

Manning, M. L., & Baruth, L. G. (2009). *Multicultural education of children and adolescents* (5th ed.). Boston: Pearson.

March, J., Gershwin, D., Kirby, S., & Xia, N. (2009). *Retaining students in grade: Lessons learned regarding policy design and implementation.* Arlington, VA: RAND.

March, T. (2005/2006). The new www: Whatever, whenever, wherever. *Educational Leadership, 63*(4), 14–19.

Marcia, J. E. (1991). Identity and self-development. In R. M. Lerner, A. C. Petersen, & E. J. Brooks-Gunn (Eds.), *Encyclopedia of adolescence* (Vol. 1, pp. 527–531). New York: Garland.

Marks, H., Doane, K., & Secada, W. (1998). Support for student achievement. In F. Newmann et al. (Eds.), *Restructuring for student achievement: The impact of structure and culture in 24 schools.* San Francisco: Jossey-Bass.

Marks, H. M. (2000). Student engagement in instructional activity: Patterns in the elementary, middle, and high school years. *American Educational Research Journal, 37*(1), 153–184.

Marsh, E., Roediger, H., Bjork, R., & Bjork, E. (2007). The memorial consequences of multiple-choice testing. *Psychonomic Bulletin & Review, 14,* 194–199.

Marsh, H. W. (1993). The multidimensional structure of academic self-concept: Invariance over gender and age. *American Educational Research Journal, 30,* 841–860.

Martella, R. C., Nelson, J. R., & Marchand-Martella, N. E. (2003). *Managing disruptive behaviors in the schools.* Boston: Allyn & Bacon.

Martin, A. (2008). Enhancing student motivation and engagement: The effects of a multidimensional intervention. *Contemporary Educational Psychology, 33*(2), 239–269.

Martin, A., & Dowson, M. (2009). Interpersonal relationships, motivation, engagement, and achievement: Yields for theory, current issues, and educational practice. *Review of Educational Research, 79*(1), 327–365.

Martin, A. J., Marsh, H. W., & Debus, R. L. (2001). Self-handicapping and defensive pessimism: Exploring a model of predictors and outcomes from a self-protection perspective. *Journal of Educational Psychology, 93*(1), 87–102.

Martinez, M. (2006). What is metacognition? *Phi Delta Kappan, 87*(9), 696–699.

Martinez, S., & Harper, D. (2008). Working with tech-savvy kids. *Educational Leadership, 66*(3), 64–70.

Marx, R., & Harris, C. (2006). No Child Left Behind and science education: Opportunities, challenges, and risks. *The Elementary School Journal, 106*(5), 467–478.

Marzano, R. (2003). Using data: Two wrongs and a right. *Educational Leadership, 60*(5), 56–60.

Marzano, R. (2009). Six steps to better vocabulary instruction. *Educational Leadership, 67*(1), 83.

Marzano, R. (2010). When students track their progress. *Educational Leadership, 67*(4), 87–88.

Marzano, R., & Kendall, J. (2007). *The new taxonomy of educational objectives.* Thousand Oaks, CA: Corwin.

Marzano, R., & Kendall, J. (2009). The new taxonomy of educational objectives (2nd ed.). Thousand Oaks, CA: Corwin.

Marzano, R., & Pickering, D. (2007). The case for and against homework. *Educational Leadership, 64*(6), 74–79.

Marzano, R. J. (2000). *Transforming classroom grading.* Alexandria, VA: ASCD.

Marzano, R. J., Pickering, D. J., & Pollock, J. E. (2001). *Classroom instruction that works: Research-based strategies for increasing student achievement.* Alexandria, VA: ASCD.

Mash, E. J., & Wolfe, D. A. (2003). Disorders of childhood and adolescence. In G. Stricker & T. A. Widiger (Eds.), *Handbook of psychology: Vol. 8. Clinical psychology* (pp. 27–64). Hoboken, NJ: Wiley.

Maslow, A. H. (1954). *Motivation and personality.* New York: Harper & Row.

Mason, D. A. (1995). Grouping students for elementary school mathematics: A survey of principals in 12 states. *Educational Research and Evaluation, 1*(4), 318–346.

Mason, D. A., & Good, T. L. (1993). Effects of two-group and whole-class teaching on regrouped elementary students' mathematics achievement. *American Educational Research Journal, 30*(2), 328–360.

Mason, L. H. (2004). Explicit self-regulated strategy development versus reciprocal questioning: Effects on expository reading comprehension among struggling readers. *Journal of Educational Psychology, 96*(2), 283–296.

Massey, C. (2008). Development: PreK–2. In T. L. Good (Ed.), *21st century learning* (Vol. 1, pp. 73–81). Thousand Oaks, CA: Sage.

Mastropieri, M. A., Scruggs, T. E., & Berkeley, S. (2007). *Educational Leadership, 64*(5), 54–60.

Mather, N., & Goldstein, S. (2001). *Learning disabilities and challenging behaviors.* Baltimore: Brookes.

Mathes, P., & Babyak, A. (2001). The effects of peer-assisted literacy strategies for first-grade readers with and without additional mini-skills lessons. *Learning Disabilities Research & Practice, 16*(1), 28–44.

Mathes, P. G., Denton, C. A., Fletcher, J. M., Anthony, J. L., Francis, D. J., & Schatschneider, C. (2005). The effects of theoretically different instruction and student characteristics on the skills of struggling readers. *Reading Research Quarterly, 40*(2), 148–182.

Mathes, P. G., Torgeson, J. K., & Allor, J. H. (2001). The effects of peer-assisted literacy strategies for first-grade readers with and without additional computer-assisted instruction in phonological awareness. *American Educational Research Journal, 38*(2), 371–410.

Mathes, P. G., Torgesen, J. K., Clancy-Menchetti, J., Santi, K., Nicholas, K., Robinson, C., & Grek, M. (2003). A comparison of teacher-directed versus peer-assisted instruction to struggling first-grade readers. *The Elementary School Journal, 103*(5), 461–479.

Matthews, J., Ponitz, C., & Morrison, F. (2009). Early gender differences in self-regulation and academic achievement. *Journal of Educational Psychology, 101*(3), 689–704.

Mattingly, D. J., Prislin, R., McKenzie, T. L., Rodriguez, J. L., & Kayzar, B. (2002). Evaluating evaluations: The case of parent involvement programs. *Review of Educational Research, 72*(4), 549–576.

Mayer, R. (2008a). Applying the science of learning: Evidence-based principles for the design of multimedia instruction. *American Psychologist, 63*(8), 757–769.

Mayer, R. (2008b). Information processing. In T. L. Good (Ed.), *21st century learning: Vol. 1* (pp. 168–174). Thousand Oaks, CA: Sage.

Mayer, R. E. (2001). *Multimedia learning.* New York: Cambridge University Press.

Mayer, R. E. (2009). *Multimedia learning* (2nd ed). New York: Cambridge University Press.

Mayer, R. E., & Wittrock, M. C. (1996). Problem-solving transfer. In D. C. Berliner & R. C. Calfee (Eds.), *Handbook of educational psychology* (pp. 47–62). New York: Macmillan.

McCaffrey, D. F., Lockwood, J. R., Koretz, D., Louis, T. A., & Hamilton, L. (2004). Models for value-added modeling of teacher effects. *Journal of Educational and Behavioral Statistics, 29*(1), 67–101.

McCaleb, J., & White, J. (1980). Critical dimensions in evaluating teacher clarity. *Journal of Classroom Interaction, 15,* 27–30.

McCallum, R. S., & Bracken, B. A. (1993). Interpersonal relations between school children and their peers, parents, and teachers. *Educational Psychology Review, 5*(2), 155–176.

McCarthey, S. J. (2008). Writing. In T. L. Good (Ed.), *21st century learning* (Vol. 1, pp. 336–342). Thousand Oaks, CA: Sage.

McClelland, D. C., & Atkinson, J. W. (1948). The projective expression of needs: II. The effect of different intensities of the hunger drive on thematic apperception. *Journal of Experimental Psychology, 38,* 643–658.

McComb, E. M., & Scott-Little, C. (2003). *After-school programs: Evaluations and outcomes.* Greensboro, NC: SERVE.

McCombs, J. S., Kirby, S. N., & Mariano, L. T. (2009). *Ending social promotion without leaving children behind: The case of New York City.* Arlington, VA: RAND.

McCormick, C. B. (2003). Metacognition and learning. In W. M. Reynolds & G. E. Miller (Eds.), *Handbook of psychology: Vol. 7. Educational psychology* (pp. 79–102). Hoboken, NJ: Wiley.

McDaniel, M., Roediger, H., & McDermott, K. (2007). Generalized test-enhanced learning from the laboratory to the classroom. *Psychonomic Bulletin and Review, 14,* 200–206.

McDaniel, M. A., & Dannelly, C. M. (1996). Learning with analogy and elaborative interrogation. *Journal of Educational Psychology, 88*(3), 508–519.

McDermott, K. (2007). "Expanding the moral community" or "Blaming the victim"? The politics of state education accountability policy. *American Educational Research Journal, 44*(1), 77–111.

McDonnell, J., Hardman, M., & McDonnell, A. (2003). *An introduction to persons with moderate and severe disabilities.* Boston: Allyn & Bacon.

McElvany, N., & Artelt, C. (2009). Systematic reading training in the family: Development, implementation, and initial evaluation of the Berlin Parent-Child Reading Program. *Learning and Instruction, 19*(1), 79–95.

McGill-Franzen, A., & Allington, R. (2006). Contamination of current accountability systems. *Phi Delta Kappan, 87*(10), 762–766.

McHale, S. M., Dariotis, J. K., & Kauh, T. J. (2003). Social development and social relationships in middle childhood. In R. M. Lerner, M. A. Easterbrooks, & J. Mistry (Eds.), *Handbook of psychology: Vol. 6. Developmental psychology* (pp. 241–265). Hoboken, NJ: Wiley.

McKenna, M., & Walpole, S. (2007). Assistive technology in the reading clinic: Its emerging potential. *Reading Research Quarterly, 42*(1), 140–145.

McKenzie, G. (1979). Effects of questions and testlike events on achievement and on-task behavior in a classroom concept learning presentation. *Journal of Educational Research, 72,* 348–350.

McKenzie, G. R., & Henry, M. (1979). Effects of testlike events on on-task behavior, test anxiety, and achievement in a classroom rule-learning task. *Journal of Educational Psychology, 71,* 370–374.

McKeown, M. G., & Beck, I. L. (1998). Talking to an author: Readers taking charge of the reading process. In R. Calfoe & N. Nelson (Eds.), *The reading–writing connection* (pp. 112–130). Chicago: National Society for the Study of Education.

McKeown, M. G., & Beck, I. L. (2004). Transforming knowledge into professional development resources: Six teachers implement a model of teaching for understanding text. *The Elementary School Journal, 104*(5), 391–408.

McLeskey, J., & Waldron, N. L. (2002). School change and inclusive schools: Lessons learned from practice. *Phi Delta Kappan, 84*(1), 65–72.

McLoyd, V. C. (1998). Economic disadvantage and child-development. *American Psychologist, 53*(2), 185–204.

McMillan, J. (2008). *Assessment essentials for standards-based education.* Thousand Oaks, CA: Corwin.

McMillan, J. H. (2007). *Classroom assessment* (4th ed.). Boston: Allyn & Bacon.

McNeely, C. A., Nonnemaker, J. M., & Blum, R. W. (2002). Promoting school connectedness. *Journal of School Health, 72*(4), 138–146.

McPartland, J. M., Balfanz, R., Jordan, W. J., & Legters, N. (2002). Promising solutions for the least productive American high schools. In S. Stringfield & D. Land (Eds.), *Educating at-risk students* (pp. 148–170). Chicago: National Society for the Study of Education.

McVee, M., Dunsmore, K., & Gavelek, J. (2005). Schema theory revisited. *Review of Educational Research, 75*(4), 531–566.

Mead, S. (2006). *The truth about boys and girls.* Washington, DC: Education Sector.

Means, B. (2001). Technology use in tomorrow's schools. *Educational Leadership, 58*(4), 57–61.

Meek, C. (2003). Classroom crisis: It's about time. *Phi Delta Kappan, 84*(8), 592–595.

Meichenbaum, D. (1977). *Cognitive behavior modification: An integrative approach.* New York: Plenum.

Mellard, D., & Johnson, E. (2008). *RTI: A practitioner's guide to implementing Response to Intervention.* Thousand Oaks, CA: Corwin.

Mercer, J. (2010). *Child development.* Thousand Oaks, CA: Sage.

Merickel, A., Linquanti, R., Parrish, T. B., Pérez, M., Eaton, M., & Esra, P. (2003). *Effects of the implementation of Proposition 227 on the education of English language learners, K–12: Year 3 report.* San Francisco: WestEd.

Merrill, D. C., Reiser, B. J., Merrill, S. K., & Landes, S. (1995). Tutoring: Guided learning by doing. *Cognition and Instruction, 13*(3), 315–372.

Mertler, C. A., & Charles, C. M. (2011). *Introduction to educational research* (7th ed.). Boston: Pearson.

Metsala, J. L., Stanovich, K. E., & Brown, G. D. A. (1998). Regularity effects and the phonological deficit model of reading disabilities: A meta-analytic review. *Journal of Educational Psychology, 90*(2), 279–293.

Metzger, M. (2002). Learning to discipline. *Phi Delta Kappan, 84*(1), 77–84.

Mevarech, Z. R. (1991). Learning mathematics in different mastery environments. *Journal of Educational Research, 84,* 225–231.

Meyer, A., & Rose, D. H. (2000). Universal design for individual differences. *Educational Leadership, 58*(3), 39–43.

Meyer, L. A. (1984). Long-term academic effects of the Direct Instruction Project follow through. *The Elementary School Journal, 84*(4), 380–394.

Meyers, J., Gelzheiser, L., Yelich, G., & Gallagher, M. (1990). Classroom, remedial and resource teachers' views of pullout programs. *Elementary School Journal, 90*(5), 531–545.

Mickelson, R. A. (2002). Race and education. In D. L. Levinson, P. W. Cookson, Jr., & A. R. Sadovnik (Eds.), *Education and sociology: An encyclopedia* (pp. 485–494). New York: Routledge Falmer.

Midgley, C., & Urdan, T. (2001). Academic self-handicapping and achievement goals: A further examination. *Contemporary Educational Psychology, 26*(1), 61–75.

Midgley, C. M. (1993). Motivation and middle level schools. In M. L. Maehr & P. R. Pintrick (Eds.), *Advances in motivation and achievement* (Vol. 8, pp. 217–274). Greenwich, CT: JAI Press.

Miller, D., Partelow, L., & Sen, A. (2004, April). *Self-regulatory reading processes in relation to fourth-graders' reading literacy.* Paper presented at the annual meeting of the American Educational Research Association, San Diego, CA.

Miller, D. J., Glover, D., Averis, D., & Door, V. (2005). The interactive whiteboard—a literature survey. *Technology, Pedagogy, and Education, 14*(2), 155–170.

Miller, P. H. (1993). *Theories of developmental psychology* (3rd ed.). New York: Freeman.

Mills, G. E. (2007). *Action research: A guide for the teacher researcher* (3rd ed.). Upper Saddle River, NJ: Pearson.

Miltenberger, R. G. (2001). *Behavior modification: Principles and procedures* (2nd ed.). Belmont, CA: Wadsworth.

Minke, K. M., & Bear, G. C. (Eds.). (2000). *Preventing school problems—promoting school success.* Bethesda, MD: National Association of School Psychologists.

Mishel, L., & Roy, J. (2006). Accurately assessing high school graduation rates. *Phi Delta Kappan, 88*(4), 287–292.

Mitchell, K. J., & Johnson, M. K. (2009). Source monitoring 15 years later: What have we learned from fMRI about the neural mechanisms of source memory? *Psychological Bulletin, 135*(4), 638–677.

Mock, D. R., & Kauffman, J. M. (2005). The delusion of full inclusion. In J. W. Jacobson, J. A. Mulick, & R. M. Foxx (Eds.), *Fads: Dubious and improbable treatments for developmental disabilities* (pp. 113–128). Mahwah, NJ: Erlbaum.

Moors, A., & De Houwer, J. (2006). Automaticity: A theoretical and conceptual analysis. *Psychological Bulletin, 132*(2), 297–326.

Mora, J. (2009). From the ballot box to the classroom. *Educational Leadership, 66*(7), 14–19.

Moran, S., Kornhaber, M., & Gardner, H. (2006). Orchestrating multiple intelligences. *Educational Leadership, 64*(1), 22–29.

Morgan, M. (1984). Reward-induced decrements and increments in intrinsic motivation. *Review of Educational Research, 54,* 5–30.

Morris, D., Tyner, B., & Perney, J. (2000). Early steps: Replicating the effects of a first-grade reading intervention program. *Journal of Educational Psychology, 92,* 681–693.

Morris, J. E. (1999). What is the future of predominantly black urban schools? The politics of race in urban education policy. *Phi Delta Kappan, 81*(4), 316–319.

Morrow, L. M. (2009). *Literacy development in the early years: Helping children read and write* (6th ed.). Boston: Pearson.

Mosenthal, J., Lipson, M., Torncello, S., Russ, B., & Mekkelsen, J. (2004). Contexts and practices of six schools successful in obtaining reading achievement. *The Elementary School Journal, 104*(5), 343–368.

Moss, P., Girard, B., & Haniford, L. (2006). Validity in educational assessment. *Review of Research in Education, 30,* 109–162.

Mosteller, F., & Boruch, R. (Eds.). (2002). *Evidence matters: Randomized trials in educational research.* Washington, DC: Brookings.

Muñoz, M. A., Dossett, D., & Judy-Gullans, K. (2004). Educating students placed at risk: Evaluating the impact of Success for All in urban settings. *Journal of Education for Students Placed at Risk, 9*(3), 261–277.

Murawski, W., Lockwood, J., Khalili, A., & Johnston, A. (2010). A bully-free school. *Educational Leadership, 67*(4), 75–78.

Murayama, K., & Elliot, A. (2009). The joint influence of personal achievement goals and classroom goal structures on achievement-relevant outcomes. *Journal of Educational Psychology, 101*(2), 432–447.

Murdock, T. B., & Anderman, E. (2006). Motivational perspectives on student cheating: Toward an integrated model of academic dishonesty. *Educational Psychologist, 41*(3), 129–145.

Murdock, T. B., Hale, N. M., & Weber, M. J. (2001). Predictors of cheating among early adolescents: Academic and social motivations. *Contemporary Educational Psychology, 26*(1), 96–115.

Murji, S., & DeLuca, J. W. (1998). Preliminary validity of the cognitive function checklist: Prediction of tower of London performance. *Clinical Neuropsychologist, 12,* 358–364.

Murphy, K. P., & Alexander, P. A. (2000). A motivated exploration of motivation technology. *Contemporary Educational Psychology, 25*(1), 3–53.

Murphy, S., & Underwood, T. (2000). *Portfolio practices: Lessons from schools, districts, and states.* Norwood, MA: Christopher-Gordon.

Murray, H., Olivier, A., & Human, P. (1992). The development of young students' division strategies. In W. Geeslin & K. Graham (Eds.), *Proceedings of the sixteenth international conference for the psychology of mathematics instruction* (Vol. 2, pp. 152–159). Durham, NH.

Nasir, N., & Hand, V. (2006). Exploring sociocultural perspectives on race, culture, and learning. *Review of Educational Research, 76*(4), 449–476.

National Assessment of Educational Progress. (2008). *NAEP 2008 trends in academic progress.* Washington, DC: U.S. Department of Education.

National Center for Education Statistics (NCES). (2004). *Language minorities and their educational and labor market indicators—recent trends.* Washington, DC: U.S. Department of Education.

National Center for Education Statistics (NCES). (2007). *The condition of education*. Washington, DC: U.S. Department of Education.

National Education Commission on Time and Learning. (1994). *Prisoners of time: Schools and programs making time work for students and teachers*. Washington, DC: Author.

National Governors' Association. (1993). *Ability grouping and tracking: Current issues and concerns*. Washington, DC: Author.

National Information Center for Children and Youth with Disabilities. (1998). *Office of Special Education Programs' IDEA amendments of 1997 curriculum*. Retrieved December 1, 1998, from www.nichcy.org/Trainpkg/trainpkg.htm

National Institute for Literacy. (2008). *Developing early literacy*. Jessup, MD: Author.

National Institute of Allergy and Infectious Diseases. (2002). *HIV infection in adolescents: Fact sheet*. Rockville, MD: National Institutes of Health.

National Institute on Drug Abuse. (2005). *Marijuana abuse*. Bethesda, MD: Author

National Joint Committee on Learning Disabilities. (1988). (Letter to NJCLD member organization). Washington, DC: Author.

National Reading Panel. (2000). *Teaching children to read: An evidence-based assessment of the scientific research literature on reading and its implications for reading instruction*. Rockville, MD: National Institute of Child Health and Human Development.

National Research Council. (1995). *Losing generations: Adolescents in high-risk settings*. Hyattsville, MD: American Psychological Association.

National Research Council. (2000). *Improving intergroup relations among youth*. Washington, DC: Author.

National Research Council. (2001). *Non-technical strategies to reduce children's exposure to inappropriate material on the Internet*. Washington, DC: National Academies Press.

Natriello, G. (2002). At-risk students. In D. L. Levinson, P. W. Cookson, Jr., & A. R. Sadovnik (Eds.), *Education and sociology: An encyclopedia* (pp. 49–54). New York: Routledge Falmer.

Navaez, D., Getz, I., Rest, J. R., & Thoma, S. J. (1999). Individual moral judgment and cultural ideologies. *Developmental Psychology, 35,* 478–488.

Neale, D. C., Smith, D., & Johnson, V. G. (1990). Implementing conceptual change teaching in primary science. *Elementary School Journal, 91,* 109–131.

Neill, M. (2003). Leaving children behind: How No Child Left Behind will fail our children. *Phi Delta Kappan, 85*(3), 225–228.

Neill, M., & Gaylor, K. (2001). Do high-stakes graduation tests improve learning outcomes? Using state-level NAEP data to evaluate the effects of mandatory graduation tests. In G. Orfield & M. L. Kornhaber (Eds.), *Raising standards or raising barriers? Inequality and high-stakes testing in public education* (pp. 107–126). New York: Century Foundation Press.

Neisser, U., Boodoo, G., Bouchard, T. J., Boykin, A. W., Brody, N., Ceci, S. J., Halpern, D. F., Loehlin, J. C., Perloff, R., Sternberg, R. J., & Urbina, S. (1996). Intelligence: Knowns and unknowns. *American Psychologist, 51,* 77–101.

Nelson, J., & Stage, S. (2007). Fostering the development of vocabulary knowledge and reading comprehension through contextually-based multiple meaning vocabulary instruction. *Education and Treatment of Children, 30*(1), 1–22.

Nelson, J. R., & Carr, B. A. (2000). *The Think Time Strategy for schools*. Denver, CO: Sopris West.

Nesbit, J., & Adesope, O. (2006). Learning with concept and knowledge maps: A meta-analysis. *Review of Educational Research, 76*(3), 413–448.

Neufield, B., & Roper, D. (2003). *Coaching: A strategy for developing instructional capacity*. Providence, RI: Annenberg Institute.

Neuman, S. (2007). Changing the odds. *Educational Leadership, 65*(2), 16–21.

Neuman, S. B. (1995). Reading together: A community-based parent tutoring program. *The Reading Teacher, 49*(2), 120–129.

Neuman, S. B., & McCormick, S. (1995). *Single-subject experimental research*. Newark, DE: International Reading Association.

Nevin, A. (1998). Curriculum and instructional adaptations for including students with disabilities in cooperative groups. In J. W. Putnam (Ed.), *Cooperative learning and strategies for inclusion* (pp. 49–66). Baltimore: Paul H. Brookes.

Newbern, D., Dansereau, D. F., Patterson, M. E., & Wallace, D. S. (1994, April). *Toward a science of cooperation*. Paper presented at the annual meeting of the American Educational Research Association, New Orleans, LA.

Newcomb, A. F., & Bagwell, C. L. (1998). The developmental significance of children's friendship relations. In W. M. Bukowski, A. F. Newcomb, & W. W. Hartup (Eds.), *The company they keep: Friendships in childhood and adolescence* (pp. 289–312). New York: Cambridge University Press.

Newell, A., & Simon, H. (1972). *Human problem solving*. Englewood Cliffs, NJ: Prentice-Hall.

Ng, J., Lee, S., & Park, Y. (2007). Contesting the model minority and perpetual foreigner stereotypes: A critical review of literature on Asian Americans in education. *Review of Research in Education, 31,* 95–130.

Niaz, M. (1997). How early can children understand some form of "scientific reasoning"? *Perceptual and motor skills, 85,* 1272–1274.

NICHD Early Child Care Research Network. (2005). A day in third grade: A large-scale study of classroom quality and teacher and student behavior. *The Elementary School Journal, 105,* 305–323.

Nieto, S. (2009). From surviving to thriving. *Educational Leadership, 66*(5), 8–13.

Nieto, S., & Bode, P. (2008). *Affirming diversity: The sociopolitical context of multicultural education* (5th ed.). Boston: Pearson.

Niguidula, D. (2005). Documenting learning with digital portfolios. *Educational Leadership, 63*(3), 44–47.

Nitsch, K. E. (1977). *Structuring decontextualized forms of knowledge*. Unpublished doctoral dissertation, Vanderbilt University.

Noddings, N. (2008). All our students thinking. *Educational Leadership, 65*(5), 8–13.

Noonan, M. J., & McCormick, L. (1993). *Early intervention in natural environments*. Pacific Grove, CA: Brooks/Cole.

Northcutt, N., & McCoy, D. (2004). *Interactive qualitative analysis*. Thousand Oaks, CA: Sage.

Nucci, L. (1987). Synthesis of research on moral development. *Educational Leadership, 44,* 86–92.

Nucci, L. P. (2009). *Nice is not enough: Facilitating moral development*. Columbus, OH: Merrill Pearson.

Nussbaum, E. (2008). Collaborative discourse, argumentation, and learning: Preface and literature review. *Contemporary Educational Psychology, 33*(3), 345–359.

NWEA (Northwest Evaluation Association). (2003). *The state of state standards: Research investigating proficiency levels in fourteen states*. Seattle, WA: Author.

Nzinga-Johnson, S., Baker, J., & Aupperlee, J. (2009). Teacher–parent relationships and school involvement among racially and educationally diverse parents of kindergartners. *The Elementary School Journal, 110*(1), 81–91.

Oakes, J. (1985). *Keeping track: How schools structure inequality*. New Haven, CT: Yale University Press.

Oakes, J. (1995). Two cities: Tracking and within-school segregation. In L. Miller (Ed.), *Brown plus forty: The promise.* New York: Teachers College Press.

Oakes, J., & Guiton, G. (1995). Matchmaking: The dynamics of high school tracking decisions. *American Educational Research Journal, 32*(1), 3–33.

Oakes, J., & Lipton, M. (1994). Tracking and ability grouping: A structural barrier to access and achievement. In J. I. Goodlad & P. Keating (Eds.), *Access to knowledge: The continuing agenda for our nation's schools.* New York: The College Board.

Oakes, J., Quartz, K., Ryan, S., & Lipton, M. (2000). *Becoming good American schools: The struggle for civic virtue in school reform.* San Francisco: Jossey-Bass.

Oakes, J., & Wells, A. S. (1998). Detracking for high student achievement. *Educational Leadership, 55*(6), 38–41.

O'Connor, C., & Fernandez, S. D. (2006). Race, class, and disproportionality: Reevaluating the relationship between poverty and special education placement. *Educational Researcher, 35*(6), 6–11.

O'Connor, C., Hill, L., & Robinson, S. (2009). Who's at risk in school and what's race got to do with it? *Review of Research in Education, 33,* 1–34.

O'Connor, K. (2007). *A repair kit for grading: 15 fixes for broken grades.* Princeton, NJ: Educational Testing Services.

O'Connor, K. (2009). *How to grade for learning, K–12* (3rd ed.). Thousand Oaks, CA: Corwin.

O'Connor, M. C. (1998). Can we trace the "efficacy of social constructivism"? In P. D. Pearson & A. Iran-Nejad (Eds.), *Review of research in education* (pp. 25–72). Washington, DC: American Educational Research Association.

Odden, A. (2009). *IO strategies for doubling student performance.* Thousand Oaks, CA: Sage.

Odden, A., & Archibald, S. J. (2009). *Doubling student performance and finding the resources to do it.* Thousand Oaks, CA: Corwin.

O'Donnell, A. M., & Dansereau, D. F. (1992). Scripted cooperation in student dyads: A method for analyzing and enhancing academic learning and performance. In R. Hertz-Lazarowitz & N. Miller (Eds.), *Interaction in cooperative groups: The theoretical anatomy of group learning* (pp. 120–144). New York: Cambridge University Press.

O'Donnell, A. M., Dansereau, D. F., & Hall, R. H. (2002). Knowledge maps as scaffolds for cognitive processing. *Educational Psychology Review, 14*(1), 71–86.

O'Donnell, J., Hawkins, J. D., Catalano, R. F., Abbott, R. D., & Day, L. E. (1995). Preventing school failure, drug use, and delinquency among low-income children: Long-term intervention in elementary schools. *American Journal of Orthopsychiatry, 65*(1), 87–100.

Ogbu, J. (2004). Collective identity and the burden of "acting white" in black history, community, and education. *The Urban Review, 36*(1), 1–35.

Ogletree, C. J. (2004). *All deliberate speed: Reflections on the first half-century of Brown v. Board of Education.* New York: Norton.

Ohler, J. (2006). The world of digital storytelling. *Educational Leadership, 63*(4), 44–47.

Ohler, J. (2009). Orchestrating the media collage. *Educational Leadership, 66*(6), 8–13.

O'Leary, K. D., & O'Leary, S. G. (1972). *Classroom management: The successful use of behavior modification.* New York: Pergamon.

Olson, A. (2005). Improving schools one student at a time. *Educational Leadership, 62*(5), 37–41.

Olszewski-Kubilius, P. (2003). Gifted education programs and procedures. In W. M. Reynolds & G. E. Miller (Eds.), *Handbook of psychology: Vol. 7. Educational psychology* (pp. 487–510). Hoboken, NJ: Wiley.

Olweus, D. (1994). Bullying at school: Basic facts and effects of a school-based intervention program. *Journal of Child Psychology and Psychiatry, 35,* 1171–1190.

Olweus, D., & Limber, S. (1999). *Blueprints for violence prevention: Bullying prevention program.* Boulder: Institute of Behavioral Science, University of Colorado.

Oosterhof, A. (2009). Developing and using classroom assessments (4th ed.). Upper Saddle River, NJ: Pearson.

Orfield, G., & Frankenberg, E. (2007). The integration decision. *Education Week, 26*(43), 34, 44.

Orfield, G., Frankenberg, E., & Lee, C. (2003). The resurgence of school segregation. *Educational Leadership, 60*(4), 16–21.

Orfield, G., & Kornhaber, M. L. (Eds.). (2001). *Raising standards or raising barriers? Inequality and high-stakes testing in public education.* New York: Century Foundation Press.

Orfield, G., & Lee, C. (2004). *Brown at 50: King's dream or Plessy's nightmare?* Cambridge, MA: The Civil Rights Project, Harvard University.

Osguthorpe, R. T., & Scruggs, T. E. (1986). Special education students as tutors: A review and analysis. *Remedial and Special Education, 7*(4), 15–25.

Osher, D., Dwyer, K., & Jackson, S. (2004). *Safe, supportive and successful schools step by step.* Longmont, CO: Sopris West.

Osher, D., & Fleischman, S. (2005). Positive culture in urban schools. *Educational Leadership, 62*(6), 84–86.

Packard, B., & Babineau, M. E. (2008). Development: 9–12. In T. L. Good (Ed.), *21st century learning* (Vol. 1, pp. 103–112). Thousand Oaks, CA: Sage.

Padrón, Y. N., Waxman, H. C., & Rivera, H. H. (2002). Issues in educating Hispanic students. In S. Stringfield & D. Land (Eds.), *Educating at-risk students* (pp. 66–88). Chicago: National Society for the Study of Education.

Page, R. N. (1991). *Lower track classrooms: A curricular and cultural perspective.* New York: Teachers College Press.

Page, S. W. (2000). When changes for the gifted spur differentiation for all. *Educational Leadership, 58*(1), 62–65.

Page-Voth, V., & Graham, S. (1999). Effects of goal setting and strategy use on the writing performance and self-efficacy of students with writing and learning problems. *Journal of Educational Psychology, 91*(2), 230–240.

Pajares, F., Britner, S. L., & Valiante, G. (2000). Relation between achievement goals and self-beliefs of middle school students in writing and science. *Contemporary Educational Psychology, 25*(4), 406–422.

Palincsar, A. S., & Brown, A. L. (1984). Reciprocal teaching of comprehension fostering and comprehension monitoring activities. *Cognition and Instruction, 2,* 117–175.

Pallas, A. M. (2002). High school dropouts. In D. L. Levinson, P. W. Cookson, Jr., & A. R. Sadovnik (Eds.), *Education and sociology: An encyclopedia* (pp. 315–320). New York: Routledge Falmer.

Panskeep, J. (1998). Attention deficit hyperactivity disorders, psychostimulants, and intolerance of childhood playfulness: A tragedy in the making? *Current Directions in Psychological Science, 7*(3), 91–97.

Parillo, V. N. (2008). *Understanding race and ethnic relations* (3rd ed.). Boston: Allyn & Bacon.

Paris, S., Cross, D., & Lipson, M. (1984). Informal strategies for learning: A program to improve children's reading awareness and comprehension. *Journal of Educational Psychology, 76,* 1239–1252.

Paris, S. G., & Paris, A. H. (2001). Classroom applications of research on self-regulated learning. *Educational Psychologist, 36*(2), 89–101.

Parkay, F. W. (2006). *Social foundations for becoming a teacher.* Boston: Allyn & Bacon.

Parker, W. D. (1997). An empirical typology of perfectionism in academically talented children. *American Educational Research Journal, 34*(3), 545–562.

Parkhurst, J. T., & Asher, S. R. (1992). Peer rejection in middle school: Subgroup differences in behavior, loneliness, and interpersonal concerns. *Developmental Psychology, 28,* 231–241.

Parten, M. (1932). Social participation among preschool children. *Journal of Abnormal and Social Psychology, 27,* 243–269.

Partnership for 21st Century Skills. (2009). *Framework for 21st century learning.* Retrieved May 1, 2010, from www.21stcenturyskills.org

Patall, E., Cooper, H., & Robinson, J. (2008). Parent involvement in homework: A research synthesis. *Review of Educational Research, 78*(4), 1039–1101.

Patchin, J., & Hinduja, S. (2006). Bullies move beyond the schoolyard: A preliminary look at cyberbullying. *Youth Violence and Juvenile Justice, 4*(2), 148–169.

Patrick, B., Hisley, J., & Kempler, T. (2000). "What's everybody so excited about?": The effects of teacher enthusiasm on student intrinsic motivation and vitality. *Journal of Experimental Education, 68,* 217–236.

Pavan, B. N. (1992). The benefits of nongraded schools. *Educational Leadership, 50*(2), 22–25.

Pawlowski, K. F. (2001). The instructional support team concept in action. In B. Sornson (Ed.), *Preventing early learning failure.* Alexandria, VA: ASCD.

Pea, R. D. (1993). Learning scientific concepts through material and social activities: Conversational analysis meets conceptual change. *Educational Psychologist, 28*(3), 265–277.

Pearl, R., Farmer, T. W., Van Acker, R., Rodkin, P. C., Bost, K. K., Coe, M., & Henley, W. (1998). The social integration of students with mild disabilities in general education classrooms: Peer group membership and peer-assessed social behavior. *The Elementary School Journal, 99*(2), 167–185.

Pellegrini, A. D. (2002). Bullying, victimization, and sexual harassment during the transition to middle school. *Educational Psychologist, 37*(3), 151–163.

Pellegrini, A. D., & Bartini, M. (2000). A longitudinal study of bullying, victimization, and peer affiliation during the transition from primary school to middle school. *American Educational Research Journal, 37*(3), 699–725.

Pendarvis, E., & Howley, A. (1996). Playing fair: The possibilities of gifted education. *Journal for the Education of the Gifted, 19,* 215–233.

Perfetti, C. A. (2003). The universal grammar of reading. *Scientific Studies of Reading, 7*(1), 3–24.

Perfetto, G. A., Bransford, J. D., & Franks, J. J. (1983). Constraints on access in a problem solving context. *Memory and Cognition, 11,* 24–31.

Perkins, D. F., & Borden, L. M. (2003). Positive behaviors, problem behaviors, and resiliency in adolescence. In R. M. Lerner, M. A. Easterbrooks, & J. Mistry (Eds.), *Handbook of psychology: Vol. 6. Developmental psychology* (pp. 373–394). Hoboken, NJ: Wiley.

Perkins-Gough, D. (2006). Do we really have a "boy crisis"? *Educational Leadership, 64*(1), 93–94.

Perry, K., & Weinstein, R. (1998). The social context of early schooling and children's school adjustment. *Educational Psychologist, 33*(4), 177–194.

Persell, C. H. (1997). Social class and educational equality. In J. A. Banks & C. A. M. Banks (Eds.), *Multicultural education: Issues and perspectives* (pp. 87–107). Boston: Allyn & Bacon.

Peterson, L. R., & Peterson, M. J. (1959). Short-term retention of individual verbal items. *Journal of Experimental Psychology, 58,* 193–198.

Petrill, S. A., & Wilkerson, B. (2000). Intelligence and achievement: A behavioral genetic perspective. *Educational Psychology Review, 12*(2), 185–199.

Pettig, K. L. (2000). On the road to differentiated practice. *Educational Leadership, 58*(1), 14–18.

Peverly, S., Ramaswamy, V., Brown, C., Sumouski, J., Alidoust, M., & Garner, J. (2007). What predicts skill in lecture note taking? *Journal of Educational Psychology, 99*(1), 167–180.

Phelan, P., Yu, H. C., & Davidson, A. L. (1994). Navigating the psychosocial pressures of adolescence: The voices and experiences of high school youth. *American Educational Research Journal, 31,* 415–447.

Phillips, J. L. (1975). *The origins of intellect: Piaget's theory* (2nd ed.). San Francisco: Freeman.

Piaget, J. (1952a). *The language and thought of the child.* London: Routledge and Kegan-Paul.

Piaget, J. (1952b). *The origins of intelligence in children.* New York: Basic Books.

Piaget, J. (1964). *The moral judgment of the child.* New York: Free Press.

Piaget, J., & Inhelder, B. (1956). *The child's conception of space.* Boston: Routledge and Kegan-Paul.

Pietsch, J., Walker, R., & Chapman, E. (2003). The relationship among self-concept, self-efficacy, and performance in mathematics during secondary school. *Journal of Educational Psychology, 95*(3), 589–603.

Pine, J., & Aschbacher, P. (2006). Students' learning of inquiry in "inquiry" curricula. *Phi Delta Kappan, 88*(4), 308–313.

Pinker, S. (1997). *How the mind works.* New York: Norton.

Pinnell, G. S., DeFord, D. E., & Lyons, C. A. (1988). *Reading Recovery: Early intervention for at-risk first graders.* Arlington, VA: Educational Research Service.

Pinnell, G. S., Lyons, C. A., DeFord, D. E., Bryk, A. S., & Seltzer, M. (1994). Comparing instructional models for the literacy education of high risk first graders. *Reading Research Quarterly, 29,* 8–38.

Pintrich, P. (2000). Multiple goals, multiple pathways: The role of goal orientation in learning and achievement. *Journal of Educational Psychology, 92*(3), 544–555.

Pintrich, P. R. (2003). A motivational science perspective on the role of student motivation in learning and teaching contexts. *Journal of Educational Psychology, 95*(4), 667–686.

Pintrich, P. R., & Schunk, D. H. (2002). *Motivation in education: Theory, research, and applications* (2nd ed.). Upper Saddle River, NJ: Merrill/Prentice-Hall.

Pittard, V., Bannister, P., & Dunn, J. (2003). *The big picture: The impact of ICT on attainment, motivation, and learning.* London: Department for Education and Skills.

Plucker, J. A., Beghetto, R. A., & Dow, G. T. (2004). Why isn't creativity more important to educational psychologists? Potential, pitfalls, and future directions in creativity research. *Educational Psychologist, 39*(2), 83–96.

Poel, E. (2007). Enhancing what students can do. *Educational Leadership, 64*(5), 64–67.

Polite, L., & Saenger, E. B. (2003). A pernicious silence: Confronting race in the elementary classroom. *Phi Delta Kappan, 85*(4), 274–278.

Pomerantz, E., Moorman, E., & Litwack, S. (2007). The how, whom, and why of parents' involvement in children's academic lives: More is not always better. *Review of Educational Research, 77*(3), 373–410.

Pomerantz, E. M., Altermatt, E. R., & Saxon, J. L. (2002). Making the grade but feeling distressed: Gender differences in academic performance and internal distress. *Journal of Educational Psychology, 94*(2), 396–404.

Pool, H., & Page, J. A. (Eds.). (1995). *Beyond tracking: Finding success in inclusive schools*. Bloomington, IN: Phi Delta Kappan Educational Foundation.

Pope, A. W., & Bierman, K. L. (1999). Predicting adolescent peer problems and antisocial activities: The relative roles of aggression and dysregulation. *Developmental Psychology, 35,* 335–346.

Popham, J. (2005). How to use PAP to make AYP under NCLB. *Phi Delta Kappan, 86*(10), 787–791.

Popham, W. (2009). Diagnosing the diagnostic test. *Educational Leadership, 66*(6), 90–91.

Popham, W. J. (2003). *Teach better, test better: The instructional role of assessment.* Alexandria, VA: ASCD.

Popham, W. J. (2004). "Teaching to the test": An expression to eliminate. *Educational Leadership, 62*(3), 82–83.

Popham, W. J. (2006). Diagnostic assessment: A measurement mirage? *Educational Leadership, 64*(2), 90–93.

Popham, W. J. (2008). *Classroom assessment: What teachers need to know* (5th ed.). Boston: Pearson.

Potter, E. F. (1977, April). *Children's expectancy of criticism for classroom achievement efforts.* Paper presented at the annual convention of the American Educational Research Association, New York.

Poulin, F., Cillessen, A. H. N., & Coie, J. D. (1997). Children's friends and behavioral similarity in the social contexts. *Social Development, 6,* 224–236.

Powell, D. R. (1995). *Enabling young children to succeed in school.* Washington, DC: American Educational Research Association.

Premack, D. (1965). Reinforcement theory. In D. Levine (Ed.), *Nebraska symposium on motivation.* Lincoln: University of Nebraska Press.

Prensky, M. (2005/2006). Listen to the natives. *Educational Leadership, 63*(4), 8–13.

Pressley, M. (2003). Psychology of literacy and literacy instruction. In W. M. Reynolds & G. E. Miller (Eds.), *Handbook of psychology: Vol. 7. Educational psychology* (pp. 333–355). Hoboken, NJ: Wiley.

Pressley, M., & Harris, K. R. (1994). Increasing the quality of educational intervention research. *Educational Psychology Review, 6*(3), 191–208.

Pressley, M., Harris, K. R., & Marks, M. B. (1992). But good strategy instructors are constructivists! *Educational Psychology Review, 4,* 3–31.

Pressley, M., Raphael, L., & Gallagher, J. (2004). Prodience, St. Mel School: How a school that works for African American students works. *Journal of Educational Psychology, 96*(2), 216–235.

Pressley, M., Roehrig, A. D., Raphael, L., Dolezal, S., Bohn, C., Mohan, L., Wharton-McDonald, R., Bogner, K., & Hogan, K. (2003). Teaching processes in elementary and secondary education. In W. M. Reynolds & G. E. Miller (Eds.), *Handbook of psychology: Vol. 7. Educational psychology* (pp. 153–175). Hoboken, NJ: Wiley.

Pressley, M., Tannenbaum, R., McDaniel, M. A., & Wood, E. (1990). What happens when university students try to answer prequestions that accompany textbook material? *Contemporary Educational Psychology, 15,* 27–35.

Pressley, M., & Yokoi, L. (1994). Motion for a new trial on transfer. *Educational Researcher, 23*(5), 36–38.

Prichard, J., Bizo, L., & Stratford, R. (2006). The educational impact of team skills training: Preparing students to work in groups. *British Journal of Educational Psychology, 76,* 119–148.

Pugh, K., & Bergin, D. (2006). Motivational influences on transfer. *Educational Psychologist, 41*(3), 147–160.

Puma, M. J., Jones, C. C., Rock, D., & Fernandez, R. (1993). *Prospects: The congressionally mandated study of educational growth and opportunity* (Interim Report). Bethesda, MD: Abt Associates.

Puma, M. J., Karweit, N., Price, C., Ricciuti, A., Thompson, W., & Vaden-Kiernan, M. (1997). *Prospects: Final report on student outcomes.* Cambridge, MA: Abt Associates.

Puntambekar, S., & Hübscher, R. (2005). Tools for scaffolding students in a complex learning environment: What have we gained and what have we missed? *Educational Psychologist, 40*(1), 1–12.

Putnam, J. W. (Ed.). (1998). *Cooperative learning and strategies for inclusion* (2nd ed.). Baltimore: Paul H. Brookes.

Quay, H. C., & Werry, J. S. (Eds.). (1986). *Psychopathological disorders of childhood* (3rd ed.). New York: Wiley.

Radosevich, D., Vaidyanathan, V., Yeo, S., & Radosevich, D. (2004). Relating goal orientation to self-regulatory processes: A longitudinal field test. *Contemporary Educational Psychology, 29*(3), 207–229.

Radziewicz, C., & Antonellis, S. (2002). Considerations and implications for habilitation of hearing-impaired children. In D. K. Bernstein & E. Tiegerman-Farber (Eds.), *Language and communication disorders in children* (5th ed.). Boston: Allyn & Bacon.

Rafoth, M. A., Leal, L., & De Fabo, L. (1993). *Strategies for learning and remembering: Study skills across the curriculum.* Washington, DC: National Education Association Professional Library.

Raison, J., Hanson, L. A., Hall, C., & Reynolds, M. C. (1995). Another school's reality. *Phi Delta Kappan, 76*(6), 480–484.

Ramey, C. T., & Ramey, S. L. (1992). *At risk does not mean doomed.* Birmingham: Civitan International Research Center, University of Alabama.

Ramey, C. T., & Ramey, S. L. (1998). Early intervention and early experience. *American Psychologist, 53*(2), 109–120.

Ramirez, A., & Soto-Hinman, I. (2009). A place for all families. *Educational Leadership, 66*(7), 79–82.

Ramirez-Smith, C. (1995). Stopping the cycle of failure: The Comer model. *Educational Leadership, 52*(5), 14–19.

Raudenbush, S. W., Rowan, B., & Cheong, Y. F. (1993). Higher order instructional goals in secondary schools: Class, teacher, and school influences. *American Educational Research Journal, 30*(3), 523–553.

Ready, D., LoGerfo, L., Burkam, D., & Lee, V. (2005). Explaining girls' advantage in kindergarten literacy learning: Do classroom behaviors make a difference? *The Elementary School Journal, 106*(1), 21–38.

Rebell, M., & Hunter, M. (2004). "Highly qualified" teachers: Pretense or legal requirement? *Phi Delta Kappan, 85*(9), 690–696.

Reed, S. (2006). Cognitive architectures for multimedia learning. *Educational Psychologist, 41*(2), 87–98.

Reeves, D. (2003). *High performance in high poverty schools: 90/90/90 and beyond.* Cambridge, MA: Center for Performance Assessment, Harvard Graduate School of Education.

Reeves, D. (2005). "If I said something wrong I was afraid." *Educational Leadership, 62*(4), 72–75.

Reeves, D. (2006). Preventing 1,000 failures. *Educational Leadership, 64*(3), 88–89.

Reeves, D. (2008). Effective grading practices. *Educational Leadership, 65*(5), 85–87.

Reeves, D. (2009). Three challenges of web 2.0. *Educational Leadership, 66*(6), 87–88.

Reeves, D. B. (Ed.) (2007). *Ahead of the curve: The power of assessment to transform teaching and learning.* Bloomington, IN: Solution Tree.

Reid, D., & Knight, M. (2006). Disability justifies exclusion of minority students: A critical history grounded in disability studies. *Educational Researcher, 35*(6), 18–23.

Reid, R., & Lienemann, T. O. (2006). Self-regulated strategy development for written expression with students with attention deficit hyperactivity disorder. *Exceptional Children, 73,* 53–68.

Reimann, P., & Schult, T. J. (1996). Turning examples into cases: Acquiring knowledge structures for analogical problem solving. *Educational Psychologist, 31,* 123–132.

Rekrut, M. D. (1992, April). *Teaching to learn: Cross-age tutoring to enhance strategy acquisition.* Paper presented at the annual meeting of the American Educational Research Association, San Francisco.

Renkl, A. (2002). Learning from worked-out examples: Instructional explanations supplement self-explanations. *Learning & Instruction, 12,* 149–176.

Renzulli, J. S., & Reis, S. M. (1997). The schoolwide enrichment model: New directions for developing high-end learning. In N. Colangelo & G. A. Davis (Eds.), *Handbook of gifted education* (2nd ed., pp. 136–154). Boston: Allyn & Bacon.

Renzulli, J. S., & Reis, S. M. (2000). The schoolwide enrichment model. In K. A. Heller, F. J. Mönks, R. Subotnik, & R. J. Sternberg (Eds.), *International handbook of giftedness and talent* (2nd ed., pp. 367–382). New York: Pergamon.

Reschly, D. J. (2003). School psychology. In W. M. Reynolds & G. E. Miller (Eds.), *Handbook of psychology: Vol. 7. Educational psychology* (pp. 431–453). Hoboken, NJ: Wiley.

Resnick, L. (1998, April). *From aptitude to effort: A new foundation for our schools.* Paper presented at the annual meeting of the American Educational Research Association, San Diego, CA.

Rest, J., Edwards, L., & Thoma, S. (1997). Designing and validating a measure of moral judgment: Stage preference and stage consistency approaches. *Journal of Educational Psychology, 89*(1), 5–28.

Reynolds, A. (2009). Why every student needs critical friends. *Educational Leadership, 67*(3), 54–57.

Reynolds, A., Temple, J., Robertson, D., & Mann, E. (2002). Age 21 cost-benefit analysis of the Title I Chicago child–parent centers. *Educational Evaluation and Policy Analysis, 24*(4), 267–303.

Reynolds, A., & Wolfe, B. (1999). Special education and school achievement: An exploratory analysis with a central-city sample. *Educational Evaluation and Policy Analysis, 21*(3), 249–269.

Reynolds, A. J. (1991). Early schooling of children at risk. *American Educational Research Journal, 28*(2), 392–422.

Reynolds, W. M., & Miller, G. E. (2003). Current perspectives in educational psychology. In W. M. Reynolds & G. E. Miller (Eds.), *Handbook of psychology: Vol. 7. Educational psychology* (pp. 3–20). Hoboken, NJ: Wiley.

Rhode, G., Jenson, W. R., & Reavis, H. K. (1993). *The tough kid book.* Longmont, CO: Sopris West.

Rice, E. P. (1996). *The adolescent: Development, relationships, and culture.* Boston: Allyn & Bacon.

Rice, F. P., & Dolgin, K. G. (Eds.). (2008). *The adolescent: Development, relationships, and culture* (12th ed.). Boston: Pearson Education Group.

Richardson, W. (2008). Footprints in the digital age. *Educational Leadership, 66*(3), 16–19.

Richardson, W. (2009). Becoming network-wise. *Educational Leadership, 66*(6), 26–31.

Riehl, C. (2006). Feeling better: A comparison of medical research and education research. *Educational Researcher, 35*(5), 24–29.

Riehl, C. J. (2000). The principal's role in creating inclusive schools for diverse students: A review of normative, empirical, and critical literature on the practice of educational administration. *Review of Educational Research, 70*(1), 55–81.

Rifkin, J. (1998). The sociology of the gene. *Phi Delta Kappan, 79*(9), 649–657.

Ritchhart, R., & Perkins, D. (2008). Making thinking visible. *Educational Leadership, 65*(5), 57–63.

Roach, A., & Elliott, S. (2006). The influence of access to general education curriculum on alternate assessment performance of students with significant cognitive disabilities. *Educational Evaluation and Policy Analysis, 28*(2), 181–194.

Robinson, D. H., Katayama, A. D., Beth, A., Odom, S., & Hsieh, Y. P. (2004). *Training students to take more graphic notes: A partial approach.* Austin: University of Texas.

Robinson, D. H., Robinson, S. L., & Katayama, A. D. (1999). When words are represented in memory like pictures: Evidence for spatial encoding of study materials. *Contemporary Educational Psychology, 24*(1), 38–54.

Robinson, D. H., & Skinner, C. H. (1996). Why graphic organizers facilitate search processes: Fewer words or computationally efficient indexing. *Contemporary Educational Psychology, 21*(2), 166–180.

Robinson, F. P. (1961). *Effective study.* New York: Harper & Row.

Robinson, T., Smith, S., Miller, M., & Brownell, M. (1999). Cognitive behavior modification of hyperactivity-impulsivity and aggression: A meta-analysis of school-based studies. *Journal of Educational Psychology, 91*(2), 195–203.

Roderick, M., & Engel, M. (2001). The grasshopper and the ant: Motivational responses of low-achieving students to high-stakes testing. *Educational Evaluation and Policy Analysis, 23*(3), 197–227.

Roderick, M., & Nagaoka, J. (2005). Retention under Chicago's high-stakes testing program: Helpful, harmful, or harmless? *Evaluation and Policy Analysis, 27*(4), 309–340.

Roeber, E., & Dutcher, P. (1989). Michigan's innovative assessment of reading. *Educational Leadership 46*(7), 64–69.

Roediger, H., & Karpicke, J. (2006). The power of testing memory: Basic research and implications for educational practice. *Perspectives on Psychological Science, 1,* 181–210.

Roeser, R., Eccles, J., & Sameroff, A. (2000). School as a context of early adolescents' academic and social-emotional development: A summary of research findings. *The Elementary School Journal, 100*(5), 443–472.

Rogers, K. B. (2009, April). *Academic acceleration and giftedness: The research from 1990 to the present: A best-evidence synthesis.* Paper presented at the annual meeting of the American Educational Research Association, San Diego, CA.

Rogoff, B. (2003). *The cultural nature of human development.* London: Oxford University Press.

Rogoff, B., & Chavajay, P. (1995). What's become of research on the cultural basis of cognitive development? *American Psychologist, 50,* 859–877.

Rogow, S. M. (1988). *Helping the visually impaired child with developmental problems: Effective practice in home, school, and community.* New York: Teachers College Press.

Rohrbeck, C. A., Ginsburg-Block, M. D., Fantuzzo, J. W., & Miller, T. R. (2003). Peer-assisted learning interventions with elementary school students: A meta-analytic review. *Journal of Educational Psychology, 94*(2), 240–257.

Rose, A., & Rudolph, K. (2006). A review of sex differences in peer relationship processes: Potential tradeoffs for the emotional and behavioral development of girls and boys. *Psychological Bulletin, 132*(1), 98–131.

Rosenberg, M., Wilson, R., Maheady, L., & Sindelar, P. (2004). *Educating students with behavioral disorders.* Boston: Pearson.

Rosenfeld, D., Folger, R., & Adelman, H. F. (1980). When rewards reflect competence: A qualification of the overjustification effect. *Journal of Personality and Social Psychology, 39,* 368–376.

Rosenfield, S. A., & Gravois, T. A. (1996). *Instructional consultation teams: Collaborating for change.* New York: Guilford.

Rosenshine, B. (2008). Systematic instruction. In T. L. Good (Ed.), *21st century learning* (Vol. 1, pp. 235–243). Thousand Oaks, CA: Sage.

Rosenshine, B., & Meister, C. (1994). Reciprocal teaching: A review of research. *Review of Educational Research, 64,* 479–530.

Rosenshine, B., Meister, C., & Chapman, S. (1996). Teaching students to generate questions: A review of the intervention studies. *Review of Educational Research, 66*(2), 181–221.

Rosenshine, B.V. (1980). How time is spent in elementary classrooms. In C. Denham & A. Lieberman (Eds.), *Time to learn*. Washington, DC: National Institute of Education.

Roseth, C., Johnson, D., & Johnson, R. (2008). Promoting early adolescents' achievement and peer relationships: The effects of cooperative, competitive, and individualistic goal structures. *Psychological Bulletin, 134*(2), 223–246.

Ross, J. A., Rolheiser, C., & Hogaboam-Gray, A. (1998, April). *Impact of self-evaluation training on mathematics achievement in a cooperative learning environment*. Paper presented at the annual meeting of the American Educational Research Association, San Diego, CA.

Ross, S. M., Smith, L. J., Casey, J., & Slavin, R. E. (1995). Increasing the academic success of disadvantaged children: An examination of alternative early intervention programs. *American Educational Research Journal, 32,* 773–800.

Ross, S. M., Smith, L. J., Lohr, L., & McNelis, M. (1994). Math and reading instruction in tracked first grade classes. *The Elementary School Journal, 95*(2), 105–119.

Rosser, R. A. (1994). *Cognitive development: Psychological and biological perspectives*. Boston: Allyn & Bacon.

Rosser, R. A. (2003). Scientific reasoning. *Encyclopedia of cognitive science*. London: Nature Publishing Group.

Rosser, R. A., Stevens, S., & Ruiz, B. (2006). Cognitive markers of adolescent risk taking: A correlate of drug abuse in at-risk individuals. *The Prison Journal, 85,* 83–96.

Rossi, R. J., & Stringfield, S. C. (1995). What we must do for students placed at risk. *Phi Delta Kappan, 71*(1), 73–76.

Rossman, G. B., & Rallis, S. F. (2003). *Learning in the field: An introduction to qualitative research* (2nd ed.). Thousand Oaks, CA: Sage.

Rotberg, I. C. (2001). A self-fulfilling prophecy. *Phi Delta Kappan, 83*(2), 170–171.

Roth, W.-M., & Lee, Y.-J. (2007). "Vygotsky's neglected legacy": Cultural-historical activity theory. *Review of Educational Research, 77*(2), 186–232.

Rotherham, A., & Willingham, D. (2009). 21st century skills: The challenges ahead. *Educational Leadership, 67*(1), 16–21.

Rothstein, R. (Ed.). (2004). *Class and schools: Using social, economic, and educational reform to close the black-white achievement gap*. Washington, DC: Economic Policy Institute.

Rothstein, R., & Jacobsen, R. (2009). Measuring social responsibility. *Educational Leadership, 66*(8), 14–19.

Rotter, J. (1954). *Social learning and clinical psychology*. Englewood Cliffs, NJ: Prentice-Hall.

Rowan, B., Correnti, R., & Miller, R. (2002). *What large-scale, survey research tells us about teacher effects on student achievement: Insights from the Prospects study of elementary schools*. Philadelphia: Consortium for Policy Research in Education, University of Pennsylvania.

Rowan, B., & Miracle, A. (1983). Systems of ability grouping and the stratification of achievement in elementary schools. *Sociology of Education, 56,* 133–144.

Rowe, M. B. (1974). Wait time and rewards as instructional variables, their influence on language, logic, and fate control. I: Wait time. *Journal of Research in Science Teaching, 11,* 81–94.

Rubie-Davies, C. (2008). Teacher expectations. In T. L. Good (Ed.), *21st century learning:* (Vol. 1, pp. 254–264). Thousand Oaks, CA: Sage.

Rubie-Davies, C. M. (2007, September). *Teacher expectations, student achievement, and perceptions of student attitudes*. Paper presented at the Biennial Conference of the Educational Association for Research in Learning and Instruction, Budapest, Hungary.

Rubin, B. C. (2003). Unpacking detracking: When progressive pedagogy meets students' social worlds. *American Educational Research Journal, 40*(2), 539–573.

Rubin, D. (2007). A basic-systems model of episodic memory. *Perspectives on Psychological Science, 1,* 277–311.

Ruble, D. N., Eisenberg, R., & Higgins, E. T. (1994). Developmental changes in achievement evaluation: Motivational implications of self-other differences. *Child Development, 65,* 1095–1110.

Ruder, S. (2000). We teach all. *Educational Leadership, 58*(1), 49–51.

Rummel, N., Levin, J. R., & Woodward, M. M. (2002). Do pictorial mnemonic text-learning aids give students something worth writing about? *Journal of Educational Psychology, 94*(2), 327–334.

Rust, F. (2008). Early childhood education: Curriculum and programs. In T. L. Good (Ed.), *21st century learning* (Vol. 1, pp. 388–395). Thousand Oaks, CA: Sage.

Ryan, A. M., & Patrick, H. (2001). The classroom social environment and changes in adolescents' motivation and engagement during middle school. *American Educational Research Journal, 38*(2), 437–460.

Ryan, K., & Ryan, A. (2005). Psychological processes underlying stereotype threat and standardized math test performance. *Educational Psychologist, 40*(1), 53–63.

Ryan, K., & Shepard, L. (2008). *The future of test-based educational accountability*. New York: Routledge.

Ryan, R. M., & Deci, E. L. (2000). Intrinsic and extrinsic motivations: Classic definitions and new directions. *Contemporary Educational Psychology, 25*(1), 54–67.

Sachs, J. (2000). The activist professional. *Journal of Educational Change, 1*(1), 77–95.

Sackett, P., Kuncel, N., Arneson, J., Cooper, S., & Waters, S. (2009). Does socioeconomic status explain the relationship between admissions tests and post-secondary academic performance? *Psychological Bulletin, 135*(1), 1–22.

Sadker, D., & Sadker, M. (2003). *Teachers, schools, and society* (6th ed.). New York: McGraw-Hill.

Sadker, M., & Sadker, D. (1994). *Failing at fairness: How America's schools cheat girls*. New York: Charles Scribner's Sons.

Sadker, M., & Sadker, D. (2006). Questioning skills. In J. Cooper (Ed.), *Classroom teaching skills* (8th ed., pp. 104–150). Boston: Houghton Mifflin.

Sadker, M., Sadker, D., & Long, L. (1997). Gender and educational equality. In J. A. Banks & C. A. M. Banks (Eds.), *Multicultural education: Issues and perspectives* (pp. 131–149). Boston: Allyn & Bacon.

Sadker, M., & Zittleman, L. (2004). Test anxiety: Are students failing tests or are tests failing students? *Phi Delta Kappan, 85*(10), 740–744.

Safer, N., & Fleischman, S. (2005). How student progress monitoring improves instruction. *Educational Leadership, 62*(5), 81–83.

Saffran, E. M., & Schwartz, M. F. (2003). Language. In M. Gallagher & R. J. Nelson (Eds.), *Handbook of psychology: Vol. 3. Biological psychology* (pp. 595–627). Hoboken, NJ: Wiley.

Saleh, M., Lazonder, A., & de Jon, T. (2007). Structuring collaboration in mixed-ability groups to promote verbal interaction, learning, and motivation of average-ability students. *Contemporary Educational Psychology, 32*(3), 314–331.

Salend, S. (2009). *Classroom testing and assessment for ALL students*. Thousand Oaks, CA: Corwin.

Saleno, S., & Garrick-Duhaney, L. (1999). The impact of inclusion on students with and without disabilities and their educators. *Remedial and Special Education, 20*(2), 114–126.

Salganik, M.W. (1980, January 27). Teachers busy teaching make city's 16 "best" schools stand out. *Baltimore Sun,* p. A4.

Salinger, T., & Fleischman, S. (2005). Teaching students to interact with text. *Educational Leadership, 64*(1), 90–93.

Salomon, G., & Perkins, D. N. (1998). Individual and social aspects of learning. In P. D. Pearson & A. Iran-Nejad (Eds.), *Review of research in education* (pp. 1–24). Washington, DC: American Educational Research Association.

Sampson, R. (2002). *Bullying in schools.* Washington, DC: U.S. Department of Justice.

San Antonio, D., & Salzfass, E. (2007). How we treat one another in school. *Educational Leadership, 64*(8), 32–39.

Sanders, M. G., Allen-Jones, G. L., & Abel, Y. (2002). Involving families and communities in the education of children and youth placed at-risk. In S. Stringfield & D. Land (Eds.), *Educating at-risk students* (pp. 171–188). Chicago: National Society for the Study of Education.

Sanders, W.L. (2000). Value-added assessment from student achievement data: Opportunities and hurdles. *Journal of Personnel Evaluation in Education, 14*(4), 329–339.

Sandoval, J. (1995). Teaching in subject matter areas: Science. *Annual Review of Psychology, 46,* 355–374.

Sanford, J. P., & Evertson, C. M. (1981). Classroom management in a low SES junior high: Three case studies. *Journal of Teacher Education, 32,* 34–38.

Sansone, C., & Harackiewicz, J. M. (Eds.). (2000). *Intrinsic and extrinsic motivation.* Orlando, FL: Academic Press.

Sapon-Shevin, M. (2001). Schools fit for all. *Educational Leadership, 58*(4), 34–39.

Sapon-Shevin, M. (2003). Inclusion: A matter of social justice. *Educational Leadership, 61*(2), 25–28.

Sato, M., & Atkin, J. (2006/2007). Supporting change in classroom assessment. *Educational Leadership, 64*(4), 76–79.

Savell, J. M., Twohig, P. T., & Rachford, D. L. (1986). Empirical status of Feuerstein's "Instrumental Enrichment" (FIE) technique as a method of teaching thinking skills. *Review of Educational Research, 56,* 381–409.

Sax, C. L., & Thoma, C. A. (2002). *Transition assessment: Wise practices for quality lives.* Baltimore: Brookes.

Schacter, D. L. (2001). *The seven sins of memory: How the mind forgets and remembers.* Boston: Houghton Mifflin.

Schacter, J. (2000). Does individual tutoring produce optimal learning? *American Educational Research Journal, 37*(3), 801–829.

Schafer, W. D., Swanson, G., Bené, N., & Newberry, G. (2001). Effects of teacher knowledge of rubrics on student achievement in four content areas. *Applied Measurement in Education, 14,* 151–170.

Schafer, W. E., & Olexa, C. (1971). *Tracking and opportunity.* Scranton, PA: Chandler.

Scharf, M., & Hertz-Lazarowitz, R. (2003). Social networks in the school context: Effects of culture and gender. *Journal of Personal Relationships, 20*(6), 843–859.

Scherer, M. (2001). How and why standards can improve student achievement: A conversation with Robert J. Marzano. *Educational Leadership, 59*(1), 14–19.

Scheurich, J., Skrla, L., & Johnson, J. (2000). Thinking carefully about equity and accountability. *Phi Delta Kappan, 82*(4), 293–299.

Schiff, M., & Lewontin, R. (1986). *Education and class: The irrelevance of IQ genetic studies.* New York: Oxford University Press.

Schifter, D. (1996). A constructivist perspective on teaching and learning mathematics. *Phi Delta Kappan, 77*(7), 492–499.

Schirmer, B., & McGough, S. (2005). Teaching reading to children who are deaf: Do the conclusions of the National Reading Panel apply? *Review of Educational Research, 75*(1), 84–117.

Schmidt, W., & Cogan, L. (2009). The myth of equal content. *Educational Leadership, 67*(3), 44–47.

Schmoker, M. (1999). *Results: The key to continuous school improvement.* Alexandria, VA: ASCD.

Schmoker, M. (2006). *Results now: How we can achieve unprecedented improvements in teaching and learning.* Alexandria, VA: ASCD.

Schneider, B. (2002). Social capital: A ubiquitous emerging conception. In D. L. Levinson, P. W. Cookson, Jr., & A. R. Sadovnik (Eds.), *Education and sociology: An encyclopedia* (pp. 545–550). New York: Routledge Falmer.

Schneider, W. (1993). Domain-specific knowledge and memory performance in children. *Educational Psychology Review, 5,* 257–273.

Schneider, W., Roth, E., & Ennemoser, M. (2000). Training phonological skills and letter knowledge in children at risk for dyslexia: A comparison of three kindergarten intervention programs. *Journal of Educational Psychology, 92*(2), 284–295.

Schnotz, W. (2002). Towards an integrated view of learning from text and visual displays. *Educational Psychology Review, 14*(1), 101–120.

Schofield, J. W. (1995). Review of research on school desegregation's impact on elementary and secondary school students. In J. A. Banks & C. A. M. Banks (Eds.), *Handbook of research on multicultural education.* New York: Macmillan.

Schraw, G., Flowerday, T., & Lehman, S. (2001). Increasing situational interest in the classroom. *Educational Psychology Review, 13*(3), 211–224.

Schunk, D. (2000). *Learning theories* (3rd ed.). Upper Saddle River, NJ: Merrill/Prentice-Hall.

Schunk, D. (2005). Self-regulated learning: The education legacy of Paul R. Pintrich. *Educational Psychologist, 40*(2), 85–94.

Schunk, D. H. (2004). *Learning theories: An educational perspective* (4th ed.). Columbus, OH: Merrill/Prentice-Hall.

Schunk, D. H., & Pajares, F. (2004, April). *Self-efficacy in education: Issues and future directions.* Paper presented at the annual meeting of the American Educational Research Association, San Diego, CA.

Schunk, D. H., & Zimmerman, B. J. (1997). Social origins of self-regulatory competence. *Educational Psychologist, 32*(4), 195–208.

Schunk, D. H., & Zimmerman, B. J. (2003). Self-regulation and learning. In W. M. Reynolds & G. E. Miller (Eds.), *Handbook of psychology: Vol. 7. Educational psychology* (pp. 59–78). Hoboken, NJ: Wiley.

Schutz, A. (2006). Home is a prison in a global city: The tragic failure of school-based community engagement strategies. *Review of Educational Research, 76*(4), 691–744.

Schutz, P. A., & Davis, H. A. (2000). Emotions and self-regulation during test taking. *Educational Psychologist, 35*(4), 243–246.

Schwartz, N. H., Ellsworth, L. S., Graham, L., & Knight, B. (1998). Assessing prior knowledge to remember text: A comparison of advance organizers and maps. *Contemporary Educational Psychology, 23*(1), 65–89.

Schweinhart, L. J., & Weikart, D. P. (1998). High/Scope Perry Preschool Program effects at age twenty-seven. In J. Crane (Ed.), *Social programs that work* (pp. 148–162). New York: Russell Sage Foundation.

Scriffiny, P. (2008). Seven reasons for standards-based grading. *Educational Leadership, 66*(2), 70–74.

Scruggs, T. E., White, K. R., & Bennion, K. (1986). Teaching test-taking skills to elementary-grade students: A meta-analysis. *Elementary School Journal, 87,* 69–82.

Secada, W. G., Chavez-Chavez, R., Garcia, E., Munoz, C., Oakes, J., Santiago-Santiago, I., & Slavin, R. (1998). *No more excuses: The final report of the Hispanic dropout project.* Washington, DC: U.S. Department of Education.

Selman, R. L. (1981). The child as a friendship philosopher. In S. R. Asher & J. M. Gottman (Eds.), *The development of children's friendships* (pp. 242–272). Cambridge, UK: Cambridge University Press.

Semb, G. B., & Ellis, J. A. (1994). Knowledge taught in school: What is remembered? *Review of Educational Research, 24*, 253–286.

Semmel, M. I., Gerber, M. M., & MacMillan, D. L. (1994). Twenty-five years after Dunn's article: A legacy of policy analysis research in special education. *Journal of Special Education, 27*, 481–495.

Sénéchal, M., & Young, L. (2008). The effect of family literacy interventions on children's acquisition of reading from kindergarten to grade 3: A meta-analytic review. *Review of Educational Research, 78*(4), 880–907.

Senko, C., & Miles, K. (2008). Pursuing their own learning agenda: How master-oriented students jeopardize their class performance. *Contemporary Educational Psychology, 33*(4), 561–583.

Sethi, S., Drake, M., Dialdin, D. A., & Lepper, M. R. (1995, April). *Developmental patterns of intrinsic and extrinsic motivation: A new look.* Paper presented at the annual meeting of the American Educational Research Association, San Francisco.

Shaffer, D., Squire, K., Halverson, R., & Gee, J. (2005). Video games and the future of learning. *Phi Delta Kappan, 87*(2), 104–111.

Shanahan, T. (1998). On the effectiveness and limitations of tutoring reading. In P. D. Pearson & A. Iran-Nejad (Eds.), *Review of research in education* (pp. 217–234). Washington, DC: American Educational Research Association.

Shanker, A. (1994/1995). Full inclusion is neither free nor appropriate. *Educational Leadership, 52*(4), 18–21.

Sharan, S., Kussell, P., Hertz-Lazarowitz, R., Bejarano, Y., Raviv, S., & Sharan, Y. (1984). *Cooperative learning in the classroom: Research in desegregated schools.* Hillsdale, NJ: Erlbaum.

Sharan, S., & Shachar, C. (1988). *Language and learning in the cooperative classroom.* New York: Springer.

Sharan, Y., & Sharan, S. (1992). *Expanding cooperative learning through group investigation.* New York: Teachers College Press.

Shavelson, R. J., Baxter, G. P., & Pine, J. (1992). Performance assessments: Political rhetoric and measurement reality. *Educational Researcher, 21*(4), 22–27.

Shaywitz, S. (2003). *Overcoming dyslexia: A new and complete science-based program for reading problems at any level.* New York: Knopf.

Shaywitz, S., & Shaywitz, B. (2004). Reading disability and the brain. *Educational Leadership, 61*(3), 7–11.

Shaywitz, S., & Shaywitz, B. (2007). What neuroscience really tells us about reading instruction: A response to Judy Willis. *Educational Leadership, 64*(5), 74–78.

Shepard, L. (2005). Linking formative assessment to scaffolding. *Educational Leadership, 63*(3), 66–71.

Shepard, L. A. (1995). Using assessment to improve learning. *Phi Delta Kappan, 52*(5), 38–43.

Shepard, L. A. (2000). The role of assessment in a learning culture. *Educational Researcher, 29*(7), 4–14.

Shih, M., & Sanchez, D. (2005). Perspectives and research on the positive and negative implications of having multiple racial identities. *Psychological Bulletin, 131*(4), 569–591.

Shih, S. (2005). Taiwanese sixth graders' achievement goals and their motivation, strategy use, and grades: An examination of the multiple goal perspective. *The Elementary School Journal, 106*(1), 39–58.

Shih, S., & Alexander, J. (2000). Interacting effects of goal setting and self- or other-referenced feedback on children's development of self-efficacy and cognitive skill within the Taiwanese classroom. *Journal of Educational Psychology, 92*(3), 536–543.

Shore, R. (2008). *The power of pow! Wham!* New York: Sesame Workshop.

Shuler, C., (2007). *D is for digital.* New York: Sesame Workshop.

Shulman, J., Lotan, R. A., & Whitcomb, J. A. (1998). *Groupwork in diverse classrooms: A cookbook for educators.* New York: Teachers College Press.

Shulman, L. S. (2000). Teacher development: Roles of domain expertise and pedagogical development. *Journal of Applied Developmental Psychology, 21*, 129–135.

Siegel, L. S. (2003). Learning disabilities. In W. M. Reynolds & G. E. Miller (Eds.), *Handbook of psychology: Vol. 7. Educational psychology* (pp. 455–486). Hoboken, NJ: Wiley.

Siegler, R. (2006). Microgenetic analyses of learning. In D. Kuhn & R. Siegler (Eds.), *Handbook of child psychology: Vol. 2* (6th ed., pp. 464–510). Hoboken, NJ: Wiley.

Siegler, R. S. (1998). *Children's thinking* (3rd ed.). Upper Saddle River, NJ: Prentice Hall.

Silver-Pacuilla, H., & Fleischman, S. (2006). Technology to help struggling students. *Educational Leadership, 63*(5), 84–85.

Simmons, D. C., Fuchs, L. S., Fuchs, P., Mathes, P., & Hodge, J. P. (1995). Effects of explicit teaching and peer tutoring on the reading achievement of learning-disabled and low-performing students in regular classrooms. *The Elementary School Journal, 95*(5), 387–408.

Simpkins, M., Cole, K., Tavalin, F., & Means, B. (2002). *Increasing student learning through multimedia projects.* Alexandria, VA: ASCD.

Sinclair, M. F., Christenson, S. L., Evelo, D. L., & Hurley, C. (1998). Dropout prevention for high-risk youth with disabilities: Efficacy of a sustained school engagement procedure. *Exceptional Children, 65*(1), 7–21.

Singer, J., Marx, R. W., Krajcik, J., & Chambers, J. C. (2000). Constructing extended inquiry projects: Curriculum materials for science education reform. *Educational Psychologist, 35*(4), 165–178.

Sins, P., va Joolingen, W., Savelsbergh, E., & van Hout-Wolters, B. (2008). Motivation and performance within a collaborative computer-based modeling task: Relations between students' achievement goal orientation, self-efficacy, cognitive processing, and achievement. *Contemporary Educational Psychology, 33*(1), 58–77.

Sio, U., & Ormerod, T. (2009). Does incubation enhance problem solving? A meta-analytic review. *Psychological Bulletin, 135*(1), 94–120.

Sireci, S., Scarpati, S., & Li, S. (2005). Test accommodations for students with disabilities: An analysis of the interaction hypothesis. *Review of Educational Research, 75*(4), 457–490.

Sirin, S. (2005). Socioeconomic status and academic achievement: A meta-analytic review of research. *Review of Educational Research, 75*(3), 417–453.

Sirotnik, K. A. (2002). Promoting responsible accountability in schools and education. *Phi Delta Kappan, 83*(9), 662–673.

Skiba, R. (2000). *Zero tolerance, zero evidence: An analysis of school disciplinary practice.* Bloomington: Indiana Education Policy Center.

Skinner, E., & Greene, T. (2008). Perceived control, coping, and engagement. In T. L. Good (Ed.), *21st century learning* (Vol. 1, pp. 121–130). Thousand Oaks, CA: Sage.

Slavin, R., & Lake, C. (2008). Effective programs in elementary mathematics; A best-evidence synthesis. *Review of Educational Research, 78*(3), 427–515.

Slavin, R. E. (1986). The Napa evaluation of Madeline Hunter's ITIP: Lessons learned. *Elementary School Journal, 87*, 165–171.

Slavin, R. E. (1987a). Ability grouping and student achievement in elementary schools: A best-evidence synthesis. *Review of Educational Research, 57*, 293–336.

Slavin, R. E. (1987b). Grouping for instruction in the elementary school. *Educational Psychologist, 22*, 109–127.

Slavin, R. E. (1990). Ability grouping and student achievement in secondary schools: A best-evidence synthesis. *Review of Educational Research, 60*, 471–499.

Slavin, R. E. (1991). Cooperative learning and group contingencies. *Journal of Behavioral Education, 1,* 105–115.

Slavin, R. E. (1994a). *Using student team learning* (4th ed.). Baltimore: Johns Hopkins University, Center for Research on Elementary and Middle Schools.

Slavin, R. E. (1994b). School and classroom organization in beginning reading: Class size, aides, and instructional grouping. In R. E. Slavin, N. L. Karweit, B. A. Wasik, & N. A. Madden (Eds.), *Preventing early school failure: Research on effective strategies.* Boston: Allyn & Bacon.

Slavin, R. E. (1995a). *Cooperative learning: Theory, research, and practice* (2nd ed.). Boston: Allyn & Bacon.

Slavin, R. E. (1995b). Cooperative learning and intergroup relations. In J. Banks (Ed.), *Handbook of research on multicultural education.* New York: Macmillan.

Slavin, R. E. (1996). Neverstreaming: Preventing learning disabilities. *Educational Leadership, 53*(5), 4–7.

Slavin, R. E. (1997/1998). Can education reduce social inequality? *Educational Leadership, 55*(4), 6–10.

Slavin, R. E. (2002). The intentional school: Effective elementary education for all children. In S. Stringfield & D. Land (Eds.), *Educating at-risk students* (pp. 111–127). Chicago: National Society for the Study of Education.

Slavin, R. E. (2003). A reader's guide to scientifically based research. *Educational Leadership, 60*(5), 12–16.

Slavin R. E. (2008a). Comprehensive school reform. In C. Ames, D. Berliner, J. Brophy, L. Corno, & M. McCaslin (Eds.), *21st century education: A reference handbook* (pp. 259–266). Thousand Oaks, CA: Sage.

Slavin, R. E. (2008b). What works? Issues in synthesizing educational program evaluations. *Educational Researcher, 37*(1), 5–14.

Slavin, R. E. (2009). Cooperative learning. In G. McCulloch & D. Crook (Eds.), *International encyclopedia of education.* Abington, UK: Routledge.

Slavin, R. E. (2010). Cooperative learning. In P. Peterson, E. Baker, & B. McGaw (Eds.), *International encyclopedia of education* (3rd ed.). Oxford, UK: Elsevier.

Slavin, R. E. (in press). Classroom applications of cooperative learning. In K. Harris, S. Graham, & T. Urdan (Eds.), *APA educational psychology handbook.*

Slavin, R. E., & Cheung, A. (2005). A synthesis of research on language of reading instruction. *Review of Educational Research, 75*(2), 247–284.

Slavin, R.E., Cheung, A., Groff, C., & Lake, C. (2008). Effective reading programs for middle and high schools: A best evidence synthesis. *Reading Research Quarterly, 43*(3), 290–322.

Slavin, R. E., & Fashola, O. S. (1998). *Show me the evidence: Proven and promising programs for America's schools.* Thousand Oaks, CA: Corwin.

Slavin, R. E., Holmes, G., Madden, N., Chamberlain, A., & Cheung, A. (2010). *Effects of a data-driven district-level reform model.* Baltimore: Center for Research and Reform in Education, Johns Hopkins University.

Slavin, R. E., & Karweit, N. L. (1982, August). *School organizational vs. developmental effects on attendance among young adolescents.* Paper presented at the annual convention of the American Psychological Association, Washington, DC.

Slavin, R. E., & Karweit, N. L. (1984, April). *Within-class ability groupings and student achievement: Two field experiments.* Paper presented at the annual convention of the American Educational Research Association, New Orleans, LA.

Slavin, R. E., Karweit, N. L., & Wasik, B. A. (1994). *Preventing early school failure: Research on effective strategies.* Boston: Allyn & Bacon.

Slavin, R. E., Lake, C., Chambers, B., Cheung, A., & Davis, S. (2009). Effective reading programs for the elementary grades: A best-evidence synthesis. *Review of Educational Research, 79*(4), 1391–1465.

Slavin, R. E., Lake, C., Davis, S., & Madden, N. (2009). *Effective programs for struggling readers: A best-evidence synthesis.* Manuscript submitted for publication.

Slavin, R. E., Lake, C., & Groff, C. (2009). Effective programs in middle and high school mathematics: A best-evidence synthesis. *Review of Educational Research, 79*(2), 839–911.

Slavin, R. E., & Madden, N.A. (1987, April). *Effective classroom programs for students at risk.* Paper presented at the annual convention of the American Educational Research Association, Washington, DC.

Slavin, R. E., & Madden, N.A. (Eds.). (2001). *One million children: Success for All.* Thousand Oaks, CA: Corwin.

Slavin, R. E., Madden, N. A., Chambers, B., & Haxby, B. (Eds.). (2009). *Two million children: Success for All.* Thousand Oaks, CA: Corwin.

Slavin, R. E., Madden, N.A., & Karweit, N. L. (Eds.). (1989). *Effective programs for students at risk.* Boston: Allyn & Bacon.

Slavin, R. E., Madden, N. A., & Leavey, M. (1984a). Effects of team assisted individualization on the mathematics achievement of academically handicapped and nonhandicapped students. *Journal of Educational Psychology, 76,* 813–819.

Slavin, R. E., Madden, N. A., & Leavey, M. B. (1984b). Effects of cooperative learning and individualized instruction on mainstreamed students. *Exceptional Children, 84,* 409–422.

Slavin, R. E., Madden, N. A., & Stevens, R. J. (1994). Cooperative integrated reading and composition: Applications for the language arts classroom. In R. J. Stahl (Ed.), *Cooperative learning in language arts: A handbook for teachers.* Boston: Addison-Wesley.

Slavin, R. E., & Stevens, R. J. (1991). Cooperative learning and mainstreaming. In J. W. Lloyd, N. N. Singh, & A. C. Repp (Eds.). *The regular education initiative: Alternative perspectives on concepts, issues, and models* (pp. 177–191). Sycamore, IL: Sycamore.

Slotte, V., & Lonka, K. (1999). Review and process effects of spontaneous note-taking on text comprehension. *Contemporary Educational Psychology, 24*(1), 1–20.

Smagorinsky, P., & Smith, M. W. (1992). The nature of knowledge in composition and literary understanding: The question of specificity. *Review of Educational Research, 62*(3), 279–305.

Smith, D. D., (2001). *Introduction to special education: Teaching in an age of opportunity.* Boston: Allyn & Bacon.

Smith, D. D., & Tyler, N. C. (Eds.). (2010). *Introduction to special education* (7th ed.). Upper Saddle River, NJ: Merrill.

Smith, H., Higgins, S., Wall, K., & Miller, J. (2005). Interactive whiteboards: Boon or bandwagon? A critical review of the literature. *Journal of Computer-Assisted Learning, 21,* 91–101.

Smith, K. (2009). From test takers to test makers. *Educational Leadership, 67*(3), 26–31.

Smith, L., & Land, M. (1981). Low-interference verbal behaviors related to teacher clarity. *Journal of Classroom Interaction, 17,* 37–42.

Smith, L. J., Ross, S. M., & Casey, J. P. (1994). *Special education analyses for Success for All in four cities.* Memphis, TN: University of Memphis, Center for Research in Educational Policy.

Smith, S. S. (2002). Desegregation. In D. L. Levinson, P. W. Cookson, Jr., & A. R. Sadovnik (Eds.), *Education and sociology: An encyclopedia* (pp. 141–149). New York: Routledge Falmer.

Smith, T. E. C., Polloway, E. A., Patton, J. R., & Dowdy, C. A. (2008). *Teaching students with special needs in inclusive settings* (5th ed.). Boston: Allyn & Bacon.

Smutny, J. (2003). *Gifted education: Promising practices.* Bloomington, IN: Phi Delta Kappan.

Snell, M. E., & Janney, R. (2000). *Collaborative teaming.* Baltimore: Brookes.

Snow, C. (2006). Cross-cutting themes and future research directions. In D. August and T. Shanahan (Eds.), *Developing literacy in second-language learners* (pp. 631–652). Mahwah, NJ: Erlbaum.

Snow, C. E., Burns, S. M., & Griffin, P. (Eds.). (1998). *Preventing reading difficulties in young children.* Washington, DC: National Academies Press.

Snow, R. E. (1992). Aptitude theory: Yesterday, today, and tomorrow. *Educational Psychologist, 27*(1), 5–32.

Snowman, J. (1984). Learning tactics and strategies. In G. Phye & T. Andre (Eds.), *Cognitive instructional psychology.* New York: Academic Press.

Snyderman, M., & Rothman, S. (1987). Survey of expert opinion on intelligence and aptitude testing. *American Psychologist, 42,* 137–144.

Solso, R. L. (2001). *Cognitive psychology* (6th ed.). Boston: Allyn & Bacon.

Somekh, B., Haldane, M., Jones, K., Lewin, C., Steadman, S., Scrimshaw, P., Sing, S., et al. (2007). *Evaluation of the primary schools whiteboards expansion project: Report to the Department for Education and Skills.* Manchester, UK: Manchester Metropolitan University.

Sornson, N. (2001). Vision and learning. In B. Sornson (Ed.), *Preventing early learning failure.* Alexandria, VA: ASCD.

Sorrells, A. M., Rieth, H., & Sindelar, P. (2004). *Critical issues in special education: Access, diversity, and accountability.* Boston: Pearson.

Sousa, D. (2001). *How the brain learns* (2nd ed.). Boston: Allyn & Bacon.

Sousa, D. (2005). *How the brain learns to read.* Thousand Oaks, CA: Corwin.

Sousa, D. (2008). *How the brain learns mathematics.* Thousand Oaks, CA: Corwin.

Specht, L. B., & Sandling, P. K. (1991). The differential effects of experiential learning activities and traditional lecture classes in accounting. *Simulation and Games, 2,* 196–210.

Spector, J. E. (1992). Predicting progress in beginning reading: Dynamic assessment of phonemic awareness. *Journal of Educational Psychology, 84*(3), 353–363.

Speece, D., Case, L., & Molloy, D. (2003). Responsiveness to general education as the first gate to learning disabilities identification. *Learning Disabilities: Research and Practice, 18*(3), 147–156.

Spencer, M. B., Noll, E., Stoltzfus, J., & Harpalani, V. (2001). Identity and school adjustment: Revisiting the "acting white" assumption. *Educational Psychologist, 36*(1), 21–30.

Sperling, G. A. (1960). The information available in brief visual presentations. *Psychological Monographs, 74*(498).

Spiegel, D. L. (2005). *Classroom discussion: Strategies for enhancing all students, building higher-level thinking skills, and strengthening reading and writing across the curriculum.* New York: Scholastic.

Spielberger, C., & Vagg, P. (Eds.). (1995). *Test anxiety: Theory, assessment, and treatment.* Washington, DC: Taylor & Francis.

Sprenger, M. (2009). Focusing the digital brain. *Educational Leadership, 67*(1), 34–39.

Squires, D. A. (2009). *Curriculum alignment: Research based strategies for increasing student achievement.* Thousand Oaks, CA: Corwin Press.

Stahl, K. A. D., Keane, A., & Vukovic, R. (2009, April). *Investigating the effects of a Response to Intervention framework in New York City.* Paper presented at the meeting of the American Educational Research Association, San Diego, CA.

Stallings, J., & Krasavage, E. M. (1986). Program implementation and student achievement in a four-year Madeline Hunter follow-through project. *Elementary School Journal, 87,* 117–138.

Stallings, J. A., & Kaskowitz, D. (1974). *Follow-through classroom observation evaluation 1972–73.* Menlo Park, CA: Standard Research Institute.

Stanovich, K. E., Siegel, L. S., & Gottard, A. (1997). Converging evidence for phonological and surface subtypes of reading disability. *Journal of Educational Psychology, 89*(10), 114–127.

Stansbury, M. (2009, July 21). *What educators can learn from brain research.* Retrieved July 27, 2009, from www.eschoolnews.com

Starfield, B. (1997). *Quality of primary care: A services perspective.* Primary Care Center Policy White Paper.

Starnes, B. A. (2006). Montana's Indian education for all: Toward an education worthy of American ideals. *Phi Delta Kappan, 88*(3), 184–189.

Starratt, R. (2003). Opportunity to learn and the accountability agenda. *Phi Delta Kappan, 85*(4), 298–303.

Stecher, B., Hamilton, L., & Gonzalez, G. (2003). *Working smarter to leave no child behind.* Santa Monica, CA: RAND.

Steel, P. (2007). The nature of procrastination: A meta-analytic and theoretical review of quintessential self-regulatory failure. *Psychological Bulletin, 133*(1), 65–94.

Stein, B. S., Littlefield, J., Bransford, J. D., & Persampieri, M. (1984). Elaboration and knowledge acquisition. *Memory and Cognition, 12,* 522–529.

Stein, M. K., Leinhardt, G., & Bickel, W. (1989). Instructional issues for teaching students at risk. In R. E. Slavin, N. L. Karweit, & N. A. Madden (Eds.), *Effective programs for students at risk.* Boston: Allyn & Bacon.

Stein, N. (2000). Listening to—and learning from—girls. *Educational Leadership, 57*(4), 18–20.

Steiner, H. H., & Carr, M. (2003). Cognitive development in gifted children: Toward a more precise understanding of emerging differences in intelligence. *Educational Psychology Review, 15*(3), 215–246.

Stephan, W. G., & Vogt, W. P. (Eds.). (2004). *Education programs for improving intergroup relations.* New York: Teachers College.

Sternberg, R. (2008). Applying psychological theories to educational practice. *American Educational Research Journal, 45*(1), 150–165.

Sternberg, R., Jarvin, L., & Grigorenko, E. (2009). *Teacing for wisdom, intelligence, creativity, and success.* Thousand Oaks, CA: Corwin.

Sternberg, R. J. (2002). Raising the achievement of all students: Teaching for successful intelligence. *Educational Psychology Review, 14*(4), 383–393.

Sternberg, R. J. (2003). Contemporary theories of intelligence. In W. M. Reynolds & G. E. Miller (Eds.), *Handbook of psychology: Vol. 7. Educational psychology* (pp. 23–45). Hoboken, NJ: Wiley.

Sternberg, R. J. (2007). Who are the bright children? The cultural context of being and acting intelligent. *Educational Researcher, 36*(3), 148–155.

Sternberg, R. J., & Bhana, K. (1986). Synthesis of research on the effectiveness of intellectual skills programs: Snake-oil remedies or miracle cures? *Educational Leadership, 44*(2), 60–67.

Stevens, R., Van Meter, P., Garner, J., Warcholak, N., Bochna, C., & Hall, T. (2008). Reading and Integrated Literacy Strategies (RAILS): An integrated approach to early reading. *Journal of Education for Students Placed at Risk, 13*(4), 357–380.

Stevens, R. J., Madden, N. A., Slavin, R. E., & Farnish, A. M. (1987). Cooperative Integrated Reading and Composition: Two field experiments. *Reading Research Quarterly, 22,* 433–454.

Stevens, R. J., & Slavin, R. E. (1995a). The cooperative elementary school: Effects on students' achievement, attitudes, and social relations. *American Educational Research Journal, 32,* 321–351.

Stevens, R. J., & Slavin, R. E. (1995b). The effects of Cooperative Integrated Reading and Composition (CIRC) on academically handicapped and non-handicapped students' achievement, attitudes, and metacognition in reading and writing. *Elementary School Journal, 95*(3), 241–262.

Stiggins, R. (2004). New assessment beliefs for a new school mission. *Phi Delta Kappan, 86*(1), 22–27.

Stiggins, R. (2007). Assessment through the student's eyes. *Educational Leadership, 64*(8), 22–26.

Stiggins, R. J. (2000). *Student-involved classroom assessment* (3rd ed.). Bloomington, IN: Phi Delta Kappan.

Stinson, D. (2006). African American male adolescents, schooling (and mathematics): Deficiency, rejection, and achievement. *Review of Educational Research, 76*(4), 477–506.

Stipek, D. (2002). *Motivation to learn: Integrating theory and practice* (4th ed.). Boston: Allyn & Bacon.

Stipek, D. (2006). No Child Left Behind comes to preschool. *The Elementary School Journal, 106*(5), 455–466.

Stipek, D., de la Sota, A., & Weishaupt, L. (1999). Life lessons: An embedded classroom approach to preventing high-risk behaviors among preadolescents. *The Elementary School Journal, 99*(5), 433–452.

Strand, S., Deary, I. J., & Smith, P. (2006). Sex differences in cognitive abilities test scores: A UK national picture. *British Journal of Educational Psychology, 76*, 463–480.

Streifer, P. (2002). *Using data to make better educational decisions.* Lanham, MD: Scarecrow Education & American Association of School Administrators.

Stringer, E. (2008). *Action research in education* (2nd ed.). Upper Saddle River, NJ: Pearson.

Stringfield, S., Millsap, M. A., Herman, R., Yoder, N., Brigham, N., Nesselrodt, P., Schaffer, E., Karweit, N., Levin, M., & Stevens, R. J. (1997). *Special strategies studies final report.* Washington, DC: U.S. Department of Education.

Strong, R. W., Silver, H. F., & Perini, M. J. (2001). *Teaching what matters most.* Alexandria, VA: ASCD.

Strout, M. (2005). Positive behavioral support on the classroom level: Considerations and strategies. *Beyond Behavior, 14*, 3–8.

Struzziero, P. (2009, April). *Does RTI help first graders at risk for reading problems?* Paper presented at the annual meeting of the American Educational Research Association, San Diego, CA.

Stuebing, K. K., Fletcher, J. M., LeDoux, J. M., Lyon, G. R., Shaywitz, S. E., & Shaywitz, B. A. (2002). Validity of IQ discrepancy classifications of reading disabilities: A meta-analysis. *American Educational Research Journal, 39*(2), 469–518.

Stumpf, H., & Stanley, J. C. (1996). Gender-related differences on the College Board's advanced placement achievement tests 1982–1992. *Journal of Educational Psychology, 88*(2), 353–364.

Summers, J. (2006). Effects of collaborative learning in math on sixth graders' individual goal orientations from a socioconstructivist perspective. *The Elementary School Journal, 106*(3), 273–290.

Summers, J. (2008). Cognitive approaches to motivation in education. In T. L. Good (Ed.), *21st century learning* (Vol. 1, pp. 113–120). Thousand Oaks, CA: Sage.

Supovitz, J. A., & Brennan, R. T. (1997). Mirror, mirror on the wall, which is the fairest test of all? An examination of the equitability of portfolio assessment relative to standardized tests. *Harvard Educational Review, 67*(3), 474–505.

Supovitz, J. A., Poglinco, S. M., & Snyder, B. A. (2001). *Moving mountains: Successes and challenges of the America's Choice comprehensive school reform design.* Philadelphia: University of Pennsylvania, Consortium for Policy Research in Education.

Susman, E. J., Dorn, L. D., & Schiefelbein, V. L. (2003). Puberty, sexuality, and health. In R. M. Lerner, M. A. Easterbrooks, & J. Mistry (Eds.), *Handbook of psychology: Vol. 6. Developmental psychology* (pp. 295–324). Hoboken, NJ: Wiley.

Sutherland, K., Wehby, J., & Copeland, S. (2000). Effect of rates of varying behavior-specific praise on the on-task behavior of students with EBD. *Journal of Emotional and Behavioral Disorders, 8*, 2–8, 26.

Suzuki, L. A., Ponterotto, J. G., & Meller, P. J. (Eds.). (2000). *Handbook of multicultural assessment* (2nd ed.). San Francisco: Jossey-Bass.

Swann, W., Chang-Schneider, C., & McClarty, K. (2007). Do people's self-views matter? *American Psychologist, 62*(2), 84–94.

Swanson, H. (2001). Research on interventions for adolescents with learning disabilities: A meta-analysis of outcomes related to higher-order processing. *The Elementary School Journal, 101*(3), 331–348.

Swanson, H., & Jerman, O. (2006). Math disabilities: A selective meta-analysis of the literature. *Review of Educational Research, 76*(2), 249–274.

Swanson, H. L., & Hoskyn, M. (1998). Experimental intervention research on students with learning disabilities: A meta-analysis of treatment outcomes. *Review of Educational Research, 68*(3), 277–321.

Swanson, H. L., Mink, J., & Bocian, K. (1999). Cognitive processing deficits in poor readers with symptoms of reading disabilities and ADHD: More alike than different? *Journal of Educational Psychology, 91*(2), 321–333.

Swanson, M. C., Mehan, H., & Hubbard, L. (1995). The AVID classroom: Academic and social support for low-achieving students. In J. Oakes & K. H. Quartz (Eds.), *Creating new educational communities.* Chicago: University of Chicago Press.

Swartz, E. (2009). Diversity: Gatekeeping knowledge and maintaining inequalities. *Review of Educational Research, 79*(2), 1044–1083.

Sweeney, D., & Hoffman, L. (2004). Research issues in autism spectrum disorders. In R. Rutherford, M. Quinn, & S. Mathur (Eds.), *Handbook of research on emotional and behavioral disorders* (pp. 302–317). New York: Guilford.

Sweller, J., van Merrienboer, J. J. G., & Paas, F. G. W. C. (1998). Cognitive architecture and instructional design. *Educational Psychology Review, 10*(3), 251–296.

Swisher, K., & Schoorman, D. (2001). Learning styles: Implications for teachers. In C. F. Diaz (Ed.), *Multicultural education in the 21st century.* New York: Longman.

Tangney, J., & Dearing, R. (2002). Gender differences in morality. In R. Bornstein & J. Masling (Eds.), *The psychodynamics of gender and gender role.* Washington, DC: American Psychological Association.

Tate, M. L. (2003). *Worksheets don't grow dendrites: 20 instructional strategies that engage the brain.* Thousand Oaks, CA: Corwin.

Tate, W., IV. (2008). "Geography of opportunity": Poverty, place, and educational outcomes. *Educational Researcher, 37*(7), 397–411.

Taylor, B., Pearson, P., Clark, K., & Walpole, S. (2000). Effective schools and accomplished teachers: Lessons about primary-grade reading instruction in low-income schools. *The Elementary School Journal, 101*(2), 121–166.

Taylor, C. (1994). Assessment for measurement or standards: The peril and promise of large-scale assessment reform. *American Educational Research Journal, 31*(2), 231–262.

Taylor, D., & Lorimer, M. (2003). Helping boys succeed. *Educational Leadership, 60*(4), 68–70.

Teeter, P. A. (2000). *Interventions for ADHD.* New York: Guilford.

Tenenbaum, H., & Ruck, M. (2007). Are teachers' expectations different for racial minority than for European American students? A meta-analysis. *Journal of Educational Psychology, 99*(2), 253–273.

Tennyson, R. D., & Park, O. (1980). The teaching of concepts: A review of instructional design literature. *Review of Educational Research, 50*, 55–70.

Terman, L. M., & Oden, M. H. (1959). The gifted group in mid-life. In *Genetic studies of genius* (Vol. 5). Stanford, CA: Stanford University Press.

Texas Center for Educational Research. (2007). *Evaluation of the Texas technology immersion pilot: Findings from the second year.* Austin, TX: Author.

Theodore, L., Bray, M., Kehle, T., & Jenson, W. (2001). Randomization of group contingencies and reinforcers for reducing classroom disruptive behavior. *Journal of School Psychology, 39,* 267–277.

Thoma, S. J., & Rest, J. R. (1999). The relationship between moral decision making and patterns of consolidation and transition in moral judgment development. *Developmental Psychology, 35*(2), 323–334.

Thomas, D., & Stevenson, H. (2009). Gender risks and education: The particular classroom challenges for urban low-income African American boys. *Review of Research in Education, 33,* 160–180.

Thomas, E. L., & Robinson, H. A. (1972). *Improving reading in every class: A sourcebook for teachers.* Boston: Allyn & Bacon.

Thomas, M. D., & Bainbridge, W. L. (2001). "All children can learn": Facts and fallacies. *Phi Delta Kappan, 82*(9), 660–662.

Thompson, R. A., Easterbrooks, M. A., & Padilla-Walker, L. M. (2003). Social and emotional development in infancy. In R. M. Lerner, M. A. Easterbrooks, & J. Mistry (Eds.), *Handbook of psychology: Vol. 6. Developmental psychology* (pp. 91–112). Hoboken, NJ: Wiley.

Thompson, R. A., & Wyatt, J. M. (1999). Current research on child maltreatment: Implications for educators. *Educational Psychology Review, 11*(3), 173–202.

Thompson, R. F. (2000). Memory: Brain systems. In A. E. Kazdin (Ed.), *Encyclopedia of psychology* (Vol. 5, pp. 175–178). Washington, DC: American Psychological Association.

Thompson, S. (2001). The authentic standards movement and its evil twin. *Phi Delta Kappan, 82*(5), 358–362.

Thompson, W., & Hickey, J. (2008). *Society in focus.* Boston: Pearson.

Thorkildsen, T. A. (1993). Those who can, tutor: High-ability students' conceptions of fair ways to organize learning. *Journal of Educational Psychology, 85*(1), 182–190.

Thorkildsen, T. A., & Nicholls, J. G. (1998). Fifth graders' achievement orientations and beliefs: Individual and classroom differences. *Journal of Educational Psychology, 90*(2), 179–201.

Thornburg, D. (2002). *The new basics: Education and the future of work in the telematic age.* Alexandria, VA: ASCD.

Thorsen, C. (2009). *Tech tactics: Technology for teachers* (3rd ed). Boston: Pearson.

Thousand, J. S., & Villa, R. A. (1994). *Creativity and collaborative learning: A practical guide to empowering students and teachers.* Baltimore: Paul H. Brookes.

Tileston, D., & Darling, S. (2008). *Teaching strategies that prepare students for high-stakes tests.* Thousand Oaks, CA: Corwin.

Tingley, J. (2001). Volunteer programs: When good intentions are not enough. *Educational Leadership, 68*(7), 53–55.

Tishman, S., Perkins, D. N., & Jay, E. (1995). *The thinking classroom.* Boston: Allyn & Bacon.

Tobias, S. (1992). The impact of test anxiety cognition in school learning. In K. A. Hagtvet & T. B. Johnsen (Eds.), *Advances in test anxiety research* (Vol. 7, pp. 18–31). Amsterdam: Swets & Zeitlinger.

Tobin, K. (1986). Effects of teacher wait time on discourse characteristics in mathematics and language arts classes. *American Educational Research Journal, 23,* 191–200.

Tobin, K. (1987). The role of wait time in higher cognitive level learning. *Review of Educational Research, 57,* 69–95.

Tobin, K. G., & Capie, W. (1982). Relationships between classroom process variables and middle-school science achievement. *Journal of Educational Psychology, 74,* 441–454.

Toga, A. W., & Thompson, P. M. (2005). Genetics of brain structure and intelligence. *Annual Review of Neuroscience, 28,* 1–23.

Tollefson, N. (2000). Classroom applications of cognitive theories of motivation. *Educational Psychology Review, 12*(1), 63–84.

Tomlinson, C. (2002). Invitation to learn. *Educational Leadership, 60*(1), 6–11.

Tomlinson, C. (2007/2008). Learning to love assessment. *Educational Leadership, 65*(4), 8–13.

Tomlinson, C. (2008). The goals of differentiation. *Educational Leadership, 66*(3), 26–31.

Tomlinson, C. A. (2004). Differentiating instruction: A synthesis of key research and guidelines. In T. L. Jetton & J. A. Dole (Eds.), *Adolescent literacy, research and practice* (pp. 228–250). New York: The Guilford Press.

Tomlinson, C. A., Kaplan, S. N., & Renzulli, J. S. (2001). *The parallel curriculum: A model for planning curriculum for gifted students and whole classrooms.* Thousand Oaks, CA: Corwin.

Tong, F., Lara-Alecio, R., Irby, B., Mathes, P., & Kwok, O. (2008). Accelerating early academic oral English development in transitional bilingual and structured English immersion programs. *American Educational Research Journal, 45*(4), 1011–1044.

Top, B. L., & Osguthorpe, R. T. (1987). Reverse-role tutoring: The effects of handicapped students tutoring regular class students. *Elementary School Journal, 87,* 413–423.

Topping, K., & Ehly, S. (Eds.). (1998). *Peer-assisted learning.* Mahwah, NJ: Erlbaum.

Topping, K., Samuels, J., & Paul, T. (2007). Does practice make perfect? Independent reading quantity, quality, and student achievement. *Learning and Instruction, 17*(3), 253–264.

Torrance, M., Fidalgo, R., & Garcia, J.-N. (2007). The teachability and effectiveness of cognitive self-regulation in sixth-grade writers. *Learning and Instruction, 17*(3), 265–285.

Towne, L., Wise, L., & Winters, T. (2005). *Advancing scientific research in education.* Washington, DC: National Academies Press.

Trammel, D. L., Schloss, P. J., & Alper, S. (1994). Using self-recording evaluation and graphing to increase completion of homework assignments. *Journal of Learning Disabilities, 27,* 75–81.

Trautwein, U. (2007). The homework–achievement relation reconsidered: Differentiating homework time, homework frequency, and homework effort. *Learning and Instruction, 17*(3), 372–388.

Trawick-Smith, J. (1997). *Early childhood development: A multicultural perspective.* Upper Saddle River, NJ: Merrill/Prentice-Hall.

Trawick-Smith, J. (Ed.). (2010). *Early childhood development: A multicultural perspective* (5th ed.). Upper Saddle River, NJ: Merrill/Prentice-Hall.

Trefil, J., & O'Brien-Trefil, W. (2009). The science students need to know. *Educational Leadership, 67*(1), 28–33.

Trent, W. T. (1997). Outcomes of school desegregation: Findings from longitudinal research. *Journal of Negro Education, 66*(3), 255–257.

Triandis, H. (1995). *Individualism and collectivism.* Boulder, CO: Westview.

Troop, W. R., & Asher, S. R. (1999). Teaching peer relationship competence in schools. In R. J. Stevens (Ed.), *Teaching in American schools.* Upper Saddle River, NJ: Merrill/Prentice-Hall.

Trotter, A. (2009, January 6). Students turn their cellphones on for classroom lessons. *Education Daily.* Retrieved February 1, 2009, from www.csun.edu/~krowlands/Content/Academic_Resources/Technology/cell%20phones%20in%20classroom.pdf

Trumbull, E., & Farr, B. (2000). *Grading and reporting student progress in an age of standards.* Norwood, MA: Christopher-Gordon.

Tschannen-Moran, M., & Woolfolk Hoy, A. (2001). Teacher efficacy: Capturing an elusive construct. *Teaching and Teacher Education, 17,* 783–805.

Tucker, J. A. (2001). Instructional support teams: It's a group thing. In B. Sornson (Ed.), *Preventing early learning failure.* Alexandria, VA: ASCD.

Tulving, E., & Craik, F. I. M. (Eds.). (2000). *The Oxford handbook of memory.* New York: Oxford University Press.

Turiel, E. (2006). The development of morality. In N. Eisenberg (Ed.), *Handbook of Child Psychology, Vol. 3* (6th ed., pp. 789–857). Hoboken, NJ: Wiley.

Turkeltaub, P. E., Gareau, L., Flowers, D. L., Zeffiro, T. A., & Eden, G. F. (2003). Development of neural mechanisms for reading. *Nature Neuroscience, 6,* 767–773.

Turner, L. A., & Johnson, B. (2003). A model of mastery motivation for at-risk preschoolers. *Journal of Educational Psychology, 95*(3), 495–505.

Turner, S., & Alborz, A. (2003). Academic attainments of children with Down's syndrome: A longitudinal study. *British Journal of Educational Psychology, 73*(4), 563–583.

Tyson, K., Darity, J., & Castellino, D. (2005). It's not a "black thing": Understanding the burden of acting white and other dilemmas of high achievement. *American Sociological Review, 70*(4), 582–605.

U.S. Census Bureau. (2001). *Population projections.* Retrieved January 1, 2010, from www.census.gov

U.S. Department of Education. (1994). *Sixteenth annual report to Congress on the implementation of the Individuals with Disabilities Education Act.* Washington, DC: Author.

U.S. Department of Education. (2000). *The 22nd annual report to Congress on the implementation of the Individuals with Disabilities Education Act.* Washington, DC: U.S. Government Printing Office.

U.S. Department of Education. (2002). *No Child Left Behind: A desktop reference.* Washington, DC: Author. Available at www.ed.gov/offices/OESE/reference

U.S. Department of Education. (2003). *Identifying and implementing educational practices supported by rigorous evidence: A user-friendly guide.* Washington, DC: Author.

U.S. Department of Education. (2005). *Annual report to Congress on the implementation of the Individuals with Disabilities Act.* Washington, DC: Author.

U.S. Department of Education. (2006). *Annual report to Congress on the implementation of the Individuals with Disabilities Act.* Washington, DC: Author.

U.S. Department of Education, Office of Special Education and Rehabilitation Services. (1998, September). *IDEA '97 general information.* Retrieved May 2, 2010, from www.ed.gov/offices/OSERS/IDEA/overview.html

University of Wisconsin-Madison. (2009, June 2). Culture, not biology, underpins math gender gap. *Science Daily.* Retrieved June 10, 2009, from www.sciencedaily.com/releases/2009/090601182655.htm

Unsworth, N., & Engle, R. (2007). On the division of short-term and working memory: An examination of simple and complex span and their relation to higher order abilities. *Psychological Bulletin, 133*(6), 1038–1066.

Urdan, T., & Mestas, M. (2006). The goals behind performance goals. *Journal of Educational Psychology, 98*(2), 354–365.

Usher, E., & Pajares, F. (2008). Sources of self-efficacy in school: Critical review of the literature and future directions. *Review of Educational Research, 78*(4), 751–796.

Usher, E., & Pajares, F. (2009). Sources of self-efficacy in mathematics: A validation study. *Contemporary Educational Psychology, 34*(1), 89–101.

Vacca, R. (2006). They can because they think they can. *Educational Leadership, 63*(5), 56–59.

Vadasy, P. F., Sanders, E. A., & Tudor, S. (2007). Effectiveness of paraeducator-supplemented individual instruction: Beyond basic decoding skills. *Journal of Learning Disabilities, 40*(6), 508–525.

Valencia, S. W., Pearson, P. D., Peters, C. W., & Wixson, K. K. (1989). Theory and practice in statewide reading assessment: Closing the gap. *Educational Leadership, 46*(7), 57–63.

Valenza, J. (2005/2006). The virtual library. *Educational Leadership, 63*(4), 54–59.

Vamosi, R. (2005, February 18). *Alarm over pharming attacks: Identity theft made even easier.* Retrieved October 6, 2005, from http://reviews.cnet.com/4520-3513_7-5670780-1.html

van Goozen, S., Fairchild, G., Snoek, H., & Harold, G. (2007). The evidence for a neurobiological model of childhood antisocial behavior. *Psychological Bulletin, 133*(1), 149–182.

van IJzendoorn, M. H., Juffer, F., & Klein Poelhuis, C. W. (2005). Adoption and cognitive development: A meta-analytic comparison of adopted and nonadopted children's IQ and school performance. *Psychological Bulletin, 131*(2), 301–316.

Van Keer, H. (2004). Fostering reading comprehension in fifth grade by explicit instruction in reading strategies and peer tutoring. *British Journal of Educational Psychology, 74*(1), 37–70.

Van Laar, C. (2001). Understanding the impact of disadvantage on academic achievement. In F. Salili & R. Hoosain (Eds.), *Multicultural education: Issues, policies, and practices.* Greenwich, CT: Information Age Publishing.

Van Meter, P. (2001). Drawing construction as a strategy for learning from text. *Journal of Educational Psychology, 93*(1), 129–140.

Van Patten, J., Chao, C. I., & Reigeluth, C. M. (1986). A review of strategies for sequencing and synthesizing instruction. *Review of Educational Research, 56,* 437–471.

Van Sickle, R. L. (1986, April). *A quantitative review of research on instructional simulation gaming: A twenty-year perspective.* Paper presented at the annual convention of the American Educational Research Association, San Francisco.

Vansteenkiste, M., Lens, W., & Deci, E. (2006). Intrinsic vs. extrinsic goal contents in self-determination theory: Another look at the quality of academic motivation. *Educational Psychologist, 41*(1), 19–31.

Van Tassel-Baska, F. S. (1989). Appropriate curriculum for gifted learners. *Educational Leadership 46*(6), 13–15.

Varma, S., McCandliss, B., & Schwartz, D. (2008). Scientific and pragmatic challenges for bridging education and neuroscience. *Educational Researcher, 37*(3), 140–152.

Vaughn, S., Bos, C. L., & Schumm, J. S. (2007). *Teaching students who are exceptional, diverse, and at risk* (4th ed.). Boston: Pearson.

Vaughn, S., Levy, S., Coleman, M., & Bos, C. S. (2002). Reading instruction for students with LD and EBD: A synthesis of observation studies. *Journal of Special Education, 36*(1), 2–13.

Vavrus, M. (2008). Culturally responsive teaching. In T. L. Good (Ed.), *21st century learning* (Vol. 2, pp. 49–57). Thousand Oaks, CA: Sage.

Veenman, S. (1995). Cognitive and noncognitive effects of multi-grade and multi-age classes: A best evidence synthesis. *Review of Educational Research, 65*(4), 319–381.

Veenman, S. (1997). Combination classrooms revisited. *Educational Research and Evaluation, 3*(3), 262–276.

Vekiri, I. (2002). What is the value of graphical displays in learning? *Educational Psychology Review, 14*(3), 261–312.

Vellutino, F. R., Scanlon, D. M., Sipay, E. R., Small, S. G., Chen, R., Pratt, A., & Denckla, M. B. (1996). Cognitive profiles of difficult-to-remediate and readily remediated poor readers: Early intervention as a vehicle for distinguishing between cognitive and experimental deficits as basic causes of specific reading disability. *Journal of Educational Psychology, 88*(4), 601–638.

Vernez, G. (1998). *Projected social context for education of children.* Washington, DC: RAND.

Villa, R., & Thousand, J. (2003). Making inclusive education work. *Educational Leadership, 61*(2), 19–23.

Villegas, A., & Lucas, T. (2007). The culturally responsive teacher. *Educational Leadership, 64*(6), 28–33.

Vispoel, W. P., & Austin, J. R. (1995). Success and failure in junior high school: A critical incident approach to understanding students' attributional beliefs. *American Educational Research Journal, 32,* 277–412.

Vokoun, M., & Bigelow, T. (2008). Dude, what choice do I have? *Educational Leadership, 66*(3), 70–74.

Volkmar, F., & Pauls, D. (2003). Autism. *Lancet, 362,* 1133–1141.

Volman, M., & van Eck, E. (2001). Gender equity and information technology in education: The second decade. *Review of Educational Research, 71*(4), 613–634.

Von Drehle, D. (2007, July 26). The myth about boys. *Time.* Retrieved June 4, 2010, from www.time.com/time/magazine/article/0,9171,1647452,00.html

von Glaserfeld, E. (1996). Footnotes to the "many faces of constructivism." *Educational Researcher, 25*(6), 19.

Vuilleumeir, P. (2005). How brains beware: Neural mechanisms of emotional attention. *Trends in Cognitive Sciences, 9,* 585–594.

Vygotsky, L. S. (1978). *Mind in society.* (M. Cole, V. John-Steiner, S. Scribner, & E. Souberman, Eds.). Cambridge, MA: Harvard University Press.

Wade, S. E. (2001). Research on importance and interest: Implications for curriculum development and future research. *Educational Psychology Review, 13*(3), 243–261.

Wadsworth, B. (2004). *Piaget's theory of cognitive and affective development* (5th ed.). Boston: Pearson.

Wagmeister, J., & Shifrin, B. (2000). Thinking differently, learning differently. *Educational Leadership, 58*(3), 45–48.

Wainer, H. (2000). *Computerized adaptive testing: A primer* (2nd ed.). Mahwah, NJ: Erlbaum.

Waitoller, F., Artiles, A., & Cheney, D. (2010). The miner's canary: A review of overrepresentation research and explanations. *The Journal of Special Education, 44*(1), 29–49.

Walker, H., Colvin, G., & Ramsey, E. (2003). *Antisocial behavior in school: Evidence-based practice.* Pacific Grove, CA: Brooks-Cole.

Walker, H., Ramsey, E., & Gresham, F. (2003a). Heading off disruptive behavior. *American Educator, 27*(4), 6–21.

Walker, H., Ramsey, E., & Gresham, F. (2003b). How disruptive students escalate hostility and disorder—and how teachers can avoid it. *American Educator, 27*(4), 22–27.

Walker, H. M., & Gresham, F. M. (2003). School-related behavior disorders. In W. M. Reynolds & G. E. Miller (Eds.), *Handbook of psychology: Vol. 7. Educational psychology* (pp. 511–530). Hoboken, NJ: Wiley.

Walker, J., & Hoover-Dempsey, K. V. (2008). Parent involvement. In T. L. Good (Ed.), *21st century learning* (Vol. 2, pp. 382–391). Thousand Oaks, CA: Sage.

Walker, J. E., Shea, T. M., & Bauer, A. M. (2004). *Behavior management: A practical approach for educators* (5th ed.). Upper Saddle River, NJ: Merrill.

Walker, J. E., Shea, T. M., & Bauer, A. M. (2007). *Behavior management: A practical approach for educators* (9th ed.). Upper Saddle River, NJ: Pearson.

Walker, J. M. T., & Hoover-Dempsey, K. V. (2001, April). *Age-related patterns in student invitations to parental involvement in homework.* Paper presented at the annual meeting of the American Educational Research Association, Seattle, WA.

Walker, L. J. (2004). Progress and prospects in the psychology of moral development. *Merrill-Palmer Quarterly, 50,* 546–557.

Wallace, R. (2004). A framework for understanding teaching with the internet. *American Educational Research Journal, 41*(2), 447–448.

Wallace-Broscious, A., Serafica, F. C., & Osipow, S. H. (1994). Adolescent career development: Relationships to self-concept and identity status. *Journal of Research on Adolescence, 4*(1), 122–149.

Wallis, C., & Steptoe, S. (2007, June 4). How to fix No Child Left Behind. *Time, 169*(3), 34–41.

Walsh, J. A., & Sattes, B. D. (2005). *Quality questioning: Research-based practice to engage every learner.* Thousand Oaks, CA: Corwin.

Wang, A. Y., & Thomas, M. H. (1995). Effect of keywords on long-term retention: Help or hindrance? *Journal of Educational Psychology, 87,* 468–475.

Warger, C. L., & Pugach, M. C. (1996). Forming partnerships around curriculum. *Educational Leadership, 53*(5), 62–65.

Warikoo, N., & Carter, P. (2009). Cultural explanations for racial and ethnic stratification in academic achievement: A call for a new and improved theory. *Review of Educational Research, 79*(1), 366–394.

Warrick, P. D., & Naglieri, J. A. (1993). Gender differences in planning, attention, simultaneous, and successive (PASS) cognitive processes. *Journal of Educational Psychology, 85*(4), 693–701.

Wartella, E., & Jennings, N. (2000). Children and computers: New technology—old concerns. *Children and Computer Technology, 10*(2), 31–43.

Wasley, P. A. (2002). Small classes, small schools: The time is now. *Educational Leadership, 59*(3), 6–10.

Waterhouse, L. (2006). Multiple intelligences, the Mozart Effect, and emotional intelligence: A critical review. *Educational Psychologist, 4*(4), 207–225.

Watkins, D., & Wentzel, K. (2008). Training boys with ADHD to work collaboratively: Social and learning outcomes. *Contemporary Educational Psychology, 33*(4), 625–646.

Watkins, M., & Canivez, G. (2004). Temporal stability of WISC-III composite strengths and weaknesses. *Psychological Assessment, 16,* 6–16.

Watt, K. M., Powell, C. A., & Mendiola, I. D. (2004). Implications of one comprehensive school reform model for secondary school students underrepresented in higher education. *Journal of Education for Students Placed at Risk, 9*(3), 241–259.

Waxman, H., Padrón, Y., & Arnold, K. (2001). Effective instructional practices for students placed at risk of academic failure. In G. Borman, S. Stringfield, & R. Slavin (Eds.), *Title I: Compensatory education at the crossroads.* Mahwah, NJ: Erlbaum.

Waxman, H. C., Gray, J. P., & Padron, N. (2002). Resiliency among students at risk of academic failure. In S. Stringfield & D. Land (Eds.), *Educating at-risk students* (pp. 29–48). Chicago: National Society for the Study of Education.

Wayne, A. J., & Youngs, P. (2003). Teacher characteristics and student achievement gains: A review. *Review of Educational Research, 73*(1), 89–122.

Weaver-Hightower, M. (2003). The "boy turn" in research on gender education. *Review of Educational Research, 73*(4), 471–498.

Webb, N., & Mastergeorge, A. (2003). Promoting effective helping behavior in peer-directed groups. *International Journal of Educational Research, 39,* 73–97.

Webb, N. M. (1992). Testing a theoretical model of student interaction and learning in small groups. In R. Hertz-Lazarowitz & N. Miller (Eds.), *Interaction in cooperative groups: The theoretical anatomy of group learning* (pp. 102–119). New York: Cambridge University Press.

Webb, N. M. (2008). Learning in small groups. In T. L. Good (Ed.), *21st century learning* (Vol. 1, pp. 203–211). Thousand Oaks, CA: Sage.

Webb, N. M., & Mastergeorge, A. M. (2003). The development of students' learning in peer-directed small groups. *Cognition and Instruction, 21,* 361–428.

Webb, N. M., & Palincsar, A. S. (1996). Group processes in the classroom. In D. C. Berliner & R. C. Calfee (Eds.), *Handbook of educational psychology.* New York: Simon & Schuster Macmillan.

Webb, N. M., Trooper, J. D., & Fall, R. (1995). Constructive activity and learning in collaborative small groups. *Journal of Educational Psychology, 87,* 406–423.

Webber, J., Scheuermann, B., McCall, C., & Coleman, M. (1993). Research on self-monitoring as a behavior management technique in special education classrooms: A descriptive review. *Remedial and Special Education, 14*(2), 38–56.

Wechsler, D. (1955). *Wechsler Adult Intelligence Scale.* New York: Psychological Corporation.

Wehmeyer, M. L. (2001). *Teaching students with mental retardation: Providing access to the general curriculum.* Baltimore: Brookes.

Weigel, M., & Gardner, H. (2009). The best of both literacies. *Educational Leadership, 66*(6), 38–41.

Weinberger, E., & McCombs, B. L. (2001, April). *The impact of learner-centered practices on the academic and non-academic outcomes of upper elementary and middle school students.* Paper presented at the annual convention of the American Educational Research Association, Seattle, WA.

Weiner, B. (1992). *Human motivation: Metaphors, theories, and research.* Newbury Park, CA: Sage.

Weiner, B. (2000). Intrapersonal and interpersonal theories of motivation from an attributional perspective. *Educational Psychology Review, 12*(1), 1–14.

Weinert, F. E., & Helmke, A. (1995). Interclassroom differences in instructional quality and interindividual differences in cognitive development. *Educational Psychologist, 30*(1), 15–20.

Weinstein, C., & Mignano, A. (1993). *Organizing the elementary school classroom: Lessons from research and practice.* New York: McGraw-Hill.

Weinstein, C., & Mignano, A. (2007). *Elementary classroom management: Lessons from research and practice* (4th ed.). New York: McGraw-Hill.

Weinstein, C. E., & Hume, L. M. (1998). *Study strategies for lifelong learning.* Washington, DC: American Psychological Association.

Weinstein, C. S. (2003). *Secondary classroom management: Lessons from research and practice* (2nd ed.). New York: McGraw-Hill.

Weinstein, C. S. (2007). *Middle and secondary classroom management: Lessons from research and practice* (3rd ed.). New York: McGraw-Hill.

Weinstein, C. S., & Mignano, A. (2003). *Elementary classroom management: Lessons from research and practice* (3rd. ed.). New York: McGraw-Hill.

Weinstein, R. S. (1996). High standards in a tracked system of schooling: For which students and with what educational supports? *Educational Researcher, 25*(8), 16–19.

Weinstein, R. S., Madison, S. M., & Kuklinski, M. R. (1995). Raising expectations in schooling: Obstacles and opportunities for change. *American Educational Research Journal, 32,* 121–159.

Wells, A. S. (1995). Reexamining social science research on school desegregation. *Teachers College Record, 96*(4), 681–690.

Wells, A. S., & Crain, R. L. (1997). *Stepping over the color line.* New Haven, CT: Yale University Press.

Wells, A. S., Hirshberg, D., Lipton, M., & Oakes, J. (1995). Bounding the case within its context: A constructivist approach to studying detracking reform. *Educational Researcher, 24*(5), 18–24.

Welner, K. (2006). K–12 race-conscious student assignment policies: Law, social science, and diversity. *Review of Educational Research, 76*(3), 349–382.

Wentzel, K. R. (1993). Does being good make the grade? Social behavior and academic competence in middle school. *Journal of Educational Psychology, 85*(2), 357–364.

Wentzel, K. R. (2000). What is it that I'm trying to achieve? Classroom goals from a content perspective. *Contemporary Educational Psychology, 25*(1), 105–115.

Wentzel, K. R. (2003). School adjustment. In W. M. Reynolds & G. E. Miller (Eds.), *Handbook of psychology: Vol. 7. Educational psychology* (pp. 235–258). Hoboken, NJ: Wiley.

Wentzel, K. R., & Asher, S. R. (1995). The academic lives of neglected, rejected, popular, and controversial children. *Child Development, 66,* 754–763.

Wentzel, K. R., Barry, C. M., & Caldwell, K. A. (2004). Friendships in middle school: Influences on motivation and school adjustment. *Journal of Educational Psychology, 96*(2), 195–203.

Wentzel, K. R., & Erdley, C. A. (1993). Strategies for making friends: Relations to social behavior and peer acceptance in early adolescence. *Developmental Psychology, 29,* 819–826.

Wessler, S. L. (2001). Sticks and stones. *Educational Leadership, 58*(4), 28–33.

Westwater, A., & Wolfe, P. (2000). The brain-compatible curriculum. *Educational Leadership, 58*(3), 49–52.

Wheatley, G. H. (1991). Constructivist perspectives on science and mathematics learning. *Science Education, 75,* 9–21.

White, A. G., & Bailey, J. S. (1990). Reducing disruptive behaviors of elementary physical education students with sit and watch. *Journal of Applied Behavior Analysis, 3,* 353–359.

White, B. Y., & Frederiksen, J. R. (1998). Inquiry, modeling, and metacognition: Making science accessible to all students. *Cognition and Instruction, 16*(1), 3–118.

White, K. J., & Kistner, J. (1992). The influence of teacher feedback on young children's peer preferences and perceptions. *Developmental Psychology, 28,* 933–940.

Whitehurst, G., Crone, D., Zevenbergen, A., Schultz, M., Velting, O., & Fischel, J. (1999). Outcomes of an emergent literacy intervention from Head Start through second grade. *Journal of Educational Psychology, 91*(2), 261–272.

Whitman, S., Williams, C., & Shah, A. (2004). *Sinai Health System's community health survey: Report 1.* Chicago: Sinai Health System.

Wigfield, A., Byrnes, J., & Eccles, J. (2006). Development during early and middle adolescence. In P. Alexander & P. Winne (Eds.), *Handbook of educational psychology* (2nd ed., pp. 87–114). Mahwah, NJ: Erlbaum.

Wigfield, A., & Eccles, J. (1989). Test anxiety in elementary and secondary students. *Educational Psychologist, 24,* 159–183.

Wigfield, A., & Eccles, J. (2000). Expectancy-value theory of achievement motivation. *Contemporary Educational Psychology, 25*(1), 68–81.

Wigfield, A., Eccles, J. S., & Rodriguez, D. (1998). The development of children's motivation in school contexts. In P. D. Pearson & A. Iran-Nejad (Eds.), *Review of research in education* (pp. 73–118). Washington, DC: American Educational Research Association.

Wigfield, A. L. (1995, April). *Relationship of children's competence beliefs and achievement values to their performance and choice of different activities.* Paper presented at the annual meeting of the American Educational Research Association, San Francisco.

Wiggan, G. (2007). Race, school achievement, and educational inequality: Toward a student-based inquiry perspective. *Review of Educational Research, 77*(3), 310–333.

Wiggins, G. (1993). Assessment: Authenticity, context, and validity. *Phi Delta Kappan, 75*(3), 200–214.

Wiggins, G., & McTighe, J. (2006). Examining the teaching life. *Educational Leadership, 63*(6), 26–30.

Wilcox, R. T. (1993). Rediscovering discovery learning. In K. M. Cauley, F. Linder, & J. H. McMillan (Eds.), *Annual editions: Educational psychology 93/94.* Guilford, CT: Dushkin.

Wilens, T. E. (1998). *Straight talk about psychiatric medications for kids.* New York: Guilford.

Wiliam, D. (2007). Content then process: Teacher learning communities in the service of formative assessment. In D. B. Reeves (Ed.), *Ahead of the curve: The power of assessment to transform teaching and learning.* Bloomington, IN: Solution Tree.

Wiliam, D. (2007/2008, December /January). Informative assessment. *Educational Leadership, 65*(4), 36–42.

Wilkins, J. (2000). *Group activities to include students with special needs.* Thousand Oaks, CA: Corwin.

Willard-Holt, C. (2003). Raising expectations for the gifted. *Educational Leadership, 61*(2), 72–75.

Williams, J. E. (1995, April). *Use of learning and study skills among students differing in self-regulated learning efficacy.* Paper presented at the annual meeting of the American Educational Research Association, San Francisco, CA.

Williams, R. (2009). Black-white biracial students in American schools: A review of the literature. *Review of Educational Research, 79*(2), 776–804.

Willingham, D. (2002). Allocating student study time. *American Educator, 26*(2), 37–39.

Willingham, D. (2003). Students remember what they think about. *American Educator, 27*(2), 37–41.

Willingham, D. T. (2004). Practice makes perfect—but only if you practice beyond the point of perfection. *American Educator, 28*(1), 31–33.

Willingham, D. T. (2006). Brain-based learning: More fiction than fact. *American Educator, 30*(3), 30–37.

Willis, J. (2007). *Research-based strategies to ignite student learning: Insights from a neurologist and classroom teacher.* Reston, VA: ASCD.

Willis, J. A. (2006). Research-based teaching strategies for improving learning success. California Association of Independent Schools (CAIS) Faculty Newsletter.

Willoughby, T., Porter, L., Belsito, L., & Yearsley, T. (1999). Use of elaboration strategies by students in grades, two, four, and six. *The Elementary School Journal, 99*(3), 221–232.

Winebrenner, S. (2000). Gifted students need an education, too. *Educational Leadership, 58*(1), 52–56.

Winett, R. A., & Winkler, R. C. (1972). Current behavior modification in the classroom: Be still, be quiet, be docile. *Journal of Applied Behavior Analysis, 5,* 499–504.

Winne, P. (2006). How software technologies can improve research on learning and bolster school reform. *Educational Psychologist, 41*(1), 5–17.

Wittrock, M. C. (1991). Generative teaching of comprehension. *Elementary School Journal, 92,* 169–184.

Wittrock, M. C., & Alesandrini, K. (1990). Generation of summaries and analogies and analytic and holistic abilities. *American Educational Research Journal, 27,* 489–502.

Wittwer, J., & Renkl, A. (2008). Why instructional explanations often do not work: A framework for understanding the effectiveness of instructional explanations. *Educational Psychologist, 43*(1), 49–64.

Wong, H., & Wong, R. (2004). *The first days of school: How to be an effective teacher.* Mountain View, CA: Harry K. Wong Publications.

Wong, L. Y. S. (1995). Research on teaching: Process-product research findings and the feeling of obviousness. *Journal of Educational Psychology, 87,* 504–511.

Wood, D. J., Bruner, J. S., & Ross, G. (1976). The role of tutoring in problem solving. *Journal of Child Psychology and Psychiatry, 17,* 89–100.

Wragg, E. C., & Brown, C. (2001). *Explaining in the primary school.* London: Routledge.

Wright, J. C., Huston, A. C., Murphy, C., St. Peters, M., Pinon, M., Scantlin, R. M., & Kotler, J. A. (2001). The relations of early television viewing to school readiness and vocabulary of children from low-income families: The early window projects. *Child Development, 72,* 1347–1366.

Wulczyn, F., Smithgall, C., & Chen, L. (2009). Child well-being: The intersection of schools and child welfare. *Review of Research in Education, 33,* 35–62.

Wyra, M., Lawson, M., & Hungi, N. (2007). The mnemonic keyword method: The effects of bidirectional retrieval training and of ability to image on foreign language vocabulary recall. *Learning and Instruction, 17*(3), 360–371.

Xu, J., & Corno, L. (2003). Family help and homework management reported by middle school students. *The Elementary School Journal, 103*(5), 503–517.

Yeung, J., Linver, M., & Brooks-Gunn, J. (2002). How money matters for young children's development: Human capital and family process. *Child Development, 73,* 1861–1879.

Yonezawa, S., Wells, A. S., & Serna, I. (2002). Choosing tracks: "Freedom of choice" in detracking schools. *American Educational Research Journal, 39*(1), 37–67.

York-Barr, J., Sommerness, J., & Hur, J. (2008). Teacher leadership. In T. L. Good (Ed.), *21st century learning* (Vol. 1, pp. 12–20). Thousand Oaks, CA: Sage.

Zellermayer, M., Salomon, G., Globerson, T., & Givon, H. (1991). Enhancing writing-related metacognitions through a computerized writing partner. *American Educational Research Journal, 28,* 373–391.

Zettergren, P. (2003). School adjustment in adolescence for previously rejected, average and popular children. *British Journal of Educational Psychology, 72*(3), 207–221.

Zhao, Y. (2009). Needed: Global villagers. *Educational Leadership, 67*(1), 60–65.

Zhao, Y., & Frank, K. A. (2003). Factors affecting technology uses in schools: An ecological perspective. *American Educational Research Journal, 40*(4), 807–840.

Zigler, E., & Gilman, E. (1998). *The legacy of Jean Piaget.* Mahwah, NJ: Erlbaum.

Zigmond, M. (2003). Where should students with disabilities receive special education services? Is one place better than another? *The Journal of Special Education, 37*(3), 193–199.

Zimmerman, B. (2000). Self-efficacy: An essential motive to learn. *Contemporary Educational Psychology, 25*(1), 82–91.

Zimmerman, B. (2008). Investigating self-regulation and motivation: Historical background, methodological developments, and future prospects. *American Educational Research Journal, 45*(1), 166–183.

Zimmerman, B. J. (1995). Self-regulation involves more than metacognition: A social cognitive perspective. *Educational Psychologist, 30,* 217–221.

Zimmerman, B. J. (1998, April). *Achieving academic excellence: The role of perceived efficacy and self-regulatory skill.* Paper presented at the annual meeting of the American Educational Research Association, San Diego, CA.

Zimmerman, B. J., & Kitsantas, A. (2002). Acquiring writing revision and self-regulatory skill through observation and emulation. *Journal of Educational Psychology, 94*(4), 660–668.

Zimmerman, B. J., & Schunk, D. H. (2001). *Self-regulated learning and academic achievement* (2nd ed.). Mahwah, NJ: Erlbaum.

Zimmerman, B. J., & Schunk, D. H. (Eds.). (2003). *Educational psychology: A century of contributions.* Mahwah, NJ: Erlbaum.

Zimmerman, S., Rodriguez, M., Rewey, K., & Heidemann, S. (2008). The impact of an early literacy initiative on the long term academic success of diverse students. *Journal of Education for Students Placed at Risk, 13*(4), 452–481.

Zittleman, K., & Sadker, D. (2003). The unfinished gender revolution. *Educational Leadership, 60*(4), 59–62.

Ziv, A. (1988). Teaching and learning with humor: Experiment and replication. *Journal of Experimental Education, 57,* 5–18.

Zmuda, A. (2008). Springing into active learning. *Educational Leadership, 66*(3), 38–43.

Zohar, A., & Peled, B. (2008). The effects of explicit teaching of metastrategic knowledge on low- and high-achieving students. *Learning and Instruction, 18*(4), 337–353.

Zwiers, J. (2005). The third language of academic English. *Educational Leadership, 62*(4), 60–63.

Name Index

Subject Index